HTML:
The Complete Reference,
Second Edition

About the Author ...

Thomas Powell has been professionally involved in the Internet community since 1987. His career began with network support at UCLA's PICnet, followed by several years at CERFnet. In 1994, he founded Powell Internet Consulting, LLC (www.pint.com), a firm specializing in advanced Web design and development.

Powell is the author of two other popular Web development books: *Web Site Engineering* (with Dominique Cutts and David Jones) and the *HTML Programmer's Reference* (with Dan Whitworth). He has written extensively about the Web and development technologies for *NetGuide*, *Internet Week*, *Interactive Age*, *Communications Week*, and *Network World*.

Mr. Powell teaches Web publishing classes through the Information Technologies program at UCSD Extension. He holds a B.S. in Math Applied Science from UCLA and an M.S. in Computer Science from UCSD.

HTML:
The Complete Reference, Second Edition

Thomas A. Powell

Osborne/**McGraw-Hill**

Berkeley New York St. Louis San Francisco
Auckland Bogotá Hamburg London Madrid
Mexico City Milan Montreal New Delhi Panama City
Paris São Paulo Singapore Sydney
Tokyo Toronto

Osborne/**McGraw-Hill**
2600 Tenth Street
Berkeley, California 94710
U.S.A.

For information on translations or book distributors outside the U.S.A., or to arrange bulk purchase discounts for sales promotions, premiums, or fund-raisers, please contact Osborne/**McGraw-Hill** at the above address.

HTML: The Complete Reference, Second Edition

234567890 AGM AGM 90198765432109

ISBN 0-07-211977-2

Publisher
Brandon A. Nordin

Associate Publisher and Editor-in-Chief
Scott Rogers

Acquisitions Editor
Megg Bonar

Project Editor
Emily Rader

Editorial Assistant
Stephane Thomas

Copy Editors
William F. McManus
Gary Morris
Vicki Van Ausdall

Technical Editor
Alan Herrick

Proofreaders
Linda Medoff
Karen Mead

Indexer
David Heiret

Computer Designers
Jani Beckwith
Ann Sellers

Illustrators
Beth Young
Bob Hansen

Series Design
Peter Hancik

Contents

Part I
Web Basics

Part II

Presentation and Layout

Part III

Programming and HTML

Part VI

Appendixes

Acknowledgments

Writing a comprehensive book about a topic as large as HTML is a daunting task. As my business partner, Jimmy Tam, often says, "Don't let anybody tell you that HTML is easy." This is more true than any of us would like to admit. Even though I have taught HTML for years at UCSD Extension, written numerous articles on the subject, and been involved in the construction of dozens of corporate sites, I am just as guilty as anybody else of underestimating the details and complexities of the language when you get beyond layout. The specifications aren't perfect, documentation varies between browser vendors, and there is a great deal of misconception and oral history floating around the Web. Worst of all, it's a continuously moving target. The HTML 4.0 specification represents a significant change in the flavor of HTML from previous versions. With the potential rise of a new form of HTML in light of XML, more changes are in the offing. I and many others tried as hard as we could to clarify everything to the best of our understanding. I would like to thank those who made the extra effort to try to make this more than just another HTML book.

First I would like to thank all of the staff members at PINT who put up with their grumpy boss and his big book project. PINT's editor, writer, and overall HTML expert, Dan Whitworth, was indispensable and did a great job of fixing what I thought were complete sentences, as well as putting everything else together. Other PINT staff members, including Jimmy Tam, Francesca Weisser, Nikos Ioannou, Eric Raether, Rob McFarlane, Mark Robertson, Cory Ducker, Keith Mar, and many others, always helped keep things running smoothly enough so I could have a few minutes to work in peace.

Megg Bonar at Osborne/McGraw-Hill, who graciously allowed me to write this book and this new edition, provided the appropriate motivation to keep things running. Stephane Thomas made sure all the manuscript was in order, and Emily Rader made sure everything was edited and put together properly. Technical editor Alan Herrick, as well as the original technical editor, MegaZone, made sure to keep our HTML code to spec as much as possible.

My family and friends, particularly my sister Diana Powell, provided moral support as well as a few chili dog deliveries that ensured eventual completion of this project. Special thanks to my good friends at Datanet in Mexico City (particularly Tony Rihan) who have always shown support and friendship when I have needed it. Last but not least, the staff and students at UCSD Extension deserve thanks for giving me the wonderful opportunity to teach HTML and Web publishing for the past four years. The feedback from students has much to do with any improvements in this new edition.

Thomas A. Powell

Preface

Sitting down to write the new edition of this book shows just how fast things move in Internet time. Since the first edition was published, HTML 4 has become a standard, Dynamic HTML (DHTML) has started to take hold, and style sheets are reasonably well supported by both of the major browsers. The Web is getting even more complex. Vestigial elements of the past, such as proprietary HTML tags, are disappearing rapidly. And finally, we are beginning to realize the immense scope of the implications of the Extensible Markup Language (XML).

Despite these rapid changes, many people seem to believe that the future of HTML is dire. At the time of the first edition, many pundits had already predicted that the need for intimate knowledge of HTML would soon disappear. This doesn't seem ridiculous when you consider WYSIWYG editors such as Microsoft's FrontPage. These tools provide the illusion that we are a mere drag-and-drop away from creating a "killer" Web site. Eventually we will get there; but, for the moment, things are often complex. WYSIWYG tools may be useful in a limited fashion, but the instability of HTML and the lack of control over layout still requires a great deal of custom coding. If anything, authoring Web pages is becoming *more* complex, not less.

HTML provides the framework for all Web pages and will continue to be an important technology for at least the next few years. Fortunately, for now, learning the basics of HTML isn't difficult. If you arm yourself with a good informational tool, you can produce decent HTML code relatively quickly. As a teacher of Web publishing classes at the University of California at San Diego Extension, I know that after only a few classes some students can produce very nice Web pages. On the other hand, mastering HTML is still a daunting task. Errors creep into pages, particularly across browsers, and new elements are invented all the time. Coding techniques have become very important. Furthermore, the latest version of HTML represents a serious increase in the number of attributes available for modifying HTML elements.

This book attempts to incorporate the ideas of HTML 4, Netscape, Microsoft, and even WebTV, along with new technologies that affect HTML, such as Cascading Style Sheets (CSS), DHTML, and XML. Don't forget that there is more to making Web pages than HTML. I'll hint at that where I can; but, rather than try to talk about everything related to Web design, I want to do one thing the best I can: cover HTML. This book isn't meant to be *only* about learning HTML. I want this to be a book you can come back to if you forget an element's syntax or just want to look something up. I want it to be current and cover Netscape, Microsoft, WebTV, and any other important HTML viewing platform. I want it to show the relationship of HTML to emerging technologies such as style sheets and present the open issues facing HTML. I would even like it to stimulate some thought about your authoring techniques. If I've done a good job, this book will be true to its name—a *complete* reference.

Thomas A. Powell
tpowell@pint.com
January, 1999

The Complete Reference

Part I

Web Basics

The
Complete
Reference

HTML

Chapter 1

Introduction to HTML

ypertext Markup Language (HTML) is the text markup language currently used on the World Wide Web. If you have ever written a school report or business memo, you have encountered text markup. Your documents probably came back to you covered in red ink, courtesy of your teacher or boss. The symbols and acronyms used in those editorial markups suggested changes for you to interpret or implement (see Figure 1-1). In that scenario, markup is separate from the actual content of your document. When you create a document with a word processing program, such as Microsoft Word or WordPerfect, the program uses markup language to indicate the structure and formatting of that electronic document. What you see on your screen looks like a page of formatted text; the rest is done "behind the scenes." HTML is the not-so-behind-the-scenes markup language that is used to tell Web browsers how to display Web pages.

Basic HTML Concepts

In the case of HTML, markup commands applied to your Web-based content tell the browser software the structure of the document and, when appropriate, how you want the content to be displayed. For example, if you want to display a section of text in boldface, you surround the corresponding text with the boldface markup tags, **<B>** and **</B>**, as shown here:

```
<B>This is important text.</B>
```

When the browser reads a document that has HTML markup in it, it determines how to render it onscreen by considering the HTML elements embedded within the document (see Figure 1-2). Be aware that browsers don't always render things in the way that you think they will. This is due partially to the design of HTML and partially to the differences in the variety of Web browsers currently in use.

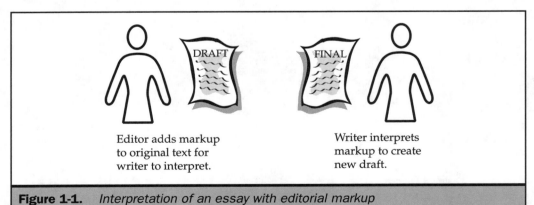

Editor adds markup to original text for writer to interpret.

Writer interprets markup to create new draft.

Figure 1-1.   *Interpretation of an essay with editorial markup*

Figure 1-2. *Interpretation of a Web page with HTML markup*

An HTML document is simply a text file that contains the information you want to publish. It also contains embedded instructions, called *elements*, that indicate how a Web browser should structure or present the document. In the following listing, the HTML elements are highlighted in a bold font. The elements are explained in greater detail later in this chapter in the section "Overview of HTML Markup."

```
<!DOCTYPE HTML PUBLIC "-//W3C//DTD HTML 4.0 Transitional//EN">
<HTML>
<HEAD>
<TITLE>Big Company's Big Home Page</TITLE>
</HEAD>

<BODY>
<H1 ALIGN="CENTER">Big Company, Inc.</H1>

<P>Welcome to Big Company, Inc.-your best source for HTML examples.
We do examples right!</P>
```

```
<UL>
     <LI><A HREF="new.htm">What's New</A>
     <LI><A HREF="products.htm">Products</A>
     <LI><A HREF="contact.htm">Contact</A>
</UL>
<HR>

<ADDRESS>E-mail:
<A HREF="mailto:webmaster@bigcompany.com">
webmaster@bigcompany.com</A>
</ADDRESS>

</BODY>
</HTML>
```

As this listing demonstrates, HTML elements generally consist of a pair of angle-bracketed tags surrounding some text. The *end tag* (**</TAG>**) is just like the *start tag* (**<TAG>**), except that it has a slash (*/*) in it, as shown here:

```
<TAG>          ◄─────────  Start tag

     . . .
     Content that the tag pair affects
     . . .
</TAG>         ◄─────────  End tag
```

The HTML elements may indicate the meaning of the enclosed information (for example, a citation) or how the text should be rendered (for example, in italics). Given the following HTML code,

```
<I>This is interesting.</I>
```

a Web browser should render the phrase "This is interesting" in italics.

HTML elements normally consist of a pair of tags that enclose some textual content or other HTML elements. However, some elements, such as the horizontal rule tag, **<HR>**, do not have a corresponding end tag; that is, they don't actually "contain" anything. These elements are termed *empty* elements. The end tag for some elements is optional, so an element may appear to be empty, even though it isn't, because its end tag is missing. For example, with the paragraph element, **<P>**, the end tag may be omitted. However, for such elements, the Web browser actually infers the presence of the end tag. For clarity's sake and to protect your pages against future changes to the HTML specification, using the end tag for an element is always a good idea, if one is defined.

HTML: A Structured Language

As the preceding discussion indicates, HTML tags have a well-defined syntax and HTML documents have a formal structure. The World Wide Web Consortium (W3C), at http://www.w3.org, is the primary organization that attempts to standardize HTML (as well as many other technologies used on the Web). To provide a standard, the W3C must carefully specify all aspects of the technology. In the case of HTML, this means precisely defining the elements in the language. The W3C has defined HTML as an application of the *Standard Generalized Markup Language (SGML)*. In short, SGML is a language used to define other languages by specifying the allowed document structure in the form of a *document type definition (DTD)*—a document that indicates the syntax that can be used for elements.

From the DTD, a basic template can be derived for an HTML document. First, you indicate the particular variant of HTML that you are using. As you'll learn later, numerous versions of HTML exist, and thus you must make sure to author your documents with the HTML standard (or nonstandard) that makes the most sense for your user base.

To indicate the particular variant of HTML that you are using, you need to specify the particular DTD to which the HTML file conforms. To accomplish this, all HTML files should begin with a **<!DOCTYPE>** indicator. Unfortunately, **<!DOCTYPE>** is rarely used correctly, and HTML's relationship to SGML is not well understood by many HTML authors. Furthermore, most browsers don't seem to care whether a document type is indicated. The benefits of using the **<!DOCTYPE>** statement are discussed in Chapter 3.

While all proper HTML files should begin with a **<!DOCTYPE>** declaration, this is generally omitted. Instead, most HTML files begin with the **<HTML>** element, which indicates that the content of the file includes markup. This is an essential element that should not be omitted.

The file should end with the **<HTML>** element's end tag, **</HTML>**. Within the **<HTML>** element are two primary sections—the head and the body. Occasionally, special framing documents contain a head and a frameset. The concept of frames is discussed in depth in Chapter 8.

The head, which is enclosed within the **<HEAD>** element (consisting of the **<HEAD>** and **</HEAD>** tags), includes supplementary information about the document, such as the title of the document, which most browsers display in a title bar at the top of the browser window. The title is indicated between the **<TITLE>** and **</TITLE>** tags. The document title is required under the current HTML specification. While some browsers may not require the inclusion of the **<TITLE>** element, you should always include it—for correctness, book marking, and the sake of good HTML style.

The information in the head of an HTML document is very important, because it is used to describe or augment the content of the document. The head of an HTML document is like the front matter or cover page of a document. In many cases, the information contained within the **<HEAD>** element is information about information, which is generally referred to as *meta-information*. This is a very important and often-overlooked aspect of HTML documents. Search engines, such as Lycos and HotBot, use meta-information to index Web pages. Besides meta-information, the **<HEAD>** element can include author contact information, scripts, style sheets, and comments.

The body, which is enclosed between **<BODY>** and **</BODY>** tags, contains the actual content and the appropriate markup tags needed to render the page. A basic HTML template is shown here:

```
<!DOCTYPE HTML PUBLIC "-//W3C//DTD HTML 4.0 Transitional//EN">
<HTML>
<HEAD>
<TITLE>Document Title Goes Here</TITLE>
...Other supplementary information goes here....
</HEAD>

<BODY>
...Document content and markup go here....
</BODY>
</HTML>
```

Note   *In the preceding template, the HTML 4 document type indicator is used. Other HTML standard conformance indicators are also possible, as discussed in Chapter 3.*

Some of the most common elements used in HTML documents are listed here:

- The **<HTML>**, **<HEAD>**, and **<BODY>** tag pairs are used to structure the document.
- The **<TITLE>** and **</TITLE>** tag pair specifies the title of the document.
- The **<H1>** and **</H1>** header tag pair creates a headline.
- The **<HR>** element, which has no end tag, inserts a horizontal rule, or bar, across the screen.
- The **<P>** and **</P>** paragraph tag pair indicates a paragraph of text.

Now that you have a template, take a look at the following sample HTML document, which uses these seven elements:

```
<!DOCTYPE HTML PUBLIC "-//W3C//DTD HTML 4.0 Transitional//EN">
<HTML>
<HEAD>
```

```
<TITLE>HTML First Example</TITLE>
</HEAD>

<BODY>
<HEAD>
<H1>Welcome to HTML</H1>
<HR>

<P>This really isn't so hard!</P>
<P>You can put in lots of text if you want to. In fact, you
could keep on typing and make up more sentences and continue
on and on.</P>
</BODY>
</HTML>
```

If you are using a word processing program, you can type the example and save it with a filename, such as first.htm or first.html. For a browser to read your file properly, it must end in either the .htm or .html extension. If you don't save your file with the appropriate extension, the browser won't attempt to interpret the HTML markup. When this happens, the codes appear in the browser window as shown here:

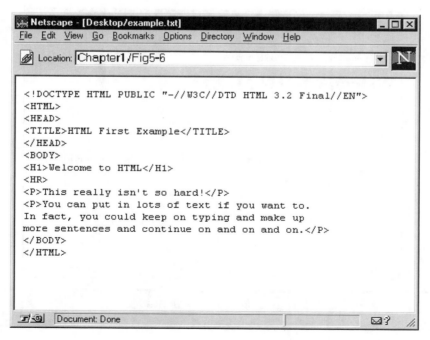

For this quick example, use a simple text-editing tool, such as Notepad in Windows 95/NT, SimpleText on the Macintosh, or vi in UNIX. While such simple programs may not give you all the features that you want, you'll avoid accidentally saving the file in the wrong format, possibly with a .txt extension, or even saving it in a proprietary word processing format that the browser cannot read.

After you save the example file on your system, use your browser to open it by using the Open, Open Page, or Open File command. After your browser reads the file, it should render a page like the one shown in Figure 1-3.

If your page does not display properly, review your file to make sure that you typed the page correctly. If you find a mistake and make a change to the file, save the file, go back to your browser, and click the Reload or Refresh button. Keeping the browser and text editor open simultaneously is a good idea, to avoid constantly reopening one or the other. Once you get the hang of HTML design, you'll see that, at this raw level, it is much like the edit, compile, and run cycle so familiar to programmers. This manual process probably isn't the way that you want to develop Web pages, because it can be tedious, error prone, and not helpful when thinking of visual design. For illustrative purposes, however, it works fine.

Based on this simple example, you might guess that learning HTML is merely a matter of learning the multitude of markup tags, such as **<B>**, that specify the format and structure of documents to browsers. While that is true in some sense, such a

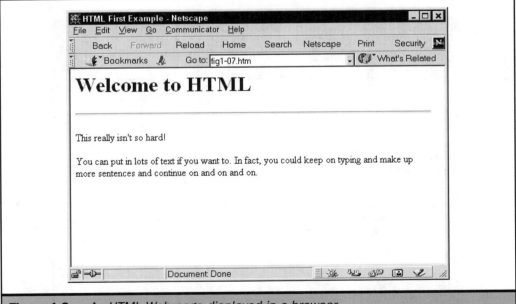

Figure 1-3.   *An HTML Web page displayed in a browser*

simplistic approach is like trying to learn print publishing by understanding only the various commands available in Microsoft Word, while disregarding paper types, document structure, and issues of style. In addition to learning the various markup tags, you need to consider the intent of HTML, its purpose, and the medium in which HTML is used—the World Wide Web.

Overview of HTML Markup

A markup language such as HTML is simply a collection of codes—*elements* in this case— that are used to indicate the structure and format of a document. The codes have meaning that is interpreted by a formatting program, often a Web browser, which renders the document. Elements in HTML consist of alphanumeric tags within angle brackets. These tags usually come in pairs, but exceptions do exist. The following table shows a few HTML elements:

Start Tag	End Tag	Description
<H1>	</H1>	The most important headline
<B>	</B>	Bold text
<CITE>	</CITE>	A citation
<P>	</P> (optional)	A paragraph of text
<HR>	None	A horizontal rule

The alphanumeric tags are case-insensitive, which means that as far as Web browsers are concerned, **<H1>** is equivalent to **<h1>**, and **<cite>** is equivalent to **<CiTe>**. For stylistic reasons, however, you should use case consistently.

Tip   *Using all uppercase elements makes distinguishing markup from document content easier. For future compatibility with XML, which is case-sensitive, lowercase might be preferable. For more on XML, see Chapter 17. Many HTML editing tools provide tag-coloring features that make maintaining documents with complex tagging structures easier.*

HTML elements often have attributes that affect the rendering of the element's content by modifying the function of the element. Attributes are very common with complex elements such as **<IMG>**, which specifies an image to load into a Web page. The name and location of the particular image are set via the **SRC** attribute, which indicates the "source" of the image file. **<IMG SRC="logo.gif">** tells the browser to display the file called logo.gif. An element may have many attributes with quoted values that are separated by one space, as shown here:

```
<IMG SRC="logo.gif" ALT="Big Company Logo" HEIGHT="100" WIDTH="200">
```

Attribute values should be enclosed within double quotes. Many browsers allow you to use single quotes or no quotes at all, particularly for values that consist of a single word. Situations also exist in which single quotes may be used within attribute values. This occurs when JavaScript is used, or when the value of the attribute includes special characters, such as spaces or punctuation. Attributes are discussed in more detail in Chapter 3.

Although HTML elements such as **<IMG>** aren't case-sensitive, the contents of attributes often are case-sensitive. For example, **<IMG SRC="logo.gif ">** isn't necessarily equivalent to **<IMG SRC="LOGO.GIF">**, because the **SRC** value follows casing rules specific to the attribute. With regard to filenames, some operating systems are case-sensitive; for example, LOGO.GIF doesn't necessarily specify the same file as logo.gif.

HTML files generally aren't sensitive to spacing. Browsers tend to collapse multiple spaces or tabs into a single space. For example,

```
<B>This is a test.</B>
```

displays the same way in a browser as does the following:

```
<B>This    is     a
        test.</B>
```

Spaces, tabs, and returns collapse when HTML files are displayed in a browser, unless they are included within elements, such as the preformatted element **<PRE>**. Because HTML allows judicious spacing, you should space out content with white space for easy reading of the source document, particularly by separating markup from content. Additional spacing does not affect the browser's rendering of the document.

In the future, when tools generate the majority of HTML, spacing and tagging styles may not be as big of an issue; but, until people stop editing HTML files directly, formatting your documents for human reading is wise.

Another aspect of HTML elements is *nesting,* which means that HTML elements can surround each other. If you have some text that you want to make bold and italic, you can apply both the **<B>** and the **<I>** elements to the text, as shown in the following illustration. In this example, the tags are nested and do not cross.

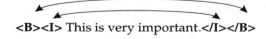

<B><I> This is very important.</I></B>

The idea of crossing tags is shown here:

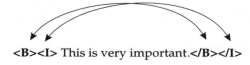

<B><I> This is very important.</B></I>

You can always determine whether tags cross, by connecting arcs from start tag to end tag, to see whether the arcs cross each other.

The preceding is only a brief introduction to some of the "rules" that HTML documents tend to follow. Unfortunately, the benefit of following the rules isn't always apparent to new Web developers, because most browsers don't strictly enforce the standards. For example, although the nesting rule agrees with the formal definition of HTML, most browsers have no problem with crossed tags, or even with tags being used totally improperly. The reason for the browsers' laxity in enforcement is actually very logical: a browser would display nonstop error messages if it displayed a message every time that it encountered a slightly miscoded Web page! Nevertheless, don't use the browsers' laxity in enforcing HTML's "rules" as an excuse to misuse HTML or sloppily code a page. Standards impose specific structural requirements on documents, and as the Web becomes increasingly more complicated and technologies such as the Extensible Markup Language (XML) are adopted, following the standards may become much more important.

Unfortunately, many document authors are unfamiliar with standards. Thus, they might not pay attention to the structure, because they don't understand the philosophy of HTML; or, they may think of HTML as a physical page-description language, such as PostScript, rather than a logical, structure-oriented markup language. Browsers don't discourage this view, and may even encourage the physical view.

Logical and Physical HTML

No introduction to HTML would be complete without a discussion of the logical versus physical markup battle at the heart of HTML. *Physical HTML* refers to using HTML to make pages look a particular way; *logical HTML* refers to using HTML to specify the structure of a document, and using another technology, such as cascading style sheets (see Chapter 10), to designate the look of the page.

Most people are already very familiar with physical document design, because they normally use WYSIWYG (*what you see is what you get*) text editors, such as Microsoft Word. When Word users want to make something bold, they simply select the appropriate button, and the text is made bold. In HTML, you can make something bold simply by enclosing it within the **<B>** and **</B>** tags, as shown here:

```
<B>This is important.</B>
```

This can easily lead people to believe that HTML is nothing more than a simple formatting language. WYSIWYG HTML editors (such as Microsoft FrontPage) also reinforce this view; but as page designers try to use HTML in this simplistic fashion, sooner or later they must face the fact that HTML is *not* a physical page-description language. Page authors can't seem to make the pages look exactly the way they want; and when they can, doing so often requires heavy use of **<TABLE>** tags, giant images, and even trick HTML. Other technologies, such as style sheets, may provide a better solution for formatting text than a slew of inconsistently supported tricks and proprietary HTML elements.

According to many experts, HTML was not designed to provide most of the document layout features people have come to expect, and it shouldn't be used for that purpose. Instead, HTML should be used as a logical, or generalized, markup language that defines a document's structure, not its appearance. For example, instead of defining the introduction of a document with a particular margin, font, and size, HTML just labels it as an introduction section and lets another system, such as Cascading Style Sheets, determine the appropriate presentation. In the case of HTML, the browser or a style sheet has the final say on how a document looks.

HTML already contains many logical elements. An example of a logical element is **<STRONG>**, which indicates something of importance, as shown here:

```
<STRONG>This is important.</STRONG>
```

The **<STRONG>** element says nothing about how the phrase "This is important" will actually appear, although it will probably be rendered in bold. While most of the logical elements are relatively underutilized, others, such as headings (**<H1>** through **<H6>**) and paragraphs, are used regularly.

The benefits of logical elements may not be obvious to those comfortable with physical markup. To understand the benefits, it's important to realize that on the Web, many browsers render things differently. In addition, predicting what the viewing environment will be is difficult. What browser does the user have? What is his or her monitor's screen resolution? Does the user even have a screen? Considering the extreme of the user having no screen at all, how would a speaking browser render the **<BOLD>** element? What about the **<STRONG>** element? Text tagged with **<STRONG>** might be read in a firm voice, but boldfaced text doesn't have a meaning outside the visual realm.

Many realistic examples exist of the power of logical elements. Consider the multinational or multilingual aspects of the Web. In some countries, the date is written with the day first, followed by the month and year. In the United States, the date generally is written with the month first, and then the day and year. A **<DATE>** element, if it existed, could tag the information and let the browser localize it for the appropriate viewing environment. Another example is the problem of screen sizes that, theoretically, could be reduced by logical structuring concepts. For example, logical elements could allow for different renderings based on the screen size of the computer running the browser. This would allow the creation of documents that look good on laptop screens as well as on large workstation monitors. In short, separation of the logical structure from the physical presentation allows multiple physical displays to be applied to the same content. This is a powerful idea that, unfortunately, is rarely taken advantage of.

Whether you subscribe to the physical or logical viewpoint, HTML is not purely a physical *or* logical language, yet. In other words, currently used HTML elements come in both flavors: physical and logical. Elements that specify fonts, type sizes, type styles, and so on, are physical. Elements that specify content or importance, such as **<CITE>** and **<H1>**, and let the browser decide how to do things are logical. A quick look at Web pages across the Internet suggests that logical elements often go unused, because Web developers want more layout control than raw HTML provides, and style sheets are relatively new and still buggy. Furthermore, many designers just don't think in the manner required for logical markup, and WYSIWYG page editors generally don't encourage such thinking.

So, like it or not, to achieve the look that they want, page designers will probably continue to abuse elements, such as **<TABLE>** and **<FRAME>**, and use tricks to implement layouts in the way that they want them. This is the struggle that currently exists between what people want out of HTML and what HTML actually provides. With the rise of HTML 4 and Cascading Style Sheets, this struggle may eventually go away; but the uptake is still slow, and millions of documents will continue to be authored with no concept of logical structuring. Web page development continues to provide an interesting study of the difference between what theorists say and what people want.

What HTML Is Not

HTML is a powerful technology, but many misconceptions exist about it. Understanding what HTML is *not* will certainly help page developers avoid common mistakes.

HTML Is Not a WYSIWYG Design Language

HTML isn't a specific, screen- or printer-precise formatting language like PostScript. Many people struggle with HTML on a daily basis, trying to create perfect layouts by using HTML elements inappropriately or by using images to make up for HTML's lack of screen- and font-handling features. Other technologies, such as style sheets, are far better than HTML for handling presentation issues.

HTML Is Not a Programming Language

Many people think that making HTML pages is similar to programming. However, HTML is unlike programming in that it does not specify logic. It specifies the structure and often the layout of a document. With the introduction of scripting languages such as JavaScript, however, the concept of dynamic HTML (DHTML) is becoming more and more popular and is used to create highly interactive Web pages. Simply put, DHTML provides scripting languages with the capability to modify HTML elements and their content before, and possibly after, the page has been loaded.

DHTML blurs the lines between HTML as a layout language and HTML as a programming environment. However, the line should be distinct, because HTML isn't a programming language. Heavily intermixing code with HTML markup in the ad hoc manner that many DHTML authors do is far worse than trying to use HTML as a WYSIWYG markup language. Programming logic can be cleanly separated in HTML in the form of script code, as discussed in Chapters 13 and 14. Unfortunately, if this separation isn't heeded, the page maintenance nightmare that results from tightly binding programming logic to content will dwarf the problems caused by misuse of HTML code for presentation purposes.

HTML Is Not Truly Standardized Yet

Although the W3C defines the HTML specification, in practical terms browser vendors and users often define their own, de facto standards or decide what aspects of the standards they support. While this may sound like heresy, it is true. Until recently, when a new browser supporting a new feature was released, many companies and individuals would rush to use it, regardless of whether the feature was included in the W3C HTML standard. Today, rather than adopting new tags as often as in the past, the tags already defined in the specification are being consistently supported.

Presently, no single browser supports all HTML 4 features, which is unfortunate, because the browsers themselves—quirks and all—are currently considered the final arbiters of the meaning of HTML elements (as far as end users are concerned). In this sense, HTML resembles English. New elements and technologies are the "slang" of HTML: they may not be correct; but eventually, many slang terms become an accepted part of the language. Many ways exist to "speak" HTML, but the key issue is whether the browser understands the markup, just as the key issue in English is whether one person understands another person's slang. Hopefully, browsers will stop being so varied in their interpretation of certain elements and will begin to offer full support of standards, such as HTML 4. But for now, the practice of building pages around "common HTML" usage may be more appropriate than implementing standard HTML usage.

HTML Is Not Extensible

Some people feel that changing HTML is easy as long as the language is simple enough for browser vendors and standards groups to determine new elements easily. A long battle has been waged to implement features correctly. Truly extensible markup environments (such as SGML and XML), in conjunction with style sheets, allow users to invent elements and renderings for those elements without compromising the experience for other users. This is currently impossible with HTML.

HTML Is Not Complete

HTML is not finished. The language does not provide all the facilities that it should, even as a logical markup language. However, work is presently focused on implementing the current HTML standards under a new language, called Extensible Markup Language (XML). Future versions of HTML will almost certainly be defined as a subset of XML. Theoretically, this is a wise decision, but the ubiquitous nature of HTML and its huge installed base suggest that considering how to extend HTML or fill in its small gaps is an incredibly important task. The W3C's current HTML *Activity Statement* can be found on its Web site (http://www.w3.org/MarkUp/Activity.html).

HTML Is Not All You Need to Know to Create Good Web Pages

Whereas HTML is the basis for Web pages, you need to know a lot more than HTML to build useful Web pages (unless the page is very simple). Document design, graphic design, and even programming often are necessary to create sophisticated Web pages. HTML serves as the foundation environment for all of these tasks, and a complete understanding of HTML technology can only aid document authors.

HTML's lack of support for certain features leads to a general problem with how people use the language. Much of the tension surrounding HTML and HTML's abuse stem from the "logical versus physical markup" debate (discussed earlier in this chapter in the section "Logical and Physical HTML") and the desire for absolute positioning of text and graphics within Web pages. These themes recur throughout this book.

Summary

HTML is neither a programming language nor a physical page-description language. It is a markup language that combines physical and logical structuring ideas. Elements— in the form of tags, such as **<B>** and **</B>**—are embedded within text documents to indicate to browsers how to render pages. The rules for HTML are fairly simple, but these rules are not strictly enforced. Browsers are still the final arbiters of page layout.

The rapid development of HTML and the laxity of its use have created a great deal of misunderstanding about how to use the language. This is due in part to the chaotic nature of the Web publishing environment and in part to HTML's inability to address all the needs of its users. Currently, HTML does not provide all the features necessary to build modern Web pages, nor should it. Developers need to use other technologies properly, such as scripting and style sheets, to build complete Web pages. In this sense, HTML will continue to be the bedrock upon which the information superhighway is built.

Chapter 3 will return to the specifics of HTML; but, first, Chapter 2 takes a look at the history of Web publishing and how HTML fits into the Web development process.

The Complete Reference

Chapter 2

Web Publishing

One of the problems with discussing the creation of Web pages is that mastery of HTML is often mistakenly equated with mastery of the process of Web design and publishing. HTML is only one part of the process. Graphic design and programming technologies are also important aspects of the process. "Web publishing" is a more appropriate term to describe the overall process of planning and putting together a Web site, particularly when some degree of forethought, skill, and artistry is employed. Knowledge of HTML alone does not provide all the facilities required to make appealing, usable Web sites. Before you get too caught up in the details of markup tags, you need to understand the Web process and how HTML works in that process.

What Is Good Web Design?

Before you read about the process of building Web pages, this section helps you define your goal clearly. What, exactly, is good Web design? Some people discuss what *isn't* good Web design (www.webpagesthatsuck.com), but this really doesn't demonstrate how to create good Web sites. Others like to discuss aesthetics and layout (www.highfive.com). This may be appropriate on a superficial level, but beauty is often in the eye of the beholder. Looks aren't everything. Function is important, too, and some people even claim that the answer to what constitutes good Web design is purely a matter of function. If it isn't usable (www.useit.com), then it isn't reasonable—but function without motivating form is boring.

Some talk too much about success, citing numerous visitors as true validation of a site's design. This assumes that the Web is primarily about popularity. Who cares how many visitors come to a page, unless it has some benefit? Think about quality and success. If serving the most burgers says anything about making good hamburgers, then McDonald's makes the world's best hamburger. This kind of logic gets people in trouble on the Web all the time. Consider whether economically successful or trendy Web pages are well designed. Characterizing good Web design is not easy, especially because it depends largely on your target audience.

Most Web discussions lose sight of the big picture, placing too much emphasis on how pages look, and not enough emphasis on their content, purpose, functionality, or the user's experience. Web design is not just graphic design. Web design *includes* graphic design. Other important aspects of the Web design process may include such areas as the following:

- Artistic style, color theory, typography, and other visual concerns
- Information design, which specifies how information should be organized and linked
- Hypertext theory
- Technical writing

- System design
- Programming
- Network and server design
- Business issues and project management

Obviously, many disciplines are part of Web design. The first requirement, however, is a clear understanding of the site's ultimate purpose. The goal of a Web designer is to produce a usable and appealing visual design for a software system, in the form of a Web site that helps a user fulfill some goal. In other words, the goal is to develop a site that can be delivered to the user in a satisfactory manner, be interpreted correctly by the user, and induce the desired outcome. Web design should be concerned not only with the aesthetic qualities of a Web site, but also with the user's overall experience in the context of a specific task or problem. The focus is on how something can be done, not just on how it looks.

It is easy to throw out expressions like "perception is reality" or "content is king" as arguments for or against focusing on the visual nature of the Web. However, the reality is a balance between these extreme points of view. If you skimp on graphics, the site may seem boring. If you provide a wonderful interface, but skimp on content, the user may leave to find a site with more information. If you forget to debug, you may send the user angrily away, facing error dialog boxes. Remember: experience is vital. Always consider what feeling the user will take away after visiting your site. A sense of accomplishment? Frustration? Understanding? Disgust?

The best approach to Web design is a holistic one, in which content, presentation, and interactivity work in harmony.

So, how can you make a Web site that is both functional and visually appealing, without exceeding the constraints of the Internet and Web technologies? Focusing on the technology and then decorating a Web page leads to the dreaded "Christmas tree" design, shown in Figure 2-1. Putting a page together with HTML and then sprucing it up with a few colored balls, a rainbow-color bar, and animated clip art doesn't help. The page looks slapped together, and the graphics provide little more than extra eye-catching glitz. In this case, the background plain interferes with the user's ability to read the text.

On the other hand, focusing too much on the visual aspects leads to online brochures with slow-downloading, full-screen images. Everything is created with graphic composition tools, such as Photoshop, which provide nearly absolute layout control, but result in huge files. Text on such a page can't be changed without a graphic designer, let alone be indexed by a Web search engine. This design also excludes those who surf with images turned off, use a text browser, or are disabled and simply can't see your images. Even worse, the site may not scale on a high-resolution monitor, causing it to be so small that it's unreadable. The full-screen-image design style, shown in Figure 2-2, may produce nice-looking pages, but it tends to relegate Web sites to fancy digital brochures. Many large sites fall into this trap because they never test their pages over a dial-in link. A page that seems to work well over the local ethernet

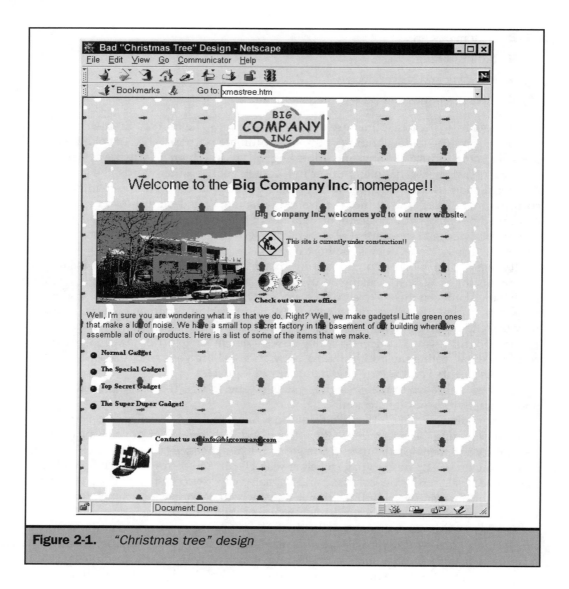

Figure 2-1. *"Christmas tree" design*

network may take ages to load over a 56Kbps modem connection. The average modem user still connects at that speed (or a lower speed), and most users are not willing to wait forever for your page to load before they give up and move on to less-bandwidth-intensive sites.

Figure 2-2.   *A full-screen-image design*

Again, balance is the issue. Sometimes, stark pages are okay. Other times, full-screen images make sense. The form of a site depends on its goals. Figuring out the site's audience and what its ultimate goals are before diving into HTML coding seems obvious, but it isn't always the approach adopted. Unfortunately, once the simplicity of HTML is revealed, many eager authors quickly mark up pages and then try to improve them by adding graphics. At the other extreme, designers may ruin the site just by thinking more about the user interface than about what is actually delivered. Creating Web sites requires a process, not an ad hoc decision to focus more on visuals or more on content.

The Process of Web Publishing

Planning, organizing, and visualizing Web sites and pages may be more important than knowing HTML. Unfortunately, these are very difficult things to teach and tend to be learned only by experience. The biggest mistake in Web development is not having a clear goal for a Web site. Even if the site is launched on time and under budget, how can you understand whether you did a good job if you had no goal in the first place? Often goals are vague. Initially, many corporate Web site projects were fueled by

FUD—fear, uncertainty, and doubt. With the hype surrounding the Web, it was important to get on the Web before the competition. If the competition was already online, having a Web site appeared even more crucial to corporate success. This is a dangerous situation to be in. Even if budget is not an issue, the benefit of the site will eventually be questioned. Web professionals may find their jobs on the line. Thus, the first step in the Web publishing process is defining the purpose of a site.

Determining Purpose

Finding a purpose for a Web site isn't necessarily very hard. The Web can be very useful, and many common reasons exist to put up a Web site, a few of which are listed here:

- Commerce
- Entertainment
- Information
- Marketing
- Personal pleasure
- Presence
- Promotion
- Research and education
- Technical support

One problem with Web sites is that they may have multiple purposes. A corporate Web site may include demands for marketing, public relations, investor relations, technical support, commerce, and human resource services such as job recruiting. Trying to meet all of these needs while thinking about the Web site as one entity can be difficult. Much like a large-scale software system with many functions, a Web site with many different goals probably should be broken into modules, or subprojects, that constitute parts of a larger whole. This leads to the idea of a *microsite*—a very specific subsite that is part of a larger site and that may be built separately. Microsites have the advantage of allowing the focus, look, or technology of a portion of a site to change without having to change the site as a whole.

No matter how the site is structured, keeping it cohesive and logical is important. For example, establishing a consistent look and feel for the site as a whole is still important, regardless of the multitude of functions. People should feel comfortable moving from your support pages to your marketing pages to your employment pages. A consistent user interface breeds familiarity and generates a united front. The user doesn't need to know that the site is constructed in modules. An inconsistent interface can lead to a user becoming lost and confused while exploring. It helps to have one person (or at least a small group) designated as the overall decision maker on a Web project. The Webmaster, or more appropriately termed *Webmanager*, coordinates the work efforts and helps keep the project on track. The Webmanager's role is basically the same as a project manager on a large software project. Without such careful management, a Web site with many goals may quickly become a mess, built to satisfy the needs and desires of its builders rather than its viewers.

Who Is the Audience?

Of course, just having a purpose for a site isn't enough: you need to consider a site's audience. Notice how often sites reflect the organizational structure of a company rather than the needs of the customer. The goal is always to keep the user at the center of the discussion. Before building a site, make sure to answer some simple audience questions:

- Are the users coming from within your organization, or from outside?
- Are they young or old?
- What language do they speak?
- When do they visit the site?
- What technologies do they support?
- What browsers do they use?

Figuring out an audience doesn't have to be that hard, but don't assume that your audience is too large. People from South America or the Sudan can visit your Web page—but do they? Should they? It is important to be realistic about the audience of the Web. The Web has millions of users, but they aren't all going to visit a particular Web site. If they did, things probably wouldn't work well. When the idea of a site's audience is discussed, don't think in terms of a nameless, faceless John Q. Cybercitizen with a modem and an America Online account. When thinking about users, try to get as specific as possible, and even ask users, if possible.

If you already have a site set up, you have a wealth of information about your users—your server logs. Logs can tell you quite a bit about your user base. Depending on the server and its configuration, you can learn the time of day that you get the most hits, the pages visited the most, the browsers and versions being used, the domains your visitors come from, and even the pages that referred visitors to your site. From the logs, you can even infer connection speeds, based on delivery time between pages. If you do not have a server running yet, begin with your best estimate of the kinds of visitors you expect. Once the site is running, check the logs against your estimates—you may find that your audience is different than you expected. An important point in Web design is that you must be willing to revise your designs, even going as far as throwing away your favorite ideas, if they do not fit with your actual audience.

Who Will Pay for It?

Sites cost money to produce, so they generally have to produce some benefit to continue. While people do put up sites for personal enjoyment, even this type of site has limits in terms of an individual's investment of time and money. It is very important to understand the business model of the site. Only a year or two ago, many corporate Web budgets were not always the first concern, due to the novelty of the technology. Today, however, Web sites often have to prove that they're "worth it." The money has to come from somewhere.

A site's creator could pay for everything, but that probably isn't reasonable unless the Web site is for pure enjoyment or is nonprofit. Typically, some funds have to be collected, probably indirectly, to support the site. For example, while a promotional site for a movie may not directly collect revenues, it can influence the audience and have some impact on the success or failure of the film. Interestingly, many Web sites are nearly as indirect as a movie promotion site. Measuring the direct benefit of having such sites can be very difficult. More directly measurable sites are those on which leads are collected or goods are sold. Some value can be put on these transactions, and an understanding of the benefit of the site can be determined.

Harder to track, but no less valuable, are Web sites for customer service and support. Placing product information or manuals online, or posting URLs for Frequently Asked Questions (FAQs) lists on your products, enables your customers to answer many of their own questions. Not only can this directly reduce the load on your customer service and support organizations, it also fosters good will among your customer base. When a customer is shopping around, the vendor who makes it easiest for them to obtain the information they are looking for tends to have an immediate advantage.

Another possible business model for a Web site is to have viewers pay, as in a subscription model. This model's problem is that viewers must be given a convincing reason to pay for the information or service available at the Web site. Making a Web site valuable to a user is tricky, especially considering that value often is both psychological and real. When looking at the value of the information available in an encyclopedia, think about its form. If the encyclopedia's information is in book form, the cost might be as high as $1,000. Put the same information on a CD-ROM, and see if the information can be sold for the same cost. What if the same information is on a Web site? On a CD-ROM, the information probably can be sold for $50 to $100. On a Web site, it goes for even less, particularly if the user only wants to buy a specific piece of information.

Users often place more value on the *delivery* of a good or service than on the good itself. Consider software, for which the design and production of packaging often costs more than reproducing the software itself. The bottom line is that packaging does count. It is no wonder that users often mistakenly overvalue the graphic aspect of a site.

Note   *As information services become more pervasive, consumers will probably begin to value content on the Internet, despite its lack of tangibility.*

Another business model involves getting someone other than the owner or the intended audience of the site to pay. This model typically comes in the form of an advertising-driven site. However, what is interesting about advertising is that a good is actually being sold—the audience. Advertisers are interested in reaching a particular audience and are willing to pay for an advertisement based on the effectiveness of that ad reaching the intended audience. The question is, how can an audience be attracted, measured, and then sold to the advertisers? The obvious approach is to provide some reason for an audience to come to a Web site and identify themselves. This is very difficult. Furthermore, the audience must be accurately measured, so that advertisers have a way to compare audience size from one site to the next and know how to spend their advertising dollars. People often discuss the number of visitors to their site as an indication of value to an advertiser. The advertisers, however, may not care about the number of visitors, unless those visitors are in their target audience.

Regardless of who is paying for the site, some understanding of the costs and benefits of the site is necessary. How much does each visitor actually cost, and what benefit does he or she produce? Understand that the number of visitors doesn't count, even when using the advertising model. The value of the site transcends this figure and addresses the effectiveness of the visitation. In other words, many visits don't necessarily mean success. Having many visitors to an online store who nonetheless make few purchases may mean huge losses, particularly if it costs more to reach each visitor. Even the form of the Web site may affect the cost. For example, because the amount of data delivered from a Web site is generally related directly to the site's variable costs, sending video costs more than sending regular HTML text. High costs for Web site development isn't always bad, particularly if it produces a big payoff. Goals must be set to measure success and understand how to budget Web sites.

Defining Goals

A goal for a site is not the same as its purpose. A *purpose* gives a general idea of what the site is for, whereas a *goal* is very specific. A goal can help define how much should be spent, but goals must be measurable. What is a measurable goal of the site? Selling x dollars worth of product directly via the Web site is a measurable goal, as is selling x dollars of product or service indirectly through leads. Reaching a certain usage level per day, week, or month can be a goal. So is lowering the number of incoming technical support phone calls by a certain amount. Many ways exist to measure the success or failure of a Web project, but measurements generally come in two categories: soft and hard. Hard measurements are those that are easily measured, such as the number of visitors per day. Soft measurements are a little less clear. For example, with a promotional site for a movie, it might be difficult to understand whether the site had any effect on the box office sales.

Why are measurements so important? From a manager's perspective, measurements can be used to determine how much to spend. If a Web site's goal is to produce $10,000 of new sales, then spending $500,000 on the site is not acceptable, unless the site has some other nonmeasurable value that can make up the other $490,000. While this seems like common sense, a clear return on investment or cost benefit is seldom determined for corporate Web sites. Soft measurements can make things difficult, because the effect the Web site may have is unclear. In the advertising industry, certain rules of thumb apply, such as spending ten percent of overall sales on advertising. A percentage of that would obviously go toward a Web site. Due to the hype surrounding the Web, very little business sense is exhibited toward Web development. Even if sites were considered as little more than online brochures, it is obvious that the more brochures printed on paper, the more expensive. The more pages, the more expensive. The more complicated, the more expensive. Web sites are the same way.

Note *Both on paper and on the Web, economies of scale do reduce the per-unit cost; but a point of diminishing returns still exists. Web sites often have diminishing returns that are ignored. For example, the expense of making a site engineered perfectly for every situation and every browser provides only a little more benefit than one engineered for most users, from a financial point of view. Interestingly, Web experts tend to get somewhat religious on the point of how a site should be implemented. However, in the face of managerial and financial realities, things can't always be done perfectly.*

Defining Scope

After you define a site's goals, you need to define what is necessary to reach your goals. You might call this *defining scope*. One thing to remember, though—scope equals money. Because of the flexible nature of the Web, many developers want to add as much as possible to the Web site. However, more isn't always better. The more that is added to the Web site, the more it costs. Furthermore, having too much information makes finding essential information difficult.

To think about scope, return to one of the first steps in the process. What is the main purpose of the site? Shouldn't the information of the site reflect this purpose? Looking at the Web, this doesn't always seem to be the case. Have you ever gone to a site and not understood its point?

Finding the essentials of a Web site might not be easy, particularly if it has many purposes or many parties involved in its development. One approach is to have a brainstorming session, in which users provide ideas. Each idea is then written down on a 3×5 card. After all the cards have been created, ask the users to sort the cards into piles. First, sort the cards into similar piles to see how things are related. Next, sort the piles in order of importance. What is important can eventually be distilled out of the cards. Remember to cut down the number of cards, to make people focus on what is truly important.

Instead of coming up with ideas of what should go into a site to meet a particular goal or goals, you may be tempted to take existing materials, such as marketing pieces, and convert them to the Web. Unfortunately, creating the content of the site based solely on text and pictures from manuals, brochures, and other support materials rarely works. Migrating text from print to the Web is troublesome, because the media are so different. Reading onscreen has been proven to be much slower than reading from paper. In practice, people tend not to read information online carefully. They tend to scan it quickly and then print what they need. In this sense, writing for paper tends to go against screen reading. Think about newspaper or TV news stories: the main point is stated first and then discussed. This goes against the slow buildup of many paper documents, which carefully spell out a point. With visitors skimming the site, key bullet points tend to be read while detailed information is skipped. The main thing is to keep the points obvious and simple. Even if information is presented well, poor organization can ruin all the hard work in preparing the information. If a viewer can't find the information, who cares how great it looks or how well it reads?

Organization of Information

Organizing the information at a Web site is often just as important as the information itself. If visitors to a Web site can't find what they are looking for, they may get frustrated and leave. Organizing information is a matter of grouping similar items in the same place. The card-sorting discussion in the previous section helps define what items should go together.

Tree Structure

Site designers often use a *tree structure* or hierarchy for their sites, as shown in Figure 2-3.

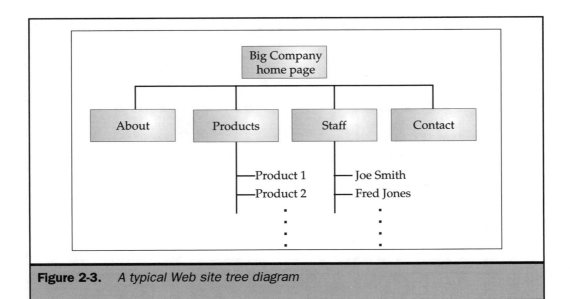

Figure 2-3. *A typical Web site tree diagram*

While the tree structure seems the most appropriate choice for Web sites, you still need to decide how many choices should be at the top level, and how wide versus how deep the tree should be. If too many choices are at the top level, the structure is flat and may be confusing. Forcing people farther down the tree can be frustrating, because it requires them to keep moving, level by level, to find the appropriate information. The depth versus breadth issue is illustrated in Figure 2-4.

From the initial studies on hypertext, the following are the three "golden rules":

- Hypertext is a body of information organized into numerous fragments. By definition, most Web sites—unless they are a single page—should fit this rule.

- These fragments relate to each other somehow. If the site doesn't have a clear goal, the relationship between pages might not be obvious.

- The user needs only a small fraction of the information presented at any time.

Sites that are too flat and provide all the choices all the time confuse the user by presenting too many choices. How many choices are okay? Studies suggest that the optimal number of choices is between five and nine, because users can retain the choices in short-term memory fairly easily. Too many choices make the selection process suboptimal, and the user may focus on extremes, such as the first item, last item, or center item. Too few choices may indicate that you are creating a needless layer; a long sequence of pages with only two choices on each may simply slow things down. Combining some of those choices on fewer pages might be better. Structuring the site appropriately may help improve a user's interaction with information. Unfortunately, sometimes the hierarchy is considered the only structure appropriate for a Web site.

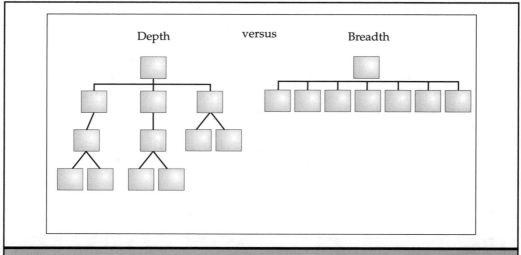

Figure 2-4.   *Depth versus breadth in a tree structure*

Pure Linear Structure

Web-based information doesn't necessarily have to be structured in the form of a tree. Sometimes, a *pure linear* organization, with one page after another, makes sense. A slide show, tour, or presentation probably should be in the form of a linear progression. (At one level, because of the browser's Back button, linear Web sites are always bidirectional as well.) The basic idea of a linear structure is shown in Figure 2-5.

Linear Structure with Alternatives

Another approach might be a *linear progression with alternatives*: a series of yes and no questions that eventually lead to the next question in the sequence. An effective application of the linear with alternatives structure comes in the form of an AIDS awareness site that discusses risk factors in a yes and no question fashion, but eventually leads to the next risk category, regardless of the choice. This gives the site a false sense of interactivity, which engages the viewer more than a pure linear structure. The linear form with alternatives is shown in Figure 2-6.

Linear Structure with Options

Another form of organization is the *linear with options* structure. This structure, shown in Figure 2-7, is good for a set of information that is sometimes optional. For example, in many surveys, the survey taker is asked to skip a set of questions, depending on his or her answer. A Web form of such a survey would be a perfect candidate for linear with options, because it allows the reader to skip over questions that are not relevant, while still preserving the general path of the information.

Linear Structure with Side Trips

The *linear with side trips* structure is perfect for a body of information that may have useful supplementary information. For example, a linear Web presentation about flowers may lead to a side trip about beekeeping that the user can view, but later return to the main discussion, as shown in Figure 2-8. This form of site provides diversion while still preserving the path. Linear with side trips is a form of tree structure—just turn the structure on its side. When used with linear content, it warrants its own discussion.

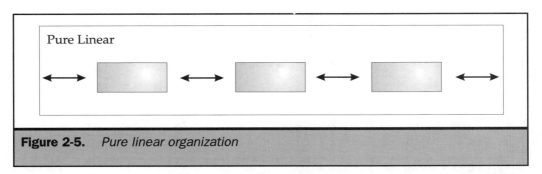

Figure 2-5.   *Pure linear organization*

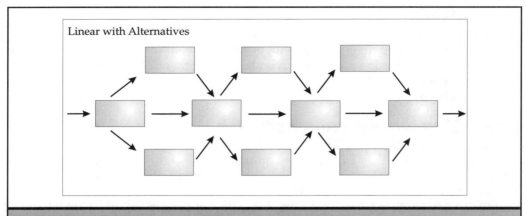

Figure 2-6. *Linear structure with alternatives*

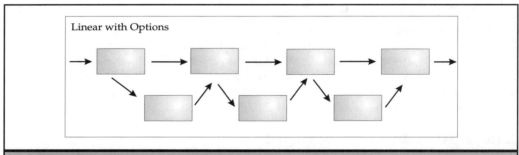

Figure 2-7. *Linear structure with options*

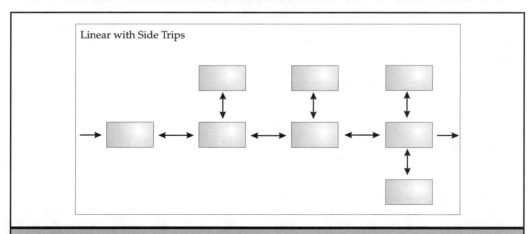

Figure 2-8. *Linear structure with side trips*

Grid-Style Structure

One uncommon form of structuring information, at least on the Web, is the *grid style*. The grid style has a great degree of spatial organization, as do many of the linear forms. The grid provides a sense of up, down, left, and right. Because of its regular structure, the grid form is good for related items and organization, such as items that might be found in a catalog. Imagine the columns of the grid being associated with a particular product line, and the nodes representing the products in that particular product line. Moving across columns might be like moving among equivalent products between product lines. The basic idea of the grid is shown in Figure 2-9.

The tree structure or hierarchy is much less structured than the grid. A narrow hierarchy provides few choices for the user, but requires many clicks to get to the destination. On the other hand, the wide hierarchy provides many choices, so it requires fewer clicks to get to the destination information, assuming the user makes the correct decisions. This is the same discussion illustrated earlier in Figure 2-4. Both forms of the tree provide some spatial organization, but there is a question of how much. The wider the tree, the less structured the information.

Mixed Hierarchy

To balance the problems of hierarchies, many developers consider a mixed form. The idea of skips ahead or alternatives was previously discussed in relationship to the linear structure. How about adding a skip ahead to a tree structure? A special link from the top of the tree could lead directly to an important piece of information. This often is seen in Web sites in which a special button on the home page links directly to the free download or another important item. Deeper in the site, it may be useful to provide a catalog, so the grid structure makes sense. Perhaps in another part of the site, a presentation should be used, so the linear style makes sense. Most complex Web sites are actually mixed hierarchies, as shown in Figure 2-10.

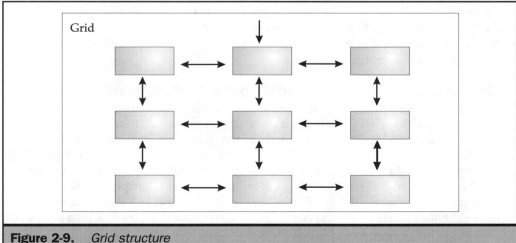

Figure 2-9. *Grid structure*

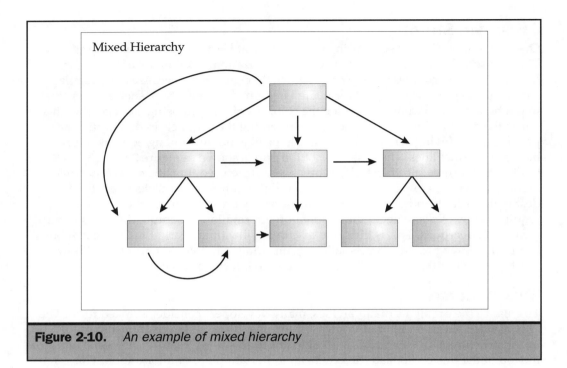

Mixed Hierarchy

Figure 2-10.   *An example of mixed hierarchy*

Pure Web Structure

The problem with the mixed hierarchy is that it can easily degrade into the pure Web form, which is a tangled mess of links in which the organization is unclear. All sense of spatiality is lost in the pure Web form. The only navigational sense is "signpost based," whereby the viewer recognizes landmarks in the site, such as the home page. The benefit of the pure Web form is obvious if the user is familiar with the data, because navigating among items that are fully connected is easy. However, the organization may be so unclear that the confusion factor drives users away. An example of a pure Web structure is shown in Figure 2-11.

Balancing Linear and Web Information Structures

When organizing information, the aim is to achieve a balance between predictability and expressiveness. Although the Web form may be very expressive, it may be completely unpredictable as far as the user is concerned. On the other hand, the linear form is very predictable, but not terribly expressive. The balance of these forms is shown in Figure 2-12. A temptation is to add links anywhere you *can*. This was commonly seen in early Web sites, wherein any word that referred to a different topic became a hyperlink. Resist this temptation. When you are adding a link, ask yourself "Does this link add value to the audience?" If the answer is "No," then the link is inappropriate. Every link is an invitation for the user to break away from the content on that page.

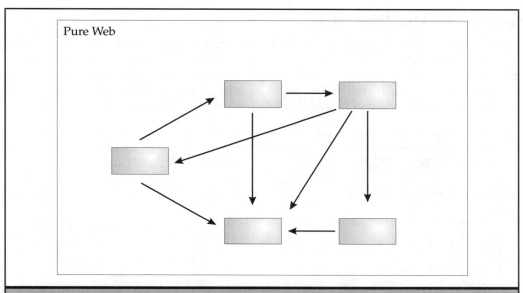

Figure 2-11.   *An example of pure Web structure*

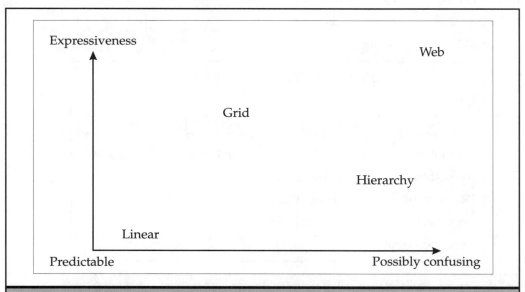

Figure 2-12.   *A balance of linear and Web information structures*

Determining the Site Plan

After you determine the purpose, content, and structure of the site, you can develop a plan. The plan should consist of a time line, a document that describes what is needed and how the site will be put together, and a flow chart of the site, as shown in Figure 2-13.

For small projects, this formality might be overkill. On larger projects, however, approaching the task without a sense of where the project is going is foolish. If the site

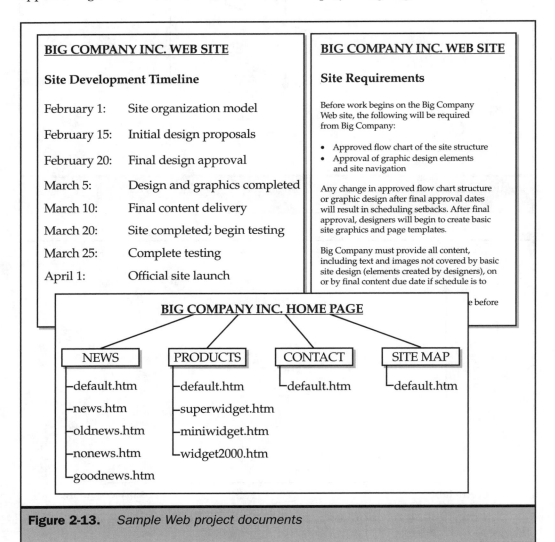

BIG COMPANY INC. WEB SITE

Site Development Timeline

February 1:	Site organization model
February 15:	Initial design proposals
February 20:	Final design approval
March 5:	Design and graphics completed
March 10:	Final content delivery
March 20:	Site completed; begin testing
March 25:	Complete testing
April 1:	Official site launch

BIG COMPANY INC. WEB SITE

Site Requirements

Before work begins on the Big Company Web site, the following will be required from Big Company:

- Approved flow chart of the site structure
- Approval of graphic design elements and site navigation

Any change in approved flow chart structure or graphic design after final approval dates will result in scheduling setbacks. After final approval, designers will begin to create basic site graphics and page templates.

Big Company must provide all content, including text and images not covered by basic site design (elements created by designers), on or by final content due date if schedule is to

BIG COMPANY INC. HOME PAGE

NEWS
- default.htm
- news.htm
- oldnews.htm
- nonews.htm
- goodnews.htm

PRODUCTS
- default.htm
- superwidget.htm
- miniwidget.htm
- widget2000.htm

CONTACT
- default.htm

SITE MAP
- default.htm

Figure 2-13.   *Sample Web project documents*

is developed commercially, such planning is mandatory. Without a sense of what goes into the site, how can a vendor price the site? People often ask Web developers how much a site costs, but this depends on the size, scope, and technology that goes into the site, among other factors. A company with a comprehensive site plan can send the project out for bids. Without a plan, comparing proposals from competing firms provides little information of value. Notice that, up until this point, no specific discussion of what the site will look like or how it works has been addressed. These tasks are part of the implementation phase.

Implementation

Readers might assume that the implementation phase of the Web publishing process is the most difficult; but, depending on how well the site was planned, it may be very straightforward. With a clear plan in hand, a site can be built very quickly. When the various parts of the site are well defined, many people can work on the site simultaneously. Even so, the implementation phase of a Web project does involve potential problems.

Gathering and Creating the Content

One of the first signs of trouble is when content isn't ready for the Web, or you have too much content. When planning a Web site, people often provide ideas for things that would be nice to put in, with no consideration of the cost. Information can be formatted quickly—but if the information doesn't exist, formatting can't take place. While this sounds like common sense, it is probably the second-most common problem on the Web, beyond purpose.

Just ask yourself what "under construction" means. Why do so many sites have many choices, but 90 percent of the pages are "under construction"? Wouldn't these sites be better if only the working areas were available? This highlights the problem of not having the content ready. The cost of developing the content often outweighs the cost of preparing it for the Web. A good plan pares the site down to what it should do and considers the cost of creating the content. Without content, the site goes nowhere. Navigation buttons and yellow-and-black animated pictures of men digging up a road don't make a good site. The client's inability to produce content on time causes commercial Web design projects to be late more often than does the firm's inability to finish the technology or graphics in a timely manner.

While we're on the subject, don't place "under construction" images on your pages. All Web sites are either under construction or stagnant. If an area of the site isn't ready for visitors, don't place the links to that area online yet. If users are unaware that an area exists, they won't be disappointed that it isn't ready. Finding a link to something you need, only to discover that it is "under construction" is highly frustrating.

Visual Design

After you have the content in hand, you can produce the visual design. Why can't visual design come before content generation? One simple reason: the visual style of the site should reflect the content of the site. Until the content is close to being finished, any developed visual style can only provide decoration. It won't add any real value to the content. Consider product literature on a Web site. What happens if the visual design is developed first, in a very corporate style, but the copy is written in a sarcastic, unprofessional tone? The site won't make much sense.

Visuals should be discussed early to set the tone of the site, but the specifics of exactly what shade of red to use or what size an image should be must wait until the implementation phase. The visual design phase generally requires that paper designs first be explored. Then, image composites can be created by using a tool such as Adobe Photoshop. The choice of a particular look and feel depends on the purpose of the site, the look and feel of related materials, technological considerations such as download time, and personal taste.

Another reason not to approach visual design too early in the development process is that the goals of the site may change. It is very frustrating to put together a visual design that is based on having five choices on the home page, only to have the number of sections increased to eight later on. Although accounting for changes that occur later in a project is impossible, by not developing graphics and navigation until after the structure and content of the site is set, you usually can avoid a great deal of rework.

Graphic designers are generally the best people to approach to make a good-looking site. Unfortunately, designers often attempt to imitate directly the existing print materials. This doesn't always work well. Subtle textures will be lost onscreen, complex gradients will translate into large-byte–sized images, and bleeds generally won't work.

Often, the best approach is to keep the spirit of existing materials and fit them to suit the needs of the Web. This doesn't give Web designers license to reinvent the corporate look and feel, but it does enable them to modify an approach so that it creates a visually stimulating page that downloads quickly. This balance between visual appeal and download speed—combined with the imprecise layout afforded by HTML and unpredictable viewing environments—is what makes Web design so challenging. The best Web designers know enough about Web technology to work within its constraints. Web designers with graphics backgrounds occasionally undervalue the sense of organization that may have been applied to a site, and want to move sections around. Be careful not to let the visual designer disrupt labeling and organization schemes based on his or her personal taste.

Technology Design

Far too many Web sites are developed as glorified brochures with big pictures. However, the best modern sites often *do* something and are more like software than printed documents. Many sites provide searching features, and some sites enable users to purchase products or even play games. Very advanced sites automatically configure themselves according to the visitor's preferences or browser type.

After adding technology—such as a database, interactive forms, or programmed objects like Java applets—to the mixture, the Web becomes more like software and less like print media. In this sense, some effort must be made to select the appropriate technology for the job and to integrate the look and content properly. As sites become more complex, appearance will still be important, but much of the effort will go into the technology. The shift from a page paradigm of Web sites to a program paradigm is fast becoming a reality. How programming ideas relate to HTML, the core Web technology, is discussed in depth starting in Chapter 12.

Producing the HTML

While visuals and technical elements are very important to Web design, the heart of nearly every modern Web page is still HTML. Although it is possible to use an embedded media type to build a complex Web page that consists of a single HTML element, such as **<EMBED SRC="bigbinary.dcr" HEIGHT="200" WIDTH="500">**, HTML is still required. In the strictest sense, all Web pages must contain *some* HTML, regardless of whether the focus and content are in an embedded binary object.

As discussed in Chapter 1, HTML is a text markup language that is used to describe the structure of a page. Until recently, HTML was also used to describe the appearance of the page. This is no longer the preferred way to do things. Presentation should be left to style sheets, as discussed in Chapter 10, but that isn't how most pages have been created to date. HTML often serves as the bridge between the content of a page and the interactive objects (such as scripts and programmed objects) that may also be part of the Web site.

In many ways, HTML provides the framework on which a Web page is built. The images, text content, and programming are equally important, but HTML is necessary to bring it all together. Because of this, some people view putting together a Web site as being similar to putting together a puzzle—just assemble the pieces. This analogy would be appropriate if the puzzle had to be designed and the pieces had to be created, broken apart, and then put back together. Given the pieces of a site, how can HTML be used to create the pages?

The creation of an HTML document for publishing on the Web is as simple as using the text editor of your choice (vi, Microsoft Word, Notepad, and so on) to insert into the text the markup tags that indicate the format and links. Or, you could use a conversion program that converts files into HTML automatically. For example, you can quickly convert Word 97 files or Rich Text Format (RTF) documents into HTML. The conversion program preserves paragraphs, character formatting, and so on. However, the translated file may have to be checked and cleaned up. Furthermore, the translation program may not add links and other items that are necessary for Web publishing, if they weren't indicated in the original document.

Today, HTML editors are commonplace. Some editors for Windows, such as HoTMetaL Pro (http://www.softquad.com), HomeSite (http://www.allaire.com), and Hot Dog (http://www.sausage.com), show the insertion of the actual HTML tags into the document directly. Some of these tools are very simple tag-insertion programs, while others are sophisticated markup tools that are similar to programmers' editing tools, such as Allaire's HomeSite, shown in Figure 2-14.

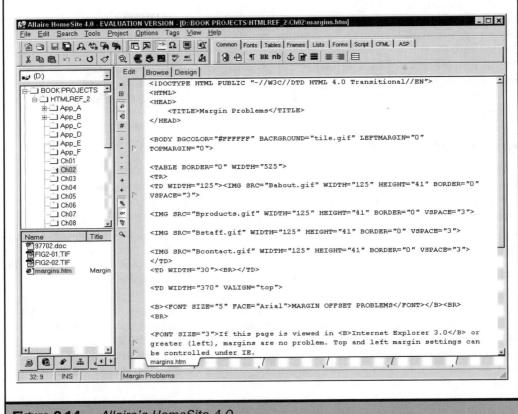

Figure 2-14.   *Allaire's HomeSite 4.0*

Other editing environments provide WYSIWYG (what you see is what you get) editing of pages, which keeps the HTML tags hidden behind the scenes. These products include Netscape Composer (http://www.netscape.com), GoLive CyberStudio (http://www.golive.com), and Microsoft FrontPage (http://www. microsoft.com/frontpage). Traditional WYSIWYG desktop publishing tools, such as PageMaker, QuarkXPress, and Microsoft Word, also now support automatic HTML output.

Although Figure 2-15 makes Web page development with a WYSIWYG editor seem much easier than a tagging-oriented editor, the entire concept of WYSIWYG Web page design is somewhat flawed. As stated in Chapter 1, the browser is the final determinant of how a page will look. If a page is composed in one program and rendered under its internal display engine, no guarantee exists that it will appear the same way under another browser's rendering engine. This idea is illustrated in Figure 2-16.

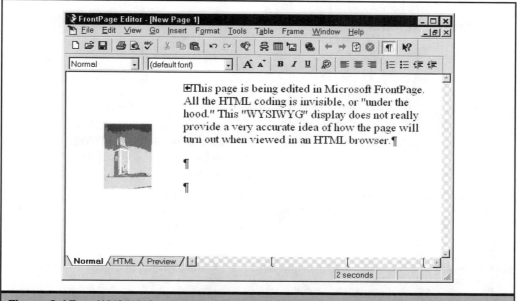

Figure 2-15. *WYSIWYG editing under FrontPage 98*

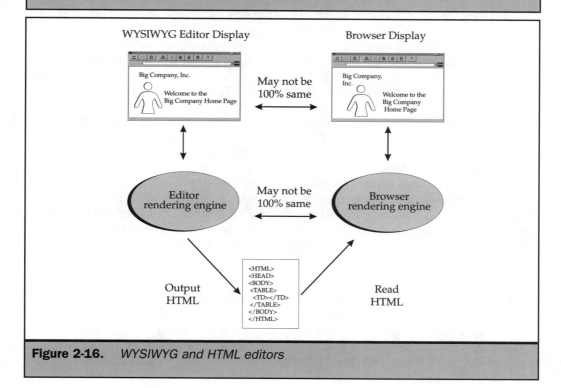

Figure 2-16. *WYSIWYG and HTML editors*

Method	Pros	Cons
By hand	Allows strict control Allows use of latest tags	Error prone Slow Requires knowledge of HTML
Translator	Provides fast translation of existing documents	Requires manual editing
Tag editor	Provides tight control Faster than by hand	Requires knowledge of HTML Makes previsualization of the page difficult
WYSIWYG editor	Easy to use Requires no knowledge of HTML	Often behind in tag support May make manual editing or generated pages difficult Not really WYSIWYG

Table 2-1.   *HTML Creation Issues*

Choosing the right Web tool for the job is not easy. In many cases, HTML tools are useful only to get a "first cut" of an HTML document. Manual editing of a Web document may still be necessary, to create superior hypermedia documents using the latest HTML features. Furthermore, HTML tools tend to take a "one-page-at-a-time" view of the world. In the case of large-scale sites, it might be better to create a template of a standard page and flow content into it directly. Table 2-1 compares the pros and cons of using particular methods to create Web pages.

The tool that you use to compose your HTML is a matter of both taste and applicability. In some cases, a WYSIWYG editor provides a good enough solution, particularly considering the ease with which the page can be created. For situations in which tight control is demanded, a tagging editor may be in order. If a quick change to fix a typo is all that is needed, then a text editor works just fine. A large volume of files might warrant a translation tool. In practicality, no single tool fits all jobs. Don't dismiss WYSIWYG tools for editors because they are easy. Many large Web firms still generate Web pages by hand, though the pages are populated automatically with a database. Just remember that creation of the HTML is only part of the job.

Testing

After you create a site or page, you must test it. Testing, in the basic sense, requires checking the page under a particular set of browsers to see whether it looks proper. Unfortunately, Web page authors often mistakenly assume that if a page looks fine under their own browsers, then it will look fine under other browsers. The same page under WebTV and Netscape Navigator might appear very different. So, on which browsers should the site look perfect? This gets back to the issue of audience. If the primary audience is AOL users, then obviously the site should be heavily tested under such conditions. The idea is to make sure that you don't lock out people from viewing your site.

Unfortunately, some HTML pundits take the idea of "audience" to an extreme. "The site should be available to everyone" is their rallying cry. While this is true in theory, in reality, limited budgets often make this ideal difficult, given other project goals. The sad fact is that the Web isn't nearly as open as people like to think. Many sites don't work well under certain browsers, particularly more esoteric browsers or those made for users with accessibility issues, such as blind users. However, a little effort can go a long way to improve a site, such as using alternative text for browsers that can't render images or ensuring that the site works under the more common browsers.

Getting past the basics can be difficult, though. For example, testing a site for compatibility with all browsers is one problem. HTML theory says that if a page conforms to standard HTML, it works. But browsers don't always work properly and don't always conform to HTML standards. Even among the same brand of browser, "slight problems" creep in that can cause huge problems. For example, under Netscape 3, each platform (Macintosh, Windows, and UNIX) has a different margin offset. For designers attempting to place an image on a background, these differences are infuriating, as shown in Figure 2-17.

Testing is a big issue, particularly as the paradigm moves closer to a programming one. Under a true programming paradigm, sloppy coding and lax testing—which previously may have resulted in an odd-looking page, a broken link, or a strangely colored image—may result in a user's system crashing. Making sure that a complex page works under all situations can be very difficult. Even if the world only consisted of two browsers, how many permutations exist? For example, Netscape Navigator has generations 1.x, 2.x, 3.x, 4.x, and 4.5x, each of which is available on three major platforms (Mac, UNIX, and Windows), as well as numerous beta versions. And this doesn't even take into account a "professional" or Gold edition, the numerous other ports (such as the one for OS/2), or foreign-language versions. All of these permutations may have subtle differences. Now, add in Internet Explorer, with 2.x, 3.x, 4.x, and 5.x generations on Mac, Windows, and UNIX, and you find that literally dozens of test possibilities exist.

In most cases, things aren't so bad, but you can learn some real lessons from browser testing. A simple JavaScript program works fine on Netscape 3 under Windows, but crashes the Macintosh every time. The UNIX version doesn't even support the calls used, while Internet Explorer 3 works fine, but under a new beta, exhibits strange behavior. These are just a few examples of real problems.

Browser and system testing isn't the end of testing. User testing is probably the most important part of testing a site. Do the users know what to do? Do they like the site? Getting some users to evaluate a site and make suggestions for improvements is probably the single most-important thing that a site developer can do. A site may seem okay to its developers, but they are too close to it to know what's wrong. Customers are rarely as familiar with a product line as the people selling it, so it is no wonder they don't know that part number XG57-6 is the "Super Widget." Having the site looked

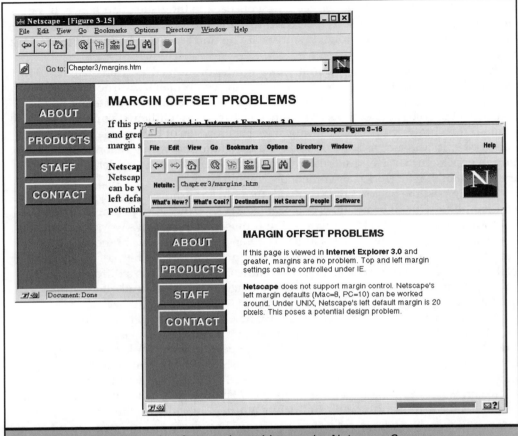

Figure 2-17.   *An example of a margin problem under Netscape 3*

over by a variety of people removes many embarrassing gaffes. The good thing about the Web is that, unlike print, it is easy to fix. This shouldn't be used as an excuse to put up subpar work first and plan to fix it later; but, instead, it should be viewed as an acknowledgment of the medium's flexibility and the reality that sites change over time.

Maintenance

Sites are born, live, and die. Far too often, sites are born full grown and slowly die due to neglect. A Web site is not a building that is rarely expanded once it's finished. It's more like a tree. Most sites continually grow and change. Occasionally, whole sections might be pruned, while other sections grow out of control like a sucker at the trunk of the tree. Many times, the original creators of a site don't think about the future, and stunt the growth of a site by not designing with room to expand. The original creators may move on to other sites or get bored of the task and assign it to another person. Sometimes, the new owners rip up the site and start fresh. Other times, they take the site in a whole new direction.

For the long life of a Web site, you must realize early that the site is always under construction and always growing. The original budget to develop a site might be a fraction of the overall cost to keep the site running, even if little new material is added. As the site continues, needs change. The purpose of the site may have to be reevaluated. A future phase of the Web site may require a whole new look or a section to sell goods online. This suggests that the whole process needs to start over with planning, implementation, and all the other steps.

The Phases of Web Site Development

The following are the four basic phases of Web site development (professionals versed in software engineering should note the basic similarity to the well-known, but not always followed, process of software development):

- **Planning**   Setting goals, specifying content, organizing content, and setting the user interface to navigate content

- **Implementing**   Creating content, implementing navigation and the user interface, and coding the site, which may include HTML, programming, and database development

- **Testing**   User, browser, and system testing

- **Maintenance**   Maintaining and updating the site, questioning old goals, and returning to the planning stage

Each phase listed has distinct subphases that can be expanded to provide more detail. For example, planning could include determining an audience, setting a budget, and performing other project-oriented tasks. Following the software-engineering comparison inevitably leads to a discussion of CASE (Computer Aided Software Engineering) tools, which in many ways are similar to emerging tools for Web development, such as Microsoft's Visual InterDev and Allaire's ColdFusion Studio. HTML tools alone provide only a small bit of help in a much larger process.

HTML's Role in the Web

As emphasized in the previous sections, HTML is just one part of a larger process for building and delivering Web pages. The Web includes the pages themselves, built with technologies such as HTML, the software and hardware that serve up the pages, the Internet and its connectivity issues, and the browsers that render the pages. When you get right down to it, the document author has very little control over anything other than the structure of the page. How quickly it gets to an end user, and what it looks like on the end user's browser, can vary over time and from browser to browser. This is a very aggravating aspect of publishing on the Web. The Web also allows open access to any platform, which is what makes it so powerful. An interesting exercise is to look at the Web as a community and try to understand why HTML is used the way that it is. Reviewing the history of the Web reveals the fundamental aspects of HTML's role on the Web and the issues facing this technology.

Historical Roots of HTML

When you consider why HTML is the way that it is, ask a simple question: do you know for sure what kind of computers, screens, or browser types people viewing your Web page have? The answer is no. So many different screen sizes, operating systems, color palettes, and other factors exist that creating software on all systems would be a nightmare.

Imagine, then, the problem faced by Tim Berners-Lee, a researcher at the Conseil Europeen pour Recherche Nucleaire (CERN) laboratory in Geneva, Switzerland. In 1989, Berners-Lee had the task of creating a hypertext delivery environment that could be used as an interface to scientific information, and that could render this information equally well on Macintosh systems with small screens, NeXT Workstations, IBM PCs, and a variety of other platforms. Rather than give up because of the variations in screen support, Berners-Lee developed the first versions of HTML, opting to concentrate on providing the content and structure first and worry about the presentation later. This made sense, because the group for whom he was designing the environment consisted of scientists looking at technical information—hardly a group looking for the latest in fonts and graphic design techniques. The presentation would be left up to the browser.

The HTML language eventually was defined as an application of Standard Generalized Markup Language (SGML), which serves as a base for defining markup languages. Much of the flavor of HTML as a structured language (instead of a presentation language) comes from this relationship with SGML.

> **Note** *Nothing indicates that the original designers of the Web didn't care about presentation—plenty of evidence suggests that they did. But the project was intended to evolve over time and fundamental issues, such as linking, structure, and network delivery, had to be resolved first.*

Deployed by late 1991, the Web grew slowly at first. In its infancy, it was characterized by a textual interface that was unattractive and somewhat difficult to use. However, much of the infrastructure necessary to make the Web work— including basic HTML, HTTP, and MIME—was in place long before the Web took off.

Mosaic: The Web Community Changes

While the division of structure and style suggested by HTML was a good design decision, it has proven to be a huge point of contention in the Web community. At first, the Web community was a homogenous bunch of folks, mostly researchers and academics. As the Web matured and its community expanded, however, calls arose to make it easier to use and for it to provide multimedia facilities.

In 1993, Marc Andreessen, an undergraduate working for the National Center for Supercomputing Applications (NCSA) in Illinois, was involved, with others, in developing a graphical browser for the Web. This graphical browser, called Mosaic, made the Web much easier to use. The most influential aspect of the Mosaic browser was its introduction of inline images, making the Web a visual experience. Mosaic took the Internet world by storm. The number of Web servers exploded into the hundreds, and then thousands, within months of the browser's release. Soon, the Web landscape was dominated by media, marketing, entertainment, and commercial Web sites of all shapes and sizes. In a matter of a few years, the Web community changed significantly to encompass many groups, fewer of which had academic interests.

Commercial and entertainment professionals can agree on one important point: presentation matters. In these arenas, how something looks is nearly as important as what it is. As originally designed, the Web did not fit well with these requirements. The first-generation Web provided relatively stark pages, with gray backgrounds and left alignment. In first-generation (Mosaic) pages, centering text was even impossible. Figure 2-18 shows an abstract view of a Web page generated in Mosaic.

Figure 2-18.   *A Mosaic-generated Web page*

The Rise of Netscape

By the spring of 1994, Andreessen and many of his colleagues left NCSA and joined Dr. James Clark, the founder of Silicon Graphics, to form a company originally called Mosaic Communications Corporation. The firm, which later changed its name to Netscape due to legal problems with NCSA, released a preliminary version of its next-generation browser in the fall of 1994. The program, later to be called Netscape Navigator, was nicknamed Mozilla (after Mosaic and Godzilla), because it was intended to be the "monster browser" that would kill Mosaic—and so it did.

By early 1995, Netscape was well entrenched in the marketplace. The reason Netscape dominated the market so easily was that it made significant enhancements to its browser and to HTML in order to improve the performance and look of the Web. For example, Netscape introduced background colors and limited font sizing. It introduced improved page layout, with text flowing around images, centering, and the much-maligned and nearly universally despised **<BLINK>** element. An early Netscape-style page is shown in Figure 2-19.

Many longtime Web professionals complained of Netscape's general disregard for HTML standards and argued in favor of the more standards-based process they felt

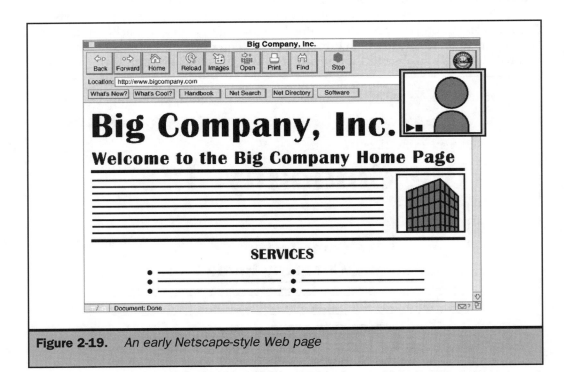

Figure 2-19.   *An early Netscape-style Web page*

should be used to expand the Web. The market, largely oblivious to such concerns, responded well to the improvements. According to most estimates, Netscape was used by nearly 80 percent of the Internet market in 1995. The elements it introduced were used on many Web sites.

The Market Matures: Microsoft Enters

The Web underwent other significant changes during 1995. Larger content producers, including the movie industry and media conglomerates like Time-Warner, embraced the Web. Advertising dollars soon followed. The phenomenal growth of the content on the Web led to the development of such services as Yahoo!, which provide directories or search facilities to navigate the flood of incoming data. Many new browsers were developed in 1995, but none except Microsoft's Internet Explorer posed a serious threat to Netscape Navigator's dominance of the market. Microsoft initially introduced its own features and HTML tags, such as **<MARQUEE>**, in an attempt to extend the presentation of the Web and gain market share. This worked to some degree, but Microsoft later decided to return to its normal approach of "embrace and extend," taking World Wide Web Consortium (W3C) ideas—such as style sheets—and implementing them first.

By 1996, the Web world had turned into a two-party system, with mostly Microsoft and Netscape browsers in use. Still, many other browsers were in use by limited numbers of people. Designers faced with supporting a variety of standards often gave up on cross-platform compatibility and focused on making pages look good under one browser or another. This was an unfortunate turn of events. To this day, many sites lock out users by requesting them to download one browser or another to view proprietary HTML tags on a page. To further complicate the Web, print designers started to force HTML to render pages the way they wanted them rendered. Pixel-level control was the graphic designer's goal, and with tables and graphics layout tricks (discussed in Chapters 6 and 7), they almost achieved it, at times. Of course, pages became increasingly complicated. The HTML being used became more confusing and proprietary. Even now, the Web continues to change.

From Pages to Programs

Many people view the Web simply as a way to deliver documents, or as a digital print distribution system. This is a very narrow view. People want to order things online, play, and communicate through the Web. The Web can do these things, but it means thinking about the Web not as a collection of documents but as a software system. The page view of the Web world is quickly being replaced with a program view of Web sites. Common Gateway Interface (CGI) programs were introduced at the dawn of the Web and are still widely in use. Plug-ins, Java, JavaScript, and ActiveX controls have helped the Web become more and more programmed.

Why have a button on a page to click for a Netscape version or a Microsoft version of the site, when a program can sense the browser type and build the appropriate page? Why design around 640 × 480 screen displays as a minimum, when the resolution can be sensed and the appropriate graphics provided? This is the idea of programmed sites, with pages that are dynamically generated from database information. Pages are no longer just collections of words. They are collections of media objects glued together with programming logic in sophisticated, windowed user interfaces. An example of a multipaned page with multimedia elements is shown in Figure 2-20.

The programmed page introduces new issues for HTML and Web development. With new programming facilities available, pages are more complex. With the rise in complexity, it is unrealistic to expect one person to have all the talents to build a Web site. Furthermore, complex Web sites need a rigorous approach to building Web sites. As this approach to Web site creation becomes more common, the concept of Web site publishing will likely be supplanted by the idea of "Web site engineering."

Figure 2-20.   *Advanced Web page style*

Issues Facing HTML and the Web

The common issue of HTML always seems to be one of structure and style. HTML can be used to structure documents, but it doesn't yet provide all the features necessary to make them look the way the author wants. This is one of the inherent compromises of the Web, but it isn't the only issue facing HTML and the Web:

- *The Web and HTML are still relatively new.* In the commercial sense, the Web is only a few years old. Many things remain to be worked out. Users expect perfect presentation and CD-ROM–like interfaces. HTML doesn't provide these features, but extensions, style sheets, and binary formats will. However, with an increasing arena of different browsing options, compatibility across platforms may be an issue for a long time to come.

- *A Web browser is easy to use, but finding things isn't so simple.* The Web needs more organization. Web search facilities, metadata, linking features, and addressing need to be improved.

- *The Web needs to be more responsive.* This isn't so much an issue with HTML or Web servers, but with the medium of delivery. The protocols and the network have to be improved so that people are satisfied with the responsiveness of Web sites. The introduction of multimedia elements and CD-ROM–like interfaces only worsens the hunger for bandwidth.

- *The Web has to be useful.* Programmed pages are useful. Ordering tickets, playing games, communicating, and finding information is what the Web is all about. HTML will have to support programming technologies, so that pages are more dynamic and sites that interact with the user become easier to build.

Summary

The process of creating a large Web site is more than just putting together some text with images and HTML. While a simple site with a few pages might not take a great deal of forethought, a little planning can go a long way, even for a small site. What is the site supposed to do? How should it look? What should it say? What is its goal? Who is the target audience? What is the site's value? Setting a goal can help ensure the future success of the site, particularly if the value of the site can be measured. Determining what the site should do, given a particular goal, might be hard, particularly with many competing purposes. Isolating the core essence of the site is possible, using some known techniques. Once content and purpose are determined, the shape and structure of the site can be set. At this point, the Web page author has a blueprint to follow while gathering the raw materials that make it up (images, text, and other content). The content and navigation can then be assembled by using Web technologies such as HTML.

After the site is built, it must be thoroughly tested, because it is created for the benefit of users, not authors. Web sites are not static—they evolve. The mission of the site may change over time. Its look and technology may become dated. The process of Web publishing is an endless loop. HTML plays only a small role in the overall development of a site, but it is an important role. The history of the Web shows that at the core of every Web page is HTML. While the future moves the Web in the direction of programmed sites, no reason exists to think that HTML will become extinct. If anything, understanding the language, its syntax, and its purpose is integral to Web mastery. Chapter 3 begins the discussion of HTML with an overview of commonly used aspects of the language.

Chapter 3

Introduction to Common HTML

This chapter provides a detailed introduction to common HTML, the form of HTML used in most Web pages. HTML 4 and its predecessors, HTML 3.2 and 2, are the starting point for this chapter, which discusses the specifications and official rules. How the rules are often broken is also discussed, particularly when the workarounds are useful, although there are reasons why you should avoid breaking the rules. As new Web technologies appear with increasing regularity, however, workarounds may no longer be necessary. This chapter is at the introductory level, but it does not provide "cookbook" HTML. Seasoned HTML authors might want to read on, because the inline notes and some of the explanations might present previously unknown nuances of the elements.

HTML Overview

As mentioned in Chapter 1, Hypertext Markup Language (HTML) is a structured markup language that is used to create Web pages. A markup language such as HTML is simply a collection of codes, called *elements*, that are used to indicate the structure and format of a document. A user agent, usually a Web browser that renders the document, interprets the meaning of these codes to figure how to structure or display a document. Elements in HTML consist of alphanumeric tokens within angle brackets, such as **<B>**, **<HTML>**, **<IMG>**, and **<HR>**.

Most elements consist of paired tags: a *start tag* and an *end tag*. The start tag is simply a mnemonic symbol for the element surrounded by angle brackets. For example, the symbol for bold text is **B** and its start tag is **<B>**. An end tag is identical to a start tag, except that the symbol for an end tag is preceded by a forward slash: **</B>**. An element's instruction applies to whatever content is contained between its start and end tags:

```
<B>This text is bold</B> but this text is not.
```

While most tags come in pairs, exceptions exist. Some elements don't require an end tag because they don't enclose content. These elements are referred to as *empty elements*. One example is the break element, **
, which indicates a line break. Finally, for some elements, such as the paragraph element, **<P>, an end tag is optional—though highly encouraged.

The HTML specification defines the type of content that an element can enclose. This is known as an element's *content model*. The content that may be enclosed by an element may include other elements, text, a mixture of elements and text, or nothing at all. For example, the **<HEAD>** element provides general information about an HTML document. Its content model allows it to contain only a small number of related elements, such as **<TITLE>** and **<META>**. The content model for the bold element, **<B>**, allows it to enclose text and some elements, such as the one for italic, **<I>**, but not others, such as **<HEAD>**. The content model of the break element, **
**, is *empty*, as mentioned earlier, because it encloses no content. Content models define the relationships that are possible between elements and content in valid HTML documents. The content model should suggest that HTML is actually a very structured language, despite how it is often coded.

An HTML start tag can sometimes contain attributes that modify the element's meaning. Attributes within a tag's brackets must be separated from the element's name by at least one space. Some attributes indicate an effect simply by their existence. An example is adding the **COMPACT** attribute to the ordered list element: **<OL COMPACT>**. Other attributes indicate a modification to the tag by assigned values. For example, **<OL TYPE="I">** assigns the bullet type of an ordered list to uppercase roman numerals. An element may contain multiple attributes, if those attributes are separated by at least one space, as in **<OL COMPACT TYPE="I" START="3">**. The order of the attributes with a start tag is not fixed, but some HTML authors like to group attributes by meaning, sort attributes alphabetically, or use some other combination of rules.

A complete HTML element is defined by a start tag, an end tag (where applicable), possible attributes, and a content model. Figure 3-1 shows an overview of the syntax of a typical HTML element.

HTML Rules and Guidelines

As discussed in Chapter 1, the following are some rules to remember when writing HTML:

- *HTML documents are structured documents.* HTML documents have a well-defined structure. The idea of a content model says that certain HTML elements should occur only within others. For example, list items (**<LI>**) should be the only items that directly nest within unordered list elements defined by **<UL>**. The structure of an HTML document is specified by a *document type definition (DTD)*. A DTD defines what elements a document can contain, their possible relationships to one another inside a document, and their possible attributes and values. If the elements in a particular HTML document agree with this formal definition, the document is said to be *valid*. Validation of HTML documents is discussed later in this chapter.

- *Element names are not case-sensitive.* An element such as **<hTml>** is equivalent to **<html>** or **<HTML>**. Element case doesn't matter to a browser. However, writing elements consistently in upper- or lowercase makes HTML documents easier to understand and maintain by people. Using all uppercase in tags makes them stand out more.

Note   *Some document authors who manually code documents may find lowercase easier to type. Modern HTML editing tools can convert tag case automatically.*

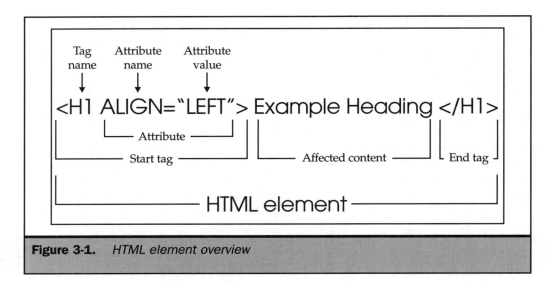

Figure 3-1. *HTML element overview*

■ *Attribute names aren't case-sensitive.* Just as **<hr>** is equivalent to **<HR>**, **<HR NOSHADE>** is equivalent to **<HR noshade>** or **<HR NoShade>**. As with elements, consistent use of case improves legibility, and uppercase is preferred.

■ *Attribute values may be case-sensitive.* The value of an attribute may be case-sensitive, especially if it refers to a file. The filename in **<IMG SRC="filename.gif">** may not be the same as the filename in **<IMG SRC="FILENAME.GIF">**; it depends on whether or not case matters to the operating system of the server delivering the file. For example, UNIX systems are case-sensitive, so FILENAME.GIF and filename.gif are two different files; on a Windows system, they would be the same. For best results, always specify a filename exactly as it has been saved. If you plan to move files from server to server, you should always use lowercase file names in attribute values.

■ *Attribute values should be quoted.* The actual attribute value may contain spaces or other special characters if it is enclosed by quotes. Some attributes require a known value, usually a string, such as **LEFT**, **RIGHT**, or **CENTER**. These values don't require surrounding quotes unless they contain embedded spaces. In common HTML, regardless of whether an attribute is user-defined or can contain only a specified value, it doesn't require quotes unless spaces or special characters occur within the value. For example, the values for the **SRC** and **ALT** attributes in the following element contain no spaces and therefore require no quotes:

```
<IMG SRC=dog.gif ALT=Rover>
```

Changing the value for the **ALT** attribute to My dog Rover introduces spaces into the value, and thus quotes must be added:

```
<IMG SRC=dog.gif ALT="My dog Rover">
```

Omitting quotes in the previous example assigns My to the **ALT** attribute and causes **dog** and **Rover** to be treated as two undefined attributes. Surrounding a value with quotes has no negative consequences if quotes aren't required. HTML authors are well advised to quote attribute values if any chance of misinterpretation exists. For stylistic reasons, as well as to make an HTML document conform to strict XML rules, quoting everything is always better. Specifically, remember to quote any values that contain any characters other than alphanumeric characters [a–z, A–Z, 0–9], dashes [-], or periods [.]. Be especially careful to quote any so-called "special characters."

- *Element names cannot contain spaces.* Browsers treat the first space encountered inside an element as the end of an element's name and the beginning of its attributes. For example, **<I M G>** doesn't mean **<IMG>**, the image element. It means **<I>**, the italic element, with two undefined attributes, **M** and **G**.

- *Browsers collapse and ignore space characters in HTML content.* Browsers collapse any sequence of spaces, tabs, and returns in an HTML document into a single space character. These characters convey no formatting information, unless they occur inside a special preformatting element, such as **<PRE>**, which preserves their meaning. Extra spacing can be used liberally within an HTML document to make it more legible to HTML authors.

Note *Authors may be interested in taking advantage of this rule by compressing HTML files filled with scripting code and extra markup. Links to a variety of HTML compression tools can be found at http://www.htmlref.com/Reference/resources.*

- *HTML documents may contain comments.* HTML supports comments that are not displayed within a browser window. Comments are denoted by a start value of **<!--** and an end value of **-->**. Comments can be many lines long. For example,

```
<!--

        Document Name: My HTML Document
        Creation Date: 1/5/99

        © 1999 Big Company, Inc.
   -->
```

is a valid comment. Be careful not to put spaces between the dashes or an exclamation point in the comment. Comments may also include HTML elements. This is very useful in hiding new HTML elements from older browsers, and is commonly used with **<STYLE>** and **<SCRIPT>** elements, discussed in Chapters 10 and 13, respectively. Readers should be aware that some very old browsers may have problems when commenting out HTML tags. For more information about comments, see Appendix A.

■ *Elements should nest.* Elements often contain other elements inside the document section that they enclose. Any element that starts within a section enclosed by another element must also end within that section. In other words, an element's tag pairs should be nested within one another, and their end tags shouldn't cross. To make some text bold and italic, use **<B><I>Correct</I></B>** and not **<B><I>Not correct</B></I>**.

Some readers may view this as primarily a stylistic issue, because no commonly used browsers have a problem with this. Authors are still advised to nest tags rather than cross them. Incorrect nesting may result in incompatibilities with emerging technologies, such as Extensible Markup Language (XML) and Dynamic HTML (DHTML).

■ *Browsers ignore unknown elements.* Browsers ignore elements they do not understand. They do, however, attempt to interpret any content enclosed by an unknown element. If a browser doesn't understand the **<STORY>** element in **<STORY>**A Tale of Two Cities**</STORY>**, it ignores it. It does, however, render the words "A Tale of Two Cities" as normal text.

■ *Browsers ignore unknown attributes.* As with elements, browsers ignore any attributes that they don't understand. Technically, the imaginary **CLOWN** attribute in the following example is well-formed HTML. Unless a browser happens to understand it, however, it is ignored.

```
<IMG CLOWN="BOZO" SRC="bozo.gif">
```

In a pragmatic sense, the final arbiter of an HTML document's correctness is the browser that is used to view it. Browsers rarely enforce formally defined HTML. Instead, most browsers liberally interpret what they treat as acceptable. They make guesses about unusual constructs and attempt to render whatever they receive. Few authors understand all the rules for composing HTML according to a DTD. Unfortunately, permissive browsers provide little incentive to learn. This is an important lesson for HTML authors. As permissiveness varies from browser to browser, and even between different versions of the same browser, simply testing pages in a browser doesn't ensure portability of documents.

Authoring HTML to a recognized DTD and using a *validator,* a program that checks that written code meets the specification, may ensure that documents are open to the widest possible audience. Many editors, such as Allaire's HomeSite, provide built-in validation services, and some Web sites (http://validator.w3.org) can validate Web documents. Most end users, however, don't concern themselves with syntax specifics, but draw their beliefs about appropriate code from how their browsers render that code. For example, even if a validator states that a document is correct, things may not work in a browser, due to bugs in the software.

As noted in Chapter 2, it is always a good idea to test documents under an assortment of browsers, such as Microsoft Internet Explorer, Netscape Navigator, Opera, WebTV, and even Lynx. The documents should also be tested on multiple platforms, such as Windows and Macintosh, when available. Even rigorous testing may not ensure that pages will work the way that you want—that is the challenge of the Web.

Note   *Permissive HTML interpretation by browsers serves a practical purpose. Imagine if browsers treated HTML errors like syntax errors in a programming language. If this were the case, a document could not be successfully viewed unless it was absolutely correct. If browsers had followed this model, the Web wouldn't have gotten very far. Relatively few complex documents on the Web today would pass extremely strict validation.*

Understanding and following a formal HTML definition takes time and practice. However, the benefits to cross-platform rendering and document maintenance make it worthwhile. This is essential for large corporations with many documents. Fortunately, the path toward writing well-formed HTML documents doesn't require an intimate understanding of the language's nuances. Well-formed documents share a common, easily comprehended document structure.

The Structure of HTML Documents

Regardless of document content, all well-written HTML documents share a common structure. Figure 3-2 provides a template for this. An HTML document begins with a **<!DOCTYPE>** declaration, indicating the version of HTML used by the document. Following this, the **<HTML>** element encloses the actual document. It contains two primary sections, the head and the body, enclosed by the **<HEAD>** and **<BODY>** elements, respectively. The *head* can contain identifying and other supplementary information about the document, or *meta-information.* The head always contains the document's title, enclosed by the **<TITLE>** element. The *body* contains the actual document content and the HTML markup used to structure the document.

```
<!DOCTYPE HTML PUBLIC "html version">
<HTML>
<HEAD>
<TITLE>Document Title</TITLE>
...Other supplementary information goes here....
</HEAD>

<BODY>
...Marked-up text goes here....
</BODY>
</HTML>
```

Figure 3-2.   *HTML document template*

Document Types

HTML follows the SGML notation for defining structured documents. From SGML, HTML inherits the requirement that all documents begin with a **<!DOCTYPE>** declaration. In an HTML context, this identifies the HTML "dialect" used in a document by referring to an external *document type definition,* or *DTD.* A DTD defines the actual elements, attributes, and element relationships that are valid in the document. The **<!DOCTYPE>** declaration allows validation software (discussed earlier) to identify the HTML DTD being followed in a document, and verify that the document is syntactically correct. Technically, any HTML construct not defined in the document's DTD should not occur. Some common **<!DOCTYPE>** declarations are shown here:

■ Document containing HTML 2 as standardized by the Internet Engineering Task Force:

```
<!DOCTYPE HTML PUBLIC "-//IETF//DTD HTML//EN">
```

■ Document containing HTML 3.2 as defined by the World Wide Web Consortium (W3C):

```
<!DOCTYPE HTML PUBLIC "-//W3C//DTD HTML 3.2 Final//EN">
```

- Document containing HTML 2 with Netscape Navigator extensions as defined by a third party:

```
<!DOCTYPE HTML PUBLIC "-//WebTechs//DTD Mozilla HTML 2.0//EN">
```

- Document containing Internet Explorer 3 HTML as defined by Microsoft Corporation:

```
<!DOCTYPE HTML PUBLIC "-//Microsoft//DTD Internet Explorer 3.0 HTML//EN">
```

- Document conforming to the transitional or loose definition of HTML 4 as defined by W3C:

```
<!DOCTYPE HTML PUBLIC "-//W3C//DTD HTML 4.0 Transitional//EN"
"http://www.w3.org/TR/REC-html40/loose.dtd">
```

- Document conforming to the strict definition of HTML 4 as defined by W3C:

```
<!DOCTYPE HTML PUBLIC "-//W3C//DTD HTML 4.0//EN"
"http://www.w3.org/TR/REC-html40/strict.dtd">
```

The HTML document template suggests always using a **<!DOCTYPE>** declaration. In some cases, this may not be practical. Including a DTD declaration conveys the intention to follow it. Unfortunately, not every HTML dialect has a DTD. Unlike the W3C, browser vendors have historically favored innovation over standardization. For an HTML author, it is better to omit a **<!DOCTYPE>** declaration than to include one that will not be followed. Misuse is pervasive.

Some HTML authoring tools automatically insert a **<!DOCTYPE>** declaration while also encouraging the use of elements not found in the related DTD. Several mass media Web sites support advanced features, such as frames in documents, declared according to the conservative HTML 2.0 specification.

At the time of this book's writing, Netscape doesn't provide DTDs. Many interested third parties have written DTDs that address Netscape Navigator extensions, in case an author wants to validate a Navigator document.

The <HTML> Element

The **<HTML>** element delimits the beginning and the end of an HTML document. It contains only the **<HEAD>** element and the **<BODY>** element. The HTML document template shown in Figure 3-2, earlier in the chapter, shows the **<HTML>** element's typical use in a document, as a container for all other elements. The **<HEAD>** element is optional. The HTML 4.0 DTD doesn't require its use, nor do popular browsers. Including it, however, makes a document more legible.

The <HEAD> Element

The **<HEAD>** element encloses a document section that contains identification and supplementary information about the document. Browsers don't generally display this information. Including the **<HEAD>** element in a document isn't technically necessary, because the boundaries of the head can always be inferred. Nevertheless, the **<HEAD>** element should always be included, for document style and legibility. In the HTML 4.0 transitional DTD, the elements allowed within the **<HEAD>** element include **<BASE>**, **<ISINDEX>**, **<LINK>**, **<META>**, **<OBJECT>**, **<SCRIPT>**, **<STYLE>**, and **<TITLE>**. The **<TITLE>** element must always occur. A brief discussion of these elements follows. Complete information is available in the cross-referenced chapters and reference section.

The **<BASE>** element specifies an absolute URL address that is used to provide server and directory information for partially specified URL addresses, called *relative URLs*, used within the document. Relative URLs are discussed in Chapter 4, which covers linking.

The **<ISINDEX>** element indicates that the document contains a searchable index. It causes the browser to display a query prompt and a field for entering a query. This element usually is used with simple site searching mechanisms, but is rarely used today, having been mostly replaced by forms. Under the HTML 4.0 strict definition, **<ISINDEX>** is deprecated. The element is discussed solely in Appendix A, as its use isn't encouraged.

The **<LINK>** element specifies a special relationship between the current document and another document. One use concerns hypertext navigational relationships. This is discussed in Chapter 4. Another use, which concerns linking to a style sheet, is discussed in Chapter 10.

The **<META>** element uses name/value pairs to provide meta-information about a document. The **<META>** element often provides descriptive information targeted by Web search engines. In a very different use, the **<META>** element can define an HTTP request header that causes one page to automatically load another page after a specified time interval. These and other uses are discussed in Chapter 4.

Note   *A document's head section contains all the descriptive information about the document. Traditionally, this section was much smaller than the document's body and could be retrieved independently from a Web server. Because of this, Web indexing robots often place special emphasis on the document head. Authors often provide various forms of "spider bait" to increase indexing relevance. With the introduction of the **<SCRIPT>** and **<STYLE>** elements, the amount of information in the head has exploded. What impact this may have on document structuring and strategies for automatic document indexing is unclear.*

The **<OBJECT>** element allows programs and other binary objects to be directly embedded in a Web page. The most popular current approaches use Java applets, plug-ins, or ActiveX controls. This approach to making Web pages more interactive is known as *client-side programming*. The **<OBJECT>** element and associated usage is discussed in Chapter 15.

The **<SCRIPT>** element allows programs written in a scripting language to be directly embedded in a Web page. The two most popular scripting languages are JavaScript and VBScript, a form of Visual Basic. This approach to making Web pages more interactive is known as *client-side scripting*. The **<SCRIPT>** element and associated usage of scripts, which is often called *Dynamic HTML (DHTML)*, is discussed in Chapter 14.

The **<STYLE>** element encloses style specifications covering fonts, colors, positioning, and other aspects of content presentation. These styles can be associated with document elements. Use of the **<STYLE>** element is discussed in Chapter 10.

> **Note**   *Comments may occur anywhere in an HTML document. They are especially valuable in the head section to assist document maintenance. Useful head comments include the document's purpose, authorship, required resources, and modification history. The form of HTML comments was discussed earlier in the chapter.*

The **<TITLE>** element, discussed next, is the only element that is absolutely required in the head of a document.

The <TITLE> Element

The **<TITLE>** element must be used in every HTML document. It gives an HTML document a title by which it is known to browsers and indexing robots. Browsers display the document title while the document is being viewed, and may also use the title in bookmark lists.

> **Note**   *Most browsers attempt to deduce a title for a document that is missing the **<TITLE>** element. The browser often uses the URL of the document being viewed, which may indicate nothing about the document's content. However, this behavior isn't guaranteed. For example, Classic WebTV simply lists the document as "untitled document." The example in Figure 3-3 shows an untitled document rendered in a browser.*

A document title may contain standard text as well as character entities (for example, **©**), which are discussed later in the chapter. However, HTML markup isn't permitted in the **<TITLE>** element and doesn't produce the expected result. So, according to the rules of the **<TITLE>** element,

```
<TITLE><B>Home Page</B></TITLE>
```

is not valid, while

```
<TITLE>The Exciting Story of HTML &copy; 1999</TITLE>
```

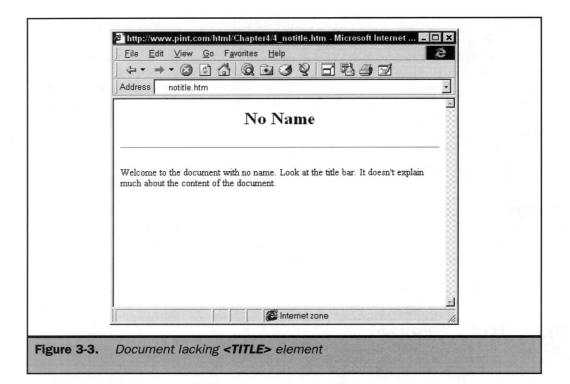

Figure 3-3.   *Document lacking **<TITLE>** element*

is valid. However, a well-formed title is not necessarily a meaningful title. Remember that a user sees a title in his or her bookmark list if the page is bookmarked. Robots and spiders that index the Web often place special meaning on the contents of the **<TITLE>** element when determining what a page is about. Because of this, a title should indicate the contents of a page, without ambiguity. Titles such as "My Page" or "Home Page" don't make much sense; "John Smith's Page" and "Big Company" do. A well-formed title can actually add navigational value to a site by showing an implicit hierarchy among a group of pages. While "Widget X-103 Datasheet" seems to be a reasonable title, "Big Company: Products: Widget X-103 Datasheet" is a better title. It not only indicates the company the product is related to, but implies a hierarchy in the site.

Note   *Initially, using characters such as colon (:), slash (/), or backslash (\) in titles was a problem. An operating system may have a problem with these titles if the document is saved to the local system. For example, the colon isn't allowed within Macintosh filenames, and slashes generally aren't allowed within filenames, because they indicate directories. Although this appears to be a problem, most browsers remove the suspect characters and reduce them to spaces during the Save process. To be on the safe side, dashes or underscores can be used to delimit sections in the title.*

While titles should be descriptive, they should also be concise. Authors should limit title length to a reasonable number of characters. Netscape Navigator and Internet Explorer display around 20 to 30 characters of a title in their bookmark lists. One way to limit the length of titles is to remove words such as *a*, *an*, and *the*, which provide little extra value.

Browsers are very sensitive to the **<TITLE>** *element. According to the HTML 3.2 and 4.0 specifications, the* **<TITLE>** *element is mandatory, while the* **<BODY>**, **<HEAD>**, *and* **<HTML>** *elements are not. In some versions of Navigator, using a poorly formed* **<TITLE>** *element causes a document not to display. So, if you get a bunch of junk on your screen (see Figure 3-4), check the* **<TITLE>** *element right away.*

According to the HTML 4.0 specification, only one **<TITLE>** element should appear in every document. The title should appear in the head of the document. Until Netscape Navigator 1.1 was released, multiple **<TITLE>** elements were often used within documents to create an animated title. This was a bug, not a Netscape innovation. More recent browsers don't support this capability, and it shouldn't be used.

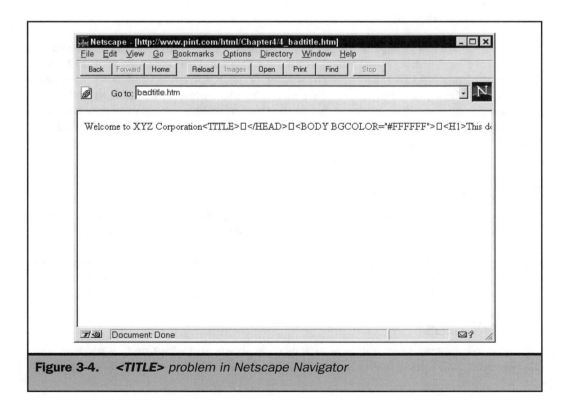

Figure 3-4. *<TITLE> problem in Netscape Navigator*

*If you do have multiple instances of the **<TITLE>** element in your document, HTML doesn't define what will happen, so different browsers handle them differently. Internet Explorer uses the last **<TITLE>** defined; Navigator uses the first. This may change with version numbers and platform types, and should never be assumed.*

The <BODY> Element

As previously shown in the HTML document template in Figure 3-2, the body of a document is delimited by **<BODY>** and **</BODY>**. Under the HTML 4.0 specification and most browsers, the **<BODY>** element is optional, but should always be included. Only one **<BODY>** element can appear per document.

Note *Under an older version of Navigator, the browser read multiple **<BODY>** elements within a document. In combination with the **BGCOLOR** attribute of the **<BODY>** element, HTML authors were able to exploit this bug to produce a document that loaded after flipping through a variety of colors. Often, this hack was used to create a fade-in or fade-out effect for a page. This bug has been fixed, so multiple **<BODY>** elements no longer provide any benefit. If multiple **<BODY>** elements are encountered in a file, typically the browser pays attention to either the first or last **<BODY>** element encountered.*

Common attributes for the **<BODY>** element affect the colors for a document's text, background, and links. These attributes include **TEXT** for text color, **BGCOLOR** for background color, **ALINK** for active link color, **VLINK** for visited link color, and **LINK** for unvisited link color. These and other **<BODY>** attributes, both standard and browser-specific, are discussed in Chapter 6. The **<BODY>** element may contain many other HTML elements. The rest of the chapter introduces the basic HTML elements that may be found in a document's body.

HTML Elements

The rest of the chapter introduces the basic HTML elements common to nearly every browser, as defined by the HTML 4.0 transitional specification. These elements fall into three distinct groups: block-level elements, text-level elements, and character entities. The elements are presented from top to bottom, from larger, block-oriented structures (such as paragraphs), to smaller units (such as the actual character entities). First, however, the attributes that are common to all HTML elements are reviewed.

Core Attributes

To accommodate new technologies such as style sheets and scripting languages, some important changes have been made to HTML 4. A set of four core attributes has been added that nearly all HTML elements support. At this stage, the purpose of these attributes may not be obvious, but it is important to address their existence, before discussing the various HTML elements.

HTML 4's core attributes are **ID**, **CLASS**, **STYLE**, and **TITLE**. The **ID** attribute is used to set a unique name for a tag in a document. For example, using the paragraph element, **<P>**,

```
<P ID="FirstParagraph">This is the first paragraph of text.</P>
```

names the bound tag **FirstParagraph**. Naming a tag is useful for manipulating the enclosed contents with a style sheet, as discussed in Chapter 10, or providing a scripting hook, as discussed in Chapter 13.

The **CLASS** attribute is used to indicate the class or classes that a tag may belong to. Like **ID**, **CLASS** is used to associate a tag with a name, so

```
<P ID="FirstParagraph" CLASS="important">
This is the first paragraph of text.
</P>
```

not only names the paragraph uniquely as **FirstParagraph**, but also indicates that this paragraph belongs to a class grouping called **important**. Class names don't have to be unique to a document.

The **STYLE** attribute is used to add style sheet information directly to a tag. For example,

```
<P STYLE="font-size: 18pt">This is the first paragraph of text.</P>
```

sets the font size of the paragraph to be 18 point. Style properties are discussed in Chapter 10.

The **TITLE** is used to provide advisory text about a tag or its contents. In the case of

```
<P TITLE="Introductory paragraph">
This is the first paragraph of text.
</P>
```

the **TITLE** attribute is set to indicate that this particular paragraph is the introductory paragraph. Browsers (currently, only Internet Explorer 4 and higher) may display this advisory text in the form of a tool tip, which may be useful to provide context-sensitive help, extra information, or other advice to the user, as shown here:

The core attributes may not make a great deal of sense at this time, because they are generally useful mostly with scripting and style sheets, but keep in mind that these four attributes are assumed with every tag that is introduced for the rest of the chapter.

Language Attributes

One major goal of HTML 4 was to provide better support for languages other than English. The use of other languages may require that text direction be changed from left to right across the screen to right to left. Nearly all HTML elements now support the **DIR** attribute, which can be used to indicate text direction as either **LTR** (left to right) or **RTL** (right to left). For example,

```
<P DIR="RTL">This is a right-to-left paragraph.</P>
```

Furthermore, mixed-language documents may become more common after support for non-ASCII-based languages is improved within browsers. The use of the **LANG** attribute enables document authors to indicate, down to the tag level, the language being used. For example,

```
<P LANG="fr">C'est Francais.</P>
```

```
<P LANG="en">This is English.</P>
```

While the language attributes should be considered part of nearly every HTML element, in reality, these attributes are poorly supported by browsers currently available.

Core Events

The last major change made in HTML 4 was to improve the possibility of adding scripting to HTML documents. In preparation for a more dynamic Web, a set of core events has been associated with nearly every HTML element. Most of these events are associated with a user doing something. For example, the user clicking an object is associated with an **onclick** event attribute. So,

```
<P onclick="alert('Ouch!')">Press this paragraph.</P>
```

would associate a small bit of scripting code with the paragraph event, which would be triggered when the user clicks the paragraph. In reality, the event model is not fully supported by all browsers for all tags, so the previous example may not do much of anything. A much more complete discussion of events is presented in Chapters 13 and 14, as well as in Appendix A. For now, just remember that a multitude of events may be associated with any tag, paving the way for a much more dynamic Web experience. The next section looks at the large, document-structuring elements, called *block-level elements*.

Block-Level Elements

Block-level elements define structural content blocks, such as paragraphs or lists. If a document is written carefully in a block style, it may be possible to improve its machine readability. The basic idea of a document that follows a block structure is shown in Figure 3-5.

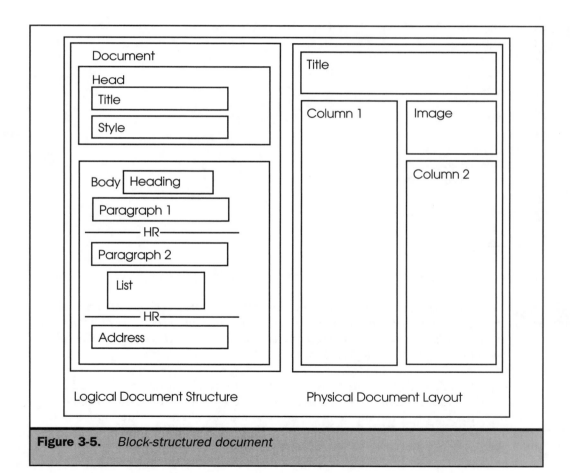

Figure 3-5. *Block-structured document*

Headings

The heading elements are used to create "headlines" in documents. Six different levels of headings are supported: **<H1>**, **<H2>**, **<H3>**, **<H4>**, **<H5>**, and **<H6>**. These range in importance from **<H1>**, the most important, to **<H6>**, the least important. Most browsers display headings in larger and/or bolder font than normal text. This causes many HTML authors to think erroneously of heading elements as formatting that makes text bigger or bolder. Actually, heading elements (such as headings themselves) convey logical meaning about a document's structure. Sizing and weight are relative to the importance of the heading, so **<H1>** level headings are larger than **<H3>** headings. As headings, text included is displayed in an alternative style (bigger and/or bold) and on a line of its own. In addition, an extra line is generally inserted after the heading. The following example markup demonstrates the heading elements:

```
<!DOCTYPE HTML PUBLIC "-//W3C//DTD HTML 4.0 Transitional//EN">
<HTML>
<HEAD>
<TITLE>Heading Example</TITLE>
</HEAD>

<BODY>
<H1>Heading 1</H1>
<H2>Heading 2</H2>
<H3>Heading 3</H3>
<H4>Heading 4</H4>
<H5>Heading 5</H5>
<H6>Heading 6</H6>
</BODY>
</HTML>
```

A sample rendering of this heading example is shown in Figure 3-6.

The Lynx text browser renders headings very differently than commercial graphical browsers. Lynx can't display larger fonts, so it may attempt to bold them or align them. <H1> headings are aligned in the center, while each lower-level heading is indented more than the next-highest-level heading.

An attribute that aligns the text left, right, or center can be added to the heading elements. By default, headings are usually left-aligned, but by setting the **ALIGN** attribute of the various heading elements, the text may be aligned to the right, left, or center of the screen. The following example markup and the result shown in Figure 3-7 show the usage and rendering of the **ALIGN** attribute for headings:

```
<!DOCTYPE HTML PUBLIC "-//W3C//DTD HTML 4.0 Transitional//EN">
<HTML>
<HEAD>
<TITLE>Heading Alignment Example</TITLE>
</HEAD>

<BODY>
<H1 ALIGN="left">Aligned Left</H1>
<H1 ALIGN="center">Aligned Center</H1>
<H1 ALIGN="right">Aligned Right</H1>
</BODY>
</HTML>
```

Under the strict version of HTML 4, the **ALIGN** attribute has been deprecated.

HTML authors often use headings to make text large. As with all HTML elements, size is a relative concept, not an absolute concept. The actual size of the heading depends on the browser, the browser's setting, and the platform on which it is running. An **<H1>** header under Navigator on a UNIX system appears a different size than the same **<H1>** header on a Windows 3.1 machine running Internet Explorer. The headlines are relatively bigger, but the exact size is unknown, making consistent layout

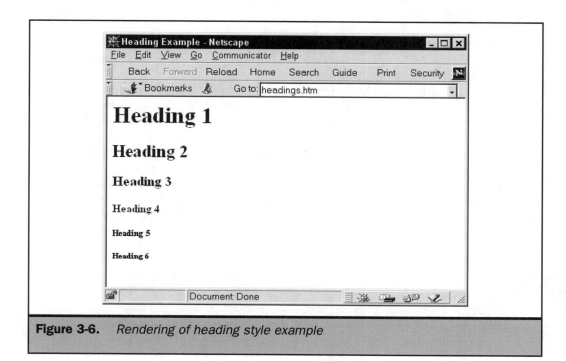

Figure 3-6. *Rendering of heading style example*

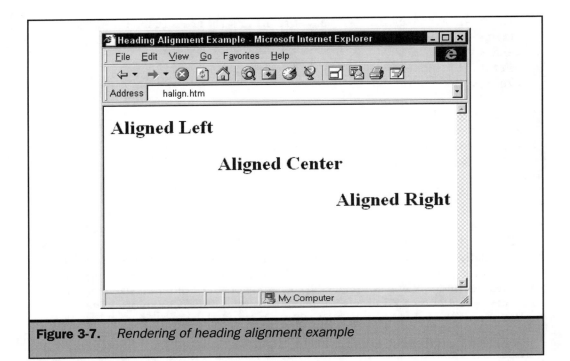

Figure 3-7.   *Rendering of heading alignment example*

difficult. Furthermore, headlines have an implied logical meaning, and typically do more than simply make something big.

Headings actually have a logical meaning. While HTML doesn't enforce the use of headings in a hierarchical, ordered way, some people feel that this use is implied; that is, documents generally have headlines ordered so that **<H3>** doesn't appear before **<H1>** and less important headings are nested within more important ones or occur after them. Given the logical use of headings, a page may support indexing features or allow for navigation schemes that currently aren't available in browsers without using scripting. For example, a browser might allow a user to view an outline of a Web document by showing the headings, and then allow the user to expand relevant headings (as shown in Figure 3-8). Although an outline view isn't built into most browsers, you can create this type of navigation by using programming facilities such as Java or Dynamic HTML. More information about this is presented in Chapter 14.

| Note | *A quick survey of heading use on the Web should reveal that headings beyond **<H3>** are rarely used. Why? Partially because people use headings in a visual fashion. The effects of **<H4>**, **<H5>**, and **<H6>** can be achieved with other elements. Furthermore, it is unusual for documents to have sections nested more than three levels deep.* |

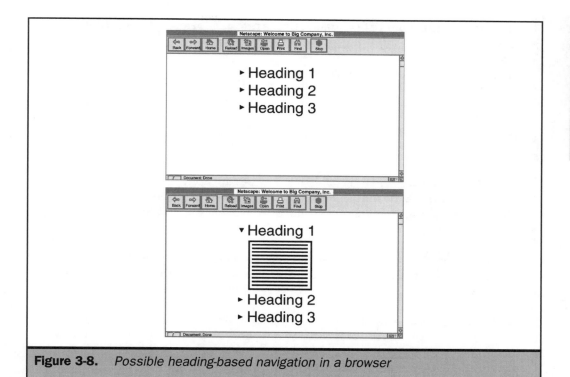

Figure 3-8.   *Possible heading-based navigation in a browser*

Paragraphs and Breaks

Unlike documents in word processors, HTML documents ignore multiple spaces, tabs, and carriage returns. Word wrapping can occur at any point in your source file, and multiple spaces are collapsed into a single space. To preserve some semblance of text formatting, elements are introduced to sectionalize the document. One of the most important structuring elements is the paragraph element. Surrounding text with the **<P>** and **</P>** tags indicates that the text is a logical paragraph unit. Normally, the browser places a blank line or two before the paragraph, but the exact rendering of the text depends on the browser. Text within the **<P>** is normally rendered flush left, with a ragged right margin. The **ALIGN** attribute makes it possible to specify a left, right, or center alignment. Under HTML 4, you also can set an **ALIGN** value of **justify**, to justify all text in the paragraph. Due to the poor quality of justification in some browsers and lack of support, this value seems to be rarely used. Also note that because left is the default value, **ALIGN="left"** is often omitted entirely. The following example shows four paragraphs with alignment, the rendering of which is shown in Figure 3-9.

```
<!DOCTYPE HTML PUBLIC "-//W3C//DTD HTML 4.0 Transitional//EN">
<HTML>
<HEAD>
<TITLE>Paragraph Example</TITLE>
</HEAD>

<BODY>
<P>This is the first paragraph in the example about the P tag.
There really isn't much to say here.</P>

<P ALIGN="center">This is the second paragraph. Again, more of
the same. This time the paragraph is aligned in the center. This
might not be such a good idea as it makes the text hard to
read.</P>

<P ALIGN="right">Here the paragraph is aligned to the right.
Right-aligned text is also troublesome to read. The rest of the
text of this paragraph is of little importance.</P>

<P ALIGN="justify">Under HTML 4.0-compliant browsers, you are
able to justify text. As you may notice, the way browsers tend to
justify text is sometimes imprecise. Furthermore, not all browsers
support this attribute value.</P>
</BODY>
</HTML>
```

Because the **<P>** element generally causes a blank line, some HTML authors attempt to insert blank lines into a document by using multiple **<P>** elements. This rarely results in the desired outcome. The browser collapses empty **<P>** elements, because they represent logical text units, not physical formatting.

Note   *Many WYSIWYG HTML editors and some page authors try to get around the collapsing paragraph problem by using a nonbreaking space character within a paragraph, to keep the element from collapsing, as shown here* **<P> </P>**. *This approach isn't recommended, because it doesn't reduce markup used and it further obscures the meaning of the document.*

To insert returns or blank lines in a document, the **
** element must be used. The **
** element is a text-level element that inserts a single carriage return or break into a document. It contains no content and has no end tag. The one attribute commonly used with **
** is **CLEAR**. This attribute allows **
** to affect how text flows around

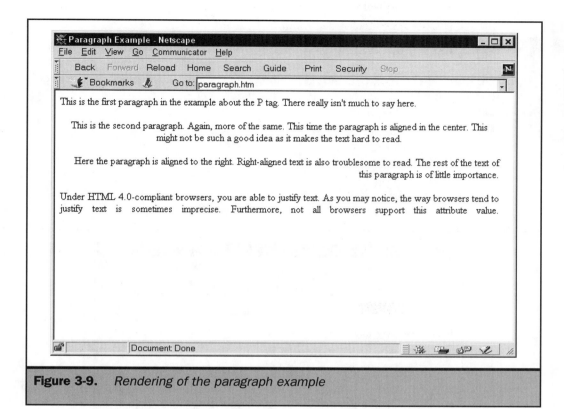

Figure 3-9. *Rendering of the paragraph example*

images or embedded objects. The use of **
** in this fashion is discussed in Chapter 5. Because of its relationship with the **<P>** element, the basic use of **
** must be presented here. The following code fragment shows how **
** might be used both within and outside paragraphs. An example screen rendering is shown in Figure 3-10.

```
<!DOCTYPE HTML PUBLIC "-//W3C//DTD HTML 4.0 Transitional//EN">
<HTML>
<HEAD>
<TITLE>Break Example</TITLE>
</HEAD>

<BODY>
<P>This is the first paragraph.<BR>
Not much to say here.
</P>
```

```
<BR><BR><BR>

<P>This is the second paragraph. Notice all the extra space between
these paragraphs. That's from the BR tags.</P>
</BODY>
</HTML>
```

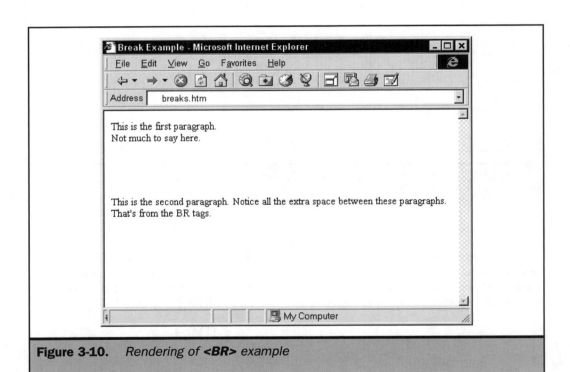

Figure 3-10. *Rendering of <BR> example*

The following code fragment shows that **<P>** and **
** are not equivalent, despite their physical rendering similarities (screen renderings appear in Figure 3-11):

```
<!DOCTYPE HTML PUBLIC "-//W3C//DTD HTML 4.0 Transitional//EN">
<HTML>
<HEAD>
<TITLE>Break Example</TITLE>
</HEAD>

<BODY>
<P>This is the first paragraph.<BR>
Not much to say here, either.
</P>

<P><P><P>

<P>This is the second paragraph. Notice that the three P tags are
treated as empty paragraphs and ignored. </P>
</BODY>
</HTML>
```

Tip   *Users looking for blank lines have to insert multiple **
** elements into their document. A single **
** element merely goes to the next line rather than inserting a blank line.*

<CENTER> as a Block Element

In the original HTML 2–based browsers, centering text was impossible. One of the major additions introduced by Netscape was the **<CENTER>** element. HTML 3.2 adopted this element because of its widespread use. To center text or embedded objects (such as images), simply enclose the content within **<CENTER>** and **</CENTER>**. In this sense, **<CENTER>** appears to be a text-formatting style element, but under the HTML 3.2 and transitional 4.0 specifications (and beyond), **<CENTER>** is defined as an alias for a block-level structuring element. Under the HTML 4.0 DTD, **<CENTER>** is

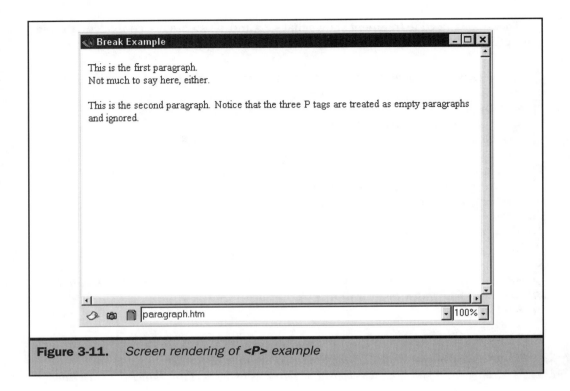

Figure 3-11. *Screen rendering of <P> example*

simply an alias for **<DIV ALIGN="CENTER">** and is treated exactly the same way. The **<CENTER>** element is unlikely to go away, considering its simplicity and widespread use. But according to specifications, two preferred ways exist to center content: the **<DIV>** element with a **center** alignment attribute, or the **ALIGN** attribute used in conjunction with some elements.

Divisions

The **<DIV>** element is used to structure HTML documents into unique sections or divisions. Adding the **ALIGN** attribute enables you to align a portion of the document to the left, right, or center. By default, content within the **<DIV>** element is left-aligned. Divisions are also useful when used in conjunction with style sheets (see Chapter 10). The following example shows the use of **<CENTER>** and **<DIV>** (Figure 3-12 shows their screen rendering):

```
<!DOCTYPE HTML PUBLIC "-//W3C//DTD HTML 4.0 Transitional//EN">
<HTML>
<HEAD>
```

```
<TITLE>Center and Division Example</TITLE>
</HEAD>

<BODY>
<CENTER>
<H1>This heading is centered.</H1>
<P>This paragraph is also centered.</P>
</CENTER>
<BR><BR>

<DIV ALIGN="right">
<H1>Division Heading</H1>
<P>Many paragraphs and other block elements
can be affected by a DIV at once.</P>
<P>Notice all the paragraphs are right aligned.</P>
</DIV>
</BODY>
</HTML>
```

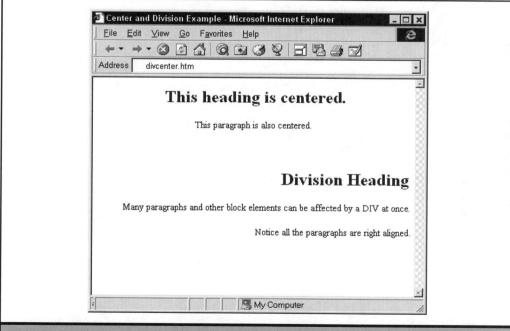

Figure 3-12.   *Example rendering of* ***<DIV>*** *and* ***<CENTER>***

Block Quotes

Occasionally, you may want to quote a large body of text to make it stand out from the other text. The **<BLOCKQUOTE>** element provides a facility to enclose large block quotations from other works within a document. Though the element is logical in nature, enclosing text within **<BLOCKQUOTE>** and **</BLOCKQUOTE>** usually indents the blocked information. Like a **<P>** element, text within beginning and ending **<BLOCKQUOTE>** elements ignores all spacing, tabs, and returns, and requires the use of **
** or other elements to modify line wrapping and spacing. The following shows an example of **<BLOCKQUOTE>** (rendered in Figure 3-13):

```
<!DOCTYPE HTML PUBLIC "-//W3C//DTD HTML 4.0 Transitional//EN">
<HTML>
<HEAD>
<TITLE>Blockquote Example</TITLE>
</HEAD>

<BODY>
<H1 ALIGN="center">Big Company Press Quote</H1>
<P>See the comments the press has about Big Company, Inc.
and our great green gadgets:</P>

<BLOCKQUOTE>
"Big Company's Green Gadget is by far the best fictitious product
ever produced! Gadget lovers and haters alike will marvel at the
sheer uselessness of the Green Gadget. It's a true shame that the
Green Gadget is limited only to HTML examples."
<BR><BR>
--Matthew J. Foley, Useless Products Magazine
</BLOCKQUOTE>

<P>With kudos like this, you need to make sure to buy your Green
Gadget today!</P>
</BODY>
</HTML>
```

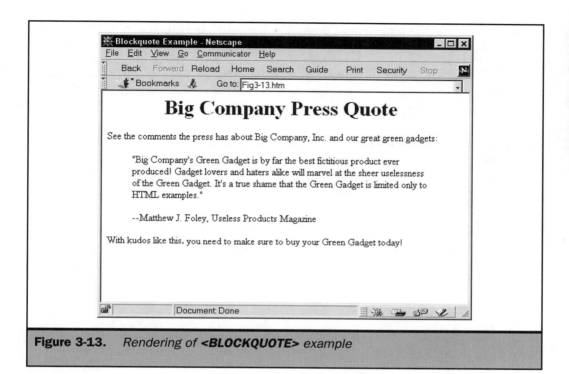

Figure 3-13.   *Rendering of* **<BLOCKQUOTE>** *example*

Note *The first HTML 2–compliant browsers did not provide any indentation or tab facility in regular text. Many HTML authors use* **<BLOCKQUOTE>** *to provide indentation. Text within* **<BLOCKQUOTE>** *may be indented on both sides of a page. It may render in an alternative style (for example, italics). For this reason, the list elements, particularly the unordered list, are common workarounds to provide indentation in Web pages. In fact, many HTML editors insert these elements to create indentation. Until style sheets become more common, these workarounds will continue.*

Preformatted Text

Occasionally, spacing, tabs, and returns are so important in text that HTML's default behavior of disregarding them would ruin the text's meaning. In such cases, you may want to preserve the intended formatting by specifying the text to be preformatted. Imagine that programming source code or poetry needs to be inserted into a Web page. In both cases, the spacing, returns, and tabs in the document must be preserved to ensure proper meaning. This situation requires an HTML directive that indicates the preservation of format. The **<PRE>** and **</PRE>** tags can be used to surround text that shouldn't be formatted by the browser. The text enclosed within the **<PRE>** tags retains all spacing and returns, and doesn't reflow when the browser is resized. Scroll bars and horizontal scrolling are required if the lines are longer than the width of the window. The browser generally renders the preformatted text in a monospaced font, usually Courier. Some text formatting, such as bold, italics, or links, can be used within the **<PRE>** tags. The following sample, displayed in Figure 3-14, uses the **<PRE>** element and compares it to regular paragraph text:

```
<!DOCTYPE HTML PUBLIC "-//W3C//DTD HTML 4.0 Transitional//EN">
<HTML>
<HEAD>
<TITLE>PRE Example</TITLE>
</HEAD>

<BODY>
<PRE>
This is P   R   E   F   O   R   M   A   T   T   E   D

   T
      E
        X
          T.

SPACES      are ok!  So are

   RETURNS!
</PRE>

<BR><BR>

<P>
This is NOT P   R   E   F   O   R   M   A   T   T   E   D

    T
      E
        X
          T.

SPACES       and
RETURNS are lost.
</P>
</BODY>
</HTML>
```

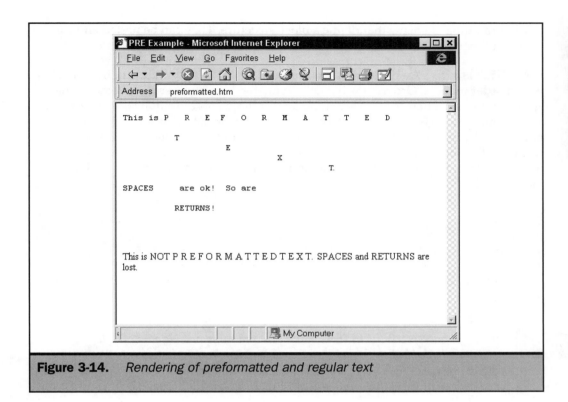

Figure 3-14.   *Rendering of preformatted and regular text*

Note   *According to the HTML 4.0 specification, other HTML elements are allowed within the **<PRE>** element, but some elements, such as **<IMG>**, are excluded. Most browsers allow any elements, even those beyond the stated specification, to appear within the **<PRE>** elements, and render these as expected. Authors should not, however, rely on this.*

Authors should be careful about using the **<PRE>** element to create simple tables or preserve spacing. Unpredictable differences in browser window sizes may introduce horizontal scrolling for wide preformatted content. In these cases, other elements may provide better formatting control.

Lists

Modern HTML has three basic forms of lists: ordered lists (**<OL>**), unordered lists (**<UL>**), and definition lists (**<DL>**). Two other rarely used list elements, **<MENU>** and **<DIR>**, are sparsely supported and are usually treated as an unordered list. Lists are block formatting elements that define a block structure. They can be nested and can contain other block-level structures, such as paragraphs.

ORDERED LISTS   An ordered list, as enclosed by <OL> and </OL>, defines a list in which order matters. Ordering is typically rendered by a numbering scheme, using Arabic numbers, letters, or Roman numerals. Ordered lists are suitable for creating simple outlines or step-by-step instructions, because the list items are numbered automatically by the browser. List items in ordered and other lists are defined by using the list item element, <LI>, which doesn't require an end tag. List items are usually indented by the browser. Numbering starts from 1. A generic ordered list looks like this:

```
<OL>
<LI>Item 1
<LI>Item 2
 . . .
<LI>Item n
</OL>
```

Note   *In many browsers, the <LI> element has some meaning outside a list. It often renders as a nonindented bullet. Some books recommend using <LI> in this way, but it isn't correct practice. While many browsers assume an unordered bullet list, this use of <LI> is undefined in the HTML specification. This hack shouldn't be used.*

The <OL> element has three basic attributes, none of which are required. These are **COMPACT**, **START**, and **TYPE**. The **COMPACT** attribute requires no value. It simply suggests that the browser attempt to compact the list, to use less space onscreen. In reality, most browsers ignore the **COMPACT** attribute.

The **TYPE** attribute of <OL> can be set to **a** for lowercase letters, **A** for uppercase letters, **i** for lowercase roman numerals, **I** for uppercase Roman numerals, or **1** for regular numerals. The numeral **1** is the default value. Remember that the **TYPE** attribute within the <OL> element sets the numbering scheme for the whole list, unless it is overridden by a **TYPE** value in an <LI> element. Each <LI> element may have a local **TYPE** attribute set to **a**, **A**, **i**, **I**, or **1**. Once an <LI> element is set with a new type, it overrides the numbering style for the rest of the list, unless another <LI> sets the **TYPE** attribute.

The <OL> element also has a **START** attribute that takes a numeric value to begin the list numbering. Whether the **TYPE** attribute is a letter or a numeral, the **START** value must be a number. To start ordering from the letter *j*, you would use <OL TYPE="a" START="10">, because *j* is the tenth letter. An <LI> element within an ordered list can override the current numbering with the **VALUE** attribute, which is also set to a numeric value. Numbering of the list should continue from the value set.

The use of ordered lists and their attributes is shown next, the rendering of which is shown in Figure 3-15:

```
<!DOCTYPE HTML PUBLIC "-//W3C//DTD HTML 4.0 Transitional//EN">
<HTML>
<HEAD>
<TITLE>Ordered List Example</TITLE>
</HEAD>

<BODY>
<P>Ordered lists can be very simple.</P>

<OL>
   <LI>Item 1
   <LI>Item 2
   <LI>Item 3
</OL>

<P>Ordered lists can have a variety of types.</P>

<OL>
   <LI TYPE="a">Lowercase letters
   <LI TYPE="A">Uppercase letters
   <LI TYPE="i">Lowercase Roman numerals
   <LI TYPE="I">Uppercase Roman numerals
   <LI TYPE="1">Arabic numerals
</OL>

<P>Ordered lists can start at different values
and with different types.</P>

<OL START="10" TYPE="a">
   <LI>This should be j.
   <LI VALUE="3">This should be c.
   <OL>
      <LI>Lists can nest.
         <OL>
            <LI>Nesting depth is unlimited.
         </OL>
      </OL>
</OL>
</BODY>
</HTML>
```

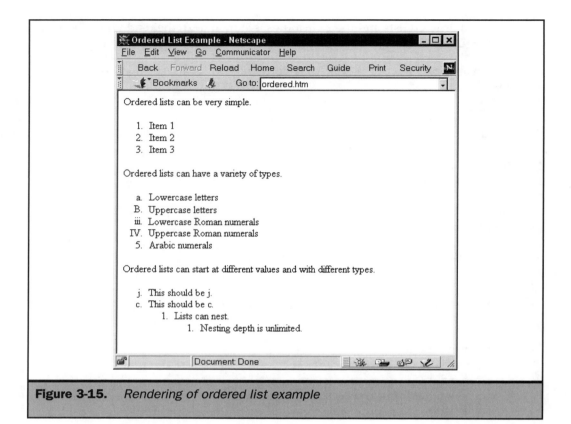

Figure 3-15.   *Rendering of ordered list example*

Note *When dealing with extremes, numbering should be used with caution. Negative values or very large values produce unpredictable results. While Navigator ignores negative numbers, Internet Explorer numbers up toward zero. Browsers may allocate a fixed width to the left of a list item to display its number. Under Navigator, a list not embedded in another block structure can accommodate only about four digits; larger numbers may overwrite list elements. A list indented by nesting in another block structure may have more space. Numbering in both Navigator and Internet Explorer loses meaning with large integer values around 10 to 100 billion, most likely due to limitations with the operating environment.*

UNORDERED LISTS   An unordered list, signified by **<UL>** and **</UL>**, is used for lists of items in which the ordering is not specific. This might be useful in a list of features and benefits for a product. A browser typically adds a bullet of some sort (a filled circle, a square, or an empty circle) for each item and indents the list.

Unordered lists can be nested. Each level of nesting indents the list further, and the bullet changes accordingly. Generally, a filled circle or solid round bullet is used on the first level of lists. An empty circle is used for the second-level list. Third-level nested lists generally use a square. These renderings for bullets are common to browsers, but shouldn't be counted on. Starting with Netscape Navigator 1.*x*–level browsers, it became possible to set the bullet type with the **TYPE** attribute; this was later added to the HTML specification. The **TYPE** attribute may appear within the **<UL>** element and set the type for the whole list, or it may appear within each **<LI>**. A **TYPE** specification in an **<LI>** element overrides the value for the rest of the list, unless it is overridden by another **TYPE** specification. The allowed values for **TYPE**, as suggested by the default actions, are **disc**, **circle**, or **square**. This change isn't consistently supported across browsers. In the case of WebTV, a triangle bullet type is also available. For the greatest level of cross-browser compatibility, authors are encouraged to set the bullet type only for the list as a whole.

Note   *Internet Explorer 3–level browsers under Windows don't render* **TYPE** *settings for unordered lists. This has been fixed under Internet Explorer 4.*

The following is an example of unordered lists, various renderings of which are shown in Figure 3-16:

```
<!DOCTYPE HTML PUBLIC "-//W3C//DTD HTML 4.0 Transitional//EN">
<HTML>
<HEAD>
<TITLE>Unordered List Example</TITLE>
</HEAD>

<BODY>
<UL>
   <LI>Unordered lists
   <UL>
      <LI>can be nested.
      <UL>
         <LI>Bullet changes on nesting.
      </UL>
   </UL>
</UL>

<P>Bullets can be controlled with the TYPE attribute. Type can be
set for the list as a whole or item by item.</P>
```

```
<UL TYPE="square">
   <LI>First item bullet shape set by UL
   <LI TYPE="disc">Disc item
   <LI TYPE="circle">Circle item
   <LI TYPE="square">Square item
</UL>
</BODY>
</HTML>
```

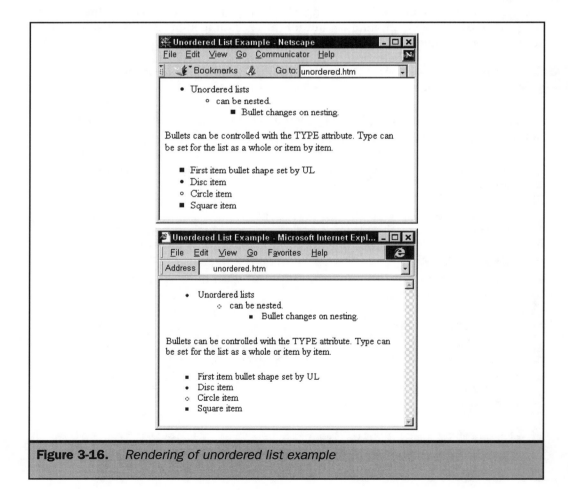

Figure 3-16. *Rendering of unordered list example*

DEFINITION LIST   A definition list is a list of terms paired with associated definitions—in other words, a glossary. Definition lists are enclosed within **<DL>** and **</DL>** tags. Each term being defined is indicated by a **<DT>** element, which is derived from *definition term*. Each definition itself is defined by **<DD>**. Neither the **<DT>** nor the **<DD>** element requires a close tag, but for long definitions, it may be helpful. The following is a basic example using **<DL>**, the rendering of which is shown in Figure 3-17:

```
<!DOCTYPE HTML PUBLIC "-//W3C//DTD HTML 4.0 Transitional//EN">
<HTML>
<HEAD>
<TITLE>Definition List Example</TITLE>
</HEAD>

<BODY>
<H1 ALIGN="center">Definitions</H1>
<DL>
    <DT>Gadget</DT>
    <DD>A useless device used in many HTML examples.</DD>

    <DT>Gizmo</DT>
    <DD>Another useless device used in a few HTML examples.</DD>
</DL>
</BODY>
</HTML>
```

Because definition lists don't add numbering or bullets, many HTML writers have used this element to indent text. While logically this is the most appropriate way to achieve some rudimentary indentation, the unordered list is often used instead. Looking at the use of **<UL>** and the output of HTML tools suggests that the use of **<UL>** instead of **<DL>** to indent text quickly is very common. The reason for the preference for **<UL>** is that it requires fewer elements to achieve indentation. Remember that lists can be nested, so a varying degree of indentation can be achieved. Users desiring a fine degree of control should avoid using lists to move things around. How far something is moved away from the left margin isn't precise, and may depend

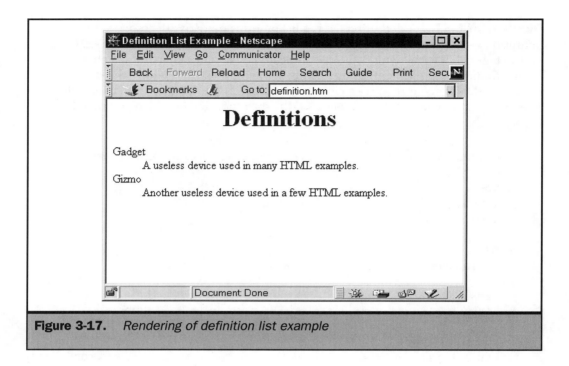

Figure 3-17. *Rendering of definition list example*

on the font size of the browser. A simple example of indenting with lists is shown next, with its rendering shown in Figure 3-18:

```
<!DOCTYPE HTML PUBLIC "-//W3C//DTD HTML 4.0 Transitional//EN">
<HTML>
<HEAD>
<TITLE>List Indent Example</TITLE>
</HEAD>

<BODY>
<DL><DD>This paragraph is indented. Watch out for
the left edge. Get too close and you'll hurt yourself!</P>
</DL>


<BR><BR>


<UL><UL>
<P>This paragraph is even further indented. Most HTML authors
```

```
and authoring tools tend to use this style to indent because
it takes fewer tags.</P>
</UL></UL>
</BODY>
</HTML>
```

*Some HTML purists are offended by the use of **<UL>** to indent. HTML authors might consider using the definition list, or tables, if possible, to indent text. However, with WYSIWYG editors spitting out **<UL>** elements in mass numbers, this may be more of a fine point than a real issue. The rise of style sheets and other technologies should, in time, put an end to this issue.*

VESTIGIAL LISTS: <DIR> AND <MENU>   Beyond basic ordered, unordered, and definition lists, two other lists are specified in HTML: **<MENU>** and **<DIR>**. These rarely used elements generally appear as unordered lists in most browsers. These elements are presented for completeness. HTML authors are warned not to use them, because they have been dropped from the strict version of HTML 4.

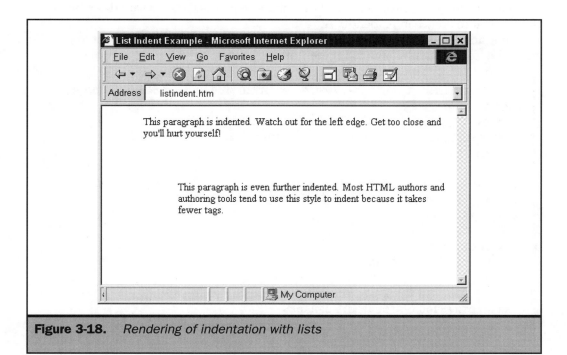

Figure 3-18.   *Rendering of indentation with lists*

Horizontal Rules

As sections are added to an HTML document, breaking up the document into visually distinct regions often is useful. A horizontal rule, indicated by the **<HR>** element, is a block-level element that serves this purpose. Under HTML 2, horizontal rules generally were rendered as an etched bar or line across a browser window. With HTML 3.2 and beyond, more control over the horizontal rule's look and size was added. The exact look of the line is still left to the browser rendering the page.

*Though it looks like a physical element, **<HR>** can have some logical meaning as a section break. For example, under an alternative browser, such as a speech-based browser, a horizontal rule might theoretically be interpreted as a pause. A hand-held browser with limited resolution might use it as a device to limit scrolling of the text.*

The **<HR>** element is an empty element, because it has no close tag and encloses no data. Adding an **<HR>** element between two paragraphs provides a simple way to put a horizontal rule between two sections.

Netscape Navigator, and later Internet Explorer, added several attributes to the **<HR>** element. **SIZE** sets the bar's thickness (height). **WIDTH** sets the bar's width. **ALIGN** sets its vertical alignment. **NOSHADE** renders the bar without a surrounding shadow. The HTML 3.2 and transitional 4.0 specification supports these basic attributes. Additional, browser-specific attributes (such as **COLOR**) are described in the element reference in Appendix A.

An example of horizontal rules and their basic attributes is shown next, the browser rendering for which is shown in Figure 3-19:

```
<!DOCTYPE HTML PUBLIC "-//W3C//DTD HTML 4.0 Transitional//EN">
<HTML>
<HEAD>
<TITLE>Horizontal Rule Example</TITLE>
</HEAD>

<BODY>
<P>Size of 10</P>
<HR SIZE="10">

<P>Width of 50% and no shading</P>
<HR WIDTH="50%" NOSHADE>

<P>Width of 200 pixels, size of 3 pixels, and no shading</P>
<HR WIDTH="200" SIZE="3" NOSHADE>
```

```
<P>Width of 100, aligned right</P>
<HR ALIGN="right" WIDTH="100">

<P>Width of 100, aligned left</P>
<HR ALIGN="left" WIDTH="100">

<P>Width of 100, aligned center</P>
<HR ALIGN="center" WIDTH="100">
</BODY>
</HTML>
```

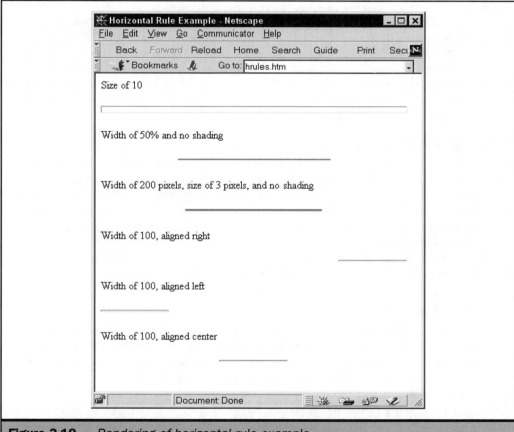

Figure 3-19.   *Rendering of horizontal rule example*

Address

The **<ADDRESS>** element is used to surround information, such as the signature of the person who created the page, or the address of the organization the page is about. For example,

```
<ADDRESS>
Big Company, Inc.<BR>
1122 Big Company Court<BR>
San Diego, CA 92109<BR>
619.555.2086<BR>
info@bigcompany.com<BR>
</ADDRESS>
```

might be inserted toward the bottom of every page throughout a Web site.

The **<ADDRESS>** element tends to act like a logical formatting element and results, typically, in italicized text. The HTML specification treats **<ADDRESS>** as an idiosyncratic block-level element. Like other block-level elements, it inserts a blank before and after the block. It may enclose many lines of text, formatting elements to change the font characteristics, and even images. According to the specification, it isn't supposed to enclose other block-level elements, such as **<UL>**. Browsers generally allow this, particularly with the **<P>** element.

Other Block-Level Elements

HTML has many other block-level elements, most notably tables and forms. Many other elements are available under Navigator and Internet Explorer, including frames, layers, and a variety of other formatting and structuring features. These elements could be introduced in this chapter, but because of their complexity, it makes more sense to discuss them in later chapters. Tables are discussed in depth in Chapter 7, and forms are discussed in Chapter 11.

The remaining sections of this chapter describe text-level elements and the many miscellaneous elements that are difficult to categorize.

Text-Level Elements

Text elements in HTML come in two basic flavors: physical and logical. *Physical elements*, such as **<B>** for bold and **<I>** for italic, are used to specify how text should be rendered. *Logical elements*, such as **<STRONG>** and **<EM>**, indicate what text is, but not necessarily how it should look. Although common renderings exist for logical text elements, the ambiguity of these elements and the limited knowledge of this type of document structuring have minimized their use. However, the rise of style sheets and the growing diversity of user agents mean using logical elements makes more sense than ever.

Physical Character-Formatting Elements

Sometimes, you may want to use bold, italics, or other font attributes to set off certain text, such as computer code. Common HTML supports various elements that can be used to influence physical formatting. The elements have no meaning other than to make text render in a particular way. Any other meaning is assigned by the reader. The common physical elements are listed in Table 3-1.

The following example code shows the basic use of the physical text-formatting elements:

```html
<!DOCTYPE HTML PUBLIC "-//W3C//DTD HTML 4.0 Transitional//EN">
<HTML>
<HEAD>
<TITLE>Physical Text Elements</TITLE>
</HEAD>

<BODY>
<H1 ALIGN="center">Physical Text Elements</H1>
<HR>
This is <B>Bold</B>                               <BR>
This is <I>Italic</I>                             <BR>
This is <TT>Monospaced</TT>                        <BR>
This is <U>Underlined</U>                          <BR>
This is <STRIKE>Strike-through</STRIKE>            <BR>
This is also <S>Strike-through</S>                 <BR>
This is <BIG>Big</BIG>                             <BR>
This is even <BIG><BIG>Bigger</BIG></BIG>          <BR>
This is <SMALL>Small</SMALL>                       <BR>
This is even <SMALL><SMALL>Smaller</SMALL></SMALL> <BR>
This is <SUP>Superscript</SUP>                     <BR>
This is <SUB>Subscript</SUB>                       <BR>
</BODY>
</HTML>
```

Physical elements can be combined in arbitrary ways. However, just because text *can* be made monospaced, bold, italic, and superscript doesn't mean that various types of formatting *should* be applied to text. Figure 3-20 shows the rendering of the physical text elements under Internet Explorer.

Several physical text-formatting elements—particularly <U>, <BIG>, and <SMALL>—present certain problems that warrant extra discussion.

Element	Element Type
<I> ... </I>	Italics
<B> ... </B>	Bold
<TT> ... </TT>	Typewriter (monospaced)
<U> ... </U>	Underline
<STRIKE> ... </STRIKE>	Strikethrough
<S> ... </S>	Alternative element form of strikethrough
_{...}	Subscript
^{...}	Superscript
<BIG> ... </BIG>	Bigger font (one font size bigger)
<SMALL> ... </SMALL>	Smaller font (one font size smaller)

Table 3-1.   *Table of Common Physical Text-Formatting Elements*

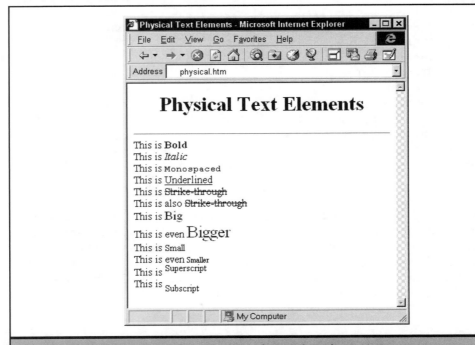

Figure 3-20.   *Rendering of physical text-formatting elements*

CONFUSION CAUSED BY UNDERLINING   Most browsers support the <U> element, which underlines text. It was not initially defined under HTML 2, and for good reason. The meaning of underlined text can be unclear to people who use the Web. In most graphical browsers, clickable hypertext links are represented as blue underlined text. (Link color may vary.) Users instinctively think of underlined text as something that can be clicked. Some feel that the link color sufficiently distinguishes links from text that is underlined purely for stylistic purposes. However, this doesn't take into consideration monochrome monitors or people who are colorblind. Because the underline element may introduce more trouble than it is worth, it should be avoided.

USING <BIG> AND <SMALL>   What do the **<BIG>** and **<SMALL>** elements actually do? On the face of it, putting the **<BIG>** element around something makes it bigger. Putting the **<SMALL>** element around something makes it smaller. What about when multiple **<BIG>** and **<SMALL>** elements are nested? HTML has relative fonts ranging from size 1, very small, to size 7, very large. Every application of **<BIG>** generally bumps up the font one notch to the next level. The default font for a document is usually relative size 3, so two applications of **<BIG>** would raise the font size to 5. Multiple occurrences of **<SMALL>** do the opposite—they make things one size smaller.

What happens when the maximum or minimum size is reached? Ideally, the browser just ignores extra applications. Depending on the browser, however, this may or may not happen. Some Web browser versions, notably Internet Explorer 3, handle multiple occurrences of the **<BIG>** and **<SMALL>** elements in an unpredictable manner. While this has been fixed under Internet Explorer 4, HTML authors are warned to use only one **<BIG>** or **<SMALL>** element at a time. Other font-sizing changes should be handled with the **<FONT>** element, discussed in Chapter 6.

Logical Elements

Logical elements indicate the type of content that they enclose. The browser is relatively free to determine the presentation of that content, although expected renderings for these elements exist that are followed by nearly all browsers. While this practice conforms to the design of HTML, there are issues about perception. Will a designer think **<STRONG>** or **<B>**? As mentioned previously, HTML pundits push for **<STRONG>**, because a browser for the blind could read strong text properly. For the majority of people coding Web pages, however, HTML is used as a visual language, despite its design intentions. Furthermore, how do you indicate something is **<STRONG>** in a WYSIWYG editor?

Seasoned experts know the beauty and intentions behind logical elements, and hopefully with style sheets, logical elements may catch on more. For now, a quick survey of sites will show that logical text elements are relatively rare. In fact, many HTML editors make it downright difficult to add logical elements to a page, which only furthers the reasons why most logical elements are rarely used. When style sheets become more commonplace, HTML authors should reexamine their use of these elements. Table 3-2 illustrates the logical text-formatting elements generally supported by browsers.

Element	Element Type
<ABBR> ... </ABBR>	Abbreviation
<CITE> ... </CITE>	Citation
<CODE> ... </CODE>	Source code
<DFN> ... </DFN>	Definition
<EM> ... <EM>	Emphasis
<KBD> ... </KBD>	Keystrokes
<SAMP> ... </SAMP>	Sample (example information)
<STRONG> ... </STRONG>	Strong emphasis
<VAR> ... </VAR>	Programming variable

Table 3-2.   *Table of Logical Text-Formatting Elements*

The following example uses all the logical elements in a test document (shown in Figure 3-21 under common browsers):

```
<!DOCTYPE HTML PUBLIC "-//W3C//DTD HTML 4.0 Transitional//EN">
<HTML>
<HEAD>
<TITLE>Logical Text Elements</TITLE>
</HEAD>

<BODY>
<H1 ALIGN="center">Logical Text Elements</H1>
<HR>
This is <EM>Emphasis</EM>                 <BR>
This is <STRONG>Strong</STRONG>           <BR>
This is <CITE>Citation</CITE>             <BR>
This is <CODE>Code</CODE>                 <BR>
This is <DFN>Definition</DFN>             <BR>
This is <KBD>Keyboard</KBD>               <BR>
This is <SAMP>Sample</SAMP>               <BR>
This is <VAR>Variable</VAR>               <BR>
</BODY>
</HTML>
```

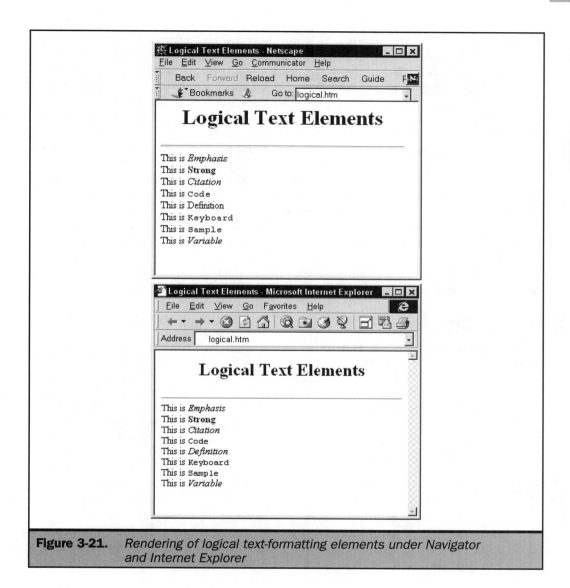

Figure 3-21.   *Rendering of logical text-formatting elements under Navigator and Internet Explorer*

Note that subtle differences may occur in rendering. For example, **<VAR>** results in monospaced text under Internet Explorer 4, but yields italicized text under Navigator 3. There is no guarantee of rendering, and older versions of browsers may vary on other logical elements, including even **<EM>**.

Probably the biggest question HTML authors have about logical elements is where to use them. This really is a philosophical question. Does the author want to define content presentation strictly or let the browser decide on a presentation appropriate for the element's logical meaning? Advocates of logical document structuring note that if a browser doesn't support bolding, the **<B>** element has no effect. Instead, the logical **<STRONG>** element, usually rendered as bold, would be rendered in some appropriate alternative. Whether this type of reasoning justifies logical structure is an open question.

With the proliferation of Web-browsing devices, such as cellular phones, personal digital assistants, WebTV, and popular browsers, logical document structuring may yet catch on. In conjunction with style sheets (discussed in Chapter 10), this approach to structure may become commonplace, because it allows different presentations for different situations. A cellular phone browser might require a different style than Navigator on a PC with a high-resolution monitor. Although this may happen, an inspection of published pages shows that few people currently use logical text elements. From a presentation perspective, why use the ambiguous **<STRONG>** element when you can use the precise **<B>** element? In addition, many HTML development tools make it difficult to insert logically oriented HTML.

Character Entities

After covering the basic text-formatting elements, you may think that nothing remains to talk about—but one more level exists to HTML documents: the characters themselves.

Sometimes, you need to put special characters within a document, such as accented letters, copyright symbols, or even the angle brackets used to enclose HTML elements. To use such characters in an HTML document, they must be "escaped" by using a special code. All character codes take the form **&*code*;**, in which *code* is a word or numeric code indicating the actual character that you want to put onscreen. Some of the more commonly used characters are shown in Table 3-3.

Note   *The character entity ™ may not always be acceptable as trademark. On many UNIX platforms, and potentially on Macs or Windows systems using various other character sets, this entity doesn't render as trademark. Because &153; may be undefined, HTML authors should try to avoid it, even though it tends to coincide with ™ on the default Windows platform and some character sets. Trademarks are important legally, so they are often needed. A future version of HTML likely will include a trademark element, but for now, the commonly used workaround is to use ^{<SMALL>TM</SMALL>}. This code creates a superscript trademark symbol (™) in a slightly smaller font. Because it's standard HTML, it works on nearly every platform.*

Numeric Value	Named Value	Symbol	Description
&#034;	&quot;	"	Quotation mark
&#038;	&amp;	&	Ampersand
&#060;	&lt;	<	Less than
&#062;	&gt;	>	Greater than
&#153;	N/A	TM	Trademark
			Nonbreaking space
&#169;	&copy;	©	Copyright symbol
&#174;	&reg;	®	Registered trademark

Table 3-3.   *A Few Common Character Entities*

The following example shows some basic uses of HTML character entities, while Figure 3-22 shows how the example might render:

```
<!DOCTYPE HTML PUBLIC "-//W3C//DTD HTML 4.0 Transitional//EN">
<HTML>
<HEAD>
<TITLE>Character Entities Example</TITLE>
</HEAD>

<BODY>
<H1 ALIGN="center">Big Company Inc.'s Tagging Products</H1>
<HR>

<P>Character entities like &amp;copy; allow users to insert special
characters like &copy;.</P>

<P>One entity that is both useful and abused is the nonbreaking
space.</P>

<BR><BR>
```

```
Inserting spaces is easy with  <BR>
Look:   S       P      
A       C       E  
    S.<BR>

<HR>
<ADDRESS>
Contents of this page &copy; 1999 Big Company, Inc.<BR> The
<B>Wonder Tag</B> &lt;P&gt; &#153; is a registered trademark
of Big Company, Inc.
</ADDRESS>
</BODY>
</HTML>
```

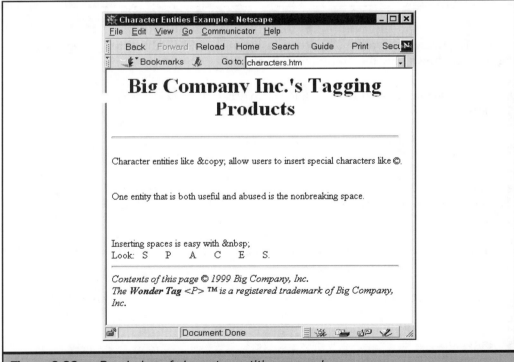

Figure 3-22. *Rendering of character entities example*

Note   *The use of the nonbreaking space to push text or elements around the screen is an overused crutch. Many HTML editors overuse this technique in an attempt to preserve a certain look and feel. This entity is discussed further in Chapter 6.*

Note   *Excessive use of character entities can make HTML source documents difficult to read if the character entities aren't well spaced.*

The character set currently supported by HTML is the ISO Latin-1 character set. Many of its characters, such as accents and special symbols, cannot be typed on all keyboards. They must be entered into HTML documents by using the appropriate code. Even if the character in question is supported on the keyboard (for example, the copyright symbol), simply typing in the symbol probably will not produce the correct encoding. Of course, many HTML editors make the appropriate insertion for you. A complete list of the character entities is presented in Appendix C.

Note   *HTML is capable of representing the standard ASCII characters and all the extended characters defined by the ISO Latin-1 character set. However, for non-Western characters, such as Japanese, Russian, or Arabic alphabets, special encoding and a special browser are needed.*

Summary

Common HTML includes the basic elements that HTML authors tend to use from the specification. Ideally, HTML is a formally defined, structured language with rules governing correct element usage. Pragmatically, however, browsers determine correct HTML usage by the HTML constructs that they successfully render. Browsers are lax in their interpretation of HTML rules, which encourages some authors to break those rules frequently. Well-written HTML documents begin with a **<!DOCTYPE>** declaration, followed by an **<HTML>** element. This encloses the document and divides it into a **<HEAD>** section, followed by a **<BODY>** section. The **<HEAD>** element contains descriptive information and must contain one **<TITLE>** element. The **<BODY>** element contains the document's displayed content. It may be structured using block-level elements, text-level elements, and special-character entities. Some text-level elements assign content a logical purpose. Others assign a physical presentation.

The elements presented so far are common across nearly all systems. Whether or not they are used, they are simple and widely understood. Yet, despite their simplicity, many of these basic elements are still abused to achieve a particular document look, which continues the struggle between the logical and physical nature of HTML. Despite some manipulation, these elements are generally used in a reasonable manner. More-complex formatting elements and programming elements are introduced in later chapters. The simplicity of this chapter should provide you with some assurance that HTML rests on a stable core.

A great number of elements have been left out of this discussion. No mention was made of layout-oriented elements, and graphics have been completely avoided. These topics and others are covered in upcoming chapters. First, we'll deal with the *H* in HTML, namely hypertext, and present the concept of linking documents and objects in the next chapter.

Chapter 4

Links and Addressing

revious chapters have shown how HTML can be used as a document formatting and structuring language, but little has been said about the hypertext aspect of the language. HTML makes it possible to define hyperlinks to other information items located all over the world, then allowing documents to join the global information space known as the World Wide Web. Linking is possible because every document on the Web has a unique address, known as a *uniform resource locator (URL)*. The explosive growth of documents on the Web has created a tangled mess, even when document locations are named consistently. The disorganized nature of the Web often leaves users lost in cyberspace. Finding information online can feel like trying to find the proverbial needle in a worldwide haystack. However, things don't have to be this way. Application of logical structure to sites; new ideas such as *uniform resource names (URNs)*; and *uniform resource characteristics (URCs)* in the form of meta-data, such as *Platform for Internet Content Selection (PICS)* labels, may eventually lead to a more understandable and organized Web.

Linking Basics

In HTML, the main way to define hyperlinks is with the anchor element, **<A>**. A *link* is simply a unidirectional pointer from the source document that contains the link to some destination. In hypertext, the end points of a link typically are called *anchors*, thus the use of the anchor nomenclature in HTML documentation.

For linking purposes, the **<A>** element requires one attribute: **HREF**. The **HREF** attribute is set to the URL of the target resource, which is basically the address of the document to link to, such as http://www.yahoo.com. The text enclosed by the **<A>** elements specifies a "hot spot" to activate the hyperlink. Anchor content may include text, images, or a mixture of the two. A general link takes the form **<A HREF="URL">**Visit our site**</A>**. The text "Visit our site" is the link. The URL specified by the **HREF** attribute is the destination, if the link is activated. Here is an example of simple **<A>** element usage; the text "Yahoo!" is the first link:

```
<!DOCTYPE HTML PUBLIC "-//W3C//DTD HTML 4.0 Transitional//EN">
<HTML>
<HEAD>
<TITLE>Simple Link Example</TITLE>
</HEAD>

<BODY>
<H1 ALIGN="center">Lots of Links</H1>
<HR>
```

```
<UL>
   <LI>Visit <A HREF="http://www.yahoo.com">Yahoo!</A>
   <LI>Conduct powerful searches with
       <A HREF="http://www.hotbot.com">HotBot</A>
   <LI>Go to the <A HREF="http://www.w3.org">W3C</A>
</UL>
</BODY>
</HTML>
```

When the preceding example is loaded into a Web browser, the links generally are indicated by underlined text, typically in a different color—usually blue or purple, depending on whether the link object has been viewed before. Link objects are displayed in a different color after you visit the linked page, so that you know in the future which links you have already followed. Status information in the browser may change when a mouse is positioned over a link. The pointer may also change, as well as other indicators showing that the information is a link. Examples of link feedback in various browsers is shown in Figure 4-1. Note that the cursor over the HotBot link in the upper-left corner now looks like a pointing finger, and the URL for the HotBot home page appears in the status area in the lower-left corner of the browser frame.

Note   *Under some browsers, link underlining can be turned off. This may cause usability problems for some users, but many find pages rendered in this way more esthetically pleasing.*

The actual rendering of links depends on the browser or other user agent. If you are using HTML style sheets, the links that you create may have different decoration. For example, a color may change for a link that has been visited previously.

Note   *You can underline any text in an HTML document by tagging it with the underline element, <U>. This practice may lead to confusion between hyperlinks and text that is underlined for stylistic purposes only. This is particularly evident if the link is viewed in a black-and-white environment or by a color-blind individual. Therefore, use the <U> element for nonlinked items with caution, so that you don't confuse users.*

In the simplest example, all the <A> elements refer to an address that contains only an external server address in the form of a URL. In many cases, however, links are made within a Web site. In this situation, a shortened URL is used, called a *relative URL*, which includes only the filename or directory structure. The following example links to several other documents: a document in the same directory, called specs.htm; a

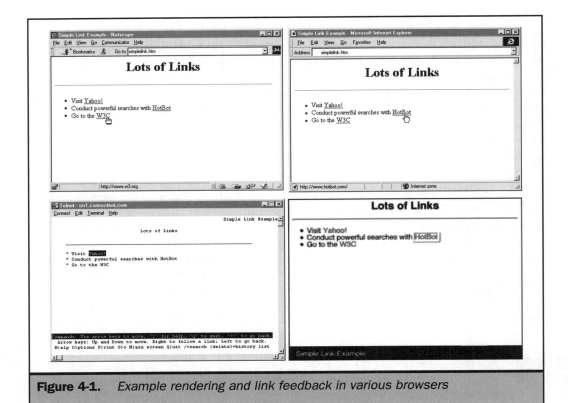

Figure 4-1. *Example rendering and link feedback in various browsers*

document in the "extras" subdirectory, called access.htm; and a link back to a home page:

```
<!DOCTYPE HTML PUBLIC "-//W3C//DTD HTML 4.0 Transitional//EN">
<HTML>
<HEAD>
<TITLE>Simple Link Example 2</TITLE>
</HEAD>

<BODY>
<H1 ALIGN="center">Green Gadgets</H1>
<HR>
```

```
<P ALIGN="center">Information about the mysterious Green
Gadget--the wonder tool of the millennium.</P>
  <UL>
    <LI><A HREF="specs.htm">Specifications</A>
    <LI><A HREF="extras/access.htm">Accessories</A>
  </UL>
<P ALIGN= center >
    <A HREF="../index.htm">Back to Big Company Home Page</A>
</P>
</BODY>
</HTML>
```

These basic examples show that the use of links, at least within text, is simple. Specifying the destination URL may not be so obvious. HTML authors often are tempted to use only very simple relative URLs, such as a filename, or fully qualified URLs, but without a sense of what URLs really can provide. Later in this chapter, the discussion returns to the HTML syntax for forming links. First, take a closer look at URLs, because thoroughly understanding URLs is quite important for forming links.

What Are URLs?

A URL is a uniform way to refer to objects and services on the Internet. Even novice users should be familiar with typing a URL, such as http://www.yahoo.com/, in a browser dialog box to get to a Web site. Internet users use URLs to invoke other Internet services, such as transferring files via FTP or sending e-mail. HTML authors use URLs in their documents to define hyperlinks to other Web documents. Despite its potentially confusing collection of slashes and colons, the URL syntax is designed to provide a clear, simple notation that people can easily understand. The designers intended URLs to be useful as information for books, business cards, and even the backs of paper napkins, not just computers, in that they are easily transmittable in forms outside the Internet. Some people might counter that saying http:// or www all the time is troublesome. The following concepts will help you to understand the major components of a URL address.

Note   *Some people call URLs* universal *resource locators. Except for a historical reference to* universal resource locators *in documentation from a few years ago, the current standard wording is* uniform *resource locator.*

Basic Concepts

To find any arbitrary object on the Internet, you need to find out the following information:

1. First, you need to locate and access the machine on the Internet (or intranet) on which the object resides. Locating the site might be a matter of specifying its domain name or IP address, while accessing the machine might be a matter of providing a username and password.

2. After you access the machine, you need to determine the name of the desired file, where the file is located, and what protocol will be used to retrieve the information or access the object.

The URL describes where something is and how it will be retrieved. The *how* is specified by the protocol (for example, HTTP). The *where* is specified by the machine name, the directory name, and the filename. Slashes and other characters are used to separate the parts of the address into machine-readable pieces. The basic structure of the URL is shown here:

protocol://site address/directory/filename

The next several sections look at the individual pieces of a URL in significant detail.

Site Address

Every Web document exists on some server computer somewhere on the global Internet or within a private intranet. The first step in finding a document is to identify its server. The most convenient way to do this on a TCP/IP-based network is with a symbolic name, called a *domain name*. On the Internet at large, a fully qualified domain name (FQDN) typically consists of a machine name, followed by a domain name. For example, www.microsoft.com specifies a machine named *www* in the microsoft.com domain. On an intranet, however, things may be a little different, because you can avoid using a domain name. For example, a machine name of hr-server may be all that you need to access the human resources server within your company's intranet.

> **Note**   *A machine name indicates the local, intra-organizational name for the actual server. A machine name can be just about any name, because machine naming has no mandated rules. Conventions exist, however, for identifying servers that provide common Internet resources. Servers for Web documents usually begin with the www prefix. However, many local machines have names similar to the user's own name (for example, jsmith), his or her favorite cartoon character (for example, homer), or even an esoteric machine name (for example, dell-p6-200-a12). Machine naming conventions are important because they allow users to form URLs without explicitly spelling them out. A user who understands domain names and machine naming conventions should be able to guess that Toyota's Web server is http://www.toyota.com/.*

The other part of most site addresses, the domain name, is fairly regular. Within the United States, a domain name consists of the actual domain or organization name, followed by a period, and then a domain type. An example is sun.com. The domain itself is sun, which represents Sun Microsystems. The sun domain exists within the commercial zone, because of Sun's corporate status, so it ends with the domain type of *com*. In the U.S., most domain identifiers currently use a three-character code that indicates the type of organization that owns the server. The most common codes are *com* for commercial, *gov* for government, *org* for nonprofit organization, *edu* for educational institution, *net* for network, and *mil* for military. Recently, some debate has occurred regarding the extent of the domain name space. Soon, a variety of new domain endings may be added, such as *firm*, *web*, and *nom*. Table 4-1 sets forth a basic listing of U.S. domain types.

Domain space beyond the United States is somewhat more complicated. An FQDN, including a country code, is generally written as follows:

machine name.domain name.domain type.country code

Zone identifiers outside the U.S. use a two-character code to indicate the country hosting the server. These include *ca* for Canada, *mx* for Mexico, and *jp* for Japan. Within each country, the local naming authorities may create domain types at their own discretion, but these domain types can't correspond to American extensions. For

Domain Type	Domain Description	Example
com	Commercial entities and individuals	apple.com
net	Networks and network providers	cerf.net
org	Nonprofit and other organizations	greenpeace.org
edu	Four-year colleges and universities	ucla.edu
gov	United States federal government agencies	whitehouse.gov
mil	United States federal government military entities	nosc.mil
us	Used for a variety of organizations and individuals, including K through 12 education, libraries, and city and county governments	co.san-diego.ca.us

Table 4-1.   *Domain Types in the United States*

example, www.sony.co.jp specifies a Web server for Sony in the *co* zone of Japan. In this case, *co*, rather than *com*, indicates a commercial venture. In the United Kingdom, the educational domain space has a different name, *ac*. Oxford University's Web server is www.ox.ac.uk, whereby ac indicates *academic*, compared to the U.S. *edu* extension for *education*. Despite a flattening of geographical name use for large, multinational companies (such as Sony), regional naming differences are very much alive. Web page authors linking to non-native domains are encouraged to understand the naming conventions of those environments. One special top-level domain, *int*, is reserved for organizations established by international treaties between governments, such as the European Union (eu.int). Top-level domains, such as *com*, *net*, and any upcoming new domains, may not necessarily correspond to a particular geographic area.

Note   *Symbolic names make it convenient for people to refer to Internet servers. A server's real address is its Internet Protocol (IP) numeric address. Every accessible server on the Internet has a unique IP address by which it can be located using the TCP/IP protocol. An IP address is a numeric string that consists of four numbers between 0 and 255, separated by periods (for example, 213.6.17.34). This number may then correspond to a domain name, such as www.bigcompany.com. Note that a server's symbolic name must be translated, or resolved, into an IP address before it can be used to locate a server. An Internet service known as Domain Name Service (DNS) automatically performs this translation. You can use an IP address instead of a symbolic name to specify an Internet server, but doing so gives up mnemonic convenience. In some cases, using an IP address may be necessary because, although every server has an IP address, not all servers have symbolic names.*

Investigating all aspects of the domain name structure is beyond the scope of this book. However, it should be noted that domain name formats and the domain name lookup service are very critical to the operation of the Web. If the domain name server is unavailable, it is impossible to access a Web server. To learn more about machine and domain names, explore the following Web sites:

- http://rs.internic.net/rs-internic.html
- http://www.iana.org
- http://www.gtld-mou.org

Note   *Domain names are not case-sensitive. For example, you could write www.BigCompany.com or www.BIGCOMPANY.com. A browser should handle both properly. Case is typically changed for marketing or branding purposes. Directory values following the domain name may be case-sensitive, depending on the operating system that the Web server is running on. For example, UNIX systems are case-sensitive, while Windows machines are not. Trouble can arise if casing is used randomly. As a rule of thumb, keep everything in lowercase, or consistently use uppercase for just the first letters in directories and filenames.*

After you specify the machine, either by its domain name or its IP address, you may need to specify the particular directory on the particular machine, as described next.

Directory

Servers may contain hundreds, if not thousands, of files. For practical use, files need to be organized into manageable units, analogous to the manila folders traditionally used to organize paper documents. This unit is known as a *file directory*. After you know on which server a document resides, the next step toward identifying its location is to specify the directory that contains the file. Just as one manila folder can contain other folders, directories can contain other directories. Directories contain other directories in a nested, hierarchical structure that resembles the branches of a tree. The directory that contains all others is known as the *root directory*. Taken together, all the directories and files form a file tree, or *file system*. A file is located in a file system by specifying its *directory path*. This is the nested list of all directories that contain the file—from the most general, the root directory—to the most specific. Similar to the UNIX operating system, directories hosted on Web servers are separated by forward slashes (/) rather than backslashes (\), as in DOS. Figure 4-2 shows a sample file tree for a Web site, where directories are organized within (or above and below) one another. For example, the directory called **special** is within the **products** directory, which is within the root directory, as indicated by the forward slash. The full path should be written as /products/special/ to indicate that **special** is an actual directory, not a file in the **products** directory. When linking to other files, you may need to refer to a directory above the current directory, or to the current directory itself. In the scheme presented, ./ means the current directory, while ../ means one directory up in the hierarchy. A document in the **special** directory with a link path of ../ will link up to the **products** directory.

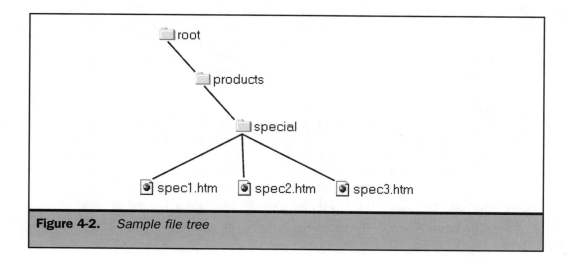

Figure 4-2.   *Sample file tree*

> **Note** *Directory names may follow conventions specific to an operating system, including being case-sensitive. Authors are cautioned to look carefully at directory casing. Furthermore, directories may follow popular usage conventions (for example, tmp), or they may be arbitrary. Usually, directory names reflect aspects of media types, subject matter, or access privileges of their content. For example, a directory called "images" might be the name of a directory containing images.*

Filename

After you specify the server and directory path for a document, the next step toward locating it is to specify its filename. This step typically has two parts: a filename, followed by a standard file extension. Filenames can be any names that are applicable under the server's operating system. Special characters such as spaces, colons, and slashes might play havoc if used in names of Web-available files. A file named test:1.htm would present problems on a Macintosh system, whereas test/1.htm might be legal on a Macintosh but problematic on a PC or UNIX machine.

A dot separates the filename and the *extension*, which is a code, usually three letters, that identifies the type of information contained in the file. For example, HTML source files have an .htm or .html extension. JPEG images have a .jpg extension. A file's extension is critically important for Web applications, because it usually is the only indication of the information type that a file contains. A Web server reads a file extension and uses it to determine which headers, in the form of a MIME type (discussed in Chapter 16), to attach to a file when delivering it to a browser. If file extensions are omitted or misused, the file may be interpreted incorrectly. When browsers read files directly, they also look at file extensions to determine how to render the file. If the extension is missing or incorrect, a file generally will not be properly displayed in a Web browser.

> **Note** *While many operating systems support four or more letters for file extensions, using a three-letter extension (.htm) versus a four-letter extension (.html) ensures that cross-platform incompatibilities are minimized. Spaces, uppercasing, and special characters should also be avoided, to provide the greatest flexibility. Authors and users should particularly be aware of case sensitivity in filenames and directory names.*

Protocol

It may seem that nothing more is needed to locate a document than its server, directory, and filename. However, one component is missing—the protocol. The Internet supports a standard set of resources, each with its own associated protocol. A *protocol* is the structured discussion that computers follow to negotiate resource-specific services. For example, the protocol that makes the Web possible is the Hypertext Transfer Protocol (HTTP). When you click a hyperlink in a Web document, your browser uses the HTTP protocol to contact a Web server and retrieve the appropriate document.

> **Note** *Although HTTP stands for Hypertext Transfer Protocol, it doesn't specify how a file is transported from a server to a browser, only how the discussion between the server and browser will take place to get the file. The actual transport of files is usually up to a lower-layer network protocol, such as the Transmission Control Protocol (TCP). On the Internet, the combination of TCP and IP makes raw communication possible. Although a subtle point, many Web professionals are unaware of lower-level protocols below application protocols, such as HTTP, which are part of URLs.*

Although less frequently used than HTTP and TCP/IP, several other protocols are important to HTML authors, because they can be invoked by hyperlinks. Here are some examples:

Protocol	Description
File	Enables a hyperlink to access a file on the local file system
File Transfer Protocol (FTP)	Enables a hyperlink to download files from remote systems
Gopher	Enables a hyperlink to access a Gopher server
mailto	Calls the *Simple Mail Transfer Protocol (SMTP)*, the Internet mail protocol, and enables a hyperlink to send an addressed e-mail message
Network News Transport Protocol (NNTP)	Enables a hyperlink to access a USENET news article
news	Enables a hyperlink to access a USENET newsgroup
telnet	Enables a hyperlink to open a telnet session on a remote host

These are the common protocols, but a variety of new protocols and URL forms are being debated all the time. Someday, such things as LDAP (Lightweight Directory Access Protocol), IRC (Internet Relay Chat), phone, fax, and even TV might be used to reference how data should be accessed. More about the future of URLs and other naming ideas is discussed toward the end of this chapter.

Beyond the protocol, server address, directory, and filename, URLs often include a username and password, port number, and sometimes a fragment identifier. Some

URLs, such as mailto, might even contain a different form of information altogether, such as an e-mail address rather than a server or filename.

User and Password

FTP and telnet are protocols for *authenticated services*. Authenticated services may assume access by authorized users, and the protocols may require a username and password as parameters. A username and password precede a server name, like this: *username:password@server-address*. The password may be optional or unspecified in the URL, making the form simply *username@server-address*.

HTML authors are warned not to include password information in URLs, because the information will be readily viewable in a Web page or within the browser's URL box.

Port

Although the situation is rare, the communication port number used in a URL also can be specified. Browsers speaking a particular protocol communicate with servers through entry points, known as *ports*, which generally are identified by numeric addresses. Associated with each protocol is a default port number. For example, an HTTP request defaults to port number 80. A server administrator can configure a server to handle protocol requests at ports other than the default numbers. Usually, this occurs for experimental or secure applications. In these cases, the intended port must be explicitly addressed in a URL. To specify a port number, place it after the server address, separated by a colon: for example, *site-address*:8080. Web administrators are forewarned not to change port numbers arbitrarily, because it confuses users and may result in them having difficulty accessing a site, particularly if access comes from behind a firewall. In short, users coming from sites with well-defined security policies may not be set up to access sites running on nonstandard port numbers.

Some Web development systems may require users to log in on nonstandard ports. A common example is an Administrator that needs to access a nonstandard port to configure a Web server using a Web browser.

Fragment

After a user specifies a file, the user may want to go directly to a particular point in the file. Because you can set up named links under HTML, you can provide links directly to different points in a file. To jump to a particular named link, the URL must include the link name, preceded by a pound symbol (#), which indicates that the value is a fragment identifier. To specify a point called "contents" in a file called test.htm, you would use test.htm#contents. Elsewhere in the file, the fragment name would be set using a named anchor, such as **<A NAME="contents"></A>**. This will be discussed later in the chapter.

Encoding

When writing the components of a URL, take care that they are written using only the displayable characters in the US-ASCII character set. Even when using characters within this basic keyboard character range, you will find certain unsafe characters, or reserved characters that may have special meaning within the context of a URL or the operating system on which the resource is found. If any unsafe, reserved, or nonprintable characters occur in a URL, they must be encoded in a special form. Failure to encode these characters may lead to errors.

The form of encoding consists of a percent sign and two hexadecimal digits corresponding to the value of the character in the ASCII character set. Within many intranet environments, filenames often include user-friendly names, such as "first quarter earnings 1997.doc." Such names contain unsafe characters. If this file were to live on a departmental Web server, it would have a URL with a file portion of first%20quarter%20earnings%201997.doc. Notice how the spaces have been mapped to **%20** values—the hex value of the space character in ASCII. Other characters that will be troublesome in URLs include the slash character (/), which encodes as **%2F**, the question mark, which maps to **%3F**, and the percent itself, which encodes as **%25**. Only alphanumeric values and some special characters ($ – _ . + ! * '), including parentheses, may be used in a URL. Other characters should be encoded. In general, special characters such as accents, spaces, and some punctuation marks have to be encoded. HTML authors are encouraged to name files with encoding in mind, so that encoding can be avoided whenever possible. Table 4-2 shows the reserved and potentially dangerous characters for URLs.

Character	Encoding Value
Space	%20
/	%2F
?	%3F
:	%3A
;	%3B
&	%26
@	%40
=	%3D

Table 4-2. *Common Character Encoding Values*

Character	Encoding Value
#	%23
%	%25
>	%3E
<	%3C
{	%7B
}	%7D
[	%5B
]	%5D
"	%22
`	%27
´	%60
^^	%5E
~	%7E
\	%5C
|	%7C

Table 4-2.   *Common Character Encoding Values* (continued)

 Many of the characters in Table 4-2 don't have to be encoded; but encoding a character never causes problems, so when in doubt, encode it.

With this brief discussion of all the various components coming to a close, the next section presents a formula for creating URLs, as well as some examples.

Formula for a URL

All URLs share the same basic syntax: a protocol name, followed by a colon, followed by a protocol-specific resource description:

```
protocol_name:resource_description
```

Beyond this basic syntax, enough variation exists between protocol specifics for each to merit a separate discussion.

HTTP

A minimal HTTP URL simply gives a server name. It provides no directory or file information. A minimal HTTP formula commonly occurs for corporate addresses used in advertising:

- **Formula** `http://server/`
- **Example** `http://www.bigcompany.com/`

A minimal HTTP URL implicitly requests the home directory of a Web site. Even when a trailing slash isn't used, it is assumed and added either by the user agent or the Web server, making an address such as http://www.bigcompany.com become http://www.bigcompany.com/. By default, requesting a directory often results in the server returning a default file from the directory, termed the *index file*. Usually, index files are named index.htm or default.htm (or index.html and default.html, respectively), depending on the server software being used. This is only a convention; Web administrators are free to name default index files whatever they like. Interestingly, many people put special importance on the minimal HTTP URL form when, like all other file-retrieval URLs, this form simply specifies a particular directory or default index file to return, although this isn't always explicitly written out.

Note *Some sites are now renaming their systems so that the use of www is optional. For example, http://pint.com/ is the same as http://www.pint.com. Although browsers often provide similar shorthand functionality, users should be careful not to assume such forms are valid. For example, in some browsers, typing bigcompany by itself may resolve to http://www.bigcompany.com. This is a browser usability improvement and can't be used as a URL in an HTML document. Because of misunderstandings with URLs, site managers are encouraged to add as many variable forms as possible, so that the site works regardless of browser improvements or slight mistakes in linking.*

Making the HTTP URL example slightly more complex, a formula is presented to retrieve a specific HTML file that is assumed to exist in the default directory for the server:

- **Formula** `http://server/file`
- **Example** `http://www.bigcompany.com/hello.htm`

An alternate, incremental extension adds directory information without specifying a file. Although the final slash should be provided, servers imply its existence if it is omitted and look for a "home" document in the given directory. In practice, the final slash is optional, but recommended:

- **Formula** `http://server/directory/`
- **Example** `http://www.bigcompany.com/products/`

An HTTP URL can specify both a directory and file:

- **Formula** `http://server/directory/file`
- **Example** `http://www.bigcompany.com/products/greeting.htm`

On some systems, special shorthand conventions may be available for directory use. For example, a UNIX-based Web server may support many directories, each owned by a specific user. Rather than spelling out the full path to a user's root directory, the user directory can be abbreviated by using the tilde character (~), followed by the user's account, followed by a slash. Any directory or file information that follows this point will be relative to the user's root directory:

- **Formula** `http://server/~user/`
- **Example** `http://www.bigisp.com/~jsmith/`

User directories indicated by the tilde are somewhat similar to the convention used on the UNIX operating system, though other Web servers on different operating systems may provide similar shortcut support.

A URL can refer to a named location inside an HTML document, which is called a *marker*, or *named link*. How markers are created is discussed later in the chapter; but for now, to refer to a document marker, follow the target document's filename with the pound character (#) and then with the marker name:

- **Formula** `http://server/directory/file#marker`
- **Example** `http://www.bigcompany.com/profile.htm#introduction`

In addition to referring to HTML documents, an HTTP URL can request any type of file. For example, http://www.bigcompany.com/images/logo.gif would retrieve from a server a GIF image rather than an HTML file. Authors should be aware that the flexibility of Web servers and URLs is often overlooked, due to the common belief that a Web-based document must be in the HTML format for it to be linked to.

To the contrary, even an HTTP URL can reference and execute a server program. These server-side programs are typically termed *Common Gateway Interface (CGI)* programs, referring to the interface standard that describes how to pass data in and out of a program. CGI and similar server-side programming facilities are discussed in Chapter 12. Quite often, server-side programs are used to access databases and then generate HTML documents in response to user-entered queries. Parameters for such programs can be directly included in a URL by appending a question mark, followed by the actual parameter string. Because the user may type special characters in a query, characters normally not allowed within a URL are encoded. Remember that the formula for special-character encoding is a percent sign, followed by two hex numbers representing the character's ASCII value. For example, a blank character can be represented by **%20**.

- **Formula**   `http://server/directory/file?parameters`
- **Example**   `http://www.bigcompany.com/products/`
                `search.cgi?cost=400.00&name=Super%20Part`

Forming complex URLs with encoding and query strings looks very difficult. In reality, this is rarely done manually. Typically, the browser generates such a string on-the-fly based on data provided via a file form. A more detailed discussion of HTML interaction with programming facilities appears in Chapters 11 through 14.

Finally, any HTTP request can be directed to a port other than the default port value of 80 by following the server identification with a colon and the intended port number:

- **Formula**   `http://server:port/directory/file`
- **Example**   `http://www.bigcompany.com:8080/products/greetings.htm`

In the preceding example, the URL references a Web server running on port 8080. Although any unreserved port number is valid, using nonstandard port numbers on servers is not good practice. To access the address in the example, a user would need to include the port number in the URL. If it is omitted, accessing www.bigcompany.com will be impossible.

One case of HTTP exists that is, in a sense, a different protocol: secured Web transactions using the Secure Sockets Layer (SSL). In this case, the protocol is referenced as https, and the port value is assumed to be 443. An example formula for Secure HTTP is shown here; other than the cosmetic difference of the *s* and the different port value, it is identical to other HTTP URLs:

- **Formula**   `https://server:port/directory/file`
- **Example**   `https://www.wellsfargo.com`

An HTTP URL for a Web page is probably the most common URL, but users may find file or similar types of URLs growing in popularity, due to the rise of intranets and serverless-style access.

file

The file protocol specifies a file residing somewhere on a computer or locally accessible computer network. it does not specify an access protocol and has limited value except for one important case: it enables a browser to access files residing on a user's local computer, an important capability for Web page development. In this usage, the server name is omitted or replaced by the keyword *localhost*, which is followed by the local directory and file specification:

- **Formula**   `file://drive or network path/directory/file`
- **Example**   `file:///dev/web/testpage.html`

In some environments, the actual drive name and path to the file is specified. On a Macintosh, a URL might be the following:

```
file:///Macintosh%20HD/Desktop%20Folder/Bookmarks.html
```

On a PC, a file URL such as the following might exist, to access a file on the C drive of a PC on the local network, pc1:

```
file://\\pc1\C\Netlog.txt
```

Depending on browser complexity, file URLs might not be required, as with Internet Explorer 4, in which the operating system is tightly coupled with the user agent.

Interestingly, in the case of intranets, many drives may be mapped or file systems mounted so that no server is required to deliver files. In this "Web-serverless" environment, accessing network drives with a file URL may be possible. This idea demonstrates how simple a Web server is. In fact, to some people, a Web server is merely a very inefficient, though open, file server. Thus, alternative file delivery systems, such as those that use the Network File System (NFS) protocol, might soon be possible—or even preferable to HTTP-based servers. Already, work is being done on WebNFS and other alternative Web-oriented technologies for remote file access. This realization regarding file transfer leads logically to the idea of the FTP URL, discussed next.

FTP

The File Transfer Protocol, which predates the browser-oriented HTTP protocol, transfers files to and from a server. It generally is geared toward transferring files that are to be locally stored rather than immediately viewed. A browser may allow files to be viewed immediately. Today, because of its efficiency, FTP is most commonly used to download large files, such as complete applications. These URLs share with HTTP the formula for indicating a server, port, directory, and file:

■ **Formula** `ftp://server:port/directory/file`

■ **Example** `ftp://ftp.bigcompany.com:9978/info/somefile.exe`

A minimal FTP URL specifies a server and then lists the following directory: ftp://ftp.bigcompany.com. Generally, however, FTP URLs are used to access by name and directory a particular file in an archive, as shown in this formula:

■ **Formula** `ftp://server/directory path/file`

■ **Example** `ftp://ftp.bigcompany.com/info/somefile.exe`

FTP is an *authenticated* protocol, which means that every valid FTP request requires a defined user account on the server downloading the files. In practice, many FTP resources are intended for general access, and defining a unique account for every potential user is impractical. Therefore, an FTP convention known as *anonymous FTP* handles this common situation. The username "anonymous" or "ftp" allows general access to any public FTP resource supported by a server. As in the previous example, the anonymous user account is implicit in any FTP URL that does not explicitly provide account information.

An FTP URL can specify the name and password for a user account. If included, it precedes the server declaration, according to the following formula:

- **Formula** `ftp://user:password@server/directory/file`
- **Example** `ftp://jsmith:harmony@ftp.bigcompany.com/products/list`

This formula shows the password embedded within the URL. Including an account password in a public document (such as an HTML file) is a dangerous proposition, because it is transmitted in plain text and viewable both in the HTML source and browser address bar. Only public passwords should be embedded in any URL for an authenticated service. Furthermore, if you omit the password, the user agent typically prompts you to enter one if a password is required. Thus, it is more appropriate to provide a link to the service and *then* require the user to enter a name and password, or just provide the user ID and have the user agent prompt for a password, as happens in this example:

- **Formula** `ftp://user@server/directory/file`
- **Example** `ftp://jsmith@ftp.bigcompany.com/products/sales`

The FTP protocol assumes that a downloaded file contains binary information. You can override this default assumption by appending a type code to an FTP URL. The following are three common values for type codes:

- An **a** code indicates that the file is an ASCII text file.
- The **i** code, which is also the default, indicates that the file is an image/binary file.
- A **d** code causes the URL to return a directory listing of the specified path instead of a file.

An example formula is presented here for completeness:

- **Formula** `ftp://server/directory/file;type=code`
- **Example** `ftp://ftp.bigcompany.com/products;type=d`

In reality, the type codes are rarely encountered, because the binary transfer format generally does not harm text files, and the user agent is usually smart enough to handle FTP URLs without type codes. Like many other URLs, the port accessed can be changed to something besides the default port of 21, but this is not recommended.

Gopher

The Gopher system, the first popular document-based technology on the Internet, arose in the early 1990s as client/server architecture appropriate for campus information systems. Gopher provided a way to organize and navigate documents hierarchically. Some Gopher servers continue to operate, but most have been replaced by the more popular HTML-based Web content. However, for backward compatibility, you may find it important to link a Web page to Gopher-based information using a Gopher-style URL.

A Gopher URL follows the same formula used by other protocols to specify a server and optional port address. However, compared to HTTP or FTP, Gopher URLs differ in the way that they specify resources on a server. This specification begins with a single-digit code that indicates the resource type referred to. The default code is 1, which indicates a directory list. Following this is a *selector string*, which corresponds to the directory and file specification found in other URL formulas. The following table lists common codes used in Gopher URLs:

Code	Resource Type
0	Text file
1	Directory listing
2	CSO phone book server
3	Error
4	Macintosh binhex file
5	DOS binary file
6	UNIX-uuencoded file
7	Full-text index search
8	telnet session
9	Binary file

The following formula and example show how these codes might be used:

- **Formula**   `gopher://server:port/type+directory path/file`
- **Example**   `gopher://gopher.bigcompany.com/4mac/somefile.hqx`

Because of the encoding and the use of the file type numbers, a Gopher URL can look extremely complex. In the preceding example, 4 indicates a Macintosh BinHex file. Normally, users see 00 or 0 for files, and 1 or 11 for directories. The numbers are often repeated, because some Gopher strings begin with a copy of the content type. Readers may wonder why Web pages do not use such numeric codes to indicate content type. MIME types (discussed in Chapter 16) provide a far better solution. Beyond the file types and encoded characters, Gopher is very similar to other file-retrieval URLs. Gopher may also include electronic forms for searching that, like HTTP, add a query string after a question mark. For example, gopher://mudhoney.micro.umn.edu:4326/7?Mexico. Notice the use of the 7 code to indicate that the type of data is a full-text index search. Also notice that, like many other protocols, Gopher may run on another port than its standard port of 70. This may be specified in the URL. As noted earlier, this is not recommended.

mailto

Atypically, the mailto protocol does not locate and retrieve an Internet resource. Instead, it opens a window for editing and sending a mail message to a particular user address:

- **Formula**   `mailto:user@server`
- **Example**   mailto:president@whitehouse.gov

This rather simple formula shows standard Internet mail addressing; other, more-complex addresses may be just as valid. Using mailto URLs is very popular in Web sites to provide a basic feedback mechanism. Note that if the user's browser hasn't been set up properly to send e-mail, this type of URL may produce error messages when used in a link, prompting the user to set up mailing preferences. Because of this problem, page authors are warned not to rely solely on mailto-based URL links to collect user feedback.

Some browsers have introduced proprietary extensions to the mailto protocol, such as the subject extension. These extensions currently aren't standard and will cause other browsers to be unable to send e-mail using the link. Work is underway to standardize extensions to the mailto protocol; but, for now, use of the proprietary extensions is discouraged.

news

A news URL invokes a news browser that allows access to USENET newsgroups. A news URL can take one of the following two alternative approaches, each of which has limitations:

- **Request a named newsgroup**   Like the mailto URL, in this form, the URL doesn't specify which news server to use to fulfill the request. A default news server address is usually set as a Web browser preference. Unfortunately, not all news servers may carry the same groups. News archives are large and tend to be distributed across multiple servers. If the requested newsgroup does not exist on the default news server, it will not be found.

■ **Formula**   `news:newsgroup`

■ **Example**   `news:alt.get-rich-quick`

■ **Request a message on a particular news server, using a server-specific message identifier, such as 13c65a7a**   Because messages generally have an expiration date, this approach has limited value. In addition, the message identifier obviously varies from server to server, so it is not easily transferable.

■ **Formula**   `news:message@server`

■ **Example**   `13c65a7a@news.bigcompany.com`

Both the second form of the news URL and the NNTP URL (to be discussed next) show the limitations of URLs when dealing with time-sensitive information. Very little URL technology exists to deal with data that changes as rapidly as USENET news. News URLs generally are used simply to access a group rather than a particular message.

NNTP

The *Network News Transport Protocol (NNTP)* allows the retrieval of individual USENET articles, qualified by server, newsgroup, and article number. Like many protocols, an optional port value can be specified to direct a user agent to a specific server port. The NNTP URL has a limitation in that a particular article number is referenced. Article numbers will vary from server to server so this URL is not transportable. Furthermore, articles generally expire rather quickly, so fully specified NNTP URLs are of somewhat limited value.

■ **Formula**   `nntp://server:port/newsgroup/article-number`

■ **Example**   `nntp://news.bigcompany.com/alt.get-rich-quick/118`

The default port value of nntp is 118, but another port value may be set in the URL. A special version of NNTP that adds security runs on port 563. The form of the URL is nntps://secnews.bigcompany.com/alt.get-rich-quick/118.

In general, the news URL appears to be more commonly used on the Web.

telnet

The telnet protocol allows a user to open an interactive terminal session on a remote host computer. A minimal telnet URL, shown next, simply gives the remote system's name. After a connection is made, the system prompts for an account name and password.

■ **Formula**   `telnet://server`

■ **Example**   `telnet://host.bigcompany.com`

As an authenticated protocol, telnet generally requires a defined user account on the remote system. When this is unspecified, the user agent or helper application handling telnet prompts for such information. Like FTP, a telnet URL can also contain an account name and password as parameters. But, as with FTP URLs, be careful about including passwords in public access documents, such as HTML files on the Web. Because of the risk of password interception, the password is optional in the formula:

- ■ **Formula**   `telnet://user:password@server`
- ■ **Example**   `telnet://jsmith:harmony@host.bigcompany.com`
- ■ **Example**   `telnet://jsmith@host.bigcompany.com`

Finally, any telnet URL can direct a request to a specific port by appending the port address to the server name:

- ■ **Formula**   `telnet://server:port`
- ■ **Example**   `telnet://host.bigcompany.com:94`

Some telnet information sources may be configured to run on a particular port other than port 23, the standard telnet port. Consequently, use of the port within a telnet URL is more common than with other URLs.

Other Protocols

A wide variety of other protocols can be used. However, a browser may not support many of these URL forms. Some protocols, such as the wais protocol, have historical interest. Little evidence suggests that people actually use this protocol much on the Web, despite its presence in books that are only one or two years old. Beyond old protocols like wais, other protocols include operating-biased protocols, such as finger, and esoteric protocols for things like VEMMI video text services. New protocols are being added all the time. In fact, dozens of proposed or even implemented protocols exist that can be referenced with some form of nonstandard URL. If you are interested in other URL forms, visit http://www.w3.org/pub/WWW/Addressing/schemes or http://www.ics.uci.edu/pub/ietf/uri/ for more information.

Relative URLs

Up to this point, the discussion has focused on a specific form of URL, typically termed an *absolute URL*. Absolute URLs completely spell out the protocol, host, directory, and filename. Providing such detail can be tedious and unnecessary, which is where a shortened form of URL, termed a *relative URL*, comes in to use. With relative URLs, the various parts of the address—the site, directory, and protocol—might be inferred by the URL of the current document, or via the **<BASE>** element. The best way to illustrate the idea of relative URLs is by example.

If a Web site has an address of www.bigcompany.com, a user may access the home page with a URL like http://www.bigcompany.com/. A link to this page from an outside system would also contain the address http://www.bigcompany.com/. Once at the site, however, no reason exists to continue spelling out the full address of the site. A fully qualified link from the home page to a staff page in the root directory called staff.html would be http://www.bigcompany.com/staff.html. The protocol, address, and directory name can be inferred, so all that is needed is the address staff.html. This relative scheme works because http://www.bigcompany.com/ is inferred as the base of all future links, thus allowing for the shorthand relative notation. The relative notation can be used with filename and directories, as shown by the examples in Table 4-3.

When relative URLs are used within a Web site, the site becomes transportable. By not spelling out the server name in every link, you can develop a Web site on one server and move it to another. Contrarily, if you use absolute URLs, all links have to be changed if a server changes names or the files are moved to another site.

Of course, using relative URLs also has a potential downside: they can become confusing in a large site, particularly if centralized directories are used for things such as images. Imagine having URLs like ../../../images/logo.gif in files deep in a site structure. Some users might be tempted to simply copy files to avoid such problems, but then updating and caching issues arise. One solution is to use the **<BASE>** element. Another solution is to use symbolic links on the Web server to reference one copy of the file from multiple locations. However, because HTML is the subject here, the focus is the former solution, using the **<BASE>** element.

The **<BASE>** element defines the base for all relative URLs within a document. Setting the **HREF** attribute of this element to a fully qualified URL allows all other relative references to use the defined base. For example, **<BASE HREF="http://www.bigcompany.com/">** sets all the anchors later that aren't fully qualified to prefix http:// www.bigcompany.com / to the destination URL. The **<BASE>** element may occur only once in an HTML document—within its head—so creating sections of a document with different base URL values is impossible. Such a feature might someday

Current Page Address	Destination Address	Relative URL
http://www.bigcompany.com/index.htm	http://www.bigcompany.com/staff.htm	staff.htm
http://www.bigcompany.com/index.htm	http://www.bigcompany.com/products/gadget1.htm	products/gadget1.htm
http://www.bigcompany.com/products/gadget1.htm	http://www.bigcompany.com/index.htm	../index.htm

Table 4-3.   *Relative URL Formation Examples*

be added to the **<DIV>** element or a similar sectioning element; but, until then, HTML authors have to deal with shorthand notation being useful in some places but not in others.

Linking in HTML

The discussion thus far has focused solely on the forms of URLs. Little has been said about how to link objects together on the Web. Later in this chapter, the discussion returns to URLs and their counterparts, URIs, URCs, and URNs.

The Anchor Element

Using a URL enables you to specify the location of many types of information resources, both on the Internet and within a local area network. But how, exactly, is HTML used to specify a hyperlink that links one document to another? The most common way to define hyperlinks is with the anchor element, **<A>**. In its most basic form, this element needs two pieces of information: the URL of the target resource and the document content needed to activate the hyperlink. Assigning a URL value to an **<A>** element's **HREF** attribute specifies the target resource. Most defined hyperlinks probably use an HTTP URL to link one HTML document to another. Remember, however, that URLs to other information resources are also possible.

The **<A>** element's content specifies a document's "hot spot" for activating the hyperlink. Anchor content may include text, images, or a mixture of the two. By enclosing some text or other content with the **<A>** and **</A>** tags, you make the item into a link that, when selected, requests a new object to be accessed. In the following code fragment, the text "Linked content" will load the URL referenced by the **HREF** attribute when it's selected:

```
<A HREF="URL">Linked content</A>
```

> **Note** *An <A> element may not enclose another <A> element. The code <A HREF= "URL1">Linked<A HREF="URL2">More linked</A></A> makes no sense.*

The simplest hyperlink combines an **<A>** element with a URL that contains only a Web server address. Implicitly, the referenced document is the server's home page, which is the default document returned from the Web server's root directory. Many more-complex examples of links are also possible. The following are various examples of HTTP links, each of which is followed by a short description:

```
<A HREF="http://www.whitehouse.gov/">Visit the President</A>
```

Adding a link to the home page of a Web site with a basic HTTP URL references the home page of the Web site.

```
<A HREF="http://www.microsoft.com/gallery/">MS Web Gallery</A>
```

Adding a directory path to the URL references the default document in a specific directory.

```
<A HREF="http://www.pint.com/Staff/thomas.htm">Thomas Bio</A>
```

Adding a filename to a URL fully describes the document location.

```
<A HREF="http://www.bigcompany.com/spec.htm#top">Go to top</A>
```

Adding a fragment to a filename describes a particular location within a document.

```
<A HREF="staff/index.htm">Staff</A>
```

Anchors may use relative URLs.

```
<A HREF="../../index.htm">Back to home</A>
```

Relative URLs may be complex.

```
<A HREF="ftp://ftp.cdrom.com">Access FTP archive</A>
```

Anchors are not limited to HTTP URLs.

```
<A HREF="mailto:info@pint.com">More information?</A>
```

Beyond retrieving files, anchors may trigger e-mail or even run programs.

The following example shows a complete example of relative and absolute URLs and their use within an HTML document:

```
<!DOCTYPE HTML PUBLIC "-//W3C//DTD HTML 4.0 Transitional//EN">
<HTML>
```

```
<HEAD>
<TITLE>Link Example 3</TITLE>
</HEAD>

<BODY>
<H1 ALIGN="center">Green Gadgets</H1>
<HR>

<P ALIGN="center">Information about the mysterious Green Gadget--the
wonder tool of the millenium.</P>

<UL>
   <LI><A HREF="specs.htm">Specifications</A>
   <LI><A HREF="extras/access.htm">Accessories</A>
   <LI><A HREF="http://www.bigcompany.com">Distributors</A>
   <LI><A HREF="ftp://ftp. bigcompany.com/order.pdf">Download order form</A>
</UL>

<P ALIGN="center">

<A HREF="../index.htm">Back to Big Company Home Page</A>
</P>
<HR>

<ADDRESS>
Questions?
   <A HREF="mailto:info@gadget.com">info@bigcompany.com</A>
</ADDRESS>
</BODY>
</HTML>
```

A rendering of the link example is shown in Figure 4-3.

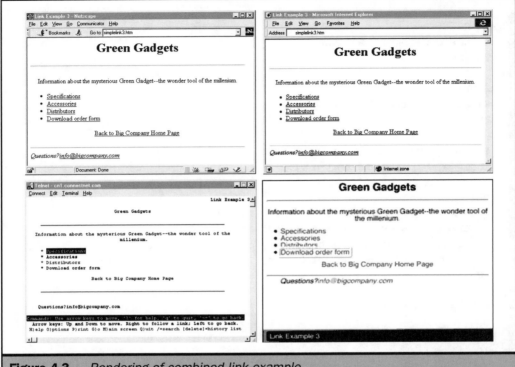

Figure 4-3. *Rendering of combined link example*

Link Renderings

In most browsers, text links are indicated by underlined text. Coloring the text—blue if the destination has never been visited, purple if it has been visited—is another common convention. If a link includes an image, the border of the image will also be blue or purple, unless the border attribute has been set to zero. HTML authors can override these default link colors with changes to the **LINK**, **ALINK**, and **VLINK** attributes of the **<BODY>** element. The **LINK** attribute changes the color of all unvisited links; the **VLINK** attribute changes all visited links. The **ALINK** attribute changes the color of the active link, which is the brief flash that appears when a link is pressed. By using an HTML style sheet, authors can also change the decoration of links to turn off underlining, or even display links in another fashion. These two changes are shown in the following example markup:

```
<!DOCTYPE HTML PUBLIC "-//W3C//DTD HTML 3.2 Final//EN">
<HTML>
<HEAD>
<TITLE>Link Style Changes</TITLE>
<STYLE TYPE="text/css">
<!--A        {text-decoration: none} /* avoid underlining links */-->
</STYLE>
</HEAD>

<BODY LINK="blue" ALINK="red" VLINK="red">
<A HREF="http://www.yahoo.com">Test Link to Yahoo!</A>
</BODY>
</HTML>
```

More information on the body attributes can be found in the element reference in Appendix A, and in Chapter 6, which covers layout facilities in HTML.

Aesthetically and logically, changing link colors or removing underlining makes sense. It may also confuse readers who have come to expect a standard color scheme for links. Occasionally, authors may try to encourage return visits by changing the setting for visited links to remain blue, or may reverse colors for layout consistency. Such changes can significantly impair the usability of the site by thwarting user expectations.

Like it or not, the standard Web experience has taught users to click underlined text that is blue or purple. Such user habits suggest that underlining for emphasis be used sparingly, if at all, in HTML documents. Furthermore, HTML text probably shouldn't be colored blue or purple, unless it obviously isn't a link. Controlling link colors is very important, but it is only one of many aspects of anchors that can be controlled.

Anchor Attributes

The **<A>** element has many possible attributes that are specific to it, besides **HREF**, as shown in Table 4-4. The more important attributes are discussed in the sections to follow, along with the concepts of binding scripts to anchors, using anchors with images, and creating a special type of image link called an *image map*. Refer to the element reference (Appendix A) to see a complete listing of all possible attributes for the **<A>** element.

Attribute Name	Possible Value	Description
HREF	A URL	Sets the URL of the destination object for the anchor
NAME	Text	Names the anchor so that it may be a target of another anchor
ID	Text	Identifies the anchor for target by another anchor, style sheet access, and scripting exposure
TARGET	A frame name	Defines the frame destination of the link
TITLE	Text	Sets the hint text for the link
ACCESSKEY	A character	Sets the key for keyboard access to the link
TABINDEX	A numeric value	Sets the order in the tabbing index for using the TAB key to move through links in a page
REL	Text	Defines the relationship of the object being linked to
REV	Text	Defines the relationship of the current object to the object being linked to

Table 4-4. *Common Anchor Attributes*

Note

*In HTML 4, the **<A>** element may also support the **SHAPE** and **COORDS** attributes, which can be used with the **<OBJECT>** element to create a generalized form of image maps. These extensions to **<A>** are discussed in the element reference in Appendix A, as well as in Chapter 5, which discusses the **<OBJECT>** element in relation to images. Today, however, these attributes of **<A>** are not widely supported. HTML authors are encouraged to use client-side image maps, which are discussed later in this chapter.*

Using the NAME Attribute

The <A> element usually defines a hyperlink's source location: where the link goes and what you click to go there. One possible destination for a hyperlink is a named location inside an HTML document. The **<A>** element is also used to define these locations in a special usage known as *setting a fragment*, though the term *marker* might make more sense. To set a marker, the **NAME** attribute replaces the **HREF** attribute. The value of the **NAME** attribute is an arbitrary, symbolic name for the marker location that must be unique within the document. Wherever the marker is placed within an HTML document becomes a named candidate destination for hyperlinks. For example, the HTML markup **<A NAME="marker">**This is a marker**</A>** sets the text "This is a marker" to be associated with the fragment identifier **#marker**.

> **Note**   *Unlike hyperlink anchors, a marker location is not underlined or in any way visually distinguished.*

In practice, when an **<A>** element is used solely as a marker, it often doesn't enclose any text, though this doesn't suggest that the close tag should be omitted, as it often is. Setting a marker such as **<A NAME="top">** is accepted by most browsers, but **<A NAME="top"></A>** is the valid form.

An **<A>** element can serve both as a destination and a link at the same time. For example,

```
<A NAME="yahoo_link" HREF="http://www.yahoo.com/">Yahoo!</A>
```

creates a link to a site and names the anchor so that it may be referenced by other links. The dual use of the **<A>** element may cause some confusion, but it is valid HTML.

> **Note**   *As discussed in Chapter 3, under the current version of HTML, the **ID** attribute is also available for nearly every element. It can also be used to set a marker. The preceding example could have been written **<A ID="yahoo_link" HREF="http:// www.yahoo.com">Yahoo!</A>**, thus exposing the anchor for targeted linking, style sheets, and dynamic manipulation via a scripting language. For backward compatibility, the **NAME** attribute should also be used, because many browsers do not support **ID** fully.*

The need for named anchors isn't always obvious. Thanks to the unidirectional nature of links on the Web, they can be used to navigate to locations within the same document. This is especially useful in lengthy reference works. Such link usage can be accomplished by using markers to define named locations and anchors that refer to them. Remember that the URL formula to refer to a location within the current document is simply the pound symbol (#), followed by a marker name. Thus, code such as **<A HREF="#top">**Top of the document**</A>** could be used if a marker called "top" was set at the start of the document. Be careful to always use the # symbol with marker names. Otherwise, the user agent will probably interpret the link as referencing a file rather than a marker.

In the more general case, a marked location in any HTML document can be referenced by placing # and a marker name after its normal URL. For example,

```
<A HREF="http://www.bigcompany.com/products.htm#spec">Specification Section</A>
```

will link to a named marker called "spec" in the products.htm file. A complete example of linking within a file and to markers outside the file is shown here:

```
<!DOCTYPE HTML PUBLIC "-//W3C//DTD HTML 4.0 Transitional//EN">
<HTML>
<HEAD>
<TITLE>Name Attribute Example</TITLE>
</HEAD>

<BODY>
<A NAME="top"></A>
Go to the <A HREF="#bottom">bottom</A> of this document.<BR> Link right
to a <A HREF="document1.htm#marker1">marker</A> in another document.

<P>To make this work we need to simulate the document being very long by
using many breaks.</P>
<BR><BR><BR><BR><BR><BR><BR><BR><BR>
<BR><BR><BR><BR><BR><BR><BR><BR><BR>
<A NAME="middle"><STRONG ID="middle">The Middle</STRONG></A>
<BR><BR><BR><BR><BR><BR><BR><BR><BR>
<BR><BR><BR><BR><BR><BR><BR><BR><BR>
<HR>
<A NAME="bottom" HREF="#top">Return to Top</A>
<A HREF="#middle">Go to middle</A>
</BODY>
</HTML>
```

Note *Named values must be unique, whether they are set by using the **NAME** attribute or the **ID** attribute.*

TITLE Attributes for Anchors

Normally, the **TITLE** attribute, as discussed in Chapter 3, may not seem terribly helpful to a user, because it provides only basic advisory information about the use of a particular element. In the case of anchors, however, **TITLE** is very useful, because it can be used to provide tool tip information or help balloons for the link. In browsers such as Internet Explorer, if a user holds the mouse over the link long enough, a tool tip showing the information specified by the **TITLE** attribute will be displayed. The following code fragment provides some helpful information for the link:

```
<A HREF="staff/index.htm"
    TITLE="Resumes and information about our staff">Staff</A>
```

If the **TITLE** attribute is not used, the destination URL generally is displayed. Figure 4-4 shows a tool tip for a link under Internet Explorer 4.

Note   *Although the **TITLE** attribute is usable in nearly every HTML element under Internet Explorer, using it makes sense mainly for links, images, binary objects, and forms.*

The **TITLE** attribute serves another purpose: it provides the title information for a bookmark when a link is bookmarked before the destination page is visited. While this may not be intuitive, with many browsers, you can right-click a link to access a menu that enables you to bookmark the link before it is visited. Then, when the page is visited, the information enclosed within the **<TITLE>** element of the destination page is used in the bookmark instead of the information in the **TITLE** attribute of the anchor that loaded the page. (Note that the **TITLE** attribute and the **<TITLE>** element are two entirely different things.)

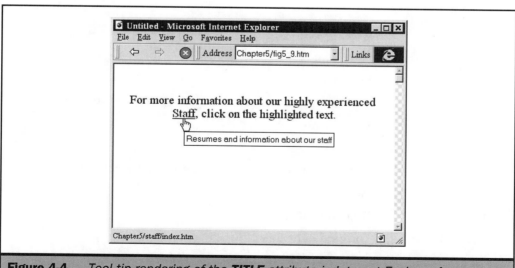

Figure 4-4.   *Tool tip rendering of the **TITLE** attribute in Internet Explorer 4*

Accelerator Keys

The HTML 4 proposed specification adds the **ACCESSKEY** to the **<A>** element, as well as to various form elements. This currently is supported primarily by Internet Explorer. With this attribute, you can set a key to invoke an anchor, without requiring a pointing device to select the link. The link is activated with the combination of the accelerator key, usually ALT, and the key specified by the attribute. So,

```
<A HREF="http://www.yahoo.com/" ACCESSKEY="Y">Yahoo!</A>
```

makes a link to Yahoo!, which can be activated by pressing ALT+Y. So far, many browsers do not appear to support fully this upgrade to link access.

Although adding keyboard access to a Web page seemingly would be a dramatic improvement, HTML authors are cautioned to be aware of access key bindings in the browsing environment. Under Internet Explorer 4 and above, eight keys are already reserved for browser functions. Netscape's Communicator 4 and above differ in one accelerator key. Assuming that both browsers will eventually support this function (Netscape doesn't at the time of this update), authors are cautioned to stay away from accelerators that use the keys in Table 4-5.

One other problem with accelerator keys is how to show them in the page. In most software, underlining indicates the letter of the accelerator key. Links are generally

Key	Mapping	Notes
F	File menu	
E	Edit menu	
C	Communicator menu	Netscape Communicator only
V	View menu	
G	Go menu	
A	Favorites menu	Internet Explorer only
H	Help	
LEFT ARROW	Back in history	
RIGHT ARROW	Forward in history	

Table 4-5.   *Reserved Browser Key Bindings*

underlined in browsers, so this approach isn't feasible. Style sheets can be used to change link direction, so underlining the first letter is possible; but then the user may be disoriented, expecting links to be fully underlined. Another approach to indicating the accelerator keys might be to set the access key letter of a text link in bold or a slightly larger size.

TABINDEX Attribute

The **TABINDEX** attribute of the **<A>** element (which is defined in HTML 4, but poorly supported by browsers) defines the order in which links will be tabbed through in a browser that supports keyboard navigation. The value of **TABINDEX** is usually a positive number. Browsers tab through links in order of increasing **TABINDEX** values, but generally skip over those with negative values. So, **<A HREF="about.htm" TABINDEX="1">** sets this anchor to be the first thing tabbed to by a browser. If the **TABINDEX** attribute is undefined, the browser tends to tab though links in the order in which they are found within an HTML document.

Note   *WebTV supports a usability improvement similar to **TABINDEX**: the **SELECTED** attribute. When you add the word **SELECTED** as an attribute to an anchor, the WebTV browser preselects the anchor with the yellow highlight rectangle. If two or more anchors are selected in a page, the last one appearing in the document will be selected. Although it seems that the browser would scroll to the first item selected if it did not appear in the first screen, in practice, the WebTV browser does not do this.*

TARGET Attribute

The **TARGET** attribute is used in conjunction with frames, which are discussed in Chapter 8. The attribute is also part of the HTML 4 proposal. To target a link so that the result loads in a particular frame, the **TARGET** attribute is added to the **<A>** element. Generally, a frame has a name, so setting the **TARGET** equal to the frame name results in the link loading in the frame named in the attribute. For example, when selected, a link such as

```
<A HREF="http://www.yahoo.com/" TARGET="display_frame">
```

loads the object referenced by the URL into the frame named **"display_frame"**. If the **TARGET** attribute is left out, the current window or frame the document is in is used. Besides author-named frames, the following are several reserved names for frames that, when used with the **TARGET** attribute, have special meaning: **_blank**, **_self**, **_parent**, and **_top**. For more information about frames, as well as instructions on how to use the **<A>** element with frames and the various reserved frame names, refer to the element reference (Appendix A) and Chapter 8.

Anchors and Link Relationships

The **<A>** element has the following two attributes, whose meanings are often misunderstood (and these attributes aren't widely supported by browsers):

- **REL** Used to describe the relationship between the document and the destination document referenced by the anchor's **HREF** attribute. For example, if the destination of the link specifies the glossary associated with a document, the anchor might read

  ```
  <A HREF="words.htm" REL="glossary">
  ```

- **REV** Defines the reverse of the relationship that **REL** defines—in this case, what the relationship is from the destination document's perspective. An example is a linear set of documents in which the **REL** attribute is set to **"next"** and the **REV** attribute is set to **"prev"**, as shown in the following code fragment:

  ```
  <A HREF="page2.htm" REL="next" REV="prev">Page 2</A>
  ```

Although the **REL** and **REV** attributes might seem very useful, few, if any, browsers support them. Currently, the only major use of these attributes is to document the relationship of links with the **<A>** elements themselves. The **<LINK>** element (discussed later in this chapter), which has semantic-link purposes similar to the **REL** and **REV** attributes, is actually supported in a limited manner by some browsers. A list of many of the proposed values for the **REL** and **REV** attributes can be found in this chapter's upcoming section about link relationships.

Scripting and Anchors

Adding logic to anchors is possible through the use of client-side scripting languages, such as JavaScript or VBScript. Under HTML 4, core event attributes have been added to the **<A>** element and include **onclick**, **onmouseover**, **onmouseout**, and other attributes, which can be bound to scripting events. The events named correspond to an anchor being clicked (**onclick**), a pointer being positioned on a link (**onmouseover**), and a pointer leaving a link (**onmouseout**). One obvious use of such events is to animate links so that when a mouse passes over the link, the text changes color, and when the link is clicked, the system issues a click sound. Generically, this is the idea of a *rollover button*. Besides the basic events that might be useful to create rollover links or trigger programming logic, event models from Microsoft and Netscape may include a variety of other events, such as the assigned Help key on the keyboard (generally F1) being pressed or other keys on the keyboard being pressed or released. HTML authors interested in scripting anchor activities should consult Chapters 13 and 14. Combined with images, anchor scripting additions can be used to create very persuasive Web pages.

Images and Anchors

As mentioned earlier, **<A>** elements may enclose text and other content, including images. When an anchor encloses an image, the image becomes *hot*. A hot image can activate the link and provide a basic mechanism for a graphic button. Normally, a browser shows an image to be part of an anchor by putting a colored border around the image—generally, the same color as the colored link text—either blue or purple. The browser may also indicate the image is a link by changing the pointer to a different shape (such as a finger) when the pointer is positioned over an image link. If combined with scripting, the anchor may also modify the size or content of the image, creating a form of animated button. The following HTML markup code shows how an anchor can be combined with the **<IMG>** element, as discussed in Chapter 5, to create a button:

```
<!DOCTYPE HTML PUBLIC "-//W3C//DTD HTML 4.0 Transitional//EN">
<HTML>
<HEAD>
<TITLE>Anchors and Images</TITLE>
</HEAD>

<BODY>
<B>Button with a border</B><BR>
<A HREF="about.htm">
<IMG SRC="about.gif" ALT="About Button" HEIGHT="55" WIDTH="55">
</A>
<BR><BR>

<B>Same button without a border</B><BR>
<A HREF="about.htm">
<IMG SRC="about.gif" ALT="About Button" BORDER="0" HEIGHT="55"
WIDTH="55">
</A>

</BODY>
</HTML>
```

Notice how the **BORDER** attribute is set to **"0"** to turn off the image's border. Further, note that the code contains a small but significant error. When a space exists between the close of an **<IMG>** element and the closing **</A>** element, a small blue or purple line, or "tick," may occur, as shown in Figure 4-5. To remove a tick, make certain that no space is between the **<IMG>** element and the closing **</A>** tag.

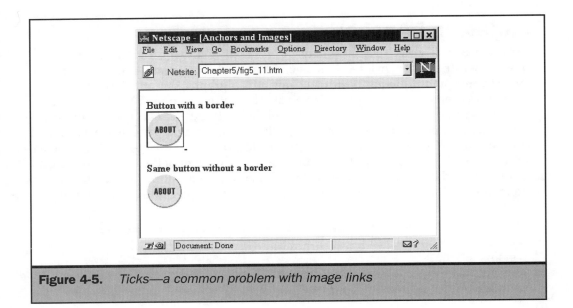

Figure 4-5. Ticks—a common problem with image links

Note

Although ticks aren't the worst offense on the Web, they indicate a lack of attention to detail in Web page coding. In print literature, spelling errors or small nicks or ticks on an image would be cause for serious alarm. Eventually, the same level of standards will be applied to Web pages, so HTML authors should begin to look for such small mistakes. Be careful when looking for ticks, though. Some browsers, such as Internet Explorer, may actually try to fix such small spacing problems for you, leading you to believe there isn't a tick if you look at it only under one browser. Testing in many browsers and validation of HTML markup should help catch subtle errors like ticks.

All the examples given so far show images with only one destination. Wherever a user clicks on the image link, the destination remains the same. In another class of image links, called *image maps*, different regions of the image can be made hot links for different destinations.

Image Maps

An *image map* is an image that contains numerous hot spots that may result in a different URL being loaded, depending on where the user clicks. The two basic types of image maps are *server-side image maps* and *client-side image maps*. In the server-side image map, the following process is followed:

1. The user clicks somewhere within the image.

2. The browser sends a request to the Web server, asking for the URL of the document associated with the area clicked. The coordinates clicked are sent to a program on the server, usually called imagemap, which decodes the information.

3. After consulting a file that shows which coordinates map to which URL, the server sends back the information requested.

4. After receiving the response, the browser requests the new URL.

The concept of server-side image maps has some major downsides. First, users really don't have a sense, URL-wise, where a particular click will take them. All that users see as they run a mouse over the image is a set of coordinates showing the current x, y value. The second—and more significant—major problem is that the server must be consulted to go to the next page. This can be a major bottleneck that slows down the process of moving between pages. The slow speed of decoding, combined with the possibility that a user can click a hot spot that is not mapped and have nothing happen, makes client-side image maps preferable to server-side maps.

With client-side image maps, all the map information—which regions map to which URLs—can be specified in the same HTML file that contains the image. Including the map data with the image and letting the browser decode it has several advantages, including

■ A server doesn't need to be visited to determine the destination, so links are resolved faster.

■ Destination URLs can be shown as the user's pointer moves over the image.

■ Image maps can be created and tested locally, without requiring a server or system administration support.

While this discussion makes it obvious that client-side image maps are far superior to their server-side cousins, very old browsers may not support this feature. This doesn't have to be a problem, however, because you can include simultaneous support for both types of image maps.

Server-Side Image Maps

To specify a server-side image map, you use the **<A>** element to enclose a specially marked **<IMG>** element. The **<A>** element **HREF** attribute should be set to the URL of a program or map file to decode the image map. The **<IMG>** element must contain the attribute **ISMAP** so that the browser can decode the image appropriately.

Note

Depending on the Web server being used, support for server-side image maps may or may not be built in. If image maps are supported directly, the **<A>** *element simply must point to the URL of the map file directly and it will be decoded. This is shown in the example in Figure 4-6. On some older servers, however, the anchor may have to point to an image map program in that server's cgi-bin directory.*

As with all linked images, turning off the image borders may be desirable, by setting the **<IMG>** element's **BORDER** attribute equal to 0. A simple example showing the syntax of a server-side image map is shown here, a rendering of which is shown in Figure 4-6:

```
<!DOCTYPE HTML PUBLIC "-//W3C//DTD HTML 4.0 Transitional//EN">
<HTML>
<HEAD>
<TITLE>Server-side Image Map Example</TITLE>
</HEAD>

<BODY>
<H1 ALIGN="center">Server-side Imagemap Test</H1>

<DIV ALIGN="center">
   <A HREF="shapes.map">
   <IMG SRC="shapes.gif" ISMAP BORDER="0" WIDTH="400"
       HEIGHT="200"></A>
</DIV>
</BODY>
</HTML>
```

As previously mentioned, server-side image maps do not provide adequate feedback to the user and may incur performance penalties. Figure 4-6 shows that the browser provides image coordinate information in the status bar, rather than a destination URL with a server-side image map.

HTML authors are encouraged to prefer client-side image maps, and to use server-side image maps only as needed.

Client-Side Image Maps

The key to using a client-side image map is to add the **USEMAP** attribute to the **<IMG>** element and have it reference a **<MAP>** element that defines the image map's active areas. An example of the **<IMG>** element syntax is **<IMG SRC="controlbar.gif" USEMAP="#controlmap">**. Note that, like server-side image maps, the image will be indicated as a link regardless of the lack of the **<A>** element surrounding the **<IMG>**. The **BORDER** attribute should be set to zero, if necessary.

The **<MAP>** element generally occurs within the same document, although support for it may exist outside of the current document. This is similar, in a sense, to the way server-side maps work. The **<MAP>** element may occur anywhere within the body of an HTML document, although it is usually found at the end of an HTML document.

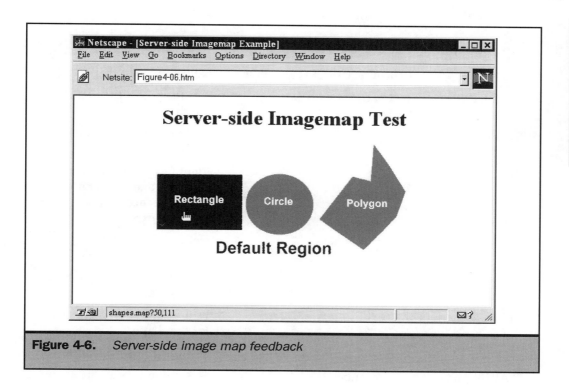

Figure 4-6. *Server-side image map feedback*

> **Note** *Theoretically, a client-side image map file may exist within another file, but most browsers do not support such a feature.*

The **<MAP>** element has one attribute, **NAME**, which is used to specify the identifier associated with the map. The map name is then referenced within the **<IMG>** element, using the **USEMAP** attribute and the associated fragment identifier. The **<MAP>** element must have a closing **</MAP>** tag. Within the **<MAP>** and **</MAP>** elements are defined shapes that are mapped onto an image, defining the hot spots for the image map. Shapes are defined by the **<AREA>** element, which is found only within the **<MAP>** element. The **<AREA>** element requires no closing element and has a variety of attributes, as shown in Table 4-6.

The most important attributes of an **<AREA>** entity are **HREF**, **SHAPE**, and **COORDS**. The **HREF** attribute defines the destination URL for the browser, if that particular region of the image is selected. The **SHAPE** and **COORDS** attributes define the particular region in question. When the **SHAPE** attribute is set to **RECT**, it defines a rectangular region, and the coordinates should be set to provide the top-left and bottom-right coordinates of the image. If the **SHAPE** attribute is set to **CIRCLE**, the **COORDS** attribute must provide the x, y coordinates of the center of the circle, followed by its radius. If the shape is set to **POLY**, it indicates that the area defined is

Attribute Name	Possible Values	Description
SHAPE	RECT, CIRCLE, and POLY	Sets the type of shape
COORDS	*x, y* coordinate pairs	Sets the points that define the shape
HREF	A URL	Defines the destination of the link
ID	Text	Identifies the anchor for target by another anchor, style sheet access, and scripting exposure
TARGET	A frame name	Defines the frame destination of the link
NOHREF	N/A	Indicates that the region has no destination
ALT	Text	Defines the alternative text for the shape
TITLE	Text	Sets the hint text for a shape
TABINDEX	A number	Sets numeric order in tabbing sequence
onclick	A script	Relates the click event of a link with a script
onmouseover	A script	Relates mouse over event with a script
onmouseout	A script	Relates mouse out event with a script

Table 4-6.   *Attributes for <AREA>*

an irregular polygon; each coordinate makes up a point in the polygon, with lines between each successive point, and the last point connected to the first. Areas of the image not assigned values can be assigned a value of **default**.

Note   *If the SHAPE attribute is not set or omitted, RECT is assumed.*

WEB AND HTML BASICS

Table 4-7 summarizes the possibilities for the **AREA** element and provides examples.

 *Under many browsers, the **SHAPE** attribute also supports **RECTANGLE**, **CIRC**, and **POLYGON**. HTML authors are encouraged to use only **RECT**, **CIRCLE**, and **POLY**, because they are defined by the standard.*

The various x and y coordinates are measured in pixels from the top-left corner (0,0) of the mapped image. Percentage values of the image's height and width also may be used. For example, **<AREA SHAPE=RECT COORDS="0,0,50%,50%">** defines a rectangular region from the upper-left corner to a point halfway up and down and halfway across. While percentage-style notation might allow the image to resize, it generally isn't useful for any but the most basic image maps. The biggest difficulty with image maps is how to determine the coordinates for the individual shapes within the image. Rather than measuring these values by hand, HTML authors are encouraged to use an image mapping tool. Many HTML editing systems include image-mapping facilities. Mapedit (http://www.boutell.com/mapedit) for Windows and UNIX, and MapMaker (http://www.kickinit.net/mapmaker/) for Macintosh also provide basic mapping facilities. A small list of image map software can be found at http://www.htmlref.com/.

*Using any **HEIGHT** and **WIDTH** values besides the actual sizes for a mapped image isn't recommended. Once a map has been mapped, resizing will ruin it.*

Shape	Coordinate Format	Example
RECT	left-x, top-y, right-x, bottom-y	**<AREA SHAPE="RECT" COORDS="0,0,100,50" HREF="about.htm">**
CIRCLE	center-x, center-y, radius	**<AREA SHAPE="CIRCLE" COORDS="25,25,10" HREF="products.htm">**
POLY	$x1, y1, x2, y2, x3, y3,\ldots$	**<AREA SHAPE="POLY" COORDS= "255,122,306,53,334,62,255,122" HREF="contact.htm">**

Table 4-7. *Shape Format and Examples*

The following is an example of using a client-side image map, the results of which are rendered in Figure 4-7:

```
<!DOCTYPE HTML PUBLIC "-//W3C//DTD HTML 4.0 Transitional//EN">
<HTML>
<HEAD>
<TITLE>Client-side Image Map Example</TITLE>
</HEAD>

<BODY>
<H1 ALIGN="CENTER">Client-side Imagemap Test</H1>

<DIV ALIGN="CENTER">
    <IMG SRC="shapes.gif" USEMAP="#shapes" BORDER="0" WIDTH="400"
        HEIGHT="200">
</DIV>

<!-- Start of Client-Side Image Map -->

<MAP NAME="shapes">
  <AREA SHAPE="RECT" COORDS="6,50,140,143" HREF="rectangle.htm"
        ALT="Rectangle">
  <AREA SHAPE="CIRCLE" COORDS="195,100,50" HREF="circle.htm"
        ALT="Circle">
  <AREA SHAPE="POLY"
        COORDS="255,122,306,53,334,62,338,0,388,77,374,116,323,171,255,122"
        HREF="polygon.htm" ALT="Polygon">
  <AREA SHAPE="default" HREF="defaultreg.htm">
</MAP>
</BODY>
</HTML>
```

You can combine support for both server-side and client-side image maps into one file. The browser typically overrides the server-side support with the improved client-side style. This approach guarantees backward compatibility with older browsers. To support both image maps, use the **ISMAP** and **USEMAP** attributes in

WEB AND HTML BASICS

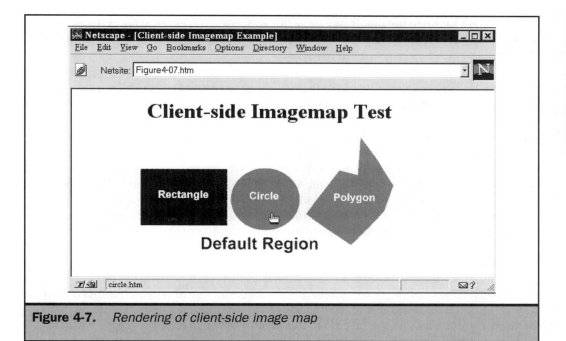

Figure 4-7.   *Rendering of client-side image map*

conjunction with an embedded map and a remote map, as shown by the following code fragment:

```
<A HREF="shapes.map">
<IMG SRC="shapes.gif" USEMAP="#shapes" BORDER="0" ISMAP WIDTH="400"
    HEIGHT="200"></A>
```

Image Map Attributes

Client-side image maps have a variety of attributes that can be used with the **<AREA>** element. Server-side image maps have no attributes other than those normally associated with the **<IMG>** element, such as **BORDER**. The important attributes are discussed here, as well as the issues of adding scripting facilities to image maps.

TARGET

The **<AREA>** element for client-side image maps has been extended to support a **TARGET** attribute, much like the addition to the **<A>** element. The **TARGET** value should be set to the name of a frame or window. Generally, a frame has a name, so setting **TARGET** to the frame name results in the link loading in the frame named in the attribute. When selected, a link such as

```
<AREA SHAPE="RECT" COORDS="0,0,50%, 50%" HREF="http://www.yahoo.com"
     TARGET="display_frame">
```

loads the page referenced by the URL set by **HREF** into the frame that is named **"display_frame"**. If the **TARGET** attribute is omitted, the current window or frame that the document is in is used. Besides author-named frames, the following are several reserved names for frames that, when used with the **TARGET** attribute, have special meaning: **_blank**, **_self**, **_parent**, and **_top**. For more information about frames, as well as instructions for how the **<AREA>** element is used with frames and the various reserved frame names, refer to the element reference (Appendix A) and Chapter 8.

NOHREF

The **NOHREF** attribute appears to have little use, but it can be used to set a region in the map that does nothing when clicked. This might be useful when attempting to cut a hole in something. For example, an image of a donut might make a great image map, particularly if the hole in the middle of the donut isn't an active, clickable area. The **NOHREF** attribute makes this simple. Just define a large click region for the whole image and then declare the middle of the image nonclickable with the **NOHREF** attribute. An example of this is shown here:

```
<!DOCTYPE HTML PUBLIC "-//W3C//DTD HTML 4.0 Transitional//EN">
<HTML>
<HEAD>
<TITLE>NOHREF Example</TITLE>
</HEAD>

<BODY>
<IMG SRC="donut.gif" WIDTH="300" HEIGHT="300" BORDER="0"
     ALT="Donut Widget" USEMAP="#donut">

<MAP NAME="donut">
  <AREA SHAPE="circle" COORDS="150,150,81" NOHREF>
  <AREA SHAPE="circle" COORDS="150,150,146" HREF="donut.htm">
  <AREA SHAPE="default" NOHREF>
</MAP>
</BODY>
</HTML>
```

When this code is rendered under Netscape, the hand cursor, indicating a clickable area, disappears when it passes over the nonclickable area; under Internet Explorer, the cursor appears the same, but the area still isn't clickable.

Given that **NOHREF** creates an inactive region that sits on top of another, what happens when one region overlaps another? According to the specification, if two or more regions overlap, the region defined first within the **<MAP>** element takes precedence over subsequent regions. This rule implies that **<AREA>** elements with the **NOHREF** attribute should be placed before **<AREA>** elements that are active, so that clicking the **<AREA>** element with the **NOHREF** attribute doesn't take the user to a new URL as a result of a previously placed, overlapping active **<AREA>** element.

ALT and TITLE

Image maps have some major drawbacks, even in their client-side aspect, with text-based browsers. The **ALT** attribute can be used, as shown in the previous examples, and should provide text labels that are displayed in the status line when the pointer passes over the hot spots. Although the **TITLE** attribute can be added to all elements and can provide a function similar to **ALT** in graphical browsers, in practice, browsers seem to pick up **ALT** before **TITLE**. To be on the safe side, you can use both attributes simultaneously. One unfortunate problem with the **ALT** attribute and client-side image maps is that nongraphical browsers don't always pick up the **ALT** attributes and build meaningful renderings. Instead of a set of links, the viewer might only see a cryptic message, as shown in Figure 4-8.

HTML authors are encouraged to provide secondary navigation that mirrors the choices available in the image map. This secondary navigation should consist of text links located below the image, which makes the site accessible for nongraphical user agents and may improve the site's usability. Users on slow connections may opt to select text links before the image is completely downloaded. An example of text links in conjunction with an image map is shown in Figure 4-9. Also, when using server-side image maps, you can make the inactive, or default, area link to a new page that contains a text menu of the choices provided via the image map. In this way, a user who selects the **ISMAP** provided by an older browser receives the menu, not the map.

Discussion of the design and navigation issues surrounding image maps is left to books that focus on site design. When possible, HTML authors should avoid relying too heavily on single-image–style image maps for navigation purposes.

TABINDEX

Under the HTML 4 proposed specification, you can use the **TABINDEX** attribute of the **<AREA>** element to define the order in which hot spots in a client-side image map are tabbed through in a browser that supports keyboard navigation. The value of **TABINDEX** typically is a positive number. A browser tabs through links in order of

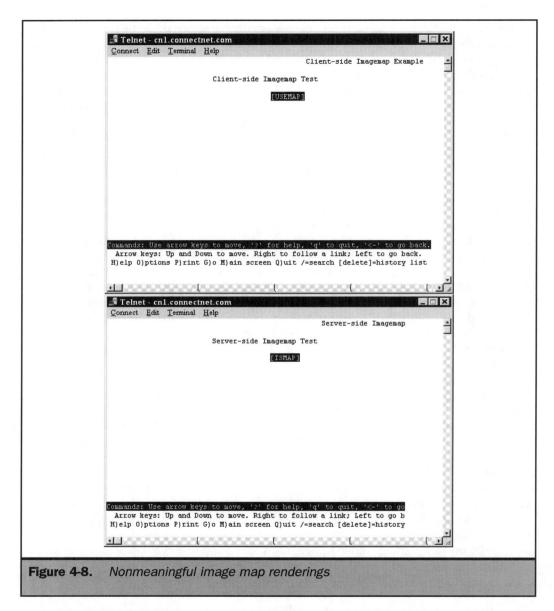

Figure 4-8. *Nonmeaningful image map renderings*

increasing **TABINDEX** values, but generally skips over those with negative values. So, the following line sets this anchor to be the first thing tabbed to:

```
<AREA SHAPE="RECT" COORDS="0,0,50%,50%" HREF="http://www.yahoo.com/"
    TABINDEX="1">
```

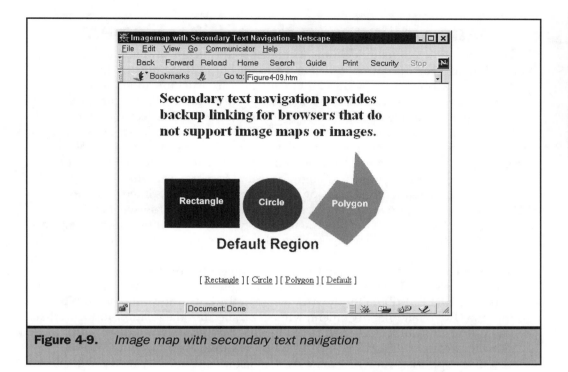

Figure 4-9.   *Image map with secondary text navigation*

If the **TABINDEX** attribute is undefined, the browser tends to tab though links in the order in which they are found within an HTML document. Currently, browser support of **TABINDEX** within image maps is sparse.

SCRIPTING

As already noted, you can add logic to image maps with client-side scripting languages, such as JavaScript or VBScript. Three extensions to the **<AREA>** element—**onclick**, **onmouseover**, and **onmouseout**—can be bound to scripting events that provide feedback when a mouse passes over a link. This is the rollover idea discussed earlier. However, the **<AREA>** element is less flexible than using anchors in conjunction with single images, because replacing only a portion of the image on-the-fly is impossible. Most rollover-style Web interfaces do not use image maps, but rely instead on images cut up and pieced together to resemble an image map.

Semantic Linking with the <LINK> Element

Syntactically, a link to another document created by an anchor says nothing about the relationship between the current document and the object being pointed to. You can use the **TITLE** attribute to provide a hint or advisory information about the link, so that the viewer of a page may associate meaning with a link. The linked image or text might also give some clue about what happens when the link is selected, but in HTML itself, links lack any semantic meaning. The **<LINK>** element, however, does provide a way to define the relationship between linked objects. The concept of the **<LINK>** element is that a document may have predefined relationships that can be specified, and that some of these relationships might be useful to a browser when offering navigation choices, rendering a page, or preparing a page to be printed. Although **<LINK>** has been around for several years, until recently, few browsers have supported **<LINK>** in any way. With the rise of style sheets, scripting, and proprietary extensions, **<LINK>** is finally being supported by browsers, at least in a limited manner.

The **<LINK>** element is found in the head of an HTML document, where it may occur more than once. The two most important attributes of the element are **HREF** and **REL**. Like the **HREF** attribute for the **<A>** element, the **HREF** attribute for **<LINK>** specifies the URL of another document, while **REL** specifies the relationship with that document. The value of **REL** is often called the *link type*. The basic syntax of the **<LINK>** element is **<LINK HREF="URL" REL="relationship">**. Under HTML 4, **<LINK>** also supports a reverse semantic relationship, indicated by the **REV** attribute, as well as the **TITLE** attribute, which can be used to set advisory information for the link. The most mysterious aspect of the **<LINK>** element is the value of the **REL** and **REV** attributes.

Link Relationships in Detail

Like the **REL** attribute for the **<A>** element, the **REL** attribute for **<LINK>** defines the relationship between the current document and the linked object. The value of the **REL** attribute is simply a text value, which can be anything the author desires. However, a browser might interpret standardized relationships in a particular way. For example, a browser might provide special icons or navigation features when the meaning of a link is understood. Currently, no standard set of document relationship values exists, but the HTML 4 specification lists some proposed relationship values, as shown in Table 4-8. Note that these values are not case-sensitive.

Beyond the HTML 4 proposed relationships, various other relationships are being discussed. In fact, HTML authors can make up their own relationships if they desire, but should be careful to avoid using **PREV** or **NEXT** as **REL** or **REV** values, because they tend to hold special meaning for browsers. Table 4-9 shows some proposed **REL** values.

The most interesting of the proposed relationships are those that are actually supported by a browser. Otherwise, they serve as little more than comments to a document's reader about the meaning of a link.

REL Value	Explanation	Example
ALTERNATE	The link references an alternative version of the document that the link is in. This may be a translated version of the document, as suggested by the **LANG** attribute.	`<LINK HREF="frenchintro.htm" REL="ALTERNATE" LANG="fr">`
APPENDIX	The link references a document that serves as an appendix for a document or site.	`<LINK HREF="intro.htm" REL="APPENDIX">`
BOOKMARK	The link references a document that serves as a bookmark; the **TITLE** attribute may be used to name the bookmark.	`<LINK HREF="index.htm" REL="BOOKMARK" TITLE="homepage">`
CHAPTER	The link references a document that is a chapter in a site or collection of documents.	`<LINK HREF="Ch01.htm" REL="CHAPTER">`
CONTENTS	The link references a document that serves as a table of contents, most likely for the site, though it might be for the document. The meaning is unclear.	`<LINK HREF="toc.htm" REL="CONTENTS">`
INDEX	The link references a page that provides an index for the current document.	`<LINK HREF="docindex.htm" REL="INDEX">`
GLOSSARY	The link references a document that provides a glossary of terms for the current document.	`<LINK HREF="glossary.htm" REL="GLOSSARY">`
COPYRIGHT	The link references a page that contains a copyright statement for the current document.	`<LINK HREF="copyright.htm" REL="COPYRIGHT">`
NEXT	The link references the next document to visit in a linear collection of documents. It can be used, for example, to "pre-fetch" the next page, as in the WebTV browsers.	`<LINK HREF="page2.htm" REL="NEXT">`

Table 4-8.   *REL* Values Proposed by HTML 3.2

REL Value	Explanation	Example
PREV	The link references the previous document in a linear collection of documents.	`<LINK HREF="page1.htm" REL="PREVIOUS">`
SECTION	The link references a document that is a section in a site or collection of documents.	`<LINK HREF="Sect07.htm" REL="SECTION">`
START	The link references the first document in a set of documents.	`<LINK HREF="begin.htm" REL="START">`
STYLESHEET	The link references an external style sheet.	`<LINK HREF="style.css" REL="STYLESHEET">`
SUBSECTION	The link references a document that is a subsection in a collection of documents.	`<LINK HREF="Sect07a.htm" REL="SUBSECTION">`
HELP	The link references a help document for the current document or site.	`<LINK HREF="help.tm" REL="HELP">`

Table 4-8. *REL Values Proposed by HTML 3.2* (continued)

REL Value	Explanation	Example
NAVIGATE	The target document contains information, such as an image map, that helps users gain a sense of how to navigate the site.	`<LINK HREF="navbar.gif" REL="NAVIGATE">`
CHILD	Many Web sites have a hierarchical or tree structure. The child relationship identifies a subordinate or subdocument in the hierarchy. Any document may have multiple **CHILD** documents within the same hierarchy.	`<LINK HREF="subpage.htm" REL="CHILD">`

Table 4-9. *Some Proposed REL Values*

REL Value	Explanation	Example
PARENT	The opposite of the child relationship, the parent relationship identifies the superior or container node in a hierarchical environment.	`<LINK HREF="index.htm" REL="PARENT">`
SIBLING	Another hierarchical relationship, the sibling relationship identifies a sibling in the current hierarchy. Any document can have multiple **SIBLING** documents in the same hierarchy.	`<LINK HREF="product2.htm" REL="SIBLING">`
BEGIN or FIRST	The **BEGIN** or **FIRST** relationship identifies the start of a sequence of documents of which the current document is part. The obvious meaning of this relationship is to reference the first document in a linear sequence.	`<LINK HREF="page1.htm" REL="BEGIN">`
END or LAST	The **END** or **LAST** relationship identifies the end of a sequence of documents of which the current document is a part. The obvious meaning of this relationship is to reference the last document in a linear sequence.	`<LINK REL="END" HREF="conclusion.htm">`
BIBLIOENTRY	The **BIBLIOENTRY** relationship identifies a bibliographic entry.	`<LINK HREF="biblio.htm#doc1" REL="BIBLIOENTRY">`
BIBLIOGRAPHY	The **BIBLIOGRAPHY** relationship identifies a bibliography.	`<A HREF="biblio.htm" REL="BIBLIOGRAPHY">...</A>`

Table 4-9.   *Some Proposed **REL** Values* (continued)

REL Value	Explanation	Example
CITATION	The **CITATION** relationship identifies a bibliographic citation. Typically, this is used with anchors rather than the **<LINK>** element, and possibly in conjunction with the **<CITE>** element.	<A REL="CITATION" HREF="#Sources">Smith [1]</A>

DEFINITION	The **DEFINITION** relationship identifies a definition of a term. The meaning of the term may be found in the document referenced by the **GLOSSARY** relationship.	<A REL="DEFINITION"
		    HREF="glossary.htm#widget">
		     Widget</A>

FOOTNOTE	The **FOOTNOTE** relationship identifies a footnote. This relationship is generally used with the **<A>** element. Theoretically, a browser may open a small pop-up window to display the footnote.	<A REL="FOOTNOTE" HREF="note1.htm">Extra info</A>

MADE	The **MADE** relationship has been used to identify the author or "maker" of an HTML document. The maker might include a tool if this is used with the **<LINK>** element.	<A REV="MADE"
		    HREF=
		    "mailto:webmaster@bigcompany.com">
		     Webmaster</A>

AUTHOR	The **AUTHOR** relationship identifies a link to information about the author of the current document, or a method to contact the author.	<LINK REL="AUTHOR" HREF="author.htm">

Table 4-9. *Some Proposed **REL** Values* (continued)

REL Value	Explanation	Example
EDITOR	The **EDITOR** relationship identifies a hypertext link to an editor. It may include a mailto URL or a link to an editor's personal home page.	`<LINK REL="EDITOR" HREF= "mailto:editor@bigcompany.com">`
PUBLISHER	The **PUBLISHER** relationship identifies a link to information about a document's publisher or a way to contact the publisher via a mailto URL.	`<LINK REL="PUBLISHER" HREF= "http://www.osborne.com">`
DISCLAIMER	The **DISCLAIMER** relationship identifies a link to a legal disclaimer applying to the document.	`<LINK REL="DISCLAIMER" HREF="legal.htm">`
TRADEMARK	The **TRADEMARK** relationship identifies a link to a trademark notice concerning the current document.	`<LINK REL="TRADEMARK" REF="trademark.htm">`
META	The **META** relationship identifies a link to a document containing meta-information (information about information) related to the current document. This is a very general relationship. The information linked to could be just about anything.	`<LINK REL="META" HREF="descript.htm">`
TRANSLATION	The **TRANSLATION** relationship specifies a link to a document with a translation to another language.	`<LINK REL="TRANSLATION" HREF="japanese.htm">`
STYLESHEET	The **STYLESHEET** relationship identifies a style sheet for the current document.	`<LINK REL="STYLESHEET" HREF="corporate.css">`

Table 4-9. *Some Proposed **REL** Values* (continued)

WebTV Support for <LINK>

The only fairly common browser to support **<LINK>** is WebTV. In the WebTV environment, **<LINK>** is used to improve performance. If the **REL** attribute is set with the value of **next** and an **HREF** is specified, the browser will "prefetch" the page in question. If the content of the next page is stored in a memory cache, the page loads much faster than if the page has to be requested from the server. If a WebTV user is being presented a brief set of pages in a linear fashion, like a slide-show or tour, the next page could be preloaded with the **<LINK>** element. For example, **<LINK REL="next" HREF="second.htm">** loads the next page, called second.htm, in advance. This technique assumes that the user is going to a predictable next page. This may not be easy to determine for all possible Web site organizations.

Note
HTML authors not using WebTV who are interested in prefetching pages can use Microsoft's preloader ActiveX control. Images also can be prefetched by setting both their **HEIGHT** *and* **WIDTH** *attributes to 1:* **<IMG SRC="image_on_nextpage.gif" HEIGHT="1" WIDTH="1">**. *This technique loads an image into the page, but the image appears as a barely perceptible dot. Then, when the next page loads, the image will have been precached by the browser. Combined with a scripting language, the loading of images can be handled after the current page has loaded, by using the* **onload** *event attribute for the* **<BODY>** *element.*

<LINK> and Style Sheets

A variety of attributes are defined for the **<LINK>** element, including **TYPE**, **MEDIA**, and **TARGET**. These new attributes are already supported in browsers such as Internet Explorer and Netscape for handling style sheets. The **<LINK>** element allows a style sheet for a document to be referenced from a separate file. If the markup code **<LINK REL="stylesheet" HREF="corpstyle.css">** is inserted in the head of an HTML document, it associates the style sheet corpstyle.css with the current document. The **REL** value of **STYLESHEET** indicates the relationship.

The **ALTERNATE STYLESHEET** relationship, which would allow users to pick from a variety of styles, has also been suggested. To define several alternative styles, the **TITLE** attribute must be set to group elements belonging to the same style. All members of the same style must have exactly the same value for **TITLE**. For example, the following fragment defines a standard style called basestyle.css, while two alternative styles, titled 640by480 and 1024by768, have been added; these refer to style sheets to improve layout at various screen resolutions:

```
<LINK REL="alternate stylesheet" TITLE="640by480"
      HREF="small-1.css">
<LINK REL="alternate stylesheet" TITLE="640by480"
      HREF="small-2.css">
<LINK REL="alternate stylesheet" TITLE="1024by768" HREF="big.css">
<LINK REL="stylesheet" HREF="basestyle.css">
```

A Web browser should provide a method for users to view and pick from the list of alternative styles, where the **TITLE** attribute might be used to name each choice. Currently, this alternative choice for style sheets is not supported by any popular browser.

Because the potential exists for many different kinds of linked objects, the **TYPE** attribute was added to the **<LINK>** element to indicate the data type of the related object. **TYPE** can be especially helpful when used to indicate the type of style sheet being used, because many style sheet technologies currently exist. **TYPE** is used by browsers to indicate the type of the linked style, as in this example:

```
<LINK REL="STYLESHEET" HREF="corpstyle.css" TYPE="text/css">
```

For style sheets, **TYPE** usually takes a MIME type, which indicates the format of the style sheet being linked to.

The **MEDIA** attribute is another new attribute for the **<LINK>** element, but it isn't widely supported. For style sheets, this attribute would indicate what type of media the style sheet should be used with. The same document could thus reference one style when it is viewed on a computer screen and a different style sheet when it is printed. This would allow a different style for printing versus screen. The browser is then responsible for filtering out those style sheets that aren't appropriate for the current environment. The following code fragment shows an example of this idea:

```
<LINK REL="STYLESHEET" MEDIA="PRINT" HREF="corp-print.css">
<LINK REL="STYLESHEET" MEDIA="SCREEN" HREF="corp-screen.css">
```

A variety of values have been proposed for the **MEDIA** attribute, including **PRINT**, **PROJECTION**, **SCREEN**, **BRAILLE**, **AURAL**, and **ALL**. When not specified, **ALL** would be the default type, suggesting that the style be used in all output environments.

Meta-Information

Meta-information is simply information about information. Information on the Web often involves many pieces of associated, descriptive information that isn't always explicitly represented in the resource itself. Examples of meta-information include the creator of a document, the document's subject, the publisher, the creation date, and even the title. When used properly, descriptive meta-information has many benefits. It can make information easier to locate, by providing search engines with more-detailed indexing information, rate information to protect minors from viewing certain content, and a variety of other things. As already discussed, meta-information is related to linking, because it helps provide meaning for a document's role in a global or local information space. Meta-information can also provide room for miscellaneous information related to the document. HTML's primary support for meta-information is through the **<META>** element, which allows authors to add arbitrary forms of metadata.

<META> and the NAME Attribute

A **<META>** element that uses the **NAME** attribute is the easiest to understand. The **NAME** attribute specifies the type of information. The **CONTENT** attribute is set to the content of the meta-information itself. For example,

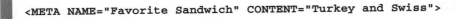

```
<META NAME="Favorite Sandwich" CONTENT="Turkey and Swiss">
```

defines meta-information indicating the document author's favorite lunch. While meta-data can be inserted into a document and list characteristics limited only by an author's imagination, some well-understood values exist that have meaning for Web search tools, such as AltaVista, HotBot, and Infoseek. Many search robots understand the **AUTHOR**, **DESCRIPTION**, and **KEYWORDS** values for the **NAME** attribute. By setting the **NAME** and **CONTENT** attributes, HTML authors can add meta-information to the head of their documents and improve the indexing of their pages by Web search robots. The following code sets the description of a Web page for a fictitious company that makes Green Gadgets:

```
<HTML>
<HEAD>
<TITLE>Big Company, Inc. Home Page</TITLE>
<META NAME="AUTHOR" CONTENT="Big Company, Inc.">
<META NAME="DESCRIPTION" CONTENT="#1 vendor of Green Gadgets.">
<META NAME="KEYWORDS" CONTENT="Big, Company, Gadgets, Green, San Diego">
</HEAD>

<BODY>
...
</BODY>
</HTML>
```

As this example demonstrates, HTML authors can improve the indexing of their pages simply by providing the appropriate keywords in the correct **<META>** element format and alerting the search robot to the site's existence. In many cases, the site may already be indexed, without submission. Authors who don't want search robots indexing their sites can put in their Web server's root directory a file called robots.txt, which provides information regarding which directories or files shouldn't be indexed. All well-behaved Web robots should request the robots.txt file first, before deciding what to index on a site. If a site is known as http://www.bigcompany.com/, a well-behaved robot will begin by requesting http://www.bigcompany.com/robots.txt and analyzing that file. After analyzing the file, the robot will index part, all, or none of the site. The format of the robots.txt file is relatively simple. It includes a field for specifying a user agent, followed by a **Disallow** field, which indicates what is disallowed. For example, if a robots.txt file contains

```
User-agent: *
Disallow: /
```

then every robot is barred from indexing anything from the root directory on down. In other words, the whole site would be skipped. A robots.txt file has only one User-agent field. Wildcards such as * may be used, or particular agents can be named directly. There may be multiple **Disallow** fields that specify different relative URLs that should not be visited, so you can name each directory separately. For example, **Disallow: /staff** bars robots from a file named staff, as well as any information in the subdirectory called staff.

Note *The robots.txt file must reside in the Web server's root directory and must be named in lowercase. Blank lines aren't permitted in the file. Errors in the file may result in the file being ignored.*

You can also put a **<META NAME="ROBOT" CONTENT="NOINDEX, NOFOLLOW">** element in the head of nonindexed documents, but this isn't as widely supported as using a robots.txt file. The robot version of the **<META>** element allows **CONTENT** values of **ALL**, **INDEX**, **NOINDEX**, and **NOFOLLOW**.

Although many Web-searching services freely publish their formats for indexing, others do not. The reason for this secrecy of indexing rules is that many HTML authors attempt to attract traffic to their site by putting an excessive amount of "spider bait" and **<META>** elements in their page, hoping to get higher rankings in search results. Loading a **<META>** element with excessive keywords may backfire, however, and result in the page being dropped from search engines. Most search engines take a few dozen words, approximately 1,024 characters at most.

Even if people didn't try to defeat search engine indexing algorithms, the current approach to cataloging the Web is far from sufficient. Most search engines return far too much information, with no sense as to the value, quality, or decency of the links returned. Many groups are already working on standard sets of meta-data for Web documents. When more-standardized meta-information is established, the organization of the Web should significantly improve, and browsers should be able to provide better decisions about content appropriateness.

META and HTTP-EQUIV

The other form of the **<META>** element uses the **HTTP-EQUIV** attribute, which directly allows the document author to insert HTTP header information. The browser can access this information during read time. The server may also access it when the document is sent, but this is rare. The **HTTP-EQUIV** attribute is set to a particular

HTTP header type, while the **CONTENT** value is set to the value associated with the header. For example,

```
<META HTTP-EQUIV="Expires" CONTENT="Wed, 04 Jun 1999 22:34:07 GMT">
```

placed in the head of a document sets the expiration date to be June 4, 1999. A variety of HTTP headers can be placed in the **<META>** element. The most useful headers are those for two concepts, known as client-pull and site filtering.

Client-Pull

Beginning with Netscape, an extension was made that allows a page to be automatically loaded after a certain period of time. This concept is called *client-pull*. For example, you can build an entry page, or *splash page,* that welcomes visitors to a site and then automatically follows with a second page after a certain period of time. The following example **<META>** element loads a page called secondpage.htm ten seconds after the first page loads:

```
<META HTTP-EQUIV="REFRESH" CONTENT="10;URL=secondpage.htm">
```

Using the client-pull form of the **<META>** element is easy. Just set the content equal to the desired number of seconds, followed by a semicolon and the URL (full or relative) of the page to load. Note, however, that not all browsers support this form of meta-refresh.

Note   *The client-pull concept is often discussed with a related idea called server-push, which primarily is used to create simple animations. However, server-push animation and other such tricks no longer need to be addressed, because they are more easily accomplished by using animated GIF images or JavaScript.*

The **<META>** element is very open-ended. The World Wide Web Consortium (W3C) is already developing more sophisticated approaches for representing meta-data. The most interesting approach is probably PICS, described next, which provides a standard for site filtering.

Site Filtering

One major use of meta-information for links and pages is *site filtering.* At its base level, a filter can be used to restrict access to certain files or types of information. As a technology, this sounds rather innocuous, but when extended, site filtering can lead quickly to censorship. Whether filtering information on the Internet is right or wrong is an area of great debate. Obviously, parents and educators are extremely concerned with the availability of pornographic, violent, or other "inappropriate" types of information on the Internet. Deciding what is inappropriate is the key to the censorship problem, because definitions of what should be allowed vary from person to person. Regardless of how "inappropriate" is defined, few people would disagree that information considered inappropriate by just about everyone does exist on the Internet. The perceived extent of this information tends to be directly related to a person's belief system. The W3C has proposed the *Platform for Internet Content Selection*, or PICS (http://www.w3.org/pub/WWW/PICS/), as a way to address the problem of content filtering on the Web.

The idea behind PICS is relatively simple. A rated page or site will include a **<META>** element within the head of an HTML document. This **<META>** element indicates the rating of the particular item. A rating service, which can be any group, organization, or company that provides content ratings, assigns the rating. Rating services range from independent, nonprofit groups such as the *Recreational Software Advisory Council (RSAC)* (http://www.rsac.org), which already implements a rating system for video games, to software vendors such as Net Sheperd (http://www.netshepherd.com), which sells rating services and software. The rating label used by a particular rating service must be based on a well-defined set of rules that describes the criteria for rating, the scale of values for each aspect of the rating, and a description of the criteria used in setting a value. Usually, the specification of a rating is found in a RAT file that can be accessed by browser or filtering software. Figure 4-10

```
((PICS-version 1.0)
(rating-system "http://www.rsac.org/Ratings/Description/")
(rating-service "http://www.rsac.org/ratingsv01.html")
(name "RSACi")
(description "The Recreational Software Advisory Council
rating service for the Internet. Based on the work of Dr.
Donald F. Roberts of Stanford University, who has studied
the effects of media for nearly 20 years.")

(category
(transmit-as "v")
(name "Violence")
(label
(name "Level 0: No violence")
(description "No aggressive violence; No natural or
accidental violence.")
(value 0) )
(label
```

Figure 4-10.   *RSACi rating system RAT file*

shows a RAT file for the violence category of RSAC-based (RSACi) PICS ratings. Other categories not shown include sex, nudity, and language.

To add rating information to a site or document, a PICS label in the form of a **<META>** element must be added to the head of an HTML file. This **<META>** element must include the URL of the rating service that produced the rating, some information about the rating itself (such as its version, submitter, or date of creation), and the rating itself. Many rating services, such as RSACi, the Internet rating system from RSAC, allow free self-rating. Filling out a form and answering a few questions about a site's content is all that is required to generate an RSACi PICS label, as shown in Figure 4-11.

After you complete and submit the questionnaire in Figure 4-11, you receive an e-mail containing the appropriate meta-information, which can then be placed in the head of your HTML documents. An example of a PICS label using the RSACi rating is shown here:

```
<!DOCTYPE HTML PUBLIC "-//W3C//DTD HTML 3.2 Final//EN">
<HTML>
<HEAD>
<TITLE>PICS Meta Tag Example</TITLE>
<META http-equiv="PICS-Label"
      content='(PICS-1.1 "http://www.rsac.org/ratingsv01.html"
      l gen true comment "RSACi North America Server"
      by "webmaster@bigcompany.com" for
    "http://www.bigcompany.com" on
    "1997.05.26T13:05-0500" r (n 0 s 0 v 0 l 1))'>
</HEAD>

<BODY>
<H1 ALIGN="center">Big Company, Inc.</H1>

<HR>
There's nothing offensive at this site.
</BODY>
</HTML>
```

Under the RSACi rating system, information is rated based on nudity, sex, violence, and language, on a five-category scale from 0 to 4. In this case, the rating is for a typical corporate site that generally has little "inappropriate" information concerning sex and violence, but may use slang or jargon that could be misconstrued out of context.

Note *The **<META>** element with PICS information must occur within the head of the document. Otherwise, it will not be recognized. More than one **<META>** element may be included within the head, so that multiple rating services can be used simultaneously.*

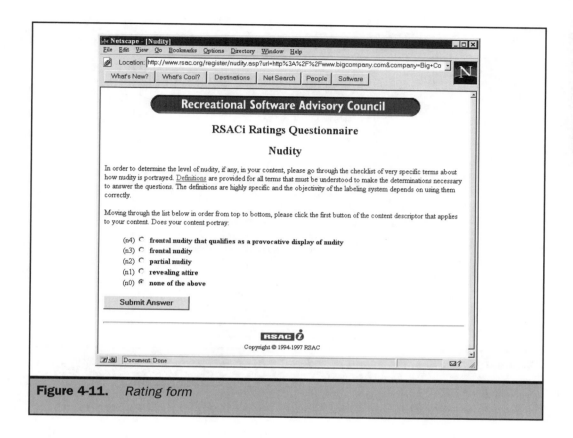

Figure 4-11. *Rating form*

When filtering software reads a file that contains a rating, it determines whether the information should be allowed or denied. Very strict filtering environments may deny all sites that have no rating, so sites with a broad audience are encouraged to use ratings, to avoid restricting readership.

Filtering technology that supports PICS is beginning to achieve widespread acceptance and use. Internet Explorer 3 and 4 already include PICS-based rating filtering, as shown in Figure 4-12.

Many filtering software packages, like SurfWatch (http://www.surfwatch.com) software, are extremely popular both with parents and corporate users trying to limit employee Web abuse. Of course, the technology itself can't cure the problem. Trust in a particular ratings system is a major stumbling block in adoption of the filtering idea. Even when trust is gained, if the rating system seems confusing or arbitrary, its value is lowered. In the "real world," Hollywood's MPAA movie rating system has a single value of G, PG, PG-13, R, or NC-17 for each movie. The assignment of a particular movie rating is based on many factors that often seem arbitrary to casual observers. When considering movies, parents may wonder how scenes of a dinosaur ripping a man to shreds merits a PG or PG-13 rating, while the use of certain four-letter words

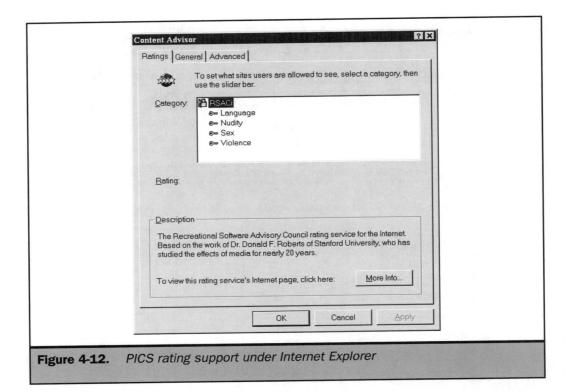

Figure 4-12.   *PICS rating support under Internet Explorer*

indicates an R rating. Certainly similar situations occur on the Internet. Because of the imprecise nature of ratings, the topic is a loaded one, both off and on the Internet.

Beyond simple content rating, some potential benefits of PICS aren't immediately obvious. With PICS-based environments, employers could limit employee access to Web sites that are used for day-to-day business. The idea of PICS can be extended not just to deny or allow information, but to prefer it. Imagine a filtering service for search engines that could return sites that have a particular quality of content or level of accuracy. In the general sense, labels are important, because they allow documents to move beyond a mere description of where the document *is* to what the document is *about*.

Linking Issues

One of the biggest problems with linking documents together with **<A>**, **<AREA>**, or **<LINK>** is that the link often breaks. Authors and users alike are already familiar with links to outside sites that change, resulting in the annoying **404 Not Found** messages so common on the Web. Unfortunately, documents do move around. Some have a very limited lifetime. Even if a link is good, intermittent problems on the Internet can make outside links temporarily stall or break. Clicking a link only to have the browser slowly attempt to resolve the host can be a frustrating interruption for a user. As you'll see next, document authors can do a great deal to ensure that outside linking and broken link problems are the exception rather than the norm.

While it is impossible to keep other sites from changing addresses, you can be a good network citizen and not move linked files around carelessly. Most Web servers are equipped to provide referrer information that indicates the URL of a linking document. If you must move a document, you can alert the Webmasters of the referring URLs about the move and have them update their links. An even better idea is to forward documents to a new location rather than remove them. Web servers can be set up to redirect users to new sites or directories if things must be moved around. In some cases, however, a user may eventually click a broken link to the site, regardless of what precautions you take. For such eventualities, rather than provide a vague error message, you can create a custom message that helps the user locate the document sought. For example, a "404 Not Found" message could be returned with a link included to a site map, table of contents, or search engine that the user can access to search for the specific document. An example of a customized server error message is shown in Figure 4-13.

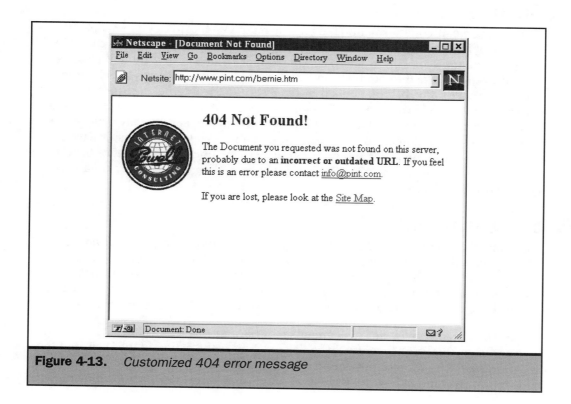

Figure 4-13.   *Customized 404 error message*

The other aspect of linking that can be troublesome often occurs when a user moves from a site to an outside link. Because of conditions on the Internet or at the end server, outside sites might not always respond right away—if at all. To warn users that they are leaving the site and accessing an outside server, a small icon can be placed next to a link, such as the one Microsoft uses with great success, shown here:

The chaotic nature of the Internet means that links will break and documents will move. Unfortunately, URLs themselves provide very little infrastructure to alleviate these problems. New ideas, such as uniform resource names (URNs), might help improve this situation.

Beyond Location

An amazing wealth of information is available on the Web. Although many people complain of information overload, the real problem isn't volume. It's relevance. How can a particular piece of information be located quickly and easily? If the Web were ideal, it would be like the computer on *Star Trek*, which always seems to deliver in a matter of seconds any information a user requests. On the Internet, a request to a search tool often yields an overwhelming list of tens of thousands of entries. Some of these entries may be outdated, the documents to which others refer may have moved, or the server specified in an entry may be unreachable. While the Web isn't science fiction, many of the computer and information systems presented in science fiction represent valid goals for the Web. The key problem with building a more organized Web is URL-based addressing.

Problems with URLs

The primary problem with URLs is that they define location rather than meaning. URLs specify where something is located on the Web, not what it is or anything about it. URLs specify where to go, not what to get. URLs blur the line between what a document is and where it is actually located. This may not seem to be a big deal, but it is. This issue becomes obvious when the problems with URLs are enumerated:

■ *URLs aren't persistent.*   Documents move around, servers change names, and documents might eventually be deleted. This is the nature of the Web, and the reason why the **404 Not Found** message is so common. When users hit a broken link, they might be at a loss to determine what happened to the document and how to locate its new home. Wouldn't it be nice if, no matter what happened, a unique identifier indicated where to get a copy of the information?

■ *URLs tend to be long and confusing.*   People often have to transcribe addresses. For example, the following is quite a lot to write on a piece of literature:

> http://www.bigcompany.com/products/supergadget/specsheets/prod1.htm

Marketing firms already are scrambling for short domain names and site structures that use short URLs, such as http://www.bigcompany.com/prod1. Advertisers often omit http:// in their promotional material. Although most browsers fill in http://, omitting it could cause problems with older browsers that require complete URLs.

■ *URLs create an artificial bottleneck and extreme reliance on DNS services, by specifying location rather than meaning.*   For example, the text of the HTML 4 specification is a useful document and certainly has an address at the W3C Web site. But does it live other places on the Internet? It probably is mirrored in a variety of locations, but what happens if the W3C server is unreachable, or DNS services fail to resolve the host? In this case, the resource is unreachable. URLs create a point source for information. Rather than trying to find a particular document, wherever it might be on the Internet, Web users try to go to a particular location. Rather than talking about where something is, Web users should try to talk about *what* that something is.

URNs, URCs, and URIs

Talking about what a document is rather than where it is makes sense when you consider how information is organized outside the Internet. Nobody talks about which library carries a particular book, or what shelf it is on. The relevant information is the title of the book, its author, and perhaps some other information. But what happens if two or more books have the same title, or two authors have the same name? This is actually quite common. Generally, a book should have a unique identifier (such as an ISBN number) that, when combined with other descriptive information (such as the author, publisher, and publication date) uniquely describes the book. This naming scheme enables people to specify a particular book and then hunt it down.

The Web, however, isn't as ordered as a library. On the Web, people name their documents whatever they like, and search robots organize their indexes however they like. Categorizing things is difficult. The only unique item for documents is the URL, which simply says where the document lives. But how many URLs does the HTML 4 specification have? A document may exist in many places. Even worse than a document with multiple locations, what happens when the content at the location changes? Perhaps a particular URL address points to information about dogs one day and cats the next. This is how the Web really is. However, a great deal of research is being done to address some of the shortcomings of the Web and its addressing schemes.

URN

A new set of addressing ideas, including URNs, URCs, and URIs, are emerging to remedy some of the Web's shortcomings. A *uniform resource name (URN)* can locate a resource by giving it a unique symbolic name rather than a unique address. Network services analogous to the current DNS services will transparently translate a URN into the URL (server IP address, directory path, and filename) needed to actually locate a resource. This translation could be used to select the closest server, to improve document delivery speed, or to try various backup servers in case a server is unavailable. The benefit of the abstraction provided by URNs should be obvious from this simple idea alone.

To better understand the idea behind URNs, consider the idea of domain names, such as www.xyz.com. These names are already translated into numeric IP addresses, like 192.102.249.3, all the time. This mapping provides the ability to change a machine's numeric address or location without seriously disrupting access to it, because the name stays the same. Furthermore, numeric addresses provide no meaning to a user, while domain names provide some indication of the entity in question. Obviously, the level of abstraction provided by a system like DNS would make sense on the Web. Rather than typing some unwieldy URL, a URN would be issued that would be translated to an underlying URL. Some experts worry that using a resolving system to translate URNs to URLs is inherently flawed and will not scale well. Because the DNS system is fairly fragile, some truth may lie behind this concern. Another problem with this idea is that, in reality, URNs probably won't be something that is easy to remember, such as urn: *booktitle*, but instead be something more difficult, such as urn:isbn: 0-12-518408-5.

URC

A *uniform resource characteristic (URC)*, also known as a *uniform resource citation*, describes a set of attribute/value pairs that defines some aspect of an information resource. URCs are somewhat like the **<META>** data items or the PICS labels associated with a Web document. The form of a URC is still under discussion, but many of the ideas of URCs are already in use.

Combined, a URL, URN, and a collection of URCs describe an information resource. For example, the document "Big Company Corporate Summary" might have a unique URN such as urn://corpid:55127.

The syntax of the preceding URN is fictional. It simply shows that URNs probably won't have easily remembered names and that many naming schemes might be used, such as ISBN numbers or corporate IDs.

The "Big Company Corporate Summary" would also have a set of URCs that describes the rating of the file, the author, the publisher, and so on. In addition, the document would have a location(s) on the Web where the document lives, such as one of the following:

http://www.bigcompany.com/about/corp.htm
http://www.bigcompany.com.jp/about/corp.htm.

URI

Taken all together, a particular information resource has been identified. The collection of information, which is used to identify this document specifically, is termed a *uniform resource identifier (URI)*.

Note   *Occasionally, URI is used interchangeably with URL. Although this is acceptable, research into the theories behind the names suggests that URI is more generic than URLs, and serves to encompass the idea of an information resource. Currently, a URL is the only common way to identify an information resource on the Internet. Although technically a URL could be considered a URI, this confuses the issue and obscures the ultimate goal of trying to talk about information more generally than a network location.*

While many of the ideas covered here are still being discussed, some systems, such as Persistent URLs, or PURLS (http://www.purl.org), and Handles (http://www.handle.net), already implement many of the features of URNs and URCs. Furthermore, many browser vendors and large Web sites are implementing special keyword navigation schemes that mimic many of the ideas of URNs and URCs. Unfortunately, as of the writing of this book, none of these approaches are widely implemented or accepted. Although any of these approaches probably can be considered as true URIs when compared to the URLs used today, for the near future, URLs are likely to remain the most common way to describe information on the Web. Therefore, the system has to be extended to deal with new types of information and access methods.

New URL Forms

URLs are here to stay; but, as new ideas are added to the Internet, URLs will evolve into new forms. For example, as telephones and televisions are joined with desktop computers and the Internet, addressing schemes for telephone numbers and TV channels will become necessary. WebTV, video game consoles, and cellular phone browsers already demonstrate that the Web is reaching users beyond the personal computer or workstation. On these devices, some of the URL schemes described early in the chapter are inappropriate. Many of these devices lack local storage, so the file protocol, discussed earlier in this chapter, is of little use. On the other hand, many of these devices usually have access to other sources of information, such as television channels and telephone services. A television channel URL form might look like tv://*channel*, where *channel* is either an alphanumeric name (like nbc or nbc7-39) or a numeric channel number. Similar to the news URL form, differentiating between nbc in one area and another would be unnecessary, because the system would be configured to get the information locally. A phone URL might look like phone://*phone-number*, with a numeric value for the phone number and any extra digit information required, such as the country code or calling card information. For example, phone://+1-619-270-2086 might dial a phone number in the United States. An instruction to send a fax could be written in a similar way, except with fax://*phone-number*.

New content types and URL schemes bring new challenges, particularly in the way links and fragment identifiers are used within HTML documents. For example, how will a particular scene in a video stream be addressed? Random access to large audio and video files is very useful, particularly considering the download requirements for such data. Subsections or "clips" of a data stream must be addressable via URLs that describe a time range. How can a URL describe the idea of accessing an audio file called mozart.audio and playing a ten-second clip starting at time 2:05? Once into clips, particularly video clips, some mechanism will be needed to link from the data stream to other data streams or objects on the Web. Some experimental systems already show video with hot spots that work like image maps. Given that video will certainly be an important media form on the Web of tomorrow and that other media forms also will have to be added as well, it should be obvious that current URL schemes are far from complete. Many new schemes are being proposed all the time. A variety of esoteric schemes are out there already. If you are interested in new URL schemes, take a look at the W3 area on addressing (http://www.w3.org/Addressing/) for more information.

Summary

Linking documents on the Web requires a consistent naming scheme. URLs provide the basic information necessary to locate an object on the Internet, by including the host name, directory, filename, and access protocol. URLs are written in a regular format, so that an address can be written for any object. A common shorthand notation, relative URLs, is particularly useful when creating links within a Web site. If a document's URL can be determined, whether it's relative or fully spelled out, it can be specified in the <A> element to create an anchor from one document to another. Links within HTML documents can be made with text or with images. A special type of clickable image, called an *image map*, allows areas of an image to be defined as "hot."

Simply linking documents together is the most basic form of hypertext. By using the <LINK> element, as well as the **REL** and **REV** attributes of the <A> element, you can create relationships between documents. So far, the <LINK> element is primarily used with style sheets. Once documents are linked together, providing extra information about the document can be very useful. HTML provides such a facility through the use of the <META> element. But even if Web authors master all aspects of linking, a bigger picture remains to worry about. The Web is a chaotic environment, and navigating among documents and linking documents presents serious challenges to the HTML author. In the future, some of these problems may be solved by URNs, URCs, and improved URLs, which, taken together, make up the uniform resource identifier (URI). However, until URNs or similar technologies are more readily available, HTML authors should be cautious about linking, and should consistently check links in their sites.

The
Complete
Reference

Chapter 5

HTML and Images

Until recently, HTML (Hypertext Markup Language) has been true to the "text" in its name. However, text alone wasn't what made the Web popular. While the Web dates from the early 1990s, the environment didn't take off until Mosaic appeared with support for inline images using the **<IMG>** element. Today, images and other binary objects are everywhere on the Web. The modern Web is more about hypermedia than plain hypertext, but it is unlikely that the language will be renamed HMML anytime soon. While images have played an important role in the success of the Web, they must be used carefully. They should not be used just for decoration. They should provide benefit, but at what cost? When used carelessly, Web visuals may require the user to wait a long time for a page to render. Images can improve the message delivered, but when abused they may confuse or hide a message as easily as they improve it. While this is not a book about design and image use, the intersection of HTML and images is important enough to warrant some discussion.

The Role of Images on the Web

When Mosaic first came out, the ability to view an image within the browser window was a huge improvement. Gopher, the popular information system at the time, was primarily textual. It didn't support multimedia and navigation to the same degree as the Web. At first, images often were used to show the logo of the company or present a graph. Today, however, some sites seem to be more about the images than about textual information. So what are images on the Web good for?

Web images can be used to illustrate an idea, show strictly visual information, provide navigation, and serve as decoration. The saying "a picture is worth a thousand words" is very true when illustrating an idea. Images can be used to show procedures, product applications, design styles, and a variety of other concepts. Think about a Web site that teaches people to dance. While it might be possible to explain the various dance steps in writing, a diagram is far easier to understand. People may complain about byte count and download time, but in terms of communication, a picture can be worth a thousand bytes.

Beyond illustrating ideas, there are some topics that require visuals. If a photographer puts up a Web site, how can that person illustrate what he or she does without pictures? For things that are intrinsically visual in nature, pictures are mandatory. Images can also be used for navigation. Visual cues can make it easier for users to find their way around the tangled Web. Even a unique home page image can serve as a consistent beacon, helping the user find his or her way back to a familiar point of reference. Last but not least, images can provide decoration for a site. Pictures make things more interesting, even if they just break up the monotony of page after page of text. A splash of color and a few images can be pleasing. Too much decoration, however, can turn a page into the online equivalent of an overdecorated Christmas tree complete with pink snow flocking.

The basic problem with images on the Web relates to confusion about their value. Far too often the quality of a Web site is judged solely on its look and feel—but what are sites really for? While perception and experience are important, ultimately the user will not focus solely on the interface. The site must provide information or some other beneficial function. In this sense, sites become like software. In a traditional software product, what is most important: the look, the functionality, or both? The answer is both, but over time the functionality far outweighs the look. Nevertheless, don't forget how important the user interface is. A good-looking, logical user interface improves a site, while a poorly designed user interface negatively affects the best content. Navigation is important and should look graphically appropriate, but the logic behind it is what really matters. While textured backgrounds, beveled buttons, and full-screen image maps may look great, they don't ensure that a site is logically organized. Pleasing graphics that reflect well-thought-out site architecture can facilitate navigation throughout the site. Confusing graphical navigation, on the other hand, may actually ruin a site.

In the long run, purely decorative images are not terribly valuable. Rainbow bars and multicolored bullets may make the site appear more exciting initially, but they may eventually irritate the user by hindering speedy navigation of the site. The first time a "What's New" animated GIF runs, the action may catch the user's eye. But what about the twentieth time? Decorating the page just for the sake of having images is not a good reason.

Images are most important when they enhance the content of the Web site. An image that provides more information than would be conveyed with plain text is truly valuable. Even if the image significantly increases the download time of the page, the supplementary information provided may be well worth it. What better way to describe the body style of a car than with a visual? A text description of a low-profile sports car with smooth curves doesn't sell nearly as many cars as an actual picture. Maps, diagrams, specifications, product pictures, portraits, and other visual content—this is what Web images are for. About the only people who should be adding pictures for their own sake to the Web site are those who create them for a living—graphic artists, photographers, and so on. Even then, what the image presents is still important.

| Note | *Software products or Web sites that are entertainment driven may have a different perspective on presentation because the presentation may actually be the content.* |

Image Preliminaries

Before discussing image use on the Web, consider how images are represented in a computer. Images on a computer screen are made up of thousands of *pixels* (shorthand for picture elements). A pixel is a tiny dot, the smallest unit of measure on a screen. The number of pixels that can be displayed on a screen is termed the *screen resolution*. Screen resolution equals the number of pixels across by the number of pixels down.

The more pixels onscreen or in an image, the greater the detail or resolution of the image. Some common screen resolutions are listed here:

640 × 480
800 × 600
1,024 × 768
1,280 × 1,024
1,600 × 1,200

The number of pixels is only one part of a digital image. Images also have color. Every monitor supports a certain number of colors that can be displayed at once. The more colors used, the more realistic the image will look. Color support is measured by the number of bits used to store the color information for each pixel. Common color resolutions are listed here:

- **Standard VGA**   4 bits per pixel = 16 colors
- **Super VGA**   8 bits per pixel = 256 colors
- **High resolution**   16 bits per pixel = 65,536 colors, or simply thousands of colors
- **True color**   24 bits per pixel = 16.7 million colors, generally referred to as millions of colors

Computer-based images come in two basic flavors: *vector images* and *bitmapped images*. Figure 5-1 illustrates the basic idea behind these images.

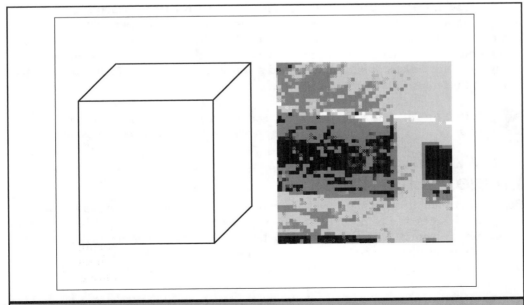

Figure 5-1.   *Idea of vector images versus bitmap images*

A vector image is described mathematically as a set of curves. When a computer reads a vector image, it evaluates the mathematical information and draws the resulting information on the screen. Because the image is defined mathematically, it is very compact. For example, a vector image of a red circle might be described simply as a circle with a radius of 50 pixels filled with red. While vector images are very useful to describe shapes, lines, and other forms of illustration, photographic and similar imagery are better described by a bitmap. A bitmap image is specified as a collection of pixels of different color values. Because of the large number of pixels that may be in an image, as well as the color information that must be described, bitmaps can be very large. For example, an uncompressed bitmap image at 640 × 480 pixels—the typical screen size—with 24 bits of color information would take up nearly 1MB. Bitmaps are the most common image formats. They include images made up of a collection of dots or pixels, such as photographs and television pictures.

The main problem with bitmaps is that the file sizes can be very large. Their excessive size makes it impractical to transmit raw bitmaps across a network like the Internet. One approach to dealing with the size problem is to compress the images. In general, there are two forms of image compression: *lossless* and *lossy*. Lossless image compression means that the compressed image is identical to the uncompressed image. Because all the data in the image must be preserved, the degree of compression, and the corresponding savings, is relatively minor. Lossy compression, on the other hand, does not preserve the image exactly, but does provide a much higher degree of compression. With lossy compression, the image quality is compromised for a smaller byte count. Because the human eye may barely notice the loss, the trade-off may be acceptable.

Image compression depends on the image file format. There are a variety of image formats in the computer world, including vector image formats like Encapsulated PostScript (EPS) and bitmap formats like GIF, TIFF, and JPEG. While the HTML standard says nothing about what image formats can be used on the Web, the browser vendors tend to support the same image types. On the Web, the primary image formats are GIF (Graphics Interchange Format) and JPEG (Joint Photographic Experts Group). A new format called PNG (Portable Network Graphics), which likely will eventually become a Web image standard, is being heavily endorsed by the World Wide Web Consortium (W3C); but, so far, browser support is spotty at best. Given the historical association between UNIX and the Internet, the X image formats—XBM (X Bitmaps) and XPM (X Pixelmaps)—are often supported natively by browsers. Page designers are warned to use only GIF and JPEG images, as these are the most commonly supported formats. Table 5-1 provides an overview of basic file types.

 Internet Explorer also supports the bitmap (BMP) file type popular with Windows users. This format has not been adopted widely on the Web.

GIF Images

GIF images are used extensively on the Web. They are probably the most widely supported image format in browsers that handle graphics. GIF images come in two basic types: *GIF87* and *GIF89a*. Both forms of GIF support 8-bit color (256 colors), use

File Type	File Extension
GIF (Graphics Interchange Format)	.gif
JPEG (Joint Photographic Experts Group)	.jpg or .jpeg
XBM (X Bitmaps)	.xbm
XPM (X Pixelmaps)	.xpm
PNG (Portable Network Graphics)	.png

Table 5-1. *Selected Internet Image File Types*

the LZW (Lempel-Ziv-Welch) lossless compression scheme, and generally have the file extension .gif. GIF 89a supports transparency and animation, both of which will be discussed in this section. All references in this text refer to the more modern 89a form.

Note *There is some concern about the use of GIF images due to the patent on the LZW algorithm held by Unisys that would require payment for use of the proprietary scheme. This concern is unsubstantiated. Nevertheless, the PNG format described in this chapter has been positioned as a substitute for the GIF format.*

The run-length encoding compression scheme used by GIF works well with large areas of continuous color, so GIF is very efficient in compression of flat-style illustration. Figure 5-2 shows the GIF compression scheme in practice. Notice in the figure how the images with large horizontal continuous areas of color compress highly, while those with variation do not. Simply taking a box filled with lines and rotating it shows how dramatic the compression effect can be.

As mentioned earlier, GIF images support 8-bit color for a maximum of 256 colors in the image. Consequently, some degree of loss is inevitable when representing true-color images such as photographs. Typically, when an image is remapped from a large number of colors to a smaller color palette, *dithering* occurs. Dithering attempts to imitate colors by placing similar colors near each other. It also produces a speckling or banding effect that may cause images to appear rough or fuzzy. Web authors should be careful to use GIF images appropriately. Netscape and Microsoft currently use a so-called "browser-safe" color palette of 216 colors that are common across systems like the Macintosh or Windows. If a GIF image using a color outside this color palette is displayed on an 8-bit system, dithering will occur. Authors looking to avoid image problems such as dithering are invited to visit www.htmlref.com.

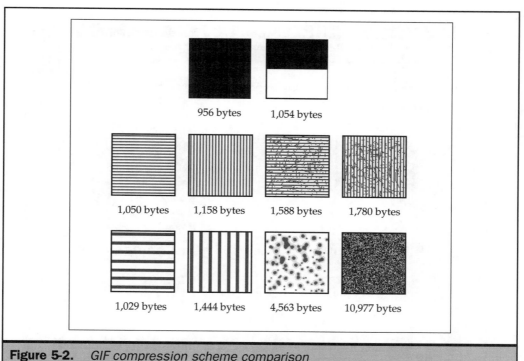

Figure 5-2. *GIF compression scheme comparison*

Note *According to the GIF specification, layering can be used to create a GIF image that supports more than 256 colors. However, not all browsers support this little-known feature. Layering also allows for an interesting form of color interlacing, which can bring in one set of colors before another.*

GIF images also support a concept called *transparency*. One bit of transparency is allowed, which means that one color can be set to be transparent. Transparency allows the background that an image is placed upon to show through, making a variety of complex effects possible. Transparency is illustrated in Figure 5-3.

GIF transparency is far from ideal, as it can result in a halo effect in certain situations. For example, in order to smooth images, a technique called *anti-aliasing* is used. Anti-aliased images appear smooth because the image is progressively made light to fade into the background. However, because only one color of transparency can

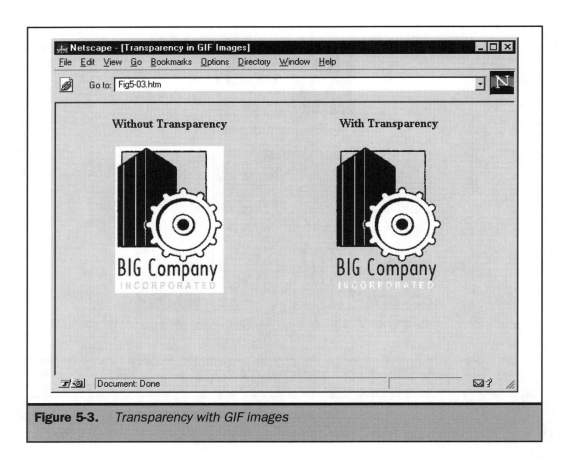

Figure 5-3. *Transparency with GIF images*

be set in an image, the anti-aliasing colors may show up as a halo or residue around the image. The idea of anti-aliasing is shown in Figure 5-4.

GIF images also support a feature called *interlacing*. Interlacing allows an image to load in a venetian-blind fashion rather than from top to bottom a line at a time. The interlacing effect allows a user to get an idea of what an image looks like before the entire image has downloaded. The idea of interlacing is shown in Figure 5-5. Only 26 percent of this 163K image is loaded, producing an indistinct, highly pixelated image. Once the image is completely loaded, it will present a clear image of an office building; at this point in its progress, however, it already gives the user a good idea of what is being downloaded. The previsualization benefit of interlacing is very useful on the Web, where download speed is often an issue. While interlacing a GIF image is

Figure 5-4.   *Anti-aliased image versus aliased image*

generally a good idea, occasionally it comes with a downside. First, interlaced images may be slightly larger than noninterlaced images. Second, an interlaced image may not always provide its intended previsualization benefit. For example, if the GIF image is of graphic text, the text will probably not be readable until the image is fully loaded.

Starting with the GIF89a format, which was supported first by Netscape 2, animation has been possible on the Web. The GIF89a format supports a series of GIF images that act as the individual frames of animation. The animation can be set up so one image is displayed after another, similar to a little flipbook. The animation extension also allows timing and looping information to be added to the image. Today, animated GIFs are one of the most popular ways to add simple animation to a Web page because nearly every browser supports them. Browsers that do not support the animated GIF format generally display the first frame of the animation in its place. Even though plug-ins or other browser facilities are not required, authors should not rush out to use animation on their pages. Excessive animation can be distracting as well as inefficient to download, particularly when frames are not used efficiently. One

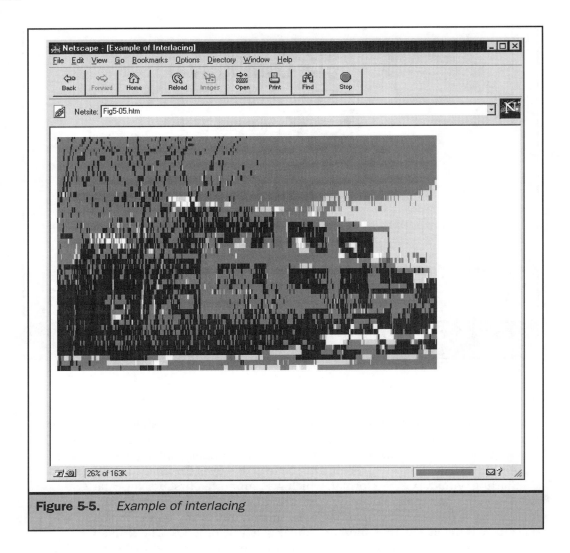

Figure 5-5. *Example of interlacing*

approach to combat file bloat is to replace only the moving parts of an individual animation frame. This may result in a dramatic saving of file size, as shown in Figure 5-6.

In summary, because of their compression scheme and support for 8-bit color, GIF images tend to be best suited for illustrations. GIF images do support interlacing, which may provide previsualization for Web-based imagery. Because of the nature of

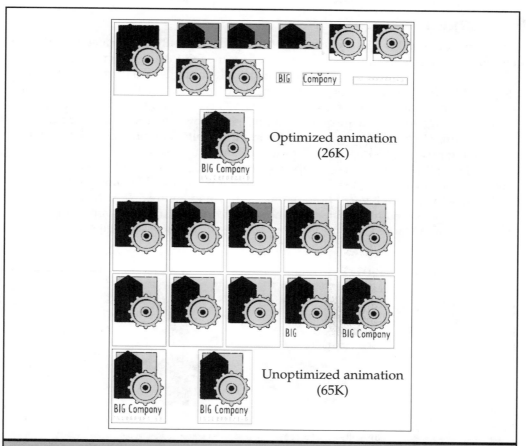

Figure 5-6.   *Example of animated GIF frames and optimization*

their image compression, GIF images may not be suitable for photographic-style imagery, which is probably better left to the JPEG format discussed in the next section. In their favor, GIF images are the most widely supported image format, and do have advanced features such as transparency and animation. Probably the only controversial aspect of the image format, besides its compression issues, is its pronunciation with either a hard *g* or a *j* sound. The author prefers the hard *g* as the other pronunciation sounds like a popular brand of peanut butter, but this sticky issue will probably never be settled.

JPEG Images

The other common Web image format is JPEG, which usually is indicated by a filename ending with .jpg or .jpeg. JPEG, which stands for the Joint Photographic Experts Group—the name of the committee that wrote the standard—is a lossy image format designed for compressing photographic images that may contain thousands, or even millions, of colors or shades of gray. Because JPEG is a lossy image format, there is some trade-off between image quality and file size. However, the JPEG format stores high-quality, 24-bit color images in a significantly smaller amount of space than GIF, thus saving precious disk space or download time on the Web.

While the JPEG format may compress photographic images well, it is not well suited to line drawings or text. The degree of compression in JPEG images, which shows how the format favors photographs, is shown in Figure 5-7. Note that when illustrations are saved in JPEG format, they may acquire extraneous information, often in the form of unwanted dots or other residue. Because JPEG is so well suited to

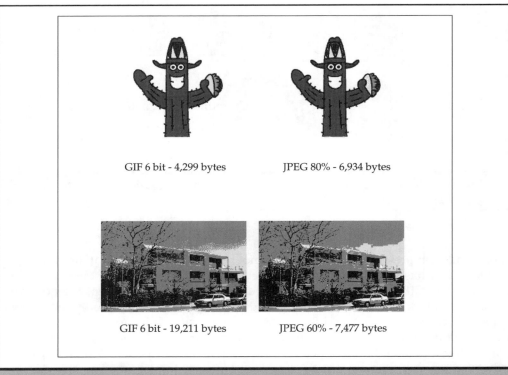

Figure 5-7.   *Comparison between GIF and JPEG formats*

photographs and GIF to illustrations, it's no wonder that both are used on the Web. JPEG images do not support animation, nor do they support any form of transparency. Web designers needing such effects must turn to another image format, such as GIF. JPEG images do support a form of interlacing in a format called *progressive JPEG*. Progressive JPEGs fade in from a low resolution to a high resolution, going from fuzzy to clear. Like interlaced GIFs, progressive JPEG images are slightly larger than their nonprogressive counterparts. One minor problem with progressive JPEGs is that very old browsers, particularly those before Netscape 2, do not support them.

PNG Images

The Portable Network Graphics (PNG) format has all of the features of GIF89a in addition to several other features. Notable features include greater color depth support, color and gamma correction, and 8-bit transparency. In addition, the compression algorithm for PNG is nonproprietary, making PNG a likely successor to GIF. Internet Explorer 4 supports inline PNG images in a limited way. Some versions of Netscape Communicator require a plug-in, while later versions provide limited support. No 4.*x*-generation browser supports PNG well enough to rely on the format, so Web designers are warned to avoid the format unless browser sensing is used to guarantee images will render properly.

Other Useful Image Formats

There are many image formats beyond GIF, JPEG, and PNG that may be used on the Web. These include vector formats like Illustrator and Flash (with the file extension .swf); compressed Freehand files; AutoCAD files (often used for architecture sites); and images that require heavy compression, such as fractals. Most of the less common image formats may require a helper application or plug-in to the browser to allow the image to be displayed. Unless you have a specific need, you should probably avoid special image types requiring browser add-ons; users may become frustrated by the work involved in obtaining the extra software.

Image Downloading Issues

One major criticism of using images on a Web page is the time they take to download and the frustration this may cause the user. The speed of the Web has prompted some to dub it the World Wide Wait. Inevitably, it takes time to transmit data across the Internet. The amount of data that can be transmitted across a link in a certain period of time is termed *bandwidth* and is often measured in bits per second (bps), kilobits per second (Kbps), or megabits per second (Mbps). The higher the bandwidth, the more data can be transmitted quickly. Unfortunately, users accessing the Internet via a modem often have very limited bandwidth available. Some common speeds and the approximate time it takes to transmit 1MB of data are shown in Table 5-2. As you can

Connection Speed	Download Time
14.4Kbps	10 minutes
28.8Kbps	5 minutes
56Kbps	2.5 minutes
ISDN	Approximately 1 minute
Cable modem	Varies from 5–30 seconds
T1	5 seconds

Table 5-2. *Bandwidth and Comparison for 1MB of Data*

see, the faster the data connection, the faster the Web will appear to load. Currently, cable modems provide the fastest connections for most home users. However, several reports indicate that the average modem speed today is still between 28.8Kbps and 56Kbps, primarily due to the very large number of users still using older modems. Designers who create for wide audiences might want to keep this in mind.

Note *The time for all connections will vary dramatically in real life. The numbers in Table 5-2 are theoretical; conditions such as provider congestion and line conditions may significantly taint download times. Furthermore, the speed of cable modems varies dramatically due to the use of proxy servers and the fact that bandwidth may be shared at the neighborhood level.*

Given that users have only so much bandwidth available, one way to reduce wait time is to reduce the amount of data that must be sent. In a typical Web page, the majority of the data transmitted tends to be binary, particularly in the form of images. Given this observation, one approach to improving Web page accessibility is to reduce the file size of the images in your Web page.

The size of a graphic file is determined first by its physical pixel size and then by the color information. The larger the physical image, the larger it tends to be bytewise. Also, the more bits used to represent color information for a particular image, the larger the file size. One approach to decreasing file size would be to reduce the physical size of an image file, possibly by creating thumbnail images that could be clicked to download the full-sized image. Another approach to decreasing file size is to reduce the number of colors in the image. Oftentimes, particularly with GIF images, there are far more bits used to represent color information than there are actual colors in the image. For example, reducing the bit depth from 8 bits (256 colors) to 5 bits (32 colors) can result in significant byte savings without greatly compromising the image.

Another approach to reducing the byte count in an image is through compression. As discussed previously, image compression is handled by the image file format, so choosing the correct format for a particular image is integral to reducing byte count. A basic rule of thumb is to use GIF images for illustrations and JPEGs for photographs. Also, by setting the degree of compression when using a JPEG image, you can reduce file size, at a small sacrifice in image quality. Because the human eye can't often perceive the difference between an image of high quality and one of medium quality, at least on the Web, tuning the image can often result in significant file size savings without penalty.

While image size is certainly important to improving the loading time of Web pages, designers shouldn't get carried away with optimizing images without consideration for the rest of the Web process. For example, while a designer may compress images to their minimum size, the user may still perceive the Web page to be slow. This occurs because there are many aspects to the delivery of a Web page, including the Web server, the links traveled on the Internet, the traffic on the Internet, the protocols, the software being used, and even the processing speed of the computer at the other end. All of these factors affect the user's experience. There is little reason to optimize images for a Web site that will be hosted on a slow or poorly connected server. No matter what, always consider stopwatch time over file size or any other measurement for download rate. What the user experiences is what counts, not the bytes transferred or the number of connections made.

Obtaining Images

One of the first problems many novice Web designers face is where to get images for their Web pages. This shouldn't be any more difficult than getting images for a different type of project. One way to obtain images is simply to make them. There are a variety of vector drawing programs, such as Adobe Illustrator, and bitmap editing or paint programs, such as Adobe Photoshop. With such tools, you can create images directly in the computer and then save them to the appropriate Web image format, such as GIF or JPEG. Images do not have to be made within the computer, however. You could scan drawings with a flatbed scanner, or take pictures with a traditional camera and scan them with a flatbed scanner, slide scanner, or even a drum scanner. Digital cameras are also very useful for capturing imagery and avoiding the scanning process altogether.

Another approach to obtaining images to use on the Web is to buy them. You may be aware of the many clip art CD-ROMs available for sale. High-quality images also can be licensed from traditional stock photography companies, such as Comstock (http://www.comstock.com). Some page authors who believe that clip art is not of high enough quality prefer to piece together images. Outlets such as Eyewire (http://www.eyewire.com) license professional-grade imagery. CD-ROMs with 100,000 images for $100 aren't always the best deal considering the quality of the imagery and the fact that you might only need one image. You truly get what you pay for with image clip art.

Not all stock photography houses understand the Web. A few still charge exorbitant prices for imagery if it will be used online. Given the popularity of the Web, this situation will probably change as they lose business to their more open-minded competitors.

The expense of licensing images and the ease with which images can be copied have convinced many people that they can simply appropriate whatever images they need. Unfortunately, this is stealing the work of others. While there are stiff penalties for copyright infringement, it can be difficult to enforce these laws. Also, some page designers tend to bend the rules thanks to the legal concept called *fair use*, which allows the use of someone else's copyrighted work under certain circumstances.

There are four basic questions used to define the fair-use concept. First, is the work in question being appropriated for a nonprofit or profit use? The fair use defense is less likely to stand up if the "borrowed" work has been used to make money for someone other than its copyright holder.

Second, is the work creative (for example, a speculative essay on the impact of a recent congressional debate) or factual (a straightforward description of the debate without commentary)? Fair use would cover use of the factual work more than use of the creative one.

Third, how much of the copyrighted work has been used? It is possible to use someone else's image if it is changed substantially from the original. The problem is determining what constitutes enough change in the image to make it a new work. Simply using a photo-editing tool to flip an image or change its colors is not enough. There is a fine line between using portions of another person's work and outright stealing. Even if you don't plan on using uncleared images, be careful of using images from free Internet clip art libraries. These so-called free images may have been submitted with the belief that they are free, but some of them may have been appropriated from a commercial clip art library somewhere down the line. Be particularly careful with high-quality images of famous individuals and commercial products. While such groups may often appreciate people using their images, the usage is generally limited to noncommercial purposes.

The third fair use question leads to the fourth. What impact does the image have on the economic value of the work? While unauthorized use of a single *Star Trek*–related image might not substantially affect the money earned by Paramount Pictures in a given fiscal year, Paramount's lawyers take a dim view of such use. In fact, some entertainment organizations have taken steps to make it very difficult for Web page designers to use such images.

One could, perhaps, add a fifth question to the list: who owns the original work, and how vigorously will the owner defend it? This whole discussion begs many legal questions that are far beyond the scope of this book. Suffice it to say that in the long run, it's always safer to create original work, license images, or use material in the public domain. Just because many Web designers skirt the law doesn't mean you should.

HTML Image Basics

To insert an image into a Web page, use the **<IMG>** element and set the **SRC** attribute of the element equal to the URL of the image. As discussed in Chapter 4, the form of the URL may be either an absolute URL or a relative URL. Most likely, the image element will use a relative URL to an image found locally. To insert a GIF image called logo.gif residing in the same directory as the current document, use

```
<IMG SRC="logo.gif">
```

Of course, an absolute URL could also be used to reference an image on another server, for example

```
<IMG SRC="http://www.bigcompany.com/images/logo.gif">
```

Using an external URL is not advised since images may move and cause the page to load at an uneven pace.

> **Note**   *The SRC attribute must be included. Otherwise, browsers that support images may display a placeholder or broken image icon.*

To set up a simple example, first create a directory to hold your images. It is usually a good idea to store all your image media in a directory named *images*. This will help you keep your site contents organized as you build the Web site. Now place a GIF format image named photo.gif in that directory. To retrieve an image off the Internet, you can simply right-click with your mouse on an image and save the file to your directory. Macintosh users will have to hold the mouse button down on an image to access the menu for saving the image. Once you have a GIF image, you should be able to use a short piece of HTML markup to experiment with the use of **<IMG>**, as shown here:

```
<!DOCTYPE HTML PUBLIC "-//W3C//DTD HTML 4.0 Transitional//EN">
<HTML>
<HEAD>
<TITLE>Image Example</TITLE>
</HEAD>

<BODY>
<H2 ALIGN="CENTER">Image Example</H2>
<IMG SRC="images/photo.gif" WIDTH="234" HEIGHT="150" BORDER="0">
</BODY>
</HTML>
```

A possible rendering of the image example is shown in Figure 5-8.

Under the original HTML 2.0 specification, besides **SRC**, there were only three other attributes to the **<IMG>** element: **ISMAP, ALIGN,** and **ALT**. Later on, Netscape and Microsoft added numerous attributes, many of which have been incorporated into the HTML 4.0 specification that is currently in progress. The next few sections cover the basic attributes. A more complete rundown of the image options available will follow.

ALT Attribute

The **ALT** attribute was set to provide alternative text for user agents that do not display images, or for graphical browsers when the user has turned image rendering off. The **ALT** attribute's value may display in place of the image, or be used as a tool tip or placeholder for information in image-based browsers. The **ALT** attribute's value is typically enclosed in double quotes and may include spaces and other characters.

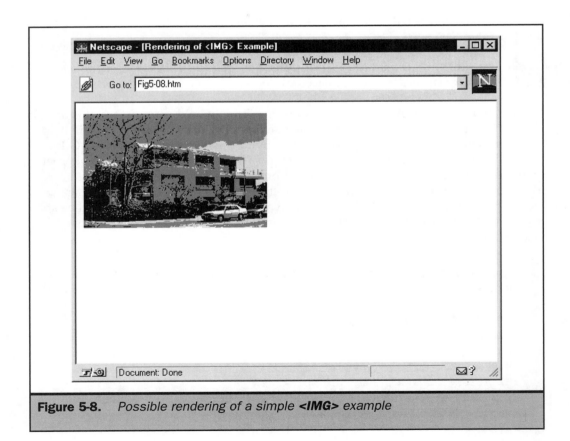

Figure 5-8.   *Possible rendering of a simple **<IMG>** example*

However, any HTML markup found in the **ALT** element will be rendered as plain text. If the option to display images is turned off, the browser will display the alternative text, as shown in Figure 5-9.

Many modern graphical browsers will also display the **ALT** text as the tool tip for the image once the pointer is positioned over the image for a period of time, as shown in Figure 5-10. A browser may also show the **ALT** text as images load, giving the user something to read as the page renders.

While some sources suggest that **ALT** text be limited to 1,024 characters, there is no limit to the text that may theoretically be used. However, anything more than a few hundred characters may become unwieldy. Furthermore, some browsers, including some versions of Netscape 4, do not handle long tool tips properly and may not wrap the descriptive text.

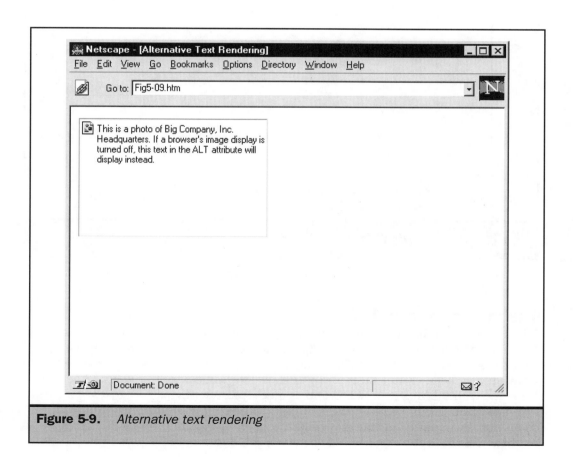

Figure 5-9.   *Alternative text rendering*

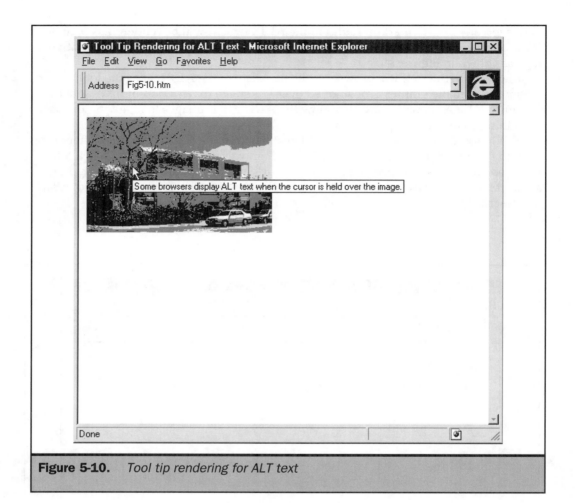

Figure 5-10. *Tool tip rendering for ALT text*

The Importance of ALT

It is easy to forget that many different types of browsers can be used to access the Web.
While much of the world may access a page via Netscape or Microsoft products, what
about everyone else out there? There are many people who have access to the Web
from a text-only environment. Figure 5-11 shows the same page two ways: under
Netscape with the image turned on and as rendered under Lynx.

In addition to those who choose to access the Web via a text-only environment,
some visually impaired people may require a different type of browser. Blind people
might access the Web using a text mode browser fed into a speaking machine or using

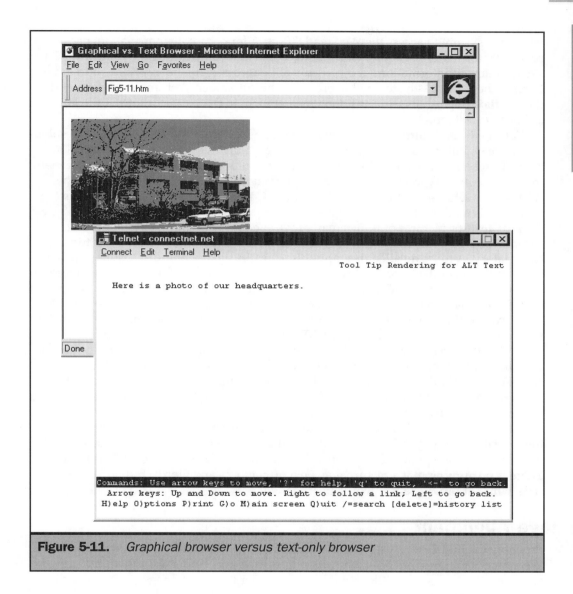

Figure 5-11.   *Graphical browser versus text-only browser*

a browser such as pwWebSpeak (http://www.prodworks.com), which can integrate with a voice synthesizer. Other users may access the Web via a telephone or other automated system just for ease of use or quick information. Already, systems like the Web-on-Call Voice Browser (http://www.netphonic.com) can be used to provide automated phone access to Web sites. Imagine a situation in which an automated telephone system to access the Web read, "Press 1 for corporate information, press 2 for product information." Finally, what about robots that come through and index a Web site for relevant information? The contents of images provide no information to index. In all of these cases—the text mode browser, the automated Web access system, and the site indexing robots—images don't mean much. In these cases, the **ALT** attribute can be very valuable.

Setting the **ALT** attribute to provide alternative information for an image can solve many accessibility problems, but simply setting alternative text is not adequate. The biggest problem with alternative text is that it often does not really provide any benefit. Imagine a company logo on a page for a company called Big Company. Should the **ALT** text be set to something like **"Logo of Big Company, Inc."**? Imagine a person hearing this read out loud. Doesn't just **"Big Company, Inc."** make more sense?

ALT text for pictures of things may prove even more cryptic. A picture of the corporate office with **ALT** text set to read "Picture of Corporate Office" is not terribly explanatory. A more detailed description such as "A picture of the exterior of the Big Company Corporate office—a three-story building with beach-flavored architecture surrounded by large trees" is much more useful. In this case, there is some added value even for the sighted user. A general rule is that if an image conveys information, the **ALT** text should convey the same information; and, if an image is simply decoration, you can set the **ALT** text to nothing: **ALT=" "**.

Last is the famous case of the bullet item. Many users add small red or blue circles or bullets to their pages. In many cases, the **ALT** text for these objects is set to be **"bullet"**. Now think about the aggravation of seeing the word *bullet* over and over again on a page, not to mention hearing it read aloud. Maybe putting an asterisk would be more appropriate for **ALT** text in this instance.

While a lot of people might argue that the Web wasn't popular until graphics were integrated or that the Web is inherently a visual medium, the value of textual content on the Web is indisputable. Consequently, it should be made as accessible as possible. There is no arguing that a picture may be worth a thousand words; but if that is the case, why not provide a few words in exchange?

Image Alignment

Probably the first thing a user wants to do after he or she is able to put an image in a Web page is to figure out how to position it on the page. Under the HTML 2.0 standard, there was very little that allowed the user to format image layout on a page. Initially, the **ALIGN** attribute could be set to a value of **TOP**, **BOTTOM**, or **MIDDLE**. When an image was included within a block structure of text, the next line of text would be aligned at the top, middle, or bottom of the image, depending on the value of the **ALIGN** attribute. If the attribute wasn't set, it would default to the bottom. The example that follows illustrates basic image alignment as first defined in HTML 2. The rendering of the image alignment example is shown in Figure 5-12.

```
<!DOCTYPE HTML PUBLIC "-//W3C//DTD HTML 4.0 Transitional//EN">
<HTML>
<HEAD>
<TITLE>Basic Image Alignment</TITLE>
</HEAD>

<BODY>
<P><IMG SRC="images/aligntest1.gif" ALIGN="TOP" BORDER="1">
This text should be aligned at the top of the image.</P>

<P><IMG SRC="images/aligntest1.gif" ALIGN="MIDDLE" BORDER="1">
This text should be aligned at the middle of the image.</P>

<P><IMG SRC="images/aligntest1.gif" ALIGN="BOTTOM" BORDER="1">
This text should be aligned at the bottom of the image.</P>
</BODY>
</HTML>
```

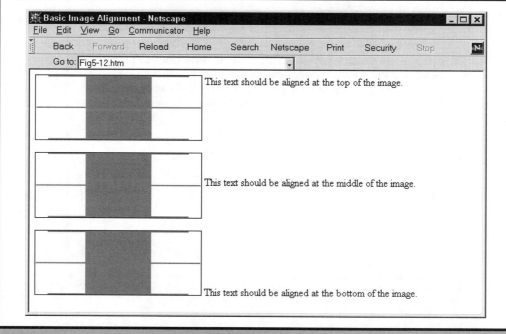

Figure 5-12.   *Image alignment rendering*

One of the problems with initial image alignment in early HTML was that the text really didn't flow around the image. In fact, only one line of text was aligned next to the image, which meant the inline images had to be very small or the layout looked somewhat strange, as shown in Figure 5-13.

Netscape introduced the **LEFT** and **RIGHT** values for **ALIGN**, which allowed text to flow around the image. When setting an image element like **<IMG SRC="logo.gif" ALIGN="LEFT">**, the image is aligned to the left and the text flows around to the right. Correspondingly, when you are using markup like **<IMG SRC="logo.gif" ALIGN="RIGHT">**, the image is aligned to the right and the text flows around to the left. It is even possible to flow the text between two objects if things are done carefully.

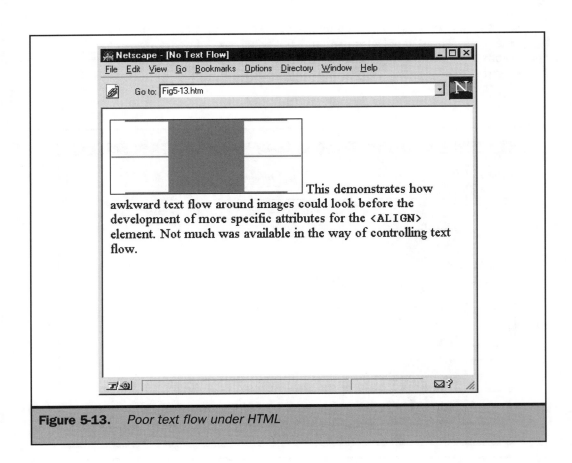

Figure 5-13. *Poor text flow under HTML*

The HTML presented here shows how the **ALIGN** attribute would be used to flow text around images. The rendering of this example is shown in Figure 5-14.

```
<!DOCTYPE HTML PUBLIC "-//W3C//DTD HTML 4.0 Transitional//EN">
<HTML>
<HEAD>
<TITLE>Improved Text Flow</TITLE>
</HEAD>

<BODY>
<IMG SRC="images/redsquare.gif" ALIGN="LEFT">
The top image has its ALIGN attribute set to "left," so the text
flows around it to the right. The top image has its ALIGN attribute
set to "left," so the text flows around it to the right. The top
image has its ALIGN attribute set to "left," so the text flows
around it to the right.

<BR CLEAR="LEFT"><BR><BR>

<IMG SRC="images/redsquare.gif" ALIGN="right">
The top image has its ALIGN attribute set to "right," so the text
flows around it to the left. The top image has its ALIGN attribute
set to "right," so the text flows around it to the left. The top
image has its ALIGN attribute set to "right," so the text flows
around it to the left.
</BODY>
</HTML>
```

Notice in this example that there is a special attribute of the **
** element. This is necessary to force the text to flow properly and will be discussed shortly. However, there are still some aspects of the **ALIGN** attribute that should be discussed. There is some confusion regarding the use of the value **CENTER** with the **ALIGN** attribute for the **<IMG>** element. Typically, this attribute value acts the same as the **MIDDLE** value and should be avoided. To actually center an image in the middle of the screen requires enclosing the image within **<P ALIGN="CENTER">**, **<DIV ALIGN="CENTER">**, or a plain **<CENTER>** element.

Netscape and Microsoft also support four other values for **ALIGN**: **TEXTOP**, **BASELINE**, **ABSMIDDLE**, and **ABSBOTTOM**. All these attributes should be avoided in most cases, since they may not be supported identically across browsers and are not

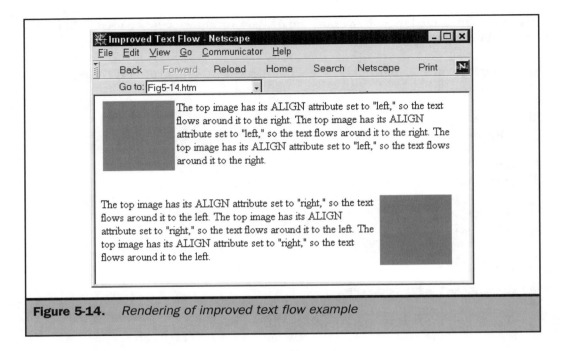

Figure 5-14. *Rendering of improved text flow example*

yet part of any standards. Positioning is handled more precisely by technologies like style sheets, which are discussed in Chapter 10. The basic meaning of these attribute values is discussed here.

Setting the **ALIGN** attribute to **TEXTTOP** aligns the top of an image with the top of the tallest character in the current line; this attribute works erratically under various browsers. The **BASELINE** value aligns the bottom of an image with the baseline of the text in the current line. (The baseline is the unseen line that all the characters sit on.) **ABSMIDDLE** aligns the middle of an image with the middle of the text in the current line, which means in the actual middle of the characters themselves. The value **ABSBOTTOM** aligns the bottom of an image with the bottom of the lowest item in the current line of text, including descender characters, such as lowercase y and g, that go below the baseline. Unlike **ABSBOTTOM, BASELINE** does not include the descenders in a character. For example, in a lowercase g, the lower half of the letter will sit below the baseline.

HSPACE and VSPACE

Just floating an image and allowing text to wrap around it may not be adequate. There is also the issue of how to position the image more precisely with the text and make sure that text breaks where it ought to. Initially introduced by Netscape and made official in HTML 3.2, the **HSPACE** and **VSPACE** attributes can be used to introduce "runaround" or buffer space around an inland image. The **HSPACE** attribute is used to insert a buffer of horizontal space on the left and right of an image, while the **VSPACE** attribute is used to insert a buffer of vertical space in between the top and bottom of the image and other objects. The value of both attributes should be a positive number of pixels. While under some browsers it may be possible to set the attribute values to percentage values, this is inadvisable, because very high values may produce strange results. However, the most problematic aspect of the **HSPACE** and **VSPACE** attributes is the amount of buffer space that occurs on both sides of the image. Take a look at the HTML markup shown here to see how **HSPACE** and **VSPACE** work. Figure 5-15 displays a possible browser rendering of the example code.

```html
<!DOCTYPE HTML PUBLIC "-//W3C//DTD HTML 4.0 Transitional//EN">
<HTML>
<HEAD>
<TITLE>HSPACE and VSPACE Example</TITLE>
</HEAD>

<BODY>
<P>The image below has its <TT><B>&lt;HSPACE&gt;</B></TT> and
<TT><B>&lt;VSPACE&gt;</B></TT> attributes set to 50 pixels, so the
text will flow around it at a distance of 50 pixels. The rest of
this text is dummy text. If it said anything interesting you would
certainly be the first to know.

<IMG SRC="images/redsquare.gif" ALIGN="LEFT" HSPACE="50" VSPACE="50">
This is dummy text.  If it said anything interesting you would certainly
be the first to know. There's really no point in reading the rest of it.
This is dummy text.  If it said anything interesting you would certainly
be the first to know. There's really no point in reading the rest of it.
This is dummy text.  If it said anything interesting you would certainly
be the first to know. There's really no point in reading the rest of it.
This is dummy text.  If it said anything interesting you would certainly
be the first to know. There's really no point in reading the rest of it.
This is dummy text.  If it said anything interesting you would certainly
be the first to know. There's really no point in reading the rest of it.
This is dummy text.  If it said anything interesting you would certainly
be the first to know. There's really no point in reading the rest of it.</P>
</BODY>
</HTML>
```

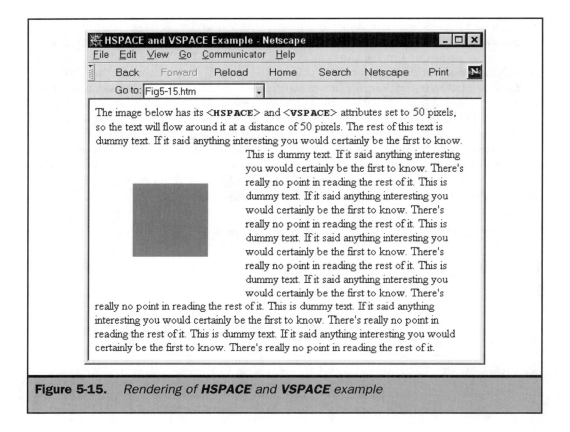

Figure 5-15. *Rendering of* **HSPACE** *and* **VSPACE** *example*

It turns out that in the future, by using style sheets (discussed in Chapter 10), it may be possible to avoid these somewhat imprecise layout features altogether. The **HSPACE** and **VSPACE** attributes have been very useful, albeit occasionally abused by Web designers. How these attributes can be used in conjunction with the so-called invisible *pixel gif* to force layouts will be discussed in Chapter 6.

Extensions to

In flowing text around an image, there may be a situation in which the designer wants to clear the text flow around the image. For example, creating an image with a caption like the one shown in Figure 5-16 might be problematic because the text may reflow. To deal with such problems, a new attribute called **CLEAR** was added to the **
** element; this extension is now part of the HTML standard. The **CLEAR** attribute can be set to **LEFT, RIGHT, ALL,** or **NONE** and will clear the gutter around an inline object like an image. For example, imagine the fragment **<IMG SRC="photo. gif"**

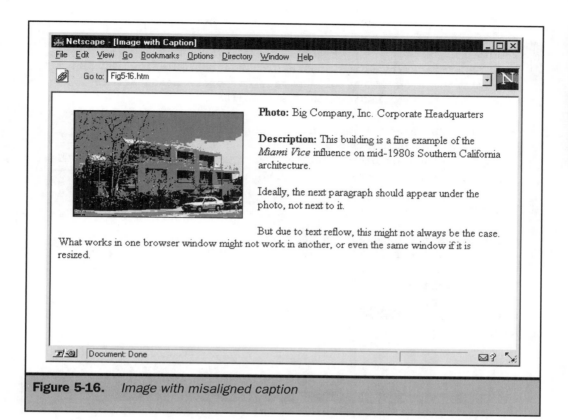

Figure 5-16.   *Image with misaligned caption*

ALIGN="LEFT"> with text wrapping around it. If **<BR CLEAR="LEFT">** is included in the text and the wrapped text is still wrapping around the image, the text will be cleared to pass the image. The **CLEAR="RIGHT"** attribute to **
** works for text flowing around right-aligned images. Of course, setting the attribute to **NONE** makes the element act as it normally would and is implied when using the **
** by itself. An example of the use of this attribute is shown here; a rendering appears in Figure 5-17.

```
<!DOCTYPE HTML PUBLIC "-//W3C//DTD HTML 4.0 Transitional//EN">
<HTML>
<HEAD>
<TITLE><BR CLEAR> Example</TITLE>
</HEAD>
```

```
<BODY>
<IMG SRC="images/building.jpg" WIDTH="234" HEIGHT="150" BORDER="2"
     ALT="Outside of the Big Company corporate headquarters"
     ALIGN="LEFT"  HSPACE="20" VSPACE="10">

<B>Photo:</B> Big Company, Inc. Corporate Headquarters<BR><BR>

<B>Description:</B> This building is a fine example of the <I>Miami
Vice</I> influence on mid-80s southern California architecture.

<BR><BR>

The next paragraph should appear under the photo, not next to it,
thanks to the <TT>&lt;BR CLEAR=LEFT&gt;</TT>.

<BR CLEAR="LEFT">
<I>Photo copyright &copy; 1999 by Big Company, Inc.</I>
</BODY>
</HTML>
```

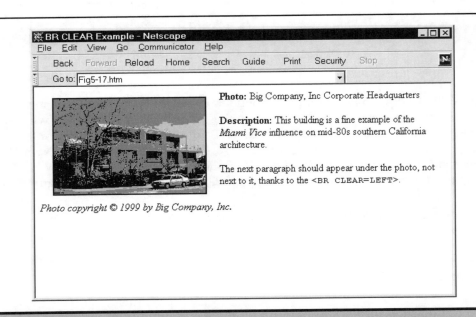

Figure 5-17.   *Rendering of <BR CLEAR> example*

HEIGHT and WIDTH

The **HEIGHT** and **WIDTH** attributes of the **<IMG>** element, introduced in HTML 3.2, are used to set the dimensions of an image. The value for these attributes is either a positive pixel value or a percentage value from 1 to 100 percent. While an image can be stretched or shrunk with this attribute, the main purpose is actually to reserve space for images that are being downloaded. As pages are requested by a browser, each individual image is requested separately. However, the browser can't lay out parts of the page, including text, until the space that the image takes up is determined. This may mean waiting for the image to download completely. By telling the browser the height and width of the image, the browser can go ahead and reserve space with a bounding box into which the image will load. Setting the height and width thus allows a browser to download and lay out text quickly while the images are still loading. For an image called test.gif that has a height of 10 and width of 150, use **<IMG SRC="test.gif" HEIGHT="10" WIDTH="150">**. The improvement in usability with the **HEIGHT** and **WIDTH** attributes for images is significant, and they should always be included.

Note *Many people wonder what the measurements of a particular image are. Using Netscape, it is possible to view the dimensions quite easily. First, load the image into the browser by itself without any accompanying HTML. Now look at the title bar of the browser, which should display the dimensions. Also, using the option to view document information for the image within the browser should reveal the dimensions.*

Beyond the prelayout advantages, the **HEIGHT** and **WIDTH** attributes can also be used to size images. This is rarely a good idea, as the image may end up being distorted. One way to avoid distortion is to shrink images in a proportional manner. However, if the image is to be made smaller, it is a better idea to size the image appropriately in a graphics program. Shrinking the image with the **HEIGHT** and **WIDTH** attributes does not affect the file size, while resizing the image beforehand will shrink the file and hence reduce the download time. Another use of **HEIGHT** and **WIDTH** sizing might be to increase the size of a simple image. For example, imagine an image of a single green pixel, and set the height and width alike: **<IMG SRC="greenpixel.gif" HEIGHT="100" WIDTH="100">**. The resulting image is a large green box with very little download penalty. A few sites even use the **HEIGHT** and **WIDTH** attributes with percentage values like 100 percent to create interesting effects such as full-screen images or vertical or horizontal color bars.

One other interesting use of the **HEIGHT** and **WIDTH** attributes would be to help preload images. With the desire for fast-loading pages, preloading can be used to create the illusion of a quick download. Imagine that during the idle time on a page, the images on the next page are being downloaded so that they are precached when the user goes to the next page. A significant perceived performance improvement is achieved. One way to perform this prefetching is by putting an image that will appear later on the current page with **HEIGHT** and **WIDTH** both set to **1**. In this case, the image won't really be visible but will be fully loaded into the browser's cache. Once the user visits the next page, the image can be fetched off the local disk and displayed quickly.

One potential problem with this approach is that the browser doesn't load images at the same rate or in the same order. Because of this, some logic should be added to the page so that the image to preload only loads after the page has finished. Another issue occurs if the user chooses a page that doesn't use the prefetched image. Because of these potential problems, a linear order of pages is probably the only structure that can benefit from this trick.

LOWSRC

Another potential speed improvement introduced by Netscape and still not part of the HTML 4.0 standard is the **LOWSRC** attribute. The **LOWSRC** attribute should be set to the URL of an image to load in first, before the so-called high source image indicated by the **SRC** attribute. In this sense, the attribute can be set to the address of a low-resolution or black-and-white file, which can be downloaded first and then followed by a high-resolution file. For example,

```
<IMG SRC="hi-res-photo.gif" LOWSRC="bw-photo.gif" HEIGHT="100"
     WIDTH="100" ALT="Outside of building photograph">
```

The **LOWSRC** attribute can provide significant usability improvement when large full-screen images must be used.

One interesting aspect of the **LOWSRC** attribute is that the browser tends to use the image dimensions of the **LOWSRC** file to reserve space within the Web page if the **HEIGHT** and **WIDTH** attributes are not set. Because of this, some strange distortion could happen if the high-resolution image is not the same size as the low-resolution image. This problem actually occurs under versions of Netscape.

Another interesting aspect of the **LOWSRC** attribute is the possibility for simple animation. For example, the **LOWSRC** attribute could be set to a picture of a closed book and the regular **SRC** attribute set to a picture of an open book. When loaded, it appears as a small two-frame animation. However, this method of animation is very simplistic and lacks timing; so while it might look good on a relatively slow connection, the effect may be lost over a T1 connection where the images load rapidly. For animation, an animated GIF should be used, as discussed earlier in the chapter. Animated GIFs require no special syntax and may be used for either **SRC** or **LOWSRC**. If more complex animation is required, using an **<EMBED>** or **<OBJECT>** element to reference a Flash file might be called for, as discussed in Chapter 9.

These are only the most basic attributes for the **<IMG>** element. A more complete listing of **<IMG>** element attributes can be found in the element reference in Appendix A.

Images as Buttons

One of the most important aspects of images, as discussed in Chapter 4, is how they can be combined with the **<A>** element to create buttons. To make an image "pressable," simply enclose it within an anchor.

```
<A HREF="http://www.bigcompany.com"><IMG SRC="logo.gif"></A>
```

When the page is rendered in the browser, clicking on the image will take the user to the anchor destination specified. Generally, to indicate that an image is pressable, the browser will put a border around the image and provide some feedback to the user when the cursor or pointing device is over the hot area, such as turning the pointer to a finger or highlighting the text. For some basic feedback types, note the example in Figure 5-18, which shows a border, finger pointer, and URL destination, all indicating that the image is pressable.

Figure 5-18.   *Image as link feedback*

One issue that may be troublesome for page designers is the border that appears around the image when it is made pressable. It is possible to turn this border off by setting the **BORDER** attribute of the image equal to **0**. For example,

```
<A HREF="http://www.bigcompany.com"><IMG SRC="logo.gif"
   BORDER="0"></A>
```

Of course, without the border it might be difficult to determine which images on a page are links and which are not. This can cause users to play a little game of finding the active click region by running the mouse all over the screen. One way to avoid such usability problems is to provide visual cues in images that are made pressable. These might include embossing, beveling, or drop shadows. Examples of such buttons are shown in Figure 5-19.

While from a design perspective some of the effects, particularly drop shadows, are a little overused, there are tangible benefits to adding feedback information to button graphics. Another approach to providing feedback about what images are clickable is to animate the buttons. Using a very simple piece of JavaScript, it is possible to animate a button so that when a mouse passes over an image it comes alive. A brief discussion about how HTML pages can be made more dynamic using a scripting language like JavaScript can be found in Chapters 13 and 14.

Figure 5-19. *Sample button styles for usability improvement*

One non-button-oriented use of the **BORDER** attribute is to put a simple stroke around an image. Many times people will use a graphics tool to create a frame on an image, but the **BORDER** attribute is a bandwidth-cheap way to get much of the same effect. Try setting the **BORDER** attribute equal to a positive value on a nonclickable image—for example, **<IMG SRC="portrait.gif" BORDER="5">**. This little change provides an easy way to frame an image and might even lend itself to interesting design ideas.

Image Maps

Another form of clickable images, discussed previously in Chapter 4, is the idea of an image map. An image map is a large image that contains numerous hot spots that can be selected, sending the user to a different anchor destination. There are two basic forms of image maps: *server side* and *client side*. In the server-side image map, the user clicks on an image but the server must decode where the user clicked before the destination page (if any) is loaded. With client-side image maps, all of the map information—which regions map to which URLs—can be specified in the same HTML file that contains the image. Including the map data with the image and letting the browser decode it has several advantages, including

1. There is no need to visit a server to determine the destination, so links are resolved faster.
2. Destination URLs can be shown in the status box as the user's pointer moves over the image.
3. Image maps can be created and tested locally, without requiring a server or system administration support.
4. Client-side image maps can be created so that they present an alternative text menu to users of text-only browsers.

While this discussion makes it obvious that client-side image maps are far superior to their server-side cousins, very old browsers may not support this feature. This does not have to be a problem, since it is possible to include support for both types of image maps at once.

Server-Side Image Maps

To specify a server-side image map, the **<A>** element is used to enclose a specially marked **<IMG>** element. The **<A>** element's **HREF** attribute should be set to the URL of the program or map file to decode the image map. The **<IMG>** element must contain the attribute **ISMAP** so the browser can decode the image appropriately. As with all linked images, it may be desirable to turn the image borders off by setting the **<IMG>** element's **BORDER** attribute equal to **0**. As mentioned in Chapter 4, server-side image maps do not provide adequate feedback to the user because they show coordinates and may incur performance penalties. HTML authors are encouraged to use client-side image maps.

Client-Side Image Maps

The key to using a client-side map is to add the **USEMAP** attribute to the <IMG> element and have it reference a <MAP> element that defines the image map's active areas. An example of the <IMG> element syntax is **<IMG SRC="controlbar.gif" USEMAP="#controlmap">**. Note that, like server-side image maps, the image will be indicated as a link regardless of the lack of the <A> element surrounding the <IMG>. The **BORDER** attribute should be set to **0** if necessary.

The <MAP> element generally occurs within the same document, though support for it outside of the current document is sparse at best. This is similar, in a sense, to the way server-side maps work. The <MAP> element may occur anywhere within the body of an HTML document, though it is usually found at the end of an HTML document.

The <MAP> element has one attribute, **NAME**, which is used to specify the identifier associated with the map. The map name is then referenced within the <IMG> element using the **USEMAP** attribute and the associated fragment identifier. The <MAP> element must have a closing **</MAP>** element. Within the <MAP> and </MAP> tags are defined "shapes" that are mapped onto an image and define the hot spots for the image map. Shapes are defined by the <AREA> element, which is found only within the <MAP> element. The format of the mapping tags is discussed in Chapter 4. However, memorizing or creating client- or server-side image maps by hand is not advised. Page designers should be able to find tools to automate the creation of image hot spots. A popular tool for doing this is MapEdit, which can be retrieved from http://www.boutell.com/mapedit.

It is possible to combine support for both server-side and client-side image maps into one file. The browser will typically override the server-side support with the improved client-side style. This approach will guarantee backward compatibility with older browsers. To support both, use the **ISMAP** and **USEMAP** attributes in conjunction with an embedded map and a remote map, as shown in the following code fragment:

```
<A HREF="shapes.map">
<IMG SRC="shapes.gif" USEMAP="#shapes" BORDER="0" ISMAP WIDTH="400"
    HEIGHT="200"></A>
```

Client-side image maps have a variety of attributes that can be used with the <AREA> element. Server-side image maps really have no attributes other than those normally associated with the <IMG> element, such as **BORDER**. The important attributes supported in HTML 3.2 and 4 are discussed in Chapter 4, as well as in the element reference in Appendix A.

Advanced Image Considerations: Scripting, Style, and <OBJECT>

While most of the basic uses of images have been discussed, there are some issues that should be mentioned for later discussion. First, because an image may be referenced by a style sheet or by a scripting environment, it may be very important to provide a name or identifier for it. The **CLASS**, **ID**, and **NAME** attributes can be used to provide names for images so they can be referenced and manipulated by scripting or style information that is usually found in the head of the document. Names should be unique and in the proper HTML form. The **TITLE** attribute may also be set to provide advisory text about what the image is. While with other elements a browser may render the **TITLE** information as a tool tip, most browsers appear to use the **ALT** attribute instead, as shown earlier in this chapter.

It is possible to include inline scripting or style information directly with an image. For example, setting the **STYLE** attribute allows an inline style to bind to the particular <IMG> element. Style sheets are discussed in Chapter 10. Furthermore, it is possible to have images bound to a particular event using an event attribute such as **onmouseover** and tying it to a script. A very simple but motivating use of tying an event with an image is to have the image change state depending on the user's action. The most basic use would be to create animated buttons or buttons that make a sound when clicked, but the possibilities are endless. A more detailed discussion and examples of how to bind JavaScript to create animated buttons is presented in Chapter 13.

The last advanced comment to make about the <IMG> element is that under HTML 4 it is supposed to be possible to include images using the <OBJECT> element. For example,

```
<OBJECT DATA="images/logo.gif">Picture of the Big Company
building</OBJECT>
```

Similar to the <IMG> tag, the **DATA** attribute is set to the URL of the included image while the alternative rendering is placed within the <OBJECT> element. Although this new syntax may create some interesting possibilities, the reality is that browsers currently don't support this form of image inclusion. This generic <OBJECT> tag for image support makes sense given that an image is no different than any other included binary object, but the fact is that until browser vendors implement it properly, it should be avoided. A more complete discussion of included media objects can be found in Chapter 9, as well as in Appendix A, which provides the full syntax of the <OBJECT> element.

Summary

Like them or not, inline images are what helped popularize the Web. However, just because images can be used to improve the look and feel of a Web page doesn't mean that they should be the primary content. While presentation is important to the Web, it is still fundamentally about the communication of information, some of which does well in image form and some of which does not. Adding images to a Web page is accomplished using the **<IMG>** element, which has numerous attributes. Many of the attributes of the **<IMG>** element—including **ALT, HEIGHT, WIDTH**, and **LOWSRC**—are useful in improving the accessibility and usability of Web pages.

As always, the eternal struggle between nice-looking pages and download time continues, and knowledge of HTML features is helpful to combat excessive wait time. Many of the other attributes for the **<IMG>** element were developed with layout in mind, particularly **ALIGN**. Images can be used in conjunction with colors to create motivating layouts, including tiled backgrounds. This will be discussed in the next chapter. In the future, style sheets and the **<OBJECT>** element may take over many of the duties of the **<IMG>** element and its attributes; but for the moment, the use of the latter is very important.

The Complete Reference

Part II

Presentation and Layout

The Complete Reference

Chapter 6

Introduction to Layout: Backgrounds, Colors, and Text

Web page designers strive to create attractive Web pages; but, until recently, it hasn't been easy. HTML was not created with design features in mind. Even a simple layout technique like centering text has only been possible for a few years. Browser vendors have added many HTML attributes and elements in order to provide page developers with more control over the look and feel of their pages. Standardized elements such as <UL> were pressed into service as structuring and layout tools. New font facilities have also provided more design capabilities in HTML. Despite all these advances, tricks and workarounds are still occasionally required to create visually appealing pages. While it's best to avoid these nonstandard techniques, they often are a reality of page design—at least until technologies such as style sheets become more widely deployed and understood.

Design Requirements

In the best of all possible Web worlds, what would the designer want? The Web was created for a cross-platform environment with little support for screen presentation, but today's Web requires better positioning control. The ability to design for every platform is the ideal situation, but the reality of designing for a particular audience is becoming more accepted. By understanding a user's environment, the designer has more control over presentation. Designers also want more control over font use. Initially, there was no way to specify what font to use in a document, whether or not the user actually had the font. Other complex layout features common to electronic composition, such as more complex color control and layers, might also be desirable. At the very least, pixel-level control and font selection are necessary to bring the Web closer to a level equal with print design.

Simply providing features to allow pixel-level placement of objects and text on the screen doesn't make Web design a straightforward process, any more than font selection does. It is still difficult to understand exactly what kind of display environment the end user has. Web displays range from small liquid crystal screens on cellular phones and pocket organizers to 20-inch monitors, or larger. Each display may have different types of color support, ranging from four shades of gray on a typical hand-held machine to millions of colors on a high-end graphic designer's system. There may not even be a screen at all, as in the case of voice-based browsers. If a guess is made about what screen configuration the user might have, or some programming facilities are provided to determine the same, a better layout could be provided.

The challenges of designing for the Web are significant. In the past, they have only been exacerbated by the lack of technology and tools, not to mention problems associated with bandwidth or usability.

HTML Approach to Web Design

While HTML was not designed with layout in mind, it has been abused and extended to support layout as best it can. Today, there are many elements, both standard and nonstandard, that can provide layout control. These include the various **ALIGN** values for elements, browser-specific proprietary elements like **<SPACER>** and **<MULTICOL>**, and tables. This section covers some of the basic HTML elements used to control text and screen layout.

Text Alignment with Traditional HTML Elements

The first thing to consider in the HTML approach to layout is all the elements and attributes used to position text and objects on a page. Web page designers have long tended to abuse elements like **<UL>** to move text around the page, as shown in the following example.

```
<!DOCTYPE HTML PUBLIC "-//W3C//DTD HTML 4.0 Transitional//EN">
<HTML>
<HEAD>
<TITLE>Unordered List Layout</TITLE>
</HEAD>

<BODY>
<UL>
This is indented text.
</UL>

<UL><UL>
This text is indented more.
</UL></UL>

<UL><UL><UL><UL><UL><UL><UL><UL><UL><UL><UL>
<UL><UL><UL><UL><UL>
This is indented heavily, but may not produce
the effect you expect.
</UL></UL></UL></UL></UL></UL></UL></UL></UL>
</UL></UL></UL></UL></UL></UL></UL>
</BODY>
</HTML>
```

Many HTML page development tools still use this approach to move things around the screen. A rendering of formatting using the unordered list element is shown in Figure 6-1.

Another approach to control text layout is the use of the **<PRE>** tag. As discussed in Chapter 3, any text enclosed by **<PRE>** preserves returns, tabs, and spaces. Using **<PRE>**, it is possible to force text to lay out the way the page author requires, even forcing the browser to scroll to the right to read text. Generally speaking, the browser changes the typeface of any preformatted text to a fixed-width font such as Courier. This font change may not be desired. How can spaces be inserted to improve text layout without a font change? Using the character entity ** ** or **&160;** should insert a nonbreaking space that will not be collapsed by the browser. To enter three spaces between words, use **   **. This leads many people to force text layout like so:

```
          
Now we are ten spaces from the left!
```

While use of this nonbreaking space is somewhat a crutch, it is interesting to note how many of these character entities will be entered into a document when using a WYSIWYG page editor.

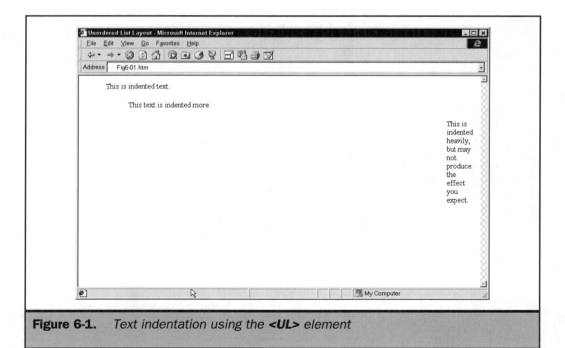

Figure 6-1. *Text indentation using the **<UL>** element*

The <CENTER> Element

In the early days of the Web it was difficult, if not impossible, to control screen layout. Netscape eventually introduced a few elements and attribute changes useful for positioning, including the **<CENTER>** element.

The **<CENTER>** element can enclose any form of content, which is then centered in the browser window. In early HTML, text could be centered using the following code:

```
<CENTER>Welcome to Big Company</CENTER>
```

<CENTER> can be used around an arbitrary amount of content in many different forms, including images and text. Use of the **<CENTER>** element is common on the Web, and it has been included in the HTML 4 standard. However, the element is shorthand for **<DIV ALIGN="CENTER">**. Later, the **ALIGN** attribute (discussed in the next few paragraphs) was added to many elements.

Alignment Attributes

Beyond **<CENTER>**, there are many elements under HTML 3.2 and 4 that support the **ALIGN** attribute. The **<DIV>** element, which is used to create a division in a document, may have the **ALIGN** attribute set to **LEFT**; **CENTER**; **RIGHT**; or, under 4, **JUSTIFY**. If the **ALIGN** attribute is not set, text generally is aligned to the left when language direction is set to **LTR** (left to right) and to the right when the language direction is set to **RTL** (right to left). Until recently, the **JUSTIFY** attribute did not work in most browsers; now it is supported by the latest versions of the two major browsers. The **<P>** paragraph element, the **<TABLE>** element, and the headings **<H1>**, **<H2>**, **<H3>**, **<H4>**, **<H5>**, and **<H6>** also support the **ALIGN** attribute, with the same basic values and meaning. Note that, as discussed in Chapter 5, the **ALIGN** attribute on the **<IMG>** element serves a different purpose.

Word Hinting with <NOBR> and <WBR>

Under many current browsers, it is possible to control text layout beyond simple alignment. Because font size and browser widths may be different, word wrapping may occur in strange ways. Microsoft and Netscape, as well as many other browsers, support the **<NOBR>** and **<WBR>** elements as a way to provide browser hints for text layout.

The **<NOBR>** element makes sure that a line of text does not wrap to the next line, regardless of browser width. This element is useful for words or phrases that must be kept together on one line. If the line of text is long, it may extend beyond the browser window, obliging the user to scroll in order to view the unbroken text. A simple example of using the **<NOBR>** element is shown here:

```
<NOBR>This is a very important long line of text, so it should not be
allowed to break across two lines.</NOBR>
```

It is possible to use the **<NOBR>** element in conjunction with images, but the browser window may need to be scrolled for all the images to be seen.

In some cases, the browser may attempt to rescale the images in order to fit them all on one line. In the case of WebTV, the browser will scale down to 80 percent of the image's original size before moving the image to the next line. **<NOBR>** acts differently under WebTV because WebTV does not allow for any horizontal scrolling.

In contrast to the **<NOBR>** element, which is quite firm in its word wrapping, the **<WBR>** element allows the page designer to suggest a soft break within text enclosed by the **<NOBR>** element. (**<WBR>** is not part of the HTML standard, but many browsers support it.) In essence, the **<WBR>** element marks a spot where a line break can take place. The element is an advisory one, unlike **
** and **<NOBR>**, which force layout. Depending on the situation, the browser may choose to ignore the **<WBR>** element because there is no need for it. **<WBR>** is an empty element that does not require a closing tag. Here's a simple example showing how it works:

```
<NOBR>This is a very important long line of text that should not
break across two lines. If the line must be split, it should happen
here <WBR> and nowhere else.</NOBR>
```

The **<WBR>** element should only exist within a **<NOBR>** element, although it may work outside of it. This element does not have any major attributes, though **CLASS**, **ID**, **STYLE**, and **TITLE** are typically specified as being allowed with the element. It is unlikely that any attribute but **ID** would be used; applying a style to a **<WBR>** element would have no effect, since it encloses no text. The **ID** attribute could be used to manipulate the element, perhaps to remove it using a scripting language. The basic point, and a very useful one, of this element, is simply to suggest a line break point.

Alignment with Images

As discussed in Chapter 5, under HTML 2 the **<IMG>** element specified the **ALIGN** attribute with allowed values of **TOP**, **BOTTOM**, or **MIDDLE**. When an image was included within a block structure of text, the next line of text would be aligned at the top, middle, or bottom of the image, depending on the value of the **ALIGN** attribute. If the attribute were not set, it would default to the bottom.

One problem with image alignment in early HTML was that the text didn't flow around the image. Only one line of text was aligned next to the image. Netscape introduced the **LEFT** and **RIGHT** values for **ALIGN**, which allowed text to flow around the image. When setting an image element like **<IMG SRC="logo.gif" ALIGN="LEFT">**, the image is aligned to the left and the text flows around to the right. Correspondingly, when using code such as **<IMG SRC="logo.gif" ALIGN="RIGHT">**, the image is aligned at the right and the text flows around to the left.

Netscape and Microsoft also support four other values for **ALIGN: TEXTTOP**, **BASELINE**, **ABSMIDDLE**, and **ABSBOTTOM**. Avoid these attributes in most cases, since they may not be supported identically across browsers and are not yet part of any standards. For more information on these attributes, see Chapter 5, as well as the element reference (Appendix A).

Because text may flow in undesirable ways around images, extensions to the **
** element were developed. The **
** element now takes a **CLEAR** attribute, which can be set to **LEFT, RIGHT, ALL**, or **NONE**. By default, the **CLEAR** attribute is set to **NONE**, which makes the element produce a carriage return. When an image is aligned at the **LEFT**, it may be useful to return past the image to start a new section of text. Placing another object using **<BR CLEAR="LEFT">** causes the browser to go clear down a column until the left side of the window is clear. **<BR CLEAR="RIGHT">** does the same thing in regard to right-aligned images. When trying to pass multiple images that may be aligned both on the **LEFT** and **RIGHT**, use **<BR CLEAR="ALL">**.

While the **ALIGN** attribute and the extensions to **
** provide some degree of page layout control (discussed in Chapter 10), technologies such as style sheets handle positioning with greater precision. Until style sheets become more common, there are certain instances in which the **<IMG>** element and its attributes (including **HSPACE, VSPACE**, and **ALIGN**) can be used to create interesting page layouts.

Invisible Images and Layout

Another way to push text around in a layout is by using an image. This approach is well known to users of the desktop publishing program QuarkXPress. With this program, users can create invisible regions and run text around them to achieve specific layout effects. This can be done under HTML by using an invisible image in combination with the **ALIGN, HSPACE**, and **VSPACE** attributes. Given a transparent 1-pixel image, the designer can perform a variety of interesting tricks. For example, take a clear pixel and set the **HSPACE** value to **5**. Now put this at the front of a paragraph, as shown here:

```
<P><IMG SRC="pixel.gif" HSPACE="5">This is the start of a paragraph.</P>
```

Given this fragment, the first line of the paragraph is indented 11 pixels (5 pixels on either side of the 1-pixel image). Imagine doing the same thing between lines using the **VSPACE** attribute. By setting the **VSPACE** attribute and using hard carriage returns, the designer could achieve arbitrary line spacing.

Imagine creating a much larger region with an invisible pixel by setting the **HEIGHT** and **WIDTH** attributes of the **<IMG>** element and using **ALIGN** to flow text around the invisible region. For example, **<IMG SRC="pixel.gif" HEIGHT="100" WIDTH="50" ALIGN="LEFT">** could create a large invisible block to run text around.

The pixel trick can be a useful workaround; but, in certain situations, it has its drawbacks. One potential use for it is to force line space between lines. For example, the code **<IMG SRC="pixel.gif" VSPACE="10">** could allow the designer to create line spacing. Similarly, a designer might decide to use an invisible pixel to create a paragraph indent using something like **<IMG SRC="pixel.gif" HSPACE="5">**. But what happens when the page is viewed with the images turned off or the stop button is pressed early? The resulting page might look like the one in Figure 6-2.

Despite their problems, image layout tricks are still very common on the Web. They are considered so useful that Netscape introduced a special element called **<SPACER>** that mimics much of the functionality of invisible images.

The <SPACER> Element

The proprietary **<SPACER>** element, introduced with Netscape 3, allows users to create invisible regions to push text and other objects around the browser screen. In many ways, this element is a response to the invisible single-pixel GIF trick discussed in the previous section. While **<SPACER>** does an adequate job of reproducing this hack for screen design, its lack of cross-platform support suggests that using the single-pixel image or a style sheet is more appropriate.

<SPACER> is an empty element and is used to insert an invisible region to force layout. Its main attribute is **TYPE**, which specifies the form of the invisible region as **HORIZONTAL**, **VERTICAL**, or **BLOCK**. The other attributes are used to set the size

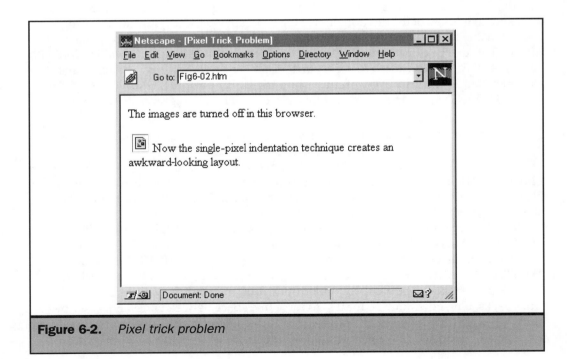

Figure 6-2.   *Pixel trick problem*

of the spacer. Example code to create a horizontal space of 75 pixels between words in a sentence is shown here:

```
This is the start of the sentence <SPACER ALIGN="LEFT"
TYPE="HORIZONTAL" SIZE="75">and this is the end.
```

As with invisible pixels, it is possible to push lines apart. In the next example, the **<SPACER>** element is set to create a vertical region of 24 pixels to give the appearance of double spacing. Notice how the vertical spacer induces line breaks.

```
This is line one.
<SPACER ALIGN="LEFT" TYPE="VERTICAL" SIZE="24">
This is line two.
```

The **<SPACER>** element can only be one type at a time. It is not possible to have a vertical and horizontal spacer. If such functionality is required, use the **BLOCK** type. The **<SPACER>** element can also be used to flow text around invisible blocks. The following HTML code creates an invisible runaround region 150 pixels high and 100 pixels across.

```
...text...
<SPACER TYPE="BLOCK" HEIGHT="150" WIDTH="100" ALIGN="LEFT">
...text...
```

Notice how the **ALIGN** attribute is used just as it would be with an image, with a default alignment value of **BOTTOM**, and so on. The element could also be combined with **<BR CLEAR="LEFT">** to avoid the spacing element affecting text that may follow.

Be careful not to make layouts rely on **<SPACER>**, as it is a somewhat all-or-nothing element that is completely unsupported beyond Netscape browsers. If it is just hinting, or providing browser tips, page layout such as line spacing can be used and will safely be ignored by other browsers. Invisible images, on the other hand, may show up under text-only browsers if you do not set the **ALT** text to no value. When using block forms to create runaround space, the invisible-pixel trick may still provide a better workaround than **<SPACER>**, because it will be picked up by most graphical browsers.

Note   *Some WYSIWYG editors seem to like to use* **<SPACER>** *in conjunction with table-based layouts. As the tag will probably be deprecated over time, designers should avoid its use.*

The <MULTICOL> Element

Like **<SPACER>**, the **<MULTICOL>** element is unique to Netscape browsers starting with Navigator 3. This element allows page designers to specify text in multiple columns, which are rendered with equal width. The element is not supported in previous versions of Netscape or Internet Explorer; it will not degrade gracefully if layout depends on it.

The most important attribute of the **<MULTICOL>** element is **COLS**, which is set to the number of text columns to display. The browser should attempt to flow the text evenly across columns and make the columns the same height, except for the last column, which may be shorter depending on the amount of text in the columns. The element also supports the attribute **GUTTER**, which is used to specify the gutter space between columns in pixels. By default, the gutter width (if unspecified) is 10 pixels. The last attribute supported by **<MULTICOL>** is **WIDTH**, which specifies the width of each column in pixels. All columns are the same width; there is no way to directly adjust a particular column's width. If the **WIDTH** attribute is not set, its value is determined by subtracting from the display width the number of pixels that constitute the gutter and then dividing by the number of columns set in the **COLS** attribute. The syntax is summarized here:

```
<MULTICOL
    COLS="number of columns"
    GUTTER="gutter width in pixels or percentage"
    WIDTH="column width in pixels or percentage">

    Text to put in column form

</MULTICOL>
```

An example showing how **<MULTICOL>** can be used is shown here; renderings of the example are shown in Figure 6-3. Notice how the layout is not preserved in Internet Explorer.

```
<HTML>
<HEAD>
<TITLE>MULTICOL Example</TITLE>
</HEAD>

<BODY>
<MULTICOL COLS="2" GUTTER="50" WIDTH="80%">
The rain in Spain falls mainly on the plain. Now is the time for all good
men to come to the aid of the country. There's no business like show
business. The rain in Spain falls mainly on the plain. Now is the time
for all good men to come to the aid of the country. There's no business
```

```
like show business. The rain in Spain falls mainly on the plain. Now is
the time for all good men to come to the aid of the country. There's no
business like show business. The rain in Spain falls mainly on the plain.
Now is the time for all good men to come to the aid of the country.
There's no business like show business. The rain in Spain falls mainly
on the plain. The rain in Spain falls mainly on the plain.
</MULTICOL>
</BODY>
</HTML>
```

When including other objects within the **<MULTICOL>** element, particularly tables and images with alignment information, the element will be unpredictable, as shown in Figure 6-4.

Because browsers are generally unable to set hyphenation, page authors may need to manually insert **<WBR>** elements between words that may overrun column size. A further problem with **<MULTICOL>** is that it will degrade when too many columns are set, so try to keep the value for **COLS** around six or less. An example showing the problem of too many columns is shown in Figure 6-5.

Use the **<MULTICOL>** element only in an all-Netscape environment. This element is only a somewhat more flexible shorthand notation for what can be accomplished with tables, except for text reflow. In reality, except for an occasional use of invisible pixels or nonbreaking spaces, most modern HTML-based page layouts are accomplished using the **<TABLE>** element, which is discussed in Chapter 7.

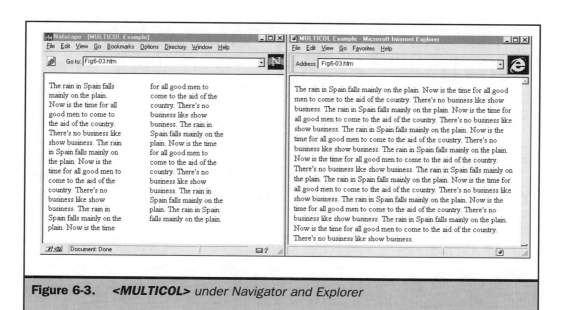

Figure 6-3.   *<MULTICOL> under Navigator and Explorer*

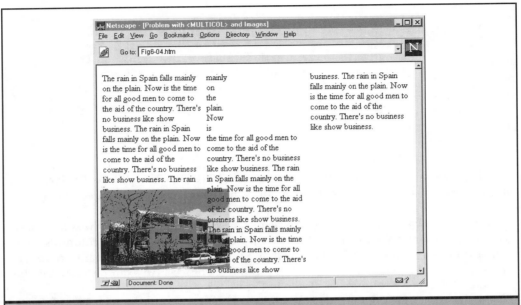

Figure 6-4.   *Problem with **<MULTICOL>** and images*

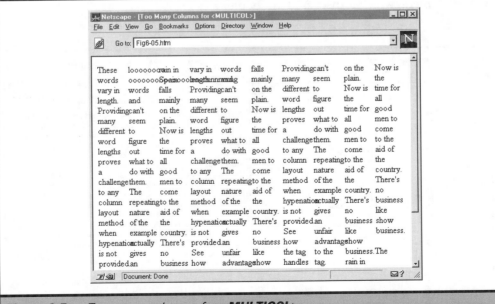

Figure 6-5.   *Too many columns for **<MULTICOL>***

Fonts

Besides better support for layout, Web page designers have long desired to be able to specify fonts in their documents. HTML 2 only supported two fonts, a proportional font and a fixed-width font. Under browsers such as Netscape and Internet Explorer, the proportional font was usually Times or Times New Roman, while the fixed-width font was Courier. To set text to Courier, page authors would use an element like **<TT>**. Otherwise, all text on the page was generally in the proportional font unless it was preformatted with the **<PRE>** element. There was also little control over the size of the font, even in relative terms. The font size of the browser was generally 12 point for the variable-width font and 10 point for the fixed-width font, but end users were free to change font size as they pleased.

There wasn't much control over typography in early browsers. In fact, the only way to use a new font or control the precise layout of text was to make it a graphic. To this day, many page designers still embed a great deal of text as graphics in order to precisely control spacing and to use fonts that the user may not have. Because of download and accessibility issues, this should not be the de facto approach to dealing with fonts.

With Netscape Navigator 1.1, it became possible to control fonts a little more. Netscape introduced the **<FONT>** element, which was used to specify the size and, starting with Navigator 2, color of text using the **SIZE** and **COLOR** attributes. Microsoft later added an attribute called **FACE** to indicate which font type should be used. Both **SIZE** and **COLOR** were introduced to the standard in HTML 3.2. Today, all of these attributes are considered part of the HTML 4 transitional standard. However, like many layout facilities, the use of the **<FONT>** element should be phased out in the future in favor of style sheets.

Under HTML 4, it is possible to make a certain portion of text a particular color by enclosing it within the **<FONT>** element and setting the **COLOR** attribute equal to a valid color name such as **red** or an equivalent value such as **#FF0000**. RGB hexadecimal equivalent codes are discussed later in this chapter and are also presented in Appendix E. So the code

```
<FONT COLOR="red">This is important.</FONT>
```

sets the text *This is important.* in red. The **<FONT>** element can contain a great deal of text or very little, so it is possible to control the colors of individual letters, though such resulting rainbow effects might be hard on the eyes.

It is also possible to set the relative size of type by setting the **SIZE** attribute of the **<FONT>** element. In a Web page, there are seven relative sizes for text numbered from **1** to **7**, where **1** is the smallest text in a document and **7** is the largest. To set some text into the largest size, use **<FONT SIZE="7">This is big</FONT>**. By default, the typical size of text is **3**; this can be overridden with the **<BASEFONT>** element, discussed later in this chapter in the section "Document-Wide Font Settings." If the font size is not known but the text should just be made one size bigger, the author can use an alternative sizing value such as **<FONT SIZE="+1">** instead of specifying the size directly. The + and – nomenclature makes it possible to bring the font size up or down a specified number of settings. The values for this form of the **SIZE** attribute should range from **+1** to **+6** and **–1** to **–6**. It is not possible to specify **<FONT SIZE="+10">** because there are only seven sizes. If the increase or decrease goes beyond acceptable sizes, the font generally defaults at the largest or smallest size, respectively.

Microsoft introduced the **FACE** attribute to the **<FONT>** element that has come to be supported by nearly all browsers, as well as the HTML 4.0 specification. The **FACE** attribute can be set to the name of the font to render the text. So a page designer who wants to render a particular phrase in Britannic Bold could use the following code:

```
<FONT FACE="Britannic Bold">This is important.</FONT>
```

The browser would then read this HTML fragment and render the text in the different font—but only for users who have the font installed on their systems. This raises an interesting problem: what happens if a user doesn't have the font specified? Using the **FACE** attribute, it is possible to specify a comma-delimited list of fonts to try one by one before defaulting to the normal proportional or fixed-width font. The fragment shown here would try first Arial, then Helvetica, and finally a generic sans-serif font before giving up and using whatever the current browser font is.

```
<FONT FACE="Arial, Helvetica, Sans-Serif">This should be in a different
font.</FONT>
```

While it is impossible to know what fonts users may have on their systems, the previous example shows how a little guesswork can be applied to take advantage of the **FACE** attribute. Most Macintosh, Windows, and UNIX users have a standard set of fonts. If equivalent fonts are specified, it may be possible to provide similar page renderings across platforms. Table 6-1 shows some of the fonts that can be found on Macintosh, Windows, and UNIX systems. The table does not attempt to cross-reference the fonts. In fact, while Windows does not always have Helvetica, Arial is fairly similar.

Most users may have many other fonts beyond the ones shown in the table. Users of Microsoft's Office will probably also have access to fonts like Algerian, Book Antiqua, Bookman Old Style, Britannic Bold, Desdemona, Garamond, Century Gothic, Haettenschweiller, and many others. The various browsers are also trying to make new fonts available. Under Internet Explorer 4, Microsoft has introduced a new font called WebDings, which provides many common icons for use on the page. Some of these icons would be useful for navigation, like arrows, while others look like audio or video symbols that could provide indication of link contents before selection. Just using

Windows	Macintosh	UNIX*
Arial	Chicago	Charter
Comic Sans MS	Courier	Clean
Courier New	Geneva	Courier
Impact	Helvetica	Fixed
Times New Roman	Monaco	Helvetica
Symbol	New York	Lucida
Verdana	Palatino	Sans Serif
Wingding	Symbol	Serif
	Times	Symbol
		Times
		Utopia

*UNIX fonts vary; this is just meant to show most of the common fonts under a standard X Window environment.

Table 6-1.   *Sample System Fonts by Platform Type*

font sizing, colors, and simple layout, it is possible to make interesting layouts with WebDings as shown in Figure 6-6.

A common set of icons for the Web is actually not a new idea. The W3C has a working draft covering a predefined set of icon-like symbols. The Microsoft font actually includes many of these symbols, but does not use the same naming convention. It may eventually be possible to include **&audio;** to add an audio icon to a Web page; but, for now, setting the WebDings value or inserting a GIF is the best choice.

Document-Wide Font Settings

In some cases, it may be appropriate to change the font size, color, or face, document-wide. To do this, use the **<BASEFONT>** element in the **<HEAD>** of the document. The **<BASEFONT>** should only occur once in the document and has major attributes **COLOR**, **FACE**, and **SIZE**. Like the **<FONT>** element, **COLOR** should be set to an RGB hexadecimal equivalent value or color name. **FACE** should be set to a font name or comma-delimited list of fonts. **SIZE** should be set to a size value between **1** and **7**. Relative sizing for the **SIZE** attribute does not generally make any sense. To set the font

Figure 6-6.   *Example page using Microsoft's WebDings font*

of the document in red Arial or Helvetica with a relative size of **6**, use **<BASEFONT COLOR="RED" FACE="Arial, Helvetica" SIZE="6">** within the **<HEAD>** element of the document.

Downloadable Fonts

While one Microsoft solution to type on the Web attempts to promote a common set of faces, it isn't a very flexible approach outside the Windows world. Though many Windows, Macintosh, and UNIX systems have similar fonts, what about when the page author wants to use a customized font? In this case, the page author is forced to create a static image of the font. This could take a great deal of time to download and gives up the ability to easily index the text, let alone copy and paste it.

The best solution for fonts on the Web would be to come up with some cross-platform form of font that could be downloaded to the browser on-the-fly. While this sounds easy enough, the problem with downloadable fonts is that they must be highly compact. Page viewers must not be able to steal the font from the page and install it on their own machines. Both of the major browser vendors have been working on downloadable fonts. Microsoft's solution for Web type is called OpenType (http://www.microsoft.com/typography). Netscape's solution, called Dynamic Fonts, is based on TrueDoc (http://www.truedoc.com). Currently, only Netscape 4 and Internet

Explorer 4 and above support downloadable fonts, so be careful not to rely too heavily on the font being available or your page layout may fall apart.

Netscape's Dynamic Fonts

To use a dynamic font under Netscape, the page author simply uses the **FACE** attribute of the **<FONT>** element or a style sheet attribute, as discussed in Chapter 10, to set the font face. If the user does not have the font installed on the system, a downloadable font linked to the page can be fetched and used to render the page. To include a link to a Netscape font definition file in Portable Font Resource (PFR) format, use the **<LINK>** element by setting the **REL** attribute to **fontdef** and the **SRC** attribute equal to the URL in which the font definition file resides. The **<LINK>** element must be found within the **<HEAD>** of the document. An example of how this element would be used is shown here:

```
<HTML>
<HEAD>
<TITLE>Netscape Font Demo</TITLE>
<LINK REL="fontdef" SRC="http://www.bigcompany.com/fonts/customfonts.pfr">
</HEAD>

<BODY>
<FONT FACE="newfont">
Content rendered in the font "newfont," which is part of the .pfr file
</FONT>
</BODY>
</HTML>
```

Note that there may be many fonts in the same font definition file. There is no limit to how many fonts can be used on a page. Once the font is accessed, it is used just as if it were installed on a user's system. Two attributes available under Netscape 4 are useful when dealing with dynamic fonts. The first extension to the **<FONT>** element is **POINT-SIZE**, which can be set to the point size of the font. The other extension to **<FONT>** is the **WEIGHT** attribute, which can be set to a value between **100** and **900** in increments of **100**. The value of the **WEIGHT** attribute determines the weight or boldness of the font. A value of **100** is the lightest weight, while **900** indicates to make the font as bold as it can be. If the **<B>** element is used, the **WEIGHT** attribute is equivalent to **900**. If dynamic fonts are to be used, it is more likely that style sheets will be the preferred way to interact with them, rather than these proprietary extensions. The only obstacle to using dynamic fonts is that the .pfr file describing the font must be created. Otherwise, they are no more troublesome than attempting to guess the font on the end user's system or rasterizing the font into a GIF image.

One drawback to the Netscape approach to dynamic fonts is that it may cause screen flashing in many versions of Netscape. This can be disorienting for the user and has somewhat limited the use of this technology.

Microsoft's Dynamic Fonts

Microsoft also provides a way to embed fonts in a Web page. To include a font, you must first build the page using the **<FONT>** element or style sheet rules that set fonts, as discussed in Chapter 10. When creating your page, don't worry about whether or not the end user has the font installed; it will be downloaded. Next, use Microsoft's Web Embedding Fonts Tool or a similar facility to analyze the font usage on the page. The program should create an .eot file that contains the embedded fonts. The font use information will then be added to the page in the form of CSS (Cascading Style Sheets) style rules, as shown here:

```
<HTML>
<HEAD>
<TITLE>Microsoft Font Test</TITLE>

<STYLE TYPE="text/css">
<!--
@font-face {
  font-family: Ransom;
  font-style: normal;
  font-weight: normal;
  src: url(fonts/ransom.eot);
 }
-->
</STYLE>
</HEAD>

<BODY>
<FONT FACE="Ransom" SIZE="6">Example Ransom Note Font</FONT>
</BODY>
</HTML>
```

A possible rendering of font embedding is shown in Figure 6-7.

Like the Netscape approach, you must first create a font file and reference it from the file that uses the font. It may be useful to define a fonts directory within your Web site to store font files, similar to storing image files for site use.

The use of the **@font-face** acts as a pseudoelement that allows you to bring any number of fonts into a page. The form of the font embedding supported by Microsoft conforms to the initial W3C specification for font embedding. For more information on

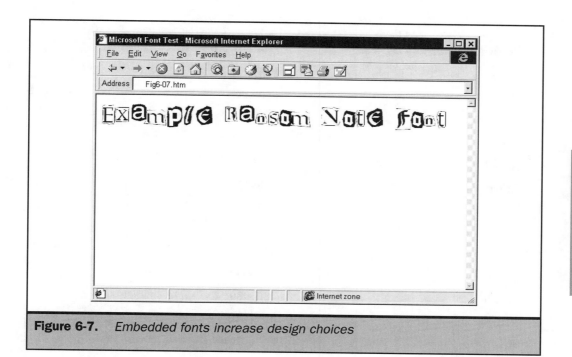

Figure 6-7.   *Embedded fonts increase design choices*

embedded fonts under Internet Explorer and links to font file creation tools like WEFR, see the Microsoft Typography site (http://www.microsoft.com/typography).

> **Note**   *It is possible to provide both links to both Microsoft and Netscape font technology in the same page. This really adds only one line or a few style rules as the rest of the document would continue to use the same **<FONT FACE="">** statements. TrueDoc technology also supports an ActiveX control to allow Internet Explorer users to view their style of embedded fonts. Given the extra download involved, the double font statement approach is preferred.*

Colors in HTML

HTML 4 supports color settings both for text and for the background of the document, or even individual table cells. With style sheets we will see it is also possible to set both foreground and background color at any time. There are 16 widely known color names defined in HTML 4. These names and their associated HEX RGB values are shown in Table 6-2.

To set a particular section of text yellow, simply surround the content with **<FONT COLOR="yellow">** and **</FONT>**. Similarly, you can also use the HEX value **#FFFF00** for the **COLOR** attribute.

Color Name	Hexadecimal RGB Value
Aqua	#00FFFF
Black	#000000
Blue	#0000FF
Fuchsia	#FF00FF
Gray	#808080
Green	#008000
Lime	#00FF00
Maroon	#800000
Navy	#000080
Olive	#808000
Purple	#800080
Red	#FF0000
Silver	#C0C0C0
Teal	#008080
White	#FFFFFF
Yellow	#FFFF00

Table 6-2. *Common HTML 4 Color Names and HEX Values*

Most browsers should recognize the common color values such as **white**, **red**, and **black** and render accordingly. Determining the HTML hexadecimal value for a particular color isn't difficult when following the basic formula of *#RRGGBB*, where *RR* equals the hex value for red, *GG* equals the hex value for green, and *BB* equals the hex value for blue. If the hex value for all off, or zero, is **00**, and the hex value for all on is **FF**, then the color **#FF0000** is red. All the red in the image is turned on in this case. A value of **#000000** would be black, **#0000FF** would be blue, and so on. Of course there are many colors and hex values, some of which seem to have been invented by the browser vendors; these are listed in Appendix E. The problem with using browser vendor–defined colors is that they don't always do what they are supposed to do. Under Netscape 4, the color aliceblue doesn't look very close to the Internet Explorer color. Even worse, you can invent your own colors. Try setting the following and viewing it under Netscape and Microsoft Internet Explorer:

```
<BODY BGCOLOR="HTML COLOR NAMES ARE TROUBLESOME">
```

This color name is totally invalid, but it still results in a shade of green that is very distinct in each browser. It is possible to make up colors like chilidog brown or stale beer yellow, but this is no more recommended than using the Netscape-defined color Dodgerblue. The hex color values are the preferred way of setting colors, since many nonstandard color names may not be supported correctly across browsers.

Document-Wide Color Attributes for <BODY>

The **<BODY>** element has numerous attributes that can be used to affect the display of content in the body of the document, including setting the background color, the color of text, and the color of links. One of the most commonly used **<BODY>** element attributes, **BGCOLOR** defines the document's background color. This was a distinct improvement over the default gray (or white under Macintosh) of Mosaic, although it and the other **<BODY>** attributes have led to a multitude of design sins. Employed wisely, they can enhance a page's appearance; misused, they have been known to induce migraines. Hexadecimal RGB values and color names can be used with **BGCOLOR** and the four attributes to follow. To create a white background, the attribute could be set to **<BODY BGCOLOR="#FFFFFF">** (hexadecimal) or simply **<BODY BGCOLOR="white">**.

The **TEXT** attribute of the **<BODY>** element defines the color of text in the entire document. The attribute takes a color in the form of either a hex code or color name. So **<BODY BGCOLOR="white" TEXT="green">** would create a white page with green text.

Note that the text color can be overridden in the text by applying the **<FONT>** element to selected text with its **COLOR** attribute, as discussed earlier in the chapter in the section "Fonts."

Besides the body text, it is also possible to define the colors of links by setting the **<BODY>** element attributes: **LINK**, **ALINK**, and **VLINK**.

LINK defines the color of unvisited links in a document. For example, if you've set your background color to **black**, it might be more useful to use a light link color instead of the standard blue. **ALINK** defines the color of the link as it is being clicked. This is often too quick to be noticed, but can create a flash effect, if desired. For a more subdued Web experience, it might be better to set the **ALINK** attribute to match either the **LINK** attribute or the next one, **VLINK**. **VLINK** defines the color of a link after it has been visited, which is purple under many user agents. Many authors wish to set the value of the **VLINK** attribute to **red**, which makes sense given standard color interpretation. So, using the last attributes, creating a white page with green text, red links, and fuchsia-colored visited links could be accomplished using the code presented here:

```
<!DOCTYPE HTML PUBLIC "-//W3C//DTD HTML 4.0 Transitional//EN">
<HTML>
<HEAD>
<TITLE>Colors</TITLE>
</HEAD>

<BODY BGCOLOR="#FFFFFF" TEXT="#008000" LINK="#FF0000"
      VLINK="#FF00FF" ALINK="#FF0000">
...Content to color...
</BODY>
</HTML>
```

Users should be forewarned not to choose link colors that might confuse their viewers. For example, reversing link colors so that visited links are blue and nonvisited links are red could confuse a user. While it is unlikely that a page author would do such a thing, it has been seen more than once—particularly in situations in which the look and feel is the driving force of the site. Other common problems with link color changes include the idea of setting all link values to **blue** with the belief that users will revisit sections thinking they haven't been there before. While this may make sense from a marketing standpoint, the frustration factor due to the lost navigation cues may override any potential benefit from extra visits. As the last example showed, setting all the link colors to **red** could have a similar effect of encouraging users to think they have seen the site already.

Page authors must also be extremely careful when setting text and background colors so that readability is preserved. Page designers are often tempted to use light colors on light backgrounds or dark colors on dark backgrounds. For example, a gray text on a black background might look cool, but will it look cool on every person's monitor? If the gamma value of some other person's monitor is much different than on yours, it may be unreadable. White and black always make a good pairing and red is certainly useful. The best combination, in terms of contrast, is actually yellow and black; but imagine the headache from reading a page that looks like a road sign. Despite the high contrast, designers should be careful of white text on a black background when font sizes are very small, particularly on poor-resolution monitors.

Note   Gamma *is a term used to describe the relationship between the input and output for a particular image device. Different monitors have inherently different gamma settings. As a result, the same image on two different monitors may appear significantly different. While the gamma of a monitor cannot be changed by the user, monitor settings such as contrast, brightness, and color can be adjusted.*

Background Images

Besides setting background colors, you can also change the appearance of a Web page by setting a background image using the **BACKGROUND** attribute of the **<BODY>** element. The value of **BACKGROUND** should be the URL for a GIF or JPEG file, usually one in the image directory of the Web site in question (for example, **<BODY BACKGROUND="images/tile.gif">**). The value could just as easily include a complete URL to access an image at another site, but this would be a rather unwieldy approach to the task at hand. Images accessed in this fashion repeat, or *tile*, in the background of a Web page. This can make or break a Web page design. Imagine someone who used the **BACKGROUND** attribute to place a 200 × 300 pixel JPEG of a favorite dog on his or her home page. The dog's image would repeat, both vertically and horizontally, in the background of the page. This would make the dog's owner very happy—and make the page very difficult to read. Figure 6-8 shows an example of a bothersome repeating background.

In general, complex background images tend to be a poor design decision. Taking the subtle approach can backfire as well. Some users attempt to create a light background like a texture or watermark thinking that, like paper, it will create a classy effect. The problem with this is that under many monitors, the image may be difficult to make out at all, or the texture may even blur the text on top of it slightly. As with setting background colors, the most important consideration is the degree of contrast. Always attempt to

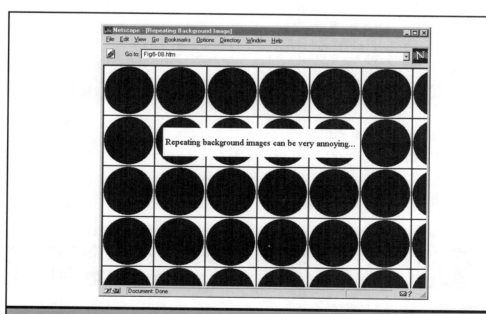

Figure 6-8.   *Repeating background image*

keep the foreground and background at a high level of contrast so that users can read the information. What good is an impressive layout if nobody can read it?

If a background is desired, image-manipulation programs such as Photoshop can be used to create seamless background tiles that are more pleasing to the eye and show no seam. Figure 6-9 demonstrates the idea of a repeating background tile.

Background images, or tiles, can also be used to create other effects. A single GIF, 5 pixels high and 1,200 pixels wide, could be used to create a useful page layout. The first 200 horizontal pixels of the GIF could be black, while the rest could be white. Assuming 1,200 pixels as the maximum width of a browser, this tile would only repeat vertically, thus creating the illusion of a two-tone background. This has become a very common concept on the Web. Many sites use the left-hand color for navigation buttons, while the remaining area is used for text, as shown in Figure 6-10. However, to guarantee that content appears on top of the appropriate section of the background image, you may be forced to use tables. Make sure to read Chapter 7 thoroughly before trying this style of page design.

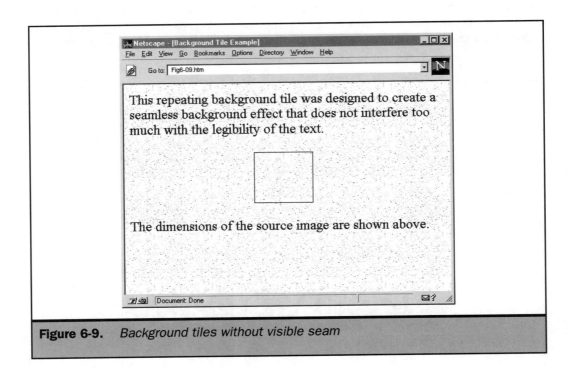

Figure 6-9. *Background tiles without visible seam*

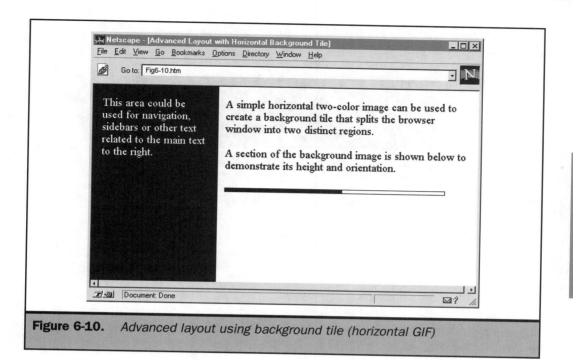

Figure 6-10.   *Advanced layout using background tile (horizontal GIF)*

Be very careful when segmenting the screen using a background tile. For example, many people are tempted to create page layout with vertical sectioning, as shown in Figure 6-11. However, there is a problem with this layout. Won't the black bar repeat? Quite possibly, because the length of the content is hard to determine. Viewers may find the black bar repeating over and over with content being lost on top. A solution might be to make the background tile very tall. However, this not only increases file size, but begs a question of how tall is enough? Because content may vary from page to page and increase or decrease over time, determining the width is next to impossible. It would appear that the same problem would occur with sidebar style tiles. This is generally not the case, given that pages usually do not scroll left to right, and monitor sizes tend to not exceed 1,200 pixels. In either case, the problem of background tile repeats is solved with style sheets as they provide a way to set the direction and frequency of a tile's repeat pattern. This is discussed further in Chapter 10. There are a few HTML-specific solutions to these and other background layout problems that are touched on briefly here.

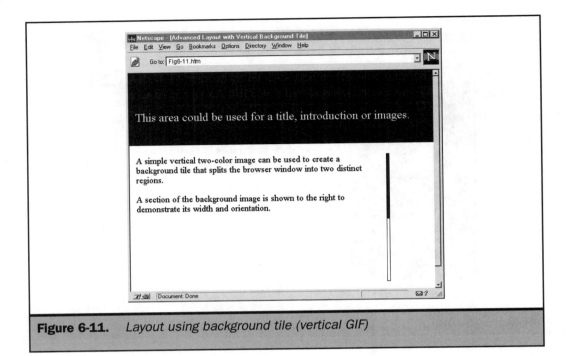

Figure 6-11.   *Layout using background tile (vertical GIF)*

Note Another problem with background tiles is that some designers try to minimize file size and download time. For example, a designer may make the background images a single pixel tall, which may cause screen painting problems because the background will have to be tiled as many times as the screen is high in pixels. With a slow video card, this may produce an annoying sweeping effect. To avoid the background painting problem, consider balancing physical file size and download size. A background image can be 5 pixels or taller, depending on how many colors are used. If colors are kept to a minimum, there is no harm in making the image 20 or 30 pixels high.

Internet Explorer Background Attributes

Internet Explorer supports a few special attributes for the **<BODY>** element that may solve background image and layout problems without resorting to style sheets. The **BGPROPERTIES** attribute offers a solution to the problem of scrolling background images. At present, however, it is only supported by Internet Explorer 3 and above. The **<BODY>** element's attribute and value **BGPROPERTIES="fixed"** will, under Internet Explorer, allow text and images to scroll while the background image accessed with the **BACKGROUND** attribute remains in place. The only value for this attribute is **fixed**.

The <BODY> element also allows the setting of margins; but, so far, this is only realized under Internet Explorer. There are two <BODY> attributes that affect margins: **LEFTMARGIN** and **TOPMARGIN**. Each is set with a number value. For example, **LEFTMARGIN="25"** will create a margin of 25 pixels between the left edge of the browser window and its content; **TOPMARGIN="15"** will create a 15-pixel margin between the top of the browser window and its content, as well as at the bottom if the content extends that far.

While many of the body properties discussed in the last few sections are useful to set the color and image attributes of a page, many of them are browser-specific or are deprecated under HTML 4. It is too soon to tell if users will embrace image layout via style sheets or continue to use the elements previously discussed. For backward-compatibility, it may be necessary to use both layout forms for another year or two.

Summary

While HTML does not provide a great deal of support for layout, it really wasn't meant to. While it is easy to say that people shouldn't use HTML to lay out pages, the fact is that they wanted and needed to. Designers desperately want pixel-level layout control of Web pages and support for fonts. The need for improved page design gave rise to the occasional abuse of HTML elements, "cheats" like the invisible-pixel GIF trick, and to proprietary elements such as <SPACER>. Despite the improvement in layout capabilities, fonts are still an open issue in HTML; but, with some assumptions regarding the use of downloadable font technology, font use is becoming a reality on the Web. Chapter 7 presents tables that make it possible to create fairly precise layouts using HTML. However, later chapters reveal that many of the problems raised in this chapter and Chapter 7 will cease once style sheets become more prevalent. Then the elements discussed in this chapter may be eliminated or may return to their original purpose.

PRESENTATION AND
LAYOUT

The
Complete
Reference

Chapter 7

Layout with Tables

243

The **<TABLE>** element and its associated elements have become one of the most commonly used means of creating Web page layouts. While positioning through style sheets (Chapter 10) should provide more precise layout capacities, browser support is inconsistent, and the issue of backward-compatibility remains a concern. For better or worse, this leaves the table approach to page layout as the only one likely to work across multiple browsers. Tables are not limited to layout, however, as the later portions of this chapter will discuss.

Introduction to Tables

A table represents information in a tabular way, like a spreadsheet: distributed across a grid of rows and columns. In printed documents, tables commonly serve a subordinate function, illustrating some point described by an accompanying text. Tables still perform this illustrative function in HTML documents. Because HTML does not offer the same layout capacities available to print designers, Web-based tables have also become a common way to create document layout and design. But unlike printed tables, HTML tables can contain information that is *dynamic*, or interactive, such as the results of a database query. To address this use, the databinding feature allows an HTML table template to be directly connected with a database source. A table is dynamically generated using the template and the results of a particular database query. Taken together, these capabilities make tables one of HTML's most useful and sophisticated resources.

Simple Tables

In its simplest form, a table places information inside the cells formed by dividing a rectangle into rows and columns. Most cells contain data. Some cells, usually on the table's top or side, contain headings. HTML represents a basic table using four elements. In HTML, a table, **<TABLE>** ... **</TABLE>**, contains one or more rows, **<TR>** ... **</TR>**. Each row contains cells holding a heading, **<TH>** ... **</TH>**, or data, **<TD>** ... **</TD>**. The following code example illustrates a basic table. Note that the only attribute used in this example is **BORDER**, which is used to specify a 1-pixel border so it is clear what the table looks like. The rendering for the simple table under various browsers is shown in Figure 7-1.

```
<!DOCTYPE HTML PUBLIC "-//W3C//DTD HTML 4.0 Transitional//EN">
<HTML>
<HEAD>
<TITLE>Simple Table Example</TITLE>
</HEAD>

<BODY>
<TABLE BORDER="1">
```

```
<CAPTION>Basic Fruit Comparison Chart</CAPTION>
<TR>
    <TH>Fruit</TH>
    <TH>Color</TH>
</TR>

<TR>
    <TD>Apple</TD>
    <TD>Red</TD>
</TR>

<TR>
    <TD>Avocado</TD>
    <TD>Green</TD>
</TR>

<TR>
    <TD>Watermelon</TD>
    <TD>Pink</TD>
</TR>
</TABLE>
</BODY>
</HTML>
```

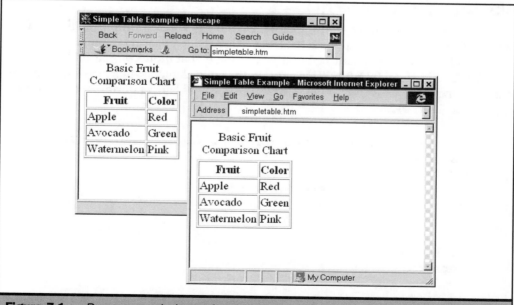

Figure 7-1.   *Browser renderings of a simple example*

This simple table example shows the use of the most basic table elements: headings, rows, and data cells.

Again, a table is made up of rows enclosed within **<TR>** . . . **</TR>**. The number of rows in the table is determined by the number of occurrences of the **<TR>** element. What about columns? Generally, the number of columns in a table is determined by the maximum number of data cells indicated by **<TD>** . . . **</TD>**, or headings indicated by **<TH>** . . . **</TH>** within the table. It may be useful to hint to the browser at the number of columns in the table by setting the **COLS** attribute, introduced in HTML 4, for the **<TABLE>** element equal to the number of columns in the table (for example, **<TABLE BORDER="1" COLS="2">**, as in the last example).

The headings for the table are set using the **<TH>** element. Generally, the browser renders the style of headings differently, possibly centering the contents of the heading and placing the text in bold type. The actual cells of the table are indicated by the **<TD>** element. Both the **<TD>** and **<TH>** elements may enclose an arbitrary amount of data of just about any type. In the previous example, a full paragraph of text could be enclosed in a table cell along with an image, lists, and links. Last, the table may have a caption enclosed within **<CAPTION>** . . . **</CAPTION>**, whose contents are generally rendered above or below the table indicating what the table contains.

The closing tags for the **<TR>**, **<TH>**, and **<TD>** tags are optional under the HTML specification. While this may make for cleaner-looking code in your HTML documents, HTML writers are still encouraged to use the closing tags, as well as indentation. This will assure that table cells and rows are clearly defined, particularly for nested tables, and avoid problems with Netscape, which often "breaks" tables that don't use closing tags for these elements.

ROWSPAN and COLSPAN

While the previous example shows that it is possible to create a simple table with a simple structure, what about when the table cells need to be larger or smaller? The HTML code that follows creates tables that are somewhat more complicated. By adding the **ROWSPAN** and **COLSPAN** attributes to the table elements, it is possible to create data cells that span a given number of rows or columns. The rendering of this code appears in Figure 7-2.

```
<!DOCTYPE HTML PUBLIC "-//W3C//DTD HTML 4.0 Transitional//EN">
<HTML>
<HEAD>
<TITLE>ROWSPAN and COLSPAN Example</TITLE>
</HEAD>

<BODY>
<TABLE BORDER="1">
<CAPTION>ROWSPAN Example</CAPTION>
<TR>
    <TD ROWSPAN="2">Element 1</TD>
    <TD>Element 2</TD>
</TR>
```

```
<TR>
    <TD>Element 3</TD>
</TR>
</TABLE>
<BR><BR>

<TABLE BORDER="1">
<CAPTION>COLSPAN Example</CAPTION>
<TR>
    <TD COLSPAN="3">Element 1</TD>
</TR>

<TR>
    <TD>Element 2</TD>
    <TD>Element 3</TD>
    <TD>Element 4</TD>
</TR>
</TABLE>
</BODY>
</HTML>
```

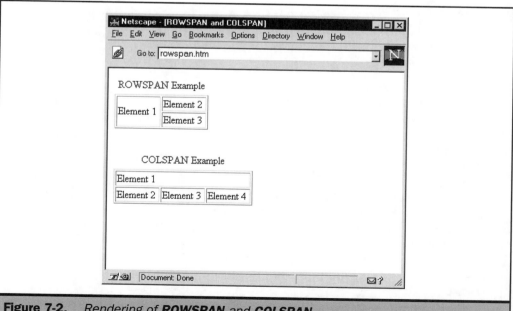

Figure 7-2.   *Rendering of **ROWSPAN** and **COLSPAN***

The basic idea of the **ROWSPAN** and **COLSPAN** attributes for **<TD>** and **<TH>** is to extend the size of the cells across two or more rows or columns, respectively. To set a cell to span three rows, use **<TD ROWSPAN="3">**; to set a heading to span two columns, use **<TH COLSPAN="2">**. Setting the value of **ROWSPAN** to more than the number of rows in the table does not extend the size of the table. Browsers should not add rows or columns when attributes suggest that there are more.

Besides being able to span rows and columns, the **<TABLE>** element, as well as its enclosed elements **<TD>**, **<TH>**, and **<CAPTION>**, supports a variety of attributes for alignment, sizing, and layout. The following example shows a more complex kind of table.

```
<!DOCTYPE HTML PUBLIC "-//W3C//DTD HTML 4.0 Transitional//EN">
<HTML>
<HEAD>
<TITLE>Complex Table Example</TITLE>
</HEAD>

<BODY>
<P>Notice how the text of a paragraph
<TABLE ALIGN="left" BORDER="1" WIDTH="300">
<CAPTION ALIGN="bottom">The Super Widget
<TR>
    <TD ROWSPAN="2"><IMG SRC="widget.gif" ALT="Super Widget"
    WIDTH="100" HEIGHT="120"></TD>
    <TH BGCOLOR="lightgreen">Specifications</TH>
</TR>

<TR>
    <TD>
    <UL>
        <LI>Diameter: 10 cm
        <LI>Composition: Kryptonite
        <LI>Color: Green
    </UL>
    </TD>
</TR>
</TABLE>
can flow around a table just as it would any other embedded
object form. Notice how the text of a paragraph can flow
around a table just as it would any other embedded object
form. Notice how the text of a paragraph can flow around
a table just as it would any other embedded object form.</P>
</BODY>
</HTML>
```

The preceding example shows that it is possible to place any form of content in a cell, as well as control the individual size of the cells and the table itself. The logical step is to control page layout by creating a grid with the **<TABLE>** element.

Tables for Layout

In themselves, tables do not seem that interesting to many people. They are, however, a very important tool for HTML page layout. The foundation of graphic design is the ability to spatially arrange visual elements in relation to each other. Tables can be used to define a layout grid for just this purpose. Prior to the advent of style sheets supporting positioning, tables were the only reliable way to accomplish this. They remain the most commonly used technique.

The key to using a table in order to create a precise page grid is the use of the **WIDTH** attribute. The **WIDTH** attribute for the **<TABLE>** element specifies the width of a table in pixels, or as percentage value, such as **80%**. It is also possible to set the individual pixel widths of each cell within the table, using a **WIDTH** attribute for the **<TD>** or **<TH>** elements. Imagine trying to create a 400-pixel column of text down the page with a buffer of 50 pixels on the left and 100 pixels on the right. With older HTML, this would be literally impossible without making the text a giant image. With a table, it is easy, as shown by the markup code here:

```
<!DOCTYPE HTML PUBLIC "-//W3C//DTD HTML 4.0 Transitional//EN">
<HTML>
<HEAD>
<TITLE>Table Layout</TITLE>
</HEAD>

<BODY>
<TABLE BORDER="0">
<TR>
   <TD WIDTH="50"><BR></TD>
   <TD WIDTH="400">
     <H1 ALIGN="center">Layout is here!</H1>
     <HR>
     <P>This is a very simple layout that would have
     been nearly impossible to do without tables.</P>
   </TD>

   <TD WIDTH="100"> </TD>
</TR>
</TABLE>
</BODY>
</HTML>
```

In the preceding code, the **BORDER** value is set to zero. This attribute isn't necessary; if the browser does not see a **BORDER** attribute in the **<TABLE>** element, it won't draw a border. It may be convenient to keep the attribute in but set to zero, so the border can be turned on and off to check to see what is going on with a particular layout. When creating empty table cells, it is a good idea to put a line break **
** or a nonbreaking space (** **) into the cell so it doesn't collapse vertically.

Tables might also be used to provide more precise layout in relation to a background. One popular design concept employs a vertical strip of colored background on the left of the page that contains navigation controls; the rest of the document contains the main text. Without tables, it is difficult to keep body content from going on top of the background image. An example of the HTML markup code to create a two-column design that works on top of a 100-pixel-wide color background is shown here:

```
<!DOCTYPE HTML PUBLIC "-//W3C//DTD HTML 4.0 Transitional//EN">
<HTML>
<HEAD>
<TITLE>Table Layout with Background</TITLE>
</HEAD>

<BODY BACKGROUND="yellowtile.gif">
<TABLE WIDTH="550">
<TR>
   <TD WIDTH="100">
       <A HREF="about.htm">About</A><BR><BR>
       <A HREF="prodcuts.htm">Products</A><BR><BR>
       <A HREF="staff.htm">Staff</A><BR><BR>
       <A HREF="contact.htm">Contact</A><BR><BR>
   </TD>

   <TD WIDTH="450">
       <H1 ALIGN="center">Welcome to Big Company, Inc.</H1>
       <HR>
       <P>This text is positioned over a white background;
       the navigation links are over a colored background.
       This layout combines a table with a background image.
       </P>
   </TD>
</TR>
</TABLE>
</BODY>
</HTML>
```

The rendering of this layout appears in Figure 7-3. Note how the foreground content (the **<BODY>** content) is aligned over the **BACKGROUND** image. Another way to achieve such effects is to set the **BGCOLOR** attribute for the table cells. **BGCOLOR** was introduced in Netscape Navigator 3 and is also supported in Internet Explorer. Background shading can also be controlled via style sheets, as discussed in Chapter 10. While such techniques would appear to help get rid of the headaches of aligning foreground and background elements, there is an issue of backward-compatibility.

In HTML documents, tables have many nontraditional uses for graphic design and layout. These extend beyond creating grids; even single-cell tables can be put to many uses. As a simple example, consider using a table to define a pastel-colored "sticky" note. These can be inserted throughout HTML documents to draw attention to important ideas. An example HTML fragment to insert a single-cell, colored table is shown here:

```
<TABLE ALIGN="left" BGCOLOR="#FFFFCC" CELLPADDING="20" HSPACE="15"
       VSPACE="15">
<TR><TD>This is an important point!</TD></TR>
</TABLE>
```

Notice that this example contains only a single data item—certainly unusual for a conventional table. It also demonstrates two more **<TABLE>** attributes. The **BGCOLOR** attribute sets the background color for a table using either a standard color name or hexadecimal RGB value. The given value indicates a light pastel yellow.

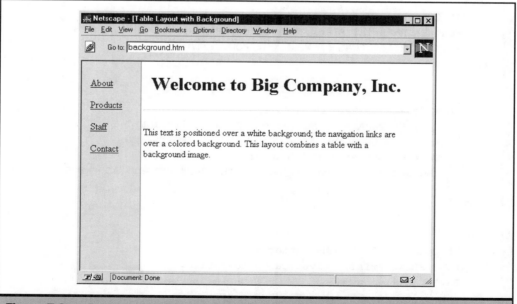

Figure 7-3.   *Rendering of foreground/background layout*

The **CELLPADDING** attribute sets the distance in pixels between a table cell's outer border and the point at which content begins. Besides "sticky" notes and other forms of colored tables to draw out information, there are various uses for single-cell tables. When combined with width, this might just be a good way to constrain the text within a page.

Advanced Layout Using Tables

Creating more sophisticated layouts with tables can be relatively simple. The following code example shows how a table can be used to create a two-column layout with text and an image. Text in the code example has been truncated to preserve space. The **COLSPAN** attribute is used to create table cells (**<TD>**) that contain headlines and subheaders that run across the width of the entire table. The **CELLPADDING** attribute for **<TABLE>** is set to **10** to prevent the text in the columns from running too close together. The rendering of this code is shown in Figure 7-4.

```
<!DOCTYPE HTML PUBLIC "-//W3C//DTD HTML 4.0 Transitional//EN">
<HTML>
<HEAD>
<TITLE>2-Column Document Layout with Table</TITLE>
</HEAD>

<BODY>
<TABLE CELLSPACING="0" CELLPADDING="10" BORDER="1" WIDTH="550">
<TR>
   <TD COLSPAN="2" ALIGN="center">
   <FONT FACE="Arial Black, Helvetica, Sans-serif" SIZE="+2">
   FEZ: IMPERIAL JEWEL OF MOROCCO</FONT></TD>
</TR>

<TR>
   <TD WIDTH="50%" VALIGN="middle">
      <FONT FACE="Arial, Helvetica, Sans-serif"SIZE="+1">
      <B>Beyond the Bou Jeloud Gate...</B></FONT></TD>
      <TD WIDTH="50%" ALIGN="center">
      <IMG SRC="boujeloud002.jpg" WIDTH="240" HEIGHT="185" BORDER="0">
   </TD>
</TR>

<TR>
   <TD COLSPAN="2" ALIGN="center">
   <FONT FACE="Arial, Helvetica, Sans-serif">
   <B><I>Luckily, a major UNESCO restoration project
   is now underway...</I></B></FONT></TD>
</TR>
```

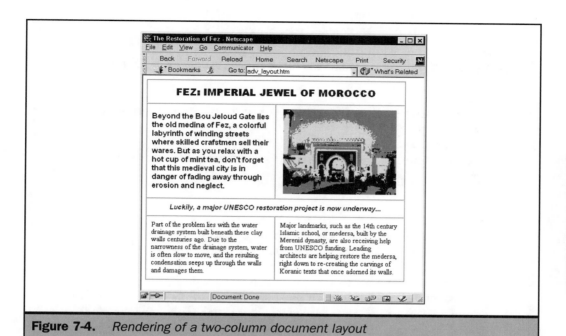

Figure 7-4.   *Rendering of a two-column document layout*

```
<TR>
   <TD WIDTH="50%" VALIGN="top">Part of the problem...</TD>
   <TD WIDTH="50%" VALIGN="top">Major landmarks...</TD>
</TR>
</TABLE>
</BODY>
</HTML>
```

It is also possible to apply tables to layout in a more complicated fashion. Layouts combining text and images can be created using large graphics that incorporate text, but this approach produces pages that are slow to download. The code example that follows shows a more complicated layout that breaks up an image and reassembles it like a jigsaw puzzle, using a table as an invisible "frame" to hold it in place. Note that links have not been applied to the graphic links in this code (for example, widgets.gif) in order to simplify the code example.

```
<!DOCTYPE HTML PUBLIC "-//W3C//DTD HTML 4.0 Transitional//EN">
<HTML>
<HEAD>
<TITLE>Big Company, Inc. Home Page</TITLE>
</HEAD>
```

```
<BODY>
<TABLE BORDER="0" CELLPADDING="0" CELLSPACING="0" WIDTH="570">
<TR>
   <TD>
      <IMG SRC="roof.gif" BORDER="0" HEIGHT="45" WIDTH="124">
   </TD>
   <TD COLSPAN="4">
      <IMG SRC="logo.gif" BORDER="0" HEIGHT="45" WIDTH="446">
   </TD>
</TR>

<TR>
   <TD VALIGN="top" ROWSPAN="7" WIDTH="124">
      <IMG SRC="building.gif" BORDER="0" HEIGHT="248" WIDTH="124">
   </TD>
   <TD ROWSPAN="7" VALIGN="top" WIDTH="185">
      <IMG SRC="headline.gif" BORDER="0" HEIGHT="45" WIDTH="185">
      And now, thanks to our merger with Massive Industries, we are
      now the world's largest manufacturer of Gadgets&#153; and
      other useless products.
      <BR><BR>
      To learn more about our products or our growing monopoly,
      click on any of the links to the right.
   </TD>

   <TD ROWSPAN="3" WIDTH="68" VALIGN="top">
      <IMG SRC="curve.gif" BORDER="0" HEIGHT="108" WIDTH="68">
   </TD>
   <TD COLSPAN="2" WIDTH="193" VALIGN="top">
      <IMG SRC="blank.gif" BORDER="0" HEIGHT="35" WIDTH="193">
   </TD>
</TR>

<TR>
   <TD COLSPAN="2" WIDTH="193" VALIGN="top">
      <IMG SRC="widgets.gif" BORDER="0" HEIGHT="35" WIDTH="193">
   </TD>
</TR>

<TR>
   <TD COLSPAN="2" WIDTH="193" VALIGN="top">
      <IMG SRC="gadgets.gif" BORDER="0" HEIGHT="38" WIDTH="193">
   </TD>
</TR>
```

```
<TR>
   <TD COLSPAN="2" ROWSPAN="4" WIDTH="136" VALIGN="top">
      <IMG SRC="gear.gif" BORDER="0" HEIGHT="140" WIDTH="136">
   </TD>

   <TD VALIGN="top" WIDTH="125">
      <IMG SRC="sales.gif" BORDER="0" HEIGHT="29" WIDTH="125">
   </TD>
</TR>

<TR>
   <TD VALIGN="top" WIDTH="125">
      <IMG SRC="about.gif" BORDER="0" HEIGHT="36" WIDTH="125">
   </TD>
</TR>

<TR>
   <TD VALIGN="top" WIDTH="125">
      <IMG SRC="history.gif" BORDER="0" HEIGHT="35" WIDTH="125">
   </TD>
</TR>

<TR>
   <TD VALIGN="top" WIDTH="125">
      <IMG SRC="map.gif" BORDER="0" HEIGHT="40" WIDTH="125">
   </TD>
</TR>

<TR>
   <TD COLSPAN="2" WIDTH="309"> </TD>
   <TD WIDTH="68"> </TD>
   <TD WIDTH="68"> </TD>
   <TD VALIGN="top" WIDTH="125">
      <IMG SRC="lowcurve.gif" BORDER="0" HEIGHT="31" WIDTH="125">
   </TD>
</TR>
</TABLE>
</BODY>
</HTML>
```

When creating a layout like this, it is very important to set the **CELLPADDING**
and **CELLSPACING** attributes to **0**. Table cell widths should correspond to the width

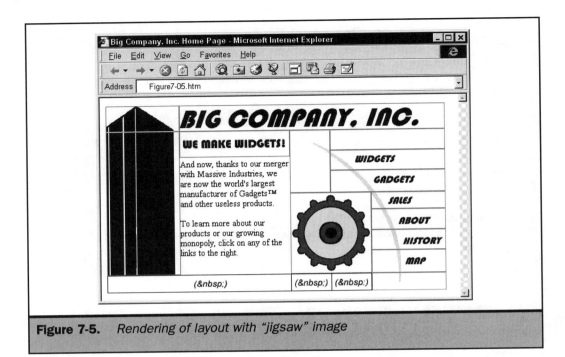

Figure 7-5. Rendering of layout with "jigsaw" image

of the image inside the cell, and the width of the table should be the sum of the cells in a table row. It is also important to include the **HEIGHT** and **WIDTH** attributes of the images used. Figure 7-5 shows a browser rendering of this layout, with an overlay to show where the image is broken up.

Note that the image consists of GIFs and JPEGs. "Photographic" areas of the image have been saved as JPEGs, while areas with limited color, such as simple text, have been saved as GIFs. By saving each area in the appropriate format, it is possible to reduce the overall file size and optimize performance. (This is discussed in more detail in Chapter 5.)

Tables in HTML 4

So far, the discussion of tables has mentioned five elements: **<TABLE>**, **<CAPTION>**, **<TR>**, **<TH>**, and **<TD>**. These are the most commonly used elements. HTML 4 introduces several new elements that provide increased control over table formatting: **<COL>**, **<COLGROUP>**, **<THEAD>**, **<TFOOT>**, and **<TBODY>**. An HTML table as defined by the HTML 4.0 specification has the following structure:

- An opening **<TABLE>** element.
- An optional caption specified by **<CAPTION>** . . . **</CAPTION>**.
- One or more groups of rows. These may consist of a header section specified by **<THEAD>**, a footer section specified by **<TFOOT>**, and a body section specified

by **<TBODY>**. While all these elements are optional, the table must at least contain a series of rows specified by **<TR>**. The rows themselves must contain at least one header or data cell, specified by **<TH>** and **<TD>**, respectively.

■ One or more groups of columns specified by **<COLGROUP>** with individual columns within the group indicated by **<COL>**.

■ A closing **</TABLE>** element.

The main difference between HTML 4 tables and the more basic table form is that rows and columns may be grouped together. The advantage to grouping is that it conveys structural information about the table that may be useful for rendering the table more quickly, or keeping it together when displaying on the screen. For example, specifying the **<THEAD>** or **<TFOOT>** may allow a consistent header or footer to be used across larger tables when they span many screens (or sheets of paper when printed). The use of these elements is mandatory when working with dynamically populated tables that incorporate databinding as introduced by Microsoft and discussed later in this chapter. The following example explains the use of the new HTML 4 table elements.

```
<!DOCTYPE HTML PUBLIC "-//W3C//DTD HTML 4.0 Transitional//EN">
<HTML>
<HEAD>
<TITLE>HTML 4 Tables</TITLE>
</HEAD>

<BODY>
<TABLE BORDER="1" FRAME="BOX" RULES="GROUPS">
<CAPTION>Fun with Food</CAPTION>
<COLGROUP>
    <COL>
</COLGROUP>

<COLGROUP>
    <COL ALIGN="CENTER">
    <COL ALIGN="CHAR" CHAR=".">
</COLGROUP>

<THEAD>
    <TR>
        <TH BGCOLOR="yellow">Fruit</TH>
        <TH BGCOLOR="yellow">Color</TH>
        <TH BGCOLOR="yellow">Cost per pound</TH>
    </TR>
</THEAD>
```

```
<TBODY>
    <TR>
        <TD>Grapes</TD>
        <TD>Purple</TD>
        <TD>$1.45</TD>
    </TR>

    <TR>
        <TD>Cherries</TD>
        <TD>Red</TD>
        <TD>$1.99</TD>
    </TR>

    <TR>
        <TD>Kiwi</TD>
        <TD>Brown</TD>
        <TD>$11.50</TD>
    </TR>
</TBODY>

<TFOOT>
    <TR>
        <TH COLSPAN="3">This has been another fine table example.</TH>
    </TR>
</TFOOT>
</TABLE>
</BODY>
</HTML>
```

The first thing to notice in this code is the use of the **FRAME** and **RULES** attributes for the **<TABLE>** element. The **FRAME** attribute specifies which sides of the frame that surrounds the table will be visible. In this example, the value is set to **BOX**, which means that the frame around the outside of the table is on. Other values for this attribute include **ABOVE, BELOW, HSIDES, VSIDES, LHS, RHS, VOID,** and **BORDER**. The meaning of all these values is discussed in the table syntax sections that follow.

Do not confuse the idea of the **FRAME** attribute with that of **RULES**. The **RULES** attribute defines the rules that may appear between the actual cells in the table. In the example, the value of **RULES** is set to **GROUPS**; this displays lines between the row or column groupings of the table. The **RULES** attribute also takes a value of **NONE, GROUPS, ROWS, COLS,** and **ALL**.

The other major difference in the HTML code for the table shown above is the inclusion of the **<THEAD>** and **<TBODY>** elements. **<THEAD>** contains the rows (**<TR>**), headings (**<TH>**), and cells (**<TD>**) that make up the head of the table. Beyond organization and the application of styles, the advantage of grouping these items is that it may be possible to repeat the elements over multiple pages (under certain browsers). Imagine printing out a large table and having the headers for the rows appear on every page of the printout. This is what **<THEAD>** may be able to provide. Similarly, the **<TFOOT>** element creates a footer to use in the table, which may also run over multiple pages. Last, **<TBODY>** indicates the body of the table, which contains the rows and columns that make up the inner part of a table. While there should be only one occurrence of **<THEAD>** and **<TFOOT>**, there may be multiple occurrences of **<TBODY>**. Multiple bodies in a document may seem confusing, but these elements are more for grouping purposes than anything else. When a table is specified without **<THEAD>**, **<TFOOT>**, or **<TBODY>**, it is assumed to have one body by default.

While tables are becoming more difficult to code, you can take heart from the variety of tools that can be used to create them. Most HTML editing tools can easily add the elements needed to make tables. This is good, since the combination of HTML 4's new table elements with various proprietary extensions introduced by Microsoft, Netscape, and WebTV results in a dizzying array of elements, and attributes for the individual table elements. The next few sections specify a complete syntax for the various table elements.

<TABLE> Elements

Every table is defined by the **<TABLE>** element, which must have a corresponding **</TABLE>** element. These elements indicate that the contained content is organized into a table with rows and columns as specified by the **<TR>**, **<TD>**, and **<TH>** elements. It is also possible to use the **<CAPTION>**, **<COL>**, **<COLGROUP>**, **<THEAD>**, **<TBODY>**, **<TFOOT>**, and **<THEAD>** elements to organize a table and apply attributes to numerous columns, rows, and data cells at once. Appendix A lists the complete syntax for all of these elements.

Databinding: Tables Generated from a Data Source

Tables often contain row after row of identically formatted data that originates in a database. There are two basic methods to create these data-dependent tables. Neither one is ideal:

- If the table data is relatively static, it is common to build a long table by hand or with a tool, individually coding each data cell.

- If the table data is dynamic, it is common to generate the entire page containing the table using a server-side CGI (Common Gateway Interface) technology.

The first approach is difficult for an HTML author. The second, which does not really qualify as HTML authoring, usually requires programming. *Databinding* is a technology recently introduced by Microsoft to dynamically bind HTML elements to data coming from an external source. While not technically restricted to HTML tables, it does represent a simpler, more powerful approach for generating large data-dependent tables.

In HTML databinding, a data source that provides information is associated with a data consumer that presents it. The data source is a control with some means to access external information that is embedded in an HTML document using the **<OBJECT>** element. This element, briefly introduced in Chapter 9, is further explained in Chapter 15. For now, it will be useful to understand that **<OBJECT>** adds a small program to the page that can be used to access an external data source. The document also contains a data consumer, an HTML element that uses special attributes to ask the ActiveX control for data that the element subsequently displays. Data consumers come in two sorts: those that present single data values, and those that present tabular data. Tables fall into the latter category.

Creating an HTML table using databinding is a very simple process. It is only necessary to define one table row. The rest are generated automatically according to the template defined by the first row. Think of each row in a tabular data set as corresponding to a database record, and each column as corresponding to a database field. A template table row is defined in HTML that associates **<TD>** or **<TH>** elements with field names in the data set. A table will subsequently be generated with one row for each record in the data set, and with cell values filled in from the appropriate record fields. The data source control may support processing capabilities such as sorting or filtering the data set. If so, the table can be dynamically regenerated on the client side in response to update information from the data source.

For example, a data source may contain a tabular data set for product price information. One field may contain the name of the product, another its price. By default, a table could present this information sorted alphabetically by product name. In response to a button on an HTML page, the data source could sort the data set by price. The table that displays the information would be dynamically regenerated. The following is a simple databinding example.

An external data file contains two or more columns of comma-delimited data. The first line contains the names of the data set fields corresponding to the columns. The following lines contain the actual data for the appropriate fields. A sample file called alphabet.txt is shown here:

```
Letter, Thing
A, Apple
B, Boy
C, Cat
D, Dog
E, Elephant
F, Fox
G, Girl
H, Hat
```

To access the data, an HTML document references an object for a data source control and a related table definition. An example of how this would be accomplished is shown here:

```
<!DOCTYPE HTML PUBLIC "-//W3C//DTD HTML 4.0 Transitional//EN">
<HTML>
<HEAD>
<TITLE>Data Binding Example</TITLE>
</HEAD>

<BODY>
<OBJECT ID="alphabet"
        CLASSID="clsid:333C7BC4-460F-11D0-BC04-0080C7055A83">
   <PARAM NAME="DataURL" VALUE="alphabet.txt">
   <PARAM NAME="UseHeader" VALUE="True">
</OBJECT>

<TABLE DATASRC="#alphabet" BORDER="1">
<THEAD>
   <TR BGCOLOR="yellow">
      <TH>Letter</TH>
      <TH>Reminder</TH>
   </TR>
</THEAD>

<TBODY>
   <TR ALIGN="center">
      <TD><SPAN DATAFLD="Letter"></SPAN> </TD>
      <TD><SPAN DATAFLD="Thing"></SPAN></TD>
   </TR>
</TBODY>
</TABLE>
</BODY>
</HTML>
```

This HTML code generates a table from the file alphabet.txt in which each table row contains a letter of the alphabet and the name of a thing that can remind the reader of that letter. The rendering of this example under Internet Explorer 4 is shown in Figure 7-6.

Examine a little more closely the pieces needed to make this databinding example work. First, the data source. This example uses the Tabular Data Control (TDC) object: an ActiveX control provided by Microsoft and identified by the lengthy class identifier. This particular control locates and manipulates text data files in a tabular format. Other controls supporting databinding could have been used instead. These might support

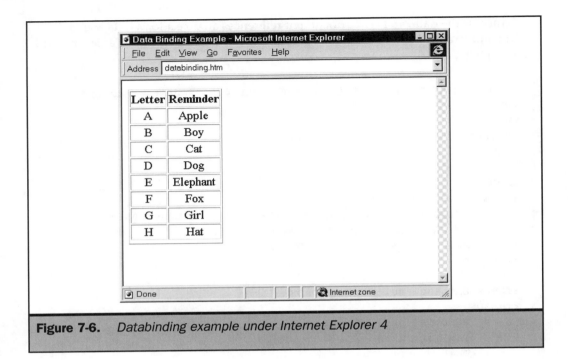

Figure 7-6.   *Databinding example under Internet Explorer 4*

different data access capabilities such as access to remote relational databases. The Microsoft ActiveX Data Objects control (ADO), however, is a representative example. The TDC supports several parameters of which two are used in this example. The **"DataURL"** parameter tells the TDC the name and location of the data file it is to use. In this case, since only a filename is provided, the TDC looks in the same directory containing the Web page. By default, the TDC treats every line in a data file as data. The **"UseHeader"** parameter tells the TDC that the first line in the data file does not contain data but rather the names of data fields.

As a data consumer, the **<TABLE>** element uses its **DATASRC** attribute to connect to a data source. Note in the example how this attribute is set to the name of the **<OBJECT>** tag invoking the data source control. The name must be preceded by the # symbol. The **<OBJECT>** element must declare a name using the **ID** attribute in order to be accessed by a data consumer. In summary, the **DATASRC** attribute identifies a data source to be used in generating a table.

The next step is to associate cells in the template table row with particular fields in the data set. This is done using the **DATAFLD** attribute of appropriate elements. It contains the name of the field in the data set that its element is to be bound to. If data set–specific names are not defined, fields can be identified using default positional names such as **Column1, Column2**, and so on. The **<TD>** tag, commonly used for cell data, does not support the **DATAFLD** attribute. To bind a field to a table cell, the **<TD>** tag needs to contain one of the elements that do support **DATAFLD**. The elements that make the most sense in the context of a table are **<SPAN>, <DIV>, <OBJECT>**, and **<IMG>**. The latter two tags illustrate that databinding is not confined to textual data. For example, a column of images can be created by using a tag declaration such as **<IMG DATAFLD="Picture">** inside a table cell. Note that the usual **SRC** attribute is not required. Instead, the **DATAFLD** attribute identifies a field inside the data set that contains a valid image filename, such as mypict.gif, and binds the image to that value.

If a table does not explicitly declare header or footer section elements, then implicitly all table content is in the body section. In static tables, this does not usually have visual consequences, but it does in tables generated by databinding. All body rows are included in the template for table row generation, not just the rows containing databound fields. To prevent header or footer information from being repeated for every row in the table, it is necessary to enclose it with the **<THEAD>** or **<TFOOT>** element. The **<TBODY>** element can then be used to signal the beginning of the template to be databound.

Such a brief example scratches the surface of databinding and merely shows the importance of tables in relation to dynamic data. For more information on databinding, visit Microsoft Sitebuilder, at http://www.microsoft.com/sitebuilder, and the Remote Data Service site, at http://www.microsoft.com/data/ado/rds/.

Summary

The development of tables was the first step toward effective layout of HTML pages. Tables provide a useful structure in which to place text and images, but they will likely be superceded by positioning with style sheets (discussed in Chapter 10); however, that will have to wait until style sheets are more widely supported by browsers. At that time, tables will continue to be important for use with dynamic data, as discussed in the preceding section. Chapter 8 addresses two more options for page layout—frames and layers—and weighs the pros and cons of both.

PRESENTATION AND LAYOUT

The Complete Reference

Chapter 8

Advanced Layout: Frames and Layers

Tables and the other HTML techniques introduced in Chapters 6 and 7 provide a significant improvement in Web page layout. Many designers want even more design facilities, including multiple windows and layers. Such expectations aren't unreasonable, because these features are common in design programs and computer interfaces. Such power comes at a price, however. Frames and layers may provide significant layout flexibility, but when misused, these structures can confuse users—or even lock them out of your site completely.

Frames

A framed document divides a browser window into multiple panes, or smaller window frames. Each frame may contain a different document. The benefits of this approach are obvious. Users can view information in one frame while keeping another frame open for reference, instead of moving back and forth between pages. The contents of one frame can be manipulated, or *linked*, to the contents of another. This enables designers to build sophisticated interfaces. For example, one frame can contain links that produce a result in another frame. An example of such an interface is shown in Figure 8-1.

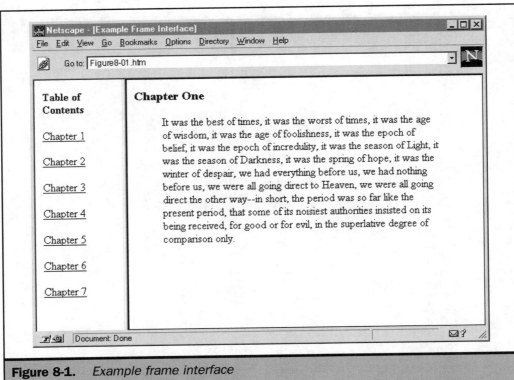

Figure 8-1.   *Example frame interface*

Frames offer many possibilities. They can contain tables of contents, site indexes, and lists of links. Frames offer *fixed-screen navigation*—whereby certain information is always at the forefront—and other options not found in the single-window approach. However, framed documents can be difficult to deal with. When Netscape 2 introduced the concept of frames, many users were very confused by framed Web sites. Frames couldn't be printed, sites were hard to bookmark, and the Back button of browsers didn't work as expected. Regardless, many site designers, excited by a new approach, rushed to develop framed pages. Then, they removed them just as quickly, due to navigation problems and user complaints.

Today, many of the problems associated with frames have been fixed at the browser level, and users have become more comfortable understanding and working with frames. Used properly in the right situation, as discussed in this chapter, frames are an important tool in the Web designer's toolbox. No longer considered proprietary browser extensions, frames are included in the HTML 4.0 standard.

Overview of Frames

A *frame* is an independent scrolling region, or window, of a Web page. Every Web page may be divided into many individual frames, which can even be nested within other frames. Fixed screen sizes limit how many frames can realistically be used simultaneously. Each frame in a window may be separated from the others with a border; in this way, a framed document may resemble a table. However, frames aren't a fancy form of tables. Each separate frame may contain a different document, indicated by a unique URL. Because the documents included in a framed region may be much larger than the room available onscreen, each frame may provide a scroll bar or other controls to manipulate the size of the frame. Individual frames usually are named, so that they may be referenced through links or scripting, allowing the contents of one frame to affect the contents of another. This referencing capability is a major difference between tables and frames. Frames provide layout facilities *and*, potentially, navigation. Figure 8-2 provides a visual overview of the components of a framed document.

Simple Frame Example

The first point to remember is that a framed document is composed of several documents. To illustrate, a page with two frames actually involves three files:

- The framing document that defines the framing relationship
- The file that contains the contents of frame one
- The file that contains the contents of frame two

Consider the simple two-frame document shown in Figure 8-3. The first frame, on the left, covers about 20 percent of the screen and contains a table of contents. The larger column on the right, which takes up the other 80 percent of the screen, displays the actual contents. For the purposes of this example, the left frame is named Controls, and the right frame is named Display.

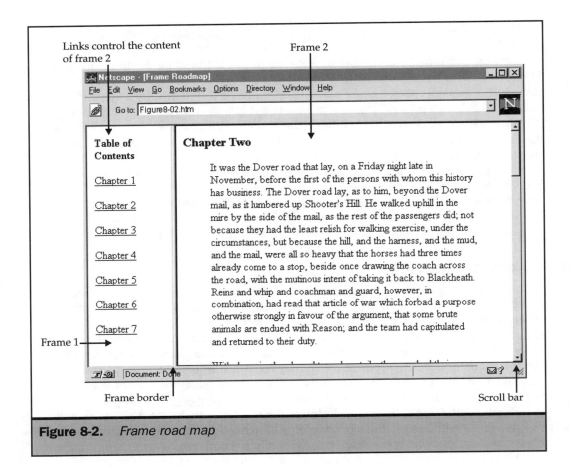

Figure 8-2. Frame road map

To specify the framing document, you need to create a file that uses the **<FRAMESET>** element instead of the **<BODY>** element. The **<FRAMESET>** element defines the set of frames that makes up the document. The major attributes for this element are the **ROWS** or **COLS** attributes. In this case, two columns take up set percentages of the total screen, so the code reads **<FRAMESET COLS="20%, 80%">**. Setting up something like **<FRAMESET ROWS="10%, 80%, 10%">** would be just as easy, which sets up three rows across the screen.

The **ROWS** and **COLS** attributes can also be set to pixel values, so that **<FRAMESET COLS="200, 400">** defines a column 200 pixels wide, followed by a column 400 pixels wide. Because determining the exact size of the screen is difficult, setting these attributes to exact values might be dangerous. If absolute pixels are used and the screen is larger than the area specified, an empty space appears in the browser window. If the screen is smaller than the specified frame values, scrolling may be required. Because of this, use absolute pixel values only when they make sense.

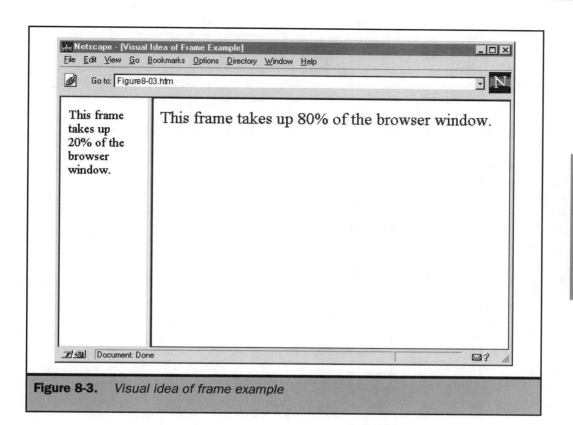

This frame takes up 20% of the browser window.

This frame takes up 80% of the browser window.

Figure 8-3.   *Visual idea of frame example*

If you know that the Controls frame contains a graphic that is 150 pixels across, consider setting the size of the first frame to 175 pixels, to fit the graphic plus some white space. If the frame were any smaller than this size, the graphic would be clipped, so using an absolute pixel value makes sense when you know the size of the contents. But what should the size of the other frame be? To simply take up the rest of the screen with whatever is left over after 175 pixels, use the wildcard character (*) to specify use of the rest of the screen. The code for such a frame set is **<FRAMESET COLS="175,*">**.

In summary, the **ROWS** and **COLS** attributes may be set to pixels, percentages, or a wildcard value. You may use multiple occurrences of wildcards, and you may mix and match values. However, you should stick with all percentages or all pixels, and use wildcards only where needed.

After you specify the frame layout with the **<FRAMESET>** element, the contents of each frame must be specified by using the **<FRAME>** element in the order that the frames are defined in the **ROW** or **COL** attribute. In the case of **<FRAMESET COLS="175, 100, *">**, the contents of the first **<FRAME>** element encountered are loaded in the 175-pixel column, the contents of the second **<FRAME>** element are loaded in the 100-pixel column, and so on. The primary attribute of the **<FRAME>** element is **SRC**, which is set to the URL of the document to load into the frame. The **NAME** attribute should be set to indicate the name of the frame. Naming of frames is important, because it allows each frame to be targeted by links and manipulated by scripting languages. A very simple example of a framing document follows:

```
<!DOCTYPE HTML PUBLIC "-//W3C//DTD HTML 4.0 Frameset//EN">
<HTML>
<HEAD>
<TITLE>Simple Frame Example</TITLE>
</HEAD>


<FRAMESET COLS="250,*">

<FRAME SRC="fileone.htm" NAME="Controls">
<FRAME SRC="filetwo.htm" NAME="Display">

<NOFRAMES><P>This document uses frames. Please follow this link
to a <A HREF="noframes.htm">noframes</A> version.
</NOFRAMES>


</FRAMESET>
</HTML>
```

The preceding example uses the **<NOFRAMES>** ... **</NOFRAMES>** element within the frame set. This element provides information to be displayed in browsers that don't support frames. Although this approach seems like a good idea, you may need to maintain both a frame and a no-frame version of a site, to accommodate different browsers. You also need to define the individual documents, in this case fileone.htm and filetwo.htm, which are loaded into the frames. Fileone.htm is shown here:

```
<!DOCTYPE HTML PUBLIC "-//W3C//DTD HTML 4.0 Transitional//EN">
<HTML>
<HEAD>
<TITLE>File One</TITLE>
</HEAD>

<BODY>
<H2>File 1</H2>
</BODY>
</HTML>
```

This is the code for filetwo.htm:

```
<!DOCTYPE HTML PUBLIC "-//W3C//DTD HTML 4.0 Transitional//EN">
<HTML>
<HEAD>
<TITLE>File Two</TITLE>
</HEAD>

<BODY>
<H2>File 2</H2>
</BODY>
</HTML>
```

Putting all three files in the same directory and loading the framed example into a browser should produce a rendering similar to the one shown in Figure 8-4.

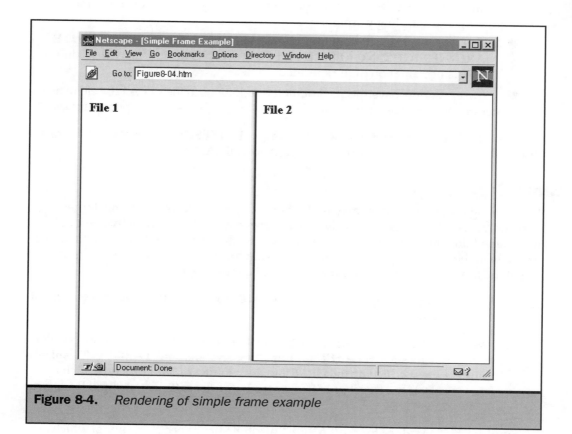

Figure 8-4. *Rendering of simple frame example*

To summarize, the **<FRAMESET>** and **<FRAME>** elements constitute the HTML needed for frames. The **<FRAMESET>** element:

- Encloses the **<FRAME>** element and defines the structure of the framed document.

- Must have a **</FRAMESET>** close tag.

- May be nested within other **<FRAMESET>** elements, to create a nested frame structure.

- Should be used in place of the **<BODY>** element in the document that defines the frame relationships. However, you can provide a **<BODY>** element after the **<FRAMESET>** in place of the **<NOFRAMES>** element as an alternative way to provide information for browsers that do not support frames.

The **<FRAME>** element, which must occur within the **<FRAMESET>** element, has the following attributes:

- The primary attributes are the **SRC** attribute, which indicates the URL of the frame content, and the **NAME** attribute, which sets a name for the frame for linking and scripting purposes.

- The HTML 4 specification defines the **FRAMEBORDER, MARGINWIDTH, MARGINHEIGHT, NORESIZE,** and **SCROLLING** attributes, which control the basic presentation of the specified frame.

- Browser vendors have specified numerous additions to the **<FRAME>** element to control its presentation and provide hooks to style sheets and scripting languages.

The complete syntax for the **<FRAME>** and **<FRAMESET>** elements, as well as a discussion of their attributes, is presented in Appendix A.

Frame Targeting

When using frames, you often may find that making the links in one frame target another frame is beneficial. This way, when a user clicks a button or activates a link in one framed document, the requested page loads in another frame. In the simple frame example in the preceding section, you might want to have the frame named Controls target the frame named Display. Link targeting has two steps:

1. Ensure frame naming by setting the **NAME** attribute in the **<FRAME>** element to a unique name.

2. Use the **TARGET** attribute in the **<A>** element to set the target for the anchor. For example, a link such as **<A HREF="http://www.yahoo.com" TARGET="Display">** loads the site specified by the **HREF** into the window called Display, if such a frame exists. If the target specified by the name doesn't exist, the link loads over the window it is in.

Some particular values for the **TARGET** attribute have special meaning, which are summarized in Table 8-1.

Value	Meaning
_blank	Load the page into a new, generally unnamed, window.
_self	Load the page over the current frame.
_parent	Load the link over the parent frame.
_top	Load the link over all the frames in the window.

Table 8-1. *Reserved **TARGET** Values*

The **_top** value for the **TARGET** attribute may be useful for "frame busting." Many page authors don't want their sites to be viewed under a framed environment. Setting the **TARGET** attribute of the links within a site to **_top** ensures that any frames being used are removed after a link is followed.

The **_blank** value for **TARGET** is also useful, because it opens another window in which to display the link. The only problem with this action is that the window may tile directly on top of the previous browser window, and the user may not know that multiple windows are open.

The **_parent** value isn't encountered often, because it is useful only when frames are nested to a great degree. The **_parent** value enables you to overwrite the parent frame that contains the nested frame, without destroying any frames that the parent may be nested within.

The **_self** value for **TARGET**, which loads a page over its current frame, duplicates the typical default action for most browsers. It may be useful, however, to accommodate browsers whose default actions are set differently.

Note *According to the HTML 4 specification, frame names beginning with an underscore are discouraged, because they may be reserved for values such as **_top**.*

The following is an example for the file named fileone.htm. This HTML document uses frame targeting with the names defined in the previous simple frame example:

```
<!DOCTYPE HTML PUBLIC "-//W3C//DTD HTML 4.0 Transitional//EN">
<HTML>
<HEAD>
<TITLE>Framed Document One</TITLE>
</HEAD>

<BODY>
<H1>Framed Document One</H1>
<HR>
```

```
<H2 ALIGN="center">Test Links</H2>

<UL>
  <LI><A HREF="http://www.yahoo.com" TARGET="Display">
  Yahoo in frame named display</A>
  <LI><A HREF="http://www.hotbot.com" TARGET="_new">
  HotBot in new window</A>
  <LI><A HREF="http://www.infoseek.com" TARGET="_self">
  Infoseek in this frame</A>
  <LI><A HREF="http://www.excite.com" TARGET="_top">
  Excite over whole window</A>
</UL>
</BODY>
</HTML>
```

Note *When using this example, you should consider naming it fileone.htm and using it within a frameset that defines a frame named Display. Otherwise, you may find that the browser simply creates a new window or overwrites the current window when the link that targets the undefined frame is selected.*

The Use of <NOFRAMES>

The **<NOFRAMES>** element is used to enclose the HTML and text that should be displayed when a browser that doesn't support frames accesses the Web page. The **<NOFRAMES>** element should be found only within the **<FRAMESET>** element. Nevertheless, **<NOFRAMES>** is often found directly outside the **<FRAMESET>** element. Because of the permissive nature of browsers, this tends to be interpreted correctly.

The contents of the **<NOFRAMES>** element should be correct HTML, potentially including the **<BODY>** element, which can be used as an alternative form for browsers that don't support frames. The following example provides the links that occur in the Controls frame for browsers that don't support frames:

```
<!DOCTYPE HTML PUBLIC "-//W3C//DTD HTML 4.0 Frameset//EN">
<HTML>
<HEAD>
<TITLE>Simple Frame Example</TITLE>
</HEAD>
```

```
<FRAMESET COLS="250,*">

<FRAME SRC="fileone.htm" NAME="Controls">
<FRAME SRC="filetwo.htm" NAME="Display">

<NOFRAMES>
  <B>No Frame Navigation</B>
<BR>
  <A HREF="http://www.yahoo.com">Yahoo</A>
<BR>
  <A HREF="http://www.microsoft.com">Microsoft</A>
<BR>
  <A HREF="http://www.netscape.com">Netscape</A>
</NOFRAMES>

</FRAMESET>
</HTML>
```

Notice that the approach of putting a second copy of site content within **<NOFRAMES>** makes the site usable across browsers, but results in having to update two copies of the same content. Because of this difficulty, many people simply put a statement in the **<NOFRAMES>** element that indicates the site requires a frame-supporting browser for viewing. This doesn't make the site very accessible, but does cut down on content duplication.

Floating Frames

Up to this point, all the frames shown have been attached to the sides of the browser (left, right, top, or bottom). Another form of frame, called a *floating frame* (introduced by Microsoft), has been incorporated into the HTML 4 standard. The idea of the floating frame is to create an inline framed region, or window, that acts similarly to any other embedded object, insofar as text can be flowed around it. An inline frame is defined by the **<IFRAME>** element and may occur anywhere within the **<BODY>** element of an HTML document. Compare this to the **<FRAME>** element, which should occur only within the **<FRAMESET>** element; remember that the **<FRAMESET>** element should preclude the **<BODY>** element.

The major attributes to set for the **<IFRAME>** element include **SRC, HEIGHT,** and **WIDTH**. The **SRC** is set to the URL of the file to load, while the **HEIGHT** and **WIDTH** are set to either the pixel or percentage value of the screen that the floating-frame region should consume. Like an **<IMG>** element, floating frames should support **ALIGN, HSPACE,** and **VSPACE** attributes for basic positioning within the flow of text. Note that, unlike the **<FRAME>** element, the **<IFRAME>** element comes with a close tag. **<IFRAME>** and **</IFRAME>** should contain any HTML markup code and text that is supposed to be displayed in browsers that don't support floating frames. A simple example of floating frames is shown here:

```
<!DOCTYPE HTML PUBLIC "-//W3C//DTD HTML 4.0 Frameset//EN">
<HTML>
<HEAD>
<TITLE>Floating Frame Example</TITLE>
</HEAD>

<BODY>
<H1 ALIGN="center">Floating Frame Example</H1>

<IFRAME NAME="float1" SRC="fileone.htm" WIDTH="350" HEIGHT="200"
ALIGN="LEFT">
There would be a floating frame here if your browser supported it.
</IFRAME>

<P>This is a simple example of how floating frames are used. Notice
that in many ways the floating frame acts very similar to an inline
image. Floating frames act like embedded objects in many ways.</P>
</BODY>
</HTML>
```

The rendering of this example code is shown in Figure 8-5. Note how the Netscape browser does not support the **<IFRAME>** element, but renders the enclosed text instead.

The complete syntax for **<IFRAME>** is strikingly similar to the **<IMG>** element, as well as to other elements, such as **<OBJECT>**, that are used to insert other forms of content inline. The **<IFRAME>** element, defined under HTML 4, includes many of the attributes that are expected. The most important attributes are **SRC**, which defines the content of the floating frame, and **NAME**, which is used for link targeting. Because the floating frame is an inlined object, it also supports the **ALIGN**, **HEIGHT**, and **WIDTH** attributes, which can be useful for content layout. The complete syntax of the **<IFRAME>** element is provided in Appendix A.

Using Frames

One of the biggest problems with frames is that they initially were used simply because they existed. Framed documents can provide considerable benefit, but at a price. A potential benefit of frames is that they allow content to be fixed onscreen. As demonstrated in previous examples, one frame may contain a table of contents, while

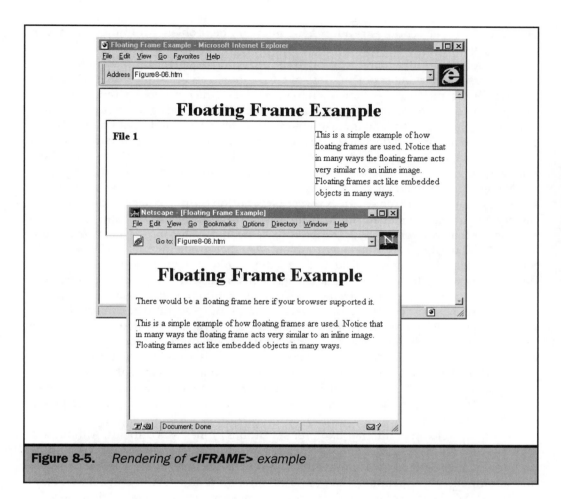

Figure 8-5.   *Rendering of* **<IFRAME>** *example*

the other frame contains the actual information. Keeping the table of contents onscreen provides a convenient way to navigate the body of information. Furthermore, if one frame has fixed navigation, the user may perceive the Web interface to be more responsive, because only part of the screen needs to update between selections. The primary benefit of frames is to present two or more things simultaneously, but this extra window of information has its costs, as explained in the next section.

Frame Problems

Many usability experts, such as Jakob Nielsen (http://www.useit.com), are extremely critical of frames. Given the current implementation of frames, and designers who don't understand the potential drawbacks of framed documents, the statement that "frames can give designers more rope to hang themselves with" has some truth to it.

However, browser vendors are addressing many of the problems of frames. With luck, designers will learn to use frames only when they provide added benefit.

The problems with frames are numerous, including design issues, navigation confusion, bookmarking problems, loss of URL context, and printing issues. Designers may not like frames because they often have borders, which can look strange in a design. However, modern frame implementations allow the designer to turn off frame borders, so this really isn't an issue anymore. The only potential design issue is the possibility that a framed document may sacrifice valuable screen real estate because of scroll bars, which could pose trouble for people with lower-resolution monitors. The only way to get around this problem is to limit the number of frames used on a page.

Navigation confusion is still a big issue with frames. Under Netscape 2, the first browser to implement frames, the browser Back button didn't go back in the frame history, but instead went back in the page history. Because Netscape 2 and subsequent versions of the browser do things differently, some lingering confusion may exist about what "Back" means in a framed environment. Another problem involves the sense of what happens when a link is clicked. Unless the framing is kept very simple, determining which frames will change when a link is clicked may not be obvious to users. In some sites, numerous frames are updated simultaneously, which may cause users to lose their sense of navigation. Even worse, if users want to bookmark the current page, they actually have to bookmark the top-level entry frame rather than the deeper level to which they have progressed. If users bookmark the actual frame content, they may lose any navigation needed to navigate the site upon return.

Additional navigational problems include loss of context, because the URL of the document tends not to change, which accounts for why bookmarking doesn't work as expected. Many people use URLs as a way to orient themselves at a site; frames give up this clue to location.

Before the release of Internet Explorer 4, printing frames was difficult. Although the contents of individual frames could be printed, printing an entire document consisting of many frames generally was impossible. The newer versions of the Microsoft browser allow complete frame printing, but page authors should understand that content may be clipped. While none of the problems with frames are insurmountable, designers should approach the technology with caution, and not just use it to show off their technical prowess.

Layers

Netscape introduced the **<LAYER>** element starting with the Communicator (Netscape 4) release of its browser. The layer function enables the page designer to define precisely positioned, overlapping layers of transparent or opaque content in a page. Besides being able to stack layers on top of each other to create complex layouts, authors can bind the layers to code that can move them around or change the order of overlap. Scripting combined with absolute positioning can truly make pages more dynamic. Although the **<LAYER>** element does sound very useful, page authors should use positioning with style sheets (discussed in Chapter 10) as the primary way to control page layout absolutely. The **<LAYER>** element is still relevant to this discussion, however, because some users prefer using **<LAYER>** in Netscape 4 to implement positioned pages, due to bugs with CSS implementation in that iteration of the browser. Layers are too Netscape-specific at this point to recommend their use. The W3C doesn't include layers in the HTML 4 specification, and isn't considering layers for inclusion in future versions. The use of layers (as defined with this proprietary HTML element) should be approached with extreme caution. However, you may find it helpful to know more about layering, so this section provides that information.

The basic idea of a layer is similar to the idea of a frame, except that layers may overlap. They generally are defined in the same document, unlike frames, which require multiple documents. A layer defines a region or portion of the browser window that can be manipulated, and may overlap other layers. Layers come in two basic forms:

- **Positioned layers**   Defined by the **<LAYER>** element
- **Inflow layers**   Defined by the **<ILAYER>** element

This discussion focuses first on positioned layers, which are slightly easier to understand.

Positioned Layers

To define a section of a document as a layer to position, enclose it within **<LAYER>** and **</LAYER>**. The layer should be named, just as a frame is named, so that it can be manipulated later. To name a layer, set the **ID** attribute of the element to a unique identifier. For a positioned layer, specify the upper corner of the layer by setting the **TOP** and **LEFT** attributes to the pixel coordinates of the upper-left corner of the layer, relative to the browser window. You may also want to set the **WIDTH** and **HEIGHT** attributes of the layer. These take pixel values, so the actual size of the layer can be controlled, regardless of its content. A simple example showing how absolutely positioned layers work is presented here:

```
<HTML>
<HEAD>
<TITLE>Layer Example</TITLE>
</HEAD>

<BODY>
<H1 ALIGN="center">Simple Layer Example</H1>
```

```
<LAYER ID="Layer1" TOP="100" LEFT="50" BGCOLOR="lightgreen">
<H2>This is a layer.</H2>
<UL>
      <LI>This layer is positioned at 100,150.
   </UL>
</LAYER>

<LAYER ID="Layer2" TOP="180" LEFT="250" BGCOLOR="orange">
<H2>This is another layer.</H2>
   <UL>
<LI>This layer is positioned at 180,250.
   </UL>
</LAYER>
</BODY>
</HTML>
```

Note that the **BGCOLOR** attribute is used with the layers to show how the layers clip each other. The rendering of the layer example is shown in Figure 8-6. To see how this code looks on a browser that does not support layers, see Figure 8-7.

Because the position of layers is defined absolutely, you don't need to define how they fall on a page; but it makes sense to define layers in a logical order, based on a left-to-right, top-to-bottom flow of the page.

For browsers that don't support layers, the **<NOLAYER>** element may be useful. Content placed between **<NOLAYER>** and **</NOLAYER>** tags is ignored by a browser such as Netscape 4, which understands layers, but renders normally on all other browsers that don't comprehend layers. The **<NOLAYER>** element enables you to add extra information to the page, for nonlayering browsers that view your site. Because browsers that don't understand the **<LAYER>** element will attempt to display the contents of the **<LAYER>** element, as shown in Figure 8-7, you should use the **SRC** attribute to include the contents of the layer from another file, as shown here:

```
<LAYER ID="Layer1" SRC="layercontents.htm" TOP="100" LEFT="100">
</LAYER>
<NOLAYER>
. . .standard HTML. . .
</NOLAYER>
```

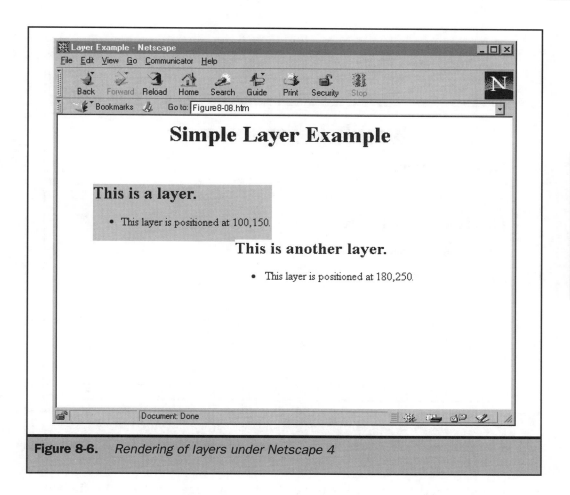

Figure 8-6.   *Rendering of layers under Netscape 4*

With this technique, you can use layers without ruining the layout for other browsers. As with frames, this may require keeping two separate forms of the site, which may be unreasonable.

Inflow Layers

Inflow layers are different than positioned layers, because inflow layers fall naturally within the flow of a document, much as an inlined object is positioned, such as an image. To indicate that content is part of an inflow layer, enclose it within **<ILAYER>** and **</ILAYER>** tags. Unlike positioned layers, where the inflow layer is defined

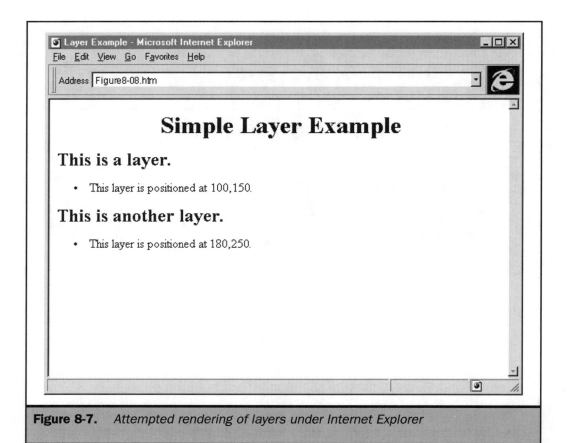

Figure 8-7. *Attempted rendering of layers under Internet Explorer*

matters, and it affects where the content ends up on the page. Similar to the **<LAYER>** element, a name is probably required for the layer and should be set by using the **ID** attribute. You also can set the **LEFT** and **TOP** values for the layer, but this positions the layer relative to the content that the layer is within, not within the upper-left corner of the browser window or enclosing layer. This positioning may be useful to move content around by a certain number of pixels, relative to text in the document. A simple example of inflow layers is shown here:

```
<HTML>
<HEAD>
<TITLE>Inflow Layer Example</TITLE>
```

```
</HEAD>

<BODY>
<P>An inflow layer can be found

<ILAYER ID="Layer1" BGCOLOR="yellow">
within the flow</ILAYER> of text.</P>

<P>This <ILAYER ID="Layer2" BGCOLOR="yellow" LEFT="25">
is positioned 25 pixels from the left</ILAYER> of the current
flow of the content.</P>

<P>This <ILAYER ID="Layer3" BGCOLOR="yellow" TOP="15">
is positioned 15 pixels below</ILAYER> the current flow of
content.</P>
</BODY>
</HTML>
```

The **BGCOLOR** attribute is used again, so that when the example is rendered, the location of the layers can be determined. The rendering of this example is shown in Figure 8-8. Note how the second inflow layer clips the text that follows it. Page authors must be very careful with layers, because layers will clip other objects onscreen. This is their nature, by design.

Interesting Uses of Layers

Although they are very proprietary, layers can be used to create a variety of interesting effects. The next chapter shows how to create similar effects by using style sheets, which is the preferred way of doing things. One major aspect of layers is that, by default, they are transparent, unless the content in the layer covers the layer entirely, as might happen with a layer's background image. Because layers are normally transparent, you can overlay text on top of images. Before layers evolved, this was difficult to do. (While background images and table cells offered some degree of

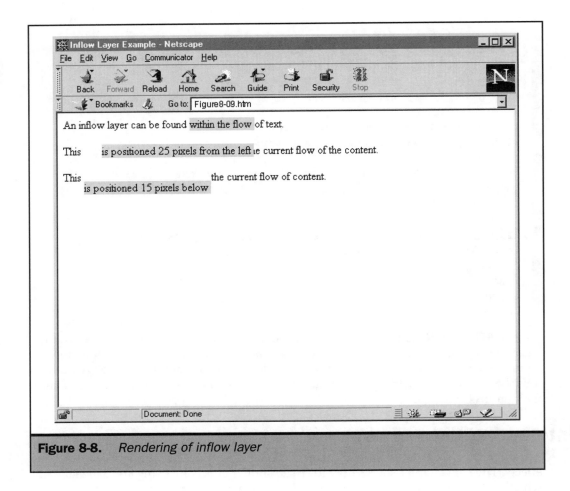

Figure 8-8. *Rendering of inflow layer*

control, it was very limited; the positioning of text on top of the image was far from precise.) The following example shows how text may be positioned over an image:

```
<HTML>
<HEAD>
<TITLE>Text Over Image</TITLE>
</HEAD>

<BODY>
<LAYER TOP="100" LEFT="100">
<IMG SRC="bclogonotext.gif" WIDTH="141" HEIGHT="197" BORDER="0">
</LAYER>
```

```
<LAYER TOP="200" LEFT="40">
   <FONT COLOR="red">
   <H2>Big Company, Inc.</H2>
   </FONT>
</LAYER>
</BODY>
</HTML>
```

In case you are skeptical of this newfound ability, a rendering of the example under Netscape 4 is shown in Figure 8-9.

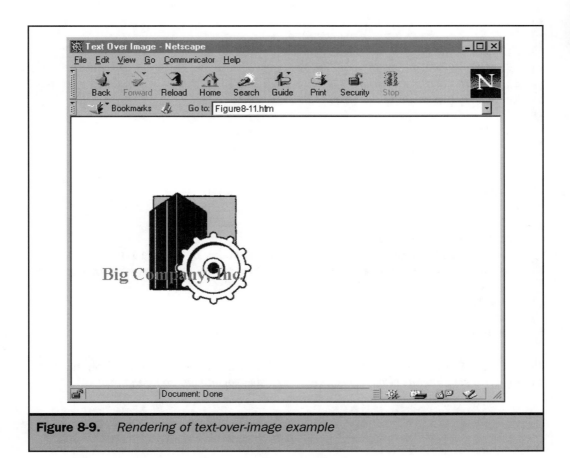

Figure 8-9.   *Rendering of text-over-image example*

Programming Layers

Layers become very interesting when they are combined with JavaScript. The clipping region of a layer can be changed incrementally so that, at first, none of the layer shows, only to gradually appear in a matter of seconds. This effect is known as a *wipe*. This simple transition effect is an example of *Dynamic HTML (DHTML)*, discussed in Chapter 14. The original direction of Netscape's DHTML focused heavily on layers, but now the preferred method is to use style sheets, discussed in Chapter 10. For old-time's sake, a layer example that creates a simple wipe is shown here:

```
<HTML>
<HEAD>
<TITLE>Curtain Layers</TITLE>
<SCRIPT LANGUAGE="JavaScript">
function wipe(alayer,xinc,inctime,stopwidth)
 {
alayer.clip.left += -(xinc/2)
alayer.clip.right += (xinc/2)
if (alayer.clip.width < 0) {lyr.clip.width = 0}
if (((xinc < 0) && (alayer.clip.width > stopwidth)) || ((xinc > 0) &&
(alayer.clip.width < stopwidth)))
 {
 setTimeout('wipe(document.layers["'+alayer.name+'"],
'+xinc+','+inctime+','+stopwidth+')',inctime)
 }
}
</SCRIPT>
</HEAD>

<BODY BGCOLOR="WHITE"
      onLoad="wipe(document.layers['lasthurrah'],-2,10,0)">
<LAYER NAME="lasthurrah" TOP="100" LEFT="100" BGCOLOR="YELLOW">
<H1>Goodbye, cruel world. I am the last layer!</H1>
</LAYER>
</BODY>
</HTML>
```

Be careful with this example. It only works in Netscape 4 and above. The line that begins with *setTimeout belongs on one line, regardless of any wrapping in the print.*

Summary

Web page layout using HTML tags is not appropriate but, until recently, that was the only available layout option. Frames are often used as a layout tool, and while the **<FRAME>** element can afford great power in making sophisticated layouts, it comes with a great price. Navigation confusion, printing mishaps, and design problems may all result from misuse of frames. However, when frames are used properly (for example, to provide a fixed table of contents or navigation aid), they are a valuable addition to the page designer's arsenal. Because of their power and popularity, frames are finally included in the HTML specification (in version 4), so you shouldn't have to worry about their future use. However, more advanced page layout tags that are highly proprietary to Netscape browsers, such as the **<LAYER>** and **<ILAYER>** elements, should be approached with caution. Although these elements can be used to create impressive and dynamic layouts, similar effects can be created by using standardized technology—particularly style sheets, which are discussed in Chapter 10.

PRESENTATION AND
LAYOUT

The Complete Reference

Chapter 9

HTML and Other Media Types

Adding images to a Web page is just the tip of the iceberg. Web pages can support a variety of media forms, including animation, sound, video, virtual reality, and other binary forms. Browser vendors have introduced special extensions to handle these new media types, but the long-term solution is to handle all media types in a similar fashion, as plain binary objects. When programming elements and true interactivity are mixed, things can become even more complicated. This chapter ties up some loose ends regarding binary object support and miscellaneous vendor-specific elements. It also previews many of the issues that arise during the discussion of interactivity on the Web.

HTML and Binary Objects

As discussed in Chapter 5, images are not directly part of HTML. Images are binary objects that are included, or pulled into, a Web page. Other objects, such as videos, animations, sound files, and programs, also can be pulled into Web pages. Initially, because no way existed to insert inline into a Web page an object such as a video, the only option was to link to it. By creating a link to a movie file, **<A HREF= "trailer.avi">** View Movie Trailer**</A>** for example, the viewer could click the link and launch a helper application to view the movie. Combining linked data with helper applications is certainly an easy approach, similar to the way images were supported on the Web before Mosaic introduced support for inline images.

So, how can objects be inserted and supported inline? Three basic approaches exist:

- Use a plug-in and reference the data by using the **<EMBED>** tag. This is primarily a Netscape approach.

- Use an ActiveX control and reference it with the **<OBJECT>** tag. This is Microsoft's approach for adding media elements to a page.

- Use the **<APPLET>** tag to add multimedia with Java.

Combining all three approaches may enable you to create a page that works under all conditions. Each approach is briefly considered next, respectively, before discussing specific methods of inserting audio, video, and other media forms.

Plug-Ins and <EMBED>

First-generation browsers displayed static HTML pages and offered the ability to launch helper applications to view different media and file types. Helper applications still run in separate windows from the browser, providing a nonintegrated experience. In contrast, plug-ins enable users to experience content such as Shockwave files or QuickTime movies directly within a Web page. The plug-in HTML syntax developed by Netscape is also supported by Internet Explorer.

The plug-in approach of extending a browser's features does have drawbacks. Users must locate and download plug-ins, install them, and restart their browsers. Many users find this rather complicated. Netscape 4 may offer some installation relief with its *self-installing plug-ins* and other features; but, for now, plug-ins remain troublesome. Furthermore, plug-ins aren't available on every machine; a plug-in binary must be compiled for each particular operating system. Because of this machine-specific approach, many plug-ins work only on Windows 95 and Windows NT. A decreasing number of plug-ins work on Windows 3.1, Macintosh, or UNIX operating systems. Finally, each plug-in installed on a system is a persistent extension to the browser, which means that it needs to be downloaded only once, but takes up memory and disk space thereafter. Having more plug-ins on your system equals increased memory requirements. A Macintosh running ten common plug-ins may need 20MB of RAM to operate. Plug-ins are a *fat-client approach*: the more functionality added, the fatter the client application becomes.

On the upside, Netscape already bundles audio, video, and Flash plug-ins in the browser. Other widely used plug-ins include Real Audio/Video and Adobe's Acrobat format. Adding support for binary objects (sounds, videos, or multimedia files) is a matter of learning the appropriate syntax for the **<EMBED>** element. In general, the **<EMBED>** element takes an **SRC** attribute to specify the URL of the included binary object. **HEIGHT** and **WIDTH** attributes often are used to indicate the pixel dimensions of the included object, if it is visible. To embed a short Audio Video Interleaved (AVI) format movie called welcome.avi to be viewed by the Netscape LiveVideo plug-in, use the following HTML fragment:

```
<EMBED SRC="welcome.avi" HEIGHT="100" WIDTH="100">
```

Beyond this simple example, things get a little more problematic. Other than **HEIGHT** and **WIDTH**, common attributes include **ALIGN**, **HIDDEN**, **ID**, **HSPACE**, **PALETTE**, **PLUGINSPAGE**, **TITLE**, and **VSPACE**. Some of these attributes, such as **ALIGN**, **HSPACE**, and **VSPACE**, work just like the same attributes for the **<IMG>** element. These elements may not be supported by all plug-ins. Many other vendor-defined attributes may also be very important. Plug-in vendors are free to define their own attributes, which makes dealing with plug-ins difficult from a developer's point of view. This chapter discusses built-in Netscape plug-ins and similar Microsoft features. A more generalized discussion of plug-ins—how they work and how to deal with them—is presented in Chapter 15.

<NOEMBED>

One important aspect of plug-ins is the **<NOEMBED>** element. Some browsers do not understand Netscape's plug-in architecture or the **<EMBED>** element. Rather than lock these browsers out of a Web page, the **<NOEMBED>** element enables you to provide some alternative text or marked up content. In the short example presented here, an AVI video is embedded in the page. The **<NOEMBED>** element contains an image, which in turn has an alternative text reading set with the **ALT** attribute. Note how the example degrades from a very sophisticated setting, all the way down to a text-only environment.

```
<EMBED SRC="welcome.avi" HEIGHT="100" WIDTH="100">

<NOEMBED>
    <IMG SRC="welcome.gif" ALT="Welcome to Big Company, Inc.">
</NOEMBED>
```

One big problem with the **<NOEMBED>** approach occurs when a browser supports plug-ins but lacks the specific plug-in to deal with the included binary object. In this case, the user is presented with a broken puzzle-piece or similar icon, and may be directed to a page from which to download the missing plug-in. This level of user interaction is inappropriate for novice users who do not understand how to download plug-ins. A better approach is for the page author to attempt to provide pages that don't require setup. (Chapter 15 presents more information on the accessibility aspects of plug-ins.)

ActiveX Controls and <OBJECT>

Microsoft's ActiveX technology is another approach to inserting binary objects (such as movie and audio players) into a Web page. ActiveX controls are small, binary components that are downloaded to a user's system and that can be accessed from within the Web page. Compared to plug-ins, installation is fairly straightforward for the user. It may even be automatic. However, this technology has some security issues that can be very problematic. Because of security and design, the ActiveX control is very different from plug-ins or Java, though the basic way to access Microsoft's form of binaries is similar as far as HTML is concerned.

Microsoft uses the **<OBJECT>** element to insert an ActiveX control in a page. The **<OBJECT>** element acts like the **<EMBED>** element insofar as it has attributes such as **ALIGN**, **HEIGHT**, and **WIDTH**. Beyond this, the two elements are very different. Using **<OBJECT>** with an ActiveX control requires the page author to specify the **CLASSID** value that corresponds to the object to insert. This unique code might be something like **CLSID:99B42120-6EC7-11CF-A6C7- 00AA00A47DD2**—not exactly easy to remember. Furthermore, a variety of data items must be passed to the ActiveX control via the **<PARAM>** element, which is included numerous times within the **<OBJECT>** element. The **<PARAM>** element usually has an attribute called **NAME** (used to set the name of the parameter) and a **VALUE** parameter (which sets the value of the particular argument to the control). For example, the following code fragment is used to insert a simple graphical label; notice how the **FontName** is set to **Arial** by using the **<PARAM>** element:

```
<OBJECT ID="IeLabel1" WIDTH="122" HEIGHT="57"
        CLASSID="CLSID:99B42120-6EC7-11CF-A6C7-00AA00A47DD2">
    <PARAM NAME="_ExtentX" VALUE="2582">
    <PARAM NAME="_ExtentY" VALUE="1207">
    <PARAM NAME="Caption" VALUE="Test Label">
    <PARAM NAME="Alignment" VALUE="4">
    <PARAM NAME="Mode" VALUE="1">
    <PARAM NAME="FontName" VALUE="Arial">
    <PARAM NAME="FontSize" VALUE="12">
Sorry, you don't have ActiveX support.
</OBJECT>
```

As this example shows, using the **<OBJECT>** element is less than straightforward. Depending on the object being inserted, the parameters may vary widely. Because of this, Microsoft has provided a variety of tools, such as the ControlPad (http://www.microsoft.com/workshop/misc/cpad), that can be used to insert ActiveX controls into a page and set their parameters.

While ActiveX controls were the first binary forms to use the **<OBJECT>** element, in the future, all binary objects—including images—will probably use this form. The W3C is attempting to standardize the method for including binary data by adopting a generalized approach of using the **<OBJECT>** element. (This approach is discussed in depth in Chapter 15.) For the rest of this discussion, simply note that because the syntax of the **<OBJECT>** element is so variable when it is used in this manner, using tools to generate the syntax, even to include Microsoft controls, is the best approach.

Java Applets

New media forms also can be inserted into a Web page by using Sun Microsystems' Java technology. Java (http://www.javasoft.com) is an attractive, revolutionary approach to cross-platform, Internet-based development. Java promises a platform-neutral development language that allows programs to be written once and deployed on any machine, browser, or operating system that supports the Java virtual machine (JVM). It uses small Java programs, called *applets*, that were introduced by Sun's HotJava browser. Today, many popular browsers, including Navigator and Internet Explorer, support Java. When applets are referenced in a Web page by using the **<APPLET>** element, they are downloaded and run directly within a browser to provide new functionality or media forms such as animation or video.

Applets are written in the Java language and compiled to a machine-independent byte code that is downloaded automatically to the Java-capable browser and run within the browser environment. But even with a fast processor, the end system runs the byte code slowly compared to a natively compiled application, because the JVM must interpret the byte code. Even with recent Just-In-Time (JIT) compilers in newer browsers, Java can't deliver ideal performance. Even if compilation weren't an issue, Java applets currently are not persistent; they must be downloaded for each use. Java browsers act like thin-client applications: they add code only when they need it.

Security in Java has been a serious concern from the outset. Because programs are downloaded and run automatically, a malicious program could be downloaded and run without the user being able to stop it. Java applets actually have little access to resources outside the browser's environment. Within Web pages, applets can't write to local disks or perform other harmful functions. This framework has been referred to as the "Java Sandbox." Developers who want to provide Java functions outside the sandbox must write Java applications, which run as separate applications from browsers. Other Internet programming technologies (plug-ins, ActiveX, and so on) provide little or no safety from damaging programs. Oddly, Java developers often want to add just these types of unsecure features, as well as powerful features such as persistence and interobject communication. Most of the features are already far along in development, and should soon become commonplace.

As far as HTML is concerned, a Java applet is yet another object to insert into a Web page. Rather than using the **<EMBED>** or **<OBJECT>** element, a special **<APPLET>** element is used to insert a Java applet. Like the **<EMBED>** element, **<APPLET>** will most likely be replaced by the **<OBJECT>** element. You need to know how **<APPLET>** works, in case you need to insert Java media objects, particularly for Netscape support.

The **<APPLET>** element specifies the Java applet to run by providing a URL to a class file containing the Java byte code. To set the applet to run, set the **CODE** attribute equal to the URL of the Java class. The **CODEBASE** attribute can also be used to set a base URL reference for the **CODE** attribute. Other basic attributes to the **<APPLET>** element are similar to those for **<IMG>**, such as **ALIGN**, **HEIGHT**, **WIDTH**, **HSPACE**, **VSPACE**, and **ALT**. Within the **<APPLET>** and **</APPLET>** elements, the user can specify parameters or arguments to the applet by using the **<PARAM>** element, in a similar fashion to how data is passed to ActiveX controls. Plain text may also appear between the **<APPLET>** and **</APPLET>** elements. Such text can be used to provide alternative text in situations in which the element is not understood at all. A small example of how **<APPLET>** might be used is shown here:

```
<APPLET CODE="http://www.bigcompany.com/java/test.class" ALIGN="LEFT"
        HEIGHT="100" WIDTH="100" HSPACE="10" VSPACE="10">
    <PARAM NAME="caption" value="Hello World">
</APPLET>
```

Depending on the Java applet being accessed, many different parameters may exist that can be passed to it. A general discussion of Java applets and how they can be used is presented in Chapter 15, so the discussion here is meant to show only that many forms of binary formats exist that can be included in Web pages.

The three elements that are useful for inserting nonimage binary objects are **<APPLET>**, **<EMBED>**, and **<OBJECT>**. In most cases, spelling out all the aspects of the **<APPLET>** and **<OBJECT>** elements is too tedious, because so many variations exist. A few plug-ins are commonly available within browsers to support media types, such as audio, video, and VRML. Furthermore, some media forms, such as Acrobat and Flash, are so common that they deserve a brief discussion regarding how they are handled within HTML. The rest of the chapter reviews common plug-ins and controls for dealing with audio, video, multimedia, and Acrobat. First, however, take a closer look at a media element that defies classification—the **<MARQUEE>** element.

Media-Like Element: <MARQUEE>

One approach to adding new support for objects is to add new elements and build in support to the browser for the object. This approach used to be very popular with browser vendors, and is partially responsible for the proliferation of browser-specific tags. **<MARQUEE>** is one example of a media-like tag that is fairly common on the Web. Although **<MARQUEE>** isn't an embedded binary object, it tends to act like one in its support for **HSPACE**, **VSPACE**, **HEIGHT**, and **WIDTH** attributes. In the proprietary HTML extension wars, Microsoft is the culprit for introducing the dreaded **<MARQUEE>** element, which is certainly as annoying as **<BLINK>**. Thanks to **<MARQUEE>**, HTML authors now can create messages that scroll and slide across a viewer's screen in a variety of different ways. Like Netscape's **<BLINK>** element, **<MARQUEE>** degrades fairly well and can be used by HTML authors who understand the ramifications of using such proprietary tags. However, the bottom line is that, in good conscience, authors shouldn't recommend more than very occasional use of the **<MARQUEE>** element.

Internet Explorer, as well as WebTV, supports the **<MARQUEE>** element. The element requires a closing **</MARQUEE>** tag. The text included between the tags is transformed into a scrolling ticker tape, similar to the one found at Times Square. A very simple continuous marquee could be set with the following HTML fragment:

```
<MARQUEE>
Welcome to Big Company, Inc. -- the biggest fake company in the world!
</MARQUEE>
```

Under Internet Explorer and other browsers that support the **<MARQUEE>** element, the enclosed text scrolls repeatedly from right to left. Under browsers that don't support **<MARQUEE>**, the text is displayed simply as plain text.

The following is a more complex example that illustrates some of the more common attributes supported by **<MARQUEE>**; the rendering is shown Figure 9-1:

```
<HTML>
<HEAD>
<TITLE>Marquee Example</TITLE>
</HEAD>

<BODY>
<DIV ALIGN="CENTER">
<MARQUEE BGCOLOR="YELLOW" BEHAVIOR="ALTERNATE" DIRECTION="RIGHT"
        LOOP="6" SCROLLAMOUNT="1" SCROLLDELAY="40"
        TITLE="Silly tags aren't just for Netscape anymore."
        WIDTH="80%">
Welcome to Big Company, the biggest fake company of them all!
</MARQUEE>
</DIV>
</BODY>
</HTML>
```

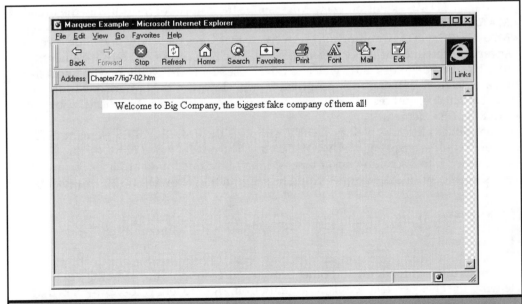

Figure 9-1.   *Rendering of the* **<MARQUEE>** *example under Internet Explorer*

Changing the attributes in this example will adjust the presentation of the marquee. For example, the **BEHAVIOR** attribute can be set to **ALTERNATE**, **SCROLL**, or **SLIDE**. This attribute determines how the scrolling text behaves. By default, a marquee scrolls text from left to right, unless the **DIRECTION** is set. The scrolled text, if it is looped, must first disappear before reappearing on the other side. When the attribute is set to **ALTERNATE**, the text bounces across the scroll region. When the attribute is set to **SLIDE**, the text slides into position, based on direction, and stays put once onscreen.

The **DIRECTION** attribute is used to set the direction in which the scrolled text moves. The allowed values for this attribute are **DOWN**, **LEFT**, **RIGHT**, and **UP**. Using Dynamic HTML (DHTML) features, you may be able to create interesting effects with <MARQUEE> by modifying the **DIRECTION** attribute.

The **LOOP** attribute is used to set the number of times that the message loops in the scroll region. By default, unless the **BEHAVIOR** is set to **SLIDE**, a marquee scrolls forever. The value of the **LOOP** attribute should be a positive integer.

Setting **SCROLLAMOUNT** to a particular number of pixels allows the smoothness of the scroll to be controlled. The value of the **SCROLLAMOUNT** attribute is set to the number of pixels between each drawing of the scrolled message in the display area. The larger the value in pixels, the jerkier the scroll.

SCROLLDELAY is used to set the number of milliseconds between each rendering of the scrolled message. A higher value for this attribute slows the scrolling. A reasonable value for this attribute is **50** or greater. Lower values for **SCROLLDELAY** tend to produce marquees that are very difficult to read.

Last, because the <MARQUEE> element represents a rectangular region, just like an image (or, for that matter, any binary included object), it has attributes such as **ALIGN**, **HSPACE**, **VSPACE**, **HEIGHT**, and **WIDTH**.

Appendix A provides a complete discussion of the <MARQUEE> element and its numerous attributes. Although the <MARQUEE> element is certainly interesting, as a simple form of animated text, it doesn't hold a candle to more persuasive media forms such as sound or video.

Audio Support in Browsers

Few things are as persuasive as sound. Just try watching television with the volume muted. It's not terribly interesting. Sound is a vital element of true multimedia Web pages—but how should sound be used? What Web audio technology is appropriate for the job? Just adding a MIDI file to a site to provide continuous background sound may turn your page into the online equivalent of an in-store electronic organ demonstration. The latest audio technologies on the Internet cover a lot of ground, from traditional download-and-play systems in a variety of formats to *streaming audio,* which plays close to real time. Surprisingly, the most advanced technologies, and the most popular, may not be the best solution.

Digital Sound Basics

This section provides a very brief overview of digital sound. Digital sound is measured by the frequency of *sampling*, or how many times the sound is digitized during a specific time period. Sampling frequencies are specified in Kilohertz (KHz), which indicate the sound sampling rate per second. CD-quality sound is approximately 44.1KHz, or 44,100 samples every second. For stereo, two channels are required, each at 8 bits; at 16 bits per sample, that yields 705,600 bits of data for each second of CD-quality sound. In theory, the bits of data on a CD could be delivered over the Internet, creating high-quality music at the end user's demand. In reality, transmitting this amount of data would take nearly half a T1 network's bandwidth. Obviously, this type of bandwidth is not available to the average Web user. Another approach must be taken.

One approach is to lower the sampling rate when creating digital sound for Web delivery. A sampling rate of 8KHz in mono might produce acceptable playback results for simple applications, such as speech, particularly considering that playback hardware often consists of a combination of a simple sound card and a small speaker. Low-quality audio requires a mere 64,000 bits of data per second, but the end user still has to wait to download the sound. For modem users, even in the best of conditions, each second of low-quality sound takes a few seconds to be delivered, making continuous sound unrealistic.

Audio File Formats and Compression

Like graphics files, audio files can be compressed to reduce the amount of data being sent. The software on the serving side compresses the data, which is decompressed and played back on the receiving end. The compression/decompression software is known together as a *codec*. Just like image formats, audio compression methods are either lossy or lossless. *Lossy* data compression doesn't perfectly represent what was compressed, but is close enough, given the size savings. Because *lossless* compression techniques guarantee that what goes in one end comes out the other, most techniques can't compress files to any significant degree. Compression always involves a tradeoff between sound quality and file size; larger file sizes mean longer download times.

When dealing with sounds, you don't really select different forms of compression. You select file formats. Many standard file formats are available, as shown in Table 9-1.

Downloading and Playing Audio

Early approaches to delivering sound via the Internet followed the "download and play" model. In this scenario, users must download sounds completely before they can play them. This takes up valuable hard drive space, even if a user wants to hear only the first few seconds of a file. Sounds must be degraded significantly in this situation, which may not be acceptable for content that requires flawless playback. Even at very low sampling rates, these sounds must be fairly short to spare impatient users the agony of prolonged download times. Download time can be reduced by creating smaller audio files, which only accentuates the drawbacks of this method.

File Format	Description
WAV	Waveform (or simply *wave*) files are the most common sound format on Windows platforms. WAVs can also be played on Macs and other systems with player software.
AU	Sparc-audio, or u-law format, is one of the oldest Internet sound formats. A player for nearly every platform is available.
AIFF	*Audio Interchange File Format* is very common on Macs. Widely used in multimedia applications, it is not very common on the Web.
MIDI	*Musical Instrument Digital Interface* format is not a digitized audio format. It represents notes and other information so that music can be synthesized. MIDI is well supported and files are very small, but it is useful for only certain applications due to its sound quality when reproduced on PC hardware.
MPEG	*Motion Pictures Experts Group* format is a standard format that has significant compression capabilities. It isn't as standardized as many people might think: it lacks widespread playing and encoding acceptance, despite its quality.

Table 9-1.   *Standard Internet Sound Formats*

Using HTML, the simplest way to support the download-and-play approach is by linking to a sound file and letting another application deal with it, such as a helper or plug-in. If no helper or plug-in is configured, the user is prompted to deal with the sound. For example, to link to an audio file in WAV format, insert a link such as this:

```
<A HREF="starspangled.wav">Star Spangled Banner (6 second WAV - 900K)</A>
```

A good idea with the download-and-play approach is to put the decision to download the file in the hands of users. Warn them about the file format and size, so that the user has some indication of how long download will take. Another helpful bit of information might be how long the sound is going to be.

For download-and-play delivery, WAV and AU are the safest formats for low-quality music or speech. MPEG—particularly MPEG level 3 (MP3)—is really the only choice for high-quality playback. Download-and-play–based audio delivery is recommended when a quick bit of sound, such as an entrance gong, is required. AU and WAV files are supported via helper applications and plug-ins. They are even supported natively by some recent Web browsers, including Netscape with its LiveAudio plug-in, and Microsoft Internet Explorer with its proprietary **<BGSOUND>** tag. Both browsers also support MIDI sound files. However, MIDI files played back via PC sound cards (such as SoundBlaster) often sound like cheap, synthesized music, which is more a reflection of the playback hardware than the protocol itself.

LiveAudio

Starting with Netscape 3, the LiveAudio plug-in was included with the Netscape browser. The LiveAudio plug-in supports AU, AIFF, WAV, and MIDI sound files in the download-and-play fashion. Adding support for audio with LiveAudio simply requires using the appropriate form of the **<EMBED>** element to access the LiveAudio plug-in. For example, to set LiveAudio to include a sound called test.wav and a panel to control the sound, use the following HTML fragment:

```
<EMBED SRC="test.wav" HEIGHT="60" WIDTH="144">
```

Including the **HEIGHT** and **WIDTH** values is important; otherwise, the browser may clip the console. The default size for the LiveAudio control is 60 pixels high and 144 pixels across. Other control styles have different default sizes. If you want to create a background sound for a page, you may find this line more appropriate:

```
<EMBED SRC="test.wav" HIDDEN="TRUE" AUTOSTART="TRUE">
```

The LiveAudio plug-in has a variety of features that can be controlled with **ATTRIBUTE** settings for the **<EMBED>** element. The syntax for the LiveAudio plug-in is shown here:

```
<EMBED SRC="URL of sound file to play"
       ALIGN="top | bottom | center | baseline | left | right |
             texttop | middle | absmiddle | absbottom"
       AUTOSTART="true | false"
       CONTROLS="console | smallconsole | playbutton | pausebutton |
               stopbutton | volumelever"
       ENDTIME="minutes:seconds"
       HEIGHT="pixels or percentage"
       HIDDEN="true | false"
       LOOP="true | false | positive integer"
       MASTERSOUND
       NAME="unique name"
       STARTTIME="minutes:seconds"
       VOLUME="number from 0 to 100"
       WIDTH="pixels or percentage"
   >
```

Like the **<IMG>** element, the LiveAudio plug-in must have an **SRC** attribute setting. The **SRC** value is a URL to a sound file supported by the plug-in. These formats include AU, AIFF, WAV, and MIDI. Remember to take the same precautions for using a complete URL to an outside file, compared to using a locally referenced file with a relative URL.

The **AUTOSTART** attributes can take one of two values, **true** or **false**. When set to **true**, the sound file begins playing as soon as it is downloaded. By default, if unspecified, **AUTOSTART** is set to **false**.

The **LOOP** attribute can take one of three values, **true**, **false**, or a positive integer. Setting the value to **true** loops the sound continuously until the Stop button is pressed. When combined with the **AUTOSTART** attribute, infinite looping could become very annoying, particularly if the Stop button is unavailable. By default, the value of **LOOP** is set to **false**. The **LOOP** attribute can also be set to a positive integer, which plays the sound a specified number of times or until the Stop button is pressed.

The **STARTTIME** attribute can be set to a time value within a sound file, to determine from where to begin playback. For example, to start playback two seconds into the sound, the attribute can be set to **00:02**.

The **ENDTIME** attribute is similar to the **STARTTIME** attribute, but instead determines the time value to end playback, and is written in the same way.

STARTTIME and ENDTIME provide little benefit without using scripting technology, because the whole sound must be downloaded, regardless. Why a user wouldn't simply edit a sound to avoid starting and stopping at a certain time index is curious. If the controls in the LiveAudio plug-in supported a fast-forward and a reverse feature, these attributes would be far more useful.

The **VOLUME** attribute can be set to an integer between 0 and 100, where **0** sets the sound to be completely off and **100** sets it at maximum volume. Values outside this range generally default to the extreme, so a value of **200** would set the volume to maximum. When the **VOLUME** attribute is combined with the **MASTERVOLUME** setting for the **NAME** attribute, you can set volume for other sounds. The default volume level is the current system volume or, typically, a value of **50**.

The **WIDTH** attribute sets the width, in pixels, for the audio controls. You should set this value unless the **HIDDEN** attribute is used. The width for the default console is 144 pixels and should be set explicitly. When the **CONTROLS** attribute is set to **SMALLCONSOLE**, the **WIDTH** attribute should also be set to 144 pixels. If the **CONTROLS** attribute is set to **VOLUMELEVER**, the **WIDTH** attribute should be set to 74 pixels; and if the **CONTROLS** attribute is set to any of the buttons, such as **PLAYBUTTON**, the **WIDTH** attribute should be set to 37 pixels. The values for the **WIDTH** attribute are summarized in Table 9-2.

CONTROLS Setting	Suggested WIDTH Value	Suggested HEIGHT Value
CONSOLE (default)	144	60
SMALLCONSOLE	144	15
VOLUMELEVER	74	20
PLAYBUTTON	37	22
PAUSEBUTTON	37	22
STOPBUTTON	37	22

Table 9-2. *Suggested **HEIGHT** and **WIDTH** values for LiveAudio*

The **HEIGHT** attribute is used to set the height, in pixels, for the audio controls. As with the **WIDTH** attribute, you should make sure to set this value, unless the **HIDDEN** attribute is used. The height for the default console is 60 pixels, while the small console is only 15 pixels high. Each button, such as the Play button, is 22 pixels up and down, and the volume lever has a height of 22 pixels. All the suggested **HEIGHT** values are summarized in Table 9-2.

The **ALIGN** attribute acts just like the **ALIGN** attribute for the **<IMG>** element. The **CONTROLS** attribute sets the type of control objects to include for the sound file. By default, the value of the **CONTROLS** attribute is set to **CONSOLE**, which includes a volume lever, Play button, and Stop button. If space is an issue, the **CONTROLS** value can be set to **SMALLCONSOLE**, which provides the same functionality in much less space. Each button—including the **PLAYBUTTON**, **PAUSEBUTTON**, and **STOPBUTTON**—can be set independently, as can the **VOLUMELEVEL**.

The **HIDDEN** value can be set to **true** if the page author wants the audio file to act as a background sound. The user can't control the sound if this attribute is set to **true**. When **HIDDEN** is set, **HEIGHT** and **WIDTH** attributes are unnecessary. By default, the **HIDDEN** attribute is set to **false**.

The **NAME** attribute is used to group together a set of individual controls that control one sound. The attribute value must be a unique identifier for all the controls. For example, the group could be called SoundGroup1. All the **<EMBED>** elements that reference the same sound should then have their **NAME** attribute value set to **SoundGroup1**. One particular **<EMBED>** occurrence must be set to be the "master sound" by setting an attribute **MASTERSOUND**, which requires no value. The master sound must point to a real sound file. However, the other occurrences of the **<EMBED>** element within the group need to point only to a dummy sound file, called a *stub file* in the Netscape documentation. The stub file is simply a file that is named appropriately to look like a sound file (for example, stub1.wav). The file itself doesn't need to contain any information, and can be a blank text file, as long as it has the appropriate name. This is somewhat of a hack but is required for the LiveAudio plug-in to work, because it must see a value for the **SRC** attribute. While it isn't obvious what use the **NAME** and **MASTERSOUND** attributes might have, the following HTML example shows how a small page could be built that uses three buttons separately to control the same sound:

```
<!DOCTYPE HTML PUBLIC "-//W3C//DTD HTML 4.0 Transitional//EN">
<HTML>
<HEAD>
<TITLE>LiveAudio Control Group Example</TITLE>
</HEAD>

<BODY>
<H1 ALIGN="CENTER">LiveAudio</H1>
<HR>

<EMBED SRC="sound1.wav" CONTROLS="PLAYBUTTON" HEIGHT="22"
       WIDTH="37" NAME="SoundGroup1" MASTERSOUND
       ALIGN="MIDDLE">

<B> -- Press this button to play the sound.</B><BR>

<EMBED SRC="stub1.wav" CONTROLS="STOPBUTTON" HEIGHT="22"
       WIDTH="37" NAME="SoundGroup1" ALIGN="MIDDLE">

<B> -- Press this button to stop the sound.</B><BR>

<EMBED SRC="stub2.wav"
       CONTROLS="PAUSEBUTTON" HEIGHT="22" WIDTH="37"
       NAME="SoundGroup1" ALIGN="MIDDLE">

<B> -- Press this button to pause the sound.</B><BR>
</BODY>
</HTML>
```

Importantly, you should not point all the **SRC** attributes for the stub files to the same dummy file. The stubs must be unique filenames and must all exist, though they may have a zero length. You can simply create blank text files and rename them stub1.wav and stub2.wav. A rendering of the last example is shown in Figure 9-2.

Note   *Under some versions of Netscape, this example may have rendering problems, even though the sound and groups will still work.*

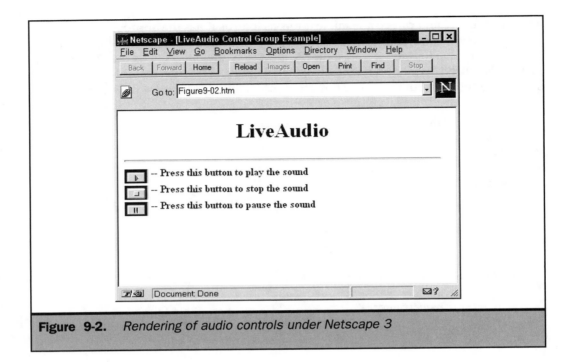

Figure 9-2.   *Rendering of audio controls under Netscape 3*

By dividing up the controls, the page author has more possibilities for integrating the audio control into the page without resorting to programming. However, the real power with the **NAME** attribute comes with the introduction of LiveConnect and other forms of DHTML. With JavaScript, you can create new buttons to control sound playing, defer sounds to play later, and play sound when clicked.

Although Netscape's LiveAudio isn't an official standard by any means, it is common enough that it could be used carefully within a Netscape environment. In a most basic form, it is also possible to support both Netscape and Microsoft browsers with LiveAudio itself or with Microsoft-specific elements, such as **<BGSOUND>**, discussed next.

Microsoft's **<BGSOUND>**

Microsoft Internet Explorer 2 and later supports WAV and MIDI files with the **<BGSOUND>** element, which plays a sound in the background after it is loaded. The user has no control over the volume or the playback of the sound, which can be annoying. The element takes an **SRC** attribute that is set to the URL of the sound file to play. A **LOOP** attribute, which can be set to an integer value indicating how many times the sound should play, is also available. The **LOOP** attribute can also be set to the value **infinite**, to keep playing over and over. A simple example to play a sound called test.wav two times under Internet Explorer could be written as **<BGSOUND SRC="test.wav" LOOP="2">**.

The **<BGSOUND>** element also supports other attributes, such as **TITLE**; but, currently, the support of programming for the **<BGSOUND>** element under Dynamic HTML is not well developed. While this element is in fairly heavy use, other approaches are suggested, particularly with Microsoft taking a more standards-oriented approach. Microsoft also supports the ActiveMovie format that can be used to insert sound-only movies. (See the section "Microsoft's ActiveMovie," later in this chapter.)

Cross-Browser Background Sounds

You can include both the **<BGSOUND>** and Netscape LiveAudio syntax in one page, as follows:

```
<EMBED SRC="test.wav" HIDDEN="TRUE" AUTOSTART="true">
<BGSOUND SRC="test.wav" LOOP="2">
```

In this case, Internet Explorer should ignore the first statement, while Netscape should ignore the second. Note that using JavaScript to control which form is inserted into the document is preferable. With both forms of sound support enabled, conflicts can occur, so page authors are advised to test their documents thoroughly.

Proprietary Audio Formats

Many proprietary audio formats exist, including RealAudio, ToolVox, TrueSpeech, and others. Of these, RealAudio is by far the most popular. But why use RealAudio if audio is built into the browser? Proprietary audio formats offer one thing that many standard digital audio formats lack: the possibility of *streaming data*. As a rule of thumb, a 28.8Kbps modem user receives approximately 2K of data per second. If one second of sound could be represented in 2K, and the data could get to the end user at a rate of 2K every second, then the data would effectively *stream*, or play in real time. Streaming seems to make a whole lot of sense. Why wait for an hour-long speech to download before playing when you care only about the current second of data being listened to? Streamed data doesn't take up hard drive space, and it opens up random access to any position in an audio file. However, streaming audio has a few potential serious drawbacks. First, to compress audio far enough for streaming, you have to sacrifice a certain degree of sound quality. Second, the Internet protocols themselves do not readily support the requirements of streaming.

Why the Internet and Streaming Don't Mix

As you may know, the Internet is frequently subject to bursts and traffic delays. Here are a couple of key points to remember. The TCP/IP protocols used on the Internet were designed for robustness and scalability. The Internet is a packet-switched network that breaks up data into little chunks and sends them separately, to be reassembled at the other end. Because these packets may be lost along their journeys or arrive out of order, the *Transmission Control Protocol (TCP)* guarantees the integrity of the data. This way, many users can share a fixed circuit that allows for economies of scale. However, packet-switched networks have one serious problem—they can't guarantee delivery time without special modifications. This makes streamed audio, video, and other "real time" applications on packet-switched networks very difficult.

Packet-switched networks can be augmented with protocols such as *Real Time Transport Protocol (RTP)* and *Resource Reservation Setup Protocol (RSVP)*, which help guarantee delivery times by making a bandwidth reservation, when needed. These protocols can improve real-time data delivery, but they are not widely supported yet. They also raise the question of how to limit reservations, because a user would always want reservations in order to have maximum bandwidth. Some experts argue that once these protocols are in place, fee structures based on bandwidth will become commonplace. For the moment, this is pure speculation, because the various real-time protocols are still very much in the developmental stages. Another solution to real-time data on the Internet is necessary.

One potential solution to real-time data on the Internet is really just an assumption—you hope the end user has the end-to-end bandwidth to receive the file in real time. (Remember the 2K per second rule for 28.8Kbps modems.) If audio compression can get one second of data to fit within those ranges, real-time data can be served to 28.8Kbps users—when the assumption holds. When the assumption doesn't hold, a glitch called a *drop-out* occurs in the audio stream. If too much drop-out occurs, the user turns off the audio stream.

One way to avoid drop-out is to *buffer* data. This process gives you a head start by preloading a certain amount of data into a buffer, so that rough spots can be overcome. An initial buffering delay of 10 or 15 seconds is acceptable for long audio clips; buffering short sounds is counterproductive. Many Internet audio solutions use a combination of intensive compression, buffering, and some level of bandwidth assumption to achieve streaming. More-complex audio solutions use servers to control the process. Both approaches to streaming audio have their pros and cons.

RealAudio

The first—and still the most popular—approach to streaming audio was developed by RealNetworks. RealAudio (http://www.real.com) uses a special server to send continuous audio data to a browser helper application, Netscape plug-in, Shockwave Xtra, or ActiveX control. With players available for all major platforms, RealAudio is the most common streaming audio format on the Internet. Putting data in RealAudio format is fairly easy if the files exist in WAV or other common audio formats. Simply use the RealAudio production tools, which can be downloaded from RealNetworks, and the data is ready to publish. But despite RealAudio's wide support, it has certain drawbacks, which mostly revolve around the use of a special server.

Servers can provide a higher degree of control. For example, they can limit or control the number of audio streams delivered and allow for easy access to specified points in an audio stream. With simpler "serverless" audio-streaming solutions, the virtual fast forward button provided by random access is sacrificed. Some sophisticated servers could potentially upgrade data quality as bandwidth becomes available. Less-complex systems give the same quality of data, regardless of the end-to-end access speed.

Server-based systems are expensive and require computing resources beyond the basic Web server. RealAudio-based streaming audio servers have a per-stream cost for high-end sites that keeps some users from adopting this solution. Fortunately, entry-level RealAudio systems with a few streams are still free or very inexpensive. Already, many organizations are using the RealAudio platform, which is a testament to the quality of the system.

Note   *One technical problem with RealAudio that bothers many users is that the server sends audio data by using the User Datagram Protocol (UDP) rather than the more common and reliable TCP protocol that is used for standard Internet data transmission. UDP is fast and helps provide data to the end user quickly, but lost packets are much more common with UDP. To get around lost packets, RealAudio data is delivered in an interleaved fashion, so that single drop-outs are not noticeable. Although UDP may help avoid TCP's link-use problems, when mixed with a firewall, RealAudio's UDP link becomes a liability. Most firewalls filter out UDP, so people accessing the Internet through a firewall may find it difficult, if not impossible, to access a UDP-based service such as RealAudio.*

From an HTML point of view, using RealAudio is really no different from using LiveAudio or any other plug-in. Similar to LiveAudio, the **SRC** attribute can be set to a RealAudio file ending in .ram. The appearance of the player, as well as how the sound should start, is also configurable using a variety of other attributes. A portion of the RealAudio syntax is shown here. Note that this syntax changes rapidly. An **<OBJECT>**-based syntax is also available for Internet Explorer support.

```
<EMBED
      SRC="URL of RealAudio stream or file"
      AUTOSTART="true | false"
      CONTROLS="ALL | ControlPanel | InfoVolumePanel | InfoPanel |
               StatusBar | PlayButton | StopButton | VolumeSlider |
               PositionSlider | PositionField | StatusField"
      HEIGHT="pixels or percentage"
      NAME="identifier for sound file"
      WIDTH="pixels or percentage">
```

The following lists and describes the key attributes in the preceding RealAudio syntax:

■ **SRC**   Sets the source of the RealAudio clip. The **SRC** should be set to a URL, which can be in the form of a full URL using the pnm:, file:, or http: protocol; or it can be a relative URL to the appropriate file type. This is required.

■ **CONTROLS**   Sets the visible control components of the player in a similar manner to LiveAudio. The default value is **ALL**, but the attribute also individually controls the aspects **ControlPanel**, **InfoVolumePanel**, **InfoPanel**, **StatusBar**, **PlayButton**, **StopButton**, **VolumeSlider**, **PositionSlider**, **PositionField**, and **StatusField**.

- **NAME**   Specifies the identifier associated with the RealAudio plug-in and clip. This value can then be used to reference and control the clip from Java, JavaScript, or other programming technologies.

- **HEIGHT**   Sets the height, in pixels, of the control panel used.

- **WIDTH**   Sets the width, in pixels, of the control panel used.

- **AUTOSTART**   Sets whether or not the RealAudio plug-in automatically starts playing once the source data is available. Valid values for this attribute are **true** and **false**.

Provided that the user has access to the appropriate audio stream, using a proprietary audio technology such as RealAudio is no more difficult than using LiveAudio. For more specific information about how to use RealAudio technology, see RealNetworks' Web site (http://www.real.com).

Sound Conclusions

The future of audio on the Internet ultimately lies in integration. People will resist downloading dozens of plug-ins for numerous data formats. They prefer single technologies that integrate into one whole presentation, such as animation or video with sound, because the uses of background music on the Internet are limited. While more advanced technologies such as RealAudio allow simple embedding of URLs and other forms of synchronization, a controlled environment is required. With programming technologies such as JavaScript and Macromedia's Shockwave or Flash, which have streaming audio support, full integration is available.

Adding sound to a Web site shouldn't be an infuriating experience for Webmasters or Web users. Using a simple download-and-play sound format built into a browser might be better than streaming data that requires special encoding or download of a special plug-in. If streaming is required, RealAudio is probably the best bet (if it's affordable). For a complete Web page solution requiring tight integration between technologies, Shockwave or Flash with streaming audio is the only choice beyond some custom integration using programming technologies such as JavaScript. Regardless of how sound is included, don't expect CD quality for Internet-based audio. And remember: a little sound can go a long way.

Video Support

The holy grail of Internet multimedia is certainly high-quality, 30-frames-per-second, real-time video. Many companies are working toward the idea of television on the Web, but most of their solutions just don't work well within the bandwidth limitations faced by the average Internet user. Sooner or later, video will be used extensively on Web pages—but what Web video technology, if any, is appropriate for the job and how can video be accessed via HTML? The latest Internet video technologies range from low-quality streaming audio with an occasional picture to traditional download-and-play systems for a variety of file formats. As with audio, the most popular technologies—and the most advanced—may not offer the best solutions for simple Web video needs.

Digital Video Basics

Digital video is measured by the number of frames per second of video, and by the size and resolution of these frames. The total size requirement for video is huge, particularly if you want NTSC (TV-quality) video. A 640 × 480 image with 24 bits of data representation for color and a frame rate of 30 frames per second takes up a staggering 27MB per second—and that's without sound. Add CD-quality audio (705,600 bits of data for each second of data) and the file size increases proportionately. In theory, the bits of data necessary to deliver TV-quality video could be transmitted over the Internet, creating the long-sought-after interactive TV. In the real world, transmitting this amount of data generally isn't feasible, even after compression.

One approach to video on the Internet is breathtakingly simple: just don't do it. A simple frame of movement every once in a while or a static picture with continuous audio can provide the illusion required for simple "talking head" applications. Frame rates and image size can be reduced enough to make download sizes seem plausible, but even a simple slide show with audio narration is nearly impossible to do in real time without compression.

Video File Formats and Compression

Like audio files, video files can be compressed to reduce the amount of data being sent. Because of the degree of compression required by video, most video codecs use a lossy approach that involves a trade-off between picture/sound quality and file size, with larger file sizes obviously resulting in longer download times.

Three standardized video file formats are used on the Web: AVI, QuickTime, and MPEG, as summarized in Table 9-3. The file format usually determines which compression technique is used. However, some file formats, such as QuickTime, allow different codecs to be selected. In some ways, this makes QuickTime the most flexible video format.

For download-and-play delivery, AVI and QuickTime are the safest formats for short video clips. Regardless of length, MPEG is typically the only choice for high-quality playback. AVI and QuickTime files are commonly supported via helper applications. They're even supported natively by many modern Web browsers in a download-and-play style.

Waiting for Video

As with audio, many online video delivery systems follow the download-and-play model, whereby users must download video clips completely before they can play

Video Format	Description
AVI	*Audio Video Interleaved.* The Video for Windows file format for digital video and audio is very common and easy to specify. A growing number of video files in AVI format are being used on the Internet, but file size of AVI is significant. Both Netscape and Internet Explorer are capable of dealing with AVIs easily.
MOV (QuickTime)	*Movie.* MOV is the extension that indicates the use of Apple's QuickTime format. Probably the most common digital video format, it continues its popularity on the Internet. QuickTime has a strong following in the multimedia development community. Various codecs and technology enhancements make QuickTime a strong digital video solution that may work in conjunction with MPEG.
MPEG	*Motion Picture Experts Group* video format is generally considered the standard format for digital video. Although compression and image quality of MPEG files are impressive, this format can be expensive and difficult to work with.

Table 9-3.   *Standard Internet Video Formats*

them. Some Web video solutions enable the user to see the video as it downloads, despite the slow speed; this allows users to cancel the download before it ends. Shortening video clips and reducing frame rates help users from giving up during download time, but these techniques may not be acceptable for content that requires flawless playback. Even at very low frame rates with no audio, video clips that are more than a few seconds long tend to exceed the patience of the average user. With download-and-play video, you should stick to common formats (such as AVI, QuickTime, or MPEG), unless the proprietary format has a wide degree of industry acceptance or provides a really motivating feature, such as compression that is high enough to allow streaming.

LiveVideo

Netscape's LiveVideo plug-in, which was introduced with Netscape 3, supports AVI on Windows. The plug-in is rather simplistic and doesn't even include controls to show, pause, or rewind a video, let alone any sort of volume control. The user must click the embedded video to start it, unless the video has an auto-play feature enabled. The basic syntax for the **<EMBED>** element as related to LiveVideo is shown here:

```
<EMBED
        SRC="URL of video file"
        ALIGN="top | bottom | center | baseline | left | right | texttop
              |middle | absmiddle | absbottom"
        AUTOSTART="true | false"
        HEIGHT="pixels or percentage"
        HSPACE="pixels"
        LOOP="true | false"
        VSPACE="pixels"
        WIDTH="pixels or percentage">
```

The following lists and describes the key attributes in the preceding syntax:

- **SRC**   Must be set to the URL of a valid AVI file.

- **ALIGN**   Acts similarly to the same attribute for the **<IMG>** element and accepts the same values.

- **AUTOSTART**   Can be set to **true** to begin play immediately after the entire AVI file downloads. The default is **false** and thus requires the user to click the video to begin its play.

- **HEIGHT**   Specifies the pixel height of the video. This attribute also takes a percentage value.

- **HSPACE**   Creates around an image a horizontal buffer region of a specified number of pixels.

- **LOOP**   Can be set to **true** to loop the video continuously (the default is **false**). Currently, no way exists to set the plug-in to loop the video a particular number of times, which seems a likely modification to this attribute.

- **VSPACE**   Can be set to a pixel value to create a vertical buffer area above and below the embedded media.

- **WIDTH**   Is set to either a pixel value or a screen percentage to specify the width of the embedded AVI file.

The following is a brief example of how LiveVideo is used to include an AVI video in a page; a rendering of the example is shown in Figure 9-3:

```
<!DOCTYPE HTML PUBLIC "-//W3C//DTD HTML 4.0 Transitional//EN">
<HTML>
<HEAD>
<TITLE>LiveVideo Rendering Under Netscape</TITLE>
```

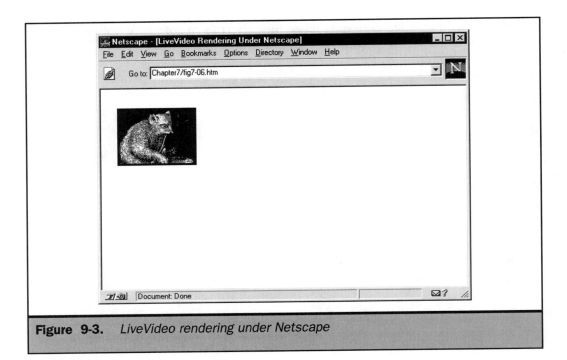

Figure 9-3. *LiveVideo rendering under Netscape*

```
<BODY>
<EMBED SRC="critter.avi" LOOP="TRUE" AUTOSTART="TRUE" HEIGHT="90"
       WIDTH="120" ALIGN="LEFT" HSPACE="15" VSPACE="15">
</BODY>
</HTML>
```

QuickTime

QuickTime videos offer a lot more benefits than simply tending to be smaller than AVI files. QuickTime is designed to provide the framework for the synchronization of time-based data in a variety of formats, including video, sound, MIDI, and even text. An interesting aspect of QuickTime is that it can work with different video compression codecs, such as Cinepack, Indeo, MPEG, and even exotic fractal compression codecs. By itself, QuickTime with standard Cinepack encoding lacks the small file size of MPEG or proprietary video files, but the quality of QuickTime files is high. Creating or editing QuickTime files is also relatively easy when using tools such as the popular Adobe Premiere package.

Starting with Netscape 3, QuickTime is supported in Macintosh and Windows versions of Netscape. Although the plug-in is available on both systems, Windows users are required to install QuickTime services for their operating systems. The way to include QuickTime media into a Web page is similar to the way in which you include LiveVideo support. Keep in mind, however, that QuickTime provides support for many forms of media and is really more of a generic media architecture than AVI.

The basic syntax for the **<EMBED>** statement for the Netscape QuickTime plug-in is shown here:

```
<EMBED
        SRC="URL of QuickTime object"
        ALIGN="top | bottom | center | baseline | left |
                right | texttop | middle | absmiddle | absbottom"
        AUTOPLAY="true | false"
        CACHE="true | false"
        CONTROLLER="true | false"
        CORRECTION="none | partial | full"    (QuickTime VR Only)
        FOV="5.0 to 85.0"                      (QuickTime VR Only)
        HEIGHT="pixels or percentage"
        HIDDEN
        HOTSPOT hotspot-id="URL of page to load"
        HREF="URL of page to load"
        HSPACE="pixels"
        LOOP="true | false | palindrome"
        NODE="node number"                     (QuickTime VR Only)
        PAN="0.0 to 360.0"                     (QuickTime VR Only)
        PLUGINSPAGE="URL of page with plug-in information"
        PLAYEVERYFRAME="true | false"
        TARGET="valid frame name"
        TILT="-42.5 to 42.5"                   (QuickTime VR Only)
        VOLUME="0 - 256"
        VSPACE="pixels"
        WIDTH="pixels or percentage">
```

The following lists and describes the key attributes in the preceding syntax:

- **SRC**   Required, and should be set to the URL of a valid QuickTime file.

- **ALIGN**   Acts similarly to same attribute for the **<IMG>** element and accepts the same values.

- **AUTOPLAY**   Can be set to **true** or **false** (default); indicates whether the movie should be played as soon as possible. Attribute has no meaning when embedding a QuickTime VR (Virtual Reality) file.

- **CACHE**   Can be set to **true** or **false**. Providing the attribute by itself implies a **true** value. Under Netscape 3 and above, a **CACHE** value of **true** causes the browser to treat the information just like other information and keep it in a local disk cache, so that it does not need to be downloaded again. When set to **false**, the movie must be downloaded again.

- **CONTROLLER**   Can be set to **true** or **false**; determines whether the movie controller is visible. The controller provides standard stop, play, pause, rewind, frame selection, and volume controls. The controller is 24 pixels high, so the **HEIGHT** value should be set to account for this. By default, the value of **CONTROLLER** generally is set to **true**, unless a QuickTime VR file is being embedded. The QuickTime VR object does not use the same style of controls.

- **CORRECTION**   Can be set to **NONE**, **PARTIAL**, or **FULL** (default); used to set the display correction for a QuickTime VR object. Has no meaning beyond a QuickTime VR scene.

- **FOV**   Specifies the initial field of view angle for a QuickTime movie. Typical values for this attribute range from **5.0** to **85.0** degrees. Has no meaning outside of QuickTime VR objects.

- **HEIGHT**   Set like the **WIDTH** attribute, with a pixel value or percentage. The value specifies the **HEIGHT** of the object and is cropped or expanded in the same method as **WIDTH**. For example, if a supplied height is greater than the movie's height, the movie is centered within this height. If the value is smaller, the object is cropped. Avoid values of **0** or **1** for the **HEIGHT** attribute, because they may cause unpredictable results. Be aware that controls for the movie are 24 pixels high, which must be added to the **HEIGHT** value for the object to display properly.

- **HIDDEN**   Takes no parameters and its presence determines whether the movie should be visible. By default, the **HIDDEN** value is **off**. In most cases, such as embedding a QuickTime video or QuickTime VR object, this is not an appropriate attribute to use. However, if a sound-only movie is being inserted, this can provide a background sound-like function, assuming that **AUTOPLAY** has been set to **true**. The **HIDDEN** attribute typically sets the **CONTROLLER** attribute to **false**; but, to make sure, the attribute can be set directly by the page author.

- **HOTSPOT**   Comes in a strange format. By setting the hot spot identifier to a URL, you can link the hot spot to a Web object. Hot spots in a movie can be defined by using a QuickTime VR authoring tool. Attribute makes sense only within a QuickTime panorama.

- **HREF**   Indicates the URL of a page to load when the movie is clicked. The meaning of this attribute is somewhat troublesome if the **CONTROLLER** attribute is set to **false**. The problem revolves around the click having two meanings, one to start the movie and the other to go to the page. Page authors should either use the autoplay feature or provide controls when using this attribute. This attribute is not appropriate when using QuickTime VR objects that may have included their own hot links.

- **HSPACE**   Sets the horizontal pixel buffer for the plug-in and acts the same way as the **HSPACE** attribute for the **<IMG>** element.

■ **LOOP**   Indicates whether the movie should play in a looped fashion. Setting the attribute to **true** loops the movie until the user stops it. The default value is **false**. When the **LOOP** value is set to **PALINDROME**, the movie loops back and forth. Setting this value produces interesting effects with movies and even reverses the soundtrack. This parameter is not appropriate for QuickTime VR objects, because they have no distinct time order.

■ **NODE**   An optional attribute that has meaning to a multinode QuickTime VR movie. In many QuickTime VR situations, setting multiple areas or viewpoints, called *nodes,* is desirable. Setting the **NODE** attribute to the integer value of a node in the scene loads the movie at the particular scene. This attribute has no meaning for non-QuickTime VR objects.

■ **PAN**   An optional attribute for QuickTime VR objects; allows the author to specify the initial pan angle in degrees. The range for the **PAN** attribute is between 0 and 360 degrees. This attribute has no meaning for other forms of QuickTime objects.

■ **PLAYEVERYFRAME**   Can be set to either **true** or **false**. When set to **true**, instructs the plug-in to play every frame, even if it requires the movie to play at a slower rate. In some sense, this is appropriate in case the processor drops frames that may be valuable. Setting this value to **true** is not advisable for movies with audio tracks; it has the side-effect of turning off the sound. Furthermore, this attribute should not be used when embedding QuickTime VR objects.

■ **PLUGINSPAGE**   Sets the URL of the page that contains information about the required plug-in and how it can be downloaded and installed, if it is not currently installed. This feature is supported by Netscape; it is also documented to work under Internet Explorer. Be careful when using this attribute. It generally should be set to http://quicktime.apple.com, unless special instructions are included beyond standard QuickTime information.

■ **SCALE**   Takes a value of **TOFIT**, **ASPECT**, or a number corresponding to the desired scaling factor, such as **1.5**. The default **SCALE** value is **1**, which is a normally scaled movie. Setting the attribute to **ASPECT** scales the movie to fit the bounding box set by the **HEIGHT** and **WIDTH** attributes. A value of **TOFIT** scales the movie to fit the **HEIGHT** and **WIDTH** attribute, with no regard to aspect ratio. Be careful when scaling movies, because it may degrade the playback performance and image quality.

■ **TARGET**   Used in conjunction with the **HREF** attribute to set the name of a frame into which to load the page indicated by the **HREF** attribute. The normal reserved frame names, such as _blank, as well as explicitly named frames are available as valid targets. More information on frames can be found in Chapter 8.

■ **TILT**   Can be set when using QuickTime VR objects to specify the initial tilt angle (up or down) for the scene. The value of the attribute is specified in degrees and typically ranges from around **–42.5** to **42.5** degrees. The parameter has no meaning outside of QuickTime VR objects.

- **VOLUME** Can be set to a value from **0** to **256**. The higher the value, the louder the audio track on the QuickTime movie. A value of **0** effectively mutes the soundtrack, whereas **256** sets the volume at the maximum level. If the attribute is not set, the default is **256**. This option does not have meaning with QuickTime VR. This is a newer attribute and will not be supported under older versions of the QuickTime plug-in.

- **VSPACE** Set to the number of vertical pixels to buffer between the embedded object and surrounding content. Used in the same way as the corresponding attribute for the **<IMG>** element.

- **WIDTH** Set to a pixel value or percentage. Be aware that the plug-in may not necessarily stretch the video image to take up the space. As mentioned previously, setting the **SCALE** attribute to **ASPECT** scales the movie to fit the bounding box set by the **HEIGHT** and **WIDTH** attributes. If the value supplied for the object width is smaller than the object's true width, it is cropped to fit the dimensions provided. The **WIDTH** value must be set, unless the **HIDDEN** attribute is used. Be careful when using small widths, such as 0 and 1 pixels, because this can cause problems.

The QuickTime plug-in for Netscape is quite complex. The following example illustrates only the most basic use of the plug-in, a rendering of which is shown in Figure 9-4:

```
<!DOCTYPE HTML PUBLIC "-//W3C//DTD HTML 4.0 Transitional//EN">
<HTML>
<TITLE>QuickTime Support Under Netscape</TITLE>

<BODY>
<FONT SIZE="4">This example shows a frame from a promotional
clip for QuickTime, as viewed in a Netscape browser.</FONT>

<EMBED SRC="quicktime.mov" WIDTH="180" HEIGHT="178"
       AUTOPLAY="TRUE" ALIGN="LEFT" HSPACE="12" VSPACE="20">
</BODY>
</HTML>
```

Interested readers should check Apple's QuickTime site, which is located at http://www.quicktime.apple.com, for more information about using QuickTime and QuickTime VR on the Web.

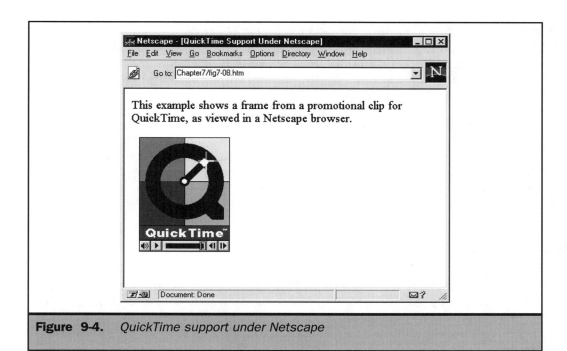

Figure 9-4.   *QuickTime support under Netscape*

Microsoft's ActiveMovie

Microsoft's media technology comes under many guises, but the main effort is called
ActiveMovie. It provides services for the playback of multimedia streams from local files
or network-based servers. Specifically, ActiveMovie allows playback of video and
audio content, compressed in various formats. ActiveMovie supports the following
formats:

- MPEG-1 and MPEG-2 (.mpg, .mpeg, .mpv, .mp2, .mpa)
- Audio Video Interleaved (.avi)
- Nonproprietary QuickTime files (.mov)
- Wave (.wav)
- AU (.au, .snd)
- AIFF (.aif, .aiff)

> **Note**   *If QuickTime is already available on a system, ActiveMovie keeps existing relationships. This is particularly useful because ActiveMovie doesn't support proprietary QuickTime features, such as QuickTime VR. However, you may find that ActiveMovie (as well as other video technologies) occasionally overrides existing file relationships, which may make viewing movies difficult.*

ActiveMovie-supported files can be played in one of two ways: either embedded within a Web page or externally, in a window displayed separately. External support of active content is handled through use of a linked object with the **<A>** element, as discussed earlier in the chapter. However, the following are the three HTML elements that you can use to embed ActiveMovie content:

```
<OBJECT>
<EMBED>
<IMG DYNSRC="movie.avi">
```

ACTIVEMOVIE WITH THE OBJECT ELEMENT   Using the **<OBJECT>** element, the **CLASSID** attribute must be set to the appropriate ActiveMovie class identifier (**CLSID**) so that a control to be used for playback is specified. The following short code fragment sets this control explicitly and uses the **<PARAM>** element to specify the address of the file to play:

```
<OBJECT CLASSID="CLSID:05589FA1-C356-11CE-BF01-00AA0055595A">
   <PARAM NAME="FileName" VALUE="test.avi">
</OBJECT>
```

The **CLASSID** value should not be entered by hand unless absolutely necessary. This may change some day, though it is very unlikely. The various **PARAM** values that can be set for the **<OBJECT>** element are too numerous to discuss. As discussed earlier in the chapter, a tool such as Microsoft's ControlPad should be used to set the **PARAM** values. To illustrate, some sample parameter values are shown here:

```
<OBJECT ID="TestMovie " HEIGHT="200" WIDTH="200"
        CLASSID="CLSID:05589FA1-C356-11CE-BF01-00AA0055595A">
   <PARAM NAME="Version" VALUE="1">
   <PARAM NAME="EnableContextMenu" VALUE="-1">
   <PARAM NAME="ShowDisplay" VALUE="-1">
   <PARAM NAME="ShowControls" VALUE="-1">
   <PARAM NAME="ShowPositionControls" VALUE="0">
   <PARAM NAME="ShowSelectionControls" VALUE="0">
   <PARAM NAME="EnablePositionControls" VALUE="-1">
```

```
        <PARAM NAME="EnableSelectionControls" VALUE="-1">
        <PARAM NAME="ShowTracker" VALUE="-1">
        <PARAM NAME="EnableTracker" VALUE="-1">
        <PARAM NAME="AllowHideDisplay" VALUE="-1">
        <PARAM NAME="AllowHideControls" VALUE="-1">
        <PARAM NAME="MovieWindowSize" VALUE="0">
        <PARAM NAME="FullScreenMode" VALUE="0">
        <PARAM NAME="MovieWindowWidth" VALUE="200">
        <PARAM NAME="MovieWindowHeight" VALUE="200">
        <PARAM NAME="AutoStart" VALUE="0">
        <PARAM NAME="AutoRewind" VALUE="-1">
        <PARAM NAME="PlayCount" VALUE="1">
        <PARAM NAME="Appearance" VALUE="1">
        <PARAM NAME="BorderStyle" VALUE="1">
        <PARAM NAME="FileName"
                VALUE="http://www.bigcompany.com/movies/test.mpg">
        <PARAM NAME="DisplayMode" VALUE="0">
        <PARAM NAME="AllowChangeDisplayMode" VALUE="-1">
        <PARAM NAME="DisplayForeColor" VALUE="16777215">
        <PARAM NAME="DisplayBackColor" VALUE="0">
</OBJECT>
```

USING THE <EMBED> ELEMENT   You can also insert an ActiveMovie file by using the Netscape-style **<EMBED>** syntax. The **<EMBED>** element works identically to the **<OBJECT>** element when used with Internet Explorer 3 or greater, because the browser simply figures out what the content is and launches the ActiveMovie control with the appropriate parameters. An example of using ActiveMovie is shown here:

```
<EMBED SRC="test.avi" AUTOSTART="FALSE" LOOP="FALSE" HEIGHT="100"
       WIDTH="100">
```

If ActiveMovie is available, this HTML fragment works under both Netscape and Internet Explorer. Microsoft pushes the **<OBJECT>** element, and the HTML 4.0 specification favors this syntax. Nevertheless, for the time being, to guarantee support across browsers, you should enclose an **EMBED** element inside of the **<OBJECT>** element, to allow for fallback.

USING THE <IMG> ELEMENT WITH THE DYNSRC ATTRIBUTE   The **DYNSRC** attribute for the **<IMG>** element originated in Internet Explorer 2 and allowed AVI files to be played within a Web page. Although the syntax is currently maintained for backward compatibility, using the **<OBJECT>** or **<EMBED>** elements is preferable.

Originally, the **DYNSRC** attribute supported only AVI files, but testing shows that any ActiveMovie-supported data can be included with this syntax. The basic attributes for **<IMG>** are all valid; however, the following additions are also available:

- This attribute should be set to the URL, either relative or absolute, of the content to play.

  ```
  DYNSRC="URL of Active content"
  ```

- If this attribute is present, controls are presented below the content, if possible. The attribute does not need a value.

  ```
  CONTROLS
  ```

- This attribute is used to set the number of times to loop the included content. When set to a positive integer, the content loops the specified number of times. When set to –1 or the keyword **INFINITE**, the content loops continuously.

  ```
  LOOP="value"
  ```

- This attribute to the **<IMG>** element is used with **DYNSRC** to specify how the content should be played. Setting the value to **FILEOPEN** plays the content as soon as the data file has finished opening. Setting the value equal to **MOUSEOVER** delays playing the content until the mouse is positioned over it. The default action for active content is **FILEOPEN**.

  ```
  START=FILEOPEN | MOUSEOVER
  ```

An example of using the **DYNSRC** attribute with the image element for an AVI movie is shown here. Figure 9-5 shows the rendering of the example under Internet Explorer 4.

```
<!DOCTYPE HTML PUBLIC "-//W3C//DTD HTML 4.0 Transitional//EN">
<HTML>
<HEAD>
<TITLE>DYNSRC Viewed Under Internet Explorer</TITLE>
</HEAD>

<BODY>
<FONT SIZE="4">
```

```
This example shows use of the DYNSRC element, with the CONTROL
attribute, as viewed in an Internet Explorer browser.</FONT>

<IMG SRC="critter.gif" DYNSRC="critter.avi" CONTROLS ALIGN="left"
     VSPACE="20">
</BODY>
</HTML>
```

In terms of browser support, it is difficult to come up with a best bet for simple Web video. Netscape 3 and Internet Explorer both support AVI in their Windows incarnations, but Macintosh users don't even get a consolation prize. For QuickTime, Internet Explorer and Netscape for Windows users without QuickTime installed on their operating systems are left out in the cold. AVI apparently might be less of a problem, but the size and synchronization quality of AVI video files makes the format far from ideal. In some sense, you probably should stick with a video format such as RealVideo, given its wide acceptance and streaming approach.

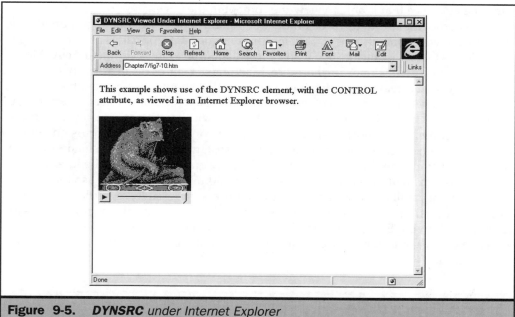

Figure 9-5.   *DYNSRC under Internet Explorer*

Other Video Formats

Like their audio compatriots, proprietary video formats offer one thing that many standard digital video formats lack: the possibility of truly streaming data. Remember that a 28.8Kbps modem user receives approximately 2K of data per second. If one second of video and sound could be represented in 2K, and that data could be delivered to the end user in time to play it, the video could effectively "stream" over the Internet. Still, a few potential drawbacks exist to streaming audio. First, to compress video far enough for streaming, you have to sacrifice a certain degree of quality. Second, the Internet protocols themselves do not readily support the requirements of streaming, as discussed in the section "Audio File Formats and Compression," earlier in this chapter.

The main streaming video format is RealNetworks' RealVideo (http://www.real.com). Like its audio counterpart, this technology uses different attributes with the **<EMBED>** and **<OBJECT>** elements to support RealAudio's own video protocol. Although most video formats share common attributes, such as **HEIGHT** and **WIDTH**, make sure to check the appropriate site for information about the particular syntax to support a proprietary video format. Fortunately, RealNetworks provides a production tool that should insert most of the syntax to handle video.

While proprietary formats may offer many benefits with respect to streaming or image quality, page authors should carefully consider the lack of built-in support before rushing out to use a new technology. Choosing the wrong technology could limit the audience that is able to view the content in the page.

Like audio, the future of video on the Internet ultimately lies in integration. People will resist downloading dozens of plug-ins for numerous data formats. They prefer single technologies that integrate into one whole presentation, and QuickTime and ActiveMovie show how this can be done. Furthermore, Macromedia supports a variety of extras for Shockwave, and integrating video into a presentation should also be possible.

Even with better integration of video into a Web page, compression and performance guarantees will be the key points—unless the bandwidth problem is resolved. More exotic compression technologies, such as fractal or wavelet video compression, will certainly become more commonplace as people struggle to stream the smallest files to users and provide the closest semblance to the holy grail of Web TV. The Internet, however, is a difficult place to broadcast information. With single sites as video stream sources, latency will make streaming to distant users impossible, regardless of how much compression is used. Unless a wide range of video and audio mirror services are deployed, allowing European users the same access to video clips as users in North America or Asia, real-time broadcasting of video on the Internet will remain restricted to a select few.

Other Binary Formats

Besides audio and video, many other data objects can be inserted into a Web page. The most common binary object besides those discussed in this chapter are Adobe Acrobat files, which are cross-platform documents, and Macromedia Shockwave and Flash files, which are complex multimedia files. Both of these technologies can be included in a Web page by using either the **<EMBED>** syntax popularized by Netscape or the **<OBJECT>** syntax to reference an ActiveX control. The **<EMBED>** syntax is the safest until **<OBJECT>** is finally cleared up as the standard way to include a file. Of course, the **<OBJECT>** element syntax enables authors to include an **<EMBED>** element to provide backward compatibility for browsers that don't yet support **<OBJECT>**. Fortunately, obtaining canned scripts is becoming easier, which can provide HTML markup for all the various browser, plug-in, and control situations.

Flash

One of the most popular new media formats on the Internet is Macromedia's Flash (http://www.macromedia.com). The Flash format is a powerful vector-based animation format that includes sound and interactivity. One of the nicest things about the format is that it is very bandwidth friendly.

Creating a Flash file requires using Macromedia's Flash tool. After you assemble the animation, you can save it in the form of a SWF file and reference it from a Web page. To reference a Flash file, you can use the **<EMBED>** syntax to use a Netscape plug-in, as shown in this example:

```
<EMBED SRC="test.swf" swLiveConnect="FALSE" WIDTH="320"
       HEIGHT="240" QUALITY="autohigh" BGCOLOR="#FFFFFF"
       TYPE="application/x-shockwave-flash"
       PLUGINSPAGE="http://www.macromedia.com/shockwave/download/
                    index.cgi?P1_Prod_Version=ShockwaveFlash">

<NOEMBED>
   <IMG SRC="test.gif" HEIGHT="250" WIDTH="320">
</NOEMBED>
```

You also can use the **<OBJECT>** syntax to reference an ActiveX control, as follows:

```
<OBJECT classid="clsid:D27CDB6E-AE6D-11cf-96B8-444553540000"
        codebase="http://active.macromedia.com/flash2/cabs/
                  swflash.cab#version=3,0,0,0"
        ID="test" WIDTH="320" HEIGHT="240">

   <PARAM NAME="movie" VALUE="test.swf">
   <PARAM NAME="quality" VALUE="autohigh">
   <PARAM NAME="bgcolor" VALUE="#FFFFFF">

   <IMG SRC="test.gif" WIDTH="320" HEIGHT="240">
</OBJECT>
```

You can even use an **<APPLET>** tag to reference a Java version of the Flash player, as shown here:

```
<APPLET CODE="Flash.class" ARCHIVE="Flash.jar" WIDTH="320"
        HEIGHT="240">
<APPLET CODE="Flash.class" ARCHIVE="Flash.zip" WIDTH="320"
        HEIGHT="240">
   <PARAM NAME="cabbase" VALUE="Flash.cab"> ');
   <PARAM NAME="movie" VALUE="test.swf"> ');
   <PARAM NAME="quality" VALUE=autohigh> ');
</APPLET>
```

Alternative renderings may be provided, and you can logically assume that forms can be combined to support any situation. Because of the complexity of doing this, Macromedia has created a tool called AfterShock, which outputs the appropriate HTML syntax and JavaScript code to ensure that the Flash file is properly supported in most every situation. A brief discussion of this is presented in Chapter 15, in the section "Cross-Platform Support with Plug-Ins and ActiveX Controls." A rendering of a Flash file in action is shown in Figure 9-6.

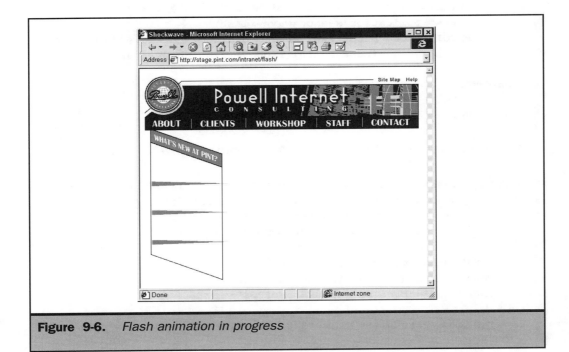

Figure 9-6.   *Flash animation in progress*

> **Note** *Before Flash, the Macromedia Director format, in a compressed form called Shockwave for Director, was very popular. The biggest problem with Director-built animations was that they tended to be very large. While Shockwave for Director files (.dcr) still exist online, they are most appropriate for complex multimedia applications rather than the simple animations and presentations that Flash is often used for. Naming confusion does exist and people seem to use Shockwave and Flash interchangeably at times. They are actually different technologies, though they are merging as time passes.*

If you are interested in adding animation to your Web pages, you should check into Flash, at http://www.macromedia.com/flash. Now that many browsers such as Netscape are shipping with the Flash format, use of this technology should skyrocket.

Acrobat

Adobe's Acrobat technology is one approach to the distribution of electronic documentation. Originally proposed to help implement the mythical ideal of the paperless office, Acrobat has now matured into a product with uses both on and off the Web. Adobe Acrobat provides the capability to deliver an electronic document to an end user without requiring the reader to have the authoring environment to open the file. Visually, Acrobat preserves the exact look and feel of the document, both onscreen and in print. For design-oriented Web publishers, Acrobat provides a highly motivating alternative to HTML that easily surpasses HTML's relatively simplistic and imprecise layout features, as shown in Figure 9-7.

Acrobat files are created by using a combination of traditional text authoring tools (word processors and desktop publishing software) and special Acrobat authoring software (Adobe Exchange or Distiller). The files are then saved in a file format aptly named *Portable Document Format*, or *PDF*. PDF files are small, self-contained documents that can be transported in a variety of ways: via disk, CD-ROM, or network. The end user then reads the files by using special Adobe Acrobat Reader software. Thus, by its very nature, Acrobat reader technology must be cross-platform. Acrobat Reader software is currently available for the following operating systems: Microsoft Windows 3.1, Windows 95, and Windows NT; Macintosh; Linux; Sun Microsystems' Sun SPARC Solaris and Sun SPARC SunOS; Hewlett-Packard's HP-UX; Silicon Graphic's IRIX; IBM's AIX and OS/2; and Digital's VMS.

With regard to HTML, inserting an Acrobat file in a page is a choice between linking to the document with the **<A>** element or using the **<EMBED>** or **<OBJECT>** element to insert the document inline. The format of the **<EMBED>** element is very straightforward, as shown by the following HTML fragment:

```
<EMBED SRC="spec.pdf" ALIGN="LEFT" HSPACE="20" HEIGHT="300"
       VSPACE="20" WIDTH="480">
```

The only thing to worry about is how the **HEIGHT** and **WIDTH** attributes are handled with the Acrobat Reader. Be careful not to use widths smaller than around

PRESENTATION AND LAYOUT

Figure 9-7.   *Sample Acrobat document*

480 pixels; otherwise, some of the controls on the reader will be chopped off. It seems like the controls should be settable with attributes or even eliminated, but any support for that appears to be undocumented. For more information about Acrobat and more details on how Acrobat might be included in a Web page, visit Adobe's Web site (http://www.adobe.com).

Summary

Many different binary objects are available that can be inserted into a Web page. Most all of these objects use the **<EMBED>**, **<APPLET>**, or **<OBJECT>** element. In some proprietary browsers, special elements or attributes have been invented in a few instances to deal with new media types. A prime example is the **DYNSRC** attribute to the **<IMG>** element, introduced by Microsoft. Although the specific attributes vary from one media type to another, most of these elements share common attributes, such as **HEIGHT**, **WIDTH**, **ALIGN**, **HSPACE**, **VSPACE**, and so on. For the most common media types, such as audio and video, browsers often provide built-in support either with a plug-in or a control. The syntax for these common forms is discussed in detail in this chapter. For other important media types, such as Flash and Acrobat, the syntax is currently in a state of flux. However, the W3C is actively moving all included binary objects to a common object format, using the **<OBJECT>** element.

Chapter 10

Style Sheets

H TML is a poor language for page formatting, but this isn't a failing of the technology. As mentioned throughout this book, HTML elements are not supposed to be used to represent layout. Even so, people often use HTML as a visual design environment. They tend to think visually, rather than organizationally, when building Web pages. Why? Well, not very many choices were available in the past. Everybody wanted the same thing—a high degree of control over the layout of their Web pages. Until recently, this control required using tables, HTML tricks, and images for layout; or embedding a binary form, such as Acrobat, in a page. These solutions generally were unsatisfactory, however.

A better solution is emerging. Finally, style sheets, in the form of *Cascading Style Sheets (CSS)*, are available in the major browsers. Style sheets offer what designers have been clamoring for over the years: more control over layout. Arguably, style sheets are the best approach for creating attractive pages. Although style sheets are still relatively new, they are likely to become the dominant way to format Web pages in the near future. Netscape and Microsoft Internet Explorer fall short in some areas of CSS1 (the first specification) support, but both browsers seem to be trending toward improved support. Another browser, Opera 3.5 (http://www.operasoftware.com/), already approaches full CSS1 compliance. As you'll see in this chapter, designers should begin transitioning away from HTML layout, which relies heavily on tables, and toward using style sheets. Furthermore, CSS2, the newest style sheet specification, is laying the groundwork for expanded media possibilities for Web pages. Although CSS2 isn't supported by many browsers yet, it will be soon, so this chapter discusses some of its more interesting features. The chapter ends with a section that covers some proprietary style sheet properties introduced by Microsoft.

The Rise of Style

Basically, style sheets separate the structure of a document from its presentation. Dividing layout and presentation has many theoretical benefits; most importantly, it can provide for flexible documents that display equally well across many types of output devices. In general, Web-based style sheets contain information that describes how documents are presented, whether on a computer monitor, in print, or perhaps even pronounced by a speech-based system for the visually impaired. Although, in some ways, this doesn't sound much different from what many people consider to be the function of HTML, in fact, it is fundamentally different than the intended function of HTML.

As early as 1993, people have been interested in adding more layout control to HTML. Many approaches have been discussed and many continue to be used. As mentioned earlier, these approaches include misuse of HTML tags and embedded binary object formats (such as Adobe's Acrobat). Because of the theoretical benefits of style sheets, they have been the favorite solution of the standards bodies. However, work on a style sheet standard for the Web didn't begin until Bert Bos of the World

Wide Web Consortium (W3C) wrote a charter to do so in 1995. Eventually, Hkon Lie, also of the W3C, introduced a proposal for cascading style sheets; in December 1996, this proposal became the W3C's recommendation of Cascading Style Sheets Level 1 (CSS1). The cascading style sheet approach of the W3C provides a chain of precedence, so that local style may override global style, and a document creator's style might even override reader styles.

But cascading isn't the most interesting aspect of CSS1. These newly introduced style rules move a step closer toward device independence, and reduce reliance on proprietary HTML elements and tricks to force layout. As previously discussed, many of these HTML layout tags and tricks are not supported across the multitude of browsers. The motivation of style sheets to divide the semantic meaning of a page from its physical presentation may seem a bit grandiose, but style sheets are gaining acceptance rapidly. The greater degree of layout control than was previously possible is the main reason that Web developers may start to use style sheets. For example, style sheets can be used to create a paragraph with a half-inch margin, 100 pixels between lines, and text rendered in 48-point green Impact font. Try doing that in HTML.

Style sheets might sound wonderful, but the fact remains that they still aren't widely supported. Internet Explorer 3 and 4, Netscape 4, and later versions of both browsers all support CSS1-based style sheets to some degree, but no widely used browser supports all aspects of the W3C CSS definition. And now the W3C has finalized the CSS Level 2 (CSS2) specification, which incorporates many of the features introduced by browser vendors—notably positioning features—and introduces new features to support aural processing of styles and printing features. Other than outside positioning, most of CSS2 is unsupported in any 4.*x* generation browser (although forthcoming 5.*x*-generation browsers probably will include more CSS2 support).

To further complicate matters, more than one type of style sheet exists. Many industry pundits support a type of sheet known as *Document Style Semantics and Specification Language (DSSSL)*, developed by the SGML community. The most recent addition is *Extensible Style Language (XSL)*, an industry proposal based on DSSSL that uses Extensible Markup Language (XML) syntax. XSL provides more-complex style manipulation, but is more complicated to use than CSS1. Whether XSL will achieve industry acceptance is an open question.

Fortunately, despite industry confusion and the browser vendors' slow adoption of style sheets, you can take advantage of what style sheets offer without causing problems for browsers that are not "style aware."

Style Sheet Basics

CSS1 style sheets rely on an underlying markup structure, such as HTML. They are not a replacement for HTML. Without a binding to an element, a style really doesn't mean anything. The purpose of a style sheet is to create a presentation for a particular element or set of elements. Binding an element to a style specification is very simple; it consists of an element, followed by its associated style information within curly braces:

```
element    {style specification}
```

Suppose that you want to bind a style rule to the **<H1>** element so that a 28-point Impact font is always used. The following rule would result in the desired display:

```
H1    {font-family: Impact;
       font-size:    28pt}
```

In general, a style specification or style sheet is simply a collection of *rules*. These rules include a *selector*—an HTML element, a **CLASS** name, or an **ID** value—which is bound to a style *property* such as **font-family**, followed by a colon and the value(s) for that style property. Multiple style rules may be included in a style specification by separating the rules with semicolons. You can also use many shorthand notations and grouping rules that are available, as discussed in "Advanced Style Rules: Contextual Selection, Grouping, and Inheritance," later in this chapter. Style sheets alone do nothing; first, you must bind the rule to a tag(s) or class of HTML objects. Currently, more than 50 properties are specified under CSS1 that affect the presentation of an HTML document, and more than 50 more properties are defined under CSS2. Unfortunately, not all of them are supported consistently across the major browsers. Even worse, most of the newer style properties defined by CSS2 are not supported by any browser. The full CSS1 specification can be found at the following address: http://www.w3.org/TR/REC-CSS1.

Note   *The style sheet information itself is not HTML. Style information may be included within an HTML document or outside it, but it isn't necessarily subject to the same rules as HTML pages. Many of the basic ideas do apply. Like HTML, style sheet rules are case-insensitive, except for the aspects of the rule that are outside the control of the style sheet language; these aspects include font family names (such as Britannic Bold) and URLs (such as http://www.bigcompany.com/Staff/thomas.htm), both of which may be case-sensitive.*

Adding Style to a Document

Style information may be included in an HTML document in any one of three basic ways:

- Use an outside style sheet, either by importing it or by linking to it.
- Embed a document-wide style in the **<HEAD>** element of the document.
- Provide an inline style exactly where the style needs to be applied.

Each of these style sheet approaches has its own pros and cons, as listed in Table 10-1.

	External Style Sheets	Document-Wide Style	Inline Style
Pros	*Can set style for many documents with one style sheet	*Can control style for a document in one place *No additional download time for style information	*Can control style to a single character instance *Overrides any external or document styles
Cons	*Require extra download time for the style sheet, which may delay page rendering	*Need to reapply style information for other documents	*Need to reapply style information throughout the document and outside documents *Bound too closely to HTML—difficult to update

Table 10-1.   *Comparison of Style Sheet Approaches*

Linking to a Style Sheet

An external style sheet is simply a plain text file containing the style specifications for HTML tags or classes. The extension indicating that the document provides style sheet information is .css, for Cascading Style Sheets.

The following CSS1 style rules might be found in a file called corpstyle.css, which defines a corporate style sheet for a large Web site:

```
BODY            {font: 10pt;
                 font-family: Serif;
                 color: black;
                 background: white}

H1              {font: 24pt;
                 font-family: Sans-Serif;
                 color: black}
```

```
H2              {font: 16pt;
                 font-family: Sans-Serif;
                 color: black}


P               {text-indent: 0.5in;
                 margin-left: 50px;
                 margin-right: 50px}


A:link:         {color: blue;
                 text-decoration: none}


A:visited:      {color: red;
                 text-decoration: none}


A:active:       {color:red;
                 text-decoration: none}


.important      {background: yellow;
                 font-weight: extra-bold}


#note           {background: orange}
```

An HTML file that uses this style sheet could reference it by using the **<LINK>** tag within the **<HEAD>** element of the document. Recall from Chapter 4 that the **<LINK>** element isn't exclusive to style sheets and has a variety of possible relationship settings that can be set with the **REL** attribute. The following is an example of how style sheet linking is used:

```
<HTML>
<HEAD>
<TITLE>Style Sheet Linking Example</TITLE>
<LINK REL="STYLESHEET" HREF="corpstyle.css" MEDIA="screen"
      TYPE="text/css">
</HEAD>

<BODY>
...Content affected by style sheet...
</BODY>
</HTML>
```

In this example, the relationship for the **<LINK>** element as indicated by the **REL** attribute is set to be **STYLESHEET**; then, the **HREF** attribute is used to indicate the URL of the style sheet to use. In this case, the style sheet resides in the same directory as the referencing file and is known as **corpstyle.css**. However, a remote style sheet could also be referenced by using a URL, such as http://www.bigcompany.com/styles/test-style1.css. Note that linking to an external style sheet has the same problems as linking to an external object insofar as the object may no longer be available or the speed of acquiring that object may inhibit performance of the page.

The **MEDIA** attribute is used under CSS2 to provide an indication of which media the style sheet should apply to. This attribute enables the page designer to define one style for computer screens, one for print, and perhaps one for personal digital assistants (PDAs). For example, a document could include two links, one for screen and one for print, as shown here:

```
<LINK REL="STYLESHEET" HREF="screenstyle.css" MEDIA="screen"
      TYPE="text/css">

<LINK REL="STYLESHEET" HREF="printstyle.css" MEDIA="print"
      TYPE="text/css">
```

Multiple values may also be set for the attribute. These should be separated by commas, to show that the style may apply to many media forms—for example, **MEDIA="screen,print"**. Currently, the **MEDIA** attribute isn't widely understood by browsers. For a discussion of media types defined by CSS2, see "CSS2: New Feature Summary," later in this chapter.

The last thing to note in the linked style sheet example is the use of the **TYPE** attribute in the **<LINK>** element, which is set to the MIME type **"text/css"**. This value indicates that the linked style sheet is a cascading style sheet, but another form of style sheet certainly could be linked. A style sheet type may be defined both inline and document wide. To avoid having to use the **TYPE** attribute, you may want to set a default style sheet language in the **<HEAD>** element of the document by using the **<META>** element, as shown here:

```
<META HTTP-EQUIV="Content-Style-Type" Content="text/css">
```

As it stands, by default, most browsers assume that CSS1 is being used; the **TYPE** setting may have little effect, regardless of how it is applied.

Embedding and Importing Style Sheets

The second way to include an external style sheet is to embed it. When you embed a style sheet, you write the style rules directly within the HTML document. You could separate the style rules into another file and then import these rules, much as an *include* file is used in a programming language such as C. However, imported style sheets are not supported consistently by browsers and are merely shorthand for pulling in all of the style information without typing it directly.

Document-wide style is a very easy way to begin using style sheets. It involves using the **<STYLE>** element found within the **<HEAD>** element of an HTML document. You enclose the style rules within the **<STYLE>** and **</STYLE>** tag pair and place this pair within the head section of the HTML document. Because multiple forms of style sheets may be included (beyond the standard CSS format), you should still include the **TYPE** attribute to indicate which format of style sheet you are using, regardless of the browser's support for other style sheet technologies. You can have multiple occurrences of the **<STYLE>** element within the head of the document, and you may even import some styles, link to some style rules, and specify some styles directly. Dividing style information into multiple sections and forms may be very useful, but a way must exist to determine which style rules apply. This is the idea of the cascade, which is discussed in more detail later in the chapter.

One concern when including style sheets within an HTML document is that not all browsers understand style information. To avoid problems, comment out the style information by using an HTML comment, such as **<-- -->**, so that the comments aren't displayed onscreen or misinterpreted by older browsers. A complete example of a document-wide style sheet, including hiding rules from older browsers, is shown here:

```
<HTML>
<HEAD>
<TITLE>Document-Wide Style Sheets</TITLE>
<STYLE TYPE="text/css" MEDIA="PRINT">

<!--
BODY    {background: white;
         margin-left: 1in;
         margin-right: 1.5in}

H1      {font-size: 24pt;
         font-family: sans-serif;
         color: red;
         text-align: center}

P       {font-size: 12pt;
         font-family: Serif;
         text-indent: 0.5in;
         color: black}
-->
```

```
</STYLE>
</HEAD>

<BODY>
...Content affected by style sheet...
</BODY>
</HTML>
```

Importing a style into a document is another way to use a document-wide style rather than provide the style directly. The idea is similar to linking. An external style sheet is referenced; but, in this case, the reference is similar to a macro expansion inline. The syntax for the rule for importing a style sheet is **@import** followed by the URL of the style sheet to include. This rule must be included within the **<STYLE>** element; it has no meaning outside that element, as compared to the linked style sheet. An example of how to import a style sheet is shown here:

```
<!DOCTYPE HTML PUBLIC "-//W3C//DTD HTML 4.0 Final//EN">
<HTML>
<HEAD>
<TITLE>Imported Style Sheets</TITLE>
<STYLE TYPE="text/css">
<!--
@import "http://www.bigcompany.com/styles/corpstyle.css";
@import "docstyle.css";
H1    {font-size: 24pt;
       color: red;
       text-align: center} /* local rules
       that may override import */
-->
</STYLE>
</HEAD>

<BODY>
...Content affected by style sheet...
</BODY>
</HTML>
```

Although imported style sheets may seem to provide a great advantage for organizing style information, their use currently is limited by the fact that none of the browsers support this form of style sheet access. Page designers should stick to the **<LINK>** form of accessing external style sheets until this form has more support.

Using Inline Style

Beyond using a style sheet for the whole document, you can add style information right down to the single element. The simplest way to add style information, but not necessarily the best, is to add style rules to the particular HTML element. Here's how it works. Suppose you want to set one particular **<H1>** tag to render in 48-point, green, Arial font. You could apply that style to all **<H1>** elements, or to a class of them (discussed in the next section), by applying a document-wide style. On the other hand, you could apply the style to only the tag in question; this is done with the **STYLE** attribute, which can be used within nearly any HTML element. For example, the following example shows how style rules could be applied to a particular **<H1>** element:

```
<H1 STYLE="font-size: 48pt; font-family: Arial; color: green">CSS1
Test</H1>
```

This sort of style information doesn't need to be hidden from a browser that isn't style-sheet–aware, because browsers ignore any attributes that they don't understand.

By using inline style, you can easily apply a style to a certain section or division of a document by using the **<DIV>** element. Setting a two-paragraph portion of a document to have a yellow background with bold, black text is fairly simple, as shown here:

```
<DIV STYLE="background: yellow; font-weight: bold; color: black">
<P>Style sheets separate the structure of a document from its
presentation. Dividing layout and presentation has many
theoretical benefits and can provide for flexible documents
that display equally well on large graphically rich systems
and palmtop computers.</P>

<P>This is another paragraph describing the wonderful benefits of
style sheets.</P>
</DIV>
```

If you want to provide style information solely for a few words, or even a few letters, the best approach is to use the **<SPAN>** element. As a block element, the **<DIV>** element works well to surround other block elements, such as paragraphs; but, when setting a localized style within a paragraph, **<SPAN>** is the correct element to bind style information. For example, notice how **<SPAN>** is used here to call attention to a particular section of text:

```
<P>Calling out <SPAN STYLE="background: yellow; font-weight: bold;
color: black">special sections of text</SPAN> isn't hard with
SPAN.</P>
```

Although putting style inline with the elements may seem like the best way to get started with style sheets, it isn't; instead, you can add style to a particular set of elements or even to a single, unique occurrence of a **<P>** element.

Using Classes and IDs

In the previous examples, the style rules were bound to a particular element or included directly within the tag in the form of an attribute. While inlining style seems easy, it gives up much of the benefit of separating the structure of the document from the style. But without inline styles, how can a particular style be applied to one occurrence of the **<H1>** element, or to only a few particular **<H1>** elements? The solutions to these problems are the **CLASS** and **ID** attributes.

As discussed in Chapter 4, you can name a particular tag with the **ID** attribute so that it can be made a destination for a link. For example,

```
<H1 ID="FirstHeading">Welcome to Big Company, Inc.</H1>
```

assigns a name of "**FirstHeading**" to the **<H1>** element so that it can be referenced from an anchor element:

```
<A HREF="#FirstHeading">Go to Heading 1</A>
```

The **ID** attribute is common to nearly all HTML elements. **ID** and **CLASS** should be available to most HTML elements, except for a few, such as **<HTML>**, **<HEAD>**, and **<BODY>**. Style sheets can also use **ID** values as selectors for the style rules, enabling you to affect a particular element with a rule without creating an inline style for it. The following markup shows how a green background is applied to the **<P>** element with the **ID** value of "**SecondParagraph**", while no style is applied to the other paragraph:

```
<HTML>
<HEAD>
<TITLE>ID Style Sheet Example</TITLE>
<STYLE TYPE="text/css">
#SecondParagraph    {background: green}
</STYLE>
</HEAD>

<BODY>
<P>This is the first paragraph.</P>
<P ID="SecondParagraph">This is the second paragraph</P>
```

```
<P>This is the third paragraph. </P>
</BODY>
</HTML>
```

Because almost every element can have an **ID** attribute, the style information doesn't need to be put within the tag. To write a style rule for an **ID** value, simply include a rule with the name of the **ID**, preceded by a pound symbol, as the selector for the rule. For example, to create a simple rule for an element with an **ID** value of **FirstHeading**, use the following syntax:

```
#FirstHeading    {color: blue}
```

The only worry that a page designer might have with using the **ID** attribute is the idea of naming, because every **ID** value must be unique. So, how can a style be applied to some occurrence of an element, but not to others? In the preceding markup example, how can the same style be applied to the first and third **<P>** elements but not the second? The answer is simple: use a class rule.

The **CLASS** attribute is referenced throughout the book when discussing the syntax of various elements, because it defines the name of the class to which a particular element belongs. **CLASS** values don't have to be unique. Many elements can be members of the same class; in fact, elements don't even have to be of the same type to be in a common class. The idea of using **CLASS** is illustrated here:

```
<HTML>
<HEAD>
<TITLE>ID Style Sheet Example</TITLE>
<STYLE TYPE="text/css">
 .important    {background: yellow}
</STYLE>
</HEAD>

<BODY>
<H1 CLASS="important">Example</H1>
<P CLASS="important">This is the first paragraph.</P>

<P>This is the second paragraph.</P>

<P CLASS="important">This is the third paragraph.</P>
</BODY>
</HTML>
```

This example has three elements, each of which has its **CLASS** attribute set to **important**. According to the style sheet information, all members of the **important** class, as indicated by the period, have a yellow background color. Writing rules for classes is easy: simply specify the class name, with a period before it as the selector:

```
.main-item    {font-size: 150%}
```

Other variations on class rules are possible. For example, setting all **<H1>** elements of the class **important** to have a background of orange could be written like this:

```
H1.important    {background: orange}
```

Classes can be used to reduce significantly the number of style rules necessary in a document. Other forms, such as contextual selection, grouping, and inheritance, which are described next, may also be useful in certain situations.

Advanced Style Rules: Contextual Selection, Grouping, and Inheritance

While the **CLASS** and **ID** attributes provide a great deal of flexibility for creating style rules, many other types of rules of equal value exist. For example, it might be useful to specify that all **<STRONG>** elements that occur within a **<P>** element get treated in a certain way, as compared to the same elements occurring elsewhere within the document. To create such a rule, the concept of *contextual selection* must be used. Contextual selectors are created by showing the order in which the attributes must be nested for the rule to be applied:

```
P STRONG    {background: yellow}
```

This rule would set all occurrences of the **<STRONG>** element within a **<P>** element to have a yellow background. Other occurrences of **<STRONG>** might not necessarily have the yellow background, because potential issues of inheritance may creep in.

HTML documents have an implicit structure. They all have an **<HTML>** element. Within this element lie the **<HEAD>** and **<BODY>** elements, which might contain the **<TITLE>** and **<P>** elements, respectively. The structure of the document looks somewhat like a family tree. For example, the document shown here would have a parse tree, as shown in Figure 10-1:

```
<HTML>
<HEAD>
<TITLE>Test File</TITLE>
</HEAD>
```

```
<BODY>
<H1>Test</H1>
<P>This is a <B>Test</B>.</P>
</BODY>
</HTML>
```

In the example parse tree, note how the **<B>** element is enclosed within the **<P>** element, which is in the **<BODY>**, which is in the **<HTML>** element. What happens if you set a style rule to the **<P>** element? Wouldn't this rule also apply to the **<B>** element? Sometimes it would; this is the idea of inheritance. Not all items inherit, so be careful when making any assumptions about inheritance.

In some cases, applying similar rules to several different elements may be more useful than rewriting the rule for each separate element or creating a special grouping class. In such a situation, you can provide a shorthand notation known as *element*

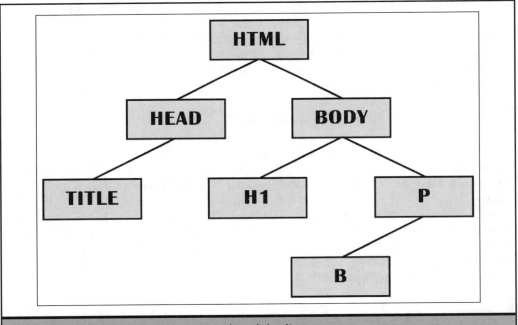

Figure 10-1.   *Simple parse tree to show inheritance*

grouping. If you want **<H1>**, **<H2>**, and **<H3>** to have the same basic background and color, you could apply the following rule:

```
H1, H2, H3    {background: yellow; color: black}
```

If it turns out that each particular heading should have a different size, you can represent that by adding other rules:

```
H1    {font-size: 200%}
H2    {font-size: 150%}
H3    {font-size: 125%}
```

When the grouping rule and the other rules are encountered, they are combined. The resulting rules create the whole style. But, what happens in the following situation?

```
H1, H2, H3    {background: yellow; color: black}
H1            {background: green}
```

What's the background color for the **<H1>** element supposed to be, green or yellow? Some might say green because it is second. But what happens if the rules are swapped? This idea, called the *cascade*, is the key to powerful style sheet rules.

The general idea of the cascade, in effect, is that it provides a system to sort out which rules apply to a document that has many style sheets. For example, a document may include a linked style sheet, embedded style definition, and inline style information for a particular element. It may even include a special style definition assigned by the user in his or her browser. With all of these different style rules in the document, one rule—perhaps a compound rule—eventually takes precedence. Under CSS, the browser's style is the least important, the user's style is next, and the designer's specified style is the most important. From a designer's point of view, this seems appropriate. Beyond this basic priority scheme, within the document itself, inline styles, such as those set with a **STYLE** attribute, take precedence over document styles, which take precedence over linked or included styles. Essentially, the closer to the element, the more priority the style has.

The cascade concept, combined with the idea of inheritance, makes style sheets very flexible. Imagine that you need to set a corporate-wide style in one document and link it to every file in a Web site, except for one particular document that requires some special changes. Why redo the corporate style when a local style can be added to take precedence over the global style? However, all of this theorizing about the cascade concept isn't really necessary, because all that you need to know can be revealed simply by using style sheets. Thus, the next section provides an example that you can follow.

PRESENTATION AND LAYOUT

Style Sheet Example

The example shown here uses two forms of style: document wide and inline. The example also illustrates the use of the **CLASS** and **ID** attributes. Most of the properties should make sense, particularly after seeing the rendering. If you don't get it, don't worry; basic CSS properties and examples are covered later in the chapter.

```
<!DOCTYPE HTML PUBLIC "-//W3C//DTD HTML 4.0 Transitional//EN">
<HTML>
<HEAD>
<TITLE>Simple CSS Example</TITLE>
<STYLE TYPE="text/css">
<!--
BODY            {background: black}
DIV.PAGE        {background: #FFD040;
                 color: black;
                 margin: 50px 10px 50px 10px;
                 padding: 10px 10px;
                 width: 100%;
                 height: 100%}

H1              {font-size: 24pt;
                 font-family: Comic Sans Ms, Cursive;
                 text-align: center}
                .black {color: black; background: white}
                .white {color: white; background: black}

P               {font-family: Arial, Sans-serif;
                 font-size: 16pt;
                 line-height: 200%;
                 text-align: justify;
                 text-indent: 20px; }

.style          {color: blue; font-family: Arial;
                 font-style: oblique}
.size           {font-size: x-large}
#letterspace    {letter-spacing: 15pt}
-->
</STYLE>
</HEAD>
```

```
<BODY>
<DIV CLASS="PAGE">
<H1><SPAN CLASS="black">CSS</SPAN>
<SPAN CLASS="white">Fun</SPAN></H1>
<HR>
<P>
With style sheets, you will be able to control the presentation
of Web pages with greater precision. Style sheets can be used to
set everything from <SPAN CLASS="style">font styles</SPAN> and
<SPAN CLASS="size">sizes</SPAN> to <SPAN ID="letterspace">letter
spacing</SPAN> and line heights.
</P>
</DIV>
</BODY>
</HTML>
```

Figure 10-2 shows how the preceding CSS example is rendered by Internet Explorer 4.

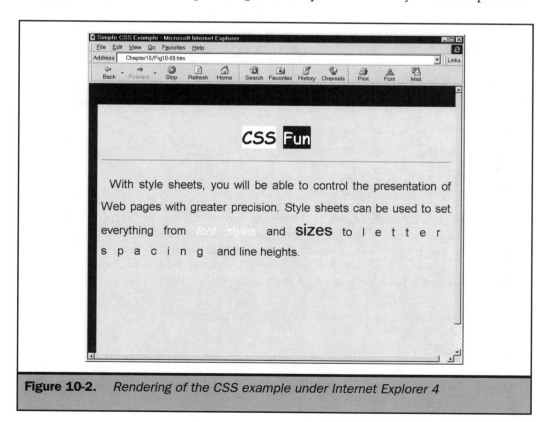

Figure 10-2.   *Rendering of the CSS example under Internet Explorer 4*

Style Sheet Properties

The basic idea of *how* rules are formed in style sheets was discussed earlier in this chapter (refer to "Style Sheet Basics"), but what *are* the various properties that can be set? CSS1 defines more than 50 different properties and values, and the browser vendors are busy inventing new ones all the time. This section covers the standard CSS1 properties, which should work in all browsers. Although they *should* work, some properties may not work in your browser. Although CSS1 promises a lot more flexibility than HTML, you still have the issues regarding lack of support across browsers and minor rendering differences.

Font Properties

CSS1 provides numerous font-oriented properties to set the family, style, size, and variations of the font used within a Web page. Beyond font properties, you also can combine these rules with rules for color, background, margin, and spacing to create a variety of interesting typographic effects.

font-family

The **font-family** property is used to set the font family that is used to render text. The **font-family** property may be set to a specific font, such as Arial, or to a generic family, such as sans serif. You have to quote any font family names that contain white space, such as **"Britannic Bold"**, and you may have to capitalize font values for a match.

According to the CSS1 specification, the following generic families should be available on all browsers that support CSS1:

- Serif (e.g., Times)
- Sans-serif (e.g., Helvetica)
- Cursive (e.g., Zapf-Chancery)
- Fantasy (e.g., Western)
- Monospace (e.g., Courier)

Like the **<FONT>** element, when setting the **font-family**, you can provide a prioritized list of names, separated by commas, that will be checked in order. Remember to always provide a backup generic font family at the end of the **font-family** list in case the user's browser doesn't support the fonts suggested. To set a document-wide font, use a rule such as the following:

```
BODY    {font-family: Arial, Helvetica, Sans-serif}
```

The end of this chapter discusses how downloadable fonts are handled with style sheets and includes a discussion of other important font properties, as well as a complete example.

font-size

The **font-size** property is used to set the relative or physical size of the font used. The value for the property may be a value that is mapped to a physical point size or to a relative word describing the size. Physical point-size values include **xx-small**, **x-small**, **small**, **medium**, **large**, **x-large**, and **xx-large**, or a relative word such as **larger** or **smaller**. Physical sizes also may include examples, such as **48pt**, **2cm**, or **.25in**. Percentage values, such as **150%**, are also valid for relative sizing; negative percentages or point sizes are not allowed. A few example rules are shown here:

```
P          {font-size: 18pt}
STRONG     {font-size: larger}
H1         {font-size: 200%}
```

One suggestion with the **font-size** property is to avoid setting point sizes, when possible, because users who can't see well may have a hard time adjusting size. On certain monitors, a 10-point font might look fine; but, on others, it might be microscopic. If you use exact point size, remember that **large** often is better as far as readability is concerned.

font-style

The **font-style** property is used to specify **normal**, **italic**, or **oblique** font style for the font being used. A few examples are shown here:

```
H1         {font-style: oblique}
.first     {font-style: italic}
.plain     {font-style: normal}
```

Don't try to override HTML elements with this property. Setting a rule whereby the **<B>** element has an italic rendering may not work. When it does, it makes for confusing markup.

font-weight

The **font-weight** property selects the weight, or darkness, of the font. Values for the property range from **100** to **900**, in increments of 100. Keywords are also supported, including **bold**, **bolder**, and **lighter**, which are used to set relative weights. Some browsers may also provide keywords such as **extra-light**, **light**, **demi-light**, **medium**, **demi-bold**, **bold**, and **extra-bold**, which correspond to the **100** to **900** values. Because font families also include **bold** values, and the meaning within them varies, the numeric scheme is preferred. A few examples are shown here:

```
STRONG     {font-weight:   bolder}
H1         {font-weight:   900}
.special   {font-weight:   extra-bold}
```

Typically, the value **bold** is the same as **700**, while the **normal** font value is **400**.

font-variant

The **font-variant** property is used to select a variation of the specified (or default) font family. The only current variants supported with this property are **small-caps**, which displays as small uppercase letters, and **normal**, which doesn't do anything. A simple rule is shown here:

```
EM     {font-variant: small-caps}
```

font

The **font** property provides a concise way to specify all of the font properties with one style rule. One attribute that is included within **font** is **line-height**, which specifies the distance between two lines of text. Each font attribute can be indicated on the line, separated by spaces, except for **line-height**, which is used with **font-size** and separated by a slash. You can use as few or as many font rules in this shorthand notation as you want. The general form of the font rule is shown here:

```
font: font-style font-variant font-weight font-size/line-height
      font-family
```

The following is an example of using a compact font rule:

```
P    {font:italic small-caps 600 18pt/24pt "Arial, Helvetica"}
```

The shorthand notation does not require all of the properties, so the next example is just as valid as the complete notation:

```
P    {font: italic 18pt/24pt}
```

Two other properties, **text-transform** and **text-decoration**, also affect type, so they are discussed next, before a complete example is presented.

text-decoration

The **text-decoration** property is used to define an effect on text. The standard values for this property include **blink**, **line-through**, **overline**, **underline**, and **none**. The meaning of these values is obvious, except for **overline**, which creates a line above text. The following examples show possible uses for this property:

```
.struck         {text-decoration: line-through}
SPAN.special    {text-decoration: blink}
H1              {text-decoration: overline}
A               {text-decoration: none}
#author         {text-decoration: underline}
```

As the fourth example shows, the **text-decoration** property often is used with the <A> element and its associated pseudoclasses, which include **A:link**, **A:active**, and **A:visited**. Make sure to note the colon in the pseudoclass. The following example sets unselected links to be underlined, turns off the underlining during the click, and puts a line through already-visited links:

```
A:link      {text-decoration: underline}
A:active    {text-decoration: none}
A:visited   {text-decoration: line-through}
```

Using grouping, or just applying the rule to the <A> element, itself, might be more appropriate if the same style is to be applied to all states of a link. For example,

```
A:link, A:active, A:visited    {text-decoration: none}
```

text-transform

The **text-transform** property determines the capitalization of the text that it affects. The possible values for this property are **capitalize**, **uppercase**, **lowercase**, and **none**. Note that the value **capitalize** may result in capitalizing every word. Here are some possible uses of the **text-transform** property:

```
P         {text-transform: capitalize}
.upper    {text-transform: uppercase}
.lower    {text-transform: lower}
```

The following is a complete style sheet example that uses all of the font rules, as well as **text-transform** and **text-decoration**:

```
<HTML>
<HEAD>
<TITLE>CSS Font Attributes Example</TITLE>
<STYLE TYPE="text/css">
<!--
BODY              {font-size: 14pt}
.serif            {font-family: serif}
.sans-serif       {font-family: sans-serif}
.cursive          {font-family: cursive}
.fantasy          {font-family: fantasy}
.comic            {font-family: Comic Sans MS}
.xx-small         {font-size: xx-small}
.x-small          {font-size: x-small}
.small            {font-size: small}
.medium           {font-size: medium}
.large            {font-size: large}
.x-large          {font-size: x-large}
.xx-large         {font-size: xx-large}
.smaller          {font-size: smaller}
.larger           {font-size: larger}
.points           {font-size: 18pt}
.percentage       {font-size: 200%}
.italic           {font-style: italic}
.oblique          {font-style: oblique}
.weight           {font-weight: 900}
.smallcaps        {font-variant: small-caps}
.uppercase        {text-transform: uppercase}
.lowercase        {text-transform: lowercase}
.capitalize       {text-transform: capitalize}
.underline        {text-decoration: underline}
.blink            {text-decoration: blink}
.line-through     {text-decoration: line-through}
.overline         {text-decoration: overline}
-->
</STYLE>
</HEAD>

<BODY>
<H2>Font Family</H2>
This text is in <SPAN CLASS="serif">Serif.</SPAN><BR>
This text is in <SPAN CLASS="sans-serif">Sans-Serif.</SPAN><BR>
```

```
This text is in <SPAN CLASS="cursive">Cursive.</SPAN><BR>
This text is in <SPAN CLASS="fantasy">Fantasy.</SPAN><BR>
Actual fonts can be specified like <SPAN CLASS=comic>
Comic Sans MS</SPAN><BR>

<H2>Font Sizing</H2>
This is <SPAN CLASS="xx-small">xx-small text.</SPAN><BR>
This is <SPAN CLASS="x-small">x-small text.</SPAN><BR>
This is <SPAN CLASS="small">small text.</SPAN><BR>
This is <SPAN CLASS="medium">medium text.</SPAN><BR>
This is <SPAN CLASS="large">large text.</SPAN><BR>
This is <SPAN CLASS="x-large">x-large text.</SPAN><BR>
This is <SPAN CLASS="xx-large">xx-large text.</SPAN><BR>
This is <SPAN CLASS="smaller">smaller text</SPAN>than the rest.<BR>
This is <SPAN CLASS="larger">larger text</SPAN>than the rest.<BR>
This is <SPAN CLASS="points">exactly 18 point text.</SPAN><BR>
This is <SPAN CLASS="percentage">200% larger text.</SPAN><BR>

<H2>Font Style, Weight, and Variant</H2>
This text is <SPAN CLASS="italic">italic.</SPAN><BR>
This text is <SPAN CLASS="oblique">oblique.</SPAN><BR>
This text is <SPAN CLASS="weight">bold.</SPAN><BR>
This text is in <SPAN CLASS="smallcaps">smallcaps.</SPAN><BR>

<H2>Text Transformation</H2>
The next bit of text is transformed <SPAN CLASS="uppercase">to all
uppercase.</SPAN><BR>
The next bit of text is transformed <SPAN CLASS="lowercase">to
all lowercase.</SPAN><BR>
<SPAN CLASS="capitalize">This text is all capitalized. It doesn't
do what you think, does it?</SPAN><BR>

<H2>Text Decoration</H2>
This text should <SPAN CLASS="blink">blink under Netscape.</SPAN>
<BR><BR>
This text should be <SPAN CLASS="underline">underlined.</SPAN>
<BR><BR>
This text should be <SPAN CLASS="line-through">struck.</SPAN>
<BR><BR>
This text should be <SPAN CLASS="overline">overline.</SPAN><BR><BR>
</BODY>
</HTML>
```

The rendering of the font and text example is shown in Figure 10-3. Note that small differences still exist between Netscape and Microsoft style sheet implementations.

Downloadable fonts and other changes to font support under style sheets are discussed later in this chapter. The next section covers colors and backgrounds.

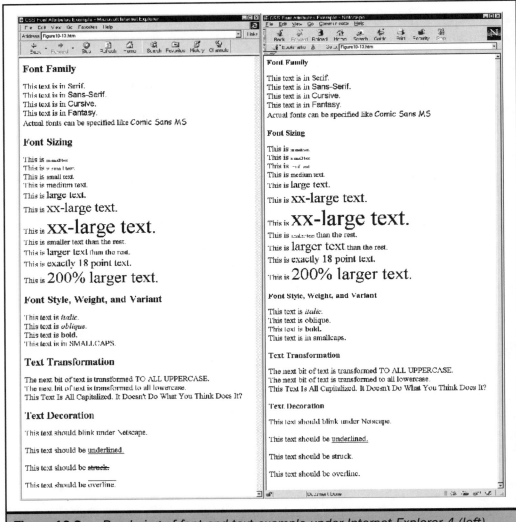

Figure 10-3.   *Rendering of font and text example under Internet Explorer 4 (left) and Netscape Navigator 4 (right)*

Color and Background Properties

CSS1 supports a variety of properties that can be used to control the colors and backgrounds in a document. With style sheets, you can create arbitrary regions with different background colors and images. In the past, such designs were difficult to accomplish without turning to tables or proprietary HTML extensions.

CSS1 style sheets support three basic forms of color specifications:

- **Color names**   The suggested keyword colors supported by browsers are a set of 16 color names taken from the Windows VGA palette. The colors include **Aqua, Black, Blue, Fuchsia, Gray, Green, Lime, Maroon, Navy, Olive, Purple, Red, Silver, Teal, White,** and **Yellow**. These are the same predefined colors from the HTML specification.

- **Hexadecimal values**   Support for the standard, six-digit color form #*RRGGBB* as used with the **<FONT>** and **<BODY>** elements. A shortened, three-digit color form, in which R, G, and B are hex digits, is also supported under CSS, but currently is an uncommon form of color specification and thus isn't suggested.

- **RGB values**   The RGB format is also specified in the form *rgb (R,G,B)*, whereby the values for R, G, and B range from 0 to 255. This format should be very familiar to users of Adobe Photoshop. Currently, most browsers don't support the *rgb (R,G,B)* color format, so use it with caution.

color

CSS supports the **color** property, which is used to set the text color. Its use is illustrated in the following examples:

```
BODY    {color: green}
H1      {color: #FF0088}
.fun    {color: #0f0}
#test   {color: rgb(0,255,0)}
```

background-color

The **background-color** property sets an element's background color. The default value is **none**, which allows any underlying content to show through. This state is also specified by the keyword **transparent**. The **background-color** property is often used in conjunction with the **color** property that sets text color. With block elements, **background-color** colors content and *padding,* the space between an element's contents and its margins. With inline elements, **background-color** colors a box that wraps with the element if it occurs over multiple lines. This property takes colors in the same format as the **color** property. A few example rules are shown here:

```
P         {background-color: yellow}
BODY      {background-color: #0000FF}
.fun      {background-color: #F00}
#test     {background-color: rgb(0,0,0)}
```

The second example is particularly interesting, because it sets the background color for the entire document. Given this capability, the **BGCOLOR** attribute of the **<BODY>** element isn't needed.

background-image

The **background-image** property associates a background image with an element. If the image contains transparent regions, underlying content shows through. To prevent this, designers often use the **background-image** property in conjunction with the **background-color** property. The color is rendered beneath the image and provides an opaque background. The **background-image** property requires a URL to the appropriate image to use as a background. Images that can be used as backgrounds include whatever the browser supports for the **BACKGROUND** attribute of the **<BODY>** element, typically GIF and JPEG. A few examples are shown here, including some that work in conjunction with the **background-color** property:

```
B         {background-image: url(donut-tile.gif);
           background-color: white}
BODY      {background-image: url(funtile.gif)}
.brick    {background-image: url(brick.gif)}
#prison   {background-image: url(bars.gif)}
```

Notice that you can set a background for a small element, such as **<B>**, just as easily as you can for the whole document, by applying the rule to the **<BODY>** element.

background-repeat

The **background-repeat** property determines how background images tile in cases in which they are smaller than the canvas space used by their associated elements. The default value is **repeat**, which causes the image to tile in the horizontal and vertical dimensions. A value of **repeat-x** for the property limits tiling to the horizontal dimension. The **repeat-y** value behaves similarly for the vertical dimension. The **no-repeat** value prevents the image from tiling.

```
P       {background-image: url(donut-tile.gif);
         background-repeat: repeat-x}
BODY    {background-image: url(donut-tile.gif);
         background-repeat: no-repeat}
```

*By using the **background-repeat** property, you can avoid some of the undesirable tiling effects from HTML-based backgrounds. As discussed in Chapter 6, designers often must resort to making very wide or tall background tiles so that users won't notice the repeat. Because the direction of **repeat** can be controlled, designers can now use much smaller background tiles.*

The second example may present an issue of what happens when the user scrolls the screen: should the background be fixed or scroll off screen? It turns out that this behavior is specified by the next property, **background-attachment**.

background-attachment

The **background-attachment** property determines whether a background image should scroll like the element content with which it is associated scrolls, or whether the image should stay fixed on the screen while the content scrolls. The default value is **scroll**. The alternative value, **fixed**, can implement a watermark effect, similar to the proprietary attribute **BGPROPERTIES** of the **<BODY>** element that was introduced by Microsoft. An example of how a watermark effect might be used is shown here:

```
BODY    {background-image:url(logo.gif);
         background-attachment: fixed}
```

background-position

The **background-position** property specifies how a background image, not a color, is positioned within the canvas space used by its element. Three ways exist to specify a position:

- The top-left corner of the image can be specified as an absolute distance.
- The position can be specified as a percentage along the horizontal and vertical dimensions.
- The position can be specified with keywords to describe the horizontal and vertical dimensions. The keywords for the horizontal dimension are **left**, **center**, and **right**. The keywords for the vertical dimension are **top**, **center**, and **bottom**. When keywords are used, the default for an unspecified dimension is assumed to be **center**.

The first example shows how to specify the top-left corner of the background by using an absolute distance:

```
P    {background-image:url(picture.gif);
      background-position: 10px 10px}
```

Remember that this distance is relative to the element and not to the document as a whole, unless, of course, the property is being set for the **<BODY>** element.

The next example shows how to specify a background image position by using percentage values along the horizontal and vertical dimensions:

```
P    {background-image:url(picture.gif);
      background-position: 20% 40%}
```

If you forget to specify one percentage value, the other value is assumed to be **50%**.

Specifying an image position by using keywords is an easy way to do simple placement of an image. When you set a value, the keyword pairs have the following meanings:

Keyword Pair	Horizontal Position	Vertical Position
top left	0%	0%
top center	50%	0%
top right	100%	0%
center left	0%	50%
center center	50%	50%
center right	100%	50%
bottom left	0%	100%
bottom center	50%	100%
bottom right	100%	100%

An example of using keywords to position a background image is shown here:

```
BODY    {background-image: url(picture.gif);
          background-position: center center}
```

Remember that if only one keyword is set, the second keyword defaults to **center**. Thus, in the preceding example, the keyword **center** was needed only once.

background

The **background** property is a comprehensive property that allows any or all of the specific background properties to be set at once, not unlike the shorthand **font** property. Property order does not matter. Any property not specified uses the default value. A few examples are shown here:

```
P          {background: white url(picture.gif) repeat-y center}
BODY       {background: url(tile.jpg) top center fixed}
.bricks    {background: repeat-y top top url(bricks.gif)}
```

A complete example of all of the background properties in cascading style sheets is shown here:

```
<!DOCTYPE HTML PUBLIC "-//W3C//DTD HTML 4.0 Transitional//EN">
<HTML>
<HEAD>
<TITLE>CSS Background Attributes Example</TITLE>
<STYLE TYPE="text/css">
<!--
P    {background: yellow url(logo.gif) repeat-y }
-->
</STYLE>
</HEAD>

<BODY>
<P>This is a paragraph of text. The left side will probably be hard to
read because it is on top of an image that repeats along the y axis.
Notice that the area not covered by the background image is filled with
the background color. This is more text just to illustrate the idea.
This is even more text. This is more text just to illustrate the idea.
This is even more text. This is more text just to illustrate the idea.
This is even more text. This is more text just to illustrate the idea.
This is even more text. This is more text just to illustrate the idea.
This is even more text.
</P>
</BODY>
</HTML>
```

Notice that multiple background types with a variety of elements may be included. A similar layout is possible under pure HTML, but the required **<TABLE>** element would be somewhat complicated. A rendering of the background style sheet example is shown in Figure 10-4.

Text Properties

Text properties are used to affect the spacing and layout of text inline, namely, the text within block elements such as paragraphs. The basic properties enable the page designer to set indentation, word spacing, letter spacing, spacing between lines, and horizontal and vertical text alignment. Although these would seem to be very useful properties, they currently aren't well supported in browsers.

When you manipulate text and other objects with a style sheet, you often must specify a length or size. CSS1 supports a variety of measurement forms. For fonts, the most familiar form of measurement is probably points (**pt**). The CSS1 specification also supports measurements such as inches (**in**), centimeters (**cm**), and millimeters (**mm**), as

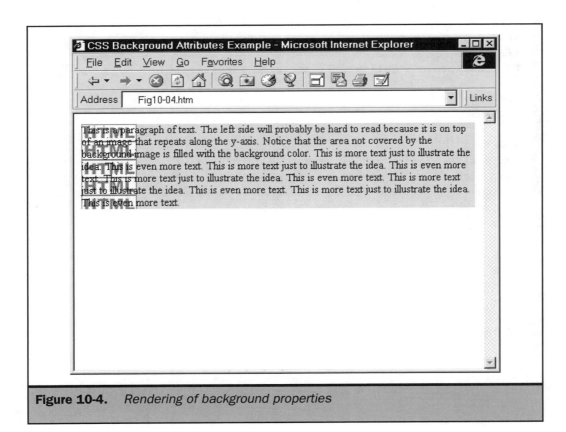

Figure 10-4.   *Rendering of background properties*

well as picas (**pc**), the em measurement (**em**), the ex unit (**x-height**), and (under certain measurement situations), pixels (**px**). In other cases, relative measurements, such as **150%**, may be specified. Page designers who are used to electronic layout tools will probably stick to the measurements most familiar to them, such as points or pixels.

 *Currently, the major browsers have only limited support, if any, for measurements using **em** or **x-height**.*

word-spacing

The **word-spacing** property specifies the amount of space between words. The default value, **normal**, uses the browser's word-spacing default. Designers are free to specify the distance between words in a variety of measurements, including inches (**in**), centimeters (**cm**), millimeters (**mm**), points (**pt**), picas (**pc**), the em (**em**) measurement, and pixels (**px**). A few examples are shown here:

```
P        {word-spacing: 1em}
BODY     {word-spacing: 10pt}
```

At the time of this writing, neither of the major browsers supports the **word-spacing** property. Page designers should check to make sure this property works in their target audience's browser(s) before relying on this property.

letter-spacing

The **letter-spacing** property specifies the amount of space between letters. The default value, **normal**, uses the browser's letter-spacing default. Like the **word-spacing** property, a variety of measurements may be used to set word spacing, from pixels to em values. A few examples of this property are shown here:

```
P        {letter-spacing: 0.2em}
BODY     {letter-spacing: 2px}
.wide    {letter-spacing: 10pt}
#Fun     {letter-spacing: 2cm}
```

vertical-align

The **vertical-align** property controls the vertical positioning of text and images with respect to the baseline currently in effect. The possible values for the **vertical-align** property include **baseline**, **sub**, **super**, **top**, **text-top**, **middle**, **bottom**, **text-bottom**, and percentage values. Compare these values with the **ALIGN** attribute for the **<IMG>** element, as well as alignment options for table cells, and things should begin to make sense. The flexibility of style sheets enables you to set element values on individual characters. When not specified, the default value of **vertical-align** is **baseline**. The following are a few examples:

```
P               {vertical-align: text-top}
.superscript    {vertical-align: super; font-size: smaller}
.subscript      {vertical-align: sub; font-size: 75%}
```

Notice in the example how **vertical-align** can be used with other properties to create an interesting contextual class, like **.superscript**.

text-align

The **text-align** property determines how text in a block-level element, such as the **<P>** element, is horizontally aligned. The allowed values for this property are **left**, **right**, **center**, and **justify**. The default value for the property is **left**. This property should act similar to most of the **ALIGN** attributes, which are available on certain block-level elements in HTML. Be aware that justification of a block element may be very noticeable when the font is very large, and may show the added spaces. A few examples are shown here:

```
P          {text-align: justify}
DIV        {text-align: center}
.goright   {text-align: right}
```

text-indent

The **text-indent** property sets the indentation for text in the first line of a block-level element. Its value can be given either as a length value (**.5cm**, **15px**, **12pt**, and so on) or as a percentage of the width of the block, such as **10%**. The default value for the property is **0**, which indicates no indentation. A few examples of how **text-indent** might be used are shown here:

```
P          {text-indent: 2em}
P.heavy    {text-indent: 50px}
```

One interesting effect is the use of negative values to create a hanging indent, wherein the text within the block element expands outside of the block. The following rule creates a paragraph with a yellow background, in which the first line of text starts left of the text:

```
P   {text-indent: -10px; background: yellow}
```

Combining the hanging indent with a large first letter for the paragraph creates an interesting effect.

line-height

The **line-height** property sets the height between lines in a block-level element, such as a paragraph. The basic idea is to set the line spacing, known more appropriately as *leading*. The value of the attribute may be specified as the number of lines (**1.4**), a length (**14pt**), or as a percentage of the line height (**200%**). So, double spacing could be written as

```
P.double     {line-height: 2}
```

as well as

```
P.double2    {line-height: 200%}
```

Other examples of using **line-height** are shown here:

```
P            {font-size: 12pt; line-height: 18pt}
P.carson     {font-size: 24pt;   line-height: 6pt}
```

Notice in the second example how the **line-height** property is much smaller than the **font-size** property. A browser generally should render the text on top of the other text, creating a hard-to-read, but potentially "cool" effect.

A complete example showing the HTML and cascading style sheet markup for text properties is shown here:

```
<!DOCTYPE HTML PUBLIC "-//W3C//DTD HTML 4.0 Transitional//EN">
<HTML>
<HEAD>
<TITLE>CSS Text Attributes Example</TITLE>
<STYLE TYPE="text/css">
<!--
.letterspaced    {letter-spacing: 10pt}
.sub             {vertical-align: sub}
.super           {vertical-align: super}
.right           {text-align: right}
.left            {text-align: left}
.center          {text-align: center}
P.indent         {text-indent: 20px;
                  line-height: 200%}
```

```
P.negindent       {text-indent: -10px;
                   background: yellow}


#BIGCHAR          {background: red;
                   color: white;
                   font-size: 28pt;
                   font-family: Impact;
                   }


P.carson          {font-size: 12pt;
                   font-family: Courier;
                   letter-spacing: 4pt;
                   line-height: 5pt}
-->
</STYLE>
</HEAD>

<BODY>
<H2>Letter Spacing and Vertical Alignment</H2>
<P>This is a paragraph of text. <SPAN CLASS="letterspaced">Spacing
letters is possible but word spacing is not.</SPAN> Vertical
alignment can be used to make <SPAN CLASS="sub">Subscript</SPAN>
and <SPAN CLASS="super">Superscript</SPAN> text, but the real use of
the property is for aligning text next to images and objects.</P>

<H2>Alignment</H2>
<P CLASS="LEFT">
It is possible to set paragraphs to align left.
</P>

<P CLASS="RIGHT">
It is possible to align paragraphs to the right.
</P>
<SPAN CLASS="CENTER">Even lines can be set to center.</SPAN>

<H2>Indentation and Line Height</H2>
<P CLASS="indent">
With style sheets it is possible to set indentation as well as line
```

```
height. Now double spacing is a reality. This is just dummy text to
show the effects of the indentation and spacing. This is just dummy
text to show the effects of the indentation and spacing.</P>

<P CLASS="negindent"><SPAN ID="BIGCHAR">T</SPAN>his is another
paragraph which has negative indenting. Notice how you can pull a
character outside the paragraph for interesting effects. This is
just dummy text to show the effect of the indent. This is just
dummy text to show the effect of the indent.</P>

<H2>Surf Gun</H2>
<P CLASS="carson">Don't get carried away with your newfound powers.
You may be tempted to show how cool you can be using text on top of
other text. While this may be good for certain situations, it may
also confuse the viewer.</P>
</BODY>
</HTML>
```

The rendering of the text properties example is shown in Figure 10-5.

Box Properties

Block-level elements, such as the **<P>** element, can be thought of as occupying rectangular boxes on the screen. Three aspects of these boxes can be controlled with style properties. The box properties that can be controlled include the following:

- **Margin properties** Determine the distance between edges of an element's box and the edges of adjacent elements.

- **Border properties** Determine the visual characteristics of a border surrounding an element's edges.

- **Padding properties** Determine the distance inside an element between its edges and its actual content.

- **Height, width, and positioning properties** Determine the size and position of the box that the element creates.

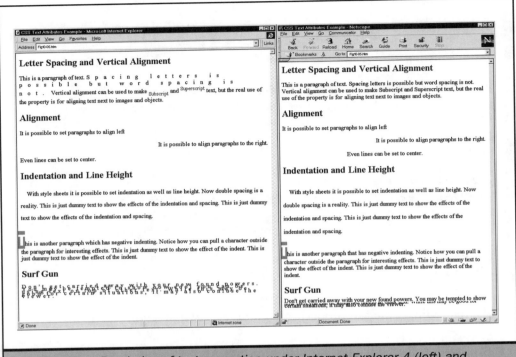

Figure 10-5.   *Rendering of text properties under Internet Explorer 4 (left) and Netscape Navigator 4 (right)*

The box properties are equivalent to attributes such as **BORDER**, **HEIGHT**, and **WIDTH** when used with block elements such as <**IMG**>, but the box properties provide even more power than is available under standard HTML.

Margin Properties

Four margin properties are available to set individually each of an element's four margins. A fifth margin property allows all of the margins to be set together. Individual margins for a block element can be set by using **margin-top**, **margin-right**, **margin-bottom**, or **margin-left** properties. The values for the margins should be a length (such as **15pt** or **2em**), a percentage value of the block element's width (such as **20%**), or the value **auto**, which attempts to figure out the appropriate margin automatically:

```
BODY        {margin-top: 20px;
             margin-bottom: 20px;
             margin-left: 30px;
             margin-left: 50px}
```

```
P            {margin-bottom: 20mm}
DIV.fun      {margin-left: 1.5cm; margin-right: 1.5cm}
```

One interesting use of margin properties is to set negative margin values. Of course, negative margins may clip the content of the block element in the browser window, if you aren't careful. Try an example such as

```
P    {margin-left: -2cm; background: green}
```

to get an idea of how negative margins work.

The last few examples show that you can set one or many margins. To make setting multiple margins even easier, a shorthand notation is available that enables page designers to set all of the margins at once. Using the **margin** property, one to four values can be assigned to affect the block element margins. If a single value is specified, it is applied to all four margins. For example,

```
P    {margin: 1.5cm}
```

sets all of the margins equal to 1.5 cm. If multiple values are specified, they are applied in clockwise order: first the top margin, followed by (in order) the right, bottom, and left margins. For example,

```
P    {margin: 10px, 5px, 15px, 5px}
```

sets the top margin to 10 pixels, the right to 5 pixels, the bottom to 15 pixels, and the left to 5 pixels. If only two or three values are specified in the rule, the missing values are determined from the opposite sides. For example,

```
P    {margin: 10px, 5px}
```

sets the top margin to 10 pixels and the right margin to 5 pixels. The opposite sides are then set accordingly, making the bottom margin 10 pixels and the left margin 5 pixels.

A complete example using the margin properties is shown here. Notice that the example uses one negative margin. The background color makes it easier to see the effect.

```
<!DOCTYPE HTML PUBLIC "-//W3C//DTD HTML 4.0 Transitional//EN">
<HTML>
<HEAD>
```

```
<TITLE>CSS Margin Example</TITLE>
<STYLE TYPE="text/css">
<!--
#ONE          {background: yellow;
               margin: 1cm 1cm;
              }

#TWO          {background: orange;
               margin-top: 1cm;
               margin-bottom: 1cm;
               margin-right: .5cm;
               margin-left: -10px;
              }

#BIGCHAR      {background: red;
               color: white;
               font-size: 28pt;
               font-family: Impact;
              }
-->
</STYLE>
</HEAD>

<BODY>
<P ID="ONE">This is a paragraph of text that has margins set for
all sides to 1 cm. This is just dummy text to show the effects of
the margins. This is just dummy text to show the effects of the margins.</P>

<P ID="TWO"><SPAN ID="BIGCHAR">T</SPAN>his is another paragraph that has
negative margins on one side. Be careful not to clip things with negative
margins. This is just dummy text to show the effect of the
margins. This is just dummy text to show the effect of the margins.</P>
</BODY>
</HTML>
```

The rendering of the cascading style sheet margin example under Internet Explorer 4 is shown in Figure 10-6.

Border Properties

Elements may be completely or partially surrounded by borders placed between their margins and their padding. The border properties control the edges of block elements by setting whether they should have a border—what the borders look like—their width, their color, and so on. Borders are supposed to work with both block-level and inline elements; you may, however, see browsers automatically convert elements with borders to block elements by adding preceding and following carriage returns.

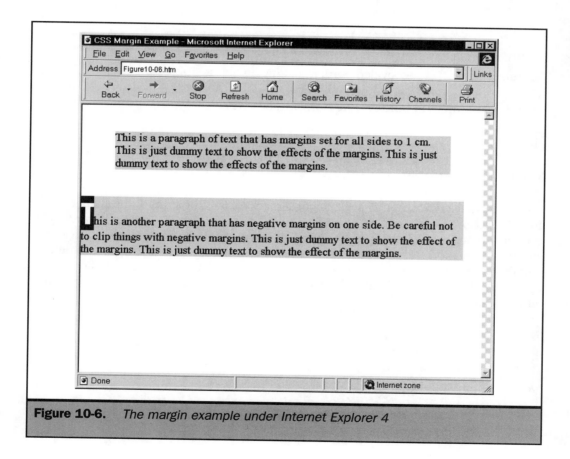

Figure 10-6. *The margin example under Internet Explorer 4*

border-style The **border-style** property is used to set the appearance of the borders. The default value for the property is **none**, which means no border is drawn, regardless of any other setting. The values for **border-style** include

Value	Intended Rendering
dotted	A dotted border
dashed	A dashed-line border
solid	A normal solid-line border
double	A double-line border
groove	An etched border
ridge	An extruded border
inset	An inset border, making an object look like it is set into the page
outset	A beveled border, making an object look raised

A few examples of **border-style** rules are shown here:

```
H1        {border-style: solid}
P.boxed   {border-style: double}
.button   {border-style: outset}
```

The **border-style** property sets the borders for each of the sides of the element. Individual border styles can be controlled with **border-top-style**, **border-bottom-style**, **border-left-style**, and **border-right-style**. The **border-style** property can also act as a shorthand notation and may take up to four values starting from top, right, bottom, and then left. Like the **margin** property, when less than four values are set, the opposite sides are set automatically. To set double borders on the top and bottom, use either of the following rules:

```
P       {border-style: double none}
P.one   {border-style: double none double none}
P.two   {border-top-style: double;
         border-bottom-style: double;
         border-left-style: none;
         border-right-style: none}
```

border-width   Numerous properties are used to set the width of borders. Four properties set the width for specific borders: **border-top-width**, **border-right-width**, **border-bottom-width**, and **border-left-width**. Similar to the **border-style** property, the **border-width** property sets all four borders at once and takes from one to four values. Multiple values are applied to borders in a clockwise order: top, right, bottom, left. If only two or three values are used, the missing values are determined from the opposite sides, just as with margins and border styles.

Width can be specified by using the keywords **thin**, **medium**, and **thick** as values indicating the size of the border, or by using an absolute measurement such as 10 pixels. The following examples illustrate how border widths can be set:

```
P                  {border-style: solid; border-width: 10px}
P.double           {border-style: double; border-width: thick}
P.thickandthin     {border-style: solid; border-width: thick thin}
.fun               {border-style: double none; border-width: thick}
```

border-color   Borders may be assigned a color by using the **border-color** property. Color values are specified by using either a supported color name or a numeric RGB specification. The **border-color** property sets all four borders and takes from one to four values. Multiple values are applied to borders in a clockwise order: top, right, bottom, left. If only two or three values are used, the missing values are determined from the opposite sides. As with border widths and styles, you can use a property for each border's color by using **border-top-color**, **border-right-color**, **border-bottom-color**, and **border-left-color**. The following examples illustrate the basic ways to set a border's colors:

```
P      {border-style: solid; border-color: green}
P.all  {border-style: solid; border-top-color: green;
        border-right-color: #FF0000;
        border-bottom-color: yellow;
        border-left-color: blue}
```

border shorthand   Several border properties allow any combination of width, color, and style information to be set in a single property. The **border-top**, **border-right**, **border-bottom**, and **border-left** properties support this for their respective borders. For example, to set the top border or paragraph elements to be red, double-line style, and 20 pixels thick, use

```
P    {border-top: double 20px red}
```

The order of the property values to set the style, width, and color is arbitrary, but according to the specification, designers should probably set the style, and then the width, followed by the color. Multiple properties can be combined in one rule to set the borders differently, as shown in the following example:

```
#RainbowBox    {background: yellow;
                 border-top: solid 20px red;
                 border-right: double 10px blue;
                 border-bottom: solid 20px green;
                 border-left: dashed 10px orange}
```

Besides a shorthand notation for each individual border side, you can use a shorthand notation for all sides by using the **border** property. For example, to set all borders of a paragraph to be red, double-line style, and 20 pixels thick, use

```
P    {border: double 20px red}
```

Note that it is impossible to set the individual border sides with this shorthand notation. The actual properties to set the various borders must be used, such as **border-top** or, even more specifically, **border-top-style**.

The following brief example shows all of the border properties used so far. Notice that both compact and explicit notations are used in the example.

```
<!DOCTYPE HTML PUBLIC "-//W3C//DTD HTML 4.0 Transitional//EN">
<HTML>
<HEAD>
<TITLE>CSS Border Example</TITLE>
<STYLE TYPE="text/css">
<!--
#OUTER     {background: orange;
            border-style: solid;
            border-width: 5px;
            padding: 10px 10px
            }

#ONE       {background: yellow;
            border-style: double;
            border-width: medium;
            }
```

```
#TWO        {background: yellow;
             border-style: double solid;
             border-color: red green purple blue;
             border-width: thin medium thick .25cm;
            }
-->
</STYLE>
</HEAD>

<BODY>
<DIV ID="outer">
<P ID="one">This is a paragraph of text that has a red double border
around it. Notice how the text creeps up on the edges. Padding values
will help you avoid this problem.</P>

<P ID="two">This is another paragraph that has its borders set in a
very bizarre way!</P>
Notice that the paragraph blocks can be within a large boxed block
structure.
</DIV>
</BODY>
</HTML>
```

The rendering of the border property example under Internet Explorer 4 is shown in Figure 10-7.

Padding Properties

The space between an element's border and its content can be specified by using the padding properties. An element's four padding regions can be set by using the **padding-top**, **padding-right**, **padding-bottom**, and **padding-left** properties. As with borders and margins, you can use a shorthand notation property, called **padding**, to set the padding for all sides at once. This example illustrates some basic uses of padding properties:

```
DIV     {padding-top: 1cm}
P       {border-style: solid;
         padding-left: 20mm;
         padding-right: 50mm}
```

PRESENTATION AND LAYOUT

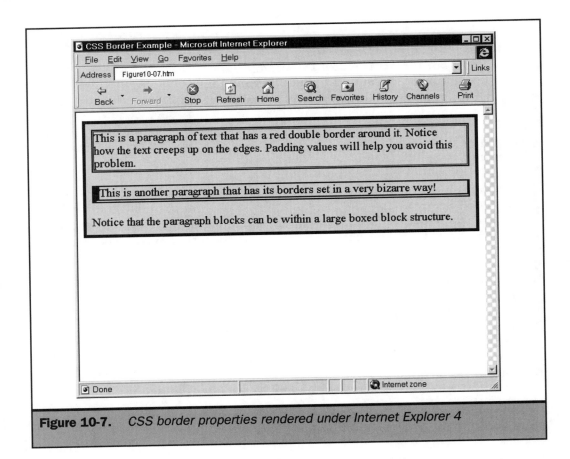

Figure 10-7. CSS border properties rendered under Internet Explorer 4

The shorthand notation property **padding** allows a single property assignment to specify all four padding regions. It can take from one to four values. A single value is applied to all four padding areas. Multiple values are applied to padding regions in a clockwise order: top, right, bottom, left. If only two or three values are used, the missing values are determined from the opposite sides. So,

```
DIV    {border-style: solid; padding: 1cm}
```

sets a region with a solid border, but with contents padded 1 cm from the border on all sides. The following sets padding on the top and bottom to 2 mm and the right and left to 4 mm for all paragraphs:

```
P    {padding: 2mm 4mm}
```

An example showing padding and borders to help you better understand padding values is shown here:

```
<!DOCTYPE HTML PUBLIC "-//W3C//DTD HTML 4.0 Transitional//EN">
<HTML>
<HEAD>
<TITLE>CSS Padding Example</TITLE>
<STYLE TYPE="text/css">
<!--
#ONE        {background: yellow;
             border-style: double;
             border-width: medium;
             padding-left: 1cm;
             padding-right: .5cm;
             }

#TWO        {background: yellow;
             border-style: double;
             border-width: medium;
             padding-top: 1cm;
             padding-bottom: 1cm;
             }

#THREE      {background: yellow;
             border-style: double;
             border-width: medium;
             padding: 1cm 1cm;
             margin: .5cm 4cm;
             }
-->
</STYLE>
</HEAD>

<BODY>
<P ID="one">This paragraph of text has padding on the left and
right,but not on the top and bottom.</P>

<P ID="two">This paragraph has padding, but this time only on the
top and bottom.</P>
```

```
<P ID="three">Be careful when using margins. They don't necessarily
apply to the text within the box, but to the box itself.</P>
</BODY>
</HTML>
```

The rendering of the padding example is shown in Figure 10-8.

width and height

The **width** property sets the width of an element's content region (the width of the area actually filled with content as opposed to its padding, border, or margin). The following example sets a paragraph with a width of 300 pixels:

```
P    {width: 300px;
      padding: 10px;
      border: solid 5px;
      background: yellow;
      color: black}
```

You can also use percentage values for the width. With the **width** property, tables apparently aren't necessary under CSS. This is true, but given the current level of support for these style sheets, relying on this feature for layout probably isn't a good idea.

Similar to **width**, the **height** property sets the height of an element's content region. When thinking about elements in Web pages other than images, setting the **height** property might seem unusual. In most cases, it is probably best to leave the **height** property alone, so that the default value, **auto**, is used. The most legitimate use of this property is to set the height for objects, such as images. An absolute value or a percentage is supported for the **height** property, just as it is for **width**. The following examples show how these properties might be used:

```
IMG    {height: 10cm; width: 10%}
P      {height: 100px; width: 300px}
```

float and clear

The **float** property influences the horizontal alignment of elements. It causes them to "float" toward either the left or right margins of their containing element. This is especially useful for placing embedded media objects (such as images and similar support) into a Web page. Similar floating capabilities under vanilla HTML can be found with the **ALIGN** attribute settings. As with HTML, the values available for the **float** property include **left**, **right**, or **none**. The value of **none** is the default. To imitate

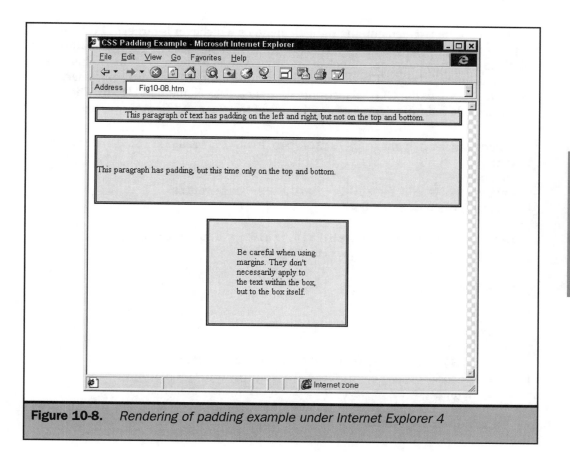

Figure 10-8.   *Rendering of padding example under Internet Explorer 4*

the HTML code **<IMG SRC="logo.gif" ALIGN="RIGHT">**, apply a style sheet rule such as this to the element:

```
IMG.LOGO    {float: right}
```

The previous example might raise a few questions. How can the **HSPACE** and **VSPACE** of the item be set by using style sheets? You have a great deal of control over the border, margin, padding, height, and width of any object, so you shouldn't have difficulty achieving the layout that you want. One thing that may not be obvious is how to clear the content that may flow around an object.

The use of floating elements creates a need to position vertically those elements that immediately follow them in an HTML document. Should the content flow continue at the floating element's side or after its bottom? If floating elements are defined on the right and left margins of the page, should content flow continue between them, after the bottom of the left element, the right element, or whichever is larger? The **clear** property allows this to be specified. A value of **left** for the property clears floating objects to the left, a value of **right** clears floating objects to the right, and the **both** value clears whichever is larger. The default value is **none**. Notice that this is extremely similar to the use of the **CLEAR** attribute with the **
** element in HTML. The following code example demonstrates the use of the **clear** and **float** properties:

```
<!DOCTYPE HTML PUBLIC "-//W3C//DTD HTML 4.0 Transitional//EN">
<HTML>
<HEAD>
<TITLE>Image and Layout Control under CSS</TITLE>
<STYLE TYPE="text/css">
<!--
IMG.aligned-right    {width: 150; height: 150; float:right}
BR.clear-text        {clear:both}
-->
</STYLE>
</HEAD>

<BODY>
<P>This is some dummy text.
<IMG CLASS="aligned-right" SRC="bluecircle.gif">
This is some dummy text. This is some dummy text.
This is some dummy text. This is some dummy text.
This dummy text should stop flowing here.
<BR CLASS="clear-text">
This text should appear after the picture.
</P>
</BODY>
</HTML>
```

The rendering of the image alignment and text flow example is shown in Figure 10-9.

Classification Properties

Cascading style sheets contain several classification properties that determine the display classification of an element. Is it a block-level element or an inline element? Does it preserve or collapse white-space characters? Is it a list element? If so, what list style does it use? The following attributes are some of the miscellaneous items in cascading style sheets.

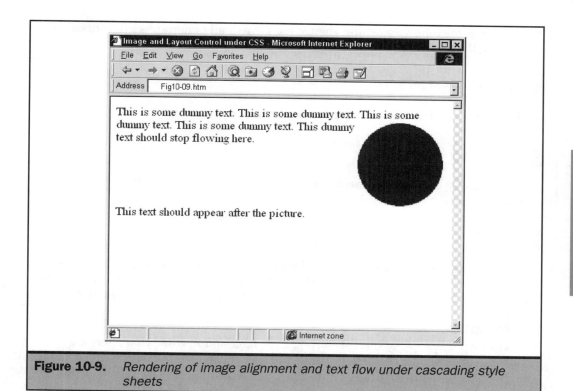

Figure 10-9.   *Rendering of image alignment and text flow under cascading style
sheets*

display

The CSS model recognizes three types of displayed elements: block elements, inline
elements, and lists. The **display** property allows an element's display type to be
changed to one of four values: **block**, **inline**, **list-item**, and **none**. The **none** value
causes an element not to display or use canvas space. This differs from the property
setting **visibility** (discussed later in this chapter), which also prevents an element from
displaying, but may reserve canvas space. To turn off a paragraph, try a rule such as
the following:

```
P.remove    {display:none}
```

Besides turning off elements, the browser should be able to turn a block element
(such as a paragraph) into an inline element, thus keeping it from adding a new line.

For example, the following would change the form of all paragraphs in the document; overriding the known action of the element is not suggested:

```
P    {display:inline}
```

Browsers may be able to turn an inline element into a block:

```
EM    {display:block}
```

You can also coerce an element to act somewhat like a list by casting it with the display property, as shown here:

```
B    {display: list-item}
```

In very few cases, other than setting display to **none**, does type overriding make sense. While you might be able to dream up interesting uses for element form changing, it upsets the improved simplicity of HTML files provided by cascading style sheets.

white-space

The **white-space** property controls how spaces, tabs, and newline characters are handled in an element. The default value, **normal**, collapses white-space characters into a single space and automatically wraps lines, just as normal HTML. When a value of **pre** is used for the property, white-space formatting is preserved, similar to how the **<PRE>** element works in HTML. The **nowrap** value prevents lines from wrapping if they exceed the element's content width. This short example shows how the **white-space** property would be used to simulate the **<PRE>** element:

```
<!DOCTYPE HTML PUBLIC "-//W3C//DTD HTML 4.0 Transitional//EN">
<HTML>
<HEAD>
<STYLE TYPE="text/css">
<!--
P.pre    {white-space:pre}
-->
</STYLE>
</HEAD>

<BODY>
<P CLASS="pre"> This     will     be    preformatted.</P>
</BODY>
</HTML>
```

Like many of the display attributes already discussed, the **nowrap** and **pre** values are not well supported in browsers at the time of this writing.

List Properties

As discussed in Chapter 4, HTML supports three major forms of lists: ordered lists, unordered lists, and definition lists. Cascading style sheets provide some list manipulation, including three style properties that can be set for lists: **list-style-type**, **list-style-image**, and **list-style-position**. A general property, **list-style**, provides a shorthand notation to set all three properties at once.

list-style-type   The items in ordered or unordered lists are labeled with a numeric value or a bullet, depending on the list form. These list labels can be set in cascading style sheets by using the **list-style-type** property. Six values are appropriate for ordered lists: **decimal**, **lower-roman**, **upper-roman**, **lower-alpha**, and **upper-alpha**. Three values are appropriate for unordered lists: **disc**, **circle**, and **square**. The value **none** prevents a label from displaying. These values are similar to the **TYPE** attribute for the list elements in HTML. Setting the following

```
OL    {list-style-type: upper-roman}
```

is equivalent to **<OL TYPE="I">**, while the following is equivalent to **<UL TYPE="square">**:

```
UL    {list-style: square}
```

Nested lists can be controlled by using context selection rules. For example, to set an outer order list to uppercase roman numerals, an inner list to lowercase roman numerals, and a further embedded list to lowercase letters, use the following rules:

```
OL          {list-style-type:upper-roman}
OL OL       {list-style-type:lower-roman}
OL OL OL    {list-style-type:lower-alpha}
```

The **list-style-type** property can also be associated with the **<LI>** element, but be aware that setting individual list elements to a particular style might require the use of the **ID** attribute, or even inline styles.

list-style-image   The **list-style-type** property provides little functionality that is different from HTML lists, but the **list-style-image** property can assign a graphic image to a list label; this is awkward to do under plain HTML. The value of the property is either the URL of the image to use as a bullet or the keyword **none**. So, to use the lovely red 3-D balls with your list, use a rule such as this:

```
UL    {list-style-image: url("ball.gif")}
```

Although setting the **list-style-image** for an ordered list may be possible, be careful, because the meaning of the list is then lost.

list-style-position   Display elements in cascading style sheets are treated as existing inside a rectangular box. Unlike other elements, the labels for list items can exist outside and to the left of the list element's box. The **list-style-position** property controls where a list item's label is displayed in relation to the element's box. The values allowed for this property are **inside** or **outside**. The **outside** value is the default. The following example tightens up a list by bringing the bullets inside the box for the list:

```
UL.COMPACT    {list-style-position: inside}
```

list-style   Like margin, padding, and other shorthand notation, the **list-style** property allows a list's type, image, or position properties to all be set by a single property. The properties may appear in any order and are determined by value. The following is an example of the shorthand notation that sets an unordered list with a bullet image that appears within the list block:

```
UL.special    {list-style: inside url("bullet.gif")}
```

Up to this point, this chapter has discussed the basic CSS1 standard, but a few things are still missing. Already, new style sheet properties are being introduced. One extension in particular, positioning, bears closer inspection.

Positioning with Style Sheets

The W3C finalized the CSS2 specification on May 12, 1998. The complete specification can be viewed online at http://www.w3.org/TR/REC-CSS2/. Currently, few important CSS2 features have been implemented by browser vendors, with one major exception: *positioning*. The rest of this chapter covers positioning in detail; summarizes new, unimplemented features in CSS2; and ends with a discussion of some proprietary style sheet effects introduced by Microsoft.

Positioning was originally developed as a separate specification called CSS-P, which has now been incorporated into the CSS2 specification. Even before finalization of CSS2, the major browsers supported style sheet–based positioning. When combined with elements such as **<DIV>**, the functionality of proprietary elements (such as **<LAYER>**) can be achieved with style sheets.

Positioning and Sizing of Regions

The first property to discuss for layout is the **position** property, which has three values:

- **static**   Places elements according to the natural order in which they occur in a document (the default).

- **absolute**   Defines a coordinate system independent from the usual block and inline element placement common in HTML documents. An element whose position is **absolute** becomes a visual container for any elements enclosed in its content. If the element is repositioned, all of the elements defined inside it move with it. If any of those contained elements are assigned coordinates outside of their parent's dimensions, they disappear.

- **relative**   Makes the element's position relative to its natural position in document flow. This can be confusing, so most designers tend to use absolute values.

After you specify how to position the region (**absolute** or **relative**), the actual location of positioned elements should be specified by using their top-left corner. The position is set with the **left** and **top** style properties. The coordinate system for positioned elements uses the upper-left corner as the origin point, namely, 0,0. Values for the x coordinate increase to the right; y values increase going down from the origin. A value such as **10,100** would be 10 units to the right and 100 units down from the origin. Values may be specified as a length in a valid CSS measurement (such as pixels) or as a percentage of the containing object's (parent's) dimension. You may find that elements contain other elements, so 0,0 isn't always the upper-left corner of the browser.

After you position the region, you may want to set its size. By default, the **height** and **width** of the positioned region are set to fit the enclosed content, but the **height** and **width** properties, as discussed earlier in this chapter, can be used to specify the region's size.

The following example uses an inline style to set a **<DIV>** element to be 120 pixels from the left and 50 pixels down from the top-left corner of the browser:

```
<DIV STYLE="{position:absolute;
            left: 120px; top: 50px;
            height: 100px; width: 150px;
            background: yellow}">
At last, absolute positioning!
</DIV>
```

Although using the inline style form isn't the best way to do things, it serves its purpose here.

Before you rush off and position elements all over the screen, be aware of the nuances of nested items. For example, look at the following markup. Notice how the position of the second area is relative to the first. If you read the coordinate values numerically, the inner area should be positioned to the left and above where it shows onscreen. Remember, the coordinates are relative to the containing box.

```
<!DOCTYPE HTML PUBLIC "-//W3C//DTD HTML 4.0 Transitional//EN">
<HTML>
<HEAD>
<TITLE>Positioning Nested Items</TITLE>
<STYLE TYPE="text/css">
<!--
#outer    {position:absolute;
           left: 100px;
           top: 50px;
           height: 100px;
           width: 150px;
           background: yellow}

#inner    {position:absolute;
           left: 75px;
           top: 50px;
           height: 30px;
           width: 40px;
           background: orange}
-->
</STYLE>
</HEAD>

<BODY>
<DIV ID="outer">
This is the outer part of the nest.
<SPAN ID="inner">This is the inner part of the nest.</SPAN>
</DIV>
</BODY>
</HTML>
```

The rendering of this example is shown in Figure 10-10.

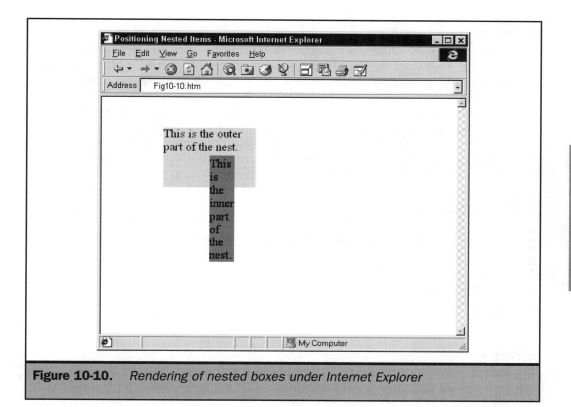

Figure 10-10.   *Rendering of nested boxes under Internet Explorer*

Clipping Regions

For elements whose position type is **absolute**, a *clipping rectangle* defines the subset of the content rectangle that is actually shown. The property **clip** can be used to set the coordinates of the clipping rectangle that houses the content. The form of the property is

```
clip: rect( top right bottom left)
```

where **top**, **right**, **bottom**, and **left** are the coordinate values that set the clipping region:

```
<DIV STYLE="{position:absolute;
            left:20; top:20;
            width:100; height:100;
            clip: rect(10 90 90 10)}">
This<BR>is<BR>a<BR>case<BR>of<BR>lines<BR>going<BR>
outside<BR>the<BR>box, which may be clipped.
</DIV>
```

overflow

Sometimes, an element's content is greater than the space allocated for it. Most browsers allocate space for content, unless size is set explicitly or a clipping region is set. The **overflow** property determines how an element should handle the situation when content doesn't fit. A value of **clip** for the property clips content to the size defined for the container. The **scroll** value allows content to scroll using a browser-dependent mechanism, such as scroll bars. The default value is **none**, which does nothing and may clip the content. The following example, which mimics the functionality of a floating frame, creates a positioned region that allows scrolling if content goes beyond its defined size:

```
<DIV STYLE="{position:absolute;
            left:20; top:20;
            width:100; height:100;
            clip: rect(10 90 90 10);
            overflow: scroll}">
This<BR>is<BR>a<BR>case<BR>of<BR>lines<BR>going<BR>
outside<BR>the<BR>box, which may be clipped.
</DIV>
```

z-index

Absolute and relative positioning allow element content to overlap. By default, overlapping elements stack in the order in which they are defined in an HTML document. The most recent elements go on top. This default order can be redefined by using an element's **z-index** property. Absolute- or relative-positioned elements define a **z-index** context for the elements that they contain. The containing element has an index of 0; the index increases with higher numbers stacked on top of lower numbers. The following example forces all images inside a container to overlap, and it uses the top class to position one image on top. Notice how the elements stack in the specified order rather than as defined:

```
<HTML>
<HEAD>
<TITLE>Z-order Example</TITLE>
<STYLE TYPE="text/css">
<!--
DIV.one    {position:absolute;
            top:20;left:20;
            height: 50; width: 50;
            color: white;
            background-color:blue;
            z-index: 2}
```

```
DIV.two        {position:absolute;
                top:30;left:30;
                height: 25; width: 100;
                background-color:orange;
                z-index: 1}

DIV.three      {position:absolute;
                top:40;left:40;
                height: 25; width: 25;
                background-color:yellow;
                z-index: 3}
-->
</STYLE>
</HEAD>

<BODY>
<DIV CLASS="one">
This is section one.
</DIV>

<DIV CLASS="two">
This is section two.
</DIV>

<DIV CLASS="three">
This is section three.
</DIV>
</BODY>
</HTML>
```

The rendering of this example is shown in Figure 10-11.

visibility

The **visibility** property determines whether an element is visible. The values for the property are **hidden**, **visible**, or **inherit**. The **inherit** value means that a property inherits its visibility state from the element that contains it. If an element is **hidden**, it still occupies the full canvas space, but is rendered as transparent. This simple example shows how the item is made invisible, but is not removed:

```
<P>This is a <EM STYLE="visibility: hidden">test</EM> of the
visibility property.
```

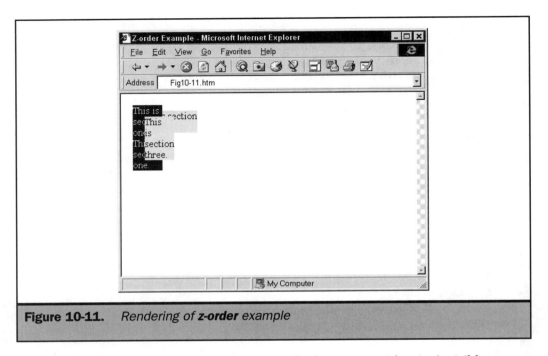

Figure 10-11. Rendering of **z-order** example

Figure 10-12 shows how the word "test" still takes up space, but isn't visible.

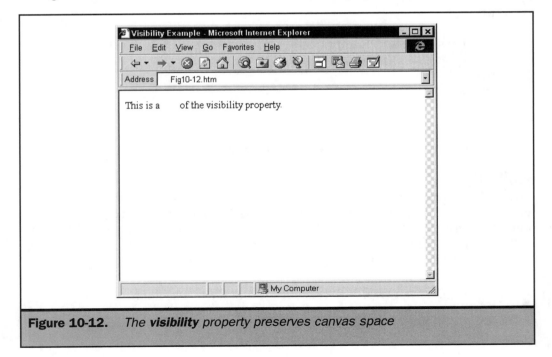

Figure 10-12. The **visibility** property preserves canvas space

Changing the visibility of different portions of the document may not seem that important, but imagine if the visibility could be controlled. If you could turn the visibility on and off, you could make content appear and disappear. A brief example of how this might be accomplished with a little scripting is shown here:

```html
<HTML>
<HEAD>
<TITLE>Visibility and Scripting</TITLE>
<STYLE TYPE="text/css">
<!--
#peek      {background: red;
            color: white;
            font-family: Comic Sans Ms, Fantasy;
            font-size: 64pt;
            position: absolute;
            top: 50px;
            text-align: center;
            visibility: hidden}

#button    {background: yellow;
            color: black;
            border-style: outset;
            border-width: thin;
            text-align: center;
            font-family: Arial, Sans-serif;
            font-size: 12pt;
            position: absolute;
            top: 10px;
            left: 10px;}
-->
</STYLE>
</HEAD>

<BODY>
<DIV ID="button" onClick="peek.style.visibility='visible'">
Press me!
</DIV>

<SPAN ID="peek">
Gotcha!
```

```
</SPAN>
</BODY>
</HTML>
```

Note that you can manipulate style values on-the-fly. By changing the look and feel of items depending on a user action, a variety of effects are possible. Look at the small code fragment here:

```
<A HREF="http://www.yahoo.com" onmouseover="this.style.color='red'"
   onmouseout="this.style.color='black'">
```

Note | *This style of link roll effect can also be implemented by using the pseudoclass **hover**, which is implemented by Microsoft. For example, a style rule such as **A:hover {color: yellow}** would change links to yellow when the user passes over them under Internet Explorer 4 and above. This low-bandwidth rollover effect would degrade gracefully under Netscape browsers, because it would ignore the pseudoclass.*

The markup for the link is modified so that the color of the item is changed to red and then back to black as a user passes a mouse over it.

Dynamic styles present many possibilities. Both Netscape and Microsoft support access to style sheets from a scripting language, though in different ways and to a different degree. See Chapter 14 for more on scripting style sheet properties, in which particular emphasis is given on the movement of layered objects.

Before looking at browser-specific style changes, an overview of the W3C CSS2 specification is important, because it promises even more future possibilities for using style sheets, including expanded media options, discussed in the next section.

CSS2: New Feature Summary

This section is not a detailed examination of the CSS2 specification, but rather a summary of some of its new features. Bear in mind that *none* of these properties are supported by any browsers at the time of this writing; in fact, the major browser vendors are only just beginning to fulfill the promises of CSS1.

Media Types

The CSS2 specification defines numerous media types, listed in Table 10-2. Until browser vendors or developers of other user agents begin to support these media types, these definitions may have no meaning outside of the specification.

Media Type	Definition
All	For use with all devices
aural	For use with speech synthesizers
braille	For use with tactile Braille devices
embossed	For use with Braille printers
handheld	For use with handheld devices
print	For use with printed material and documents viewed onscreen in print preview mode
projection	For use with projected media (direct computer-to-projector presentations), or printing transparencies for projection
screen	For use with color computer screens
tty	For use with low-resolution teletypes, terminals, or other devices with limited display capabilities
tv	For use with television-type devices

Table 10-2. *Media Types Defined Under CSS2*

Media-Dependent Style Sheets

Under the CSS2 specification, certain style sheet properties are supported only by specific media types. In other cases, more than one media type supports a property but may call for different values. For example, when font-related properties are used for both computer display and for printing, two different media may require different font styles or sizes.

CSS2 provides two main ways to define media types for style sheets. The first method simply uses the HTML language to define the media type. The other method uses either the **@import** rule or the **@media** rule.

The following code example shows how style sheet media types are defined using HTML:

```
<!DOCTYPE HTML PUBLIC "-//W3C//DTD HTML 4.0 Transitional//EN">
<HTML>
<HEAD>
<TITLE>CSS Media Type Example</TITLE>
```

```
<LINK REL="stylesheet" TYPE="text/css" MEDIA="print, handheld"
    HREF="newstyle.css">
</HEAD>

<BODY>
...Body content...
</BODY>
</HTML>
```

The **@import** rule has already been discussed in this chapter (refer to "Embedding and Importing Style Sheets"). Defining a media type under CSS2 simply requires the addition of an appropriate media type after defining the URL with the **@import** rule, as shown in this code fragment:

```
@import url("braille.css") braille;
```

The **@media** rule is used to define style rules for multiple media types in a single style sheet. For example, you may want to have a document display in a large, sans-serif font when viewed on a monitor, but display in a smaller, serif font when printed. Multiple media types should be separated by commas, as shown in the following code fragment:

```
<STYLE TYPE="text/css">
<!--
@media screen          {BODY
                        {font-family: sans-serif;
                         font-size: 18 pt}
                        }

@media print           {BODY
                        {font-family: serif;
                         font-size: 9 pt}
                        }

@media screen, print   {BODY
                        {line-height: 150%}
                        }

-->
</STYLE>
```

If implemented by a browser or another user agent, this code would cause the body of the Document to display in an 18-point, sans-serif font on a computer monitor, to print out as a 9-point, serif font, and to have a line height of 150 percent in both media.

User Interface Changes

The CSS2 specification also promises more options for user interfaces, allowing page designers to implement various contextual display options for cursors, colors, and fonts, many of which can be set to match the end user's system settings.

cursor

The **cursor** property determines how the cursor displays when passed over the affected element. The **auto** value leaves the display to be determined by the user agent, so the cursor will display according to either the browser default settings or the user settings. The **crosshair** value renders the cursor as a simple cross, whereas **default** displays the system's default cursor (usually an arrow). Various other values listed in the CSS2 specification may indicate that something is a link (**pointer**), that text can be selected (**text**), that something may be resized in various directions (**e-resize, ne-resize, nw-resize, n-resize, se-resize, sw-resize, s-resize, w-resize**), or that the user must wait while a program is busy (**wait**). One value, **uri**, can be used to reference a cursor source; multiple cursor sources may be listed, as shown in this example from the CSS2 specification:

```
P    {cursor : url("mything.cur"), url("second.csr"), text; }
```

As with fonts, the user agent should attempt to render the first cursor listed, try the second one if necessary, and ultimately default to the generic cursor value listed last. Internet Explorer already supports this property to a limited degree, as discussed later in this chapter.

Integrating Colors with User Preferences

Under CSS2, authors will be able to provide color values that match preexisting settings on the end user's system. This may be particularly useful in providing pages that are set to accommodate a user's visual impairment or other disability. These values may be used with any CSS color properties (**color, background-color**, and so on). The CSS2 specification recommends using the mixed-case format of the values shown in Table 10-3, even though they are not, in fact, case-sensitive.

Color Value	Intended Rendering
ActiveBorder	Color of user's active window border setting
ActiveCaption	Color of user's active window caption setting
AppWorkspace	Background color of user's multiple document interface setting
Background	Color of user's desktop background setting
ButtonFace	Face color of user's 3-D display elements setting
ButtonHighlight	Highlight color of user's 3-D display elements setting
ButtonShadow	Shadow color of user's 3-D display elements setting
ButtonText	Color of user's push button text setting
CaptionText	Color of user's text settings for captions, size box, and scroll bar arrow box
GrayText	Color of user's disabled text setting; if system doesn't display gray, defaults to black
Highlight	Background color of user's control-selected items setting
HighlightText	Text color of user's control-selected items setting
InactiveBorder	Color of user's inactive window border setting
InactiveCaption	Color of user's inactive window caption setting
InactiveCaptionText	Text color of user's inactive caption setting
InfoBackground	Background color of user's tool tip control setting
InfoText	Text color of user's tool tip control setting
Menu	Color of user's menu background setting
MenuText	Text color of user's menus setting
Scrollbar	Color of user's scroll bar setting (gray area)
ThreeDDarkShadow	Dark-shadow color of user's setting for edges of 3-D display elements
ThreeDFace	Face color of user's 3-D display elements setting
ThreeDHighlight	Highlight color of user's 3-D display elements setting

Table 10-3.   *User Color Preferences Under CSS2*

ThreeDLightShadow	Light-shadow color of user's setting for edges of 3-D display elements
ThreeDShadow	Dark-shadow color of user's setting for 3-D display elements
Window	Background color of user's window setting
WindowFrame	Frame color of user's window setting
WindowText	Text color of user's window setting

Table 10-3.   *User Color Preferences Under CSS2* (continued)

The following code fragment shows how these values could be used to make a paragraph display with the same foreground and background colors as the user's system:

```
P    {color: WindowText; background-color: Window}
```

Coordinating Fonts with User Preferences

Under CSS2, designers will have the option of coordinating fonts with the fonts defined by the end user's system. These system font values may be used only with the shorthand **font** property, *not* with **font-family**. Table 10-4 lists these values and their related system font values.

Font Value	System Font Referenced
Caption	System font used to caption buttons and other controls
Icon	System font used to label icons
Menu	System font used for drop-down menus and menu lists
Message-box	System font used in dialog boxes
small-caption	System font used for labeling small controls
status-bar	System font used in window status bars

Table 10-4.   *Using CSS2 to Match an End-User's System Fonts*

Thus, to make level-three headers in a document display in the same font as a user's system uses to display window status bars, you would use the following code fragment in a style sheet:

```
H3    {font: status-bar}
```

Outline Properties

Outlines are a new CSS2 feature that resemble borders but take up no additional space, and may be set to a shape different from that of the image, form field, or other element to which they are applied. Outlines are drawn over an item, rather than around it, thus causing no reflow. Outlines may be used dynamically, to indicate what element in a page has focus. Outline properties include **outline-width**, **outline-style**, **outline-color**, and the shorthand property **outline**. Table 10-5 lists the values associated with these properties.

Aural Improvements

The CSS2 specification contains numerous properties designed to provide aural rendering of Web documents. While not yet implemented, these properties represent one of the most forward-looking aspects of CSS2, targeted primarily for the sight-impaired, but offering expanded media possibilities for the Web, as well. While the use of a speech-based interface may seem like science fiction, the advances made in both speech synthesis and speech recognition suggest that practical use of this technology is not far away. This is a brief summary of the aural properties defined in CSS2. Again, these properties haven't been implemented, so any references to them in the present tense are based on their definition within the CSS2 specification, not on their actual use.

Outline Property	Values Accepted
outline-width	Same values as **border-width**
outline-style	Same values as **border-style**, except **hidden**
outline-color	All color values, including **invert**
outline	Sets all three values

Table 10-5.　*CSS2 Outline Properties and Values*

Basically, aural style sheets allow synthetic speech sources to be associated with paragraphs and other elements. Timing and the spatial relationships between sounds will also be subject to control by style sheets. Presumably, various synthetic voices will function in a way analogous to fonts on a computer screen; different "voices" may be assigned to different elements or classes of elements, or the qualities of any given voice may be altered to suit an element (more emphasis for headers, and so forth).

speech-rate The **speech-rate** property is used to determine the rate of speech. Values include numeric values, **x-slow**, **slow**, **medium**, **fast**, **x-fast**, **faster**, **slower**, and **inherit**. Numeric values determine the number of words spoken per minute (wpm). Speeds range from 80 wpm for the value **x-slow**, to 500 wpm for the value **x-fast**. The relative value **faster** increases the speech rate by 40 wpm, while **slower** reduces it by 40 wpm. The default value is **medium**. The value **inherit** may also be used with this property.

voice-family The **voice-family** property works much like the **font-family** property insofar as it can be set to reference a specific voice "font," generic voice "fonts," or a combination thereof, using a comma-separated list. A sample might look like this:

```
P.1    {voice-family: "bill gates", executive, male}
P.2    {voice-family: "jewel", singer, female}
```

In this hypothetical example, the first voice name is a specific voice based on a public figure, the second is a specific voice meant to suggest a similar character, and the final voice is a generic voice. According to the CSS2 specification, names may be quoted, and should be quoted if they contain white space. The value **inherit** may also be used with this property.

pitch The **pitch** property defines the average pitch of a voice. Values include numeric values, which determine the voice's frequency in hertz, as well as **x-low**, **low**, **medium**, **high**, and **inherit**. The default value is **medium**. The values **x-low** through **high** are dependent on the pitch of the voice family in use (as determined by the **voice-family** property). The value **inherit** may also be used with this property.

pitch-range The **pitch-range** property determines the range of pitch variation of a voice's average pitch, as defined through the **voice-family** and **pitch** properties. Values are either inherited (**inherit**) or defined by a numeric value between **0** and **100**. The value **0** produces no pitch variation, **50** approximates normal pitch variation, and **100** produces an exaggerated pitch range. The value **inherit** may also be used with this property.

stress   The **stress** property assigns stress, or peaks, in a voice's intonation. Used in conjunction with **pitch-range**, this may allow the creation of more-detailed vocal ranges. The rendering of numeric values may be dependent on the voice's gender and the language spoken. Values are numeric, ranging from **0** to **100**; the default value is **50**. The value **inherit** may also be used with this property.

richness   The **richness** property determines the richness of a voice. Numeric values range from **0** to **100**, with a default value of **50**. The higher the number, the more the voice carries. The value **inherit** may also be used with this property.

volume   The **volume** property determines the average volume of a voice. Numeric values range from **0** to **100**. A value of **0** produces the lowest audible volume, and **100** the loudest comfortable volume. Values may also be set to a percentage of the inherited volume. Other values include **silent** (no sound), **x-soft** (equivalent to **0**), **soft** (equivalent to **25**), **medium** (equivalent to **50**), **loud** (equivalent to **75**), and **x-loud** (equivalent to **100**). The only other value is **inherit**. These values will depend largely on the speech-rendering system used and on user settings, such as speaker volume.

speak   The **speak** property determines whether text is spoken, and how. The value **none** prevents text from being spoken. The default value **normal** renders text in a "normal" speaking voice, as determined by other properties and the user agent. The value **spell-out** causes the user agent to speak text as individual letters, useful when dealing with acronyms. The only other value is **inherit**.

pause-before   The **pause-before** property defines a pause to take place before an element's content is spoken. Values can be expressed as time, measured in seconds (the default) or milliseconds (**ms**), or as a percentage. Percentages define pause length in relation to the average length of a word, as determined by the **speech-rate** property. (For a **speech-rate** of **100wpm**, each word takes an average time of 600 milliseconds; a **pause-before** value of **100%** creates a pause of 600 ms, while a value of **50%** creates a pause of 300 ms.) The CSS2 specification recommends the use of relative (percentage) units. This property is not inherited.

pause-after   The **pause-after** property defines a pause to take place before an element's content is spoken. Values can be expressed as time, measured in seconds (the default) or milliseconds (**ms**), or as a percentage. Percentages define pause length in relation to the average length of a word, as determined by the **speech-rate** property. (For a **speech-rate** of **100wpm**, each word takes an average time of 600 milliseconds; a **pause-after** value of **100%** creates a pause of 600 ms, while a value of **50%** creates a 300 ms pause.) The CSS2 specification recommends the use of relative (percentage) units. This property is not inherited.

pause   The **pause** property is a shorthand notation for the **pause-before** and **pause-after** properties, just discussed. A style rule of

```
P    {pause: 12 ms}
```

creates a 12-second pause before and after rendering an element; a style rule of

```
P    {pause: 12 ms   20 ms}
```

creates a 12-second pause before the element and a 20-second pause after it.

cue-before   The **cue-before** property sets an audio icon to be played before an element. One example might be a musical tone at the start of a paragraph, or a voice stating "begin paragraph." In some sense, this may be similar to the page-turning noise that often is used in children's books with an accompanying tape, record, or CD; this would serve as an attention cue for the listener. The value can be set to the URI of an audio file, as shown here:

```
P    {cue-before: url("ding.wav")}
```

This would play the sound file ding.wav just before speaking the contents of the paragraph. The value of the property may also be set to **none**. If a URI is used that doesn't reference a viable audio file, the property renders as if the value were **none**. The CSS2 specification recommends that user agents reference a default sound file if the file referenced is not valid. This property is not inherited, but the value can be set to inherit from a parent element.

cue-after   The **cue-after** property sets an audio icon to be played after an element. Values are the same as for **cue-before**:

```
P    {cue-after: url("ding.wav")}
```

cue   The **cue** property provides shorthand notation for **cue-before** and **cue-after**. A single value sets both properties to the same value; the properties can also be set separately:

```
P    {cue: url("ding.wav")}
```

play-during   The **play-during** property allows a background sound (music, sound effects, and such) to play while an element is being rendered. The sound is determined by the URI of an audio file. Additional values include the following:

- **mix**   Causes the sound set by a parent element's **play-during** property to continue playing while the child element is being spoken; otherwise, the sound determined by the child element's **play-during** property plays.

- **repeat**   Causes the sound to repeat if its duration is less than the time needed to render the element's content; if the rendering time of content is shorter than the sound file's duration, the sound is clipped.

- **auto**   Causes the parent element's sound to keep on playing.

- **none**   Terminates the parent element's background sound until the child element has finished rendering, at which time it should resume. The **play-during** property is not inherited unless the value is set to **inherit**.

- **inherit**   Causes the parent element's background sound to start over for the child element, rather than continue to play as determined by the **mix** and **auto** values.

azimuth   The **azimuth** property determines the horizontal location of a sound. How this renders will depend largely on the user agent and the audio system used with it. Values can be set to specific angles, based on the concept of 360-degree surround sound. A value of **0deg** places a sound dead center, as if originating directly in front of the listener. A value of **180deg** places a sound directly behind a listener; **90deg** indicates dead right, while **270deg** or **–90deg** indicates dead left. Named values include **left-side** (270 degrees), **far-left, left, center-left, center** (0 degrees), **center-right, right, far-right**, and **right-side** (90 degrees). The default value is **center**. The relative value **leftwards** moves the sound 20 degrees counterclockwise, while **rightward** moves it 20 degrees clockwise. The CSS2 specification notes that these values indicate a desired result, but that how this will work must be determined by user agents. The **azimuth** property is inherited.

elevation   The **elevation** property determines the vertical location of a sound relative to the listener. Angle values range from **90deg** (directly above) to **–90deg** (directly below). A value of **0deg** locates the sound on the same level as the listener. Named values include **above** (90 degrees), **level** (0 degrees), and **below** (–90 degrees). The relative value **higher** adds 10 degrees of elevation, while **lower** subtracts 10 degrees. The **elevation** property is inherited.

speak-punctuation   The **speak-punctuation** property affects how punctuation is rendered. The value **code** causes punctuation to render as literal speech (in other words, **,** is spoken as "comma" and **?** is spoken as "question mark," much as a person giving dictation might speak the name of the punctuation out loud). A value of **none**

(the default) renders punctuation as it would sound in ordinary speech—as short and long pauses, proper inflection of questions, and so on. The only other value is **inherit**. The **speak-punctuation** property is inherited.

speak-numeral   The **speak-numeral** property provides two options for the rendering of numbers. The value **digits** causes numbers to render as a sequence of digits (**1001** renders as one, zero, zero, one). A value of **continuous** (the default) causes numbers to render as complete numbers (**1001** renders as one thousand and one). The only other value is **inherit**. The **speak-numeral** property is inherited.

speak-header   The **speak-header** property provides options for speech rendering of table headers relative to table data. Values include **once**, **always**, and **inherit**. The value **once** causes the content of a table header to be spoken once before the content of all associated table cells is rendered ("Animal: dog, cat, cow…"). The value **always** causes the table header content to render before each associated table cell is rendered ("Animal: dog; Animal: cat; Animal: cow…"). The **speak-header** property is inherited.

This is just a brief overview of many of the defined aural properties under CSS2. While the exact syntax is well defined in the CSS2 specification, at the time of this writing, no browsers actually support this technology for testing purposes. Syntax may vary when the style properties are finally implemented. The next section covers some properties that are implemented by browser vendors, but that may or may not be part of the CSS specification.

Microsoft-Specific Style Sheet Properties

Browser vendors are already making new additions to cascading style sheets. Microsoft has added a variety of multimedia filters and transitions that can be accessed via a style sheet. Under Internet Explorer, you can also change the cursor of an object, control the printing of a document to a limited degree, and even use downloadable fonts. Undoubtedly, these additions are just the beginning of a slew of new proprietary changes introduced into style sheets. For definitive information on the latest style sheet extensions, check the browser vendor's developer information.

Filters

Microsoft initially supported a variety of multimedia filters, such as ActiveX controls, that were included with the Internet Explorer browser. Use of these multimedia effects was somewhat limited due to the proprietary nature of ActiveX, as well as the public's lack of familiarity with the technology. Instead of using controls directly, Microsoft has taken an approach to make these multimedia effects available via style sheets. What is interesting about this approach is that Microsoft did it in a very generalized manner,

PRESENTATION AND LAYOUT

thus showing how other filters might be added by other vendors. The basic form of a filter rule is shown here:

```
Filter: filtername(filtervalue1, filtervalue2,...)
```

Each of the possible values for *filtername* is shown in Table 10-6. Note that each filter might have many values that must be set in order for it to work properly. See the Microsoft documentation available at http://www.microsoft.com/sitebuilder/ for a complete discussion of the possible values for the various filters.

Filter Name	Description
Alpha	Sets a uniform transparency level
Blur	Creates the impression of moving at high speed
Chroma	Makes a specific color transparent
DropShadow	Creates a solid silhouette of the object
FlipH	Creates a horizontal mirror image
FlipV	Creates a vertical mirror image
Glow	Adds radiance around the outside edges of the object
Grayscale	Drops color information from the image
Invert	Reverses the hue, saturation, and brightness values
Light	Projects a light source onto an object
Mask	Creates a transparent mask from an object
Shadow	Creates an offset solid silhouette
Wave	Creates a sine wave distortion along the X axis
Xray	Shows just the edges of the object

Table 10-6. *Filter Names Supported in Internet Explorer 4*

An example that illustrates how the filters may be used with some text is shown here:

```
<!DOCTYPE HTML PUBLIC "-//W3C//DTD HTML 4.0 Transitional//EN">
<HTML>
<HEAD>
<TITLE>Microsoft Filter Test</TITLE>
<STYLE TYPE="text/css">
<!--
.glow          {height: 10; width: 400;
                filter: Glow(Color=#00FF00, Strength=4)}
.blur          {height: 10; width: 400;
                filter: Blur(Add = 1, Direction = 90, Strength = 10);}
.dropshadow    {height: 10; width: 400;
                filter:DropShadow(Color=#FF0000, OffX=2, OffY=2,
                Positive=1)}
.fliph         {height: 10; width: 400; filter: fliph()}
.flipv         {height: 10; width: 400; filter: flipv()}
.shadow        {height: 10; width: 400; filter: Shadow(color=#00FF00)}
.wave          {height: 10; width: 400;
                filter: Wave(Add=1, Freq=4, LightStrength=50,
                        Phase=50, Strength=10)}
-->
</STYLE>
</HEAD>

<BODY>
<H1 ALIGN="CENTER">Microsoft Multimedia Filters</H1>

<DIV CLASS="blur">This is the blur filter.</DIV>
<DIV CLASS="dropshadow">This is the dropshadow filter.</DIV>
<DIV CLASS="fliph">This is the flip horizontal filter.</DIV>
<DIV CLASS="flipv">This is the flip vertical filter.</DIV>
<DIV CLASS="glow">This is the glow filter.</DIV>
<DIV CLASS="shadow">This is the shadow filter.</DIV>
<DIV CLASS="wave">This is the wave filter.</DIV>
</BODY>
</HTML>
```

Playing with the values for the various filter properties may change the effects dramatically. A rendering of the text filters from this example is shown in Figure 10-13.

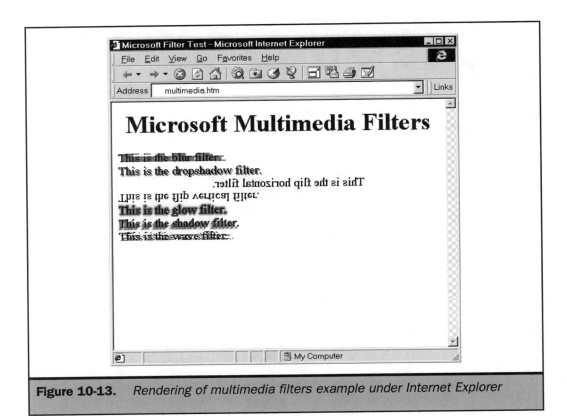

Figure 10-13. *Rendering of multimedia filters example under Internet Explorer*

Remember that a visual filter can be applied to any visible element on the HTML page that supports the filter property, ranging from a single spanned character to the entire body of the document. It is even possible to apply a visual filter to a **<DIV>** tag to utilize a single set of filter effects on all of the visual objects in that region and even stack up effects on enclosed objects.

Reveal Transition Filter

The reveal transition filter allows objects to be revealed by using a variety of transitions, such as box-ins or wipes. These transitions are similar to those found in presentation programs, such as Microsoft's PowerPoint. The form of the filter property for **revealtrans** is shown here:

```
filter: revealtrans(duration=duration, transition=transition#)
```

The value of **duration** is the time it should take to reveal or hide the object in seconds.milliseconds. The transition number is a numeric value from **0** to **24**, which corresponds to one of the predefined patterns to reveal objects. The following table shows the values and their corresponding meanings:

Value	Meaning
0	Box in
1	Box out
2	Circle in
3	Circle out
4	Wipe up
5	Wipe down
6	Wipe right
7	Wipe left
8	Vertical blinds
9	Horizontal blinds
10	Checkerboard across
11	Checkerboard down
12	Random dissolve
13	Split vertical in
14	Split vertical out
15	Split horizontal in
16	Split horizontal out
17	Strips left down
18	Strips left up
19	Strips right down
20	Strips right up
21	Random bars horizontal
22	Random bars vertical
23	Random

PRESENTATION AND LAYOUT

A rule such as the following would set all paragraph elements of the class **intro** to reveal themselves by using an expanding circle:

```
P.intro    {filter: revealtrans(duration=4.0, transition=3)}
```

It may be required to trigger the transition with script code, so don't just throw a bunch of transitions on the page and hope that the page starts animating. These transitions might be of little use on a set page, but what about between pages?

Interpage Transitions

Interpage transitions enable you to provide multimedia effects while a Web page is loading or exiting. Interpage transitions are not handled with style sheets, but instead are handled by using the **<META>** element within the **<HEAD>** section of a Web page. However, the syntax of the transitions is the same as the reveal transition, so covering it here seems appropriate.

The syntax for transitions consists of three parts: specifying when the event should be played, the duration of the transition, and what kind of transition effect to use. The following two examples show how to set transitions upon entry and exit of a page. To make a checkerboard entrance that lasts three seconds, use a **<META>** element, such as the following:

```
<META http-equiv="Page-Enter"
      CONTENT="RevealTrans(Duration=3.0,Transition=10)">
```

To make a big exit, you could set a wipe effect that lasts two seconds:

```
<META http-equiv="Page-Exit"
      CONTENT="RevealTrans(Duration=2.0,Transition=7)">
```

Of course, leaving the page would require a link from the page to another destination.

Experiment with all of the different transition effects by setting the transition number anywhere from **0** to **23**. While transitions seem pretty interesting, don't get carried away. They can be even more annoying than **<BLINK>**.

Setting the Cursor

Starting with Internet Explorer 4, Microsoft has added the capability to set the form of the cursor when it is placed over an object. Because you can make everything on the page capable of being pressed, resetting the cursor is certainly very useful. To set the cursor, create a rule like this:

```
P    {cursor: hand}
```

Now, whenever the user places the mouse over a paragraph element, the cursor shows up as a hand.

The possible values for the **cursor** property are **crosshair**, **default**, **hand**, **move**, **e-resize**, **ne-resize**, **nw-resize**, **n-resize**, **se-resize**, **sw-resize**, **s-resize**, **w-resize**, **text**, **wait**, and **help**. The default value of **auto** sets the cursor to whatever it should be, based on the element it is over.

Setting Page Breaks

In the future, style sheets will certainly be extended to support more printing capabilities, but Microsoft has already provided the **page-break-before** property and **page-break-after** property under Internet Explorer 4. These properties can be used to set a page break on the printer. By using these properties, you can set the printer to go to a new page before or after a particular element. The default value for either of the properties is **auto**. Other possible values include **always**, **left**, and **right**. Most likely, the value **always** will be used to tell the printer to always insert a page break. Imagine a rule such as this:

```
BR.newpage    {page-break-after: always}
```

Adding this rule would always cause a page break wherever the rule is inserted into a document.

If an issue of the newline showing onscreen arises, you can use a nonbreaking element, such as **<SPAN>**, to set the page break. Ongoing work for standardizing CSS Printing Extensions can be found at http://www.w3.org/TR/WD-print.

Downloadable Fonts

As with the font technology discussed in Chapter 6, fonts can be embedded in a Web page by using style sheet syntax. To embed fonts in a Web document under Microsoft Internet Explorer, use the **@font-face** property. This property allows the designer to specify fonts in the document that might not be available on the viewer's system.

To embed a font, first specify the **font-family** property. Then, specify the **src** property and set it equal to the URL of an embedded OpenType file, which should have an .eot extension. When the file is downloaded, it is converted to a TrueType font and then displayed on the screen. By putting a rule such as the following in the style sheet, the font named GhostTown can be used elsewhere on the page by using the **font-family** property:

```
@font-face    {font-family:GhostTown;
              src:url(http://www.bigcompany.com/fonts/ghost.eot);}
```

One big question is, how can a special embedded font file be created? The designer has to run the font through a tool to create the font definition file and then place that file on the Web server. Another potential issue is having to make changes to the Web server so that the file is delivered correctly. See the Microsoft Typography Web site, at http://www.microsoft.com/typography, for information about font creation tools and other deployment issues.

To embed fonts by the Netscape definition, use the **@fontdef** rule in a style sheet to indicate the downloadable font. You will also need to create an embedded font file for Netscape-based dynamic fonts—in this case, a PFR file. So, to bring in GhostTown, use

```
@fontdef url(http://www.bigcompany.com/fonts/ghosttown.pfr);
```

or, as discussed in Chapter 6, a **<LINK>** element could also be used in the **<HEAD>** of the document, as shown here:

```
<LINK REL="FONTDEF"
      SRC="http://www.bigcompany.com/fonts/ghosttown.pfr">
```

These style sheet and HTML font solutions work for Netscape. The Microsoft style of adding an **SRC** rule for **@font-face** is the proposed solution from the W3C and should eventually be supported by Netscape. More information about Netscape's current font and style sheet syntax, as well as links to dynamic font tools, can be found at http://www.truedoc.com.

Summary

Cascading style sheets provide better control over the look and feel of Web pages. Style sheets aren't just useful for making attractive pages. By dividing structure and style, they make documents simpler, and easier to manipulate. While style sheets provide a great deal of flexibility in creating pages, they are not fully implemented yet in today's browsers. Some inconsistencies exist between implementations. When used in a nonobtrusive manner, style sheets are a great way to improve the layout of pages, without locking into a proprietary solution.

Despite the open nature of style sheets, extensions are already being made by browser vendors, so this open nature of the technology might not be quite what it has been built up to be. Pixel-level layout control and downloadable fonts are almost here, but the innovations don't stop. Why just strive for a print style layout when fully programmed pages are possible? Chapter 11 starts the transition from static Web pages to programmed pages, beginning with forms.

The Complete Reference

Part III

Programming and HTML

Chapter 11

Basic Interactivity and HTML: Forms

One of the most dynamic aspects of the Web is that it offers the ability to include interactive features. Up to this point, the discussion has focused on the Web as a static publishing environment. Adding a way for the end viewer to submit information makes the Web more powerful than traditional media. At the simplest level, you could create a link with a mailto URL, covered in Chapter 4, and have visitors send in e-mail comments. There are other times when creating a fill-out form would make more sense. With fill-out forms and the appropriate programs to handle the submitted information, it is possible to create an interactive environment ranging from an order entry system to a dynamically created Web site.

How Are Forms Used?

There are many uses for forms on the Web. The most common ones include comment response forms, order entry forms, subscription forms, registration forms, and customization forms:

- A *comment response* is generally used as a way to collect comments from Web site viewers and have people suggest improvements.

- *Order entry forms,* which are now common on the Web, provide a way for viewers to order goods from online stores. Order entry forms typically require the user to provide an address, credit card number, and other information necessary to facilitate online commerce.

  Such forms are often used to access database-hosted information; for example, looking up information in a catalog. Many e-commerce sites rely on forms and databases to provide order entry services.

Note   *People worry about the interception of credit card numbers when they are sending them to firms they may know very little about. There are facilities to encrypt data transmitted between Web browser and server, but users should be very cautious about who is at the other end of the connection. A little common sense can remove much of the fear around sensitive data transmission.*

- Many sites, particularly those that attempt to generate revenue through direct subscriptions or by selling advertising space, are adopting a subscriber model using *subscription forms*.

- *Registration forms* are used to collect information about a user and often are tied to an authentication system, which limits access to the site.

- Some sites allow the user to select the look and feel for the site itself, literally creating a custom site for each visitor. A *customization form* might allow users to specify what topics they are interested in within an online magazine. When tied to an authentication system, a user accessing the site views a version set according to his or her tastes.

There are many other examples of how forms might be used on the Web. The point here is to illustrate the kind of interactivity provided by forms.

Form Preliminaries

Making forms is easy. Just add the **<FORM>** element and associated tags for the form fields to the document, as you'll learn more about in the next section. But how can the contents of a form be processed once the user submits the information? After a form is filled in, it is sent somewhere (as specified by a URL); generally, a program on a remote Web server will then parse the submitted information and do something with it. The programs that handle the incoming form data are usually Common Gateway Interface (CGI) programs. They can also utilize ColdFusion, or NSAPI (Netscape Server API) programs, or ISAPI (Internet Information Server API) filters. A basic overview of how the relationship works is shown in Figure 11-1.

The point here isn't to get into the complications of how to make a CGI program or other programs to handle form submitted data, just to understand that the form itself is only part of the equation. There still must be some way to make the form do something, but this may not be your responsibility. CGI can get complicated, since it usually involves real programming in languages like C, Perl, or even Applescript. It may be beyond the skill set of the page designer. It is possible to use off-the-shelf CGI programs in many cases.

But why worry about these issues? Does the person who creates the IRS tax form know how the program that calculates things works? Why should you worry about how the CGI for the database query form you created is written? This division of labor is far too often missing in Web projects. The people who build the back end of the Web site that the form interacts with probably aren't the best ones to code the form. The person who codes the form isn't necessarily always the best person to write the back-end CGI program. Think about how the form works in the grand scheme of things, but worry mostly about making your end of the site work.

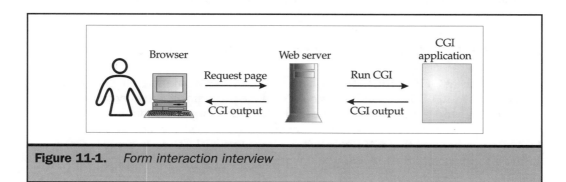

Figure 11-1.   *Form interaction interview*

The <FORM> Element

A form in HTML is enclosed between the **<FORM>** and **</FORM>** tags. The form itself contains regular text; other HTML elements such as tables; and form elements such as check boxes, pull-down menus, and text fields. The W3C specification calls these form elements *controls*. This is somewhat confusing, because Microsoft also refers to ActiveX objects as controls. To avoid confusion, we'll call form elements either form fields or form controls, not just controls. The form controls are set by a user to indicate the contents of the form. Once the user has finished filling out the form, it must be submitted for processing. Completed forms are generally passed to a remote program that handles the data. The contents may even be mailed to a user for further inspection. To make the form work, you must specify two things, and potentially two other important features. First, specify the address of the program that will handle the form contents using **ACTION**. Next, specify the method in which the form data will be passed using the **METHOD** attribute. The **NAME** attribute is also very important to set a name for the form so it can be later manipulated by a scripting language such as JavaScript. Finally, in some cases you may have to specify how the form will be encoded using the **ENCTYPE** attribute.

ACTION Attribute

How an HTML form is to be handled is set using the **ACTION** attribute for the form element. The **ACTION** attribute is usually set to a URL of the program that will handle the form data. This URL will usually point to a CGI script to decode the form results. For example, the code

```
<FORM ACTION="http://www.bigcompany.com/cgi-bin/post-query"
    METHOD="POST">
```

would be for a script called post-query in the cgi-bin directory on the server www.bigcompany.com. It is also possible to use a relative URL for the **ACTION** attribute if the form is delivered by the same server that houses the form-handling program:

```
<FORM ACTION="../cgi-bin/post-query" METHOD="POST">
```

Setting the **ACTION** immediately begs this question: what program should the data be passed to? This depends on who writes the program. There may be canned programs to handle the contents of the form. But what happens if there is no way to use a remote program? It is possible to create a "poor man's" form using the mailto URL. Remember that the **ACTION** attribute is set to a URL. Thus, in some cases, a form element such as the following will work.

```
<FORM ACTION="mailto:formtest@bigcompany.com" METHOD="POST"
     ENCTYPE="text/plain">
```

It is even possible to use an extended form of mailto URL, which is supported by Netscape browsers. For example:

```
<FORM ACTION="mailto:formtest@bigcompany.com?
Subject=Comment%20Form%20Result">
```

Although the mailto form seems the best way to do things, not all browsers support this style. There are also potential security issues. Even if the browser supports the mailto style, the data should be passed using the **POST** method. It may be useful to encode the data differently by setting it to use text/plain encoding rather than the default style, which is a cryptic encoding style similar to how URLs look. The next section discusses the methods and the encoding type.

METHOD Attribute

It is also necessary to specify how the form will be submitted to the address specified by the **ACTION** attribute. How data will be submitted is handled by the **METHOD** attribute. There are two acceptable values for the **METHOD** attribute: **GET** and **POST**. These are the HTTP methods that a browser uses to "talk" to a server. We'll find out more about that in a moment, as well as in Chapter 12. Note that if the **METHOD** attribute remains unspecified, most browsers will default to the **GET** method. While much of the following discussion is more applicable to the people writing the programs that handle form data, it is important to understand the basic idea of each method.

GET Method

The **GET** method is generally the default method for browsers to submit information. In fact, HTML documents are generally retrieved by requesting a single URL from a Web server using the **GET** method, which is part of the HTTP protocol. When you type a URL such as http://www.bigcompany.com/staff/thomas.htm into your Web browser, it is translated into a valid HTTP **GET** request such as this:

```
GET /staff/thomas.htm HTTP/1.0
```

This request is then sent to the server www.bigcompany.com. What this request says, essentially, is "Get me the file thomas.htm in the staff directory. I am speaking the 1.0 dialect of HTTP." How does this relate to forms? You really aren't getting a file *per se* when you submit a form, are you? In reality, you are running a program to handle the form data. For example, the **ACTION** value might specify a URL like

PROGRAMMING AND HTML

http://www.bigcompany.com/cgi-bin/comment.exe, which is the address of a program that can parse your comment form. So wouldn't the HTTP request be something like the one shown here?

```
GET /cgi-bin/comment.exe HTTP/1.0
```

Not quite. You need to pass the form data along with the name of the program to run. To do this, all the information from the form is appended onto the end of the URL being requested. This produces a hundred-character URL with the actual data in it, as shown here:

```
http://www.bigompany.com/cgi-bin/comments.exe?
Name=Al+Smith&Age=30&Sex=male
```

The **GET** method isn't very secure, since the data input appears in the URL. Furthermore, there is a limitation to just how much data can be passed with the **GET** method. It would be impossible to append a 10,000-word essay to the end of a URL, as most browsers limit a URL to several thousand characters. Further problems with **GET** become obvious when dealing with foreign language environments. Would it be possible to deal with Japanese Kanji characters in the URL using the GET method? Maybe not. Under the HTML 4.0 specification, the **GET** method has been deprecated. Despite the fact that **GET** is not recommended, it is still the default method when the **METHOD** attribute is not specified.

With all these problems, why use **GET**? First, **GET** is easy to deal with. An example URL such as the following should make it obvious that the **Name** field is set to **"Al Smith"**, the **Age** field is set to **"30"**, and the **Sex** field is set to **"male"**:

```
http://www.bigompany.com/cgi-bin/
comments.exe?Name=Al+Smith&Age=30&Sex=male
```

Form field names are set to values that are generally encoded with plus signs instead of spaces. Nonalphanumeric characters are replaced by *%nn*, where *nn* is the hexadecimal ASCII code for the character, similar to the URL encoding, as described in Chapter 4. The individual form field values are separated by ampersands. It would be trivial to write a parsing program to recover data out of this form.

The other method, **POST**, is just as easy, so this is not a motivating reason to use **GET**. Perhaps the best reason to use **GET** is that it comes in the form of a URL, so it can be set as a link or bookmarked. **GET** is used well in search engines. When a user submits a query to a search engine, the engine runs the query and then returns page upon page of result. It is possible to bookmark the query results and rerun the query later. It is also possible to create anchors that fire off canned CGI programs. This is particularly useful in certain varieties of dynamic Web sites. For example, the link shown next fires off a CGI program written in the ColdFusion Markup (CFM) language and passes it a value setting—setting the ExecutiveID to 1.

```
<A HREF="displayexec.cfm?ExecutiveId=1">John Kowalski</A>
```

The query is built into the link; when the link is clicked, the CGI program will access the appropriate database of executives and bring up information about John Kowalski.

While the **GET** method is far from perfect, there are certain situations where it makes a great deal of sense. It is unlikely that **GET** will be truly deprecated for quite some time.

POST Method

In situations in which a large amount of information must be passed back, the **POST** method is more appropriate than **GET**. The **POST** method transmits all form input information immediately after the requested URL. In other words, once the server has received a request from a form using **POST**, it knows to continue "listening" for the rest of the information. In some sense, this method requires making two contacts to the Web server. The **GET** method only requires one, because the method comes with the data to use right in the request. The encoding of the form data is handled in the same general way as the **GET** method by default; spaces become plus signs and other characters are encoded in the URL fashion. A sample form might send data that would look like

```
Name=Al+Smith&Age=30&Sex=male
```

The data will still have to be broken up to be used by the handling program. The benefit of using the **POST** method is that a large amount of data can be submitted this way because the form contents are not in the URL. It is even possible to send the contents of files using this method. In the case of the **POST** example, the encoding of the form data is the same as **GET**. It is possible to change the encoding method using the **ENCTYPE** attribute.

NAME Attribute

It is often desirable to check data before it is sent into the Web server. Users find it very frustrating to fill out a form and submit it to a server only to have the server return a page indicating data problems or omissions. Checking data before submission, often termed *form validation,* requires the use of JavaScript, which is discussed in Chapters 13 and 14. Key to using JavaScript is making sure to give the form an alphanumeric identifier. The **NAME** attribute can be set to an alphanumeric value such as "orderform." As with all form elements, you should be sure to always set the **NAME** attribute for a **<FORM>** element for future manipulation by a scripting language.

There many be some confusion on the use of **NAME** since the HTML 4.0 specification provides the **ID** attribute as a core attribute. However, browsers, including Netscape 2 and 3, depend on the occurrence of **NAME** to provide access to the form. Page authors looking to use **ID** instead should consider setting **NAME** and **ID** to the same value. Note that while many browsers will handle this just fine, it is not allowed according to the specification, since the **NAME** and **ID** attributes share namespace. This example is one of these specification-versus-practice problems so common on the Web.

ENCTYPE Attribute

When data is passed from a form to a Web server, it is typically encoded just like a URL. In this encoding, spaces are replaced by the + symbol and nonalphanumeric characters are replaced by %*nn*, where *nn* is the hexadecimal ASCII code for the character. The form of this is described in the special MIME file format *application/x-www-form-urlencoded*. By default, all form data is submitted in this form. It is possible, however, to set the encoding method for form data by setting the **ENCTYPE** attribute. When using a mailto URL in the **ACTION** attribute, the encoding type of **text/plain** might be more desirable. The result would look like the example shown here:

```
First Name=Joe
Last Name=Smith
Sex=Male
Submit=Send it
```

Each form field is on a line of its own. Even with this encoding form, nonalphanumeric characters may be encoded in the hexadecimal form.

Another form of encoding is also important: **multiform/form-data**. When passing files back via a form, it is important to designate where each file begins and ends. A value of **multipart/form-data** for the **ENCTYPE** is used to indicate this style. In this encoding, spaces and nonalphanumeric characters are preserved; data elements are separated by special delimiter lines. The following file fragment shows the submission of a form with **multipart/form-data** encoding, including the contents of the attached files:

```
Content-type: multipart/form-data;
boundary=-------------------------2988412654262
Content-Length: 5289
-------------------------2988412654262
Content-Disposition: form-data; name="firstname"
Homer
```

```
----------------------------2988412654262
Content-Disposition: form-data; name="lastname"
Simpson
----------------------------2988412654262
Content-Disposition: form-data; name="myfile";
filename="C:\WINNT\PROFILES\ADMINISTRATOR\DESKTOP\TEST.HTM"
Content-Type: text/html
<html><head><title>Test File</title></head><BODY><BR>
<center>Test File</center><hr></BODY></html>
----------------------------------------
8/12/99 4:47:45 PM--SF_NOTIFY_PREPROC_HEADERS
URL=/clients/postit.cfm?
----------------------------------------
8/12/99 4:47:45 PM--SF_NOTIFY_URL_MAP
URL=/clients/postit.cfm
Physical Path=C:\InetPub\wwwroot\clients\postit.cfm
----------------------------------------
```

Simple <FORM> Syntax

Given that we have a destination for the form contents as specified by the **ACTION** attribute and possibly a **METHOD**, either **GET** or **POST**, and maybe an encoding form, we can write a simple stub example for a form as shown here:

```
<!DOCTYPE HTML PUBLIC "-//W3C//DTD HTML 4.0 Transitional//EN">
<HTML>
<HEAD>
<TITLE>Form Stub</TITLE>
</HEAD>

<BODY>
<FORM ACTION="/cgi-bin/post-query" METHOD="POST">
Form field controls and standard HTML markup
</FORM>
</BODY>
</HTML>
```

While this syntax is adequate to build the form framework in most cases, there are other attributes for the **<FORM>** element that may be useful for frame targeting, scripting, and style sheets. Before discussing the individual form controls, let's review the complete syntax for the **<FORM>** element.

Complete <FORM> Syntax

The **<FORM>** element is a block-level structure used to define a fill-in form. Form contents are enclosed within the **<FORM>** and **</FORM>** tags, both of which are mandatory. The **<FORM>** element has a variety of attributes, as shown here:

```
<FORM
     ACCEPT-CHARSET="list of supported characters sets"
     ACTION="URL"
     CLASS="class name(s)"
     DIR="LTR | RTL"
     ENCTYPE="application/x-www-form-urlencoded |
             multipart/form-data | text/plain |
             Media Type as per RFC 2045"
     ID="unique alphanumeric identifier"
     LANG=language code
     METHOD="GET | POST"
     STYLE="style information"
     TARGET="frame name | _blank | _parent | _self | _top"
             (transitional)
     TITLE=advisory text

     eventhandler="script">

     Form controls and HTML markup

</FORM>
```

Two additional attributes for the **<FORM>** element are defined by Internet Explorer 4. The **NAME** attribute is also supported by most Web browsers.

```
     NAME="unique alphanumeric identifier"
     LANGUAGE="JAVASCRIPT | JSCRIPT | VBSCRIPT | VBS"
```

Attributes

The **<FORM>** element has a variety of attributes. Most of these are common to the HTML 4.0 standard or the major browsers.

ACCEPT-CHARSET   This attribute specifies the list of character encoding values for input data that must be accepted by the server processing the form. The value is a space- or comma-delimited list of character sets defined in RFC 2045 (http://ds. internic.net/rfc/rfc2045.txt). The default value for this attribute is the reserved value **UNKNOWN**.

ACTION   This attribute specifies the address to which the form contents will be sent. This is usually the URL of a server-side program that handles the form content. It may also be a mailto URL. The **ACTION** value is required for working forms, though on some browsers a value similar to the base URL of the document will be assumed if the **ACTION** is left out.

CLASS   This attribute is used to specify the class name for the form so that it can be used as a subclass from a style sheet, as discussed in Chapter 10.

DIR   This attribute is intended to specify the direction of text (left-to-right or right-to-left) with the values **LTR** and **RTL**.

ENCTYPE   This attribute is used to specify the encoding form of the form data. By default, the encoding value is **application/x-www-form-urlencoded**, where spaces are translated to plus signs and other nonalphanumeric values are translated into hexadecimal values just as URLs are encoded. As discussed earlier, other possible values for this attribute include **plain/text**, which is useful when mailing form contents to people, and **multipart/form-data**, which is used to upload files via forms.

ID   This attribute is used to specify a unique name for the **<FORM>** element. It can also serve as the destination of a link or be manipulated by a style sheet. The **ID** value also makes the form available for scripting; but, for now, for backward-compatibility, you may want to stick to specifying only the **NAME** attribute, as older browsers will recognize it.

LANG   This attribute is used to specify the language being used in the form. The language is specified by setting the attribute to the ISO-standard language abbreviation form.

LANGUAGE   The Internet Explorer–specific **LANGUAGE** attribute is used to specify the language of the script associated with the **<FORM>** element. In particular, this attribute applies to the script handlers bound to the various events handled in the **<FORM>** element itself. This attribute has no bearing on the language of scripts called by form controls or the functions that may be called via the event handlers. The value for the **LANGUAGE** attribute is JavaScript by default, but **JSCRIPT**, **VBS**, and **VBSCRIPT** are also possible.

METHOD   This attribute indicates how the form data should be sent to the address specified by the **ACTION** attribute. The possible values for this attribute are **GET** and **POST**. **GET** sends the information within the URL of the request, while **POST** sends it following the request. Under HTML 4, the **GET** element is considered deprecated; however, it is still the default value when this method is unspecified. When using a mailto **ACTION** value, be sure to set the **METHOD** to **POST**.

NAME   This attribute is used to provide a name for the form for manipulation from a scripting language. While the HTML 4.0 specification may prefer the **ID** attribute, browsers—including Netscape 2 and 3—depend on the occurrence of **NAME** to provide access to the form. Page authors looking to use **ID** instead should consider setting **NAME** and **ID** to the same value. However, note that while many browsers will handle this just fine, it is not allowed according to the specification, since the **NAME** and **ID** attributes share namespace. This example is another one of those specification-versus-practice problems so common on the Web.

STYLE   This attribute is used to specify an inline style rule for the **<FORM>** element.

TARGET   This attribute is used to set the window or frame that should display any results returned by the form action. As with all frame-oriented extensions, values of **_blank**, **_parent**, **_self**, and **_top** have special meaning. When the value is not specified, the form loads over itself.

TITLE   This attribute is used to set advisory text for the form. The contents of the **TITLE** attribute might be rendered onscreen as a tool tip when the user's mouse hovers over the form or may simply act as a note to readers of the HTML text. **TITLE** will also benefit users of speech browsers or other alternative access media. The use of the **TITLE** attribute generally makes more sense for the individual form controls than for the form itself.

Event Handlers

A variety of events can be associated with the form. HTML 4 defines **onsubmit** and **onreset** as the primary events that correspond to the submission of the form and the resetting of the form's fields to their defaults, respectively. Other events defined include **onclick**, **ondblclick**, **onkeydown**, **onkeypress**, **onkeyup**, **onmousedown**, **onmousemove**, **onmouseout**, **onmouseover**, **onmouseup**, **onreset**, and **onsubmit**. Microsoft Internet Explorer 4 also supports **ondragstart**, **onhelp**, and **onselectstart** as events for a form. A more detailed discussion of how events are used with forms is presented later in the section "Forms and Events."

Form Controls

A form is made up of fields or controls, as well as the markup necessary to structure the form and control its presentation. The controls are the items filled in or manipulated by the user to indicate the state of the form. Form controls include text fields, password fields, multiple-line text fields, pop-up menus, scrolled lists, radio buttons, check boxes, and buttons. Hidden form controls are also possible. The most common element used to specify a form control is the **<INPUT>** element. However, **<SELECT>**, in conjunction with the **<OPTION>** element and the **<TEXTAREA>** elements, is also common in forms. Rather than discuss the syntax of the particular elements, let's first approach learning forms by exploring the form controls, and then look at the complete syntax for the elements. This discussion only covers basic form controls. Newer form items, represented by **<BUTTON>**, **<LABEL>**, **<FIELDSET>**, and **<LEGEND>**, are discussed in the section "New and Emerging Form Elements, later in this chapter."

Text Controls

Text controls are form fields, generally one line long, that take text input like a person's name and address, and other information. These fields are specified with the **<INPUT>** element, but it is possible to specify a multiple-line text field using the **<TEXTAREA>** element.

Simple Text Entry

The simplest type of form control is the text entry type. To set a text entry control, use the **<INPUT>** element and set the **TYPE** attribute equal to **TEXT**:

```
<INPUT TYPE="TEXT" NAME="CustomerName">
```

All form elements should be named. **NAME="CustomerName"** is used to create a text field to collect a customer's name on an order form.

This example creates a one-line text entry field that will be associated with the name **CustomerName**:

Customer Name: Bob Smith

Customer Name: Bob Smith_

Customer Name: Bob Smith

Remember to pick a name that makes sense and is unique to the form. The name will be used when the form is submitted, as well as for manipulation by scripting languages.

The last example does not specify the size of the field or the maximum number of characters that can be entered into the field. By default, unless specified, this field generally will be a width of 20 characters. To set the size of the field in characters, use the **SIZE** attribute. For example,

```
<INPUT TYPE="TEXT" NAME="CustomerName" SIZE="40">
```

The value of the **SIZE** field for an **<INPUT>** element is the number of characters to be displayed. It is possible for the user to type more characters than this value. The text will just scroll by. If you want to limit the size of the field, you need to set the value of the **MAXLENGTH** attribute to the maximum number of characters allowed in the field. The browser will prevent the user from typing more than the number of characters specified. Browser feedback may include beeping or may just overstrike the last character. To set a text field that shows 30 characters but has a maximum of 60 characters that can be entered, use something like

```
<INPUT TYPE="TEXT" NAME="CustomerName" SIZE="30" MAXLENGTH="60">
```

The last attribute that is useful to set with a text entry field is the **VALUE** attribute. With this attribute, you can specify the default text you want to appear in the field when the form is first loaded. For example, in the following code fragment, a value of **"Enter your name here"** is provided as a prompt to the user to fill in the field properly:

```
<INPUT TYPE="TEXT" NAME="CustomerName" SIZE="30" MAXLENGTH="60"
       VALUE="Enter your name here">
```

A very simple example of the basic text field type is shown here:

```
<!DOCTYPE HTML PUBLIC "-//W3C//DTD HTML 4.0 Transitional//EN">
<HTML>
<HEAD>
<TITLE>Text Field Example</TITLE>
</HEAD>

<BODY>
<H1 ALIGN="center">Gadget Order Form</H1>
<HR>
```

```
<FORM ACTION="http://www.bigcompany.com/cgi-bin/post-query"
      METHOD="POST">


<B>Customer Name:</B>
<INPUT TYPE="text"
       NAME="CustomerName"
       SIZE="25"
       MAXLENGTH="35">
</FORM>
<HR>
</BODY>
</HTML>
```

Password Fields

The password style of form control is the same as the simple text entry field, except that the input to the field is not revealed. In many cases, the browser may render each character as an asterisk or dot to avoid people seeing the password being entered, as shown here:

Not echoing the password onscreen is appropriate. It discourages the idea of "shoulder surfing," where an unscrupulous user looks on your screen to see what secret data you input. To set a password form control, use the **<INPUT>** element, but set the **TYPE** attribute equal to **PASSWORD**. As with the text entry field, it is possible to specify the size of the field in characters with **SIZE**, the maximum entry with **MAXLENGTH** in characters. In the case of the password control, it is probably wise to limit the length of the field so users don't become confused about how many characters they have entered.

The password form is very similar to the single-line text entry field. However, setting a default value for the password field with the **VALUE** attribute doesn't make much sense since the user can see it by viewing the HTML source of the document. A complete example of the password field's use within the form is shown here:

```
<!DOCTYPE HTML PUBLIC "-//W3C//DTD HTML 4.0 Transitional//EN">
<HTML>
<HEAD>
<TITLE>Password Field Example</TITLE>
</HEAD>

<BODY>
<H1 ALIGN="center">Gadget Order Form</H1>
<HR>

<FORM ACTION="http://www.bigcompany.com/cgi-bin/post-query"
      METHOD="POST">

<B>Customer Name:</B>
<INPUT TYPE="text"
       NAME="CustomerName"
       SIZE="25"
       MAXLENGTH="35">
<BR>

<B>Customer ID:</B>
<INPUT TYPE="PASSWORD"
       NAME="CustomerID"
       SIZE="10"
       MAXLENGTH="10">
</FORM>
<HR>
</BODY>
</HTML>
```

Multiple-Line Text Input

When it is necessary to enter more than one line of text in a form field, the **<INPUT>** element must be abandoned in favor of the **<TEXTAREA>** element. Like the text input field, there are similar attributes to control the size of the data entry area as well as the default value and the name of the control. For example, to set the number of rows in the text entry area, set the **ROWS** attribute equal to the number of rows desired. To set the number of characters per line, set the **COLS** attribute. So, to define a text area of five rows of 80 characters each, use the following:

```
<TEXTAREA ROWS="5" COLS="80" NAME="CommentBox">
</TEXTAREA>
```

Because there may be many lines of text within the **<TEXTAREA>** element, it is not possible to set the default text for the area using the **VALUE** attribute. Instead, place the default text between the **<TEXTAREA>** and **</TEXTAREA>** tags:

```
<TEXTAREA ROWS="5" COLS="80" NAME="CommentBox">
Please fill in your comments here.
</TEXTAREA>
```

The information enclosed within the **<TEXTAREA>** element must be plain text and should not include any HTML markup. In fact, the contents of the element act like the **<PRE>** element by preserving spaces, returns, and other characters. HTML elements entered within the form control will not be interpreted. A complete example of a multiple-line text field is shown here:

```
<!DOCTYPE HTML PUBLIC "-//W3C//DTD HTML 4.0 Transitional//EN">
<HTML>
<HEAD>
<TITLE>Multiple-line Text Field Example</TITLE>
</HEAD>

<BODY>
<H1 ALIGN="center">Gadget Order Form</H1>
<HR>

<FORM ACTION="http//www.bigcompany.com/cgi-bin/post-query"
      METHOD="POST">

<B>Special Instructions:</B><BR>
<TEXTAREA ROWS="10" COLS="40" NAME="Instructions">
Enter any special gadget ordering instructions in this space.
</TEXTAREA>
</FORM>
<HR>
</BODY>
</HTML>
```

A rendering of the text area example is shown in Figure 11-2.

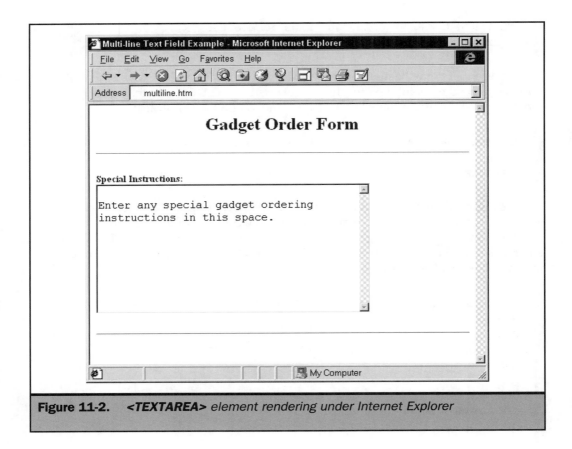

Figure 11-2. *<TEXTAREA>* element rendering under Internet Explorer

Netscape supports a special **WRAP** attribute for the **<TEXTAREA>** element. The values for this attribute are **OFF**, **HARD**, and **SOFT**. A value of **OFF** disables word wrapping in the form control. Any text users enter is displayed exactly as is, though users may insert hard returns of their own. A value of **HARD** allows word wrapping, and the actual break points are included when the form is submitted. A value of **SOFT** allows word wrapping in the form control, but the line breaks are not sent with the form's contents. A value of **SOFT** is the default, and this mimics how other browsers deal with the **<TEXTAREA>** element. These are the only unique attributes for **<TEXTAREA>**; but, like most elements under HTML 4, **<TEXTAREA>** also supports **ID, CLASS, STYLE, TITLE, LANG, DIR,** and a multitude of event handler attributes like **onclick**. See Appendix A for more information about these. The **<TEXTAREA>** element has three important accessibility attributes—**DISABLED, TABINDEX,** and

READONLY—which are described in the section "Form Accessibility Enhancements," later in this chapter.

Pull-Down Menus

HTML form controls include pull-down menus. A pull-down menu lets the user select one choice out of many possible choices. One nice aspect of pull-down menus is that all choices do not have to be seen on the screen and are normally hidden. The following illustration shows the rendering of a pull-down menu under different browsers:

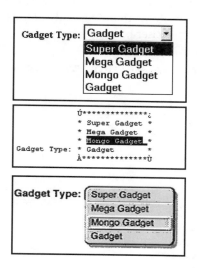

To create a pull-down menu, use the **<SELECT>** element. This element must include both a start and an end tag. It should only contain zero or more occurrences of the **<OPTION>** element. The **<OPTION>** elements specify the actual choices on the menu, and generally do not use a close tag (similar to how the **<LI>** element is used). In many ways, the structure of a pull-down menu looks similar to a list structure, as shown in the following code fragment:

```
<SELECT NAME="GadgetType">
    <OPTION>Super Gadget
    <OPTION>Mega Gadget
    <OPTION>Mongo Gadget
    <OPTION>Plain Gadget
</SELECT>
```

As shown in the code fragment, like all form controls, the **<SELECT>** element has a **NAME** attribute that is used to set a unique name for the control for purposes of decoding the user selection. It is also possible to set attributes for the **<OPTION>** element. An occurrence of the attribute **SELECTED** in the **<OPTION>** element sets the form control to select this item by default. If no value is selected, typically the field remains undefined. Some user agents may preselect the first item specified with the **<OPTION>** element. Normally, the value submitted when the form is sent is the value enclosed by the **<OPTION>** element. However, it is possible to set the **VALUE** attribute for the element that will be returned instead. This might be important when the user has different names for items than "official" names. A complete example of a simple pull-down menu is shown here:

```
<!DOCTYPE HTML PUBLIC "-//W3C//DTD HTML 4.0 Transitional//EN">
<HTML>
<HEAD>
<TITLE>Pull-down Menu Example</TITLE>
</HEAD>

<BODY>
<H1 ALIGN="center">Gadget Order Form</H1>

<FORM ACTION="mailto:test@bigcompany.com" METHOD="POST">

<B>Gadget Type:</B>
<SELECT NAME="GadgetType">
    <OPTION VALUE="SG-01">Super Gadget
    <OPTION VALUE="MEG-G5">Mega Gadget
    <OPTION VALUE="MO-45">Mongo Gadget
    <OPTION SELECTED>Gadget
</SELECT>
</FORM>
</BODY>
</HTML>
```

Scrolled Lists

The **<SELECT>** element also may contain the **SIZE** attribute, which is used to specify the number of items showing on the screen at once. The default value for this attribute is 1, which specifies a normal pull-down menu. Setting a positive number creates a list in a window of the specified number of rows, as shown here:

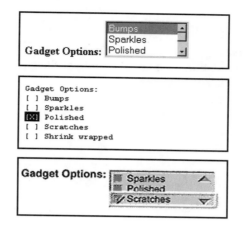

In many cases, scrolled lists act just like pull-down menus. However, if the <SELECT> element contains the attribute **MULTIPLE**, it becomes possible to select more than one entry. How multiple items are selected depends on the browser; but, generally, it requires holding down some modifier key such as ALT, COMMAND, or SHIFT and selecting the appropriate items with the mouse.

Note *Many novice users have a hard time with the scrolled list control and multiple entries. Depending on your target audience, it might be wise to provide instructions near the control to assist the user.*

Because it is possible to select more than one entry in a scrolled list when the multiple option is applied, it is then possible to use the **SELECTED** attribute multiple times in the enclosed <OPTION> elements. A complete example illustrating how the scrolled list is used is shown here:

```
<!DOCTYPE HTML PUBLIC "-//W3C//DTD HTML 4.0 Transitional//EN">
<HTML>
<HEAD>
<TITLE>Scrolled List Example</TITLE>
</HEAD>

<BODY>
<H1 ALIGN="center">Gadget Order Form</H1>

<FORM ACTION="mailto:order@bigcompany.com" METHOD="POST">
```

```
<B>Gadget Options:</B>
<SELECT NAME="GadgetOptions" MULTIPLE SIZE="3">
    <OPTION VALUE="Hit with hammer" SELECTED>Bumps
    <OPTION VALUE="Add glitter">Sparkles
    <OPTION VALUE="Buff it">Polished
    <OPTION SELECTED>Scratches
    <OPTION>Shrink wrapped
</SELECT>
</FORM>
<HR>
</BODY>
</HTML>
```

Check Boxes

With the scrolled list, it is possible to select many items out of a large group of items. Unfortunately, not all the items are presented at once for the user to choose. If there are a few options to select from that are not mutually exclusive, it is probably better to use a group of check boxes that the user can check off. Check boxes are best used to toggle choices on and off. While it is possible to have multiple numbers of check boxes and let the user select as many as he or she wants, if there are too many it may be difficult to deal with. Don't forget about scrolled lists.

To create a check box, use the **<INPUT>** element and set the **TYPE** attribute equal to **CHECKBOX**. The check box should also be named by setting the **NAME** attribute. For example, to create a check box asking if a user wants cheese, use some markup like

```
Cheese: <INPUT TYPE="CHECKBOX" NAME="Cheese">
```

In this example, the label to the left is arbitrary. It could be to the right as well. The label could say "Put cheese on it," but there will be no indication to the receiving program of this label. In this simple example, if the check box is selected, a value of **Cheese=on** will be transmitted to the server. Setting a value for the check box might make more sense. Values to be transmitted instead of the default value can be set with the **VALUE** attribute. The code

```
Cheese: <INPUT TYPE="Checkbox" NAME="Extras" VALUE="Cheese">
```

would send a response like **Extras=Cheese** to the server. It is also possible to have multiple check box controls with the same name. The code

```
Cheese: <INPUT TYPE="CHECKBOX"  NAME="Extras" VALUE="Cheese">
Pickles: <INPUT TYPE="CHECKBOX"  NAME="Extras" VALUE="Pickles">
```

would send multiple entries like the following to the server when both extras were selected:

```
Extras=Cheese&Extras=Pickels
```

It is possible to set a check box to be selected by default by using the **CHECKED** attribute within the **<INPUT>** element. The **CHECKED** attribute requires no value. A complete example using check box controls is shown here:

```
<!DOCTYPE HTML PUBLIC "-//W3C//DTD HTML 4.0 Transitional//EN">
<HTML>
<HEAD>
<TITLE>Check Box Example</TITLE>
</HEAD>

<BODY>
<H1 ALIGN="center">Gadget Order Form</H1>
<HR>

<FORM ACTION="mailto:order@bigcompany.com" METHOD="POST">
   <B>Gadget Bonus Options:</B>
   <BR>
   Super-magneto:
   <INPUT TYPE="CHECKBOX" NAME="BONUS" VALUE="Magnetize">
   <BR>
   Kryptonite Coating:
   <INPUT TYPE="CHECKBOX" NAME="BONUS" VALUE="Anti-Superman" CHECKED>
   <BR>
   Anti-gravity:
   <INPUT TYPE="CHECKBOX" NAME="BONUS" VALUE="Anti-gravity">
   <BR>
</FORM>
<HR>
</BODY>
</HTML>
```

Radio Buttons

Radio buttons use a similar notation to check boxes, but only one option may be chosen among many. This is an especially good option for choices that don't make sense when selected together. In this sense, radio buttons are like pull-down menus that allow only one choice. The main difference is that all options are shown at once with radio buttons.

Like check boxes, this form control uses the standard **<INPUT TYPE="">** format. In this case, set **TYPE** equal to **RADIO**. Setting the **NAME** field is very important in the case of radio buttons because it groups together controls that share the radio functionality. The radio functionality says that when an item is selected, it deselects the previously pressed item. If the names are different for each radio button, the functionality becomes that of a check box, but with a different shape. Possible renderings of the radio button form control are shown here:

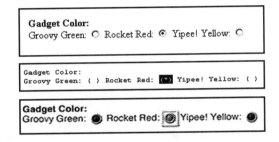

Another important attribute is **VALUE**. It is important to set each individual radio button to a different value entry. Otherwise, it will be impossible to decipher which button was selected. Like check boxes, the occurrence of the **SELECTED** attribute in the **<INPUT>** element will preselect the item. Only one item may be selected as a default out of a radio group. If the **SELECTED** attribute does not occur, the browser typically will not display any items as selected. A complete example using radio buttons is shown here:

```
<!DOCTYPE HTML PUBLIC "-//W3C//DTD HTML 4.0 Transitional//EN">
<HTML>
<HEAD>
<TITLE>Radio Button Example</TITLE>
</HEAD>

<BODY>
<H1 ALIGN="center">Gadget Order Form</H1>
<HR>
```

```
<FORM ACTION="mailto:order@bigcompany.com" METHOD="POST">

<B>Gadget Color:</B><BR>
Groovy Green: <INPUT TYPE="RADIO" NAME="Color" VALUE="Green">
Rocket Red: <INPUT TYPE="RADIO" NAME="Color" VALUE="Red" CHECKED>
Yipee! Yellow: <INPUT TYPE="RADIO" NAME="Color" VALUE="Yellow">
</FORM>
<HR>
</BODY>
</HTML>
```

Reset and Submit Buttons

Once a form has been filled in, there must be a way to send it on its way, whether it is submitted to a program for processing or simply mailed to an e-mail address. The **<INPUT>** element has two values, **RESET** and **SUBMIT**, for the **TYPE** attribute; these can create common buttons that are useful for just about any form. Setting the **TYPE** attribute for the **<INPUT>** element to **RESET** creates a button that allows the user to clear or set to default all the form controls at once. Setting the **TYPE** attribute for **<INPUT>** to **SUBMIT** creates a button that triggers the browser to send the contents of the form to the address specified in the **ACTION** attribute of the **<FORM>** element. Common renderings of the **SUBMIT** and **RESET** form controls are shown here:

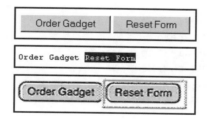

The buttons themselves take two basic attributes: **VALUE** and **NAME**. The **VALUE** attribute sets both the value of the button when pressed and the wording of the button. The **NAME** value associates an identifier with the form control. A complete example showing a small form with submit and reset buttons is shown here:

```
<!DOCTYPE HTML PUBLIC "-//W3C//DTD HTML 4.0 Transitional//EN">
<HTML>
<HEAD>
```

```
<TITLE>Complete Form Example</TITLE>
</HEAD>

<BODY>
<H1 ALIGN="center">Gadget Order Form</H1>
<HR>

<FORM ACTION="mailto:order@bigcompany.com"
      METHOD="POST" ENCTYPE="text/plain">


<B>Customer Name:</B>
<INPUT TYPE="TEXT"
       NAME="CustomerName"
       SIZE="25"
       MAXLENGTH="35">
<BR><BR>


<B>Customer ID:</B>
<INPUT TYPE="PASSWORD"
       NAME="CustomerID"
       SIZE="10"
       MAXLENGTH="10">
<BR><BR>


<B>Gadget Type:</B>
<SELECT NAME="GadgetType">
   <OPTION VALUE="SG-01">Super Gadget
   <OPTION VALUE="MEG-G5">Mega Gadget
   <OPTION VALUE="MO-45">Mongo Gadget
   <OPTION SELECTED>Gadget
</SELECT>
<BR><BR>

<INPUT TYPE="SUBMIT" VALUE="Order Gadget" NAME="SubmitButton">
<INPUT TYPE="RESET" VALUE="Reset Form" NAME="ResetButton">
</FORM>
<HR>
</BODY>
</HTML>
```

Because the submit and reset buttons cause an action, either form submission or field reset, it would not seem obvious why the **VALUE** or **NAME** field might be useful. While having multiple reset buttons might not be useful, multiple submit buttons are useful because the value of the button is sent to the address specified in the **<FORM>** element's **ACTION** attribute. One possible use might be to have three submit buttons: one for add, one for delete, and one for update.

```
<INPUT TYPE="SUBMIT" VALUE="Place Order" NAME="Add">
<INPUT TYPE="SUBMIT" VALUE="Delete Order" NAME="Delete">
<INPUT TYPE="SUBMIT" VALUE="Update Order" NAME="Update">
<INPUT TYPE="RESET" VALUE="Reset Form" NAME="ResetButton">
```

When the form is submitted, the value of the button is sent to the form-handling program, which will decide what to do with the submitted data based upon its contents. This use of a submit button hints at a more generalized form of button, which is discussed in the next section.

If you have two buttons next to each other, it is useful to separate the two with nonbreaking spaces ( ). Otherwise, the buttons will probably render too closely together. Another approach would be to use a small table around the buttons and provide some cell padding or a blank cell between the buttons.

Additional <INPUT> Types

There are a few forms of the **<INPUT>** element that have not been discussed. These form elements hint at the potential complexity of using forms. Some of these elements, particularly the file selection form element, are not supported in older browsers.

Hidden Text and Its Uses

The usefulness of this form control is not always obvious to the new user. By setting the **TYPE** attribute of the **<INPUT>** element to a value of **HIDDEN**, it is possible to transmit default or previously specified text that is hidden from the user to the handling program. If there were many versions of the same form all over a Web site, then the hidden text could be used to specify where the form came from, as shown in this example:

```
<INPUT TYPE="hidden" NAME="SubmittingFormName" VALUE="Form1">
```

Because this field is not shown on the page, it is impossible for the user to modify it. Thus, it must have its **VALUE** attribute set. While this last example seems rather contrived, there is actually a very important use for hidden form controls.

When filling in forms, there is often an issue of remembering information from one form to the next. Imagine a form in which the user fills in his or her personal information on one page and the ordering information on the next page. How will the two pages be related to each other? This presents the state-loss problem. The protocols of the Web, primarily HTTP, do not support a "memory." In other words, they don't preserve state. One way to get around this is to use hidden text. Imagine that, in the last example, the personal information is passed to the next page by dynamically embedding it in the ordering page as hidden text. Then state has been preserved—or has it? When users are finished ordering, they submit the whole form at once as a complete transaction. This idea of using hidden text to get around the state-loss problem is illustrated in Figure 11-3.

There are other approaches to saving state, including extended path information and cookies. These ideas are briefly discussed in Chapter 12.

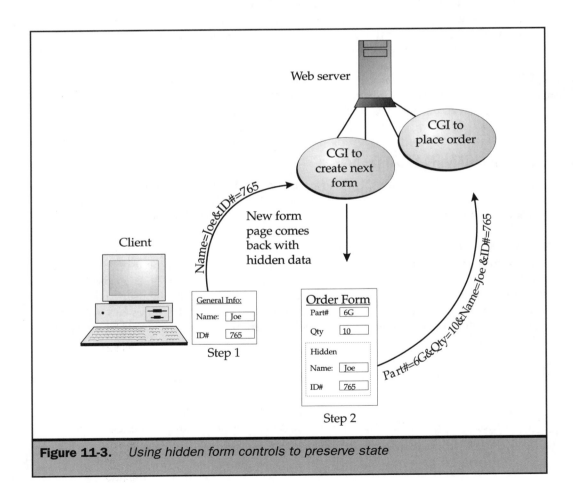

Figure 11-3.   *Using hidden form controls to preserve state*

Image Type

One form of the **<INPUT>** element that is somewhat strange is the image type, as specified by setting **TYPE="IMAGE"**. This form of **<INPUT>** creates a graphical version of the submit button, which not only submits the form but transmits coordinate information about where the user clicked in the image. The image is specified by the **SRC** attribute. Many of the attributes used for the **<IMG>** element may be valid for this form of **<INPUT>** as well. The specification defines **ALT** and **ALIGN**. Other attributes like **BORDER**, **HSPACE**, or **VSPACE** may or may not be supported by browsers. Like all other forms of **<INPUT>**, the **NAME** attribute is a very important part of how the coordinate information is transmitted. The example use of **<INPUT>** shown next could be used to insert a map of the United States, allowing users to click the regional office in which they want to submit their order forms.

```
<INPUT TYPE="IMAGE" SRC="usamap.gif" NAME="Sales"
       ALT="Sales Region Map">
```

When clicked, the form values would be submitted, along with two extra values, **Sales.x** and **Sales.y**. **Sales.x** and **Sales.y** would be set equal to the x and y coordinates of where the image was clicked. The x and y coordinates are relative to the image with an origin in the upper left-hand corner of the image. You may notice a similarity to image maps. Indeed, much of the functionality of this form control could be imitated with a client-side image map in conjunction with some scripting code. A future extension to this form of the **<INPUT>** element would be to make it less server-side dependent, possibly even allowing the page author to set a map name to decode coordinates or set function. Except for specialized needs, page designers should probably look to provide the functionality of the image form control in some other way.

File Form Control

A recent addition to the **<INPUT>** element that is now part of the HTML 4.0 specification is the possibility of setting the **TYPE** attribute to **FILE**. This form control is used for file uploading. The field generally consists of a text entry box for a filename that can be manipulated with the **SIZE** and **MAXLENGTH** attributes, as well as a button immediately to the right of the field, which is usually labeled Browse. Pressing the Browse button allows the user to browse the local system to find a file to specify for upload. The logistics of how a file is selected depend on the user agent.

Following is an example of the file form control syntax, in which the **ENCTYPE** value has been set to **multipart/form-data** to allow the file to be attached to the uploaded form:

```
<!DOCTYPE HTML PUBLIC "-//W3C//DTD HTML 4.0 Transitional//EN">
<HTML>
<HEAD>
```

```
<TITLE>File Upload Test</TITLE>
</HEAD>

<BODY>
<H1 ALIGN="CENTER">File Upload System</H1>
<HR>

<FORM ACTION="http://www.bigcompany.com/cgi-bin/uploadfile.pl"
      METHOD="POST" ENCTYPE="mutipart/form-data">

<B>File Description:</B><BR>
<INPUT TYPE="TEXT" NAME="Description" SIZE="50"
       MAXLENGTH="100"><BR>

<B>Specify File to Post:</B><BR>
<INPUT TYPE="FILE" NAME="FileName">

<BR><BR>
<HR>

<DIV ALIGN="center">
   <INPUT TYPE="SUBMIT" NAME="Submit" VALUE="Send it">
</DIV>
</FORM>
</BODY>
</HTML>
```

A rendering of the file upload example showing the browsing mechanism is given in Figure 11-4.

While it is possible to set the **SIZE** and **MAXLENGTH** values of the file entry box, this is not suggested, since the path name may be larger than the size specified. (This depends on how the user has set up his or her system.) The file form control is not supported by all browsers. HTML 4 also specifies the **ACCEPT** attribute for the **<INPUT TYPE="FILE">** element, which can be used to specify a comma-separated list of MIME types that the server receiving the contents of the form will know how to handle properly. Browsers could use this attribute to keep users from uploading files that are unacceptable to a server (for example, executable files). It is not known if browsers actually pay any attention to this attribute.

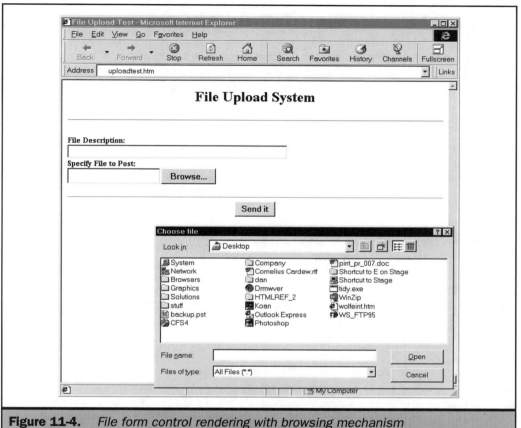

Figure 11-4. *File form control rendering with browsing mechanism*

PROGRAMMING
AND HTML

Generalized Buttons

One last form of the **<INPUT>** element, hinted at earlier, is the generalized button. By using **<INPUT TYPE="BUTTON">**, it is possible to create a button in the style of the submit or reset buttons that, unlike the submit or reset buttons, has no predetermined actions. Inserting something like the following doesn't really do much:

```
<INPUT TYPE="BUTTON" VALUE="Press Me!" NAME="mybutton">
```

If you click the rendering of this button, no action is triggered, and no value will be submitted. So what's the point? By using a scripting language, it is possible to tie an event to the button and create an action. At the end of this chapter, as well as in Chapter 13, you'll see how forms can be tied to scripting languages to create powerful interactive documents.

New and Emerging Form Elements

At the time of this writing, the W3C has proposed adding several form-related tags and attributes to the next version of HTML. These are intended to address limitations in the current forms and to make them more interactive. Microsoft has already implemented several of these proposed extensions in Internet Explorer 4.

<BUTTON> Element

This element provides a way to add generic buttons to forms. The text enclosed by the tags is the button's label. In its simplest usage, the **<BUTTON>** element is functionally equivalent to **<INPUT TYPE="BUTTON">**, which is not supported by the official HTML 3.2 definition. In newer browsers like Internet Explorer 4 that support both button forms, the following two statements render identically.

```
<INPUT TYPE="BUTTON" VALUE="Press Me">
<BUTTON>Press Me</BUTTON>
```

The **<BUTTON>** usage is more versatile because its content can include most inline and block-level elements. The following example illustrates a button element containing text, an embedded image, and the use of a cascading style sheet rule to change the background and text color.

```
<BUTTON NAME="HomePage" VALUE="Test Button"
        STYLE="{background-color:blue; color:yellow}">
   <IMG SRC="images/logonotext.gif" WIDTH="141" HEIGHT="197">
   <BR>BigCompany Home Page
</BUTTON>
```

What is interesting about this element is that the browser should render the button in a relief style and even present a pushing effect, just like a submit or reset button, so it is not quite the same as **<INPUT TYPE="IMAGE">**. Another key difference between the image button previously described and the new **<BUTTON>** element is that the new element does not submit any coordinate information, nor is it strictly a submit button. In fact, it is possible to tie this style of button to a general action using the **TYPE** attribute. Allowed values for this attribute are **BUTTON** (default), **SUBMIT**, and **RESET**. The HTML 4.0 documentation suggests that **SUBMIT** is the default value, but this does not make sense, nor is it supported by the browsers that understand the **<BUTTON>** element.

 It is incorrect to associate an image map with any image enclosed by a <BUTTON> element.

While the **<BUTTON>** element seems a more generalized way to deal with images as form buttons, it is not widely supported yet—only by Internet Explorer 4. Older browsers may require an alternative approach.

Labels

Another new form element introduced in HTML 4 and supported by advanced browsers is the **<LABEL>** element. One motivation for this tag is to better support speech-based browsers that can read descriptions next to form fields. However, a more common use of the **<LABEL>** element is to associate the labeling text of form controls with the actual controls they describe.

The **<LABEL>** element can be associated with a form control by enclosing it as shown here:

```
<LABEL>First Name:
   <INPUT TYPE="TEXT" NAME="FirstName" SIZE="20" MAXLENGTH="30">
</LABEL>
```

A **<LABEL>** element can also be associated with a control by referring to the control's **ID** with the **FOR** attribute. In this usage, the label does not need to enclose the control. This allows labels to be positioned in tables with their own cells. It is common to use tables to make better-looking forms. Far too often, form elements snake down a page and are not aligned very well. The following code fragment illustrates how the **<LABEL>** element with the **FOR** attribute would be used.

```
<TABLE>
   <TR>
      <TD ALIGN="RIGHT">
         <LABEL FOR="CustName">Customer Name : </LABEL>
      <TD ALIGN="LEFT">
         <INPUT TYPE="TEXT" ID="CustName" SIZE="25" MAXLENGTH="35">
   </TR>
</TABLE>
```

The **<LABEL>** element also supports the **ID, CLASS, STYLE, TITLE, LANG,** and **DIR** attributes, as well as numerous event handlers. These are used in the same way as on any other HTML element. The **DISABLED** and **ACCESSKEY** are also supported attributes for this element and are discussed further in the section on form accessibility enhancements, later in the chapter.

<FIELDSET>

This proposed element groups related form elements similar to the way the **<DIV>** element groups general body content. Like **<DIV>**, the **<FIELDSET>** element can be nested; it can also have an associated **<LEGEND>** element to describe the enclosed items. The **<FIELDSET>** element itself has no special attributes besides those common to all elements, like **ID, CLASS, LANG, DIR, TITLE, STYLE,** and event handlers. However, the **<LEGEND>** element does support the **ALIGN** attribute, which can be used to specify where the description will be rendered in relation to the group of form items; its values are **TOP** (the default value), **BOTTOM, LEFT,** or **RIGHT**. In addition to **ALIGN, <FIELDSET>** supports the common attributes to most elements under HTML 4—**ID, CLASS, STYLE, TITLE, LANG, DIR,** and the numerous event handlers. See the element reference in Appendix A for more information about these. The example shown here illustrates how the **<FIELDSET>** and **<LEGEND>** elements are used:

```
<!DOCTYPE HTML PUBLIC "-//W3C//DTD HTML 4.0 Transitional//EN">
<HTML>
<HEAD>
<TITLE>Fieldset and Legend Example</TITLE>
</HEAD>

<BODY>
<FORM ACTION="mailto:order@bigcompany.com" METHOD="POST">
<FIELDSET>
    <LEGEND>Customer Identification</LEGEND>
    <BR>

    <LABEL>Customer Name:
        <INPUT TYPE="TEXT" ID="CustomerName" SIZE="25"
    </LABEL>
    <BR><BR>

    <LABEL>Customer ID:
        <INPUT TYPE="PASSWORD" ID="CustomerID" SIZE="8" MAXLENGTH="8">
    </LABEL>
    <BR>
</FIELDSET>
</FORM>
</BODY>
</HTML>
```

The W3C proposal recommends that a **<FIELDSET>** be enclosed by a box. This rendering is supported by Internet Explorer 4, as shown in the rendering in Figure 11-5.

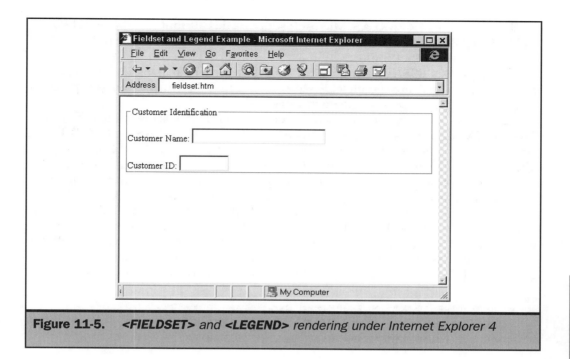

Figure 11-5. *<FIELDSET> and <LEGEND> rendering under Internet Explorer 4*

Form Accessibility Enhancements

One of the most important changes made to forms under HTML 4 is the improved support for accessibility. HTML 4 defines the **ACCESSKEY** attribute for the **<LABEL>**, **<INPUT>**, **<BUTTON>**, and **<LEGEND>** elements. Setting the value of the key to a character creates an accelerator key that can activate the form control associated with the element. Generally, the key must be pressed in combination with the CONTROL, ALT, or OPTION key in order to activate the field. An example of how this attribute might be used is shown in the following code example:

```
<LABEL ACCESSKEY="N">Customer <U>N</U>ame:
   <INPUT TYPE="TEXT" ID="CustName" SIZE="25">
</LABEL>
```

Notice how the **<U>** element is used to highlight the letter that will activate the field. This is the common practice to indicate accelerator keys in a Windows GUI. According to the HTML 4.0 specification, browsers should provide their own form of highlighting for an access key, but in practice this isn't very common.

The HTML 4.0 standard defines the **ACCESSKEY** attribute for the **<LABEL>**, **<INPUT>**, **<LEGEND>**, and **<BUTTON>** elements, though it leaves off support for

<SELECT> and **<TEXTAREA>**. Microsoft supports this attribute for the **<SELECT>** and **<TEXTAREA>** elements. It seems likely that this will eventually be rolled into the final HTML 4.0 specification.

While the **ACCESSKEY** attribute can improve a form by making it more keyboard access friendly, there are certain letters to avoid because they map to browser functions in the two major browsers, as shown in Table 11-1.

Another accessibility improvement introduced in HTML 4 is the use of the **TABINDEX** attribute for the **<INPUT>**, **<SELECT>**, **<TEXTAREA>**, and **<BUTTON>** elements. This attribute allows the tab order between fields to be defined. In the Microsoft implementation, elements with **TABINDEX** values greater than zero are selected in increasing order. Generally, if a browser supports tabbing through form fields it is by the order in which they are defined. However, with the **TABINDEX** set the tabbing order goes from the lowest positive **TABINDEX** value to the highest. Any elements with a **TABINDEX** of **0** are selected in the order they are encountered after the rest of the tabbing controls have been exhausted. Fields with negative **TABINDEX** values should be left out of the tabbing order. So, in the next fragment, the last field gets selected first and then the first, and the second field is completely skipped over.

```
<INPUT TYPE="TEXT" NAME="First Name" TABINDEX="2">
<INPUT TYPE="TEXT" NAME="Middle Name" TABINDEX="-1">
<INPUT TYPE="TEXT" NAME="Last Name" TABINDEX="1">
```

Key	Mapping	Notes
F	File menu	
E	Edit menu	
C	Communicator menu	Netscape Communicator only
V	View menu	
G	Go menu	
A	Favorites menu	Internet Explorer only
H	Help	
LEFT ARROW	Back in history	
RIGHT ARROW	Forward in history	

Table 11-1.   *Reserved Browser Key Bindings*

Be careful when setting the **TABINDEX** value with radio buttons, as the browser may use arrow keys to move among a group of radio buttons rather than the TAB key.

Page designers are encouraged to set **ACCESSKEY** and **TABINDEX** attributes to their documents immediately as they will have no harmful side effects in older browsers and will simply be ignored.

Miscellaneous HTML 4 Form Attributes

The HTML 4.0 specification also adds two other attributes to certain form controls: **DISABLED** and **READONLY**. When the **DISABLED** attribute is present in a form control element, it turns off the field. Disabled elements will not be submitted, nor may they receive any focus from the keyboard or mouse. The browser may also gray out the disabled form. The point of the **DISABLED** attribute might not be obvious, but imagine being able to disable the form submission button until the appropriate fields have been filled in. Of course, being able to dynamically turn the **DISABLED** attribute for a form control on or off implies scripting support that not all browsers have.

When the **READONLY** attribute is present in a form control element, it prevents the control's value from being changed. A form control set to **READONLY** can be selected by the user but cannot be changed. Selection may even include the inclusion of the form control in the tabbing order. Unlike disabled controls, the values of read-only controls are submitted with the form. In some sense, a read-only form control can be thought of as a visible form of **<INPUT TYPE="HIDDEN">**. According to the HTML 4.0 specification, the **READONLY** attribute is defined for the elements **<INPUT TYPE="TEXT">**, **<INPUT TYPE="PASSWORD">**, and **<TEXTAREA>**, but some browser vendors may also support the **<SELECT>** element or even check boxes. Like a disabled form control, read-only controls can only be changed through the use of a script.

Form Presentation

Up to this point, most of the form elements in the HTML 4.0 specification, as well as those supported by the major browsers, have been presented. Some special considerations for the WebTV environment will be considered in a moment. However, let's first turn our attention to making forms more presentable. Unfortunately, on the Web, little attention seems to be paid to making logical or even presentable-looking forms. For example, take a look at the form in Figure 11-6. Notice that nothing is grouped or lined up.

Form designers are reminded that other HTML markup elements can be used within forms, so there is no excuse for having a poorly laid-out form. For example, a form can be vastly improved by using a table, as shown in Figure 11-7.

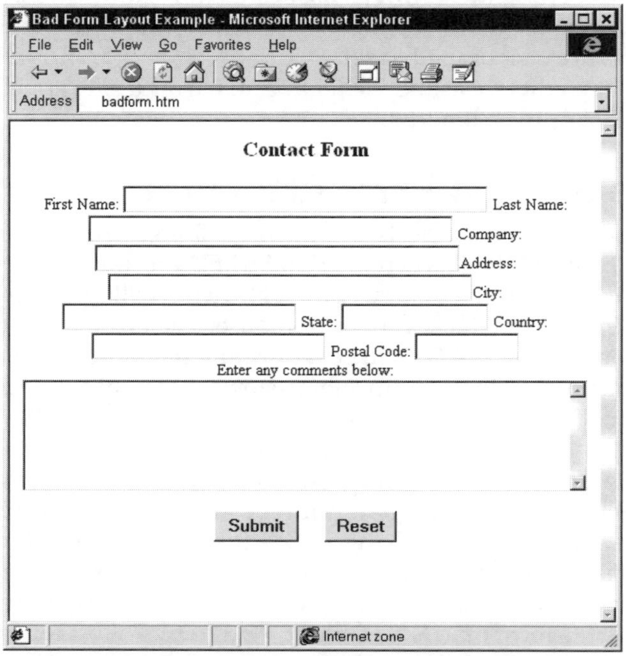

Figure 11-6. *Example of a poorly laid-out form*

The markup for the form using a table in Figure 11-7 is shown here:

```
<!DOCTYPE HTML PUBLIC "-//W3C//DTD HTML 4.0 Transitional//EN">
<HTML>
<HEAD>
<TITLE>Table and Form Example</TITLE>
</HEAD>

<BODY>
<DIV ALIGN="center">
<H2>Contact Form</H2>

<FORM ACTION="mailto: info@bigcompany.com" METHOD=POST>
<TABLE BORDER="1">
```

```
<TR>
   <TD>First Name:</TD>
   <TD><INPUT NAME="firstname" SIZE="40"></TD>
</TR>

<TR>
   <TD>Last Name:</TD>
   <TD><INPUT NAME="lastname" SIZE="40"></TD>
</TR>

<TR>
   <TD>Company:</TD>
   <TD><INPUT NAME="company" SIZE="40"></TD>
</TR>

<TR>
   <TD>Address:</TD><TD><INPUT NAME="address" SIZE="40"></TD>
</TR>

<TR>
   <TD>City:</TD>
   <TD><INPUT NAME="city" SIZE="25"></TD>
</TR>

<TR>
   <TD>State:</TD>
   <TD><INPUT NAME="state" SIZE="15"></TD>
</TR>

<TR>
   <TD>Country:</TD>
   <TD><INPUT NAME="country" SIZE="25"></TD>
</TR>

<TR>
   <TD>Postal Code:</TD>
   <TD><INPUT NAME="zip" SIZE="10"></TD>
</TR>

<TR>
   <TD COLSPAN="2"><BR>Enter any comments below:<BR>
   <TEXTAREA NAME="text" ROWS="5" COLS="50"></TEXTAREA></TD>
</TR>
```

```
    <TR>
       <TD COLSPAN="2" ALIGN="center"><BR>
          <INPUT TYPE="submit" VALUE="Submit"> <INPUT TYPE="reset"><BR><BR>
       </TD>
    </TR>
</TABLE>
</FORM>
</DIV>
</BODY>
</HTML>
```

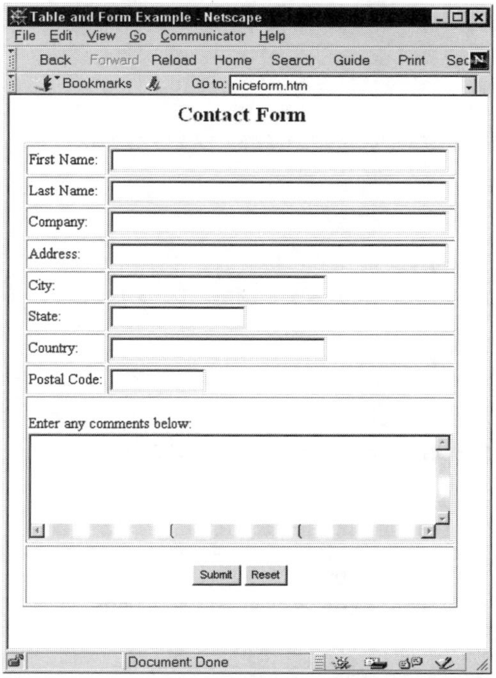

Figure 11-7. *Form layout improved with table*

Besides laying out a form with tables, it might be nice to use the **<FIELDSET>** element to group and box form controls. However, until this element is widely supported, it should not be relied on. Tables should be used instead. Adding a light background color to the different sections of the table could help improve the organization of the form as well.

Page authors might wonder if it is possible to improve the look and feel of forms using style sheets. Under the HTML 4.0 specification, both the **<FORM>** element and the form control elements support the **CLASS, ID,** and **STYLE** attributes to allow access from style sheets. For backward compatibility, particularly with scripting environments, they also support the **NAME** attribute. One interesting aspect of forms and style sheets is that style rules applied to the **<FORM>** element do not seem to be inherited by controls inside the form. This is contrary to the normal case, in which style specifications are inherited by contained elements. In other words, the text inside **<INPUT>** control in the following example will appear as black, not red, when viewed in a browser.

```
<FORM STYLE="{color:red}">
This text is red.
   <INPUT TYPE="TEXT" VALUE="but this text is black">
</FORM>
```

In theory, style sheets should be well supported in forms. In practice, support varies widely from browser to browser. Under Internet Explorer 4, the **CLASS, ID,** and **STYLE** attributes work for **<FORM>, <INPUT>,** and **<SELECT>**. Under Netscape 4 and above, style specifications are not very well supported. The following example demonstrates some of Netscape 4's shortcomings.

```
<FORM STYLE="{color:red}">
This text is red.

<INPUT TYPE="TEXT" VALUE="but this text is blue"
       STYLE="font-family: Arial; color: blue;
              font-size: 12px; background: lightblue">
<BR><BR>

<INPUT VALUE="Submit" TYPE="Submit" STYLE="color: white;
              background: green; font-style;
              bold; font-size: 22px">
</FORM>
```

Under Internet Explorer 4 and above, all of the style information is displayed, including blue 12-pixel Arial text against a light blue background in the input field and large bold white text on a green button. Netscape 4 and above will render the font-family and font-size information properly, but all of the color and background information in this and the previous example are ignored. Many of these problems are bugs or oversights; but, until these issues are cleared up for commonly used browsers, page authors should carefully explore the use of style sheets with form elements before using them.

Special Form Considerations for WebTV

The WebTV browser introduces many attributes to form elements specifically designed to enhance TV-based interaction. This section covers some of these actions. For the latest extensions, visit the WebTV developer's site at http://developer.webtv.net.

While the **<FORM>** element itself is not modified under WebTV, the **<INPUT>** element has many proprietary extensions. Because it is difficult to fill in forms using the onscreen keyboard, WebTV provides some attributes that can be used to make form input a little easier. Because it may be difficult to see the text onscreen, you can set the background color (**BGCOLOR**) as well as the cursor color (**CURSOR**) for individual **<INPUT TYPE="TEXT">** elements. WebTV has introduced many other form extensions. The purpose here is only to illustrate that forms may present issues unique to the viewing environment. This makes extensions worthwhile. However, for the future, such presentational controls are better suited to style sheet developments. Perhaps **"tv"** will become a valid media type for style sheets.

Forms and Events

As presented here, forms really don't finish the job. It is easy to create a form that asks users for their names and the number of gadgets they want to order. It is also easy to write a CGI program (assuming you're a programmer) that can take submitted form data and do something with it. However, it is not easy to make sure that the submitted data is correct. Why should you let the user enter a quantity of –10 (negative ten) gadgets in the form and submit it when that is obviously wrong? Sure, the CGI could catch this, but it's best to try to catch this at the browser level before submitting the form for processing. This is one of the main reasons for client-side scripting.

Starting with Netscape 2 and continuing until today, it has been possible to use a scripting language like JavaScript to associate scripts with user-generated events in a browser. The way to handle events for a form control is by setting an event handler using an attribute that corresponds to the name of the event. If you want to trigger a script when a button is pressed, you could insert some script code associated with the event attribute, as shown in the following dummy form:

```
<FORM>
<INPUT TYPE="BUTTON" VALUE="Don't Press Me!"
      onclick="alert('Danger! Danger!');">
</FORM>
```

Events are added to form controls using attribute declarations such as **onclick**, **onsubmit**, **onreset**, and so on. The number of events has grown significantly and now applies to elements outside forms. In fact, under Dynamic HTML, the trend is for every displayed HTML element to have events associated with it. Let's look at a short example of how forms may be validated using a small amount of scripting code and follow with an overview of the form-related events supported in current HTML dialects. Chapters 13 and 14 provide more details on scripting in general.

Already you have learned that one possible use of form events is to validate form data before it is sent in. In the following example, a form collects a customer name, a customer identification value, and the quantity of gadgets requested. In this example, all values should be entered and a positive number of gadgets ordered. To perform this check, create a simple validation script that looks at the fields and prompts the user to fix any errors. The validation is triggered by the click of a generalized button. When everything checks out, the browser submits the form.

```html
<!DOCTYPE HTML PUBLIC "-//W3C//DTD HTML 4.0 Transitional//EN">
<HTML>
<HEAD>
<TITLE>Basic Form Validation</TITLE>
<SCRIPT LANGUAGE="JavaScript">
<!--
function validate ()
{
    if (document.forms.order.CustomerName.value == "") {
        alert("Please enter your name.")
        return false;
    }

    if (document.forms.order.CustomerID.value == "") {
        alert("Please enter your Customer ID.")
        return false;
    }

    if (document.forms.order.Qty.value <= 0) {
        alert("Please enter a positive number of gadgets.")
        return false;
    }

    return true;
}
// -->
```

```
</SCRIPT>
</HEAD>

<BODY>
<H1 ALIGN="center">Gadget Order Form</H1>
<HR>
<FORM NAME="order" METHOD="POST"
      ACTION="mailto:order@bigcompany.com"
      onsubmit="return validate()">

<B>Customer Name: </B>
<INPUT TYPE="TEXT"
      NAME="CustomerName"
      SIZE="25"
      MAXLENGTH="35">
<BR><BR>

<B>Customer ID:</B>
<INPUT TYPE="PASSWORD"
      NAME="CustomerID"
      SIZE="8"
      MAXLENGTH="9">
<BR><BR>

<B>Quantity of Gadgets:</B>
<INPUT TYPE="TEXT"
      NAME="Qty"
      SIZE="2"
      MAXLENGTH="2">
<HR>

<INPUT TYPE="BUTTON"
      VALUE="Order"
      onclick="validate()">

<INPUT TYPE="RESET" VALUE="Reset">
</FORM>
</BODY>
</HTML>
```

There are a few things to point out in this example. First, the form has been assigned a name. Giving the form a name allows it to be referred to by name in the validation script. Another thing to notice is the use of the **onclick** event attribute. This connects an event the button can respond to with a script to handle the event.

```
<INPUT TYPE="BUTTON" VALUE="Order" onclick="validate()">
```

The value for the **onclick** attribute is the name of the JavaScript function, defined elsewhere, that validates the form. The validation function is declared in the document head inside the **<SCRIPT>** element. Don't worry if the scripting issues, particularly the events, don't make complete sense. They are covered in great detail in Chapters 13 and 14.

Summary

HTML forms provide a basic interface for adding interactivity to a Web site. HTML supports traditional graphical user interface controls like check boxes, radio buttons, pull-down menus, scrolled lists, multi- and single-line text areas, and buttons. These controls can be used to build a form that can be submitted via e-mail to a server-side program for processing. While making a rudimentary form isn't terribly difficult, laying out the form is often overlooked. Using tables and improved grouping elements like **<LABEL>**, **<FIELDSET>**, and **<LEGEND>** can improve a form dramatically. Other features new to HTML 4, such as accelerator keys and tabbing order specification, can also improve how a form may be used. Yet even if a nice form can be developed, it is missing the spark that makes it go. The logic of the form needs to be added either by a server-side program or through a client-side technology like JavaScript. Until then, forms only provide a simple way to collect information.

The Complete Reference

HTML

Chapter 12

Introduction to Server-Side Programming

453

The last chapter hinted at the move from static Web pages to a more dynamic paradigm. The Web is undergoing a shift from a page-oriented view of the world to a more program-oriented view. Although there is increased focus on the programmed elements of a Web page, this doesn't mean that HTML is going away any time soon. Knowing how to author well-formed HTML documents may become more important than ever with the rise of Dynamic HTML. Yet, even before the rise of client-side technologies, HTML has intersected with programming ideas. Server-side computing on the Web has often had an HTML flavor to it, particularly when server-side includes and parsed HTML solutions like Microsoft's Active Server Pages (ASP) or Allaire's ColdFusion are involved. These technologies blur the lines between HTML and programming, because they appear in the form of special markup tags that include information or perform programming tasks. These topics may not seem to be part of HTML and are not official in the standards sense, but they do illustrate how programming and HTML interact.

This chapter will examine the general concept of the programmed Web site and some of the technologies that can be used on the server side to add interactivity to Web pages. The next two chapters will continue the discussion, but with a focus on client-side scripting technologies and object technologies, respectively.

Overview of Client/Server Programming on the Web

When it comes right down to it, the Web is just a form of client/server interaction. Web browsers make requests of Web servers to do some processing or to return a file that is sent back and displayed in the browser. This basic idea is shown in Figure 12-1.

In this basic printed-page idea of the Web, a Web server acts as a file server that delivers HTML files to a Web browser. As shown in the last chapter, thinking about the Web as a digital paper medium is somewhat limiting and does not take advantage of the potential of interactivity.

The most basic form of interactivity on the Web, beyond link selection, is using fill-out forms that are handled by programs, typically Common Gateway Interface (CGI) applications, running on a Web server. The way a user interacts with a CGI-based Web site is easy to describe. First, the user requests a dynamic page or fills out a form to perform a task, such as ordering a product. The request is sent to the Web server, which runs the CGI program, which then outputs information to return to the Web browser, as shown in Figure 12-2.

In this sense, the Web can be used to run programs on a remote server, which then returns a result. When described this way, the Web begins to look more and more like a client/server application environment.

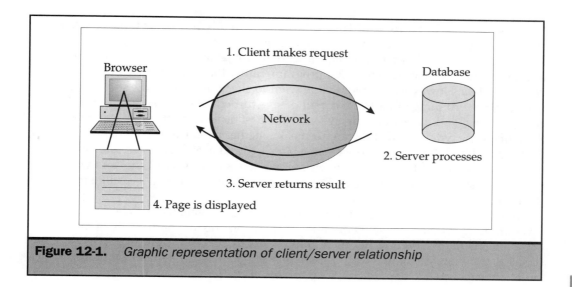

Figure 12-1.   *Graphic representation of client/server relationship*

The diagram in Figure 12-2 suggests two questions. First, where should the computing happen? And second, using what technology? On the early Web, the browser tended to do very little computing. It was solely responsible for rendering pages on the screen. Now, with the rise of client-side technologies like Java, ActiveX, JavaScript, and DHTML, it is possible to perform a great deal of computation from within the browser. Put all the pressure on the server, and it might bog down, or the user might get frustrated with poor responsiveness. Doing most of the computing on the client might cause problems with compatibility, since it's difficult to know what kinds of clients are out there.

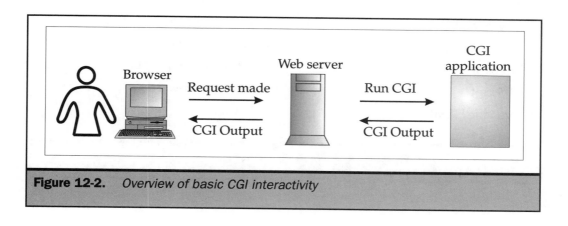

Figure 12-2.   *Overview of basic CGI interactivity*

PROGRAMMING
AND HTML

Security may also be a problem. The best solution is a mixture: some things are better suited for the client; some are better suited for the server.

As discussed in Chapter 11, it makes sense to use JavaScript to check the contents of a form before it is submitted to a CGI program, rather than have the CGI program check the data. However, you would still want to check the data at the server side for users who are running older clients or who have turned off client-side scripting. Things can go wrong, and users don't always have the best browser with all the right settings. And, of course, you would still want to check whether a malicious user has deliberately sent the CGI bad data. A developer who wants to build a Web-based application must choose where to host the logic of the program (client side or server side) and which technology should be used to do it. The decision isn't always obvious, as illustrated by the numerous choices in Table 12-1.

What's interesting about the numerous technologies available for Web programming is that developers often focus solely on one tool or one side of the equation (client or server) rather than thinking about how the applications they are trying to build are going to work. This chapter will look at the server side of the equation; subsequent chapters will focus on the client side.

Client Side	Server Side
Helpers	CGI programs
Plug-ins	NSAPI/ISAPI programs
Active-X controls	Server-side scripting
Java applets	Server-side includes
Scripting languages	Active Server pages
JavaScript	Server-side JavaScript (LiveWire)
VBScript	Database middleware
Dynamic HTML	ColdFusion

Table 12-1. *Web Programming Technology Choices*

Server-Side Programming

When adding interactivity to a Web page, it often makes sense to add all functionality on the server side. There are two basic reasons for doing this. First, the server side is the only part of the equation that can be completely controlled. If we only rely on the browser to render HTML pages, life is simple. If we assume users have JavaScript, Java, or a particular plug-in, things become less predictable. Why is this, given that most modern browsers come with many of these technologies? There are too many variables and too many bugs. Users often turn off support for Java, JavaScript, or ActiveX due to fear of security breaches. Even when turned on, these technologies are often far from robust. For example, JavaScript comes in two basic flavors, Microsoft and Netscape, and has more than three versions running on at least four major operating systems (Mac, Windows 3.1, 95/NT, and UNIX). Each of these implementations has some subtle and not-so-subtle differences, including feature disparity and bugs. It is no wonder we would want to move computation to the server, where these issues are more controllable.

The second reason that server-side computation makes sense is that the server is where much of the data required actually "lives." Consider a database. A common requirement of the Web is to act as a front end to access a database. Imagine a Web site where the user wants to query a system to see if a particular product is available. A form could be developed for the user to submit the query. The contents of the form could be passed to a program on a Web server, which would parse the form data and produce a database query. Such a program is called *middleware*, because it sits between the back-end database server and the client-accessible Web server. A CGI program is one form of middleware. After the database completes the query, the result is passed back to the middleware, which formats the result as an HTML page and passes the result back to the browser. The Web server acts as the coordinator for this whole process, including interacting with and possibly even starting the middleware. This process is illustrated in Figure 12-3.

One potential downside to adding interactivity via server-side programs should be mentioned: too much reliance on the server. In the last examples, the browser was relatively simple, because the computation took place almost entirely on the server side. The client browser was only responsible for rendering the entry form and the resulting pages. Choosing the appropriate approach to deal with a problem like database access is beyond the scope of this book, but remember that there can be disadvantages to putting all the computing responsibility on the server—namely, speed and scalability. For now, our discussion turns to the approaches to server-based interactivity and how it intersects with HTML.

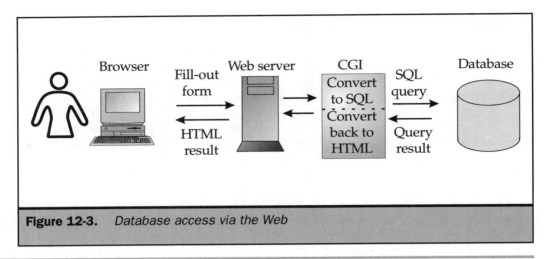

Figure 12-3. *Database access via the Web*

Common Gateway Interface (CGI)

Probably the most common way to add interactivity to a Web page is through a CGI program. *Common Gateway Interface (CGI)* is a protocol standard that specifies how information can be passed from a Web page via a Web server, to a program, and back from the program to a browser in the proper format. Many people confuse the program that does this with the CGI protocol. In reality, the program is just a program. It just happens to be a CGI program since it was written to pass information back and forth using the CGI specification.

The following steps summarize how CGI interacts with a form:

1. The user submits a form.
2. The form is sent to the server and eventually to the CGI program, using the following steps:
   a. The server determines if the request is a document or program request by examining execution settings and path.
   b. The server locates the program (in the cgi-bin directory on the server or elsewhere) and determines if the program can be executed.
   c. The server starts the program and prepares the data, and any extra information from the environment, to be sent to the program from the form fields.
   d. The program runs.
   e. The server waits for the program to produce output (optional) and then passes back the properly formatted result to the client or, potentially, an error message.
3. The CGI program processes the data and responds to the server.
4. The Web server passes the CGI response back to the client.

Note *Server launching of the program (step 2c) is operating system–dependent and may require starting a new process.*

It is possible to create anything, including games, with CGI; but complex tasks are often limited by the state problem. The common uses of CGI include

- Form processing
- Database access
- Counters
- Custom document generation
- Browser-specific page delivery
- Banner ad serving
- Guest book and authentication
- Threaded discussion
- Games

Understanding how CGI works requires an understanding of how the HTTP protocol works. The only magic behind CGI is knowing how to read data in and write data out to talk to a Web browser. Writing data out is the easiest. The key to writing data out for Web browsers is understanding the headers so the browser knows what it is getting, namely, MIME types. MIME stands for *Multipurpose Internet Mail Extension*. The MIME content type of a file tells a browser how to process it.

The following example, which shows how a Web browser and a Web server communicate, should help us better understand exactly what CGI programs do.

You can access a Web server directly by using a telnet program to literally log in to the TCP service port for HTTP. To do this, use a telnet program to access a Web server and set the port number to 80. In UNIX, you might type

```
telnet www.bigcompany.com 80
```

This could also be performed via Windows 95/NT, which has telnet built into it. Just make sure to set the port value to 80.

Once connected to the Web server, type in the proper HTTP request. A simple request would be

```
GET / HTTP/1.0
```

Then press ENTER twice to send a blank line, without which the operation won't work.

PROGRAMMING AND HTML

Once the server processes the request, the result should look something like the listing shown here:

```
HTTP/1.0 200 OK
Date:     Monday, 01-January-99 09:00:00 GMT
Server:   NCSA/1.3.1
MIME-version: 1.0
Content-type: text/html
Content-length: 1200


<HTML>
<HEAD>
<TITLE>Sample HTML Document</TITLE>
</HEAD>

<BODY>
...content...
</BODY>
```

If a Web browser were reading this data stream, it would read the **Content-type** line. The browser would then determine what to do with the data. Browsers have a mapping that takes a MIME type and then determines what to do with it. Figure 12-4 shows the mapping file from Netscape Navigator 3's helper application.

Notice in the preceding code that the content-type is **text/html**. This has the action of a browser, which would render the HTML within the browser window. Remember that Web servers can serve just about any type of data and pass that data to a plug-in or helper, or query the user to save the file.

CGI Output

Given that you have now seen the manual execution of an HTTP request, what is important to the Web browser? The simple answer is the MIME type and its associated data. In most cases, the pages being delivered are HTML based, so the MIME type should be **text/html** and any HTML you want on your screen. With this idea in mind, it should be easy to write a CGI program that fakes an HTML page. To do this, you need to print out the MIME type indication **Content-type: text/html**, followed by a series of HTML codes. The following small Perl program shows how this might be done. Any language, including C, Pascal, or BASIC, could also be used to make such an example.

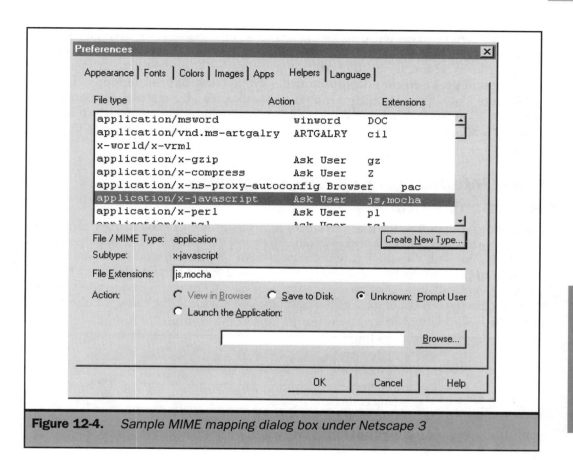

Figure 12-4. *Sample MIME mapping dialog box under Netscape 3*

```
#!/usr/bin/perl# Note the path to perl may vary.
# Really simple CGI program
#
print "Content-type: text/html\n\n"

print "<HTML>\n<HEAD><TITLE>First CGI</TITLE></HEAD>\n"

print "<BODY>\n<H1>I was created by a CGI
program!</H1>\n</BODY>\n</HTML>"
```

If this example were typed and set to run on a Perl-capable Web server, it could be accessed directly by a user to print out the simple page shown in Figure 12-5. To see the program in action, try the URL http://www.htmlref.com/cgi-bin/firstcgi.pl.

In summary: To create a document on the fly, you have to print a group of headers. Make sure to do this in the correct format. Other than that, the rest of the program is up to you. This section only covers getting information from the server, which is just half of the CGI equation. The following section discusses getting information to your program.

Passing Information to a CGI Program: Environment Variables

In order to get information into a CGI program, you generally need to use a form. The CGI program itself can actually read some information from the HTTP request and the local environment. This information can be used in conjunction with form data to understand the environment the program is running. Environment variables are actually very valuable. They can be used to help the CGI program decide what kind of pages to prepare. A list of most of the common CGI environment variables is provided in Table 12-2.

Figure 12-5.   *Output of simple CGI program*

Variable Name	Description
GATEWAY_INTERFACE	The version number of CGI supported by the server; for example, CGI/1.1.
SERVER_NAME	The domain name or IP address of the Web server running the CGI program.
SERVER_SOFTWARE	Information about the Web server, typically the name and version number of the software—for example, Netscape-Commerce/1.12.
SERVER_PROTOCOL	The version number of the HTTP protocol being used in the request—for example, HTTP/1.1.
SERVER_PORT	The port on which the Web server is running, typically 80.
REQUEST_METHOD	The method by which the information is being passed, in either **GET** or **POST**.
CONTENT_TYPE	For queries that have attached information, because they use the **POST** or **PUT** method; contains the content type of the passed data in MIME format.
CONTENT_LENGTH	The length of any passed content (**POST** or **PUT**) as given by the client, typically as length in bytes.
PATH_INFO	Any extra path information passed in with the file request. This would usually be associated with the **GET** request.
SCRIPT_NAME	The relative path to the script that is running.
QUERY_STRING	Query information passed to the program.
DOCUMENT_ROOT	The document root of the Web server.
REMOTE_USER	If the server supports user authentication and the script is protected, this variable holds the user name that the user has authenticated.
AUTH_TYPE	This variable is set to the authentication method used to validate the user if the script being run is protected.

Table 12-2.   *Common CGI Variables*

PROGRAMMING
AND HTML

Variable Name	Description
REMOTE_IDENT	If the Web server supports RFC 931–based identification, then this variable will be set to the remote username retrieved from the server. This is rarely used.
REMOTE_HOST	The remote host name of the browser passing information to the server—for example, sun1.bigcompany.com.
REMOTE_ADDR	The IP address of the browser making the request.
HTTP_ACCEPT	A list of MIME types the browser can accept.
HTTP_USER_AGENT	A code indicating the type of browser making the request.
HTTP_REFERER	The URL of the linking document (the document that linked to the CGI being run). If the user types in the address of the program directly, the **HTTP_REFERER** value will be unset.

Table 12-2. *Common CGI Variables* (continued)

Figure 12-6 shows the results of a CGI program that prints out the environment information. Try to execute the program at http://www.htmlref.com/cgi-bin/printenv.cgi to see if the results are different.

Depending on the Web server and browser, there may be other useful environment variables. These include **HTTPS**, which is used to indicate if Secure Sockets Layer (SSL) security is on; **HTTP_CONNECTION**, which is used to indicate to the server to keep a connection open for improved performance; and **HTTP_ACCEPT_LANGUAGE**, which is used to indicate what language the server accepts data in. There are other potential values available, so be certain to check the Web server programming documentation.

The Perl code for the result in Figure 12-6 is shown here:

```
#!/usr/bin/perl

&print_HTTP_header;
&print_head;
&print_body;
&print_tail;
```

```perl
# print the HTTP Content-type header

sub print_HTTP_header {
    print "Content-type: text/html\n\n";
}

#Print the start of the HTML file

sub print_head {
    print <<END;
<HTML>
<HEAD>
<TITLE>CGI Environment Variables</TITLE>
</HEAD>

<BODY>
<H1 ALIGN="CENTER">Environment Variables</H1>
<HR>
END
}

#Loop through the environment variable

#associative array and print out its values.

sub print_body {
    foreach $variable (sort keys %ENV) {
        print "<B>$variable:</B> $ENV{$variable}<BR>\n";
    }

}

#Print the close of the HTML file

sub print_tail {
        print <<END;

</BODY>
</HTML>
END
}
```

Notice that the code is written to make the printing of the appropriate headers, the start of the HTML file, the results, and the close of the file more straightforward. Code libraries, which do much of the work of CGI, are commonly available.

Browser Sensing with CGI

At first glance, the environment variables might not seem very useful. When used properly, however, they are indispensable. One of the most important uses of CGI is to sense the browser being used so that customized pages can be delivered for different browser types. Using a small program, it would be possible to sense a user's browser type and redirect him or her automatically to another page.

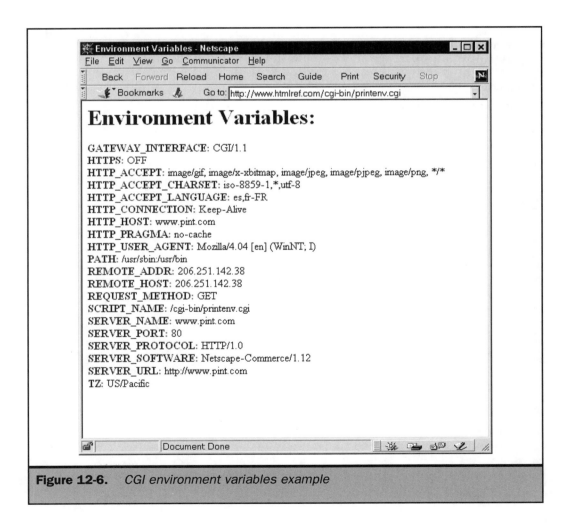

Figure 12-6. CGI environment variables example

Note

To make browser sensing work, the server may have to be configured to run the CGI program automatically. This may just require putting a file called index.cgi in the root directory or performing some similar renaming.

Here is how browser sensing works. The CGI environment variable called **HTTP_USER_AGENT** is read in by the CGI program using a simple call available from a Perl CGI library. Once the value is set, a set of conditions determines which page to send, depending on the browser accessing the page. In the following example, the file netscapehome.htm is sent if the browser is Netscape 3 or above. If the browser is Microsoft Internet Explorer 3 or above, the file mshome.htm is sent. Otherwise, the file home.htm is sent.

```perl
#!/usr/local/bin/perl

require '/usr/local/ns-home/cgi-bin/cgi-lib.pl';

# pulls in special library for easy reading of
# environment variables
&ReadParse;
$agent = $ENV{'HTTP_USER_AGENT'};

if ($agent =~ /Mozilla\/3.0|Mozilla\/4.0/i) {
    $file = "netscapehome.htm";
}
if ($agent =~ /MSIE 3.0|MSIE 4.0/i) {
    $file = "mshome.htm";
}

else {
    $file = "home.htm";
}
print "Location: http://www.bigcompany.com/$file", "\n\n";
```

What's interesting is that this file was used to sort out what form of animation could be used. The people who received the mshome.htm file could read Macromedia Flash files, Netscape 3 and 4 users could use JavaScript rollover animations, and everyone who could do neither received a static page. When a site is done well, there isn't an entrance page that says "Click here for Netscape" and "Click here for other browsers." Things just work, because the site has browser-aware pages. Of course, one huge problem with this idea is having to keep different files for the same page. Parsed HTML, as discussed later in the chapter, may offer a better solution to browser-aware pages.

Passing Information to a CGI Program: Form Data

Forms are a good way to collect user input such as a survey result or a comment. They can also start database queries or launch programs. Creating HTML forms was discussed in Chapter 11. For a quick refresher on how HTML forms are used, take a look at the following example:

```
<!DOCTYPE HTML PUBLIC "-//W3C//DTD HTML 4.0 Final//EN">
<HTML>
<HEAD>
<TITLE>Meet and Greet</TITLE>
</HEAD>

<BODY>
<H1 ALIGN="CENTER">Welcome to CGI!</H1>
<HR>

<FORM METHOD="POST"
      ACTION="http://www.pint.com/cgi-bin/helloworld.pl">

<B>What's your name?</B>
<INPUT TYPE="TEXT" NAME="user_name" SIZE="25">
<BR><BR>
<INPUT TYPE="SUBMIT" VALUE="Hi I am...">
<INPUT TYPE="RESET" VALUE="RESET">

</FORM>
</BODY>
</HTML>
```

If this example is typed and run, it will greet the user by whatever name he or she types in. The **<FORM>** element is the key to this example, because it has an action to perform (as indicated by the **ACTION** attribute when the form is submitted). The action is to launch a CGI program indicated by the URL value of the **ACTION** attribute. The **<FORM>** element also has an attribute, **METHOD**, which indicates how information will be passed to the receiving CGI program. There are two basic methods to pass data in via a form: **GET** and **POST**. **GET** appends information on the end of the submitting URL, so the URL accessed in the previous example might be something like

```
http://www.pint.com/cgi-bin/hello.pl?user_name=Joe+Smith
```

The data sent will be encoded. Long strings may have **+** or **%*nn*** hex-encoded values. Name/value pairs will be separated by ampersands. (The format of URL-encoded data is discussed in Chapter 11.) The problem with the **GET** method is that, besides being ugly, it is limited to the amount of data that can be easily sent in. **GET** does have two advantages: it is easy to understand and provides the possibility for canned queries. The more common approach for larger forms is to use the **POST** method, which sends the form data as a separate data stream—in other words, a file—to the server. The data stream (essentially a file) consists of many lines, such as **name=Joe%20Smith**. These lines can be parsed by the receiving program for later processing. Given how data is encoded, a skilled programmer could easily determine how to parse data and access the values. The following simple helloworld.pl example shows how this might be done in a brute force manner that does no error checking:

```perl
#! /usr/bin/perl

# Print the HTTP headers

print "Content-type: text/html\n";
print "\n";

read (STDIN, $GN_QUERY, $ENV{CONTENT_LENGTH});

# This statement will split data into different fields

@QUERY_LIST = split( /&/, $GN_QUERY);

foreach $item (@QUERY_LIST) {

    # First convert plus signs into spaces

    $item =~ s/\+/ /g;

    # Now convert $nn encoded data to characters

    $item =~ s/%(..)/pack("c",hex($1))/ge;

    # Now put the result into the QueryArray

    $loc=index($item,"=");
    $param=substr($item, 0, $loc);
    $value=substr($item, $loc+1);
    $QUERY_ARRAY{$param} .= $value;
}
```

```
# Now get the users name

$name = "$QUERY_ARRAY{user_name}";

# Print Return HTML
print "<HTML><HEAD><TITLE>Hello</TITLE></HEAD>\n<BODY>\n";
print "<H1>Hello $name. Welcome to CGI!</H1>\n";
print "</BODY></HTML>";
```

Writing CGI Programs

The previous examples might seem to suggest that writing CGI programs is trivial. This is true if data is only to be read in and written out. In fact, this part of CGI is so mechanical that page designers are encouraged not to attempt to parse the data themselves. There are many scripting libraries available for Perl. These include cgic (http://www.boutell.com/cgic/) for ANSI programs, cgi++ (http://www.webthing.com/cgiplusplus/) for C++, and CGI.pm (http://stein.cshl.org/WWW/software/CGI/cgi_docs.html) for Perl 5. These libraries, and others available on the Internet, make the reading of environment variables and parsing of encoded form data a simple process.

The difficult part of CGI isn't the input and output of data. It is the logic of the code itself. Given that the CGI program can be written in nearly any language, Web programmers might wonder what language to use. Performance, Web suitability, and string handling are important criteria for selecting a language for CGI authoring. Performancewise, compiled CGI programs typically will have better performance than interpreted programs written in a scripting language like Perl. However, it is probably easier to write a simple CGI in a scripting language like Perl or AppleScript than to use C or C++.

Some programming languages may have better interfaces to Web servers and HTTP than others. For example, Perl has a great number of CGI libraries and operating system facilities readily available. Because much of CGI is about reading and writing text data, ease of string handling may also be a big consideration in selecting the language. The bottom line is that scripting language choice mainly depends on the server the script must run on and the programmer's preference. It is even possible to use an old version of FORTRAN or some obscure language to write a CGI program, though it would be easier to pick a language that works well with the Web server and use it to access some other program. CGI lives up to its name as a gateway.

Table 12-3 lists the common languages for CGI coding based on the Web server's operating system. Notice that Perl is common to most of the platforms due to its ease of use and long-standing use on the Web.

Web Server Operating System	Common CGI Languages
UNIX	Perl, C, C++, Java, Shell script languages (csh, ksh, sh), Python
Windows	Visual Basic, C, C++, Perl
Macintosh	AppleScript, Perl, C, C++

Table 12-3.   *Common CGI Language Choices*

Don't rush around and get ready to code your own form handlers. Consider how many other people in the world need to access a database or e-mail a form. Given these common needs, it may be better to borrow or buy a canned CGI solution than to build a new one.

Buying or Borrowing CGI Programs

Most CGI programs are similar to one another. There are a great deal of shareware, freeware, or commercial packages available to do most of the common Web tasks. Matt's Script Archive (http://www.worldwidemart.com/scripts) and the CGI Resource Index (http://www.cgi-resources.com) are good places to start looking for these. There are many scripts for form handling, bulletin boards, counters, and countless other things available for free on the Internet. There are also compiled commercial CGI programs made to perform a particular task. Site developers are urged to consider the cost of developing custom solutions versus buying premade solutions, particularly when time is an important consideration in building the site.

NSAPI/ISAPI

One serious problem with CGI programs is their slowness. There are two reasons why CGI programs can be slow. The first is that the launch of the CGI program by the Web server can be slow. Once launched, the program may run relatively slowly, because it is written in an interpreted language like Perl. Solving the second problem is easy: simply rewrite the program in a compiled language like C. Performance should quickly improve. What about the launch problem? One approach would be to prelaunch the main CGI program so that it is running all the time and have smaller CGI programs launch when needed. While this would help, the server would still have to communicate with an external program, which might be time consuming. If speed is of the essence, migrating the functionality of the CGI program into the server is required. This is the idea behind the Netscape Server Application Programming Interface (NSAPI) and the Internet Server Application Programming Interface (ISAPI).

In short, NSAPI and ISAPI programs are like plug-ins for a server. A program, typically written in C or C++, that conforms to the NSAPI/ISAPI can be plugged into the server to add functionality to the system. Obviously, writing such a solution is much more difficult than writing a simple CGI program. There are other drawbacks as well. For example, a misbehaving ISAPI/NSAPI program may bring a whole server down. Developers who write an application programming interface (API)–based solution may also be stuck using a particular server platform, while CGI programs are generally portable from server to server. Regardless of their drawbacks, NSAPI/ISAPI programs have the advantage of speed and the ability to share data across sessions and users very easily. With this power, many third-party developers have created server extensions to allow fast and easy database access, threaded discussion capability, and many other features. While most developers are about as likely to use NSAPI or ISAPI programs as they are to write browser plug-ins, the technology has enabled the creation of server-side parsing technology, which is useful to almost every Web page developer.

Parsed HTML Solutions: Server-Side Scripting

CGI and NSAPI/ISAPI programs are beyond the technical understanding of some Web page developers. However, adding interactivity to a site does not always have to be difficult. Another form of server-based programming, generically termed *parsed HTML*, provides much of the sophistication of general CGI with the ease of HTML. The idea of parsed HTML is simple. First, code a page using standard HTML. Then add special new elements or directives to indicate what to do in particular cases. Imagine if you wanted to print out different HTML headings for Netscape users, Microsoft Internet Explorer, and other browser users. Using parsed HTML, you might put statements in a parsed HTML language in your file, like this:

```
$if browser = Netscape
     <H1><BLINK>Hey Netscape User!</BLINK></H1>
$else if browser = IE
     <MARQUEE>Hey Microsoft User!</MARQUEE>
$else
     <H1>Hey User!</H1>
$endif
```

To indicate that the file is a special parsed HTML file, end its name with the extension .parsedhtml. Next, configure the server to parse and execute the special statements you have added to the file. In this case, the server will then output only the HTML, depending on the particular browser being used. An overview of parsed HTML solutions is shown in Figure 12-7.

While parsed HTML solutions are very easy for people to deal with, they can put an excessive load on the server. Use them wisely. The next few sections describe three common parsed HTML technologies used on the Web: server-side includes (SSI), ColdFusion, and Active Server Pages (ASP).

Server-Side Includes (SSIs)

Server-side includes are the simplest form of parsed HTML. SSIs are short directives you can embed in an HTML document to indicate files to be read and included in the final output. This might be useful if the designer wants to make one file with footer information, such as an address and copyright, and then append it to all pages dynamically. To do this, create a file called footer.htm and then include it dynamically using SSI. The contents of footer.htm might look something like this:

```
<HR NOSHADE>
<CENTER>
<FONT SIZE="-1">
Copyright 1997 Big Company<BR>
2105 Garnet Ave, Suite E, San Diego, CA 92109</FONT>
```

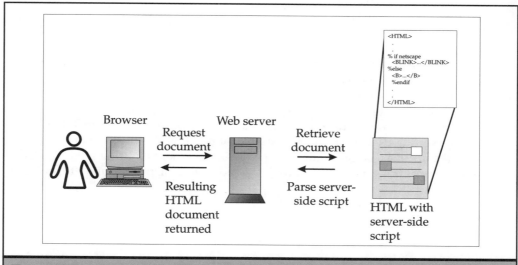

Figure 12-7. *Overview of parsed HTML solutions*

To include this file in another file, you would need an SSI directive like this:

```
<!--#include file="footer.htm" -->
```

Notice that this is just a special form of an HTML comment with an **#include** command and a parameter file, which is set to the file you want to include. To indicate to the server that the page contains SSI commands, use the .shtml extension. If the server is properly configured, it should pick up the file and execute it before sending the result.

Besides including external files, SSI can also be used to show the results of programs, including CGI programs. Thus, it can provide a way to query databases and make a page counter, among other things. The simple example that follows shows how the **echo** SSI command can be used to access the environment variables to which CGI programs have access.

```
<HTML>
<HEAD>

<BODY>

<H2 ALIGN="CENTER">Welcome <!--#echo var="REMOTE_HOST" -->
to my server <!--#echo var="SERVER_NAME" --></H2>
<HR>

You are using <!--#echo var="HTTP_USER_AGENT" -->.

</BODY>
</HTML>
```

One possible result of this example is shown in Figure 12-8. Remember that your result will be different since the page is dynamically generated and must be run from a server with SSI turned on.

The environment variables that are accessible from SSI are similar to those that can be accessed by any CGI program. They also include the variables listed in Table 12-4.

Besides inserting CGI environment variable values, it is also possible to use SSI to embed the results of a CGI program into an HTML document by using the EXEC CGI command. For example, it would be possible to add a simple page counter to an HTML

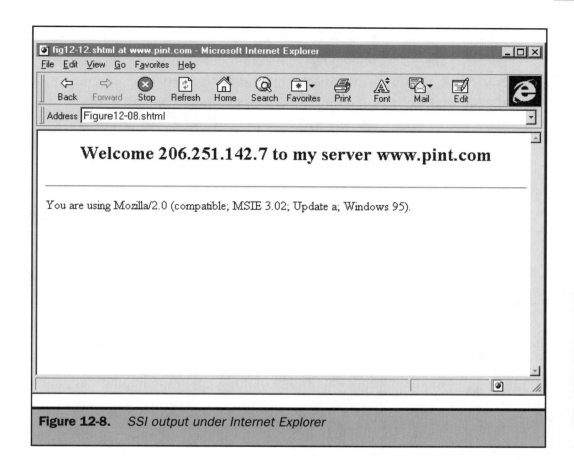

Figure 12-8. *SSI output under Internet Explorer*

Variable Name	Description
DATE_GMT	This value references the current server local date, same as **DATE_LOCAL**, but in Greenwich mean time. This variable is subject to formatting from the **CONFIG** SSI command.
DATE_LOCAL	The current date, local time zone. Subject to formatting from the **CONFIG** SSI command.

Table 12-4. *SSI-Available Variables Potentially Outside the CGI Set*

Variable Name	Description
DOCUMENT_NAME	The variable holds the current filename.
DOCUMENT_URI	The variable contains the virtual path to the current document—for example, /about/bigcompany/contact.shtml.
LAST_MODIFIED	The last modification date of the current document. This variable is subject to the date formatting set by the **CONFIG** SSI command.
QUERY_STRING_ UNESCAPED	This variable contains the "unescaped" version of any search query (**GET**) sent by the browser. Any special characters are escaped using the \ character.

Table 12-4.   *SSI-Available Variables Potentially Outside the CGI Set* (continued)

document by using an SSI command to execute the counter program and display its results in the page. Assuming there were a program called counter.cgi in the cgi-bin directory on the server, you could use a simple SSI statement like the following to add the page count:

```
<!--#exec cgi="cgi-bin/counter.cgi"-->
```

In general, SSI consists of a special comment form that indicates the SSI command, as well as any parameters to modify the command in the general format, as follows:

```
<!-- #command parameter=value -->
```

Following are some of the common SSI commands and their associated parameters.

ECHO

PARAMETERS   VAR

DESCRIPTION   Used to insert the values of special SSI variables and environment variables into the page.

```
<!--#ECHO VAR="REMOTE_HOST"-->
```

INCLUDE

PARAMETERS   FILE, VIRTUAL

DESCRIPTION   Used to insert the contents of a document into the current file. This pathname of the file can be either relative or virtual. Relative files paths are relative to the current directory, while virtual filenames may access other directories using the ../ directory style or an absolute path.

```
<!--#INCLUDE FILE="footer.htm"-->
<!--#INCLUDE VIRTUAL="../templates/footer.htm"-->
```

FSIZE

PARAMETERS   FILE

DESCRIPTION   Inserts the size of a given file.

```
<!--#FSIZE FILE="index.htm"-->
```

FLASTMOD

PARAMETERS   FILE

DESCRIPTION   Inserts the last modification date of a given file.

```
<!--#FLASTMOD FILE="index.htm"-->
```

EXEC

PARAMETERS   CMD, CGI

DESCRIPTION   Allows you to execute external programs, either an application on the host or a CGI program.

```
<!--#EXEC CMD="/usr/bin/ls"-->
<!--#EXEC CGIi="cgi-bin/counter.cgi"-->
```

PROGRAMMING AND HTML

CONFIG

PARAMETERS   ERRMSG= *string,* **SIZEFMT**= bytes | abbrev, **TIMEFMT**= *format string*

DESCRIPTION   Allows you to configure SSI output options for error output, file size output, and data output. The value for **ERRMSG** is simply a string value for the error message. **SIZEFMT** may be set to bytes or abbrev, while **TIMEFMT** can be set to a UNIX date format string in the form compatible with the strftime library.

```
<!--#CONFIG ERRMSG="[SSI Statement Failed!]"-->
<!--#CONFIG SIZEFMT="bytes"-->
<!--#CONFIG TIMEFM="%A %b %d %j"-->
```

Depending on the server, there may be more SSI statements, including **ODBC** and **EMAIL**, which are used to access a database and send e-mail, respectively. These commands are the ones most common across most SSI-capable servers.

While SSI looks appealing, it has two potential problems: security and performance. SSI's security problem is mainly due to the EXEC command, which can be used to execute a program on the server. With this command, security breaches are possible. For example, it might be possible to insert a command to launch a remote session. Even if security isn't a big issue, depending on how SSI and the Web server are configured, the executing command may have a great deal of permissions and be able to remove values. Web administrators are advised to limit use of this SSI command.

The other problem with SSI, performance, is typical with any parsed HTML solution. Because all SSI files have to be parsed, they may cause a performance hit. If a site has serious performance requirements, parsed HTML solutions may be inappropriate. Fortunately, it is possible to limit parsed HTML or mix it with standard HTML by having only certain files, for example those ending in .shtml, parsed by the server. When used in a limited fashion, SSI can provide powerful features that are within the technical ability of any HTML writer. However, SSI is limited. Page designers may find other parsed HTML solutions, such as ColdFusion or ASP, more appropriate.

ColdFusion

One of the most popular server-parsed HTML solutions is Allaire's ColdFusion (http://www.allaire.com). ColdFusion is a complete Web application development tool that allows developers to create dynamic database-driven Web site applications with an easy-to-use, server-side markup language similar to HTML. Getting started with ColdFusion requires learning a few new markup tags that look like HTML but make up what is called ColdFusion Markup Language (CFML). Since one of its primary functions is database access, ColdFusion uses the Open Database Connectivity

(ODBC) standard to connect to popular database servers like Microsoft SQL Server, Access, Sybase, Oracle, and others. ColdFusion is not dependent on a particular database or Web server, and it works well on a variety of Windows NT- and Unix-based servers. While ColdFusion is not a W3C defined standard, it is widely used. It is presented here to illustrate an example of parsed HTML and to show how HTML might be used to interact with a database.

Web applications built with ColdFusion use dynamic pages composed of a mixture of CFML and HTML markup. When the page is requested, the ColdFusion application running on the server preprocesses the page, interacts with a database or other server-side technologies, and returns a dynamically generated HTML page. It is probably better to refer to ColdFusion–enabled pages as templates since the actual page output varies.

Using CFML

Here is how to use CFML to select and output data in a dynamic Web page. This section will show how to use a number of CFML tags to query data from a database, take the results of the query, and populate a Web page.

Database Overview

A database is simply a collection of data that is organized in a regular fashion, typically in the form of a table. Imagine you want to create a Web site to post the various job openings in your company. The first thing you need to do is to decide what information is relevant: position number, job title, location, brief description, hiring manager, and posting date. This information could be organized in the form of a database table, called Positions, as shown in Table 12-5.

Position-Num	JobTitle	Location	Description	Hiring Manager	PostDate
343	Gadget Sales	Austin	Requires an aggressive sales person to sell gadgets to guys and gals	M. Spacely	01/20/99
525	Office Manager	San Jose	Responsible for running the entire office single-handedly	P. Mohta	01/24/99

Table 12-5.   *Simple Database Table Called Positions*

PROGRAMMING AND HTML

Position-Num	JobTitle	Location	Description	Hiring Manager	PostDate
2585	President	San Diego	Figurehead position requiring daily golf games and nightly poker parties	T. Powell	01/30/99
3950	Groundskeeper	San Diego	Must like outdoor work and long hours in the sun with no sunscreen	J. Tam	01/30/99
1275	HTML Hacker	Seattle	Must be able to recite HTML specifications by heart and code HTML by hand; long hours, low pay	D. Whitworth	01/27/99
2015	Game Tester	Los Angeles	Must be able to play games all day long; poor posture and junk food diet essential	J. Daffyd	01/18/99

Table 12-5. *Simple Database Table Called Positions* (continued)

The example is populated with some simple data, but how can the data be retrieved to be displayed in a Web page automatically?

Selecting the Data

The first step is to define a database query using Structured Query Language (SQL). SQL is the language used to retrieve or modify data from the tables in a database. The language is relatively simple, at least as far as mastering the basics. If you were interested in making a query to the database table called Positions, you would use a SQL statement like

```
SELECT * FROM Positions
```

This query simply says to select all items indicated by the wildcard (*) in the table called Positions. If you just want to list all the positions in Austin, you could qualify the query by adding a **WHERE** modifier, indicating you only want entries for which the location is Austin.

```
SELECT * FROM Positions WHERE Location="Austin"
```

Using the **WHERE** modifier, it is possible to create complex queries. For example, you could query all jobs in Austin, or in Los Angeles, for which the position is Game Tester.

```
SELECT *
    FROM Positions
    WHERE ((Location="Austin" OR
        (Location="Los Angeles") AND
        (Position="Game Tester"))
```

This brief discussion should reveal the flavor of SQL. While the basic language is simple, queries can be more complicated. A full discussion of SQL is well beyond the scope of this book. For sake of this discussion, only simple queries are used in the examples.

In order to pull data out of the database, write a SQL query, and then place it within a **<CFQUERY>** element. The following example illustrates the use of **<CFQUERY>**. A select SQL query called **ListJobs**, as specified by the **NAME** attribute, will query a database and retrieve all the records in the Positions table. The syntax for this example is shown here.

```
<CFQUERY NAME="ListJobs"
        DATASOURCE="CompanyDataBase">
SELECT * FROM Positions
</CFQUERY>
```

Notice that the **DATASOURCE** attribute is set equal to CompanyDataBase, which is the ODBC data source that contains a database called Company, which contains the Positions table from which data is pulled.

PROGRAMMING
AND HTML

Open Database Connectivity (ODBC) is a standardized way to access data from a variety of different databases. ODBC provides a layer of abstraction that protects the developer from having to learn the particulars of a specific database system. To query the Positions table, your server might connect to a simple Microsoft Access database or a powerful Oracle system. In order to access a database, a developer needs to set up an ODBC data source. This requires that developer to select an ODBC driver, name the data source, and configure any specific settings for the database. A complete discussion of how to set up ODBC drivers and configure data sources can be found in the documentation for ColdFusion.

Besides **NAME** and **DATASOURCE**, the **<CFQUERY>** element has a variety of attributes, as described in Table 12-6.

Attribute	Description
NAME	Required. This attribute is used to assign a name to the SQL query. The name is used later in the template to reference the query results.
DATASOURCE	Required. This attribute is used to specify the name of the ODBC data source that will be used to access the database.
MAXROWS	Optional. This attribute is used to specify the maximum number of rows as a positive integer number that should be returned by the query. More output rows beyond this value will be dropped.
USERNAME	Optional. Since many databases have login features, this attribute is used to set the username to access the data source. This attribute overrides the default settings in the ColdFusion Administrator.
PASSWORD	Optional. This attribute is used to set the password associated for the username that will access the database. This value overrides the default settings in the ColdFusion Administrator.
TIMEOUT	Optional. This attribute can be set to a time, in milliseconds, for a query to successfully execute. Queries that take longer than this value will fail.
DEBUG	Optional. When present, this attribute turns on the tracing and debugging features for the file.

Table 12-6.   *<CFQUERY> Attribute Summary*

Outputing the Data

Using the **<CFOUTPUT>** element, it is possible to display the data retrieved from a previously defined **<CFQUERY>** element. For example, in order to output the query called ListJobs, you would use a code fragment, as shown here:

```
<CFOUPUT QUERY="ListJobs">

    <HR NOSHADE><BR>
    Position Number: #PostionNum#<BR><BR>
    Title: #JobTitle#<BR><BR>
    Location: #Location#<BR><BR>
    Description: #Description#

</CFOUPUT>
```

Notice the use of the **#** symbols throughout this code fragment. These values are used to delimit the areas in which you wish to place the data from the database. For example, **#PositionNum#** will be populated with data from the column **PositionNum**, while **#JobTitle#** will get the values for the **JobTitle** column in the database. Notice also that normal HTML markup can be used within the query.

The primary attribute for the **<CFOUTPUT>** element is **QUERY**, but there are numerous other attributes, as shown in Table 12-7.

Attribute	Description
QUERY	Required. This is set to the name of the **<CFQUERY>** that will be used to query the database.
MAXROWS	Optional. This attribute is used to specify the maximum number of rows in the query: a positive integer, which should be displayed.
GROUP	Optional. This attribute is used to group output and is useful for nested reporting.
STARTROW	Optional. This attribute is used to specify an integer row from which to start output; for example, setting this attribute to 5 would start the output with the fifth row returned by the query.

Table 12-7. *<CFOUTPUT> Attribute Summary*

PROGRAMMING
AND HTML

By putting both the **<CFQUERY>** and the **<CFOUTPUT>** elements together in a complete CFML template file, which you could call example1.cfm, and putting this on a server that understands ColdFusion, you could create a dynamically generated page. A complete listing showing the two primary ColdFusion elements is shown here:

```
<!DOCTYPE HTML PUBLIC "-//W3C//DTD HTML 4.0 Transitional//EN">
<!-- SQL statement to select jobs available from the database-->

<CFQUERY NAME="ListJobs" DATASOURCE="CompanyDataBase">
SELECT * FROM Positions
</CFQUERY>

<HTML>
<HEAD>
<TITLE>Big Company Job Listings</TITLE>
</HEAD>

<BODY>
<H2 ALIGN="center">Big Company Job Listings</H2>
<HR>

<CFOUTPUT QUERY="ListJobs">
<HR NOSHADE><BR>
Position Number: #PositionNum#<BR><BR>
Title: #JobTitle#<BR><BR>
Location: #Location#<BR><BR>
Description: #Description#
</CFOUTPUT>
<HR>

<ADDRESS>
Big Company, Inc.
</ADDRESS>
</BODY>
</HTML>
```

Figure 12-9 shows a dynamically generated ColdFusion page under Netscape. Note that there are no browser-side requirements for ColdFusion. In other words, this application would work equally well under Internet Explorer, Lynx, WebTV, or any other browser.

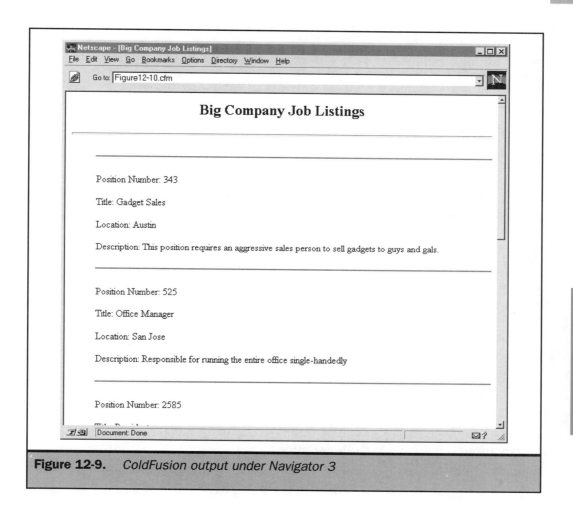

Figure 12-9.   *ColdFusion output under Navigator 3*

Conditional Statements

When creating dynamic pages, things don't always work out as expected. What happens, for example, if there are no jobs in the database to print out? Should the user get a blank page or one that says "Sorry, no jobs available?" ColdFusion provides a number of facilities to take care of just such problems. Using the **<CFIF>** element, simple comparison conditions can be added to the page and simple applications can be built. The basic syntax for the **<CFIF>** element is shown here.

```
<CFIF expression>

HTML and CFML tags

<CFELSE>

HTML and FML tags

</CFIF>
```

An expression is a comparison condition. For example, **IS NOT ""** would be an expression to see if something is not set. So

```
<CFIF ListJobs.PostionNum IS NOT "">

Print the query here.

</CFIF>
```

would only do the section "Print the query here." if the **PostionNum** field were not empty. Note that, as shown in this example, the **<CFELSE>** element is optional.

The expression used in the **<CFIF>** element can be complex and may consist of one or many of the operators shown in Table 12-8.

Operator	Description
IS	Performs a case-insensitive comparison of two values and returns **TRUE** if the values are identical
IS NOT or **NEQ**	Performs the opposite function of the **IS** operator returning **TRUE** only if the values are not equal
CONTAINS	Performs a check to determine if the value on the left of the operator is contained in the value on the right of the operator and returns **TRUE** if it is
DOES NOT CONTAIN	Opposite of the **CONTAINS** operator

Table 12-8. *<CFIF> Operators Summary*

Operator	Description
GREATER THAN or **GT**	Checks whether the value on the left is greater than the value on the right and returns **TRUE** if it is
LESS THAN *or* **LT**	Checks whether the value on the left is less than the value on the right and returns **TRUE** if it is
GREATER THAN OR EQUAL TO or **GTE**	Checks whether the value on the left is greater than or equal to the value on the right and returns **TRUE** if it is
LESS THAN OR EQUAL TO or **LTE**	Checks whether the value on the left is less than or equal to the value on the right and returns **TRUE** if it is

Table 12-8.   *<CFIF> Operators Summary* (continued)

Using the conditional capabilities provided by the **<CFIF>** element, it is possible to create an improved example that checks whether the table has open positions. If not, it prints out a statement indicating that no jobs are available, as shown here:

```
<!-- SQL statement to select jobs available from the database-->

<CFQUERY NAME="ListJobs" DATASOURCE="CompanyDataBase">
SELECT * FROM Positions
</CFQUERY>

<CFIF ListJobs.PositionNumber IS NOT "">

<HTML>
<HEAD>
<TITLE>Big Company Job Listings</TITLE>
</HEAD>

<BODY>
<H2 ALIGN="CENTER">Big Company Job Listings</H2>
<HR>
```

```
<CFOUTPUT QUERY="ListJobs">
   <UL>
   <HR NOSHADE><BR>
   Position Number: #PositionNum#<BR><BR>
   Title: #JobTitle#<BR><BR>
   Location: #Location#<BR><BR>
   Description: #Description#
   </UL>
</CFOUTPUT>


<HR>
<ADDRESS>
Big Company, Inc.
</ADDRESS>
</BODY>
</HTML>


<CFELSE>
<CFLOCATION URL="nojobs.htm">
</CFIF>
```

The **<CFIF>** statement in this example checks to see if the **PositionNum** field is empty in the database. If the field is not empty, then it proceeds to populate the Web page. If the field is empty, it redirects to a page called nojobs.htm, which indicates that there are no positions currently available at the company.

CFML Summary

It should be obvious from the examples presented that ColdFusion can be used to create dynamic Web pages. When using conditional operators, as well as other CFML elements that can be used to loop or set variables, it is even possible to create full-fledged applications with ColdFusion. ColdFusion and other HTML-like, server-parsed languages are great, because they are relatively easy to get started with. There are fewer than two dozen CFML elements to learn. Some of these provide very powerful features like file upload, cookie manipulation, file inclusion, automatic HTML table creation, and mailing. A brief summary of the CFML elements available in ColdFusion is presented in Table 12-9.

The previous discussion is just a sample of what ColdFusion can do. It is only meant to illustrate what a server-side HTML language can do. For more detailed

Element	Description
<CFABORT>	Aborts the processing of the CFML application or template at the specified location
<CFAPPLICATION>	Defines the CFML application name and activates the client variables
<CFCOL>	Defines a table column header, including setting width and alignment of the column
<CFCONTENT>	Defines the content type and the name of the file to be uploaded from the application
<CFCOOKIE>	Defines and sets a cookie, which can be used to preserve state information
<CFERROR>	Customizes HTML error pages
<CFFILE>	Allows the developer to define file-handling tasks within the CFML application
<CFHEADER>	Generates HTTP headers in the application, which may be useful to avoid having the page be cached
<CFIF>	Creates a conditional expression that is useful for catching error conditions or setting up more output logic
<CFINCLUDE>	Includes a ColdFusion template file in the application (useful for keeping routines in separate files)
<CFINSERT>	Inserts records into an ODBC database.
<CFLOCATION>	Opens a ColdFusion template or HTML file (most often used for redirection of output)
<CFLOOP>	"Loops" or repeats a set of instructions or displays conditional output
<CFMAIL>	Sends SMTP e-mail from the CFML application
<CFOUTPUT>	Displays the results of a database query as specified by the **<CFQUERY>** element
<CFPARAM>	Assigns a parameter an initial value

Table 12-9. *CFML Language Summary*

Element	Description
<CFQUERY>	Passes a SQL statement, typically a query to an ODBC-connected database
<CFREPORT>	Embeds a report from Crystal Reports into the page
<CFSET>	Defines a variable within the CFML application that can be accessed later using a **<CFIF>** or similar construct
<CFTABLE>	Builds a quick HTML table to hold the output of a query
<CFUPDATE>	Updates records in an ODBC data source

Table 12-9.   *CFML Language Summary* (continued)

information on the syntax of ColdFusion, as well as examples of its use, see the ColdFusion Language Reference at Allaire's Web site (http://www.allaire.com). While ColdFusion is somewhat tag oriented, there are other server-side parsed HTML solutions, such as Microsoft's ASP, that may provide more scripting style functionality.

Active Server Pages (ASP)

Microsoft's ASP is a server-side scripting environment primarily for the Microsoft Internet Information Server (IIS) Web server, although third-party vendors have recently ported ASP to other Web servers, such as the Netscape Enterprise server. Using ASP, it is possible to combine HTML, scripting code, and server-side ActiveX components to create dynamic Web applications. The ability to write scripts in standard scripting languages such as VBScript, JavaScript, and other scripting languages such as Perl, enables developers to create applications with almost any type of functionality. This makes the ASP approach to server-side scripting very generalized for a broad range of applications. Server-side scripts can also access server-side objects in the form of ActiveX controls for a variety of functions, such as database access via ODBC. Like other parsed HTML solutions, an ASP-enabled page is parsed by the Web server to generate the dynamic HTML that is sent to the Web browser. This means that ASP-enabled pages work equally well on every browser.

Creating ASP Pages

To get started using ASP, the developer needs to have a working knowledge of HTML, as well as knowledge of a scripting language like VBScript or JavaScript. Files created for ASP have an .asp file extension. When an ASP-enabled server sees a file with such an extension, it will execute it before delivering it to the user. For example, the simple VBScript embedded into the file shown here is used to display the current date on a Web page dynamically:

```
<SCRIPT LANGUAGE="VBScript" RUNAT="Server">
</SCRIPT>
<HTML>
<HEAD>
<TITLE>ASP Display Date Example</TITLE>
<HEAD>

<BODY>
<H1>Welcome to News of the Day</H1>
<% = date %>

<P>
Today the stock of a major software company<BR> reached an all time
high, making the bigcompany.com's CEO<BR> the world's first and
only trillionaire.<BR>
</BODY>
</HTML>
```

The **<SCRIPT>** element is used to indicate the primary scripting language being employed. This element also tells the Web server to execute the script code on the server rather than the client with the **RUNAT** attribute. This can be abbreviated as **<@ LANGUAGE =** *script_language***>**. Notice how the **<% %>** is used to delimit the script code that is run. ASP is a generalized technology. It can be used to do whatever a user dreams up. Since people commonly want to do things on the Web like access a database, it has been enhanced to do this well.

DATABASE ACCESS IN ASP   In the following discussion, ASP will be used to access the Positions database described earlier in the chapter. While this could probably be done more easily using ColdFusion, the point here is to introduce the idea of object access from ASP. The first step in this example is to create an instance of the database component by adding the following line to an ASP file, which might be named example.asp.

```
<OBJECT RUNAT="Server" ID="Conn"
        PROGID="ADODB.Connection"></OBJECT>
```

This statement creates an instance of a database access object called **Conn** that can be used with a server-side script.

Later on, the file will open a connection to the database and execute a SQL command to select job positions and return a set of records. The small code fragment shown next does this. The code is enclosed within **<%** and **%>** so that the server knows to execute this rather than display it on the screen.

```
<%
Conn.Open Session("ConnectionString")
SQL = "SELECT * FROM Positions"
Set RS = Conn.Execute(SQL)
Do While Not RS.EOF
%>
```

The code between the **<% %>** statements is VBScript, which is interpreted by the Web server when this page is requested. The Do While statement is a standard VBScript looping statement, which is used here to loop through the record set until an end of file (EOF) marker is reached, signifying the end of the records. While looping through each record, the output is displayed in the context of regular HTML code, such as displaying the Job Department field in a table cell:

```
<TD>
<%= RS("JobDepartment")%>
</TD>
```

Putting this all together in a file called example.asp provides a complete ASP database access example:

```
<!DOCTYPE HTML PUBLIC "-//W3C//DTD HTML 3.2 Final//EN">
<OBJECT RUNAT="Server" ID="Conn"
        PROGID="ADODB.Connection"></OBJECT>
<%@ LANGUAGE = VBScript %>
<HTML>
<HEAD>
<TITLE>Open Positions</TITLE>
</HEAD>
```

```
<BODY>
<H2 ALIGN="CENTER">Open Positions</H2>
<BR><BR>

<TABLE WIDTH="100%" BORDER="1" CELLSPACING="0" CELLPADDING="4">
<TR>
   <TH>Position Number</TH>
   <TH>Location</TH>
   <TH>Description</TH>
   <TH>Hiring Manager</TH>
   <TH>Data Posted</TH>
</TR>

<!-- Open Database Connection
     Execute SQL query statement
     Set RS variable to store results of query
     Loop through records while still records to process
-->

<%
Conn.Open Session("ConnectionString")
SQL = "SELECT JobTitle, Location, Description, HiringManager,
PostDate FROM Positions"
Set RS = Conn.Execute(SQL)
Do While Not RS.EOF
%>

<!--  Display database fields in table cells -->
<TR>
   <TD>
   <%= RS("JobTitle") %>
   </TD>

   <TD>
   <%= RS("Location")%>
   </TD>

   <TD>
   <%= RS("Description")%>
   </TD>
```

PROGRAMMING
AND HTML

```
    <TD>
    <%= RS("HiringManager")%>
    </TD>

    <TD>
    <%= RS("PostDate") d%>
    </TD>
</TR>

<!-- Move to next record and continue loop -->

<%
RS.MoveNext
Loop
%>
</TABLE>
</BODY>
</HTML>
```

From this example, you can see the advantages of ASP for generating dynamic pages. The actual data to be displayed is a database that the server can access with an ASP script using a database access object. The dynamically created page is built from a combination of VBScript that uses a small amount of programming and HTML. The result can be served to different browsers without any client-side compatibility problems, because the pages are generated on the server. While this example showed a more complicated way to access data from a database, it hints at the generalized power of ASP. Active Server Pages are useful for creating applications rather than just dynamic pages. With ASP, it is possible to determine the user's browser, keep track of the user's progress through a set of pages, and manage all the data that is passed back and forth from the user (including cookies and form fields). The key to this power is the server-side objects provided with ASP.

Built-In ASP Objects

What makes ASP so powerful is that the technology includes five built-in objects for global use:

- Application
- Request
- Response
- Server
- Session

The application object is used to share common information within an application. An example would be a page counter. You can store the number of times a page has been accessed and use this object to display it on the page. The application object supports locking, since multiple users may be using the Web application at the same time and could possibly corrupt data.

The request object is used to get information from the user, including form data, cookies, or standard HTTP request variables such as browser type (user agent). The request object contains collections of information that can be used in scripts. The request object supports the following collections:

- **ClientCertificate**   The values of fields stored in the client certificate that is sent in the HTTP request
- **Cookies**   The values of cookies sent in the HTTP request
- **Form**   The values of the fields sent from a form submission
- **QueryString**   The values of the variables sent in an HTTP query string
- **ServerVariables**   HTTP server information, such as server name, type, and version

The response object is used to send information to the user. It could be used to set the type of content to be sent to a browser, such as HTML; Word files; or other formats, such as graphics. It could also send and retrieve cookie values to a client to determine user preferences for creating customized pages.

The server object provides access to server methods and properties, including setting how long a script should run and asking for server-side objects, such as database objects.

The session object, one of the most useful objects, is used to store information for a particular user session. This means that information is maintained as the user jumps from page to page, thus preserving state. The basic property for this object sets an ID for the session while the events deal with the start or end of a session.

A generalized language like VBScript or JavaScript, combined with server-side objects to do common tasks like maintaining user state, makes complex server-side applications possible. Many other technologies, such as Netscape's LiveWire with its server-side JavaScript, take a similar approach. When it comes right down to it, the differences between ColdFusion and ASP are somewhat cosmetic. Programmers may find ASP comfortable, while skilled HTML authors may find ColdFusion more suitable. The choice of any server-side technology should be a logical process rather than a blind acceptance of a single vendor's solution.

This discussion introduces ASP and is by no means complete. It illustrates a much-generalized method of parsed HTML that utilizes the power of popular scripting languages and access to server-side objects with common and powerful functions, such as database access and session tracking. Complete information on ASP can be found on the Microsoft Internet Information Server Web site (http://www.microsoft.com/iis/) or in the ASP Roadmap documentation that is included when ASP is installed on a Web server.

Summary

Server-side programming is one way to add interactivity to a Web page. CGI is the traditional way to do this. Writing a CGI program isn't difficult if you use libraries, but the price to pay for ease is often speed. Because so many CGI programs are very similar, some are rewritten as faster server-side plug-ins called NSAPI or ISAPI programs. While these types of server modules tend to be beyond most developers, it is easy to buy one to solve a common problem like database access. Some server engines now support a form of server-side scripting known generically as parsed HTML. Parsed HTML solutions such as SSIs, ColdFusion, and ASP provide an easy way for HTML authors to add functionality to Web pages. While server-side technologies provide a great deal of power for the Web developer, they are only half the picture. It is also possible to add interactivity using a client-side technology like JavaScript or Java. The next two chapters discuss these technologies and their intersection with HTML.

Chapter 13

Introduction to Scripting and HTML

Adding interactivity to a Web site is not limited to server-side programs. The client side of the Web, the browser, can generally execute code in the form of scripting or embedded programmed objects. For HTML writers, the easiest way to begin adding dynamic aspects to a Web page is through client-side scripting, using JavaScript or VBScript. This chapter discusses the intersection between scripting and HTML, but does not attempt to teach scripting techniques in depth. The idea of scripting requires the page designer to think more carefully about how the user will interact with the page. If scripting is not used carefully, errors may creep in and cause problems for the viewer.

As it stands now, scripting languages such as JavaScript are often relegated to small embellishments such as the ubiquitous rollover button. However, Dynamic HTML (DHTML) and the Document Object Model (DOM) show how the idea of a page may change forever because of client-side scripting (discussed in Chapter 14). Beyond these new dynamic features, scripting has an even bigger role to play on a Web page. Whereas HTML may provide the structure, scripting may act as the glue, providing a link between static content and user actions, and between various embedded objects (discussed in Chapter 15).

The Purpose of Scripting

How do Web scripting languages relate to full-fledged Web programming languages such as Java? In general, scripting languages are used in small doses, for specific tasks. Scripting has a very limited domain. Some people use scripting languages for tasks such as loan calculators. Such simple tasks illustrate basic features of the scripting language. The basic uses of scripting include

- Form validation
- Page embellishment, including rollover buttons and animation
- Dynamic page generation
- Interobject communication "glue"

HTML developers tend to be comfortable with scripting languages, because they can simply enter script commands into the HTML file along with the text markup. In fact, some developers simply cut and paste scripts to add scrolling marquees, dialog boxes, and other customized features to their pages. This form of quick embellishment comes at a cost. If testing is not rigorous, serious problems—even crashes—may creep in. With the rise of so many scripting languages, such as JavaScript versions 1, 1.1, 1.2, 1.3, and various versions of JScript (Microsoft's interpretation of JavaScript), bugs are becoming more common. Hopefully, the rise of ECMAScript, a standardized form of JavaScript, may help solve some of these problems. Beyond compatibility issues, scripting occasionally has some security problems, mostly related to browser implementation bugs. Some more cautious users may even turn off script interpretation in their browsers, potentially causing the page to render improperly. If scripting makes sense for your site, you must choose between JavaScript and VBScript.

JavaScript

JavaScript is a scripting language developed by Netscape. Microsoft also supports JavaScript in the form of JScript, a clone language used in Internet Explorer. The language was turned over to the international standards body *European Computer Manufacturers Association (ECMA)*, which announced during the summer of 1997 the approval of ECMA-262, or ECMAScript, as a cross-platform Internet standard for scripting. Browser vendors will comply with the specification but will still use the commonly recognized JavaScript name.

> **Note**   *At the time of this writing, neither Netscape nor Internet Explorer fully support ECMAScript—quite a few "gaps" in implementation still exist. Opera is the only browser currently supporting ECMAScript in full.*

As a scripting language, JavaScript is meant to be easy to use, noncompiled (interpreted), and useful in small chunks. This sets it apart from Java and other languages that might be used on the Internet, which tend to be compiled and relatively hard to master for the nonprogrammer. The syntax of JavaScript is somewhat like C or Java with Perl-style regular expression handling, and the language has basic object-oriented capabilities. JavaScript is not, however, a true object-oriented programming language, and it retains features (such as weak typing) that are common to simple scripting languages.

JavaScript is useful for small jobs, such as checking form data; adding small bits of HTML code to a page on-the-fly; and performing browser-, time-, and user-specific computation. JavaScript is also a powerful means of controlling events in browsers and accessing the DOM for programming DHTML, which is discussed in the next chapter. An important potential function of JavaScript is to act as the glue between different technologies, such as plug-ins, Java applets, and HTML pages. An example of JavaScript code being used to greet the user is shown here; a rendering of the script in action is shown in Figure 13-1:

```
<!DOCTYPE HTML PUBLIC "-//W3C//DTD HTML 4.0 Transitional//EN">
<HTML>
<HEAD>
<TITLE>First JavaScript Example</TITLE>

<SCRIPT LANGUAGE="JavaScript">
<!--
```

```
  function Greet()
    {
      alert("Hello user! Welcome to JavaScript.");
    }
//-->
</SCRIPT>
</HEAD>

<BODY>
<H1 ALIGN="CENTER">First JavaScript Example</H1>

<DIV ALIGN="CENTER">

<FORM>
    <INPUT TYPE="BUTTON" VALUE="Press Me" onclick="Greet()">
</FORM>

</DIV>
</BODY>
</HTML>
```

This is a simple example of how JavaScript may be included in an HTML file. The form button triggers the function called **Greet()**, which greets the user. The event handler attribute **onclick** is used to tie the HTML to the JavaScript that is contained in the head of the document within the **<SCRIPT>** element. While this example is very easy, remember that it is also a trivial example; this is a real programming language that has many nuances. During its short lifetime, JavaScript has undergone many changes. Not all browsers support it to the same degree, if at all. JavaScript has a few major dialects, including JavaScript 1 (Netscape 2.x), JavaScript 1.1 (Netscape 3.x), and JavaScript 1.2 (Netscape 4.x). JScript in Internet Explorer 3 is approximately equivalent to JavaScript 1; it doesn't support JavaScript 1.1 features, such as dynamic image replacement. Internet Explorer 4 appears to support JavaScript 1.1, but with a richer object model. Finally, there is the ECMAScript standard, the latest variation of JavaScript.

Table 13-1 shows the JavaScript versions supported by different browsers.

For more information on JavaScript, visit Netscape's developer site, located at http://developer.netscape.com/. Information about Microsoft's implementation of JavaScript, called JScript, can be found at http://msdn.microsoft.com/scripting/.

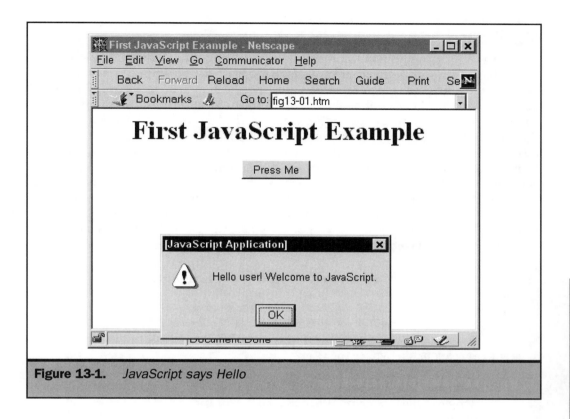

Figure 13-1.   *JavaScript says Hello*

Browser	JavaScript Support
Netscape Navigator 2.*x*	JavaScript 1
Netscape Navigator 3.*x*	JavaScript 1.1
Netscape Navigator 4–4.05	JavaScript 1.2
Netscape Navigator 4.06, 4.5*x*	JavaScript 1.3
Internet Explorer 2.*x*	None
Internet Explorer 3.*x*	JScript (JavaScript 1)
Internet Explorer 4.*x*	JScript (JavaScript 1.1), ECMAScript-compliant

Table 13-1.   *JavaScript Support by Browser Release*

VBScript

Visual Basic Scripting Edition, generally called VBScript, is a subset of the popular
Visual Basic language. Because of its Visual Basic heritage, VBScript is somewhat more
well defined and seems to have a more stable specification than JavaScript. VBScript is
less prevalent than JavaScript on the Internet, largely because VBScript is fully
supported only in Internet Explorer 3 and above. The language can be used to provide
the same functionality as JavaScript and is just as capable as accessing the various
objects that compose a Web page (termed a browser's *Document Object Model*). Avoid
trying to use VBScript as a cross-platform scripting solution. Used with ActiveX
controls in a more controllable environment, such as an intranet, VBScript might just be
what the Microsoft-oriented developer needs. When dealing with ActiveX controls
(discussed in Chapter 14), VBScript may provide more functionality. The following is a
sample of VBScript to give you a flavor of its syntax; this example has the same
functionality as the JavaScript example given previously:

```
<!DOCTYPE HTML PUBLIC "-//W3C//DTD HTML 4.0 Transitional//EN">
<HTML>
<HEAD>
<TITLE>VBSscript Example</TITLE>

<SCRIPT LANGUAGE="VBScript">
<!--
Sub Greet_onclick
        MsgBox "Hello user! Welcome to VBScript."
End Sub
'-->
</SCRIPT>
</HEAD>

<BODY>
<H1 ALIGN="CENTER">First VBScript Example</H1>

<DIV ALIGN="CENTER">

<FORM>
<INPUT TYPE="BUTTON" VALUE="Press Me" NAME="Greet">
</FORM>

</DIV>
</BODY>
</HTML>
```

This is a simple example of how VBScript may be included in an HTML file. It produces a rendering similar to the one shown in Figure 13-2.

As in the first example, the form button named Greet triggers an alert box that greets the user. Notice that rather than using an explicit HTML attribute such as **onclick**, as was used in the JavaScript example, the VBScript example names the subroutine in a certain way to associate it with the button event, in this case **Greet_onclick**.

Other subtle differences in VBScript include the use of the **MsgBox** function to create the alert window, as well as other syntactical differences, such as use of parentheses. Readers familiar with Visual Basic should find this example very easy, because this language is just a subset of Visual Basic proper. Unfortunately, as a client-side technology, VBScript is not very useful, other than for use on an intranet. Because it is limited to Internet Explorer, relying on VBScript locks out all Netscape users, which is unacceptable for a public Web site. Because of this, VBScript is often limited to being used within a Microsoft-oriented intranet or on the server side, in the form of Active Server Page code (as discussed in Chapter 12). No significant discussion of VBScript occurs during this client-side discussion. However, readers interested in

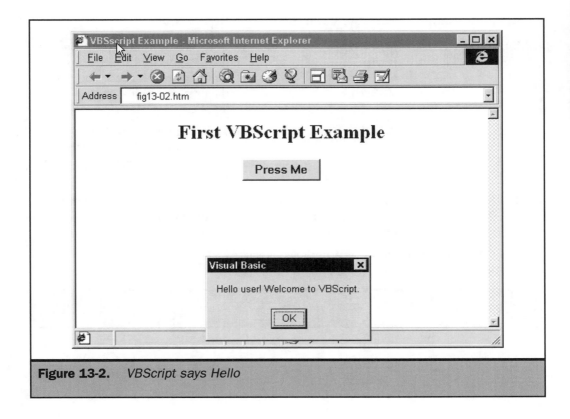

Figure 13-2. *VBScript says Hello*

more information about the syntax of VBScript, as well as examples, are encouraged to visit Microsoft's VBScript site (http://msdn.microsoft.com/scripting/).

Including Scripts in an HTML Document

As suggested by the last two examples, the main way to include in a Web page scripts written in any language is primarily with the **<SCRIPT>** element. The **<SCRIPT>** element is used to delimit the script code; anything that is found within this element is treated as a script, not HTML, by a scripting-capable browser. This is an important statement for HTML writers to ponder. Script code tends to be sensitive to returns and capitalization, whereas HTML is not. The HTML rules that you know and love may not be valid once you are within the **<SCRIPT>** element.

While the contents of the **<SCRIPT>** element may be very complex, the syntax of the element is relatively simple. The **<SCRIPT>** element has only three major attributes, as shown in Table 13-2.

Attribute Name	Possible Value(s)	Description
LANGUAGE	**JavaScript** **Jscript** **VBS** **VBScript**	The value of this attribute is used to specify the scripting language being used. The two major possibilities are JavaScript or VBScript.
SRC	A URL	This attribute is used to indicate the URL of a file that contains an external script to load.
TYPE	**application/x-javascript*** **text/javascript** **text/vbscript**	Indicates the MIME type of the script to run.

*The **TYPE** value of **application/x-javascript** is not encouraged, although it is common for older browsers that support JavaScript.

Table 13-2.   *<SCRIPT> Element Attributes*

The actual script to execute should be placed between the **<SCRIPT>** and **</SCRIPT>** tags, as shown here:

```
<SCRIPT LANGUAGE="JavaScript">
Script goes here.
</SCRIPT>
```

Remember that what is between these tags is script, not HTML markup. A very different syntax may be involved, depending on the scripting language used.

The **<SCRIPT>** element can be used multiple times in the **<HEAD>**, as well as in the **<BODY>** element. Because HTML pages are read sequentially, a lot of scripting code may appear in the head section of a document. Much of this script code could be termed *deferred script*, because it may be read in the head but not executed until later in the script. This script code can be called later by immediate scripts or by user-action scripts within the body of the HTML document. The type of script that tends to go into the **<HEAD>** element is similar to a function or procedure definition, as shown in the following example:

```
<!DOCTYPE HTML PUBLIC "-//W3C//DTD HTML 4.0 Transitional//EN">
<HTML>
<HEAD>
<SCRIPT LANGUAGE="JavaScript">
<!--
function AlertTest( ){
alert("Danger JavaScript ahead!");
}
// -->
</SCRIPT>
</HEAD>

<BODY>
    HTML tags that eventually may trigger JavaScript code in head
</BODY>
</HTML>
```

As previously stated, the **<SCRIPT>** element may also occur in the **<BODY>** element. Generally, it is used to create immediate scripts that are executed as soon as the browser reads them. For example, the following markup includes JavaScript code that adds the document modification time automatically to the end of the document:

```
<!DOCTYPE HTML PUBLIC "-//W3C//DTD HTML 4.0 Transitional//EN">
<HTML>
<HEAD>
<TITLE>Immediate Script</TITLE>
</HEAD>

<BODY>
<H1 ALIGN="CENTER">Big Company, Inc.</H1>
<HR>

<P>Interesting text goes here.</P>
<HR>

<SCRIPT LANGUAGE="JavaScript">
<!--
document.write("Last updated on: "+document.lastModified);
//-->
</SCRIPT>
</BODY>
</HTML>
```

Besides using the **<SCRIPT>** element, you can also embed script code directly into HTML tags. Typically, scripts for handling user-triggered events are the common way that scripts are referenced outside the **<SCRIPT>** element. HTML elements generally have special attributes, called *script handlers,* for particular user events. For example, a click event to a button is handled by a special **onclick** event. While HTML attributes tend to be written in uppercase, event handlers are often written in mixed case or lowercase, to distinguish the fact that the handler is concerned with scripting, as shown in the following example using the **<INPUT>** element:

```
<FORM>
   <INPUT TYPE="BUTTON" NAME="TestButton" VALUE="Don't push me!"
          onclick="AlertTest()">
</FORM>
```

By combining deferred scripts with user-triggered events, you can make dynamic documents. The following example presents a button that, when clicked, opens a small alert dialog box by using JavaScript (which is the same as the first example presented in the chapter):

```
<!DOCTYPE HTML PUBLIC "-//W3C//DTD HTML 4.0 Transitional//EN">
<HTML>
<HEAD>
<SCRIPT LANGUAGE="JavaScript">
<!--
Function AlertTest( ) {
 alert("Danger! JavaScript ahead! ");
 }
// -->
</SCRIPT>
</HEAD>

<BODY>
<DIV ALIGN="CENTER">

<FORM>
   <INPUT TYPE="BUTTON" NAME="TestButton"
          VALUE="Don't push me!" onclick="AlertTest()">
</FORM>

</DIV>
</BODY>
</HTML>
```

In summary, the following are the primary ways that you can add JavaScript code to an HTML document:

■ To the head of the document, within the **<SCRIPT>** element

■ To the body of a document, within the **<SCRIPT>** element

■ Within the elements themselves, as values of event handler attributes such as **onclick**

Two more ways exist to add JavaScript code to an HTML document. The first way involves a URL scripting pseudoprotocol. Netscape browsers introduced the use of a new URL style in the form of **javascript:**, which can be used with links. For example,

```
<A HREF='javascript:alert("Danger! JavaScript ahead!")'>Script
me!</A>
```

creates a link that, when clicked, executes the specified JavaScript code. Internet Explorer also supports this style. The other, very uncommon way to add JavaScript code to a Web page is with a character entity. (Remember that using **©** would include a copyright symbol.) JavaScript code can be inserted inside of a special entity of the form **&{javascript code};**. The JavaScript code must be included within braces; it may even call functions or perform numerous statements. This entity form can only be used as an attribute value. This style could be used as a form of macro in Netscape 4 or Internet Explorer 4 pages. Imagine inserting in the head of the document a bunch of identifiers for colors and font style, and then referencing them by name later, as shown in the following example:

```
<!DOCTYPE HTML PUBLIC "-//W3C//DTD HTML 4.0 Transitional//EN">
<HTML>
<HEAD>
<TITLE>Entity Script</TITLE>

<SCRIPT LANGUAGE="JavaScript">
<!--
  textColor='green';
//-->
</SCRIPT>
</HEAD>

<BODY>
   <FONT COLOR=&{textColor;};>This should be green.</FONT>
</BODY>
</HTML>
```

This example would probably be better handled by a style sheet, but it is presented here solely to show how the entity script style works. The entity and pseudo-URL style for adding JavaScript is specific to this particular scripting language. As more scripting languages are used online, other ways to add script to a page may very well arise. For now, the two standard ways are in the form of the **<SCRIPT>** element and as values of the attribute event handlers for individual elements such as **onclick**, which is discussed in greater detail later in the chapter (see "Script Events and HTML").

Specifying the Scripting Language

By default, most browsers assume that the script language being used is JavaScript. The **LANGUAGE** attribute can be used to specify other languages, including VBScript and many others. The HTML 4.0 specification deprecates the **LANGUAGE** attribute in favor of the **TYPE** attribute. The **TYPE** attribute is used to indicate the MIME type of the script to run; for example, **text/javascript**. This indication of scripting dialect is not often used; it may not provide the flexibility of **LANGUAGE**.

Not all versions of JavaScript support the same features. The object relied upon by animated buttons wasn't available until JavaScript 1.1; it causes errors in older browsers if it isn't accounted for. The **LANGUAGE** attribute can be used to indicate the version of JavaScript being used. The attribute can be set to **JavaScript1.1** or **JavaScript1.2**, rather than simply **JavaScript**. Only browsers that understand the particular dialect of JavaScript will execute the enclosed script code. With this idea, you can make a fall-through situation with multiple versions of similar code, as shown here:

```
<SCRIPT LANGUAGE="JavaScript">
Simple version
</SCRIPT>

<SCRIPT LANGUAGE="JavaScript1.1">
Netscape 3
</SCRIPT>

<SCRIPT LANGUAGE="JavaScript1.2">
Netscape 4
</SCRIPT>
```

One final way exists to indicate a scripting language: use the **<META>** element in the **<HEAD>**. For example,

```
<META http-equivv="Content-Script-Type" content="text/javascript">
```

sets the default scripting language for the whole document to JavaScript, unless overridden by a local occurrence of the **LANGUAGE** attribute. A Web server may also be configured to issue such a header.

External Scripts

You also can place the script code in a separate file and specify that file by using the **SRC** attribute that specifies the URL of the script to include. For example,

```
<SCRIPT SRC="http://www.bigcompany.com/scripts/myscript.js">
</SCRIPT>
```

loads a script called myscript.js, specified by the URL for the **SRC** attribute.

PROGRAMMING AND HTML

When including an external script in a page by setting the **SRC** attribute, the **LANGUAGE** attribute may not be used. While JavaScript is assumed anyway, the file extension of the file is used by the Web server to specify the scripting language. The Web server should map the extension to the appropriate MIME type—in this case, **application/x-javascript**—so that the browser receiving the file knows what to do with it. Older servers may require a MIME type that is configured to allow remote inclusion of script files.

Note *One major advantage of external scripts is that a browser may cache the script file locally. If the same script code is used over and over again, the files that reference it would require only the simple <SCRIPT> statement and would be able to reuse the cached copy. Considering how much script code is inserted in many pages, this could improve site efficiency.*

Scripting and Non-Script-Aware Browsers

One advantage to referencing external script files is that it provides compatibility for older, non-JavaScript-aware browsers. A browser simply ignores any tags that it doesn't understand, so nothing happens when an older browser reads a **<SCRIPT>** element that uses an **SRC** attribute. If the script is used inline, as shown here, older browsers that don't understand JavaScript will display the statement **alert ("I am a Script.");** onscreen instead of executing it:

```
<SCRIPT LANGUAGE="JavaScript">
alert("I am a script.");
</SCRIPT>
```

To improve compatibility with non-JavaScript-aware browsers, scripting code should be commented out. In JavaScript, this would be accomplished as shown here:

```
<SCRIPT LANGUAGE="JavaScript">
<!--
alert("I am a script.");
//-->
</SCRIPT>
```

Notice how the HTML comment starts the exclusion of JavaScript, but **//-->** is used to close the comment. This is because JavaScript interprets lines with **//** as comments and does not attempt to run a command **-->** as a command.

Commenting out VBScript code is similar, requiring only a simple comment, as shown here:

```
<SCRIPT LANGUAGE="VBScript">
<!--
    MsgBox "Hello World!", 0, ""
' -->
</SCRIPT>
```

Other languages may have different commenting styles for hiding the script code from the non-script-aware browser.

<NOSCRIPT>

Like other extensions to HTML, the **<SCRIPT>** element supports a special element to deal with browsers that don't execute a script. The **<NOSCRIPT>** element is used to enclose alternative text and markup for browsers that don't interpret a script. Furthermore, users can turn off support for a scripting language in their browsers. The **<NOSCRIPT>** content renders onscreen, as shown in the following example, if the user has turned off scripting support or is using a browser that doesn't understand JavaScript:

```
<!DOCTYPE HTML PUBLIC "-//W3C//DTD HTML 4.0 Transitional//EN">
<HTML>
<HEAD>
<TITLE>JavaScript and NOSCRIPT</TITLE>
</HEAD>

<BODY>

<SCRIPT LANGUAGE="JavaScript">
<!--

document.write('<H1 ALIGN="CENTER">JavaScript is ON</H1>');
//-->
</SCRIPT>

<NOSCRIPT>
<B>Please turn on JavaScript if you have it and reload this
page!</B>
</NOSCRIPT>

</BODY>
</HTML>
```

Although this example works, some confusion currently exists between the specification and current browser actions in relation to **<NOSCRIPT>** when the language is not understood. According to the HTML 4.0 specification, browsers should evaluate the content in **<NOSCRIPT>** when the scripting language used earlier in the **<SCRIPT>** statement is not understood. In the case of the imaginary language named BozoScript, the browser should evaluate the content in **<NOSCRIPT>** in the markup shown here:

```
<SCRIPT LANGUAGE="BozoScript">
This is bozo language.
</SCRIPT>

<NOSCRIPT>
I don't understand BozoScript.
</NOSCRIPT>
```

Unfortunately, this is not how browsers act in all cases. In fact, browsers may ignore the **<NOSCRIPT>** statement in this case. Furthermore, **<NOSCRIPT>** has a major problem when you consider that multiple occurrences of the **<SCRIPT>** element can occur in a document. This raises an important question: which **<NOSCRIPT>** occurrence matches which **<SCRIPT>**? The natural assumption is that the first **<NOSCRIPT>** element following a particular **<SCRIPT>** element would match that **<SCRIPT>** element; but is this, or should this, be the way things work?

Script Events and HTML

Earlier in this chapter, the section "Including Scripts in an HTML Document" mentioned that script code could be added to HTML documents through special attributes called *event handlers*. What are events? Events occur as the result of a user action or, potentially, an external event, such as a page loading. Examples of events include a user clicking a button, pressing a key, moving a window, or even simply moving the mouse around the screen. HTML provides a way to bind a script to the occurrence of a particular event, through an *event handler attribute*. This is the name of the event, prefixed by the word *on*; for example, **onclick**. The following code shows how the **onclick** event handler attribute is used to bind some script to a button click occurrence:

```
<FORM>
<BUTTON onclick='alert("Hey this is JavaScript")' VALUE="Press Me">
</FORM>
```

Under HTML 4, event handler attributes can be added to quite a number of HTML elements. In practice, event handler attributes are most commonly associated with form controls specified by the **<INPUT>**, **<SELECT>**, **<TEXTAREA>**, and **<BUTTON>** elements, though this is changing with the rise of DHTML. As Table 13-3 shows, HTML 4 defines a wide range of events for nearly all the elements.

Event Attribute	Event Description	Elements Allowed Under HTML 4
onblur	Occurs when a form element loses focus, meaning that a user has entered into another form field, either typically—by clicking the mouse on it—or by tabbing to it	**<A>** **<AREA>** **<BUTTON>** **<INPUT>** **<LABEL>** **<SELECT>** **<TEXTAREA>**
onchange	Signals both that the form control has lost user focus and that its value has been modified during its last access	**<INPUT>** **<SELECT>** **<TEXTAREA>**
onclick	Indicates the element has been clicked	Most elements
ondblclick	Indicates the element has been double-clicked	Most elements
onfocus	Describes when a form control has received focus, namely that it has been selected for manipulation or data entry	**<A>** **<AREA>** **<BUTTON>** **<INPUT>** **<LABEL>** **<SELECT>** **<TEXTAREA>**
onkeydown	Indicates a key is being pressed	Most elements
onkeypress	Describes a key being pressed and released	Most elements
onkeyup	Indicates a key is being released	Most elements
onload	Indicates when a window or frame finishes loading a document	**<BODY>** **<FRAMESET>**

Table 13-3.   *Events defined in HTML 4*

Event Attribute	Event Description	Elements Allowed Under HTML 4
onmousedown	Indicates the press of a mouse button	Most elements
onmousemove	Indicates the mouse has moved	Most elements
onmouseout	Indicates the mouse has moved away from an element	Most elements
onmouseover	Indicates the mouse has moved over an element	Most elements
onmouseup	Indicates the release of a mouse button	Most elements
onreset	Indicates the form is being reset, possibly by the click of a reset button	<FORM>
onselect	Indicates the selection of text by a user, typically by highlighting the text	<INPUT> <TEXTAREA>
onsubmit	Indicates a form submission, generally by clicking a submit button	<FORM>
onunload	Indicates that the browser is leaving the current document and unloading it from the window or frame	<BODY> <FRAMESET>

Table 13-3.   *Events defined in HTML 4* (continued)

The core event model according to HTML 4 includes **onclick, ondblclick, onkeydown, onkeypress, onkeyup, onmousedown, onmousemove, onmouseout, onmouseover,** and **onmouseup**. These core events are defined for nearly all HTML elements in which the element is displayed onscreen. As used in Table 13-3, the expression "Most elements" is meant to include the following:

<A>	<CAPTION>	<DIR>
<ACRONYM>	<CENTER>	<DIV>
<ADDRESS>	<CITE>	<DL>
<AREA>	<CODE>	<DT>
<B>	<COL>	<EM>
<BIG>	<COLGROUP>	<FIELDSET>
<BLOCKQUOTE>	<DD>	<FORM>
<BODY>	<DEL>	<H1>
<BUTTON>	<DFN>	<H2>

<H3>	<MENU>	<STRONG>
<H4>	<NOFRAMES>	<SUB>
<H5>	<NOSCRIPT>	<SUP>
<H6>	<OBJECT>	<TABLE>
<HR>	<OL>	<TBODY>
<I>	<OPTION>	<TD>
<IMG>	<P>	<TEXTAREA>
<INPUT>	<PRE>	<TFOOT>
<INS>	<Q>	<TH>
<KBD>	<S>	<THEAD>
<LABEL>	<SAMP>	<TR>
<LEGEND>	<SELECT>	<TT>
<LI>	<SMALL>	<U>
<LINK>	<SPAN>	<UL>
<MAP>	<STRIKE>	<VAR>

Obviously, certain structuring or miscellaneous elements do not make any sense for events. Under the HTML 4.0 specification, these include the following elements:

<APPLET>	<HTML>
<BASE>	<IFRAME>
<BASEFONT>	<ISINDEX>
<BDO>	<META>
 	<PARAM>
<FONT>	<SCRIPT>
<FRAME>	<STYLE>
<FRAMESET>	<TITLE>
<HEAD>	

Note   *The HTML 4.0 specification indicates that **<APPLET>** and **<FONT>** do not take the core events. However, some browsers do define events for them.*

Certain elements under HTML 4 have their own special events outside this core event model. For example, the **<BODY>** and **<FRAMESET>** elements have an event for loading and unloading pages, so both elements also have the **onload** and **onunload** event attributes. In the case of the **<FRAMESET>** element, the load and unload events don't fire until all the frames have been loaded or unloaded, respectively. The **<FORM>** element itself also has two special events that are typically triggered when the user clicks the submit or reset button. These events are **onsubmit** and **onreset**. Of course, with scripting, these events may fire for other reasons. Last, the primary form

PROGRAMMING
AND HTML

element types under HTML 4 are **<BUTTON>**, **<INPUT>**, **<LABEL>**, **<SELECT>**, and **<TEXTAREA>**. For text fields set with the **<INPUT>** element, you can catch the focus and blur events with **onfocus** and **onblur**. These events fire when the user accesses the field and moves on to another one. You can also watch for the select event with **onselect**, which is triggered when a user selects some text, as well as the change event (**onchange**), which is triggered when a field's value changes and loses focus.

The following markup illustrates simple use of the HTML 4 event attributes with form elements and links:

```
<!DOCTYPE HTML PUBLIC "-//W3C//DTD HTML 4.0 Transitional//EN">
<HTML>
<HEAD>
<TITLE>HTML 4.0 Events</TITLE>
</HEAD>

<BODY onload='alert("Event demo loaded")'
      onunload='alert("Leaving demo")'>

<H1 ALIGN="CENTER">HTML 4.0 Events</H1>

<FORM onreset='alert("Form reset")'
      onsubmit='alert("Form submit");return false;'>

<UL>

<LI>onblur: <INPUT TYPE="TEXT" VALUE="Click into field and then leave"
                    SIZE="40" onblur='alert("Lost focus")'><BR><BR>

<LI>onclick: <INPUT TYPE="BUTTON" VALUE="Click Me"
                    onclick='alert("Button click")'><BR><BR>

<LI>onchange: <INPUT TYPE="TEXT" VALUE="Change this text then leave"
                    SIZE="40" onchange='alert("Changed")'><BR><BR>

<LI>ondblclick: <INPUT TYPE="BUTTON" VALUE="Double-click Me"
                       ondblclick='alert("Button double-clicked")'>
<BR><BR>

<LI>onfocus: <INPUT TYPE="TEXT" VALUE="Click into field"
                    onfocus='alert("Gained focus")'><BR><BR>
```

```
<LI>onkeydown: <INPUT TYPE="TEXT"
                    VALUE="Press key and release slowly here"
                    SIZE="40"
                    onkeydown='alert("Key down")'><BR><BR>

<LI>onkeypress: <INPUT TYPE="TEXT" VALUE="Type here" SIZE="40"
                    onkeypress='alert("Key pressed")'><BR><BR>

<LI>onkeyup: <INPUT TYPE="TEXT" VALUE="Type and release" SIZE="40"
                    onkeyup='alert("Key up")'><BR><BR>

<LI>onload:    Alert presented on initial document load.<BR><BR>

<LI>onmousedown: <INPUT TYPE="BUTTON" VALUE="Click and hold"
                    onmousedown='alert("Mouse down")'><BR><BR>

<LI>onmousemove: Move mouse over this
<A HREF=""onmousemove='alert("Mouse moved")'>link</A><BR><BR>

<LI>onmouseout: Position mouse
<A HREF=""onmouseout='alert("Mouse out")'>here</A> and now leave.<BR><BR>

<LI>onmouseover: Position mouse over this
<A HREF=""onmouseover='alert("Mouse over")'>link</A><BR><BR>

<LI>onmouseup: <INPUT TYPE="BUTTON" VALUE="Click and release"
                    onmouseup='alert("Mouse up")'><BR><BR>

<LI>onreset: <INPUT TYPE="RESET" VALUE="Reset Demo"><BR><BR>

<LI>onselect: <INPUT TYPE="TEXT" VALUE="Select this text" SIZE="40"
                    onselect='alert("Selected")'><BR><BR>

<LI>onsubmit: <INPUT TYPE="Submit" VALUE="Test Submit"><BR><BR>

<LI>onunload: Try to leave document by following this
<A HREF="http://www.yahoo.com">link</A>.<BR><BR>

</UL>
```

PROGRAMMING
AND HTML

```
</FORM>

</BODY>
</HTML>
```

*You may encounter problems with the **onfocus** demo under some versions of Netscape, because it may not release the focus event. This does not occur under all versions of the browser and, hopefully, will be fixed in the version that you are testing under.*

While the example events should work equally well under Internet Explorer 4 and Netscape 4 browsers, the extent to which the events can be used in various elements varies from browser to browser. For example, the **onclick** handler is defined for nearly all elements, including **<B>**, **<SPAN>**, and even **<HR>**. However, only Internet Explorer 4 and above currently support markup such as the following:

```
<B onclick='alert("You clicked the bold text")'>Click here</B>
```

As of the time of this writing, Netscape does not provide as rich an event or object model as the HTML 4.0 specification defines, but future versions such as 5 promise to support the full HTML 4 event model. Interestingly, both the browsers *do* support other events not in the current specification.

Extended Event Models

While HTML 4 specifies numerous events, Netscape and Internet Explorer support many more events. Some of the events, such as **onabort**, have been around since Netscape 3 and are well understood. The **onabort** handler fires when a download of an image is not completed:

```
<IMG SRC="reallybigimportantimage.gif"
     onabort='alert("Please reload page")'>
```

Other events, such as the numerous data binding events, are not nearly as well understood, and are supported only in Internet Explorer 4. Table 13-4 lists these extended events, as well as their compatibility.

Event Attribute	Description	Associated Elements	Compatibility
onabort	Fires when user aborts image load with stop button or similar effect	**\<IMG\>**	Netscape 3 Netscape 4 Internet Explorer 4
onafterupdate	Fires after the transfer of data from the element to a data provider, namely, a data update	**\<APPLET\>** **\<BODY\>** **\<BUTTON\>** **\<CAPTION\>** **\<DIV\>** **\<EMBED\>** **\<IMG\>** **\<INPUT\>** **\<MARQUEE\>** **\<OBJECT\>** **\<SELECT\>** **\<TABLE\>** **\<TD\>** **\<TEXTAREA\>** **\<TR\>**	Internet Explorer 4
onbeforeunload	Fires just prior to a document being unloaded from a window	**\<BODY\>**	Internet Explorer 4
onbeforeupdate	Fires before the transfer of data from the element to the data provider; may fire explicitly or by loss of focus or page unload, forcing data update	**\<APPLET\>** **\<BODY\>** **\<BUTTON\>** **\<CAPTION\>** **\<DIV\>** **\<EMBED\>** **\<HR\>** **\<IMG\>** **\<INPUT\>** **\<OBJECT\>** **\<SELECT\>** **\<TABLE\>** **\<TD\>** **\<TEXTAREA\>** **\<TR\>**	Internet Explorer 4

Table 13-4.   *Extended Event Model*

Event Attribute	Description	Associated Elements	Compatibility
onbounce	Fires when bouncing contents of a marquee touch one side or another	\<MARQUEE\>	Internet Explorer 4
ondataavailable	Fires when data arrives from data sources that transmit information asynchronously	\<APPLET\> \<OBJECT\>	Internet Explorer 4
ondatasetchanged	Fires when the initial data is made available from data source or when the data changes	\<APPLET\> \<OBJECT\>	Internet Explorer 4
ondatasetcomplete	Fires when all data is available from the data source	\<APPLET\> \<OBJECT\>	Internet Explorer 4
ondragstart	Fires when a user begins to drag a highlighted selection	\<A\> \<APPLET\> \<AREA\> \<BODY\> \<BUTTON\> \<DIV\> \<EMBED\> \<HR\> \<IMG\> \<INPUT\> \<MARQUEE\> \<OBJECT\> \<SELECT\> \<TABLE\> \<TD\> \<TEXTAREA\> \<TR\>	Internet Explorer 4

Table 13-4. *Extended Event Model* (continued)

Event Attribute	Description	Associated Elements	Compatibility
ondragdrop	Fires when a user drags an object onto the browser window to attempt to load it	**\<BODY>** (window)	Netscape 4
onerror	Fires when the loading of a document, particularly the execution of a script, causes an error; used to trap syntax errors	**\<BODY>** (window)	Netscape 3 Netscape 4 Internet Explorer 4
onerrorupdate	Fires if a data transfer has been canceled by the **onbeforeupdate** event handler	**\<A>** **\<APPLET>** **\<OBJECT>** **\<SELECT>** **\<TEXTAREA>**	Internet Explorer 4
onfilterchange	Fires when a page filter changes state or finishes	Nearly all elements	Internet Explorer 4
onfinish	Fires when a looping marquee finishes	**\<MARQUEE>**	Internet Explorer 4
onhelp	Fires when a user presses F1 key or similar help button in user agent	Nearly all elements	Internet Explorer 4
onmove	Fires when a user moves a window	**\<BODY>**	Netscape 4
onreadystatechange	Similar to **onload**; fires whenever the ready state for an object has changed	**\<APPLET>** **\<BODY>** **\<EMBED>** **\<FRAME>** **\<FRAMESET>** **\<IMG>** **\<LINK>** **\<OBJECT>** **\<SCRIPT>** **\<STYLE>**	Internet Explorer 4

Table 13-4. *Extended Event Model* (continued)

PROGRAMMING AND HTML

Event Attribute	Description	Associated Elements	Compatibility
onresize	Fires whenever an object is resized; can only be bound to the window under Netscape, as set via the \<BODY\> element	\<BODY\>* \<APPLET\> \<BUTTON\> \<CAPTION\> \<DIV\> \<EMBED\> \<HR\> \<IMG\> \<MARQUEE\> \<OBJECT\> \<SELECT\> \<TABLE\> \<TD\> \<TEXTAREA\> \<TR\>	Netscape 4* Internet Explorer 4
onrowenter	Fires when a bound data row has changed and new data values are available	\<APPLET\> \<BODY\> \<BUTTON\> \<CAPTION\> \<DIV\> \<EMBED\> \<HR\> \<IMG\> \<MARQUEE\> \<OBJECT\> \<SELECT\> \<TABLE\> \<TD\> \<TEXTAREA\> \<TR\>	Internet Explorer 4

Table 13-4.   *Extended Event Model* (continued)

Event Attribute	Description	Associated Elements	Compatibility
onrowexit	Fires just before a bound data source control changes the current row	<APPLET> <BODY> <BUTTON> <CAPTION> <DIV> <EMBED> <HR> <IMG> <MARQUEE> <OBJECT> <SELECT> <TABLE> <TD> <TEXTAREA> <TR>	Internet Explorer 4
onscroll	Fires when a scrolling element is repositioned	<BODY> <DIV> <FIELDSET> <IMG> <MARQUEE> <SPAN> <TEXTAREA>	Internet Explorer 4
onselectstart	Fires when a user begins to select information by highlighting	Nearly all elements	Internet Explorer 4
onstart	Fires when a looped marquee begins or starts over	<MARQUEE>	Internet Explorer 4

Table 13-4.   *Extended Event Model* (continued)

The following markup demonstrates a few of the extended events for Netscape 4 and Internet Explorer 4.

```
<HTML>
<HEAD>
<TITLE>Extended Events</TITLE>
</HEAD>

<BODY onhelp='alert("Going to help now")'
      ondragdrop='alert("Drag and drop.")'
      onmove='alert("Moving")'
      onresize='alert("Resizing")'>

<H1 ALIGN="CENTER">Extended Events Example</H1>

<UL>

<LI>onbounce, onfinish, onstart: Watch marquee events fire.
(IE4 Only)<BR>

<MARQUEE BEHAVIOR="ALTERNATE"
        BGCOLOR="yellow" LOOP="2" WIDTH="400"
        onstart='alert("Marquee start!")'
        onbounce='alert("Bounced!")'
        onfinish='alert("Marquee done!")'>
Bouncing message
</MARQUEE>
<BR><BR>

<LI>ondragdrop: Try dragging a file onto the browser window.
(N4 Only)

<LI>ondragstart: Try selecting text and dragging. (IE4 Only)<BR>

<FORM>
<TEXTAREA ROWS="1" COLS="80"
          ondragstart='alert("Going to drag")'>
Select this text and attempt to drag
</TEXTAREA>
</FORM><BR>

<LI>onhelp: Click in window and press F1 key for help. (IE4 Only)

<LI>onmove: Try moving the browser window.  (N4 Only)
```

```
<LI>onresize: Try resizing the window.

<LI>onscroll: Scroll the textarea. (IE4 Only)<BR>

<FORM>
<TEXTAREA ROWS="1" COLS="80" onscroll='alert("Scrolled")'>
Type some text in here and scroll this.
</TEXTAREA>
</FORM><BR>

<LI>onselectstart:
<SPAN onselectstart='alert("Select starting")'>
Try selecting this text. (IE4 Only)</SPAN>

</UL>
</BODY>
</HTML>
```

As shown here, events currently vary from browser to browser. How these events can be captured also varies. Netscape currently supports a concept called *event capturing*, while Microsoft supports *event bubbling*. The basic idea of event bubbling is that an event "bubbles up" through the document structure, starting from where it occurred. If a user clicks a **<B>** element, it may be passed up to an enclosing **<P>** element, and then to the **<BODY>** element, and then disappear. Netscape takes the opposite approach, offering the event first to the highest-level structure and then on down. Such differences make coding cross-platform scripts somewhat difficult. Furthermore, the extent of elements that support particular events is changing rapidly. Only some elements under Netscape can respond to events, but this will probably change quickly.

Internet Explorer 5 Event Preview

At the time of this writing, Internet Explorer 5 is nearing release stage. This browser introduces even more events for JavaScript. Notably, IE 5 introduces events dealing with the transfer of data within a page and from other applications by using the cut, copy, and paste functions of a browser or application. These event handlers, which are fairly self-explanatory, include **oncopy**, **onbeforecopy**, **oncut**, **onbeforecut**, **onpaste**, and **onbeforepaste**. IE 5 also provides a rich model for drag and drop, with event handlers for **ondrag**, **ondragend**, **ondragenter**, **ondragleave**, **ondragover**, and **ondrop**.

Internet Explorer 5 also introduces the ability to sense printing using the event handlers **onafterprint** and **onbeforeprint**. These may be useful to change the style of a page or its content before printing.

One potentially useful new event handler for Internet Explorer 5 is **oncontextmenu**, which can be triggered when a user trys to bring up the context menu for an object. This is generally invoked by a right mouse click by the user. Imagine having a Web interface in which the user could right click objects to trigger pop-up menus. With the addition of these events to the existing proprietary and standard events, Web interfaces are nearly as rich as any modern graphical user interface environment. However, to guarantee compatibility, page authors should consider staying with events associated with form controls, as defined in the HTML 4.0 specification.

Error Handlers

One interesting event handler that warrants special consideration is **onerror**. An **onerror** event handler executes scripting code when an error (typically a scripting error) occurs while loading a document. The benefit to the **onerror** handler is that you can use it to turn off the annoying and often numerous error messages that may pester a user when reading a misbehaving script. When used properly, you might even provide the user with a simple feedback message, instructing the user what to do to rectify the problem, or even how to report the bug. To display the entire error message in JavaScript and replace it, set **window.onerror** to the name of your special error handler. Make sure to return **true** to suppress any normal scripting alerts. The following example shows this idea in use:

```
<HTML>
<HEAD>
<TITLE>Error Handler</TITLE>

<SCRIPT Language="JavaScript">
<!--
window.onerror=displaySorry

  function displaySorry(message, url, line)
{
    var msg="There has been a scripting error.\n"
    msg +="Please contact bugs@bigcompany.com\n";
    msg +="Reference file: " + url

    alert(msg);
    return true;
}
//-->
```

```
</SCRIPT>
</HEAD>

<BODY>
<SCRIPT>
bad script code;
</SCRIPT>
</BODY>
</HTML>
```

The preceding "bad script code" will invoke a dialog box, as shown here:

Many sites would benefit from adding such facilities to their pages to suppress and help clean up the numerous scripting errors that occur.

 Because of the confusion of JavaScript error messages, starting with version 4.5, the Netscape browser suppresses most messages to a separate console.

Microsoft Event-Handling Extensions

Typically, event handlers are specified as attributes for the particular element with which the event is associated. For example,

```
<INPUT TYPE="BUTTON" onclick="script">
```

However, Microsoft also supports a different form of event handler, first in the form of an extension to the **<SCRIPT>** element, and second as a naming convention for VBScript. Under Internet Explorer, the **<SCRIPT>** element also has an **EVENT** and a **FOR** attribute. The **EVENT** attribute is used to define a particular event that should be reacted to. The **FOR** attribute is used to define the name or ID of the element that the event is tied to. Notice in the following example how the **FOR** attribute is associated with the particular button named myButton, and the **EVENT** attribute is used to specify the event to respond to—in this case, **onclick**:

```
<HTML>
<HEAD>
<TITLE>Microsoft Alternate Event Form</TITLE>

<SCRIPT FOR="myButton" EVENT="onclick" LANGUAGE="JavaScript">
<!--
 alert("I've been clicked!");
//-->
</SCRIPT>
</HEAD>

<BODY>
<FORM>
    <INPUT TYPE="BUTTON" NAME="myButton" VALUE="Click me">
</FORM>
</BODY>
</HTML>
```

This form of **<SCRIPT>** handler is specific to Microsoft and will either run incorrectly or even cause errors with Netscape browsers. Using VBScript, this style is very common. VBScript also supports a naming convention style for event handling:

```
<HTML>
<HEAD>
<TITLE>Microsoft Alternate Event Form</TITLE>

<SCRIPT LANGUAGE="VBScript">
<!--
Sub myButton_onclick
msgBox "I've been clicked!"
End Sub
'-->
</SCRIPT>
</HEAD>
```

```
<BODY>
<FORM>
  <INPUT TYPE="BUTTON" NAME="myButton" VALUE="Click me">
</FORM>
</BODY>
</HTML>
```

Notice that the name of the subroutine has the event handler name in it and requires no hooks into HTML. In some sense, this is the cleanest way to integrate scripts with HTML, but JavaScript does not support this style of event handling. The extensions introduced by Microsoft for event handling should be avoided, except when trying to access ActiveX controls, which tend to require the **FOR/EVENT** style for JScript or the VBScript naming idea.

Form Validation in JavaScript

So far, this chapter has looked at very simple changes to pages, such as writing out the last modification date of a page dynamically or creating a button that greets the user. The basic examples are meant only to show the intersection of JavaScript with HTML. However, before moving on to more advanced forms of scripting, it is important to look at a very useful application of JavaScript—form validation.

Form validation is the process of checking the validity of user-supplied data in an HTML form before it is submitted to a server-side program, such as a CGI program. By prevalidating data before it is sent to a server, you can avoid a lot of user frustration and reduce communication time between the Web browser and the server.

The key to checking form data is naming the various form fields. Take a look at the example HTML markup shown here:

```
<!DOCTYPE HTML PUBLIC "-//W3C//DTD HTML 4.0 Transitional//EN">
<HTML>
<HEAD>
<TITLE>Reading a Form Field</TITLE>
</HEAD>

<BODY>
<FORM NAME="myform" ACTION="cgi-bin/dosomething.pl" METHOD="POST">
<B>Name:</B>
```

```
<INPUT TYPE="TEXT" NAME="username" SIZE="25" MAXLENGTH="25"><BR><BR>
<INPUT TYPE="BUTTON" VALUE="CHECK NAME"
        onclick="alert('You entered '+document.myform.username.value)">
</FORM>
</BODY>
</HTML>
```

This example has a form named **myform** and a text field named **username** inside the form. In both cases, the names were set by using the **NAME** attribute, which is being phased out in HTML 4 in favor of **ID**. For backward compatibility, **NAME** will always be used in this book for form validation. Next, notice that the **onclick** event handler creates an alert that references **document.myform.username.value**. This small piece of JavaScript references the form named **myform** in the current document; its field called **username**; and, finally, that object's value property. So, if you run the simple example, you can see that reading the contents of any field that a user may fill out is easy.

Note *Under newer browsers, you may be able to use simply **username.value** or **myform.username.value**. Be very careful, because although this will work under the latest browsers, older JavaScript-aware browsers such as Netscape Navigator 2 and 3 will fail. It would be ironic if your code to keep the user from making errors ended up causing a different form of frustration. Remember, it is always best to reference your object explicitly so it will work in all situations.*

Suppose that you want to make sure that the user enters something in each text field before submitting a form. Checking the contents of the field, as shown in this example, is fairly easy.

```
<!DOCTYPE HTML PUBLIC "-//W3C//DTD HTML 4.0 Transitional//EN">
<HTML>
<HEAD>
<TITLE>Reading a Form Field</TITLE>

<SCRIPT>
<!--
function validate()
  {
  if (document.myform.username.value == "")
    alert('Please enter your name');
```

```
  else
    alert('You entered '+document.myform.username.value)
 }
// -->
</SCRIPT>
</HEAD>

<BODY>
<FORM NAME="myform" ACTION="cgi-bin/dosomething.pl" METHOD="POST">
<B>Name:</B>
   <INPUT TYPE="TEXT" NAME="username" SIZE="25"
          MAXLENGTH="25"><BR><BR>
   <INPUT TYPE="BUTTON"
          VALUE="CHECK NAME"
          onclick="validate()">
</FORM>
</BODY>
</HTML>
```

In this example, the function **validate()** is called and the contents of the field **username** is checked to see whether it is blank or contains information. If the field is left blank when the user clicks the button, the user is told to complete the field; otherwise, the data entered is printed in the alert box. By making some simple modifications to the preceding example, you can change the button to a submit button and have the validation function **validate()** return a **true** or **false** value to indicate whether the form submission is allowed to continue, as shown here:

```
<!DOCTYPE HTML PUBLIC "-//W3C//DTD HTML 4.0 Transitional//EN">
<HTML>
<HEAD>
<TITLE>Reading a Form Field</TITLE>

<SCRIPT>
<!--
function validate()
 {
  if (document.myform.username.value == "")
   {
```

```
        alert('Please enter your name');
        return false;
      }
    else
    {
    alert('Thanks for your submission '+document.myform.username.value);
    return true;
  }
 }
// -->
</SCRIPT>
</HEAD>

<BODY>
<FORM NAME="myform" ACTION="cgi-bin/dosomething.pl"
      METHOD="POST" onSubmit="return validate()">
<B>Name:</B>
   <INPUT TYPE="TEXT" NAME="username" SIZE="25"
          MAXLENGTH="25"><BR><BR>
   <INPUT TYPE="SUBMIT" VALUE="CHECK NAME">
</FORM>
</BODY>
</HTML>
```

This example uses the HTML event handler attribute **onsubmit**, which is triggered when the user clicks the submit button. The submission will occur unless the event returns a **false** value. Notice how the validation function **validate()** returns a **true** or **false** value, based upon the user's input. Expanding this example to check more fields is not difficult, as was shown in the larger example at the end of Chapter 11.

Note
Another approach to form field validation is to catch errors as users move from field to field. By using the onblur attribute, you can sense when a user has deselected a field and is trying to select another field. Be careful: many users may be annoyed by form validation using onblur, and it may not even always work, because of bugs in JavaScript implementations.

The previous discussion is meant to serve only as a basic introduction to the concept of form validation. Even if you are an experienced programmer, it is not suggested that you go out and attempt to create your own validation scripts for e-mail addresses, credit card numbers, ZIP codes, and so on. Many libraries already exist that perform these tasks; these libraries are available from JavaScript archive sites such as http://www.javascripts.com; http://javascript.internet.com; and Netscape's original form validation library, located at the following address:

> http://developer.netscape.com/docs/examples/javascript/formval/overview.html

Form validation is only one example of how JavaScript may be useful in a Web page. The next chapter looks at how to embellish pages by using JavaScript and focuses on the idea of DHTML, which enables you to manipulate the very elements of your page.

Summary

Client-side technologies have their place in a Web site. The evolution of scripting technologies has off-loaded some of the processing that traditionally occurred on the server. For example, validating form field entries by using JavaScript or VBScript on the client makes more sense than relegating this processing to the server. Integrating scripts into a Web page comes in two major forms: within the **<SCRIPT>** element and as event handlers in the form of HTML attributes. By using JavaScript or VBScript, you can create simple interface changes or even perform useful tasks such as form validation. The intersection between HTML and scripting was originally very distinct; but, as the next chapter explains, a script now can be used to modify the very elements in a page by accessing the Document Object Model. When combining this approach to scripting Web pages with improved page layout facilities, such as style sheets, you can make your pages come alive with interaction and movement: thus, DHTML is born.

PROGRAMMING
AND HTML

The Complete Reference

Chapter 14

Dynamic HTML (DHTML)

The previous chapter discussed how scripting languages such as JavaScript could be added to HTML documents. One of the only reasonable applications discussed was form validation. However, many Web developers are more interested in making their buttons light up or making their pages come alive with movement. This chapter discusses the idea of Dynamic HTML, or DHTML, which is the popular expression to describe interactive HTML pages. We'll look at how to make rollover buttons and even how to animate positioned layers on a page. However, before diving into the effects, it is important to understand what DHTML is all about. You'll see that entire Web pages, right down to the individual HTML elements and their content, soon will become changeable through a scripting language. True Dynamic HTML won't just be about moving the content around the screen, but changing it dynamically based on user desires.

Dynamic HTML and the Document Object Model

Dynamic HTML (DHTML) is not about new tags or attributes that can animate pages. Dynamic HTML actually extends the current set of HTML elements, and a few other things like style sheet properties, by allowing them to be accessed and modified by a scripting language like JavaScript or VBScript. Dynamic facilities can be added by exposing tags to a scripting language; this allows pages to come alive with movement and interactivity. The tags in a page are accessed through the Document Object Model (DOM).

Every Web document is made up of a variety of elements like **<B>**, **<IMG>**, and **<FORM>**. Browsers read pages in a regular fashion because they understand the extent of the objects that are possible in a page. A page might be composed of three image elements, two paragraphs, an unordered list, and the text within these elements. The DOM describes each document as a collection of individual objects like images, paragraphs, and forms, all the way down to the individual characters. Each particular object may have properties associated with it, typically in the form of HTML attributes. For example, the paragraph element has an alignment attribute that may be set to left, right, or center. In the object model, this attribute is called a property of the object. An object may have methods that are associated with it, and events that may occur and affect it. An image tag may have an **onmouseover** event that is triggered when a user places the cursor over the image. A form may have a submit method that can be used to trigger the submission of the form and its contents to a server-based CGI program.

The best way to explain the DOM is with an example. Look at this simple HTML file:

```
<!DOCTYPE HTML PUBLIC "-//W3C//DTD HTML 4.0 Transitional//EN">
<HTML>
<HEAD>
<TITLE>Big Company</TITLE>
</HEAD>
```

```
<BODY BGCOLOR="white">
<H1 ALIGN="CENTER">Big Company</H1>
<HR>

<P ID="para1">This is a paragraph of text.</P>

<UL>
   <LI><A HREF="about.htm">About</A>
   <LI><A HREF="products.htm">Products</A>
</UL>
</BODY>
</HTML>
```

This file could be modeled as a parse tree, as shown in Figure 14-1. The structured breakdown of HTML elements and how they enclose one another should be familiar even from the first chapter of this book.

The concept of the Document Object Model is that there is a rigid structure defined to access the various HTML elements and text items that make up a document. This model starts from the browser window itself. A typical window contains either a document or a collection of frames (basically windows) that in turn contain documents. Within a document is a collection of HTML elements. Some of these HTML elements, particularly forms, contain even more HTML elements, and some may contain text. The key to accessing the elements in a document is to understand the hierarchy and make sure to name the various elements in the page using either the **ID** or the **NAME**

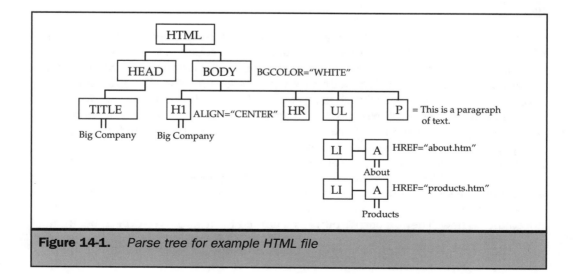

Figure 14-1.   *Parse tree for example HTML file*

attribute. In the previous example, you may want to address the first paragraph of text, which happens to have the **ID** of **para1**. It could be referenced under Internet Explorer 4 or above using a JavaScript identifier like **window.document.all['para1']**, **document.all['para1']**, or simply **para1**. Since **para1** refers to a **<P>** element, you may want to manipulate its attributes (for example, the **ALIGN** attribute). Adding the word **align** to any of the object references previously mentioned, in the form **para1.align**, should give us access to the value of this attribute. The following example, which works currently only under Internet Explorer 4 or above, shows how you could manipulate the alignment of the paragraph dynamically.

```
<!DOCTYPE HTML PUBLIC "-//W3C//DTD HTML 4.0 Transitional//EN">
<HTML>
<HEAD>
<TITLE>The Dynamic Paragraph</TITLE>
</HEAD>

<BODY BGCOLOR="white">
<H1 ALIGN="CENTER">The Dynamic Paragraph</H1>
<HR>

<P ID="para1">I am a dynamic paragraph. Watch me dance!</P>
<HR>

<SPAN onClick="para1.align='right'">[ Shift Right ]</SPAN>
<SPAN onClick="para1.align='left'">[ Shift Left ]</SPAN>
<SPAN onClick="para1.align='center'">[ Shift Center ]</SPAN>
</BODY>
</HTML>
```

In the previous example, every time the user clicks on the spanned text, the actual value of the **ALIGN** attribute for the **<P>** tag is manipulated. Of course, if you view the source of the page you won't notice anything, but this is basically what is happening. Note that the last example will not work under Netscape 4.*x*–generation browsers. The differences between the two browsers' approach to Dynamic HTML will be discussed shortly.

The DOM can be complex, but what it can do is impressive—without always requiring a great deal of work. Developers may use the object model to find an image on a page and replace it with another image when a user rolls a cursor over it. Such rollovers, or animated buttons, are already common on the Web. In conjunction with scripting, the DOM can also animate a page by moving objects around, set up an expanding tree structure to navigate a site, or create a complex application like a game or database front end. To seasoned JavaScript programmers, many of these ideas might not sound so new. They've been around in a limited form since Netscape 2. Beginning with that release, JavaScript provided an object model that allowed access to many parts of a Web page, including anchors, form elements, and images. True Dynamic HTML, however, takes the idea much further. It gets right down to the actual text, styles, tags, and scripts within a page, making the whole page modifiable.

The DOM is the core component of both browser vendors' idea of Dynamic HTML. As defined by the World Wide Web Consortium (http://www.w3.org/pub/WWW/ MarkUp/DOM/), DOM is a "platform- and language-neutral interface that will allow programs and scripts to dynamically access and update the content, structure, and style of documents." The Web standards body has already released the Level 1 specification of the DOM that includes the syntax for accessing page elements. At the time of the writing of this book, the browser vendors have gone far beyond the definition of the current DOM in some areas but still lack support for some of its basic features.

The definition of Dynamic HTML as a DOM isn't precisely what is meant by DHTML in the commercial arena. There, DHTML can include style sheets, absolute positioning, multimedia effects, database access facilities, dynamic fonts, and potentially any other thing that can make a page dynamic. This is where the confusion about Dynamic HTML arises. Netscape and Microsoft have the same basic idea about the DOM, and both companies are working jointly with the W3C to develop a standard; but when it comes down to specific details, DHTML varies (often significantly) between the two leading browser vendors. This can cause trouble for designers looking to create cross-platform dynamic pages.

Object Models

Since Netscape 2, the browser, window, document, and document contents—forms, images, links, and so on—have been modeled as a collection of objects. This is generically referred to as an *object model* or, more precisely, the Document Object Model (DOM). Both of the major browsers support the DOM idea, but each has different naming conventions and a different degree of exposure. For example, in Netscape 3, only particular items—form elements—are accessible for scripting. Figure 14-2 illustrates the object model for Netscape 3 and Internet Explorer 3.

Objects in the Netscape 3 object hierarchy provide access not only to page elements like links, anchors, frames, and forms, but to things like the browser's name, history, plug-ins, and Java classes associated with the current window.

With the introduction of Netscape 4, more elements, such as layers, are accessible. Under Internet Explorer 4, all page elements are scriptable, and it is obvious that Netscape will soon follow suit, making the entire page modifiable. Figure 14-3 shows an expanded object model. Note that many of the items in this model are available only under one browser or another.

Once the objects that make up a page are accessible, there are certain changes that must be made to HTML documents, particularly concerning correct markup and naming of elements.

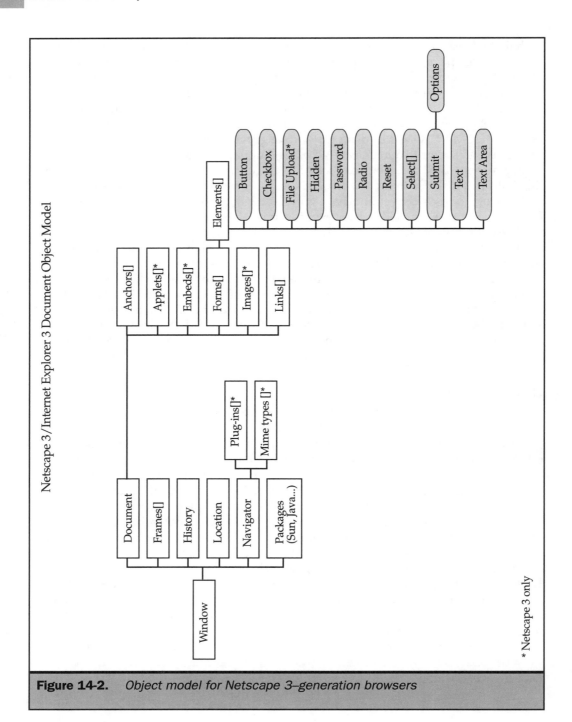

Figure 14-2. Object model for Netscape 3–generation browsers

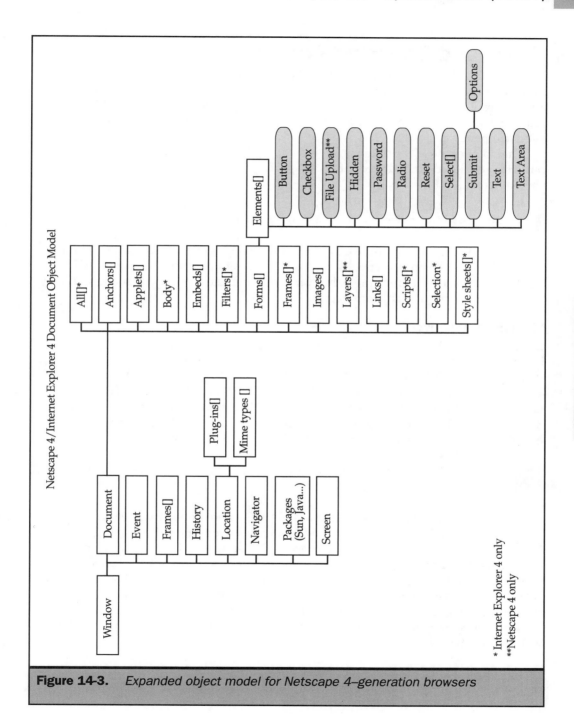

Netscape 4/Internet Explorer 4 Document Object Model

* Internet Explorer 4 only
**Netscape 4 only

Figure 14-3. *Expanded object model for Netscape 4–generation browsers*

HTML and Scripting Access

While the DOM specifies a model for all the objects and HTML elements that make a Web page, they need to be named properly to allow scripting languages to easily read and manipulate them. The basic way to attach a unique identifier to an HTML element under HTML 4 is by using the **ID** attribute. The **ID** attribute is associated with nearly every element.

The point of the **ID** attribute is to bind a unique identifier to the element. To name a particular enclosed bolded piece of text **SuperImportant**, you could use the markup shown here:

```
<B ID="SuperImportant">This is very important.</B>
```

Naming is very important. Authors are encouraged to adopt a consistent naming style and to avoid using potentially confusing names that include the names of HTML elements themselves. For example, **button** does not make a very good name, and may interfere with scripting language access.

NAME Attribute

Before HTML 4, the **NAME** attribute was often used to expose items to scripting. For backward compatibility, the **NAME** attribute is commonly defined for **<A>**, **<APPLET>**, **<BUTTON>**, **<EMBED>**, **<FORM>**, **<FRAME>**, **<IFRAME>**, **<IMG>**, **<INPUT>**, **<OBJECT>**, **<MAP>**, **<SELECT>**, and **<TEXTAREA>**. The HTML 4.0 specification does not support all of these. In particular, **<FORM>** and **<IMG>** are missing, and **<OBJECT>** has a different meaning. Notice that the occurrence of the **NAME** attribute corresponds closely to the Netscape 3 object model.

Note   *Both **<META>** and **<PARAM>** support attributes called **NAME**, but these have totally different meanings than script access.*

Page developers must be careful to use **NAME** where necessary to ensure backward compatibility with older browsers. Earlier browsers will not recognize the **ID** attribute, so use **NAME** as well. However, as **NAME** and **ID** share the same namespace, you must not use the same value for both. As **ID** is not case-sensitive, values differentiated only by case are not allowed. For example, **<A NAME="link1" ID="LINK1">** is not legal. If the names clash, what happens remains unclear; some browsers may ignore the second occurrence, while others may disable script access.

Another consideration when adding scripting to a page is whether the HTML is well formed. Simple things such as crossed elements, as shown here,

```
<B><I>Test</B></I>
```

may cause a problem with a scripting language. This has to do with the manipulation of the text within the elements. Page authors should consider it dangerous to manipulate poorly formed markup with scripts; according to the HTML 4.0 specification, the results are unpredictable.

When HTML documents are well formed, scripting languages such as JavaScript and VBScript can be used to read and manipulate the various objects in a page. DOM defines a special set of reserved names that use this notation to allow scripting languages like JavaScript to refer to entities in the browser and the document, including form elements. The basic notation uses a series of object and property names separated by dots. To access the form defined by

```
<FORM NAME="myform">
<INPUT TYPE="TEXT" NAME="username">
</FORM>
```

with a scripting language, use either **window.document.myform** or simply **document.myform**. The field and its value can be accessed in a similar fashion. To access the text field, use **document.myform.username**. To access the actual value of the **username** field, access the **value** property using **document.myform.username.value**. Note that, as shown previously, it may also be possible to use a shorthand notation such as **myform.username.value**, as supported under Internet Explorer.

This simple naming style can be used to access the properties of the various objects that make up the document. The following example, similar to those in the last chapter, shows the concept in action as the contents of a form field are accessed and displayed dynamically in an alert window:

```
<HTML>
<HEAD>
<TITLE>Meet and Greet</TITLE>
<SCRIPT LANGUAGE="JavaScript">
<!--
function sayHello()
{
 theirname=document.myform.username.value;
 if (theirname !="")
  alert("Hello "+theirname+"!");
 else
  alert("Don't be shy.");
}
// -->
</SCRIPT>
</HEAD>
```

```
<BODY>
<FORM ACTION="mailto: info@bigcompany.com"
     METHOD="POST" NAME="myform">
<B>What's your name?</B>
<INPUT TYPE="TEXT" NAME="username" SIZE="20"> <BR><BR>
<INPUT TYPE="BUTTON" VALUE="Greet" onclick='sayHello()'>
</BODY>
</HTML>
```

One potential problem to overcome with naming document objects is the **NAME** and **ID** namespace conflict. Older browsers only understand **NAME**, while the specification encourages **ID**. A likely approach would be simply to set the **NAME** and **ID** attributes to be the same values as those shown here:

```
<INPUT TYPE="TEXT" NAME="username" ID="username">
```

According to the specification, this approach is not supposed to work because **NAME** and **ID** share the namespace, creating a conflict. In practice, browsers don't seem to care. Scripting could be used to deal with different names for the same object, but that introduces needless complexity. The simple solution is to use **NAME** on all elements that support it and **ID** on the new elements.

Besides accessing the properties of various document objects, it is also occasionally possible to trigger actions called *methods*. An example of a method would be to submit a form. In the last example, **document.myform.submit()** would submit the form to the address specified by the **ACTION** attribute for the **<FORM>** element.

The previous example only scratches the surface of the DOM. It is possible to refer to forms and form elements without assigning them a name using an array notation. Forms can be referred to with a forms array that includes a number beginning at 0. Elements within a form can be referred to with an elements array that includes a number beginning at 0. The previous example contains only one form and one field, so the syntax **document.forms[0].elements[0].value** is the same as **document.myform.username.value**. Note that it is better to name elements rather than to access them via their position in a page, since any additions or movement of the HTML elements within the page may potentially break the script.

It is also possible, in some cases, to update the contents of certain elements such as form fields. The following example code shows how this might be done:

```
<HTML>
<HEAD>
<TITLE>Meet and Greet 2</TITLE>
```

```
<SCRIPT LANGUAGE="JavaScript">
<!--
function sayHello()
{
 theirname = document.myform.username.value;

 if (theirname != "")
  document.myform.response.value="Hello "+theirname+"!";
 else
  document.myform.response.value="Don't be shy.";
}
// -->
</SCRIPT>
</HEAD>

<BODY>
<FORM NAME="myform">
<B>What's your name?</B>
<INPUT TYPE="TEXT" NAME="username" SIZE="20"> <BR><BR>
<B>Greeting:</B>
<INPUT TYPE="TEXT" NAME="response" SIZE="40"> <BR><BR>
<INPUT TYPE="BUTTON" VALUE="Greet" onclick='sayHello()'>
</BODY>
</HTML>
```

Note   *You may have noted the use of **NAME** rather than **ID** in this example. Unfortunately, with form elements, browser support is inconsistent with the **ID** attribute and may cause errors. Try switching out **NAME** for **ID** if you are using a 5.x–generation browser, and you should get the same result.*

Under Netscape 3 and 4 and Internet Explorer 3, only some objects in a page are changeable, notably form elements. Starting with Internet Explorer 4, everything in a page can be modified right down to the very text and markup itself. This is the real idea of Dynamic HTML. Look at the following markup:

```
<HTML>
<HEAD>
<TITLE>Simple DHTML for IE4</TITLE>
</HEAD>
```

PROGRAMMING
AND HTML

```
<BODY>
<B ID="bold1" onclick='this.innerText="The text has changed"'>
Click me</B>
<BR><BR><BR>
<SPAN onclick="bold1.innerText='Click me'">[ Change text back ]</SPAN>
</BODY>
</HTML>
```

Notice that the **<B>** element is named **bold1**. This is later referenced by the **<SPAN>** element. Furthermore, notice that the actual text is changed when the user clicks on the text regions. It is obvious that this form of DHTML is very powerful, particularly when you consider that it can also be used to control style sheets.

Script Interaction with Style Sheets

Both Netscape and Microsoft support scripting access for style sheets. Of course, the variations between the two browsers are significant. Currently, Microsoft and Netscape differ on how style sheets can be accessed and the degree to which they can be manipulated. For example, under Netscape 4 the only style sheet properties that can be changed after the document has loaded are the absolute positioning properties **left**, **top**, **z-index**, and **visibility**.

Microsoft has shown the extent to which style sheets can be manipulated via scripting language. It is assumed that Netscape 5.*x*–generation browsers will support such manipulation as well. The following code fragment shows how events can be tied with style changes to make text that changes to red when the mouse is over it:

```
<A HREF="http://www.yahoo.com"
   onmouseover='this.style.color="#FF0000"'
   onmouseout='this.style.color="#0000FF"'>Yahoo!</A>
```

The special scripting keyword **this** is a shortcut reference to the current element, but an **ID** attribute could be used just as well, as shown here:

```
<A HREF="http://www.yahoo.com"
   ID="yahoolink"
   onmouseover='yahoolink.style.color="red";
                yahoolink.style.fontSize="larger"'
```

```
onmouseout='yahoolink.style.color="blue";
            yahoolink.style.fontSize="smaller"'
STYLE="color: blue">
Yahoo!</A>
```

It is also possible to use multiple style sheet rules, as presented in Chapter 10. In the last example, the size and color of the text are changed when the mouse rolls over it. Using positioning, style sheets, and scripting, it is possible to make some very dynamic pages with little effort, as you will see in the next two sections.

Rollover Buttons

The preceding examples demonstrate how scripting can be used to manipulate the look of a link as a user rolls over it. A feature available since Netscape called *dynamic buttons,* commonly called *rollover buttons,* is one of the first common examples of dynamic page manipulation using JavaScript, although it predates DHTML. We will first explore traditional JavaScript rollovers and then take a look at their more advanced DHTML cousins.

A *rollover button* is a button that becomes active when the user positions the mouse over it. The button may also have a special activation state when it is pressed. To create a rollover button, you will first need at least two, perhaps even three images, to represent each of the button's states—inactive, active, and unavailable. A sample set of rollover images is shown here:

In order to add this rollover image to the page, simply use the **<IMG>** tag like another image. The idea is to swap the image out when the mouse passes over the image and switch back to the original image when the mouse leaves the image. By literally swapping the value of the **SRC** attribute, you can achieve the rollover effect. This is in essence what the following script, which should work in Netscape 3 and Internet Explorer 4, would do:

```
<!DOCTYPE HTML PUBLIC "-//W3C//DTD HTML 4.0 Transitional//EN">
<HTML>
<HEAD>
<TITLE>Rollover</TITLE>
```

```
<SCRIPT LANGUAGE="JavaScript">
<!--
/* Check to ensure rollovers work */
if (document.images)
{
 /* preload the images */
 buttonoff = new Image();
 buttonoff.src = "buttonoff.gif";
 buttonon = new Image();
 buttonon.src = "buttonon.gif";
}

function On(imageName)
{
 if (document.images)
   {
    document[imageName].src = eval(imageName+"on.src");
   }
}

function Off(imageName)
{
 if (document.images)
   {
    document[imageName].src = eval(imageName+"off.src");
   }
}
// -->
</SCRIPT>
</HEAD>

<BODY>
<H1 ALIGN="CENTER">Rollover Fun</H1>
<HR>
<A HREF="http://www.yahoo.com" onmouseover="On('button')"
   onmouseout = "Off('button')">
<IMG SRC="buttonoff.gif" NAME="button" WIDTH="90" HEIGHT="20"
     BORDER="0"></A>
</BODY>
</HTML>
```

Let's take a look at how the code works. The first section of the JavaScript checks to make sure the browser supports the images part of the Document Object Model. This capability is necessary to make the rollover buttons work. If the browser supports this feature, the images are loaded in and assigned names. Once the page is loaded, the user can move the mouse over the image. The link, as indicated by the **<A>** element, has two event handlers: one for the mouse passing over the image (**onmouseover**) and one for the mouse leaving the image (**onmouseout**). These handlers call the **On()** and **Off()** functions, respectively. The **On()** function simply sets the **SRC** of the **<IMG>** element to the name of the image passed to it and appends **on.src**, which changes the image to the on state. The **Off()** function does the opposite by setting the **SRC** equal to the image name with **off.src** appended to it. The key to adding more images is the names. For example, if you wanted to add another button called **button1.gif**, you would add the following code to the **<SCRIPT>** element within the first **if** statement,

```
button1off = new Image();
button1off.src = "button1off.gif";
button1on = new Image();
buttonon1.src = "button1on.gif";
```

and the following code later on in the document:

```
<A HREF="URL to load " onmouseover="On('button1')"
   onmouseout = "Off('button1')">
<IMG SRC="buttonoff1.gif" NAME="button1" WIDTH="90"
   HEIGHT="20" BORDER="0"></A>
```

Because rollovers are so common on Web sites, there are many sites, such as http://www.webreference.com/javascript, that offer rollover tutorials. Tools such as Macromedia's Dreamweaver can create the code instantly when they are provided with two images.

Style Sheet–Based Rollovers

One potential downside to image-based rollovers is that you need numerous images for every single button on a page. If you have a menu with nine choices, you may find you are downloading 18 images for a two-state button or even 27 images for a three-state button. The number of images can certainly affect download time, so you may desire to find a way to create interesting text buttons without graphics using style sheets. The following code illustrates how we can set the color and size of a link as a mouse rolls on and off the link under Internet Explorer. It is possible to create a clunky version of this that works in Netscape, but they should eventually support this form of rollover in a future browser.

```
<!DOCTYPE HTML PUBLIC "-//W3C//DTD HTML 4.0 Transitional//EN">
<HTML>
<HEAD>
<TITLE>CSS Rollover 1</TITLE>
<STYLE TYPE="text/css">
<!--
A         {color: blue;}
.over     {color: red; font-size: larger}
-->
</STYLE>
</HEAD>

<BODY>
<A HREF="http://www.yahoo.com" onmouseover="this.className='over'"
   onmouseout="this.className=''">Visit Yahoo!</A>
<BR><BR>

<A HREF="http://www.excite.com" onmouseover="this.className='over'"
   onmouseout="this.className=''">Visit Excite</A>
</BODY>
</HTML>
```

Because text rollovers on links are so common, Microsoft even introduced a special pseudoclass for the **<A>** element called **hover**. This pseudoclass, as well as the **active** class, is now part of the CSS2 specification and is illustrated in this simple example, which works in Internet Explorer 4 and beyond:

```
<!DOCTYPE HTML PUBLIC "-//W3C//DTD HTML 4.0 Transitional//EN">
<HTML>
<HEAD>
<TITLE>CSS2 Text Rollovers</TITLE>
<STYLE TYPE="text/css">
<!--
A:link      {color: blue}      /* unvisited link */
A:visited   {color: purple}    /* visited link   */
A:hover     {color: red}       /* mouse hovers    */
A:active    {color: yellow}    /* active link     */
-->
</STYLE>
</HEAD>
```

```
<BODY>
<A HREF="http://www.yahoo.com">Visit Yahoo!</A>
</BODY>
</HTML>
```

There are many other forms of rollovers that are possible using DHTML and style sheets. One interesting approach is the use of image map rollovers. The concept here is to make a solid button bar of all off-state and a solid button bar of all on-state, and place the on-state bar behind the off-state bar using style sheet positioning. Then you can write JavaScript code to reveal a portion of the covered image as the user rolls over the button bar. The advantage to this approach is that it avoids having to download multiple images for every state of every button. This low-bandwidth rollover approach and others are detailed at many sites about DHTML and JavaScript, including this one:

http://www.webreference.com/dhtml and http://www.webreference.com/js

Moving Objects with DHTML

One of the unfortunate aspects of DHTML is that it is not supported in the same way across browsers. Many of the preceding examples work only under Internet Explorer 4 or above. However, one area in which the browsers are very similar in their support is in the positioning of regions using style sheets and in the visibility of these regions. Both browsers support the movement of regions after load time as well as setting visibility of regions. With these rudimentary features, it is possible to create a variety of interesting animation and page effects, as illustrated in the following simple example.

As discussed in Chapter 10, objects can be positioned using style sheets. To position a simple graphic with an explosion and the word *DHTML* on it, use some markup like this:

```
<DIV ID="dhtml" STYLE="position:absolute; width:200px;
    height:115px; z-index:1; left: 100px; top: 50px">
  <IMG SRC="dhtml.gif" WIDTH="275" HEIGHT="175">
</DIV>
```

Moving the object is a little more difficult. The basic idea is to change the **left** and **top** properties of the **<DIV>** element by a set number of pixels every so often. The basic problem is that Netscape and Microsoft reference the object in their object models differently. It is easy enough to detect what browser object model is in effect by using some JavaScript code such as this:

```
var NS4 = (document.layers) ? 1 : 0;
var IE4 = (document.all) ? 1 : 0;
```

Basically, this code sets a variable called **NS4** to **1** (true) if the **document.layers** object exists, as this is something unique to Netscape, and **0** (false) otherwise. The variable **IE4** is set to true (**1**) or false (**0**) based on the existence of the **document.all** structure. Once the browser is determined, you can then execute different code based on which browser is being used. This code can be messy, so it is nicer to abstract away the difference by creating yet another way to reference the various properties of a positioned region. Many libraries for doing this exist on the Web.

The following example modifies code from the Web Reference animation library and provides a simple animation; the code has been simplified for readability and to provide only the necessary features.

```
<!DOCTYPE HTML PUBLIC "-//W3C//DTD HTML 4.0 Transitional//EN">
<HTML>
<HEAD>
<TITLE>DHTML Animation</TITLE>
<SCRIPT LANGUAGE="JavaScript">
<!--
var NS4 = (document.layers) ? 1 : 0;
var IE4 = (document.all) ? 1 : 0;

function AnimationObject(elementid)
{
  this.element = (NS4) ? document[elementid] :
                        document.all[elementid].style;
  this.active = 0;
  this.timer = null;
  this.path = null;
  this.num = null;
  this.name = elementid + "Var";
  eval(this.name + " = this");
  this.animate = Animate;
  this.step = Step;
  this.left = Left;
  this.top = Top;
  this.MoveTo = MoveTo;
  this.SlideBy = SlideBy;
```

```
  this.SlideTo = SlideTo;
}

function Animate(interval)
{
 if (this.active)
 return;
 this.num = 0;
 this.active = 1;
 this.timer = setInterval(this.name + ".step()", interval);
}

function Step()
{
 this.MoveTo(this.path[this.num].x, this.path[this.num].y);
 if (this.num >= this.path.length - 1)
   {
    clearInterval(this.timer);
    this.active = 0;
    if (this.statement)
    eval (this.statement);
   }
 else
   {
    this.num++;
   }
}

/* Returns the left coordinate */
function Left()
{
 return (NS4) ? this.element.left : this.element.pixelLeft;
}

/* Returns the top coordinate */
function Top()
{
 return (NS4) ? this.element.top : this.element.pixelTop;
}
```

```
/* Move element to x,y position */
function MoveTo(x, y)
{
 this.element.left = x;
 this.element.top = y;
}

/* Slide the element by changex pixels on x axis, changey pixels on
   y axis, using a time interval specified by interval in pixel steps
   specified by steps */

function SlideBy(changex, changey, steps, interval)
{
 var startx = this.left();
 var starty = this.top();
 var finalx = startx + changex;
 var finaly = starty + changey;

 this.SlideTo(finalx, finaly, steps, interval);
}

/* Slide the element to a particular point set by finalx and finaly in
   increments of steps pixels with an interval specified by interval */

function SlideTo(finalx, finaly, steps, interval)
{
 var startx = this.left();
 var starty = this.top();
 var changex = finalx - startx;
 var changey = finaly - starty;
 var stepx = changex / steps;
 var stepy = changey / steps;
 var steparray = new Array();

 for (var i = 0; i < steps; i++)
    {
```

```
    startx += stepx;
    starty += stepy;
    steparray[i] = new position(startx, starty);
    }

 this.path = steparray;
 this.animate(interval);
}

/* Return the position as an integer value */
function position(x, y)
{
 this.x = Math.round(x);
 this.y = Math.round(y);
}
//-->
</SCRIPT>
</HEAD>

<BODY BGCOLOR="#FFFFFF" >
<DIV ID="dhtml" STYLE="position:absolute; width:200px; height:115px;
                       z-index:1; left: 100px; top: 50px">
   <IMG SRC="dhtml.gif" WIDTH="275" HEIGHT="175">
</DIV>

<SCRIPT LANGUAGE="JavaScript">
<!--
dhtmllayer = new AnimationObject("dhtml");
dhtmllayer.SlideBy(100, 150, 99, 50);
// -->
</SCRIPT>
</BODY>
</HTML>
```

Before and after renderings of this example are shown in Figure 14-4.

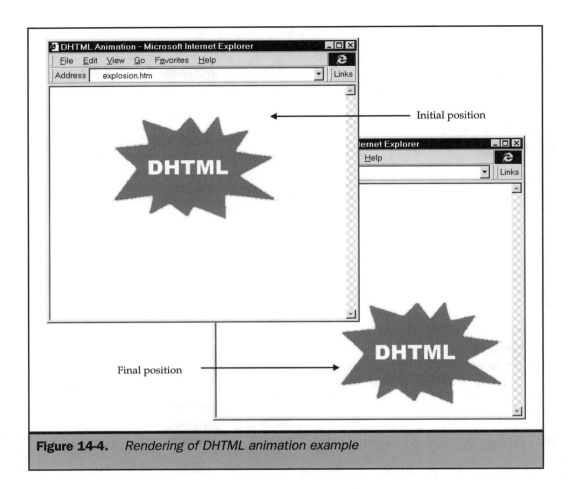

Figure 14-4. *Rendering of DHTML animation example*

If you are an experienced programmer, this code won't seem that difficult, but others might find it impossible to understand. It turns out that even using code libraries isn't the best way to animate a page. Many companies have already released products that can be used to create DHTML animation easily. Probably the most popular of these is Macromedia's Dreamweaver, shown in Figure 14-5.

Dreamweaver can generate the JavaScript to make your animation run with little fuss and is even good at rollover buttons. Unless you plan to learn to program, using a tool is a good idea.

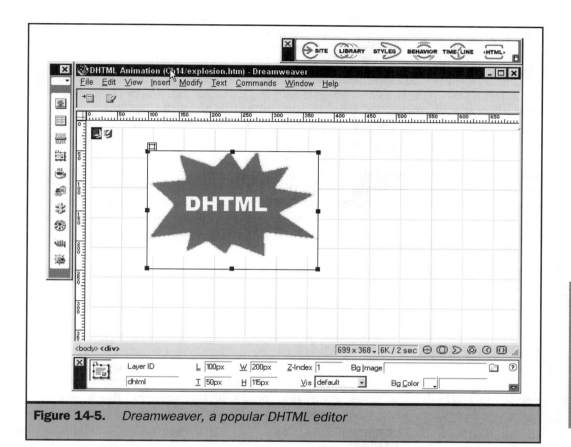

Figure 14-5.   *Dreamweaver, a popular DHTML editor*

Ramifications of DHTML

DHTML raises the requirements for Web developers significantly. First, to use DHTML, you need to make sure your pages are coded properly in HTML. Since you have been reading this book, you have a huge head start, because you have been quoting attributes, naming elements, and generating your HTML in a structured fashion. Second, you need to understand style sheets. This isn't terribly difficult either. Third, you need to understand JavaScript very well. JavaScript isn't a difficult language; but when all is said and done, those who know fundamental programming produce much better code than those who learn programming for the first time with

JavaScript. It is sad to see just how many Web scripts don't exhibit fundamental coding techniques, such as variable hiding, modularity, and even simple commenting and logical variable naming. It's no wonder script code breaks all the time. Finally, you need to understand the Document Object Model. This isn't difficult either, particularly if you think about HTML in a structured manner. If you consider all of the things you need to know to create a DHTML page, you realize that creating a DHTML page is much more complicated than creating a static HTML page. With DHTML, we have definitely moved from a page paradigm to a program paradigm, and with that comes new complications. For example, testing becomes paramount. You can't assume your page is correct just because it looks correct; the page has to be tested under numerous conditions, including displaying it under different browsers and other conditions. The bottom line is that DHTML changes Web design so that there is much more emphasis on JavaScript, and you need to be sure you understand this technology just as well as you understand HTML.

Summary

Script code can be used to modify elements within a page by accessing the Document Object Model (DOM), particularly when the HTML is well formed and named using the **ID** attribute. Modeling the document as a collection of objects has been done since Netscape 2; but under DHTML, modeling has been taken to a new extreme. Now browsers such as Internet Explorer 4 can be used to manipulate anything on a Web page from simple text elements, such as **<B>**, to style sheets, to even the very text of the page itself. DHTML shows where client-side computing is headed, but this power comes at a price. For the moment, the standard DOM as specified by the W3C isn't consistently supported by browser vendors, so defensive programming techniques and major amounts of testing are required when building script-filled Web pages. If the page designer takes proper steps, client scripting does not have to be relegated to simple embellishments. It should be considered the "glue" that is used to bind elements of a Web page together, including embedded binary objects.

The
Complete
Reference

Chapter 15

Client-Side
Programming and HTML

The last chapter discussed how scripting elements can be added to HTML pages. Scripts can manipulate a variety of form elements, and, in the case of Dynamic HTML, the page elements themselves. Scripts are also used to access embedded binary objects. As discussed in Chapter 9, embedded objects can be used to bring new media types, such as sounds and movies, to the Web. They can also be used to add small executable programs to a page. Binary objects come in many forms, including Netscape plug-ins, Java applets, and ActiveX controls. Each of these requires special HTML elements. In the future, all included media types will eventually be added with the **<OBJECT>** element. Until objects are standardized, however, it is useful to understand each individual technology and how it might intersect with HTML.

Scripting, Programming, and Objects

You might wonder why this chapter is separate from the last two. With both scripts and embedded objects, the interactivity takes place on the client side. What's the difference? Why distinguish between scripting and objects? Remember the point of Web client-side scripting—small bits of interpreted code used to add a bit of functionality to a page or fill the gaps in an application. Scripting is *not* necessarily as complex or general as programming, though it often seems like it is. Programming is more generalized than scripting; programming enables you to create just about anything that you can imagine, though it tends to be more complex in some sense than scripting. Think about checking the data fields of a form; you need only a few lines of code to make sure the fields are filled. Now consider trying to create something sophisticated, such as a Web-based, résumé-handling system that can sort through thousands of submissions a day. This takes more than a few lines of code, and should probably be programmed in a language such as Java, C/C++, or Visual Basic.

Scripting generally isn't powerful enough to build full applications, but it can be useful in tying things together. As you build your Web application, you may decide to build the logic entirely on the server, in the form of a Common Gateway Interface (CGI) program, or you may use a client-side technology (Java applets or ActiveX controls). If you choose a client-side technology, you'll probably build the Web pages with a combination of HTML, scripting, and embedded programming objects such as ActiveX controls, Netscape plug-ins, or Java applets. Building objects is not trivial. It can require significant knowledge of programming. You may be able to string together premade objects, generically called *components*, by using HTML and either JavaScript or VBScript. Consequently, for most casual Web page designers, putting together a custom object probably isn't necessary. This chapter discusses each of the object technologies, as well as how such objects can be inserted into a Web page.

Plug-Ins

Plug-ins were introduced by Netscape in Navigator 2 and above and supported by Internet Explorer 3. They address the communication and integration issues that plagued helper applications. *Plug-ins* are small helper programs (components) that run within the context of the browser itself. The plug-in approach of extending a browser's features has its drawbacks, however. Users must locate and download plug-ins, install them, and even restart their browsers. Many users find this rather complicated. Netscape 4 offers some installation relief with somewhat self-installing plug-ins and other features, but plug-ins remain troublesome. To further combat this problem, many of the most commonly requested plug-ins, such as Macromedia's Flash, are being included as a standard feature with Netscape browsers. However, even if installation were not such a problem, unfortunately, plug-ins are not available on every machine; an executable program, or *binary*, must be created for each particular operating system. Because of this machine-specific approach, many plug-ins only work on Windows 95 and NT. A decreasing number of plug-ins work on Windows 3.1, Macintosh, or UNIX. Finally, each plug-in installed on a system is a persistent extension to the browser, and takes up memory and disk space.

The benefit of plug-ins is that they can be well integrated into Web pages. They may be included by using the HTML elements **<EMBED>** or **<OBJECT>**. Typically, the **<EMBED>** syntax is used, but the **<OBJECT>** syntax is the preferred method and will eventually supplant **<EMBED>** completely. In general, the **<EMBED>** element takes an **SRC** attribute to specify the URL of the included binary object. **HEIGHT** and **WIDTH** attributes often are used to indicate the pixel dimensions of the included object, if it is visible. To embed a short Audio Video Interleaved (AVI) format movie called welcome.avi that can be viewed by the Netscape LiveVideo plug-in (generally installed with Netscape 3.*x*– and 4.*x*–generation browsers), use the following HTML fragment:

```
<EMBED SRC="welcome.avi" HEIGHT="100" WIDTH="100">
```

The **<EMBED>** element displays the plug-in (in this case a movie) as part of the HTML document in a rectangular area of the page (shown in Figure 15-1).

Although plug-ins can appear anywhere in a Web page, special limitations apply to plug-ins within a **<LAYER>** element. Plug-ins use the main window, and usually appear on top of all other content.

A browser may have many plug-ins installed. To check which plug-ins are installed in Netscape, the user may enter a strange URL, such as **about:plugins**, or look under the browser's Help menu for an entry that reads "About Plug-ins." The browser will show a list of plug-ins that are installed, the associated MIME type that will invoke each plug-in, and information as to whether that plug-in is enabled. Figure 15-2 shows an example of the plug-ins information page.

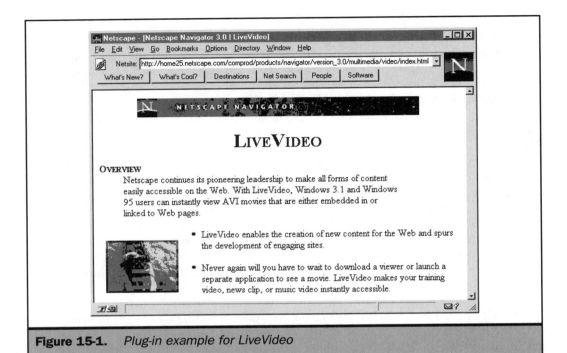

Figure 15-1. Plug-in example for LiveVideo

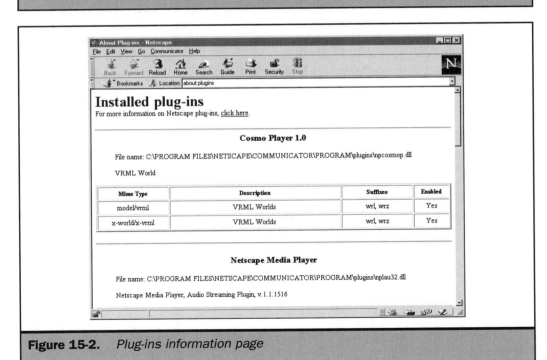

Figure 15-2. Plug-ins information page

<EMBED> Syntax

The primary way to load plug-ins for Netscape 2 and 3 and Internet Explorer 3 and is to use the HTML element **<EMBED>**, which is not part of the HTML 4.0 specification. It would be preferable to use the **<OBJECT>** element, which is part of the specification, but **<OBJECT>** works only under Internet Explorer 3 and above, and Netscape 4 and above. For backward compatibility, you may have to use both forms, as shown later in this chapter. The general syntax of the **<EMBED>** element can be found in the element reference in Appendix A.

The most important attribute for the **<EMBED>** element is probably **SRC**, which is set to the URL of the data object that is to be passed to the plug-in and embedded in the page. The browser generally determines the MIME type of the file—and thus the plug-in to pass the data to—by the filename suffix. For example, a file such as test1.dcr would be mapped to a MIME type of application/x-director and passed to a Shockwave for Director plug-in. In some cases, however, the plug-in to use with a particular **<EMBED>** tag is not obvious. The plug-in may not need to use an **SRC** attribute if it reads all of its data at run time or doesn't need any external data; if no **SRC** attribute exists, how do you determine the proper plug-in? The best way to indicate the plug-in is to use the **TYPE** attribute and set it to the MIME type, which then uses the appropriate plug-in. Don't use the **TYPE** attribute to override a MIME type or avoid using file extensions. In the following markup fragment, the file named mysteryfile has no filename suffix:

```
<EMBED SRC="mysteryfile" TYPE="application/x-director">
```

Although a **TYPE** attribute is used, this won't work, because the server will send the file with a content-type indication of plain/text or application/octet-stream, and the browser will attempt to handle it accordingly. Instead, the file should be named correctly. In general, you shouldn't need the **TYPE** attribute if the **SRC** attribute can be used to infer the type. The use of **TYPE** is mandatory if the **SRC** is not set.

Because plug-ins are rectangular, embedded objects, similar to images, the **<EMBED>** element has many of the same attributes as the **<IMG>** element:

- **ALIGN**   Use to align the object relative to the page and allow text to flow around the object. To achieve the desired text layout, you may have to use the **
** element with the **CLEAR** attribute.

- **HSPACE** and **VSPACE**   Use to set the buffer region, in pixels, between the embedded object and the surrounding text.

- **BORDER**   Use to set a border for the plug-in, in pixels. As with images, setting this attribute to zero may be useful when using the embedded object as a link.

- **HEIGHT** and **WIDTH**   Use to set the vertical and horizontal size of the embedded object, typically in pixels, although you may express them as percentage values. The **UNITS** attribute also can be used to define the unit of measurement for these attributes. **UNITS** has a pixel value, by default, but a value of **EN** can be used to indicate that half the point size should be used as the measurement unit. Values for **HEIGHT** and **WIDTH** should always be set, unless the **HIDDEN** attribute is used. Setting the **HIDDEN** attribute to **TRUE** in the **<EMBED>** element causes the plug-in to be hidden and overrides any **HEIGHT** and **WIDTH** settings, as well as any effect the object may have on layout.

Another interesting attribute for the **<EMBED>** element is **PALETTE**, which indicates the color palette for the plug-in to use. By default, the plug-in uses the background palette, but you can alternatively use the foreground color palette by setting the attribute to **FOREGROUND**. Setting this value properly may avoid the annoying color shifting that occurs under Windows environments with limited color support when switching between applications that use different color palettes.

Custom Plug-in Attributes

In addition to the standard attributes for the **<EMBED>** element, plug-ins may have custom attributes to communicate specialized information between the HTML page and the plug-in code. A movie-playing plug-in may have a **LOOP** attribute to indicate how many times to loop the movie. Remember that, under HTML, the browser ignores all nonstandard attributes when parsing the HTML. All other attributes are passed to the plug-in, allowing the plug-in to examine the list for any custom attributes that could modify its behavior. Enumerating all of the possible custom attributes isn't possible. Each particular plug-in used may have a variety of custom attributes. You should be certain to look at the documentation for whatever plug-in you are going to use.

Attributes for Installation of Plug-ins

Users often have a difficult time installing plug-ins. Under Netscape 2, plug-ins often had to be found and installed manually. Users could visit the Plug-in Plaza at Browserwatch (http://www.browserwatch.com), for example, and install the plug-ins that interested them. These plug-ins often came with installation scripts; a few required users to copy the plug-in manually to the appropriate directory. The directory, usually found in the same directory as the browser application itself, was named **plug-ins**. On the UNIX system, however, the directory could be set by using the environment variable NPX_PLUGIN_PATH, which defaulted to /usr/local/netscape/plugins, ~/netscape/plugins. This path could be different than where the browser application was installed.

Having users figure out for themselves which plug-in to install manually isn't the best solution. You can set the **PLUGINSPAGE** attribute equal to a URL that indicates the instructions for installing the plug-in. This way, if the browser encounters an **<EMBED>** element that it can't handle, it visits the specified page and provides information on how to download and install the plug-in. Starting with Netscape 4, however, this attribute automatically points to a special Netscape plug-in finder page.

The Netscape 4 browser release also simplifies the plug-in installation process by introducing the JAR Installation Manager (JIM), which is used to install Java Archive files (JARs). JAR files are a collection of files, including plug-ins, that can be automatically downloaded and installed. Set the **PLUGINURL** attribute for the **<EMBED>** element to the URL of a JAR file containing the plug-in that is needed. If the user doesn't have the appropriate plug-in already installed, the browser invokes JIM with the specified JAR file and begins the download and installation process. The user has control over this process. The downloaded objects may be signed—a type of authentication—to help users avoid downloading malicious code. Figure 15-3 shows a sample JIM window under Netscape 4.

In Netscape 4 and above, the **PLUGINURL** attribute takes precedence over **PLUGINSPAGE**. Using **PLUGINURL** rather than **PLUGINSPAGE** is recommended. If neither attribute is used, the Netscape browser defaults to a plug-in finder page. Although the JIM provides a great deal of help in dealing with plug-ins, it is very specific to Netscape. Microsoft's Internet Explorer does support the **<EMBED>** element, so any benefits of the JIM will not be experienced by Internet Explorer users.

<NOEMBED>

One important aspect of plug-ins is the idea of **<NOEMBED>**. Some browsers don't understand Netscape's plug-in architecture, or even the **<EMBED>** element. Rather than lock out these browsers from a Web page, the **<NOEMBED>** element enables

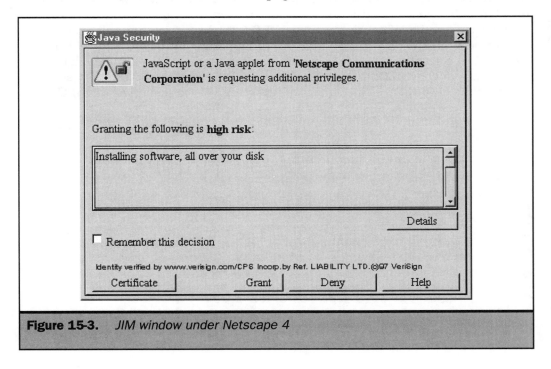

Figure 15-3.   *JIM window under Netscape 4*

you to provide some alternative text or marked-up content. In the following short example, an AVI video is embedded in the page. The **<NOEMBED>** element contains an image, which in turn has an alternative text reading set with the **ALT** attribute. Note how the example degrades from a very sophisticated setting all the way down to a text-only environment:

```
<EMBED SRC="welcome.avi" HEIGHT="100" WIDTH="100">
<NOEMBED>
   <IMG SRC="welcome.gif" ALT="Welcome to Big Company, Inc.">
</NOEMBED>
```

One potential problem with the **<NOEMBED>** approach occurs when a browser supports plug-ins but lacks the specific plug-in to deal with the included binary object. In this case, the user is presented with a broken puzzle-piece icon or a similar icon, and then is directed to a page to download the missing plug-in. You should set the **PLUGINURL** or **PLUGINSPAGE** attribute to start the user on the process of getting the plug-in needed to view the content.

<OBJECT> Syntax for Plug-Ins

Starting with Netscape 4, the **<OBJECT>** element can be used to include a variety of object types in a Web page, including Netscape plug-ins. Like the **<EMBED>** element, the **<OBJECT>** element's attributes determine the type of object to include, as well as the type and location of the plug-in. The **<OBJECT>** element supports alternative representations, if the browser isn't capable of supporting the object. The **<EMBED>** element that currently is used for plug-ins does not handle this well, although it does provide the **<NOEMBED>** syntax. The following is the syntax of **<OBJECT>** as it relates to the **<EMBED>** element (a more generalized discussion of the **<OBJECT>** element is presented in "ActiveX Controls," later in this chapter):

```
<OBJECT
     DATA="URL of Object's Data"
     ALIGN="LEFT | RIGHT | TOP | BOTTOM | MIDDLE"
     CODEBASE="URL"
     CLASSID="URL of plug-in to download"
     HEIGHT="pixels"
     ID="Unique Identifier"
     TYPE="MIME Type"
     WIDTH="pixels">

     Alternative HTML representation here

</OBJECT>
```

For the complete syntax of the **<OBJECT>** element, refer to the element reference in Appendix A.

The **DATA** attribute represents the URL of the object's data and is equivalent to the **SRC** attribute of **<EMBED>**. Like the **<EMBED>** element, the **TYPE** attribute represents the MIME type of the object's data. This may sometimes be inferred from the value of the **DATA** attribute. The **CODEBASE** attribute, which is similar to the **PLUGINSPAGE** attribute, represents the URL of the plug-in. The **CLASSID** attribute is used to specify the URL to use to install the plug-in, by using the JIM. If no **CLASSID** attribute is specified and the object can't be handled, the object is ignored, and any nested HTML is displayed. The **ID** attribute is used to set the name of the object for scripting. If the browser can't handle the type, or can't determine the type, it can't embed the object. Subsequent HTML is parsed as normal. The following is an example of using the LiveAudio plug-in under Netscape 4 with the **<OBJECT>** syntax:

```
<OBJECT DATA="click.wav" TYPE="audio/wav" HEIGHT="60" WIDTH="144"
    AUTOSTART="FALSE">
   <B>Sorry, no LiveAudio installed...</B>
</OBJECT>
```

Page authors should avoid referencing plug-ins with the **<OBJECT>** element, because compatibility issues with Microsoft Internet Explorer may arise.

Scripting and Plug-Ins

Plug-ins can be accessed from a scripting language. Each plug-in in a document can be referenced in Netscape's version of JavaScript as an element of the **embeds[ ]** collection, which is part of the document object. The **NAME** attribute should be set to a unique identifier, so that the plug-in can be accessed easily by name from a scripting language. Internet Explorer and Netscape 4 prefer the use of the **ID** attribute; the plug-in may not work well with the **NAME** attribute. For backward compatibility with Netscape 3.x–generation browsers, the **NAME** attribute should be used whenever possible. An example of how a plug-in is named is shown here:

```
<EMBED SRC="welcome.avi" NAME="WelcomeMovie" HEIGHT="100"
    WIDTH="100">
```

This example gives the LiveVideo plug-in the name WelcomeMovie. After the plug-in is named, it can be accessed from JavaScript as **document.WelcomeMovie**. If it is the second plug-in on the page, it could also be referenced as **document.embeds[1]**. Why not **document.embeds[2]**? Ordered arrays in JavaScript start numbering at zero; so **document.embeds[0]** references the first plug-in, **document.embeds[1]** references the second plug-in, and so on.

Under Netscape 3 and 4 and Internet Explorer 4, you can determine which plug-ins are available in the browser by using the **plugins[]** collection, which is part of the navigator object in JavaScript. The following markup displays the plug-ins that are installed in a Netscape browser:

```
<HTML>
<HEAD>
<TITLE>Print Plug-ins</TITLE>
</HEAD>

<BODY>
<H2 ALIGN="CENTER">Plug-ins Installed</H2>
<HR>

<SCRIPT LANGUAGE="JavaScript">
if (navigator.appName == "Microsoft Internet Explorer")
 document.write("Plug-ins[] collection not supported under IE");
else
 {
   num_plugins = navigator.plugins.length;
   for (count=0; count < num_plugins; count++)
   document.write(navigator.plugins[count].name + "<BR>");
 }
</SCRIPT>
</BODY>
</HTML>
```

Note that this example will not display the plug-ins under Internet Explorer, because that browser doesn't support the same **plugins[]** collection. Under Netscape, however, you can use some simple if-then logic to determine which HTML to use if a particular plug-in is loaded in the browser.

After you name an occurrence of a plug-in in a page, you may be able to manipulate the plug-in's actions even after you load the page. Netscape browsers, starting with the 3.x generation, include a technology called *LiveConnect* that enables JavaScript to communicate with Java applets and plug-ins. However, only those plug-ins written to support LiveConnect can be manipulated by using LiveConnect. Netscape's LiveAudio, as presented in Chapter 9, does support LiveConnect. Using LiveAudio in conjunction with LiveConnect, audio-enhanced buttons can be created. The next simple example shows how the link could play a short sound when the mouse passes over it. This example could easily be extended to create animated buttons with synchronized sounds by using LiveConnect.

```
<HTML>
<HEAD>
<TITLE>Audio Link</TITLE>
</HEAD>

<BODY>
  <EMBED SRC="click.wav" HIDDEN="TRUE" AUTOSTART="FALSE">
  <A HREF="http://www.yahoo.com"
     onmouseover="document.embeds[0].play(false)">Yahoo!</A>
</BODY>
</HTML>
```

Note   *The preceding example is very specific to Netscape. The implementation of LiveConnect is buggy and may not work under all versions of Navigator.*

Tying together plug-ins by using a scripting language in conjunction with LiveConnect hints at the power of such component models as Netscape's plug-ins. However, Netscape plug-ins are often passed over in favor of Java or ActiveX for general programming tasks, and plug-ins are often regulated to handling new media forms.

Java Applets

Sun Microsystems' Java technology (http://www.javasoft.com) is an attractive, revolutionary approach to cross-platform, Internet-based development. Java promises a platform-neutral development language that allows programs to be written once and deployed on any machine, browser, or operating system that supports the Java virtual machine (JVM). Java uses small Java programs, called *applets*, that were first introduced by Sun's HotJava browser. Also used by Netscape, Microsoft, and others, applets are downloaded and run directly within a browser to provide new functionality.

Applets are written in the Java language and compiled to a machine-independent byte code, which is downloaded automatically to the Java-capable browser and run within the browser environment. But even with a fast processor, the end system may appear to run the byte code slowly compared to a natively compiled application, because the byte code must be interpreted by the JVM. Even with recent Just-In-Time (JIT) compilers in newer browsers, Java often doesn't deliver performance equal to natively compiled applications. Even if compilation weren't an issue, current Java applets generally aren't persistent; they may have to be downloaded again in the future. Java-enabled browsers act like thin-client applications, because they add code only when they need it. In this sense, the browser doesn't become bloated with added features, but expands and contracts upon use.

Security in Java has been a serious concern from the outset. Because programs are downloaded and run automatically, a malicious program could be downloaded and run without the user being able to stop it. Under the first implementation of the technology, Java applets had little access to resources outside the browser's environment. Within Web pages, applets can't write to local disks or perform other harmful functions. This framework has been referred to as the *Java sandbox.* Developers who want to provide Java functions outside of the sandbox must write Java applications, which run as separate applications from browsers. Other Internet programming technologies (plug-ins and ActiveX) provide little or no safety from damaging programs.

Oddly, Java developers often want to add just these types of insecure features, as well as such powerful features as persistence and interobject communication. In fact, under new browsers, extended access can be requested for signed Java applets. (A *signed applet* enables users to determine who authored its code and to accept or reject the applet accordingly.) Java applets can securely request limited disk access, limited disk access and network usage, limited disk read access and unlimited disk write access, and unrestricted access. Users downloading an applet that is requesting any enhanced privileges are presented with a dialog box that outlines the requested access and presents the applet's credentials in the form of its digital signature. The user can then approve or reject the applet's request. If the user doesn't approve the request, the applet may continue to run, but it can't perform the denied actions.

Java looks very much like C++. The following code fragment shows a simple example of a Java applet:

```
import java.applet.Applet;
import java.awt.Graphics;

public class helloworld extends Applet {

    public void paint(Graphics g)
    {
        g.drawString("Hello World", 50, 25);
    }

}
```

Sending this code through a Java compiler (such as JavaSoft's javac) should produce a class file called helloworld.class, which can be used on a Web page to display the phrase "Hello World." You can use the **<APPLET>** element to add a Java applet to a Web page. As with the **<EMBED>** element, you must indicate the object to add. In this case, use the **CODE** attribute to indicate the URL of the Java class file to load. Because this is an included object, the **HEIGHT** and **WIDTH** attributes should also be set. The following example includes the HelloWorld applet in a Web page. Figure 15-4 shows the rendering of the Java example under Netscape 4 with Java turned on. Figure 15-5 shows the same example rendered with Java turned off.

```
<HTML>
<HEAD>
<TITLE>Java Hello World</TITLE>
</HEAD>

<BODY>
<H1 ALIGN="CENTER">Java Applet Demo</H1>
<HR>

<APPLET CODE="helloworld.class"
        HEIGHT="50"
        WIDTH="175">
<H1>Hello World for you non-Java-aware browsers</H1>
</APPLET>
</BODY>
</HTML>
```

In the preceding code example, between **<APPLET>** and **</APPLET>** is an alternative rendering for browsers that don't support Java or the **<APPLET>** element, or that have Java support disabled.

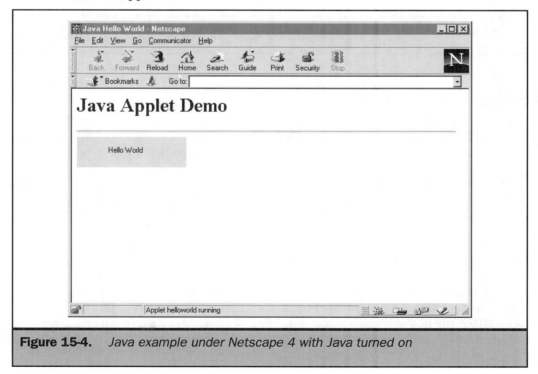

Figure 15-4.   *Java example under Netscape 4 with Java turned on*

Figure 15-5.   *Java example under Netscape 4 with Java turned off*

`<APPLET>` Syntax

Because Java applets are included objects, just like Netscape plug-ins, the syntax for the `<APPLET>` element is similar to the `<EMBED>` element, particularly for things such as alignment and sizing. The general syntax for `<APPLET>` is shown in the element reference in Appendix A.

The most important attribute for the `<APPLET>` element is probably **CODE**, which is set to the URL of the Java class to load into the page. The **CODEBASE** attribute can be set to the URL of the directory that contains the Java classes; otherwise, the current document's URL is used for any relative URLs.

Because Java applets are rectangular, embedded objects (similar to images or plug-ins), the `<APPLET>` element has many of the same attributes as images and plug-ins, including **ALIGN**, **HEIGHT**, **WIDTH**, **HSPACE**, and **VSPACE**.

The **ARCHIVE** attribute can be used to include many classes into a single archive file, which can then be downloaded to the local disk. The file specified by the **ARCHIVE** attribute may be a compressed PKZIP file (.zip) or a Java Archive (.jar), which can be made with a JAR packaging utility. For example,

```
<APPLET ARCHIVE="bunchofclasses.zip"
        CODE="sampleApp.class"
        WIDTH="560"
        HEIGHT="270">
</APPLET>
```

downloads all the classes in bunchofclasses.zip. After the file is downloaded, the **CODE** attribute is examined and the archive is checked to see whether sampleApp.class exists there. If not, it is fetched from the network. Due to the expense of downloading many class files by using HTTP, ideally you should attempt to archive all potentially used classes and send them simultaneously. You may also derive some caching benefit by using the **ARCHIVE** attribute, because it keeps class files in the user's cache or a temporary directory. According to the HTML 4.0 specification, the **ARCHIVE** attribute may take a comma-separated list of archive files. So far, however, no browsers support more than one archive file per **<APPLET>** occurrence. The **ARCHIVE** attribute is currently only supported by Netscape 3 and above.

Passing Data to Java Applets

Unlike plug-ins, Java applets don't use special attributes to pass data. Instead, they use a different element called **<PARAM>**, which is enclosed within the **<APPLET>** element as the way to pass in information. You could extend the HelloWorld applet to allow the message output to be modified by using **<PARAM>** elements to pass in a message, as shown here:

```
<APPLET CODE="helloworld.class"
        WIDTH="50"
        HEIGHT="175">
<PARAM NAME="Message" VALUE="Hello World in Java!">
<H1>Hello World for you non-Java-aware browsers</H1>
</APPLET>
```

The following is the HTML 4 syntax for **<PARAM>**; it is the same for Java applets and ActiveX controls:

```
<PARAM
    NAME="Object property name"
    VALUE="Value to pass in with object name"
    VALUETYPE="DATA | REF | OBJECT"
    TYPE="MIME Type"
    ID="document-wide unique id">

</PARAM>
```

The **NAME** attribute for **<PARAM>** is used to specify the name of the object property that is being set; in the previous example, the name is Message. If you are using a premade Java applet, the various property names should be specified in the documentation for the applet. The actual value to be assigned to the property is set by the **VALUE** attribute. The **VALUETYPE** attribute specifies the meaning of the **VALUE** attribute. The data passed to an attribute typically takes the form of a string. Setting the **VALUETYPE** attribute to **DATA** results in the default action. Setting **VALUETYPE** to **REF** indicates that the data assigned to the **VALUE** attribute is a URL that references an external file to load for the attribute. The last value for **VALUETYPE** is **OBJECT**, which indicates that **VALUE** is set to the name of an applet or object located somewhere else within the document. The data in the applet or object can be referenced to allow objects to "talk" to each other.

The **<PARAM>** elements for a particular Java applet occur within the **<APPLET>** tag; a Java applet may have many **<PARAM>** elements. The **<APPLET>** element may also enclose regular HTML markup that provides an alternative rendering for non-Java-capable browsers. When alternative content is found within the **<APPLET>** element, the **<PARAM>** elements should be placed before the other content. Note that you also can set the **ALT** attribute for the **<APPLET>** element, to provide a short description. Authors should use the text contained within the element as the alternative text, and not the **ALT** attribute.

Java and Scripting

Java applets may control scripts in a Web page. Inclusion of the **MAYSCRIPT** attribute in the **<APPLET>** element permits the applet to access JavaScript. When dealing with applets retrieved from other sources, you can use the **MAYSCRIPT** attribute to prevent the applet from accessing JavaScript without the user's knowledge. If an applet attempts to access JavaScript when this attribute has not been specified, a run-time exception should occur.

Probably more interesting for page designers is the fact that scripts can control, or even modify, Java applets that are embedded in a page. For the applet to be accessed, it should be named by using the **NAME** attribute for the **<APPLET>** element. Microsoft also supports the **ID** attribute, which has the same functionality as **NAME**. For compatibility purposes, **NAME** should be used.

Providing a unique name for the applet allows scripts to access the applet and its public interfaces. The name can also be used by other applets to allow the applets to communicate with each other. JavaScript in Netscape 3 and above, as well as in Internet Explorer 4 and above, allows access to the applets in a page via the **applets[]** collection, which is a property of the document object. When an applet is named, it can be accessed via JavaScript as **document.***appletname* (**document.myApplet**) or **document.applets["myApplet"]**. If the Java applet has public properties exposed, they can be modified from a script in a Web page. The following simple Java code takes the

Hello World example from earlier in the chapter and expands it with a **setMessage** method, which can be used to change the message displayed in the applet:

```
import java.applet.Applet;
import java.awt.Graphics;
public class newhelloworld extends Applet {

    String theMessage;

    public void init()
      {
        theMessage = new String("Hello World");
      }
    public void paint(Graphics g)
      {
        g.drawString(theMessage, 50, 25);
      }
    public void setMessage(String message)
      {
        theMessage = message;
        repaint();
      }
}
```

If this Java code is compiled into a class file, it can be included in a Web page and accessed via JavaScript, as shown next. The following example markup shows how a form could be used to collect data from the user and update the applet in real time:

```
<HTML>
<HEAD>
<TITLE>LiveConnect Java Hello World</TITLE>
</HEAD>

<BODY>
<H1 ALIGN="CENTER">LiveConnect Java Applet Demo</H1>
<HR>

<APPLET CODE="newhelloworld.class"
        NAME="NewHello"
        HEIGHT="50"
        WIDTH="175">
```

```
<H1>Hello World for you non-Java-aware browsers</H1>
</APPLET>

<FORM NAME="TestForm">

<INPUT TYPE="TEXT" SIZE="15" MAXLENGTH="15" NAME="NewMessage">
<INPUT TYPE="BUTTON" VALUE="Set Message"
        onclick="document.NewHello.setMessage(NewMessage.value)">
</BODY>
</HTML>
```

Netscape initially called this technology LiveConnect. Using this technology is similar to how you may communicate with plug-ins embedded in a Web page. Microsoft also supports the same form of applet access under Internet Explorer, so it is unclear whether LiveConnect will continue to be the name used to describe using JavaScript to communicate with Java applets. The bottom line is that this technology is not unique to Netscape.

<OBJECT> Syntax for Java Applets

The HTML 4.0 specification indicates that the **<APPLET>** element has been deprecated and that **<OBJECT>** should be used instead. Although this may be the decree, using **<OBJECT>** for Java applets has some serious problems. The following is the most basic HTML 4 syntax for inserting an object, such as a Java applet:

```
<OBJECT
    CLASSID="URL of Object to include"
    HEIGHT="pixels"
    WIDTH="pixels">

    Parameters and alternative text

</OBJECT>
```

For the complete **<OBJECT>** syntax, see the element reference in Appendix A.

Notice that the **CLASSID** attribute is used to specify the URL of the object to include. In the case of Java applets, you should use **java:**. For ActiveX controls, use **clsid:**. To rewrite a simple Java example, use the following code:

```
<OBJECT CLASSID="java:Blink.class" WIDTH="300" HEIGHT="100">
<PARAM NAME="LBL" VALUE="Java, is, fun, exciting, and new.">
<PARAM NAME="SPEED" VALUE="2">
This will display in non-Java-aware or non-Java-enabled browsers.
</OBJECT>
```

Because of the fragmentation of the Java community, JavaSoft has made some attempts to bring together the syntax of Java applets via a Java plug-in. The syntax for this plug-in under Netscape and Internet Explorer includes both **<OBJECT>** and **<EMBED>** forms. Readers interested in this syntax for applet inclusion are directed straight to JavaSoft for the latest syntax (http://www.javasoft.com), because the syntax is changing quite rapidly.

Using Java Without Programming

The broad functionality of Java can cost both time and money. Java programming assumes that you have a familiarity with an advanced programming language as well as object-oriented design. Web professionals lacking programming skills or budgets can find many free, premade applets available for reuse or sale at directories such as Gamelan (http://www.gamelan.com). Commercial vendors actively sell a variety of premade Java applets, as well as Java components called *JavaBeans*, which can be used to create powerful Web applications.

JavaBeans is a portable, platform-independent component model written in Java. Like other components, such as ActiveX controls, JavaBeans components (called *Beans* for short) are reusable software components that can be strung together to form complex applications. In one sense, Beans are just a special form of applet that are written in such a manner that tools can inspect and manipulate the Beans and the Beans can intercommunicate in a predictable manner. Beans generally are self-contained and persistent. You can analogize components such as Beans as bricks that form larger structures, like buildings. Tools such as Netscape's Visual JavaScript (see Figure 15-6) already provide some basic drag-and-drop programming capabilities by tying together JavaBeans components with JavaScript code.

While Java provides a relatively secure and powerful cross-platform development environment, it does so at the expense of speed and local operating system integration. Because of this, many Web developers, particularly those building intranet applications, have explored using ActiveX controls as Web page components.

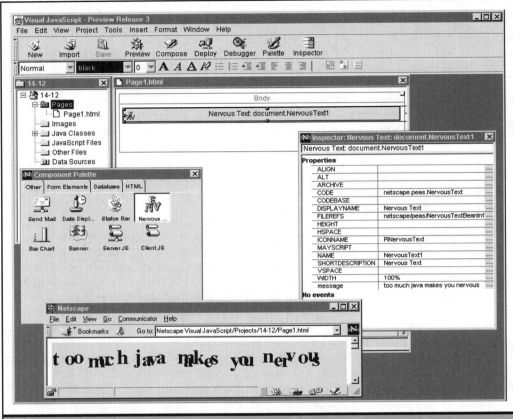

Figure 15-6.   *Netscape's Visual JavaScript uses Beans*

ActiveX Controls

ActiveX (http://www.microsoft.com/activex), which is the Internet portion of the Component Object Model (COM), is Microsoft's component technology for creating small components, or *controls*, within a Web page. ActiveX is intended for distributing these controls via the Internet in order to add new functionality to browsers such as Internet Explorer. Microsoft maintains that ActiveX controls are more similar to generalized components than they are to plug-ins, because ActiveX controls can reside beyond the browser, within container programs such as Microsoft Office. ActiveX controls are similar to Netscape plug-ins insofar as they are persistent and machine-specific. Although this makes resource use a problem, installation is not an issue: the components download and install automatically.

Security is a big concern for ActiveX controls. Because these small pieces of code could potentially have full access to a user's system, they could cause serious damage. This capability, combined with automatic installation, creates a serious problem with ActiveX. End users may be quick to click a button to install new functionality, only to accidentally get their hard drives erased. This unlimited functionality of ActiveX controls creates a gaping security hole. To address this problem, Microsoft provides authentication information to indicate who wrote a control, in the form of code signed by a certificate, as shown in Figure 15-7.

Certificates only provide some indication that the control creator is reputable; they do nothing to prevent a control from actually doing something malicious. Safe Web browsing should be practiced by accepting controls only from reputable sources.

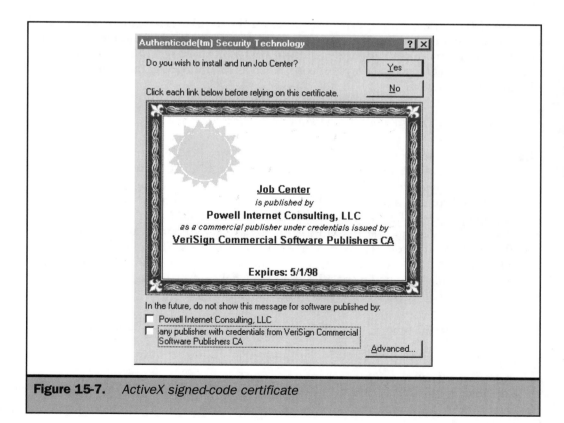

Figure 15-7.   *ActiveX signed-code certificate*

Adding Controls to Web Pages

Adding an ActiveX control to a Web page requires the use of the **<OBJECT>** element. The basic form of the **<OBJECT>** element for an ActiveX control is as follows:

```
<OBJECT
     CLASSID="CLSID:class-identifier"
     HEIGHT="pixels"
     WIDTH="pixels"
     ID="unique identifier>"

     Parameters and alternative text rendering

</OBJECT>
```

CLASSID is the most important attribute for the **<OBJECT>** element when you insert ActiveX controls. The value of **CLASSID** identifies the object to include. Each ActiveX control has a class identifier of the form CLSID:*class-identifier*, where the value for *class-identifier* is a complex string, such as the following, that uniquely identifies the control:

```
99B42120-6EC7-11CF-A6C7-00AA00A47DD2
```

This string is the identifier for the ActiveX label control.

The other important attributes for the basic form of **<OBJECT>** when used with ActiveX controls include **HEIGHT** and **WIDTH,** which are set to the pixel dimensions of the included control, and **ID**, which associates a unique identifier with the control for scripting purposes. Between the **<OBJECT>** and **</OBJECT>** tags are various **<PARAM>** elements that specify information to pass to the control, and alternative HTML markup that displays in non-ActiveX-aware browsers. The following is a complete example that uses the **<OBJECT>** element to insert an ActiveX control into a Web page. The markup shown specifies a simple label control. Figure 15-8 shows the rendering of the control under Internet Explorer 4 and Netscape 4.

```
<!DOCTYPE HTML PUBLIC "-//W3C//DTD HTML 4.0 Transitional//EN">
<HTML>
<HEAD>
<TITLE>ActiveX Label Test</TITLE>
</HEAD>

<BODY>
<H1 ALIGN="CENTER">ActiveX Demo</H1>
<HR>
```

```
<OBJECT CLASSID="CLSID:99B42120-6EC7-11CF-A6C7-00AA00A47DD2"
        ID="IeLabel1" HEIGHT="65" WIDTH="325">
   <PARAM NAME="_ExtentX" VALUE="6879">
   <PARAM NAME="_ExtentY" VALUE="1376">
   <PARAM NAME="Caption" VALUE="Hello World">
   <PARAM NAME="Alignment" VALUE="4">
   <PARAM NAME="Mode" VALUE="1">
   <PARAM NAME="ForeColor" VALUE="#FF0000">
   <PARAM NAME="FontName" VALUE="Arial">
   <PARAM NAME="FontSize" VALUE="36">
   <B>Hello World for you non-ActiveX users!</B>
</OBJECT>
</BODY>
</HTML>
```

After you look at the ActiveX Label Test code in Figure 15-8, you may have questions about how to determine the **CLASSID** value for the control and the associated **<PARAM>** values that can be set. However, providing a chart for all of the controls and their associated identifiers isn't necessary. Many Web page tools, including Microsoft Control Pad (http://www.microsoft.com/workshop/misc/cpad),

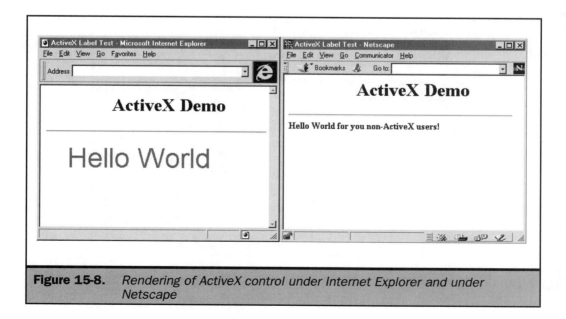

Figure 15-8.   *Rendering of ActiveX control under Internet Explorer and under Netscape*

support the automated insertion of controls into a page, as well as configuration of the various control properties. Figure 15-9 shows an example of the Control Pad and the configuration of controls.

Installing ActiveX Controls

As mentioned earlier, the most important attribute in the **<OBJECT>** syntax is probably **CLASSID**, which is used to identify the particular object to include. For example, the syntax CLSID:*class-identifier* is for registered ActiveX controls. Generally, however, when the **<OBJECT>** element supports other included items well, **CLASSID** might be set to other forms, such as **java:Blink.class**, as shown earlier in the chapter in the section "<OBJECT> Syntax for Java Applets." Microsoft also allows the use of the **CODE** attribute for the **<OBJECT>** element. **CODE** is used to set the URL of the Java class file to include.

ActiveX and plug-ins are similar in the sense that both are persistent, platform-specific components. ActiveX controls, however, are easy to download and install. This

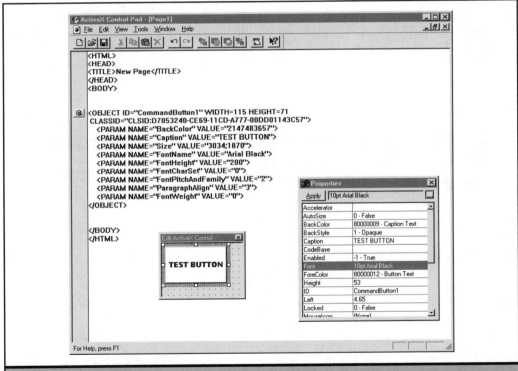

Figure 15-9. *Using Control Pad to insert and configure ActiveX controls*

installation, or running of ActiveX controls, can be described as a series of steps, as follows:

1. The browser loads an HTML page that references an ActiveX control with the **<OBJECT>** element and its associated **CLASSID** attribute.

2. The browser checks the system registry to see whether the control specified by the **CLASSID** value is installed; this control takes the following form: CLSID:*some-id-number*.

3. If the control is installed, the browser compares the **CODEBASE** version attribute stored in the registry against the **CODEBASE** version attribute in the HTML page. If a newer version is specified in the page, a newer control is needed.

4. If the control is not installed, the value of the **CODEBASE** attribute is used to determine the location of the control to download. The **CODETYPE** attribute might also be used to set the MIME type of the object to download. Most inclusions of ActiveX controls avoid this, because it tends to default to the MIME type application/octet-stream.

For security reasons, the browser checks to see whether the code is signed, before the download and installation begins. If the code is not signed, the user is warned. If the code is signed, the user is presented with an Authenticode certificate bearing the identity of the author of the control. Based on these criteria, the user can allow or deny the installation of the control on his or her system. If the user accepts the control, it is automatically downloaded, installed, and invoked in the page for its specific function. Finally, the control is stored persistently on the client machine for further invocation. This process may be avoided when the **DECLARE** attribute is present. The **DELCARE** attribute is used to indicate whether the **<OBJECT>** is being defined only and not actually instantiated until later **<OBJECT>** occurrences, which will start the installation process.

Note *The W3C HTML 4.0 specification also indicates use of the **STANDBY** attribute, which can be used to specify a message to display as the object is being downloaded. This is not currently supported by any browsers.*

Passing Data to ActiveX Controls

Like Java applets, ActiveX controls do not use special attributes to pass data. Instead, they use a different element, called **<PARAM>**, which is enclosed within the **<OBJECT>** element. You can pass parameters to the label control by using the **<PARAM>** elements, as shown here:

```
<OBJECT CLASSID="CLSID:99B42120-6EC7-11CF-A6C7-00AA00A47DD2"
        ID="IeLabel1" HEIGHT="65" WIDTH="325">
  <PARAM NAME="Caption" VALUE="Hello World">
```

```
<PARAM NAME="FontName" VALUE="Arial">
<PARAM NAME="FontSize" VALUE="36">
<B>Hello World for you non-ActiveX users!</B>
</OBJECT>
```

In this case, the **Caption** parameter is set to Hello World, the **FontName** parameter is set to Arial, and the **FontSize** parameter is set to 36 points. Recall the HTML 4 syntax for **<PARAM>** (shown earlier in this chapter in the section "Passing Data to Java Applets"), which is the same for Java applets and ActiveX controls.

The meaning of these attributes is provided in the section "Java Applets," earlier in this chapter, as well as in Appendix A. Microsoft has introduced a few changes for data binding. Internet Explorer 4 and above supports the ability to bind data dynamically from a database or text file. With data binding, the parameters for an ActiveX control can be set by using an external file or database entry. The attributes that provide this functionality include

- **DATAFLD** Sets the column name to use for the **<PARAM>** element
- **DATASRC** Bound to the identifier, which indicates the data to bind to
- **DATAFORMATS** Set to either **HTML** or **TEXT**, indicating whether the bound data is HTML or plain text

For more information on how to use data binding, see the Microsoft SiteBuilder Network (http://www.microsoft.com/sitebuilder).

Another way to pass data to ActiveX controls or other embedded objects is by using the **DATA** attribute, which should be set to a URL that references a data file to load. The type of this data may be determined by the file suffix. The **TYPE** attribute also can be used to explicitly declare the MIME type for the data to use.

Using ActiveX Without Programming

Developers can access an abundance of available controls for various purposes. Many repositories of free and commercial ActiveX controls are available on the Web, such as ActiveX.com (http://www.activex.com). Microsoft already includes a variety of controls built in to Internet Explorer; these include various form-like elements, a timer, a preloader control that allows pages and objects to be prefetched, and many others. Microsoft also promotes controls for multimedia, such as ActiveMovie and Netshow, and controls for database access, such as ActiveX Data Objects (ADO), Remote Data Services (RDS), and Tabular Data Control (TDC). Microsoft even provides a control called the *Agent control*, which can be used to add to a Web page an animated agent that the user can interact with (shown in Figure 15-10).

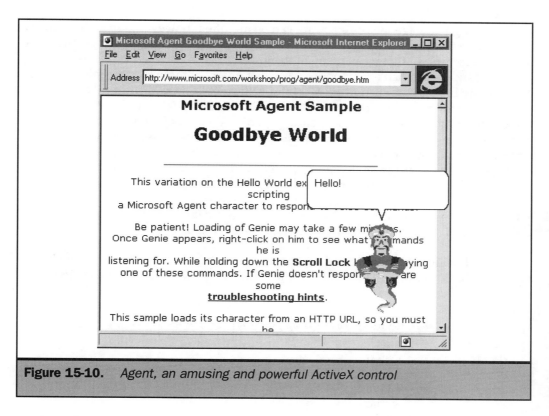

Figure 15-10.   *Agent, an amusing and powerful ActiveX control*

As with Java applets, page designers can use prebuilt controls for most functions. Many Web page development tools (such as Microsoft Control Pad) provide an easy way to string together ActiveX controls.

Page designers can also write their own ActiveX controls, though in some cases this may be like reinventing the wheel. Controls can be created by using a variety of languages, such as Visual Basic, C++, and Java. You can also convert existing Windows programs to controls. The ActiveX model is not limited to client-side controls. It is part of a larger framework known as the *Active Platform,* with server-side and distributed aspects. Although a discussion of the Active Platform is beyond the scope of this book, one of its important aspects is that client-side controls expose their interfaces through the Component Object Model, which can be accessed and controlled easily through scripting languages.

ActiveX Controls and Scripting

As with Java applets, you can control ActiveX controls by using a scripting language, such as JavaScript or VBScript. One advantage of ActiveX controls is that many premade controls with exposed properties are available that can be easily manipulated by a scripting language. Before a control can be modified, however, it must be named, by using the **ID** attribute. After it is named, scripting code for a particular event can be set for the control, so that it can respond to events. As discussed in the last chapter, Microsoft supports a rich event model. However, many of these events (noted with an asterisk) are beyond the current HTML 4.0 specification. The **<OBJECT>** element supports the following events: **onafterupdate***, **onbeforeupdate***, **onblur***, **onclick**, **ondblclick**, **ondragstart***, **onfocus***, **onhelp***, **onkeydown**, **onkeypress**, **onkeyup**, **onmousedown**, **onmousemove**, **onmouseout**, **onmouseover**, **onmouseup**, **onreadystatechange***, **onresize***, **onrowenter***, **onrowexit***, and **onselectstart***. However, these events generally aren't used directly with JavaScript as attributes to the **<OBJECT>** element. VBScript access may be more appropriate.

> **Note**
> *The events designated with an asterisk are defined for Internet Explorer and were not part of the W3C HTML 4.0 standard at the time of this writing.*

The following example, created with the Control Pad, shows how two ActiveX command buttons can be used to communicate with a label control to change its message:

```
<!DOCTYPE HTML PUBLIC "-//W3C//DTD HTML 4.0 Transitional//EN">
<HTML>
<HEAD>
<TITLE>ActiveX Scripting Demo</TITLE>
<SCRIPT LANGUAGE="VBScript">
<!--
    Sub CommandButton1_Click()
        Label1.Caption = "I've been clicked!"
    end sub

    Sub CommandButton2_Click()
        Label1.Caption = "Not Set"
    end sub
-->
</SCRIPT>
</HEAD>


<BODY>
<H1 ALIGN="CENTER">ActiveX Scripting</H1>
<HR>
<B>Label:</B>

<OBJECT CLASSID="CLSID:978C9E23-D4B0-11CE-BF2D-00AA003F40D0"
        ALIGN="TOP" ID="Label1" HEIGHT="80" WIDTH="200">
```

```
    <PARAM NAME="BackColor" VALUE="8454143">
    <PARAM NAME="Caption" VALUE="Not set">
    <PARAM NAME="Size" VALUE="4233;1212">
    <PARAM NAME="BorderColor" VALUE="8421504">
    <PARAM NAME="BorderStyle" VALUE="1">
    <PARAM NAME="FontHeight" VALUE="200">
    <PARAM NAME="FontCharSet" VALUE="0">
    <PARAM NAME="FontPitchAndFamily" VALUE="2">
    <PARAM NAME="ParagraphAlign" VALUE="3">
</OBJECT>
<HR>

<OBJECT ALIGN="TOP" ID="CommandButton1" WIDTH="168" HEIGHT="52"
        CLASSID="CLSID:D7053240-CE69-11CD-A777-00DD01143C57">
    <PARAM NAME="ForeColor" VALUE="65535">
    <PARAM NAME="BackColor" VALUE="10485760">
    <PARAM NAME="Caption" VALUE="Update Label">
    <PARAM NAME="Size" VALUE="3577;1101">
    <PARAM NAME="FontHeight" VALUE="200">
    <PARAM NAME="FontCharSet" VALUE="0">
    <PARAM NAME="FontPitchAndFamily" VALUE="2">
    <PARAM NAME="ParagraphAlign" VALUE="3">
</OBJECT>

<OBJECT ALIGN="TOP" ID="CommandButton2" WIDTH="168" HEIGHT="52"
        CLASSID="CLSID:D7053240-CE69-11CD-A777-00DD01143C57">
    <PARAM NAME="ForeColor" VALUE="65535">
    <PARAM NAME="BackColor" VALUE="10485760">
    <PARAM NAME="Caption" VALUE="Reset Label">
    <PARAM NAME="Size" VALUE="3577;1101">
    <PARAM NAME="FontHeight" VALUE="200">
    <PARAM NAME="FontCharSet" VALUE="0">
    <PARAM NAME="FontPitchAndFamily" VALUE="2">
    <PARAM NAME="ParagraphAlign" VALUE="3">
</OBJECT>
</BODY>
</HTML>
```

Note that the event handlers are written in VBScript. This file won't work in anything other than Internet Explorer 3 or above running on a Windows-based system. Although scripting is a simple but powerful tool for ActiveX controls, controls (as with plug-ins) tend to be too platform-specific to be used for external Web sites, unless pages are coded very carefully. On a Windows-centered intranet, however, the use of platform-dependent controls and VBScript might not be a problem.

Cross-Platform Support with Plug-Ins and ActiveX Controls

Although the whole point of Java applets is to deal with cross-platform compatibility issues, Microsoft ActiveX controls and Netscape plug-ins are extremely platform- and browser-dependent. However, you can provide limited support for both platforms. Netscape users interested in running ActiveX controls may want to look at the ScriptActive plug-in, available from Ncompass Labs (http://www.ncompasslabs.com). This plug-in provides general compatibility under Netscape for ActiveX controls, assuming the site using them pays attention to Ncompass conventions. The Ncompass approach is not terribly robust. A preferred method is to attempt to provide a plug-in solution in conjunction with an ActiveX solution. Consider the inclusion of Macromedia Flash media in a Web page. Internet Explorer prefers the Flash control, whereas Netscape prefers a Flash plug-in. Very old browsers or less common browsers may only be able to handle an animated GIF. All browsers can be accommodated with a little planning. For example, Macromedia's Aftershock tool (included with Flash) can generate HTML markup and JavaScript that can be used to handle all of the situations. A modified version of this tool's output for a Flash file called splashpage.swf is shown here:

```
<OBJECT classid="clsid:D27CDB6E-AE6D-11cf-96B8-444553540000"
        CODEBASE="http://active.macromedia.com/flash2/cabs/
                  swflash.cab#version=3,0,0,0"
        ID="splashpage" WIDTH="320" HEIGHT="240">
   <PARAM NAME="movie" VALUE="splashpage.swf">
   <PARAM NAME="quality" VALUE="autohigh">
   <PARAM NAME="bgcolor" VALUE="#FFFFFF">

<!-- Script code for non-ActiveX browsers like Netscape -->
<SCRIPT LANGUAGE="JavaScript">
<!--
   var ShockMode = 0;
   if (navigator.mimeTypes &&
       navigator.mimeTypes["application/x-shockwave-flash"] &&
       navigator.mimeTypes["application/x-shockwave-flash"].enabledPlugin)
   {
   if (navigator.plugins && navigator.plugins["Shockwave Flash"])
       ShockMode = 1;
   }
   if ( ShockMode )
```

```
      {
        document.write('<EMBED SRC="splashpage.swf"');
        document.write(' swLiveConnect="FALSE" WIDTH="320" HEIGHT="240"');
        document.write(' QUALITY="autohigh" BGCOLOR="#FFFFFF"');
        document.write(' TYPE="application/x-shockwave-flash"
                        PLUGINSPAGE="http://www.macromedia.com/
                                     shockwave/download/index.cgi?P1
                        Prod Version=ShockwaveFlash">');
        document.write('</EMBED>');
      }
      else
      if (!(navigator.appName && navigator.appName.indexOf("Netscape")>=0
          && navigator.appVersion.indexOf("2.")>=0)
        {
          document.write('<IMG SRC="splashpage.gif" WIDTH="320" HEIGHT="240"
                          BORDER="0">');
        }
//-->
</SCRIPT>

<NOEMBED>
   <IMG SRC="splashpage.gif" WIDTH="320" HEIGHT="240" BORDER="0">
</NOEMBED>

<NOSCRIPT>
   <IMG SRC="splashpage.gif" WIDTH="320" HEIGHT="240" BORDER="0">
</NOSCRIPT>
</OBJECT>
```

In this example, the browser should try to use an ActiveX control. If the browser can't handle the ActiveX control, it should go for a plug-in. As a last resort, if scripting is turned off, the plug-in isn't present, or the browser doesn't support plug-ins, the browser should end up with an animated GIF. Of course, the plug-in part of the example doesn't provide an accurate reference to a JAR file for automatic download of the plug-in, but it gets the point across. This code can be added by using the Macromedia Aftershock tool. Careful thought, combined with some server- or client-side scripting, should enable you to deal with the various browser conditions that may occur. Until the syntax for including objects is straightened out, this is the only reasonable approach to handling cross-browser issues, short of locking users out of a page or falling back to less interactive or less motivating technology.

The Future of <OBJECT>

According to the HTML 4.0 specification, **<OBJECT>** will be the main way to add any form of object to a Web page, whether it's an image, image map, sound, video, ActiveX control, Java applet, or anything else. This approach seems appropriate, but before rushing out to use **<OBJECT>**, understand the ramifications. Even though **<OBJECT>** can be used in some browsers, the syntax is not consistent. **<OBJECT>** is still mostly used to include ActiveX controls in a page. Other meanings are not fully supported, if at all. According to the HTML 4.0 specification, the **<OBJECT>** element can be used to include HTML from another file by using the **DATA** attribute. Any file included must not introduce elements that would ruin the syntax of the document. For example, including a file that already has a **<HEAD>** and **<BODY>** element may result in an ill-formed document with multiple **<HEAD>** and **<BODY>** elements. Imagine specifying a header file called header.htm with the contents shown here:

```
<H1 ALIGN="CENTER">Big Company, Inc.</H1>
<HR>
```

This file could then be included in a Web page by using the **<OBJECT>** element, like so:

```
<OBJECT DATA="header.htm">
Header not included
</OBJECT>
```

This example should pull in the contents of the file header.htm in browsers that support this feature and display "Header not included" in all others. No major browser appears to support this functionality for the **<OBJECT>** element, so this should be avoided in favor of technologies such as server-side includes (Chapter 12) and dynamic documents generated with JavaScript.

Eventually, the **<OBJECT>** element will be used in a generalized sense. For now, HTML page authors should use the **<APPLET>**, **<IMG>**, and **<EMBED>** elements to include binary forms beyond ActiveX controls in pages.

Summary

With the inclusion of programmed objects such as ActiveX controls, Java applets, and Netscape plug-ins, Web pages can become complex, living documents. Choosing the appropriate component technology is not very straightforward. Netscape plug-ins are very popular for including media elements such as Shockwave movies, video, or sound files, but they are platform-specific and somewhat specific to Netscape browsers.

Microsoft supports the **\<EMBED\>** element syntax to include plug-ins in a page, but the preferred solution in the Microsoft world is ActiveX controls. ActiveX controls are just as platform-specific as Netscape plug-ins and have some potential security issues. Solving the cross-platform problem requires complex page scripting or the use of Java applets that provide cross-platform object support, typically at the expense of performance. Either way, the page rendering should degrade gracefully if the user can't support the particular object technology. Eventually, the syntax for all included media will be handled with the **\<OBJECT\>** element; but, for now, **\<EMBED\>** and **\<APPLET\>** should be used within **\<OBJECT\>** to provide backward compatibility for including plug-ins and Java applets in a Web page.

The Complete Reference

Part IV

Site Delivery

Chapter 16

Putting It All Together:
Delivering the Web Site

595

So far, this book has said nothing about how to deliver Web pages. Even if developers master the creation of Web pages using HTML, they can still fall flat on their faces if they don't pay careful consideration to how they deliver the pages to the user. As far as the viewer of a page is concerned, the Web is one big system. If a page is slow because of a server, the user still views the site in a negative light no matter how compelling the content or inspiring the design. Ignoring such site delivery issues as outsourcing, Web server choice, and protocol issues may doom a Web project to failure.

Publishing the Site

There are two basic choices for publishing your HTML documents on the Internet. One way involves having a dedicated connection to the Internet and running your own server. The other approach involves renting space or bandwidth from an outside vendor to place your server or pages outside your organization.

While running your own Web server and connection to the Internet might seem like the way to go, it can be quite expensive. A common leased line such as a T1 with Internet services may cost thousands of dollars a year. When factoring in labor, server, facilities, and other expenses, the total cost starts to approach six figures. Often, many of these facilities are already available within the organization and should be used. Yet using someone else's server may be the only choice for people who want to publish Web documents but can't afford a huge fee. Even those firms that have capable staffs should consider outsourcing because it provides many benefits. Figure 16-1 gives a basic overview of the two hosting approaches.

Outsourcing Web Hosting

As Web sites become more critical to the information infrastructure of companies, there is a growing need to provide high-quality, high-availability solutions. However, it is expensive for companies to develop in-house Talents and facilities to run a mission-critical Web site. Because of this, many firms have decided to outsource their Web facilities. Web server outsourcing comes in two basic flavors: *shared or virtual hosting* and *colocation*.

Web hosting involves using the shared server facilities of a hosting vendor. This means that the site will share Web server resources and bandwidth with other hosted sites. Sharing can be problematic. Server responsiveness may be significantly affected because of other hosted Web sites, particularly if those sites become popular. Furthermore, many customers are wary of sharing a server with others, because security often cannot be guaranteed on these shared systems. Despite its drawbacks, hosting is still relatively inexpensive. Shared hosting prices are dependent on the extra services offered and the traffic expected. Consumer-grade hosting can cost as little as $20 per month. High-availability, and possibly mirrored, hosting can run into thousands,

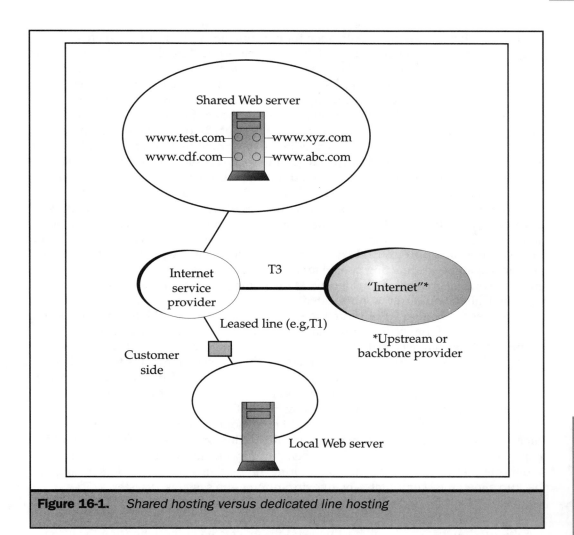

Figure 16-1. *Shared hosting versus dedicated line hosting*

if not tens of thousands, of dollars a month. Many Internet Service Providers (ISPs) and specialized hosting companies offer professional-quality shared Web hosting services.

The other Web server outsourcing option is often called colocation. This describes the use of a dedicated server, often owned by the organization purchasing the service. Colocation provides a greater degree of autonomy than shared Web services. In fact, the colocated machine typically only shares physical facilities, and possibly network bandwidth, with other customers. Colocation is generally more expensive than hosting; it may cost anywhere from around a thousand dollars to tens of thousands per month. Many of the large ISPs offer colocation services as well as specialized data center providers.

Price is often the essential motivation for outsourcing Web services. Research suggests that Web server outsourcing takes as much as one-third the cost of providing an equivalent service in-house. Yet the cost differences don't always add up, since a great deal of control and security will be lost. Looking beyond cost, there are major benefits from Web server outsourcing, including bandwidth, security, and facilities issues.

Having enough bandwidth available can be important for mission-critical Web sites. Regardless of server bottlenecks, a mere fractional T1 or full T1 leased line might not provide enough bandwidth to deal with the bursty nature of Web access. However, installing multiple T3 leased lines just to deal with the occasional flash crowd that may swamp a site seems wasteful given the significant investment required. Rather than bringing bandwidth to the server, why not move the server to the bandwidth?

Even if bandwidth is not an issue, there may be some issue of network closeness. Because there will always be a site that is far away, using a provider that can provide mirrors of the site around the world and automatically redirect the Web browser to the closest site seems appropriate. Many high-end providers are beginning to use products that are capable of redirecting people to the network's closest or least busy server to provide some degree of load balancing. Many of the popular sites on the Internet such as Yahoo! already use such sophisticated techniques.

Another motivation for outsourcing Web services is security. Many companies are still very afraid of the security problems associated with the Internet. Firewalls and security policies can help; but, if a public Web server is located on the firm's LAN, allowing Web viewers to access it is similar to asking potential robbers to come knock on your door. Putting public use information on outsourced Web servers keeps casual intruders away from a firm's network access point and allows stronger security policies to be put into place at the corporate firewall.

Facilities are often an overlooked benefit of outsourced Web services. With high-end data centers, colocation or hosting the facility provides benefits that would be expensive to replicate otherwise. These benefits may include around-the-clock live monitoring rather than automated monitoring, high-quality power services including backup generators, computer-sensitive fire suppression systems, disaster recovery–oriented construction, and sophisticated physical security.

Despite all the benefits of Web server outsourcing, there are some potentially significant drawbacks. Not all hosting vendors are created equal. Choosing the wrong vendor can lead to serious problems. While ISPs have more than enough bandwidth to host Web sites or colocate machines, many providers are more knowledgeable about networks than servers. This shows when they are questioned about available development tools and server maintenance policies. Data center vendors may be more on top of the server aspect of the puzzle, but they often come at a much higher price. If the correct vendor can be isolated, the only sacrifices facing the outsourced site are security and control.

While outsourcing Web service can help separate a sensitive network from the Internet, it also begs the question of the security of the Web server. If the outsourced site contains sensitive information, there is always the possibility this information may be compromised. Hosting vendors generally do not provide complete guarantees of data integrity. Careful reading of the fine print of hosting contracts indicates, at most, a "best effort" to protect data. In some cases, there is no guarantee whatsoever. Even if the hosting vendors protect against outside intrusion internally, security is often very lax. Security itself is just an example of the general problem of Web server outsourcing—a lack of control.

The biggest problem with many outsourced Web services, particularly hosting, is control. Most hosting vendors do not necessarily allow customers to do what they want. The choice of Web server, server software, development tools such as database development tools, and statistics packages are often up to the discretion of the hosting vendor. Particularly with lower-priced hosting services, use of a particular database, operating system, and statistics package may be forced on the customer. While customization is still often available, it may come at a significantly higher price. The ramifications of control go far beyond choice of operating system. Don't be surprised if a hosting vendor decides to upgrade its Web server during the middle of the day. It is the vendor's server, after all; and, logically or not, the vendor decides how to run it. With colocation, control is generally more in the customer's hand, since the vendor only provides network access, power, and safe facilities.

Companies looking to save money on Web hosting find outsourcing very attractive, but some flexibility and security may have to be sacrificed. With less experienced hosting companies, this lack of control can be disastrous, resulting in hidden costs in site redevelopment or problems with reliability. Those who want more control over their Web services should consider colocation or running their own servers locally. This is a more viable option than shared hosting, but it will certainly cost more.

Virtual Hosting

Hosting on a shared Web server often provides support for the feature known as *virtual hosting*. In essence, this feature enables multiple domain names to be hosted on the same server, yet appear as if each were running on its own server. Each machine on the Internet has an address such as http://www.bigcompany.com; this address maps to a particular IP (Internet Protocol) address such as 192.102.249.3. In the case of virtual hosting, the operating system the Web server runs on has the capability of mapping multiple IP addresses to a single-network interface card installed in the server hardware. In turn, multiple domain names can be mapped to these IP addresses.

Different types of virtual hosting are offered. Most hosting services offer a true virtual hosting service, where the URL for a customer's Web site is as would normally be expected; that is, http://www.bigcompany.com automatically goes to the customer's home page. The address is mapped to a single IP address. However, in some implementations of virtual hosting, multiple domain names may be mapped to only a single IP address. In this case, customers are given an address with a notation such as http://www.bigcompany.com/~bigco, where /~bigco indicates the actual username of the customer on the Web server. The common ~ notation is a server setting that enables all users on a particular server to have Web pages in their home directories and have a URL based on their usernames.

A step up from this, but still not true virtual hosting, comes in the form of having an address such as http://www.bigcompany.com/bigco, where /bigco is a specific directory assigned to a customer for hosting a Web page. In selecting a shared Web server hosting provider, potential customers should be careful to ask hosting companies the type of address provided in their virtual hosting services. The HTTP 1.1 protocol, as discussed in the section "How Web Servers Work," later in the chapter, supports virtual hosting using a single IP address, and will make managing virtual hosting services easier from the server administrator's point of view once most browsers support this extension.

If you are looking to run a small Web site, you may want to consider getting a local ISP or a low-cost, high-volume national hosting vendor such as HiWay Technologies (http://www.hway.com). Because of the competitive nature of the hosting business, pricing and services vary widely. Be sure to visit sites such as http://www.webhostlist.com before making a quick decision about where to host your site. Remember, the user won't be able to tell if the server is slow or the site is designed poorly.

Running a Local Web Server

Besides outsourcing hosting, it is also possible to pull in a full-time connection to the Internet and run your own Web server. When doing this, consider what Web servers actually do. In some sense, a Web server is a glorified file server, and occasionally an application server. Browsers make requests to the Web server for files. These files are located on the disk drive and then copied out to the network. In the case of running Common Gateway Interface (CGI) programs or similar server-side technology, a request is made to the server to run a program. The program is then loaded from disk and run, and the result is sent out to the network. To make the best Web server possible, you should pay careful attention to the disk and network interface. While many are quick to fault the processor speed or amount of memory, the disk is often the greatest bottleneck for a Web server. The big question is how to pick the best possible hardware platform, operating system, and Web server software combination to serve pages. Of course, all of these decisions must consider budget.

Selecting a Web Server

Price and performance are the basic issues for choosing a Web server. First, you need to understand what kind of activity to expect and what type of data you will serve. Then you need to set a budget for your server. A personal Web server might use freeware or shareware and run on a low-cost personal computer such as a PC or Macintosh. A large corporate system might use a powerful UNIX workstation running commercial-grade Web server software. There is no single correct hardware/software combination for Web page serving. One of the main considerations for a Web server will be the operating system used. Each operating system popular for Web service has its own pros and cons, summarized in Table 16-1.

 A variant of UNIX, called Linux, has recently become very popular as a Web hosting platform. Many of the pricing issues and hardware costs associated with traditional UNIX solutions are not as problematic under Linux.

While Table 16-1 presents a good overview of the issues involved in choosing one operating system over another for a Web server, the decision may often be made on the basis of familiarity or personal taste. There is nothing wrong with this. While one person may argue about the merits of UNIX, introducing a UNIX server into an environment with heavy Macintosh investment would be foolish. The bottom line is to always remember suitability. A small Web server for a school might do well on a Macintosh, while a Windows NT system might make a great departmental server, and a Sun server might be used for a high-performance Web site. Once the hardware and operating system are selected, you should consider which Web server software to use.

Only a few years ago, there were only two major Web servers available: NCSA's httpd server for UNIX and CERN's httpd server for UNIX. Both of these servers are free to use, but both require users to compile and install the software themselves. Today there are dozens of different Web servers available on a variety of machines. If you are interested in learning about all of the servers, go to the Serverwatch home page, at http://www.serverwatch.com, which provides links and reviews of most of the Web servers currently available. Rather than considering all Web servers in your decision, it might be wise to look at the most common Web servers used. Based upon surveys and analysis of reachable servers on the Internet, these servers are well agreed upon, though their exact market percentage is a topic of hot debate.

These are the major Web servers:

- Apache
- Microsoft's IIS
- Netscape Web servers
- WebSite
- WebStar

These popular Web servers are discussed in the following sections. This should by no means be considered as approval of these products, just a synopsis of each product and some of its known issues.

SITE DELIVERY

Operating System	Pros	Cons
UNIX	Tends to run on fast hardware such as UltraSparc and Alpha systems Very flexible High-end applications are available	Can be complicated to use and difficult to maintain Labor costs may be high Buy-in costs for hardware and software are relatively high
Windows NT	Can run on both high- and low-end systems, from Intel to Alpha systems Relatively robust Fairly easy to administer and may have lower maintenance costs Numerous high-end applications being ported to this operating system	May require more high-end hardware for adequate performance May not be as flexible or robust as UNIX for some Internet-related tasks
Windows 95/98	Easy to run Low equipment and labor costs Inexpensive Web server and development software	Not as robust as Windows NT or UNIX; prone to crashes May require a fast system for adequate performance Not as much server software ported to Windows 95/98 as to Windows NT Not as flexible as UNIX or Windows NT
Macintosh	Easy to run Fairly low equipment and labor costs Inexpensive software	Operating system architecture's inhibiting of performance Relatively little Web software available Not as flexible as Windows NT or UNIX Not robust and prone to crashes like Windows 95/98

Table 16-1.   *Operating System Summary*

Apache (http://www.apache.org)

A descendant of NCSA's httpd server, Apache is probably the first or second most popular Web server on the Internet. Apache's popularity stems from the fact that it is free and fast. It is also very powerful, supporting features such as HTTP 1.1, extended server-side includes (SSIs), a module architecture similar to NSAPI/ISAPI, and numerous free modules that perform functions such as server-based Perl interpretation or interpretation of parsed HTML. However, Apache is not for everyone. The main issue with Apache is that it isn't a commercial package. While there is generally support available on the Internet, many firms may be hesitant to run their mission-critical systems on a user-supported product. However, as with operating systems such as Linux, various third parties offer commercial support for Apache.

Another potential limiting factor for Apache is that the system currently is mainly for UNIX, although a port to Windows 95/Windows NT was recently developed. This may limit the use of Apache to high-use external and not-for-profit Web sites rather than intranets. Last, Apache might require modification of configuration files or even compilation in order to install. If you like to tinker, have a UNIX system, and don't have a lot of money, then Apache might just be for you. You'll be in good company: some of the largest Web sites on the Internet swear by this product.

 For Web trivia buffs, the name Apache is derived from the description of the software as a patched version of NCSA. Think "a patchy NCSA server."

Microsoft Internet Information Server (http://www.microsoft.com/iis)

IIS is Microsoft's server for Windows NT. Windows 95 also supports a similar but much less powerful version of IIS called the Personal Web Server (PWS). While PWS is certainly popular, of the two, most organizations favor IIS. One very important aspect of IIS is that it is very tightly integrated with the Windows NT environment. Unfortunately, being so Windows NT specific is also considered one of the problems with IIS. Because of hardware and clustering issues, it hasn't proved quite as scalable as some UNIX-based servers. With new Microsoft clustering technologies and integration with a transaction processor, this scalability problem is likely to change. For an intranet environment, particularly one with heavy Microsoft investment, it is difficult to beat the services offered by IIS—particularly its integration with other Microsoft products such as the SQL-Server database system. The price for IIS is currently a big selling point for the software: it's free.

Netscape Web Servers (http://home.netscape.com/servers)

Netscape has a growing line of Web servers, ranging from its FastTrack system to its Enterprise server. Netscape Web servers run on most major variants of UNIX (Solaris, SunOS, AIX, HP-UX, Digital UNIX, and IRIX), as well as Windows 95 and Windows NT. The systems are advanced, supporting hooks with databases, content management, HTTP 1.1, and a variety of other features. Netscape has attempted to make the software more commercial grade, including Web-based installation and administration. The only gripe people tend to make about these servers is that they sometimes perform sluggishly. Otherwise, if you are in a cross-platform environment, consider using Netscape servers. Netscape Web software is available for evaluation, but it is commercial and requires payment.

WebSite (http://website.ora.com)

A very easy-to-use Web server for Window 95 and Windows NT, O'Reilly's WebSite is one of the only robust Web servers available for Windows 95. Though it lacks the performance of Netscape or Microsoft servers running on more powerful systems, WebSite is considered one of the easiest servers to install and administer. Furthermore, the system provides many nice development features such as integration with Cold Fusion, advanced SSI, and special APIs for server extensions. For intranets or sites that don't need the performance of Windows NT or UNIX, WebSite is a great choice.

WebStar (http://www.starnine.com)

The most popular Web server for the Macintosh was originally based on MacHTTPD. WebStar integrates well with the Macintosh. It supports AppleScript and other Macintosh-specific tools and ideas such as automatic binhexing of files. The system supports UNIX-style CGI programs, a Java virtual machine for server-side Java, and extended SSI. The performance of WebStar often leaves much to be desired, though claims have been made that this has been improved. WebStar is probably more than adequate for intranets or small Web sites.

   In the Web server software discussion, people often don't consider that different packages will have different performance characteristics. Using the same hardware, one Web server software package may far outperform another. When planning to build a Web server, start either from the hardware and build up, or from the particular software and build down, picking the best possible hardware. If you make good software and hardware choices, the performance of the site can be significantly improved. However, be sure to base your build-out on requirements. It is always possible to design your Web server to handle a certain number of users or requests per second or minute.

How Web Servers Work

When it comes to the physical process of publishing documents, the main issues are whether to run your own server or to host elsewhere in conjunction with Web server software and hardware. An understanding of how Web servers do their job is important to understanding potential bottlenecks and leads to an in-depth understanding of how the Web works. In some sense, all that a Web server does is listen for requests from browsers or, as they are called more generically, *user agents*. Once the server receives a request, typically to deliver a file, it determines if it should do it. If so, it copies the file from the disk out to the network. In some cases, the user agent may ask the server to execute a program, but the idea is the same: eventually, some data is transmitted back to the browser for display. This discussion between the user agent, typically a Web browser, and the server takes place using the HTTP protocol.

HTTP

The Hypertext Transfer Protocol (HTTP) is the basic underlying application-level protocol used to facilitate the transmission of data to and from a Web server. HTTP provides a simple, fast way to specify the interaction between client and server. The protocol actually defines how a client must ask for data from the server and how the server returns it. HTTP does not specify how the data is actually transferred; this is up to lower-level network protocols such as TCP.

The first version of HTTP, known as version 0.9, was used as early as 1990. The current version of HTTP 1, as defined by RFC 1945, is supported by most servers and clients (Web browsers). However, HTTP 1 does not properly handle the effects of hierarchical proxies and caching, or provide features to facilitate virtual hosts. More important, HTTP 1 has significant performance problems due to the opening and closing of many connections for a single Web page.

HTTP 1.1 solves many of these problems. It is currently supported by newer, version 4–generation Web browsers as well as servers. There are still many limitations to HTTP, however. It is used increasingly in applications that need more sophisticated features, including distributed authoring, collaboration, and remote procedure calls. The Protocol Extension Protocol (PEP) is a proposed extension to HTTP designed to address the tension between browser, server, and proxy vendor enhancement agreements and public specifications. PEP allows the software to introduce new protocols during communication, negotiate protocols or content, or even switch between protocols on-the-fly. For now, such protocols are still in development. This discussion will deal with HTTP 1 and 1.1.

The process of a Web browser or other user agent such as a Web spider or robot requesting a document from a web—or, more correctly, an HTTP server—is simple and has been discussed throughout the book. The overall process is diagrammed in Figure 16-2.

In Figure 16-2, the user first requests a document from a Web server by specifying the URL of the document desired.

Note *During this step, a domain name lookup may occur, which translates a machine name such as www.bigcompany.com to an underlying IP address such as 192.102.249.3. If the domain name lookup fails, an error message such as "No such host" or "The server does not have a DNS entry" will be returned. Certain assumptions, such as the default service port to access for HTTP requests (80), may also be made. This is transparent to the user, who simply uses a URL to access a page.*

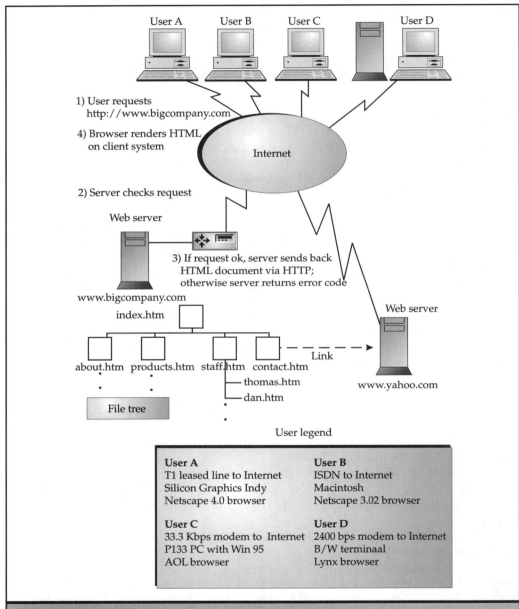

Figure 16-2.   *Overview of Web client/server relationship*

The browser then forms the proper HTTP request and sends the request to the server residing at the address specified by the URL. A typical HTTP request consists of

```
HTTP-Method Identifier HTTP-version
<Optional additional request headers>
```

In this example, the HTTP-Method would be **GET** or **POST**. An identifier might correspond to the file desired (for example, **/reports/latest.html**), and the HTTP-version indicates the dialect of HTTP being used (for example, **HTTP/1.0**).

If a user requests a document with the URL http://www.bigcompany.com/reports/lastest.html, the browser might generate a request such as the one shown here to retrieve the object from the server:

```
GET /reports/latest.html HTTP/1.0
If-Modified-Since: Tuesday, 12-Aug-99 01:39:39 GMT;
Referer: http://www.bigcompany.com/reports/index.html
Connection: Keep-Alive
User-Agent: Mozilla/4.02 [en] (X11; I; SunOS 5.4 sun4m)
Accept: image/gif, image/x-xbitmap, image/jpeg, image/pjpeg, */*
Accept-Language: en
Accept-Charset: iso-8859-1,*,utf-8
```

People often ask why the complete URL is not shown in the request. It isn't necessary in most cases, except when using a proxy server. The use of a relative URL in the header is adequate. The server knows where it is; it just needs to know what document to get from its own file tree. In the case of using a proxy server, which requests a document on behalf of a browser, a full URL is passed to it that is later made relative by the proxy. Besides the simple **GET** method, there are various other methods specified in HTTP. Not all are commonly used. Table 16-2 provides a summary of the HTTP 1.1 request methods.

Within an HTTP request, there is a variety of optional fields for creating a complete request. The common fields and an example for each are shown in the following sections.

Accept: *MIME-type/MIME-subtype*

This field indicates the data types accepted by the browser. An entry of */* indicates anything is accepted; however, it is possible to indicate particular content types such as **image/jpeg** so the server can make a decision on what to return. This facility could

Method	Description
GET	Returns the object specified by the identifier
HEAD	Returns information about the object specified by the identifier, such as last modification data, but does not return the actual object
OPTIONS	Returns information about the capabilities supported by a server if no location is specified, or the possible methods that can be applied to the specified object
POST	Sends information to the address indicated by the identifier; generally used to transmit information from a form using the **METHOD="POST"** attribute of the **<FORM>** element to a server-based CGI program
PUT	Sends data to the server and writes it to the address specified by the identifier overwriting previous content; in basic form, can be used for file upload
DELETE	Removes the file specified by the identifier; generally disallowed
TRACE	Provides diagnostic information by allowing the client to see what is being received on the server

Table 16-2.   *Summary of HTTP 1.1 Request Methods*

be used to introduce a form of content negotiation so that a browser could be served only data it understands or prefers, although this approach is not widely understood or implemented.

```
Accept: image/gif, image/x-xbitmap, image/jpeg, image/pjpeg, */*
```

Accept-Charset: *charset*
This field indicates the character set that is accepted by the browser, such as ASCII or foreign character encodings.

```
Accept-Charset: iso-8859-1,*,utf-8
```

Accept-Encoding: *encoding-type*

This field instructs the server as to what type of encoding the browser understands. Typically, this field is used to indicate to the server that compressed data can be handled.

```
Accept-Encoding: x-compress
```

Accept-language: *language*

This field lists the languages preferred by the browser and could be used by the server to pass back the appropriate language data.

```
Accept-Language: en
```

Authorization: *authorization-scheme authorization-data*

This field is typically used to indicate the userid and "encrypted" password if the user is returning authorization information.

```
Authorization: user joeblow:testpass
```

Content-length: *bytes*

This field gives the length in bytes of the message being sent to the server, if any. Remember that the browser may upload or pass data using the **PUT** or **POST** method.

```
Content-length: 1805
```

Content-type: *MIME-type/MIME-subtype*

This field indicates the MIME type of a message being sent to a server, if any. The value of this field would be particularly important in the case of file upload.

```
Content-type: text/plain
```

Date: *date-time*

This field indicates the date and time in Greenwich Mean Time (GMT) that a request was made. GMT time is mandatory for time consistency, given the worldwide nature of the Web.

```
Date: Thursday, 15-Jan-99 01:39:39 GMT
```

SITE DELIVERY

From: *e-mail address*

If given, this field may contain an e-mail address for the requesting browser. For privacy reasons, this request header often is not sent.

```
From: joe@bigcompany.com
```

Host

This field indicates the host and port of the server to which the request is being made.

```
Host: www.bigcompany.com
```

If-Modified-Since: *date-time*

This field indicates file freshness to improve the efficiency of the **GET** method. When used in conjunction with a **GET** request for a particular file, the requested file is checked to see if it has been modified since the time specified in the field. If the file has not been modified, a "Not Modified" code (304) is sent to the client so a cached version of the document can be used; otherwise, the file is returned normally.

```
If-Modified-Since: Thursday, 15-Jan-99 01:39:39 GMT
```

If-Match: *selector-string*

This field makes a request conditionally only if the items match some selector value passed in. Imagine only using **POST** to add data once it has been moved to a file called olddata.

```
If-Match: "olddata"
```

If-None-Match: *selector-string*

This field does the opposite of **If-Match**. The method is conditional only if the selector does not match anything. This might be useful for preventing overwrites of existing files.

```
If-None-Match: "newfile"
```

If-Range: *selector*

If a client has a partial copy of an object in its cache and wishes to have an up-to-date copy of the entire object there, it could use the **Range** request header with this conditional **If-Range** modifier to update the file. Modification selection can take place on time as well.

```
If-Range: Thursday, 15-Jan-99 01:39:39 GMT;
```

If-Unmodified-Since

This field makes a conditional method. If the requested file has not been modified since the specified time, the server should perform the requested method; otherwise, the method should fail.

```
If-Unmodified-Since: Thursday, 15-Jan-99 01:39:39 GMT
```

Max-Forwards: *integer*

This field is used with the **TRACE** method to limit the number of proxies or gateways that can forward the request. This would be useful to determine failures if a request moves through many proxies before reaching the final server.

```
Max-Forwards: 6
```

MIME-version: *version-number*

This field indicates the MIME protocol version, understood by the browser, that the server should use when fulfilling requests.

```
MIME-Version: 1.0
```

Proxy-Authorization: *authorization information*

This field allows the client to identify itself or the user to a proxy that requires authentication.

```
Proxy-Authorization: joeblow: testpass; Realm: All
```

Pragma: *server-directive*

This field passes information to a server; for example, this field can be used to inform a caching proxy server to fetch a fresh copy of a page.

```
Pragma: no-cache
```

Range: *byte-range*

This field requests a particular range of a file such as a certain number of bytes. The example shows a request for the last 500 bytes of a file.

```
Range: bytes=-500
```

Referrer: *URL*

This field indicates the URL of the document from which the request originates (in other words, the linking document). This value may be empty if the user has entered the URL directly rather than by following a link.

```
Referrer: http://www.bigcompany.com/reports/index.html
```

User-Agent: *agent-code*

This field indicates the type of browser making the request.

```
User-Agent: Mozilla/3.0 (Windows 95; Internet Explorer)
```

Note that all of these request headers seem very familiar. They constitute the same environment variables that you can access from within a CGI program. Now it should be clear how this information is obtained.

After receiving a request, the Web server attempts to process the request. The result of the request is indicated by a server status line that contains a response code, for example, the ever-popular "Not Found" (404). The server response status line takes this form:

```
HTTP-version Status-code Reason-String
```

For a successful query, a status line might read as follows:

```
HTTP/1.0   200   OK
```

while in case of error the status line might read

```
HTTP/1.0   404   Not Found
```

The status codes for the emerging HTTP 1.1 standard are listed in Table 16-3.

After the status line, the server responds with information about itself and the data being returned. There are various selected response headers, but the most important indicates the type of data in the form of a MIME-type and subtype that will be returned. Like request headers, many of these codes are optional and depend on the status of the request.

Status Code	Reason String	Description
Informational Codes (Process Continues After This)		
100	Continue	An interim response issued by the server that indicates the request is in progress but has not been rejected or accepted. This status code is in support of the persistent connection idea introduced in HTTP 1.1.
101	Switching Protocols	Can be returned by the server to indicate that a different protocol should be used to improve communication. This could be used to initiate a real-time protocol.
Success Codes (Request Understood and Accepted)		
200	OK	Indicates the successful completion of a request.
201	Created	Indicates the successful completion of a PUT request and the creation of the file specified.
202	Accepted	This code indicates that the request has been accepted for processing, but that the processing has not been completed and the request may or may not actually finish properly.
203	Non-Authoritative Information	Indicates a successful request, except that returned information, particularly meta-information about a document, comes from a third source and is unverifiable.

Table 16-3. *HTTP 1.1 Status Codes*

SITE DELIVERY

Status Code	Reason String	Description
204	No Content	Indicates a successful request, but there is no new data to send to the client.
205	Reset Content	Indicates that the client should reset the page that sent the request (potentially for more input). This could be used on a form page that needs consistent refreshing, rather than reloading as might be used in a chat system.
206	Partial Content	Indicates a successful request for a piece of a larger document or set of documents. This response typically is encountered when media is sent out in a particular order, or byte-served, as with streaming Acrobat files.

Redirection Codes (Further Action Necessary to Complete Request)

300	Multiple Choices	Indicates that there are many possible representations for the requested information, so the client should use the preferred representation, which may be in the form of a closer server or different data format.
301	Moved Permanently	Requested resource has been assigned a new permanent address and any future references to this resource should be done using one of the returned addresses.
302	Moved Temporarily	Requested resource temporarily resides at a different address. For future requests, the original address should still be used.
303	See Other	Indicates that the requested object can be found at a different address and should be retrieved using a **GET** method on that resource.

Table 16-3. *HTTP 1.1 Status Codes* (continued)

Status Code	Reason String	Description
304	Not Modified	Issued in response to a conditional **GET**; indicates to the agent to use a local copy from cache or similar action as the request object has not changed.
305	Use Proxy	Indicates that the requested resource must be accessed through the proxy given by the URL in the **Location** field.

Client Error Codes (Syntax Error or Other Problem Causing Failure)

Status Code	Reason String	Description
400	Bad Request	Indicates that the request could not be understood by the server due to malformed syntax.
401	Unauthorized	Request requires user authentication. The authorization has failed for some reason, so this code is returned.
402	Payment Required	Obviously in support of commerce, this code is currently not well defined.
403	Forbidden	Request is understood but disallowed and should not be reattempted, compared to the 401 code, which may suggest a reauthentication. A typical response code in response to a query for a directory listing when the latter are disallowed.
404	Not Found	Usually issued in response to a typo by the user or a moved resource, as the server can't find anything that matches the request nor any indication that the requested item has been moved.
405	Method Not Allowed	Issued response to a method request such as **GET**, **POST**, or **PUT** on an object for which such a method is not supported. Generally an indication of what methods are supported will be returned.

Table 16-3.   *HTTP 1.1 Status Codes* (continued)

SITE DELIVERY

Status Code	Reason String	Description
406	Not Acceptable	Indicates that the response to the request will not be in one of the content types acceptable by the browser, so why bother doing the request? This is an unlikely response given the */* acceptance issued by most, if not all, browsers.
407	Proxy Authentication Required	Indicates that the proxy server requires some form of authentication to continue. This code is similar to the 401 code.
408	Request Time-Out	Indicates that the client did not produce or finish a request within the time that the server was prepared to wait.
409	Conflict	The request could not be completed because of a conflict with the requested resource; for example, the file might be locked.
410	Gone	Indicates that the requested object is no longer available at the server and no forwarding address is known. Search engines may want to add remote references to objects that return this value since it is a permanent condition.
411	Length Required	Indicates that the server refuses to accept the request without a defined **Content-length** header. This may happen when a file is posted without a length.
412	Precondition Failed	Indicates that a precondition given in one or more of the request header fields, such as **If-Unmodified-Since**, evaluated to false.

Table 16-3. *HTTP 1.1 Status Codes* (continued)

Status Code	Reason String	Description
413	Request Entity Too Large	Indicates that the server is refusing to return data because the object may be too large or the server may be too loaded to handle the request. The server may also provide information indicating when to try again if possible, but just as well may terminate any open connections.
414	Request-URI Too Large	Indicates that the Uniform Resource Identifier (URI), generally a URL, in the request field is too long for the server to handle. This is unlikely to occur since browsers will probably not allow such transmissions.
415	Unsupported Media Type	Indicates the server will not perform the request because the media type specified in the message is not supported. This code might be returned when a server receives a file it is not configured to accept via the **PUT** method.

Server Error Codes (Server Can't Fulfill a Potentially Valid Request)

Status Code	Reason String	Description
500	Internal Server Error	A serious error message indicating that the server encountered an internal error that keeps it from fulfilling the request.
501	Not Implemented	This response is to a request that the server does not support or may be understood but not implemented.
502	Bad Gateway	Indicates that the server acting as a proxy encountered an error from some other gateway and is passing the message along.

Table 16-3.   *HTTP 1.1 Status Codes* (continued)

Status Code	Reason String	Description
503	Service Unavailable	Indicates the server is currently overloaded or is undergoing maintenance. Headers may be sent to indicate when the server will be available.
504	Gateway Time-Out	Indicates that the server, when acting as a gateway or proxy, encountered too long a delay from an upstream proxy and decided to time out.
505	HTTP Version Not Supported	Indicates that the server does not support the HTTP version specified in the request.

Table 16-3. *HTTP 1.1 Status Codes* (continued)

An example server response for the request shown earlier in the chapter follows:

```
HTTP/1.0 200 OK
Server: Netscape-Commerce/1.12
Date: Thursday, 01-Aug-98 13:05:08 GMT
Content-type: text/html
Last-modified: Thursday, 01-Aug-98 10:09:00 GMT
Content-length: 205

<HTML>
<HEAD>
<TITLE>Report 1</TITLE>
</HEAD>

<BODY>
<H1>Report About Important Things</H1>
<HR>
<P>Here is some information about important things. </P>
</BODY>
</HTML>
```

The common server response headers for HTTP 1.1 are given next.

Age

This header shows the sender's estimate of the amount of time since the response was generated at the origin server. Age values are nonnegative decimal integers, representing time in seconds.

```
Age: 10
```

Content-encoding

This header indicates the encoding type in which the data is returned.

```
Content-encoding: x-compress
```

Content-language

This header indicates the language used for the data returned by the server.

```
Content-language: en
```

Content-length

This header indicates the number of bytes returned by the server.

```
Content-length: 205
```

Content-range

This header indicates the range of the data being sent back by the server.

```
Content-range: -500
```

Content-type

This header is probably the most important; it indicates in the form of a MIME type what type of content is being returned by the server.

```
Content-type: text/html
```

Expires

This header gives the date and time after which the returned data should be considered stale and should not be returned from a cache.

```
Expires: Thu, 04 Dec 1997 16:00:00 GMT
```

SITE DELIVERY

Last-modified

This header is used to indicate the date on which the content returned was last modified. It can be used by caches to decide whether or not to keep local copies of objects.

```
Last-modified: Thursday, 01-Aug-96 10:09:00 GMT
```

Location

This header is used to redirect the browser to another page. Occasionally, scripts use this method for browser redirection based on capability.

```
Location: http://www.bigcompany.com/netscapehome.htm
```

Proxy-authenticate

This header is included with a "Proxy Authentication Required" (407) response. Its value consists of a challenge that indicates the authentication scheme and parameters applicable to the proxy for the request.

```
Proxy-authenticate: GreenDecoderRing: 0124.
```

Public

This header lists the set of methods supported by the server. The purpose of this field is strictly to inform the browser of the server's capabilities when new or unusual methods are encountered.

```
Public: OPTIONS, MGET, MHEAD, GET, HEAD
```

Retry-after

This header can be used in conjunction with a "Service Unavailable" (503) response to indicate how long the service is expected to be unavailable to the requesting client. Its value can be either an HTTP-date or an integer number of seconds after which to retry.

```
Retry-after: Fri, 31 Dec 1999 23:59:59 GMT Retry-after: 60
```

Server

This header contains information about the Web software used.

```
Server: Netscape-Commerce/1.12
```

Warning

This header is used to carry additional information about the status of a response that may not be found in the status code.

```
Warning: 10 Response is stale
```

WWW-authenticate

This header is included with an "Unauthorized" (401) response message. Its value consists of at least one challenge that indicates the authentication scheme and parameters applicable to the request made by the client.

```
WWW-authenticate: Magic-Key-Challenge=555121, DecoderRing= Green
```

The most important header response field is the **Content-type** field. The MIME type indicated by this field is a device by which the browser is able to figure out what to do with the data being returned.

MIME

MIME (Multipurpose Internet Mail Extensions) was originally developed as an extension to the Internet mail protocol that allows for the communication of multimedia. The basic idea of MIME is transmission of text files with headers that indicate binary data that will follow. Each MIME header is composed of two parts that indicate the data type and subtype in the following format:

```
Content-type: type/subtype
```

where *type* can be image, audio, text, video, application, multipart, message, or extension-token; and *subtype* gives the specifics of the content. Some samples are listed here:

```
text/html
application/x-director
application/x-pdf
video/quicktime
video/x-msvideo
image/gif
audio/x-wav
```

Beyond these basic headers, you may also include information such as the character-encoding language. For more information about MIME, refer to RFC 1521, available from many sites including http://www.faqs.org/rfcs, or the list of registered MIME types at ftp://ftp.isi.edu/in-notes/iana/assignments/media-types.

When a Web server delivers a file, the header information is intercepted by the browser and questioned. The MIME type, as mentioned earlier, is specified by the **Content-type** server response field. For example, if a browser receives a basic HTML file, the **text/html** header indicates what to do and typically renders the file in the browser window. If the browser receives a type it does not understand—for example, **application/x-director**—it may ask the user to pick a helper, save it, or delete it, as shown by the familiar dialog box shown here:

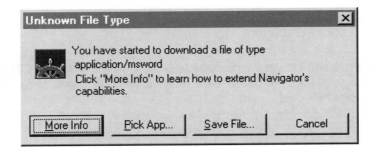

Normally, users hope that helper applications or plug-ins will intercept any MIME typed data that their browser doesn't understand and deal with it. It is interesting to note how little is said about MIME, but how important it is in the discussion between the browser and the server.

Speed and State Problems with HTTP

HTTP is a very simple protocol. That is, in a sense, its problem: it may be too simple. As a simple request-response protocol, HTTP can sometimes be very inefficient. Consider a Web page with five images on it. In order to fetch this Web page, it may take six or seven individual requests to pull down all of the files. These may include one request for the HTML text, five for the images, and perhaps even a redirect request for a partially formed URL. Each HTTP request has a little overhead with it. Do you see a potential problem? HTTP 1 suffered from this performance problem. HTTP 1.1, however, attempts to get around it by keeping connections open and pipelining responses. Browser vendors are also worried about performance issues and enable their browsers to request multiple objects at once to get around performance drags. Because HTTP is so important to the performance of Web sites, many advanced versions of HTTP are being discussed, most notably HTTP-NG. More information on this upcoming protocol can be found at http://www.w3.org/Protocols/HTTP-NG.

The other problem with HTTP is that it is stateless. After a Web server has finished fulfilling a client request, the server retains no "memory" of the request that just took place, except in the form of an entry in a log file, which records the request. An example of this lack of memory is how a user may partially fill in a form on a Web page, leave the site, and then come back and find the form cleared. As discussed in Chapter 11, the state problem is one of the biggest challenges to building complex applications on the Web. Not having to preserve state is what keeps HTTP relatively simple and fast.

The Realities of Publishing and Maintaining a Web Site

While understanding how Web servers work and the issues in choosing an in-house or outsourced server appears easy enough, it does not hint at the challenges of actually running a Web site. Far too often, Web professionals are quick to start a Web project but slow to continue it. The fun is often in the development of the site, setting the structure, designing the navigation, creating the look and feel, and then coding the page. But what happens next? The site is released to its intended audience, but you can't abandon it now. Web sites need care and feeding. Depending on the site, there may be daily, weekly, or monthly maintenance to perform. Adding new information, checking for broken links, continually testing under new browsers, upgrading HTML or script code to modern standards, running statistics, and performing various server-related activities such as upgrading software or running backups are all vital tasks. The real work of the site comes after it is released. The site was built for some purpose, and now it is time to fulfill it.

Summary

Site development should address the need of hosting pages on a Web server. Developers can choose to host sites on servers within companies; obtain the necessary hardware, software, Internet connection, and labor required to do hosting themselves; or elect to outsource hosting to an ISP or Web hosting company. Because of the costs and complications involved in trying to provide sufficient resources to do your own hosting, it often makes sense to outsource. This approach presents the options of renting space on a shared server or the colocation of a dedicated server at a hosting facility. There is more flexibility in running your own server, rather than being at the mercy of what a shared hosting provider makes available. Running your own server requires selection and evaluation of server software and hosting platform, as well as consideration of performance requirements. In addition to server and hosting choices, an understanding of how Web servers work using the HTTP and MIME protocols can be essential to monitoring and improving server performance for better Web page delivery.

The Complete Reference

HTML

Part V

New Horizons

The Complete Reference

Chapter 17

XML: Beyond HTML

With much fanfare, Extensible Markup Language (XML) has emerged rapidly as a new approach to delivering structured data over the Web. Why XML? Simply put, using this Web-efficient version of Standard Generalized Markup Language (SGML), the mother language used to define HTML, will enable authors to define their own elements. Although much of the full XML vision is not widely supported in currently shipping browsers, and important features have yet to be finalized, the effects of XML can already be felt.

Microsoft, Sun, and Netscape are furiously working to make XML real, under the aegis of the World Wide Web Consortium (W3C). And, as usual, browser vendors are attempting to support XML documents or ideas even before standards are put in place. For example, Microsoft's push technology, Channel Definition Format (CDF), as well as Open Software Description (OSD) format, are both based on an XML data format. But why XML? What's so wrong with HTML? Quite simply, HTML isn't flexible enough to meet the document-structuring requirements of specific industries or new viewing environments. In the short term, XML isn't necessarily going to replace HTML, but it may change the way that HTML is defined and used, after it is supported by major browsers.

Relationship Among HTML, SGML, and XML

To understand what all of the XML excitement is about, you need to understand the connection between HTML, SGML, and XML. XML is defined as an application profile, or restricted form, of SGML that is designed to support the efficient use of SGML documents over the Web. Informally, an *application profile* is a subset of a standard that has been given a little twist to accommodate real-world use. Understanding the twist that XML gives to SGML requires that you understand the strengths and weaknesses of SGML and its most famous application, HTML. However, the goal of XML is not to replace either technology, but to complement and augment them as appropriate.

The first question that needs to be addressed is why XML is even necessary when HTML is already available. Any technology that is used globally by tens of millions of people must be doing something right. As a general-purpose technology, HTML meets an extraordinarily broad set of user needs. However, it doesn't fit very well with applications that rely upon specialized information, either as data files or as complex, structured documents. This is particularly true for applications such as automated data interchange, which requires data to be structured in a consistent manner. Imagine trying to format a complex mathematical formula in HTML. The only choices are to make an image out of the formula, embed a special math technology, or use another document-formatting technology, such as Adobe's Acrobat.

As you have seen already, by itself, HTML can't realistically accommodate the structuring and formatting needs of documents that require more than paragraphs, sections, and lists. HTML can't deal with more-complex application-specific problems, because its elements are fixed. The language contains no provision for extending itself, namely, it has no provision for defining new elements. Although browser vendors used to add new elements all the time, any proposed extension now entails lengthy advocacy before the W3C.

Regardless, adding more element types to HTML doesn't make sense at this point. The language is already large enough. It is meant to be a general-purpose language that is capable of handling a large variety of documents. Thus, HTML needs some mechanism so that its general-purpose framework can be augmented to accommodate specialized content.

SGML seems like a reasonable candidate to increase HTML's flexibility. SGML is a *meta-language*, a language that is used to define other languages. Although HTML is the best-known SGML-defined language, SGML itself has been used successfully to define special document types ranging from aviation maintenance manuals to scholarly texts. SGML can represent very complex information structures, and it scales well to accommodate enormous volumes of information. SGML is extremely complex, however, and wasn't built with today's online applications in mind. The language first appeared in the 1970s, the golden age of batch processing, and wasn't designed to be used in networked, interactive applications. Without resolving these issues, the full SGML language can't be efficiently used over the Web.

Thus, XML is an attempt to define a subset of SGML that is specifically designed for use in a Web context. As such, it will be influenced both by its SGML parent and by HTML. The exact way that XML will fit into Web documents is still a topic of great debate, but the general role of the language is clear. Initially, it will be used to represent specialized data to augment HTML documents. In fact, it is already being used to do this. For example, Microsoft's Channel Definition Format, which specifies documents for "push" delivery on the Internet, is actually an application of XML. (*Push* is a technology in which data, such as news, is sent to users on a scheduled basis, saving them the trouble of hunting for it on the Web.)

Such purpose-specific extensions to Web documents will be the first use of XML; but, at some point, XML will be used in its own right to design Web documents, instead of using HTML. XML is already being used to add data to HTML documents, such as forms of meta-data that describe the document.

What's unusual about these specific examples of XML use is that the core language syntax hasn't been finalized yet. It is still in the working-draft stage. Leave it to the browser vendors to implement first and ask questions later. The features that will make XML a document platform in its own right are even more tentative. For example, linking models are at the draft stage, and style sheet use and Document Object Model relationships are still at the discussion stage.

So, is XML just a work in progress? Yes, as much as HTML is. XML is already arriving in various forms, such as CDF, OSD, Synchronized Multimedia Integration Language (SMIL), Mathematical Markup Language (MathML), and Chemical Markup Language (CML). Other possible XML-based languages are being discussed, as well, including such languages as Hand-held Device Markup Language (HDML), Resource

Description Framework (RDF), and Platform for Internet Content Selection–Next Generation (PICS-NG). Given the overwhelming interest in XML, it is wise to look at the current state of its syntax, as well as its likely future directions.

Basic XML

Because XML is a subset of SGML, it should be somewhat familiar, as HTML itself is an application of SGML. However, to support efficient Web usage, XML doesn't allow the use of many SGML constructs that are used to define documents. The eliminated constructs are either infrequently used or add a performance penalty to document parsing. Writing XML sounds like a daunting task, requiring an esoteric knowledge of SGML beyond the capabilities of most HTML authors. Actually, writing simple XML documents is fairly easy. For example, suppose that you have a compelling need to define some elements to represent a fast-food restaurant's combination meals, which contain a burger, drink, and fries. How might you do this in XML? You would simply create a file such as burger.xml that contains the following markup:

```
<?xml version="1.0"?>
<COMBOMEAL>
    <BURGER>
    <NAME>Tasty Burger</NAME>
    <BUN BREAD="WHITE">
        <MEAT />
        <CHEESE />
        <MEAT />
    </BUN>
    </BURGER>

    <FRIES SIZE="LARGE" />
    <DRINK SIZE="LARGE" FLAVOR="Cola" />
</COMBOMEAL>
```

A rendering of this example under a preview version of Internet Explorer 5 is shown in Figure 17-1.

Notice that the browser shows a structural representation of the file, not a screen representation. You'll see how to make this file actually look like something later in sthe chapter. First, take a look at the document syntax. In many ways, this example "Meal Markup Language" (or MML, if you like) looks similar to HTML—but how do you know to name the element **<COMBOMEAL>** instead of **<MEALDEAL>** or **<LUNCHSPECIAL>**? You don't need to know, because the decision is completely up to you. Simply choose any element and attribute names that meaningfully represent

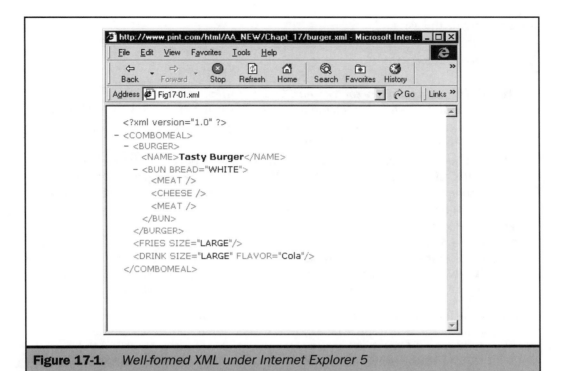

Figure 17-1.   *Well-formed XML under Internet Explorer 5*

the domain that you want to model. Does this mean that XML has no rules? It has rules, but they are few, simple, and relate only to syntax:

- Just like well-written HTML, *all elements must be properly nested.* For example,

```
<OUTER><INNER>ground zero</INNER></OUTER>
```

is correct, while this isn't:

```
<OUTER><INNER>ground zero</OUTER></INNER>
```

- *All attribute values must be quoted.* In HTML, quoting is good authoring practice, but it is required only for values that contain characters other than letters (A–Z and a–z), numbers (0–9), hyphens (-), or periods (.). For example, under XML,

```
<BLASTOFF COUNT="10">
```

is correct, while this isn't:

```
<BLASTOFF COUNT=10>
```

- *All elements with empty content must be self-identifying,* by ending in **/>** instead of the familiar **>**. An empty element is one such as the HTML **
, **<HR>, or **<IMG>** elements. In XML, these would be represented, respectively, as **
, **<HR/>, and **<IMG SRC="test.gif" />**.

- *All elements must be cased consistently.* If you start a new element such as **<BURGER>**, you must close it as **</BURGER>**, not **</burger>**. Later in the document, if the element is in lowercase, you actually are referring to a new element known as **<burger>**. Attribute names are also case-sensitive.

- *A valid XML file may not contain certain characters that have reserved meanings.* These include characters such as **&**, which indicates the beginning of a character entity such as ** **, and **<**, which indicates the start of an element name such as **<SUNNY>**. These characters must be coded as **&** and **<**, respectively. They can, however, occur in a section marked off as character data.

A document constructed according to the previous simple rules is known as a *well-formed document*. SGML purists may find this notion eccentric and somewhat troubling. Although SGML itself is currently being revised, traditional SGML has no notion of well-formed documents—documents that are in some sense okay because they conform to some basic syntax guidelines. Instead, conventional SGML uses the notion of *valid* documents—documents that adhere to a formally defined document type definition (DTD). Although this concept is also part of HTML, it often is lost on many page authors. For anything beyond casual applications, defining a DTD and validating documents against that definition are real benefits. XML supports both well-formed and valid documents. The well-formed model should encourage those not schooled in the intricacies of SGML to begin authoring XML documents, thus making XML as accessible as HTML has been. The valid model is available for applications in which a document's logical structure needs to be verified.

Valid Documents

Most HTML authors are familiar with basic elements and attributes. Now, due to the rising complexity of pages, they are becoming more familiar with the importance of making an HTML document conform to the rules of a DTD, such as HTML 4. As noted in the previous paragraph, a document that conforms to a DTD is said to be *valid*. Unlike most HTML authors, SGML authors normally concern themselves with producing valid documents. Many also concern themselves with writing the DTDs that HTML authors usually take for granted. With the appearance of XML, HTML authors can look forward to mastering a new skill: writing DTDs. The following example illustrates how XML might be used to track student performance in an instructional management system. A definition of the sample language to accomplish this task can be found within the document, although this definition can be kept outside the file, as well. The students.xml file shown here includes both the DTD and an occurrence of a document that conforms to the language in the same document:

```xml
<?xml version="1.0"?>
<!DOCTYPE GRADES [
<!ELEMENT GRADES  (STUDENT+)>
<!ELEMENT STUDENT (COURSE+)>
<!ATTLIST STUDENT  NAME   CDATA    #REQUIRED
          SEX   (M | F)          #REQUIRED
          LEVEL  (6 | 7 | 8)    #REQUIRED>

<!ELEMENT COURSE EMPTY>
<!ATTLIST COURSE TITLE   CDATA    #REQUIRED
          GRADE   (PASS | FAIL)  #REQUIRED>
]>

<!-- the document instance -->
<GRADES>
   <STUDENT NAME="WILLIE" SEX="M" LEVEL="7">
      <COURSE TITLE="MATH" GRADE="PASS" />
      <COURSE TITLE="ENGLISH"  GRADE="FAIL" />
   </STUDENT>

   <STUDENT NAME="FIONA" SEX="F" LEVEL="7">
      <COURSE TITLE="MATH"  GRADE="PASS" />
      <COURSE TITLE="ART" GRADE="PASS" />
   </STUDENT>
</GRADES>
```

The meaning of this language is straightforward. A document is enclosed by the **<GRADES>** element, which in turn contains **<STUDENT>** elements that have **NAME**, **SEX**, and **GRADE** attributes. The **NAME** attribute can be any character data (**CDATA**); the **SEX** attribute can be **M** or **F**; and the **LEVEL** can be **6**, **7**, or **8**. The **<STUDENT>** element may contain one or more **<COURSE>** elements. The **<COURSE>** element is an empty element. However, each **<COURSE>** element has a **TITLE** attribute, which can contain character data, and a **GRADE** attribute, which can have a value of either **PASS** or **FAIL**. The example document shows the use of these new elements. A rendering of the document under Internet Explorer 5 is shown in Figure 17-2.

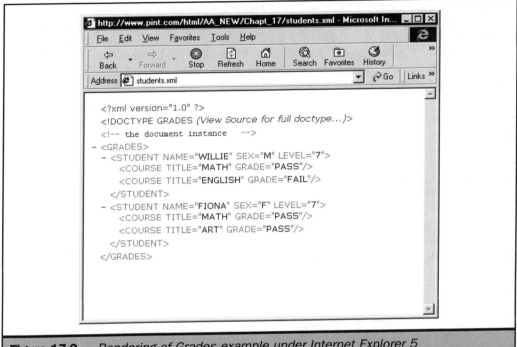

Figure 17-2.   *Rendering of Grades example under Internet Explorer 5*

One interesting aspect of using a DTD with an XML file is that the correctness of the document can be checked. For example, changing the value of the **LEVEL** attribute on the first **<STUDENT>** element to **4** should cause the XML parser to reject the document, as shown in Figure 17-3.

Writing a DTD might seem like an awful lot of trouble; but, without one, the value of XML is limited. If you can guarantee conformance to the specification, you can start to allow automated parsing and exchange of documents. Writing a DTD is going to be a new experience for most HTML authors, and not everybody will want to write one. Fortunately, although not apparent from the DTD rules in this brief example, XML significantly reduces the complexity of full SGML. A couple of measurements may help you appreciate the extent of this reduction. First, the full SGML standard is about 500 pages. The XML 1.0 specification is only around 30 pages. Second, XML removes about 30 constructs that SGML uses to define DTDs. The constructs are either infrequently used or introduce ambiguities that would make efficient document parsing difficult.

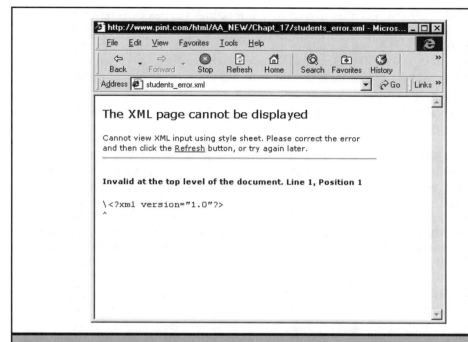

Figure 17-3.   *Validation Error message under IE 5*

The following valid SGML declaration for an HTML 4 **<BODY>** element can be used to illustrate some of the features removed from SGML:

```
<!ELEMENT BODY O O (%block) -BODY +(INS | DELS) - - the body tag - ->
```

Note the following syntax differences:

- **O O** following the **BODY** identifier indicates that the start and end tags are optional and can be omitted. Their presence can be contextually inferred. XML doesn't allow omitted tags.

- **–BODY** is a type of identifier known as an *exclusion*. It modifies the basic content model for the **<BODY>** element by specifying that it can't include another **<BODY>** element. XML doesn't support exclusions.

■ **+(INS | DELS)** specifies an *inclusion*. It modifies the basic content model of the **<BODY>** element by specifying that it can additionally use the **<INS>** or **<DELS>** elements anywhere inside its content. XML doesn't support inclusions. **(INS | DELS)** is also known as a *name group,* a construct—not supported by XML—that is used to indicate that a declaration applies to multiple elements.

■ **- - the body tag - -** is an embedded comment. XML supports comments, but not inside declarations.

Although XML will not support some SGML capabilities, it will retain powerful SGML capabilities that are not found in standard HTML. For example, XML *general entities,* which essentially are macros that associate an identifier with replacement text defined either inside the declaration or in an external file. HTML authors may be familiar with character entities, such as **"**, which are used to insert special characters. XML general entities are used in the same way, except that the replacement text can be arbitrarily long. Anyone who has ever needed to modify something that is used repeatedly in a document will appreciate entities. By using the entity name throughout the document, the replacement text can be modified in a single place, the entity declaration. For example, the **GRAMMAR** entity acts as a shorthand notation for a longer course name:

```
<?xml version="1.0"?>
<!DOCTYPE GRADES [
<!-- An entity whose replacement text is immediately defined -->
<!ENTITY   GRAMMAR    "Language Studies: Introduction to English
                      Grammar">
<!ELEMENT GRADES (STUDENT+)>
<!ELEMENT STUDENT (COURSE+)>
<!ATTLIST STUDENT  NAME      CDATA      #REQUIRED
          SEX     (M | F)              #REQUIRED
          LEVEL   (6 | 7 | 8)          #REQUIRED

<!ELEMENT COURSE EMPTY>
<!ATTLIST COURSE TITLE        CDATA    #REQUIRED
          GRADE         (PASS | FAIL)  #REQUIRED>
]>

<!-- the document instance -->
<GRADES>
   <STUDENT NAME="WILLIE"   SEX="M" LEVEL="7">
      <COURSE TITLE= "MATH" GRADE="PASS" />
      <COURSE TITLE="&GRAMMAR;"  GRADE="FAIL" />
   </STUDENT>
```

```
   <STUDENT NAME="FIONA"   SEX="F"   LEVEL="7">
     <COURSE TITLE="MATH"   GRADE="PASS" />
     <COURSE TITLE="&GRAMMAR;" GRADE="PASS" />
   </STUDENT>
</GRADES>
```

A few more things can be defined in an XML DTD; but, at this point, you may be wondering whether you are required to include a full DTD every time that you author an XML document. The answer is no. Just as an HTML file is supposed to start with a DTD that references an external document type, so, too, is an XML file supposed to start with a DTD. In the following example, the definition of the **GRADES** language has been put in a file called grades.dtd:

```
<!-- Grades DTD -->
<!ELEMENT GRADES   (STUDENT+)>
<!ELEMENT STUDENT (COURSE+)>
<!ATTLIST STUDENT   NAME   CDATA   #REQUIRED
          SEX   (M | F)          #REQUIRED
          LEVEL   (6 | 7 | 8)    #REQUIRED>

<!ELEMENT COURSE EMPTY>
<!ATTLIST COURSE TITLE   CDATA   #REQUIRED
          GRADE   (PASS | FAIL)  #REQUIRED>
```

Notice that you don't have to enclose the various rules in a **DOCTYPE** statement. You then would reference the external DTD with the **<!DOCTYPE>** element. The use of the **SYSTEM** keyword and URL indicates that the DTD is external to this file. The next example shows how you could reference the external definition grades.dtd:

```
<?xml version="1.0"?>
<!DOCTYPE GRADES SYSTEM "grades.dtd">
<!-- the document instance -->

<GRADES>
   <STUDENT NAME="BILLIE" SEX="M" LEVEL="7">
     <COURSE TITLE="MATH" GRADE="PASS" />
     <COURSE TITLE="ENGLISH"   GRADE="FAIL" />
   </STUDENT>
```

```
<STUDENT NAME="FIONA" SEX="F"  LEVEL="7">
  <COURSE TITLE="MATH"  GRADE="PASS" />
  <COURSE TITLE="ART" GRADE="PASS" />
</STUDENT>
</GRADES>
```

Linking to an external document type is very useful. In the future, you should be able to obtain DTDs from other organizations.

Ways to Use XML

While creating XML documents doesn't seem particularly hard, you may wonder how to actually use this technology. At least three distinct application models are on the horizon:

- Using XML for special data files that support HTML applications
- Embedding XML elements into HTML documents
- Using XML by itself as the basis for interactive documents

The third approach, using XML by itself, begs a question of how a page will actually render. Three approaches are designed to solve this problem. The first approach is to convert XML into HTML, or HTML plus style sheets. This is the only solution for browsers that are not XML-aware. At the time that this edition was being written, only Internet Explorer 5 prerelease versions support XML to any major degree. However, assuming that browsers eventually support XML, you may be able to use one of the other two approaches: rendering XML by binding your tags to CSS rules or using XSL, another style sheet technology used with XML to translate the XML document to HTML or CSS.

XML for Data Files

The first pervasive use of XML is to define special data files that support HTML applications. This use is already in place in newer browser releases. Microsoft Internet Explorer 4 relies upon an XML-based language to support *push functionality*, the ability of viewers to subscribe to Web sites that are automatically updated on a scheduled basis. The language, known as *Channel Definition Format*, is the most publicized of several other "helper" languages that have suddenly appeared recently. A related language is *Open Software Description*, used to support the automatic downloading of software. The slogan that Microsoft uses to describe the HTML/XML relationship is "HTML is for presentation, while XML is for data."

Operationally, these XML-based language documents are identified by a special file extension, such as .cdf, that is analogous to the special extensions used for GIF (.gif) and JPEG (.jpeg) files. XML files are retrieved like files for HTML media inserts, but are processed in a special way. Instead of being handled by a browser extension for visual rendering, they are handled by an extension that parses the document and uses the information that it contains to control the browser's behavior. This use requires only those few XML features that are needed to define data and doesn't approach the full XML vision. Because these documents are not directly viewed, they can function quite well without the XML capabilities that are still under development.

The CDF language illustrates the characteristics of the "XML as data" model. It contains neither linking information, other than the common **HREF** attribute used in HTML, nor any style information for rendering CDF elements in an HTML browser. It contains only the information-building blocks needed to define a channel. The small CDF document shown next presents an example of some of the more common CDF elements. The **<CHANNEL>** element defines the channel and points to an initial HTML document. It contains a **<SCHEDULE>** element to update the channel and several **<ITEM>** elements to define viewable items, such as pages and even a screen saver. Viewable pages have an **<ABSTRACT>** element to summarize their content and may have both a large and a small graphic logo associated with them, as specified by the empty **<LOGO/>** element.

```
<?xml version="1.0"?>
<CHANNEL HREF="http://www.bigcompany.com/">
<TITLE>Big Company Channel</TITLE>
<ABSTRACT>
Welcome to the Big Company channel, a comprehensive
guide to the latest book examples.
</ABSTRACT>

<LOGO HREF="http://www.bigcompany.com/imageslogo.ico"
      STYLE="ICON"/>

<LOGO HREF="http://www.bigcompany.com/images/logo.gif"
      STYLE="IMAGE"/>

<SCHEDULE ENDDATE="1998.12.31">
   <INTERVALTIME DAY="1"/>
</SCHEDULE>

<ITEM HREF="http://www.bigcompany.com/p1.html">
   <LOGO HREF="http://www.bigcompany.com/images/pagelogo.ico"
         STYLE="ICON"/>
```

NEW HORIZONS

```
    <LOG VALUE="document:view"/>
    <TITLE>Page 1</TITLE>
    <ABSTRACT>Abstract for Page 1</ABSTRACT>
</ITEM>

<ITEM HREF="http://www.bigcompany.com/page2.html">
    <LOGO HREF="http://www.bigcompany.com/images/pagelogo.ico"
        STYLE="ICON"/>
    <LOG VALUE="document:view"/>
    <TITLE>Page 2</TITLE>
    <ABSTRACT>Abstract for Page 2</ABSTRACT>
</ITEM>

<ITEM HREF="http://www.bigcompany.com/scrnsave.html">
    <USAGE VALUE="ScreenSaver"></USAGE>
</ITEM>
</CHANNEL>
```

The point of this example isn't to explain the CDF syntax, but to show how XML represents data in a real application. Readers interested in making a CDF channel can visit Microsoft's Sitebuilder network (http://www.microsoft.com/sitebuilder/) for the latest CDF syntax. Here's one other point about CDF to consider: this file format is external to HTML files. Like any other media type (fractal images, Shockwave, and so on), CDF could be handled by an external helper application or even a plug-in. But can you consider putting a language such as CDF right into an HTML document?

Embedding XML into HTML Documents

Although the "official" XML syntax remains unclear, the expectation exists for a means to embed XML elements into HTML documents. One approach is to use a special element such as **<XML>** to indicate sections of XML content. This approach is the idea behind Microsoft's XML *data islands*. The **<XML>** element can be used anywhere within an HTML document to enclose XML content, which might work as follows:

```
<HTML>
<HEAD>
<TITLE>XML Data Islands</TITLE>
</HEAD>
```

```
<BODY>
<H1>Regular HTML Here</H1>
<XML ID="tasty">
<COMBOMEAL>
   <BURGER>
      <NAME>Tasty Burger</NAME>
      <BUN BREAD="WHITE">
         <MEAT />
         <CHEESE />
         <MEAT />
      </BUN>
   </BURGER>

   <FRIES SIZE="LARGE" />
   <DRINK SIZE="LARGE" FLAVOR="Cola" />
</COMBOMEAL>
</XML>
</BODY>
</HTML>
```

Under Internet Explorer 5, this markup and content will be hidden, though it is exposed for scripting manipulation. Other browsers may ignore the **<XML>** and newly defined tags but still render onscreen content, such as the phrase "Tasty Burger," as shown in Figure 17-4.

To avoid the rendering of unknown markup onscreen, you could use the **SRC** attribute for the **<XML>** element:

```
<XML SRC="combomeal.xml"></XML>
```

Older browsers will safely ignore this markup.

Besides using the **<XML>** element, you could use the **<SCRIPT>** element to include HTML. For example,

```
<SCRIPT LANGUAGE="XML" TYPE="text/xml">
<WEATHER>
   <SUNNY />
</WEATHER>
</SCRIPT>
```

NEW HORIZONS

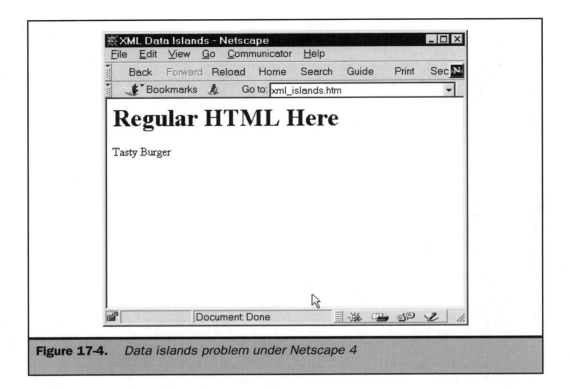

Figure 17-4. *Data islands problem under Netscape 4*

You could also use the **SRC** attribute for the **<SCRIPT>** element to reference an external XML file, like so:

```
<SCRIPT SRC="http://www.bigcompany.com/combomeal.xml"></SCRIPT>
```

Regardless of the particular syntax, proposing to use XML inside HTML documents creates the expectation that XML elements will integrate into the HTML application environment. But how exactly should this happen? The previous example shows that embedding XML content in the **<BODY>** element may cause a problem. What about the **<HEAD>** of the document? Placing XML elements inside an HTML document's **<HEAD>** element is consistent with the "XML as data" model. After all, the purpose of the head of the document is to house the document's meta-data, as illustrated by the following example:

```
<HTML>
<HEAD>
<TITLE>Widget Wonders</TITLE>
```

```
<XML ID="xmlmetaone">
<DESCRIPTION>
   <AUTHOR>Thomas A. Powell</AUTHOR>
   <SUMMARY>A sample document about widgets</SUMMARY>

   <KEYWORDS>
      <KEYWORD RANK="1">Widget</KEYWORD>
      <KEYWORD RANK="2">Sample</KEYWORD>
   </KEYWORDS>

   <CREATION>January 5, 1999</CREATION>
   <EXPIRES>December 31, 1999</EXPIRES>
</DESCRIPTION>
</XML>
</HEAD>

<BODY>
<H1 ALIGN="CENTER">Widget Sample Document</H1>
<HR>
<P>This is some sample text about widgets.</P>
</BODY>
</HTML>
```

The XML code in this example will not render on older browsers, though you could potentially render or manipulate it with an XML-aware browser. A more likely approach would be to use a server-side program to index the documents more carefully, instead of using a traditional, free text-search engine. Although the use of XML data islands may not seem obvious, if raw XML documents could be displayed, the improved structure that the language provides over HTML surely could be harnessed.

Converting XML to HTML for Display

As you have already seen, simply including new XML elements in the body of a document can cause problems, because most browsers will want to display the contents of the elements. Of course, no formatting will be applied to raw XML elements because (unlike HTML) XML elements have no default appearance; they must be assigned one. The most basic way to render XML is to translate it into HTML. All browsers support HTML, at least to some degree, so you can use a server-side program to translate your XML documents to HTML documents at delivery time. You may wonder what benefit this may have, given that HTML doesn't provide the rich structuring that XML does. The most obvious benefit is the abstraction provided.

Imagine if you had a press release that you marked up in a simple press-release language. It might look something like the following file, called pressrelease1.xml:

```
<?xml version="1.0"?>
<!DOCTYPE PRESSRELEASE SYSTEM "pressrelease.dtd">
<!-- the document instance -->
<PRESSRELEASE>
    <DATE>January 5, 1999</DATE>
    <HEADING>Big Company Releases Super Widget</HEADING>

    <RELEASEBODY>
    This is a sample press release. This is just some dummy text.
    </RELEASEBODY>

    <IMG SRC="widget.gif" />
    <CONTACT TYPE="PHONE">619-555-1212</CONTACT>
    <CONTACT TYPE="FAX">619-444-1212</CONTACT>
    <CONTACT TYPE="EMAIL">info@bigcompany.com</CONTACT>
</PRESSRELEASE>
```

Assume that all the elements are used appropriately according to the referenced DTD. Obviously, you can't deliver this file as-is, but you could write a server-side program that would take these tags and convert them into HTML fragments, to assemble an HTML file to be delivered. Maybe this file would look something like this:

```
<HTML>
<HEAD>
<TITLE>Big Company Releases Super Widget</TITLE>
</HEAD>

<BODY>
<H3 ALIGN="RIGHT" ID="DATE">January 5, 1999</H3>
<H1 ALIGN="CENTER" ID="HEADING">Big Company Releases Super
Widget</H1>
<HR>

<DIV ID="RELEASEBODY">
    <P>This is a sample press release this is just sample text.
    <IMG SRC="widget.gif" ALIGN="RIGHT" ID="IMG">
    </P>
</DIV>
<HR>
```

```
<!--Contact block -->
<ADDRESS>
E-mail: <A HREF="mailto: info@bigcompany.com">
info@bigcompany.com</A><BR>
Phone: 619-555-1212<BR>
FAX: 619-444-1212<BR>
</ADDRESS>
</BODY>
</HTML>
```

You can tell by the use of the **ID** attributes and comments how the fragments might map into the resulting HTML file. You could also use CSS rules to improve the look of the press release, but the preceding example should illustrate the basic concept. The benefit to this XML-translated-to-HTML approach is the abstraction provided. Because the HTML or HTML/CSS fragments are stored separately from the content, you could change the fragments without necessarily changing the actual content itself, which is stored in the XML file. You potentially could also provide different fragments depending on the browser accessing the page. This is a very powerful idea and might make the possibility of delivering multiple versions of a page a little more realistic.

Note   *The concept being described here isn't unique to XML; you could create the same effect by using a database. This idea may actually be more appropriate as a database-driven page.*

Displaying XML Documents by Using CSS and XSL

The conversion from XML to HTML seems awkward; it would be preferable to deliver a native XML file and display it. By using Cascading Style Sheets (CSS) or a new technology called *Extensible Stylesheet Language* (XSL), you should be able to deliver XML documents right to the screen. Note that neither of these technologies is well defined in relation to XML, so these examples may require significant rework to render in your browser. However, both examples should provide the flavor of how native XML may be presented.

The following file is a well-formed XML document representing a catalog of small parts:

```
<?xml version="1.0"?>
<?xml-stylesheet href="catalog.css" type="text/css" ?>
<CATALOG>
   <PART>
      <NAME>Super Widget</NAME>
      <DESCRIPTION>
```

```
        The Super Widget is the most powerful widget in the world.
      </DESCRIPTION>
      <PRICE>$1.95</PRICE>
    </PART>

    <PART>
      <NAME>Deluxe Widget</NAME>
      <DESCRIPTION>
      The Deluxe Widget is the fanciest widget in the world.
      </DESCRIPTION>
      <PRICE>$2.95</PRICE>
    </PART>
  </CATALOG>
```

Notice that the second line of the file references a style sheet in the same directory, called catalog.css. The content of this file is shown here:

```
CATALOG        {font-family: Arial; font-size: 14pt;}
PART           {background: orange; display: block}
NAME           {font-size: larger; font-style: italic;
                display: block}
DESCRIPTION    {text-indent: 10px; display: block;}
PRICE          {color: #009900; text-align: right;
                font-weight: bold; display: block}
```

Notice that the syntax for the style sheet is the same as the syntax discussed for CSS in Chapter 10, except that the element names are the XML elements that were defined in the previous example. One small issue with this approach to formatting XML is that positioning objects with style sheets is difficult unless you either use CSS-P extensions for absolute positions or assign a display property to the XML element. Notice that the rule **display** assigns a value of **block** to each of the elements. This makes the example XML act like an HTML block element, and thus induces a return in the document. The rendering of this rudimentary example under Internet Explorer 5 is shown in Figure 17-5.

The lack of flow objects in CSS makes properly displaying this XML document very difficult. In some sense, CSS still relies heavily on HTML for basic document structure. Because of its potential shortcomings, many Web experts look to XSL as a possible solution. XSL, a much more complex language than CSS, is based on a style sheet technology called Document Style Semantics and Specification Language (DSSSL) that was used in the SGML community. Fortunately, XSL doesn't retain much of the complexity and awkward parentheses notation of DSSSL. One of the most interesting

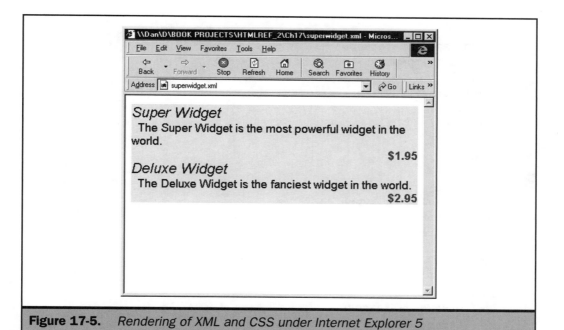

Figure 17-5.   *Rendering of XML and CSS under Internet Explorer 5*

aspects of XSL is its complex pattern matching. You can write XSL rules that match various pieces of an XML file and then output the appropriate HTML and/or CSS markup to display the information. Using the previous simple Parts example, you could link instead to an XSL file by using the following statement:

```
<?xml-stylesheet href="catalog.xsl" type="text/xsl" ?>
```

The catalog.xsl file shown here contains a variety of pattern-matching rules that would output HTML and style rules:

```
<?xml version="1.0"?>
<xsl>
<rule>
   <root />
   <HTML>
   <HEAD>
     <TITLE>Parts Catalog</TITLE>
   </HEAD>
```

```
     <BODY BGCOLOR="orange">
     <H1 ALIGN="CENTER">Product Catalog</H1>
     <HR/>
     <children/>
     <BR/>
     </BODY>
     </HTML>
</rule>

<rule>
   <target-element type="PART" />
   <DIV STYLE="margin: 50px; background: yellow">
     <children />
   </DIV>
</rule>

<rule>
   <element type="PART">
      <target-element type="NAME" />
   </element>

   <B>
   <children />
   </B><BR/>
</rule>

<rule>
   <element type="PART">
      <target-element type="DESCRIPTION" />
   </element>

   <DIV STYLE="text-indent: 20px; font-style: italic">
      <children/>
   </DIV>
   <BR/>
</rule>

<rule>
   <element type="PART">
      <target-element type="PRICE" />
   </element>
```

```
   <DIV ALIGN="RIGHT" STYLE="color: green;">
      <children/>
   </DIV><BR/>
</rule>
</xsl>
```

One interesting aspect of XSL is that it actually is defined in XML. Note the precise nesting, quoting, case consistency, and self-identifying in the document, as required by XML. The basic purpose of this example XSL file is to define numerous rules to match XML elements to HTML markup. The various rules are defined by the **<rule>** element, which contains matching statements such as **<target-element type="PRICE" />**. This would look for an element called **<PRICE>**. You can make the rule more specific by including the **<target-element>** tag within an **<element>** tag that indicates which tag must enclose the tag that you are trying to match. The second part of the **<rule>** element is the actual markup that should be output when the rule works. You may notice the continued use of the **<children/>** element, which indicates that the contents of the element should be processed or output if necessary.

 The last example doesn't work properly under Internet Explorer 5. However, a JavaScript-based XSL parse utility was able to parse the file properly and output the appropriate HTML code.

The example provided only begins to touch on the richness of XSL, which provides complex pattern matching and basic programming facilities. Unfortunately, at the time of this new edition's writing, XSL is still in a draft form; even the latest browsers have only partial support for this technology. Readers interested in the latest developments in XSL are directed to the W3C Web site (http://www.w3.org/Style/XSL/), as well as Microsoft's XML site (http://www.microsoft.com/xml).

Rewriting HTML as XML

As you read about XML, you may wonder how this technology is going to affect HTML. Already, XML is being used in a fashion that complements HTML. For example, the concept of XML data islands, as introduced by Microsoft, allows XML elements to be added to an HTML document based on need. The use of XML as a data format language outside the realm of HTML shouldn't affect HTML either. Already, CDF is being used with HTML files to define push channels for Internet Explorer, and SMIL is being used by Real Platform (http://www.real.com) to define presentations. However, XML is not going to stay quietly behind the scenes for long. This chapter has

NEW HORIZONS

already shown examples of how XML could be displayed natively in a browser, or even translated into HTML for display. XML goes beyond this and may totally change the flavor of HTML forever.

In late 1998, the W3C released its first draft of how HTML could be rewritten in light of XML. Code-named Voyager, this form of HTML broke the language into modules and applied all XML rules to HTML elements. Although these rules were discussed earlier in this chapter in the section "Basic XML," they are significant and should be mentioned again with specific focus on HTML syntax:

- *All elements must be nested.* For example, ****Ok**** is okay, but ****Bad**** is not.

- *End tags are always required.* For example, **<p>** must always have a corresponding **</p>**.

- *Empty elements must include a trailing slash.* For example, **
** isn't valid, but **
** is.

- *Attributes must not be minimized.* For example, **<ol compact>** is not allowed, but **<ol compact="compact">** is.

- *All tags and attributes must be lowercase.* Because XML is case-sensitive, Voyager is case-sensitive, too. **<P>** and **<p>** are different tags. The W3C has decided, for the moment, that **<p>** is the official way to denote a paragraph.

Some other rules have been added to make HTML more precise. First, you must indicate the particular set of XML-defined HTML tags that you are using. This is defined not by a **<!DOCTYPE>**, but by the **xmlns** attribute for the **<html>** element. For example,

```
<html xmlns="http://www.w3.org/Profiles/voyager-strict">
```

specifies the URL that defines the namespace and document profile for this new form of HTML. A namespace is a new idea added to XML that enables you to indicate where elements are defined. The use of namespaces allows more than one author to define an element, such as **<title>**, without having to worry about another person somewhere else in the world causing a problem with their document. As long as a namespace is indicated, you can always reference the proper definition.

The last important rule is that the first element within the **<head>** of a document must be the **<title>** element and it must be followed by the **<base>** element, if one is used.

Many of these rules are simply the same good HTML practices that have been promoted throughout this book. However, the consequences for not following the rules under Voyager are a little stricter than under HTML. With HTML, browsers pretty much render anything, even if it doesn't conform to any known DTD. Under Voyager, if the document breaks any of the previously discussed rules or uses elements that are undefined in Voyager, the document will not render at all. This seriously changes the flavor of HTML, both in good and bad ways.

Predicting the Future of XML

Predicting the future of XML or its effects on HTML is difficult. One thing is for certain: HTML isn't going away in its present form any time soon. Simply too many people are writing HTML documents for it to go away overnight. Furthermore, the definition of HTML as an XML language may not have much effect in the short term. Unfortunately, people just don't seem to follow the rules with HTML, suggesting that all existing documents have to be rewritten in order to render is unlikely. More likely, browsers will contain some sort of compatibility mode to deal with old HTML markup, which will water down the effect of Voyager in the short term. Because Voyager is so precisely defined, over time, you will see tools developed that guarantee the production of precise HTML. The strictness of Voyager will also spare browsers from having to make assumptions about markup, which may help resolve browser compatibility issues to some degree. Hopefully, this will lead to a much more stable Web.

XML clearly provides significant benefits. The technology is simple to describe, yet provides the power to create data that can be passed between programs or people without loss of meaning. With its structure, XML will enable Web-based automation, improved search engines, and a host of motivating e-commerce applications. However, before you get too excited, consider that to achieve the dream of an XML-enabled Web, many diverse groups need to get together and agree on data formats. Just because XML *could* be used to write a special language to be used to automate data interchange in a particular industry doesn't mean that people *will* accept it. Remember that XML is based on SGML, and SGML has promised similar benefits during its history. Getting groups to agree upon a common data format and actually use it isn't always feasible, given the competitive nature of business. Anyone can define their own XML-based language. McDonald's could define FFML (Fast Food Markup Language). But does this mean that Burger King will accept it as standard? With people defining languages for their own special needs, the chaos of the Web could multiply into a markup Tower of Babel.

Don't underestimate the simplicity of HTML. It may be ill defined and misused, but it is commonly known and understood. In some sense, HTML is the English of the Web. Unfortunately, this analogy might make Voyager the equivalent of Esperanto—the supposed well-defined perfect common language. Only one thing is certain about HTML and XML: change will happen. But consider the requirements to move the Web from an HTML-centered approach to an XML-centered one, and you'll see that the widespread adoption of XML is going to take some time.

Summary

This discussion of XML's core syntax and extension only scratches the surface of what remains an emerging technology. The best way to track XML's rapid evolution is to closely monitor the XML activity at the W3C site, http://www.w3.org. The implications of XML are enormous. Just as a meta-data definition language, XML has some wonderful uses for extending the Web. CDF shows how XML is used to define a push language. Other languages are certainly possible, including markup to help search engines more accurately index Web pages. However, eventually, a demand will arise to include XML directly into HTML pages to augment the functionality of the page, or maybe even replace the page outright.

As it stands, XML is still missing well-defined and well-implemented linking and style definitions. As a middle-ground language, XML attempts to provide much of the power of SGML while keeping the application oriented to the Web and within the easy-to-use spirit of HTML. What XML will eventually bring, if it can be used directly within Web pages, is the power to make data more regular and more specific to particular applications or industries. With improved structure, migrating Web data to and from databases, exchanging documents with other parties, and navigating large collections of documents could get significantly easier.

Like many new hot technologies, XML will go through a "hype phase" that suggests it is good for everything. However, at least in the short term, XML will augment HTML and address its weaknesses rather than replace it outright. Just as Windows relied on DOS and did not quickly supplant it, the market-driven nature of Web technologies in conjunction with the existing heavy investment in HTML-based information will probably spur an XML evolution rather than XML revolution.

Chapter 18

Future Directions

653

Where HTML is heading isn't always easy to predict. The Web has been rocked by rapid commercialization and the introduction of numerous new technologies. However, the evolution of Web technology is far from finished. Only a few years ago it was hard to imagine the types of multimedia and programmed sites that are common on the Web today. Current trends in presentation, programming, page structure, and the Web in general suggest what might happen to HTML and the Web in the near future.

Presentation Issues

Getting pages to look a particular way is one of the chief goals of Web page designers. With the rise of Cascading Style Sheets (CSS1) and the CSS positioning extensions (CSS-P), which are now part of CSS2, style sheets provide many of the layout features that page designers want. However, the CSS language is far from perfect; it is particularly lacking in adequate support for tables, multimedia, and fonts. One approach to dealing with tables is not to have CSS address them, and leave that for HTML. HTML 4 already provides a rich table model, so this may be adequate. Other style sheet technologies such as DSSSL (Document Style Semantics and Specification Language), which is now recast in the form of XSL (Extensible Style Language), show that it is possible to address table support at the style sheet level. It is unclear in which direction table support will go. For now, as style sheets grow in acceptance, tables will probably continue to serve double duty both as traditional tables and as positioning devices to create well-laid-out Web pages.

Another aspect of presentation that isn't perfectly clear yet is fonts. It is critical that downloadable fonts come to the Web. Having page designers rely on certain fonts being installed on the end user's computer or attempting to embed fonts as pictures is not reasonable. Microsoft and Netscape have already demonstrated that Web fonts are possible. Even so, the issue of fonts isn't solved. As the difference between the desktop and the Web shrinks, an issue of font compatibility arises. On the desktop, we use TrueType and PostScript fonts. On the Web, we use TrueDoc or OpenType fonts. There is a conflict here when moving documents back and forth. Microsoft's OpenType is intended to format for both the Web and the desktop. This seems logical. Netscape however, is looking to create a Web-specific font technology. Despite logic, which font format will win is still far from clear. The World Wide Web Consortium (W3C) is working hard on font-embedding specifications, including defining a way to create fonts from font objects so that it is possible to avoid downloading complete font sets for very similar fonts.

A great deal of the discussion about Web presentation is based on the desire to reach print standards, but are we really looking to mimic print? The Web is more about multimedia than about paper. Things like multiple windows, or frames, animated buttons, and page transitions are inevitable additions to Web pages. How should these features be added? In some cases, new HTML elements have been introduced to support these features, such as the **<MARQUEE>** element. This definitely isn't the best way to introduce these technologies. Small embedded binaries should probably be used to add new multimedia features, but how will they be referenced from HTML and style sheets? Microsoft has shown that it is possible to add numerous multimedia features, in the form of filters, to style sheets. Many more features for multimedia will undoubtedly be added. The **<OBJECT>** element may serve as the generic way to add new binary forms. Which binary forms will dominate the Web is hard to predict, but it is unlikely that more than two formats will be viable in sound, animation, video, and 3-D. At this point it seems that Macromedia's Flash and RealNetwork's RealAudio and RealVideo are quickly gaining industry support. However, new forms may be on the horizon. Forms that some might expect to go away, such as Adobe Acrobat, will continue to thrive online in areas where style sheets and HTML come up short, such as electronics specifications.

Programming Issues

The Web isn't just about print. A transition is already underway from a page-oriented view of the Web to a more program-oriented view of Web sites. Think of a complex system like a job postings Web site. The site must be able to provide dynamic listings of various jobs, support keyword searches, accept résumés, schedule interviews, and perform a variety of other tasks. It should do this within the constraints of the different browsers that might access the site. Described this way, Web sites sound more like software. The truth is, many sites *are* like software.

Adding interactivity to Web sites is now commonplace. There are various new technologies to choose from. Some of these, such as CGI, NSAPI/ISAPI, and server-side scripting, are server side. Others, such as plug-ins, are client side. And still others, such as JavaScript, VBScript, and Java, are used on both ends of the transaction. The rise of so-called Dynamic HTML (DHTML) and the Document Object Model (DOM) show just how intermixed HTML and programming languages are becoming. Choosing which technology to use, and when, is a challenge. Too much emphasis on the server can slow the site down and keep it from scaling. Placing too much responsibility on the client side can also be problematic, since it is often difficult to ensure that all clients support the technology properly. Because the client is beyond the page designer's control, it may be hard to ensure that things don't go wrong, even with careful design and rigorous testing. There is a balance between what should be done on the client side and what should be done on the server.

The chief problems with programming facilities being added to Web sites include standardization, scalability, and methodology. Web programming technologies like Java and JavaScript are far from standardized. There seems to be a growing rift between one browser's idea of Java and another's. Netscape's JavaScript and Microsoft's JScript have major differences despite conformance to the ECMAScript standard. These issues will have to be sorted out soon if there is to be any hope for a true cross-platform programming environment. Otherwise, it may be necessary to use platform-specific technologies like ActiveX controls or Netscape plug-ins in conjunction with server-side technologies, regardless of what makes sense in theory.

As more and more users get on the Internet, some programmed sites are going to face a critical problem of scalability. Imagine an airline reservation system on the Web. How is it going to handle tens or hundreds of thousands of people who use it nearly at the same time to order cheap tickets for the holidays? Another example of the problem of scalability was when, in the fall of 1997, trading and related news sites were quickly swamped after the stock market took a plunge. The problems continued in 1998 when shopping sites were overwhelmed during the Christmas rush and electronic auction sites went up and down due to huge traffic spikes. The need to build large, robust systems will increase as electronic commerce develops. Today, however, most systems simply won't scale. The applications aren't distributed across many servers, and it is difficult to create distributed systems. Many industry pundits like to discuss how programming objects will be flung far over the Internet, and how corporate networks will be served out from various application servers to help solve scalability problems. These objects should help when you think of many application servers distributing ordering objects to airline ticket buyers. In this sense, the Web turns into a giant distributed system. The question arises of how well these objects are going to interact. Even on a single-user's computer, the idea of having objects communicate with each other has been less than straightforward. Doing this over a network only makes things worse. The battle for the object world, already in progress, pits a loose alliance of Common Object Request Broker Architecture (CORBA) and Java against Microsoft's Distributed Component Object Model (DCOM). Which of these particular object technologies will dominate the Internet is unclear. One may be popular on intranets, while the other is common outside the corporation. The true answer might be neither, as XML-based formats provide a way for applications to interact with each other over the Internet. Already companies like Allaire (http://www.allaire.com), with its WDDX format, and others show that this can be done today.

With the rise of complexity in programming systems, particularly those that must be built to scale, rigorous development methodologies must be adopted. The current state of affairs on the Web overemphasizes the look and feel of a site. Back end work on databases and programming often take a backseat to visuals. Testing is poorly considered. Sites are often built without solid plans, in a mad rush to get on the Web or outdo the competition. This has to change. To build complex systems, the ideas of software engineering will have to be applied to Web pages. The ad hoc approaches used to date won't work. Principles adopted from software engineering, which may be dubbed Web site engineering, may help curb problems, but there is still a great deal of work left to do in order to develop the best practices for Web site development. Don't be fooled: tools won't save the developer facing a complex task. Methodology is required as well.

The idea of using simple what-you-see-is-what-you-get (WYSIWYG) development tools to link components in a Rapid Application Development (RAD) style is a tempting idea, but it doesn't work. RAD is widely practiced on the Web, but in a form that often causes more harm than benefit. The key to RAD is the idea of prototype-driven design. On the Web, this would mean creating a Web site and then working over the site in numerous iterations with user input, including design meetings, until the final design falls out. In this sense, RAD means building the wrong site multiple times until the right site falls out of the process. How far is the rapidly developed Web site from what the users actually want? Will there be repercussions if a subpar site is launched for public use? Looking at all the sites with "under construction" signs on them, it seems that RAD is very popular on the Web. It is not, however, a safe approach to building Web sites, least of all complex ones.

RAD grew from the maturity of the software engineering discipline. Before RAD came a variety of structured design paradigms that helped developers understand the systems they were developing. How can one create a RAD-based tool or philosophy for an environment that is still in its infancy? RAD will work, and it will certainly have its place on the Web, but it is too soon for Web RAD. Many Web page developers are hardly schooled in software development, let alone structured software development. Ask yourself if the HTML code, not to mention the scripts, of many Web site files exhibits strict coding standards. Naming conventions, organization, and coding rules are not widely promoted on the Web.

No more evidence of the Web's lack of software development maturity is required than the state of testing. Vague references to "test your site under other browsers" are the typical depth of this discussion, which invariably omits test plans and matrices, test types, regression testing, and so on. Even if browser testing were the only aspect to Web testing, just how many versions of browsers are there? There are literally hundreds. The payoff of making a site work under the Commodore 64 browser (there is one) is generally minor. How many versions of Netscape are there? A quick survey shows ports to Macintosh, Windows 3.1, Windows 95/NT, OS/2, and numerous flavors of UNIX. The browser itself has gone through numerous major releases at the time of this writing (1.x, 2.x, 3.x, 4, 4.5, and soon 5.x), and there are various beta versions still floating around. So what? you might ask. The problem is that these browsers act differently when it comes to programming facilities. Serious bugs exist, programmingwise, under different versions of the browser, such as JavaScript support. Ad hoc "looks right so it must be right" testing by example could spell disaster for complex programmed Web sites. This is not a proclamation of doom and gloom for Web development, simply a wakeup call to the requirements of programmed sites.

There should be no doubt that, when appropriate, the programming paradigm of Web sites is here. Many of the more interesting sites that do something have sophisticated back end systems, and often tie in with databases. Scripting and objects have made it to the client. The idea of Dynamic HTML (DHTML) makes the page a dynamic document rather than a print-oriented one. However, these changes come with a potential price. Remember how mixing the structure of a Web page with presentation by forcing layout with HTML was considered a bad idea? Now add in a heavy amount of scripting. Without careful decomposition in pages to keep content separate in a structured fashion from presentation and logic, can pages live on past the current state?

Structure

One of a Web designer's chief roles is bringing order to the chaos, simply to provide structure. As mentioned throughout this book, the original intent of HTML was as a structuring language, but its purpose was often misunderstood. The structure that HTML provides for documents is not enough, particularly when considering the site as a whole. While it is easy enough to collect documents, how do they relate, and how will the documents be managed? Many Web sites manage their information as a collection of files in directories. This won't work as the site scales unless very strict rules are followed. The keys to solving many of the problems of document management and site structure are databases and XML. A database can be used to hold content that is pulled out of a database and flowed into HTML templates. The HTML templates are then combined with style sheets, binary objects, and programming logic to form a complex Web-based application. An overview of this separation is shown in Figure 18-1.

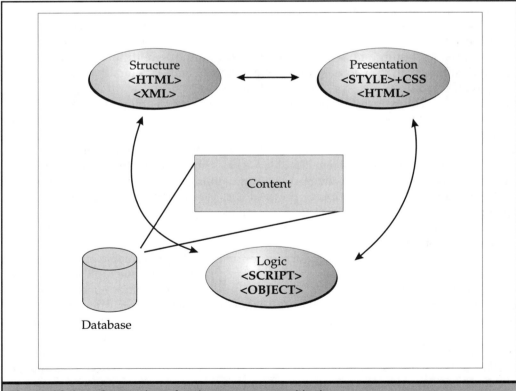

Figure 18-1.   *Separation of style, structure, and logic*

The benefits of such harsh borders are not always obvious. Using a database as a centralized repository for information can provide significant benefits. Imagine the knowledge of a company stored in a document repository that can be mined to pull data out and flowed into various different presentation formats like PageMaker files, HTML files, and so on. These files can then be distributed in a variety of fashions: paper, Web, or even CD-ROM. Figure 18-2 provides an overview of this idea.

While all this makes sense, few people are really doing it. In many cases, HTML is the primary form of the data; the structure and the content of the document are tightly bound. Is this such a wise idea? Think back to just one year ago. Are last year's HTML facilities considered passé? How easy is it to retrofit these documents and bring them up to the latest features? In some cases, certain HTML elements have been deprecated. The way HTML is being used today does not promote long document life. While this may keep Web professionals in business, it really isn't the best approach. Document

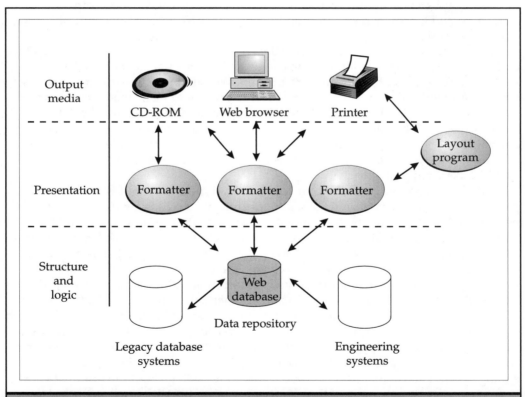

Figure 18-2.   *Content and preservation separation in action*

form should be dependent on the purpose and life expectancy of the information. Certain documents might not work well in HTML. Adobe Acrobat, which allows the display of more complicated documents in a Web browser, might be a great solution, particularly as it also permits easier printing of those documents. Translating certain low-priority documents from Microsoft Word to the Web might be totally wasteful given the possibility of using word processing files on the Web. HTML does bring structure, but there are other ways to do things.

XML may provide the structure that HTML does not, particularly for industry-specific applications. HTML is a generalized markup language that provides structures like headings, lists, and paragraphs. However, data often has a much richer meaning than simply being a paragraph. Imagine a summary paragraph for a technical paper. Perhaps you would want to indicate such a structure with a **<SUMMARY>** tag. In XML, it would be possible to deploy such specific markup. XML already has been used to develop a special push-technology markup language called Channel Definition Format (CDF), as well as a software distribution language called Open Software Description (OSD), a Chemical Markup Language (CML), and a Mathematical Markup Format (MathML). The structure such languages provide is not just helpful for particular industries; it can help migrate data in and out of databases. Imagine creating a special markup language for electronics parts with elements like **<PRODUCTID>**, **<DESCRIPTION>**, **<PRICE>**, and **<DIESIZE>**. Wouldn't it be easy to have database table definitions with similar names? Such structure would make managing complex data collections on the Web much easier. The answer depends on what the data is doing. If data is to be interchanged between systems, XML makes sense as it is a neutral form. However, XML-based flat file systems will never be able to provide the searching and query mechanisms databases are good at, so XML won't solve all the Web's structuring problems.

HTML does not provide all the structuring that is necessary, but when it's used properly, it's a start. That's why the idea of document structuring with HTML should be taken to heart. Eventually, XML might be required. Exactly how XML and HTML will interact is unclear. How databases and HTML/XML should work together is also uncertain. Microsoft has already shown that, using data binding, it is possible to provide direct interaction between Web pages and databases. Databases are mandatory. Structure is mandatory. If you are unconvinced, look at the history of hypermedia. Numerous papers written about hypertext have discussed a three-layer model consisting of a presentation layer, a linking layer, and a database layer. The Web has presentation in the form of the browser, style sheets, and certain HTML features. The Web also has the hypertext abstract layer in the form of URLs and HTML linking constructs. But what about the database layer? The Web itself really does not have such a thing, though individual sites often do. What's interesting about the future of HTML is that it intersects with many of the grand problems of the Web, such as the lack of regular structure for Web documents.

Web-Wide Problems

Many Web-wide problems intersect HTML every day. One major problem involves searching the Web. It is very difficult to find things on the Internet using a search engine. Why this is a problem is obvious if you consider how search engines work. A search engine looks at a Web page and indexes the words it sees there. The engine determines what the page is about based upon a heuristic that combines how many times a particular word occurs, the value of the keywords specified by the **<META>** elements in the document, and the title of the document. This is terribly imprecise, as anyone who has searched the Web knows. A Web page that contains the word *Intel* in it may have nothing to do with the Intel Corporation. Typing this word in a search engine might return hundreds of thousands of responses. You should hope to see a site like http://www.intel.com listed first, but this rarely happens. The robots or spiders that index Web pages really have no idea what they are indexing. They can provide no value to the indexing that a human might. For the search engines to understand the information they are looking at, wouldn't they have to possess artificial intelligence? Yes, if data is unstructured. If structure can be added to data, then it is very easy to index information. HTML elements like **<META>** and new meta-data formats written in XML should bring such order. However, this is actually more difficult than it sounds. Getting people to agree on the structure of more complex meta-data, the allowable words in the data, and the organizations that will certify the correctness of the meta-data will be very difficult.

As searching suggests, navigating around the Web is less than straightforward. People are perpetually lost in cyberspace; the back button is their only way to safety. The linking mechanisms of the Web will certainly be improved. Eventually, even some type of uniform naming scheme, like a uniform resource name (URN), will arise. HTML will have to be extended to deal with a richer linking structure, because the **<A>** element provides only limited functionality as it stands. The **<META>** element provides some relief; but after looking at complex timing and linking technologies used with SGML, such as HyTime, there are many other extensions that may have to be made to HTML or XML.

Another Web-wide problem is that of accessibility. Lack of accessibility comes in many forms: an international user dealing with an English-only environment, a visually impaired user dealing with a site that has too much visual emphasis, or a technology-poor user unable to run Netscape to enter the latest and greatest site. The bottom line is that the Web and HTML should not intentionally lock people out. There may be cases where the designers of the site want to limit access based upon their own views, but the technology itself should not be designed to do such a thing.

The first example of accessibility is internationalization. The Web is supposed to be the World Wide Web, but it seems as if a U.S.-centric viewpoint often dominates the landscape. The Web needs to be improved to support other languages' character sets and reading directions. HTML 4 is already moving toward a more international approach, but there is still a long way to go. English will probably continue to serve as the dominant language, but Web documents in French, Spanish, German, Japanese, Chinese, Korean, and Russian are already commonplace. Undoubtedly, more languages will be used online. There will need to be facilities to provide friendly help to those with a less-than-perfect mastery of a given language.

Much can also be said about how unfriendly the Web can be for those who have handicaps. Many Web sites completely lock out those users who are sight impaired because such sites provide no meaningful **ALT** text and rely heavily on graphics. (You may recall that the **ALT** attribute provides alternative text for user agents that do not display images, or for graphical browsers where the user has turned image rendering off.) While the Web will continue to be a medium rich in visuals, the W3C is making sure that many users are not left out of the experience by extending HTML to help make pages more accessible via keyboard, voice, and Braille.

Last, there are those users who, because of limited bandwidth or computing technology, don't often receive the complete picture. HTML does not always degrade gracefully when older or less common browsers view pages. More work, both in standards and development techniques, will be required to keep the Web open to those people who don't always use the latest and greatest gadgets or applications.

Despite all the problems with accessibility, the biggest gripe with the Web is performance. The Internet is growing at such a wild pace that traffic snarls are an everyday occurrence. New protocols like HTTP 1.1, image formats with better compression schemes like Portable Network Graphics (PNG), and new technologies like DSL and cable modems will help speed the delivery of Web pages in the future. However, the amount of data that users want is quickly increasing. Bandwidth-hungry media forms like video don't work reliably on the Internet. Delivering reasonable-quality video over today's Web is impossible. Even still images can seem to take an eternity to download. HTML has been extended to help improve the usability of multimedia-laden pages. Remember the **HEIGHT**, **WIDTH**, and **LOWSRC** attributes for the **<IMG>** element? Other approaches that have been considered are the ideas of suggesting which pages will be visited next so that they can be pre-fetched for the user. WebTV shows one way HTML can be used to provide such functionality.

Other approaches that will help speed the Web experience include alternative transport protocols, caches, and page-level compression. However, delivery always breaks down because of the idea of point sources. With single Web servers delivering data, eventually there is going to be a bottleneck. Content must be replicated around caches and delivered from mirror sites, or even broadcast. One technique is the use of intelligent hardware devices to balance distribution of pages among different Web servers based on how busy the servers are or by determining which server is closest to the user requesting pages. Another approach is with the proposed Distribution and Replication Protocol (DRP). DRP distributes updates to content such as Web pages in a differential fashion, meaning that if only part of a file has been changed, just that part will be sent, instead of the whole file. These and other approaches to better content distribution models are just now being determined, but many sites (including Yahoo!) already use some of these techniques to provide a high level of performance. While the

Web may be slow, the problems are being addressed at the network level with improvements in the Internet infrastructure and better protocols such as IP Multicast and IPv6, which address inefficiencies in the current TCP/IP protocol, and protocols based on it, such as HTTP. The idea of multicast, for example, enables the broadcast delivery of a single file to multiple destinations, instead of sending the same file many times to multiple destinations. Some of these solutions will certainly affect HTML. Remember that the network is the medium of the Web; its effect is significant. How people access the Web will certainly affect the direction HTML takes.

Application-Specific Presentation

As the Internet and the Web become more mainstream, the way they are used will certainly change. In just a few years, the Web has gone from being an environment of engineers and academics to being a very commercial environment dominated by consumers. The major change is still to come. Many people are not on the Web, and the potential uses of the medium have not been fully explored.

The Web is very computer-centered, but this may change somewhat. Many people do not have computers, but many want to get one just to get on the Web. Because of such interest, consumer-oriented devices such as WebTV have been developed. While none of these devices is as common as VCRs or CD players, the adoption rate of WebTV is higher than the initial adoption rate of VCRs. People often forget that consumer electronics may take five or ten years to become mainstream. The CD player was initially considered a status symbol in the early '80s before it finally caught on and all but replaced cassettes and LPs in the consumer market. It is obvious that consumer Web devices will not be the way that most people will access the Internet for the near term. However, their development and initial acceptance points to an interesting trend toward nontraditional, computer-based Web use. This has some interesting ramifications for HTML.

HTML may have to become more of an application specification. At the very least, new languages will be developed to deal with such applications. This book has mentioned numerous WebTV extensions. Regardless of your particular slant on whether vendors should make such extensions to HTML, television-based Web viewing is very different from computer-based browsing. People tend to browse Web sites by themselves, close up to a computer with a high-resolution monitor. They may not read information onscreen; they may print it instead. Now think of using a WebTV. The WebTV uses a large screen with relatively low resolution. People, often many of them at once, tend to sit far away from the screen they are viewing. They probably will not read large amounts of text on a TV screen. They may use a remote or a wireless keyboard to interact with information. A traditional mouse pointer is out of the question when you are sitting on the couch. Given WebTV's unique environment, it seems obvious that less text in bigger size would probably work better. The dimensions of the screen are different as well. Other considerations arise. Won't people have to consume the information onscreen? How much information can be positioned onscreen? How should the navigation work? Many of the HTML extensions made by WebTV address some of these problems, though in subtle ways. These extensions make it easier to fill out forms and constrain pages not to scroll left to right, among other things. WebTV shows that applications will influence what features will have to be included.

Other application-specific environments that may need special extensions or HTML-like languages include voice browsing and cellular phone browsing. Devices that allow you to view a Web page with a telephone or pocket organizer, such as a Windows-CE hand-held device, are already available. These systems are very different from traditional computer screens; they often have tiny screens with only four shades of gray. Furthermore, many hand-held devices have slower access rates to the Internet, even as low as 4800 bps via a wireless network. Traditional HTML may not be well suited to these low-speed, small-screen environments. A language called HDML (Hand-held Device Markup Language) has already been submitted to the W3C as a proposed standard. Whether special languages are implemented as new languages, subsets of HTML, supersets of HTML, or as new languages written as applications of XML remains unclear. The current thought is that HTML will be written with conformance profiles like TV, phone, computer, and so on. Various devices will then be able to request pages that meet a particular conformance profile. With the rise of network computers, hand-held personal information managers, sophisticated digital cellular phones, and consumer-oriented network devices, the ideas of HTML will certainly have to be modified to fit a radically different application environment.

What Is the Future of HTML?

After all this discussion, we might wonder what can be said for sure about the future of HTML. One thing is certain: page designers won't do things the way they do now. Hacking around in HTML is a throwback to the days of page-setting languages such as troff or LaTeX. With the rise of PostScript and the tools that could output it, document designers stopped editing files directly in most cases. While older page-setting technologies are still used, and some people even program directly in PostScript, most do not. Using a tool to output PostScript, whether a word processor or a page layout program tool, is the way most designers create documents. As HTML settles down and becomes more standardized, tools will certainly be developed that can output pages appropriately. Right now, with standards and browsers in flux, tool vendors have a nearly impossible time creating such tools. For the moment, HTML designers often have to resort to doing tweaks, if not the whole page, by hand. This won't last long. If HTML can be written in a precise way as an XML application, it should be a lot easier to create machine-readable and editable markup. At this point we should be able to focus less on tag syntax and more on document design and content. What does this mean? Simply that within five years, HTML coders will be in about as much demand as typesetting machine operators.

With the rise of electronic and improved mechanical printing technologies, the demand for these skills quickly went away. However, HTML as a print formatting language is not the point. The migration to a dynamic program-like environment should already be clear. Dynamic HTML, databases, and embedded objects all point the way to the Web of tomorrow. Knowledge of HTML will serve as a backbone for accessing these technologies. The benefit of short-term mastery of HTML will be early access to these ideas and a fundamental understanding of how the Web works.

Summary

While standards and the open philosophy of the Web are important, there is one big lesson to be learned from the past, present, and future of HTML: there is no single correct solution to the Web puzzle. What is cutting edge today will be trivial tomorrow. Tools will eventually make intimate knowledge of HTML obsolete. So why did you even read this book? Because today you have to build Web pages, and HTML is one of the primary tools for this task. Don't lose perspective: HTML and the other technologies are just tools to help people accomplish goals for disseminating information and providing services. Not everybody has the same goals. This book has discussed how things can be done and provided some information on why, but the real answer to the why question is up to you. Many of the ideas and the syntax presented here will undoubtedly be outdated in a few years, but that doesn't matter. Implementing a site today and reaching your goals is the main point of the Web. Today most people will not judge a site by its conformance to the document type definition, but by whether it was useful or enjoyable. This is often forgotten when talking about HTML. Knowing the particular syntax of an HTML element or the correct structure for HTML documents is very important, just as the rules and standards are important. But these rules are not well enforced. This doesn't mean you should break the rules; it means you should design for today with an eye on tomorrow. Remember that in the future with the rise of XML, the rules will matter. Making a transition will be easy if you understand how HTML is supposed to be written. Tools should make the transition easier, but until then, actually knowing HTML completely and precisely will be invaluable when authoring Web pages.

The Complete Reference

Part VI

Appendixes

The
Complete
Reference

HTML

Appendix A

HTML Element
Reference

This appendix provides a complete reference of the elements in the HTML 4.0 specification and the elements commonly supported by Internet Explorer, Netscape, and WebTV. Some elements presented here may be nonstandard or deprecated, but are included because browser vendors continue to support them or they are still in common use. The standard used in this text is the final version of HTML 4 as defined on December 18, 1997, and is available at http://www.w3.org/TR/REC-html40/.

Core Attributes Reference

The HTML 4.0 specification provides four main attributes, which are common to nearly all elements and have the same meaning for all elements. These elements are **CLASS**, **ID**, **STYLE**, and **TITLE**.

CLASS

This attribute is used to indicate the class or classes that a particular element belongs to. A class name is used by a style sheet to associate style rules to multiple elements at once. For example, it may be desirable to associate a special class name called "important" with all elements that should be rendered with a yellow background. Since class values are not unique to a particular element, **<B CLASS="important">** could be used as well as **<P CLASS="important">** in the same document. It is also possible to have multiple values for the **CLASS** attribute separated by white space; **<STRONG CLASS="important special-font">** would define two classes with the particular **<STRONG>** element. Currently, most browsers recognize only one class name for this attribute.

ID

This attribute specifies a unique alphanumeric identifier to be associated with an element. Naming an element is important to being able to access it with a style sheet, a link, or a scripting language. Names should be unique to a document and should be meaningful, so while **ID="x1"** is perfectly valid, **ID="Paragraph1"** might be better. Values for the **ID** attribute must begin with a letter (A–Z and a–z) and may be followed by any number of letters, digits, hyphens, and periods.

One potential problem with the **ID** attribute is that for some elements, particularly form controls and images, the **NAME** attribute already serves its function. Values for **NAME** should not collide with values for **ID**, as they share the same naming space. For example, the following would not be allowed:

```
<B ID="elementX">This is a test.</B>
<IMG NAME="elementX" SRC="image.gif">
```

There is some uncertainty about what to do to ensure backward compatibility with browsers that understand **NAME** but not **ID**. Some people suggest that the following is illegal:

```
<IMG NAME="image1" ID="image1" SRC="image.gif">
```

Since **NAME** and **ID** are naming the same item, there should be no problem; the common browsers do not have an issue with such markup. Complex scripting necessary to deal with two different names for the image, like

```
<IMG NAME="image1name" ID="imageid" SRC="image.gif">
```

is possible, but may not be necessary.

Page designers are encouraged to pick a naming strategy and use it consistently. Once elements are named, they should be easy to manipulate with a scripting language.

Like the **CLASS** attribute, the **ID** attribute is also used by style sheets for accessing a particular element.

For example, an element named **Paragraph1** can be referenced by a style rule in a document-wide style using a fragment identifier:

```
#Paragraph1    {color: blue}
```

Once an element is named using **ID**, it is also a potential destination for an anchor. In the past an **<A>** element was used to set a destination; now any element may be a destination. For example,

```
<A HREF="#firstbolditem">Go to first bold element.</A>
<B ID="firstbolditem">This is important.</B>
```

STYLE

This attribute specifies an inline style (as opposed to an external style sheet) associated with the element. The style information is used to determine the rendering of the affected element. Because the **STYLE** attribute allows style rules to be used directly with the element, it gives up much of the benefit of style sheets that divide the presentation of an HTML document from its structure. An example of this attribute's use is shown here:

```
<STRONG STYLE="font-family: Arial;
          font-size: 18pt">Important text</STRONG>
```

TITLE

This attribute supplies advisory text for the element that may be rendered as a tool tip when the mouse is over the element. A title may also simply provide information that alerts future document maintainers to the meaning of the element and its enclosed content. In some cases, such as the **<A>** element, the **TITLE** attribute may provide additional help in bookmarking. Like the title for the document itself, **TITLE** attribute values as advisory information should be short, yet useful. For example, **<P TITLE="paragraph1">** provides little information of value, while **<P TITLE="HTML Programmer's Reference: Chapter 1, Paragraph 10">** provides much more detail. When combined with scripting, it may provide facilities for automatic index generation.

Language Reference

One of the main goals of the HTML 4.0 specification is better support for other languages besides English. The use of other languages in a Web page may require that text direction be changed from left to right or right to left. Furthermore, once supporting non-ASCII languages becomes easier, it may be more common to see documents in mixed languages. Thus, there must be a way to indicate the language in use.

LANG

This attribute indicates the language being used for the enclosed content. The language is identified using the ISO standard language abbreviation such as *fr* for French, *en* for English, and so on. RFC 1766 (ftp://ds.internic.net/rfc/rfc1766.txt) describes these codes and their format.

DIR

This attribute sets the text direction as related to the **LANG** attribute. The accepted values under the HTML 4.0 specification are **LTR** (left to right) and **RTL** (right to left). It should be possible to override whatever direction a user agent sets by using the **<BDO>** element. No browsers yet support this attribute; Internet Explorer 5 may support **DIR**, but not in the beta version available for testing at the time of this edition.

Events Reference

In preparation for a more dynamic Web, the W3C (World Wide Web Consortium) has defined a set of core events that are associated with nearly every HTML element. Most of these events cover simple user interaction such as the click of a mouse button or a key being pressed. A few elements, such as form controls, have some special events associated with them, signaling that the field has received focus from the user or that the form was submitted. Intrinsic events like a document loading and unloading are also described. The core events are summarized in the Table A-1. Note that, in the table, Internet Explorer 4 and 5 and Netscape 4 and 4.5 are abbreviated to IE4, IE5, N4, and N4.5, respectively.

Note   *In Table A-1, "most display elements" means all elements except <APPLET>, <BASE>, <BASEFONT>, <BDO>, <BR>, <FONT>, <FRAME>, <FRAMESET>, <HEAD>, <HTML>, <IFRAME>, <ISINDEX>, <META>, <PARAM>, <SCRIPT>, <STYLE>, and <TITLE>.*

This event model is far from complete, and it is still not fully supported by browsers. The event model should be considered a work in progress. It will certainly change as the Document Object Model (DOM) is more carefully defined. More information about the DOM can be found at http://www.w3.org/DOM/.

Extended Events

Browsers may also support other events than those defined in the preliminary HTML 4.0 specification. Microsoft in particular has introduced a variety of events to capture more complex

Event Attribute	Event Description	Elements Allowed Under HTML 4	Additional Elements (IE4 and IE5)	Additional Elements (N4 and N4.5)
onblur	Occurs when an element loses focus, meaning that the user has moved focus to another element, typically either by clicking it or tabbing to it	<A> <AREA> <BUTTON> <INPUT> <LABEL> <SELECT> <TEXTAREA>	<BODY> <APPLET> <DIV> <EMBED> <HR> <IMG> <MARQUEE> <OBJECT> <SPAN> <TABLE> <TD> <TR>	<BODY> <FRAMESET> <ILAYER> <LAYER>
onchange	Signals that the form control has lost user focus and its value has been modified during its last access	<INPUT> <SELECT> <TEXTAREA>		
onclick	Indicates that the element has been clicked	*Most display elements*	<APPLET> <FONT>	
ondblclick	Indicates that the element has been double-clicked	*Most display elements*	<APPLET> <FONT>	
onfocus	Describes when an element has received focus, namely when it has been selected for manipulation or data entry	<A> <AREA> <BUTTON> <INPUT> <LABEL> <SELECT> <TEXTAREA>	<APPLET> <BODY> <DIV> <EMBED> <HR> <IMG> <MARQUEE> <OBJECT> <SPAN> <TABLE> <TD> <TR>	<BODY> <FRAMESET> <ILAYER> <LAYER>
onkeydown	Indicates that a key is being pressed with focus on the element	*Most display elements*	<APPLET> <FONT>	

Table A-1.   *Core Events*

Event Attribute	Event Description	Elements Allowed Under HTML 4	Additional Elements (IE4 and IE5)	Additional Elements (N4 and N4.5)
onkeypress	Describes the event of a key being pressed and released with focus on the element	*Most display elements*	<APPLET> <FONT>	
onkeyup	Indicates that a key is being released with focus on the element	*Most display elements*	<APPLET> <FONT>	
onload	Indicates the event of a window or frame set finishing the loading of a document	<BODY> <FRAMESET>	IE4 only: <APPLET> <EMBED> <LINK> <SCRIPT> <STYLE> IE4 and IE5: <ILAYER> <IMG> <LAYER>	<ILAYER> <IMG> <LAYER>
onmousedown	Indicates the click of a mouse button with focus on the element	*Most display elements*	<APPLET> <FONT>	
onmousemove	Indicates that the mouse has moved while over the element	*Most display elements*	<APPLET> <FONT>	
onmouseout	Indicates that the mouse has moved away from an element	*Most display elements*	<APPLET> <FONT>	<ILAYER> <LAYER>
onmouseover	Indicates that the mouse has moved over an element	*Most display elements*	<APPLET> <FONT>	<ILAYER> <LAYER>
onmouseup	Indicates the release of a mouse button with focus on the element	*Most display elements*	<APPLET> <FONT>	

Table A-1. *Core Events* (continued)

APPENDIXES

Event Attribute	Event Description	Elements Allowed Under HTML 4	Additional Elements (IE4 and IE5)	Additional Elements (N4 and N4.5)
onreset	Indicates that the form is being reset, possibly by the click of a reset button	\<FORM\>		
onselect	Indicates the selection of text by the user, typically by highlighting the desired text	\<INPUT\> \<TEXTAREA\>		
onsubmit	Indicates a form submission, generally by clicking a submit button	\<FORM\>		
onunload	Indicates that the browser is leaving the current document and unloading it from the window or frame	\<BODY\> \<FRAMESET\>		

Table A-1.   *Core Events* (continued)

mouse actions like dragging, element events like the bouncing of **\<MARQUEE\>** text, and data-binding events signaling the loading of data. (Mouse events may be bound to data in a database.) The events are described in more detail in Table A-2.

Caution   *Documentation errors may exist. Microsoft currently documents events in the object model, not in the HTML reference. On inspection, some events are obviously not supported or may have been omitted. Events were tested by the author for accuracy, but for an accurate, up-to-date event model for these browsers, visit http://developer.netscape.com or http://www.microsoft.com/sitebuilder.*

Note   *Microsoft introduced a number of new proprietary event handlers in the Internet Explorer 5 browser. For a brief discussion of these new event handlers, see the section "Internet Explorer 5 Event Preview" in Chapter 13.*

Event Attribute	Event Description	Compatibility					Associated Elements
		IE4	IE5	N3	N4	N4.5	
onabort	Triggered by the user aborting the image load with a stop button or similar effect.	✓	✓	✓	✓	✓	<IMG>
onafterupdate	Fires after the transfer of data from the element to a data provider, namely a data update.	✓	✓				<APPLET> <BODY> <BUTTON> <CAPTION> <DIV> <EMBED> <IMG> <INPUT> <MARQUEE> <OBJECT> <SELECT> <TABLE> <TD> <TEXTAREA> <TR>
onbeforeunload	Fires just prior to a document being unloaded from a window.	✓	✓				<BODY> <FRAMESET>
onbeforeupdate	Triggered before the transfer of data from the element to the data provider. May be triggered explicitly or by a loss of focus or a page unload forcing a data update.	✓	✓				<APPLET> <BODY> <BUTTON> <CAPTION> <DIV> <EMBED> <HR> <IMG> <INPUT> <OBJECT> <SELECT> <TABLE> <TD> <TEXTAREA> <TR>

Table A-2.   *Extended Event Model*

Event Attribute	Event Description	Compatibility					Associated Elements
		IE4	IE5	N3	N4	N4.5	
onbounce	Triggered when the bouncing contents of a marquee touch one side or another.	✓	✓				\<MARQUEE\>
ondataavailable	Fires when data arrives from data sources that transmit information asynchronously.	✓	✓				\<APPLET\> \<OBJECT\>
ondatasetchanged	Triggered when the initial data is made available from data source or when the data changes.	✓	✓				\<APPLET\> \<OBJECT\>
ondatasetcomplete	Indicates that all the data is available from the data source.	✓	✓				\<APPLET\> \<OBJECT\>
ondragdrop	Triggered when the user drags an object onto the browser window to attempt to load it.	✓	✓		✓	✓	\<BODY\> \<FRAMESET\> (*window*)
ondragstart	Fires when the user begins to drag a highlighted selection.	✓	✓				\<A\> \<ACRONYM\> \<ADDRESS\> \<APPLET\> \<AREA\> \<B\> \<BIG\> \<BLOCKQUOTE\> \<BODY\> (*document*) \<BUTTON\> \<CAPTION\> \<CENTER\> \<CITE\> \<CODE\> \<DD\> \<DEL\> \<DFN\> \<DIR\> \<DIV\> \<DL\>

Table A-2. *Extended Event Model* (continued)

Event Attribute	Event Description	Compatibility					Associated Elements
		IE4	IE5	N3	N4	N4.5	
							<DT> <EM> <FONT> <FORM> <FRAMESET> *(document)* <H1> <H2> <H3> <H4> <H5> <H6>
onerror	Fires when the loading of a document, particularly the execution of a script, causes an error. Used to trap syntax errors.	✓	✓	✓	✓	✓	<BODY> <FRAMESET> *(window)* <IMG> IE4: <LINK> <OBJECT> <SCRIPT> <STYLE>
onerrorupdate	Fires if a data transfer has been canceled by the **onbeforeupdate** event handler.	✓	✓				<A> <APPLET> <OBJECT> <SELECT> <TEXTAREA>
onfilterchange	Fires when a page filter changes state or finishes.	✓	✓				*Nearly all elements*
onfinish	Triggered when a looping marquee finishes.	✓	✓				<MARQUEE>
onhelp	Triggered when the user presses the F1 key or similar help button in the user agent.	✓	✓				*Nearly all elements under IE4 only*
onmove	Triggered when the user moves a window.				✓	✓	<BODY> <FRAMESET>

Table A-2. *Extended Event Model* (continued)

Event Attribute	Event Description	Compatibility					Associated Elements
		IE4	IE5	N3	N4	N4.5	
onreadystatechange	Similar to onload. Fires whenever the ready state for an object has changed.	✓	✓				\<APPLET\> \<BODY\> \<EMBED\> \<FRAME\> \<FRAMESET\> \<IFRAME\> \<IMG\> \<LINK\> \<OBJECT\> \<SCRIPT\> \<STYLE\>
onresize	Triggered whenever an object is resized. Can only be bound to the window under Netscape as set via the \<BODY\> element.	✓			✓*	✓*	\<APPLET\> \<BODY\> \<BUTTON\> \<CAPTION\> \<DIV\> \<EMBED\> \<FRAMESET\> \<HR\> \<IMG\> \<MARQUEE\> \<OBJECT\> \<SELECT\> \<TABLE\> \<TD\> \<TEXTAREA\> \<TR\>
onrowenter	Indicates that a bound data row has changed and new data values are available.	✓	✓				\<APPLET\> \<BODY\> \<BUTTON\> \<CAPTION\> \<DIV\> \<EMBED\> \<HR\> \<IMG\> \<MARQUEE\> \<OBJECT\> \<SELECT\> \<TABLE\> \<TD\> \<TEXTAREA\> \<TR\>

*\<BODY\> only

Table A-2. *Extended Event Model* (continued)

APPENDIXES

Event Attribute	Event Description	Compatibility					Associated Elements
		IE4	IE5	N3	N4	N4.5	
onrowexit	Fires just prior to a bound data source control changing the current row.	✓	✓				\<APPLET\> \<BODY\> \<BUTTON\> \<CAPTION\> \<DIV\> \<EMBED\> \<HR\> \<IMG\> \<MARQUEE\> \<OBJECT\> \<SELECT\> \<TABLE\> \<TD\> \<TEXTAREA\> \<TR\>
onscroll	Fires when a scrolling element is repositioned.	✓	✓				\<BODY\> \<DIV\> \<FIELDSET\> \<IMG\> \<MARQUEE\> \<SPAN\> \<TEXTAREA\>
onselectstart	Fires when the user begins to select information by highlighting.	✓	✓				*Nearly all elements*
onstart	Fires when a looped marquee begins or starts over.	✓	✓				\<MARQUEE\>

Table A-2. *Extended Event Model* (continued)

HTML Element Reference

This appendix lists all HTML 4 elements, as well as some proprietary elements defined by different browser vendors. The element entries include all or some of the following information:

- **Syntax**   HTML 4 syntax for the element, including attributes and event handlers defined by the W3C specification
- **Attributes and events defined by browsers**   Additional syntax defined by different browsers
- **Attributes**   Descriptions of all attributes associated with the element
- **Attribute and Event Support**   Browser support of attributes and events
- **Example(s)**   A code example or examples using the element
- **Compatibility**   The element's general compatibility with HTML specifications and browser versions
- **Notes**   Additional information about the element

Listings of attributes and events defined by browser versions assume that these attributes and events remain associated with later versions of that browser; for example, attributes defined by Internet Explorer 4 are also valid for Internet Explorer 5, and attributes defined for Netscape 4 are also valid for Netscape 4.5.

<!-- ... --> (Comment)

This construct is used to include text comments that will not be displayed by the browser.

Syntax

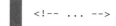

```
<!-- ... -->
```

Attributes
None.

Event Handlers
None.

Examples

```
<!-- This is an informational comment that can occur anywhere in an HTML
    document. The next example shows how a script is "commented out" to
    prevent non-script-enabled browsers from reading the script. -->

<SCRIPT>
<!--
document.write("hello world");
// -->
</SCRIPT>
```

APPENDIXES

Compatibility

> HTML 2, 3.2, and 4
> Internet Explorer 2, 3, 4, and 5
> Netscape 1, 2, 3, 4, and 4.5
> WebTV

Notes

Comments are often used to exclude content from older browsers, particularly those that do not understand client-side scripting or style sheets. Page developers should be careful when commenting HTML markup. Older browsers may or may not render the enclosed content.

<!DOCTYPE>   (Document Type Definition)

This SGML construct specifies the document type definition corresponding to the document.

Syntax

```
<!DOCTYPE "DTD identifier">
```

Attributes

None.

Event Handlers

None.

Example

```
<!DOCTYPE HTML PUBLIC "-//W3C//DTD HTML 4.0 Transitional//EN">
```

Compatibility

> HTML 2, 3.2, and 4
> Internet Explorer 2, 3, 4, and 5
> Netscape 1, 2, 3, 4, and 4.5
> WebTV

Notes

The **<!DOCTYPE>** element should be used as the first line of all HTML documents. Validation programs may use this construct when determining the correctness of an HTML document. Be certain to use the document type appropriate for the elements used in the document.

<A>   (Anchor)

This element indicates the portion of the document that is a hyperlink or the named target destination for a hyperlink.

Syntax

```
<A
     ACCESSKEY="key"
     CHARSET="character code for language of linked
              resource"
     CLASS="class name(s)"
     COORDS="comma-separated list of numbers"
     DIR="LTR | RTL"
     HREF="URL"
     HREFLANG="language code"
     ID="unique alphanumeric identifier"
     LANG="language code"
     NAME="name of target location"
     REL="comma-separated list of relationship values"
     REV="comma-separated list of relationship values"
     SHAPE="DEFAULT | CIRCLE | POLY | RECT"
     STYLE="style information"
     TABINDEX="number"
     TARGET="_blank | frame-name | _parent | _self | _top"
            (transitional)
     TITLE="advisory text"
     TYPE="content type of linked data"
     onblur="script" (transitional)
     onclick="script"
     ondblclick="script">
     onfocus="script"
     onhelp="script"
     onkeydown="script"
     onkeypress="script"
     onkeyup="script"
     onmousedown="script"
     onmousemove="script"
     onmouseout="script"
     onmouseover="script"
     onmouseup="script">

     Linked content

</A>
```

Attributes and Events Defined by Internet Explorer 4

```
DATAFLD="name of column supplying bound data"
DATASRC="ID of data source object supplying data"
LANGUAGE="JAVASCRIPT | JSCRIPT | VBS | VBSCRIPT"
METHODS="http-method"
URN="urn"
ondragstart="script"
onselectstart="script"
```

Attributes Defined by WebTV

```
NOCOLOR
SELECTED
```

Attributes

ACCESSKEY   This attribute specifies a keyboard navigation accelerator for the element. Pressing ALT or a similar key (depending on the browser and operating system) in association with the specified key selects the anchor element correlated with that key.

CHARSET   This attribute defines the character encoding of the linked resource. The value is a space- and/or comma-delimited list of character sets as defined in RFC 2045. The default value is **ISO-8859-1**.

CLASS   See "Core Attributes Reference," earlier in this appendix.

COORDS   For use with object shapes, this attribute uses a comma-separated list of numbers to define the coordinates of the object on the page.

DATAFLD   This attribute specifies the column name from that data source object that supplies the bound data. This attribute is specific to Microsoft's Data Binding in Internet Explorer 4.

DATASRC   This attribute indicates the **ID** of the data source object that supplies the data that is bound to this element. This attribute is specific to Microsoft's Data Binding in Internet Explorer 4.

DIR   See "Language Reference," earlier in this appendix.

HREF   This is the single required attribute for anchors defining a hypertext source link. It indicates the link target, either a URL or a URL fragment, that is a name preceded by a hash mark (#), which specifies an internal target location within the current document. URLs are not restricted to Web (http)-based documents. URLs may use any protocol supported by the browser. For example, file, ftp, and mailto work in most user agents.

HREFLANG   This attribute is used to indicate the language of the linked resource. See "Language Reference," earlier in this appendix for information on allowed values.

ID   See "Core Attributes Reference," earlier in this appendix.

LANG   See "Language Reference," earlier in this appendix.

LANGUAGE   This attribute specifies the language the current script is written in and invokes the proper scripting engine. The default value is **JAVASCRIPT**. **JAVASCRIPT** and **JSCRIPT** represent that the scripting language is written in JavaScript. **VBS** and **VBSCRIPT** represent that the scripting language is written in VBScript. It may also be possible to use extended names, such as **JavaScript1.1**, to hide code from JavaScript-aware browsers that don't conform to a particular version of the language.

METHODS   The value of this attribute provides information about the functions that may be performed on an object. The values are generally given by the HTTP protocol when it is used, but it may, for similar reasons as for the **TITLE** attribute, be useful to include advisory information, in advance, in the link. For example, the browser may choose a different rendering of a link as a function of the methods specified; something that is searchable may get a different icon, or an outside link may render with an indication of leaving the current site. This element is not well understood nor supported, even by the defining browser, Internet Explorer 4.

NAME   This attribute is required in an anchor defining a target location within a page. A value for **NAME** is similar to a value for the **ID** core attribute and should be an alphanumeric identifier unique to the document.

NOCOLOR   Supported only by WebTV, this attribute overrides the **LINK** color set in the **BODY** element and prevents the link from changing color.

REL   For anchors containing the **HREF** attribute, this attribute specifies the relationship of the target object to the link object. The value is a comma-separated list of relationship values. The values and their semantics will be registered by some authority that may have meaning to the document author. The default relationship, if no other is given, is **void**. The **REL** attribute should be used only when the **HREF** attribute is present.

REV   This attribute specifies a reverse link, the inverse relationship of the **REL** attribute. It is useful for indicating where an object came from, such as the author or a document.

SELECTED   Supported only in WebTV, this attribute selects the anchor with a yellow highlight box.

SHAPE   This attribute is used to define a selectable region for hypertext source links associated with a figure to create an image map. The values for the attribute are **CIRCLE**, **DEFAULT**, **POLYGON**, and **RECT**. The format of the **COORDS** attribute depends on the value of **SHAPE**. For **CIRCLE**, the value is x,y,r where x and y are the pixel coordinates for the center of the circle and r is the radius value in pixels. For **RECT**, the **COORDS** attribute should be x,y,w,h. The x,y

values define the upper-left-hand corner of the rectangle, while *w* and *h* define the width and height respectively. A value of **POLYGON** for **SHAPE** requires *x1,y1,x2,y2,...* values for **COORDS**. Each of the *x,y* pairs defines a point in the polygon, with successive points being joined by straight lines and the last point joined to the first. The value **DEFAULT** for **SHAPE** defines that the entire enclosed area, typically an image, be used.

STYLE   See "Core Attributes Reference," earlier in this appendix.

TABINDEX   This attribute uses a number to identify the object's position in the tabbing order for keyboard navigation using the TAB key.

TARGET   This attribute specifies the target window for a hypertext source link referencing frames. The information linked to will be displayed in the named window. Frames must be named to be targeted. There are, however, special name values, including **_blank**, which indicates a new window; **_parent**, which indicates the parent frame set containing the source link; **_self**, which indicates the frame containing the source link; and **_top**, which indicates the full browser window.

TITLE   See "Core Attributes Reference," earlier in this appendix.

TYPE   This attribute specifies the media type in the form of a MIME type of the link target. Generally, this is provided strictly as advisory information; however, in the future a browser may add a small icon for multimedia types. For example, a browser might add a small speaker icon when **TYPE** was set to audio/wav.

URN   See the "Notes" section for this element.

Attribute and Event Support

NETSCAPE 4   HREF, NAME, TARGET, onclick, onmouseout, and onmouseover. (CLASS, ID, LANG, and STYLE are implied.)

INTERNET EXPLORER 4   ACCESSKEY, CLASS, HREF, ID, LANG, NAME, REL, REV, STYLE, TARGET, TITLE, onblur, onclick, ondblclick, onfocus, onhelp, onkeydown, onkeypress, onkeyup, onmousedown, onmousemove, onmouseout, onmouseover, onmouseup, and all attributes and events defined by Internet Explorer 4.

WEBTV   HREF, ID, NAME, NOCOLOR, SELECTED, onclick, onmouseout, and onmouseover.

Event Handlers

See "Events Reference," earlier in this appendix.

Examples

```
<!-- anchor linking to external file -->
<A HREF="http://www.pint.com/">External link</A>
```

```
<!-- anchor linking to file on local filesystem -->
<A HREF="file:/c:\html\index.htm">Local file link</A>

<!-- anchor invoking anonymous FTP -->
<A HREF="ftp://www.kyz.com/workshop/freestuff">Anonymous FTP
Link</A>

<!-- anchor invoking FTP with password -->
<A HREF="ftp://joeuser:secretpassword@company.com/path/file">
FTP with password</A>

<!-- anchor invoking mail -->
<A HREF="mailto:fakeid@bigcompany.com">Send mail</A>

<!-- anchor used to define target destination within document -->
<A NAME="jump">Jump Target</A>

<!-- anchor linking internally to previous target anchor -->
<A HREF="#jump">Local jump within document</A>

<!-- anchor linking externally to previous target anchor -->
<A HREF="http://www.company.com/document#jump">Remote jump
within document</A>
```

Compatibility

HTML 2, 3.2, and 4
Internet Explorer 2, 3, 4, and 5
Netscape 1, 2, 3, 4, and 4.5
WebTV

Notes

- The following are reserved browser key bindings for the two major browsers and should not be used as values to **ACCESSKEY: A, C, E, F, G, H, V**, left arrow, and right arrow.
- The **URN** attribute was defined in HTML 2. Although Internet Explorer 4 and above support it, its use is unclear, particularly since URNs are not yet well defined.
- HTML 3.2 defines only **NAME, HREF, REL, REV**, and **TITLE**.
- HTML 2 defines only **NAME, HREF, METHODS, REL, REV, TITLE**, and **URN**.
- The **TARGET** attribute is not defined in browsers that do not support frames, such as Netscape 1–generation browsers.
- The **DIR** attribute is not yet supported by any browsers.

<ABBR> (Abbreviation)

This element allows authors to clearly indicate a sequence of characters that compose an acronym or abbreviation for a word (XML, WWW, and so on). See **<ACRONYM>**.

Syntax

```
<ABBR
     CLASS="class name(s)"
     DIR="LTR | RTL"
     ID="unique alphanumeric identifier"
     LANG="language code"
     STYLE="style information"
     TITLE="advisory text"
     onclick="script"
     ondblclick="script"
     onkeydown="script"
     onkeypress="script"
     onkeyup="script"
     onmousedown="script"
     onmousemove="script"
     onmouseout="script"
     onmouseover="script"
     onmouseup="script">

</ABBR>
```

Attributes

CLASS   See "Core Attributes Reference," earlier in this appendix.

DIR   See "Language Reference," earlier in this appendix.

ID   See "Core Attributes Reference," earlier in this appendix.

LANG   See "Language Reference," earlier in this appendix.

STYLE   See "Core Attributes Reference," earlier in this appendix.

TITLE   See "Core Attributes Reference," earlier in this appendix.

Attribute and Event Support

None.

Event Handlers

See "Events Reference," earlier in this appendix.

Examples

```
<ABBR TITLE="Dynamic Hypertext Markup Language">DHTML
</ABBR>

<ABBR LANG="fr" TITLE="World Wrestling Federation">WWF
</ABBR>
```

Compatibility

HTML 4

Notes

<ABBR> is a new element that is not defined under HTML 2 or 3.2. At present, no browsers appear to support the **<ABBR>** element. **<ACRONYM>** serves a similar function but is only supported by Internet Explorer 4 and later.

<ACRONYM>   (Acronym)

This element allows authors to clearly indicate a sequence of characters that compose an acronym or abbreviation for a word (XML, WWW, and so on).

Syntax

```
<ACRONYM
    CLASS="class name(s)"
    DIR="LTR | RTL"
    ID="unique alphanumeric identifier"
    LANG="language code"
    STYLE="style information"
    TITLE="advisory text"
    onclick="script"
    ondblclick="script"
    onkeydown="script"
    onkeypress="script"
    onkeyup="script"
    onmousedown="script"
    onmousemove="script"
    onmouseout="script"
    onmouseover="script"
    onmouseup="script">

</ACRONYM>
```

APPENDIXES

Attributes and Events Defined by Internet Explorer 4

```
LANGUAGE="JAVASCRIPT | JSCRIPT | VBS | VBSCRIPT"
ondragstart="script"
onhelp="script"
onselectstart="script"
```

Attributes

CLASS   See "Core Attributes Reference," earlier in this appendix.

DIR   See "Language Reference," earlier in this appendix.

ID   See "Core Attributes Reference," earlier in this appendix.

LANG   See "Language Reference," earlier in this appendix.

LANGUAGE   This attribute specifies the language the current script is written in and invokes the proper scripting engine. The default value is **JAVASCRIPT**. **JAVASCRIPT** and **JSCRIPT** represent that the scripting language is written in JavaScript. **VBS** and **VBSCRIPT** represent that the scripting language is written in VBScript. It may also be possible to use extended names, such as **JavaScript1.1**, to hide code from JavaScript-aware browsers that don't conform to a particular version of the language.

STYLE   See "Core Attributes Reference," earlier in this appendix.

TITLE   See "Core Attributes Reference," earlier in this appendix.

Attribute and Event Support

INTERNET EXPLORER 4   All attributes.

Event Handlers
See "Events Reference," earlier in this appendix.

Examples

```
<ACRONYM TITLE="Extensible Markup Language">XML</ACRONYM>

<ACRONYM LANG="fr" TITLE="Soci&eacute;t&eacute;
                    Nationale de Chemins de Fer">SNCF</ACRONYM>
```

Compatibility

HTML 4
Internet Explorer 4 and 5

Notes

<ACRONYM> is a new element that is not defined under HTML 2 or 3.2. Under Internet Explorer 4 and above, the **TITLE** attribute renders as a tool tip that can be used to define the meaning of the acronym.

<ADDRESS>   (Address)

This element marks up text indicating authorship or ownership of information. It generally occurs at the beginning or end of a document.

Syntax

```
<ADDRESS
    CLASS="class name(s)"
    DIR="LTR | RTL"
    ID="unique alphanumeric identifier"
    LANG="language code"
    STYLE="style information"
    TITLE="advisory text"
    onclick="script"
    ondblclick="script"
    onkeydown="script"
    onkeypress="script"
    onkeyup="script"
    onmousedown="script"
    onmousemove="script"
    onmouseout="script"
    onmouseover="script"
    onmouseup="script">

</ADDRESS>
```

Attributes and Events Defined by Internet Explorer 4

```
    LANGUAGE="JAVASCRIPT | JSCRIPT | VBS | VBSCRIPT"
    ondragstart="script"
    onhelp="script"
    onselectstart="script"
```

Attributes

CLASS   See "Core Attributes Reference," earlier in this appendix.

DIR   See "Language Reference," earlier in this appendix.

ID   See "Core Attributes Reference," earlier in this appendix.

LANG   See "Language Reference," earlier in this appendix.

LANGUAGE   This attribute specifies the language the current script is written in and invokes the proper scripting engine. The default value is **JAVASCRIPT**. **JAVASCRIPT** and **JSCRIPT** represent that the scripting language is written in JavaScript. **VBS** and **VBSCRIPT** represent that the scripting language is written in VBScript. It may also be possible to use extended names, such as **JavaScript1.1**, to hide code from JavaScript-aware browsers that don't conform to a particular version of the language.

STYLE   See "Core Attributes Reference," earlier in this appendix.

TITLE   See "Core Attributes Reference," earlier in this appendix.

Attribute and Event Support

NETSCAPE 4   CLASS, ID, LANG, and STYLE.

INTERNET EXPLORER 4   CLASS, ID, LANG, LANGUAGE, STYLE, TITLE, onclick, ondblclick, ondragstart, onhelp, onkeydown, onkeypress, onkeyup, onmousedown, onmousemove, onmouseout, onmouseover, onmouseup, and onselectstart.

WEBTV   No attributes.

Event Handlers

See "Events Reference," earlier in this appendix.

Example

```
<ADDRESS>Big Company, Inc.<BR>2105 Demo Street<BR>
San Diego, CA U.S.A.</ADDRESS>
```

Compatibility

HTML 2, 3.2, and 4
Internet Explorer 2, 3, 4, and 5
Netscape 1, 2, 3, 4, and 4.5
WebTV

Notes

Under HTML 2, 3.2, and WebTV there are no attributes for **<ADDRESS>**.

<APPLET>   (Java Applet)

This element identifies the inclusion of a Java applet. The strict HTML 4.0 definition does not include this element.

Syntax (Transitional Only)

```
<APPLET
     ALIGN="BOTTOM | LEFT | MIDDLE | RIGHT | TOP"
     ALT="alternative text"
     ARCHIVE="URL of archive file"
     CLASS="class name(s)"
     CODE="URL of Java class file"
     CODEBASE="URL for base referencing"
     HEIGHT="pixels"
     HSPACE="pixels"
     ID="unique alphanumeric identifier"
     NAME="unique name for scripting reference"
     OBJECT="filename"
     STYLE="style information"
     TITLE="advisory text"
     VSPACE="pixels"
     WIDTH="pixels">

     <PARAM> elements

     Alternative content

</APPLET>
```

Attributes and Events Defined by Internet Explorer 4

```
     ALIGN="ABSBOTTOM | ABSMIDDLE | BASELINE | BOTTOM |
            LEFT | MIDDLE | RIGHT | TEXTTOP | TOP"
     DATAFLD="name of column supplying bound data"
     DATASRC="ID of data source object supplying data"
     SRC="URL"
     onafterupdate="script"
     onbeforeupdate="script"
     onblur="script"
     onclick="script"
     ondataavailable="script"
     ondatasetchanged="script"
```

APPENDIXES

```
ondatasetcomplete="script"
ondblclick="script"
ondragstart="script"
onerrorupdate="script"
onfocus="script"
onhelp="script"
onkeydown="script"
onkeypress="script"
onkeyup="script"
onmousedown="script"
onmousemove="script"
onmouseout="script"
onmouseover="script"
onmouseup="script"
onreadystatechange="script"
onresize="script"
onrowenter="script"
onrowexit="script"
```

Attributes Defined by Netscape 4

```
ALIGN="ABSBOTTOM | ABSMIDDLE | BASELINE | CENTER | TEXTTOP"
MAYSCRIPT
```

Attributes

ALIGN   This attribute is used to position the applet on the page relative to content that may flow around it. The HTML 4.0 specification defines values of **BOTTOM, LEFT, MIDDLE, RIGHT,** and **TOP,** while Microsoft and Netscape may also support **ABSBOTTOM, ABSMIDDLE, BASELINE, CENTER,** and **TEXTTOP.**

ALT   This attribute causes a descriptive text alternate to be displayed on browsers that do not support Java. Page designers should also remember that content enclosed within the **<APPLET>** element may also be rendered as alternative text.

ARCHIVE   This attribute refers to an archived or compressed version of the applet and its associated class files, which may help reduce download time.

CLASS   See "Core Attributes Reference," earlier in this appendix.

CODE   This attribute specifies the URL of the applet's class file to be loaded and executed. Applet filenames are identified by a .class filename extension. The URL specified by **CODE** may be relative to the **CODEBASE** attribute.

CODEBASE   This attribute gives the absolute or relative URL of the directory where applets' .class files referenced by the **CODE** attribute are stored.

DATAFLD   This attribute, supported by Internet Explorer 4 and above, specifies the column name from the data source object that supplies the bound data. This attribute may be used to specify the various <PARAM> elements passed to the Java applet.

DATASRC   Like **DATAFLD**, this attribute is used for data binding under Internet Explorer 4. It indicates the **ID** of the data source object that supplies the data that is bound to the **<PARAM>** elements associated with the applet.

HEIGHT   This attribute specifies the height, in pixels, that the applet needs.

HSPACE   This attribute specifies additional horizontal space, in pixels, to be reserved on either side of the applet.

ID   See "Core Attributes Reference," earlier in this appendix.

MAYSCRIPT   In the Netscape implementation, this attribute allows access to an applet by programs in a scripting language embedded in the document.

NAME   This attribute assigns a name to the applet so that it can be identified by other resources, particularly scripts.

OBJECT   This attribute specifies the URL of a serialized representation of an applet.

SRC   As defined for Internet Explorer 4 and above, this attribute specifies a URL for an associated file for the applet. The meaning and use are unclear and not part of the HTML standard.

STYLE   See "Core Attributes Reference," earlier in this appendix.

TITLE   See "Core Attributes Reference," earlier in this appendix.

VSPACE   This attribute specifies additional vertical space, in pixels, to be reserved above and below the applet.

WIDTH   This attribute specifies in pixels the width that the applet needs.

Attribute and Event Support

NETSCAPE 4   ALIGN, ALT, ARCHIVE, CODE, CODEBASE, HSPACE, MAYSCRIPT, NAME, VSPACE, and WIDTH. (CLASS, ID, and STYLE are implied.)

INTERNET EXPLORER 4   ALT, CLASS, CODE, CODEBASE, HEIGHT, HSPACE, ID, NAME, STYLE, TITLE, VSPACE, WIDTH, and all attributes and events defined by Internet Explorer 4.

Event Handlers

None.

Example

```
<APPLET CODE="game.class"
        ALIGN="LEFT"
        ARCHIVE="game.zip"
        HEIGHT="250" WIDTH="350">
   <PARAM NAME="DIFFICULTY"  VALUE="EASY">
   <B>Sorry, you need Java to play this game.</B>
</APPLET>
```

Compatibility

HTML 3.2 and 4
Internet Explorer 3, 4, and 5
Netscape 2, 3, 4, and 4.5

Notes

■ The **<APPLET>** element replaces the original **<APP>** element. Parameter values can be passed to applets using the **<PARAM>** element in the applet's content area.

■ The HTML 4.0 specification does not encourage the use of **<APPLET>** and prefers the use of the **<OBJECT>** element. Under the HTML 4.0 strict specification, this element is not defined.

■ WebTV's current implementation does not support Java applets.

■ Java applets were first supported under Netscape 2–level browsers and Internet Explorer 3–level browsers.

<AREA> (Image Map Area)

<AREA> is an empty element used within the content model of the **<P>** element to implement client-side image maps. It defines a hot-spot region on the map and associates it with a hypertext link.

Syntax

```
<AREA
    ACCESSKEY="character"
    ALT="alternative text"
    CLASS="class name(s)"
```

```
COORDS="comma separated list of values"
DIR="LTR | RTL"
HREF="URL"
ID="unique alphanumeric identifier"
LANG="language code"
NOHREF
SHAPE="CIRCLE | DEFAULT | POLY | RECT"
STYLE="style information"
TABINDEX="number"
TARGET="_blank | frame-name | _parent | _self |
        _top" (transitional)
TITLE="advisory text"
onblur="script"
onclick="script"
ondblclick="script"
onfocus="script"
onkeydown="script"
onkeypress="script"
onkeyup="script"
onmousedown="script"
onmousemove="script"
onmouseout="script"
onmouseover="script"
onmouseup="script">
```

Attributes and Events Defined by Internet Explorer 4

```
LANGUAGE="JAVASCRIPT | JSCRIPT | VBS | VBSCRIPT"
SHAPE="CIRC | CIRCLE | POLY | POLYGON | RECT |
        RECTANGLE"
ondragstart="script"
onhelp="script"
onselectstart="script"
```

Attributes Defined by Netscape 4

```
NAME="filename"
SHAPE="CIRCLE | DEFAULT | POLY | POLYGON | RECT"
```

Attributes Defined by WebTV

```
NOTAB
```

Attributes

ACCESSKEY   This attribute specifies a keyboard navigation accelerator for the element. Pressing ALT or a similar key in association with the specified character selects the form control correlated with that key sequence. Page designers are forewarned to avoid key sequences already bound to browsers.

ALT   This attribute contains a text string alternative to display on browsers that cannot display images.

CLASS   See "Core Attributes Reference," earlier in this appendix.

COORDS   This attribute contains a set of values specifying the coordinates of the hot-spot region. The number and meaning of the values depend upon the value specified for the **SHAPE** attribute. For a **RECT** or **RECTANGLE** shape, the **COORDS** value is two x,y pairs: **left, top, right,** and **bottom.** For a **CIRC** or **CIRCLE** shape, the **COORDS** value is x,y,r where x,y is a pair specifying the center of the circle and r is a value for the radius. For a **POLY** or **POLYGON** shape, the **COORDS** value is a set of x,y pairs for each point in the polygon: $x1,y1,x2,y2,x3,y3$ and so on.

DIR   See "Language Reference," earlier in this appendix.

HREF   This attribute specifies the hyperlink target for the area. Its value is a valid URL. Either this attribute or the **NOHREF** attribute must be present in the element.

ID   See "Core Attributes Reference," earlier in this appendix.

LANG   See "Language Reference," earlier in this appendix.

LANGUAGE   This attribute specifies the language the current script is written in and invokes the proper scripting engine. The default value is **JAVASCRIPT**. **JAVASCRIPT** and **JSCRIPT** represent that the scripting language is written in JavaScript. **VBS** and **VBSCRIPT** represent that the scripting language is written in VBScript. It may also be possible to use extended names, such as **JavaScript1.1**, to hide code from JavaScript-aware browsers that don't conform to a particular version of the language.

NAME   This attribute is used to define a name for the clickable area so that it can be scripted by older browsers.

NOHREF   This attribute indicates that no hyperlink exists for the associated area. Either this attribute or the **HREF** attribute must be present in the element.

NOTAB   Supported by WebTV, this attribute keeps the element from appearing in the tabbing order.

SHAPE   This attribute defines the shape of the associated hot spot. HTML 4 defines the values **RECT**, which defines a rectangular region; **CIRCLE**, which defines a circular region; **POLY**, which defines a polygon; and **DEFAULT**, which indicates the entire region beyond any defined shapes. Many browsers, notably Internet Explorer 4 and above, support **CIRC, POLYGON,** and **RECTANGLE** as valid values for **SHAPE**.

STYLE   See "Core Attributes Reference," earlier in this appendix.

TABINDEX   This attribute represents a numeric value specifying the position of the defined area in the browser tabbing order.

TARGET   This attribute specifies the target window for hyperlink referencing frames. The value is a frame name or one of several special names. A value of **_blank** indicates a new window. A value of **_parent** indicates the parent frame set containing the source link. A value of **_self** indicates the frame containing the source link. A value of **_top** indicates the full browser window.

TITLE   See "Core Attributes Reference," earlier in this appendix.

Attribute and Event Support

NETSCAPE 4   COORDS, HREF, NOHREF, SHAPE, TARGET, onmouseout, and onmouseover. (**CLASS, ID, LANG,** and **STYLE** are implied but not listed for this element in Netscape documentation.)

INTERNET EXPLORER 4   ALT, CLASS, COORDS, HREF, ID, LANG, LANGUAGE, NOHREF, SHAPE, STYLE, TABINDEX, TARGET, TITLE, all W3C-defined events, and all attributes and events defined by Internet Explorer 4.

WEBTV   COORDS, HREF, ID, NAME, NOTAB, SHAPE, TARGET, onmouseout, and onmouseover.

Event Handlers
See "Events Reference," earlier in this chapter.

Example

```
<MAP NAME="primary">
  <AREA SHAPE="CIRCLE" COORDS="200,250,25"
       HREF="another.htm">
  <AREA SHAPE="DEFAULT" NOHREF>
</MAP>
```

Compatibility

HTML 3.2 and 4
Internet Explorer 2, 3, 4, and 5
Netscape 1, 2, 3, 4, and 4.5
WebTV

Notes

■ By the HTML 3.2 and 4.0 specifications, the closing tag **</AREA>** is forbidden.

■ The **ID, CLASS,** and **STYLE** attributes have the same meaning as the core attributes defined in the HTML 4.0 specification, but only Netscape and Microsoft define them.

■ Netscape 1–level browsers do not understand the **TARGET** attribute as it relates to frames.

■ HTML 3.2 defines only **ALT, COORDS, HREF, NOHREF,** and **SHAPE**.

<AUDIOSCOPE>   (Sound Amplitude Display)

This WebTV-specific element displays an audioscope for a sound resource that displays a dynamic, graphical display of a sound's amplitude.

Syntax (Defined by WebTV)

```
<AUDIOSCOPE
    ALIGN="ABSBOTTOM | ABSMIDDLE | BASELINE | BOTTOM |
          LEFT | MIDDLE | RIGHT | TEXTTOP | TOP"
    BORDER="pixels"
    GAIN="number"
    HEIGHT="pixels"
    LEFTCOLOR="color name | #RRGGBB"
    LEFTOFFSET="number"
    MAXLEVEL="TRUE | FALSE"
    RIGHTCOLOR="name | #RRGGBB"
    RIGHTOFFSET="number"
    WIDTH="pixels">
```

Attributes

ALIGN   This attribute positions the audioscope object on the page relative to text or other content that may flow around it.

BORDER   This attribute sets the width of the audioscope border in pixels. The default value is **1**.

GAIN   This attribute takes a numeric value, which is a multiplier for the amplitude display. The default value is **1**.

HEIGHT   This attribute sets the height of the audioscope in pixels. The default value is **80** pixels.

LEFTCOLOR   This attribute sets the color of the line displaying the left audio channel in the audioscope. Values can either be given as named colors or in the numeric #*RRGGBB* format. The default value is **#8ECE10**.

LEFTOFFSET   This attribute sets the vertical offset for the display of the left audio channel with positive and negative values relative to the center of the audioscope. The default value is **0**.

MAXLEVEL   This Boolean attribute specifies whether the audioscope should clip sound according to the specified gain. The default value is **FALSE**.

RIGHTCOLOR   This attribute sets the color of the line displaying the right audio channel in the audioscope. Values can either be given as named colors or in the numeric *#RRGGBB* format. The default value is **#8ECE10**.

RIGHTOFFSET   This attribute sets the vertical offset for the display of the right audio channel with positive and negative values relative to the center of the audioscope. The default value is **1**.

WIDTH   This attribute sets the width of the audioscope in pixels. The default width is **100** pixels.

Attribute and Event Support

WEBTV   All attributes.

Event Handlers
None.

Example

```
<AUDIOSCOPE BORDER="1" HEIGHT="16" WIDTH="240" GAIN="3"
        MAXLEVEL="FALSE">
```

Compatibility

WebTV

Notes
<AUDIOSCOPE> is supported only by WebTV.

<B>   (Bold)
This element indicates that the enclosed text should be displayed in boldface.

Syntax

```
<B
    CLASS="class name(s)"
    DIR="LTR | RTL"
    ID="unique alphanumeric identifier"
```

```
        LANG="language code"
        STYLE="style information"
        TITLE="advisory text"
        onclick="script"
        ondblclick="script"
        onkeydown="script"
        onkeypress="script"
        onkeyup="script"
        onmousedown="script"
        onmousemove="script"
        onmouseout="script"
        onmouseover="script"
        onmouseup="script">


</B>
```

Attributes and Events Defined by Internet Explorer 4

```
        LANGUAGE="JAVASCRIPT | JSCRIPT | VBS | VBSCRIPT"
        ondragstart="script"
        onhelp="script"
        onselectstart="script"
```

Attributes

CLASS   See "Core Attributes Reference," earlier in this appendix.

DIR   See "Language Reference," earlier in this appendix.

ID   See "Core Attributes Reference," earlier in this appendix.

LANG   See "Language Reference," earlier in this appendix.

LANGUAGE   This attribute specifies the language the current script is written in and invokes the proper scripting engine. The default value is **JAVASCRIPT**. **JAVASCRIPT** and **JSCRIPT** represent that the scripting language is written in JavaScript. **VBS** and **VBSCRIPT** represent that the scripting language is written in VBScript. It may also be possible to use extended names, such as **JavaScript1.1**, to hide code from JavaScript-aware browsers that don't conform to a particular version of the language.

STYLE   See "Core Attributes Reference," earlier in this appendix.

TITLE   See "Core Attributes Reference," earlier in this appendix.

Attribute and Event Support

NETSCAPE 4   CLASS, ID, LANG, and STYLE are implied but not explicitly listed for this element.

INTERNET EXPLORER 4   All W3C-defined attributes and events except DIR, and attributes and events defined by Internet Explorer 4.

Event Handlers

See "Events Reference," earlier in this appendix.

Example

```
This text is <B>bold</B> for emphasis.
```

Compatibility

HTML 2, 3.2, and 4
Internet Explorer 2, 3, 4, and 5
Netscape 1, 2, 3, 4, and 4.5
WebTV

Notes

HTML 2 and 3.2 do not define any attributes for this element.

<BASE>   (Base URL)

This element specifies the base URL to use for all relative URLs contained within a document. It occurs only in the scope of a <HEAD> element.

Syntax

```
<BASE
    HREF="URL"
    TARGET="_blank | frame-name | _parent | _self |
            _top" (transitional)>
```

Attributes

HREF   This attribute specifies the base URL to be used throughout the document for relative URL addresses.

TARGET   For documents containing frames, this attribute specifies the default target window for every link that does not have an explicit target reference. Besides named frames, several special values exist. A value of **_blank** indicates a new window. A value of **_parent** indicates the parent frame set containing the source link. A value of **_self** indicates the frame containing the source link. A value of **_top** indicates the full browser window.

Attribute and Event Support

NETSCAPE 4   HREF and **TARGET**.

INTERNET EXPLORER 4   HREF and **TARGET**.

WEBTV   HREF and **TARGET**.

Event Handlers
None.

Examples

```
<BASE HREF="http://www.bigcompany.com/">

<BASE TARGET="_blank" HREF="http://www.bigcompany.com/">
```

Compatibility

HTML 2, 3.2, and 4
Internet Explorer 2, 3, 4, and 5
Netscape 1, 2, 3, 4, and 4.5
WebTV

Notes
HTML 2 and 3.2 define only the **HREF** attribute.

<BASEFONT>   (Base Font)

This element establishes a default font size for a document. Font size can then be varied relative to the base font size using the **<FONT>** element. The **<BASEFONT>** element must be placed near the beginning of the body part of the page.

Syntax (Transitional Only)

```
<BASEFONT
    COLOR="color name | #RRGGBB"
    FACE="font name(s)"
    ID="unique alphanumeric identifier"
    SIZE="1-7 | +/-int">
```

Attributes Defined by Internet Explorer 4

```
CLASS="class name(s)"
LANG="language code"
```

Attributes

CLASS   Internet Explorer 4 documentation indicates that the **CLASS** can be set for the <BASEFONT> element; however, this is probably a mistake in the documentation.

COLOR   This attribute sets the text color using either a named color or a color specified in the hexadecimal *#RRGGBB* format.

FACE   This attribute contains a list of one or more font names. The document text in the default style is rendered in the first font face that the client's browser supports. If no font listed is installed on the local system, the browser typically defaults to the proportional or fixed width font for that system.

ID   See "Core Attributes Reference," earlier in this appendix.

LANG   Internet Explorer 4 documentation also mentions use of the **LANG** attribute to indicate the language used. Meaning with this element is not well defined.

SIZE   This attribute specifies the font size as either a numeric or relative value. Numeric values range from **1** to **7** with **1** being the smallest and **3** the default.

Attribute and Event Support

NETSCAPE 4   ID (implied) and **SIZE**.

INTERNET EXPLORER 4   All attributes.

WEBTV   SIZE.

Event Handlers
None.

Example

```
<BASEFONT COLOR="#FF0000" FACE="Helvetica, Times Roman"
       SIZE="+2">
```

Compatibility

HTML 3.2 and 4 (transitional)
Internet Explorer 2, 3, 4, and 5

APPENDIXES

Netscape 1.1, 2, 3, 4, and 4.5
WebTV

Notes

■ HTML 3.2 supports the **<BASEFONT>** element and the **SIZE** attribute. HTML 4.0 transitional specification adds support for **COLOR** and **FACE** as well.

■ The HTML 4.0 strict specification does not support this element.

■ The font sizes indicated by numeric values are browser dependent and not absolute.

<BDO>   (Bidirectional Override)

This element is used to override the current directionality of text.

Syntax

```
<BDO
     CLASS="class name(s)"
     DIR="LTR | RTL"
     ID="unique alphanumeric identifier"
     LANG="language code"
     STYLE="style information"
     TITLE="advisory text">

</BDO>
```

Attributes

CLASS   See "Core Attributes Reference," earlier in this appendix.

DIR   This attribute is required for the **<BDO>** element. It sets the text direction either to left to right (**LTR**) or right to left (**RTL**).

ID   See "Core Attributes Reference," earlier in this appendix.

LANG   See "Language Reference," earlier in this appendix.

STYLE   See "Core Attributes Reference," earlier in this appendix.

TITLE   See "Core Attributes Reference," earlier in this appendix.

Attribute and Event Support

None.

Event Handlers

None.

Example

```
<!-- Switch text direction -->
<BDO ID="switch1" DIR="RTL">This text will go right to left
if you can find a browser that supports this element.
</BDO>
```

Compatibility

HTML 4
Internet Explorer 5

Notes

Internet Explorer 5 is the first browser to support this element. In the beta version of Internet Explorer 5, available at the time of this edition, **<BDO>** is the only element with which the **DIR** attribute works.

<BGSOUND>   (Background Sound)

This Internet Explorer and WebTV element associates a background sound with a page.

Syntax (Defined by Internet Explorer 4)

```
<BGSOUND>
     BALANCE="number"
     CLASS="class name(s)"
     ID="unique alphanumeric identifier"
     LANG="language code"
     LOOP=number
     SRC="URL of sound file"
     TITLE="advisory text"
     VOLUME="number">
```

Attributes

BALANCE   This attribute defines a number between –10,000 and +10,000 that determines how the volume will be divided between the speakers.

CLASS   See "Core Attributes Reference," earlier in this appendix.

ID   See "Core Attributes Reference," earlier in this appendix.

LANG   See "Language Reference," earlier in this appendix.

LOOP   This attribute indicates the number of times a sound is to be played and either has a numeric value or the keyword **infinite**.

SRC   This attribute specifies the URL of the sound file to be played, which must be one of the following types: .wav, .au, or .mid.

TITLE   See "Core Attributes Reference," earlier in this appendix.

VOLUME   This attribute defines a number between –10,000 and 0 that determines the loudness of a page's background sound.

Attribute and Event Support

INTERNET EXPLORER 4   All attributes.

WEBTV   LOOP and SRC.

Event Handlers
None.

Examples

```
<BGSOUND SRC="sound1.mid">

<BGSOUND SRC="sound2.au" LOOP="INFINITE">
```

Compatibility

Internet Explorer 2, 3, 4, and 5
WebTV

Notes
Similar functionality can be achieved in Netscape using the **<EMBED>** element to invoke LiveAudio.

<BIG>   (Big Font)

This element indicates that the enclosed text should be displayed in a larger font relative to the current font.

Syntax

```
<BIG
    CLASS="class name(s)"
    DIR="LTR | RTL"
    ID="unique alphanumeric identifier"
    LANG="language code"
    STYLE="style information"
    TITLE="advisory text"
    onclick="script"
    ondblclick="script"
```

```
            onkeydown="script"
            onkeypress="script"
            onkeyup="script"
            onmousedown="script"
            onmousemove="script"
            onmouseout="script"
            onmouseover="script"
            onmouseup="script">

        </BIG>
```

Attributes and Events Defined by Internet Explorer 4

```
        LANGUAGE="JAVASCRIPT | JSCRIPT | VBS | VBSCRIPT"
        ondragstart="script"
        onhelp="script"
        onselectstart="script"
```

Attributes

CLASS   See "Core Attributes Reference," earlier in this appendix.

DIR   See "Language Reference," earlier in this appendix.

ID   See "Core Attributes Reference," earlier in this appendix.

LANG   See "Language Reference," earlier in this appendix.

LANGUAGE   This attribute specifies the language the current script is written in and invokes the proper scripting engine. The default value is **JAVASCRIPT**. **JAVASCRIPT** and **JSCRIPT** represent that the scripting language is written in JavaScript. **VBS** and **VBSCRIPT** represent that the scripting language is written in VBScript.

STYLE   See "Core Attributes Reference," earlier in this appendix.

TITLE   See "Core Attributes Reference," earlier in this appendix.

Attribute and Event Support

NETSCAPE 4   **CLASS**, **ID**, **LANG**, and **STYLE** are implied.

INTERNET EXPLORER 4   All attributes and events except **DIR**.

Event Handlers
See "Events Reference," earlier in this appendix.

Example

```
This text is regular size. <BIG>This text is larger.</BIG>
```

Compatibility

HTML 3.2 and 4
Internet Explorer 2, 3, 4, and 5
Netscape 2, 3, 4, and 4.5
WebTV

Notes

HTML 3.2 does not support any attributes for this element.

<BLACKFACE>   (Blackface Font)

This WebTV element renders the enclosed text in a double-weight boldface font. It is used for headings and other terms needing special emphasis.

Syntax

```
<BLACKFACE>  Text  </BLACKFACE>
```

Attributes

None.

Event Handlers

None.

Example

```
<BLACKFACE>Buy now!</BLACKFACE > This offer expires in five minutes.
```

Compatibility

WebTV

Notes

This element is supported only by WebTV.

<BLINK>   (Blinking Text Display)

This Netscape-specific element causes the enclosed text to flash slowly.

Syntax (Defined by Netscape)

```
<BLINK
    CLASS="class name(s)"
    ID="unique alphanumeric identifier"
    LANG="language code"
    STYLE="style information">

</BLINK>
```

Attributes

CLASS   See "Core Attributes Reference," earlier in this appendix.

ID   See "Core Attributes Reference," earlier in this appendix.

LANG   See "Language Reference," earlier in this appendix.

STYLE   See "Core Attributes Reference," earlier in this appendix.

Attribute and Event Support

NETSCAPE 4   All attributes.

Event Handlers
None.

Example

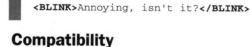

```
<BLINK>Annoying, isn't it?</BLINK>
```

Compatibility

Netscape 1, 2, 3, 4, and 4.5

Notes
While not defined explicitly in Netscape documentation, the **CLASS**, **ID**, **LANG**, and **STYLE** attributes are mentioned to be universal to all elements under Netscape 4 and above, and may have meaning here.

<BLOCKQUOTE>   (Block Quote)
This block element indicates that the enclosed text is an extended quotation. Usually this is rendered visually by indentation.

Syntax

```
<BLOCKQUOTE
    CITE="URL of source information"
    CLASS="class name(s)"
    DIR="LTR | RTL"
    ID="unique alphanumeric identifier"
    LANG="language code"
    STYLE="style information"
    TITLE="advisory text"
    onclick="script"
    ondblclick="script"
    onkeydown="script"
    onkeypress="script"
    onkeyup="script"
    onmousedown="script"
    onmousemove="script"
    onmouseout="script"
    onmouseover="script"
    onmouseup="script">

</BLOCKQUOTE>
```

Attributes and Events Defined by Internet Explorer 4

```
    LANGUAGE="JAVASCRIPT | JSCRIPT | VBS | VBSCRIPT"
    ondragstart="script"
    onhelp="script"
    onselectstart="script"
```

Attributes

CITE   The value of this attribute should be a URL of the document in which the information cited can be found.

CLASS   See "Core Attributes Reference," earlier in this appendix.

DIR   See "Language Reference," earlier in this appendix.

ID   See "Core Attributes Reference," earlier in this appendix.

LANG   See "Language Reference," earlier in this appendix.

LANGUAGE   This attribute specifies the language the current script is written in and invokes the proper scripting engine. The default value is **JAVASCRIPT**. **JAVASCRIPT** and **JSCRIPT**

represent that the scripting language is written in JavaScript. **VBS** and **VBSCRIPT** represent that the scripting language is written in VBScript.

STYLE   See "Core Attributes Reference," earlier in this appendix.

TITLE   See "Core Attributes Reference," earlier in this appendix.

Attribute and Event Support

NETSCAPE 4   CLASS, ID, LANG, and **STYLE**.

INTERNET EXPLORER 4   All attributes and events except **CITE** and **DIR**.

Event Handlers
See "Events Reference," earlier in this appendix.

Example

```
The following paragraph is taken from our March report:
<BLOCKQUOTE CITE="marchreport.htm"> ... text ...
</BLOCKQUOTE>
```

Compatibility

HTML 2, 3.2, and 4
Internet Explorer 2, 3, 4, and 5
Netscape 1, 2, 3, 4, and 4.5
WebTV

Notes

■ HTML 2 and 3.2 do not support any attributes for this element.

■ WebTV only indents the left margin of text enclosed in the **<BLOCKQUOTE>** element.

■ Some browsers understand the **<BQ>** shorthand notation.

<BODY>   (Document Body)

This element encloses a document's displayable content, in contrast to the descriptive and informational content contained in the **<HEAD>** element.

Syntax

```
<BODY
    ALINK="color name | #RRGGBB" (transitional)
    BACKGROUND="URL of background image" (transitional)
```

```
BGCOLOR="color name | #RRGGBB" (transitional)
CLASS="class name(s)"
DIR="LTR | RTL"
ID="unique alphanumeric identifier"
LANG="language code"
LINK="color name | #RRGGBB" (transitional)
STYLE="style information"
TEXT="color name | #RRGGBB" (transitional)
TITLE="advisory text"
VLINK="color name | #RRGGBB" (transitional)
onclick="script"
ondblclick="script"
onkeydown="script"
onkeypress="script"
onkeyup="script"
onload="script"
onmousedown="script"
onmousemove="script"
onmouseout="script"
onmouseover="script"
onmouseup="script"
onunload="script">

</BODY>
```

Attributes and Events Defined by Internet Explorer 4

```
BGPROPERTIES="FIXED"
BOTTOMMARGIN="pixels"
LANGUAGE="JAVASCRIPT | JSCRIPT | VBS | VBSCRIPT"
LEFTMARGIN="pixels"
RIGHTMARGIN="pixels"
SCROLL="NO | YES"
TOPMARGIN="pixels"
onafterupdate="script"
onbeforeunload="script"
onbeforeupdate="script"
ondragstart="script"
onhelp="script"
onrowenter="script"
onrowexit="script"
onscroll="script"
onselect="script"
onselectstart="script"
```

Events Defined by Netscape 4

```
onblur="script"
onfocus="script"
```

Attributes Defined by WebTV

```
CREDITS="URL"
INSTRUCTIONS="URL"
LOGO="URL"
```

Attributes

ALINK   This attribute sets the color for active links within the document. Active links represent the state of a link as it is being pressed. The value of the attribute can either be a browser-dependent named color or a color specified in the hexadecimal #*RRGGBB* format.

BACKGROUND   This attribute contains a URL for an image file, which will be tiled to provide the document background.

BGCOLOR   This attribute sets the background color for the document. Its value can either be a browser-dependent named color or a color specified using the hexadecimal #*RRGGBB* format.

BGPROPERTIES   This attribute, first introduced in Internet Explorer 2, has one value, **FIXED**, which causes the background image to act as a fixed watermark and not to scroll.

BOTTOMMARGIN   This attribute specifies the bottom margin for the entire body of the page and overrides the default margin. When set to **0** or "", the bottom margin is the bottom edge of the window or frame the content is displayed in.

CLASS   See "Core Attributes Reference," earlier in this appendix.

CREDITS   In the WebTV implementation, this attribute contains the URL of the document to retrieve when the viewer presses the credits button on the Info Panel.

DIR   See "Language Reference," earlier in this appendix.

ID   See "Core Attributes Reference," earlier in this appendix.

INSTRUCTIONS   In the WebTV implementation, this attribute contains the URL of the document to retrieve when the viewer presses the instructions button on the Info Panel.

LANG   See "Language Reference," earlier in this appendix.

LANGUAGE   This attribute specifies the language the current script is written in and invokes the proper scripting engine. The default value is **JAVASCRIPT**. **JAVASCRIPT** and **JSCRIPT**

represent that the scripting language is written in JavaScript. **VBS** and **VBSCRIPT** represent that the scripting language is written in VBScript.

LEFTMARGIN   This Internet Explorer–specific attribute sets the left margin for the page in pixels, overriding the default margin. When set to **0** or **""**, the left margin is the left edge of the window or the frame.

LINK   This attribute sets the color for hyperlinks within the document that have not yet been visited. Its value can either be a browser-dependent named color or a color specified using the hexadecimal *#RRGGBB* format.

LOGO   In the WebTV implementation, this attribute contains the URL of a 70 × 52–pixel thumbnail image for the page, which is used in the history and bookmarks for WebTV.

RIGHTMARGIN   This attribute, specific to Internet Explorer, sets the right margin for the page in pixels, overriding the default margin. When set to **0** or **""**, the right margin is the right edge of the window or the frame.

SCROLL   This attribute turns the scroll bars on or off. The default value is **YES**.

STYLE   See "Core Attributes Reference," earlier in this appendix.

TEXT   This attribute sets the text color for the document. Its value can either be a browser-dependent named color or a color specified using the hexadecimal *#RRGGBB* format.

TITLE   See "Core Attributes Reference," earlier in this appendix.

TOPMARGIN   This Internet Explorer–specific attribute sets the top margin for the document in pixels. If set to **0** or **""**, the top margin will be exactly on the top edge of the window or frame.

VLINK   This attribute sets the color for links within the document that have already been visited. Its value can either be a browser-dependent named color or a color specified using the hexadecimal *#RRGGBB* format.

Attribute and Event Support

NETSCAPE 4   ALINK, BACKGROUND, BGCOLOR, LINK, TEXT, VLINK, **onblur**, **onfocus**, **onload**, and **onunload**. (**CLASS**, **ID**, **LANG**, and **STYLE** are implied.)

INTERNET EXPLORER 4   All W3C-defined attributes and events except **DIR**, all attributes and events defined by Internet Explorer 4, and **onblur** and **onfocus**.

WEBTV   BACKGROUND, BGCOLOR, CREDITS, INSTRUCTIONS, LINK, LOGO, TEXT, VLINK, **onload**, and **onunload**.

Event Handlers
See "Events Reference," earlier in this appendix.

Example

```
<BODY BACKGROUND="checkered.gif"
      BGCOLOR="White"
      ALINK="Red"
      LINK="Blue"
      VLINK="Red"
      TEXT="Black"> ... </BODY>

<!-- myLoadFunction defined in document head in <SCRIPT> element -->
<BODY onload="myLoadFunction()"> ... </BODY>
```

Compatibility

HTML 2, 3.2, and 4
Internet Explorer 2, 3, 4, and 5
Netscape 1, 2, 3, 4, and 4.5
WebTV

Notes

- When defining text colors, it is important to be careful to specify both foreground and background explicitly so that they are not masked out by browser defaults set by the user.

- Under the HTML 4.0 strict specification, all color-setting attributes and background attributes are not allowed. This includes the **ALINK**, **BACKGROUND**, **BGCOLOR**, **LINK**, **TEXT**, and **VLINK** attributes

- This element must be present in all documents except those declaring a frame set.

<BQ>   (Block Quote)

This obsolete element signifies that the enclosed text is an extended quotation. Though it has been defined in early HTML specifications, it is currently supported only by the WebTV browser as an alias for the **<BLOCKQUOTE>** element.

Syntax (Obsolete)

```
<BQ>
</BQ>
```

Attributes
None.

Event Handlers
None.

Example

```
<BQ>HTML: The Complete Reference says "Don't use this element."</BQ>
```

Compatibility

WebTV

Notes

This element originated in the early days of HTML and is considered obsolete. It should not be used.

   (Line Break)

This empty element forces a line break.

Syntax

```
<BR
    CLASS="class name(s)"
    CLEAR="ALL | LEFT | NONE | RIGHT" (transitional)
    ID="unique alphanumeric identifier"
    STYLE="style information"
    TITLE="advisory text">
```

Attributes Defined by Internet Explorer 4

```
    LANGUAGE="JAVASCRIPT | JSCRIPT | VBS | VBSCRIPT"
```

Attributes

CLASS   See "Core Attributes Reference," earlier in this appendix.

CLEAR   This attribute forces the insertion of vertical space so that the tagged text may be positioned with respect to images. A value of **LEFT** clears text that flows around left-aligned images to the next full left margin, a value of **RIGHT** clears text that flows around right-aligned images to the next full right margin, and a value of **ALL** clears text until it can reach both full margins. The default value according to the HTML 4.0 transitional specification is **NONE**, but its meaning is generally supported as just introducing a return and nothing more.

ID   See "Core Attributes Reference," earlier in this appendix.

LANGUAGE   This attribute specifies the language the current script is written in and invokes the proper scripting engine. The default value is **JAVASCRIPT**. **JAVASCRIPT** and **JSCRIPT** represent that the scripting language is written in JavaScript. **VBS** and **VBSCRIPT** represent that the scripting language is written in VBScript.

STYLE   See "Core Attributes Reference," earlier in this appendix.

TITLE   See "Core Attributes Reference," earlier in this appendix.

Attribute and Event Support

NETSCAPE 4   CLEAR. (**CLASS**, **ID**, and **STYLE** are implied by Netscape documentation.)

INTERNET EXPLORER 4   All attributes.

WEBTV   CLEAR.

Event Handlers
None.

Examples

```
This text will be broken here <BR>and continued on a new line.

<IMG SRC="test.gif" ALIGN="RIGHT">
This is the image caption.<BR CLEAR="RIGHT">
```

Compatibility

HTML 3.2 and 4
Internet Explorer 2, 3, 4, and 5
Netscape 1, 2, 3, 4, and 4.5
WebTV

Notes

- This is an empty element. A closing tag is illegal.
- Under the HTML 4.0 strict specification, the **CLEAR** attribute is not valid. Style sheet rules provide the functionality of the **CLEAR** attribute.

<BUTTON> (Form Button)

This element defines a nameable region known as a button, which may be used together with scripts.

Syntax

```
<BUTTON
     ACCESSKEY="key"
     CLASS="class name(s)"
     DIR="LTR | RTL"
     DISABLED
     ID="unique alphanumeric identifier"
     LANG="language code"
     NAME="button name"
     STYLE="style information"
     TABINDEX="number"
     TITLE="advisory text"
     TYPE="BUTTON | RESET | SUBMIT"
     VALUE="button value"
     onblur="script"
     onclick="script"
     ondblclick="script"
     onfocus="script"
     onkeydown="script"
     onkeypress="script"
     onkeyup="script"
     onmousedown="script"
     onmousemove="script"
     onmouseout="script"
     onmouseover="script"
     onmouseup="script">

</BUTTON>
```

Attributes and Events Defined by Internet Explorer 4

```
     DATAFLD="name of column supplying bound data"
     DATAFORMATAS="HTML | TEXT"
     DATASRC="ID of data source object supplying data"
     LANGUAGE="JAVASCRIPT | JSCRIPT | VBS | VBSCRIPT"
     onafterupdate="script"
     onbeforeupdate="script"
     ondragstart="script"
     onhelp="script"
     onresize="script"
     onrowenter="script"
     onrowexit="script"
     onselectstart="script"
```

Attributes

ACCESSKEY   This attribute specifies a keyboard navigation accelerator for the element. Pressing ALT or a similar key in association with the specified key selects the anchor element correlated with that key.

CLASS   See "Core Attributes Reference," earlier in this appendix.

DATAFLD   This attribute specifies the column name from the data source object that supplies the bound data that defines the information for the **<BUTTON>** element's content.

DATAFORMATAS   This attribute indicates if the bound data is plain text or HTML.

DATASRC   This attribute indicates the **ID** of the data source object that supplies the data that is bound to the **<BUTTON>** element.

DIR   See "Language Reference," earlier in this appendix.

DISABLED   This attribute is used to disable the button.

ID   See "Core Attributes Reference," earlier in this appendix.

LANG   See "Language Reference," earlier in this appendix.

LANGUAGE   This attribute specifies the language that the current script associated with the event handlers is written in and invokes the proper scripting engine. The default value is **JAVASCRIPT. JAVASCRIPT** and **JSCRIPT** represent that the scripting language is written in JavaScript. **VBS** and **VBSCRIPT** represent that the scripting language is written in VBScript.

NAME   This attribute is used to define a name for the button so that it can be scripted by older browsers or used to provide a name for submit buttons when there is more than one in a page.

STYLE   See "Core Attributes Reference," earlier in this appendix.

TABINDEX   This attribute uses a number to identify the object's position in the tabbing order.

TITLE   See "Core Attributes Reference," earlier in this appendix.

TYPE   Defines the type of button. According to the HTML 4.0 specification, by default the button is undefined. Possible values include **BUTTON, RESET,** and **SUBMIT,** which are used to indicate the button is a plain button, reset button, or submit button respectively.

VALUE   Defines the value that is sent to the server when the button is pressed. This may be useful when using multiple **SUBMIT** buttons that perform different actions to indicate which button was pressed to the handling CGI program.

Attribute and Event Support

INTERNET EXPLORER 4   All attributes and events except **DIR, NAME, TABINDEX,** and **VALUE.**

Event Handlers

See "Events Reference," earlier in this appendix.

Examples

```
<BUTTON NAME="Submit"
        VALUE="Submit"
        TYPE="Submit">Submit Request</BUTTON>

<BUTTON TYPE="BUTTON"
        onclick="doSomething()">Click This Button</BUTTON>

<BUTTON TYPE="BUTTON">
<IMG SRC="polkadot.gif" ALT="Polkadot"></BUTTON>
```

Compatibility

HTML 4
Internet Explorer 4 and 5

Notes

- It is illegal to associate an image map with an **<IMG>** that appears as the contents of a **BUTTON** element.
- The HTML 4.0 specification reserves the data-binding attributes **DATAFLD, DATAFORMATAS,** and **DATASRC** for future use.

<CAPTION>   (Figure or Table Caption)

This element is used within both the figure and table elements to define a caption.

Syntax

```
<CAPTION
    ALIGN="BOTTOM | LEFT | RIGHT | TOP" (transitional)
    CLASS="class name(s)"
    DIR="LTR | RTL"
    ID="unique alphanumeric identifier"
    LANG="language code"
    STYLE="style information"
    TITLE="advisory text"
```

```
        onclick="script"
        ondblclick="script"
        onkeydown="script"
        onkeypress="script"
        onkeyup="script"
        onmousedown="script"
        onmousemove="script"
        onmouseout="script"
        onmouseover="script"
        onmouseup="script">

</CAPTION>
```

Attributes and Events Defined by Internet Explorer 4

```
        LANGUAGE="JAVASCRIPT | JSCRIPT | VBS | VBSCRIPT"
        VALIGN="BOTTOM | TOP"
        onafterupdate="script"
        onbeforeupdate="script"
        onblur="script"
        onchange="script"
        ondragstart="script"
        onfocus="script"
        onhelp="script"
        onresize="script"
        onrowenter="script"
        onrowexit="script"
        onselect="script"
        onselectstart="script"
```

Attributes

ALIGN   This attribute specifies the alignment of the caption. HTML 4 defines **BOTTOM, LEFT, RIGHT**, and **TOP** as legal values. Internet Explorer and WebTV also support **CENTER**. Because this does not provide the possibility of combining vertical and horizontal alignments, Microsoft has introduced the **VALIGN** attribute for the **<CAPTION>** element.

CLASS   See "Core Attributes Reference," earlier in this appendix.

DIR   See "Language Reference," earlier in this appendix.

ID   See "Core Attributes Reference," earlier in this appendix.

LANG   See "Language Reference," earlier in this appendix.

LANGUAGE   This attribute specifies the language the current script is written in and invokes the proper scripting engine. The default value is **JAVASCRIPT**. **JAVASCRIPT** and **JSCRIPT** represent that the scripting language is written in JavaScript. **VBS** and **VBSCRIPT** represent that the scripting language is written in VBScript.

STYLE   See "Core Attributes Reference," earlier in this appendix.

TITLE   See "Core Attributes Reference," earlier in this appendix.

VALIGN   This Internet Explorer–specific attribute specifies whether the table caption appears at the top or bottom.

Attribute and Event Support

NETSCAPE 4   ALIGN. (**CLASS**, **ID**, **LANG**, and **STYLE** are implied.)

INTERNET EXPLORER 4   All attributes and events except **DIR**.

WEBTV   ALIGN (**CENTER** I **LEFT** I **RIGHT**).

Event Handlers
See "Events Reference," earlier in this appendix.

Example

```
<TABLE>
    <CAPTION ALIGN="TOP">Our High-Priced Menu</CAPTION>
        <TR>
            <TD>Escargot</TD>
            <TD>Filet Mignon</TD>
            <TD>Big Mac</TD>
        </TR>
</TABLE>
```

Compatibility

HTML 3.2 and 4
Internet Explorer 2, 3, 4, and 5
Netscape 1.1, 2, 3, 4, and 4.5
WebTV

Notes

- There should be only one caption per table.
- HTML 3.2 defines only the **ALIGN** attribute with values of **BOTTOM** and **TOP**. No other attributes are defined prior to HTML 4. WebTV adds a **CENTER** value to the **ALIGN** attribute.

<CENTER>   (Center Alignment)

This element causes the enclosed content to be centered within the margins currently in effect. Margins are either the default page margins or those imposed by overriding elements such as tables.

Syntax (Transitional Only)

```
<CENTER
    CLASS="class name(s)"
    DIR="LTR | RTL"
    ID="unique alphanumeric identifier"
    LANG="language code"
    STYLE="style information"
    TITLE="advisory text"
    onclick="script"
    ondblclick="script"
    onkeydown="script"
    onkeypress="script"
    onkeyup="script"
    onmousedown="script"
    onmousemove="script"
    onmouseout="script"
    onmouseover="script"
    onmouseup="script">

</CENTER>
```

Attributes and Events Defined by Internet Explorer 4

```
    LANGUAGE="JAVASCRIPT | JSCRIPT | VBS | VBSCRIPT"
    ondragstart="script"
    onhelp="script"
    onselectstart="script"
```

Attributes

CLASS   See "Core Attributes Reference," earlier in this appendix.

DIR   See "Language Reference," earlier in this appendix.

ID   See "Core Attributes Reference," earlier in this appendix.

LANG   See "Language Reference," earlier in this appendix.

LANGUAGE   This attribute specifies the language the current script is written in and invokes the proper scripting engine. The default value is **JAVASCRIPT**. **JAVASCRIPT** and **JSCRIPT**

represent that the scripting language is written in JavaScript. **VBS** and **VBSCRIPT** represent that the scripting language is written in VBScript.

STYLE   See "Core Attributes Reference," earlier in this appendix.

TITLE   See "Core Attributes Reference," earlier in this appendix.

Attribute and Event Support

NETSCAPE 4   **CLASS**, **ID**, **LANG**, and **STYLE** are implied.

INTERNET EXPLORER 4   All attributes and events except **DIR**.

Event Handlers
See "Events Reference," earlier in this appendix.

Example

```
<CENTER>This is in the center of the page.</CENTER>
```

Compatibility

HTML 3.2 and 4 (transitional)
Internet Explorer 2, 3, 4, and 5
Netscape 1.1, 2, 3, 4, and 4.5
WebTV

Notes

- The **<CENTER>** element defined by the W3C is a shorthand notation for **<DIV ALIGN="CENTER">**. The HTML 4.0 strict specification does not include the **<CENTER>** element.
- HTML 3.2 does not support any attributes for this element.

<CITE>   (Citation)

This element indicates a citation from a book or other published source and is usually rendered in italics by a browser.

Syntax

```
<CITE
    CLASS="class name(s)"
    DIR="LTR | RTL"
    ID="unique alphanumeric identifier"
```

```
LANG="language code"
STYLE="style information"
TITLE="advisory text"
onclick="script"
ondblclick="script"
onkeydown="script"
onkeypress="script"
onkeyup="script"
onmousedown="script"
onmousemove="script"
onmouseout="script"
onmouseover="script"
onmouseup="script">

</CITE>
```

Attributes and Events Defined by Internet Explorer 4

```
LANGUAGE="JAVASCRIPT | JSCRIPT | VBS | VBSCRIPT"
ondragstart="script"
onhelp="script"
onselectstart="script"
```

Attributes

CLASS   See "Core Attributes Reference," earlier in this appendix.

DIR   See "Language Reference," earlier in this appendix.

ID   See "Core Attributes Reference," earlier in this appendix.

LANG   See "Language Reference," earlier in this appendix.

LANGUAGE   This attribute specifies the language the current script is written in and invokes the proper scripting engine. The default value is **JAVASCRIPT**. **JAVASCRIPT** and **JSCRIPT** represent that the scripting language is written in JavaScript. **VBS** and **VBSCRIPT** represent that the scripting language is written in VBScript.

STYLE   See "Core Attributes Reference," earlier in this appendix.

TITLE   See "Core Attributes Reference," earlier in this appendix.

Attribute and Event Support

NETSCAPE 4   **CLASS, ID, LANG,** and **STYLE** are implied.

INTERNET EXPLORER 4 All events and attributes except **DIR**.

Event Handlers

See "Events Reference," earlier in this appendix.

Example

This example is taken from the **<CITE>** HTML Programmer's Reference. **</CITE>**

Compatibility

HTML 2, 3.2, and 4
Internet Explorer 2, 3, 4, and 5
Netscape 1, 2, 3, 4, and 4.5
WebTV

Notes

HTML 2 and 3.2 do not indicate any attributes for this element.

<CODE>   (Code Listing)

This element indicates that the enclosed text is source code in a programming language. Usually it is rendered in a monospaced font.

Syntax

```
<CODE
     CLASS="class name(s)"
     DIR="LTR | RTL"
     ID="unique alphanumeric identifier"
     LANG="language code"
     STYLE="style information"
     TITLE="advisory text"
     onclick="script"
     ondblclick="script"
     onkeydown="script"
     onkeypress="script"
     onkeyup="script"
     onmousedown="script"
     onmousemove="script"
     onmouseout="script"
     onmouseover="script"
     onmouseup="script">

</CODE>
```

Attributes and Events Defined by Internet Explorer 4

```
LANGUAGE="JAVASCRIPT | JSCRIPT | VBS | VBSCRIPT"
ondragstart="script"
onhelp="script"
onselectstart="script"
```

Attributes

CLASS   See "Core Attributes Reference," earlier in this appendix.

DIR   See "Language Reference," earlier in this appendix.

ID   See "Core Attributes Reference," earlier in this appendix.

LANG   See "Language Reference," earlier in this appendix.

LANGUAGE   This attribute specifies the language the current script is written in and invokes the proper scripting engine. The default value is **JAVASCRIPT**. **JAVASCRIPT** and **JSCRIPT** represent that the scripting language is written in JavaScript. **VBS** and **VBSCRIPT** represent that the scripting language is written in VBScript.

STYLE   See "Core Attributes Reference," earlier in this appendix.

TITLE   See "Core Attributes Reference," earlier in this appendix.

Attribute and Event Support

NETSCAPE 4   **CLASS**, **ID**, **LANG**, and **STYLE** are implied.

INTERNET EXPLORER 4   All attributes and events except **DIR**.

Event Handlers
See "Events Reference," earlier in this appendix.

Example
To increment a variable called *count*, use

```
<CODE> count++ </CODE>
```

Compatibility

HTML 2, 3.2, and 4
Internet Explorer 2, 3, 4, and 5
Netscape 1, 2., 3, 4, and 4.5
WebTV

Notes

■ This element is best for short code fragments because it does not preserve special indentation. For multiline code fragments, page authors tend to use the **<PRE>** element.

■ HTML 2 and 3.2 do not support any attributes for this element.

<COL> (Column)

This element defines a column within a table and is used for grouping and alignment purposes. It is generally found within a **<COLGROUP>** element.

Syntax

```
<COL
    ALIGN="CENTER | CHAR | JUSTIFY | LEFT | RIGHT"
    CHAR="character"
    CHAROFF="number"
    CLASS="class name(s)"
    DIR="LTR | RTL"
    ID="unique alphanumeric identifier"
    LANG="language code"
    SPAN="number"
    STYLE="style information"
    TITLE="advisory text"
    VALIGN="BASELINE | BOTTOM | MIDDLE | TOP"
    WIDTH="column width specification"
    onclick="script"
    ondblclick="script"
    onkeydown="script"
    onkeypress="script"
    onkeyup="script"
    onmousedown="script"
    onmousemove="script"
    onmouseout="script"
    onmouseover="script"
    onmouseup="script">
```

Attributes

ALIGN   This attribute specifies horizontal alignment of a cell's contents.

CHAR   This attribute is used to set the character to align the cells in a column on. Typical values for this include a period (.) when attempting to align numbers or monetary values.

CHAROFF   This attribute is used to indicate the number of characters to offset the column data from the alignment characters specified by the **CHAR** value.

CLASS   See "Core Attributes Reference," earlier in this appendix.

DIR   See "Language Reference," earlier in this appendix.

ID   See "Core Attributes Reference," earlier in this appendix.

LANG   See "Language Reference," earlier in this appendix.

SPAN   When present, this attribute applies the attributes of the **<COL>** element to additional consecutive columns.

STYLE   See "Core Attributes Reference," earlier in this appendix.

TITLE   See Core Attributes Reference," earlier in this appendix.

VALIGN   This attribute specifies the vertical alignment of the text within the cell. Possible values for this attribute are **BASELINE**, **BOTTOM**, **MIDDLE**, and **TOP**.

WIDTH   This attribute specifies a default width for each column in the current column group. In addition to the standard pixel and percentage values, this attribute may take the special form **0***, which means that the width of each column in the group should be the minimum width necessary to hold the column's contents. Relative widths like 0.5* can also be used.

Attribute and Event Support

INTERNET EXPLORER 4   ALIGN (CENTER | LEFT | RIGHT), CLASS, ID, SPAN, STYLE, TITLE, VALIGN, and WIDTH.

Event Handlers
See "Events Reference," earlier in this appendix.

Example

```
<TABLE BORDER="1" WIDTH="400">
<COLGROUP>
<COL ALIGN="CENTER" WIDTH="150"><COL ALIGN="RIGHT">

<TR>
   <TD>This column is aligned to the center.</TD>
   <TD>This one is aligned to the right.</TD>
</TR>

<TR><TD>!</TD><TD>?</TD></TR>

<TR><TD>!</TD><TD>?</TD></TR>
</TABLE>
```

Compatibility

HTML 4
Internet Explorer 4

Notes

- As an empty element, **<COL>** does not require a closing tag.
- This element generally appears within a **<COLGROUP>** element and like that element is somewhat of a convenience feature used to set attributes with one or more table columns.

<COLGROUP>   (Column Group)

This element creates an explicit column group to access a group of table columns for scripting or formatting.

Syntax

```
<COLGROUP
      ALIGN="CENTER | CHAR | JUSTIFY | LEFT | RIGHT"
      CHAR="character"
      CHAROFF="number"
      CLASS="class name(s)"
      DIR="LTR | RTL"
      ID="unique alphanumeric identifier"
      LANG="language code"
      SPAN="number"
      STYLE="style information"
      TITLE="advisory text"
      VALIGN="BASELINE | BOTTOM | MIDDLE | TOP"
      WIDTH="column width specification"
      onclick="script"
      ondblclick="script"
      onkeydown="script"
      onkeypress="script"
      onkeyup="script"
      onmousedown="script"
      onmousemove="script"
      onmouseout="script"
      onmouseover="script"
      onmouseup="script">

      <COL> elements

</COLGROUP>
```

Attributes

ALIGN   This attribute specifies horizontal alignment of contents of the cells in the column group. The values of **CENTER, LEFT,** and **RIGHT** have obvious meanings. A value of **JUSTIFY** for the attribute should attempt to justify all the column's contents. A value of **CHAR** attempts to align the contents based on the value of the **CHAR** attribute in conjunction with **CHAROFF**.

CHAR   This attribute is used to set the character to align the cells in a column on. Typical values for this include a period (.) when attempting to align numbers or monetary values.

CHAROFF   This attribute is used to indicate the number of characters to offset the column data from the alignment characters specified by the **CHAR** value.

CLASS   See "Core Attributes Reference," earlier in this appendix.

DIR   See "Language Reference," earlier in this appendix.

ID   See "Core Attributes Reference," earlier in this appendix.

LANG   See "Language Reference," earlier in this appendix.

SPAN   When present, this attribute specifies the default number of columns in this group. Browsers should ignore this attribute if the current column group contains one or more **<COL>** elements. The default value of this attribute is **1**.

STYLE   See "Core Attributes Reference," earlier in this appendix.

TITLE   See "Core Attributes Reference," earlier in this appendix.

VALIGN   This attribute specifies the vertical alignment of the contents of the cells within the column group.

WIDTH   This attribute specifies a default width for each column and its cells in the current column group. In addition to the standard pixel and percentage values, this attribute may take the special form **0***, which means that the width of each column in the group should be the minimum width necessary to hold the column's contents.

Attribute and Event Support

INTERNET EXPLORER 4   ALIGN (CENTER | LEFT | RIGHT), CLASS, ID, SPAN, STYLE, TITLE, VALIGN, and WIDTH.

Event Handlers

See "Events Reference," earlier in this appendix.

Examples

```
<COLGROUP SPAN="10" ALIGN="CHAR" CHAR=":" VALIGN="CENTER">

<COLGROUP STYLE="{background: green}">
   <COL ALIGN="LEFT">
   <COL ALIGN="CENTER">
</COLGROUP>
```

Compatibility

HTML 4
Internet Explorer 4 and 5

Notes

Each column group defined by a **<COLGROUP>** may contain zero or more **<COL>** elements.

<COMMENT>   (Comment Information)

This nonstandard element treats enclosed text as nondisplaying comments while processing enclosed HTML. This element should not be used.

Syntax (Defined by Internet Explorer 4)

```
<COMMENT
     ID="unique alphanumeric identifier"
     LANG="language code"
     TITLE="advisory text">

     Commented information

</COMMENT>
```

Attributes

ID   See "Core Attributes Reference," earlier in this appendix.

LANG   See "Language Reference," earlier in this appendix.

TITLE   See "Core Attributes Reference," earlier in this appendix.

Attribute and Event Support

INTERNET EXPLORER 4   All attributes.

Event Handlers
None.

Example

<COMMENT>This is not the proper way to form comments.</COMMENT>

Compatibility

Internet Explorer 4 and 5
WebTV

Notes

- It is better to use the <!- -. . .- -> element, an alternate comment element that does not process enclosed HTML in all specification-conforming browsers.

- Because the **<COMMENT>** element is not supported by all browsers, commented text done in this fashion will appear in Netscape browsers. While Internet Explorer still supports this element, IE documentation recommends use of the <!- -. . .- -> element.

- While some notes indicate that the **<COMMENT>** element will render HTML included within it, in practice this does not seem to be the case.

<DD>   (Definition in a Definition List)

This element indicates the definition of a term within a list of defined terms (**<DT>**) enclosed by a definition list (**<DL>**).

Syntax

```
<DD
     CLASS="class name(s)"
     DIR="LTR | RTL"
     ID="unique alphanumeric identifier"
     LANG="language code"
     STYLE="style information"
     TITLE="advisory text"
     onclick="script"
     ondblclick="script"
     onkeydown="script"
     onkeypress="script"
     onkeyup="script"
     onmousedown="script"
     onmousemove="script"
     onmouseout="script"
     onmouseover="script"
     onmouseup="script">

</DD>
```

Attributes and Events Defined by Internet Explorer 4

```
LANGUAGE="JAVASCRIPT | JSCRIPT | VBS | VBSCRIPT"
ondragstart="script"
onhelp="script"
onselectstart="script"
```

Attributes

CLASS   See "Core Attributes Reference," earlier in this appendix.

DIR   See "Language Reference," earlier in this appendix.

ID   See "Core Attributes Reference, earlier in this appendix.

LANG   See "Language Reference," earlier in this appendix.

LANGUAGE   This attribute specifies the language the current script is written in and invokes the proper scripting engine. The default value is **JAVASCRIPT**. **JAVASCRIPT** and **JSCRIPT** represent that the scripting language is written in JavaScript. **VBS** and **VBSCRIPT** represent that the scripting language is written in VBScript.

STYLE   See "Core Attributes Reference," earlier in this appendix.

TITLE   See "Core Attributes Reference," earlier in this appendix.

Attribute and Event Support

NETSCAPE 4   CLASS, ID, LANG, and STYLE.

INTERNET EXPLORER 4   All attributes and events except **DIR**.

Event Handlers

See "Events Reference," earlier in this appendix.

Example

```
<DL>
    <DT>DOG
        <DD>A domesticated animal that craves attention all the time
    <DT>CAT
        <DD>An animal that would just as soon ignore you until it
            gets hungry
</DL>
```

Compatibility

HTML 2, 3.2, and 4
Internet Explorer 2, 3, 4, and 5
Netscape 1, 2, 3, 4, and 4.5
WebTV

Notes

- The close tag for this element is optional, though encouraged when it will help make the list more understandable.

- This element occurs within a list of defined terms enclosed by the **<DL>** element. Typically associated with it is the term it defines, indicated by the **<DT>** element that just proceeds it.

- HTML 2 and 3.2 define no attributes for this element.

<DEL> (Deleted Text)

This element is used to indicate that text has been deleted from a document. A browser may render deleted text as strikethrough text.

Syntax

```
<DEL
    CITE="URL"
    CLASS="class name(s)"
    DATETIME="date"
    DIR="LTR | RTL"
    ID="unique alphanumeric identifier"
    LANG="language code"
    STYLE="style information"
    TITLE="advisory text"
    onclick="script"
    ondblclick="script"
    onkeydown="script"
    onkeypress="script"
    onkeyup="script"
    onmousedown="script"
    onmousemove="script"
    onmouseout="script"
    onmouseover="script"
    onmouseup="script"
    onselectstart="script">

</DEL>
```

Attributes and Events Defined by Internet Explorer 4

```
LANGUAGE="JAVASCRIPT | JSCRIPT | VBS | VBSCRIPT"
ondragstart="script"
onhelp="script"
```

Attributes

CITE   The value of this attribute is a URL that designates a source document or message that may give a reason why the information was deleted.

CLASS   See "Core Attributes Reference," earlier in this appendix.

DATETIME   This attribute is used to indicate the date and time the deletion was made. The value of the attribute is a date in a special format as defined by ISO 8601. The basic date format is

```
YYYY-MM-DDThh:mm:ssTZD
```

where the following is true:

```
YYYY=four-digit year such as 1999
MM=two-digit month (01=January, 02=February, and so on)
DD=two-digit day of the month (01 through 31)
hh=two digit hour (00 to 23) (24-hour clock, not AM or PM)
mm=two digit minute (00 through 59)
ss=two digit second (00 through 59)
TZD=time zone designator
```

The time zone designator is either **Z**, which indicates UTC (Universal Time Coordinate, or coordinated universal time format), or **+hh:mm**, which indicates that the time is a local time that is *hh* hours and *mm* minutes ahead of UTC. Alternatively, the format for the time zone designator could be **-hh:mm**, which indicates that the local time is behind UTC. Note that the letter "T" actually appears in the string, all digits must be used, and **00** values for minutes and seconds may be required. An example value for the **DATETIME** attribute might be **1999-10-6T09: 15:00-05:00**, which corresponds to October 6, 1999, 9:15 A.M., U.S. Eastern Standard Time.

DIR   See "Language Reference," earlier in this appendix.

ID   See "Core Attributes Reference," earlier in this appendix.

LANG   See "Language Reference," earlier in this appendix.

LANGUAGE   In the Microsoft implementation, this attribute specifies the scripting language to be used with an associated script bound to the element, typically through an event handler attribute. Possible values may include **JAVASCRIPT**, **JSCRIPT**, **VBS**, and **VBSCRIPT**. Other values, which include the version of the language used, such as **JavaScript1.1**, may also be possible.

STYLE   See "Core Attributes Reference," earlier in this appendix.

TITLE   See "Core Attributes Reference," earlier in this appendix.

Attribute and Event Support

INTERNET EXPLORER 4   All attributes and events except **CITE**, **DATETIME**, and **DIR**.

Event Handlers

See "Events Reference," earlier in this appendix.

Example

```
<DEL CITE="http://www.bigcompany.com/changes/oct97.htm"
    DATETIME="1990-10-06T09:15:00-05:00">
The penalty clause applies to client lateness as well.
</DEL>
```

Compatibility

HTML 4
Internet Explorer 4 and 5

Notes

■ Browsers may render deleted (**<DEL>**) text in a different style to show the changes that have been made to the document. Internet Explorer 4 renders the text as strikethrough text. Eventually, a browser may have a way to show a revision history on a document. User agents that do not understand **<DEL>** or **<INS>** will show the information anyway, so there is no harm in adding information—only in deleting it. Because of the fact that **<DEL>**-enclosed text may show up, it may be wise to comment it out within the element as shown here:

```
<DEL>
<!-- This is old information. -->
</DEL>
```

■ The **<DEL>** element is not supported under the HTML 2.0 and 3.2 specifications.

<DFN>   (Defining Instance of a Term)

This element encloses the defining instance of a term. It is usually rendered as bold or bold italic text.

Syntax

```
<DFN
     CLASS="class name(s)"
     DIR="LTR | RTL"
     ID="unique alphanumeric identifier"
     LANG="language code"
     STYLE="style information"
     TITLE="advisory text"
     onclick="script"
     ondblclick="script"
     onkeydown="script"
     onkeypress="script"
     onkeyup="script"
     onmousedown="script"
     onmousemove="script"
     onmouseout="script"
     onmouseover="script"
     onmouseup="script">

</DFN>
```

Attributes and Events Defined by Internet Explorer 4

```
     LANGUAGE="JAVASCRIPT | JSCRIPT | VBS | VBSCRIPT"
     ondragstart="script"
     onhelp="script"
     onselectstart="script"
```

Attributes

CLASS   See "Core Attributes Reference," earlier in this appendix.

DIR   See "Language Reference," earlier in this appendix.

ID   See "Core Attributes Reference," earlier in this appendix.

LANG   See "Language Reference," earlier in this appendix.

LANGUAGE   This attribute specifies the language the current script is written in and invokes the proper scripting engine. The default value is **JAVASCRIPT**. **JAVASCRIPT** and **JSCRIPT** represent that the scripting language is written in JavaScript. **VBS** and **VBSCRIPT** represent that the scripting language is written in VBScript.

STYLE   See "Core Attributes Reference," earlier in this appendix.

TITLE   See "Core Attributes Reference," earlier in this appendix.

Attribute and Event Support

INTERNET EXPLORER 4   All attributes and events except **DIR**.

Event Handlers
See "Events Reference," earlier in this appendix.

Example

```
An <DFN>elephant</DFN> is too large to make
a viable pet for anyone poorer than Bill Gates.
```

Compatibility

HTML 2, 3.2, and 4
Internet Explorer 2, 3, 4, and 5
WebTV

Notes
HTML 2 and 3.2 define no attributes for this element.

<DIR>   (Directory List)

This element encloses a list of brief, unordered items, such as might occur in a menu or directory. The individual items are indicated by the **<UL>** element. Use of this element is not encouraged, as it is not part of the HTML 4.0 strict specification and provides little extra benefit over the **<UL>** element.

Syntax (Transitional Only)

```
<DIR
    CLASS="class name(s)"
    COMPACT
    DIR="LTR | RTL"
    ID="unique alphanumeric identifier"
    LANG="language code"
    STYLE="style information"
    TITLE="advisory text"
    onclick="script"
    ondblclick="script"
    onkeydown="script"
    onkeypress="script"
    onkeyup="script"
```

APPENDIXES

```
        onmousedown="script"
        onmousemove="script"
        onmouseout="script"
        onmouseover="script"
        onmouseup="script">

</DIR>
```

Attributes and Events Defined by Internet Explorer 4

```
        LANGUAGE="JAVASCRIPT | JSCRIPT | VBS | VBSCRIPT"
        ondragstart="script"
        onhelp="script"
        onselectstart="script"
```

Attributes

CLASS   See "Core Attributes Reference," earlier in this appendix.

COMPACT   This attribute reduces the white space between list items.

DIR   See "Language Reference," earlier in this appendix.

ID   See "Core Attributes Reference," earlier in this appendix.

LANG   See "Language Reference," earlier in this appendix.

LANGUAGE   This attribute specifies the language the current script is written in and invokes the proper scripting engine. The default value is **JAVASCRIPT**. **JAVASCRIPT** and **JSCRIPT** represent that the scripting language is written in JavaScript. **VBS** and **VBSCRIPT** represent that the scripting language is written in VBScript.

STYLE   See "Core Attributes Reference," earlier in this appendix.

TITLE   See "Core Attributes Reference," earlier in this appendix.

Attribute and Event Support

NETSCAPE 4   **CLASS, ID, LANG,** and **STYLE** are explicit.

INTERNET EXPLORER 4   All events and attributes except **COMPACT** and **DIR**.

WEBTV   No attributes. (Note: WebTV bolds text enclosed in the **<DIR>** element.)

Event Handlers

See "Events Reference," earlier in this appendix.

Example

```
<DIR>
  <LI>Header Files
  <LI>Code Files
  <LI>Comment Files
</DIR>
```

Compatibility

HTML 2, 3.2, and 4 (transitional)
Internet Explorer 2, 3, 4, and 5
Netscape 1, 2, 3, 4, and 4.5
WebTV

Notes

■ Because the **<DIR>** element is supposed to be used with short lists, the items in the list should have a maximum width of 20 characters.

■ The HTML 4.0 strict specification does not support this element.

■ Many browsers will not to render the **<DIR>** element any differently than the **<UL>** element.

■ Many browsers will not render the **COMPACT** list style.

■ HTML 2 and 3.2 support only the **COMPACT** attribute.

<DIV>   (Division)

This element indicates a block of document content, which should be treated as a logical unit.

Syntax

```
<DIV
    ALIGN="CENTER | JUSTIFY | LEFT | RIGHT"
          (transitional)
    CLASS="class name(s)"
    DATAFLD="name of column supplying bound data"
          (reserved)
    DATAFORMATAS="HTML | TEXT" (reserved)
    DATASRC="ID of data source object supplying data"
          (reserved)
    DIR="LTR | RTL"
```

```
ID="unique alphanumeric identifier"
LANG="language code"
STYLE="style information"
TITLE="advisory text"
onclick="script"
ondblclick="script"
onkeydown="script"
onkeypress="script"
onkeyup="script"
onmousedown="script"
onmousemove="script"
onmouseout="script"
onmouseover="script"
onmouseup="script">

</DIV>
```

Attributes and Events Defined by Internet Explorer 4

```
LANGUAGE="JAVASCRIPT | JSCRIPT | VBS | VBSCRIPT"
onafterupdate="script"
onbeforeupdate="script"
onblur="script"
ondragstart="script"
onfocus="script"
onhelp="script"
onresize="script"
onrowenter="script"
onrowexit="script"
onscroll="script"
onselectstart="script"
```

Attributes

ALIGN   This attribute indicates how the tagged text should be horizontally aligned on the page. The default value is **LEFT**. The **JUSTIFY** value is supported only by the Microsoft implementation.

CHARSET   This attribute defines the character encoding of the linked resource specified by the **HREF** attribute. The value is a space- and/or comma-delimited list of character sets as defined in RFC 2045. The default value is **ISO-8859-1**.

CLASS   See "Core Attributes Reference," earlier in this appendix.

DATAFLD   This attribute specifies the column name from the data source object that supplies the bound data.

DATAFORMATAS   This attribute indicates if the bound data is plain text or HTML.

DATASRC   This attribute indicates the **ID** of the data source object that supplies the data that is bound to this element.

DIR   See "Language Reference," earlier in this appendix.

ID   See "Core Attributes Reference," earlier in this appendix.

LANG   See "Language Reference," earlier in this appendix.

LANGUAGE   This attribute specifies the language the current script is written in and invokes the proper scripting engine. The default value is **JAVASCRIPT**. **JAVASCRIPT** and **JSCRIPT** represent that the scripting language is written in JavaScript. **VBS** and **VBSCRIPT** represent that the scripting language is written in VBScript.

STYLE   See "Core Attributes Reference," earlier in this appendix.

TITLE   See "Core Attributes Reference," earlier in this appendix.

Attribute and Event Support

NETSCAPE 4   ALIGN, CLASS, ID, LANG, and STYLE.

INTERNET EXPLORER 4   All attributes and events except **DIR**.

WEBTV   ALIGN (CENTER | LEFT | RIGHT).

Event Handlers
See "Events Reference," earlier in this appendix.

Examples

```
<DIV ALIGN="JUSTIFY">
All text within this division will be justified
(but only under Netscape 4).
</DIV>

<DIV CLASS="special" ID="div1" STYLE="background: yellow">
Get ready to animate and stylize this.
</DIV>
```

APPENDIXES

Compatibility

HTML 3.2 and 4
Internet Explorer 2, 3, 4, and 5
Netscape 2, 3, 4, and 4.5
WebTV

Notes

- Many users are confused about the proper use of the <DIV> element, since all it does is create a block element. It is very useful for binding scripts or styles to an arbitrary section of a document. In this sense, <DIV> complements <SPAN>, which is used inline.

- The HTML 4.0 specification specifies that the **DATAFLD, DATAFORMATAS**, and **DATASRC** attributes are reserved for <DIV> and may be supported in the future. Internet Explorer 4 already supports these reserved attributes.

- Under the HTML 4.0 strict specification, the **ALIGN** attribute is not supported.

- HTML 3.2 supports only the **ALIGN** attribute.

<DL> (Definition List)

This element encloses a list of terms and definition pairs. A common use for this element is to implement a glossary.

Syntax

```
<DL
     CLASS="class name(s)"
     COMPACT
     DIR="LTR | RTL"
     ID="unique alphanumeric identifier"
     LANG="language code"
     STYLE="style information"
     TITLE="advisory text"
     onclick="script"
     ondblclick="script"
     onkeydown="script"
     onkeypress="script"
     onkeyup="script"
     onmousedown="script"
     onmousemove="script"
     onmouseout="script"
     onmouseover="script"
     onmouseup="script">

</DL>
```

Attributes and Events Defined by Internet Explorer 4

```
LANGUAGE="JAVASCRIPT | JSCRIPT | VBS | VBSCRIPT"
ondragstart="script"
onhelp="script"
onselectstart="script"
```

Attributes

CLASS   See "Core Attributes Reference," earlier in this appendix.

COMPACT   This attribute reduces the white space between list items.

DIR   See "Language Reference," earlier in this appendix.

ID   See "Core Attributes Reference," earlier in this appendix.

LANG   See "Language Reference," earlier in this appendix.

LANGUAGE   This attribute specifies the language the current script is written in and invokes the proper scripting engine. The default value is **JAVASCRIPT**. **JAVASCRIPT** and **JSCRIPT** represent that the scripting language is written in JavaScript. **VBS** and **VBSCRIPT** represent that the scripting language is written in VBScript.

STYLE   See "Core Attributes Reference," earlier in this appendix.

TITLE   See "Core Attributes Reference," earlier in this appendix.

Attribute and Event Support

NETSCAPE 4   **CLASS, COMPACT, ID, LANG,** and **STYLE.**

INTERNET EXPLORER 4   All attributes and events except **DIR.**

Event Handlers

See "Events Reference," earlier in this appendix.

Example

```
<DL>
   <DT>Cat
      <DD>A domestic animal that likes fish
   <DT>Skunk
      <DD>A wild animal that needs deodorant
</DL>
```

APPENDIXES

Compatibility

> HTML 2, 3.2, and 4
> Internet Explorer 2, 3, 4, and 5
> Netscape 1, 2, 3, 4, and 4.5
> WebTV

Notes

- The items in the list comprise two parts: the term, indicated by the **<DT>** element, and its definition, indicated by the **<DD>** element.

- Some page designers may use the **<DL>** element or **<UL>** element to help create text indent. While this is a common practice on the Web, it is not advisable because it confuses the meaning of the element by making it a physical layout device rather than a list.

- Under the HTML 4.0 strict specification, the **COMPACT** attribute is not allowed.

- HTML 2 and 3.2 support only the **COMPACT** attribute for this element.

<DT>   (Term in a Definition List)

This element identifies a definition list term in a definition list term-definition pair.

Syntax

```
<DT
      CLASS="class name(s)"
      DIR="LTR | RTL"
      ID="unique alphanumeric identifier"
      LANG="language code"
      STYLE="style information"
      TITLE="advisory text"
      onclick="script"
      ondblclick="script"
      onkeydown="script"
      onkeypress="script"
      onkeyup="script"
      onmousedown="script"
      onmousemove="script"
      onmouseout="script"
      onmouseover="script"
      onmouseup="script">
```

Attributes and Events Defined by Internet Explorer 4

```
      LANGUAGE="JAVASCRIPT | JSCRIPT | VBS | VBSCRIPT"
      ondragstart="script"
```

```
onhelp="script"
onselectstart="script"
```

Attributes

CLASS   See "Core Attributes Reference," earlier in this appendix.

DIR   See "Language Reference," earlier in this appendix.

ID   See "Core Attributes Reference," earlier in this appendix.

LANG   See "Language Reference," earlier in this appendix.

LANGUAGE   This attribute specifies the language the current script is written in and invokes the proper scripting engine. The default value is **JAVASCRIPT**. **JAVASCRIPT** and **JSCRIPT** represent that the scripting language is written in JavaScript. **VBS** and **VBSCRIPT** represent that the scripting language is written in VBScript.

STYLE   See "Core Attributes Reference," earlier in this appendix.

TITLE   See "Core Attributes Reference," earlier in this appendix.

Attribute and Event Support

NETSCAPE 4   **CLASS**, **ID**, **LANG**, and **STYLE**.

INTERNET EXPLORER 4   All attributes and events except **DIR**.

Event Handlers
See "Events Reference," earlier in this appendix.

Example

```
<DL>
<DT>Rake
    <DD>A garden tool used to gather leaves and rubbish
  <DT>Trowel
    <DD>A small garden tool used to shovel earth
</DL>
```

Compatibility

HTML 2, 3.2, 4
Internet Explorer 2, 3, 4, and 5

Netscape 1, 2, 3, 4, and 4.5
WebTV

Notes

■ This element occurs within a list of defined terms enclosed by the **<DL>** element. It is generally used in conjunction with the **<DD>** element, which indicates its definition. However, **<DT>** elements do not require a one-to-one correspondence with **<DD>** elements.

■ The close tag for the element is optional but suggested when it will make things more clear, particularly with multiple-line definitions.

■ HTML 2 and 3.2 support no attributes for this element.

<EM> (Emphasis)

This element indicates emphasized text, which many browsers display as italic text.

Syntax

```
<EM
    CLASS="class name(s)"
    DIR="LTR | RTL"
    ID="unique alphanumeric identifier"
    LANG="language code"
    STYLE="style information"
    TITLE="advisory text"
    onclick="script"
    ondblclick="script"
    onkeydown="script"
    onkeypress="script"
    onkeyup="script"
    onmousedown="script"
    onmousemove="script"
    onmouseout="script"
    onmouseover="script"
    onmouseup="script">

</EM>
```

Attributes and Events Defined by Internet Explorer 4

```
    LANGUAGE="JAVASCRIPT | JSCRIPT | VBS | VBSCRIPT"
    ondragstart="script"
    onhelp="script"
    onselectstart="script"
```

Attributes

CLASS   See "Core Attributes Reference," earlier in this appendix.

DIR   See "Language Reference," earlier in this appendix.

ID   See "Core Attributes Reference," earlier in this appendix.

LANG   See "Language Reference," earlier in this appendix.

LANGUAGE   This attribute specifies the language the current script is written in and invokes the proper scripting engine. The default value is **JAVASCRIPT**. **JAVASCRIPT** and **JSCRIPT** represent that the scripting language is written in JavaScript. **VBS** and **VBSCRIPT** represent that the scripting language is written in VBScript.

STYLE   See "Core Attributes Reference," earlier in this appendix.

TITLE   See "Core Attributes Reference," earlier in this appendix.

Attribute and Event Support

NETSCAPE 4   CLASS, ID, LANG, and STYLE are implied.

INTERNET EXPLORER 4   All attributes and events except **DIR**.

Event Handlers
See "Events Reference," earlier in this appendix.

Example

```
This is an <EM>important point</EM> to consider.
```

Compatibility

HTML 2, 3.2, and 4
Internet Explorer 2, 3, 4, and 5
Netscape 1, 2, 3, 4, and 4.5
WebTV

Notes

■ As a logical element, **<EM>** is a prime candidate to bind style information to. For example, to define emphasis to mean a larger font size in the Impact font, you might use a CSS rule like the following in a document-wide style sheet.

```
EM {font-size: larger; font-family: Impact;}
```

■ HTML 2 and 3.2 support no attributes for this element.

<EMBED>   (Embedded Object)

This widely supported but nonstandard element specifies an object, typically a multimedia element, to be embedded in an HTML document.

Syntax (Defined by Internet Explorer 4)

```
<EMBED
     ALIGN="ABSBOTTOM | ABSMIDDLE | BASELINE | BOTTOM |
            LEFT | MIDDLE | RIGHT | TEXTTOP | TOP"
     ALT="alternative text"
     CLASS="class name(s)"
     CODE="filename"
     CODEBASE="URL"
     HEIGHT="pixels"
     HSPACE="pixels"
     ID="unique alphanumeric identifier"
     NAME="string"
     SRC="URL"
     STYLE="style information"
     TITLE="advisory text"
     VSPACE="pixels"
     WIDTH="pixels">

</EMBED>
```

Attributes Defined by Netscape 4

```
     BORDER="pixels"
     HIDDEN="TRUE | FALSE"
     PALETTE="BACKGROUND | FOREGROUND"
     PLUGINSPAGE="URL"
     TYPE="MIME type"
     UNITS="EN | PIXELS"
```

Attributes

ALIGN   This attribute controls the alignment of adjacent text with respect to the embedded object. The default value is **LEFT**.

ALT   This attribute indicates the text to be displayed if the applet cannot be executed.

BORDER   This attribute specifies the size in pixels of the border around the embedded object.

CLASS   See "Core Attributes Reference," earlier in this appendix.

CODE   This attribute specifies the name of the file containing the compiled Java class if the <EMBED> element is used to include a Java applet. This is a strange alternate form of Java inclusion documented by Microsoft.

CODEBASE   This specifies the base URL for the plug-in or potential applet in the case of the alternative form under Internet Explorer.

HEIGHT   This attribute sets the height in pixels of the embedded object.

HIDDEN   If this attribute is set to the value **TRUE**, the embedded object is not visible on the page and implicitly has a size of zero.

HSPACE   This attribute specifies in pixels the size of the left and right margin between the embedded object and surrounding text.

ID   See "Core Attributes Reference," earlier in this appendix.

NAME   This attribute specifies a name for the embedded object, which can be referenced by client-side programs in an embedded scripting language.

PALETTE   This attribute is used only on Windows systems to select the color palette used for the plug-in and may be set to **BACKGROUND** or **FOREGROUND**. The default is **BACKGROUND**.

PLUGINSPAGE   This attribute contains the URL of instructions for installing the plug-in required to render the embedded object.

SRC   This attribute specifies the URL of source content for the embedded object.

STYLE   See "Core Attributes Reference," earlier in this appendix.

TITLE   See "Core Attributes Reference," earlier in this appendix.

TYPE   This attribute specifies the MIME type of the embedded object. It is used by the browser to determine an appropriate plug-in for rendering the object. It can be used instead of the **SRC** attribute for plug-ins that have no content or that fetch it dynamically.

UNITS   This Netscape-specific attribute is used to set the units for measurement for the embedded object either in **EN** or in the default, **PIXELS**.

VSPACE   This attribute specifies in pixels the size of the top and bottom margin between the embedded object and surrounding text.

WIDTH   This attribute sets the width in pixels of the embedded object.

Attribute and Event Support

NETSCAPE 4   ALIGN (BOTTOM | LEFT | RIGHT | TOP), HEIGHT, SRC, WIDTH, and all Netscape-defined attributes. (**CLASS, ID, LANG,** and **STYLE** are implied.)

INTERNET EXPLORER 4   All Microsoft-defined attributes and events.

WEBTV   ALIGN (BOTTOM | LEFT | RIGHT | TOP), BORDER, HEIGHT, HIDDEN, HSPACE, NAME, SRC, VSPACE, and WIDTH.

Event Handlers

See "Events Reference," earlier in this appendix.

Examples

```
<!-- EMBED without a close tag -->
<EMBED SRC="testmovie.mov" HEIGHT="150" WIDTH="150">
<NOEMBED>
  <IMG SRC="testgif.gif" HEIGHT="150" WIDTH="150" ALT="Test Image">
</NOEMBED>

<!-- EMBED with a close tag -->
<EMBED SRC="testmovie.mov" HEIGHT="150" WIDTH="150">
<NOEMBED>
  <IMG SRC="testgif.gif" HEIGHT="150" WIDTH="150" ALT="Test Image">
</NOEMBED>
</EMBED>
```

Compatibility

Netscape 2, 3, 4, and 4.5
Internet Explorer 3, 4, and 5
WebTV

Notes

■ It is unclear whether or not the close tag for **<EMBED>** is required. Many sites tend not to use it, and documentation is not consistent. Some people claim that a close tag is required and should surround any alternative content in a **<NOEMBED>** element; others do not use a close tag. Since this element should eventually be phased out in favor of **<OBJECT>**, this may be a moot issue.

■ While WebTV may support the **<EMBED>** element, it can deal only with media types the equipment knows how to handle, such as Macromedia Flash or certain standard audio files. Other plug-ins cannot be added to the system.

■ The **<EMBED>** element is not favored by the W3C and is not part of any official HTML specification; however, it is very common. The HTML specification says to use the **<OBJECT>** element, which can be used in conjunction with the **<EMBED>** element to provide backward compatibility.

■ Embedded objects are multimedia content files of arbitrary type, which are rendered by browser plug-ins. The **TYPE** attribute uses a file's MIME type to determine an appropriate browser plug-in. Any attributes not defined are treated as object-specific parameters and passed through to the embedded object. Consult the plug-in or object documentation to determine these. The standard parameters supported by the Microsoft implementation are **HEIGHT, NAME, PALETTE, SRC, UNITS,** and **WIDTH**.

<FIELDSET>   (Form Field Set)

This element allows form designers to group thematically related controls together.

Syntax

```
<FIELDSET
    CLASS="class name(s)"
    DIR="LTR | RTL"
    ID="unique alphanumeric identifier"
    LANG="language code"
    STYLE="style information"
    TITLE="advisory text"
    onclick="script"
    ondblclick="script"
    onkeydown="script"
    onkeypress="script"
    onkeyup="script"
    onmousedown="script"
    onmousemove="script"
    onmouseout="script"
    onmouseover="script"
    onmouseup="script">

</FIELDSET>
```

Attributes and Events Defined by Internet Explorer 4

```
    ALIGN="CENTER | LEFT | RIGHT"
    LANGUAGE="JAVASCRIPT | JSCRIPT | VBS | VBSCRIPT"
    onblur="script"
    onchange="script"
    ondragstart="script"
    onfilterchange="script"
    onfocus="script"
    onhelp="script"
    onresize="script"
    onscroll="script"
    onselect="script"
    onselectstart="script"
```

Attributes

ALIGN   Internet Explorer defines the **ALIGN** attribute, which sets how the element and its contents are positioned in a table or the window.

CLASS See "Core Attributes Reference," earlier in this appendix.

DIR See "Language Reference," earlier in this appendix.

ID See "Core Attributes Reference," earlier in this appendix.

LANG See "Language Reference," earlier in this appendix.

LANGUAGE This attribute specifies the language the current script is written in and invokes the proper scripting engine. The default value is **JAVASCRIPT**. **JAVASCRIPT** and **JSCRIPT** represent that the scripting language is written in JavaScript. **VBS** and **VBSCRIPT** represent that the scripting language is written in VBScript.

STYLE See "Core Attributes Reference," earlier in this appendix.

TITLE See "Core Attributes Reference," earlier in this appendix.

Attribute and Event Support

INTERNET EXPLORER 4 All attributes and events except **DIR**.

Event Handlers
See "Events Reference," earlier in this appendix.

Example

```
<FIELDSET>
   <LEGEND>Customer Identification</LEGEND>
   <BR>
   <LABEL>Customer Name:
   <INPUT TYPE="TEXT" ID="CustName" SIZE="25">
</FIELDSET>
```

Compatibility

HTML 4
Internet Explorer 4 and 5

Notes

- Grouping controls makes it easier for users to understand the purposes of the controls while simultaneously facilitating tabbing navigation for visual user agents and speech navigation for speech-oriented user agents. The proper use of this element makes documents more accessible to people with disabilities.

- The caption for this element is defined by the **<LEGEND>** element within the **<FIELDSET>** element.

<FN>   (Footnote)

This WebTV-specific element indicates either a reference to a footnote or the footnote itself.

Syntax (Defined by WebTV)

```
<FN
    HREF="URL"
    ID="unique alphanumeric identifier">

</FN>
```

Attributes

HREF   This attribute contains a URL that references the footnote. Typically the URL is a fragment in the form of the pound sign (#) followed by the name of the footnote anchor. It indicates that the tagged text is a reference to a footnote.

ID   This attribute contains the name of the footnote anchor. It indicates that the tagged text is a footnote.

Attribute and Event Support

WEBTV   HREF and ID.

Event Handlers

None.

Example

```
This wonderful idea came from <FN HREF="#smith">Smith.</FN>

<FN ID="smith">Smith, Fred, Journal of Really Good Ideas</FN>
```

Compatibility

WebTV

Notes

■ Footnotes are implemented as internal links within a document. Use the **HREF** attribute to indicate a reference to a footnote. Use the **ID** attribute to indicate the footnote itself.

■ Footnotes are not to be used outside the WebTV environment. They are a leftover of the failed HTML 3 proposal.

APPENDIXES

<FONT> (Font Definition)

This element allows specification of the size, color, and font of the text it encloses. Use of this element is not encouraged as it is not part of the HTML 4.0 strict specification. Style sheets provide a cleaner way of providing the same functionality when they are supported.

Syntax (Transitional Only)

```
<FONT
    CLASS="class name(s)"
    COLOR="color name | #RRGGBB"
    DIR="LTR | RTL"
    FACE="font name"
    ID="unique alphanumeric identifier"
    LANG="language code"
    SIZE="1 to 7 | +1 to +6 | -1 to -6"
    STYLE="style information"
    TITLE="advisory text">

</FONT>
```

Attributes and Events Defined by Internet Explorer 4

```
LANGUAGE="JAVASCRIPT | JSCRIPT | VBS | VBSCRIPT"
onclick="script"
ondblclick="script"
ondragstart="script"
onhelp="script"
onkeydown="script"
onkeypress="script"
onkeyup="script"
onmousedown="script"
onmousemove="script"
onmouseout="script"
onmouseover="script"
onmouseup="script"
onselectstart="script"
```

Attributes Defined by Netscape 4

```
POINT-SIZE="point size for font"
WEIGHT="100 | 200 | 300 | 400 | 500 | 600 | 700 |
        800 | 900"
```

Attributes Defined by WebTV

```
EFFECT="EMBOSS | RELIEF | SHADOW"
TRANSPARENCY="number (0-100)"
```

Attributes

CLASS   See "Core Attributes Reference," earlier in this appendix.

COLOR   This attribute sets the text color using either a browser-dependent named color or a color specified in the hexadecimal *#RRGGBB* format.

DIR   See "Language Reference," earlier in this appendix.

EFFECT   In the WebTV implementation, this attribute renders the tagged text in a special way. The **RELIEF** value causes the text to appear raised off the page. The **EMBOSS** value causes the text to appear embossed into the page.

FACE   This attribute contains a list of one or more font names separated by commas. The user agent looks through the specified font names and renders the text in the first font that is supported.

ID   See "Core Attributes Reference," earlier in this appendix.

LANG   See "Language Reference," earlier in this appendix.

LANGUAGE   This attribute specifies the language the current script is written in and invokes the proper scripting engine. The default value is **JAVASCRIPT**. **JAVASCRIPT** and **JSCRIPT** represent that the scripting language is written in JavaScript. **VBS** and **VBSCRIPT** represent that the scripting language is written in VBScript.

POINT-SIZE   This Netscape 4–specific attribute specifies the point size of text and is used with downloadable fonts.

SIZE   This attribute specifies the font size as either a numeric or relative value. Numeric values range from **1** to **7** with **1** being the smallest and **3** the default. The relative values, + and −, increment or decrement the font size relative to the current size. The value for increment or decrement should range only from **+1** to **+ 6** or **−1** to **−6**.

STYLE   See "Core Attributes Reference," earlier in this appendix.

TITLE   See "Core Attributes Reference," earlier in this appendix.

TRANSPARENCY   WebTV's proprietary **TRANSPARENCY** attribute is used to set the transparency level of the text. A value of **0** indicates the text is opaque; a value of **100** indicates text is fully transparent, allowing the background to show through. The default value for this attribute is **0**.

WEIGHT   Under Netscape 4, this attribute specifies the weight of the font, with a value of **100** being lightest and **900** being heaviest.

Attribute and Event Support

NETSCAPE 4   COLOR, POINT-SIZE, SIZE, and **WEIGHT**. (CLASS, ID, LANG, and STYLE are implied.)

INTERNET EXPLORER 4   All W3C-defined attributes and events except **DIR**, and all attributes and events defined by Internet Explorer 4.

WEBTV   COLOR, EFFECT, SIZE, and **TRANSPARENCY**.

Event Handlers
See "Events Reference," earlier in this appendix.

Example

```
<FONT COLOR="#FF0000" FACE="Helvetica, Times Roman" SIZE="+1">
Relatively large red text in Helvetica or Times
</FONT>
```

Compatibility

HTML 3.2 and 4
Internet Explorer 2, 3, 4, and 5
Netscape 1.1, 2, 3, 4, and 4.5
WebTV

Notes

- The default text size for a document can be set using the **SIZE** attribute of the **<BASEFONT>** element.
- The HTML 3.2 specification supports only the **COLOR** and **SIZE** attributes for this element.
- The HTML 4.0 transitional specification supports the **CLASS, COLOR, DIR, FACE, ID, LANG, SIZE, STYLE,** and **TITLE** attributes.
- The HTML 4.0 strict specification does not support the **<FONT>** element at all.

<FORM>   (Form for User Input)

The element defines a fill-in form to contain labels and form controls, such as menus and text entry boxes that may be filled in by a user.

Syntax

```
<FORM
    ACCEPT-CHARSET="list of supported character sets"
    ACTION="URL"
    CLASS="class name(s)"
    DIR="LTR | RTL"
    ENCTYPE="application/x-www-form-urlencoded |
             multipart/form-data | text/plain |
             Media Type as per RFC 2045"
    ID="unique alphanumeric identifier"
    LANG="language code"
    METHOD="GET | POST"
    STYLE="style information"
    TARGET="_blank | frame name | _parent | _self |
            _top" (transitional)
    TITLE="advisory text"
    onclick="script"
    ondblclick="script"
    onkeydown="script"
    onkeypress="script"
    onkeyup="script"
    onmousedown="script"
    onmousemove="script"
    onmouseout="script"
    onmouseover="script"
    onmouseup="script"
    onreset="script"
    onsubmit="script">

</FORM>
```

Attributes and Events Defined by Internet Explorer 4

```
    LANGUAGE="JAVASCRIPT | JSCRIPT | VBS | VBSCRIPT"
    NAME="string"
    ondragstart="script"
    onhelp="script"
    onselectstart="script"
```

Attributes

ACCEPT-CHARSET   This attribute specifies the list of character encodings for input data that must be accepted by the server processing form. The value is a space- or comma-delimited list of character sets as defined in RFC 2045. The default value for this attribute is the reserved value **UNKNOWN**.

ACTION   This attribute contains the URL of the server program, which will process the contents of the form. Some browsers may also support a mailto URL, which may mail the results to the specified address.

CLASS   See "Core Attributes Reference," earlier in this appendix.

DIR   See "Language Reference," earlier in this appendix.

ENCTYPE   This attribute indicates how form data should be encoded before being sent to the server. The default is **application/x-www-form-urlencoded**. This encoding replaces blank characters in the data with a + and all other nonprinting characters with a % followed by the character's ASCII HEX representation. The multipart/form-data option does not perform character conversion and transfers the information as a compound MIME document. This must be used when using **<INPUT TYPE="FILE">**. It may also be possible to use another encoding like text/plain to avoid any form of hex encoding which may be useful with mailed forms.

ID   See "Core Attributes Reference," earlier in this appendix.

LANG   See "Language Reference," earlier in this appendix.

LANGUAGE   This attribute specifies the language the current script is written in and invokes the proper scripting engine. The default value is **JAVASCRIPT**. **JAVASCRIPT** and **JSCRIPT** represent that the scripting language is written in JavaScript. **VBS** and **VBSCRIPT** represent that the scripting language is written in VBScript.

METHOD   This attribute indicates how form information should be transferred to the server. The **GET** option appends data to the URL specified by the **ACTION** attribute. This approach gives the best performance, but imposes a size limitation determined by the command line length supported by the server. The **POST** option transfers data using a HTTP post transaction. This approach is more secure and imposes no data size limitation.

NAME   This attribute specifies a name for the form and can be used by client-side programs to reference form data.

STYLE   See "Core Attributes Reference," earlier in this appendix.

TARGET   In documents containing frames, this attribute specifies the target frame to display the results of a form submission. In addition to named frames, several special values exist. The **_blank** value indicates a new window. The **_parent** value indicates the parent frame set containing the source link. The **_self** value indicates the frame containing the source link. The **_top** value indicates the full browser window.

TITLE   See "Core Attributes Reference," earlier in this appendix.

Attribute and Event Support

NETSCAPE 4   ACTION, ENCTYPE, METHOD, NAME, TARGET, **onreset**, and **onsubmit**. (**CLASS**, **ID**, **LANG**, and **STYLE** are implied.)

INTERNET EXPLORER 4   All attributes and events except **ACCEPT-CHARSET** and **DIR**.

WEBTV   ACTION, METHOD, TARGET, onreset, and onsubmit.

Event Handlers
See "Events Reference," earlier in this appendix.

Example

```
<FORM ACTION="http://www.bigcompany.com/cgi-bin/processit.exe"
      METHOD="POST" NAME="testform" onsubmit="validate()">
Enter your comments here:<BR>
   <TEXTAREA NAME="comments" COLS="30" ROWS="8"></TEXTAREA>
   <BR>
   <INPUT TYPE="SUBMIT">
   <INPUT TYPE="RESET">
</FORM>
```

Compatibility

HTML 2, 3.2, and 4
Internet Explorer 2, 3, 4, and 5
Netscape 1, 2, 3, 4, and 4.5
WebTV

Notes

■ Form content is defined using the **<BUTTON>**, **<INPUT>**, **<SELECT>**, and **<TEXTAREA>** elements as well as other HTML formatting and structuring elements. Special grouping elements like **<FIELDSET>**, **<LABEL>**, and **<LEGEND>** have been introduced to provide better structuring for forms, but other HTML elements such as **<DIV>** and **<TABLE>** may also be used to improve form layout.

■ HTML 2 and 3.2 support only the **ACTION**, **ENCTYPE**, and **METHOD** attributes for the **<FORM>** element.

<FRAME>   (Window Region)

This element defines a nameable window region, known as a frame, that can independently display its own content.

Syntax (Transitional Only)

```
<FRAME
    CLASS="class name(s)"
    FRAMEBORDER="0 | 1"
```

```
ID="unique alphanumeric identifier"
LONGDESC="URL of description"
MARGINHEIGHT="pixels"
MARGINWIDTH="pixels"
NAME="string"
NORESIZE
SCROLLING="AUTO | NO | YES"
SRC="URL" of frame contents"
STYLE="style information"
TITLE="advisory text">
```

Attributes and Events Defined by Internet Explorer 4

```
BORDERCOLOR="color name | #RRGGBB"
DATAFLD="name of column supplying bound data"
DATASRC="ID of data source object supplying data"
FRAMEBORDER="NO | YES | 0 | 1"
HEIGHT="pixels"
LANG="language code"
LANGUAGE="JAVASCRIPT | JSCRIPT | VBS | VBSCRIPT"
WIDTH="pixels"
onreadystatechange="script"
```

Attributes Defined by WebTV

```
ALIGN="BOTTOM | CENTER | LEFT | RIGHT | TOP"
```

Attributes

BORDERCOLOR   This attribute sets the color of the frame's border using either a named color or a color specified in the hexadecimal *#RRGGBB* format.

CLASS   See "Core Attributes Reference," earlier in this appendix.

DATAFLD   This Internet Explorer attribute specifies the column name from the data source object that supplies the bound data.

DATASRC   This Internet Explorer attribute indicates the **ID** of the data source object that supplies the data that is bound to this element.

FRAMEBORDER   This attribute determines whether the frame is surrounded by an outlined three-dimensional border. The HTML specification prefers the use of **1** for the frame border on and **0** for off; most browsers also acknowledge the use of **NO** and **YES**.

ID   See "Core Attributes Reference," earlier in this appendix.

LANG   See "Language Reference," earlier in this appendix.

LANGUAGE   This attribute specifies the language the current script is written in and invokes the proper scripting engine. The default value is **JAVASCRIPT**. **JAVASCRIPT** and **JSCRIPT** represent that the scripting language is written in JavaScript. **VBS** and **VBSCRIPT** represent that the scripting language is written in VBScript.

LONGDESC   This attribute specifies a URL of a document that contains a long description of the frame's content. This attribute should be used in conjunction with the **<TITLE>** element.

MARGINHEIGHT   This attribute sets the height in pixels between the frame's contents and its top and bottom borders.

MARGINWIDTH   This attribute sets the width in pixels between the frame's contents and its left and right borders.

NAME   This attribute assigns the frame a name so that it can be the target destination of hyperlinks as well as be a possible candidate for manipulation via a script.

NORESIZE   This attribute overrides the default ability to resize frames and gives the frame a fixed size.

SCROLLING   This attribute determines if the frame has scroll bars. A **YES** value forces scroll bars, a **NO** value prohibits them, and an **AUTO** value lets the browser decide. When not specified, the default value of **AUTO** is used. Authors are recommended to leave the value as **AUTO**. If you turn off scrolling and the contents end up being too large for the frame (due to rendering differences, window size, etc.), the user will not be able to scroll to see the rest of the contents. If you turn scrolling on and the contents all fit in the frame, the scroll bars will needlessly consume screen space. With the **AUTO** value, scroll bars appear only when needed.

SRC   This attribute contains the URL of the contents to be displayed in the frame. If absent, nothing will be loaded in the frame.

STYLE   See "Core Attributes Reference," earlier in this appendix.

TITLE   See "Core Attributes Reference," earlier in this appendix.

Attribute and Event Support

NETSCAPE 4   **BORDERCOLOR, FRAMEBORDER, MARGINHEIGHT, MARGINWIDTH, NAME, NORESIZE, SCROLLING,** and **SRC.** (**CLASS, ID, LANG,** and **STYLE** are implied.)

INTERNET EXPLORER 4   All W3C-defined attributes except **LONGDESC** and **STYLE,** and all attributes and events defined by Internet Explorer 4. (Note: Internet Explorer 4 supports the values **NORESIZE** and **RESIZE.**)

APPENDIXES

WEBTV   **ALIGN, FRAMEBORDER (0 | 1), MARGINHEIGHT, MARGINWIDTH, NAME,** and **SRC.**

Event Handlers

See "Events Reference," earlier in this appendix.

Example

```
<FRAMESET ROWS="20%,80%">
  <FRAME SRC="controls.htm" NAME="controls" NORESIZE SCROLLING="NO">
  <FRAME SRC="content.htm">
</FRAMESET>
```

Compatibility

HTML 4
Internet Explorer 2, 3, 4, and 5
Netscape 2, 3, 4, and 4.5
WebTV

Notes

■ A frame must be declared as part of a frame set as set by the **<FRAMESET>** element, which specifies the frame's relationship to other frames on a page. A frame set occurs in a special HTML document in which the **<FRAMESET>** element replaces the **<BODY>** element. Another form of frames called *independent frames*, or *floating frames*, is also supported by Microsoft as well as the HTML 4.0 transitional specification. Floating frames can be directly embedded in a document without belonging to a frameset. These are defined with the **<IFRAME>** element.

■ Numerous browsers do not support frames and require the use of the **<NOFRAMES>** element.

■ Frames introduce potential navigation difficulties; their use should be limited to instances where they can be shown to help navigation rather than hinder it.

<FRAMESET> (Frameset Definition)

This element is used to define the organization of a set of independent window regions known as *frames* as defined by the **<FRAME>** element. This element replaces the **<BODY>** element in framing documents.

Syntax (Transitional Only)

```
<FRAMESET
    CLASS="class name(s)"
    COLS="list of columns"
```

```
       ID="unique alphanumeric identifier"
       ROWS="list of rows"
       STYLE="style information"
       TITLE="advisory text"
       onload="script"
       onunload="script">

       <FRAME> elements and <NOFRAMES>

</FRAMESET>
```

Attributes and Events Defined by Internet Explorer 4

```
       BORDER="pixels"
       BORDERCOLOR="color name | #RRGGBB"
       FRAMEBORDER="NO | YES | 0 | 1"
       FRAMESPACING="pixels"
       LANG="language code"
       LANGUAGE="JAVASCRIPT | JSCRIPT | VBS | VBSCRIPT"
```

Attributes and Events Defined by Netscape 4

```
       BORDER="pixels"
       BORDERCOLOR="color name | #RRGGBB"
       FRAMEBORDER="NO | YES | 0 | 1"
       LANG="language code"
       onblur="script"
       onfocus="script"
```

Attributes Defined by WebTV

```
       BORDER="pixels"
       FRAMEBORDER="0 | 1"
```

Attributes

BORDER   This attribute sets the width in pixels of frame borders within the frame set. Setting **BORDER="0"** eliminates all frame borders. This attribute is not defined in the HTML specification but is widely supported.

BORDERCOLOR   This attribute sets the color for frame borders within the frame set using either a named color or a color specified in the hexadecimal *#RRGGBB* format.

CLASS   See "Core Attributes Reference," earlier in this appendix.

COLS   This attribute contains a comma-delimited list, which specifies the number and size of columns contained within a set of frames. List items indicate columns, left to right. Column size is specified in three formats, which may be mixed. A column can be assigned a fixed width in pixels. It can also be assigned a percentage of the available width, such as 50 percent. Lastly a column can be set to expand to fill the available space by setting the value to *, which acts as a wildcard.

FRAMEBORDER   This attribute controls whether or not frame borders should be displayed. Netscape supports **NO** and **YES** values. Microsoft uses **1** and **0** as well as **NO** and **YES**.

FRAMESPACING   This attribute indicates the space between frames in pixels.

ID   See "Core Attributes Reference," earlier in this appendix.

LANG   See "Language Reference," earlier in this appendix.

LANGUAGE   This attribute specifies the language the current script is written in and invokes the proper scripting engine. The default value is **JAVASCRIPT**. **JAVASCRIPT** and **JSCRIPT** represent that the scripting language is written in JavaScript. **VBS** and **VBSCRIPT** represent that the scripting language is written in VBScript.

ROWS   This attribute contains a comma-delimited list, which specifies the number and size of rows contained within a set of frames. The number of entries in the list indicates the number of rows. Row size is specified with the same formats used for columns.

STYLE   See "Core Attributes Reference," earlier in this appendix.

TITLE   See "Core Attributes Reference," earlier in this appendix.

Attribute and Event Support

NETSCAPE 4   BORDER, BORDERCOLOR, COLS, FRAMEBORDER, ROWS, onblur, onfocus, onload, and onunload. (CLASS, ID, LANG, and STYLE are implied.)

INTERNET EXPLORER 4   BORDER, BORDERCOLOR, CLASS, COLS, FRAMEBORDER, ID, LANG, LANGUAGE, ROWS, and TITLE.

WEBTV   BORDER, COLS, FRAMEBORDER (0 | 1), FRAMESPACING, ROWS, onload, and onunload.

Event Handlers
See "Events Reference," earlier in this appendix.

Examples

```
<!-- This example defines a frame set of three columns. The middle column
is 50 pixels wide. The first and last columns fill the remaining space.
The last column takes twice as much space as the first. -->

<FRAMESET COLS="*,50,*">
  <FRAME SRC="column1.htm">
  <FRAME SRC="column2.htm">
  <FRAME SRC="column3.htm">
</FRAMESET>

<!-- This example defines a frame set of two columns, one of which is 20%
of the screen, and the other, 80%. -->

<FRAMESET COLS="20%, 80%">
  <FRAME SRC="controls.htm">
  <FRAME SRC="display.htm">
</FRAMESET>

<!-- This example defines two rows, one of which is 10% of the screen,
and the other, whatever space is left. -->

<FRAMESET ROWS="10%, *">
  <FRAME SRC="adbanner.htm" NAME="ad_frame">
  <FRAME SRC="contents.htm" NAME="content_frame">
</FRAMESET>
```

Compatibility

HTML 4 (transitional)
Internet Explorer 2, 3, 4, and 5
Netscape 2, 3, 4, and 4.5
WebTV

Notes

■ The **<FRAMESET>** element contains one or more **<FRAME>** elements, which are used to indicate the framed contents. The **<FRAMESET>** element may also contain a **<NOFRAMES>** element whose contents will be displayed on browsers that do not support frames.

■ The **<FRAMESET>** element replaces the **<BODY>** element in a framing document as shown here:

```
<HTML>
<HEAD>
<TITLE>Collection of Frames</TITLE>
</HEAD>

<FRAMESET COLS="*,50,*">
  <FRAME SRC="column1.htm" NAME="col1">
  <FRAME SRC="column2.htm" NAME="col2">
  <FRAME SRC="column3.htm" NAME="col3">
  <NOFRAMES>
  Please visit our <A HREF"noframes.htm">no frames</A> site.
  </NOFRAMES>
</FRAMESET>
</HTML>
```

<H1> Through <H6>   (Headings)

These tags implement six levels of document headings; **<H1>** is the most prominent, and **<H6>** is the least prominent.

Syntax

```
<H1
     ALIGN="CENTER | JUSTIFY | LEFT | RIGHT"
          (transitional)
     CLASS="class name(s)"
     DIR="LTR | RTL"
     ID="unique alphanumeric identifier"
     LANG="language code"
     STYLE="style information"
     TITLE="advisory text"
     onclick="script"
     ondblclick="script"
     onkeydown="script"
     onkeypress="script"
     onkeyup="script"
     onmousedown="script"
     onmousemove="script"
     onmouseout="script"
     onmouseover="script"
     onmouseup="script">

</H1>
```

Attributes and Events Defined by Internet Explorer 4

```
LANGUAGE="JAVASCRIPT | JSCRIPT | VBS | VBSCRIPT"
ondragstart="script"
onhelp="script"
onselectstart="script"
```

Attributes

ALIGN   This attribute controls the horizontal alignment of the heading with respect to the page. The default value is **LEFT**.

CLASS   See "Core Attributes Reference," earlier in this appendix.

DIR   See "Language Reference," earlier in this appendix.

ID   See "Core Attributes Reference," earlier in this appendix.

LANG   See "Language Reference," earlier in this appendix.

LANGUAGE   This attribute specifies the language the current script is written in and invokes the proper scripting engine. The default value is **JAVASCRIPT**. **JAVASCRIPT** and **JSCRIPT** represent that the scripting language is written in JavaScript. **VBS** and **VBSCRIPT** represent that the scripting language is written in VBScript.

STYLE   See "Core Attributes Reference," earlier in this appendix.

TITLE   See "Core Attributes Reference," earlier in this appendix.

Attribute and Event Support

NETSCAPE 4   ALIGN. (**CLASS, ID, LANG,** and **STYLE** are implied.)

INTERNET EXPLORER 4   All attributes and events except **DIR**. (Note: The **JUSTIFY** value for **ALIGN** is not supported.)

WEBTV   ALIGN (**CENTER | LEFT | RIGHT**).

Event Handlers
See "Events Reference," earlier in this appendix.

Example

```
<H1>This is a Major Document Heading</H1>
<H2 ALIGN="CENTER">Second heading, aligned to the center</H2>
```

APPENDIXES

```
<H3 ALIGN="RIGHT">Third heading, aligned to the right</H3>
<H4>Fourth heading</H4>
<H5 STYLE="{font-size: 20pt}">Fifth heading with style information</H5>
<H6>The smallest heading</H6>
```

Compatibility

HTML 2, 3.2, and 4
Internet Explorer 2, 3, 4, and 5
Netscape 1, 2, 3, 4, and 4.5
WebTV

Notes

■ In most implementations, heading numbers correspond inversely with the six font sizes supported by the **<FONT>** element. For example, **<H1>** corresponds to **<FONT SIZE="6">**. The default font size is **3**. However, this approach to layout is not encouraged and page designers should consider using styles to set even relative sizes.

■ HTML 3.2 supports only the **ALIGN** attribute. HTML 2 does not support any attributes for headings.

■ The HTML 4.0 strict specification does not include support for the **ALIGN** attribute. Style sheets should be used instead.

<HEAD>　(Document Head)

This element indicates the document head that contains descriptive information about the HTML document as well as other supplementary information such as style rules or scripts.

Syntax

```
<HEAD
    DIR="LTR | RTL"
    LANG="language code"
    PROFILE="URL">

</HEAD>
```

Attributes and Events Defined by Internet Explorer 4

```
    CLASS="class name(s)"
    ID="unique alphanumeric identifier"
    TITLE="advisory text"
```

Attributes

CLASS   See "Core Attributes Reference," earlier in this appendix.

DIR   See "Language Reference," earlier in this appendix.

ID   See "Core Attributes Reference," earlier in this appendix.

LANG   See "Language Reference," earlier in this appendix.

PROFILE   This attribute specifies a URL for a meta-information dictionary. The specified profile should indicate the format of allowed meta-data and the potential meaning of the data.

TITLE   See "Core Attributes Reference," earlier in this appendix.

Attribute and Event Support

INTERNET EXPLORER 4   CLASS, ID, and TITLE.

Event Handlers
None.

Example

```
<HEAD>
   <TITLE>Big Company Home Page</TITLE>
   <BASE HREF="http://www.bigcompany.com">
   <META NAME="Keywords" CONTENT="BigCompany, SuperWidget">
</HEAD>
```

Compatibility

HTML 2, 3.2, and 4
Internet Explorer 2, 3, 4, and 5
Netscape 1, 2, 3, 4, and 4.5
WebTV

Notes

- The **<HEAD>** element must contain a **<TITLE>** element. It may also contain the **<BASE>**, **<ISINDEX>**, **<LINK>**, **<META>**, **<SCRIPT>**, and **<STYLE>** elements. Internet Explorer 4 supports the inclusion of the **<BASEFONT>** element in the **<HEAD>** element, but **<BASEFONT>** has been deprecated under HTML 4.

- While the HTML 4.0 specification shows support for the **PROFILE** attribute, no browsers appear to support it.

APPENDIXES

■ Internet Explorer 4 defines the **<BGSOUND>** element as another legal element within **<HEAD>**.

■ HTML 2 and 3.2 support no attributes for this element.

<HR>   (Horizontal Rule)

This element is used to insert a horizontal rule to visually separate document sections. Rules are usually rendered as a raised or etched line.

Syntax

```
<HR
      ALIGN="CENTER | LEFT | RIGHT" (transitional)
      CLASS="class name(s)"
      ID="unique alphanumeric identifier"
      NOSHADE (transitional)
      SIZE="pixels" (transitional)
      STYLE="style information"
      TITLE="advisory information"
      WIDTH="percentage | pixels" (transitional)
      onclick="script"
      ondblclick="script"
      onkeydown="script"
      onkeypress="script"
      onkeyup="script"
      onmousedown="script"
      onmousemove="script"
      onmouseout="script"
      onmouseover="script"
      onmouseup="script">
```

Attributes and Events Defined by Internet Explorer 4

```
      COLOR="color name | #RRGGBB"
      LANG="language code"
      LANGUAGE="JAVASCRIPT | JSCRIPT | VBS | VBSCRIPT"
      SRC="URL"
      onbeforeupdate="script"
      onblur="script"
      ondragstart="script"
      onfocus="script"
      onhelp="script"
      onresize="script"
      onrowenter="script"
      onrowexit="script"
      onselectstart="script"
```

Attributes Defined by WebTV

INVERTBORDER

Attributes

ALIGN   This attribute controls the horizontal alignment of the rule with respect to the page. The default value is **LEFT**.

CLASS   See "Core Attributes Reference," earlier in this appendix.

COLOR   This attribute sets the rule color using either a named color or a color specified in the hexadecimal #*RRGGBB* format. This attribute is currently supported only by Internet Explorer.

ID   See "Core Attributes Reference," earlier in this appendix.

INVERTBORDER   This WebTV-specific attribute creates a horizontal rule that appears raised, as opposed to embossed, on the surface of the page.

LANG   See "Language Reference," earlier in this appendix.

LANGUAGE   This attribute specifies the language the current script is written in and invokes the proper scripting engine. The default value is **JAVASCRIPT**. **JAVASCRIPT** and **JSCRIPT** represent that the scripting language is written in JavaScript. **VBS** and **VBSCRIPT** represent that the scripting language is written in VBScript.

NOSHADE   This attribute causes the rule to be rendered as a solid bar without shading.

SIZE   This attribute indicates the height in pixels of the rule.

SRC   This attribute specifies a URL for an associated file.

STYLE   See "Core Attributes Reference," earlier in this appendix.

TITLE   See "Core Attributes Reference," earlier in this appendix.

WIDTH   This attribute indicates how wide the rule should be specified either in pixels or as a percent of screen width, such as 80 percent.

Attribute and Event Support

NETSCAPE 4   ALIGN, NOSHADE, SIZE, and WIDTH. (CLASS, ID, and STYLE are implied.)

INTERNET EXPLORER 4   All attributes and events defined by W3C and Internet Explorer 4.

WEBTV   ALIGN, INVERTBORDER, NOSHADE, SIZE, and WIDTH.

Event Handlers

See "Events Reference," earlier in this appendix.

Examples

```
<HR ALIGN="LEFT" NOSHADE SIZE="1" WIDTH="420">

<HR ALIGN="CENTER" WIDTH="100%" SIZE="3" COLOR="#000000">
```

Compatibility

HTML 2, 3.2, and 4
Internet Explorer 2, 3, 4, and 5
Netscape 1, 2, 3, 4, and 4.5
WebTV

Notes

The HTML 4.0 strict specification removes support for the **ALIGN**, **NOSHADE**, **SIZE**, and **WIDTH** attributes for horizontal rules. These effects are possible using style sheets.

\<HTML\> (HTML Document)

This element identifies a document as containing HTML-tagged content.

Syntax

```
<HTML
    DIR="LTR | RTL"
    LANG="language code"
    VERSION="URL" (transitional)>

</HTML>
```

Attributes Defined by Internet Explorer 4

```
    TITLE="advisory text"
```

Attributes

DIR   See "Language Reference," earlier in this appendix.

LANG   See "Language Reference," earlier in this appendix.

TITLE   See "Core Attributes Reference," earlier in this appendix.

VERSION   The **VERSION** attribute is used to set the URL of the location of the document type definition (DTD) that the current document conforms to. The DTD is also specified by the **<!DOCTYPE>** comment. Since few if any browsers support the **VERSION** attribute, it should be used only in conjunction with a **<!DOCTYPE>** comment and not instead of one.

Attribute and Event Support

INTERNET EXPLORER 4   LANG and TITLE.

Event Handlers
None.

Example

```
<!-- Minimal HTML document -->
<HTML>
<HEAD><TITLE>Minimal Document</TITLE></HEAD>
<BODY></BODY>
</HTML>
```

Compatibility

HTML 4
Internet Explorer 4 and 5
Netscape 4 and 4.5
WebTV

Notes
The **<HTML>** element is the first element in an **<HTML>** document. Except for comments, the only tags it directly contains are the **<HEAD>** element followed by either a **<BODY>** element or a **<FRAMESET>** element.

<I>   (Italic)
This element indicates that the enclosed text should be displayed in an italic typeface.

Syntax

```
<I
    CLASS="class name(s)"
    DIR="LTR | RTL"
    ID="unique alphanumeric identifier"
    LANG="language code"
    STYLE="style information"
    TITLE="advisory text"
```

```
     onclick="script"
     ondblclick="script"
     onkeydown="script"
     onkeypress="script"
     onkeyup="script"
     onmousedown="script"
     onmousemove="script"
     onmouseout="script"
     onmouseover="script"
     onmouseup="script">

</I>
```

Attributes and Events Defined by Internet Explorer 4

```
     LANGUAGE="JAVASCRIPT | JSCRIPT | VBS | VBSCRIPT"
     ondragstart="script"
     onhelp="script"
     onselectstart="script"
```

Attributes

CLASS   See "Core Attributes Reference," earlier in this appendix.

DIR   See "Language Reference," earlier in this appendix.

ID   See "Core Attributes Reference," earlier in this appendix.

LANG   See "Language Reference," earlier in this appendix.

LANGUAGE   This attribute specifies the language the current script is written in and invokes the proper scripting engine. The default value is **JAVASCRIPT**. **JAVASCRIPT** and **JSCRIPT** represent that the scripting language is written in JavaScript. **VBS** and **VBSCRIPT** represent that the scripting language is written in VBScript.

STYLE   See "Core Attributes Reference," earlier in this appendix.

TITLE   See "Core Attributes Reference," earlier in this appendix.

Attribute and Event Support

NETSCAPE 4   **CLASS**, **ID**, **LANG**, and **STYLE** are implied.

INTERNET EXPLORER 4   All attributes and events except **DIR**.

Event Handlers

See "Events Reference," earlier in this appendix.

Example

```
Here is some <I>italicized</I> text.
```

Compatibility

HTML 4
Internet Explorer 4 and 5
Netscape 4 and 4.5
WebTV

<IFRAME>   (Floating Frame)

This element indicates a floating frame, an independently controllable content region that can be embedded in a page.

Syntax (Transitional Only)

```
<IFRAME
    ALIGN="BOTTOM | LEFT | MIDDLE | RIGHT | TOP"
    CLASS="class name(s)"
    FRAMEBORDER="0 | 1"
    HEIGHT="percentage | pixels"
    ID="unique alphanumeric identifier"
    LONGDESC="URL of description"
    MARGINHEIGHT="pixels"
    MARGINWIDTH="pixels"
    NAME="string"
    SCROLLING="AUTO | NO | YES"
    SRC="URL of frame contents"
    STYLE="style information"
    TITLE="advisory text"
    WIDTH="percentage | pixels">

</IFRAME>
```

Attributes Defined by Internet Explorer 4

```
    ALIGN="ABSBOTTOM | ABSMIDDLE | BASELINE | TEXTTOP"
    BORDER="pixels"
    BORDERCOLOR="color name | #RRGGBB"
```

```
DATAFLD="name of column supplying bound data"
DATASRC="ID of data source object supplying data"
FRAMEBORDER="No | YES | 0 | 1"
FRAMESPACING="pixels"
HSPACE="pixels"
LANG="language code"
LANGUAGE="JAVASCRIPT | JSCRIPT | VBS | VBSCRIPT"
NORESIZE="noresize | resize"
VSPACE="pixels"
```

Attributes

ALIGN   This attribute controls the horizontal alignment of the floating frame with respect to the page. The default is **LEFT**.

BORDER   This attribute specifies the thickness of the border in pixels.

BORDERCOLOR   This attribute specifies the color of the border.

CLASS   See "Core Attributes Reference," earlier in this appendix.

DATAFLD   This attribute specifies the column name from the data source object that supplies the bound data.

DATASRC   This attribute indicates the **ID** of the data source object that supplies the data that is bound to this element.

FRAMEBORDER   This attribute determines whether the frame is surrounded by a border. The HTML 4.0 specification defines **0** to be off and **1** to be on. The default value is **1**. Internet Explorer also defines the values **NO** and **YES**.

FRAMESPACING   This attribute creates additional space between the frames.

HEIGHT   The attribute sets the floating frame's height in pixels.

HSPACE   This attribute specifies margins for the frame.

ID   See "Core Attributes Reference," earlier in this appendix.

LANG   See "Language Reference," earlier in this appendix.

LANGUAGE   This attribute specifies the language the current script is written in and invokes the proper scripting engine. The default value is **JAVASCRIPT**. **JAVASCRIPT** and **JSCRIPT** represent that the scripting language is written in JavaScript. **VBS** and **VBSCRIPT** represent that the scripting language is written in VBScript.

LONGDESC   This attribute specifies a URL of a document which contains a long description of the frame's contents. This may be particularly useful as a complement to the **<TITLE>** element.

MARGINHEIGHT   This attribute sets the height in pixels between the floating frame's content and its top and bottom borders.

MARGINWIDTH   This attribute sets the width in pixels between the floating frame's content and its left and right borders.

NAME   This attribute assigns the floating frame a name so that it can be the target destination of hyperlinks.

NORESIZE   When **NORESIZE** is included, the frame cannot be resized by the user.

SCROLLING   This attribute determines if the frame has scroll bars. A **YES** value forces scroll bars; a **NO** value prohibits them.

SRC   This attribute contains the URL of the content to be displayed in the floating frame. If absent, the frame is blank.

STYLE   See "Core Attributes Reference," earlier in this appendix.

TITLE   See "Core Attributes Reference," earlier in this appendix.

VSPACE   This attribute specifies margins for the frame.

WIDTH   This attribute sets the floating frame's width in pixels.

Attribute and Event Support

INTERNET EXPLORER 4   All attributes and events except **LONGDESC**.

Event Handlers
See "Events Reference," earlier in this appendix.

Example

```
<IFRAME SRC="http://www.bigcompany.com" HEIGHT="150" WIDTH="200"
        NAME="FloatingFrame1">
Sorry, your browser doesn't support inline frames.
</IFRAME>
```

Compatibility

HTML 4 (transitional)
Internet Explorer 3, 4, and 5

APPENDIXES

Notes

■ A floating frame does not need to be declared by the **<FRAMESET>** element as part of a frame set.

■ WebTV and Netscape 4 do not support floating frames.

■ Under the HTML 4.0 strict specification, the **<IFRAME>** element is not defined. Floating frames may be imitated using the **<DIV>** element and CSS positioning facilities.

<ILAYER>   (Inflow Layer)

This Netscape-specific element allows the definition of overlapping content layers that can be positioned, hidden or shown, rendered transparent or opaque, reordered front to back, and nested. An *inflow layer* is a layer with a relative position that appears where it would naturally occur in the document, in contrast to a *general layer*, which may be positioned absolutely regardless of its location in a document. The functionality of layers is available using CSS positioning, and page developers are advised not to use this element.

Syntax (Defined by Netscape 4)

```
<ILAYER
     ABOVE="layer"
     BACKGROUND="URL of image"
     BELOW="layer"
     BGCOLOR="color name | #RRGGBB"
     CLASS="class name(s)"
     CLIP="x1, y1, x2, y2"
     HEIGHT="percentage | pixels"
     ID="unique alphanumeric identifier"
     LEFT="pixels"
     NAME="string"
     PAGEX="pixels"
     PAGEY="pixels"
     SRC="URL of layer contents"
     STYLE="style information"
     TOP="pixels"
     VISIBILITY="HIDE | INHERIT | SHOW"
     WIDTH="percentage | pixels"
     Z-INDEX="number"
     onblur="script"
     onfocus="script"
     onload="script"
     onmouseout="script"
     onmouseover="script">

</ILAYER>
```

Attributes

ABOVE   This attribute contains the name of the layer to be rendered above the current layer.

BACKGROUND   This attribute contains the URL of a background image for the layer.

BELOW   This attribute contains the name of the layer to be rendered below the current layer.

BGCOLOR   This attribute specifies a layer's background color. Its value can be either a named color or a color specified in the hexadecimal *#RRGGBB* format.

CLASS   This attribute specifies the class name(s) for access via a style sheet.

CLIP   This attribute specifies the clipping region or viewable area of the layer. All layer content outside that rectangle will be rendered as transparent. The **CLIP** rectangle is defined by two x,y pairs: top x, left y, bottom x, and right y. Coordinates are relative to the layer's origin point, **0,0** in its top-left corner.

HEIGHT   This attribute specifies the height of a layer in pixels or percentage values.

ID   See "Core Attributes Reference," earlier in this appendix.

LEFT   This attribute specifies in pixels the horizontal offset of the layer. The offset is relative to its parent layer if it has one or to the left page margin if it does not.

NAME   This attribute assigns the layer a name that can be referenced by programs in a client-side scripting language. The **ID** attribute can also be used.

PAGEX   This attribute specifies the horizontal position of the layer relative to the browser window.

PAGEY   This attribute specifies the vertical position of the layer relative to the browser window.

SRC   This attribute is used to set the URL of a file that contains the content to load into the layer.

STYLE   This attribute specifies an inline style for the layer.

TOP   This attribute specifies in pixels the top offset of the layer. The offset is relative to its parent layer if it has one or the top page margin if it does not.

VISIBILITY   This attribute specifies whether a layer is hidden, shown, or inherits its visibility from the layer that includes it.

WIDTH   This attribute specifies a layer's width in pixels.

Z-INDEX   This attribute specifies a layer's stacking order relative to other layers. Position is specified with positive integers, with **1** indicating the bottommost layer.

Attribute and Event Support

NETSCAPE 4   All attributes.

Event Handlers
None.

Example

```
<P>Content comes before.</P>
<ILAYER NAME="background" BGCOLOR="green">
  <P>Layered information goes here.</P>
</ILAYER>
<P>Content comes after.</P>
```

Compatibility

Netscape 4 and 4.5

Notes

- This element will likely fall out of fashion because of its lack of cross-browser compatibility. The functionality of **<ILAYER>** is possible using the positioning features in CSS, and page developers are encouraged not to use this element.

- Applets, plug-ins, and other embedded media forms, generically called *objects,* may be included in a layer; however, they will float to the top of all other layers even if their containing layer is obscured.

<IMG>   (Image)

This element indicates a media object to include in an HTML document. Usually, the object is a graphic image, but some implementations support movies and animations.

Syntax

```
<IMG
     ALIGN="BOTTOM | LEFT | MIDDLE | RIGHT | TOP"
            (transitional)
     ALT="alternative text"
     BORDER="pixels" (transitional)
     CLASS="class name(s)"
     DIR="LTR | RTL"
     HEIGHT="pixels"
     HSPACE="pixels" (transitional)
     ID="unique alphanumeric identifier"
```

```
ISMAP
LANG="language code"
LONGDESC="URL of description file"
SRC="URL of image"
STYLE="style information"
TITLE="advisory text"
USEMAP="URL of map file"
VSPACE="pixels" (transitional)
WIDTH="pixels"
onclick="script"
ondblclick="script"
onkeydown="script"
onkeypress="script"
onkeyup="script"
onmousedown="script"
onmousemove="script"
onmouseout="script"
onmouseover="script"
onmouseup="script">
```

Attributes and Events Defined by Internet Explorer 4

```
ALIGN="ABSBOTTOM | ABSMIDDLE | BASELINE | TEXTTOP"
DATAFLD="name of column supplying bound data"
DATASRC="ID of data source object supplying data"
DYNSRC="URL of movie"
LANGUAGE="JAVASCRIPT | JSCRIPT | VBS | VBSCRIPT"
LOOP="INFINITE | number"
LOWSRC="URL of low-resolution image"
NAME="unique alphanumeric identifier"
onabort="script"
onafterupdate="script"
onbeforeupdate="script"
onblur="script"
ondragstart="script"
onerror="script"
onfocus="script"
onhelp="script"
onload="script"
onresize="script"
onrowenter="script"
onrowexit="script"
onselectstart="script"
```

Attributes Defined by Netscape 4

```
ALIGN="ABSBOTTOM | ABSMIDDLE | BASELINE | TEXTTOP"
LOWSRC="URL of low-resolution image"
NAME="unique alphanumeric identifier"
SUPPRESS="TRUE | FALSE"
```

Attributes Defined by WebTV

```
CONTROLS
NAME="unique alphanumeric identifier"
RELOAD="seconds"
SELECTED="x,y pair"
TRANSPARENCY="number (1-100)"
```

Attributes

ALIGN   This attribute controls the horizontal alignment of the image with respect to the page. The default value is **LEFT**. Only the Netscape, Internet Explorer 4, and WebTV implementations support the **ABSBOTTOM, ABSMIDDLE, BASELINE,** and **TEXTTOP** values.

ALT   This attribute contains a string to display instead of the image for browsers that cannot display images.

BORDER   This attribute indicates the width in pixels of the border surrounding the image.

CLASS   See "Core Attributes Reference," earlier in this appendix.

CONTROLS   Under Internet Explorer 3 and WebTV, it is possible to set the controls to show by placing this attribute in the **<IMG>** element. This attribute does not appear to be supported under Internet Explorer 4, and users are encouraged to use the **<OBJECT>** element to embed video for Internet Explorer.

DATAFLD   This attribute specifies the column name from the data source object that supplies the bound data to set the **SRC** of the **<IMG>** element.

DATASRC   This attribute indicates the **ID** of the data source object that supplies the data that is bound to this **<IMG>** element.

DIR   See "Language Reference," earlier in this appendix.

DYNSRC   In the Microsoft and WebTV implementations, this attribute indicates the URL of a movie file and is used instead of the **SRC** attribute.

HEIGHT   This attribute indicates the height in pixels of the image.

HSPACE   This attribute indicates the horizontal space in pixels between the image and surrounding text.

ID   See "Core Attributes Reference," earlier in this appendix.

ISMAP   This attribute indicates that the image is a server-side image map. User mouse actions over the image are sent to the server for processing.

LANG   See "Language Reference," earlier in this appendix.

LANGUAGE   This attribute specifies the language the current script is written in and invokes the proper scripting engine. The default value is **JAVASCRIPT**. **JAVASCRIPT** and **JSCRIPT** represent that the scripting language is written in JavaScript. **VBS** and **VBSCRIPT** represent that the scripting language is written in VBScript.

LONGDESC   This attribute specifies a URL of a document which contains a long description of the image. This attribute is used as a complement to the **ALT** attribute.

LOOP   In the Microsoft implementation, this attribute is used with the **DYNSRC** attribute to cause a movie to loop. Its value is either a numeric loop count or the keyword **INFINITE**.

LOWSRC   In the Netscape implementation, this attribute contains the URL of an image to be initially loaded. Typically, the **LOWSRC** image is a low-resolution or black-and-white image that provides a quick preview of the image to follow. Once the primary image is loaded, it replaces the **LOWSRC** image.

NAME   This common attribute is used to bind a name to the image. Older browsers understand the **NAME** field, and in conjunction with scripting languages it is possible to manipulate images by their defined names to create effects such as "rollover" buttons. The **ID** attribute under HTML 4 specifies element identifiers; for backward compatibility, **NAME** may still be used.

RELOAD   In the WebTV implementation, this attribute indicates in seconds how frequently an image should be reloaded.

SELECTED   In the WebTV implementation, this attribute indicates the initial x,y coordinate location on the image. The cursor is placed at that location when the image is loaded. It requires either the **ISMAP** or the **USEMAP** attribute.

SRC   This attribute indicates the URL of an image file to be displayed.

STYLE   See "Core Attributes Reference," earlier in this appendix.

SUPPRESS   This Netscape-specific attribute determines if a placeholder icon will appear during image loading. Values are **TRUE** and **FALSE**. **SUPPRESS="TRUE"** will suppress display of the placeholder icon as well as display of any **ALT** information until the image is loaded. **SUPPRESS="FALSE"** will allow the placeholder icon and any tool tips defined by the **ALT** information to display while the image is loading. The default value is **FALSE**. If the browser is set to not load images automatically, the **SUPPRESS** attribute is ignored.

TITLE   See "Core Attributes Reference," earlier in this appendix.

TRANSPARENCY   In the WebTV implementation, this attribute allows the background to show through the image. It takes a numeric argument indicating the degree of transparency, from fully opaque (**0**) to fully transparent (**100**).

USEMAP   This attribute makes the image support client-side image mapping. Its argument is a URL specifying the map file, which associates image regions with hyperlinks.

VSPACE   This attribute indicates the vertical space in pixels between the image and surrounding text.

WIDTH   This attribute indicates the width in pixels of the image.

Attribute and Event Support

NETSCAPE 4   ALIGN, ALT, BORDER, HEIGHT, HSPACE, ISMAP, LOWSRC, NAME, SRC, SUPPRESS, USEMAP, VSPACE, and WIDTH.

INTERNET EXPLORER 4   All W3C-defined attributes and events except **DIR** and **LONGDESC**, and all attributes and events defined by Internet Explorer 4.

WEBTV   ALIGN, BORDER, HEIGHT, HSPACE, ID, ISMAP, NAME, SELECTED, SRC, START, TRANSPARENCY, USEMAP, VSPACE, WIDTH, onabort, onerror, and onload.

Event Handlers
See "Events Reference," earlier in this appendix.

Examples

```
<IMG SRC="lakers.jpg" LOWSRC="lakersbw.jpg" ALT="Los Angeles Lakers"
    HEIGHT="100" WIDTH="300">

<IMG SRC="hugeimagemap.gif" USEMAP="mainmap" BORDER="0" HEIGHT="200"
        WIDTH="200" ALT="Image Map Here">

<A HREF="home.htm"><IMG SRC="homebutton.gif" WIDTH="50" HEIGHT="20"
   ALT="Link to Home Page"></A>
```

Compatibility

HTML 2, 3.2, and 4
Internet Explorer 2, 3, 4, and 5
Netscape 1, 2, 3, 4, and 4.5
WebTV

Notes

- No browser currently appears to support **LONGDESC**.

- Typically, when you use the **USEMAP** attribute, the URL is a fragment, such as #map1, rather than a full URL. Some browsers do not support external client-side map files.

- Under the HTML 4.0 strict specification, the **<IMG>** element does not support **ALIGN**, **BORDER**, **HEIGHT**, **HSPACE**, **VSPACE**, and **WIDTH**. The functionality of these attributes should be possible using style sheet rules.

- While the HTML 4.0 specification reserves data-binding attributes like **DATAFLD** or **DATASRC**, it is not specified for **<IMG>**, although Internet Explorer provides support for these attributes.

<INPUT> (Input Form Control)

This element specifies an input control for a form. The type of input is set by the **TYPE** attribute and may be a variety of different types, including single-line text field, multiline text field, password style, check box, radio button, or push button.

Syntax

```
<INPUT
    ACCEPT="MIME TYPES"
    ACCESSKEY="character"
    ALIGN="BOTTOM | LEFT | MIDDLE | RIGHT | TOP"
            (transitional)
    ALT="text"
    CHECKED
    CLASS="class name(s)"
    DIR="LTR | RTL"
    DISABLED
    ID="unique alphanumeric identifier"
    LANG="language code"
    MAXLENGTH="maximum field size"
    NAME="field name"
    READONLY
    SIZE="field size"
    SRC="URL of image file"
    STYLE="style information"
    TABINDEX="number"
    TITLE="advisory text"
    TYPE="BUTTON | CHECKBOX | FILE | HIDDEN | IMAGE |
            PASSWORD | RADIO | RESET | SUBMIT | TEXT"
    USEMAP="URL of map file"
    VALUE="field value"
    onblur="script"
    onchange="script"
```

```
onclick="script"
ondblclick="script"
onfocus="script"
onkeydown="script"
onkeypress="script"
onkeyup="script"
onmousedown="script"
onmousemove="script"
onmouseout="script"
onmouseover="script"
onmouseup="script"
onselect="script">
```

Attributes and Events Defined by Internet Explorer 4

```
ALIGN="CENTER"
LANGUAGE="JAVASCRIPT | JSCRIPT | VBS | VBSCRIPT"
onafterupdate="script"
onbeforeupdate="script"
ondragstart="script"
onhelp="script"
onselectstart="script"
```

Attributes Defined by Netscape 4

```
ALIGN="ABSBOTTOM | ABSMIDDLE | BASELINE | TEXTTOP"
```

Attributes Defined by WebTV

```
BGCOLOR="color name | #RRGGBB"
BORDERIMAGE="URL"
CURSOR="color name | #RRGGBB"
USESTYLE
WIDTH="pixels"
```

Attributes

ACCEPT   This attribute is used to list the MIME types accepted for file uploads when <INPUT TYPE="FILE">.

ACCESSKEY   This attribute specifies a keyboard navigation accelerator for the element. Pressing ALT or a similar key in association with the specified character selects the form control correlated with that key sequence. Page designers are forewarned to avoid key sequences already bound to browsers.

ALIGN   With image form controls (**TYPE="IMAGE"**), this attribute aligns the image with respect to surrounding text. The HTML 4.0 transitional specification defines **BOTTOM, LEFT, MIDDLE, RIGHT,** and **TOP** as allowable values. Netscape and Microsoft browsers may also allow the use of attribute values like **ABSBOTTOM** or **ABSMIDDLE**. Like other presentation-specific aspects of HTML, the **ALIGN** attribute is dropped under the HTML 4.0 strict specification.

ALT   This attribute is used to display an alternative description of image buttons for text-only browsers. The meaning of **ALT** for forms of **<INPUT>** beyond **TYPE="INPUT"** is unclear.

BGCOLOR   In the WebTV implementation, this attribute specifies the background color of a text form control (**TYPE="TEXT"**). The value of the attribute can be either a named color or a color specified in the hexadecimal *#RRGGBB* format.

BORDERIMAGE   In the WebTV implementation, this attribute allows specification of a graphical border for **RESET, SUBMIT,** and **TEXT** controls. Its value is the URL of a .bif (Border Image File) graphics file that specifies the border. Border image files tend to reside in WebTV ROM; the common values are **file://ROM/Border/ButtonBorder2.bif** and **file://ROM/Border/ButtonBorder3.bif**, though other values may be present under later versions of WebTV.

CHECKED   This attribute should be used only for check box (**TYPE="CHECKBOX"**) and radio (**TYPE="RADIO"**) form controls. The presence of this attribute indicates that the control should be displayed in its checked state.

CLASS   See "Core Attributes Reference," earlier in this appendix.

CURSOR   In the WebTV implementation, this attribute sets the cursor color for a text form control (**TYPE="TEXT"**). The attribute's value is either a named color or a color specified in the hexadecimal *#RRGGBB* format.

DIR   See "Language Reference," earlier in this appendix.

DISABLED   This attribute is used to turn off a form control. Elements will not be submitted, nor may they receive any focus from the keyboard or mouse. Disabled form controls will not be part of the tabbing order. The browser may also gray out the form that is disabled, in order to indicate to the user that the form control is inactive. This attribute requires no value.

ID   See "Core Attributes Reference," earlier in this appendix.

LANG   See "Language Reference," earlier in this appendix.

LANGUAGE   In the Microsoft implementation, this attribute specifies the scripting language to be used with an associated script bound to the element typically through an event handler attribute. Possible values may include **JAVASCRIPT, JSCRIPT, VBS** and **VBSCRIPT**. Other values that include the version of the language used, such as **JavaScript1.1**, may also be possible.

MAXLENGTH   This attribute indicates the maximum content length that can be entered in a text form control (**TYPE="TEXT"**). The maximum number of characters allowed differs from the visible dimension of the form control, which is set with the **SIZE** attribute.

NAME   This attribute allows a form control to be assigned a name so that it can be referenced by a scripting language. **NAME** is supported by older browsers such as Netscape 2–generation browsers, but the W3C encourages the use of the **ID** attribute. For compatibility purposes, both may have to be used.

READONLY   This attribute prevents the form control's value from being changed. Form controls with this attribute set may receive focus from the user but may not be modified. Since it receives focus, a **READONLY** form control will be part of the form's tabbing order. Last, the control's value will be sent on form submission. This attribute can only be used with **<INPUT>** when **TYPE** is set to **TEXT** or **PASSWORD**. The attribute is also used with the **<TEXTAREA>** element.

SIZE   This attribute indicates the visible dimension, in characters, of a text form control (**TYPE="TEXT"**). This differs from the maximum length of content, which can be entered in a form control set by the **MAXLENGTH** attribute.

SRC   This attribute is used with image form controls (**TYPE="IMAGE"**) to specify the URL of the image file to load.

STYLE   See "Core Attributes Reference," earlier in this appendix.

TABINDEX   This attribute takes a numeric value that indicates the position of the form control in the tabbing index for the form. Tabbing proceeds from the lowest positive **TABINDEX** value to the highest. Negative values for **TABINDEX** will leave the form control out of the tabbing order. When tabbing is not explicitly set, the browser may tab through items in the order they are encountered. Form controls that are disabled due to the presence of the **DISABLED** attribute will not be part of the tabbing index, though read-only controls will be.

TITLE   See "Core Attributes Reference," earlier in this appendix.

TYPE   This attribute specifies the type of the form control. A value of **BUTTON** indicates a general-purpose button with no well-defined meaning. However, an action can be associated with the button using an event handler attribute, such as **onclick**. A value of **CHECKBOX** indicates a check box control. Check box form controls have a checked and nonchecked set, but even if these controls are grouped together, they allow a user to select multiple check boxes at once. In contrast, a value of RADIO indicates a radio button control. When grouped, radio buttons allow only one of the many choices to be selected at a given time.

A form control type of **HIDDEN** indicates a field that is not visible to the viewer but is used to store information. A hidden form control is often used to preserve state information between pages. A value of **FILE** for the **TYPE** attribute indicates a control that allows the viewer to upload a file to a server. The filename can be entered in a displayed field, or a user agent may provide a special browse button allowing the user to locate the file. A value of **IMAGE** indicates a graphic image form control that a user can click on to invoke an associated action. A value of **PASSWORD** for the **TYPE** attribute indicates a password entry field. A password field will not display text entered as it is typed; it may instead show a series of dots. Note that password-entered data is not transferred to the server in any secure fashion. A value of **RESET** for the **TYPE** attribute is used to insert a button that resets all controls within a form to their default values. A value of **SUBMIT** inserts a special submission button that, when pressed, sends the contents of the form to the location indicated by the **ACTION** attribute of the enclosing **<FORM>** element. Last, a value of **TEXT** (the default) for the **TYPE** attribute indicates a single-line text input field.

USEMAP   This HTML 4 attribute is used to indicate the map file to be associated with an image when the form control is set with **TYPE="IMAGE"**. The value of the attribute should be a URL of a map file, but will generally be in the form of a URL fragment referencing a map file within the current file.

USESTYLE   In the WebTV implementation, the presence of this attribute causes control text to be rendered in the default text style for the page. This attribute requires no value.

VALUE   This attribute has two different uses, depending on the value for the **TYPE** attribute. With data entry controls (**TYPE="TEXT"** and **TYPE="PASSWORD"**), this attribute is used to set the default value for the control. When used with check box or radio form controls, this attribute specifies the return value for the control when it is turned on, rather than the default Boolean value submitted.

WIDTH   This WebTV attribute is used to set the size of the form control in pixels.

Attribute and Event Support

NETSCAPE 4   NAME, VALUE, and onclick. (CLASS, ID, LANG, and STYLE are implied.)

INTERNET EXPLORER 4   All W3C-defined attributes and events except **ACCEPT**, **CHECKED**, **DIR**, and **USEMAP**, and all attributes and events defined by Internet Explorer 4. (Note: Internet Explorer 4 supports only the **CENTER**, **LEFT**, and **RIGHT** values for the **ALIGN** attribute.)

WEBTV   ALIGN, BGCOLOR, CHECKED, CURSOR, ID, MAXLENGTH, NAME, SIZE, TYPE, USESTYLE, VALUE, WIDTH, onblur, onchange, onclick, onfocus, and onselect.

Event Handlers
See "Events Reference," earlier in this appendix.

Examples

```
<FORM>
Which is your favorite food?
  <INPUT TYPE="RADIO" NAME="favorite" VALUE="Mexican">Mexican
  <INPUT TYPE="RADIO" NAME="favorite" VALUE="Russian">Russian
  <INPUT TYPE="RADIO" NAME="favorite" VALUE="Japanese">Japanese
```

```
   <INPUT TYPE="RADIO" CHECKED NAME="favorite" VALUE="Other">Other
</FORM>

<FORM>
Enter your name: <INPUT TYPE="TEXT" MAXLENGTH="35" SIZE="20"><BR>
Enter your password: <INPUT TYPE="PASSWORD" MAXLENGTH="35" SIZE="20"><BR>
<BR>
  <INPUT TYPE="SUBMIT" VALUE="Submit">
  <INPUT TYPE="RESET" VALUE="Reset">
</FORM>
```

Compatibility

HTML 2, 3.2, and 4
Internet Explorer 2, 3, 4, and 5
Netscape 1, 2, 3, 4, and 4.5
WebTV

Notes

- The **<INPUT>** element is an empty element and requires no closing tag.
- Some documents suggest the use of **TYPE="TEXTAREA"**. Even if this style is supported, it should be avoided in favor of the **<TEXTAREA>** element, which is common to all browsers.
- The HTML 2.0 and 3.2 specifications support only the **ALIGN, CHECKED, MAXLENGTH, NAME, SIZE, SRC, TYPE,** and **VALUE** attributes for the **<INPUT>** element.
- The HTML 4.0 specification also reserves the use of the **DATAFLD, DATAFORMATAS,** and **DATASRC** data-binding attributes.
- Under the HTML strict specification, the **ALIGN** attribute is not allowed.

<INS>   (Inserted Text)

This element is used to indicate that text has been added to the document.

Syntax

```
<INS
     CITE="URL"
     CLASS="class name(s)"
     DATETIME="date"
     ID="unique alphanumeric identifier"
```

```
      LANG="language code"
      STYLE="style information"
      TITLE="advisory text"
      onclick="script"
      ondblclick="script"
      onkeydown="script"
      onkeypress="script"
      onkeyup="script"
      onmousedown="script"
      onmousemove="script"
      onmouseout="script"
      onmouseover="script"
      onmouseup="script">

</INS>
```

Attributes and Events Defined by Internet Explorer 4

```
      LANGUAGE="JAVASCRIPT | JSCRIPT | VBS | VBSCRIPT"
      ondragstart="script"
      onhelp="script"
```

Attributes

CITE   The value of this attribute is a URL that designates a source document or message for the information inserted. This attribute is intended to point to information explaining why the text was changed.

CLASS   See "Core Attributes Reference," earlier in this appendix.

DATETIME   This attribute is used to indicate the date and time the insertion was made. The value of the attribute is a date in a special format, as defined by ISO 8601. The basic date format is

```
YYYY-MM-DDThh:mm:ssTZD
```

where the following is true:

```
YYYY=four-digit year such as 1999
  MM=two-digit month (01=January, 02=February, and so on)
  DD=two-digit day of the month (01 through 31)
  hh=two-digit hour (00 to 23) (24-hour clock not AM or PM)
  mm=two-digit minute (00 to 59)
  ss=two-digit second (00 to 59)
  TZD=time zone designator
```

The time zone designator is either **Z**, which indicates UTC (Universal Time Coordinate, or coordinated universal time format), or **+hh:mm**, which indicates that the time is a local time that is *hh* hours and *mm* minutes ahead of UTC. Alternatively, the format for the time zone designator could be **-hh:mm**, which indicates that the local time is behind UTC. Note that the letter "T" actually appears in the string, all digits must be used, and **00** values for minutes and seconds may be required. An example value for the **DATETIME** attribute might be **1999-10-6T09:15:00-05:00**, which corresponds to October 6, 1999, 9:15 A.M., U.S. Eastern Standard Time.

ID   See "Core Attributes Reference," earlier in this appendix.

LANG   See "Language Reference," earlier in this appendix.

LANGUAGE   In the Microsoft implementation, this attribute specifies the scripting language to be used with an associated script bound to the element, typically through an event handler attribute. Possible values may include **JAVASCRIPT**, **JSCRIPT**, **VBS**, and **VBSCRIPT**. Other values that include the version of the language used, such as **JavaScript1.1**, may also be possible.

STYLE   See "Core Attributes Reference," earlier in this appendix.

TITLE   See "Core Attributes Reference," earlier in this appendix.

Attribute and Event Support

INTERNET EXPLORER 4   All attributes and events except **CITE** and **DATETIME**.

Event Handlers
See "Events Reference," earlier in this appendix.

Example

```
<INS CITE="http://www.bigcompany.com/changes/oct99.htm"
    DATE="1999-10-06T09:15:00-05:00">
The penalty clause applies to client lateness as well.
</INS>
```

Compatibility

HTML 4
Internet Explorer 4

Notes

■ Browsers may render inserted (**<INS>**) or deleted (**<DEL>**) text in a different style to show the changes that have been made to the document. Eventually, a browser may have a way to show a revision history on a document. User agents that do not understand **<DEL>** or **<INS>** will show the information anyway, so there is no harm in adding information, only in deleting it.

■ The **<INS>** element is not supported under the HTML 2 and 3.2 specifications.

<ISINDEX>   (Index Prompt)

This element indicates that a document has an associated searchable keyword index. When a browser encounters this element, it inserts a query entry field at that point in the document. The viewer can enter query terms to perform a search. This element is deprecated under the strict HTML 4 specification and should not be used.

Syntax (Transitional Only)

```
<ISINDEX
      CLASS="class name(s)"
      DIR="LTR | RTL"
      HREF="URL" (nonstandard but common)
      ID="unique alphanumeric identifier"
      LANG="language code"
      PROMPT="string"
      STYLE="style information"
      TITLE="advisory text">
```

Attributes Defined by Internet Explorer 4

```
LANGUAGE="JAVASCRIPT | JSCRIPT | VBS | VBSCRIPT"
```

Attributes

ACTION   This attribute specifies the URL of the query action to be executed when the viewer presses the ENTER key. While this attribute is not defined under any HTML specification, it is common to many browsers, particularly Internet Explorer 3, which defined it.

CLASS   See "Core Attributes Reference," earlier in this appendix.

DIR   See "Language Reference," earlier in this appendix.

HREF   The **HREF** attribute is used with the **<ISINDEX>** element as a way to indicate what the search document is. Another approach is to use the **<BASE>** element for the document. The HTML 2 documentation suggests that this is a legal approach and browsers appear to support it; however, it is poorly documented at best.

ID   See "Core Attributes Reference," earlier in this appendix.

LANG   See "Language Reference," earlier in this appendix.

LANGUAGE   In the Microsoft implementation, this attribute specifies the scripting language to be used with an associated script bound to the element, typically through an event handler attribute. Possible values may include **JAVASCRIPT**, **JSCRIPT**, **VBS**, and **VBSCRIPT**. Other values that include the version of the language used, such as **JavaScript1.1**, may also be possible.

PROMPT   This attribute allows a custom query prompt to be defined. The default prompt is "This is a searchable index. Enter search keywords." WebTV does not implement this attribute.

STYLE   See "Core Attributes Reference," earlier in this appendix.

TITLE   See "Core Attributes Reference," earlier in this appendix.

Attribute and Event Support

NETSCAPE 4   PROMPT. (**CLASS, ID, LANG,** and **STYLE** are implied.)

INTERNET EXPLORER 4   CLASS, ID, LANG, LANGUAGE, PROMPT, and STYLE.

Event Handlers
None.

Examples

```
<ISINDEX ACTION="cgi-bin/search" PROMPT="Enter search terms">

<ISINDEX HREF="cgi-bin/search" PROMPT="Keywords:">

<BASE HREF="cgi-bin/search">
<ISINDEX PROMPT="Enter search terms">
```

Compatibility

HTML 2, 3.2, and 4 (transitional)
Internet Explorer 2, 3, 4, and 5
Netscape 1, 2, 3, 4, and 4.5
WebTV

Notes

- As an empty element, **<ISINDEX>** requires no closing tag.
- The HTML 3.2 specification only allows the **PROMPT** attribute, while HTML 2 expected a text description to accompany the search field.
- Netscape 1.1 originated the use of the **PROMPT** attribute. WebTV does not support this attribute.
- Originally, the W3C intended this element to be used in a document's header. Browser vendors have relaxed this usage to allow the element in a document's body. Early implementations did not support the **ACTION** attribute and used the **<BASE>** element or an **HREF** attribute to specify a search function's URL.
- Older versions of Internet Explorer also support the **ACTION** attribute, which specifies the URL to use for the query rather than relying on the URL set in the **<BASE>** element.

Internet Explorer 4 does not support the **ACTION**, **DIR**, **HREF**, or **TITLE** attributes. Microsoft documentation suggests using **<INPUT>** instead of this deprecated element.

<KBD> (Keyboard Input)

This element logically indicates text as keyboard input. A browser generally renders text enclosed by this element in a monospaced font.

Syntax

```
<KBD
    CLASS="class name(s)"
    DIR="LTR | RTL"
    ID="unique alphanumeric identifier"
    LANG="language code"
    STYLE="style information"
    TITLE="advisory text"
    onclick="script"
    ondblclick="script"
    onkeydown="script"
    onkeypress="script"
    onkeyup="script"
    onmousedown="script"
    onmousemove="script"
    onmouseout="script"
    onmouseover="script"
    onmouseup="script">

</KBD>
```

Attributes and Events Defined by Internet Explorer 4

```
    LANGUAGE="JAVASCRIPT | JSCRIPT | VBS | VBSCRIPT"
    ondragstart="script"
    onhelp="script"
    onselectstart="script"
```

Attributes

CLASS   See "Core Attributes Reference," earlier in this appendix.

DIR   See "Language Reference," earlier in this appendix.

ID   See "Core Attributes Reference," earlier in this appendix.

LANG   See "Language Reference," earlier in this appendix.

LANGUAGE In the Microsoft implementation, this attribute specifies the scripting language to be used with an associated script bound to the element, typically through an event handler attribute. Possible values may include **JAVASCRIPT**, **JSCRIPT**, **VBS**, and **VBSCRIPT**. Other values that include the version of the language used, such as **JavaScript1.1**, may also be possible.

STYLE See "Core Attributes Reference," earlier in this appendix.

TITLE See "Core Attributes Reference," earlier in this appendix.

Attribute and Event Support

NETSCAPE 4 CLASS, ID, LANG, and **STYLE** are implied.

INTERNET EXPLORER 4 All attributes and events except **DIR**.

Event Handlers
See "Events Reference," earlier in this appendix.

Example

```
Enter the change directory command at the prompt as shown below:<BR>
<BR>
<KBD>CD ... </KBD>
```

Compatibility

HTML 2, 3.2, and 4
Internet Explorer 2, 3, 4, and 5
Netscape 1, 2, 3, 4, and 4.5
WebTV

Notes
The HTML 2 and 3.2 specifications support no attributes for this element.

<LABEL> (Form Control Label)
This HTML 4 element is used to relate descriptions to form controls.

Syntax

```
<LABEL
    ACCESSKEY="key"
    CLASS="class name(s)"
    DIR="LTR | RTL"
    FOR="ID of control"
```

```
        ID="unique alphanumeric identifier"
        LANG="language code"
        STYLE="style information"
        TITLE="advisory text"
        onblur="script"
        onclick="script"
        ondblclick="script"
        onfocus="script"
        onkeydown="script"
        onkeypress="script"
        onkeyup="script"
        onmousedown="script"
        onmousemove="script"
        onmouseout="script"
        onmouseover="script"
        onmouseup="script">

</LABEL>
```

Attributes and Events Defined by Internet Explorer 4

```
        DATAFLD="column name"
        DATAFORMATAS="HTML | TEXT"
        DATASRC="data source ID"
        LANGUAGE="JAVASCRIPT | JSCRIPT | VBS | VBSCRIPT"
        ondragstart="script"
        onhelp="script"
        onselectstart="script"
```

Attributes

ACCESKEY   This attribute specifies a keyboard navigation accelerator for the element. Pressing ALT or a similar key in association with the specified key selects the anchor element correlated with that key.

CLASS   See "Core Attributes Reference," earlier in this appendix.

DATAFLD   This attribute is used to indicate the column name in the data source that is bound to the content of the **<LABEL>** element.

DATAFORMATAS   This attribute indicates if the bound data is plain text (**TEXT**) or HTML (**HTML**). The data bound with **<LABEL>** is used to set the content of the label.

DATASRC   The value of this attribute is an identifier indicating the data source to pull data from.

DIR   See "Language Reference," earlier in this appendix.

FOR   This attribute specifies the **ID** for the form control element the label references. This is optional when the label encloses the form control it is bound to. In many cases, particularly when a table is used to structure the form, the **<LABEL>** element cannot enclose the associated form control, so the **FOR** attribute should be used. This attribute allows more than one label to be associated with the same control by creating multiple references.

ID   See "Core Attributes Reference," earlier in this appendix.

LANG   See "Language Reference," earlier in this appendix.

LANGUAGE   In the Microsoft implementation, this attribute specifies the scripting language to be used with an associated script bound to the element, typically through an event handler attribute. Possible values may include **JAVASCRIPT**, **JSCRIPT**, **VBS**, and **VBSCRIPT**. Other values that include the version of the language used, such as **JavaScript1.1**, may also be possible.

STYLE   See "Core Attributes Reference," earlier in this appendix.

TITLE   See "Core Attributes Reference," earlier in this appendix.

Attribute and Event Support

INTERNET EXPLORER 4   All W3C-defined attributes and events except **DIR**, **onblur**, and **onfocus**, and all attributes and events defined by Internet Explorer 4.

Event Handlers

See "Events Reference," earlier in this appendix.

Examples

```
<FORM>
   <LABEL ID="usernamelabel">Name
   <INPUT TYPE="TEXT" ID="username">
   </LABEL>
</FORM>

<FORM>
   <TABLE>
      <TR>
         <TD><LABEL FOR="username">Name</LABEL></TD>
         <TD><INPUT TYPE="TEXT" ID="username"></TD>
      </TR>
   </TABLE>
</FORM>
```

Compatibility

HTML 4
Internet Explorer 4 and 5

Notes

■ To associate a label with another control implicitly, make the control the contents of the **LABEL**. In this case, a **<LABEL>** element may only contain one other control element. The label itself may be positioned before or after the associated control. If it is impossible to enclose the associated form control, the **FOR** attribute may be used.

■ The HTML 4 specification defines the **onblur** and **onfocus** events for **<LABEL>**. However, Internet Explorer 4 does not document their use.

<LAYER>   (Content Layers)

This Netscape-specific element allows the definition of overlapping content layers that can be exactly positioned, hidden or shown, rendered transparent or opaque, reordered front to back, and nested. The functionality of layers is available using CSS positioning facilities; page developers are advised not to use the **<LAYER>** element.

Syntax (Defined by Netscape 4)

```
<LAYER
     ABOVE="layer name"
     BACKGROUND="URL of background image"
     BELOW="layer name"
     BGCOLOR="color value"
     CLASS="class name(s)"
     CLIP="clip region coordinates in x1, y1, x2, y2 form"
     HEIGHT="percentage | pixels"
     ID="unique alphanumeric identifier"
     LEFT="pixels"
     NAME="string"
     PAGEX="horizontal pixel position of layer"
     PAGEY="vertical pixel position of layer"
     SRC="URL of layer's contents"
     STYLE="style information"
     TITLE="advisory text"
     TOP="pixels"
     VISIBILITY="HIDE | INHERIT | SHOW"
     WIDTH="percentage | pixels"
     Z-INDEX="number"
     onblur="script"
     onfocus="script"
     onload="script"
     onmouseout="script"
     onmouseover="script">

</LAYER>
```

APPENDIXES

Attributes

ABOVE　　This attribute contains the name of the layer (as set with the **NAME** attribute) to be rendered directly above the current layer.

BACKGROUND　　This attribute contains the URL of a background pattern for the layer. Like backgrounds for the document as a whole, the image may tile.

BELOW　　This value of this attribute is the name of the layer to be rendered below the current layer.

BGCOLOR　　This attribute specifies a layer's background color. The attribute's value can be either a named color, such as **red**, or a color specified in the hexadecimal *#RRGGBB* format, such as **#FF0000**.

CLASS　　See "Core Attributes Reference," earlier in this appendix.

CLIP　　This attribute clips a layer's content to a specified rectangle. All layer content outside that rectangle is rendered transparent. The **CLIP** rectangle is defined by two x,y pairs that correspond to the top x, left y, bottom x, and right y coordinate of the rectangle. The coordinates are relative to the layer's origin point, **0,0** in its top-left corner, and may have nothing to do with the pixel coordinates of the screen.

HEIGHT　　This attribute is used to set the height of the layer either in pixels or as a percentage of the screen or region the layer is contained within.

ID　　See "Core Attributes Reference," earlier in this appendix.

LEFT　　This attribute specifies in pixels the left offset of the layer. The offset is relative to its parent layer, if it has one, or to the left browser margin if it does not.

NAME　　This attribute assigns the layer a name that can be referenced by programs in a client-side scripting language. The **ID** attribute can also be used.

PAGEX　　This attribute is used to set the horizontal pixel position of the layer relative to the document window rather than any enclosing layer.

PAGEY　　This attribute is used to set the vertical pixel position of the layer relative to the document window rather than any enclosing layer.

SRC　　This attribute specifies the URL that contains the content to include in the layer. Using this attribute with an empty element is a good way to preserve layouts under older browsers.

STYLE　　See "Core Attributes Reference," earlier in this appendix.

TITLE　　See "Core Attributes Reference," earlier in this appendix.

TOP　　This attribute specifies in pixels the top offset of the layer. The offset is relative to its parent layer if it has one, or the top browser margin if it is not enclosed in another layer.

VISIBILITY   This attribute specifies whether a layer is hidden (**HIDDEN**), shown (**SHOW**), or inherits (**INHERITS**) its visibility from the layer enclosing it.

WIDTH   This attribute specifies a layer's width in pixels or as a percentage value of the enclosing layer or browser width.

Z-INDEX   This attribute specifies a layer's stacking order relative to other layers. Position is specified with positive integers, with "1" indicating the bottommost layer.

Attribute and Event Support

NETSCAPE 4   All attributes.

Event Handlers

See "Events Reference," earlier in this appendix.

Examples

```
<LAYER NAME="scene" BGCOLOR="#00FFFF">
   <LAYER NAME="Shaq" LEFT="100" TOP="100">
     <IMG SRC="shaq.gif">
   </LAYER>

   <LAYER NAME="Kobe" LEFT="200" TOP="100"
         VISIBLITY="HIDDEN">
   <IMG SRC="bryant.jpg">
   </LAYER>
</LAYER>

<!-- The better way to do layers -->
<LAYER SRC="contents.htm" LEFT="20" TOP="20"
      HEIGHT="80%" WIDTH="80%">
</LAYER>
```

Compatibility

Netscape 4 and 4.5

Notes

- This element will likely fall out of fashion because it lacks cross-browser compatibility. The functionality of **<LAYER>** is possible using the positioning features in CSS; page developers are encouraged not to use the **<LAYER>** element.

- Applets, plug-ins, and other embedded media forms, generically called *objects,* may be included in a layer; however, they float to the top of all other layers even if their containing layer is obscured.

APPENDIXES

<LEGEND>   (Field Legend)

This HTML 4 element is used to assign a caption to a set of form fields, as defined by the
<FIELDSET> element.

Syntax

```
<LEGEND
     ACCESSKEY="character"
     ALIGN="BOTTOM | LEFT | RIGHT | TOP" (transitional)
     CLASS="class name(s)"
     DIR="LTR | RTL"
     ID="unique alphanumeric identifier"
     LANG="language code"
     STYLE="style information"
     TITLE="advisory text"
     onclick="script"
     ondblclick="script"
     onkeydown="script"
     onkeypress="script"
     onkeyup="script"
     onmousedown="script"
     onmousemove="script"
     onmouseout="script"
     onmouseover="script"
     onmouseup="script">

</LEGEND>
```

Attributes and Events Defined by Internet Explorer 4

```
     ALIGN="CENTER"
     LANGUAGE="JAVASCRIPT | JSCRIPT | VBS | VBSCRIPT"
     VALIGN="BOTTOM | TOP"
     ondragstart="script"
     onhelp="script"
```

Attributes

ACCESKEY   This attribute specifies a keyboard navigation accelerator for the element.
Pressing ALT or a similar key in association with the specified key selects the form section or the
legend itself.

ALIGN   This attribute indicates where the legend value should be positioned within the border
created by a **<FIELDSET>** element. The default position for the legend is the upper-left corner. It

is also possible to position the legend to the right by setting the attribute to **RIGHT**. The specification defines **BOTTOM** and **TOP** as well. Microsoft defines the use of the **CENTER** and also defines another attribute, **VALIGN**, to set the vertical alignment separately. Future support for **VALIGN** is unclear; page designers are encouraged to use only the **ALIGN** attribute and to eventually rely on style sheets for legend positioning.

CLASS   See "Core Attributes Reference," earlier in this appendix.

DIR   See "Language Reference," earlier in this appendix.

ID   See "Core Attributes Reference," earlier in this appendix.

LANG   See "Language Reference," earlier in this appendix.

LANGUAGE   In the Microsoft implementation, this attribute specifies the scripting language to be used with an associated script bound to the element, typically through an event handler attribute. Possible values may include **JAVASCRIPT**, **JSCRIPT**, **VBS**, and **VBSCRIPT**. Other values that include the version of the language used, such as **JavaScript1.1**, may also be possible.

STYLE   See "Core Attributes Reference," earlier in this appendix.

TITLE   See "Core Attributes Reference," earlier in this appendix.

VALIGN   This Microsoft-specific attribute is used to set whether the legend appears on the **BOTTOM** or the **TOP** of the border defined by the enclosing **<FIELDSET>** element. The attribute will probably be dropped, as it is nonstandard.

Attribute and Event Support

INTERNET EXPLORER 4   All attributes and events except **ACCESSKEY** and **DIR**.

Event Handlers

See "Events Reference," earlier in this appendix.

Example

```
<FORM>
   <FIELDSET>
     <LEGEND ALIGN="TOP">User Information</LEGEND>
     First Name: <INPUT TYPE="TEXT" ID="firstname"
                       SIZE="20"><BR>
     Last Name: <INPUT TYPE="TEXT" ID="lastname"
                       SIZE="20"><BR>
   </FIELDSET>
</FORM>
```

Compatibility

HTML 4
Internet Explorer 4 and 5

Notes

- The **<LEGEND>** element should occur only within the **<FIELDSET>** element. There should be only one **<LEGEND>** per **<FIELDSET>** element.
- The legend improves accessibility when the **FIELDSET** is rendered nonvisually.
- The Microsoft implementation can use the **CENTER** option in the **ALIGN** attribute. Microsoft also defines the **VALIGN** attribute for legend positioning. However, the **VALIGN** attribute does not appear to work consistently.
- WebTV and Netscape do not yet support this element.

<LI> (List Item)

This element is used to indicate a list item as contained in an ordered list (**<OL>**), unordered list (**<UL>**), or older list styles such as **<DIR>** and **<MENU>**.

Syntax

```
<LI
    CLASS="class name(s)"
    DIR="LTR | RTL"
    ID="unique alphanumeric identifier"
    LANG="language code"
    STYLE="style information"
    TITLE="advisory text"
    TYPE="CIRCLE | DISC | SQUARE | a | A | i | I | 1"
        (transitional)
    VALUE="number" (transitional)
    onclick="script"
    ondblclick="script"
    onkeydown="script"
    onkeypress="script"
    onkeyup="script"
    onmousedown="script"
    onmousemove="script"
    onmouseout="script"
    onmouseover="script"
    onmouseup="script">
```

Attributes and Events Defined by Internet Explorer 4

```
LANGUAGE="JAVASCRIPT | JSCRIPT | VBS | VBSCRIPT"
ondragstart="script"
onhelp="script"
onselectstart="script"
```

Attributes

CLASS   See "Core Attributes Reference," earlier in this appendix.

DIR   See "Language Reference," earlier in this appendix.

ID   See "Core Attributes Reference," earlier in this appendix.

LANG   See "Language Reference," earlier in this appendix.

LANGUAGE   In the Microsoft implementation, this attribute specifies the scripting language to be used with an associated script bound to the element, typically through an event handler attribute. Possible values may include **JAVASCRIPT**, **JSCRIPT**, **VBS**, and **VBSCRIPT**. Other values that include the version of the language used, such as **JavaScript1.1**, may also be possible.

STYLE   See "Core Attributes Reference," earlier in this appendix.

TITLE   See "Core Attributes Reference," earlier in this appendix.

TYPE   This attribute indicates the bullet type used in unordered lists or the numbering type used in ordered lists. For ordered lists, a value of **a** indicates lowercase letters, **A** indicates uppercase letters, **i** indicates lowercase Roman numerals, **I** indicates uppercase Roman numerals, and **1** indicates numbers. For unordered lists, values are used to specify bullet types. While the browser is free to set bullet styles, a value of **DISC** generally specifies a filled circle, a value of **CIRCLE** specifies an empty circle, and a value of **b** specifies a filled square. Browsers such as WebTV may include other bullet shapes such as triangles.

VALUE   This attribute indicates the current number of items in an ordered list, as defined by the <OL> element. Regardless of the value of **TYPE** being used to set Roman numerals or letters, the only allowed value for this attribute is a number. List items that follow continue numbering from the value set. The **VALUE** attribute has no meaning for unordered lists.

Attribute and Event Support

NETSCAPE 4   CLASS, ID, LANG, STYLE, TYPE, and VALUE.

INTERNET EXPLORER 4   All attributes and events except **DIR**.

WEBTV   TYPE and **VALUE**.

Event Handlers

See "Events Reference," earlier in this appendix.

Examples

```
<UL>
    <LI TYPE="CIRCLE">First list item is a circle
    <LI TYPE="SQUARE">Second list item is a square
    <LI TYPE="DISC">Third list item is a square
</UL>


<OL>
    <LI TYPE="I">Roman Numerals
    <LI TYPE="A" VALUE="3">Second list item is letter C
    <LI TYPE="a">Continue list in lowercase letters
</OL>
```

Compatibility

HTML 2, 3.2, and 4
Internet Explorer 2, 3, 4, and 5
Netscape 1, 2, 3, 4, and 4.5
WebTV

Notes

■ Under the strict HTML 4.0 definition, the **<LI>** element loses the **TYPE** and **VALUE** attributes, as these functions can be performed with style sheets.

■ While bullet style can be set explicitly, browsers tend to change styles for bullets when **<UL>** lists are nested. However, ordered lists generally do not change style automatically, nor do they support outline style numbers (1.1, 1.1.1, and so on).

■ The closing tag **</LI>** is optional and is not commonly used.

<LINK>   (Link to External Files or Set Relationships)

This empty element specifies relationships between the current document and other documents. Possible uses for this element include defining a relational framework for navigation and linking the document to a style sheet.

Syntax

```
<LINK
    CHARSET="charset list from RFC 2045"
```

```
CLASS="class name(s)"
DIR="LTR | RTL"
HREF="URL"
HREFLANG="language code"
ID="unique alphanumeric identifier"
LANG="language code"
MEDIA="ALL | AURAL | BRAILLE | PRINT | PROJECTION |
       SCREEN | other"
REL="relationship value"
REV="relationship value"
STYLE="style information"
TARGET="frame name" (transitional)
TITLE="advisory information"
TYPE="content type"
onclick="script"
ondblclick="script"
onkeydown="script"
onkeypress="script"
onkeyup="script"
onmousedown="script"
onmousemove="script"
onmouseout="script"
onmouseover="script"
onmouseup="script">
```

Attributes Defined by Internet Explorer 4

```
DISABLED
```

Attributes Defined by Netscape 4

```
SRC="URL"
```

Attributes

CHARSET   This attribute specifies the character set used by the linked document. Allowed values for this attribute are character set names, such as EUC-JP, as defined in RFC 2045.

CLASS   See "Core Attributes Reference," earlier in this appendix.

DIR   See "Language Reference," earlier in this appendix.

DISABLED   This Microsoft-defined attribute is used to disable a link relationship. The presence of the attribute is all that is required to remove a linking relationship. In conjunction with scripting, this attribute could be used to turn on and off various style sheet relationships.

HREF   This attribute specifies the URL of the linked resource. A URL may be absolute or relative.

HREFLANG   This attribute is used to indicate the language of the linked resource. See "Language Reference," earlier in this appendix for information on allowed values.

ID   See "Core Attributes Reference," earlier in this appendix.

LANG   See "Language Reference," earlier in this appendix.

MEDIA   This attribute specifies the destination medium for any linked style information, as indicated when the **REL** attribute is set to **STYLESHEET**. The value of the attribute may be a single media descriptor such as **SCREEN** or a comma-separated list. Possible values for this attribute include **ALL**, **AURAL**, **BRAILLE**, **PRINT**, **PROJECTION**, and **SCREEN**. Other values may also be defined, depending on the browser. Internet Explorer supports **ALL**, **PRINT**, and **SCREEN** as values for this attribute.

REL   This attribute names a relationship between the linked document and the current document. Possible values for this attribute include **ALTERNATE**, **BOOKMARK**, **CHAPTER**, **CONTENTS**, **COPYRIGHT**, **GLOSSARY**, **HELP**, **INDEX**, **NEXT**, **PREV**, **SECTION**, **START**, **STYLESHEET**, and **SUBSECTION**.

   The most common use of this attribute is to specify a link to an external style sheet. The **REL** attribute is set to **STYLESHEET**, and the **HREF** attribute is set to the URL of an external style sheet to format the page. WebTV also supports the use of the value **NEXT** for **REL** to preload the next page in a document series.

REV   The value of the **REV** attribute shows the relationship of the current document to the linked document, as defined by the **HREF** attribute. The attribute thus defines the reverse relationship compared to the value of the **REL** attribute. Values for the **REV** attribute are similar to the possible values for **REL**. They may include **ALTERNATE**, **BOOKMARK**, **CHAPTER**, **CONTENTS**, **COPYRIGHT**, **GLOSSARY**, **HELP**, **INDEX**, **NEXT**, **PREV**, **SECTION**, **START**, **STYLESHEET**, and **SUBSECTION**.

STYLE   See "Core Attributes Reference," earlier in this appendix.

TARGET   The value of the **TARGET** attribute is used to define the frame or window name that has the defined linking relationship or that will show the rendering of any linked resource.

TITLE   See "Core Attributes Reference," earlier in this appendix.

TYPE   This attribute is used to define the type of the content linked to. The value of the attribute should be a MIME type such as **text/html**, **text/css**, and so on. The common use of this attribute is to define the type of style sheet linked and the most common current value is **text/css**, which indicates a Cascading Style Sheet format.

Attribute and Event Support

NETSCAPE 4   REL, SRC, and TYPE. (CLASS, ID, LANG, and STYLE are implied.)

INTERNET EXPLORER 4   DISABLED, HREF, ID, MEDIA (ALL | PRINT | SCREEN), REL, REV, TITLE, and TYPE.

WEBTV   HREF and REL (value="NEXT").

Event Handlers

See "Event Reference," earlier in this appendix.

Examples

```
<LINK HREF="products.htm" REL="parent">

<LINK HREF="corpstyle.css" REL="stylesheet" TYPE="text/css" MEDIA="ALL">

<LINK HREF="nextpagetoload.htm" REL="next">
```

Compatibility

HTML 2, 3.2, and 4
Internet Explorer 3, 4, and 5
Netscape 4 and 4.5
WebTV

Notes

- As an empty element **<LINK>** has no closing tag.
- The **<LINK>** element can occur only in the **<HEAD>** element; there may be multiple occurrences of the element.
- HTML 3.2 defines only the **HREF, REL, REV,** and **TITLE** attributes for the **<LINK>** element.
- HTML 2 defines the **HREF, METHODS, REL, REV, TITLE,** and **URN** attributes for the **<LINK>** element. The **METHODS** and **URN** attributes were later removed from specifications.
- The HTML 4.0 specification defines event handlers for the **<LINK>** element, but it is unclear how they would be used.

<LISTING>   (Code Listing)

This deprecated element from HTML 2 is used to indicate a code listing; it is no longer part of the HTML standard. Text tends to be rendered in a smaller size within this element. Otherwise, the **<PRE>** element should be used instead of **<LISTING>** to indicate preformatted text.

Syntax (HTML 2; Deprecated)

```
<LISTING>
</LISTING>
```

Attributes and Events Defined by Internet Explorer 4

```
CLASS="class name(s)"
ID="unique alphanumeric string"
LANG="language code"
LANGUAGE="JAVASCRIPT | JSCRIPT | VBS | VBSCRIPT"
STYLE="style information"
TITLE="advisory text"
onclick="script"
ondblclick="script"
ondragstart="script"
onhelp="script"
onkeydown="script"
onkeypress="script"
onkeyup="script"
onmousedown="script"
onmousemove="script"
onmouseout="script"
onmouseover="script"
onmouseup="script"
onselectstart="script">
```

Attributes

CLASS   See "Core Attributes Reference," earlier in this appendix.

ID   See "Core Attributes Reference," earlier in this appendix.

LANG   See "Language Reference," earlier in this appendix.

LANGUAGE   In the Microsoft implementation, this attribute specifies the scripting language to be used with an associated script bound to the element, typically through an event handler attribute. Possible values may include **JAVASCRIPT**, **JSCRIPT**, **VBS**, and **VBSCRIPT**. Other values that include the version of the language used, such as **JavaScript1.1**, may also be possible.

STYLE   See "Core Attributes Reference," earlier in this appendix.

TITLE   See "Core Attributes Reference," earlier in this appendix.

Attribute and Event Support

INTERNET EXPLORER 4   All attributes.

Event Handlers

See "Events Reference," earlier in this appendix.

Example

```
<LISTING>
This is a code listing. The preformatted text element &lt;PRE&gt;
should be used instead of this deprecated element.
</LISTING>
```

Compatibility

HTML 2
Internet Explorer 2, 3, 4, and 5
Netscape 1, 2, 3, 4, and 4.5
WebTV

Notes

- As a deprecated element, this element should not be used. This element is not supported by HTML 4. It is still documented by many browser vendors, however, and does creep into some pages. The **<PRE>** element should be used instead of **<LISTING>**.

- It appears that Netscape and Internet Explorer browsers also make text within **<LISTING>** one size smaller than normal text, probably because the HTML 2.0 specification suggested that 132 characters fit to a typical line rather than 80.

- Netscape does not document support for this element, though it is still supported.

<MAP>   (Client-Side Image Map)

This element is used to implement client-side image maps. The element is used to define a map to associate locations on an image with a destination URL. Each hot region or hyperlink mapping is defined by an enclosed **<AREA>** element. A map is bound to a particular image through the use of the **USEMAP** attribute in the **<IMG>** element, which is set to the name of the map.

Syntax

```
<MAP
     CLASS="class name(s)"
     DIR="LTR | RTL"
     ID="unique alphanumeric identifier"
     LANG="language code"
     NAME="unique alphanumeric identifier"
     STYLE="style information"
     TITLE="advisory text"
     onclick="script"
     ondblclick="script"
     onkeydown="script"
     onkeypress="script"
     onkeyup="script"
     onmousedown="script"
     onmousemove="script"
     onmouseout="script"
     onmouseover="script"
     onmouseup="script">

     <AREA> elements

</MAP>
```

Events Defined by Internet Explorer 4

```
     ondragstart="script"
     onhelp="script"
     onselectstart="script"
```

Attributes

CLASS   See "Core Attributes Reference," earlier in this appendix.

DIR   See "Language Reference," earlier in this appendix.

ID   See "Core Attributes Reference," earlier in this appendix.

LANG   See "Language Reference," earlier in this appendix.

NAME   Like **ID**, this attribute is used to define a name associated with the element. In the case of the **<MAP>** element, the **NAME** attribute is the common way to define the name of the image map to be referenced by the **USEMAP** attribute within the **<IMG>** element.

STYLE   See "Core Attributes Reference," earlier in this appendix.

TITLE   See "Core Attributes Reference," earlier in this appendix.

Attribute and Event Support

NETSCAPE 4   NAME. (**CLASS, ID, LANG,** and **STYLE** are implied.)

INTERNET EXPLORER 4   All attributes and events except **DIR.**

WEBTV   NAME.

Event Handlers
See "Events Reference," earlier in this appendix.

Example

```
<MAP NAME="mainmap">
    <AREA SHAPE="CIRCLE" COORDS="200,250,25"
          HREF="file1.htm">

    <AREA SHAPE="RECTANGLE" COORDS="50,50,100,100"
          HREF="file2.htm#important">

    <AREA SHAPE="DEFAULT" NOHREF>
</MAP>
```

Compatibility

HTML 3.2 and 4
Internet Explorer 2, 3, 4, and 5
Netscape 1, 2, 3, 4, and 4.5
WebTV

Notes

- HTML 3.2 supports only the **NAME** attribute for the **<MAP>** element.
- Client-side image maps are not supported under HTML 2. They were first suggested by Spyglass and later incorporated in Netscape and other browsers.

<MARQUEE>   (Marquee Display)

This proprietary element specifies a scrolling, sliding, or bouncing text marquee. This is primarily a Microsoft-specific element, though a few other browsers, notably WebTV, support it as well.

Syntax (Defined by Internet Explorer 4)

```
<MARQUEE
      BEHAVIOR="ALTERNATE | SCROLL | SLIDE"
      BGCOLOR="color name | #RRGGBB"
      CLASS="class name(s)"
      DATAFLD="column name"
      DATAFORMATAS="HTML | TEXT"
      DATASRC="data source ID"
      DIRECTION="DOWN | LEFT | RIGHT | UP"
      HEIGHT="pixels or percentage"
      HSPACE="pixels"
      ID="unique alphanumeric identifier"
      LANG="language code"
      LANGUAGE="JAVASCRIPT | JSCRIPT | VBS | VBSCRIPT"
      LOOP="INFINITE | number"
      SCROLLAMOUNT="pixels"
      SCROLLDELAY="milliseconds"
      STYLE="style information"
      TITLE="advisory text"
      TRUESPEED
      VSPACE="pixels"
      WIDTH="pixels or percentage"
      onafterupdate="script"
      onblur="script"
      onbounce="script"
      onclick="script"
      ondblclick="script"
      ondragstart="script"
      onfinish="script"
      onfocus="script"
      onhelp="script"
      onkeydown="script"
      onkeypress="script"
      onkeyup="script"
      onmousedown="script"
      onmousemove="script"
      onmouseout="script"
      onmouseover="script"
      onmouseup="script"
      onresize="script"
      onrowenter="script"
      onrowexit="script"
      onselectstart="script"
      onstart="script">

      Marquee text

</MARQUEE>
```

Attributes Defined by WebTV

```
ALIGN="BOTTOM | CENTER | LEFT | RIGHT | TOP"
TRANSPARENCY="number (0-100)"
```

Attributes

ALIGN   This WebTV-specific attribute is used to indicate how the marquee should be aligned with surrounding text. The alignment values and rendering are similar to other embedded objects, such as images. The default value for this attribute under WebTV is **LEFT**. Microsoft Internet Explorer no longer supports this attribute.

BEHAVIOR   This attribute controls the movement of marquee text across the marquee. The **ALTERNATE** option causes text to completely cross the marquee field in one direction and then cross in the opposite direction. A value of **SCROLL** for the attribute causes text to wrap around and start over again. This is the default value for a marquee. A value of **SLIDE** for this attribute causes text to cross the marquee field and stop when its leading character reaches the opposite side.

BGCOLOR   This attribute specifies the marquee's background color. The value for the attribute can either be a color name or a color value defined in the hexadecimal *#RRGGBB* format.

CLASS   See "Core Attributes Reference," earlier in this appendix.

DATAFLD   This attribute is used to indicate the column name in the data source that is bound to the <MARQUEE> element.

DATAFORMATAS   This attribute indicates if the bound data is plain text (**TEXT**) or HTML (**HTML**). The data bound with <MARQUEE> is used to set the message that is scrolled.

DATASRC   The value of this attribute is set to an identifier indicating the data source to pull data from. Bound data is used to set the message that is scrolled in the <MARQUEE>.

DIRECTION   This attribute specifies the direction in which the marquee should scroll. The default is **LEFT**. Other possible values for **DIRECTION** include **DOWN**, **RIGHT**, and **UP**. WebTV does not support the **DOWN** and **UP** values.

HEIGHT   This attribute specifies the height of the marquee in pixels or as a percentage of the window.

HSPACE   This attribute indicates the horizontal space in pixels between the marquee and surrounding content.

ID   See "Core Attributes Reference," earlier in this appendix.

LANG   See "Language Reference," earlier in this appendix.

LANGUAGE   In the Microsoft implementation, this attribute specifies the scripting language to be used with an associated script bound to the element, typically through an event handler attribute. Possible values may include **JAVASCRIPT**, **JSCRIPT**, **VBS**, and **VBSCRIPT**. Other values that include the version of the language used, such as **JavaScript1.1**, may also be possible.

LOOP   This attribute indicates the number of times the marquee content should loop. By default, a marquee loops infinitely unless the **BEHAVIOR** attribute is set to **SLIDE**. It is also possible to use a value of **INFINITE** or **–1** to set the text to loop indefinitely.

SCROLLAMOUNT   This attribute specifies the width in pixels between successive displays of the scrolling text in the marquee.

SCROLLDELAY   This attribute specifies the delay in milliseconds between successive displays of the text in the marquee.

STYLE   See "Core Attributes Reference," earlier in this appendix.

TITLE   See "Core Attributes Reference," earlier in this appendix.

TRANSPARENCY   In the WebTV implementation, this attribute specifies the marquee's degree of transparency. Values range from **0** (totally opaque) to **100** (totally transparent). A value of **50** is optimized for fast rendering.

TRUESPEED   When this attribute is present, it indicates that the **SCROLLDELAY** value should be honored for its exact value. If the attribute is not present, any values less than 60 are rounded up to 60 milliseconds.

VSPACE   This attribute indicates the vertical space in pixels between the marquee and surrounding content.

WIDTH   This attribute specifies the width of the marquee in pixels or as a percentage of the enclosing window.

Attribute and Event Support

INTERNET EXPLORER 4   All Microsoft-defined attributes and events.

WEBTV   ALIGN, BEHAVIOR, BGCOLOR, DIRECTION, HEIGHT, HSPACE, LOOP, SCROLLAMOUNT, SCROLLDELAY, TRANSPARENCY, VSPACE, and WIDTH. (Note: WebTV supports only the **LEFT and RIGHT** values for the **DIRECTION** attribute.)

Event Handlers

The <MARQUEE> element has a few unique events. For example, an event is triggered when the text bounces off one side or another on the marquee. This can be caught with the **onbounce** event handler attribute. When the text first starts scrolling, the start event fires, which can be caught with **onstart**; when the marquee is done, a finish event fires, which can be caught with **onfinish**. The other events are common to HTML 4 elements with Microsoft extensions.

Examples

```
<MARQUEE BEHAVIOR="ALTERNATE">
SPECIAL VALUE !!! This week only !!!
</MARQUEE>

<MARQUEE ID="marquee1" BGCOLOR="RED" DIRECTION="RIGHT" HEIGHT="30"
         WIDTH="80%" HSPACE="10" VSPACE="10">
The super scroller scrolls again!!
More fun than a barrel of &lt;BLINK&gt; elements.
</MARQUEE>
```

Compatibility

Internet Explorer 3, 4, and 5
WebTV

Notes

■ The **<MARQUEE>** element is supported only by Microsoft and WebTV.

<MENU>   (Menu List)

This element is used to indicate a short list of items that might occur in a menu of choices.
Like the ordered and unordered lists, the individual items in the list are indicated by the **<LI>**
element. Most browsers render the **<MENU>** element exactly the same as the unordered
list, so there is little reason to use it. Under the HTML 4.0 strict specification, **<MENU>** is no
longer supported.

Syntax (Transitional Only)

```
<MENU
    CLASS="class name(s)"
    COMPACT
    DIR="LTR | RTL"
    ID="unique alphanumeric string"
    LANG="language code"
    STYLE="style information"
    TITLE="advisory text"
    onclick="script"
    ondblclick="script"
    onkeydown="script"
    onkeypress="script"
    onkeyup="script"
    onmousedown="script"
```

```
        onmousemove="script"
        onmouseout="script"
        onmouseover="script"
        onmouseup="script">
```

```
</MENU>
```

Events Defined by Internet Explorer 4

```
        ondragstart="script"
        onhelp="script"
        onselectstart="script"
```

Attributes

CLASS   See "Core Attributes Reference," earlier in this appendix.

COMPACT   This attribute indicates that the list should be rendered in a compact style. Few browsers actually change the rendering of the list regardless of the presence of this attribute. The **COMPACT** attribute requires no value.

DIR   See "Language Reference," earlier in this appendix.

ID   See "Core Attributes Reference," earlier in this appendix.

LANG   See "Language Reference," earlier in this appendix.

STYLE   See "Core Attributes Reference," earlier in this appendix.

TITLE   See "Core Attributes Reference," earlier in this appendix.

Attribute and Event Support

NETSCAPE 4   CLASS, ID, LANG, and STYLE.

INTERNET EXPLORER 4   All attributes and events except **COMPACT** and **DIR**.

Event Handlers
See "Events Reference," earlier in this appendix.

Example

```
    <H2>Taco List</H2>
       <MENU>
```

```
    <LI>Fish
    <LI>Pork
    <LI>Beef
    <LI>Chicken
</MENU>
```

Compatibility

HTML 2, 3.2, and 4 (transitional)
Internet Explorer 2, 3, 4, and 5
Netscape 1, 2, 3, 4, and 4.5
WebTV

Notes

- Under the HTML 4.0 strict specification, this element is not defined. Since most browsers simply render this style of list as an unordered list, using the <UL> element instead is preferable.
- Most browsers tend not to support the **COMPACT** attribute.
- The HTML 2.0 and 3.2 specifications support only the **COMPACT** attribute.

<META> (Meta-Information)

This element specifies general information about a document, which can be used in document indexing. It also allows a document to define fields in the HTTP response header when it is sent from the server. A common use of this element is for *client-pull* page loading, which allows a document automatically to load another document after a specified delay.

Syntax

```
<META
    CONTENT="string"
    DIR="LTR | RTL"
    HTTP-EQUIV="http header string"
    LANG="language code"
    NAME="name of meta-information"
    SCHEME="scheme type">
```

Attributes Defined by WebTV

```
    URL="url"
```

APPENDIXES

Attributes

CONTENT   This attribute contains the actual meta-information. The form of the actual meta-information varies greatly, depending on the value set for **NAME**.

DIR   This attribute defines the text direction (left to right or right to left) of the content of the <**META**> element, as defined by the **CONTENT** attribute.

HTTP-EQUIV   This attribute binds the meta-information in the **CONTENT** attribute to an HTTP response header. If this attribute is present, the **NAME** attribute should not be used. The **HTTP-EQUIV** attribute is often used to create a document that automatically loads another document after a set time. This is called *client-pull*. An example of a client-pull <**META**> element is

```
<META HTTP-EQUIV="REFRESH" CONTENT="10;URL='nextpage.htm'">
```

Note that the **CONTENT** attribute contains two values. The first is the number of seconds to wait, and the second is the identifier URL and the URL to load after the specified time.

LANG   This attribute is the language code associated with the language used in the **CONTENT** attribute.

NAME   This attribute associates a name with the meta-information contained in the **CONTENT** attribute. If present, the **HTTP-EQUIV** attribute should not be used.

SCHEME   The scheme attribute is used to indicate the expected format of the value of the **CONTENT** attribute. The particular scheme may also be used in conjunction with the meta-data profile as indicated by the **PROFILE** attribute for the <**HEAD**> element.

Attribute and Event Support

NETSCAPE 4   CONTENT, HTTP-EQUIV, and **NAME**.

INTERNET EXPLORER 4   All attributes except **DIR**.

WEBTV   CONTENT, HTTP-EQUIV, and **URL**.

Event Handlers
None.

Examples

```
<!-- Use of the META element to assist in document indexing -->
<META NAME="KEYWORDS" CONTENT="HTML, SCRIPTING"
      SCHEME="Lycos">

<!-- Use of the META element to implement client-pull to
     automatically load a page -->
```

```
<META HTTP-EQUIV="REFRESH"
      CONTENT="3;URL='http://www.pint.com/'">

<!-- Use of the META element to add rating information -->
<META HTTP-EQUIV="PICS-Label" CONTENT="(PICS-1.1
                  'http://www.rsac.org/ratingsv01.html'
                  1 gen true comment 'RSACi North America
                  Server' by 'webmaster@bigcompany.com'
                  for 'http://www.bigcompany.com' on
                  '1999.05.26T13:05-0500'
                  r (n 0 s 0 v 0 1 1))">
```

Compatibility

HTML 2, 3.2, and 4
Internet Explorer 2, 3, 4, and 5
Netscape 1.1, 2, 3, 4, and 4.5
WebTV

Notes

■ The **<META>** element can occur only in the **<HEAD>** element. It may be defined multiple times.

■ The **<META>** element is an empty element and does not have a closing tag nor contain any content.

■ A common use of the **<META>** element is to set information for indexing tools such as search engines. The common values for the **NAME** attribute when performing this function include **AUTHOR**, **DESCRIPTION**, and **KEYWORDS**; other attributes may also be possible.

■ Along the same line as indexing, meta-information is also used for rating pages.

■ The HTML 2.0 and 3.2 specifications define only the **CONTENT**, **HTTP-EQUIV**, and **NAME** attributes.

<MULTICOL>   (Multiple Column Text)

This Netscape-specific element renders the enclosed content in multiple columns. This element should not be used in favor of a table, which is a more standard way to render multiple columns of text across browsers. It is likely that style sheets will provide for multicolumn rendering in the future.

Syntax (Defined by Netscape)

```
<MULTICOL
      CLASS="class name(s)"
      COLS="number of columns"
```

APPENDIXES

```
       GUTTER="pixels"
       ID="unique alphanumeric identifier"
       STYLE="style information"
       WIDTH="pixels">

</MULTICOL>
```

Attributes

CLASS   See "Core Attributes Reference," earlier in this appendix.

COLS   This attribute indicates the number of columns in which to display the text. The browser attempts to fill the columns evenly.

GUTTER   This attribute indicates the width in pixels between the columns. The default value for this attribute is **10** pixels.

ID   See "Core Attributes Reference," earlier in this appendix.

STYLE   See "Core Attributes Reference," earlier in this appendix.

WIDTH   This attribute indicates the column width for all columns. The width of each column is set in pixels and is equivalent for all columns in the group. When the attribute is not specified, the width of columns is determined by taking the available window size, subtracting the number of pixels for the gutter between the columns as specified by the **GUTTER** attribute, and evenly dividing the result by the number of columns in the group as set by the **COLS** attribute.

Attribute and Event Support

NETSCAPE 4   All attributes.

Event Handlers
None.

Example

```
<MULTICOL COLS="3" GUTTER="20">
Put a long piece of text here....
</MULTICOL>
```

Compatibility

Netscape 3, 4, and 4.5

Notes

■ Do not attempt to use images or other embedded media within a multicolumn layout, as defined by **<MULTICOL>**.

■ Do not set the number of columns to high or resize the browser window very small, as this will cause text to overwrite other lines.

<NOBR>   (No Breaks)

This proprietary element renders enclosed text without line breaks. Break points for where text may wrap can be inserted using the **<WBR>** element.

Syntax

```
<NOBR
    CLASS="class name(s)"
    ID="unique alphanumeric identifier"
    STYLE="style information"
    TITLE="advisory text">

</NOBR>
```

Attributes

CLASS   See "Core Attributes Reference," earlier in this appendix.

ID   See "Core Attributes Reference," earlier in this appendix.

STYLE   See "Core Attributes Reference," earlier in this appendix.

TITLE   See "Core Attributes Reference," earlier in this appendix.

Attribute and Event Support

NETSCAPE 4   All attributes.

INTERNET EXPLORER 4   ID, STYLE, and TITLE.

Event Handlers
None.

Examples

```
<NOBR>This really long text ... will not be broken.</NOBR>

<NOBR>With this element it is often important to hint where a line may
be broken using &lt;WBR&gt;.<WBR> This element acts as a soft return.</NOBR>
```

APPENDIXES

Compatibility

Internet Explorer 2, 3, 4, and 5
Netscape 1.1, 2, 3, 4, and 4.5
WebTV

Notes

While many browsers support this attribute, it is not part of any W3C standard.

<NOEMBED>   (No Embedded Media Support)

This Netscape-specific element is used to indicate alternative content to display on browsers that cannot support an embedded media object. It should occur in conjunction with the **<EMBED>** element.

Syntax

```
<NOEMBED>

    Alternative content here

</NOEMBED>
```

Attributes

Netscape does not specifically define attributes for this element; however, Netscape documentation suggests that **CLASS, ID, STYLE,** and **TITLE** may be supported for this element.

Event Handlers

None.

Example

```
<EMBED SRC="trailer.mov" HEIGHT="150" WIDTH="150">
   <NOEMBED>
      <IMG SRC="trailer.gif">
      <BR>
   Sorry, this browser is not configured to display video.
   </NOEMBED>
</EMBED>
```

Compatibility

Netscape 2, 3, 4, and 4.5
WebTV

Notes

This element will disappear as the **<OBJECT>** style of inserting media into a page becomes more common.

<NOFRAMES>   (No Frame Support Content)

This element is used to indicate alternative content to display on browsers that do not support frames.

Syntax (Transitional Only)

```
<NOFRAMES
     CLASS="class name(s)"
     DIR="LTR | RTL"
     ID="unique alphanumeric identifier"
     LANG="language code"
     STYLE="style information"
     TITLE="advisory text"
     onclick="script"
     ondblclick="script"
     onkeydown="script"
     onkeypress="script"
     onkeyup="script"
     onmousedown="script"
     onmousemove="script"
     onmouseout="script"
     onmouseover="script"
     onmouseup="script">

     Alternative content for non-frame-supporting browsers

</NOFRAMES>
```

Attributes

CLASS   See "Core Attributes Reference," earlier in this appendix.

DIR   See "Language Reference," earlier in this appendix.

ID   See "Core Attributes Reference," earlier in this appendix.

LANG   See "Language Reference," earlier in this appendix.

STYLE   See "Core Attributes Reference," earlier in this appendix.

TITLE   See "Core Attributes Reference," earlier in this appendix.

Attribute and Event Support

NETSCAPE 4   CLASS, ID, LANG, and STYLE are implied.

INTERNET EXPLORER 4   ID, STYLE, and TITLE.

Event Handlers

It is interesting to note that while the **<NOFRAMES>** element does support the common events for nearly all HTML 4 elements, their value seems unclear. The only time that content within a **<NOFRAMES>** could be rendered is on a browser that does not support frames; however, browsers that do not support frames are unlikely to support an event model or similar features. There might be some possibility with clever scripting to access framed and nonframed content, but for now the benefit of the events seems unclear. For more information, see "Events Reference," earlier in this appendix.

Example

```
<FRAMESET ROWS="100,*">
   <FRAME SRC="controls.htm">
   <FRAME SRC="content.htm">
      <NOFRAMES>
      Sorry, this browser does not support frames.
      </NOFRAMES>
</FRAMESET>
```

Compatibility

HTML 4 (transitional)
Internet Explorer 2, 3, 4, and 5
Netscape 2, 3, 4, and 4.5
WebTV

Notes

- This element should be used within the scope of the **<FRAMESET>** element.
- The benefit of events and sophisticated attributes such as **STYLE** is unclear for browsers that would use content within **<NOFRAMES>**, given that older browsers that don't support frames would probably not support these features.

<NOSCRIPT>   (No Script Support Content)

This element is used to enclose content that should be rendered on browsers that do not support scripting or that have scripting turned off.

Syntax

```
<NOSCRIPT
    CLASS="class name(s)"
    DIR="LTR | RTL"
    ID="unique alphanumeric identifier"
    LANG="language code"
    STYLE="style information"
    TITLE="advisory text"
    onclick="script"
    ondblclick="script"
    onkeydown="script"
    onkeypress="script"
    onkeyup="script"
    onmousedown="script"
    onmousemove="script"
    onmouseout="script"
    onmouseover="script"
    onmouseup="script">

    Alternative content for non-script-supporting browsers

</NOSCRIPT>
```

Attributes

CLASS   See "Core Attributes Reference," earlier in this appendix.

DIR   See "Language Reference," earlier in this appendix.

ID   See "Core Attributes Reference," earlier in this appendix.

LANG   See "Language Reference," earlier in this appendix.

STYLE   See "Core Attributes Reference," earlier in this appendix.

TITLE   See "Core Attributes Reference," earlier in this appendix.

Attribute and Event Support

NETSCAPE 4   **CLASS**, **ID**, **LANG**, and **STYLE** are implied.

Event Handlers

As defined in the preliminary specification of HTML 4, the benefits of event handlers are not very obvious, considering that content within the **<NOSCRIPT>** element assumes the browser does not support scripting, while the script handlers themselves are for browsers that support scripting. These are standard events for nearly all HTML 4 elements. For definitions, see "Events Reference," earlier in this appendix.

Example

```
Last Updated:
<SCRIPT LANGUAGE="JAVASCRIPT">
<!-- document.writeln(document.lastodified); // -->
</SCRIPT>

<NOSCRIPT>
1999
</NOSCRIPT>
```

Compatibility

HTML 4
Internet Explorer 3, 4, and 5
Netscape 2, 3, 4, and 4.5
WebTV

Notes

Improved functionality for the **<NOSCRIPT>** element may come if it is extended to deal with the lack of support for one scripting language or another. Currently, the element is used only to indicate if any scripting is supported or not. It is also useful to "comment out" scripting information so non-scripting-aware browsers will not read it.

<OBJECT>   (Embedded Object)

This element specifies an arbitrary object to be included into an HTML document. Initially, this element was used to insert ActiveX controls, but according to the HTML 4.0 specification, an object may be any media object, document, applet, ActiveX control, or even image.

Syntax

```
<OBJECT
     ALIGN="BOTTOM | LEFT | MIDDLE | RIGHT | TOP"
           (transitional)
     ARCHIVE="URL"
     BORDER="percentage | pixels" (transitional)
     CLASS="class name(s)"
     CLASSID="ID"
     CODEBASE="URL"
     CODETYPE="MIME Type"
     DATA="URL of data"
```

```
DECLARE
DIR="LTR | RTL"
HEIGHT="percentage | pixels"
HSPACE="percentage | pixels" (transitional)
ID="unique alphanumeric identifier"
LANG="language code"
NAME="unique alphanumeric name"
STANDBY="standby text string"
STYLE="style information"
TABINDEX="number"
TITLE="advisory text"
TYPE="MIME Type"
USEMAP="URL"
VSPACE="percentage | pixels" (transitional)
WIDTH="percentage | pixels"
onclick="script"
ondblclick="script"
onkeydown="script"
onkeypress="script"
onkeyup="script"
onmousedown="script"
onmousemove="script"
onmouseout="script"
onmouseover="script"
onmouseup="script">
```

```
</OBJECT>
```

Attributes and Events Defined by Internet Explorer 4

```
ACCESSKEY="character"
ALIGN="ABSBOTTOM | ABSMIDDLE | BASELINE | TEXTTOP"
CODE="URL"
DATAFLD="column name"
DATASRC="ID for bound data"
LANGUAGE="JAVASCRIPT | JSCRIPT | VBS | VBSCRIPT"
onafterupdate="script"
onbeforeupdate="script"
onblur="script"
ondragstart="script"
onfocus="script"
onhelp="script"
onreadystatechange="script"
onresize="script"
onrowenter="script"
onrowexit="script"
onselectstart="script"
```

Attributes

ACCESSKEY   This Microsoft attribute specifies a keyboard navigation accelerator for the element. Pressing ALT or a similar key in association with the specified character selects the form control correlated with that key sequence. Page designers are forewarned to avoid key sequences already bound to browsers.

ALIGN   This attribute aligns the object with respect to the surrounding text. The default is **LEFT**. The HTML 4.0 specification defines **BOTTOM, MIDDLE, RIGHT**, and **TOP** as well. Browsers may provide an even richer set of alignment values. The behavior of alignment for objects is similar to images. Under the strict HTML 4.0 specification, the **<OBJECT>** element does not support this attribute.

ARCHIVE   This attribute contains a URL for the location of an archive file. An archive file is typically used to contain multiple object files to improve the efficiency of access.

BORDER   This attribute specifies the width of the object's borders in pixels or as a percentage.

CLASS   See "Core Attributes Reference," earlier in this appendix.

CLASSID   This attribute contains a URL for an object's implementation. The URL syntax depends upon the object's type. With ActiveX controls, the value of this attribute does not appear to be a URL but something of the form *CLSID: object-id*; for example, **CLSID: 99B42120-6EC7-11CF-A6C7-00AA00A47DD2.**

CODE   Under the old Microsoft implementation, this attribute contains the URL referencing a Java applet class file. The way to access a Java applet under the HTML 4.0 specification is to use **<OBJECT CLASSID="java<: classname.class">**. The pseudo URL *java:* is used to indicate a Java applet. Microsoft Internet Explorer 4 and beyond support this style, so **CODE** should not be used.

CODEBASE   This attribute contains a URL to use as a relative base to access the object specified by the **CLASSID** attribute.

CODETYPE   This attribute specifies an object's MIME type. Do not confuse this attribute with **TYPE**, which specifies the MIME type of the data the object may use as defined by the **DATA** attribute.

DATA   This attribute contains a URL for data required by an object.

DATAFLD   This attribute is used to indicate the column name in the data source that is bound to the **<OBJECT>** element.

DATASRC   The value of this attribute is set to an identifier indicating the data source to pull data from.

DECLARE   This attribute declares an object without instantiating it. This is useful when the object will be a parameter to another object.

DIR   See "Language Reference," earlier in this appendix.

HEIGHT   This attribute specifies the height of the object in pixels or as a percentage of the enclosing window.

HSPACE   This attribute indicates the horizontal space in pixels or percentages between the object and surrounding content.

ID   See "Core Attributes Reference," earlier in this appendix.

LANG   See "Language Reference," earlier in this appendix.

LANGUAGE   In the Microsoft implementation, this attribute specifies the scripting language to be used with an associated script bound to the element, typically through an event handler attribute. Possible values may include **JAVASCRIPT, JSCRIPT, VBS,** and **VBSCRIPT.** Other values that include the version of the language used, such as **JavaScript1.1,** may also be possible.

NAME   This attribute under the Microsoft definition defines the name of the control so scripting can access it. The HTML 4.0 specification suggests that it is a name for form submission, but this meaning is unclear and not supported by browsers.

STANDBY   This attribute contains a text message to be displayed while the object is loading.

STYLE   See "Core Attributes Reference," earlier in this appendix.

TABINDEX   This attribute takes a numeric value indicating the position of the object in the tabbing index for the document. Tabbing proceeds from the lowest positive **TABINDEX** value to the highest. Negative values for **TABINDEX** will leave the object out of the tabbing order. When tabbing is not explicitly set, the browser may tab through items in the order they are encountered.

TITLE   See "Core Attributes Reference," earlier in this appendix.

TYPE   This attribute specifies the MIME type for the object's data. This is different from the **CODETYPE,** which is the MIME type of the object and not the data it uses.

USEMAP   This attribute contains the URL of the image map to be used with the object. Typically, the URL is a fragment identifier referencing a **<MAP>** element somewhere else within the file. The presence of this attribute indicates that the type of object being included is an image.

VSPACE   This attribute indicates the vertical space in pixels or percentages between the object and surrounding text.

WIDTH   This attribute specifies the width of the object in pixels or as a percentage of the enclosing window.

Attribute and Event Support

NETSCAPE 4   ALIGN, CLASSID, CODEBASE, DATA, HEIGHT, TYPE, and WIDTH. (CLASS, ID, LANG, and STYLE are implied.)

INTERNET EXPLORER 4   ALIGN, CLASS, CLASSID, CODE, CODEBASE, CODETYPE, DATA, HEIGHT, ID, LANG, NAME, STYLE, TABINDEX, TITLE, TYPE, WIDTH, all W3C-defined events, and all attributes and events defined by Internet Explorer 4.

Event Handlers

See "Events Reference," earlier in this appendix.

Examples

```
<OBJECT ID="IeLabel1" WIDTH="325" HEIGHT="65"
        CLASSID="CLSID:99B42120-6EC7-11CF-A6C7-00AA00A47DD2">
    <PARAM NAME="_ExtentX" VALUE="6879">
    <PARAM NAME="_ExtentY" VALUE="1376">
    <PARAM NAME="Caption" VALUE="Hello World">
    <PARAM NAME="Alignment" VALUE="4">
    <PARAM NAME="Mode" VALUE="1">
    <PARAM NAME="ForeColor" VALUE="#FF0000">
    <PARAM NAME="FontName" VALUE="Arial">
    <PARAM NAME="FontSize" VALUE="36">
<B>Hello World for non-ActiveX users!</B>
</OBJECT>


<OBJECT CLASSID="java:Blink.class"
        STANDBY="Here it comes"
        HEIGHT="100" WIDTH="300">
    <PARAM NAME="LBL" VALUE="Java is fun, exciting, and new.">
    <PARAM NAME="SPEED" VALUE="2">
This will display in non-Java-aware or -enabled
browsers.
</OBJECT>


<OBJECT DATA="pullinthisfile.html">
Data not included!
</OBJECT>


<OBJECT DATA="bigimage.gif" SHAPES>
    <A HREF="page1.htm" SHAPE="RECT" COORDS="10,10,40,40">
    Page 1</A>
    <A HREF="page2.htm" SHAPE="CIRCLE" COORDS="100,90,20 ">
    Page 2</A>
</OBJECT>
```

Compatibility

HTML 4
Internet Explorer 3, 4, and 5
Netscape 4 and 4.5

Notes

■ Under the strict HTML 4.0 specification the **<OBJECT>** element loses most of its presentation attributes, including **ALIGN, BORDER, HEIGHT, HSPACE, VSPACE,** and **WIDTH**. These attributes are replaced by style sheet rules.

■ The HTML 4.0 specification reserves the **DATAFLD, DATAFORMATAS,** and **DATASRC** attributes for future use.

■ Alternative content should be defined within the **<OBJECT>** element after the **<PARAM>** elements.

■ The **<OBJECT>** element is still mainly used to include binaries in pages. While the specification defines that it can load in HTML files and create image maps, few, if any, browsers support this.

<OL>   (Ordered List)

This element is used to define an ordered or numbered list of items. The numbering style comes in many forms, including letters, Roman numerals, and regular numerals. The individual items within the list are specified by **<LI>** elements included with the **<OL>** element.

Syntax

```
<OL
    CLASS="class name(s)"
    COMPACT (transitional)
    DIR="LTR | RTL"
    ID="unique alphanumeric identifier"
    LANG="language code"
    START="number" (transitional)
    STYLE="style information"
    TITLE="advisory text"
    TYPE="a | A | i | I | 1" (transitional)
    onclick="script"
    ondblclick="script"
    onkeydown="script"
    onkeypress="script"
    onkeyup="script"
    onmousedown="script"
    onmousemove="script"
    onmouseout="script"
    onmouseover="script"
    onmouseup="script">

</OL>
```

APPENDIXES

Attributes and Events Defined by Internet Explorer 4

```
LANGUAGE="JAVASCRIPT | JSCRIPT | VBS | VBSCRIPT"
ondragstart="script"
onhelp="script"
onselectstart="script"
```

Attributes

CLASS   See "Core Attributes Reference," earlier in this appendix.

COMPACT   This attribute indicates that the list should be rendered in a compact style. Few browsers actually change the rendering of the list regardless of the presence of this attribute. The **COMPACT** attribute requires no value.

DIR   See "Language Reference," earlier in this appendix.

ID   See "Core Attributes Reference," earlier in this appendix.

LANG   See "Language Reference," earlier in this appendix.

LANGUAGE   In the Microsoft implementation, this attribute specifies the scripting language to be used with an associated script bound to the element, typically through an event handler attribute. Possible values may include **JAVASCRIPT**, **JSCRIPT**, **VBS**, and **VBSCRIPT**. Other values that include the version of the language used, such as **JavaScript1.1**, may also be possible.

START   This attribute is used to indicate the value to start numbering the individual list items from. While the ordering type of list elements may be Roman numerals such as XXXI or letters, the value of **START** is always represented as a number. To start numbering elements from the letter "C," use **<OL TYPE="A" START="3">**.

STYLE   See "Core Attributes Reference," earlier in this appendix.

TITLE   See "Core Attributes Reference," earlier in this appendix.

TYPE   This attribute indicates the numbering type: "a" indicates lowercase letters, "A" indicates uppercase letters, "i" indicates lowercase Roman numerals, "I" indicates uppercase Roman numerals, and "1" indicates numbers. Type set in the **<OL>** element is used for the entire list unless a **TYPE** attribute is used within an enclosed **<LI>** element.

Attribute and Event Support

NETSCAPE 4   CLASS, ID, LANG, START, STYLE, and TYPE.

INTERNET EXPLORER 4   All attributes and events except **COMPACT** and **DIR**.

WEBTV   START and TYPE.

Event Handlers

See "Events Reference," earlier in this appendix.

Examples

```
<OL TYPE="1">
   <LI>First step
   <LI>Second step
   <LI>Third step
</OL>

<OL COMPACT TYPE="I" START="30">
   <LI>Clause 30
   <LI>Clause 31
   <LI>Clause 32
</OL>
```

Compatibility

HTML 2, 3.2, 4
Internet Explorer 2, 3, 4, and 5
Netscape 1, 2, 3, 4, and 4.5
WebTV

Notes

■ Under the strict HTML 4.0 specification, the **<OL>** element no longer supports the **COMPACT, START,** and **TYPE** attributes. These aspects of lists can be controlled with style sheet rules.

■ The HTML 3.2 specification supports only the **COMPACT, START,** and **TYPE** attributes. The HTML 2.0 specification supports only the **COMPACT** attribute.

<OPTGROUP>   (Option Grouping)

This element specifies a grouping of items in a selection list defined by **<OPTION>** elements so that the menu choices may be presented in a hierarchical menu or similar alternative fashion to improve access via nonvisual browsers.

Syntax

```
<OPTGROUP
     CLASS="class name(s)"
     DIR="LTR | RTL"
     DISABLED
     ID="unique alphanumeric identifier"
```

```
     LABEL="text description"
     LANG="language code"
     STYLE="style information"
     TITLE="advisory text"
     onclick="script"
     ondblclick="script"
     onkeydown="script"
     onkeypress="script"
     onkeyup="script"
     onmousedown="script"
     onmousemove="script"
     onmouseout="script"
     onmouseover="script"
     onmouseup="script">

     <OPTION> elements

</OPTGROUP>
```

Attributes

CLASS   See "Core Attributes Reference," earlier in this appendix.

DIR   See "Language Reference," earlier in this appendix.

DISABLED   Occurrence of this attribute indicates that the enclosed set of options is disabled.

ID   See "Core Attributes Reference," earlier in this appendix.

LABEL   This attribute contains a short label that may be more appealing to use when the selection list is rendered as items in a hierarchy.

LANG   See "Language Reference," earlier in this appendix.

STYLE   See "Core Attributes Reference," earlier in this appendix.

TITLE   See "Core Attributes Reference," earlier in this appendix.

Attribute and Event Support
None.

Event Handlers
See "Events Reference," earlier in this appendix.

Example

```
Where would you like to go for your vacation?<BR>
<SELECT>
    <OPTION ID="ch1" VALUE="China">The Great Wall
    <OPTGROUP LABEL="Mexico">
        <OPTION ID="ch2" LABEL="Los Cabos" VALUE="Los Cabos">
        Los Cabos, Mexico

        <OPTION ID="ch3" LABEL="Leon" VALUE="Leon">Leon, Mexico

        <OPTION ID="ch4" VALUE="MXC">Mexico City
    </OPTGROUP>
    <OPTION ID="ch5" VALUE="home" SELECTED>Your backyard
</SELECT>
```

Compatibility

HTML 4

Notes

This element should only occur within the context of a **<SELECT>** element.

<OPTION>   (Option in Selection List)

This element specifies an item in a selection list defined by the **<SELECT>** element.

Syntax

```
<OPTION
    CLASS="class name(s)"
    DIR="LTR | RTL"
    DISABLED
    ID="unique alphanumeric identifier"
    LABEL="text description"
    LANG="language code"
    SELECTED
    STYLE="style information"
    TITLE="advisory text"
    VALUE="option value"
    onclick="script"
    ondblclick="script"
    onkeydown="script"
    onkeypress="script"
    onkeyup="script"
    onmousedown="script"
```

```
        onmousemove="script"
        onmouseout="script"
        onmouseover="script"
        onmouseup="script">
```

```
</OPTION>
```

Attributes and Events Defined by Internet Explorer 4

```
        LANGUAGE="JAVASCRIPT | JSCRIPT | VBS | VBSCRIPT"
        ondragstart="script"
        onselectstart="script"
```

Attributes

CLASS   See "Core Attributes Reference," earlier in this appendix.

DIR   See "Language Reference," earlier in this appendix.

DISABLED   Presence of this attribute indicates that the particular item is not selectable.

ID   See "Core Attributes Reference," earlier in this appendix.

LABEL   This attribute contains a short label that may be more appealing to use when the selection list is rendered as a hierarchy due to the presence of an **<OPTGROUP>** element.

LANG   See "Language Reference," earlier in this appendix.

LANGUAGE   In the Microsoft implementation, this attribute specifies the scripting language to be used with an associated script bound to the element, typically through an event handler attribute. Possible values may include **JAVASCRIPT, JSCRIPT, VBS,** and **VBSCRIPT.** Other values that include the version of the language used, such as **JavaScript1.1,** may also be possible.

SELECTED   This attribute indicates that the associated item is the default selection. If not included, the first item in the selection list is the default. If the **<SELECT>** element enclosing the **<OPTION>** elements has the **MULTIPLE** attribute, the **SELECTED** attribute may occur in multiple entries. Otherwise, it should occur only in one entry.

STYLE   See "Core Attributes Reference," earlier in this appendix.

TITLE   See "Core Attributes Reference," earlier in this appendix.

VALUE   This attribute indicates the value to include with the form result when the item is selected.

Attribute and Event Support

NETSCAPE 4   SELECTED and VALUE. (CLASS, ID, LANG, and STYLE are implied.)

INTERNET EXPLORER 4   CLASS, ID, LANGUAGE, SELECTED, VALUE, **ondragstart**, and **onselectstart**.

WEBTV   SELECTED and VALUE.

Event Handlers
See "Events Reference," earlier in this appendix.

Examples

```
Where would you like to go for your vacation?<BR>
<SELECT>
   <OPTION ID="choice1" VALUE="China">The Great Wall
   <OPTION ID="choice2" VALUE="Mexico">Los Cabos
   <OPTION ID="choice3" VALUE="Home" SELECTED>Your backyard
</SELECT>
```

Compatibility

HTML 2, 3.2, and 4
Internet Explorer 2, 3, 4, and 5
Netscape 1, 2, 3, 4, and 4.5
WebTV

Notes

- The closing tag for **<OPTION>** is optional.
- This element should only occur within the context of a **<SELECT>** element.
- The HTML 2.0 and 3.2 specifications define only the **SELECTED** and **VALUE** attributes for this element.

<P>   (Paragraph)
This element is used to define a paragraph of text. Browsers typically insert a blank line before and after a paragraph of text.

Syntax

```
<P
    ALIGN="CENTER | JUSTIFY | LEFT | RIGHT"
          (transitional)
```

```
CLASS="class name(s)"
DIR="LTR | RTL"
ID="unique alphanumeric identifier"
LANG="language code"
STYLE="style information"
TITLE="advisory text"
onclick="script"
ondblclick="script"
onkeydown="script"
onkeypress="script"
onkeyup="script"
onmousedown="script"
onmousemove="script"
onmouseout="script"
onmouseover="script"
onmouseup="script">

</P>
```

Attributes and Events Defined by Internet Explorer 4

```
LANGUAGE="JAVASCRIPT | JSCRIPT | VBS | VBSCRIPT"
ondragstart="script"
onhelp="script"
onselectstart="script"
```

Attributes

ALIGN   This attribute specifies the alignment of text within a paragraph. The default value is **LEFT**. The transitional specification of HTML 4.0 also defines **CENTER**, **JUSTIFY**, and **RIGHT**. However, under the strict specification of HTML 4.0 text alignment can be handled through a style sheet rule.

CLASS   See "Core Attributes Reference," earlier in this appendix.

DIR   See "Language Reference," earlier in this appendix.

ID   See "Core Attributes Reference," earlier in this appendix.

LANG   See "Language Reference," earlier in this appendix.

LANGUAGE   In the Microsoft implementation, this attribute specifies the scripting language to be used with an associated script bound to the element, typically through an event handler attribute. Possible values may include **JAVASCRIPT**, **JSCRIPT**, **VBS**, and **VBSCRIPT**. Other values that include the version of the language used, such as **JavaScript1.1**, may also be possible.

STYLE   See "Core Attributes Reference," earlier in this appendix.

TITLE   See "Core Attributes Reference," earlier in this appendix.

Attribute and Event Support

NETSCAPE 4   ALIGN. (**CLASS, ID, LANG,** and **STYLE** are implied.)

INTERNET EXPLORER 4   All attributes and events except **DIR**. (Note: The **JUSTIFY** value for **ALIGN** is not supported by Internet Explorer 4.)

WEBTV   ALIGN (**CENTER | LEFT | RIGHT**).

Event Handlers

See "Events Reference," earlier in this appendix.

Examples

```
<P ALIGN="RIGHT">A right-aligned paragraph</P>

<P ID="Para1" CLASS="defaultParagraph"
   TITLE="Introduction Paragraph">
This is the introductory paragraph for a very long paper about nothing.
</P>
```

Compatibility

HTML 2, 3.2, and 4
Internet Explorer 2, 3, 4, and 5
Netscape 1, 2, 3, 4, and 4.5
Web TV

Notes

■ Under the strict HTML 4.0 specification the **ALIGN** attribute is not supported. Alignment of text can be accomplished using style sheets.

■ The closing tag for the **<P>** element is optional.

■ As a logical element, empty paragraphs are ignored by browsers, so do not try to use multiple **<P>** elements in a row like **<P><P><P><P>** to add blank lines to a Web page. This will not work; use the **
** element instead.

■ The HTML 3.2 specification supports only the **ALIGN** attribute with values of **CENTER, LEFT,** and **RIGHT**.

■ The HTML 2.0 specification supports no attributes for the **<P>** element.

<PARAM>   (Object Parameter)

This element specifies a parameter to pass to an embedded object using the **<OBJECT>** or **<APPLET>** element. This element should occur only within the scope of one of these elements.

Syntax

```
<PARAM
    ID="unique alphanumeric identifier"
    NAME="parameter name"
    TYPE="MIME Type"
    VALUE="parameter value"
    VALUETYPE="DATA | OBJECT | REF">

</PARAM>
```

Attributes Defined by Internet Explorer 4

```
    DATAFLD="column name"
    DATAFORMATAS="HTML | TEXT"
    DATASRC="data source ID"
```

Attributes

DATAFLD   This Internet Explorer–specific attribute is used to indicate the column name in the data source that is bound to the **<PARAM>** element's value.

DATAFORMATAS   This Internet Explorer–specific attribute indicates if the bound data is plain text (**TEXT**) or HTML (**HTML**).

DATASRC   The value of this attribute is set to an identifier indicating the data source to pull data from. Bound data is used to set the value of the parameters passed to the object or applet with which this **<PARAM>** element is associated.

ID   See "Core Attributes Reference," earlier in this appendix.

NAME   This attribute contains the parameter's name. The name of the parameter depends on the particular object being inserted into the page, and it is assumed that the object knows how to handle the passed data. Do not confuse the **NAME** attribute with the **NAME** attribute used for form elements. In the latter case, the **NAME** attribute does not have a similar meaning as **ID**, but rather specifies the name of the data to be passed to an enclosing **<OBJECT>** element.

TYPE   When the **VALUETYPE** attribute is set to **REF**, the **TYPE** attribute can be used to indicate the type of the information to be retrieved. Legal values for this attribute are in the form of MIME types such as **text/html**.

VALUE This attribute contains the parameter's value. The actual contents of this attribute depend on the object and the particular parameter being passed in, as determined by the **NAME** attribute.

VALUETYPE This HTML 4–specific attribute specifies the type of the **VALUE** attribute being passed in. Possible values for this attribute include **DATA**, **OBJECT**, and **REF**. A value of **DATA** specifies that the information passed in through the **VALUE** parameter should be treated just as data. A value of **REF** indicates that the information being passed in is a URL that indicates where the data to use is located. The information is not retrieved, but the URL is passed to the object which may then retrieve the information if necessary. The last value of **OBJECT** indicates that the value being passed in is the name of an object as set by its **ID** attribute. In practice, the **DATA** attribute is used by default.

Attribute and Event Support

NETSCAPE 4 NAME and VALUE. (**ID** may be implied.)

INTERNET EXPLORER 4 NAME, DATAFLD, DATAFORMATAS, DATASRC, and VALUE.

Event Handlers
None.

Examples

```
<APPLET CODE="plot.class">
   <PARAM NAME="min" VALUE="5">
   <PARAM NAME="max" VALUE="30">
   <PARAM NAME="ticks" VALUE=".5">
   <PARAM NAME="line-style" VALUE="dotted">
</APPLET>

<OBJECT CLASSID="clsid:D27CDB6E-AE6D-11cf-96B8-444553540000"
        CODEBASE="swflash.cab#version=2,0,0,0"
        HEIGHT="100" WIDTH="100">
   <PARAM ID="param1" NAME="Movie" VALUE="SplashLogo.swf">
   <PARAM ID="param2" NAME="Play" VALUE="True">
</OBJECT>
```

Compatibility

HTML 3.2 and 4
Internet Explorer 3, 4, and 5
Netscape 2, 3, 4, and 4.5

Notes

- The closing tag for this element is forbidden.
- The HTML 3.2 specification supports only the **NAME** and **VALUE** attributes for this element.

<PLAINTEXT> (Plain Text)

This deprecated element from the HTML 2.0 specification renders the enclosed text as plain text and forces the browser to ignore any enclosed HTML. Typically, information affected by the <PLAINTEXT> element is rendered in monospaced font. This element is no longer part of the HTML standard.

Syntax (HTML 2; Deprecated Under HTML 4)

```
<PLAINTEXT>
```

Attributes and Events Defined by Internet Explorer 4

```
CLASS="class name(s)"
DIR="LTR | RTL"
ID="unique alphanumeric identifier"
LANG="language code"
LANGUAGE="JAVASCRIPT | JSCRIPT | VBS | VBSCRIPT"
STYLE="style information"
TITLE="advisory text"
onclick="script"
ondblclick="script"
ondragstart="script"
onhelp="script"
onkeydown="script"
onkeypress="script"
onkeyup="script"
onmousedown="script"
onmousemove="script"
onmouseout="script"
onmouseover="script"
onmouseup="script"
onselectstart="script"
```

Attributes

CLASS   See "Core Attributes Reference," earlier in this appendix.

DIR   See "Language Reference," earlier in this appendix.

ID   See "Core Attributes Reference," earlier in this appendix.

LANG   See "Language Reference," earlier in this appendix.

LANGUAGE   In the Microsoft implementation, this attribute specifies the scripting language to be used with an associated script bound to the element, typically through an event handler attribute. Possible values may include **JAVASCRIPT**, **JSCRIPT**, **VBS**, and **VBSCRIPT**. Other values that include the version of the language used, such as **JavaScript1.1**, may also be possible.

STYLE   See "Core Attributes Reference," earlier in this appendix.

TITLE   See "Core Attributes Reference," earlier in this appendix.

Attribute and Event Support

NETSCAPE 4   **CLASS**, **ID**, **LANG**, and **STYLE** are implied.

INTERNET EXPLORER 4   All attributes and events.

Event Handlers
See "Events Reference," earlier in this appendix.

Example

```
<HTML>
<HEAD><TITLE>Plaintext Example</TITLE></HEAD>
<BODY>
The rest of this file is in plain text.
<PLAINTEXT>
Even though this is supposed to be <B>bold</B>, the tags still show.
There is no way to turn plain text off once it is on. </PLAINTEXT>
does nothing to help. Even </BODY> and </HTML> will show up.
```

Compatibility

HTML 2
Internet Explorer 2, 3, 4, and 5
Netscape 1, 2, 3, 4, and 4.5

Notes

- No closing tag for this element is necessary, since the browser will ignore all tags after the starting tag.

- This element should not be used. Plain text information can be indicated by a file type, and information can be inserted in a preformatted fashion using the **<PRE>** element.

<PRE> (Preformatted Text)

This element is used to indicate that the enclosed text is preformatted, meaning that spaces, returns, tabs, and other formatting characters are preserved. Browsers do, however, acknowledge most HTML elements that are found with the **<PRE>** element. Preformatted text is generally rendered by the browsers in a monospaced font.

Syntax

```
<PRE
     CLASS="class name(s)"
     DIR="LTR | RTL"
     ID="unique alphanumeric value"
     LANG="language code"
     STYLE="style information"
     TITLE="advisory text"
     WIDTH="number" (transitional)
     onclick="script"
     ondblclick="script"
     onkeydown="script"
     onkeypress="script"
     onkeyup="script"
     onmousedown="script"
     onmousemove="script"
     onmouseout="script"
     onmouseover="script"
     onmouseup="script">

</PRE>
```

Attributes and Events Defined by Internet Explorer 4

```
     LANGUAGE="JAVASCRIPT | JSCRIPT | VBS | VBSCRIPT"
     ondragstart="script"
     onhelp="script"
     onselectstart="script"
```

Attributes and Events Defined by Netscape 4

```
     COL="columns"
     WRAP
```

Attributes

CLASS   See "Core Attributes Reference," earlier in this appendix.

DIR   See "Language Reference," earlier in this appendix.

ID   See "Core Attributes Reference," earlier in this appendix.

LANG   See "Language Reference," earlier in this appendix.

LANGUAGE   In the Microsoft implementation, this attribute specifies the scripting language to be used with an associated script bound to the element, typically through an event handler attribute. Possible values may include **JAVASCRIPT**, **JSCRIPT**, **VBS**, and **VBSCRIPT**. Other values that include the version of the language used, such as **JavaScript1.1**, may also be possible.

STYLE   See "Core Attributes Reference," earlier in this appendix.

TITLE   See "Core Attributes Reference," earlier in this appendix.

WIDTH   This attribute should be set to the **WIDTH** of the preformatted region. The value of the attribute should be the number of characters to display. In practice, this attribute is not supported and is dropped under the strict HTML 4.0 specification.

Attribute and Event Support

NETSCAPE 4   CLASS, COLS, ID, LANG, STYLE, and WRAP.

INTERNET EXPLORER 4   All attributes and events except **DIR** and **WIDTH**.

Event Handlers

See "Events Reference," earlier in this appendix.

Example

```
<PRE>
Within PREFORMATTED text      A L L      formatting IS      PRESERVED
NO  m    a    t    e    r how wild it is. Remember that some
<B>HTML</B> markup is allowed within the &lt;PRE&gt; element.
</PRE>
```

Compatibility

HTML 2, 3.2, and 4
Internet Explorer 2, 3, 4, and 5
Netscape 1, 2, 3, 4, and 4.5
WebTV

Notes

■ The HTML 4.0 transitional specification states that the **<APPLET>**, **<BASEFONT>**, **<BIG>**, **<FONT>**, **<IMG>**, **<OBJECT>**, **<SMALL>**, **<SUB>**, and **<SUP>** elements should not be used within the **<PRE>** element. The strict HTML 4.0 specification states that only the **<BIG>**, **<IMG>**, **<OBJECT>**, **<SMALL>**, **<SUB>**, and **<SUP>** elements should not be used within the **<PRE>** element. The other excluded elements are missing, as they are deprecated from the strict specification. While these attributes should not be used, it appears that the two most popular browsers render them anyway.

- The strict HTML 4.0 specification drops support for the **WIDTH** attribute, which was not generally supported anyway.

- The HTML 2.0 and 3.2 specifications support only the **WIDTH** attribute for **<PRE>**.

<Q> (Quote)

This element indicates that the enclosed text is a short inline quotation.

Syntax

```
<Q
    CITE="URL of source"
    CLASS="class name(s)"
    DIR="LTR | RTL"
    ID="unique alphanumeric string"
    LANG="language code"
    STYLE="style information"
    TITLE="advisory text"
    onclick="script"
    ondblclick="script"
    onkeydown="script"
    onkeypress="script"
    onkeyup="script"
    onmousedown="script"
    onmousemove="script"
    onmouseout="script"
    onmouseover="script"
    onmouseup="script">

</Q>
```

Attributes and Events Defined by Internet Explorer 4

```
    LANGUAGE="JAVASCRIPT | JSCRIPT | VBS | VBSCRIPT"
    ondragstart="script"
    onhelp="script"
    onselectstart="script"
```

Attributes

CITE   The value of this attribute is a URL that designates a source document or message for the information quoted. This attribute is intended to point to information explaining the context or the reference for the quote.

CLASS   See "Core Attributes Reference," earlier in this appendix.

DIR   See "Language Reference," earlier in this appendix.

ID   See "Core Attributes Reference," earlier in this appendix.

LANG   See "Language Reference," earlier in this appendix.

LANGUAGE   In the Microsoft implementation, this attribute specifies the scripting language to be used with an associated script bound to the element, typically through an event handler attribute. Possible values may include **JAVASCRIPT**, **JSCRIPT**, **VBS**, and **VBSCRIPT**. Other values that include the version of the language used, such as **JavaScript1.1**, may also be possible.

STYLE   See "Core Attributes Reference," earlier in this appendix.

TITLE   See "Core Attributes Reference," earlier in this appendix.

Attribute and Event Support

INTERNET EXPLORER 4   All attributes and events except **CITE** and **DIR**.

Event Handlers
See "Events Reference," earlier in this appendix.

Example

```
<Q STYLE="color: green">"A few green balls and a rainbow bar will give
you an exciting Web page Christmas tree!"</Q>
```

Compatibility

HTML 4
Internet Explorer 4 and 5

Notes

■ This element is intended for short quotations that don't require paragraph breaks, as compared to text that would be contained within **<BLOCKQUOTE>**. Microsoft documentation continues to indicate this is a block element, when it is not.

■ Internet Explorer does not make any sort of style change for quotations, but it is possible to apply a style rule.

<S> (Strikethrough)

This element renders the enclosed text with a line drawn through it.

Syntax (Transitional Only)

```
<S
    CLASS="class name(s)"
    DIR="LTR | RTL"
    ID="unique alphanumeric identifier"
    LANG="language code"
    STYLE="style information"
    TITLE="advisory text"
    onclick="script"
    ondblclick="script"
    onkeydown="script"
    onkeypress="script"
    onkeyup="script"
    onmousedown="script"
    onmousemove="script"
    onmouseout="script"
    onmouseover="script"
    onmouseup="script">

</S>
```

Attributes and Events Defined by Internet Explorer 4

```
    LANGUAGE="JAVASCRIPT | JSCRIPT | VBS | VBSCRIPT"
    ondragstart="script"
    onhelp="script"
    onselectstart="script"
```

Attributes

CLASS   See "Core Attributes Reference," earlier in this appendix.

DIR   See "Language Reference," earlier in this appendix.

ID   See "Core Attributes Reference," earlier in this appendix.

LANG   See "Language Reference," earlier in this appendix.

LANGUAGE   In the Microsoft implementation, this attribute specifies the scripting language to be used with an associated script bound to the element, typically through an event handler attribute. Possible values may include **JAVASCRIPT, JSCRIPT, VBS,** and **VBSCRIPT.** Other values that include the version of the language used, such as **JavaScript1.1,** may also be possible.

STYLE   See "Core Attributes Reference," earlier in this appendix.

TITLE   See "Core Attributes Reference," earlier in this appendix.

Attribute and Event Support

NETSCAPE 4   CLASS, ID, LANG, and STYLE are implied.

INTERNET EXPLORER 4   All attributes and events except **DIR.**

Event Handlers

See "Events Reference," earlier in this appendix.

Examples

```
This line contains a <S>misstake</S>.

<S ID="strike1"
    onmouseover="this.style.color='red'"
    onmouseout="this.style.color='black'">Fastball</S>
```

Compatibility

HTML 4 (transitional)
Internet Explorer 2, 3, 4, and 5
Netscape 3, 4, and 4.5
WebTV

Notes

- This element should act the same as the **<STRIKE>** element.
- This HTML 3 element was eventually adopted by Netscape and Microsoft and was later incorporated into the HTML 4.0 transitional specification.
- The strict HTML 4.0 specification does not include the **<S>** element or the **<STRIKE>** element. It is possible to indicate strikethrough text using a style sheet.

<SAMP>   (Sample Text)

This element is used to indicate sample text. Enclosed text is generally rendered in a monospaced font.

Syntax

```
<SAMP
    CLASS="class name(s)"
    DIR="LTR | RTL"
    ID="unique alphanumeric string"
    LANG="language code"
    STYLE="style information"
    TITLE="advisory text"
    onclick="script"
    ondblclick="script"
    onkeydown="script"
    onkeypress="script"
    onkeyup="script"
    onmousedown="script"
    onmousemove="script"
    onmouseout="script"
    onmouseover="script"
    onmouseup="script">

</SAMP>
```

Attributes and Events Defined by Internet Explorer 4

```
    LANGUAGE="JAVASCRIPT | JSCRIPT | VBS | VBSCRIPT"
    ondragstart="script"
    onhelp="script"
    onselectstart="script"
```

Attributes

CLASS   See "Core Attributes Reference," earlier in this appendix.

DIR   See "Language Reference," earlier in this appendix.

ID   See "Core Attributes Reference," earlier in this appendix.

LANG   See "Language Reference," earlier in this appendix.

LANGUAGE   In the Microsoft implementation, this attribute specifies the scripting language to be used with an associated script bound to the element, typically through an event handler attribute. Possible values may include **JAVASCRIPT**, **JSCRIPT**, **VBS**, and **VBSCRIPT**. Other values that include the version of the language used, such as **JavaScript1.1**, may also be possible.

STYLE   See "Core Attributes Reference," earlier in this appendix.

TITLE   See "Core Attributes Reference," earlier in this appendix.

Attribute and Event Support

INTERNET EXPLORER 4   All attributes and events except **DIR**.

Event Handlers
See "Events Reference," earlier in this appendix.

Example

```
Use the following salutation in all e-mail messages to the boss:
<SAMP>Please excuse the interruption, oh exalted manager.</SAMP>
```

Compatibility

HTML 2, 3.2, and 4
Internet Explorer 2, 3, 4, and 5
Netscape 1, 2, 3, 4, and 4.5
WebTV

Notes

- As a logical element, **<SAMP>** is useful to bind style rules to.
- The HTML 2.0 and 3.2 specifications supported no attributes for this element.

<SCRIPT>   (Scripting)

This element encloses statements in a scripting language for client-side processing. Scripting statements can either be included inline or loaded from an external file and may be commented out to avoid execution by non-scripting-aware browsers.

Syntax

```
<SCRIPT
    CHARSET="character set"
    DEFER
    EVENT="event name" (reserved)
    FOR="element ID" (reserved)
    LANGUAGE="scripting language name"
    SRC="URL of script code"
    TYPE="MIME type">

</SCRIPT>
```

Attributes Defined by Internet Explorer 4

```
CLASS="class name(s)"
ID="unique alphanumeric identifier"
TITLE="advisory text"
```

Attributes

CHARSET This attribute defines the character encoding of the script. The value is a space-and/or comma-delimited list of character sets as defined in RFC 2045. The default value is **ISO-8859-1**.

CLASS This Microsoft-defined attribute does not make much sense given that scripting code would not be bound by style sheet rules. Its meaning as defined in the "Core Attributes Reference" in this appendix is unclear within the context of the **<SCRIPT>** element.

DEFER The presence of this attribute indicates that the browser may defer execution of the script enclosed by the **<SCRIPT>** element. In practice, deferring code may be more up to the position of the **<SCRIPT>** element or the contents. This attribute was added very late to the HTML 4.0 specification and its support is currently minimal.

EVENT This Microsoft attribute is used to define a particular event that the script should react to. It must be used in conjunction with the **FOR** attribute. Event names are the same as event handler attributes, for example, **onclick**, **ondblclick**, and so on.

FOR The **FOR** attribute is used to define the name or ID of the element to which an event defined by the **EVENT** attribute is related. For example, **<SCRIPT EVENT="onclick" FOR="button1" LANGUAGE="VBSCRIPT">** defines a VBScript that executes when a click event is issued for an element named **button1**.

ID See "Core Attributes Reference," earlier in this appendix.

LANGUAGE This attribute specifies the scripting language being used. The Netscape implementation supports JavaScript. The Microsoft implementation supports JScript (a JavaScript clone) as well as VBScript, which can be indicated by either **VBS** or **VBSCRIPT**. Other values that include the version of the language used, such as **JavaScript1.1** and **JavaScript1.2**, may also be possible and are useful to exclude browsers from executing script code that is not supported.

SRC This attribute specifies the URL of a file containing scripting code. Typically, files containing JavaScript code have a .js extension, and a server attaches the appropriate MIME type; if not, the **TYPE** attribute may be used to explicitly set the content type of the external script file. The **LANGUAGE** attribute may also be helpful in determining this.

TITLE See "Core Attributes Reference," earlier in this appendix.

TYPE   This attribute should be set to the MIME type corresponding to the scripting language used. For JavaScript, for example, this would be **text/javascript**. In practice, the **LANGUAGE** attribute is the more common way to indicate which scripting language is in effect.

Attribute and Event Support

NETSCAPE 4   LANGUAGE and **SRC**.

INTERNET EXPLORER 4   All attributes and events except **CHARSET** and **DEFER**.

WEBTV   LANGUAGE and **SRC**.

Event Handlers

There are no events directly associated with the **<SCRIPT>** element. However, the Microsoft implementation does allow the **EVENT** attribute to be used to indicate what event a particular script may be associated with.

Examples

```
<SCRIPT LANGUAGE="JavaScript">
<!-- alert("Hello World !!!"); // -->
</SCRIPT>

<!-- code in external file -->
<SCRIPT LANGUAGE="JavaScript1.2" SRC="superrollover.js">
</SCRIPT>

<SCRIPT FOR="myButton" EVENT="onclick"
        LANGUAGE="JavaScript">
<!-- alert("I've been clicked!"); // -->
</SCRIPT>

<FORM>
   <INPUT TYPE="BUTTON" NAME="myButton" VALUE="Click me">
</FORM>
```

Compatibility

HTML 4
Internet Explorer 3, 4, and 5
Netscape 2, 3, 4, and 4.5

Notes

■ It is common practice to "comment out" statements enclosed by the **<SCRIPT>** element. Without commenting, scripts are displayed as page content by browsers that do not support scripting. The particular comment style may be dependent on the language being used. For example, in JavaScript use the following style.

```
<SCRIPT LANGUAGE="JavaScript">
<!-- JavaScript code here // -->
</SCRIPT>
```

and in VBScript use

```
<SCRIPT LANGUAGE="VBSCRIPT">
<!-- VBScript code here // -->
</SCRIPT>
```

- The HTML 3.2 specification defined a placeholder **<SCRIPT>** element, but otherwise the element is new to HTML 4.
- Refer to the **<NOSCRIPT>** element in this appendix to see how content may be identified for non-scripting-aware browsers.

<SELECT>   (Selection List)

This element defines a selection list within a form. Depending on the form of the selection list, the control allows the user to select one or more list options.

Syntax

```
<SELECT
    CLASS="class name(s)"
    DIR="LTR | RTL"
    DISABLED
    ID="unique alphanumeric identifier"
    LANG="language code"
    MULTIPLE
    NAME="unique alphanumeric name"
    SIZE="number"
    STYLE="style information"
    TABINDEX="number"
    TITLE="advisory text"
    onblur="script"
    onchange="script"
    onclick="script"
    ondblclick="script"
    onfocus="script"
    onkeydown="script"
    onkeypress="script"
    onkeyup="script"
    onmousedown="script"
    onmousemove="script"
    onmouseout="script"
    onmouseover="script"
```

```
        onmouseup="script">

    <OPTION> elements

</SELECT>
```

Attributes and Events Defined by Internet Explorer 4

```
    ACCESSKEY="character"
    ALIGN="ABSBOTTOM | ABSMIDDLE | BASELINE | BOTTOM |
          LEFT | MIDDLE | RIGHT | TEXTTOP | TOP"
    DATAFLD="column name"
    DATASRC="data source ID"
    LANGUAGE="JAVASCRIPT | JSCRIPT | VBS | VBSCRIPT"
    onafterupdate="script"
    onbeforeupdate="script"
    ondragstart="script"
    onhelp="script"
    onresize="script"
    onrowenter="script"
    onrowexit="script"
    onselectstart="script"
```

Attributes Defined by WebTV

```
    AUTOACTIVATE
    BGCOLOR="color name | #RRGGBB"
    EXCLUSIVE
    SELCOLOR="color name | #RRGGBB"
    TEXT="color name | #RRGGBB"
    USESTYLE
```

Attributes

ACCESSKEY   This Microsoft attribute specifies a keyboard navigation accelerator for the element. Pressing ALT or a similar key in association with the specified character selects the form control correlated with that key sequence. Page designers are forewarned to avoid key sequences already bound to browsers.

ALIGN   This Microsoft-specific attribute controls the alignment of the image with respect to the content on the page. The default value is **LEFT,** but other values such as **ABSBOTTOM, ABSMIDDLE, BASELINE, BOTTOM, MIDDLE, RIGHT, TEXTTOP,** and **TOP** may also be supported. The meaning of these values should be similar to inserted objects such as images.

AUTOACTIVATE   In the WebTV implementation, this attribute causes the selection list control to immediately activate when the user selects it, allowing the user to quickly use the arrow keys to move up and down. Without this attribute, the process is a two-step procedure to select the control and then move around.

BGCOLOR   In the WebTV implementation, this attribute specifies the background color of the selection list. The value for this attribute can be either a named color, such as **red**, or a color specified in the hexadecimal *#RRGGBB* format, such as **#FF0000**.

CLASS   See "Core Attributes Reference," earlier in this appendix.

DATAFLD   This attribute is used to indicate the column name in the data source that is bound to the options in the **<SELECT>** element.

DATASRC   The value of this attribute is set to an identifier indicating the data source to pull data from.

DIR   See "Language Reference," earlier in this appendix.

DISABLED   This attribute is used to turn off a form control so that elements will not be submitted, and will not receive any focus from the keyboard or mouse. Disabled form controls will not be part of the tabbing order. The browser may also gray out the form that is disabled, in order to indicate to the user that the form control is inactive. This attribute requires no value.

EXCLUSIVE   In the WebTV implementation, this attribute prevents duplicate entries in the selection list. The attribute requires no value.

ID   See "Core Attributes Reference," earlier in this appendix.

LANG   See "Language Reference," earlier in this appendix.

LANGUAGE   In the Microsoft implementation, this attribute specifies the scripting language to be used with an associated script bound to the element, typically through an event handler attribute. Possible values may include **JAVASCRIPT**, **JSCRIPT**, **VBS**, and **VBSCRIPT**. Other values that include the version of the language used, such as **JavaScript1.1**, may also be possible.

MULTIPLE   This attribute allows the selection of multiple items in the selection list. The default is single-item selection.

NAME   This attribute allows a form control to be assigned a name so that it can be referenced by a scripting language. **NAME** is supported by older browsers such as Netscape 2-generation browsers, but the W3C encourages the use of the **ID** attribute. For compatibility purposes both may have to be used.

SELCOLOR   In the WebTV implementation, this attribute specifies the background color for selected items. Its value can be either a named color, such as **green**, or a color specified in the hexadecimal *#RRGGBB* format, such as **#00FF00**. The default for this attribute in WebTV is **#EAEAEA**.

SIZE   This attribute sets the number of visible items in the selection list. When the **MULTIPLE** attribute is not present, only one entry should show; however, when **MULTIPLE** is present, this attribute is useful to set the size of the scrolling list box.

STYLE   See "Core Attributes Reference," earlier in this appendix.

TABINDEX   This attribute takes a numeric value indicating the position of the form control in the tabbing index for the form. Tabbing proceeds from the lowest positive **TABINDEX** value to the highest. Negative values for **TABINDEX** will leave the form control out of the tabbing order. When tabbing is not explicitly set, the browser may tab through items in the order they are encountered. Form controls that are disabled due to the presence of the **DISABLED** attribute will not be part of the tabbing index, though read-only controls will be.

TEXT   In the WebTV implementation, this attribute specifies the text color for items in the list. Its value can be either a named color, such as **blue**, or a color specified in the hexadecimal *#RRGGBB* format, such as **#0000FF**.

TITLE   See "Core Attributes Reference," earlier in this appendix.

USESTYLE   This WebTV-specific attribute causes text to be rendered in the style in effect for the page. The attribute requires no value.

Attribute and Event Support

NETSCAPE 4   MULTIPLE, NAME, SIZE, **onblur**, **onchange**, and **onfocus**. (CLASS, ID, LANG, and STYLE are implied.)

INTERNET EXPLORER 4   All W3C-defined attributes and events except **DIR** and **TITLE**, and all attributes and events defined by Internet Explorer 4.

WEBTV   AUTOACTIVATE, BGCOLOR, MULTIPLE, NAME, SELCOLOR, SIZE, TEXT, USESTYLE, **onblur**, **onchange**, **onfocus**, and **onclick**.

Event Handlers
See "Events Reference," earlier in this appendix.

Examples

```
Choose your favorite colors
<SELECT MULTIPLE SIZE="2">
   <OPTION>Red
   <OPTION>Blue
   <OPTION>Green
   <OPTION>Yellow
</SELECT>
```

APPENDIXES

```
Taco Choices
<SELECT NAME="tacomenu">
   <OPTION VALUE="SuperChicken">Chicken
   <OPTION VALUE="Baja">Fish
   <OPTION VALUE="RX-Needed">Carnitas
</SELECT>
```

Compatibility

HTML 2, 3.2, and 4
Internet Explorer 2, 3, 4, and 5
Netscape 1, 2, 3, 4, and 4.5
WebTV

Notes

■ The HTML 4.0 specification reserves the attributes **DATAFLD** and **DATASRC** for future use.

■ The HTML 2.0 and 3.2 specifications define only **MULTIPLE**, **NAME**, and **SIZE** attributes.

<SMALL>   (Small Text)

This element renders the enclosed text one font size smaller than a document's base font size unless it is already set to the smallest size.

Syntax

```
<SMALL
    CLASS="class name(s)"
    DIR="LTR | RTL"
    ID="unique alphanumeric string"
    LANG="language code"
    STYLE="style information"
    TITLE="advisory text"
    onclick="script"
    ondblclick="script"
    onkeydown="script"
    onkeypress="script"
    onkeyup="script"
    onmousedown="script"
    onmousemove="script"
    onmouseout="script"
    onmouseover="script"
    onmouseup="script">

</SMALL>
```

Attributes and Events Defined by Internet Explorer 4

```
LANGUAGE="JAVASCRIPT | JSCRIPT | VBS | VBSCRIPT"
ondragstart="script"
onhelp="script"
onselectstart="script"
```

Attributes

CLASS   See "Core Attributes Reference," earlier in this appendix.

DIR   See "Language Reference," earlier in this appendix.

ID   See "Core Attributes Reference," earlier in this appendix.

LANG   See "Language Reference," earlier in this appendix.

LANGUAGE   In the Microsoft implementation, this attribute specifies the scripting language to be used with an associated script bound to the element, typically through an event handler attribute. Possible values may include **JAVASCRIPT**, **JSCRIPT**, **VBS**, and **VBSCRIPT**. Other values that include the version of the language used, such as **JavaScript1.1**, may also be possible.

STYLE   See "Core Attributes Reference," earlier in this appendix.

TITLE   See "Core Attributes Reference," earlier in this appendix.

Attribute and Event Support

NETSCAPE 4   **CLASS**, **ID**, **LANG**, and **STYLE** are implied.

INTERNET EXPLORER 4   All attributes and events except **DIR**.

Event Handlers
See "Events Reference," earlier in this appendix.

Examples

```
Here is some <SMALL>small text</SMALL>.

This element can be applied <SMALL><SMALL><SMALL>multiple
times</SMALL></SMALL></SMALL>to make things even smaller.
```

Compatibility

HTML 3.2 and 4
Internet Explorer 2, 3, 4, and 5

Netscape 2, 3, 4, and 4.5
WebTV

Notes

- The **<SMALL>** element can be used multiple times to decrease the size of text to a greater degree. Using more than six **<SMALL>** elements together doesn't make sense, since browsers currently only support relative font sizes from 1 to 7. As style sheets become more common, this element may fall out of favor.

- The default base font size for a document is typically 3, although it can be changed with the **<BASEFONT>** element.

<SPACER> (Extra Space)

This proprietary element specifies an invisible region for pushing content around a page.

Syntax (Defined by Netscape 3)

```
<SPACER
    ALIGN="ABSMIDDLE | ABSBOTTOM | BASELINE | BOTTOM |
           LEFT | MIDDLE | RIGHT | TEXTTOP | TOP"
    HEIGHT="pixels"
    SIZE="pixels"
    TYPE="BLOCK | HORIZONTAL | VERTICAL"
    WIDTH="pixels">
```

Attributes

ALIGN   This attribute specifies the alignment of the spacer with respect to surrounding text. It is only used with spacers with **TYPE="BLOCK"**. The default value for the **ALIGN** attribute is **BOTTOM**. The meanings of the **ALIGN** values are similar to those used with the **<IMG>** element.

HEIGHT   This attribute specifies the height of the invisible region in pixels. It is only used with spacers with **TYPE="BLOCK"**.

SIZE   Used with **TYPE="BLOCK"** and **TYPE="HORIZONTAL"** spacers, this attribute sets the spacer's width in pixels. Used with a **TYPE="VERTICAL"** spacer, this attribute is used to set the spacer's height.

TYPE   This attribute indicates the type of invisible region. A **HORIZONTAL** spacer adds horizontal space between words and objects. A **VERTICAL** spacer is used to add space between lines. A **BLOCK** spacer defines a general-purpose positioning rectangle like an invisible image that text may flow around.

WIDTH   This attribute is used only with the **TYPE="BLOCK"** spacer and is used to set the width of the region in pixels.

Attribute and Event Support

NETSCAPE 4   All attributes.

WEBTV   All attributes.

Examples

```
A line of text with two <SPACER TYPE="HORIZONTAL" SIZE="20">words
separated by 20 pixels. Here is a line of text.<BR>
<SPACER TYPE="VERTICAL" SIZE="50">

Here is another line of text with a large space between the two
lines.<SPACER ALIGN="LEFT" TYPE="BLOCK" HEIGHT="100" WIDTH="100"> This
is a bunch of text that flows around an invisible block region. You
could have easily performed this layout with a table.
```

Compatibility

Netscape 3, 4, and 4.5
WebTV

Notes

■ This element should not be used. If the effect of this element is required and style sheets cannot be used, an invisible pixel trick may be a more appropriate choice. The invisible pixel trick requires a transparent image, which is then resized with the **HEIGHT** and **WIDTH** attributes of the **<IMG>** element:

```
<IMG SRC="pixel.gif" HEIGHT="100" WIDTH="100">
```

■ This is an empty element; no closing tag is allowed.

<SPAN> (Text Span)

This element is used to group inline text, typically so scripting or style rules can be applied to the content. As it has no preset or rendering meaning, this is the most useful inline element for associating style and script with content.

Syntax

```
<SPAN
    CLASS="class name(s)"
    DATAFLD="column name" (reserved)
    DATAFORMATAS="HTML | TEXT" (reserved)
    DATASRC="data source ID" (reserved)
```

```
DIR="LTR | RTL"
ID="unique alphanumeric string"
LANG="language code"
STYLE="style information"
TITLE="advisory text"
onclick="script"
ondblclick="script"
onkeydown="script"
onkeypress="script"
onkeyup="script"
onmousedown="script"
onmousemove="script"
onmouseout="script"
onmouseover="script"
onmouseup="script">

</SPAN>
```

Attributes and Events Defined by Internet Explorer 4

```
LANGUAGE="JAVASCRIPT | JSCRIPT | VBS | VBSCRIPT"
ondragstart="script"
onhelp="script"
onselectstart="script"
```

Attributes

CLASS   See "Core Attributes Reference," earlier in this appendix.

DATAFLD   This attribute is used to indicate the column name in the data source that is bound to the contents of the **<SPAN>** element.

DATAFORMATAS   This attribute indicates if the bound data is plain text (**TEXT**) or HTML (**HTML**). The data bound with **<SPAN>** should be used to set the content of the element and may include HTML markup.

DATASRC   The value of this attribute is set to an identifier indicating the data source to pull data from.

DIR   See "Language Reference," earlier in this appendix.

ID   See "Core Attributes Reference," earlier in this appendix.

LANG   See "Language Reference," earlier in this appendix.

LANGUAGE   In the Microsoft implementation, this attribute specifies the scripting language to be used with an associated script bound to the element, typically through an event handler attribute. Possible values may include **JAVASCRIPT, JSCRIPT, VBS,** and **VBSCRIPT.** Other values that include the version of the language used, such as **JavaScript1.1,** may also be possible.

STYLE   See "Core Attributes Reference," earlier in this appendix.

TITLE   See "Core Attributes Reference," earlier in this appendix.

Attribute and Event Support

NETSCAPE 4   CLASS, ID, LANG, and STYLE.

INTERNET EXPLORER 4   All attributes and events except **DIR.**

Event Handlers
See "Events Reference," earlier in this appendix.

Examples

```
Here is some <SPAN STYLE="font: 14pt; color: purple">very
strange</SPAN> text.

<SPAN ID="toggletext"
      onclick="this.style.color='red'"
      ondblclick="this.style.color='black'">
Click and Double Click Me
</SPAN>
```

Compatibility

HTML 4
Internet Explorer 3, 4, and 5
Netscape 4 and 4.5

Notes

- ■ The HTML 4.0 specification reserves the **DATAFLD, DATAFORMATAS,** and **DATASRC** attributes for future use. Internet Explorer 4 supports them.
- ■ Unlike <DIV>, as an inline element <SPAN> does not cause any line breaks.

<STRIKE>   (Strikeout Text)

This element is used to indicate strikethrough text, namely text with a line drawn through it. The <S> element provides shorthand notation for this element.

Syntax (Transitional Only)

```
<STRIKE
     CLASS="class name(s)"
     DIR="LTR | RTL"
     ID="unique alphanumeric string"
     LANG="language code"
     STYLE="style information"
     TITLE="advisory text"
     onclick="script"
     ondblclick="script"
     onkeydown="script"
     onkeypress="script"
     onkeyup="script"
     onmousedown="script"
     onmousemove="script"
     onmouseout="script"
     onmouseover="script"
     onmouseup="script">

</STRIKE>
```

Attributes and Events Defined by Internet Explorer 4

```
     LANGUAGE="JAVASCRIPT | JSCRIPT | VBS | VBSCRIPT"
     ondragstart="script"
     onhelp="script"
     onselectstart="script"
```

Attributes

CLASS   See "Core Attributes Reference," earlier in this appendix.

DIR   See "Language Reference," earlier in this appendix.

ID   See "Core Attributes Reference," earlier in this appendix.

LANG   See "Language Reference," earlier in this appendix.

LANGUAGE   In the Microsoft implementation, this attribute specifies the scripting language to be used with an associated script bound to the element, typically through an event handler attribute. Possible values may include **JAVASCRIPT**, **JSCRIPT**, **VBS**, and **VBSCRIPT**. Other values that include the version of the language used, such as **JavaScript1.1**, may also be possible.

STYLE   See "Core Attributes Reference," earlier in this appendix.

TITLE   See "Core Attributes Reference," earlier in this appendix.

Attribute and Event Support

NETSCAPE 4   **CLASS**, **ID**, **LANG**, and **STYLE** are implied.

INTERNET EXPLORER 4   All attributes and events except **DIR**.

Event Handlers

See "Events Reference," earlier in this appendix.

Example

```
This line contains a spelling <STRIKE>misstake</STRIKE> mistake.
```

Compatibility

HTML 3.2 and 4 (transitional)
Internet Explorer 2, 3, 4, and 5
Netscape 3, 4, and 4.5
WebTV

Notes

- This element should act the same as the **<S>** element.
- The strict HTML 4.0 specification does not include the **<STRIKE>** element nor the **<S>** element. It is possible to indicate strikethrough text using a style sheet.

<STRONG>   (Strong Emphasis)

This element indicates strongly emphasized text. It is usually rendered in a bold typeface, but is a logical element rather than a physical one.

Syntax

```
<STRONG
    CLASS="class name(s)"
    DIR="LTR | RTL"
    ID="unique alphanumeric string"
    LANG="language code"
    STYLE="style information"
    TITLE="advisory text"
    onclick="script"
    ondblclick="script"
    onkeydown="script"
```

```
    onkeypress="script"
    onkeyup="script"
    onmousedown="script"
    onmousemove="script"
    onmouseout="script"
    onmouseover="script"
    onmouseup="script">
```

```
</STRONG>
```

Attributes and Events Defined by Internet Explorer 4

```
LANGUAGE="JAVASCRIPT | JSCRIPT | VBS | VBSCRIPT"
ondragstart="script"
onhelp="script"
onselectstart="script"
```

Attributes

CLASS   See "Core Attributes Reference," earlier in this appendix.

DIR   See "Language Reference," earlier in this appendix.

ID   See "Core Attributes Reference," earlier in this appendix.

LANG   See "Language Reference," earlier in this appendix.

LANGUAGE   In the Microsoft implementation, this attribute specifies the scripting language to be used with an associated script bound to the element, typically through an event handler attribute. Possible values may include **JAVASCRIPT**, **JSCRIPT**, **VBS**, and **VBSCRIPT**. Other values that include the version of the language used, such as **JavaScript1.1**, may also be possible.

STYLE   See "Core Attributes Reference," earlier in this appendix.

TITLE   See "Core Attributes Reference," earlier in this appendix.

Attribute and Event Support

NETSCAPE 4   **CLASS**, **ID**, **LANG**, and **STYLE** are implied.

INTERNET EXPLORER 4   All attributes and events except **DIR**.

Event Handlers
See "Events Reference," earlier in this appendix.

Examples

```
It is really <STRONG>important</STRONG> to pay attention.

<STRONG STYLE="font-family: impact; font-size: 28pt">
Important Info
</STRONG>
```

Compatibility

HTML 2, 3.2, and 4
Internet Explorer 2, 3, 4, and 5
Netscape 1, 2, 3, 4, and 4.5
WebTV

Notes

■ This element generally renders as bold text. As a logical element, however, **<STRONG>** is useful to bind style rules to.

■ As compared to **<B>**, this element does have meaning and voice browsers may state **<STRONG>** enclosed text in a different voice than text that is enclosed by **<B>**.

<STYLE> (Style Information)

This element is used to surround style sheet rules for a document. This element should be found only in the **<HEAD>** of a document. Style rules within a document's **<BODY>** element should be set with the style attribute for a particular element.

Syntax

```
<STYLE
    DIR="LTR | RTL"
    LANG="language code"
    MEDIA="ALL | PRINT | SCREEN | others"
    TITLE="advisory text"
    TYPE="MIME Type">

</STYLE>
```

Attributes Defined by Internet Explorer 4

```
    DISABLED
```

Attributes

DIR   This attribute is used to set the text direction of the title for the style sheet, either left to right (**LTR**) or right to left (**RTL**).

DISABLED   This Microsoft-defined attribute is used to disable a style sheet. The presence of the attribute is all that is required to disable the style sheet. In conjunction with scripting, this attribute could be used to turn on and off various style sheets in a document.

LANG   The value of this attribute is a language code, like all other **LANG** attributes; however, this attribute defines the language of the **TITLE** attribute rather than the content of the element.

MEDIA   This attribute specifies the destination medium for the style information. The value of the attribute may be a single media descriptor such as **SCREEN** or a comma-separated list. Possible values for this attribute include **ALL, AURAL, BRAILLE, PRINT, PROJECTION**, and **SCREEN**. Other values may also be defined, depending on the browser. Internet Explorer supports **ALL, PRINT**, and **SCREEN** as values for this attribute.

TITLE   This attribute associates an informational title with the style sheet.

TYPE   This attribute is used to define the type of style sheet. The value of the attribute should be the MIME type of the style sheet language used. The most common current value for this attribute is **text/css**, which indicates a Cascading Style Sheet format.

Attribute and Event Support

NETSCAPE 4   TYPE.

INTERNET EXPLORER 4   DISABLED, MEDIA (ALL | PRINT | SCREEN), TITLE, and TYPE.

Event Handlers
None.

Example

```
<HTML>
<HEAD>
<TITLE>Style Sheet Example</TITLE>
<STYLE TYPE="text/css">
<!--
   BODY {background: black; color: white; font: 12pt Helvetica}
   H1   {color: red; font: 14pt Impact}
-->
```

```
</STYLE>
</HEAD>

<BODY>
<H1>A 14-point red Impact heading on a black background</H1>
Regular body text, which is 12 point white Helvetica
</BODY>
</HTML>
```

Compatibility

HTML 4
Internet Explorer 3, 4, and 5
Netscape 4 and 4.5

Notes

- Style information can also be specified in external style sheets, as defined by the **<LINK>** element.

- Style information can also be associated with a particular element using the **STYLE** attribute.

- Style rules are generally commented out within the **<STYLE>** element to avoid interpretation by nonconforming browsers.

<SUB>   (Subscript)

This element renders its content as subscripted text.

Syntax

```
<SUB
    CLASS="class name(s)"
    DIR="LTR | RTL"
    ID="unique alphanumeric string"
    LANG="language code"
    STYLE="style information"
    TITLE="advisory text"
    onclick="script"
    ondblclick="script"
    onkeydown="script"
    onkeypress="script"
    onkeyup="script"
```

```
      onmousedown="script"
      onmousemove="script"
      onmouseout="script"
      onmouseover="script"
      onmouseup="script">

</SUB>
```

Attributes and Events Defined by Internet Explorer 4

```
      LANGUAGE="JAVASCRIPT | JSCRIPT | VBS | VBSCRIPT"
      ondragstart="script"
      onhelp="script"
      onselectstart="script"
```

Attributes

CLASS   See "Core Attributes Reference," earlier in this appendix.

DIR   See "Language Reference," earlier in this appendix.

ID   See "Core Attributes Reference," earlier in this appendix.

LANG   See "Language Reference," earlier in this appendix.

LANGUAGE   In the Microsoft implementation, this attribute specifies the scripting language to be used with an associated script bound to the element, typically through an event handler attribute. Possible values may include **JAVASCRIPT**, **JSCRIPT**, **VBS**, and **VBSCRIPT**. Other values that include the version of the language used, such as **JavaScript1.1**, may also be possible.

STYLE   See "Core Attributes Reference," earlier in this appendix.

TITLE   See "Core Attributes Reference," earlier in this appendix.

Attribute and Event Support

NETSCAPE 4   **CLASS**, **ID**, **LANG**, and **STYLE** are implied.

INTERNET EXPLORER 4   All attributes and events except **DIR**.

Event Handlers
See "Events Reference," earlier in this appendix.

Example

```
Here is some <SUB>subscripted</SUB> text.
```

Compatibility

HTML 3.2 and 4
Internet Explorer 2, 3, 4, and 5
Netscape 2, 3, 4, and 4.5
WebTV

Notes

The HTML 3.2 specification supports no attributes for the **<SUB>** element.

<SUP> (Superscript)

This element renders its content as superscripted text.

Syntax

```
<SUP
    CLASS="class name(s)"
    DIR="LTR | RTL"
    ID="unique alphanumeric string"
    LANG="language code"
    STYLE="style information"
    TITLE="advisory text"
    onclick="script"
    ondblclick="script"
    onkeydown="script"
    onkeypress="script"
    onkeyup="script"
    onmousedown="script"
    onmousemove="script"
    onmouseout="script"
    onmouseover="script"
    onmouseup="script">

</SUP>
```

APPENDIXES

Attributes and Events Defined by Internet Explorer 4

```
LANGUAGE="JAVASCRIPT | JSCRIPT | VBS | VBSCRIPT"
ondragstart="script"
onhelp="script"
onselectstart="script"
```

Attributes

CLASS See "Core Attributes Reference," earlier in this appendix.

DIR See "Language Reference," earlier in this appendix.

ID See "Core Attributes Reference," earlier in this appendix.

LANG See "Language Reference," earlier in this appendix.

LANGUAGE In the Microsoft implementation, this attribute specifies the scripting language to be used with an associated script bound to the element, typically through an event handler attribute. Possible values may include **JAVASCRIPT**, **JSCRIPT**, **VBS**, and **VBSCRIPT**. Other values that include the version of the language used, such as **JavaScript1.1**, may also be possible.

STYLE See "Core Attributes Reference," earlier in this appendix.

TITLE See "Core Attributes Reference," earlier in this appendix.

Attribute and Event Support

NETSCAPE 4 **CLASS**, **ID**, **LANG**, and **STYLE** are implied.

INTERNET EXPLORER 4 All attributes and events except **DIR**.

Event Handlers

See "Events Reference," earlier in this appendix.

Example

```
Here is some <SUP>superscripted</SUP> text.
```

Compatibility

HTML 3.2 and 4
Internet Explorer 2, 3, 4, and 5
Netscape 2, 3, 4, and 4.5
WebTV

Notes

The HTML 3.2 specification defines no attributes for this element.

\<TABLE\>   (Table)

This element is used to define a table. Tables are used to organize data as well as to provide structure for laying out pages.

Syntax

```
<TABLE
    ALIGN="CENTER | LEFT | RIGHT" (transitional)
    BGCOLOR="color name | #RRGGBB" (transitional)
    BORDER="pixels"
    CELLPADDING="pixels"
    CELLSPACING="pixels"
    CLASS="class name(s)"
    DATAPAGESIZE="number of records to display"
    DIR="LTR | RTL"
    FRAME="ABOVE | BELOW | BORDER | BOX | HSIDES |
           LHS | RHS | VOID | VSIDES"
    ID="unique alphanumeric identifier"
    LANG="language code"
    RULES="ALL | COLS | GROUPS | NONE | ROWS"
    STYLE="style information"
    SUMMARY="summary information"
    TITLE="advisory text"
    WIDTH="percentage | pixels"
    onclick="script"
    ondblclick="script"
    onkeydown="script"
    onkeypress="script"
    onkeyup="script"
    onmousedown="script"
    onmousemove="script"
    onmouseout="script"
    onmouseover="script"
    onmouseup="script">

</TABLE>
```

Attributes and Events Defined by Internet Explorer 4

```
    BACKGROUND="URL"
    BORDERCOLOR="color name | #RRGGBB"
    BORDERCOLORDARK="color name | #RRGGBB"
```

```
BORDERCOLORLIGHT="color name | #RRGGBB"
COLS="number"
DATASRC="data source ID"
HEIGHT="percentage | pixels"
LANGUAGE="JAVASCRIPT | JSCRIPT | VBS | VBSCRIPT"
onafterupdate="script"
onbeforeupdate="script"
onblur="script"
ondragstart="script"
onfocus="script"
onhelp="script"
onresize="script"
onrowenter="script"
onrowexit="script"
onselectstart="script"
```

Attributes Defined by Netscape 4

```
BACKGROUND="URL of image" file
BORDERCOLOR="color name | #RRGGBB"
COLS="number of columns"
HEIGHT="pixels"
HSPACE="pixels"
VSPACE="pixels"
```

Attributes Defined by WebTV

```
ALIGN="BLEEDLEFT | BLEEDRIGHT | JUSTIFY"
BACKGROUND="URL of image file"
CELLBORDER="pixels"
GRADANGLE="gradient angle"
GRADCOLOR="color value"
HREF="URL"
HSPACE="pixels"
NAME="string"
NOWRAP
TRANSPARENCY="number (0-100)"
VSPACE="pixels"
```

Attributes

ALIGN This attribute specifies the alignment of the table with respect to surrounding text. The HTML 4.0 specification defines **CENTER, LEFT,** and **RIGHT**. WebTV also defines **BLEEDLEFT** and **BLEEDRIGHT**, which cause the table to bleed over the right and left margins of the page, and **JUSTIFY**, which is used to justify the table within the browser window. Some browsers may also support alignment values, such as **ABSMIDDLE**, that are common to block objects.

BACKGROUND   This nonstandard attribute, which is supported by Internet Explorer, Netscape, and WebTV, specifies the URL of a background image for the table. The image is tiled if it is smaller than the table dimensions. Netscape displays the background image in each table cell, rather than behind the complete table as Internet Explorer does.

BGCOLOR   This attribute specifies a background color for a table. Its value can be either a named color, such as **red**, or a color specified in the hexadecimal *#RRGGBB* format, such as **#FF0000**.

BORDER   This attribute specifies in pixels the width of a table's borders. A value of **0** makes a borderless table, which is useful for graphic layout.

BORDERCOLOR   This attribute, supported by Internet Explorer 4 and Netscape 4, is used to set the border color for a table. The attribute should only be used with a positive value for the **BORDER** attribute. The value of the attribute can be either a named color, such as **green**, or a color specified in the hexadecimal *#RRGGBB* format, such as **#00FF00**. Internet Explorer colors the entire table border, including cell borders; Netscape only colors the outer border of the table.

BORDERCOLORDARK   This Internet Explorer–specific attribute specifies the darker of two border colors used to create a three-dimensional effect for cell borders. It must be used with the **BORDER** attribute set to a positive value. The attribute value can be either a named color, such as **blue**, or a color specified in the hexadecimal *#RRGGBB* format, such as **#00FF00**.

BORDERCOLORLIGHT   This Internet Explorer–specific attribute specifies the lighter of two border colors used to create a three-dimensional effect for cell borders. It must be used with the **BORDER** attribute set to a positive value. The attribute value can be either a named color, such as **red**, or a color specified in the hexadecimal *#RRGGBB* format, such as **#FF0000**.

CELLBORDER   In the WebTV implementation, this attribute sets the width in pixels of the border between table cells. If this value is not present, the default border as specified by the **BORDER** attribute is used.

CELLPADDING   This attribute sets the width in pixels between the edge of a cell and its content.

CELLSPACING   This attribute sets the width in pixels between individual cells.

CLASS   See "Core Attributes Reference," earlier in this appendix.

COLS   This attribute specifies the number of columns in the table and is used to help quickly calculate the size of the table. This attribute was part of the preliminary specification of HTML 4, but was later dropped. A few browsers, notably Netscape 4, already support it.

DATAPAGESIZE   The value of this Microsoft-specific attribute is the number of records that can be displayed in the table when data binding is used.

DATASRC   The value of this Microsoft-specific attribute is an identifier indicating the data source to pull data from.

DIR   See "Language Reference," earlier in this appendix.

FRAME   This attribute specifies which edges of a table are to display a border frame. A value of **ABOVE** indicates only the top edge; **BELOW** indicates only the bottom edge; and **BORDER** and **BOX** indicate all edges, which is the default when the **BORDER** attribute is a positive integer. A value of **HSIDES** indicates only the top and bottom edges should be displayed; **LHS** indicates the left-hand edge should be displayed; **RHS** indicates the right-hand edge should be displayed; **VSIDES** indicates the left and right edges should both be displayed; and **VOID** indicates no border should be displayed.

GRADANGLE   This WebTV-specific attribute defines the gradient angle for a table, ranging from 90 to –90 degrees. **GRADANGLE="0"** yields a left-to-right gradient, while **GRADANGLE="90"** yields a top-to-bottom gradient. The beginning color of the gradient is defined by the **BGCOLOR** attribute, and the ending color is defined by the **GRADCOLOR** attribute.

GRADCOLOR   This WebTV-specific attribute defines the end color of a table's background gradient, in conjunction with the gradient angle defined by the **GRADANGLE** attribute and the starting color defined by the **BGCOLOR** attribute.

HEIGHT   For Netscape 4, this attribute allows the author to specify the height of the table in pixels. Internet Explorer 4 allows both pixels and percentages.

HREF   This WebTV-specific attribute is used to make the entire table function as a hyperlink anchor to the specified URL.

HSPACE   This Netscape-specified attribute indicates the horizontal space in pixels between the table and surrounding content. This attribute is also supported by WebTV but, oddly, not by Internet Explorer.

ID   See "Core Attributes Reference," earlier in this appendix.

LANG   See "Language Reference," earlier in this appendix.

LANGUAGE   In the Microsoft implementation, this attribute specifies the scripting language to be used with an associated script bound to the element, typically through an event handler attribute. Possible values may include **JAVASCRIPT**, **JSCRIPT**, **VBS**, and **VBSCRIPT**. Other values that include the version of the language used, such as **JavaScript1.1**, may also be possible.

NAME   This WebTV attribute is used to assign the table a unique name. It is synonymous with the **ID** attribute.

NOWRAP   This WebTV-specific attribute keeps table rows from wrapping if they extend beyond the right margin. The attribute requires no value.

RULES   This attribute controls the display of dividing rules within a table. A value of **ALL** specifies dividing rules for rows and columns. A value of **COLS** specifies dividing rules for columns only. A value of **GROUPS** specifies horizontal dividing rules between groups of table cells defined by the **<THEAD>**, **<TBODY>**, **<TFOOT>**, or **<COLGROUP>** elements. A value of **ROWS** specifies dividing rules for rows only. A value of **NONE** indicates no dividing rules and is the default.

STYLE   See "Core Attributes Reference," earlier in this appendix.

SUMMARY   This attribute is used to provide a text summary of the table's purpose and structure. This element is used for accessibility, and its presence is important for nonvisual user agents.

TITLE   See "Core Attributes Reference," earlier in this appendix.

TRANSPARENCY   This WebTV-specific attribute specifies the degree of transparency of the table. Values range from **0** (totally opaque) to **100** (totally transparent). A value of **50** is optimized for fast rendering.

VSPACE   This Netscape attribute indicates the vertical space in pixels between the table and surrounding content. This attribute is also supported by WebTV but, oddly, not by Internet Explorer.

WIDTH   This attribute specifies the width of the table either in pixels or as a percentage value of the enclosing window.

Attribute and Event Support

NETSCAPE 4   ALIGN (LEFT I RIGHT), BGCOLOR, BORDER, CELLPADDING, CELLSPACING, COLS, HEIGHT, HSPACE, VSPACE, and WIDTH. (CLASS, ID, LANG, and STYLE are implied.)

INTERNET EXPLORER 4   All W3C-defined attributes and events except **DIR** and **SUMMARY**, and all attributes and events defined by Internet Explorer 4.

WEBTV   ALIGN (BLEEDLEFT I BLEEDRIGHT I CENTER I LEFT I RIGHT), BACKGROUND, BGCOLOR, BORDER, CELLPADDING, CELLSPACING, GRADANGLE, GRADCOLOR, HSPACE, ID, NOWRAP, TRANSPARENCY, and WIDTH.

Event Handlers
See "Events Reference," earlier in this appendix.

Examples

```
<TABLE BGCOLOR="WHITE" BORDER="2">
    <TR>
        <TD>Cell 1</TD>
        <TD>Cell 2</TD>
        <TD>Cell 3</TD>
```

```
        <TD>Cell 4</TD>
    </TR>

    <TR>
        <TD>Cell 5</TD>
        <TD>Cell 6</TD>
    </TR>
</TABLE>

<TABLE RULES="ALL" BGCOLOR="YELLOW">
<CAPTION>Widgets by Area</CAPTION>
<THEAD ALIGN="CENTER" BGCOLOR="GREEN" VALIGN="CENTER">
    <TD>This is a Header</TD>
</THEAD>

<TFOOT ALIGN="RIGHT" BGCOLOR="RED" VALIGN="BOTTOM">
    <TD>This is part of the footer.</TD>
    <TD>This is also part of the footer.</TD>
</TFOOT>

<TBODY>
    <TR>
        <TD> </TD>
        <TH>Regular Widget</TH>
        <TH>Super Widget</TH>
    </TR>

    <TR>
        <TH>West Coast</TH>
        <TD>10</TD>
        <TD>12</TD>
    </TR>

    <TR>
        <TH>East Coast</TH>
        <TD>1</TD>
        <TD>20</TD>
    </TR>
</TBODY>
</TABLE>
```

Compatibility

HTML 3.2 and 4
Internet Explorer 2, 3, 4, and 5

Netscape 1.1, 2, 3, 4, and 4.5
WebTV

Notes

- In addition to displaying tabular data, tables are used to support graphic layout and design.
- The HTML 4.0 specification reserves the future use of the **DATAFLD**, **DATAFORMATAS**, and **DATASRC** attributes for the **<TABLE>** element.
- The HTML 3.2 specification defines only the **ALIGN**, **BORDER**, **CELLPADDING**, **CELLSPACING**, and **WIDTH** attributes for the **<TABLE>** element.
- The **COLS** attribute may provide an undesirable result under Netscape, which assumes the size of each column in the table is exactly the same.

<TBODY> (Table Body)

This element is used to group the rows within the body of a table so that common alignment and style defaults can be set easily for numerous cells.

Syntax

```
<TBODY   ALIGN="CENTER | CHAR | JUSTIFY | LEFT | RIGHT"
         CHAR="character"
         CHAROFF="offset"
         CLASS="class name(s)"
         DIR="LTR | RTL"
         ID="unique alphanumeric identifier"
         LANG="language code"
         STYLE="style information"
         TITLE="advisory text"
         VALIGN="BASELINE | BOTTOM | MIDDLE | TOP"
         onclick="script"
         ondblclick="script"
         onkeydown="script"
         onkeypress="script"
         onkeyup="script"
         onmousedown="script"
         onmousemove="script"
         onmouseout="script"
         onmouseover="script"
         onmouseup="script">

</TBODY>
```

Attributes and Events Defined by Internet Explorer 4

```
BGCOLOR="color name | #RRGGBB"
LANGUAGE="JAVASCRIPT | JSCRIPT | VBS | VBSCRIPT"
VALIGN="CENTER"
ondragstart="script"
onhelp="script"
onselectstart="script"
```

Attributes

ALIGN   This attribute is used to align the contents of the cells within the **<TBODY>** element. Common values are **CENTER, JUSTIFY, LEFT**, and **RIGHT**. The HTML 4.0 specification also defines a value of **CHAR**. When **ALIGN** is set to **CHAR**, the attribute **CHAR** must be present and set to the character to which cells should be aligned. A common use of this approach would be to set cells to align on a decimal point.

BGCOLOR   This attribute specifies a background color for the cells within the **<TBODY>** element. Its value can be either a named color, such as **red**, or a color specified in the hexadecimal *#RRGGBB* format, such as **#FF0000**.

CHAR   This attribute is used to define the character to which element contents are aligned when the **ALIGN** attribute is set to the **CHAR** value.

CHAROFF   This attribute contains an offset as a positive or negative integer to align characters as related to the **CHAR** value. A value of **2**, for example, would align characters in a cell two characters to the right of the character defined by the **CHAR** attribute.

CLASS   See "Core Attributes Reference," earlier in this appendix.

DIR   See "Language Reference," earlier in this appendix.

ID   See "Core Attributes Reference," earlier in this appendix.

LANG   See "Language Reference," earlier in this appendix.

LANGUAGE   In the Microsoft implementation, this attribute specifies the scripting language to be used with an associated script bound to the element, typically through an event handler attribute. Possible values may include **JAVASCRIPT, JSCRIPT, VBS**, and **VBSCRIPT**. Other values that include the version of the language used, such as **JavaScript1.1**, may also be possible.

STYLE   See "Core Attributes Reference," earlier in this appendix.

TITLE   See "Core Attributes Reference," earlier in this appendix.

VALIGN   This attribute is used to set the vertical alignment for the table cells with the <TBODY> element. HTML 4 defines **BASELINE, BOTTOM, MIDDLE,** and **TOP.** Internet Explorer replaces **MIDDLE** with **CENTER;** the effect should be the same.

Attribute and Event Support

INTERNET EXPLORER 4   All W3C-defined attributes and events except **CHAR, CHAROFF,** and **DIR.** (Note: Internet Explorer 4 does not support the **CHAR** and **JUSTIFY** values for **ALIGN,** nor the **MIDDLE** value for **VALIGN.**)

Event Handlers
See "Events Reference," earlier in this appendix.

Example

```
<TABLE RULE="ALL" BGCOLOR="YELLOW">

<TBODY ALIGN="CENTER" BGCOLOR="RED" VALIGN="BASELINE">
    <TR>
        <TD> </TD>
        <TH>Regular Widget</TH>
        <TH>Super Widget</TH>
    </TR>

    <TR>
        <TH>West Coast</TH>
        <TD>10</TD>
        <TD>12</TD>
    </TR>

    <TR>
        <TH>East Coast</TH>
        <TD>1</TD>
        <TD>20</TD>
    </TR>
</TBODY>
</TABLE>
```

Compatibility

HTML 4
Internet Explorer 4 and 5

Notes

This element is contained by the **<TABLE>** element and contains one or more table rows as indicated by the **<TR>** element.

<TD> (Table Data)

This element specifies a data cell in a table. The element should occur within a table row, as defined by the **<TR>** element.

Syntax

```
<TD
    ABBR="abbreviation"
    ALIGN="CENTER | JUSTIFY | LEFT | RIGHT"
    AXIS="group name"
    BGCOLOR="color name | #RRGGBB" (transitional)
    CHAR="character"
    CHAROFF="offset"
    CLASS="CLASS name"
    COLSPAN="number"
    DIR="LTR | RTL"
    HEADERS="space-separated list of associated header
            cells' ID values"
    HEIGHT="pixels" (transitional)
    ID="unique alphanumeric identifier"
    LANG="language code"
    NOWRAP (transitional)
    ROWSPAN="number"
    SCOPE="COL | COLGROUP | ROW | ROWGROUP"
    STYLE="style information"
    TITLE="advisory text"
    VALIGN="BASELINE | BOTTOM | MIDDLE | TOP"
    WIDTH="pixels" (transitional)
    onclick="script"
    ondblclick="script"
    onkeydown="script"
    onkeypress="script"
    onkeyup="script"
    onmousedown="script"
    onmousemove="script"
    onmouseout="script"
    onmouseover="script"
    onmouseup="script">

</TD>
```

Attributes and Events Defined by Internet Explorer 4

```
BACKGROUND="URL of image file"
BORDERCOLOR="color name | #RRGGBB"
BORDERCOLORDARK="color name | #RRGGBB"
BORDERCOLORLIGHT="color name | #RRGGBB"
LANGUAGE="JAVASCRIPT | JSCRIPT | VBS | VBSCRIPT"
VALIGN="CENTER"
onafterupdate="script"
onbeforeupdate="script"
onblur="script"
ondragstart="script"
onfocus="script"
onhelp="script"
onresize="script"
onrowenter="script"
onrowexit="script"
onscroll="script"
onselectstart="script"
```

Attributes Defined by Netscape 4

```
BACKGROUND="URL of image file"
BORDERCOLOR="color name | #RRGGBB"
```

Attributes Defined by WebTV

```
ABSHEIGHT="pixels"
ABSWIDTH="pixels"
BACKGROUND="URL of image file"
GRADANGLE="gradient angle"
GRADCOLOR="color"
MAXLINES="number"
TRANSPARENCY="number (0-100)"
```

Attributes

ABBR   The value of this attribute is an abbreviated name for a header cell. This may be useful when attempting to display large tables on small screens.

ABSHEIGHT   This WebTV-specific attribute sets the absolute height of a cell in pixels. Content that does not fit within this height is clipped.

ABSWIDTH   This WebTV-specific attribute sets the absolute width of a cell in pixels. Content that does not fit within this width is clipped.

ALIGN   This attribute is used to align the contents of the cells within the **<TBODY>** element. Common values are **CENTER, JUSTIFY, LEFT,** and **RIGHT**.

AXIS   This attribute is used to provide a name for a group of related headers.

BACKGROUND   This nonstandard attribute, which is supported by Internet Explorer, Netscape and WebTV, specifies the URL of a background image for the table cell. The image is tiled if it is smaller than the cell's dimensions.

BGCOLOR   This attribute specifies a background color for a table cell. Its value can be either a named color, such as **red**, or a color specified in the hexadecimal #*RRGGBB* format, such as **#FF0000.** (Netscape Navigator often fails to render a cell with a colored background unless a nonbreaking space, at least, is inserted in the cell.)

BORDERCOLOR   This attribute, supported by Internet Explorer and Netscape, is used to set the border color for a table cell. The attribute should only be used with a positive value for the **BORDER** attribute. The value of the attribute can be either a named color, such as **green**, or a color specified in the hexadecimal #*RRGGBB* format, such as **#00FF00.**

BORDERCOLORDARK   This Internet Explorer–specific attribute specifies the darker of two border colors used to create a three-dimensional effect for a cell's borders. It must be used with the **BORDER** attribute set to a positive value. The attribute value can be either a named color, such as **blue**, or a color specified in the hexadecimal #*RRGGBB* format, such as **#00FF00.**

BORDERCOLORLIGHT   This Internet Explorer–specific attribute specifies the lighter of two border colors used to create a three-dimensional effect for a cell's borders. It must be used with the **BORDER** attribute set to a positive value. The attribute value can be either a named color, such as **red**, or a color specified in the hexadecimal #*RRGGBB* format, such as **#FF0000.**

CHAR   This attribute is used to define the character to which element contents are aligned when the **ALIGN** attribute is set to the **CHAR** value.

CHAROFF   This attribute contains an offset as a positive or negative integer to align characters as related to the **CHAR** value. A value of **2**, for example, would align characters in a cell two characters to the right of the character defined by the **CHAR** attribute.

CLASS   See "Core Attributes Reference," earlier in this appendix.

COLSPAN   This attribute takes a numeric value that indicates how many columns wide a cell should be. This is useful to create tables with cells of different widths.

DIR   See "Language Reference," earlier in this appendix.

GRADANGLE   This WebTV-specific attribute defines the gradient angle for a table cell, ranging from 90 to –90 degrees. **GRADANGLE="0"** yields a left-to-right gradient, while **GRADANGLE="90"** yields a top-to-bottom gradient. The beginning color of the gradient is defined by the **BGCOLOR** attribute, and the ending color is defined by the **GRADCOLOR** attribute.

GRADCOLOR   This WebTV-specific attribute defines the end color of a table cell's background gradient, in conjunction with the gradient angle defined by the **GRADANGLE** attribute and the starting color defined by the **BGCOLOR** attribute.

HEADERS   This attribute takes a space-separated list of **ID** values that correspond to the header cells related to this cell.

HEIGHT   This attribute indicates the height in pixels of the cell.

ID   See "Core Attributes Reference," earlier in this appendix.

LANG   See "Language Reference," earlier in this appendix.

LANGUAGE   In the Microsoft implementation, this attribute specifies the scripting language to be used with an associated script bound to the element, typically through an event handler attribute. Possible values may include **JAVASCRIPT**, **JSCRIPT**, **VBS**, and **VBSCRIPT**. Other values that include the version of the language used, such as **JavaScript1.1**, may also be possible.

MAXLINES   This WebTV-specific attribute takes a numeric argument indicating the maximum number of content lines to display. Content beyond these lines is clipped.

NOWRAP   This attribute keeps the content within a table cell from automatically wrapping.

ROWSPAN   This attribute takes a numeric value that indicates how many rows high a table cell should span. This attribute is useful in defining tables with cells of different heights.

SCOPE   This attribute specifies the table cells that the current cell provides header information for. A value of **COL** indicates that the cell is a header for the the rest of the column below it. A value of **COLGROUP** indicates that the cell is a header for its current column group. A value of **ROW** indicates that that the cell contains header information for the rest of the row it is in. A value of **ROWGROUP** indicates that the cell is a header for its row group. This attribute may be used in place of the **HEADER** attribute and is useful for rendering assistance by nonvisual browsers. This attribute was added very late to the HTML 4.0 specification so support for this attribute is minimal.

STYLE   See "Core Attributes Reference," earlier in this appendix.

TITLE   See "Core Attributes Reference," earlier in this appendix.

TRANSPARENCY   This WebTV-specific attribute specifies the degree of transparency of the table cell. Values range from **0** (totally opaque) to **100** (totally transparent). A value of **50** is optimized for fast rendering.

VALIGN   This attribute is used to set the vertical alignment for the table cell. HTML 4 defines **BASELINE**, **BOTTOM**, **MIDDLE**, and **TOP**. Internet Explorer replaces **MIDDLE** with **CENTER**; the effect should be the same.

WIDTH   This attribute specifies the width of a cell in pixels.

Attribute and Event Support

NETSCAPE 4   ALIGN, BACKGROUND, BGCOLOR, BORDERCOLOR, COLSPAN, HEIGHT, NOWRAP, ROWSPAN, VALIGN, and WIDTH. (CLASS, ID, LANG, and STYLE are implied.)

INTERNET EXPLORER 4   All W3C-defined attributes and events except ABBR, AXIS, CHAR, CHAROFF, DIR, HEADERS and HEIGHT, and all attributes and events defined by Internet Explorer 4. (Note: Internet Explorer 4 does not support the JUSTIFY value for ALIGN, nor the MIDDLE value for VALIGN.)

WEBTV   ALIGN (CENTER | LEFT | RIGHT), BACKGROUND, BGCOLOR, COLSPAN, GRADANGLE, GRADCOLOR, HEIGHT, ROWSPAN, TRANSPARENCY, VALIGN (BASELINE | BOTTOM | MIDDLE | TOP), and WIDTH.

Event Handlers
See "Events Reference," earlier in this appendix.

Examples

```
<TABLE>
   <TR>
      <TD ALIGN="LEFT" VALIGN="TOP">
      Put me in the top left corner.
      </TD>

      <TD ALIGN="BOTTOM" BGCOLOR="RED" VALIGN="RIGHT">
      Put me in the bottom right corner.
      </TD>
   </TR>
</TABLE>

<TABLE BORDER="1" WIDTH="80%">
   <TR>
      <TD COLSPAN="3">
      A pretty wide cell
      </TD>
   </TR>

   <TR>
      <TD>Item 2</TD>
      <TD>Item 3</TD>
      <TD>Item 4</TD>
   </TR>
</TABLE>
```

Compatibility

HTML 3.2 and 4
Internet Explorer 2, 3, 4, and 5
Netscape 1.1, 2, 3, 4, and 4.5
WebTV

Notes

■ The HTML 3.2 specification defines only **ALIGN, COLSPAN, HEIGHT, NOWRAP, ROWSPAN, VALIGN,** and **WIDTH** attributes.

■ This element should always be within the **<TR>** element.

<TEXTAREA>   (Multiline Text Input)

This element specifies a multiline text input field contained within a form.

Syntax

```
<TEXTAREA
      ACCESSKEY="character"
      CLASS="class name"
      COLS="number"
      DIR="LTR | RTL"
      DISABLED
      ID="unique alphanumeric identifier"
      LANG="language code"
      NAME="unique alphanumeric identifier"
      READONLY
      ROWS="number"
      STYLE="style information"
      TABINDEX="number"
      TITLE="advisory text"
      onblur="script"
      onchange="script"
      onclick="script"
      ondblclick="script"
      onfocus="script"
      onkeydown="script"
      onkeypress="script"
      onkeyup="script"
      onmousedown="script"
      onmousemove="script"
      onmouseout="script"
      onmouseover="script"
      onmouseup="script"
      onselect="script">

</TEXTAREA>
```

Attributes and Events Defined by Internet Explorer 4

```
ALIGN="ABSBOTTOM | ABSMIDDLE | BASELINE | BOTTOM |
       LEFT | MIDDLE | RIGHT | TEXTTOP | TOP"
DATAFLD="column name"
DATASRC="data source ID"
LANGUAGE="JAVASCRIPT | JSCRIPT | VBS | VBSCRIPT"
WRAP="OFF | PHYSICAL | VIRTUAL"
onafterupdate="script"
onbeforeupdate="script"
ondragstart="script"
onhelp="script"
onresize="script"
onrowenter="script"
onrowexit="script"
onscroll="script"
onselectstart="script"
onstart="script"
```

Attributes Defined by Netscape 4

```
WRAP="HARD | OFF | SOFT"
```

Attributes Defined by WebTV

```
ALLCAPS
AUTOACTIVATE
AUTOCAPS
BGCOLOR="color name | #RRGGBB"
CURSOR="color name | #RRGGBB"
GROWABLE
NOHARDBREAKS
NOSOFTBREAKS
NUMBERS
SHOWKEYBOARD
USESTYLE
```

Attributes

ACCESSKEY   This Microsoft-specific attribute specifies a keyboard navigation accelerator for the element. Pressing ALT or a similar key in association with the specified character selects the form control correlated with that key sequence. Page designers are forewarned to avoid key sequences already bound to browsers.

ALIGN   Microsoft defines alignment values for this element. The values for this attribute should behave similarly to any included object or image.

ALLCAPS   This WebTV-specific attribute renders all viewer-entered text in capital letters. This attribute requires no value.

AUTOACTIVATE   This WebTV-specific attribute causes the text input control to immediately activate. This attribute requires no value.

AUTOCAPS   This WebTV-specific attribute renders the first letter of all viewer-entered words in a capital letter. This attribute requires no value.

BGCOLOR   This WebTV-specific attribute specifies the background color for the text input area. Its value can be either a named color, such as **red**, or a color specified in the hexadecimal *#RRGGBB* format, such as **#FF0000**. The default color for the **<TEXTAREA>** element under WebTV is **#EAEAEA**.

CLASS   See "Core Attributes Reference," earlier in this appendix.

COLS   This attribute sets the width in characters of the text area. The typical default values for the size of a **<TEXTAREA>** element when this attribute is not set is **20** characters.

CURSOR   This WebTV-specific attribute is used to indicate the cursor color for the text input area. Its value can be either a named color, such as **red**, or a color specified in the hexadecimal *#RRGGBB* format, such as **#FF0000**. The default value for the cursor color in the WebTV browser is **darkblue** (**#3333AA**).

DATAFLD   This attribute is used to indicate the column name in the data source that is bound to the content enclosed by the **<TEXTAREA>** element.

DATASRC   The value of this attribute is an identifier indicating the data source to pull data from.

DIR   See "Language Reference," earlier in this appendix.

DISABLED   This attribute is used to turn off a form control. Elements will not be submitted nor may they receive any focus from the keyboard or mouse. Disabled form controls will not be part of the tabbing order. The browser may also gray out the form that is disabled, in order to indicate to the user that the form control is inactive. This attribute requires no value.

GROWABLE   This WebTV-specific attribute allows the text input area to expand vertically to accommodate extra text entered by the user. This attribute requires no value.

ID   See "Core Attributes Reference," earlier in this appendix.

LANG   See "Language Reference," earlier in this appendix.

LANGUAGE   In the Microsoft implementation, this attribute specifies the scripting language to be used with an associated script bound to the element, typically through an event handler attribute. Possible values may include **JAVASCRIPT**, **JSCRIPT**, **VBS**, and **VBSCRIPT**. Other values that include the version of the language used, such as **JavaScript1.1**, may also be possible.

NAME   This attribute allows a form control to be assigned a name so that it can be referenced by a scripting language. **NAME** is supported by older browsers, such as Netscape 2–generation browsers, but the W3C encourages the use of the **ID** attribute. For compatibility purposes, both attributes may have to be used.

NOHARDBREAKS   This WebTV-specific attribute causes a press of the ENTER key to select the next form element rather than causing a line break in the text input area. The attribute requires no value.

NOSOFTBREAKS   This attribute removes breaks automatically inserted into the text by line wrapping when the form is submitted. The attribute requires no value.

NUMBERS   This WebTV-specific attribute causes the number "1" to be selected in the onscreen keyboard in anticipation of the viewer entering a numeric value.

READONLY   This attribute prevents the form control's value from being changed. Form controls with this attribute set may receive focus from the user but may not be modified. Since they receive focus, a **READONLY** form control will be part of the form's tabbing order. Finally, the control's value will be sent on form submission. The attribute can only be used with **<INPUT>** when **TYPE** is set to **TEXT** or **PASSWORD**. The attribute is also used with the **<TEXTAREA>** element.

ROWS   This attribute sets the number of rows in the text area. The value of the attribute should be a positive integer.

SHOWKEYBOARD   In the WebTV implementation, this attribute causes the onscreen keyboard to be displayed when the **<TEXTAREA>** element is selected.

STYLE   See "Core Attributes Reference," earlier in this appendix.

TABINDEX   This attribute takes a numeric value indicating the position of the form control in the tabbing index for the form. Tabbing proceeds from the lowest positive **TABINDEX** value to the highest. Negative values for **TABINDEX** will leave the form control out of the tabbing order. When tabbing is not explicitly set, the browser may tab through items in the order they are encountered. Form controls that are disabled due to the presence of the **DISABLED** attribute will not be part of the tabbing index, though read-only controls will be.

TITLE   See "Core Attributes Reference," earlier in this appendix.

USESTYLE   This WebTV-specific attribute causes text to be rendered in the style in effect for the page. The attribute requires no value.

WRAP   In Netscape and Microsoft browsers, this attribute controls word wrap behavior. A value of **OFF** for the attribute forces the **<TEXTAREA>** not to wrap text, so the viewer must manually enter line breaks. A value of **HARD** causes word wrap and includes line breaks in text submitted to the server. A value of **SOFT** causes word wrap but removes line breaks from text submitted to the server. Internet Explorer supports a value of **PHYSICAL**, which is equivalent to Netcape's **HARD** value, and a value of **VIRTUAL**, which is equivalent to Netscape's **SOFT** value. If the **WRAP** attribute is not included, text will still wrap under Internet Explorer, but under Netscape it will scroll horizontally in the text box. It is always a good idea to include the **WRAP** attribute.

Attribute and Event Support

NETSCAPE 4   COLS, NAME, ROWS, WRAP (HARD I OFF I SOFT), **onblur, onchange, onfocus**, and **onselect**. (**CLASS, ID, LANG**, and **STYLE** are implied.)

INTERNET EXPLORER 4   All W3C-defined events and attributes except **DIR**, and all attributes and events defined by Internet Explorer 4.

WEBTV   BGCOLOR, COLS, CURSOR, NAME, ROWS, USESTYLE, **onblur, onchange**, and **onfocus**.

Event Handlers
See "Events Reference," earlier in this appendix.

Examples

```
<TEXTAREA NAME="CommentBox" COLS="40" ROWS="8">
Default text in field
</TEXTAREA>

<TEXTAREA NAME="comment" ROWS="10" COLS="40" WRAP="virtual"
        ALIGN="center">
</TEXTAREA>
```

Compatibility

HTML 2, 3.2, and 4
Internet Explorer 2, 3, 4, and 5
Netscape 1, 2, 3, 4, and 4.5
WebTV

Notes

- Any text between the **<TEXTAREA>** and **</TEXTAREA>** tags is rendered as the default entry for the form control.
- The HTML 2.0 and 3.2 specifications define only the **COLS, NAME**, and **ROWS** attribute for this element.

■ The HTML 4.0 specification reserves the **DATAFLD** and **DATASRC** attributes for future use with the **<TEXTAREA>** element.

<TFOOT>   (Table Footer)

This element is used to group the rows within the footer of a table so that common alignment and style defaults can be set easily for numerous cells. This element may be particularly useful when setting a common footer for tables that are dynamically generated.

Syntax

```
<TFOOT
     ALIGN="CENTER | CHAR | JUSTIFY | LEFT | RIGHT"
     BGCOLOR="color name | #RRGGBB" (transitional)
     CHAR="character"
     CHAROFF="offset"
     CLASS="class name(s)"
     DIR="LTR | RTL"
     ID="unique alphanumeric identifier"
     LANG="language code"
     STYLE="style information"
     TITLE="advisory text"
     VALIGN="BASELINE | BOTTOM | MIDDLE | TOP"
     onclick="script"
     ondblclick="script"
     onkeydown="script"
     onkeypress="script"
     onkeyup="script"
     onmousedown="script"
     onmousemove="script"
     onmouseout="script"
     onmouseover="script"
     onmouseup="script">

</TFOOT>
```

Attributes and Events Defined by Internet Explorer 4

```
     LANGUAGE="JAVASCRIPT | JSCRIPT | VBS | VBSCRIPT"
     VALIGN="CENTER"
     ondragstart="script"
     onhelp="script"
     onselectstart="script"
```

Attributes

ALIGN   This attribute is used to align the contents of the cells within the **<TFOOT>** element. Common values are **CENTER, JUSTIFY, LEFT,** and **RIGHT**. The HTML 4.0 specification also defines a value of **CHAR**. When **ALIGN** is set to **CHAR**, the attribute **CHAR** must be present and set to the character to which cells should be aligned. A common use of this approach would be to set cells to align on a decimal point.

BGCOLOR   This attribute specifies a background color for the cells within the **<TFOOT>** element. Its value can be either a named color, such as **red**, or a color specified in the hexadecimal *#RRGGBB* format, such as **#FF0000**.

CHAR   This attribute is used to define the character to which element contents are aligned when the **ALIGN** attribute is set to the **CHAR** value.

CHAROFF   This attribute contains an offset as a positive or negative integer to align characters as related to the **CHAR** value. A value of **2**, for example, would align characters in a cell two characters to the right of the character defined by the **CHAR** attribute.

CLASS   See "Core Attributes Reference," earlier in this appendix.

DIR   See "Language Reference," earlier in this appendix.

ID   See "Core Attributes Reference," earlier in this appendix.

LANG   See "Language Reference," earlier in this appendix.

LANGUAGE   In the Microsoft implementation, this attribute specifies the scripting language to be used with an associated script bound to the element, typically through an event handler attribute. Possible values may include **JAVASCRIPT, JSCRIPT, VBS,** and **VBSCRIPT**. Other values that include the version of the language used, such as **JavaScript1.1**, may also be possible.

STYLE   See "Core Attributes Reference," earlier in this appendix.

TITLE   See "Core Attributes Reference," earlier in this appendix.

VALIGN   This attribute is used to set the vertical alignment for the table cells with the **<TFOOT>** element. HTML 4 defines **BASELINE, BOTTOM, MIDDLE,** and **TOP**. Internet Explorer replaces **MIDDLE** with **CENTER**; the effect should be the same.

Attribute and Event Support

INTERNET EXPLORER 4   All events and attributes except **CHAR, CHAROFF,** and **DIR**. (Note: Internet Explorer 4 does not support the **JUSTIFY** value for the **ALIGN** attribute.)

Event Handlers

None.

Example

```
<TABLE BORDER="1" BGCOLOR="YELLOW" WIDTH="80%">
<TBODY CLASS="tablebody">
   <TR>
      <TD>The contents of the table!</TD>
   </TR>
</TBODY>

<TFOOT ALIGN="CENTER" BGCOLOR="RED" CLASS="footer"
      VALIGN="BOTTOM">
   <TD>This is part of the footer.</TD>
   <TD>This is also part of the footer.</TD>
</TFOOT>
</TABLE>
```

Compatibility

HTML 4
Internet Explorer 4 and 5

Notes

This element is only contained by the **<TABLE>** element and contains table rows as delimited by **<TR>** elements.

<TH>   (Table Header)

This element specifies a header cell in a table. The element should occur within a table row, as defined by a **<TR>** element. The main difference between this element and **<TD>** is that browsers may render table headers slightly differently.

Syntax

```
<TH
     ABBR="abbreviation"
     ALIGN="CENTER | JUSTIFY | LEFT | RIGHT"
     AXIS="group name"
     BGCOLOR="color name | #RRGGBB" (transitional)
     CHAR="character"
     CHAROFF="offset"
     CLASS="CLASS name"
```

```
COLSPAN="number"
DIR="LTR | RTL"
HEADERS="space-separated list of associated header
        cells' ID values"
HEIGHT="pixels" (transitional)
ID="unique alphanumeric identifier"
LANG="language code"
NOWRAP (transitional)
ROWSPAN="number"
SCOPE="COL | COLGROUP | ROW | ROWGROUP"
STYLE="style information"
TITLE="advisory text"
VALIGN="BASELINE | BOTTOM | MIDDLE | TOP"
WIDTH="pixels" (transitional)
onclick="script"
ondblclick="script"
onkeydown="script"
onkeypress="script"
onkeyup="script"
onmousedown="script"
onmousemove="script"
onmouseout="script"
onmouseover="script"
onmouseup="script">

</TH>
```

Attributes and Events Defined by Internet Explorer 4

```
BACKGROUND="URL of image" file
BORDERCOLOR="color name | #RRGGBB"
BORDERCOLORDARK="color name | #RRGGBB"
BORDERCOLORLIGHT="color name | #RRGGBB"
LANGUAGE="JAVASCRIPT | JSCRIPT | VBS | VBSCRIPT"
VALIGN="CENTER"
ondragstart="script"
onhelp="script"
onscroll="script"
onselectstart="script"
```

Attributes Defined by Netscape 4

```
BACKGROUND="URL of image file"
BORDERCOLOR="color name | #RRGGBB"
```

Attributes Defined by WebTV

```
ABSHEIGHT="pixels"
ABSWIDTH="pixels"
BACKGROUND="URL of image" file
GRADANGLE
GRADCOLOR
MAXLINES="number"
TRANSPARENCY="number (0-100)"
```

Attributes

ABBR   The value of this attribute is an abbreviated name for a header cell. This may be useful when attempting to display large tables on small screens.

ABSHEIGHT   This WebTV-specific attribute sets the absolute height of a cell in pixels. Content that does not fit within this height is clipped.

ABSWIDTH   This WebTV-specific attribute sets the absolute width of a cell in pixels. Content that does not fit within this width is clipped.

ALIGN   This attribute is used to align the contents of the cells within the **<TBODY>** element. Common values are **CENTER, JUSTIFY, LEFT**, and **RIGHT**.

AXIS   This attribute is used to provide a name for a group of related headers.

BACKGROUND   This nonstandard attribute, which is supported by Internet Explorer, Netscape and WebTV, specifies the URL of a background image for the table cell. The image is tiled if it is smaller than the cell's dimensions.

BGCOLOR   This attribute specifies a background color for a table cell. Its value can be either a named color, such as red, or a color specified in the hexadecimal *#RRGGBB* format, such as **#FF0000**.

BORDERCOLOR   This attribute, supported by Internet Explorer and Netscape, is used to set the border color for a table cell. The attribute should only be used with a positive value for the **BORDER** attribute. The value of the attribute can be either a named color, such as **green**, or a color specified in the hexadecimal *#RRGGBB* format, such as **#00FF00**.

BORDERCOLORDARK   This Internet Explorer–specific attribute specifies the darker of two border colors used to create a three-dimensional effect for a cell's borders. It must be used with the **BORDER** attribute set to a positive value. The attribute value can be either a named color, such as **blue**, or a color specified in the hexadecimal *#RRGGBB* format, such as **#00FF00**).

BORDERCOLORLIGHT   This Internet Explorer–specific attribute specifies the lighter of two border colors used to create a three-dimensional effect for a cell's borders. It must be used with the **BORDER** attribute set to a positive value. The attribute value can be either a named color, such as **red**, or a color specified in the hexadecimal *#RRGGBB* format, such as **#FF0000**.

CHAR   This attribute is used to define the character to which element contents are aligned when the **ALIGN** attribute is set to the **CHAR** value.

CHAROFF   This attribute contains an offset as a positive or negative integer to align characters as related to the **CHAR** value. A value of **2**, for example, would align characters in a cell two characters to the right of the character defined by the **CHAR** attribute.

CLASS   See "Core Attributes Reference," earlier in this appendix.

COLSPAN   This attribute takes a numeric value that indicates how many columns wide a cell should be. This is useful to create tables with cells of different widths.

DIR   See "Language Reference," earlier in this appendix.

GRADANGLE   This WebTV-specific attribute defines the gradient angle for a table header, ranging from 90 to –90 degrees. **GRADANGLE="0"** yields a left-to-right gradient, while **GRADANGLE="90"** yields a top-to-bottom gradient. The beginning color of the gradient is defined by the **BGCOLOR** attribute, and the ending color is defined by the **GRADCOLOR** attribute.

GRADCOLOR   This WebTV-specific attribute defines the end color of a table header's background gradient, in conjunction with the gradient angle defined by the **GRADANGLE** attribute and the starting color defined by the **BGCOLOR** attribute.

HEADERS   This attribute takes a space-separated list of **ID** values that correspond to the header cells related to this cell.

HEIGHT   This attribute indicates the height in pixels of the header cell.

ID   See "Core Attributes Reference," earlier in this appendix.

LANG   See "Language Reference," earlier in this appendix.

LANGUAGE   In the Microsoft implementation, this attribute specifies the scripting language to be used with an associated script bound to the element, typically through an event handler attribute. Possible values may include **JAVASCRIPT**, **JSCRIPT**, **VBS**, and **VBSCRIPT**. Other values that include the version of the language used, such as **JavaScript1.1**, may also be possible.

MAXLINES   This WebTV-specific attribute takes a numeric argument indicating the maximum number of content lines to display. Content beyond these lines is clipped.

NOWRAP   This attribute keeps the content within a table header cell from automatically wrapping.

ROWSPAN   This attribute takes a numeric value that indicates how many rows high a table cell should span. This attribute is useful in defining tables with cells of different heights.

SCOPE   This attribute specifies the table cells that the current cell provides header information for. A value of **COL** indicates that the cell is a header for the the rest of the column below it. A value of **COLGROUP** indicates that the cell is a header for its current column group. A value of **ROW** indicates that that the cell contains header information for the rest of the row it is in. A value of **ROWGROUP** indicates that the cell is a header for its row group. This attribute may be used in place of the **HEADER** attribute and is useful for rendering assistance by nonvisual browsers. This attribute was added very late to the HTML 4.0 specification so support for this attribute is minimal.

STYLE   See "Core Attributes Reference," earlier in this appendix.

TITLE   See "Core Attributes Reference," earlier in this appendix.

TRANSPARENCY   This WebTV-specific attribute specifies the degree of transparency of the table header. Values range from **0** (totally opaque) to **100** (totally transparent). A value of **50** is optimized for fast rendering.

VALIGN   This attribute is used to set the vertical alignment for the table cell. HTML 4 defines **BASELINE**, **BOTTOM**, **MIDDLE**, and **TOP**. Internet Explorer further defines **CENTER**, which should act just like **MIDDLE**.

WIDTH   This attribute specifies the width of a header cell in pixels.

Attribute and Event Support

NETSCAPE 4   ALIGN, BACKGROUND, BGCOLOR, BORDERCOLOR, COLSPAN, HEIGHT, NOWRAP, ROWSPAN, VALIGN, and WIDTH. (CLASS, ID, LANG, and STYLE are implied.)

INTERNET EXPLORER 4   ALIGN (CENTER | LEFT | RIGHT), BGCOLOR, CLASS, COLSPAN, ID, LANG, NOWRAP, ROWSPAN, STYLE, TITLE, and VALIGN (BASELINE | BOTTOM | TOP), all W3C-defined events, and all attributes and events defined by Internet Explorer 4.

WEBTV   ALIGN (CENTER | LEFT | RIGHT), BGCOLOR, COLSPAN, GRADANGLE, GRADCOLOR, NOWRAP, ROWSPAN, TRANSPARENCY, VALIGN (BASELINE | BOTTOM | MIDDLE | TOP), and WIDTH.

Event Handlers
See "Events Reference," earlier in this appendix.

Examples

```
<TABLE BORDER="1">
   <TR>
      <TH>Names</TH>
      <TH>Apples</TH>
      <TH>Oranges</TH>
   </TR>
```

```
<TR>
    <TD>Bobby</TD>
    <TD>10</TD>
    <TD>5</TD>
</TR>

<TR>
    <TD>Ruby Sue</TD>
    <TD>20</TD>
    <TD>3</TD>
</TR>
</TABLE>
```

Compatibility

HTML 3.2 and 4
Internet Explorer 2, 3, 4, and 5
Netscape 1.1, 2, 3, 4, and 4.5
WebTV

Notes

- The HTML 3.2 specification defines only **ALIGN**, **COLSPAN**, **HEIGHT**, **NOWRAP**, **ROWSPAN**, **VALIGN**, and **WIDTH** attributes.
- This element should always be within the **<TR>** element.

<THEAD>   (Table Header)

This element is used to group the rows within the header of a table so that common alignment and style defaults can be set easily for numerous cells. This element may be particularly useful when setting a common head for tables that are dynamically generated.

Syntax

```
<THEAD
    ALIGN="CENTER | CHAR | JUSTIFY | LEFT | RIGHT"
    CHAR="character"
    CHAROFF="offset"
    CLASS="class name(s)"
    DIR="LTR | RTL"
    ID="unique alphanumeric identifier"
    LANG="language code"
    STYLE="style information"
    TITLE="advisory text"
```

```
          VALIGN="BASELINE | BOTTOM | MIDDLE | TOP"
          onclick="script"
          ondblclick="script"
          onkeydown="script"
          onkeypress="script"
          onkeyup="script"
          onmousedown="script"
          onmousemove="script"
          onmouseout="script"
          onmouseover="script"
          onmouseup="script">

</THEAD>
```

Attributes and Events Defined by Internet Explorer 4

```
          BGCOLOR="color name | #RRGGBB"
          LANGUAGE="JAVASCRIPT | JSCRIPT | VBS | VBSCRIPT"
          VALIGN="CENTER"
          ondragstart="script"
          onhelp="script"
          onselectstart="script"
```

Attributes

ALIGN   This attribute is used to align the contents of the cells within the **<THEAD>** element. Common values are **CENTER**, **JUSTIFY**, **LEFT**, and **RIGHT**. The HTML 4.0 specification also defines a value of **CHAR**. When **ALIGN** is set to **CHAR**, the attribute **CHAR** must be present and set to the character to which cells should be aligned. A common use of this approach would be to set cells to align on a decimal point.

BGCOLOR   This attribute specifies a background color for the cells within the **<THEAD>** element. Its value can be either a named color, such as **red**, or a color specified in the hexadecimal #*RRGGBB* format, such as **#FF0000**.

CHAR   This attribute is used to define the character to which element contents are aligned when the **ALIGN** attribute is set to the **CHAR** value.

CHAROFF   This attribute contains an offset as a positive or negative integer to align characters as related to the **CHAR** value. A value of **2**, for example, would align characters in a cell two characters to the right of the character defined by the **CHAR** attribute.

CLASS   See "Core Attributes Reference," earlier in this appendix.

DIR   See "Language Reference," earlier in this appendix.

ID   See "Core Attributes Reference," earlier in this appendix.

LANG   See "Language Reference," earlier in this appendix.

LANGUAGE   In the Microsoft implementation, this attribute specifies the scripting language to be used with an associated script bound to the element, typically through an event handler attribute. Possible values may include **JAVASCRIPT**, **JSCRIPT**, **VBS**, and **VBSCRIPT**. Other values that include the version of the language used, such as **JavaScript1.1**, may also be possible.

STYLE   See "Core Attributes Reference," earlier in this appendix.

TITLE   See "Core Attributes Reference," earlier in this appendix.

VALIGN   This attribute is used to set the vertical alignment for the table cells with the <THEAD> element. HTML 4 defines **BASELINE**, **BOTTOM**, **MIDDLE**, and **TOP**. Internet Explorer replaces **MIDDLE** with **CENTER**; the effect should be the same.

Attribute and Event Support

INTERNET EXPLORER 4   All attributes and events except **CHAR**, **CHAROFF**, and **DIR**. (Note: Internet Explorer 4 does not support the **JUSTIFY** value for the **ALIGN** attribute.)

Event Handlers
See "Events Reference," earlier in this appendix.

Example

```
<TABLE BORDER="1" BGCOLOR="YELLOW" WIDTH="80%">
<THEAD ALIGN="CENTER" BGCOLOR="RED" CLASS="footer"
      VALIGN="BOTTOM">
  <TD>This is the Important Table Headline</TD>
</THEAD>

<TBODY CLASS="tablebody">
  <TR>
     <TD>The contents of the table!</TD>
  </TR>
</TBODY>
</TABLE>
```

Compatibility

HTML 4
Internet Explorer 3, 4, and 5

Notes
This element is only contained by the **<TABLE>** element and contains table rows as delimited by **<TR>** elements.

<TITLE>   (Document Title)

This element encloses the title of an HTML document. It must occur within a document's <HEAD> element and must be present in all valid documents. Meaningful titles are very important since they are used for bookmarking a page and may be used by search engines attempting to index the document.

Syntax

```
<TITLE
    DIR="LTR | RTL"
    LANG="language code">

</TITLE>
```

Attributes Defined by Internet Explorer 4

```
        ID="unique alphanumeric identifier"
        TITLE="advisory text"
```

Attributes

DIR   See "Language Reference," earlier in this appendix.

ID   See "Core Attributes Reference," earlier in this appendix.

LANG   See "Language Reference," earlier in this appendix.

TITLE   See "Core Attributes Reference," earlier in this appendix.

Attribute and Event Support

INTERNET EXPLORER 4   ID and **TITLE**.

Event Handlers

None.

Example

```
<HEAD><TITLE>Big Company: Products: Super Widget</TITLE></HEAD>
```

Compatibility

HTML 2, 3.2, and 4
Internet Explorer 2, 3, 4, and 5

Netscape 1, 2, 3, 4, and 4.5
WebTV

Notes

■ Meaningful names should provide information about the document. A poor title would be something like "My Home Page," while a better title would be "Joe Smith's Home Page."

■ Older versions of Netscape allowed for multiple occurrences of the **<TITLE>** element. When multiple **<TITLE>** elements were encountered, they could be used to simulate an animated title bar. This was a bug with the Netscape browser, however, and the effect of multiple **<TITLE>** elements no longer works.

■ Browsers may be extremely sensitive with the **<TITLE>** element. If the title element is malformed or not closed, the page may not even render in the browser.

■ The HTML 2.0 and 3.2 specifications define no attributes for the **<TITLE>** element.

<TR>   (Table Row)

This element specifies a row in a table. The individual cells of the row are defined by the **<TH>** and **<TD>** elements.

Syntax

```
<TR
     ALIGN="CENTER | JUSTIFY | LEFT | RIGHT"
     BGCOLOR="color name | #RRGGBB" (transitional)
     CHAR="character"
     CHAROFF="offset"
     CLASS="class name(s)"
     DIR="LTR | RTL"
     ID="unique alphanumeric identifier"
     LANG="language code"
     STYLE="style information"
     TITLE="advisory text"
     VALIGN="BASELINE | BOTTOM | MIDDLE | TOP"
     onclick="script"
     ondblclick="script"
     onkeydown="script"
     onkeypress="script"
     onkeyup="script"
     onmousedown="script"
     onmousemove="script"
     onmouseout="script"
     onmouseover="script"
     onmouseup="script">

</TR>
```

Attributes and Events Defined by Internet Explorer 4

```
BORDERCOLOR="color name | #RRGGBB"
BORDERCOLORDARK="color name | #RRGGBB"
BORDERCOLORLIGHT="color name | #RRGGBB"
LANGUAGE="JAVASCRIPT | JSCRIPT | VBS | VBSCRIPT"
VALIGN="CENTER"
onafterupdate="script"
onbeforeupdate="script"
onblur="script"
ondragstart="script"
onfocus="script"
onhelp="script"
onresize="script"
onrowenter="script"
onrowexit="script"
onselectstart="script
```

Attributes Defined by WebTV

```
NOWRAP
TRANSPARENCY="number (0-100)"
```

Attributes

ALIGN   This attribute is used to align the contents of the cells within the **<THEAD>** element. Common values are **CENTER**, **JUSTIFY**, **LEFT**, and **RIGHT**.

BGCOLOR   This attribute specifies a background color for all the cells in a row. Its value can be either a named color, such as **red**, or a color specified in the hexadecimal #*RRGGBB* format, such as **#FF0000**.

BORDERCOLOR   This attribute, supported by Internet Explorer and Netscape, is used to set the border color for table cells in the row. The attribute should only be used with a positive value for the **BORDER** attribute. The value of the attribute can be either a named color, such as **green**, or a color specified in the hexadecimal #*RRGGBB* format, such as **#00FF00**.

BORDERCOLORDARK   This Internet Explorer–specific attribute specifies the darker of two border colors used to create a three-dimensional effect for the cell's borders. It must be used with the **BORDER** attribute set to a positive value. The attribute value can be either a named color, such as **blue**, or a color specified in the hexadecimal #*RRGGBB* format, such as **#00FF00**.

BORDERCOLORLIGHT   This Internet Explorer–specific attribute specifies the lighter of two border colors used to create a three-dimensional effect for a cell's borders. It must be used with the **BORDER** attribute set to a positive value. The attribute value can be either a named color, such as **red**, or a color specified in the hexadecimal #*RRGGBB* format, such as **#FF0000**.

CHAR   This attribute is used to define the character to which element contents are aligned when the **ALIGN** attribute is set to the **CHAR** value.

CHAROFF   This attribute contains an offset as a positive or negative integer to align characters as related to the **CHAR** value. A value of **2**, for example, would align characters in a cell two characters to the right of the character defined by the **CHAR** attribute.

CLASS   See "Core Attributes Reference," earlier in this appendix.

DIR   See "Language Reference," earlier in this appendix.

ID   See "Core Attributes Reference," earlier in this appendix.

LANG   See "Language Reference," earlier in this appendix.

LANGUAGE   In the Microsoft implementation, this attribute specifies the scripting language to be used with an associated script bound to the element, typically through an event handler attribute. Possible values may include **JAVASCRIPT**, **JSCRIPT**, **VBS**, and **VBSCRIPT**. Other values that include the version of the language used, such as **JavaScript1.1**, may also be possible.

NOWRAP   This WebTV-specific attribute keeps table rows from wrapping if they extend beyond the right margin.

STYLE   See "Core Attributes Reference," earlier in this appendix.

TITLE   See "Core Attributes Reference," earlier in this appendix.

TRANSPARENCY   This WebTV-specific attribute specifies the degree of transparency of the table. Values range from **0** (totally opaque) to **100** (totally transparent). A value of **50** is optimized for fast rendering.

VALIGN   This attribute is used to set the vertical alignment for the table cells with the **<TR>** element. HTML 4 defines **BASELINE**, **BOTTOM**, **MIDDLE**, and **TOP**. Internet Explorer replaces **MIDDLE** with **CENTER**; the effect should be the same.

Attribute and Event Support

NETSCAPE 4   ALIGN, BGCOLOR, and **VALIGN**. (CLASS, ID, LANG, and STYLE are implied.)

INTERNET EXPLORER 4   ALIGN (CENTER | LEFT | RIGHT), BGCOLOR, ID, LANG, STYLE, TITLE, and **VALIGN (BASELINE | BOTTOM | TOP)**, all W3C-defined events, and all attributes and events defined by Internet Explorer 4.

WEBTV   ALIGN (CENTER | LEFT | RIGHT), BGCOLOR, NOWRAP, TRANSPARENCY, and **VALIGN (BASELINE | BOTTOM | MIDDLE | TOP)**.

Event Handlers
See "Events Reference," earlier in this appendix.

Example

```
<TABLE WIDTH="300" BORDER="1">
    <TR BGCOLOR="RED" ALIGN="CENTER" VALIGN="CENTER">
        <TD>3</TD>
        <TD>5.6</TD>
        <TD>7.9</TD>
    </TR>
</TABLE>
```

Compatibility

HTML 3.2 and 4
Internet Explorer 2, 3, 4, and 5
Netscape 1.1, 2, 3, 4, and 4.5
WebTV

Notes

- This element is contained by the **<TABLE>**, **<THEAD>**, **<TBODY>**, and **<TFOOT>** elements. It contains the **<TH>** and **<TD>** elements.

- The HTML 3.2 specification defines only the **ALIGN** and **VALIGN** attributes for this element.

<TT> (Teletype Text)

This element is used to indicate that text should be rendered in a monospaced font similar to teletype text.

Syntax

```
<TT
    CLASS="class name(s)"
    DIR="LTR | RTL"
    ID="unique alphanumeric identifier"
    LANG="language code"
    STYLE="style information"
    TITLE="advisory text"
    onclick="script"
    ondblclick="script"
    onkeydown="script"
    onkeypress="script"
    onkeyup="script"
    onmousedown="script"
    onmousemove="script"
```

```
        onmouseout="script"
        onmouseover="script"
        onmouseup="script">

</TT>
```

Attributes and Events Defined by Internet Explorer 4

```
    LANGUAGE="JAVASCRIPT | JSCRIPT | VBS | VBSCRIPT"
    ondragstart="script"
    onhelp="script"
    onselectstart="script"
```

Attributes

CLASS   See "Core Attributes Reference," earlier in this appendix.

DIR   See "Language Reference," earlier in this appendix.

ID   See "Core Attributes Reference," earlier in this appendix.

LANG   See "Language Reference," earlier in this appendix.

LANGUAGE   In the Microsoft implementation, this attribute specifies the scripting language to be used with an associated script bound to the element, typically through an event handler attribute. Possible values may include **JAVASCRIPT**, **JSCRIPT**, **VBS**, and **VBSCRIPT**. Other values that include the version of the language used, such as **JavaScript1.1**, may also be possible.

STYLE   See "Core Attributes Reference," earlier in this appendix.

TITLE   See "Core Attributes Reference," earlier in this appendix.

Attribute and Event Support

NETSCAPE 4   CLASS, ID, LANG, and STYLE are implied.

INTERNET EXPLORER 4   All attributes and events except **DIR**.

Event Handlers
See "Events Reference," earlier in this appendix.

Example

```
Here is some <TT>monospaced text</TT>.
```

APPENDIXES

Compatibility

HTML 2, 3.2, and 4
Internet Explorer 2, 3, 4, and 5
Netscape 1, 2, 3, 4, and 4.5
WebTV

<U>   (Underline)

This element is used to indicate that the enclosed text should be displayed underlined.

Syntax (Transitional Only)

```
<U
    CLASS="class name(s)"
    DIR="LTR | RTL"
    ID="unique alphanumeric string"
    LANG="language code"
    STYLE="style information"
    TITLE="advisory text"
    onclick="script"
    ondblclick="script"
    onkeydown="script"
    onkeypress="script"
    onkeyup="script"
    onmousedown="script"
    onmousemove="script"
    onmouseout="script"
    onmouseover="script"
    onmouseup="script">

</U>
```

Attributes and Events Defined by Internet Explorer 4

```
    LANGUAGE="JAVASCRIPT | JSCRIPT | VBS | VBSCRIPT"
    ondragstart="script"
    onhelp="script"
    onselectstart="script"
```

Attributes

CLASS   See "Core Attributes Reference," earlier in this appendix.

DIR   See "Language Reference," earlier in this appendix.

ID   See "Core Attributes Reference," earlier in this appendix.

LANG   See "Language Reference," earlier in this appendix.

LANGUAGE   In the Microsoft implementation, this attribute specifies the scripting language to be used with an associated script bound to the element, typically through an event handler attribute. Possible values may include **JAVASCRIPT**, **JSCRIPT**, **VBS**, and **VBSCRIPT**. Other values that include the version of the language used, such as **JavaScript1.1**, may also be possible.

STYLE   See "Core Attributes Reference," earlier in this appendix.

TITLE   See "Core Attributes Reference," earlier in this appendix.

Attribute and Event Support

NETSCAPE 4   CLASS, ID, LANG, and **STYLE** are implied.

INTERNET EXPLORER 4   All attributes and events except **DIR**.

Event Handlers
See "Events Reference," earlier in this appendix.

Examples

```
Here is some <U>underlined text</U>.

Be careful with <U>underlined</U> text; it looks
like <A HREF="http://www.yahoo.com/">links</A>.
```

Compatibility

HTML 3.2 and 4 (transitional)
Internet Explorer 2, 3, 4, and 5
Netscape 3, 4, and 4.5
WebTV

Notes

- Under the strict HTML 4.0 specification, the <U> element is not defined. The capabilities of this element are possible using style sheets.

- Underlining text can be problematic because it looks similar to a link, especially in a black-and-white environment.

<UL>   (Unordered List)

This element is used to indicate an unordered list, namely a collection of items that do not have a numerical ordering. The individual items in the list are defined by the **<LI>** element, which is the only allowed element within **<UL>**.

Syntax

```
<UL
    CLASS="class name(s)"
    COMPACT (transitional)
    DIR="LTR | RTL"
    ID="unique alphanumeric identifier"
    LANG="language code"
    STYLE="style information"
    TITLE="advisory text"
    TYPE="CIRCLE | DISC | SQUARE" (transitional)
    onclick="script"
    ondblclick="script"
    onkeydown="script"
    onkeypress="script"
    onkeyup="script"
    onmousedown="script"
    onmousemove="script"
    onmouseout="script"
    onmouseover="script"
    onmouseup="script">

    List items specified by <LI> elements

</UL>
```

Attributes and Events Defined by Internet Explorer 4

```
    LANGUAGE="JAVASCRIPT | JSCRIPT | VBS | VBSCRIPT"
    ondragstart="script"
    onhelp="script"
    onselectstart="script"
```

Attributes

CLASS   See "Core Attributes Reference," earlier in this appendix.

COMPACT   This attribute indicates that the list should be rendered in a compact style. Few browsers actually change the rendering of the list regardless of the presence of this attribute. The **COMPACT** attribute requires no value.

DIR   See "Language Reference," earlier in this appendix.

ID   See "Core Attributes Reference," earlier in this appendix.

LANG   See "Language Reference," earlier in this appendix.

LANGUAGE In the Microsoft implementation, this attribute specifies the scripting language to be used with an associated script bound to the element, typically through an event handler attribute. Possible values may include **JAVASCRIPT**, **JSCRIPT**, **VBS**, and **VBSCRIPT**. Other values that include the version of the language used, such as **JavaScript1.1**, may also be possible.

STYLE See "Core Attributes Reference," earlier in this appendix.

TITLE See "Core Attributes Reference," earlier in this appendix.

TYPE The **TYPE** attribute is used to set the bullet style for the list. The values defined under HTML 3.2 and the transitional version of HTML 4 are **CIRCLE**, **DISC**, and **SQUARE**. A user agent may decide to use a different bullet depending on the nesting level of the list unless the **TYPE** attribute is used. The WebTV interface also supports a **TRIANGLE** bullet. The **TYPE** attribute is dropped under the strict version of HTML 4, since style sheets can provide richer bullet control.

Attribute and Event Support

NETSCAPE 4 CLASS, ID, LANG, STYLE, and TYPE.

INTERNET EXPLORER 4 All attributes and events except **COMPACT** and **DIR**.

WEBTV TYPE.

Event Handlers
See "Events Reference," earlier in this appendix.

Examples

```
<UL COMPACT TITLE="Sushi Short List" TYPE="CIRCLE">
   <LI>Maguro
   <LI>Ebi
   <LI>Hamachi
</UL>


<!-- Common but bad example -->
<UL>Indenting using lists should not be used, though it is common.
Many Web editors generate code laden with nonbreaking spaces and
unordered lists.</UL>
```

Compatibility

HTML 2, 3.2, and 4
Internet Explorer 2, 3, 4, and 5
Netscape 1, 2, 3, 4, and 4.5
WebTV

Notes

- HTML 2 supports only the **COMPACT** attribute.
- The HTML 3.2 specification supports **COMPACT** and **TYPE**.
- Under the strict HTML 4.0 specification, the **<UL>** element does not support the **COMPACT** attribute or the **TYPE** attribute. Both of these attributes can be safely replaced with style rules.
- Many Web page designers and page development tools use the **<UL>** element to indent text. Be aware that the only element that should occur within a **<UL>** element is **<LI>**, according to HTML standards, so such HTML markup does not conform to standards. However, this common practice is likely to continue.

<VAR>   (Variable)

This element is used to indicate a variable. Variables are identifiers that occur in a programming language or a mathematical expression. The element is logical, though enclosed text is often rendered in italics.

Syntax

```
<VAR
     CLASS="class name(s)"
     DIR="LTR | RTL"
     ID="unique alphanumeric value"
     LANG="language code"
     STYLE="style information"
     TITLE="advisory text"
     onclick="script"
     ondblclick="script"
     onkeydown="script"
     onkeypress="script"
     onkeyup="script"
     onmousedown="script"
     onmousemove="script"
     onmouseout="script"
     onmouseover="script"
     onmouseup="script">

</VAR>
```

Attributes and Events Defined by Internet Explorer 4

```
LANGUAGE="JAVASCRIPT | JSCRIPT | VBS | VBSCRIPT"
ondragstart="script"
onhelp="script"
onselectstart="script"
```

Attributes

CLASS   See "Core Attributes Reference," earlier in this appendix.

DIR   See "Language Reference," earlier in this appendix.

ID   See "Core Attributes Reference," earlier in this appendix.

LANG   See "Language Reference," earlier in this appendix.

LANGUAGE   In the Microsoft implementation, this attribute specifies the scripting language to be used with an associated script bound to the element, typically through an event handler attribute. Possible values may include **JAVASCRIPT**, **JSCRIPT**, **VBS**, and **VBSCRIPT**. Other values that include the version of the language used, such as **JavaScript1.1**, may also be possible.

STYLE   See "Core Attributes Reference," earlier in this appendix.

TITLE   See "Core Attributes Reference," earlier in this appendix.

Attribute and Event Support

NETSCAPE 4   CLASS, ID, LANG, and **STYLE** are implied.

INTERNET EXPLORER 4   All attributes and events except **DIR**.

Event Handlers
See "Events Reference," earlier in this appendix.

Example

```
Assign the value 5 to the variable <VAR>x</VAR>.
```

Compatibility

HTML 2, 3.2, and 4
Internet Explorer 2, 3, 4, and 5
Netscape 1, 2, 3, 4, and 4.5
WebTV

Notes

- As a logical element, **<VAR>** is a perfect candidate for style sheet binding.
- The HTML 2.0 and 3.2 specifications support no attributes for this element.

<WBR>   (Word Break)

This nonstandard element is used to indicate a place where a line break can occur if necessary. This element is used in conjunction with the **<NOBR>** element, which is used to keep text from wrapping. When used this way, **<WBR>** can be thought of as a soft line break in comparison to the **
** element. This element is common to both Netscape and Microsoft implementations, though it is not part of any HTML standard.

Syntax

```
<WBR
    CLASS="class name(s)"
    ID="unique alphanumeric value"
    LANGUAGE="JAVASCRIPT | JSCRIPT | VBS | VBSCRIPT"
    STYLE="style information"
    TITLE="advisory text">
```

Attributes

CLASS   See "Core Attributes Reference," earlier in this appendix.

ID   See "Core Attributes Reference," earlier in this appendix.

LANGUAGE   In the Microsoft implementation, this attribute specifies the scripting language to be used with an associated script bound to the element, typically through an event handler attribute. Possible values may include **JAVASCRIPT, JSCRIPT, VBS,** and **VBSCRIPT**. Other values that include the version of the language used, such as **JavaScript1.1**, may also be possible.

STYLE   See "Core Attributes Reference," earlier in this appendix.

TITLE   See "Core Attributes Reference," earlier in this appendix.

Attribute and Event Support

NETSCAPE 4   **CLASS, ID, STYLE,** and **TITLE** are implied.

INTERNET EXPLORER 4   All attributes.

Event Handlers
See "Events Reference," earlier in this appendix.

Example

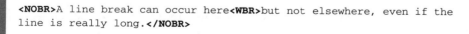
```
<NOBR>A line break can occur here<WBR>but not elsewhere, even if the
line is really long.</NOBR>
```

Compatibility

Internet Explorer 2, 3, 4, and 5
Netscape 1.1, 2, 3, 4, and 4.5

Notes

- This element was introduced in Netscape 1.1.
- This is an empty element, so no closing tag is required.

<XML> (XML Data Island)

This proprietary element introduced by Microsoft can be used to embed islands of XML (Extensible Markup Language) data into HTML documents; this only works under Internet Explorer 5. The **<XML>** element can be used to reference outside data sources using the **SRC** attribute, or to surround XML data in the HTML document itself.

Syntax (defined by Internet Explorer 5)

```
<XML
      ID="unique alphanumeric value"
      NS="URL of XML namespace"
      PREFIX="XML prefix"
      SRC="URL of XML data file"
      ondataavailable="script"
      ondatasetchanged="script"
      ondatasetcomplete="script"
      onreadystatechange="script"
      onrowenter="script"
      onrowexit="script">

      Embedded XML code

</XML>
```

Attributes

ID   See "Core Attributes Reference," earlier in this appendix.

NS   This attribute, still largely theoretical at the time of this writing, references the URL of an XML namespace.

PREFIX   This attribute references the URL of an XML namespace prefix in conjunction with the **NS** attribute.

SRC   This attribute references an external XML data file.

Event Handlers

See "Extended Events," earlier in this appendix.

Attribute and Event Support

INTERNET EXPLORER 5   ID, SRC, **ondataavailable, ondatasetchanged, ondatasetcomplete, onreadystatechange, onrowenter,** and **onrowexit.**

Examples

```
<!-- This code embeds XML data directly into a document.
     All code between the XML tags is not HTML, but a
     hypothetical example of XML. -->

<XML ID="tasty">
<COMBOMEAL>
   <BURGER>
   <NAME>Tasty Burger</NAME>
   <BUN BREAD="WHITE">
      <MEAT />
      <CHEESE />
      <MEAT />
   </BUN>
   </BURGER>
   <FRIES SIZE="LARGE" />
   <DRINK SIZE="LARGE" FLAVOR="Cola" />
</COMBOMEAL>
</XML>

<!-- This code fragment uses the SRC attribute to
     reference an external file containing XML data. -->

<XML SRC="combomeal.xml"></XML>
```

Compatibility

Internet Explorer 5

Notes

- Support of the **<XML>** element is currently exclusive to Internet Explorer 5.
- For a more detailed discussion of this element, refer to the section "Embedding XML into HTML Documents" in Chapter 17.

<XMP> (Example)

This deprecated element indicates that the enclosed text is an example. Example text is generally rendered in a monospaced font, and the spaces, tabs, and returns are preserved, as with the **<PRE>** element. As the **<XMP>** element is no longer standard, the **<PRE>** or **<SAMP>** elements should be used instead.

Syntax (Defined by HTML 2; Deprecated Under HTML 4)

```
<XMP>
</XMP>
```

Attributes and Events Defined by Internet Explorer 4

```
CLASS="class name(s)"
ID="unique alphanumeric value"
LANG="language code"
LANGUAGE="JAVASCRIPT | JSCRIPT | VBS | VBSCRIPT"
STYLE="style information"
TITLE="advisory text"
onclick="script"
ondblclick="script"
ondragstart="script"
onhelp="script"
onkeydown="script"
onkeypress="script"
onkeyup="script"
onmousedown="script"
onmousemove="script"
onmouseout="script"
onmouseover="script"
onmouseup="script"
onselectstart="script"
```

Attributes

CLASS   See "Core Attributes Reference," earlier in this appendix.

ID   See "Core Attributes Reference," earlier in this appendix.

LANG   See "Language Reference," earlier in this appendix.

LANGUAGE   In the Microsoft implementation, this attribute specifies the scripting language to be used with an associated script bound to the element, typically through an event handler attribute. Possible values may include **JAVASCRIPT**, **JSCRIPT**, **VBS**, and **VBSCRIPT**. Other values that include the version of the language used, such as **JavaScript1.1**, may also be possible.

STYLE   See "Core Attributes Reference," earlier in this appendix.

TITLE   See "Core Attributes Reference," earlier in this appendix.

Attribute and Event Support

NETSCAPE 4   CLASS, ID, STYLE, and TITLE.

INTERNET EXPLORER 4   All attributes.

Event Handlers
See "Events Reference," earlier in this appendix.

Example

```
<XMP>This is a large block of text used as an example. Note that returns
as well as    S P A C E S are preserved.</XMP>
```

Compatibility

HTML 2
Internet Explorer 2, 3, 4, and 5
Netscape 1, 2, 3, 4, and 4.5
WebTV

Notes

This element is very old, though it continues to be documented. It was first deprecated under HTML 3.2 and continues to be unsupported under HTML 4. Page designers should not use this element. Internet Explorer documentation supports this element but recommends use of **<PRE>** or **<SAMP>** instead.

The Complete Reference

Appendix B

Style Sheet Reference

C ascading style sheets, covered in Chapter 10, offer a powerful new tool for Web page layout. When used properly, style sheets also separate style from document structure, as was originally intended for HTML. Many of the style properties defined by the Cascading Style Sheets 1 (CSS1) specification are supported by major browsers, including Internet Explorer 3, 4, and 5, and Netscape Navigator 4 and 4.5. This appendix provides a concise look at style sheet rules, a listing of commonly supported CSS1 style properties and their values, and their current compatibility with the major browsers. Testing on a prerelease version of Netscape's new browser engine suggests that future Netscape browsers will support a wider range of style sheet properties. Cascading Style Sheets 2 (CSS2) positioning properties, also supported by the most recent browser versions, are included in this appendix. For a more detailed discussion of the CSS2 specification, see Chapter 10.

Style Sheet Terms

This section defines some basic terms used when working with style sheets.

Embedded Styles

Document-wide styles can be embedded in a document's **<HEAD>** element using the **<STYLE>** element. Note that styles should be commented out to avoid interpretation by non-style-aware browsers.

EXAMPLE

```
<HEAD>
<STYLE>
<!--
P  {font-size: 14pt; font-face: Times; color: blue;
    backgroundcolor: yellow}
EM {font-size: 16pt; color: green}
-->
</STYLE>
<TITLE> ... </TITLE></HEAD>
```

BROWSER SUPPORT

Internet Explorer 3, 4, and 5
Netscape 4 and 4.5

Inline Styles

Styles can be applied directly to elements in the body of a document. Rather than set document-wide values for the **<H1>** element, it is possible to set the style for an individual header, as shown here:

EXAMPLE

```
<H1 STYLE="font-size: 48pt; font-family: Arial;
          color: green">CSS1 Test</H1>
```

An **<H1>** header elsewhere in the document could be assigned a completely different style.

BROWSER SUPPORT

Internet Explorer 3, 4, and 5
Netscape 4 and 4.5

Linked Styles

Style can be contained in an external style sheet linked to a document or a set of documents (see Chapter 10), as shown in the following example. Linked information should be placed inside the **<HEAD>** element.

EXAMPLE

```
<LINK REL="stylesheet" TYPE="text/css" HREF="newstyle.css">
```

BROWSER SUPPORT

Internet Explorer 3, 4, and 5
Netscape 4 and 4.5

Imported Styles

Styles can be imported from an external file and expanded in place, similar to a macro. Importing can be used to include multiple style sheets. An imported style is defined with the **<STYLE>** element and the **TYPE** attribute, followed by the URL for the style sheet, as shown here:

EXAMPLE

```
<HEAD>
<STYLE TYPE="text/css">
@import url(newstyle.css)
<TITLE> ... </TITLE></HEAD>
```

BROWSER SUPPORT

Internet Explorer 5
Future versions of Netscape

Selectors

A selector is an HTML element, identifier, or class name associated with a style rule. In the following examples, **P** and **DIV** are the selectors.

EXAMPLES

```
P {font-size: 12pt}
DIV {font-family: Courier}
```

BROWSER SUPPORT

Internet Explorer 3, 4, and 5
Netscape 4 and 4.5

Class Selectors

Multiple classes can be defined for individual elements (selectors). To create a class selector, attach a class name to a selector; separate the selector from the class name with a period. Repeat this with the same selector, but give it a different name.

EXAMPLE

```
P.one {font-face: Arial; font-size: 12pt}
P.two {font-face: Verdana; font-size: 14pt}
```

There are now two different paragraph styles to choose from. Use the **CLASS** attribute with the **<P>** element to distinguish between them in the body of the document.

EXAMPLE

```
<P CLASS="one">This is paragraph style one.</P>
<P CLASS="two">This is paragraph style two.</P>
```

It is also possible to create stand-alone class selectors by omitting element names.

EXAMPLE

```
.one {font-face: Arial; font-size: 12pt}
.two {font-face: Verdana; font-size: 14pt}

<P CLASS="one">This is paragraph style one.</P>
<P CLASS="two">This is paragraph style two.</P>
<H1 CLASS="two">This header will also be style two.</P>
```

BROWSER SUPPORT

Internet Explorer 3, 4, and 5
Netscape 4 and 4.5

Contextual Selectors

Contextual selectors define the display of elements within other specific elements. In the following example, **<STRONG>** text within a **<DIV>** element displays as green; however, **<STRONG>** text outside the context of the **<DIV>** element is not affected by this style. Note that the contextual selectors **DIV** and **STRONG** are separated by white space, not by commas. Another way to say this is that a **<STRONG>** element with a **<DIV>** ancestor will match this style.

EXAMPLE

```
DIV STRONG {color: green}
```

BROWSER SUPPORT

Internet Explorer 3, 4, and 5
Netscape 4 and 4.5

ID Selectors

Styles can be assigned independent of elements by creating ID selectors. Create an ID selector by creating a name preceded by the character # and following it with the style to be associated with that ID.

EXAMPLE

```
#style43 {font-size: 6pt; font-face: Verdana; font-variant:
        small-caps}
```

In the body of the document, use the **ID** attribute to assign the style to an element or elements.

EXAMPLE

```
<P ID="style43">This text is hard to read.</P>
<H1 ID="style43">So is the text in this header.</H1>
```

Note *ID must be unique. Each value must appear only once in a given document.*

BROWSER SUPPORT

Internet Explorer 3, 4, and 5
Netscape 4 and 4.5

Rules

Style rules determine the styles to be associated with a selector. Style rules are enclosed within braces. A rule must include a property (**font-face**, in the following example) and a value (the font name **Impact**, in the following example).

EXAMPLE

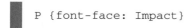
```
P {font-face: Impact}
```

Multiple rules can be included within a single style specification, but they must be separated by semicolons.

EXAMPLE

```
P {font-face: Impact; font-size: 12pt; line-height: 16pt}
```

BROWSER SUPPORT

Internet Explorer 3, 4, and 5
Netscape 4 and 4.5

Grouping

Selectors and declarations can be grouped together so that all the selectors are associated with a particular rule. Note that the listed selectors are separated by commas.

EXAMPLE

```
P, DIV, SPAN {background-color: yellow; font-face: Arial;
              color: black; font-size: 14pt}
```

BROWSER SUPPORT

Internet Explorer 3, 4, and 5
Netscape 4 and 4.5

Inheritance

In most cases, elements contained within another element inherit the property values specified for the parent element, unless those properties are defined differently for the nested elements. In the following example, the **<P>** element retains the background color and font color defined for the **<BODY>** element; only the font face changes.

EXAMPLE

```
BODY {background-color: blue; font-face: Courier; color: white}
P    {font-face: Arial}
```

BROWSER SUPPORT

Internet Explorer 3, 4, and 5
Netscape 4 and 4.5

Pseudoclasses

Elements can be assigned pseudoclasses to affect their display. There are three pseudoclasses: **A:active**, **A:link**, and **A:visited**.

A:active

This property specifies how the text in active links will display.

EXAMPLE

```
A:active {text-decoration: none}
```

BROWSER SUPPORT   Internet Explorer 5

A:link

This property specifies how text in unvisited links will display.

EXAMPLE

```
A:link {text-decoration: underline}
```

BROWSER SUPPORT

Internet Explorer 3, 4, and 5
Netscape 4 and 4.5

A:visited

This property specifies how text in visited links will display.

EXAMPLE

```
A:visited {text-decoration: line-through}
```

BROWSER SUPPORT

Internet Explorer 4 and 5
Netscape 4 and 4.5

Pseudoelements

This section discusses *pseudoelements*, which affect typographical items, such as the first line of a paragraph, rather than *structural elements*, such as the paragraph (**<P>**) itself.

first-letter

This property specifies how the first letter of text in a block-level element will display.

EXAMPLE

```
P:first-letter {font-face: Arial Black; font-size: 25pt}
```

BROWSER SUPPORT   None currently; probable in future versions of Netscape

first-line

This property specifies how the first line of text in a block-level element will display.

EXAMPLE

```
P:first-line {font-face: Arial Black; font-size: 150%;
              font-weight: bold}
```

BROWSER SUPPORT   None currently; probable in future versions of Netscape

Miscellaneous

This section discusses some miscellaneous terms associated with style sheets.

/* comments */

Comments can be placed within style sheets. HTML comment syntax (**<!-- comment -->**) does not apply. Style sheets use the comment syntax used in C programming (**/*comment*/**).

EXAMPLE

```
<STYLE>
P {font-face: Courier; font-size: 14pt; font-weight: bold;
   background-color: yellow}
/*This style sheet was created at Big Company, Inc.
All rights reserved.*/
</STYLE>
```

BROWSER SUPPORT

Internet Explorer 3, 4, and 5
Netscape 4 and 4.5

! Important

This property specifies that a style takes precedence over any different, conflicting styles. A style specified as important by an author takes precedence over a rule set by an end user.

EXAMPLE

```
DIV {font-size: 14pt; line-height: 150%; font-family: Arial ! important}
```

BROWSER SUPPORT

Internet Explorer 5
Future versions of Netscape

Fonts

The font properties are **font-family**, **font-size**, **font-style**, **font-weight**, **font-variant**, **text-transform**, **text-decoration**, and **font**. The **font** property can be used as a shorthand notation of font values.

EXAMPLE

```
{font-family: Arial, sans-serif; font-size: 18pt; font-style: italic;
  font-variant: normal; font-weight: bold; text-decoration: underline
  text-transform: capitalize;}
```

font-family

This property sets the font face for text. It is equivalent to the **FACE** attribute of the **<FONT>** element.

EXAMPLE

```
{font-family: "Arial, Helvetica, sans-serif"}
```

Fonts are read in descending order and must be separated by commas. In the preceding example, Arial is the primary font and will be displayed by browsers and systems with that font. If Arial is not available, Helvetica will be displayed. The final option, the generic font name **sans-serif**, will be used when no other listed font is available.

BROWSER SUPPORT

Internet Explorer 3, 4, and 5
Netscape 4 and 4.5

Name Values

These values define a specific font family or families.

EXAMPLES

```
{font-family: "Times New Roman"}
{font-family: "Courier"}
{font-family: "Times New Roman, Courier"}
```

BROWSER SUPPORT

Internet Explorer 3, 4, and 5
Netscape 4 and 4.5

Generic Font Names

These values can be used to set a final option in a list of fonts, generally to the default generic font on a user's system. For example, **serif** defaults to Courier on many systems. There are five generic font names currently available: **serif**, **sans-serif**, **cursive**, **fantasy**, and **monospace**.

serif   This value specifies a default serif font.

EXAMPLES

```
{font-family: "serif"}
{font-family: "Times New Roman, serif"}
```

BROWSER SUPPORT

Internet Explorer 3 (Windows only), 4, and 5
Netscape 4 and 4.5

sans-serif   This value specifies a default sans-serif font.

EXAMPLES

```
{font-family: sans-serif}
{font-family: "Arial, sans-serif"}
```

BROWSER SUPPORT

Internet Explorer 3 (Windows only), 4, and 5
Netscape 4 and 4.5

cursive   This value specifies a default cursive font.

EXAMPLE

```
{font-family: cursive}
```

BROWSER SUPPORT

Internet Explorer 3 (Windows only), 4, and 5
Future versions of Netscape

fantasy   This value specifies a default fantasy font.

EXAMPLE

```
{font-family: fantasy}
```

BROWSER SUPPORT

Internet Explorer 3 (Windows only), 4, and 5
Future versions of Netscape

monospace   This value specifies a default monospace font.

EXAMPLE

```
{font-family: monospace}
```

BROWSER SUPPORT

Internet Explorer 3, 4, and 5
Netscape 4 and 4.5

font-size

This property sets the font size of text. Options include exact sizes (point, pixel, or other values), absolute sizes, relative sizes, and percentages.

EXAMPLE

```
{font-face: Arial; font-size: 18pt}
```

BROWSER SUPPORT

Internet Explorer 3, 4, and 5
Netscape 4 and 4.5

Exact Font Size Values

These values set the font size to an exact size in points (pt) or pixels (px).

EXAMPLES

```
{font-size: 12pt}
{font-size: 30px}
```

BROWSER SUPPORT

Internet Explorer 3, 4, and 5
Netscape 4 and 4.5

Absolute Font Size Values

These values set the font size to an absolute size. There are seven possible sizes: **xx-small**, **x-small**, **small**, **medium**, **large**, **x-large**, and **xx-large**.

EXAMPLE

```
{font-size: xx-small}
```

BROWSER SUPPORT

Internet Explorer 3, 4, and 5
Netscape 4 and 4.5

xx-small   The value sets the font size to the smallest absolute font size, which is usually equivalent to one point size smaller than the HTML code **<FONT SIZE="1">**.

EXAMPLE

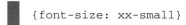

```
{font-size: xx-small}
```

BROWSER SUPPORT

Internet Explorer 3, 4, and 5
Netscape 4 and 4.5

x-small   The value sets the font size to the second-smallest absolute font size, which is equivalent to the HTML code **<FONT SIZE="1">**.

EXAMPLE

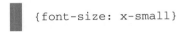

```
{font-size: x-small}
```

BROWSER SUPPORT

Internet Explorer 3, 4, and 5
Netscape 4 and 4.5

small   This value sets the font size to the third smallest absolute font size, which is equivalent to the HTML code **<FONT SIZE="2">**.

EXAMPLE

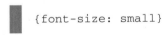

```
{font-size: small}
```

BROWSER SUPPORT

Internet Explorer 3, 4, and 5
Netscape 4 and 4.5

medium   The value sets the font size to the middle absolute font size, which is equivalent to the HTML code **<FONT SIZE="3">**.

EXAMPLE

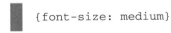

```
{font-size: medium}
```

BROWSER SUPPORT

Internet Explorer 3, 4, and 5
Netscape 4 and 4.5

large   The value sets the font size to the third-largest absolute font size, which is equivalent to the HTML code **<FONT SIZE="4">**.

EXAMPLE

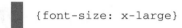

```
{font-size: large}
```

BROWSER SUPPORT

Internet Explorer 3, 4, and 5
Netscape 4 and 4.5

x-large   The value sets the font size to the second-largest absolute font size, which is equivalent to the HTML code **<FONT SIZE="5">**.

EXAMPLE

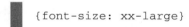

```
{font-size: x-large}
```

BROWSER SUPPORT

Internet Explorer 3, 4, and 5
Netscape 4 and 4.5

xx-large   The value sets the font size to the largest absolute font size, which is equivalent to the HTML code **<FONT SIZE="6">**.

EXAMPLE

```
{font-size: xx-large}
```

BROWSER SUPPORT

Internet Explorer 3, 4, and 5
Netscape 4 and 4.5

Percentage Font Size Values

These values set the font size to a percentage of the primary font size of a section or document. For example, if the font size for the **<BODY>** element were set to 12 points, and font size for a **<P>** element inside the body were set to 200 percent, the text inside the **<P>** element would display in 24-point type. This could be cleared on inheritance.

EXAMPLE

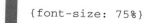

```
{font-size: 75%}
```

BROWSER SUPPORT

Internet Explorer 3 (incomplete), 4, and 5
Netscape 4 and 4.5

Relative Font Size Values

These values define the font size relative to the primary font size of a document or section.

smaller This value sets the font size one point smaller than the primary font size of a section or document. It is equivalent to the HTML code **<FONT SIZE=-1>**.

EXAMPLE

```
{font-size: smaller}
```

BROWSER SUPPORT

Internet Explorer 4 and 5
Netscape 4 and 4.5

larger This value sets the font size to one point larger than the primary font size of a section or document. It is equivalent to the HTML code **<FONT SIZE=+1>**.

EXAMPLE

```
{font-size: larger}
```

BROWSER SUPPORT

Internet Explorer 4 and 5
Netscape 4 and 4.5

font-style

This property sets the style of a font to normal, oblique, or italic. This can also be done by using a specific font (for example, Times New Roman Italic). It also allows control of style across font families.

EXAMPLES

```
{font-style: normal}
{font-style: oblique}
{font-style: italic}
```

BROWSER SUPPORT

Internet Explorer 3 (incomplete), 4, and 5
Netscape 4 and 4.5

normal

This value sets the style of a font to Roman.

EXAMPLE

```
{font-style: normal}
```

BROWSER SUPPORT

Internet Explorer 4 and 5
Netscape 4 and 4.5

italic

This value sets the style of a font to italic.

EXAMPLE

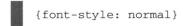

```
{font-style: normal}
```

BROWSER SUPPORT

Internet Explorer 3, 4, and 5
Netscape 4 and 4.5

oblique

This value sets the style of a font to oblique.

EXAMPLE

```
{font-style: oblique}
```

BROWSER SUPPORT

Internet Explorer 4 and 5
Netscape 4 and 4.5

font-weight

This property sets the weight, or relative boldness, of a font. Values can be set with named values (**normal, bold, bolder,** or **lighter**) or with numbered values (**100** through **900**).

EXAMPLES

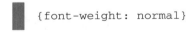

```
{font-weight: bold}
{font-weight: 300}
```

BROWSER SUPPORT

Internet Explorer 3 (incomplete), 4, and 5
Netscape 4 and 4.5 (incomplete)

normal

This value sets the weight of the font to normal.

EXAMPLE

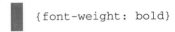

```
{font-weight: normal}
```

BROWSER SUPPORT

Internet Explorer 4 and 5
Netscape 4 and 4.5

bold

This value sets the weight of the font to bold.

EXAMPLE

```
{font-weight: bold}
```

BROWSER SUPPORT

Internet Explorer 3, 4, and 5
Netscape 4 and 4.5

bolder

his value sets the weight of the font to one that is bolder than set by the **bold** value.

EXAMPLE

```
{font-weight: bolder}
```

BROWSER SUPPORT   Internet Explorer 4 and 5

lighter

This value sets the weight of the font to one that is lighter than set by the **normal** value.

EXAMPLE

```
{font-weight: lighter}
```

BROWSER SUPPORT   Internet Explorer 4 and 5

100–900

These values set the weight of the font from lightest (**100**) to boldest (**900**) in increments of 100. In practice, under Internet Explorer 4 and Netscape 4, the values **100** through **500** display as normal text; **600** through **800** display as bold; and **900** displays as extra bold. Browser support for other values is inconsistent at best.

EXAMPLE

```
{font-weight: 600}
```

BROWSER SUPPORT

Internet Explorer 4 and 5 (Windows only, incomplete)
Netscape 4 and 4.5 (incomplete for Macs)

font-variant

This property sets a variation of the specified or default font family. Values currently supported are **normal** and **small-caps**.

EXAMPLE

```
{font-family: Courier; font-size: 14pt; font-variant: small-caps}
```

BROWSER SUPPORT

Internet Explorer 4 and 5
Future versions of Netscape

normal

This value, which is the default, or "off" value for this property, sets the display to the font's normal appearance.

EXAMPLE

```
{font-family: Arial; font-size: 12pt; font-variant: normal}
```

BROWSER SUPPORT

Internet Explorer 4 and 5
Future versions of Netscape

small-caps

This value sets text to all small capitals.

EXAMPLE

```
{font-family: Times New Roman; font-size: 20pt;
 font-variant: small-caps}
```

BROWSER SUPPORT

Internet Explorer 4 and 5
Future versions of Netscape

text-transform

This property transforms the case of the affected text. Possible values are **capitalize**, **uppercase**, **lowercase**, and **none**.

EXAMPLE

```
{text-transform: capitalize}
```

BROWSER SUPPORT

Internet Explorer 4 and 5
Netscape 4 (incomplete for Macs) and 4.5

pitalize

value capitalizes the initial letter of each word in the affected text.

EXAMPLE

```
{font-family: Times New Roman; font-size: 20pt;
 text-transform: capitalize}
```

BROWSER SUPPORT

Internet Explorer 4 and 5
Netscape 4 and 4.5

uppercase

This value capitalizes all the letters of each word in the affected text.

EXAMPLE

```
{font-family: Helvetica; font-size: 10pt; text-transform: uppercase}
```

BROWSER SUPPORT

Internet Explorer 4 and 5
Netscape 4 and 4.5

lowercase

This value sets the letters of each word in the affected text to lowercase.

EXAMPLE

```
{font-family: Verdana; font-size: 14pt; text-transform: lowercase}
```

BROWSER SUPPORT

Internet Explorer 4 and 5
Netscape 4 and 4.5

none

This value leaves text unaffected or overrides another established value.

EXAMPLE

```
{font-family: Arial; font-size: 12pt; text-transform: none}
```

BROWSER SUPPORT

Internet Explorer 4 and 5
Netscape 4 and 4.5

text-decoration

This property defines specific text effects. Possible values are **blink**, **line-through**, **overline**, **underline**, and **none**.

EXAMPLE

```
{text-decoration: underline}
```

This property is often used with the **<A>** element and its associated pseudoclasses (**A:active**, **A:link**, and **A:visited**). The following example draws a line through visited links in a page.

EXAMPLE

```
A:visited {text-decoration: line-through}
```

BROWSER SUPPORT

Internet Explorer 3 (incomplete), 4, and 5
Netscape 4 and 4.5 (incomplete)

blink

This value causes text to blink.

EXAMPLE

```
{text-decoration: blink}
```

BROWSER SUPPORT   Netscape 4 and 4.5

line-through

This value draws a line through text.

EXAMPLE

```
{text-decoration: line-through}
```

BROWSER SUPPORT

Internet Explorer 3, 4, and 5
Netscape 4 and 4.5

overline

This value draws a line over text.

EXAMPLE

```
{text-decoration: overline}
```

BROWSER SUPPORT

Internet Explorer 4 and 5
Future versions of Netscape

underline

This value draws a line under text.

EXAMPLE

```
{text-decoration: underline}
```

BROWSER SUPPORT

Internet Explorer 3, 4, and 5
Netscape 4 and 4.5

none

This value displays plain text. It can be used with **A:active**, **A:link**, and **A:visited** to turn off underlining of links.

EXAMPLE

```
{text-decoration: none}
```

BROWSER SUPPORT

Internet Explorer 3, 4, and 5
Netscape 4 and 4.5

font

This property provides a shorthand way to specify all font properties with one style rule. Properties are **font-family**, **font-size/line-height**, **font-style**, **font-weight**, and **font-variant**. It is not necessary to include all properties. The **line-height** property is discussed in the following section, "Text." Font names consisting of more than one word should be placed in quotes. Lists of variant fonts should be separated by commas and placed in quotes.

EXAMPLE

```
{font: normal small-caps bold 12pt/18pt
       "Times New Roman, Courier, serif"}
```

BROWSER SUPPORT

Internet Explorer 3 (incomplete), 4, and 5
Netscape 4 (incomplete for Macs) and 4.5

Text

This section discusses style properties that affect text-level elements.

word-spacing

This property sets the spacing between words. Values can be set in inches (**in**), centimeters (**cm**), millimeters (**mm**), points (**pt**), picas (**pc**), em spaces (**em**), or pixels (**px**); or to the default value **normal**.

EXAMPLES

```
{font-family: Arial; font-size: 16pt; word-spacing: 3pt}
{font-family: Helvetica; font-size: 12pt; word-spacing: normal}
```

BROWSER SUPPORT   None currently; probable in future versions of Netscape

normal

This value, which is the default for this property, sets word spacing to the browser's setting.

EXAMPLE

```
{font-family: Arial; font-size: 10pt; word-spacing: normal}
```

BROWSER SUPPORT   None currently; probable in future versions of Netscape

letter-spacing

This property sets the amount of spacing between letters. Values can be set in various units or to the default value **normal**.

EXAMPLE

```
{font-family: Arial; font-size: 14pt; letter-spacing: 2pt}
```

BROWSER SUPPORT

Internet Explorer 4 and 5
Future versions of Netscape

Unit Values

These values set letter spacing to a certain number of units in inches (**in**), centimeters (**cm**), millimeters (**mm**), points (**pt**), picas, (**pc**), em spaces (**em**), or pixels (**px**).

EXAMPLE

```
{font-family: Arial; font-size: 14pt; letter-spacing: 2pt}
```

BROWSER SUPPORT

Internet Explorer 4 and 5
Future versions of Netscape

normal

This value sets letter spacing to the browser's default setting.

EXAMPLE

```
{font-family: Arial; font-size: 14pt; letter-spacing: normal}
```

BROWSER SUPPORT

Internet Explorer 4 and 5
Future versions of Netscape

line-height

This property sets the height (leading) between lines of text in a block-level element such as a paragraph. Values can be specified as a number of lines, a number of units (pixels, points, and so on), or a percentage of the font size. This property is generally used in conjunction with the **font-size** property.

EXAMPLES

```
{font-family: Arial; font-size: 14pt; line-height: 2}
{font-family: Arial; font-size: 14pt; line-height: 16px}
{font-family: Arial; font-size: 14pt; line-height: normal}
{font-family: Arial; font-size: 14pt; line-height: 125%}
```

BROWSER SUPPORT

Internet Explorer 3, 4, and 5
Netscape 4 and 4.5

text-align

This property sets the horizontal alignment of block-level text elements. Values are **left**, **right**, **center**, and **justify**. The default value is **left**. This property is similar to the **ALIGN** attribute available with HTML block-level elements such as **<P>**.

BROWSER SUPPORT

Internet Explorer 3 (incomplete), 4, and 5 (Windows only; incomplete)
Netscape 4 and 4.5

left

This value sets the horizontal alignment of text in block-level elements to the left.

EXAMPLE

```
P {text-align: left}
```

BROWSER SUPPORT

Internet Explorer 3, 4, and 5
Netscape 4 and 4.5

right

This value sets the horizontal alignment of text in block-level elements to the right.

EXAMPLE

```
P {text-align: right}
```

BROWSER SUPPORT

Internet Explorer 3, 4, and 5
Netscape 4 and 4.5

center

This value sets the horizontal alignment of text in block-level elements to the center.

EXAMPLE

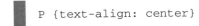
```
P {text-align: center}
```

BROWSER SUPPORT

Internet Explorer 3, 4, and 5
Netscape 4 and 4.5

justify

This value sets the horizontal alignment of text in block-level elements flush to the left and right.

EXAMPLE

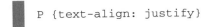
```
P {text-align: justify}
```

BROWSER SUPPORT

Internet Explorer 5
Netscape 4 and 4.5

vertical-align

This property sets the vertical positioning of text and images with respect to the baseline setting. Possible values are **baseline**, **sub**, **super**, **top**, **text-top**, **middle**, **bottom**, and **text-bottom**. Percentages can also be given as values. The default value is **baseline**.

EXAMPLE

```
P {vertical-align: baseline}
```

BROWSER SUPPORT   Internet Explorer 4 and 5 (incomplete)

baseline

This value, which is the default for this property, aligns text or images to the baseline setting.

EXAMPLE

```
P {vertical-align: baseline}
```

BROWSER SUPPORT   Not supported

sub

This value positions text or images as a subscript of the baseline setting.

EXAMPLE

```
P {vertical-align: sub}
```

BROWSER SUPPORT   Internet Explorer 4 and 5

super

This value positions text or images as a superscript of the baseline setting.

EXAMPLE

```
P {vertical-align: super}
```

BROWSER SUPPORT   Internet Explorer 4 and 5

top

This value aligns the top of text or images with the top of the tallest element, relative to the baseline.

EXAMPLE

```
P {vertical-align: top}
```

BROWSER SUPPORT   Not supported

text-top

This value aligns the top of text or images with the top of the font in the containing element.

EXAMPLE

```
P {vertical-align: text-top}
```

BROWSER SUPPORT   Not supported

middle

This value aligns the middle of text or images to the middle of the x-height of the containing element.

EXAMPLE

```
P {vertical-align: middle}
```

BROWSER SUPPORT   Not supported

bottom

This value aligns the bottom of text or images with the bottom of the lowest element, relative to the baseline.

EXAMPLE

```
P {vertical-align: bottom}
```

BROWSER SUPPORT   Not supported

text-bottom

This value aligns the bottom of text or images with the bottom of the font in the containing element.

EXAMPLE

```
P {vertical-align: text-bottom}
```

BROWSER SUPPORT   Not supported

text-indent

This property indents the text in the first line of a block-level element. Values can be defined as length values (**.5cm**, **15px**, **12pt**, and so on) or as a percentage of the width of the block element. The default value is **0**, which indicates no indentation.

EXAMPLES

```
{text-indent: 5pt}
{text-indent: 15%}
```

BROWSER SUPPORT

Internet Explorer 3, 4, and 5
Netscape 4 and 4.5

Colors and Backgrounds

This section discusses the style properties that affect backgrounds and various
concerns associated with backgrounds, such as color, images, and scrolling, as well as
the property that affects the color of text.

color

This property sets the color of text. Values can be specified as color names, hex values
in three- or six-digit format, or red-green-blue (RGB) values (numbers or percentages).
For browser support of color values, see the section "Style Sheet Color Values," later in
this appendix.

EXAMPLES

```
{color: yellow}
{color: #FFFF00}
{color: #FF0}
{color: rgb(255,255,0)}
{color: rgb(100%,100%,0%)}
```

BROWSER SUPPORT

Internet Explorer 3, 4, and 5
Netscape 4 and 4.5

background-color

This property sets an element's background color. It is often used in conjunction with
the **color** property, which sets text color (see the discussion of the **color** property under
"color," later in this appendix). Used with block elements, this property colors content
and padding but not margins. The default value, **transparent**, allows any underlying

content to show through. See "Style Sheet Color Values," later in this appendix, for browser support of color values.

EXAMPLES

```
{background-color: #00CCFF}
{background-color: orange}
{background-color: rgb(255,0,255}
```

BROWSER SUPPORT

> Internet Explorer 4 and 5
> Netscape 4 and 4.5

transparent

The value, which is the default for this property, sets the background color to allow any underlying content to show through, as it does when used with the **background** property.

EXAMPLE

```
{background-color: transparent}
```

BROWSER SUPPORT

> Internet Explorer 4 and 5
> Netscape 4 and 4.5

background-image

This property associates a background image with an element. Underlying content shows through transparent regions in the source image. The background image requires a URL (complete or relative) to link it to the source image (GIF or JPEG). The default value is **none**.

BROWSER SUPPORT

> Internet Explorer 4 and 5
> Netscape 4 and 4.5

Background Image URL Values

These values provide a URL link to a source image to be used as the background image.

EXAMPLE

```
{background-image: url(yellowpattern.gif)}
```

BROWSER SUPPORT

Internet Explorer 4 and 5
Netscape 4 and 4.5

none This value, which is the default for this property, sets the background so that it doesn't display an image (any underlying content shows through).

EXAMPLE

```
{background-image: none}
```

BROWSER SUPPORT

Internet Explorer 4 and 5
Netscape 4 and 4.5

background-repeat

This value determines how background images tile when they are smaller than the canvas space used by their associated elements. It is used in conjunction with the **background-image** property. Possible values are **repeat, repeat-x, repeat-y**, and **no-repeat**.

BROWSER SUPPORT

Internet Explorer 4 and 5
Netscape 4 and 4.5

repeat

This value, which is the default for this property, sets the background image to repeat horizontally and vertically.

EXAMPLE

```
{background-image: url(yellowpattern.gif) background-repeat: repeat}
```

BROWSER SUPPORT

Internet Explorer 4 and 5
Netscape 4 and 4.5

repeat-x

This value sets the background image to repeat horizontally only.

EXAMPLE

```
{background-image: url(yellowpattern.gif); background-repeat: repeat-x}
```

BROWSER SUPPORT

Internet Explorer 4 and 5
Netscape 4 and 4.5

repeat-y

This value sets the background image to repeat vertically only.

EXAMPLE

```
{background-image: url(yellowpattern.gif); background-repeat: repeat-y}
```

BROWSER SUPPORT

Internet Explorer 4 and 5
Netscape 4 and 4.5

no-repeat

This value prevents the background image from repeating.

EXAMPLE

```
{background-image: url(yellowpattern.gif);
 background-repeat: no-repeat}
```

BROWSER SUPPORT

Internet Explorer 4 and 5
Netscape 4 and 4.5.

background-attachment

This property sets the background image to scroll or not to scroll with its associated element's content. The default value is **scroll**. The alternate value, **fixed**, is intended to create a watermark effect similar to the proprietary attribute, **BGPROPERTIES**, of the **<BODY>** element introduced by Microsoft.

EXAMPLE

```
{background-image: url(yellowpattern.gif);
 background-attachment: scroll}
```

BROWSER SUPPORT   Internet Explorer 4 and 5

scroll

This value, the default for this property, sets the background image to scroll with associated content, such as text.

EXAMPLE

```
{background-image: url(yellowpattern.gif);
 background-attachment: scroll}
```

BROWSER SUPPORT   Internet Explorer 4 and 5

fixed

This value sets the background image to remain static while associated content, such as text, scrolls.

EXAMPLE

```
{background-image: url(yellowpattern.gif);
 background-attachment: fixed}
```

BROWSER SUPPORT   Internet Explorer 4 and 5

background-position

This property determines how a background image is positioned within the canvas space used by its associated element. The position of the image's upper-left corner can be specified as an absolute distance in pixels. It can also be specified as a percentage along the horizontal and vertical dimensions. Finally, the position can be specified as named values that describe the horizontal and vertical dimensions. The named values for the horizontal axis are **center**, **left**, and **right**; those for the vertical axis are **top**, **center**, and **bottom**. The default value for an unspecified dimension is assumed to be **center**.

EXAMPLES

```
{background-image: url(yellowpattern.gif);
 background-position: 50px 100px}
{background-image: url(yellowpattern.gif);
 background-position: 10% 45%}
{background-image: url(yellowpattern.gif);
 background-position: top center}
```

BROWSER SUPPORT   Internet Explorer 4 and 5

Background Position Numeric Values

These values set the position of the background image by specifying a specific pixel position for the upper-left corner of the image.

EXAMPLE

```
{background-image: url(picture.gif);
 background-position: 10px 10px}
```

BROWSER SUPPORT   Internet Explorer 4 and 5

Background Position Percentage Values

These values define a background's position as a percentage of its parent element's horizontal and vertical axes.

EXAMPLE

```
{background-image: url(picture.gif);
 background-position: 20% 40%}
```

BROWSER SUPPORT   Internet Explorer 4 and 5

Background Position Named Values

These values, which include **top**, **center**, **bottom**, **left**, and **right**, define the position of a background image relative to its parent element.

top   This value sets the position of the background image to the top of its associated element. It can be used in combination with the **center** value or with a horizontal value (**left** or **right**).

EXAMPLES

```
{background-image: url(picture.gif);
 background-position: top}
{background-image: url(picture.gif);
 background-position: top left}
```

BROWSER SUPPORT   Internet Explorer 4 and 5

center   This value sets the position of the background image to the center of its associated element. It can be used in combination with a vertical value (**bottom** or **top**).

EXAMPLES

```
{background-image: url(picture.gif);
 background-position: center}
{background-image: url(picture.gif);
 background-position: center bottom}
```

BROWSER SUPPORT   Internet Explorer 4 and 5

bottom   This value sets the position of the background image to the bottom of its associated element. It can be used in combination with the **center** value or with a horizontal value (**left** or **right**).

EXAMPLES

```
{background-image: url(picture.gif);
 background-position: bottom}
{background-image: url(picture.gif);
 background-position: bottom left}
```

BROWSER SUPPORT   Internet Explorer 4 and 5

left   This value sets the position of the background image to the left side of its associated element. It can be used in combination with the **center** value or with a vertical value (**bottom** or **top**).

EXAMPLES

```
{background-image: url(picture.gif);
 background-position: left}
{background-image: url(picture.gif);
 background-position: left center}
```

BROWSER SUPPORT   Internet Explorer 4 and 5

right   This value sets the position of the background image to the left side of its associated element. It can be used in combination with the **center** value or with a vertical value (**bottom** or **top**).

EXAMPLES

```
{background-image: url(picture.gif);
 background-position: right}
{background-image: url(picture.gif);
 background-position: right top}
```

BROWSER SUPPORT   Internet Explorer 4 and 5

background

This property sets any or all background properties, including images. Properties not specified use their default values. Property order does not matter, and semicolons are not required.

EXAMPLE

```
{background: white url(picture.gif) repeat-y center}
```

BROWSER SUPPORT

Internet Explorer 3, 4, and 5
Netscape 4 and 4.5 (incomplete)

transparent

This value sets the background color to a transparent setting, which allows any underlying content to show through.

EXAMPLE

```
{background: transparent}
```

BROWSER SUPPORT

Internet Explorer 3, 4, and 5
Netscape 4 and 4.5

Background URL Values

These values provide a URL link to a source image to be used as the background image using the same syntax as **background-image**.

EXAMPLE

```
{background: url(yellowpattern.gif)}
```

BROWSER SUPPORT

Internet Explorer 3, 4, and 5
Netscape 4 and 4.5

none   This value, which is the default for this property, specifies that there will be no background image.

EXAMPLE

```
{background: none}
```

BROWSER SUPPORT

Internet Explorer 3, 4, and 5
Netscape 4 and 4.5

repeat   This value sets the background image to repeat horizontally and vertically. If no value is specified, **repeat** is assumed as the default value.

EXAMPLE

```
{background: url(yellowpattern.gif) repeat}
```

BROWSER SUPPORT

Internet Explorer 3, 4, and 5
Netscape 4 and 4.5

repeat-x   This value sets the background image to repeat horizontally only.

EXAMPLE

```
{background: url(yellowpattern.gif) repeat-x}
```

BROWSER SUPPORT

Internet Explorer 3, 4, and 5
Netscape 4 and 4.5

repeat-y   This value sets the background image to repeat vertically only.

EXAMPLE

```
{background: url(yellowpattern.gif) repeat-y}
```

BROWSER SUPPORT

Internet Explorer 3, 4, and 5
Netscape 4 and 4.5

no-repeat   This value specifies that the background image does not repeat.

EXAMPLE

```
{background: url(yellowpattern.gif) no-repeat}
```

BROWSER SUPPORT

Internet Explorer 3, 4, and 5
Netscape 4 and 4.5

scroll   This value specifies that the background image scrolls with its associated content. Under Internet Explorer 3, setting the scroll value does not work; if this value is not specified, however, the background scrolls with its associated content.

EXAMPLE

```
{background: url(yellowpattern.gif) repeat scroll}
```

BROWSER SUPPORT   Internet Explorer 4 and 5

fixed   This value specifies that the background image remains stationary while its associated content scrolls.

EXAMPLE

```
{background: url(yellowpattern.gif) fixed}
```

BROWSER SUPPORT   Internet Explorer 3, 4, and 5

Background Positioning Percentage Values

These values set the position of the background image as a percentage along the horizontal and vertical dimensions. The first percentage value sets horizontal placement; the second sets vertical placement. If only one value is specified, the vertical placement value defaults to **50%**. Use of these values in a page with no content can lead to problems under Internet Explorer 3. (For example, a value of **bottom** aligns the bottom of the image with the top of the browser window, thus placing it completely out of view. This has been corrected in Internet Explorer 4, which displays the image properly at the bottom of the browser window.) If no values are set, the placement defaults to the upper-left corner of the browser window.

EXAMPLE

```
{background url(picture.gif) no-repeat 20% 50%}
```

BROWSER SUPPORT   Internet Explorer 3, 4, and 5

Background Positioning Named Values

These values sets the position of the background image. The values **top**, **middle**, and **bottom**, assign vertical positions; **center**, **left**, and **right** assign horizontal positions. Values can be combined as common sense suggests. If no values are set, the placement defaults to the upper-left corner of the browser window.

EXAMPLES

```
{background url(picture.gif) no-repeat top center}
{background url(picture.gif) no-repeat right bottom}
```

BROWSER SUPPORT   Internet Explorer 3, 4, and 5

top   This value sets the position of the background image to the top of its associated element. If no other value is set, the top-aligned image defaults to the left.

EXAMPLE

```
{background url(picture.gif) no-repeat top}
```

BROWSER SUPPORT   Internet Explorer 3, 4, and 5

center   This value sets the position of the background image to the horizontal center of its associated element. If no other value is set, the center-aligned image defaults to the vertical middle.

EXAMPLE

```
{background url(picture.gif) no-repeat center}
```

BROWSER SUPPORT   Internet Explorer 3, 4, and 5

middle   This value sets the position of the background image to the vertical middle of its associated element. If no other value is set, the middle-aligned image defaults to the left. Under Internet Explorer 4, **middle** works only when assigned a horizontal value; otherwise, the background image defaults to the upper left.

EXAMPLE

```
{background url(picture.gif) no-repeat middle}
```

BROWSER SUPPORT   Internet Explorer 3, 4, and 5

bottom   This value sets the position of the background image to the bottom of its associated element. If no other value is set, the bottom-aligned image defaults to the left.

EXAMPLE

```
{background url(picture.gif) no-repeat bottom}
```

BROWSER SUPPORT   Internet Explorer 3, 4, and 5

left   This value, which is the default horizontal position for this property, sets the position of the background image to the left of its associated element.

EXAMPLE

```
{background url(picture.gif) no-repeat left}
```

BROWSER SUPPORT   Internet Explorer 3, 4, and 5

right   This value sets the position of the background image to the right of its associated element.

EXAMPLE

```
{background url(picture.gif) no-repeat right}
```

BROWSER SUPPORT   Internet Explorer 3, 4, and 5

Layout

This section discusses style properties that affect the layout of HTML documents.

Margins

Style sheets can be used to set margins around an element with the **margin** property. Margin values can be set to a specific length (**15pt**, **2em**, and so on) or to a percentage value of the block element's width. Another value, **auto**, attempts to calculate the margin automatically. The **auto** value is not supported. Four distinct margins can be set separately from one another using the following properties: **margin-top**, **margin-bottom**, **margin-right**, and **margin-left**. By itself, **margin** sets a consistent margin on all four sides of the affected element. Margins can also be set to negative values.

BROWSER SUPPORT

Internet Explorer 3 (Windows only), 4, and 5
Netscape 4 and 4.5

margin-top

This property sets an element's top margin.

EXAMPLE

```
{margin-top: 15pt}
```

BROWSER SUPPORT

Internet Explorer 3 (Windows only), 4, and 5
Netscape 4 and 4.5

margin-bottom

This property sets an element's bottom margin.

EXAMPLE

```
{margin-bottom: 10pt}
```

BROWSER SUPPORT

Internet Explorer 3 (Windows only), 4, and 5
Netscape 4 and 4.5

margin-right

This property sets an element's right margin.

EXAMPLE

```
{margin-right: 15pt}
```

BROWSER SUPPORT

Internet Explorer 3, 4, and 5
Netscape 4 and 4.5

margin-left

This property sets an element's left margin.

EXAMPLE

```
{margin-left: 12pt}
```

BROWSER SUPPORT

Internet Explorer 3, 4, and 5
Netscape 4 and 4.5

margin

This property sets all margins for an element. Up to four values can be defined, in this order: **top**, **right**, **bottom**, and **left**. The value **auto** is not currently supported. A single value defines the same margin for all four sides.

EXAMPLE

```
{margin: 25pt}
```

If two values are specified, the first defines the top and bottom margins, while the second defines the left and right margins.

EXAMPLE

```
{margin: 15pt, 25pt}
```

If three values are specified, the first defines the top margin, the second defines the left and right margins, and the third defines the bottom margin. Note that the unspecified margin is inferred from the value defined for its opposite side.

EXAMPLE

```
{margin: 25pt, 50pt, 25pt}
```

Finally, all four margins can be set to different values if desired (**top**, **right**, **bottom**, and **left**, in that order).

EXAMPLE

```
{margin: 15pt, 25pt, 50pt, 10pt}
```

BROWSER SUPPORT

Internet Explorer 3 (incomplete), 4, and 5
Netscape 4 and 4.5

Borders

There are five properties for setting the width of borders: **border-top-width**, **border-bottom-width**, **border-right-width**, **border-left-width**, and **border-width**. The first four set the width of specific borders; **border-width** is used to set all four. Values for border widths can be set in numeric measurements or with the named values **thin**,

medium, or **thick**. Border colors and styles can be set with the properties **border-color** and **border-style**, respectively. The properties **border-top**, **border-bottom**, **border-right**, and **border-left** can be used to set width, style, and color values for different sides of a border; the **border** property sets the width, style, and color of all sides of an element's border.

border-top-width

This property sets the width of an element's top border. Values can be keywords (**thin**, **medium**, or **thick**) and numerical lengths.

EXAMPLES

```
{border-top-width: thin}
{border-top-width: 25px}
```

BROWSER SUPPORT

Internet Explorer 4 and 5
Netscape 4 and 4.5

border-bottom-width

This property sets the width of an element's bottom border. Values can be keywords (**thin**, **medium**, or **thick**) and numerical lengths.

EXAMPLES

```
{border-bottom-width: medium}
{border-bottom-width: 15px}
```

BROWSER SUPPORT

Internet Explorer 4 and 5
Netscape 4 and 4.5

border-right-width

This property sets the width of an element's right border. Values can be keywords (**thin**, **medium**, or **thick**) and numerical lengths.

EXAMPLES

```
{border-right-width: thick}
{border-right-width: 40px}
```

BROWSER SUPPORT

Internet Explorer 4 and 5
Netscape 4 and 4.5

border-left-width

This property sets the width of an element's left border. Values can be keywords (**thin**, **medium**, or **thick**) and numerical lengths.

EXAMPLES

```
{border-left-width: thin}
{border-left-width: 5px}
```

BROWSER SUPPORT

Internet Explorer 4 and 5
Netscape 4 and 4.5

border-width

This property sets the width of an element's complete border. Values can be keywords (**thin**, **medium**, or **thick**) and numerical lengths.

EXAMPLES

```
{border-width: medium}
{border-width: 5px}
```

BROWSER SUPPORT

Internet Explorer 4 and 5
Netscape 4 and 4.5

thin   This value sets the width of an element's border to thin.

EXAMPLE

```
{border-width: thin}
```

BROWSER SUPPORT

Internet Explorer 4 and 5
Netscape 4 and 4.5

thick This value sets the width of an element's border to thick.

EXAMPLE

```
{border-width: thick}
```

BROWSER SUPPORT

Internet Explorer 4 and 5
Netscape 4 and 4.5

medium This value sets the width of an element's border to medium.

EXAMPLE

```
{border-width: medium}
```

BROWSER SUPPORT

Internet Explorer 4 and 5
Netscape 4 and 4.5

border-color

This property defines the color of an element's border. See "Style Sheet Color Values," later in this appendix, for browser support of color values.

EXAMPLES

```
{border-color: blue}
{border-color: #0000EE}
```

BROWSER SUPPORT

Internet Explorer 4 and 5
Netscape 4 and 4.5

border-style

This property defines an element's border style.

EXAMPLE

```
{border-style: solid}
```

The **border-style** property defines the style of up to four different side of a border, using the values **none, dotted, dashed, solid, double, groove, ridge, inset**, and **outset**. These values are listed, in order, for the top, right, bottom, and left sides. Missing values are inferred from the value defined for the opposite side.

EXAMPLE

```
{border-style: solid, double, solid, double}
```

 Note   *Netscape 4 supports only one value for **border-style**. Use of multiple values will create erratic display under that browser.*

BROWSER SUPPORT

Internet Explorer 4 and 5
Netscape 4 (incomplete)

none   This value "turns off" the border, even if other border properties have been set.

EXAMPLE

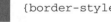
```
{border-style: none}
```

BROWSER SUPPORT

Internet Explorer 4 and 5
Netscape 4 and 4.5

dotted   This value defines a dotted border style.

EXAMPLE

```
{border-style: dotted}
```

BROWSER SUPPORT   None currently; likely in future versions of Netscape

dashed   This value defines a dashed border style.

EXAMPLE

```
{border-style: dashed}
```

BROWSER SUPPORT   None currently; likely in future versions of Netscape

solid   This value, which is the default for this property, sets the border to a solid line. It does not need to be set.

EXAMPLE

```
{border-style: solid}
```

BROWSER SUPPORT

    Internet Explorer 4 and 5
    Netscape 4 and 4.5

double   This value sets the border to two solid lines.

EXAMPLE

```
{border-style: double}
```

BROWSER SUPPORT

    Internet Explorer 4 and 5
    Netscape 4 and 4.5

groove   This value sets the border to resemble a grooved line.

EXAMPLE

```
{border-style: grooved}
```

BROWSER SUPPORT

    Internet Explorer 4 and 5
    Netscape 4 and 4.5

inset   This value sets the border to display a lighter shade of the border color on its right and bottom sides.

EXAMPLE

```
{border-style: inset}
```

BROWSER SUPPORT

Internet Explorer 4 and 5
Netscape 4 and 4.5

outset   This value sets the border to display a lighter shade of the border color on its top and left sides.

EXAMPLE

```
{border-style: outset}
```

BROWSER SUPPORT

Internet Explorer 4
Netscape 4 and 4.5

ridge   This value sets the border to resemble a raised ridge by reversing the shading of the grooved rendering.

EXAMPLE

```
{border-style: ridge}
```

BROWSER SUPPORT

Internet Explorer 4 and 5
Netscape 4 and 4.5

border-top

This property defines the width, style, and color for the top border of an element.

EXAMPLE

```
{border-top: thin solid blue}
```

BROWSER SUPPORT

Internet Explorer 4 and 5
Future versions of Netscape

border-bottom

This property defines the width, style, and color for the bottom border of an element.

EXAMPLE

```
{border-bottom: thick double #CCFFCC}
```

BROWSER SUPPORT

Internet Explorer 4 and 5
Future versions of Netscape

border-right

This property defines the width, style, and color for the right border of an element.

EXAMPLE

```
{border-right: thick solid black}
```

BROWSER SUPPORT

Internet Explorer 4 and 5
Future versions of Netscape

border-left

This property defines the width, style, and color for the left border of an element.

EXAMPLE

```
{border-left: normal inset green}
```

BROWSER SUPPORT

Internet Explorer 4 and 5
Future versions of Netscape

border

This property defines the width, style, and color for all four sides of an element's border.

EXAMPLE

```
{border: normal inset green}
```

BROWSER SUPPORT

Internet Explorer 4 and 5
Netscape 4 and 4.5

Padding

The padding properties set the space between an element's border and its content.
There are five properties for padding: **padding-top**, **padding-bottom**, **padding-right**,
padding-left, and **padding**. The **padding** value sets the padding for all four sides; the
other four set the padding for specific sides. Values can be specified as specific values
(pixels, points, and so on) or as a percentage of the element's overall width. Unlike the
margin property, the **padding** property cannot take negative values.

padding-top

This property sets the distance between an element's top border and the top of
its content.

EXAMPLE

```
{padding-top: 25px}
```

BROWSER SUPPORT

Internet Explorer 4 and 5
Netscape 4 and 4.5

padding-bottom

This property sets the distance between an element's bottom border and the bottom of
its content.

EXAMPLE

```
{padding-bottom: 15px}
```

BROWSER SUPPORT

Internet Explorer 4 and 5
Netscape 4 and 4.5

padding-right

This property sets the distance between an element's right border and the right side of
its content.

EXAMPLE

```
{padding-right: 5px}
```

BROWSER SUPPORT

Internet Explorer 4 and 5
Netscape 4 and 4.5

padding-left

This property sets the distance between an element's left border and the left side of its content.

EXAMPLE

```
{padding-left: 25px}
```

BROWSER SUPPORT

Internet Explorer 4 and 5
Netscape 4 and 4.5

padding

This property sets the distance between an element's border and its contents. A single value creates equal padding on all sides.

EXAMPLE

```
{border-style: solid; padding: 10px}
```

Up to four values can be used, in the following clockwise order: **top**, **right**, **bottom**, and **left**.

EXAMPLE

```
{border-style: solid; padding: 10px 20px 10px 50px}
```

Any missing value defaults to the value defined for the side opposite to it.

EXAMPLE

```
{border-style: solid; padding: 10px 20px 10px}
```

BROWSER SUPPORT

Internet Explorer 4 and 5
Netscape 4 and 4.5

width

This property sets the width of an element's content region (excluding padding, border, and margin). The next example sets a paragraph with a width of 400 pixels.

EXAMPLE

```
P {width: 400px; padding: 10px; border: solid 5px}
```

Percentage values, based on the width of the containing element, can also be used.

EXAMPLE

```
P {width: 80%; padding: 10px; border: solid 5px}
```

The **auto** value automatically calculates the width of an element, based on the width of the containing element and the size of the content.

EXAMPLE

```
P {width: auto; padding: 10px; border: solid 5px}
```

BROWSER SUPPORT

Internet Explorer 5
Netscape 4 and 4.5

height

This property sets the height of an element's content region (excluding padding, border, and margin). The next example sets a paragraph with a height of 200 pixels.

EXAMPLE

```
P {height: 200px; padding: 10px; border: solid 5px}
```

Percentage values, based on the height of the containing element, can also be used.

EXAMPLE

```
P {height: 80%; padding: 10px; border: solid 5px}
```

The **auto** value automatically calculates the height of an element, based on the height of the containing element and the size of the content.

EXAMPLE

```
P {height: auto; padding: 10px; border: solid 5px}
```

BROWSER SUPPORT

Internet Explorer 5
Future versions of Netscape

float

This property influences the horizontal alignment of an element, making it "float" toward the left or right margin of its containing element. Possible values are **left, right**, and **none**.

EXAMPLE

```
IMG {float: right}
```

BROWSER SUPPORT

Internet Explorer 4 and 5
Netscape 4 and 4.5

left

This value causes an element to float toward the left margin of its containing element.

EXAMPLE

```
IMG {float: left}
```

BROWSER SUPPORT

Internet Explorer 4 and 5
Netscape 4 and 4.5

right

This value causes an element to float toward the right margin of its containing element.

EXAMPLE

```
IMG {float: right}
```

BROWSER SUPPORT

Internet Explorer 4 and 5
Netscape 4 and 4.5

none

This value, which is the default for this property, prevents an element from floating.

EXAMPLE

```
IMG {float: none}
```

BROWSER SUPPORT

Internet Explorer 4 and 5
Netscape 4 and 4.5

clear

This property specifies the placement of an element in relation to floating objects. Possible values are **left, right, both,** and **none.**

EXAMPLE

```
{clear: right}
```

BROWSER SUPPORT

Internet Explorer 5
Netscape 4 and 4.5 (incomplete)

left

This value clears floating objects to the left of the element.

EXAMPLE

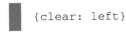

```
{clear: left}
```

BROWSER SUPPORT

Internet Explorer 5
Netscape 4 and 4.5 (incomplete)

right

This value clears floating objects to the right of the element.

EXAMPLE

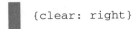

```
{clear: right}
```

BROWSER SUPPORT

Internet Explorer 5
Netscape 4 and 4.5 (incomplete)

both

This value clears floating objects to both sides of the element.

EXAMPLE

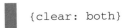

```
{clear: both}
```

BROWSER SUPPORT

Internet Explorer 5
Netscape 4 and 4.5 (incomplete)

none

This is the default value for this property. Objects around an element will not clear when **clear** is set to none.

EXAMPLE

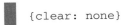

```
{clear: none}
```

BROWSER SUPPORT

Internet Explorer 5
Netscape 4 and 4.5

Layers and Positioning

This section discusses style properties that affect layering and positioning of elements.

position

This property defines how an element is positioned relative to other elements, using the values **static**, **absolute**, and **relative**. The **left** and **top** properties define the element's precise location, using the affected element's upper-left corner (0,0) as reference. Because elements can contain other elements, 0,0 is not necessarily the upper-left corner of the browser.

EXAMPLE

```
{position: relative; right: 190px; top: 30px}
```

BROWSER SUPPORT   Internet Explorer 4 and 5

static

This value, which is the default for this property, places elements according to the natural order in which they occur in a document.

EXAMPLE

```
{position: static; left: 120px; top: 50px}
```

BROWSER SUPPORT   Internet Explorer 4 and 5

absolute

This value defines a coordinate system independent from other block and inline element placement. An element whose position is absolute acts as a visual container for any elements enclosed within its content. All elements defined inside it move with it. Contained elements that are assigned coordinates outside their container's dimensions will disappear.

EXAMPLE

```
{position: absolute; left: 120px; top: 50px}
```

BROWSER SUPPORT   Internet Explorer 4 and 5

relative

This value positions elements relative to their natural position in document flow.

EXAMPLE

```
{position: relative; left: 120px; top: 50px}
```

BROWSER SUPPORT   Internet Explorer 4 and 5

left

This value defines the *x* (horizontal) coordinate for a positioned element, relative to the upper-left corner. Values can be specified as lengths (inches, pixels, and so on), as a percentage of the containing object's dimensions, or as **auto**.

EXAMPLES

```
{position: absolute; left: 120px; top: 50px}
{position: absolute; left: 30%; top: 50%}
{position: absolute; left: auto; top: auto}
```

BROWSER SUPPORT

Internet Explorer 4 and 5
Netscape 4 and 4.5

top

This value defines the *y* (vertical) coordinate for a positioned element, relative to the upper-left corner. Values can be specified as lengths (inches, pixels, and so on), as a percentage of the containing object's dimensions, or as **auto**, which lets this property function as determined by the browser or as defined by the parent element.

EXAMPLES

```
{position: absolute; left: 100px; top: 150px}
{position: absolute; left: 50%; top: 30%}
{position: absolute; left: auto; top: auto}
```

BROWSER SUPPORT

Internet Explorer 4 and 5
Netscape 4 and 4.5

width

This property defines the width of an element. Values can be specified as lengths (positive values only), percentages (relative to the containing element's width), or **auto**, which defaults to the element's natural width.

EXAMPLE

```
IMG {position: absolute; left: 120px; top: 50px; height: 200px;
    width: 400px}
```

BROWSER SUPPORT   Internet Explorer 4 and 5

height

This property defines the height of an element. Values can be specified as lengths (positive values only), percentages (relative to the containing element's height), or as **auto**, which defaults to the element's natural height.

EXAMPLE

```
IMG {position: absolute; left: 120px; top: 50px; height: 100px;
    width: 150px}
```

BROWSER SUPPORT   Internet Explorer 4 and 5

clip

This property sets the coordinates of the clipping rectangle that houses the content of elements set to a position value of **absolute**. Coordinate values are **top**, **right**, **bottom**, **left**, and **auto**. The **auto** value lets clipping occur as it will.

EXAMPLE

```
{position: absolute; left: 20; top: 20; width:100; height:100;
 clip: rect(10 90 90 10)}
```

BROWSER SUPPORT   Internet Explorer 5

overflow

This property determines an element's behavior when its content doesn't fit into the space defined by the element's other properties. Possible values are **clip**, **scroll**, and **none**.

EXAMPLE

```
{position: absolute; left: 20; top: 20; width: 100; height: 100;
 clip: rect(10 90 90 10); overflow: scroll}
```

BROWSER SUPPORT   Internet Explorer 5

clip

This value clips content to the size defined for the container.

EXAMPLE

```
{position: absolute; left: 20; top: 20; width: 100; height: 100;
 clip: rect(10 90 90 10); overflow: clip}
```

BROWSER SUPPORT   None

scroll

This value allows content to scroll using scroll bars or another browser-dependent mechanism.

EXAMPLE

```
{position: absolute; left: 20; top: 20; width: 100; height: 100;
 clip: rect(10 90 90 10); overflow: scroll}
```

BROWSER SUPPORT   Internet Explorer 5

none

This value does nothing, but can allow clipping of the content.

EXAMPLE

```
{position: absolute; left: 20; top: 20; width: 100; height: 100;
 clip: rect(10 90 90 10); overflow: none}
```

BROWSER SUPPORT   None

z-index

This property defines a layering context for elements containing other elements with relative or absolute positioning. By default, overlapping elements stack in the order in which they are defined in an HTML document. This property can override default layering by assigning numeric layering values to an element, with higher numbers layering above lower numbers. The **auto** value tries to determine the z-placement of an element automatically.

EXAMPLE

```
{position: absolute; top:20; left:20; height: 50; width: 50;
 background-color: blue; z-index: 2}
```

BROWSER SUPPORT

Internet Explorer 5
Netscape 4 and 4.5

visibility

This property determines whether or not an element is visible. Possible values are **hidden**, **visible**, and **inherit**.

EXAMPLE

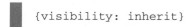
```
{visibility: inherit}
```

BROWSER SUPPORT   Internet Explorer 4 and 5

hidden

This value specifies that an element is hidden from view. A hidden element still occupies its full canvas space.

EXAMPLE

```
{visibility: hidden}
```

BROWSER SUPPORT   Internet Explorer 4 and 5

visible

This value specifies that an element is visible.

EXAMPLE

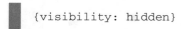
```
{visibility: visible}
```

BROWSER SUPPORT   Internet Explorer 4 and 5

inherit
This value specifies that an element inherits its visibility state from the element that contains it.

EXAMPLE

```
{visibility: inherit}
```

BROWSER SUPPORT   Internet Explorer 4 and 5

◼ Classification
This section discusses style properties that affect the display type of elements (block-level, inline, and so on) and the display of lists and white space.

display
This property specifies an element's display type. This property can override an element's defined display type. For example, block-level elements can be redefined as inline elements so that extra lines will not be placed between them.

EXAMPLE

```
P {display: inline}
```

BROWSER SUPPORT

Internet Explorer 4 and 5 (incomplete)
Netscape 4 and 4.5 (incomplete)

block
This value sets an element to display as a block element.

EXAMPLE

```
{display: block}
```

BROWSER SUPPORT

Internet Explorer 5
Netscape 4 and 4.5

inline

This value sets an element to display as an inline element.

EXAMPLE

```
P {display: inline}
```

BROWSER SUPPORT

Internet Explorer 5
Future versions of Netscape

list-item

This value sets an element to display as a list-item element.

EXAMPLE

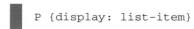
```
P {display: list-item}
```

BROWSER SUPPORT   Netscape 4 and 4.5

none

This value turns off the display of an element. Unlike the **hidden** value of the **visibility** property, **none** does not preserve an element's canvas space.

EXAMPLE

```
P {display: none}
```

BROWSER SUPPORT

Internet Explorer 4 and 5
Netscape 4 and 4.5

white-space

This property controls how spaces, tabs, and newline characters are handled in an element. Possible values are **normal**, **pre**, and **nowrap**.

EXAMPLE

```
{white-space: pre}
```

BROWSER SUPPORT Netscape 4 and 4.5 (incomplete)

normal

This value collapses white-space characters into single spaces and automatically wraps lines, as in normal HTML.

EXAMPLE

```
{white-space: normal}
```

BROWSER SUPPORT Netscape 4 and 4.5

pre

This value preserves white-space formatting, similar to the **<PRE>** element in HTML.

EXAMPLE

```
{white-space: pre}
```

BROWSER SUPPORT Netscape 4 and 4.5

nowrap

This value prevents lines from wrapping if they exceed the element's content width.

EXAMPLE

```
{white-space: nowrap}
```

BROWSER SUPPORT None currently; likely in future versions of Netscape

list-style-type

This property defines labels for ordered and unordered lists. The value **none** prevents a label from displaying.

EXAMPLES

```
OL {list-style-type: upper-roman}
UL {list-style-type: disc}
```

BROWSER SUPPORT Internet Explorer 4 and 5; Netscape 4 and 4.5

none

This value specifies that no label will be displayed for items in ordered or
unordered lists.

EXAMPLES

```
OL {list-style-type: none}
UL {list-style-type: none}
```

BROWSER SUPPORT

Internet Explorer 4 and 5
Netscape 4 and 4.5

Ordered Lists

There are five values for ordered lists: **decimal**, **lower-roman**, **upper-roman**,
lower-alpha, and **upper-alpha**.

decimal   This value specifies Arabic numerals (1, 2, 3, and so on) for the labeling of
items in an ordered list.

EXAMPLE

```
OL {list-style-type: decimal}
```

BROWSER SUPPORT

Internet Explorer 4 and 5
Netscape 4 and 4.5

lower-roman   This value specifies lowercase Roman numerals (i, ii, iii, and so on) for
the labeling of items in an ordered list.

EXAMPLE

```
OL {list-style-type: lower-roman}
```

BROWSER SUPPORT

Internet Explorer 4 and 5
Netscape 4 and 4.5

upper-roman   This value specifies uppercase Roman numerals (I, II, III, and so on) for the labeling of items in an ordered list.

EXAMPLE

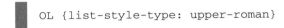
```
OL {list-style-type: upper-roman}
```

BROWSER SUPPORT

Internet Explorer 4 and 5
Netscape 4 and 4.5

lower-alpha   This value specifies lowercase letters (a, b, c, and so on) for the labeling of items in an ordered list.

EXAMPLE

```
OL {list-style-type: lower-alpha}
```

BROWSER SUPPORT

Internet Explorer 4 and 5
Netscape 4 and 4.5

upper-alpha   This value specifies uppercase letters (A, B, C, and so on) for the labeling of items in an ordered list.

EXAMPLE

```
OL {list-style-type: upper-alpha}
```

BROWSER SUPPORT

Internet Explorer 4 and 5
Netscape 4 and 4.5

Unordered Lists

There are three values for unordered lists: **disc**, **circle**, and **square**.

disc   This value specifies a black dot bullet for items in an unordered list.

EXAMPLE

```
UL {list-style-type: disc}
```

BROWSER SUPPORT

Internet Explorer 4 and 5
Netscape 4 and 4.5

circle   This value specifies a circular bullet for items in an unordered list.

EXAMPLE

```
UL {list-style-type: circle}
```

BROWSER SUPPORT

Internet Explorer 4 and 5
Netscape 4 and 4.5

square   This value specifies a square bullet for items in an unordered list.

EXAMPLE

```
UL {list-style-type: square}
```

BROWSER SUPPORT

Internet Explorer 4 and 5
Netscape 4 and 4.5

list-style-image

This property assigns a graphic image to a list label, using the URL of the image. The other value for **list-style-image** other than a URL is **none**.

EXAMPLE

```
UL {list-style-image: url(ball.gif)}
```

BROWSER SUPPORT

Internet Explorer 4 and 5
Future versions of Netscape

list-style-position

This property specifies whether the labels for an element's list items are positioned inside or outside the "box" defined by the area. By default, labels appear outside the "box."

EXAMPLE

```
OL {list-style-type: upper-roman; list-style-position: outside;
    background: yellow}
```

The **inside** value places the bullets inside the "box."

EXAMPLE

```
UL {list-style-type: square; list-style-position: inside;
    background: yellow}
```

BROWSER SUPPORT   Internet Explorer 4 and 5

list-style

This property is more concise than the other **list-style** properties. It sets type, image, and position properties for ordered and unordered lists. The properties can appear in any order. The values **inside** and **outside** are not supported.

EXAMPLES

```
UL {list-style: inside url("bullet.gif")}
UL {list-style: outside square}
OL {list-style: lower-roman inside}
```

BROWSER SUPPORT   Internet Explorer 4 and 5

Style Sheet Measurement Values

This section discusses measurement values used in association with style sheets.

%

This value defines a measurement as a percentage relative to another value.

EXAMPLE

```
P {font-size: 14pt; line-height: 150%}
```

BROWSER SUPPORT

Internet Explorer 3, 4, and 5
Netscape 4 and 4.5

cm

This value defines a measurement in centimeters.

EXAMPLE

```
DIV {margin-bottom: 1cm}
```

BROWSER SUPPORT

Internet Explorer 3, 4, and 5
Netscape 4 and 4.5

em

This value defines a measurement for the height of a font in em spaces.

EXAMPLE

```
P {letter-spacing: 5em}
```

BROWSER SUPPORT

Internet Explorer 3 (Mac only)
Netscape 4 and 4.5 (incomplete)

ex (x-height)

This value defines a measurement relative to a font's x-height. The x-height is determined by the height of the font's lowercase letter *x*.

EXAMPLE

```
P {font-size: 14pt; line-height: 2ex}
```

BROWSER SUPPORT

Internet Explorer 3 (Mac only)
Netscape 4 and 4.5 (incomplete)

in

This value defines a measurement in inches.

EXAMPLE

```
P {word-spacing: .25in}
```

BROWSER SUPPORT

Internet Explorer 3, 4, and 5
Netscape 4 and 4.5

mm

This value defines a measurement in millimeters.

EXAMPLE

```
P {word-spacing: 12mm}
```

BROWSER SUPPORT

Internet Explorer 3, 4, and 5
Netscape 4 and 4.5

pc

This value defines a measurement in picas.

EXAMPLE

```
P {font-size: 10pc}
```

BROWSER SUPPORT

Internet Explorer 3, 4, and 5
Netscape 4 and 4.5

pt

This value defines a measurement in points.

EXAMPLE

```
BODY {font-size: 14pt}
```

BROWSER SUPPORT

Internet Explorer 3, 4, and 5
Netscape 4 and 4.5

px

This value defines a measurement in pixels.

EXAMPLE

```
P {padding: 15px}
```

BROWSER SUPPORT

Internet Explorer 3, 4, and 5
Netscape 4 and 4.5

Style Sheet Color Values

This section discusses color values used in association with style sheets.

Named Color Values

Color values can be defined using 16 color names: **aqua**, **black**, **blue**, **fuchsia**, **gray**, **green**, **lime**, **maroon**, **navy**, **olive**, **purple**, **red**, **silver**, **teal**, **white**, and **yellow**. (An extended list of color names has been introduced by Netscape, but it is safer to use the hexadecimal equivalents of those names, which are listed in Appendix E.)

EXAMPLE

```
BODY {font-family: Arial; font-size: 12pt; color: red}
```

BROWSER SUPPORT

Internet Explorer 3, 4, and 5
Netscape 4 and 4.5

Six-Digit Hexadecimal Color Values

Color values can be defined using the six-digit hexadecimal color values commonly used on the Web.

EXAMPLE

```
DIV {font-family: Courier; font-size: 10pt; color: #00CCFF}
```

BROWSER SUPPORT

Internet Explorer 3, 4, and 5
Netscape 4 and 4.5

Three-Digit Hexadecimal Color Values

Color values can be defined using the three-digit hexadecimal color values, a concise version of the six-digit values just noted.

EXAMPLE

```
SPAN {font-family: Helvetica; font-size: 14pt; color: #0CF}
```

BROWSER SUPPORT

Internet Explorer 3, 4, and 5
Netscape 4 and 4.5

RGB Color Values

Color values can be defined using RGB values. Colors are defined by the letters *rgb,* followed by three numbers between 0 and 255, contained in parentheses and separated by commas, with no spaces between them.

EXAMPLE

```
P {color: rgb(204,0,51)}
```

BROWSER SUPPORT

Internet Explorer 4
Netscape 4 and 4.5

RGB Color Values Using Percentages

RGB color values can also be defined using percentages. The format is the same, except that the numbers are replaced by percentage values between **0%** and **100%**.

EXAMPLE

```
P {color: rgb(75%,10%,50%)}
```

BROWSER SUPPORT

Internet Explorer 4
Netscape 4 and 4.5

The
Complete
Reference

Appendix C

Special Characters

This appendix lists the special characters available in standard HTML and HTML 4. Note that browser support of entities is based on testing in the following browser versions: Netscape 1.22, Netscape 2.02, Netscape 3.01, Netscape Communicator 4, Netscape Communicator 4.5, Internet Explorer 3.02, Internet Explorer 4, Internet Explorer 5, and WebTV. In the tables in this appendix, the following abbreviations are used for the different Netscape and Internet Explorer versions:

N1 = Netscape 1.22
N2 = Netscape 2.02
N3 = Netscape 3.01
N4 = Netscape Communicator 4
N4.5 = Netscape Communicator 4.5
IE3 = Internet Explorer 3.02
IE4 = Internet Explorer 4
IE5 = Internet Explorer 5

"Standard" HTML Character Entities

As discussed in Chapter 4, Web browsers do not read certain characters if they appear in an HTML document. To get around this limitation, codes have been assigned to certain characters. These codes consist of numbered entities; and some, but not all, of these numbered entities have corresponding named entities. For example, the numbered entity **Ë** produces the character Ë. The named entity **Ë** produces the same character. Note that the named entity suggests the intended rendering of the character, which provides a handy mnemonic device for dedicated HTML codes. While **Ë** is widely supported, not all character entities work in all browsers. Theoretically, a browser vendor could even create arbitrary interpretations of these codes. For example, WebTV has assigned its own unique renderings for the entities numbered 128 and 129. Under the HTML specifications, 128 and 129 are not assigned characters. The codes numbered 32 through 255 (with some gaps) were assigned standard keyboard characters. Some of these codes duplicate characters that Web browsers can already interpret. The entity **5** represents the numeral 5, while **¥** represents *A*. Character entities become more practical when it is necessary to employ characters used in foreign languages, such as Œ or Å, or special characters such as ¶. The following chart lists these "standard" entities and their intended renderings, and identifies which browsers support each of them.

Named Entity	Browser Support	Numbered Entity	Browser Support	Intended Rendering	Description
		&#32;	N1, N2, N3, N4, N4.5, IE3, IE4, IE5, WebTV		Space
		&#33;	N1, N2, N3, N4, N4.5, IE3, IE4, IE5, WebTV	!	Exclamation point

Named Entity	Browser Support	Numbered Entity	Browser Support	Intended Rendering	Description
&quot;	N1, N2, N3, N4, N4.5, IE3, IE4, IE5, WebTV	&#34;	N1, N2, N3, N4, N4.5, IE3, IE4, IE5, WebTV	"	Double quotes
		&#35;	N1, N2, N3, N4, N4.5, IE3, IE4, IE5, WebTV	#	Number symbol
		&#36;	N1, N2, N3, N4, N4.5, IE3, IE4, IE5, WebTV	$	Dollar symbol
		&#37;	N1, N2, N3, N4, N4.5, IE3, IE4, IE5, WebTV	%	Percent symbol
&amp;	N1, N2, N3, N4, N4.5, IE3, IE4, IE5, WebTV	&#38;	N1, N2, N3, N4, N4.5, IE3, IE4, IE5, WebTV	&	Ampersand
		&#39;	N1, N2, N3, N4, N4.5, IE3, IE4, IE5, WebTV	'	Single quote
		&#40;	N1, N2, N3, N4, N4.5, IE3, IE4, IE5, WebTV	(	Opening parenthesis
		&#41;	N1, N2, N3, N4, N4.5, IE3, IE4, IE5, WebTV	)	Closing parenthesis
		&#42;	N1, N2, N3, N4, N4.5, IE3, IE4, IE5, WebTV	*	Asterisk
		&#43;	N1, N2, N3, N4, N4.5, IE3, IE4, IE5, WebTV	+	Plus sign
		&#44;	N1, N2, N3, N4, N4.5, IE3, IE4, IE5, WebTV	,	Comma
		&#45;	N1, N2, N3, N4, N4.5, IE3, IE4, IE5, WebTV	–	Minus sign (hyphen)
		&#46;	N1, N2, N3, N4, N4.5, IE3, IE4, IE5, WebTV	.	Period

Named Entity	Browser Support	Numbered Entity	Browser Support	Intended Rendering	Description
		&#47;	N1, N2, N3, N4, N4.5, IE3, IE4, IE5, WebTV	/	Slash/virgule/bar
		&#48;	N1, N2, N3, N4, N4.5, IE3, IE4, IE5, WebTV	0	Zero
		&#49;	N1, N2, N3, N4, N4.5, IE3, IE4, IE5, WebTV	1	One
		&#50;	N1, N2, N3, N4, N4.5, IE3, IE4, IE5, WebTV	2	Two
		&#51;	N1, N2, N3, N4, N4.5, IE3, IE4, IE5, WebTV	3	Three
		&#52;	N1, N2, N3, N4, N4.5, IE3, IE4, IE5, WebTV	4	Four
		&#53;	N1, N2, N3, N4, N4.5, IE3, IE4, IE5, WebTV	5	Five
		&#54;	N1, N2, N3, N4, N4.5, IE3, IE4, IE5, WebTV	6	Six
		&#55;	N1, N2, N3, N4, N4.5, IE3, IE4, IE5, WebTV	7	Seven
		&#56;	N1, N2, N3, N4, N4.5, IE3, IE4, IE5, WebTV	8	Eight
		&#57;	N1, N2, N3, N4, N4.5, IE3, IE4, IE5, WebTV	9	Nine
		&#58;	N1, N2, N3, N4, N4.5, IE3, IE4, IE5, WebTV	:	Colon

Named Entity	Browser Support	Numbered Entity	Browser Support	Intended Rendering	Description
		&#59;	N1, N2, N3, N4, N4.5, IE3, IE4, IE5, WebTV	;	Semicolon
&lt;	N1, N2, N3, N4, N4.5, IE3, IE4, IE5, WebTV	&#60;	N1, N2, N3, N4, N4.5, IE3, IE4, IE5, WebTV	<	Less than symbol
		&#61;	N1, N2, N3, N4, N4.5, IE3, IE4, IE5, WebTV	=	Equal sign
&gt;	N1, N2, N3, N4, N4.5, IE3, IE4, IE5, WebTV	&#62;	N1, N2, N3, N4, N4.5, IE3, IE4, IE5, WebTV	>	Greater than symbol
		&#63;	N1, N2, N3, N4, N4.5, IE3, IE4, IE5, WebTV	?	Question mark
		&#64;	N1, N2, N3, N4, N4.5, IE3, IE4, IE5, WebTV	@	At symbol
		&#65;	N1, N2, N3, N4, N4.5, IE3, IE4, IE5, WebTV	A	
		&#66;	N1, N2, N3, N4, N4.5, IE3, IE4, IE5, WebTV	B	
		&#67;	N1, N2, N3, N4, N4.5, IE3, IE4, IE5, WebTV	C	
		&#68;	N1, N2, N3, N4, N4.5, IE3, IE4, IE5, WebTV	D	
		&#69;	N1, N2, N3, N4, N4.5, IE3, IE4, IE5, WebTV	E	
		&#70;	N1, N2, N3, N4, N4.5, IE3, IE4, IE5, WebTV	F	

Named Entity	Browser Support	Numbered Entity	Browser Support	Intended Rendering	Description
		&#71;	N1, N2, N3, N4, N4.5, IE3, IE4, IE5, WebTV	G	
		&#72;	N1, N2, N3, N4, N4.5, IE3, IE4, IE5, WebTV	H	
		&#73;	N1, N2, N3, N4, N4.5, IE3, IE4, IE5, WebTV	I	
		&#74;	N1, N2, N3, N4, N4.5, IE3, IE4, IE5, WebTV	J	
		&#75;	N1, N2, N3, N4, N4.5, IE3, IE4, IE5, WebTV	K	
		&#76;	N1, N2, N3, N4, N4.5, IE3, IE4, IE5, WebTV	L	
		&#77;	N1, N2, N3, N4, N4.5, IE3, IE4, IE5, WebTV	M	
		&#78;	N1, N2, N3, N4, N4.5, IE3, IE4, IE5, WebTV	N	
		&#79;	N1, N2, N3, N4, N4.5, IE3, IE4, IE5, WebTV	O	
		&#80;	N1, N2, N3, N4, N4.5, IE3, IE4, IE5, WebTV	P	
		&#81;	N1, N2, N3, N4, N4.5, IE3, IE4, IE5, WebTV	Q	
		&#82;	N1, N2, N3, N4, N4.5, IE3, IE4, IE5, WebTV	R	

Named Entity	Browser Support	Numbered Entity	Browser Support	Intended Rendering	Description
		&#83;	N1, N2, N3, N4, N4.5, IE3, IE4, IE5, WebTV	S	
		&#84;	N1, N2, N3, N4, N4.5, IE3, IE4, IE5, WebTV	T	
		&#85;	N1, N2, N3, N4, N4.5, IE3, IE4, IE5, WebTV	U	
		&#86;	N1, N2, N3, N4, N4.5, IE3, IE4, IE5, WebTV	V	
		&#87;	N1, N2, N3, N4, N4.5, IE3, IE4, IE5, WebTV	W	
		&#88;	N1, N2, N3, N4, N4.5, IE3, IE4, IE5, WebTV	X	
		&#89;	N1, N2, N3, N4, N4.5, IE3, IE4, IE5, WebTV	Y	
		&#90;	N1, N2, N3, N4, N4.5, IE3, IE4, IE5, WebTV	Z	
		&#91;	N1, N2, N3, N4, N4.5, IE3, IE4, IE5, WebTV	[	Opening bracket
		&#92;	N1, N2, N3, N4, N4.5, IE3, IE4, IE5, WebTV	\	Backslash
		&#93;	N1, N2, N3, N4, N4.5, IE3, IE4, IE5, WebTV	]	Closing bracket
		&#94;	N1, N3, N4, N4.5, IE3, IE4, IE5, WebTV	^	Caret

Named Entity	Browser Support	Numbered Entity	Browser Support	Intended Rendering	Description
		&#95;	N1, N2, N3, N4, N4.5, IE3, IE4, IE5, WebTV	_	Underscore
		&#96;	N1, N2, N3, N4, N4.5, IE3, IE4, IE5, WebTV	'	Grave accent, no letter
		&#97;	N1, N2, N3, N4, N4.5, IE3, IE4, IE5, WebTV	a	
		&#98;	N1, N2, N3, N4, N4.5, IE3, IE4, IE5, WebTV	b	
		&#99;	N1, N2, N3, N4, N4.5, IE3, IE4, IE5, WebTV	c	
		&#100;	N1, N2, N3, N4, N4.5, IE3, IE4, IE5, WebTV	d	
		&#101;	N1, N2, N3, N4, N4.5, IE3, IE4, IE5, WebTV	e	
		&#102;	N1, N2, N3, N4, N4.5, IE3, IE4, IE5, WebTV	f	
		&#103;	N1, N2, N3, N4, N4.5, IE3, IE4, IE5, WebTV	g	
		&#104;	N1, N2, N3, N4, N4.5, IE3, IE4, IE5, WebTV	h	
		&#105;	N1, N2, N3, N4, N4.5, IE3, IE4, IE5, WebTV	i	
		&#106;	N1, N2, N3, N4, N4.5, IE3, IE4, IE5, WebTV	j	
		&#107;	N1, N2, N3, N4, N4.5, IE3, IE4, IE5, WebTV	k	

Named Entity	Browser Support	Numbered Entity	Browser Support	Intended Rendering	Description
		&#108;	N1, N2, N3, N4, N4.5, IE3, IE4, IE5, WebTV	l	
		&#109;	N1, N2, N3, N4, N4.5, IE3, IE4, IE5, WebTV	m	
		&#110;	N1, N2, N3, N4, N4.5, IE3, IE4, IE5, WebTV	n	
		&#111;	N1, N2, N3, N4, N4.5, IE3, IE4, IE5, WebTV	o	
		&#112;	N1, N2, N3, N4, N4.5, IE3, IE4, IE5, WebTV	p	
		&#113;	N1, N2, N3, N4, N4.5, IE3, IE4, IE5, WebTV	q	
		&#114;	N1, N2, N3, N4, N4.5, IE3, IE4, IE5, WebTV	r	
		&#115;	N1, N2, N3, N4, N4.5, IE3, IE4, IE5, WebTV	s	
		&#116;	N1, N2, N3, N4, N4.5, IE3, IE4, IE5, WebTV	t	
		&#117;	N1, N2, N3, N4, N4.5, IE3, IE4, IE5, WebTV	u	
		&#118;	N1, N2, N3, N4, N4.5, IE3, IE4, IE5, WebTV	v	
		&#119;	N1, N2, N3, N4, N4.5, IE3, IE4, IE5, WebTV	w	
		&#120;	N1, N2, N3, N4, N4.5, IE3, IE4, IE5, WebTV	x	

Named Entity	Browser Support	Numbered Entity	Browser Support	Intended Rendering	Description
		`&#121;`	N1, N2, N3, N4, N4.5, IE3, IE4, IE5, WebTV	y	
		`&#122;`	N1, N2, N3, N4, N4.5, IE3, IE4, IE5, WebTV	z	
		`&#123;`	N1, N2, N3, N4, N4.5, IE3, IE4, IE5, WebTV	{	Opening brace
		`&#124;`	N1, N2, N3, N4, N4.5, IE3, IE4, IE5, WebTV	|	Vertical bar
		`&#125;`	N1, N2, N3, N4, N4.5, IE3, IE4, IE5, WebTV	}	Closing brace
		`&#126;`	N1, N2, N3, N4, N4.5, IE3, IE4, IE5, WebTV	~	Equivalency symbol (tilde)
		`&#127;`	n/a		No character (Note: In the standard, the values from 127 to 159 are not assigned. Authors are advised not to use them. Many of them only work under Windows or produce different characters on other operating systems or with different default font sets.)
		`&#128;`	WebTV (nonstandard)*		No character defined

* WebTV renders `&#128;` as a right-pointing arrowhead.

Named Entity	Browser Support	Numbered Entity	Browser Support	Intended Rendering	Description
&trade;	IE3, IE4	&#129;	WebTV (nonstandard)†	™	Trademark symbol (Nonstandard numeric value; use **™** or **™** instead.)
		&#130;	N3, N2, N4, N4.5, IE3, IE4, IE5, WebTV	‚	Low-9 quote (nonstandard)
		&#131;	N3, N4, N4.5, IE3, IE4, IE5, WebTV	ƒ	Small ƒ with hook (nonstandard)
		&#132;	N2, N3, N4, N4.5, IE3, IE4, IE5, WebTV	„	Low-9 double quotes (nonstandard)
		&#133;	N2, N3, N4, N4.5, IE3, IE4, IE5, WebTV	…	Ellipsis (nonstandard)
		&#134;	N2, N3, N4, N4.5, IE3, IE4, IE5, WebTV	†	Dagger (nonstandard)
		&#135;	N2, N3, N4, N4.5, IE3, IE4, IE5, WebTV	‡	Double dagger (nonstandard)
		&#136;	N3, N4, N4.5, IE3, IE4, IE5, WebTV	^	Circumflex accent, no letter (nonstandard)
		&#137;	N2, N3, N4, N4.5, IE3, IE4, IE5, WebTV	‰	Per thousand (nonstandard)
		&#138;	N3, N4, N4.5, IE3, IE4, IE5, WebTV	Š	Uppercase S with caron (nonstandard)
		&#139;	N2, N3, N4, N4.5, IE3, IE4, IE5, WebTV	‹	Opening single angle quote (nonstandard)

† *WebTV renders*  *as a left-pointing arrowhead.*

Named Entity	Browser Support	Numbered Entity	Browser Support	Intended Rendering	Description
		&#140;	N3, N4, N4.5, IE3, IE4, IE5, WebTV	Œ	Uppercase OE ligature (nonstandard)
		&#141;	None	Ÿ	Uppercase *Y* with umlaut (nonstandard)
		&#142;	n/a		No character
		&#143;	n/a		No character
		&#144;	n/a		No character
		&#145;	N1, N2, N3, N4, N4.5, IE3, IE4, IE5, WebTV	'	Opening "smart" single quote (nonstandard)
		&#146;	N1, N2, N3, N4, N4.5, IE3, IE4, IE5, WebTV	'	Closing "smart" single quote (nonstandard)
		&#147;	N2, N3, N4, N4.5, IE3, IE4, IE5, WebTV	"	Opening "smart" double quote (nonstandard)
		&#148;	N2, N3, N4, N4.5, IE3, IE4, IE5, WebTV	"	Closing "smart" double quote (nonstandard)
		&#149;	N2, N3, N4, N4.5, IE3, IE4, IE5, WebTV	•	Bullet (nonstandard)
		&#150;	N2, N3, N4, N4.5, IE3, IE4, IE5, WebTV	–	En dash (nonstandard)
		&#151;	N2, N3, N4, N4.5, IE3, IE4, IE5, WebTV	—	Em dash (nonstandard)
		&#152;	N3, N4, N4.5, IE3, IE4, IE5, WebTV	~	Tilde (nonstandard)

Named Entity	Browser Support	Numbered Entity	Browser Support	Intended Rendering	Description
&trade;	IE3, IE4	&#153;	N2, N3, N4, N4.5, IE3, IE4, IE5, WebTV	™	Trademark symbol‡ (nonstandard numeric value; use ™ or ™ instead)
		&#154;	N3, N4, N4.5, IE3, IE4, IE5, WebTV	š	Lowercase S with caron (nonstandard)
		&#155;	N2, N3, N4, N4.5, IE3, IE4, IE5, WebTV	>	Closing single angle quote (nonstandard)
		&#156;	N3, N4, N4.5, IE3, IE4, IE5, WebTV	œ	Lowercase oe ligature (nonstandard)
		&#157;	n/a		No character
		&#158;	n/a		No character
		&#159;	N3, N4, N4.5, IE3	Ÿ	Uppercase Y with umlaut (nonstandard)
	N1, N3, N4, N4.5, IE3		N1, N2, N3, N4, N4.5, IE3, IE4		Nonbreaking space
&iexcl;	N3, N4, N4.5, IE3, IE4, IE5, WebTV	&#161;	N1, N3, N4, N4.5, IE3, IE4, IE5, WebTV	¡	Inverted exclamation point
&cent;	N3, N4, N4.5, IE3, IE4, IE5, WebTV	&#162;	N1, N3, N4, N4.5, IE3, IE4, IE5, WebTV	¢	Cent symbol
&pound;	N3, N4, N4.5, IE3, IE4, IE5, WebTV	&#163;	N1, N3, N4, N4.5, IE3, IE4, IE5, WebTV	£	Pound sterling symbol
&curren;	N3, N4, N4.5, IE3, IE4, IE5, WebTV	&#164;	N1, N2, N3, N4, N4.5, IE3, IE4, IE5, WebTV	¤	Currency symbol
&yen;	N3, N4, N4.5, IE3, IE4, IE5, WebTV	&#165;	N1, N3, N4, N4.5, IE3, IE4, IE5, WebTV	¥	Japanese Yen

‡ *Support for* ™ *(™) is inconsistent across platforms. Alternative tagging such as* ^{<SMALL>TM</SMALL>} *is recommended, at least until there is wider support for* ™ *(*™*) as standardized under the HTML 4.0 specification (see Chapter 3).*

Named Entity	Browser Support	Numbered Entity	Browser Support	Intended Rendering	Description
&brvbar;	N3, N4, N4.5, IE3, IE4, IE5, WebTV	&#166;	N2, N3, N4, N4.5, IE3, IE4, IE5, WebTV	¦	Broken vertical bar
&sect;	N3, N4, N4.5, IE3, IE4, IE5, WebTV	&#167;	N1, N2, N3, N4, N4.5, IE3, IE4, IE5, WebTV	§	Section symbol
&uml;	N3, N4, N4.5, IE3, IE4, IE5, WebTV	&#168;	N1, N3, N4, N4.5, IE3, IE4, IE5, WebTV	¨	Umlaut, no letter
&copy;	N1, N2, N3, N4, N4.5, IE3, IE4, IE5, WebTV	&#169;	N1, N2, N3, N4, N4.5, IE3, IE4, IE5, WebTV	©	Copyright symbol
&ordf;	N3, N4, N4.5, IE3, IE4, IE5, WebTV	&#170;	N1, N3, N4, N4.5, IE3, IE4, IE5, WebTV	a	Feminine ordinal indicator
&laquo;	N3, N4, N4.5, IE3, IE4, IE5, WebTV	&#171;	N1, N2, N3, N4, N4.5, IE3, IE4, IE5, WebTV	«	Opening double angle quote
&not;	N3, N4, N4.5, IE3, IE4, IE5, WebTV	&#172;	N1, N2, N3, N4, N4.5, IE3, IE4, IE5, WebTV	¬	Logical "not" symbol
&shy;	N3, N4, N4.5, IE3, IE4, IE5, WebTV	&#173;	N1, N2, N3, N4, N4.5, IE3, IE4, IE5, WebTV	-	Soft hyphen
&reg;	N1, N2, N3, N4, N4.5, IE3, IE4, IE5, WebTV	&#174;	N1, N2, N3, N4, N4.5, IE3, IE4, IE5, WebTV	®	Registration mark
&macr;	N3, N4, N4.5, IE3, IE4, IE5, WebTV	&#175;	N1, N3, N4, N4.5, IE3, IE4, IE5, WebTV	‾	Macron
&deg;	N3, N4, N4.5, IE3, IE4, IE5, WebTV	&#176;	N1, N2, N3, N4, N4.5, IE3, IE4, IE5, WebTV	°	Degree symbol
&plusmn;	N3, N4, N4.5, IE3, IE4, IE5, WebTV	&#177;	N1, N2, N3, N4, N4.5, IE3, IE4, IE5, WebTV	±	Plus/minus symbol

Named Entity	Browser Support	Numbered Entity	Browser Support	Intended Rendering	Description
&sup2;	N3, N4, N4.5, IE3, IE4, IE5, WebTV	&#178;	N1, N3, N4, N4.5, IE3, IE4, IE5, WebTV	²	Superscript 2
&sup3;	N3, N4, N4.5, IE3, IE4, IE5, WebTV	&#179;	N1, N3, N4, N4.5, IE3, IE4, IE5, WebTV	³	Superscript 3
&acute;	N3, N4, N4.5, IE3, IE4, IE5, WebTV	&#180;	N1, N3, N4, N4.5, IE3, IE4, IE5, WebTV	´	Acute accent, no letter
&micro;	N3, N4, N4.5, IE3, IE4, IE5, WebTV	&#181;	N1, N2, N3, N4, N4.5, IE3, IE4, IE5, WebTV	µ	Micron
&para;	N3, N4, N4.5, IE3, IE4, IE5, WebTV	&#182;	N1, N2, N3, N4, N4.5, IE3, IE4, IE5, WebTV	¶	Paragraph symbol
&middot;	N3, N4, N4.5, IE3, IE4, IE5, WebTV	&#183;	N1, N3, N4, N4.5, IE3, IE4, IE5, WebTV	•	Middle dot
&cedil;	N3, N4, N4.5, IE3, IE4, IE5, WebTV	&#184;	N1, N3, N4, N4.5, IE3, IE4, IE5, WebTV	¸	Cedilla
&sup1;	N3, N4, N4.5, IE3, IE4, IE5, WebTV	&#185;	N1, N3, N4, N4.5, IE3, IE4, IE5, WebTV	¹	Superscript 1
&ordm;	N3, N4, N4.5, IE3, IE4, IE5, WebTV	&#186;	N1, N3, N4, N4.5, IE3, IE4, IE5, WebTV	º	Masculine ordinal indicator
&raquo;	N3, N4, N4.5, IE3, IE4, IE5, WebTV	&#187;	N1, N2, N3, N4, N4.5, IE3, IE4, IE5, WebTV	»	Closing double angle quotes
&frac14;	N3, N4, N4.5, IE3, IE4, IE5, WebTV	&#188;	N1, N3, N4, N4.5, IE3, IE4, IE5, WebTV	¼	One-quarter fraction
&frac12;	N3, N4, N4.5, IE3, IE4, IE5, WebTV	&#189;	N1, N3, N4, N4.5, IE3, IE4, IE5, WebTV	½	One-half fraction

Named Entity	Browser Support	Numbered Entity	Browser Support	Intended Rendering	Description
&frac34;	N3, N4, N4.5, IE3, IE4, IE5, WebTV	&#190;	N1, N3, N4, N4.5, IE3, IE4, IE5, WebTV	¾	Three-fourths fraction
&iquest;	N3, N4, N4.5, IE3, IE4, IE5, WebTV	&#191;	N1, N3, N4, N4.5, IE3, IE4, IE5, WebTV	¿	Inverted question mark
&Agrave;	N1, N3, N4, N4.5, IE3, IE4, IE5, WebTV	&#192;	N1, N3, N4, N4.5, IE3, IE4, IE5, WebTV	À	Uppercase *A* with grave accent
&Aacute;	N1, N3, N4, N4.5, IE3, IE4, IE5, WebTV	&#193;	N1, N3, N4, N4.5, IE3, IE4, IE5, WebTV	Á	Uppercase *A* with acute accent
&Acirc;	N1, N3, N4, N4.5, IE3, IE4, IE5, WebTV	&#194;	N1, N3, N4, N4.5, IE3, IE4, IE5, WebTV	Â	Uppercase *A* with circumflex
&Atilde;	N1, N3, N4, N4.5, IE3, IE4, IE5, WebTV	&#195;	N1, N3, N4, N4.5, IE3, IE4, IE5, WebTV	Ã	Uppercase *A* with tilde
&Auml;	N1, N3, N4, N4.5, IE3, IE4, IE5, WebTV	&#196;	N1, N3, N4, N4.5, IE3, IE4, IE5, WebTV	Ä	Uppercase *A* with umlaut
&Aring;	N1, N3, N4, N4.5, IE3, IE4, IE5, WebTV	&#197;	N1, N3, N4, N4.5, IE3, IE4, IE5, WebTV	Å	Uppercase *A* with ring
&AElig;	N1, N3, N4, N4.5, IE3, IE4, IE5, WebTV	&#198;	N1, N3, N4, N4.5, IE3, IE4, IE5, WebTV	Æ	Uppercase *AE* ligature
&Ccedil;	N1, N3, N4, N4.5, IE3, IE4, IE5, WebTV	&#199;	N1, N3, N4, N4.5, IE3, IE4, IE5, WebTV	Ç	Uppercase *C* with cedilla
&Egrave;	N1, N3, N4, N4.5, IE3, IE4, IE5, WebTV	&#200;	N1, N3, N4, N4.5, IE3, IE4, IE5, WebTV	È	Uppercase *E* with grave accent
&Eacute;	N1, N3, N4, N4.5, IE3, IE4, IE5, WebTV	&#201;	N1, N3, N4, N4.5, IE3, IE4, IE5, WebTV	É	Uppercase *E* with acute accent

Named Entity	Browser Support	Numbered Entity	Browser Support	Intended Rendering	Description
&Ecirc;	N1, N3, N4, N4.5, IE3, IE4, IE5, WebTV	&#202;	N1, N3, N4, N4.5, IE3, IE4, IE5, WebTV	Ê	Uppercase *E* with circumflex
&Euml;	N1, N3, N4, N4.5, IE3, IE4, IE5, WebTV	&#203;	N1, N3, N4, N4.5, IE3, IE4, IE5, WebTV	Ë	Uppercase *E* with umlaut
&Igrave;	N1, N3, N4, N4.5, IE3, IE4, IE5, WebTV	&#204;	N1, N3, N4, N4.5, IE3, IE4, IE5, WebTV	Ì	Uppercase *I* with grave accent
&Iacute;	N1, N3, N4, N4.5, IE3, IE4, IE5, WebTV	&#205;	N1, N3, N4, N4.5, IE3, IE4, IE5, WebTV	Í	Uppercase *I* with acute accent
&Icirc;	N1, N3, N4, N4.5, IE3, IE4, IE5, WebTV	&#206;	N1, N3, N4, N4.5, IE3, IE4, IE5, WebTV	Î	Uppercase *I* with circumflex
&Iuml;	N1, N3, N4, N4.5, IE3, IE4, IE5, WebTV	&#207;	N1, N3, N4, N4.5, IE3, IE4, IE5, WebTV	Ï	Uppercase *I* with umlaut
&ETH;	N1, N3, N4, N4.5, IE3, IE4, IE5, WebTV	&#208;	N1, N3, N4, N4.5, IE3, IE4, IE5, WebTV	Ð	Capital eth
&Ntilde;	N1, N3, N4, N4.5, IE3, IE4, IE5, WebTV	&#209;	N1, N3, N4, N4.5, IE3, IE4, IE5, WebTV	Ñ	Uppercase *N* with tilde
&Ograve;	N1, N3, N4, N4.5, IE3, IE4, IE5, WebTV	&#210;	N1, N3, N4, N4.5, IE3, IE4, IE5, WebTV	Ò	Uppercase *O* with grave accent
&Oacute;	N1, N3, N4, N4.5, IE3, IE4, IE5, WebTV	&#211;	N1, N3, N4, N4.5, IE3, IE4, IE5, WebTV	Ó	Uppercase *O* with acute accent
&Ocirc;	N1, N3, N4, N4.5, IE3, IE4, IE5, WebTV	&#212;	N1, N3, N4, N4.5, IE3, IE4, IE5, WebTV	Ô	Uppercase *O* with circumflex
&Otilde;	N1, N3, N4, N4.5, IE3, IE4, IE5, WebTV	&#213;	N1, N3, N4, N4.5, IE3, IE4, IE5, WebTV	Õ	Uppercase *O* with tilde

Named Entity	Browser Support	Numbered Entity	Browser Support	Intended Rendering	Description
&Ouml;	N1, N3, N4, N4.5, IE3, IE4, IE5, WebTV	&#214;	N1, N3, N4, N4.5, IE3, IE4, IE5, WebTV	Ö	Uppercase O with umlaut
&times;	N3, N4, N4.5, IE3, IE4, IE5, WebTV	&#215;	N1, N3, N4, N4.5, IE3, IE4, IE5, WebTV	×	Multiplication symbol
&Oslash;	N1, N3, N4, N4.5, IE3, IE4, IE5, WebTV	&#216;	N1, N3, N4, N4.5, IE3, IE4, IE5, WebTV	Ø	Uppercase O with slash
&Ugrave;	N1, N3, N4, N4.5, IE3, IE4, IE5, WebTV	&#217;	N1, N3, N4, N4.5, IE3, IE4, IE5, WebTV	Ù	Uppercase U with grave accent
&Uacute;	N1, N3, N4, N4.5, IE3, IE4, IE5, WebTV	&#218;	N1, N3, N4, N4.5, IE3, IE4, IE5, WebTV	Ú	Uppercase U with acute accent
&Ucirc;	N1, N3, N4, N4.5, IE3, IE4, IE5, WebTV	&#219;	N1, N3, N4, N4.5, IE3, IE4, IE5, WebTV	Û	Uppercase U with circumflex accent
&Uuml;	N1, N3, N4, N4.5, IE3, IE4, IE5, WebTV	&#220;	N1, N3, N4, N4.5, IE3, IE4, IE5, WebTV	Ü	Uppercase U with umlaut
&Yacute;	N1, N3, N4, N4.5, IE3, IE4, IE5, WebTV	&#221;	N1, N3, N4, N4.5, IE3, IE4, IE5, WebTV	Ý	Uppercase Y with acute accent
&THORN;	N1, N3, N4, N4.5, IE3, IE4, IE5, WebTV	&#222;	N1, N3, N4, N4.5, IE3, IE4, IE5, WebTV	Þ	Capital thorn
&szlig;	N1, N3, N4, N4.5, IE3, IE4, IE5, WebTV	&#223;	N1, N3, N4, N4.5, IE3, IE4, IE5, WebTV	ß	*SZ* ligature
&agrave;	N1, N3, N4, N4.5, IE3, IE4, IE5, WebTV	&#224;	N1, N3, N4, N4.5, IE3, IE4, IE5, WebTV	à	Lowercase *a* with grave accent
&aacute;	N1, N3, N4, N4.5, IE3, IE4, IE5, WebTV	&#225;	N1, N3, N4, N4.5, IE3, IE4, IE5, WebTV	á	Lowercase *a* with acute accent

APPENDIXES

Named Entity	Browser Support	Numbered Entity	Browser Support	Intended Rendering	Description
&acirc;	N1, N3, N4, N4.5, IE3, IE4, IE5, WebTV	&#226;	N1, N3, N4, N4.5, IE3, IE4, IE5, WebTV	â	Lowercase *a* with circumflex
&atilde;	N1, N3, N4, N4.5, IE3, IE4, IE5, WebTV	&#227;	N1, N3, N4, N4.5, IE3, IE4, IE5, WebTV	ã	Lowercase *a* with tilde
&auml;	N1, N3, N4, N4.5, IE3, IE4, IE5, WebTV	&#228;	N1, N3, N4, N4.5, IE3, IE4, IE5, WebTV	ä	Lowercase *a* with umlaut
&aring;	N1, N3, N4, N4.5, IE3, IE4, IE5, WebTV	&#229;	N1, N3, N4, N4.5, IE3, IE4, IE5, WebTV	å	Lowercase *a* with ring
&aelig;	N1, N3, N4, N4.5, IE3, IE4, IE5, WebTV	&#230;	N1, N3, N4, N4.5, IE3, IE4, IE5, WebTV	æ	Lowercase *ae* ligature
&ccedil;	N1, N3, N4, N4.5, IE3, IE4, IE5, WebTV	&#231;	N1, N3, N4, N4.5, IE3, IE4, IE5, WebTV	ç	Lowercase *c* with cedilla
&egrave;	N1, N3, N4, N4.5, IE3, IE4, IE5, WebTV	&#232;	N1, N3, N4, N4.5, IE3, IE4, IE5, WebTV	è	Lowercase *e* with grave accent
&eacute;	N1, N3, N4, N4.5, IE3, IE4, IE5, WebTV	&#233;	N1, N3, N4, N4.5, IE3, IE4, IE5, WebTV	é	Lowercase *e* with acute accent
&ecirc;	N1, N3, N4, N4.5, IE3, IE4, IE5, WebTV	&#234;	N1, N3, N4, N4.5, IE3, IE4, IE5, WebTV	ê	Lowercase *e* with circumflex
&euml;	N1, N3, N4, N4.5, IE3, IE4, IE5, WebTV	&#235;	N1, N3, N4, N4.5, IE3, IE4, IE5, WebTV	ë	Lowercase *e* with umlaut
&igrave;	N1, N3, N4, N4.5, IE3, IE4, IE5, WebTV	&#236;	N1, N3, N4, N4.5, IE3, IE4, IE5, WebTV	ì	Lowercase *i* with grave accent
&iacute;	N1, N3, N4, N4.5, IE3, IE4, IE5, WebTV	&#237;	N1, N3, N4, N4.5, IE3, IE4, IE5, WebTV	í	Lowercase *i* with acute accent

Named Entity	Browser Support	Numbered Entity	Browser Support	Intended Rendering	Description
&icirc;	N1, N3, N4, N4.5, IE3, IE4, IE5, WebTV	&#238;	N1, N3, N4, N4.5, IE3, IE4, IE5, WebTV	î	Lowercase *i* with circumflex
&iuml;	N1, N3, N4, N4.5, IE3, IE4, IE5, WebTV	&#239;	N1, N3, N4, N4.5, IE3, IE4, IE5, WebTV	ï	Lowercase *i* with umlaut
&eth;	N1, N3, N4, N4.5, IE3, IE4, IE5, WebTV	&#240;	N1, N3, N4, N4.5, IE3, IE4, IE5, WebTV	ð	Lowercase eth
&ntilde;	N1, N3, N4, N4.5, IE3, IE4, IE5, WebTV	&#241;	N1, N3, N4, N4.5, IE3, IE4, IE5, WebTV	ñ	Lowercase *n* with tilde
&ograve;	N1, N3, N4, N4.5, IE3, IE4, IE5, WebTV	&#242;	N1, N3, N4, N4.5, IE3, IE4, IE5, WebTV	ò	Lowercase *o* with grave accent
&oacute;	N1, N3, N4, N4.5, IE3, IE4, IE5, WebTV	&#243;	N1, N3, N4, N4.5, IE3, IE4, IE5, WebTV	ó	Lowercase *o* with acute accent
&ocirc;	N1, N3, N4, N4.5, IE3, IE4, IE5, WebTV	&#244;	N1, N3, N4, N4.5, IE3, IE4, IE5, WebTV	ô	Lowercase *o* with circumflex accent
&otilde;	N1, N3, N4, N4.5, IE3, IE4, IE5, WebTV	&#245;	N1, N3, N4, N4.5, IE3, IE4, IE5, WebTV	õ	Lowercase *o* with tilde
&ouml;	N1, N3, N4, N4.5, IE3, IE4, IE5, WebTV	&#246;	N1, N3, N4, N4.5, IE3, IE4, IE5, WebTV	ö	Lowercase *o* with umlaut
&divide;	N3, N4, N4.5, IE3, IE4, IE5, WebTV	&#247;	N1, N3, N4, N4.5, IE3, IE4, IE5, WebTV	÷	Division symbol
&oslash;	N1, N3, N4, N4.5, IE3, IE4, IE5, WebTV	&#248;	N1, N3, N4, N4.5, IE3, IE4, IE5, WebTV	ø	Lowercase *o* with slash
&ugrave;	N1, N3, N4, N4.5, IE3, IE4, IE5, WebTV	&#249;	N1, N3, N4, N4.5, IE3, IE4, IE5, WebTV	ù	Lowercase *u* with grave accent

Named Entity	Browser Support	Numbered Entity	Browser Support	Intended Rendering	Description
&uacute;	N1, N3, N4, N4.5, IE3, IE4, IE5, WebTV	&#250;	N1, N3, N4, N4.5, IE3, IE4, IE5, WebTV	ú	Lowercase *u* with acute accent
&ucirc;	N1, N3, N4, N4.5, IE3, IE4, IE5, WebTV	&#251;	N1, N3, N4, N4.5, IE3, IE4, IE5, WebTV	û	Lowercase *u* with circumflex
&uuml;	N1, N3, N4, N4.5, IE3, IE4, IE5, WebTV	&#252;	N1, N3, N4, N4.5, IE3, IE4, IE5, WebTV	ü	Lowercase *u* with umlaut
&yacute;	N1, N3, N4, N4.5, IE3, IE4, IE5, WebTV	&#253;	N1, N3, N4, N4.5, IE3, IE4, IE5, WebTV	ý	Lowercase *y* with acute accent
&thorn;	N1, N3, N4, N4.5, IE3, IE4, IE5, WebTV	&#254;	N1, N3, N4, N4.5, IE3, IE4, IE5, WebTV	þ	Lowercase thorn
&yuml;	N1, N3, N4, N4.5, IE3, IE4, IE5, WebTV	&#255;	N1, N3, N4, N4.5, IE3, IE4, IE5, WebTV	ÿ	Lowercase *y* with umlaut

HTML 4 Character Entities

The HTML 4.0 specification introduces a wide array of new character entities. These include additional Latin characters, the Greek alphabet, special spacing characters, arrows, technical symbols, and various shapes. Some of these entities have yet to be supported by browser vendors. Netscape 4 supports only a few of the extended Latin characters and some entities that duplicate characters already available in the "standard" list (34 through 255). Microsoft has taken the lead in this area, with Internet Explorer 4 supporting many of these entities, including the Greek alphabet and mathematical symbols. These character entities expand the presentation possibilities of

HTML, particularly in the presentation of foreign languages. Netscape's neglect of these tags is an unfortunate oversight that ideally should be corrected as soon as possible.

Latin Extended-A

Named Entity	Browser Support	Numbered Entity	Browser Support	Intended Rendering	Description
&Oelig;	IE4, IE5	&#338;	IE4, IE5, N4, N4.5	Œ	Uppercase ligature *OE*
&oelig;	IE4, IE5	&#339;	IE4, IE5, N4, N4.5	œ	Lowercase ligature *oe*
&Scaron;	IE4, IE5	&#352;	IE4, IE5, N4, N4.5	Š	Uppercase *S* with caron
&scaron;	IE4, IE5	&#353;	IE4, IE5, N4, N4.5	š	Lowercase *s* with caron
&Yuml;	IE4, IE5	&#376;	IE4, IE5, N4, N4.5	Ÿ	Uppercase *Y* with umlaut

Latin Extended-B

Named Entity	Browser Support	Numbered Entity	Browser Support	Intended Rendering	Description
&fnof;	IE4, IE5	&#402;	IE4, IE5, N4, N4.5	ƒ	Latin small *f* with hook

Spacing Modifier Letters

Named Entity	Browser Support	Numbered Entity	Browser Support	Intended Rendering	Description
&circ;	IE4, IE5	&#710;	IE4, IE5, N4, N4.5	^	Circumflex accent
&tilde;	IE4, IE5	&#732;	IE4, IE5, N4, N4.5	~	Small tilde

General Punctuation

Named Entity	Browser Support	Numbered Entity	Browser Support	Intended Rendering	Description
	None		None		En space
	None		None		Em space
	None		None		Thin space
&zwnj;	IE4	&#8204;	IE4	|	Zero width nonjoiner
&zwj;	IE4	&#8205;	IE4	Ỷ	Zero width joiner
&lrm;	None	&#8206;	None	Unknown	Left-to-right mark
&rlm;	None	&#8207;	None	Unknown	Right-to-left mark
&ndash;	IE4, IE5	&#8211;	IE4, IE5, N4, N4.5	–	En dash
&mdash;	IE4, IE5	&#8212;	IE4, IE5, N4, N4.5	—	Em dash
&lsquo;	IE4, IE5	&#8216;	IE4, IE5, N4, N4.5	'	Left single quotation mark
&rsquo;	IE4, IE5	&#8217;	IE4, IE5, N4, N4.5	'	Right single quotation mark
&sbquo;	IE4, IE5	&#8218;	IE4, IE5, N4, N4.5	‚	Single low-9 quotation mark
&ldquo;	IE4, IE5	&#8220;	IE4, IE5, N4, N4.5	"	Left double quotation mark
&rdquo;	IE4, IE5	&#8221;	IE4, IE5, N4, N4.5	"	Right double quotation mark
&bdquo;	IE4, IE5	&#8222;	IE4, IE5, N4, N4.5	„	Double low-9 quotation mark
&dagger;	IE4, IE5	&#8224;	IE4, IE5, N4, N4.5	†	Dagger
&Dagger;	IE4, IE5	&#8225;	IE4, IE5, N4, N4.5	‡	Double dagger
&bull;	IE4, IE5	&#8226;	IE4, IE5, N4, N4.5	•	Bullet
&hellip;	IE4, IE5	&#8230;	IE4, IE5, N4, N4.5	…	Horizontal ellipsis

Named Entity	Browser Support	Numbered Entity	Browser Support	Intended Rendering	Description
&permil;	IE4, IE5	&#8240;	IE4, IE5, N4, N4.5	‰	Per thousand sign
&prime;	IE4, IE5	&#8242;	IE4, IE5	'	Prime, minutes, or feet
&Prime;	IE4, IE5	&#8243;	IE4, IE5	"	Double prime, seconds, or inches
&lsaquo;	IE4, IE5	&#8249;	IE4, IE5, N4, N4.5	‹	Single left-pointing angle quotation mark
&rsaquo;	IE4, IE5	&#8250;	IE4, IE5, N4, N4.5	›	Single right-pointing angle quotation mark
&oline;	IE4, IE5	&#8254;	IE4, IE5	‾	Overline
&frasl;	IE4, IE5	&#8260;	IE4, IE5	/	Fraction slash

Greek

Note *Testing suggests that Internet Explorer support for this set of characters only works under Windows NT, not under Windows 95.*

Named Entity	Browser Support	Numbered Entity	Browser Support	Intended Rendering	Description
&Alpha;	IE4, IE5	&#913;	IE4, IE5	A	Greek capital letter alpha
&Beta;	IE4, IE5	&#914;	IE4, IE5	B	Greek capital letter beta
&Gamma;	IE4, IE5	&#915;	IE4, IE5	Γ	Greek capital letter gamma
&Delta;	IE4, IE5	&#916;	IE4, IE5	Δ	Greek capital letter delta
&Epsilon;	IE4, IE5	&#917;	IE4, IE5	E	Greek capital letter epsilon
&Zeta;	IE4, IE5	&#918;	IE4, IE5	Z	Greek capital letter zeta
&Eta;	IE4, IE5	&#919;	IE4, IE5	H	Greek capital letter eta
&Theta;	IE4, IE5	&#920;	IE4, IE5	Θ	Greek capital letter theta
&Iota;	IE4, IE5	&#921;	IE4, IE5	I	Greek capital letter iota
&Kappa;	IE4, IE5	&#922;	IE4, IE5	K	Greek capital letter kappa

Named Entity	Browser Support	Numbered Entity	Browser Support	Intended Rendering	Description
&Lambda;	IE4, IE5	&#923;	IE4, IE5	Λ	Greek capital letter lambda
&Mu;	IE4, IE5	&#924;	IE4, IE5	M	Greek capital letter mu
&Nu;	IE4, IE5	&#925;	IE4, IE5	N	Greek capital letter nu
&Xi;	IE4, IE5	&#926;	IE4, IE5	Ξ	Greek capital letter xi
&Omicron;	IE4, IE5	&#927;	IE4, IE5	O	Greek capital letter omicron
&Pi;	IE4, IE5	&#928;	IE4, IE5	Π	Greek capital letter pi
&Rho;	IE4, IE5	&#929;	IE4, IE5	P	Greek capital letter rho
&Sigma;	IE4, IE5	&#931;	IE4, IE5	Σ	Greek capital letter sigma
&Tau;	IE4, IE5	&#932;	IE4, IE5	T	Greek capital letter tau
&Upsilon;	IE4, IE5	&#933;	IE4, IE5	Y	Greek capital letter upsilon
&Phi;	IE4, IE5	&#934;	IE4, IE5	Φ	Greek capital letter phi
&Chi;	IE4, IE5	&#935;	IE4, IE5	X	Greek capital letter chi
&Psi;	IE4, IE5	&#936;	IE4, IE5	Ψ	Greek capital letter psi
&Omega;	IE4, IE5	&#937;	IE4, IE5	Ω	Greek capital letter omega
&alpha;	IE4, IE5	&#945;	IE4, IE5	α	Greek small letter alpha
&beta;	IE4, IE5	&#946;	IE4, IE5	β	Greek small letter beta
&gamma;	IE4, IE5	&#947;	IE4, IE5	γ	Greek small letter gamma
&delta;	IE4, IE5	&#948;	IE4, IE5	δ	Greek small letter delta
&epsilon;	IE4, IE5	&#949;	IE4, IE5	ε	Greek small letter epsilon
&zeta;	IE4, IE5	&#950;	IE4, IE5	ζ	Greek small letter zeta
&eta;	IE4, IE5	&#951;	IE4, IE5	η	Greek small letter eta
&theta;	IE4, IE5	&#952;	IE4, IE5	θ	Greek small letter theta
&iota;	IE4, IE5	&#953;	IE4, IE5	ι	Greek small letter iota
&kappa;	IE4, IE5	&#954;	IE4, IE5	κ	Greek small letter kappa
&lambda;	IE4, IE5	&#955;	IE4, IE5	λ	Greek small letter lambda
&mu;	IE4, IE5	&#956;	IE4, IE5	μ	Greek small letter mu
&nu;	IE4, IE5	&#957;	IE4, IE5	ν	Greek small letter nu
&xi;	IE4, IE5	&#958;	IE4, IE5	ξ	Greek small letter xi

Named Entity	Browser Support	Numbered Entity	Browser Support	Intended Rendering	Description
&omicron;	IE4, IE5	&#959;	IE4, IE5	o	Greek small letter omicron
&pi;	IE4, IE5	&#960;	IE4, IE5	π	Greek small letter pi
&rho;	IE4, IE5	&#961;	IE4, IE5	ρ	Greek small letter rho
&sigmaf;	IE4, IE5	&#962;	IE4, IE5	ς	Greek small letter final sigma
&sigma;	IE4, IE5	&#963;	IE4, IE5	σ	Greek small letter sigma
&tau;	IE4, IE5	&#964;	IE4, IE5	τ	Greek small letter tau
&upsilon;	IE4, IE5	&#965;	IE4, IE5	υ	Greek small letter upsilon
&phi;	IE4, IE5	&#966;	IE4, IE5	φ	Greek small letter phi
&chi;	IE4, IE5	&#967;	IE4, IE5	χ	Greek small letter chi
&psi;	IE4, IE5	&#968;	IE4, IE5	ψ	Greek small letter psi
&omega;	IE4, IE5	&#969;	IE4, IE5	ω	Greek small letter omega
&thetasym;	None	&#977;	None	θ	Greek small letter theta symbol
&upsih;	None	&#978;	None	ϒ	Greek upsilon with hook symbol
&piv	None	&#982;	None	ϖ	Greek pi symbol

Letter-Like Symbols

Named Entity	Browser Support	Numbered Entity	Browser Support	Intended Rendering	Description
&weierp;	None	&#8472;	None	℘	Script capital *P*, power set
&image;	None	&#8465;	None	ℑ	Blackletter capital *I*, or imaginary part symbol
&real;	None	&#8476;	None	ℜ	Blackletter capital *R*, or real part symbol
&trade;	IE3, IE4, IE5	&#8482;	IE4, IE5, N4, N4.5	™	Trademark symbol
&alefsym;	None	&#8501;	None	ℵ	Alef symbol, or first transfinite cardinal

Arrows

 Testing suggests that Internet Explorer support for this set of characters only works under Windows NT, not under Windows 95.

Named Entity	Browser Support	Numbered Entity	Browser Support	Intended Rendering	Description
&larr;	IE4, IE5	&#8592;	IE4, IE5	←	Leftward arrow
&uarr;	IE4, IE5	&#8593;	IE4, IE5	↑	Upward arrow
&rarr;	IE4, IE5	&#8594;	IE4, IE5	→	Rightward arrow
&darr;	IE4, IE5	&#8595;	IE4, IE5	↓	Downward arrow
&harr;	IE4, IE5	&#8596;	IE4, IE5	↔	Left-right arrow
&crarr;	None	&#8629;	None	↵	Downward arrow with corner leftward
&lArr;	None	&#8656;	None	⇐	Leftward double arrow
&uArr;	None	&#8657;	None	⇑	Upward double arrow
&rArr;	None	&#8658;	None	⇒	Rightward double arrow
&dArr;	None	&#8659;	None	⇓	Downward double arrow
&hArr;	None	&#8660;	None	⇔	Left-right double arrow

Mathematical Operators

Named Entity	Browser Support	Numbered Entity	Browser Support	Intended Rendering	Description
&forall;	None	&#8704;	None	∀	For all
&part;	IE4, IE5	&#8706;	IE4, IE5	∂	Partial differential
&exist;	None	&#8707;	None	∃	There exists
&empty;	None	&#8709;	None	∅	Empty set, null set, diameter
&nabla;	None	&#8711;	None	∇	Nabla, or backward difference
&isin;	None	&#8712;	None	∈	Element of

Named Entity	Browser Support	Numbered Entity	Browser Support	Intended Rendering	Description
&notin;	None	&#8713;	None	∉	Not an element of
&ni;	None	&#8715;	None	∋	Contains as member
&prod;	IE4, IE5	&#8719;	IE4, IE5	∏	N-ary product, or product sign
&sum;	IE4, IE5	&#8721;	IE4, IE5	∑	N-ary summation
&minus;	IE4, IE5	&#8722;	IE4, IE5	−	Minus sign
&lowast;	None	&#8727;	None	∗	Asterisk operator
&radic;	IE4, IE5	&#8730;	IE4, IE5	√	Square root, radical sign
&prop;	None	&#8733;	None	~	Proportional to
&infin;	IE4, IE5	&#8734;	IE4, IE5	∞	Infinity
&ang;	None	&#8736;	None	∠	Angle
&and;	None	&#8869;	None	∧	Logical and
&or;	None	&#8870;	None	∨	Logical or
&cap;	IE4, IE5	&#8745;	IE4, IE5	∩	Intersection, cap
&cup;	None	&#8746;	None	∪	Union, cup
&int;	IE4, IE5	&#8747;	IE4, IE5	∫	Integral
&there4;	None	&#8756;	None	∴	Therefore
&sim;	None	&#8764;	None	~	Tilde operator
&cong;	None	&#8773;	None	≅	Approximately equal to
&asymp;	IE4, IE5	&#8776;	IE4, IE5	≈	Almost equal to, asymptotic to
&ne;	IE4, IE5	&#8800;	IE4, IE5	≠	Not equal to
&equiv;	IE4, IE5	&#8801;	IE4, IE5	≡	Identical to
&le;	IE4, IE5	&#8804;	IE4, IE5	≤	Less than or equal to
&ge;	IE4, IE5	&#8805;	IE4, IE5	≥	Greater than or equal to
&sub;	None	&#8834;	None	⊂	Subset of
&sup;	None	&#8835;	None	⊃	Superset of
&nsub;	None	&#8836;	None	⊄	Not a subset of
&sube;	None	&#8838;	None	⊆	Subset of or equal to
&supe;	None	&#8839;	None	⊇	Superset of or equal to

Named Entity	Browser Support	Numbered Entity	Browser Support	Intended Rendering	Description
&oplus;	None	&#8853;	None	⊕	Circled plus, direct sum
&otimes;	None	&#8855;	None	⊗	Circled times, vector product
&perp;	None	&#8869;	None	⊥	Perpendicular
&sdot;	None	&#8901;	None	:	Dot operator

Technical Symbols

Named Entity	Browser Support	Numbered Entity	Browser Support	Intended Rendering	Description
&lceil;	None	&#8968;	None	⌈	Left ceiling, apl upstile
&rceil;	None	&#8969;	None	⌉	Right ceiling
&lfloor;	None	&#8970;	None	⌊	Left floor, apl downstile
&rfloor;	None	&#8971;	None	⌋	Right floor
&lang;	None	&#9001;	None	<	Left-pointing angle bracket
&rang;	None	&#9002;	None	>	Right-pointing angle bracket

Geometric Shapes

Named Entity	Browser Support	Numbered Entity	Browser Support	Intended Rendering	Description
&loz;	IE4, IE5	&#9674;	IE4, IE5	◊	Lozenge

Miscellaneous Symbols

Named Entity	Browser Support	Numbered Entity	Browser Support	Intended Rendering	Description
&spades;	IE4, IE5	&#9824;	IE4, IE5	♠	Black spade suit
&clubs;	IE4, IE5	&#9827;	IE4, IE5	♣	Black club suit
&hearts;	IE4, IE5	&#9829;	IE4, IE5	♥	Black heart suit
&diams;	IE4, IE5	&#9830;	IE4v	♦	Black diamond suit

Appendix D

Fonts

This appendix lists fonts commonly available on most systems, as well as those that come with Internet Explorer. While other fonts may be available on users' systems, it is advisable to limit font choices to those most likely to be in use, or to provide the ones listed here as alternative fonts (as discussed in Chapter 8) in case a preferred but uncommon font is not available.

Fonts for Microsoft Platforms and Browsers

The following table lists fonts supported under various Microsoft browsers (Internet Explorer 3.02 and/or 4) and systems. Representatives of these font families are displayed in Figure D-1.

Font	Win 95	Win 3.1x	Win NT 3.x	IE 3.02	IE 4
Arial	✓	✓	✓		
Arial Black				✓	
Arial Bold	✓	✓	✓		
Arial Italic	✓	✓	✓		
Arial Bold Italic	✓	✓	✓		
Comic Sans MS				✓	✓
Comic Sans MS Bold				✓	
Courier New	✓	✓	✓		
Courier New Bold	✓	✓	✓		
Courier New Italic	✓	✓	✓		
Courier New Bold Italic	✓	✓	✓		
Impact				✓	
Lucida Sans Unicode			✓ (except 3.0)		
Lucida Console			✓ (except 3.0)		
Marlett	✓				
Symbol	✓	✓	✓		

Font	Win 95	Win 3.1x	Win NT 3.x	IE 3.02	IE 4
Times New Roman	✓	✓	✓		
Times New Roman Bold	✓	✓	✓		
Times New Roman Italic	✓	✓	✓		
Times New Roman Bold Italic	✓	✓	✓		
Verdana				✓	✓
Verdana Bold				✓	✓
Verdana Italic				✓	✓
Verdana Bold Italic				✓	✓
Webdings					✓
Wingdings	✓	✓	✓		

Win = Windows   IE = Internet Explorer

Arial

Arial Black

Comic Sans MS

Courier New

Impact

Lucida Sans

□ ✔ ✖ ⌐ ⌐ ▲ ▲ (Marlett)

Σψμβολ (Symbol)

Times New Roman

Verdana

▶ 🏛 🏨 🏤 🚒 👁 🏛 🏦 (Webdings)

✙ ✠ ■ ℣ ♌ ✠ ■ ℣ ♦ (Wingdings)

Figure D-1.   *Font families available for Microsoft browsers and systems*

Fonts for Apple Macintosh System 7

The fonts available with Macintosh System 7 are displayed in Figure D-2.

Chicago

Courier Regular

Geneva

Helvetica

Monaco

New York

Palatino

Σψμβολ   (Symbol)

Times

Figure D-2.   *Font families available with Macintosh System 7*

Fonts for Unix Systems

The fonts available for Unix systems are displayed in Figure D-3.

Charter

Clean

Courier

Fixed

Helvetica

Lucida

Lucidabright

New Century Schoolbook

Σψμβολ   (Symbol)

Terminal

Times

Utopia

Figure D-3.   *Font families available for Unix systems*

Appendix E

Color Names and Hexadecimal Codes

Table E-1 lists all the color names commonly supported by the major browsers (Netscape 3 and above, Internet Explorer 3 and above, and WebTV). Sixteen colors (aqua, black, blue, fuchsia, gray, green, lime, maroon, navy, olive, purple, red, silver, teal, white, and yellow) were introduced by Microsoft and are now part of the official W3C HTML specification; the rest were introduced by Netscape. The corresponding hexadecimal code is shown next to each color name. So, the code **<BODY BGCOLOR="lightsteelblue">** would produce the same result as **<BODY BGCOLOR="#B0C4DE">** under any browser that supported these color names. Don't forget to use the pound symbol (#) before hexadecimal values. Color names are easier to remember than numerical codes, but may cause trouble when viewed under old or uncommon browsers. It is advisable to stick with the hexadecimal approach to colors because it is generally safer, especially since only 16 of the names are officially recognized. WebTV supports the color names but displays several colors differently, as noted in the table. General WebTV color support may also vary due to essential differences between computer monitors and television screens. The RGB Equivalent column provides the RGB equivalent of each color, allowing easy reference for Web authors trying to match colors in Photoshop or in other graphics programs.

Hexadecimal Code	Name	RGB Equivalent	Notes
F0F8FF	aliceblue	240,248,255	The name aliceblue is not supported by Netscape.
FAEBD7	antiquewhite	250,235,215	
00FFFF	aqua	0,255,255	
7FFFD4	aquamarine	127,255,212	
F0FFFF	azure	240,255,255	
F5F5DC	beige	245,245,220	
FFE4C4	bisque	255,228,196	
000000	black	0,0,0	
FFEBCD	blanchedalmond	255,235,205	
0000FF	blue	0,0,255	

Table E-1. *Color Names Supported by the Popular Browsers*

Hexadecimal Code	Name	RGB Equivalent	Notes
8A2BE2	blueviolet	138,43,226	WebTV displays blueviolet the same as blue (0000EE).
A52A2A	brown	165,42,42	
DEB887	burlywood	222,184,135	
5F9EA0	cadetblue	95,158,160	
7FFF00	chartreuse	127,255,0	
D2691E	chocolate	210,105,30	
FF7F50	coral	255,127,80	
6495ED	cornflowerblue	100,149,237	
FFF8DC	cornsilk	255,248,220	
DC143C	crimson	220,20,60	
00FFFF	cyan	0,255,255	
00008B	darkblue	0,0,139	
008B8B	darkcyan	0,139,139	
B8860B	darkgoldenrod	184,134,11	
A9A9A9	darkgray	169,169,169	
006400	darkgreen	0,100,0	
BDB76B	darkkhaki	189,183,107	
8B008B	darkmagenta	139,0,139	
556B2F	darkolivegreen	85,107,47	
FF8C00	darkorange	255,140,0	
9932CC	darkorchid	153,50,204	
8B0000	darkred	139,0,0	
E9967A	darksalmon	233,150,122	

Table E-1.   *Color Names Supported by the Popular Browsers* (continued)

Hexadecimal Code	Name	RGB Equivalent	Notes
8FBC8F	darkseagreen	143,188,143	
483D8B	darkslateblue	72,61,139	
2F4F4F	darkslategray	47,79,79	
00CED1	darkturquoise	0,206,209	
9400D3	darkviolet	148,0,211	
FF1493	deeppink	255,20,147	
00BFFF	deepskyblue	0,191,255	
696969	dimgray	105,105,105	
1E90FF	dodgerblue	30,144,255	
B22222	firebrick	178,34,34	
FFFAF0	floralwhite	255,250,240	
228B22	forestgreen	34,139,34	
FF00FF	fuchsia	255,0,255	
DCDCDC	gainsboro	220,220,220	
F8F8FF	ghostwhite	248,248,255	
FFD700	gold	255,215,0	
DAA520	goldenrod	218,165,32	WebTV displays goldenrod the same as gold (FFD700).
808080	gray	127,127,127	
008000	green	0,128,0	
ADFF2F	greenyellow	173,255,47	WebTV displays greenyellow the same as green (008000).
F0FFF0	honeydew	240,255,240	

Table E-1.   *Color Names Supported by the Popular Browsers* (continued)

Hexadecimal Code	Name	RGB Equivalent	Notes
FF69B4	hotpink	255,105,180	
CD5C5C	indianred	205,92,92	
4B0082	indigo	75,0,130	
FFFFF0	ivory	255,255,240	
F0E68C	khaki	240,230,140	
E6E6FA	lavender	230,230,250	
FFF0F5	lavenderblush	255,240,245	
7CFC00	lawngreen	124,252,0	
FFFACD	lemonchiffon	255,250,205	
ADD8E6	lightblue	173,216,230	
F08080	lightcoral	240,128,128	
E0FFFF	lightcyan	224,255,255	
FAFAD2	lightgoldenrodyellow	250,250,210	
90EE90	lightgreen	144,238,144	
D3D3D3	lightgrey	211,211,211	
FFB6C1	lightpink	255,182,193	
FFA07A	lightsalmon	255,160,122	
20B2AA	lightseagreen	32,178,170	
87CEFA	lightskyblue	135,206,250	
778899	lightslategray	119,136,153	
B0C4DE	lightsteelblue	176,196,222	
FFFFE0	lightyellow	255,255,224	
00FF00	lime	0,255,0	
32CD32	limegreen	50,205, 50	WebTV displays limegreen the same as lime (00FF00).

Table E-1.   *Color Names Supported by the Popular Browsers* (continued)

Hexadecimal Code	Name	RGB Equivalent	Notes
FAF0E6	linen	250,240,230	
FF00FF	magenta	255,0,255	
800000	maroon	128,0,0	
66CDAA	mediumaquamarine	102,205,170	
0000CD	mediumblue	0,0,205	
BA55D3	mediumorchid	186,85,211	
9370DB	mediumpurple	147,112,219	
3CB371	mediumseagreen	60,179,113	
7B68EE	mediumslateblue	123,104,238	
00FA9A	mediumspringgreen	0,250,154	According to the WebTV specification, WebTV supports mediumspringgreen, but the name display does not match the numerical code display.
48D1CC	mediumturquoise	72,209,204	
C71585	mediumvioletred	199,21,133	
191970	midnightblue	25,25,112	
F5FFFA	mintcream	245,255,250	
FFE4E1	mistyrose	255,228,225	
FFE4B5	moccasin	255,228,181	
FFDEAD	navajowhite	255,222,173	
000080	navy	0, 0,128	

Table E-1.   *Color Names Supported by the Popular Browsers* (continued)

Hexadecimal Code	Name	RGB Equivalent	Notes
9FAFDF	navyblue	159,175,223	WebTV displays navyblue the same as navy (000080).
FDF5E6	oldlace	253,245,230	
808000	olive	128,128,0	
6B8E23	olivedrab	107,142,35	WebTV displays olivedrab the same as olive (808000).
FFA500	orange	255,165,0	
FF4500	orangered	255,69,0	WebTV displays orangered the same as orange (FFA500).
DA70D6	orchid	218,112,214	
EEE8AA	palegoldenrod	238,232,170	
98FB98	palegreen	152,251,152	
AFEEEE	paleturquoise	175,238,238	
DB7093	palevioletred	219,112,147	
FFEFD5	papayawhip	255,239,213	
FFDAB9	peachpuff	255,218,185	
CD853F	peru	205,133, 63	
FFC0CB	pink	255,192,203	
DDA0DD	plum	221,160,221	
B0E0E6	powderblue	176,224,230	
800080	purple	128,0,128	
FF0000	red	255,0,0	
BC8F8F	rosybrown	188,143,143	

Table E-1.   *Color Names Supported by the Popular Browsers* (continued)

Hexadecimal Code	Name	RGB Equivalent	Notes
4169E1	royalblue	65,105,225	
8B4513	saddlebrown	139,69,19	
FA8072	salmon	250,128,114	
F4A460	sandybrown	244,164,96	
2E8B57	seagreen	46,139,87	
FFF5EE	seashell	255,245,238	
A0522D	sienna	160,82,45	
C0C0C0	silver	192,192,192	
87CEEB	skyblue	135,206,235	
6A5ACD	slateblue	106,90,205	
708090	slategray	112,128,144	
FFFAFA	snow	255,250,250	
00FF7F	springgreen	0,255,127	
4682B4	steelblue	70,130,180	
D2B48C	tan	210,180,140	
008080	teal	0,128,128	
D8BFD8	thistle	216,191,216	
FF6347	tomato	255,99,71	
40E0D0	turquoise	64,224,208	
EE82EE	violet	238,130,238	
F5DEB3	wheat	245,222,179	
FFFFFF	white	255,255,255	
F5F5F5	whitesmoke	245,245,245	
FFFF00	yellow	255,255,0	

Table E-1.   *Color Names Supported by the Popular Browsers* (continued)

APPENDIXES

Hexadecimal Code	Name	RGB Equivalent	Notes
9ACD32	yellowgreen	139,205,50	WebTV displays yellowgreen the same as yellow (FFFF00).

Table E-1.   *Color Names Supported by the Popular Browsers* (continued)

Note   *Many online color references claim that further color variations can be introduced by adding the numbers 1 through 4 to color names. If this were correct, cadetblue1, cadetblue2, cadetblue3, and cadetblue4 would display as different shades of the same color, with 1 being the lightest and 4 the darkest. Some of these references also claim that gray supports up to 100 color variations (gray10, gray50, gray90, and so on). Testing reveals that this does not work under Netcape, Internet Explorer, or WebTV.*

Appendix F

Reading a Document Type Definition

T his appendix presents the document type definitions (DTDs) for HTML 4. HTML "dialects" are defined using SGML (Standard Generalized Markup Language), a complex language with many nuances. Fortunately, only a small amount of SGML needs to be understood to read the HTML DTDs. Before turning to the DTDs, this appendix examines how to read them.

Declarations

Two common types of declarations should be familiar to HTML authors: element type declarations and attribute list declarations. Beyond these, the less familiar declarations for parameter and general entities are not very complicated. They are discussed later in this appendix under the sections "Parameter Entities" and "General Entities."

Element Type Declarations

An *element type declaration* defines three characteristics:

- The element type's name, also known as its *generic identifier*
- Whether or not start and end tags are required, forbidden (end tags on empty elements), or may be omitted
- The element type's *content model,* or what content it can enclose

All element type declarations begin with the keyword **ELEMENT** and have the following form:

```
<!ELEMENT name minimization content_model>
```

The declaration for the HTML 2 **
** element type gives a simple example:

```
<!ELEMENT BR - O EMPTY>
```

Tag minimization is declared by two parameters that indicate the start and end tags. These parameters may take one of two values. A hyphen indicates that the tag is required. An uppercase **O** indicates that it may be omitted. The combination of **O**, for the end tag, and the content model **EMPTY** means that the end tag is forbidden. Thus, the **
** tag requires a start tag but not an end tag. Since the **
** tag does not contain any content, its content model is defined by the keyword **EMPTY**.

Most HTML elements enclose content. If a content model is declared, it is enclosed within parentheses and known as a *model group.* The HTML 4.0 declaration for a selection list option gives the following example:

```
<!ELEMENT OPTION - O (#PCDATA)*>
```

Note that the model group contains the keyword **#PCDATA**. PCDATA stands for *parsed character data*, character content that contains no element markup but that may contain entity symbols for special characters.

Occurrence Indicators

In the previous example, note the asterisk appended to the model group. This is an *occurrence indicator*, a special symbol that qualifies the element type or model group to which it is appended, indicating how many times it may occur. There are three occurrence indicators:

- ? means optional and at most one occurrence (zero or one occurrence).
- * means optional and any number of occurrences (zero or more occurrences).
- + means at least one occurrence is required (one or more occurrences).

So, the content model in the previous declaration says that the **<OPTION>** element may contain any amount of character content, including none.

Content models can also define an element type as containing element content, as illustrated by the HTML 2.0 declaration for a definition list (**<DL>**):

```
<!ELEMENT DL - - (DT|DL)+>
```

Logical Connectors

Note that the model group contains **DT** and **DL**, the names of element types that a **<DL>** element may enclose. Note also the vertical bar separating **DT** and **DL**. This is a *logical connector*, a special symbol indicating how the content units it connects relate to each other. There are three logical connectors:

- | means "or" (one and only one of the connected content units must occur).
- & means "and" (all of the connected content units must occur).
- , means "sequence" (the connected content units must occur in the specified order).

So, the content model in the previous declaration says that the **<DL>** element must contain either a **<DT>** or a **<DL>** element and may contain any additional number of **<DT>** or **<DL>** elements.

Model groups can be nested inside other model groups. Very flexible content models can be declared by combining this type of nesting with the ability to qualify content units with occurrence indicators and logical operators. The HTML 4.0 declaration for the **<TABLE>** element type illustrates this point:

```
<!ELEMENT TABLE - - (CAPTION?, ((COL*|COLGROUP*), THEAD?, TFOOT?,
                     TBODY+), CAPTION?)>
```

The content model for the **<TABLE>** element type reads as follows:

1. Table content must begin with zero or one **<CAPTION>** element.
2. This must be followed by a content group.
3. The content group must contain zero or more **<COL>** elements or zero or more **<COLGROUP>** elements.
4. This must be followed by zero or one **<THEAD>** element.
5. This must be followed by zero or one **<TFOOT>** element.
6. This must be followed by one or more **<TBODY>** elements.
7. The content must end with zero or one **<CAPTION>** element.

Content Exclusion

Occasionally the need arises to declare that an element type cannot contain certain other element types. This is known as a *content exclusion*. The excluded tags follow the model group, enclosed by parentheses and preceded by a minus sign:

```
(model group) -(excluded tags)
```

Content Inclusion

A related special need is the ability to declare that an element type can occur anywhere inside a content model. This is known as a *content inclusion*. The included tags follow the model group, enclosed by parentheses and preceded by a plus sign:

```
(model group) +(included tags)
```

Example of Content Exclusion and Inclusion

The HTML 4.0 declaration for the **<BODY>** element type illustrates both excluded and included elements:

```
<!ELEMENT BODY O O (%block;) -(BODY) +(INS|DEL)>
```

Why are insertions and deletions used in this declaration? The content exclusion says that a **<BODY>** element cannot contain another **<BODY>** element. This is necessary because of the curious **%block** declaration used in the model group. The leading % character identifies this as a *parameter entity*, essentially a macro symbol that refers to a longer character string declared elsewhere in the DTD. Parameter entities, which commonly occur in HTML DTDs, will be discussed shortly (see "Parameter Entities"). The **%block** entity reference is shorthand for all block element types that happen to include the **<BODY>** element. It is easier to exclude **<BODY>** from the list of block elements than to define a special purpose declaration.

The content inclusion says that the **<INS>** and **<DEL>** elements can occur anywhere within the **<BODY>** content. Pragmatically, **<INS>** and **<DEL>** are used to indicate modifications, any inserted or deleted **<BODY>** content. They need to be freed from the normal structural constraints imposed on other **<BODY>** elements.

Attribute List Declarations

All attribute list declarations begin with the keyword **ATTLIST**, followed by the name of the element type they are associated with. Following these are declarations for one or more individual attributes. Each declaration has three parts:

- The attribute's name
- The attribute's value type
- The attribute's default

Following is the syntax for an attribute list declaration:

```
<!ATTLIST element_type
  name1   type1   default1
  ...
  nameN   typeN   defaultN
>
```

The HTML 4 **<BDO>** element type illustrates a small attribute declaration:

```
<!ATTLIST BDO
lang  NAME       #IMPLIED
dir   (ltr|rtl)  #REQUIRED
>
```

SGML Keywords

The preceding example declares the **lang** attribute as having a value of type **NAME**, an alphabetic string. **NAME** is one of several SGML keywords, listed here, occurring in HTML declarations to declare an attribute's type:

- **CDATA**   Unparsed character data
- **ID**   A document-wide unique identifier
- **IDREF**   A reference to a document-wide identifier

- **NAME** An alphabetic character string, followed by a hyphen and a period
- **NMTOKEN** An alphanumeric character string, followed by a hyphen and a period
- **NUMBER** A character string containing decimal numbers

The **dir** attribute does not declare its type using a keyword. Instead, the type is specified using an enumerated list containing two possible values: **ltr** and **rtl**.

In the example, the attribute's default behavior is specified with one of the following keywords. A default value may be specified using a quoted string.

- **#REQUIRED** A value must be supplied for the attribute.
- **#IMPLIED** The attribute is optional.
- **#FIXED** The attribute has a fixed value that is declared in quotes using an additional parameter. Because the attribute/value pair is assumed to be constant, it does not need to be used in the document instance.

Parameter Entities

An entity is essentially a macro that allows a short name to be associated with replacement text. Parameter entities define replacement text used in DTD declarations. Syntactically, a parameter entity is distinguished by using the percent (%) sign. Its general form and context are shown here:

```
<!ENTITY %name "replacement text">
```

It is used in DTDs as follows, sometimes with an optional semicolon:

```
%name;
```

Parameter entities are a convenient way to define commonly occurring parts of a DTD so that changes only need to be made in one place. HTML 4 uses a parameter entity to define the core attributes common to most elements.

```
<!ENTITY % coreattrs
"id         ID        #IMPLIED
 class      CDATA     #IMPLIED
 style      CDATA     #IMPLIED
 title      CDATA     #IMPLIED"
>
```

These attributes could be added to an attribute list declaration in the following format:

```
<!ATTLIST some_element  %coreattrs;>
```

In fact, HTML 4 also uses the **coreattrs** parameter entity in a different way. Parameter entities can be used inside other parameter entity declarations. The **coreattrs** parameter entity is used with the **i18n** and **events** parameter entities to define the expansion text for an aggregate entity called **attrs**:

```
<!ENTITY % attrs "%coreattrs %i18n %events">
```

General Entities

While parameter entities are used to manipulate syntax in DTD declarations, general entities are used to associate symbols with replacement text for use in actual documents. General entities have a versatile syntax. One type is familiar to many HTML authors: the character entity used for special symbols:

```
<!ENTITY name CDATA "replacement text">
```

The **ENTITY** keyword without the % character identifies this as a general entity. For example, HTML authors needing to use the ampersand character (&) use the **&** entity. It is declared as follows:

```
<!ENTITY amp CDATA "&#38;">
```

The name of the entity is **amp**. The entity type is indicated by the **CDATA** keyword, for *character data*. This is followed by the replacement text **&**.

Comments

Comments can be embedded inside HTML declarations for explanatory purposes. Embedded comments are delimited by two dashes, like this,

```
<!-- This is a comment. -->
```

and a single declaration may contain many embedded comments, as shown here:

```
<!ATTLIST PARAM
 name                          CDATA #REQUIRED -- property name --
 value                         CDATA #IMPLIED  -- property value --
 valuetype (DATA|REF|OBJECT) DATA              -- How to interpret
                                                  value --
 type                          CDATA #IMPLIED  -- Internet media
                                                  type --
>
```

Marked Section Declaration

Some HTML DTDs use a special SGML construct to allow them to include or exclude certain declarations from a DTD, such as those supporting deprecated tags. An SGML *marked section declaration* uses keywords to indicate that the content it encloses should be treated in a special way. HTML DTDs use parameter entities to assign the **INCLUDE** and **IGNORE** keywords to marked section declarations. This causes the declarations enclosed by the sections to be included or ignored, respectively.

```
<![keyword [affected declarations]]>
<!ENTITY % HTML.Deprecated "IGNORE">
<![ %HTML.Deprecated [affected declarations]]>
```

The rest of this appendix presents the document type definitions for HTML 4, starting with the transitional DTD, which is recommended. This is followed by the strict definition, which removes the presentational elements from HTML. The last DTD listed is the frameset definition, which is identical to the traditional definition except that the **<BODY>** elelment is replaced by the **<FRAMESET>** element. The latest versions of these DTDs can be retrieved from the W3C:

- **Transitional**　http://www.w3.org/TR/REC-html40/sgml/loosedtd.html
- **Strict**　http://www.w3.org/TR/REC-html40/sgml/dtd.html
- **Frameset**　http://www.w3.org/TR/REC-html40/sgml/framesetdtd.html

These DTDs have been found to contain some errors. An updated list of errors can be found at the following Web address:

http://www.w3.org/MarkUp/html40-updates/REC-html40-19980424-errata.html

The DTDs for HTML 2 and HTML 3.2 are also available online, at the following Web addresses:

- **HTML 2**　http://www.w3.org/MarkUp/html-spec/html.dtd
- **HTML 3.2**　http://www.w3.org/TR/REC-html32#dtd

HTML 4 Transitional DTD

```
<!--
    This is the HTML 4.0 Transitional DTD, which includes
    presentation attributes and elements that W3C expects to phase out
    as support for style sheets matures. Authors should use the Strict
    DTD when possible, but may use the Transitional DTD when support
    for presentation attribute and elements is required.

    HTML 4.0 includes mechanisms for style sheets, scripting,
    embedding objects, improved support for right to left and mixed
    direction text, and enhancements to forms for improved
    accessibility for people with disabilities.

        Draft: $Date: 1998/04/02 00:17:00 $

        Authors:
            Dave Raggett <dsr@w3.org>
            Arnaud Le Hors <lehors@w3.org>
            Ian Jacobs <ij@w3.org>

    Further information about HTML 4.0 is available at:

        http://www.w3.org/TR/REC-html40
-->
<!ENTITY % HTML.Version "-//W3C//DTD HTML 4.0 Transitional//EN"
    -- Typical usage:

    <!DOCTYPE HTML PUBLIC "-//W3C//DTD HTML 4.0 Transitional//EN"
            "http://www.w3.org/TR/REC-html40/loose.dtd">
    <html>
    <head>
    ...
    </head>
    <body>
    ...
    </body>
    </html>

    The URI used as a system identifier with the public identifier allows
    the user agent to download the DTD and entity sets as needed.
```

The FPI for the Strict HTML 4.0 DTD is:

    "-//W3C//DTD HTML 4.0//EN"

and its URI is:

    http://www.w3.org/TR/REC-html40/strict.dtd

Authors should use the Strict DTD unless they need the
presentation control for user agents that don't (adequately)
support style sheets.

If you are writing a document that includes frames, use
the following FPI:

    "-//W3C//DTD HTML 4.0 Frameset//EN"

with the URI:

    http://www.w3.org/TR/REC-html40/frameset.dtd

The following URIs are supported in relation to HTML 4.0

"http://www.w3.org/TR/REC-html40/strict.dtd" (Strict DTD)
"http://www.w3.org/TR/REC-html40/loose.dtd" (Loose DTD)
"http://www.w3.org/TR/REC-html40/frameset.dtd" (Frameset DTD)
"http://www.w3.org/TR/REC-html40/HTMLlat1.ent" (Latin-1 entities)
"http://www.w3.org/TR/REC-html40/HTMLsymbol.ent" (Symbol entities)
"http://www.w3.org/TR/REC-html40/HTMLspecial.ent" (Special entities)

These URIs point to the latest version of each file. To reference
this specific revision use the following URIs:

"http://www.w3.org/TR/1998/REC-html40-19980424/strict.dtd"
"http://www.w3.org/TR/1998/REC-html40-19980424/loose.dtd"
"http://www.w3.org/TR/1998/REC-html40-19980424/frameset.dtd"
"http://www.w3.org/TR/1998/REC-html40-19980424/HTMLlat1.ent"
"http://www.w3.org/TR/1998/REC-html40-19980424/HTMLsymbol.ent"
"http://www.w3.org/TR/1998/REC-html40-19980424/HTMLspecial.ent"

-->

```
<!--=================== Imported Names =======================================-->

<!ENTITY % ContentType "CDATA"
    -- media type, as per [RFC2045]
    -->

<!ENTITY % ContentTypes "CDATA"
    -- comma-separated list of media types, as per [RFC2045]
    -->

<!ENTITY % Charset "CDATA"
    -- a character encoding, as per [RFC2045]
    -->

<!ENTITY % Charsets "CDATA"
    -- a space separated list of character encodings, as per [RFC2045]
    -->

<!ENTITY % LanguageCode "NAME"
    -- a language code, as per [RFC1766]
    -->

<!ENTITY % Character "CDATA"
    -- a single character from [ISO10646]
    -->

<!ENTITY % LinkTypes "CDATA"
    -- space-separated list of link types
    -->

<!ENTITY % MediaDesc "CDATA"
    -- single or comma-separated list of media descriptors
    -->

<!ENTITY % URI "CDATA"
    -- a Uniform Resource Identifier,
       see [URI]
    -->

<!ENTITY % Datetime "CDATA" -- date and time information. ISO date format -->
```

```
<!ENTITY % Script "CDATA" -- script expression -->

<!ENTITY % StyleSheet "CDATA" -- style sheet data -->

<!ENTITY % FrameTarget "CDATA" -- render in this frame -->

<!ENTITY % Text "CDATA">

<!-- Parameter Entities -->

<!ENTITY % head.misc "SCRIPT|STYLE|META|LINK|OBJECT" -- repeatable head
                                                       elements -->

<!ENTITY % heading "H1|H2|H3|H4|H5|H6">

<!ENTITY % list "UL | OL |  DIR | MENU">

<!ENTITY % preformatted "PRE">

<!ENTITY % Color "CDATA" -- a color using sRGB: #RRGGBB as Hex values -->

<!-- There are also 16 widely known color names with their sRGB values:

    Black  = #000000    Green  = #008000
    Silver = #C0C0C0    Lime   = #00FF00
    Gray   = #808080    Olive  = #808000
    White  = #FFFFFF    Yellow = #FFFF00
    Maroon = #800000    Navy   = #000080
    Red    = #FF0000    Blue   = #0000FF
    Purple = #800080    Teal   = #008080
    Fuchsia= #FF00FF    Aqua   = #00FFFF
 -->

<!ENTITY % bodycolors "
  bgcolor      %Color;       #IMPLIED  -- document background color --
  text         %Color;       #IMPLIED  -- document text color --
  link         %Color;       #IMPLIED  -- color of links --
  vlink        %Color;       #IMPLIED  -- color of visited links --
  alink        %Color;       #IMPLIED  -- color of selected links --
  ">
```

```
<!--================ Character mnemonic entities ===========================-->

<!ENTITY % HTMLlat1 PUBLIC
   "-//W3C//ENTITIES Latin1//EN//HTML"
   "http://www.w3.org/TR/1998/REC-html40-19980424/HTMLlat1.ent">
%HTMLlat1;

<!ENTITY % HTMLsymbol PUBLIC
   "-//W3C//ENTITIES Symbols//EN//HTML"
   "http://www.w3.org/TR/1998/REC-html40-19980424/HTMLsymbol.ent">
%HTMLsymbol;

<!ENTITY % HTMLspecial PUBLIC
   "-//W3C//ENTITIES Special//EN//HTML"
   "http://www.w3.org/TR/1998/REC-html40-19980424/HTMLspecial.ent">
%HTMLspecial;
<!--=================== Generic Attributes ===============================-->

<!ENTITY % coreattrs
  "id           ID            #IMPLIED   -- document-wide unique id --
   class        CDATA         #IMPLIED   -- space separated list of classes --
   style        %StyleSheet;  #IMPLIED   -- associated style info --
   title        %Text;        #IMPLIED   -- advisory title/amplification --"
  >

<!ENTITY % i18n
  "lang         %LanguageCode; #IMPLIED  -- language code --
   dir          (ltr|rtl)     #IMPLIED   -- direction for weak/neutral text --"
  >

<!ENTITY % events
  "onclick      %Script;       #IMPLIED  -- a pointer button was clicked --
   ondblclick   %Script;       #IMPLIED  -- a pointer button was double clicked--
   onmousedown  %Script;       #IMPLIED  -- a pointer button was pressed down --
   onmouseup    %Script;       #IMPLIED  -- a pointer button was released --
   onmouseover  %Script;       #IMPLIED  -- a pointer was moved onto --
   onmousemove  %Script;       #IMPLIED  -- a pointer was moved within --
   onmouseout   %Script;       #IMPLIED  -- a pointer was moved away --
   onkeypress   %Script;       #IMPLIED  -- a key was pressed and released --
   onkeydown    %Script;       #IMPLIED  -- a key was pressed down --
   onkeyup      %Script;       #IMPLIED  -- a key was released --"
  >
```

```
<!-- Reserved Feature Switch -->
<!ENTITY % HTML.Reserved "IGNORE">

<!-- The following attributes are reserved for possible future use -->
<![ %HTML.Reserved; [
<!ENTITY % reserved
 "datasrc        %URI;          #IMPLIED  -- a single or tabular Data Source --
  datafld        CDATA          #IMPLIED  -- the property or column name --
  dataformatas (plaintext|html) plaintext -- text or html --"
  >
]]>

<!ENTITY % reserved "">

<!ENTITY % attrs "%coreattrs; %i18n; %events;">

<!ENTITY % align "align (left|center|right|justify)  #IMPLIED"
                  -- default is left for ltr paragraphs, right for rtl --
  >

<!--==================== Text Markup ========================================-->

<!ENTITY % fontstyle
 "TT | I | B | U | S | STRIKE | BIG | SMALL">

<!ENTITY % phrase "EM | STRONG | DFN | CODE |
                   SAMP | KBD | VAR | CITE | ABBR | ACRONYM" >

<!ENTITY % special
   "A | IMG | APPLET | OBJECT | FONT | BASEFONT | BR | SCRIPT |
    MAP | Q | SUB | SUP | SPAN | BDO | IFRAME">

<!ENTITY % formctrl "INPUT | SELECT | TEXTAREA | LABEL | BUTTON">

<!-- %inline; covers inline or "text-level" elements -->
<!ENTITY % inline "#PCDATA | %fontstyle; | %phrase; | %special; | %formctrl;">

<!ELEMENT (%fontstyle;|%phrase;) - - (%inline;)*>
<!ATTLIST (%fontstyle;|%phrase;)
  %attrs;                              -- %coreattrs, %i18n, %events --
>
```

```
<!ELEMENT (SUB|SUP) - - (%inline;)*     -- subscript, superscript -->
<!ATTLIST (SUB|SUP)
  %attrs;                               -- %coreattrs, %i18n, %events --
  >


<!ELEMENT SPAN - - (%inline;)*          -- generic language/style container -->
<!ATTLIST SPAN
  %attrs;                               -- %coreattrs, %i18n, %events --
  %reserved;                            -- reserved for possible future use --
  >


<!ELEMENT BDO - - (%inline;)*           -- I18N BiDi over-ride -->
<!ATTLIST BDO
  %coreattrs;                           -- id, class, style, title --
  lang            %LanguageCode; #IMPLIED -- language code --
  dir             (ltr|rtl)      #REQUIRED -- directionality --
  >


<!ELEMENT BASEFONT - O EMPTY            -- base font size -->
<!ATTLIST BASEFONT
  id              ID             #IMPLIED -- document-wide unique id --
  size            CDATA          #REQUIRED -- base font size for FONT elements --
  color           %Color;        #IMPLIED -- text color --
  face            CDATA          #IMPLIED -- comma separated list of font
                                             names --

  >


<!ELEMENT FONT - - (%inline;)*          -- local change to font -->
<!ATTLIST FONT
  %coreattrs;                           -- id, class, style, title --
  %i18n;                                -- lang, dir --
  size            CDATA          #IMPLIED -- [+|-]nn e.g. size="+1", size="4" --
  color           %Color;        #IMPLIED -- text color --
  face            CDATA          #IMPLIED -- comma separated list of font
                                             names --

  >


<!ELEMENT BR - O EMPTY                  -- forced line break -->
<!ATTLIST BR
  %coreattrs;                           -- id, class, style, title --
  clear           (left|all|right|none) none -- control of text flow --
  >
```

```
<!--=================== HTML content models ===================================-->

<!--
    HTML has two basic content models:

        %inline;       character level elements and text strings
        %block;        block-like elements e.g. paragraphs and lists
-->

<!ENTITY % block
    "P | %heading; | %list; | %preformatted; | DL | DIV | CENTER |
     NOSCRIPT | NOFRAMES | BLOCKQUOTE | FORM | ISINDEX | HR |
     TABLE | FIELDSET | ADDRESS">

<!ENTITY % flow "%block; | %inline;">

<!--=================== Document Body =======================================-->

<!ELEMENT BODY O O (%flow;)* +(INS|DEL) -- document body -->
<!ATTLIST BODY
  %attrs;                              -- %coreattrs, %i18n, %events --
  onload          %Script;   #IMPLIED  -- the document has been loaded --
  onunload        %Script;   #IMPLIED  -- the document has been removed --
  background      %URI;      #IMPLIED  -- texture tile for document
                                          background --
  %bodycolors;                         -- bgcolor, text, link, vlink, alink --
  >

<!ELEMENT ADDRESS - - ((%inline;)|P)* -- information on author -->
<!ATTLIST ADDRESS
  %attrs;                              -- %coreattrs, %i18n, %events --
  >

<!ELEMENT DIV - - (%flow;)*           -- generic language/style
                                         container -->

<!ATTLIST DIV
  %attrs;                              -- %coreattrs, %i18n, %events --
  %align;                              -- align, text alignment --
  %reserved;                           -- reserved for possible
                                          future use --

  >
```

```
<!ELEMENT CENTER - - (%flow;)*         -- shorthand for DIV align=center -->
<!ATTLIST CENTER
  %attrs;                              -- %coreattrs, %i18n, %events --
  >


<!--================== The Anchor Element =====================================-->

<!ENTITY % Shape "(rect|circle|poly|default)">
<!ENTITY % Coords "CDATA" -- comma separated list of lengths -->

<!ELEMENT A - - (%inline;)* -(A)       -- anchor -->
<!ATTLIST A
  %attrs;                              -- %coreattrs, %i18n, %events --
  charset     %Charset;      #IMPLIED  -- char encoding of linked resource --
  type        %ContentType;  #IMPLIED  -- advisory content type --
  name        CDATA          #IMPLIED  -- named link end --
  href        %URI;          #IMPLIED  -- URI for linked resource --
  hreflang    %LanguageCode; #IMPLIED  -- language code --
  target      %FrameTarget;  #IMPLIED  -- render in this frame --
  rel         %LinkTypes;    #IMPLIED  -- forward link types --
  rev         %LinkTypes;    #IMPLIED  -- reverse link types --
  accesskey   %Character;    #IMPLIED  -- accessibility key character --
  shape       %Shape;        rect      -- for use with client-side image
                                          maps --
  coords      %Coords;       #IMPLIED  -- for use with client-side image
                                          maps --
  tabindex    NUMBER         #IMPLIED  -- position in tabbing order --
  onfocus     %Script;       #IMPLIED  -- the element got the focus --
  onblur      %Script;       #IMPLIED  -- the element lost the focus --
  >


<!--================== Client-side image maps =============================-->

<!-- These can be placed in the same document or grouped in a
     separate document although this isn't yet widely supported -->

<!ELEMENT MAP - - ((%block;)+ | AREA+) -- client-side image map -->
<!ATTLIST MAP
  %attrs;                              -- %coreattrs, %i18n, %events --
  name        CDATA          #REQUIRED -- for reference by usemap --
  >
```

```
<!ELEMENT AREA - O EMPTY                    -- client-side image map area -->
<!ATTLIST AREA
  %attrs;                                   -- %coreattrs, %i18n, %events --
  shape         %Shape;         rect        -- controls interpretation of
                                               coords --
  coords        %Coords;        #IMPLIED    -- comma separated list of lengths --
  href          %URI;           #IMPLIED    -- URI for linked resource --
  target        %FrameTarget;   #IMPLIED    -- render in this frame --
  nohref        (nohref)        #IMPLIED    -- this region has no action --
  alt           %Text;          #REQUIRED   -- short description --
  tabindex      NUMBER          #IMPLIED    -- position in tabbing order --
  accesskey     %Character;     #IMPLIED    -- accessibility key character --
  onfocus       %Script;        #IMPLIED    -- the element got the focus --
  onblur        %Script;        #IMPLIED    -- the element lost the focus --
  >

<!--=================== The LINK Element =====================================-->

<!--
  Relationship values can be used in principle:

    a) for document specific toolbars/menus when used
       with the LINK element in document head e.g.
         start, contents, previous, next, index, end, help
    b) to link to a separate style sheet (rel=stylesheet)
    c) to make a link to a script (rel=script)
    d) by stylesheets to control how collections of
       html nodes are rendered into printed documents
    e) to make a link to a printable version of this document
       e.g. a postscript or pdf version (rel=alternate media=print)
-->

<!ELEMENT LINK - O EMPTY                    -- a media-independent link -->
<!ATTLIST LINK
  %attrs;                                   -- %coreattrs, %i18n, %events --
  charset       %Charset;       #IMPLIED    -- char encoding of linked resource --
  href          %URI;           #IMPLIED    -- URI for linked resource --
  hreflang      %LanguageCode;  #IMPLIED    -- language code --
  type          %ContentType;   #IMPLIED    -- advisory content type --
  rel           %LinkTypes;     #IMPLIED    -- forward link types --
  rev           %LinkTypes;     #IMPLIED    -- reverse link types --
```

```
   media          %MediaDesc;   #IMPLIED  -- for rendering on these media --
   target         %FrameTarget; #IMPLIED  -- render in this frame --
   >


<!--==================== Images ========================================-->

<!-- Length defined in strict DTD for cellpadding/cellspacing -->
<!ENTITY % Length "CDATA" -- nn for pixels or nn% for percentage length -->
<!ENTITY % MultiLength "CDATA" -- pixel, percentage, or relative -->

<!ENTITY % MultiLengths "CDATA" -- comma-separated list of MultiLength -->

<!ENTITY % Pixels "CDATA" -- integer representing length in pixels -->

<!ENTITY % IAlign "(top|middle|bottom|left|right)" -- center? -->

<!-- To avoid problems with text-only UAs as well as
     to make image content understandable and navigable
     to users of non-visual UAs, you need to provide
     a description with ALT, and avoid server-side image maps -->
<!ELEMENT IMG - O EMPTY                 -- Embedded image -->
<!ATTLIST IMG
   %attrs;                              -- %coreattrs, %i18n, %events --
   src          %URI;        #REQUIRED -- URI of image to embed --
   alt          %Text;       #REQUIRED -- short description --
   longdesc     %URI;        #IMPLIED  -- link to long description
                                          (complements alt) --
   height       %Length;     #IMPLIED  -- override height --
   width        %Length;     #IMPLIED  -- override width --
   usemap       %URI;        #IMPLIED  -- use client-side image map --
   ismap        (ismap)      #IMPLIED  -- use server-side image map --
   align        %IAlign;     #IMPLIED  -- vertical or horizontal alignment --
   border       %Length;     #IMPLIED  -- link border width --
   hspace       %Pixels;     #IMPLIED  -- horizontal gutter --
   vspace       %Pixels;     #IMPLIED  -- vertical gutter --
   >

<!-- USEMAP points to a MAP element which may be in this document
     or an external document, although the latter is not widely supported -->
```

```
<!--==================== OBJECT ========================================-->
<!--
   OBJECT is used to embed objects as part of HTML pages
   PARAM elements should precede other content. SGML mixed content
   model technicality precludes specifying this formally ...
-->

<!ELEMENT OBJECT - - (PARAM | %flow;)*
 -- generic embedded object -->
<!ATTLIST OBJECT
   %attrs;                              -- %coreattrs, %i18n, %events --
   declare     (declare)    #IMPLIED   -- declare but don't instantiate flag --
   classid     %URI;        #IMPLIED   -- identifies an implementation --
   codebase    %URI;        #IMPLIED   -- base URI for classid, data, archive--
   data        %URI;        #IMPLIED   -- reference to object's data --
   type        %ContentType; #IMPLIED  -- content type for data --
   codetype    %ContentType; #IMPLIED  -- content type for code --
   archive     %URI;        #IMPLIED   -- space separated archive list --
   standby     %Text;       #IMPLIED   -- message to show while loading --
   height      %Length;     #IMPLIED   -- override height --
   width       %Length;     #IMPLIED   -- override width --
   usemap      %URI;        #IMPLIED   -- use client-side image map --
   name        CDATA        #IMPLIED   -- submit as part of form --
   tabindex    NUMBER       #IMPLIED   -- position in tabbing order --
   align       %IAlign;     #IMPLIED   -- vertical or horizontal alignment --
   border      %Length;     #IMPLIED   -- link border width --
   hspace      %Pixels;     #IMPLIED   -- horizontal gutter --
   vspace      %Pixels;     #IMPLIED   -- vertical gutter --
   %reserved;                          -- reserved for possible future use --
   >

<!ELEMENT PARAM - O EMPTY             -- named property value -->
<!ATTLIST PARAM
   id          ID           #IMPLIED   -- document-wide unique id --
   name        CDATA        #REQUIRED  -- property name --
   value       CDATA        #IMPLIED   -- property value --
   valuetype   (DATA|REF|OBJECT) DATA  -- How to interpret value --
   type        %ContentType; #IMPLIED  -- content type for value
                                          when valuetype=ref --
   >
```

```
<!--==================== Java APPLET =====================================-->
<!--
   One of code or object attributes must be present.
   Place PARAM elements before other content.
-->
<!ELEMENT APPLET - - (PARAM | %flow;)* -- Java applet -->
<!ATTLIST APPLET
  %coreattrs;                              -- id, class, style, title --
  codebase    %URI;           #IMPLIED  -- optional base URI for applet --
  archive     CDATA           #IMPLIED  -- comma separated archive list --
  code        CDATA           #IMPLIED  -- applet class file --
  object      CDATA           #IMPLIED  -- serialized applet file --
  alt         %Text;          #IMPLIED  -- short description --
  name        CDATA           #IMPLIED  -- allows applets to find each other --
  width       %Length;        #REQUIRED -- initial width --
  height      %Length;        #REQUIRED -- initial height --
  align       %IAlign;        #IMPLIED  -- vertical or horizontal alignment --
  hspace      %Pixels;        #IMPLIED  -- horizontal gutter --
  vspace      %Pixels;        #IMPLIED  -- vertical gutter --
  >


<!--==================== Horizontal Rule ==================================-->

<!ELEMENT HR - O EMPTY -- horizontal rule -->
<!ATTLIST HR
  %coreattrs;                           -- id, class, style, title --
  %events;
  align       (left|center|right) #IMPLIED
  noshade     (noshade)       #IMPLIED
  size        %Pixels;        #IMPLIED
  width       %Length;        #IMPLIED
  >


<!--==================== Paragraphs =======================================-->

<!ELEMENT P - O (%inline;)*              -- paragraph -->
<!ATTLIST P
  %attrs;                               -- %coreattrs, %i18n, %events --
  %align;                               -- align, text alignment --
  >
```

```
<!--==================== Headings =======================================-->

<!--
  There are six levels of headings from H1 (the most important)
  to H6 (the least important).
-->

<!ELEMENT (%heading;)  - - (%inline;)* -- heading -->
<!ATTLIST (%heading;)
  %attrs;                              -- %coreattrs, %i18n, %events --
  %align;                              -- align, text alignment --
  >


<!--==================== Preformatted Text ==============================-->

<!-- excludes markup for images and changes in font size -->
<!ENTITY % pre.exclusion "IMG|OBJECT|APPLET|BIG|SMALL|SUB|SUP|FONT|BASEFONT">

<!ELEMENT PRE - - (%inline;)* -(%pre.exclusion;) -- preformatted text -->
<!ATTLIST PRE
  %attrs;                              -- %coreattrs, %i18n, %events --
  width         NUMBER         #IMPLIED
  >


<!--===================== Inline Quotes =================================-->

<!ELEMENT Q - - (%inline;)*            -- short inline quotation -->
<!ATTLIST Q
  %attrs;                              -- %coreattrs, %i18n, %events --
  cite          %URI;          #IMPLIED -- URI for source document or msg --
  >


<!--==================== Block-like Quotes ==============================-->

<!ELEMENT BLOCKQUOTE - - (%flow;)*     -- long quotation -->
<!ATTLIST BLOCKQUOTE
  %attrs;                              -- %coreattrs, %i18n, %events --
  cite          %URI;          #IMPLIED -- URI for source document or msg --
  >
```

```
<!--==================== Inserted/Deleted Text ============================-->

<!-- INS/DEL are handled by inclusion on BODY -->
<!ELEMENT (INS|DEL) - - (%flow;)*          -- inserted text, deleted text -->
<!ATTLIST (INS|DEL)
  %attrs;                                  -- %coreattrs, %i18n, %events --
  cite         %URI;          #IMPLIED  -- info on reason for change --
  datetime     %Datetime;     #IMPLIED  -- date and time of change --
  >


<!--==================== Lists ==============================================-->

<!-- definition lists - DT for term, DD for its definition -->

<!ELEMENT DL - - (DT|DD)+               -- definition list -->
<!ATTLIST DL
  %attrs;                                  -- %coreattrs, %i18n, %events --
  compact      (compact)      #IMPLIED  -- reduced interitem spacing --
  >

<!ELEMENT DT - O (%inline;)*            -- definition term -->
<!ELEMENT DD - O (%flow;)*              -- definition description -->
<!ATTLIST (DT|DD)
  %attrs;                                  -- %coreattrs, %i18n, %events --
  >

<!-- Ordered lists (OL) Numbering style

    1    arabic numbers     1, 2, 3, ...
    a    lower alpha        a, b, c, ...
    A    upper alpha        A, B, C, ...
    i    lower roman        i, ii, iii, ...
    I    upper roman        I, II, III, ...

    The style is applied to the sequence number which by default
    is reset to 1 for the first list item in an ordered list.

    This can't be expressed directly in SGML due to case folding.
-->
```

```
<!ENTITY % OLStyle "CDATA"         -- constrained to: "(1|a|A|i|I)" -->

<!ELEMENT OL - - (LI)+                     -- ordered list -->
<!ATTLIST OL
  %attrs;                                  -- %coreattrs, %i18n, %events --
  type          %OLStyle;       #IMPLIED   -- numbering style --
  compact       (compact)       #IMPLIED   -- reduced interitem spacing --
  start         NUMBER          #IMPLIED   -- starting sequence number --
  >

<!-- Unordered Lists (UL) bullet styles -->
<!ENTITY % ULStyle "(disc|square|circle)">

<!ELEMENT UL - - (LI)+                     -- unordered list -->
<!ATTLIST UL
  %attrs;                                  -- %coreattrs, %i18n, %events --
  type          %ULStyle;       #IMPLIED   -- bullet style --
  compact       (compact)       #IMPLIED   -- reduced interitem spacing --
  >

<!ELEMENT (DIR|MENU) - - (LI)+ -(%block;) -- directory list, menu list -->
<!ATTLIST DIR
  %attrs;                                  -- %coreattrs, %i18n, %events --
  compact       (compact)       #IMPLIED
  >
<!ATTLIST MENU
  %attrs;                                  -- %coreattrs, %i18n, %events --
  compact       (compact)       #IMPLIED
  >

<!ENTITY % LIStyle "CDATA" -- constrained to: "(%ULStyle;|%OLStyle;)" -->

<!ELEMENT LI - O (%flow;)*                 -- list item -->
<!ATTLIST LI
  %attrs;                                  -- %coreattrs, %i18n, %events --
  type          %LIStyle;       #IMPLIED   -- list item style --
  value         NUMBER          #IMPLIED   -- reset sequence number --
  >
```

```
<!--=============== Forms ===============================================-->
<!ELEMENT FORM - - (%flow;)* -(FORM)    -- interactive form -->
<!ATTLIST FORM
  %attrs;                                 -- %coreattrs, %i18n, %events --
  action       %URI;           #REQUIRED -- server-side form handler --
  method       (GET|POST)      GET       -- HTTP method used to submit the form--
  enctype      %ContentType;   "application/x-www-form-urlencoded"
  onsubmit     %Script;        #IMPLIED  -- the form was submitted --
  onreset      %Script;        #IMPLIED  -- the form was reset --
  target       %FrameTarget;   #IMPLIED  -- render in this frame --
  accept-charset %Charsets;    #IMPLIED  -- list of supported charsets --
  >

<!-- Each label must not contain more than ONE field -->
<!ELEMENT LABEL - - (%inline;)* -(LABEL) -- form field label text -->
<!ATTLIST LABEL
  %attrs;                                 -- %coreattrs, %i18n, %events --
  for          IDREF           #IMPLIED  -- matches field ID value --
  accesskey    %Character;     #IMPLIED  -- accessibility key character --
  onfocus      %Script;        #IMPLIED  -- the element got the focus --
  onblur       %Script;        #IMPLIED  -- the element lost the focus --
  >

<!ENTITY % InputType
  "(TEXT | PASSWORD | CHECKBOX |
    RADIO | SUBMIT | RESET |
    FILE | HIDDEN | IMAGE | BUTTON)"
  >

<!-- attribute name required for all but submit & reset -->
<!ELEMENT INPUT - O EMPTY                -- form control -->
<!ATTLIST INPUT
  %attrs;                                 -- %coreattrs, %i18n, %events --
  type         %InputType;     TEXT      -- what kind of widget is needed --
  name         CDATA           #IMPLIED  -- submit as part of form --
  value        CDATA           #IMPLIED  -- required for radio and checkboxes --
  checked      (checked)       #IMPLIED  -- for radio buttons and check boxes --
  disabled     (disabled)      #IMPLIED  -- unavailable in this context --
  readonly     (readonly)      #IMPLIED  -- for text and passwd --
  size         CDATA           #IMPLIED  -- specific to each type of field --
  maxlength    NUMBER          #IMPLIED  -- max chars for text fields --
```

```
    src          %URI;          #IMPLIED   -- for fields with images --
    alt          CDATA          #IMPLIED   -- short description --
    usemap       %URI;          #IMPLIED   -- use client-side image map --
    tabindex     NUMBER         #IMPLIED   -- position in tabbing order --
    accesskey    %Character;    #IMPLIED   -- accessibility key character --
    onfocus      %Script;       #IMPLIED   -- the element got the focus --
    onblur       %Script;       #IMPLIED   -- the element lost the focus --
    onselect     %Script;       #IMPLIED   -- some text was selected --
    onchange     %Script;       #IMPLIED   -- the element value was changed --
    accept       %ContentTypes; #IMPLIED   -- list of MIME types for file
                                              upload --
    align        %IAlign;       #IMPLIED   -- vertical or horizontal alignment --
    %reserved;                              -- reserved for possible future use --
    >

<!ELEMENT SELECT - - (OPTGROUP|OPTION)+ -- option selector -->
<!ATTLIST SELECT
    %attrs;                                 -- %coreattrs, %i18n, %events --
    name         CDATA          #IMPLIED   -- field name --
    size         NUMBER         #IMPLIED   -- rows visible --
    multiple     (multiple)     #IMPLIED   -- default is single selection --
    disabled     (disabled)     #IMPLIED   -- unavailable in this context --
    tabindex     NUMBER         #IMPLIED   -- position in tabbing order --
    onfocus      %Script;       #IMPLIED   -- the element got the focus --
    onblur       %Script;       #IMPLIED   -- the element lost the focus --
    onchange     %Script;       #IMPLIED   -- the element value was changed --
    %reserved;                              -- reserved for possible future use --
    >

<!ELEMENT OPTGROUP - - (OPTION)+ -- option group -->
<!ATTLIST OPTGROUP
    %attrs;                                 -- %coreattrs, %i18n, %events --
    disabled     (disabled)     #IMPLIED   -- unavailable in this context --
    label        %Text;         #REQUIRED  -- for use in hierarchical menus --
    >

<!ELEMENT OPTION - O (#PCDATA)        -- selectable choice -->
<!ATTLIST OPTION
    %attrs;                                 -- %coreattrs, %i18n, %events --
    selected     (selected)     #IMPLIED
    disabled     (disabled)     #IMPLIED   -- unavailable in this context --
```

```
    label           %Text;            #IMPLIED    -- for use in hierarchical menus --
    value           CDATA            #IMPLIED    -- defaults to element content --
    >

<!ELEMENT TEXTAREA - - (#PCDATA)          -- multi-line text field -->
<!ATTLIST TEXTAREA
    %attrs;                               -- %coreattrs, %i18n, %events --
    name            CDATA            #IMPLIED
    rows            NUMBER           #REQUIRED
    cols            NUMBER           #REQUIRED
    disabled        (disabled)       #IMPLIED    -- unavailable in this context --
    readonly        (readonly)       #IMPLIED
    tabindex        NUMBER           #IMPLIED    -- position in tabbing order --
    accesskey       %Character;      #IMPLIED    -- accessibility key character --
    onfocus         %Script;         #IMPLIED    -- the element got the focus --
    onblur          %Script;         #IMPLIED    -- the element lost the focus --
    onselect        %Script;         #IMPLIED    -- some text was selected --
    onchange        %Script;         #IMPLIED    -- the element value was changed --
    %reserved;                                   -- reserved for possible future
                                                    use --

    >

<!--
    #PCDATA is to solve the mixed content problem,
    per specification only whitespace is allowed there!
    -->
<!ELEMENT FIELDSET - - (#PCDATA,LEGEND,(%flow;)*) -- form control group -->
<!ATTLIST FIELDSET
    %attrs;                               -- %coreattrs, %i18n, %events --
    >

<!ELEMENT LEGEND - - (%inline;)*          -- fieldset legend -->
<!ENTITY % LAlign "(top|bottom|left|right)">

<!ATTLIST LEGEND
    %attrs;                               -- %coreattrs, %i18n, %events --
    accesskey       %Character;      #IMPLIED    -- accessibility key character --
    align           %LAlign;         #IMPLIED    -- relative to fieldset --
    >
```

```
<!ELEMENT BUTTON - -
      (%flow;)* -(A|%formctrl;|FORM|ISINDEX|FIELDSET|IFRAME)
      -- push button -->
<!ATTLIST BUTTON
  %attrs;                               -- %coreattrs, %i18n, %events --
  name          CDATA         #IMPLIED
  value         CDATA         #IMPLIED  -- sent to server when submitted --
  type          (button|submit|reset) submit -- for use as form button --
  disabled      (disabled)    #IMPLIED  -- unavailable in this context --
  tabindex      NUMBER        #IMPLIED  -- position in tabbing order --
  accesskey     %Character;   #IMPLIED  -- accessibility key character --
  onfocus       %Script;      #IMPLIED  -- the element got the focus --
  onblur        %Script;      #IMPLIED  -- the element lost the focus --
  %reserved;                            -- reserved for possible future use --
  >


<!--======================= Tables ========================================-->

<!-- IETF HTML table standard, see [RFC1942] -->

<!--
The BORDER attribute sets the thickness of the frame around the
table. The default units are screen pixels.

The FRAME attribute specifies which parts of the frame around
the table should be rendered. The values are not the same as
CALS to avoid a name clash with the VALIGN attribute.

The value "border" is included for backwards compatibility with
<TABLE BORDER> which yields frame=border and border=implied
For <TABLE BORDER=1> you get border=1 and frame=implied. In this
case, it is appropriate to treat this as frame=border for backwards
compatibility with deployed browsers.
-->
<!ENTITY % TFrame "(void|above|below|hsides|lhs|rhs|vsides|box|border)">

<!--
The RULES attribute defines which rules to draw between cells:

 If RULES is absent then assume:
     "none" if BORDER is absent or BORDER=0 otherwise "all"
-->
```

```
<!ENTITY % TRules "(none | groups | rows | cols | all)">

<!-- horizontal placement of table relative to document -->
<ENTITY % TAlign "(left|center|right)">

<!-- horizontal alignment attributes for cell contents -->
<!ENTITY % cellhalign
  "align       (left|center|right|justify|char) #IMPLIED
   char        %Character;    #IMPLIED  -- alignment char, e.g. char=':' --
   charoff     %Length;       #IMPLIED  -- offset for alignment char --"
  >

<!-- vertical alignment attributes for cell contents -->
<!ENTITY % cellvalign
  "valign      (top|middle|bottom|baseline) #IMPLIED"
  >

<!ELEMENT TABLE - -
      (CAPTION?, (COL*|COLGROUP*), THEAD?, TFOOT?, TBODY+)>
<!ELEMENT CAPTION  - - (%inline;)*      -- table caption -->
<!ELEMENT THEAD    - O (TR)+            -- table header -->
<!ELEMENT TFOOT    - O (TR)+            -- table footer -->
<!ELEMENT TBODY    O O (TR)+            -- table body -->
<!ELEMENT COLGROUP - O (col)*           -- table column group -->
<!ELEMENT COL      - O EMPTY            -- table column -->
<!ELEMENT TR       - O (TH|TD)+         -- table row -->
<!ELEMENT (TH|TD)  - O (%flow;)*        -- table header cell, table data cell-->

<!ATTLIST TABLE                         -- table element --
  %attrs;                               -- %coreattrs, %i18n, %events --
  summary       %Text;      #IMPLIED -- purpose/structure for speech output--
  width         %Length;    #IMPLIED -- table width --
  border        %Pixels;    #IMPLIED -- controls frame width around table --
  frame         %TFrame;    #IMPLIED -- which parts of frame to render --
  rules         %TRules;    #IMPLIED -- rulings between rows and cols --
  cellspacing   %Length;    #IMPLIED -- spacing between cells --
  cellpadding   %Length;    #IMPLIED -- spacing within cells --
  align         %TAlign;    #IMPLIED -- table position relative to window --
  bgcolor       %Color;     #IMPLIED -- background color for cells --
  %reserved;                          -- reserved for possible future use --
  datapagesize CDATA        #IMPLIED -- reserved for possible future use --
  >
```

```
<!ENTITY % CAlign "(top|bottom|left|right)">

<!ATTLIST CAPTION
  %attrs;                               -- %coreattrs, %i18n, %events --
  align         %CAlign;      #IMPLIED -- relative to table --
  >


<!--
COLGROUP groups a set of COL elements. It allows you to group
several semantically related columns together.
-->
<!ATTLIST COLGROUP
  %attrs;                               -- %coreattrs, %i18n, %events --
  span          NUMBER        1         -- default number of columns in
                                           group --
  width         %MultiLength; #IMPLIED -- default width for enclosed COLs --
  %cellhalign;                          -- horizontal alignment in cells --
  %cellvalign;                          -- vertical alignment in cells --
  >


<!--
 COL elements define the alignment properties for cells in
 one or more columns.

 The WIDTH attribute specifies the width of the columns, e.g.

     width=64        width in screen pixels
     width=0.5*      relative width of 0.5


 The SPAN attribute causes the attributes of one
 COL element to apply to more than one column.
-->
<!ATTLIST COL                         -- column groups and properties --
  %attrs;                               -- %coreattrs, %i18n, %events --
  span          NUMBER        1         -- COL attributes affect N columns --
  width         %MultiLength; #IMPLIED -- column width specification --
  %cellhalign;                          -- horizontal alignment in cells --
  %cellvalign;                          -- vertical alignment in cells --
  >
```

```
<!--
    Use THEAD to duplicate headers when breaking table
    across page boundaries, or for static headers when
    TBODY sections are rendered in scrolling panel.

    Use TFOOT to duplicate footers when breaking table
    across page boundaries, or for static footers when
    TBODY sections are rendered in scrolling panel.

    Use multiple TBODY sections when rules are needed
    between groups of table rows.
-->
<!ATTLIST (THEAD|TBODY|TFOOT)         -- table section --
  %attrs;                             -- %coreattrs, %i18n, %events --
  %cellhalign;                        -- horizontal alignment in cells --
  %cellvalign;                        -- vertical alignment in cells --
  >


<!ATTLIST TR                          -- table row --
  %attrs;                             -- %coreattrs, %i18n, %events --
  %cellhalign;                        -- horizontal alignment in cells --
  %cellvalign;                        -- vertical alignment in cells --
  bgcolor     %Color;     #IMPLIED    -- background color for row --
  >


<!-- Scope is simpler than axes attribute for common tables -->
<!ENTITY % Scope "(row|col|rowgroup|colgroup)">


<!-- TH is for headers, TD for data, but for cells acting as both use TD -->
<!ATTLIST (TH|TD)                     -- header or data cell --
  %attrs;                             -- %coreattrs, %i18n, %events --
  abbr        %Text;      #IMPLIED    -- abbreviation for header cell --
  axis        CDATA       #IMPLIED    -- names groups of related headers--
  headers     IDREFS      #IMPLIED    -- list of id's for header cells --
  scope       %Scope;     #IMPLIED    -- scope covered by header cells --
  rowspan     NUMBER      1           -- number of rows spanned by cell --
  colspan     NUMBER      1           -- number of cols spanned by cell --
  %cellhalign;                        -- horizontal alignment in cells --
  %cellvalign;                        -- vertical alignment in cells --
  nowrap      (nowrap)    #IMPLIED    -- suppress word wrap --
  bgcolor     %Color;     #IMPLIED    -- cell background color --
  width       %Pixels;    #IMPLIED    -- width for cell --
  height      %Pixels;    #IMPLIED    -- height for cell --
  >
```

```
<!--================== Document Frames =======================================-->

<!--
  The content model for HTML documents depends on whether the HEAD is
  followed by a FRAMESET or BODY element. The widespread omission of
  the BODY start tag makes it impractical to define the content model
  without the use of a marked section.
-->

<!-- Feature Switch for frameset documents -->
<!ENTITY % HTML.Frameset "IGNORE">

<![ %HTML.Frameset; [
<!ELEMENT FRAMESET - - ((FRAMESET|FRAME)+ & NOFRAMES?) -- window
                                                      subdivision-->
<!ATTLIST FRAMESET
  %coreattrs;                           -- id, class, style, title --
  rows        %MultiLengths; #IMPLIED   -- list of lengths,
                                           default: 100% (1 row) --
  cols        %MultiLengths; #IMPLIED   -- list of lengths,
                                           default: 100% (1 col) --
  onload      %Script;       #IMPLIED   -- all the frames have been loaded  --
  onunload    %Script;       #IMPLIED   -- all the frames have been removed --
  >
]]>

<![ %HTML.Frameset; [
<!-- reserved frame names start with "_" otherwise starts with letter -->
<!ELEMENT FRAME - O EMPTY              -- subwindow -->
<!ATTLIST FRAME
  %coreattrs;                           -- id, class, style, title --
  longdesc     %URI;        #IMPLIED   -- link to long description
                                          (complements title) --
  name         CDATA        #IMPLIED   -- name of frame for targetting --
  src          %URI;        #IMPLIED   -- source of frame content --
  frameborder  (1|0)        1          -- request frame borders? --
  marginwidth  %Pixels;     #IMPLIED   -- margin widths in pixels --
  marginheight %Pixels;     #IMPLIED   -- margin height in pixels --
  noresize     (noresize)   #IMPLIED   -- allow users to resize frames? --
  scrolling    (yes|no|auto) auto      -- scrollbar or none --
  >
```

```
]]>

<!ELEMENT IFRAME - - (%flow;)*          -- inline subwindow -->
<!ATTLIST IFRAME
  %coreattrs;                           -- id, class, style, title --
  longdesc    %URI;          #IMPLIED  -- link to long description
                                          (complements title) --
  name        CDATA          #IMPLIED  -- name of frame for targetting --
  src         %URI;          #IMPLIED  -- source of frame content --
  frameborder (1|0)          1         -- request frame borders? --
  marginwidth %Pixels;       #IMPLIED  -- margin widths in pixels --
  marginheight %Pixels;      #IMPLIED  -- margin height in pixels --
  scrolling   (yes|no|auto)  auto      -- scrollbar or none --
  align       %IAlign;       #IMPLIED  -- vertical or horizontal alignment --
  height      %Length;       #IMPLIED  -- frame height --
  width       %Length;       #IMPLIED  -- frame width --
  >

<![ %HTML.Frameset; [
<!ENTITY % noframes.content "(BODY) -(NOFRAMES)">
]]>

<!ENTITY % noframes.content "(%flow;)*">

<!ELEMENT NOFRAMES - - %noframes.content;
 -- alternate content container for non frame-based rendering -->
<!ATTLIST NOFRAMES
  %attrs;                               -- %coreattrs, %i18n, %events --
  >

<!--================ Document Head =========================================-->
<!-- %head.misc; defined earlier on as "SCRIPT|STYLE|META|LINK|OBJECT" -->
<!ENTITY % head.content "TITLE & ISINDEX? & BASE?">

<!ELEMENT HEAD O O (%head.content;) +(%head.misc;) -- document head -->
<!ATTLIST HEAD
  %i18n;                               -- lang, dir --
  profile     %URI;          #IMPLIED  -- named dictionary of meta info --
  >
```

```
<!-- The TITLE element is not considered part of the flow of text.
     It should be displayed, for example as the page header or
     window title. Exactly one title is required per document.
     -->
<!ELEMENT TITLE - - (#PCDATA) -(%head.misc;) -- document title -->
<!ATTLIST TITLE %i18n>


<!ELEMENT ISINDEX - O EMPTY            -- single line prompt -->
<!ATTLIST ISINDEX
  %coreattrs;                          -- id, class, style, title --
  %i18n;                               -- lang, dir --
  prompt        %Text;       #IMPLIED  -- prompt message -->


<!ELEMENT BASE - O EMPTY               -- document base URI -->
<!ATTLIST BASE
  href          %URI;        #IMPLIED  -- URI that acts as base URI --
  target        %FrameTarget; #IMPLIED -- render in this frame --
  >


<!ELEMENT META - O EMPTY               -- generic metainformation -->
<!ATTLIST META
  %i18n;                               -- lang, dir, for use with content --
  http-equiv    NAME         #IMPLIED  -- HTTP response header name   --
  name          NAME         #IMPLIED  -- metainformation name --
  content       CDATA        #REQUIRED -- associated information --
  scheme        CDATA        #IMPLIED  -- select form of content --
  >


<!ELEMENT STYLE - - %StyleSheet        -- style info -->
<!ATTLIST STYLE
  %i18n;                               -- lang, dir, for use with title --
  type          %ContentType; #REQUIRED -- content type of style language --
  media         %MediaDesc;  #IMPLIED  -- designed for use with these
                                          media --
  title         %Text;       #IMPLIED  -- advisory title --
  >


<!ELEMENT SCRIPT - - %Script;          -- script statements -->
<!ATTLIST SCRIPT
  charset       %Charset;    #IMPLIED  -- char encoding of linked resource --
  type          %ContentType; #REQUIRED -- content type of script language --
```

```
    language     CDATA          #IMPLIED   -- predefined script language name --
    src          %URI;          #IMPLIED   -- URI for an external script --
    defer        (defer)        #IMPLIED   -- UA may defer execution of script --
    event        CDATA          #IMPLIED   -- reserved for possible future use --
    for          %URI;          #IMPLIED   -- reserved for possible future use --
    >

<!ELEMENT NOSCRIPT - - (%flow;)*
    -- alternate content container for non script-based rendering -->
<!ATTLIST NOSCRIPT
    %attrs;                                 -- %coreattrs, %i18n, %events --
    >


<!--================ Document Structure ======================================-->
<!ENTITY % version "version CDATA #FIXED '%HTML.Version;'">


<![ %HTML.Frameset; [
<!ENTITY % html.content "HEAD, FRAMESET">
]]>


<!ENTITY % html.content "HEAD, BODY">


<!ELEMENT HTML O O (%html.content;)      -- document root element -->
<!ATTLIST HTML
    %i18n;                                 -- lang, dir --
    %version;
    >
```

HTML 4 Strict DTD

```
<!--
    This is HTML 4.0 Strict DTD, which excludes the presentation
    attributes and elements that W3C expects to phase out as
    support for style sheets matures. Authors should use the Strict
    DTD when possible, but may use the Transitional DTD when support
    for presentation attribute and elements is required.
```

HTML 4.0 includes mechanisms for style sheets, scripting, embedding objects, improved support for right to left and mixed direction text, and enhancements to forms for improved accessibility for people with disabilities.

     Draft: $Date: 1998/04/02 00:17:00 $

     Authors:
         Dave Raggett <dsr@w3.org>
         Arnaud Le Hors <lehors@w3.org>
         Ian Jacobs <ij@w3.org>

Further information about HTML 4.0 is available at:

    http://www.w3.org/TR/REC-html40
-->
<!--

    Typical usage:

    <!DOCTYPE HTML PUBLIC "-//W3C//DTD HTML 4.0//EN"
        "http://www.w3.org/TR/REC-html40/strict.dtd">
    <html>
    <head>
    ...
    </head>
    <body>
    ...
    </body>
    </html>

    The URI used as a system identifier with the public identifier allows the user agent to download the DTD and entity sets as needed.

    The FPI for the Transitional HTML 4.0 DTD is:

        "-//W3C//DTD HTML 4.0 Transitional//EN"

    and its URI is:

        http://www.w3.org/TR/REC-html40/loose.dtd

If you are writing a document that includes frames, use
the following FPI:

```
"-//W3C//DTD HTML 4.0 Frameset//EN"
```

with the URI:

```
http://www.w3.org/TR/REC-html40/frameset.dtd
```

The following URIs are supported in relation to HTML 4.0

```
"http://www.w3.org/TR/REC-html40/strict.dtd" (Strict DTD)
"http://www.w3.org/TR/REC-html40/loose.dtd" (Loose DTD)
"http://www.w3.org/TR/REC-html40/frameset.dtd" (Frameset DTD)
"http://www.w3.org/TR/REC-html40/HTMLlat1.ent" (Latin-1 entities)
"http://www.w3.org/TR/REC-html40/HTMLsymbol.ent" (Symbol entities)
"http://www.w3.org/TR/REC-html40/HTMLspecial.ent" (Special entities)
```

These URIs point to the latest version of each file. To reference
this specific revision use the following URIs:

```
"http://www.w3.org/TR/1998/REC-html40-19980424/strict.dtd"
"http://www.w3.org/TR/1998/REC-html40-19980424/loose.dtd"
"http://www.w3.org/TR/1998/REC-html40-19980424/frameset.dtd"
"http://www.w3.org/TR/1998/REC-html40-19980424/HTMLlat1.ent"
"http://www.w3.org/TR/1998/REC-html40-19980424/HTMLsymbol.ent"
"http://www.w3.org/TR/1998/REC-html40-19980424/HTMLspecial.ent"
```

```
-->

<!--==================== Imported Names ========================================-->

<!ENTITY % ContentType "CDATA"
    -- media type, as per [RFC2045]
    -->


<!ENTITY % ContentTypes "CDATA"
    -- comma-separated list of media types, as per [RFC2045]
    -->
```

```
<!ENTITY % Charset "CDATA"
    -- a character encoding, as per [RFC2045]
    -->

<!ENTITY % Charsets "CDATA"
    -- a space separated list of character encodings, as per [RFC2045]
    -->

<!ENTITY % LanguageCode "NAME"
    -- a language code, as per [RFC1766]
    -->

<!ENTITY % Character "CDATA"
    -- a single character from [ISO10646]
    -->

<!ENTITY % LinkTypes "CDATA"
    -- space-separated list of link types
    -->

<!ENTITY % MediaDesc "CDATA"
    -- single or comma-separated list of media descriptors
    -->

<!ENTITY % URI "CDATA"
    -- a Uniform Resource Identifier,
       see [URI]
    -->

<!ENTITY % Datetime "CDATA" -- date and time information. ISO date format -->

<!ENTITY % Script "CDATA" -- script expression -->

<!ENTITY % StyleSheet "CDATA" -- style sheet data -->

<!ENTITY % Text "CDATA">

<!-- Parameter Entities -->
```

```
<!ENTITY % head.misc "SCRIPT|STYLE|META|LINK|OBJECT" -- repeatable head
                                                        elements -->


<!ENTITY % heading "H1|H2|H3|H4|H5|H6">


<!ENTITY % list "UL | OL">


<!ENTITY % preformatted "PRE">

<!--================ Character mnemonic entities ===========================-->

<!ENTITY % HTMLlat1 PUBLIC
   "-//W3C//ENTITIES Latin1//EN//HTML"
   "http://www.w3.org/TR/1998/REC-html40-19980424/HTMLlat1.ent">
%HTMLlat1;


<!ENTITY % HTMLsymbol PUBLIC
   "-//W3C//ENTITIES Symbols//EN//HTML"
   "http://www.w3.org/TR/1998/REC-html40-19980424/HTMLsymbol.ent">
%HTMLsymbol;


<!ENTITY % HTMLspecial PUBLIC
   "-//W3C//ENTITIES Special//EN//HTML"
   "http://www.w3.org/TR/1998/REC-html40-19980424/HTMLspecial.ent">
%HTMLspecial;
<!--==================== Generic Attributes ================================-->

<!ENTITY % coreattrs
  "id           ID            #IMPLIED  -- document-wide unique id --
   class        CDATA         #IMPLIED  -- space separated list of classes --
   style        %StyleSheet;  #IMPLIED  -- associated style info --
   title        %Text;        #IMPLIED  -- advisory title/amplification --"
   >


<!ENTITY % i18n
  "lang         %LanguageCode; #IMPLIED  -- language code --
   dir          (ltr|rtl)      #IMPLIED  -- direction for weak/neutral
                                            text --"

   >
```

```
<!ENTITY % events
 "onclick        %Script;        #IMPLIED  -- a pointer button was clicked --
  ondblclick     %Script;        #IMPLIED  -- a pointer button was double
                                              clicked--
  onmousedown    %Script;        #IMPLIED  -- a pointer button was pressed down --
  onmouseup      %Script;        #IMPLIED  -- a pointer button was released --
  onmouseover    %Script;        #IMPLIED  -- a pointer was moved onto --
  onmousemove    %Script;        #IMPLIED  -- a pointer was moved within --
  onmouseout     %Script;        #IMPLIED  -- a pointer was moved away --
  onkeypress     %Script;        #IMPLIED  -- a key was pressed and released --
  onkeydown      %Script;        #IMPLIED  -- a key was pressed down --
  onkeyup        %Script;        #IMPLIED  -- a key was released --"
  >

<!-- Reserved Feature Switch -->
<!ENTITY % HTML.Reserved "IGNORE">

<!-- The following attributes are reserved for possible future use -->
<![ %HTML.Reserved; [
<!ENTITY % reserved
 "datasrc        %URI;           #IMPLIED  -- a single or tabular Data Source --
  datafld        CDATA           #IMPLIED  -- the property or column name --
  dataformatas (plaintext|html) plaintext -- text or html --"
  >
]]>

<!ENTITY % reserved "">

<!ENTITY % attrs "%coreattrs; %i18n; %events;">

<!--==================== Text Markup =========================================-->

<!ENTITY % fontstyle
 "TT | I | B | BIG | SMALL">

<!ENTITY % phrase "EM | STRONG | DFN | CODE |
                   SAMP | KBD | VAR | CITE | ABBR | ACRONYM" >

<!ENTITY % special
   "A | IMG | OBJECT | BR | SCRIPT | MAP | Q | SUB | SUP | SPAN | BDO">
```

```
<!ENTITY % formctrl "INPUT | SELECT | TEXTAREA | LABEL | BUTTON">

<!-- %inline; covers inline or "text-level" elements -->
<!ENTITY % inline "#PCDATA | %fontstyle; | %phrase; | %special; |
                   %formctrl;">

<!ELEMENT (%fontstyle;|%phrase;) - - (%inline;)*>
<!ATTLIST (%fontstyle;|%phrase;)
  %attrs;                           -- %coreattrs, %i18n, %events --
  >

<!ELEMENT (SUB|SUP) - - (%inline;)*    -- subscript, superscript -->
<!ATTLIST (SUB|SUP)
  %attrs;                           -- %coreattrs, %i18n, %events --
  >

<!ELEMENT SPAN - - (%inline;)*         -- generic language/style
                                          container -->

<!ATTLIST SPAN
  %attrs;                           -- %coreattrs, %i18n, %events --
  %reserved;                        -- reserved for possible future use --
  >

<!ELEMENT BDO - - (%inline;)*          -- I18N BiDi over-ride -->
<!ATTLIST BDO
  %coreattrs;                       -- id, class, style, title --
  lang          %LanguageCode; #IMPLIED -- language code --
  dir           (ltr|rtl)       #REQUIRED -- directionality --
  >

<!ELEMENT BR - O EMPTY                 -- forced line break -->
<!ATTLIST BR
  %coreattrs;                       -- id, class, style, title --
  >

<!--==================== HTML content models ====================================-->

<!--
     HTML has two basic content models:

          %inline;     character level elements and text strings
```

```
            %block;       block-like elements e.g. paragraphs and lists
   -->


   <!ENTITY % block
        "P | %heading; | %list; | %preformatted; | DL | DIV | NOSCRIPT |
         BLOCKQUOTE | FORM | HR | TABLE | FIELDSET | ADDRESS">


   <!ENTITY % flow "%block; | %inline;">


   <!--=================== Document Body =======================================-->

   <!ELEMENT BODY O O (%block;|SCRIPT)+ +(INS|DEL) -- document body -->
   <!ATTLIST BODY
     %attrs;                              -- %coreattrs, %i18n, %events --
     onload          %Script;   #IMPLIED  -- the document has been loaded --
     onunload        %Script;   #IMPLIED  -- the document has been removed --
     >


   <!ELEMENT ADDRESS - - (%inline;)* -- information on author -->
   <!ATTLIST ADDRESS
     %attrs;                              -- %coreattrs, %i18n, %events --
     >


   <!ELEMENT DIV - - (%flow;)*           -- generic language/style
                                            container -->
   <!ATTLIST DIV
     %attrs;                              -- %coreattrs, %i18n, %events --
     %reserved;                           -- reserved for possible future use --
     >


   <!--=================== The Anchor Element ===================================-->

   <!ENTITY % Shape "(rect|circle|poly|default)">
   <!ENTITY % Coords "CDATA" -- comma separated list of lengths -->

   <!ELEMENT A - - (%inline;)* -(A)       -- anchor -->
   <!ATTLIST A
     %attrs;                              -- %coreattrs, %i18n, %events --
     charset      %Charset;     #IMPLIED  -- char encoding of linked resource --
     type         %ContentType; #IMPLIED  -- advisory content type --
     name         CDATA         #IMPLIED  -- named link end --
```

```
   href          %URI;            #IMPLIED   -- URI for linked resource --
   hreflang      %LanguageCode;   #IMPLIED   -- language code --
   rel           %LinkTypes;      #IMPLIED   -- forward link types --
   rev           %LinkTypes;      #IMPLIED   -- reverse link types --
   accesskey     %Character;      #IMPLIED   -- accessibility key character --
   shape         %Shape;          rect       -- for use with client-side image
                                                 maps --

   coords        %Coords;         #IMPLIED   -- for use with client-side image
                                                 maps --

   tabindex      NUMBER           #IMPLIED   -- position in tabbing order --
   onfocus       %Script;         #IMPLIED   -- the element got the focus --
   onblur        %Script;         #IMPLIED   -- the element lost the focus --
   >


<!--================== Client-side image maps ============================-->

<!-- These can be placed in the same document or grouped in a
       separate document although this isn't yet widely supported -->

<!ELEMENT MAP - - ((%block;)+ | AREA+) -- client-side image map -->
<!ATTLIST MAP
   %attrs;                                   -- %coreattrs, %i18n, %events --
   name          CDATA            #REQUIRED  -- for reference by usemap --
   >


<!ELEMENT AREA - O EMPTY                     -- client-side image map area -->
<!ATTLIST AREA
   %attrs;                                   -- %coreattrs, %i18n, %events --
   shape         %Shape;          rect       -- controls interpretation of coords --
   coords        %Coords;         #IMPLIED   -- comma separated list of lengths --
   href          %URI;            #IMPLIED   -- URI for linked resource --
   nohref        (nohref)         #IMPLIED   -- this region has no action --
   alt           %Text;           #REQUIRED  -- short description --
   tabindex      NUMBER           #IMPLIED   -- position in tabbing order --
   accesskey     %Character;      #IMPLIED   -- accessibility key character --
   onfocus       %Script;         #IMPLIED   -- the element got the focus --
   onblur        %Script;         #IMPLIED   -- the element lost the focus --
   >
```

```
<!--================== The LINK Element =====================================-->

<!--
   Relationship values can be used in principle:

     a) for document specific toolbars/menus when used
        with the LINK element in document head e.g.
          start, contents, previous, next, index, end, help
     b) to link to a separate style sheet (rel=stylesheet)
     c) to make a link to a script (rel=script)
     d) by stylesheets to control how collections of
        html nodes are rendered into printed documents
     e) to make a link to a printable version of this document
        e.g. a postscript or pdf version (rel=alternate media=print)
-->

<!ELEMENT LINK - O EMPTY                -- a media-independent link -->
<!ATTLIST LINK
  %attrs;                               -- %coreattrs, %i18n, %events --
  charset     %Charset;       #IMPLIED  -- char encoding of linked resource --
  href        %URI;           #IMPLIED  -- URI for linked resource --
  hreflang    %LanguageCode;  #IMPLIED  -- language code --
  type        %ContentType;   #IMPLIED  -- advisory content type --
  rel         %LinkTypes;     #IMPLIED  -- forward link types --
  rev         %LinkTypes;     #IMPLIED  -- reverse link types --
  media       %MediaDesc;     #IMPLIED  -- for rendering on these media --
  >


<========= Images ====================================================-->

<!-- Length defined in strict DTD for cellpadding/cellspacing -->
<!ENTITY % Length "CDATA" -- nn for pixels or nn% for percentage length -->
<!ENTITY % MultiLength "CDATA" -- pixel, percentage, or relative -->

<!ENTITY % MultiLengths "CDATA" -- comma-separated list of MultiLength -->

<!ENTITY % Pixels "CDATA" -- integer representing length in pixels -->

<!-- To avoid problems with text-only UAs as well as
     to make image content understandable and navigable
     to users of non-visual UAs, you need to provide
```

```
      a description with ALT, and avoid server-side image maps -->
<!ELEMENT IMG - O EMPTY                        -- Embedded image -->
<!ATTLIST IMG
  %attrs;                                      -- %coreattrs, %i18n, %events --
  src           %URI;           #REQUIRED  -- URI of image to embed --
  alt           %Text;          #REQUIRED  -- short description --
  longdesc      %URI;           #IMPLIED   -- link to long description
                                              (complements alt) --
  height        %Length;        #IMPLIED   -- override height --
  width         %Length;        #IMPLIED   -- override width --
  usemap        %URI;           #IMPLIED   -- use client-side image map --
  ismap         (ismap)         #IMPLIED   -- use server-side image map --
  >

<!-- USEMAP points to a MAP element which may be in this document
  or an external document, although the latter is not widely supported -->


<!--===================== OBJECT =========================================-->
<!--
  OBJECT is used to embed objects as part of HTML pages
  PARAM elements should precede other content. SGML mixed content
  model technicality precludes specifying this formally ...
-->

<!ELEMENT OBJECT - - (PARAM | %flow;)*
  -- generic embedded object -->
<!ATTLIST OBJECT
  %attrs;                                      -- %coreattrs, %i18n, %events --
  declare       (declare)       #IMPLIED   -- declare but don't instantiate flag --
  classid       %URI;           #IMPLIED   -- identifies an implementation --
  codebase      %URI;           #IMPLIED   -- base URI for classid, data, archive--
  data          %URI;           #IMPLIED   -- reference to object's data --
  type          %ContentType;   #IMPLIED   -- content type for data --
  codetype      %ContentType;   #IMPLIED   -- content type for code --
  archive       %URI;           #IMPLIED   -- space separated archive list --
  standby       %Text;          #IMPLIED   -- message to show while loading --
  height        %Length;        #IMPLIED   -- override height --
  width         %Length;        #IMPLIED   -- override width --
  usemap        %URI;           #IMPLIED   -- use client-side image map --
  name          CDATA           #IMPLIED   -- submit as part of form --
```

```
    tabindex    NUMBER          #IMPLIED    -- position in tabbing order --
    %reserved;                              -- reserved for possible future use --
    >


<!ELEMENT PARAM - O EMPTY               -- named property value -->
<!ATTLIST PARAM
    id          ID              #IMPLIED    -- document-wide unique id --
    name        CDATA           #REQUIRED   -- property name --
    value       CDATA           #IMPLIED    -- property value --
    valuetype   (DATA|REF|OBJECT) DATA      -- How to interpret value --
    type        %ContentType;   #IMPLIED    -- content type for value
                                               when valuetype=ref --
    >


<!--=================== Horizontal Rule ====================================-->

<!ELEMENT HR - O EMPTY -- horizontal rule -->
<!ATTLIST HR
    %coreattrs;                             -- id, class, style, title --
    %events;
    >


<!--=================== Paragraphs =========================================-->

<!ELEMENT P - O (%inline;)*          -- paragraph -->
<!ATTLIST P
    %attrs;                                 -- %coreattrs, %i18n, %events --
    >


<!--=================== Headings ===========================================-->

<!--
  There are six levels of headings from H1 (the most important)
  to H6 (the least important).
-->

<!ELEMENT (%heading;)  - - (%inline;)* -- heading -->
<!ATTLIST (%heading;)
    %attrs;                                 -- %coreattrs, %i18n, %events --
    >
```

```
<!--=================== Preformatted Text =================================-->

<!-- excludes markup for images and changes in font size -->
<!ENTITY % pre.exclusion "IMG|OBJECT|BIG|SMALL|SUB|SUP">


<!ELEMENT PRE - - (%inline;)* -(%pre.exclusion;) -- preformatted text -->
<!ATTLIST PRE
  %attrs;                                    -- %coreattrs, %i18n, %events --
  >


<!--===================== Inline Quotes =================================-->

<!ELEMENT Q - - (%inline;)*             -- short inline quotation -->
<!ATTLIST Q
  %attrs;                                -- %coreattrs, %i18n, %events --
  cite         %URI;         #IMPLIED  -- URI for source document or msg --
  >


<!--=================== Block-like Quotes =================================-->

<!ELEMENT BLOCKQUOTE - - (%block;|SCRIPT)+ -- long quotation -->
<!ATTLIST BLOCKQUOTE
  %attrs;                                -- %coreattrs, %i18n, %events --
  cite         %URI;         #IMPLIED  -- URI for source document or msg --
  >


<!--=================== Inserted/Deleted Text =============================-->

<!-- INS/DEL are handled by inclusion on BODY -->
<!ELEMENT (INS|DEL) - - (%flow;)*       -- inserted text, deleted text -->
<!ATTLIST (INS|DEL)
  %attrs;                                -- %coreattrs, %i18n, %events --
  cite         %URI;         #IMPLIED  -- info on reason for change --
  datetime     %Datetime;    #IMPLIED  -- date and time of change --
  >


<!--=================== Lists =============================================-->

<!-- definition lists - DT for term, DD for its definition -->
```

```
<!ELEMENT DL - - (DT|DD)+          -- definition list -->
<!ATTLIST DL
  %attrs;                          -- %coreattrs, %i18n, %events --
  >


<!ELEMENT DT - O (%inline;)*       -- definition term -->
<!ELEMENT DD - O (%flow;)*         -- definition description -->
<!ATTLIST (DT|DD)
  %attrs;                          -- %coreattrs, %i18n, %events --
  >


<!ELEMENT OL - - (LI)+             -- ordered list -->
<!ATTLIST OL
  %attrs;                          -- %coreattrs, %i18n, %events --
  >


<!-- Unordered Lists (UL) bullet styles -->
<!ELEMENT UL - - (LI)+             -- unordered list -->
<!ATTLIST UL
  %attrs;                          -- %coreattrs, %i18n, %events --
  >


<!ELEMENT LI - O (%flow;)*         -- list item -->
<!ATTLIST LI
  %attrs;                          -- %coreattrs, %i18n, %events --
  >


<!--================ Forms ===================================================-->
<!ELEMENT FORM - - (%block;|SCRIPT)+ -(FORM) -- interactive form -->
<!ATTLIST FORM
  %attrs;                              -- %coreattrs, %i18n, %events --
  action        %URI;          #REQUIRED -- server-side form handler --
  method        (GET|POST)     GET    -- HTTP method used to submit the
                                         form--
  enctype       %ContentType;  "application/x-www-form-urlencoded"
  onsubmit      %Script;       #IMPLIED -- the form was submitted --
  onreset       %Script;       #IMPLIED -- the form was reset --
  accept-charset %Charsets;    #IMPLIED -- list of supported charsets --
>
```

```
<!-- Each label must not contain more than ONE field -->
<!ELEMENT LABEL - - (%inline;)* -(LABEL) -- form field label text -->
<!ATTLIST LABEL
  %attrs;                              -- %coreattrs, %i18n, %events --
  for            IDREF        #IMPLIED -- matches field ID value --
  accesskey      %Character;  #IMPLIED -- accessibility key character --
  onfocus        %Script;     #IMPLIED -- the element got the focus --
  onblur         %Script;     #IMPLIED -- the element lost the focus --
  >

<!ENTITY % InputType
  "(TEXT | PASSWORD | CHECKBOX |
    RADIO | SUBMIT | RESET |
    FILE | HIDDEN | IMAGE | BUTTON)"
  >

<!-- attribute name required for all but submit & reset -->
<!ELEMENT INPUT - O EMPTY             -- form control -->
<!ATTLIST INPUT
  %attrs;                                -- %coreattrs, %i18n, %events --
  type          %InputType;   TEXT       -- what kind of widget is needed --
  name          CDATA         #IMPLIED   -- submit as part of form --
  value         CDATA         #IMPLIED   -- required for radio and checkboxes --
  checked       (checked)     #IMPLIED   -- for radio buttons and check boxes --
  disabled      (disabled)    #IMPLIED   -- unavailable in this context --
  readonly      (readonly)    #IMPLIED   -- for text and passwd --
  size          CDATA         #IMPLIED   -- specific to each type of field --
  maxlength     NUMBER        #IMPLIED   -- max chars for text fields --
  src           %URI;         #IMPLIED   -- for fields with images --
  alt           CDATA         #IMPLIED   -- short description --
  usemap        %URI;         #IMPLIED   -- use client-side image map --
  tabindex      NUMBER        #IMPLIED   -- position in tabbing order --
  accesskey     %Character;   #IMPLIED   -- accessibility key character --
  onfocus       %Script;      #IMPLIED   -- the element got the focus --
  onblur        %Script;      #IMPLIED   -- the element lost the focus --
  onselect      %Script;      #IMPLIED   -- some text was selected --
  onchange      %Script;      #IMPLIED   -- the element value was changed --
  accept        %ContentTypes; #IMPLIED  -- list of MIME types for file upload --
  %reserved;                             -- reserved for possible future use --
  >
```

```
<!ELEMENT SELECT - - (OPTGROUP|OPTION)+ -- option selector -->
<!ATTLIST SELECT
  %attrs;                              -- %coreattrs, %i18n, %events --
  name        CDATA         #IMPLIED  -- field name --
  size        NUMBER        #IMPLIED  -- rows visible --
  multiple    (multiple)    #IMPLIED  -- default is single selection --
  disabled    (disabled)    #IMPLIED  -- unavailable in this context --
  tabindex    NUMBER        #IMPLIED  -- position in tabbing order --
  onfocus     %Script;      #IMPLIED  -- the element got the focus --
  onblur      %Script;      #IMPLIED  -- the element lost the focus --
  onchange    %Script;      #IMPLIED  -- the element value was changed --
  %reserved;                          -- reserved for possible future
                                         use --
  >

<!ELEMENT OPTGROUP - - (OPTION)+ -- option group -->
<!ATTLIST OPTGROUP
  %attrs;                              -- %coreattrs, %i18n, %events --
  disabled    (disabled)    #IMPLIED  -- unavailable in this context --
  label       %Text;        #REQUIRED -- for use in hierarchical menus --
  >

<!ELEMENT OPTION - O (#PCDATA)       -- selectable choice -->
<!ATTLIST OPTION
  %attrs;                              -- %coreattrs, %i18n, %events --
  selected    (selected)    #IMPLIED
  disabled    (disabled)    #IMPLIED  -- unavailable in this context --
  label       %Text;        #IMPLIED  -- for use in hierarchical menus --
  value       CDATA         #IMPLIED  -- defaults to element content --
  >

<!ELEMENT TEXTAREA - - (#PCDATA)     -- multi-line text field -->
<!ATTLIST TEXTAREA
  %attrs;                              -- %coreattrs, %i18n, %events --
  name        CDATA         #IMPLIED
  rows        NUMBER        #REQUIRED
  cols        NUMBER        #REQUIRED
  disabled    (disabled)    #IMPLIED  -- unavailable in this context --
  readonly    (readonly)    #IMPLIED
  tabindex    NUMBER        #IMPLIED  -- position in tabbing order --
```

```
   accesskey    %Character;     #IMPLIED  -- accessibility key character --
   onfocus      %Script;        #IMPLIED  -- the element got the focus --
   onblur       %Script;        #IMPLIED  -- the element lost the focus --
   onselect     %Script;        #IMPLIED  -- some text was selected --
   onchange     %Script;        #IMPLIED  -- the element value was changed --
   %reserved;                              -- reserved for possible future use --
   >


<!--
  #PCDATA is to solve the mixed content problem,
  per specification only whitespace is allowed there!
  -->
<!ELEMENT FIELDSET - - (#PCDATA,LEGEND,(%flow;)*) -- form control group -->
<!ATTLIST FIELDSET
   %attrs;                                 -- %coreattrs, %i18n, %events --
   >


<!ELEMENT LEGEND - - (%inline;)*         -- fieldset legend -->
<!ENTITY % LAlign "(top|bottom|left|right)">


<!ATTLIST LEGEND
   %attrs;                                 -- %coreattrs, %i18n, %events --
   accesskey    %Character;     #IMPLIED  -- accessibility key character --
   >


<!ELEMENT BUTTON - -
     (%flow;)* -(A|%formctrl;|FORM|FIELDSET)
     -- push button -->
<!ATTLIST BUTTON
   %attrs;                                 -- %coreattrs, %i18n, %events --
   name         CDATA           #IMPLIED
   value        CDATA           #IMPLIED  -- sent to server when submitted --
   type         (button|submit|reset) submit -- for use as form button --
   disabled     (disabled)      #IMPLIED  -- unavailable in this context --
   tabindex     NUMBER          #IMPLIED  -- position in tabbing order --
   accesskey    %Character;     #IMPLIED  -- accessibility key character --
   onfocus      %Script;        #IMPLIED  -- the element got the focus --
   onblur       %Script;        #IMPLIED  -- the element lost the focus --
   %reserved;                              -- reserved for possible future use --
   >
```

```
<!--======================= Tables =========================================-->

<!-- IETF HTML table standard, see [RFC1942] -->

<!--
 The BORDER attribute sets the thickness of the frame around the
 table. The default units are screen pixels.

 The FRAME attribute specifies which parts of the frame around
 the table should be rendered. The values are not the same as
 CALS to avoid a name clash with the VALIGN attribute.

 The value "border" is included for backwards compatibility with
 <TABLE BORDER> which yields frame=border and border=implied
 For <TABLE BORDER=1> you get border=1 and frame=implied. In this
 case, it is appropriate to treat this as frame=border for backwards
 compatibility with deployed browsers.
-->
<!ENTITY % TFrame "(void|above|below|hsides|lhs|rhs|vsides|box|border)">


<!--
 The RULES attribute defines which rules to draw between cells:

 If RULES is absent then assume:
     "none" if BORDER is absent or BORDER=0 otherwise "all"
-->

<!ENTITY % TRules "(none | groups | rows | cols | all)">


<!-- horizontal placement of table relative to document -->
<!ENTITY % TAlign "(left|center|right)">


<!-- horizontal alignment attributes for cell contents -->
<!ENTITY % cellhalign
  "align        (left|center|right|justify|char) #IMPLIED
   char         %Character;     #IMPLIED -- alignment char, e.g. char=':' --
   charoff      %Length;        #IMPLIED -- offset for alignment char --"
  >
```

```
<!-- vertical alignment attributes for cell contents -->
<!ENTITY % cellvalign
  "valign     (top|middle|bottom|baseline) #IMPLIED"
  >


<!ELEMENT TABLE - -
      (CAPTION?, (COL*|COLGROUP*), THEAD?, TFOOT?, TBODY+)>
<!ELEMENT CAPTION   - - (%inline;)*      -- table caption -->
<!ELEMENT THEAD     - O (TR)+            -- table header -->
<!ELEMENT TFOOT     - O (TR)+            -- table footer -->
<!ELEMENT TBODY     O O (TR)+            -- table body -->
<!ELEMENT COLGROUP - O (col)*            -- table column group -->
<!ELEMENT COL       - O EMPTY            -- table column -->
<!ELEMENT TR        - O (TH|TD)+         -- table row -->
<!ELEMENT (TH|TD)   - O (%flow;)*        -- table header cell, table data
                                            cell-->


<!ATTLIST TABLE                          -- table element --
  %attrs;                                -- %coreattrs, %i18n, %events --
  summary       %Text;       #IMPLIED    -- purpose/structure for speech
                                            output--
  width         %Length;     #IMPLIED    -- table width --
  border        %Pixels;     #IMPLIED    -- controls frame width around
                                            table --
  frame         %TFrame;     #IMPLIED    -- which parts of frame to render --
  rules         %TRules;     #IMPLIED    -- rulings between rows and cols --
  cellspacing   %Length;     #IMPLIED    -- spacing between cells --
  cellpadding   %Length;     #IMPLIED    -- spacing within cells --
  %reserved;                             -- reserved for possible future
                                            use --
  datapagesize CDATA         #IMPLIED    -- reserved for possible future
                                            use --
  >


<!ENTITY % CAlign "(top|bottom|left|right)">

<!ATTLIST CAPTION
  %attrs;                                -- %coreattrs, %i18n, %events --
  >
```

```
<!--
COLGROUP groups a set of COL elements. It allows you to group
several semantically related columns together.
-->
<!ATTLIST COLGROUP
  %attrs;                              -- %coreattrs, %i18n, %events --
  span           NUMBER       1        -- default number of columns in group --
  width          %MultiLength; #IMPLIED -- default width for enclosed COLs --
  %cellhalign;                         -- horizontal alignment in cells --
  %cellvalign;                         -- vertical alignment in cells --
  >


<!--
 COL elements define the alignment properties for cells in
 one or more columns.

 The WIDTH attribute specifies the width of the columns, e.g.

     width=64         width in screen pixels
     width=0.5*       relative width of 0.5

 The SPAN attribute causes the attributes of one
 COL element to apply to more than one column.
-->
<!ATTLIST COL                          -- column groups and properties --
  %attrs;                              -- %coreattrs, %i18n, %events --
  span           NUMBER       1        -- COL attributes affect N columns --
  width          %MultiLength; #IMPLIED -- column width specification --
  %cellhalign;                         -- horizontal alignment in cells --
  %cellvalign;                         -- vertical alignment in cells --
>


<!--
    Use THEAD to duplicate headers when breaking table
    across page boundaries, or for static headers when
    TBODY sections are rendered in scrolling panel.

    Use TFOOT to duplicate footers when breaking table
    across page boundaries, or for static footers when
    TBODY sections are rendered in scrolling panel.
```

```
       Use multiple TBODY sections when rules are needed
       between groups of table rows.
-->
<!ATTLIST (THEAD|TBODY|TFOOT)          -- table section --
   %attrs;                             -- %coreattrs, %i18n, %events --
   %cellhalign;                        -- horizontal alignment in cells --
   %cellvalign;                        -- vertical alignment in cells --
   >


<!ATTLIST TR                           -- table row --
   %attrs;                             -- %coreattrs, %i18n, %events --
   %cellhalign;                        -- horizontal alignment in cells --
   %cellvalign;                        -- vertical alignment in cells --
   >


<!-- Scope is simpler than axes attribute for common tables -->
<!ENTITY % Scope "(row|col|rowgroup|colgroup)">


<!-- TH is for headers, TD for data, but for cells acting as both use TD -->
<!ATTLIST (TH|TD)                      -- header or data cell --
   %attrs;                             -- %coreattrs, %i18n, %events --
   abbr         %Text;     #IMPLIED    -- abbreviation for header cell --
   axis         CDATA      #IMPLIED    -- names groups of related headers--
   headers      IDREFS     #IMPLIED    -- list of id's for header cells --
   scope        %Scope;    #IMPLIED    -- scope covered by header cells --
   rowspan      NUMBER     1           -- number of rows spanned by cell --
   colspan      NUMBER     1           -- number of cols spanned by cell --
   %cellhalign;                        -- horizontal alignment in cells --
   %cellvalign;                        -- vertical alignment in cells --
   >


<!--================ Document Head =========================================-->
<!-- %head.misc; defined earlier on as "SCRIPT|STYLE|META|LINK|OBJECT" -->
<!ENTITY % head.content "TITLE & BASE?">


<!ELEMENT HEAD O O (%head.content;) +(%head.misc;) -- document head -->
<!ATTLIST HEAD
   %i18n;                              -- lang, dir --
   profile      %URI;      #IMPLIED    -- named dictionary of meta info --
   >
```

```
<!-- The TITLE element is not considered part of the flow of text.
       It should be displayed, for example as the page header or
       window title. Exactly one title is required per document.
    -->
<!ELEMENT TITLE - - (#PCDATA) -(%head.misc;) -- document title -->
<!ATTLIST TITLE %i18n>

<!ELEMENT BASE - O EMPTY              -- document base URI -->
<!ATTLIST BASE
   href        %URI;          #REQUIRED -- URI that acts as base URI --
   >

<!ELEMENT META - O EMPTY              -- generic metainformation -->
<!ATTLIST META
   %i18n;                               -- lang, dir, for use with content --
   http-equiv  NAME           #IMPLIED -- HTTP response header name   --
   name        NAME           #IMPLIED -- metainformation name --
   content     CDATA          #REQUIRED -- associated information --
   scheme      CDATA          #IMPLIED -- select form of content --
   >

<!ELEMENT STYLE - - %StyleSheet       -- style info -->
<!ATTLIST STYLE
   %i18n;                               -- lang, dir, for use with title --
   type        %ContentType;  #REQUIRED -- content type of style language --
   media       %MediaDesc;    #IMPLIED -- designed for use with these
                                           media --
   title       %Text;         #IMPLIED -- advisory title --
   >

<!ELEMENT SCRIPT - - %Script;         -- script statements -->
<!ATTLIST SCRIPT
   charset     %Charset;      #IMPLIED -- char encoding of linked resource --
   type        %ContentType;  #REQUIRED -- content type of script language --
   src         %URI;          #IMPLIED -- URI for an external script --
   defer       (defer)        #IMPLIED -- UA may defer execution of script --
   event       CDATA          #IMPLIED -- reserved for possible future use --
   for         %URI;          #IMPLIED -- reserved for possible future use --
   >
```

```
<!ELEMENT NOSCRIPT - - (%block;)+
  -- alternate content container for non script-based rendering -->
<!ATTLIST NOSCRIPT
  %attrs;                                  -- %coreattrs, %i18n, %events --
  >


<!--================ Document Structure ====================================-->
<!ENTITY % html.content "HEAD, BODY">


<!ELEMENT HTML O O (%html.content;)      -- document root element -->
<!ATTLIST HTML
  %i18n;                                  -- lang, dir --
  >
```

HTML 4 Frameset DTD

```
<!--
    This is the HTML 4.0 Frameset DTD, which should be
    used for documents with frames. This DTD is identical
    to the HTML 4.0 Transitional DTD except for the
    content model of the "HTML" element: in frameset
    documents, the "FRAMESET" element replaces the "BODY"
    element.

          Draft: $Date: 1997/12/11 15:31:11 $

          Authors:
              Dave Raggett <dsr@w3.org>
              Arnaud Le Hors <lehors@w3.org>
              Ian Jacobs <ij@w3.org>

    Further information about HTML 4.0 is available at:

          http://www.w3.org/TR/REC-html40.
-->
<!ENTITY % HTML.Version "-//W3C//DTD HTML 4.0 Frameset//EN"
  - Typical usage:
```

```
<!DOCTYPE HTML PUBLIC "-//W3C//DTD HTML 4.0 Frameset//EN"
        "http://www.w3.org/TR/REC-html40/frameset.dtd">
<html>
<head>
...
</head>
<frameset>
...
</frameset>
</html>
->

<!ENTITY % HTML.Frameset "INCLUDE">
<!ENTITY % HTML4.dtd PUBLIC "-//W3C//DTD HTML 4.0 Transitional//EN">
%HTML4.dtd;
```

Index

E